12th July 1986

To my own Dear Husband

Donald

on the occasion of our Silver Wedding

May our marriage go on maturing like a good wine

His own Dear wife

Isobel

Hugh Johnson's

WINE COMPANION

The New Encyclopaedia of Wines, Vineyards and Winemakers

Hugh Johnson's

WINE COMPANION

The New Encyclopaedia of Wines, Vineyards and Winemakers

MITCHELL BEAZLEY

Hugh Johnson's Wine Companion

Edited and designed by Mitchell Beazley International Ltd.,
87–89 Shaftesbury Avenue, London W1V 7AD

Executive Editor Chris Foulkes
Art Editor Heather Jackson
Editors Rachel Grenfell, Dian Taylor
Editorial Assistant Bill Martin
Associate Designer Nigel O'Gorman
Proofreader Kathie Gill
Indexer Naomi Good
Production Jean Rigby
Executive Art Editor Douglas Wilson

Illustrations Paul Hogarth
Grape Illustrations John Davis
Colour Maps Eugene Fleury

ISBN 0 85533 419 3
First edition 1983, reprinted 1984

Filmset in Garamond by Filmtype Services Limited,
Scarborough, North Yorkshire
Reproduction by Bridge Graphics, Hull, England
Printed in Holland by
Koninklijke Smeets Offset b.v.

The author and publishers will be very grateful for any information which will assist them in keeping future editions of this book up to date.

AUTHOR'S ACKNOWLEDGMENTS

A list of the many people whose help has been indispensable, and invariably most generously given, appears on page 544. Some have been so deeply involved in various parts or phases of my research that I must offer them my special thanks at the outset. First among these I count my tireless colleagues at Mitchell Beazley, especially Chris Foulkes, my deeply involved and almost unharassable editor, Heather Jackson, who personally designed every aspect and every detail of the book, Rachel Grenfell and Dian Taylor, who nursed every word and statistic into place, Adrian Webster, whose idea it was, and Valerie Dobson, who combines enthusiasm with orderliness – my ideal secretary. I am more grateful to them than I can (briefly or decently) say.

Other people whose contributions were crucial in important aspects of the work, and whom I most gratefully acknowledge, are: Miranda Alexander, Burton Anderson, Colin Anderson, M.W., Rafael Balão, the late Martin Bamford, M.W., Jean-Claude Berrouet, Gerald D. Boyd, Brigitte Brugnon, Jean-Henri Dubernet, Hubrecht Duijker, Len Evans, André Gagey, Rosemary George, M.W., Claudie Gomme, Marie-Christine Machard de Grammont, James Halliday, Ian Jamieson, M.W., Graham Knox, Tony Laithwaite, Tim Marshall, Sarah Matthews, Barbara Onderka, John Parkinson, Jan and Maite Read, Michael Rothwell, Michael Symington, Michel Tesseron, Bob and Harolyn Thompson, Michael Vaughan, Peter Vinding-Diers, Richard Vine.

CONTENTS

INTRODUCTION

To live in the Golden Age of one of life's great pleasures is something we all do, but few of us seem to realize. There never was a time when more good wine, and more different kinds of wine, were being made.

Exactly 150 years ago Cyrus Redding, a London wine merchant, wrote his great *History and Description of Modern Wines*. To him the word 'Modern' distinguished the wines of his time from those of the Ancients, still then reverentially supposed to have been, like their architecture, of a quality that could be only humbly imitated.

Redding asserted the new world of nineteenth-century wine, based on the technology of the Industrial Revolution. If the great mass of wine in his day was still made by medieval methods, the leaders were setting the styles and standards and devising the techniques that today we accept as classic.

These methods are now old. Our understanding of wine and our techniques for making it have moved into a new phase, led by sciences that were not dreamed of in the last century. It is time to use the word modern again with a new meaning to describe the brilliant new age of wine that has opened in the past generation.

The nineteenth century closed, and the twentieth opened, with crisis and calamity in the vineyards of the world. Phylloxera, mildew, war, Prohibition and slump followed in a succession that prevented the majority of wine growers from making more than a meagre living. Standards, ideas and technology marked time. For the privileged there were wonderful wines to be had – and cheap, too. But little that was new or exciting developed into commercial reality until the 1960s. Then suddenly the product and the market rediscovered one another.

There were stirrings everywhere, but it was California that led the way. The coincidence of ideal wine-growing conditions and a fast-growing, educated and thriving population were the necessary elements. A generation of inspired university researchers and teachers in California and Europe (and also in Australia) were the catalysts. In the 1970s sudden intense interest in every aspect of wine caught on in country after country.

This book is a portrait of this new world of wine: its goals, its methods, its plant of vineyards and cellars, and above all its practitioners. It is designed to be a practical companion in choices that become more varied and challenging all the time. Like any portrait, it tries to capture the reality of a single moment. The moment is past as soon as the shutter has clicked. The closer the focus and the greater the detail the more there is to change and grow out of date. Yet the detailed record of a single season in wine's long history is as close to reality as it is possible to get.

To be a practical companion I have tried to give the essential information about each wine country and wine region you are likely to encounter or which is worth making an effort to know. I have shunned a great catalogue of the legislation that surrounds the wine business increasingly each year. It casts little light and does nothing to add to the pleasure of our subject – which is, after all, either a pleasure or a failure.

The essentials, it seems to me, are the names and as far as possible (which is not very far) descriptions of the world's worthwhile wines, who makes them, how much there is of them, what they cost, how well they keep, and where they fit into our lives – which are too short, alas, to do justice to anything like all of them. You will also find answers to the recurring questions about grape varieties, production methods and the ways of the wine trade. You will not find a historical survey or a technical treatise; just enough technical information, I hope, to indicate essential differences and the trends of change in wine-making today.

The heart of the book is arranged by countries on the same system as my Pocket Encyclopaedia of Wine, with the Index as the alphabetical alternative to find a name you cannot immediately place in a national or regional context. This book will not be updated every year so it leaves the question of current vintages and their maturity to its annually revised pocket-sized stablemate. Both will be much clearer if you possess *The World Atlas of Wine*, in which the regions are graphically displayed.

Each national or regional section gives the essential background information about the wines in question, then lists with succinct details the principal producers. In a few well-trodden areas the lists make themselves. In most others a complete catalogue would be as unhelpful as it would be unmanageable. My method then has been to consult first my own experience, then the advice of friends, local brokers and officials whom I have reason to respect. I have corresponded with as many producers as possible, asking them specific questions about their properties or firms, the methods, products and philosophies. Often, unfortunately, the exigencies of space have forced me to leave out good producers I would have liked to include. In most countries I have also employed intermediaries to research, interview and pass me their findings. I have tasted as many of the wines described as I could (which is why specific tasting notes go back five years).

The enjoyment of wine is a very personal thing. Yet if you love it, and spend your life among other wine lovers, you will find a remarkable consensus about which wines have the power to really thrill and satisfy us. Prejudice and narrow-mindedness have no place; preferences are what it is all about. I have not tried to hide my preferences among the fabulous variety described in this book.

Stainless steel is one of the trademarks of modern wine-making. It is increasingly replacing wood as the material for vats and storage tanks.

Modern Wine

At its simplest, wine is made by crushing grapes and allowing the yeasts naturally present on the skins to convert the sugar in their juice to alcohol. This is the process of fermentation. No more human intervention is needed than to separate the juice from the skins by pressing. Crushed and fermented like this, white grapes make white wine and red grapes red.

The art of the wine maker can be equally simply expressed. It is to choose good grapes, to carry out the crushing, fermenting and pressing with scrupulous care and hygiene, and to prepare the wine for drinking by cleaning it of yeasts and all foreign bodies. For some sorts of wine this entails ageing it as well; for others the quicker it gets to market the better.

These are the eternal verities of wine and wine-making, well understood for hundreds of years. They can be carried to perfection with no modern scientific knowledge or equipment whatever – with luck. Great wines came to be made in the places where nature, on balance, was kindest. Given a ripe crop of grapes in a healthy state, the element that determined success more than any other was the temperature of the cellar during and after the fermentation. France (but not the south), Germany, the Alps, Hungary, had these conditions. The Mediterranean and places with a similar climate did not.

If there is one innovation that has made the most difference between old and modern wine-making it is refrigeration. Refrigeration and air conditioning have added the whole zone of Mediterranean climate to the world of potentially fine wine.

But technology has advanced on a broad front. Every aspect of grape-growing and wine-making is now under a degree of control undreamed of before. These controls are now common practice in almost all the bigger and newer plants where wine is made. Its scientific basis is widely understood even in traditional areas and among small properties.

One California professor confesses that wine makers now have more controls than they know how to use. In California white-wine making is so clinically perfected that one of the main problems is deciding what sort of wine you want to make.

On the other hand, as Professor Peynaud, the leading consultant wine maker in Bordeaux, says, 'The goal of modern oenology is to avoid having to treat the wine at all.'

HOW WINE IS MADE

Wine is simply fermented grape juice. The basic techniques are explained above, variations on the theme are listed on the right.

White wine
1) Red or white grapes are put through a crusher-stemmer that crushes the grapes and tears off the stalks.
2) The broken grapes are pumped into a horizontal press.
3) The juice falls into a trough from which it is pumped into a fermenting vat.
4) Fermentation may be arrested to produce sweet or sparkling wine, or allowed to continue until all the sugar is consumed to make dry wine.

Red wine
5) Red grapes are fed through a crusher or crusher-stemmer and pumped into a vat.
6) The grapes ferment (usually with skins) until all the sugar is consumed.
7) The free-run wine runs off.
8) The skins are pressed in a hydraulic basket press. Some

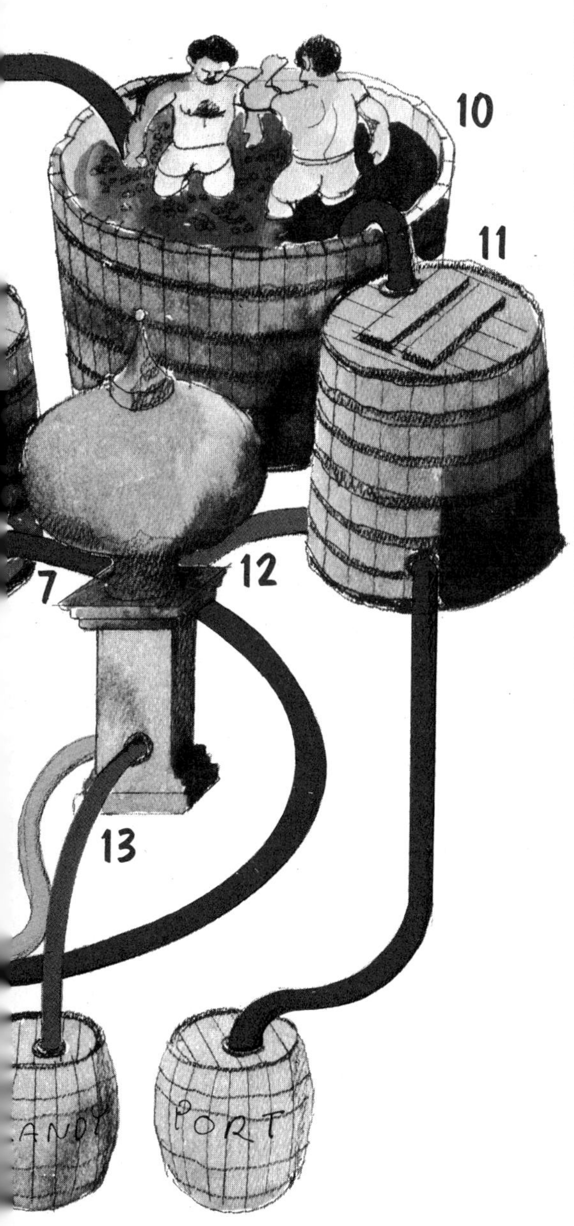

press wine is usually mixed with free-run wine.

Rosé

9) Red grapes are crushed, pumped into a fermentation vat, and almost immediately the juice is run off into another vat, having taken a pink colour from the skins.

Port

(The process is similar for other fortified wines.)

10) Red grapes are trodden in a stone trough.

11) The juice ferments in a vat until half the sugar is converted to alcohol.

12) Brandy, from a still, is added to stop fermentation.

Brandy

13) White wine is made in the normal way and distilled to produce brandy.

VARIATIONS

DRY WHITE WINES

Plain dry *or semi-dry wine of no special character, fully fermented, not intended to be aged. Usually made with non-aromatic grapes, especially in Italy, southern France, Spain, California. Outstanding examples are Muscadet and Soave. Wine-making is standard, with increasing emphasis on freshness by excluding oxygen and fermenting cool.*

Fresh, fruity, *dry to semi-sweet wines for drinking young, made from aromatic grape varieties: Riesling, Sauvignon Blanc, Gewürztraminer, Muscat Blanc, for example. Extreme emphasis on picking at the right moment, clean juice, cool fermentation and early bottling.*

Dry but full-bodied *and smooth whites usually made with a degree of 'skin contact', fermentation at a higher temperature, sometimes in barrels. Bottled after a minimum of 9 months and intended for further ageing. Chardonnay from Burgundy is the classic example. Sauvignon Blanc can be used in this way.*

SWEET WHITE WINES

Fresh, fruity, *light in alcohol, semi-sweet to sweet in the German style. Now made by fermenting to dryness and 'back-blending' with unfermented juice.*

The same style *but made by stopping fermentation while some sugar remains. Usually has higher alcohol and more winey, less obviously grapey flavour. Most French, Spanish, Italian and many New World medium-sweet wines are in this category.*

Botrytis *(noble rot) wines with balance of either low alcohol with very high sugar (German style) or very high alcohol and fairly high sugar (Sauternes style).*

Very sweet wines *made from extremely ripe or partially raisined grapes. Italian vin santo is the classic example.*

ROSE WINES

Pale rosé *from red grapes pressed immediately to extract juice with very little colour, sometimes called Vin Gris ('grey wine') or Blanc de Noirs.*

Rosé with more colour *made from red grapes crushed and saignes or 'blooded' by a short red-wine type maceration or vatting, then pressed and fermented like white wine. The more common method used for Tavel rosé, Anjou rosé, Italian Chiaretto and vin d'une nuit.*

Champagne rosé *is the only rosé traditionally made by blending red and white wines.*

RED WINES

Light, fruity *wines made with minimum tannin by short vatting on the skins. Should be drunk within a year or two as the extract, pigments and tannin necessary for maturation are absent. Can be made with aromatic grapes but are more commonly made of varieties with a simple fruity smell (e.g. Gamay) or with neutral grapes.*

Softer, richer, *more savoury and deep-coloured wines (but still low in tannin) made by macération carbonique or interior fermentation of the grapes before pressing. Heating the must is another method of producing colour and smoothness.*

Full-blooded reds *for maturing (vins de garde) made by long vatting of the skins in the juice to extract pigments, tannins, phenols, etc. All great red wines are made this way.*

FORTIFIED WINES

Vin doux naturel *is naturally very sweet wine fermented to about 15% alcohol, when further fermentation is stopped (muté) by adding spirits.*

Port *follows the vin doux naturel procedure, but fermentation is stopped earlier, at 4–6°, by a larger dose of spirits: a quarter of the volume.*

Sherry *is naturally strong white wine fully fermented to dryness. Then a small quantity of spirits is added to stabilize it while it matures in contact with air.*

Madeira *is white wine with naturally high acidity stopped with alcohol before fermentation has stopped. Then it is baked in 'stoves' before ageing in barrels or big glass jars.*

SPARKLING WINES

*White (or sometimes red) wines made to ferment a second time by adding yeast and sugar. The gas from the second fermentation dissolves in the wine. In the classic champagne method the second fermentation takes place in the bottle in which the wine is sold, involving complicated and laborious processing (**see page 174**). Less expensive methods are:*

The transfer process. *The wine is transferred, via a filter, under pressure to another bottle.*

Cuve close. *The second fermentation takes place in a tank; the wine is then filtered under pressure and bottled.*

Carbonization. *Carbon dioxide is pumped into still wine.*

The following pages summarize some of the more important modern techniques and currently held views on the many factors that affect the qualities of wine. They follow the processes of grape-growing and wine-making more or less sequentially so that they can be read as an account or referred to as a glossary. Some processes apply to white wine only, some to red, some to both.

IN THE VINEYARD

Grape Varieties

The choice of grape varieties is the most fundamental decision of all. The subject is covered, in colour and with a number of detailed distribution maps, on pages 17–32.

Source of Grapes

There are arguments both for and against growing your own grapes. Those in favour are that you have total control over the management of the vineyard and thus decide the quality of the grapes. The argument against is that an independent wine maker can pick and choose among the best grapes of specialist growers in different areas.

In France and throughout most of Europe almost all quality wine (except for most champagne) is 'home-grown'. In California the debate is more open. Wine makers who buy their grapes (almost always from the same suppliers) include some of the very best.

Virus-free Vines

Certain authorities (notably at the University of California) are convinced that the only way to achieve a healthy vineyard is to 'clean' the vine stocks in it of all virus infections. It was not appreciated until recently that the beautiful red colouring of vine leaves in autumn is generally a symptom of a virus-infected, and therefore possibly weakened, plant.

Plants can now be propagated free of virus infection by growing them very fast in a hot greenhouse, then cutting off the growing tips and using them as mini-cuttings (or micro-cuttings, growing minute pieces of the plant tissue in a nutrient jelly). The virus is always one pace behind the new growth, which is thus 'clean' and will have all its natural vigour.

It must be said on the other hand that virus elimination is not a substitute for selection of the best vines for propagation. The Office International du Vin officially declared in 1980 that 'it is a fantasy to try to establish a vineyard free of all virus diseases' and recommended its members to 'select clones resistant to dangerous virus diseases and which will still be capable, after infection, of producing a satisfactory crop both as to quality and quantity' (*see* Cloning).

Cloning

Close observation in a vineyard will tend to show that some vine branches are inherently more vigorous, bear more fruit, ripen earlier or have other desirable characteristics. These branches (and their buds) are 'mutations', genetically slightly different from the parent plant. The longer a variety has been in cultivation the more 'degenerate' and thus genetically unstable it will be, and the more mutations it will have. The Pinot family is extremely ancient and notoriously mutable.

A recent technique is to select such a branch and propagate exclusively from its cuttings. A whole vineyard can then be planted with what is in effect one identical individual plant – known as a clone. There is thus not one single Pinot Noir variety in Burgundy but scores of clones selected for different attributes. Growers who plant highly productive clones will never achieve the best-quality wine. Those who choose a shy-bearing, small-berried clone for colour and flavour must reckon on smaller crops.

One advantage of a single-clone vineyard is that all its grapes will ripen together. A disadvantage is that one problem, pest or disease will affect them all equally. Common sense seems to indicate that the traditional method of selecting cuttings from as many different healthy vines as possible (known as 'mass selection') rather than one individual, carries a better chance of long-term success.

The Choice of Rootstocks

The great majority of modern vineyards are of a selected variety of European vine grafted on to a selected American rootstock which has inbuilt resistance to the vine-killing pest phylloxera. Compatible rootstocks have been chosen and/or bred and virus-freed to be ideal for specific types of vineyard soil. Some are recommended for acid to neutral soils (such as most in California) while others flourish on the limey or alkaline soils common to most of Europe's best vineyards.

Grafting

The grafting of a 'scion' of the chosen vine variety on to an appropriate rootstock is either done at the nursery before planting ('bench grafting') or on to an already-planted rootstock in the vineyard ('field grafting'). In California recently it has become common practice for a grower to change his mind after a vine has been in production for several years, deciding that he wants (say) less Zinfandel and more Chardonnay. In this case he simply saws off the Zinfandel vine at rootstock level, just above the ground, and 'T-bud' grafts a Chardonnay scion in its place. Within two years he will have white wine instead of red.

Hybrid Vines

After the phylloxera epidemic in Europe a century ago a number of France's leading biologists started breeding hybrid vines by marrying the European classics to phylloxera-resistant American species. Once the technique of grafting the French originals on to American roots was well established the French establishment rejected these '*producteurs directes*', or 'PDs' (so-called because they produced 'directly' via their own roots). Good, hardy and productive as many of them are they are banned from all French appellation areas for fear of altering their precious identity. Their American parenthood, however, has made them highly suitable for use in the eastern United States, where hardiness is a perpetual problem (*see* page 459). They are also very popular in the new vineyards of England and New Zealand.

New Crossings of European Vines

Germany is the centre of a breeding programme quite distinct from 'hybrid' vines. Its object is to find within the genetic pool of varieties of *Vitis vinifera* a combination of desirable qualities which could supplant, in particular, the Riesling, Germany's finest vine but one that ripens relatively late, thus carrying a high risk element at vintage time. So far no cross has even remotely challenged the Riesling for flavour or hardiness – though many have for productivity, strongly aromatic juice and early ripening. The Müller-Thurgau was the first and is still the best-known example.

The University of California also has a *vinifera* breeding programme which has produced some useful additions, particularly among high-yielding grapes for hot areas which retain good aromas and acidity. The best-known examples are Ruby Cabernet (Cabernet Sauvignon × Carignan), Carnelian and Centurion (Cabernet Sauvignon × Grenache), Carmine (Cabernet Sauvignon × Merlot), Emerald Riesling (Riesling × Muscadelle) and Flora (Gewürztraminer × Semillon), all produced by Dr. Harold Olmo at Davis.

South Africa has produced the Pinotage, said to be a cross between Pinot Noir and Cinsaut (though unfortunately with none of the qualities of the former). With more than 3,000 named varieties already in circulation to choose from there seems to be a limited point in breeding for the sake of breeding.

Soil

Soil is always given pride of place in French discussions of wine quality. It is considered from two aspects: its chemical and its physical properties. Current thinking is that the latter is much the more important. Most soils contain all the chemical elements the vine needs. The physical factors that affect quality are texture, porosity, drainage, depth and even colour. In cool climates anything that tends to make the soil warm (i.e. absorb and store heat from the sun) is good. Stones on the surface store heat and radiate it at night. Darker soil absorbs more radiation. In Germany vine rows are oriented to expose the soil to the sunlight for as long as possible.

Dry soil warms up faster. Another important advantage of good deep drainage (e.g. on Médoc gravel) is the fact that it makes the vine root deep to find moisture. Deep roots are in a stable environment: a sudden downpour just before harvest will not instantly inflate the grapes with water. On the other hand experiments at Davis, California, recently have shown that where the soil is cooler than the above-ground parts of the vine the effect can be good for the grape pigments and give deep-coloured red wine. (Château Petrus on the iron-rich clay of Pomerol would seem to bear this out. St-Estèphe also has more clay and its wines often more colour than the rest of the Médoc.)

In California clay also seems to produce stable white wines that resist oxidation and therefore have a greater ability to mature. But in California over-rapid ripening often leads to wines that are low in acid and easily oxidized. The cool of clay may simply be slowing the ripening process: the very opposite of the effect required in, say, Germany.

A reasonable conclusion would be that the best soil is the soil that results in the grapes coming steadily to maturity: warm in cool areas, reasonably cool in hot areas. It should be deep enough for the roots to have constant access to moisture, since a vine under acute stress of drought closes the pores of its leaves. Photosynthesis stops and the grapes cannot develop or ripen.

Expert opinion seems to be that if the soils of the great vineyards (e.g. Bordeaux first-growths) have more available nutrients and minerals (especially potassium) it is because their owners have invested more in them. The closest scrutiny of the Côte d'Or has not revealed chemical differences between the soils of the different crus which would account for their acknowledged differences of flavour.

Sites, Slopes and Microclimates

It is conventional wisdom that wine from slopes is better. The words *côtes* and *coteaux*, meaning slopes, constantly recur in France. The obvious reasons are the increased solar radiation on a surface tipped towards the sun, meaning warmer soil, and the improved cold-air drainage, reducing the risk of frost.

A south slope is almost always the ideal, but local conditions can modify this. In areas with autumn morning fog a westerly slope is preferable, since the sun does not normally burn through the fog until the afternoon. The best slopes of the Rheingau are examples. But in Burgandy and Alsace easterly slopes have the advantage of sun all morning to warm the ground, which stores the heat while the angle of the sun decreases during the afternoon. Alsace also benefits from a particularly sunny local climate caused by the 'rain shadow' of the Vosges mountains to its west.

Many of the best Old World vineyards (e.g. in Germany, the Rhône valley, the Douro valley for port) were terraced on steep slopes to combine the advantages of the slope with some depth of soil. Being inaccessible to machinery, terraces are largely being abolished. In Germany huge earth-moving projects (known as *Fluorbereinigung*) have rebuilt whole hills to allow tractors to operate. The Douro valley is being remodelled with wide sloping terraces instead of the old narrow flat ones.

A flat valley floor (as in the Napa Valley) is the riskiest place to plant vines because cold air drains to it on spring nights when the vines have tender shoots (*see* Frost Protection).

It is noteworthy that in Burgundy the Grands Crus vineyards have a lower incidence of frost damage than the Premiers Crus – presumably because growers have observed the cold spots and lavished their attentions on the safer ones. The same is even true of the incidence of hail.

The term microclimate refers to the immediate surroundings of the vine. The slightest difference can become important in the long period between bud break and harvest. In the Rheingau wind is considered a principal enemy since it can blow out accumulated warmth from the rows – which are therefore planted across the prevailing summer southwest wind.

Another microclimatic factor is the shade and possible build-up of humidity under a dense canopy of leaves (*see* Training and Trellising). Yet another is the greater incidence of frost over soil covered with herbage than over bare earth, which makes it worth cultivating the vine rows in spring.

Irrigation

Another piece of conventional wisdom considers that any irrigation of the vines can only lower wine quality (by diluting the juice). It is hard to discern any logical distinction between rainfall and water applied by hoses or sprinklers, provided it is done within reason and at the right time (i.e. not shortly before the harvest). Irrigation is still strictly forbidden in all French appellation areas, but is standard practice in many warm countries. Australia has whole vineyard regions which would be desert without irrigation. Chile's vineyards depend on flood irrigation devised by the Incas. In California drip irrigation (by perforated hoses laid along the rows) is widely used for establishing new vine plants. The sprinkler systems installed for frost protection (q.v.) also usefully double as artificial rain in times of drought or for cooling the air in times of excessive heat. Irrigation should only take place during the period of active growth of the vine with the object of maintaining a proper balance between moisture supply to the roots and evaporation from the leaves.

Frost Control

A dormant *vinifera* vine in winter can survive temperatures down to −28°C (−18°F). In regions where lower temperatures regularly occur (in Russia and parts of eastern North America, for

Mechanical harvesting in California

example) it is common practice to bury the lower half of the vines by earthing-up in late autumn. A vine is most vulnerable to frost in spring when its new growth is green and sappy. The only old means of protection (still practised in many places) was to light stoves (sometimes called 'smudge pots') in the vineyards on clear spring nights. It was often a forlorn hope. An improvement introduced in frost-prone areas of California, for example, was a giant fan to keep the air in the vineyard moving and prevent cold air accumulating, but it has proved ineffectual without heaters as well. The latest and much the most effective protective device is the sprinkler, which simply rains heavily on the almost-freezing vine. The water freezes on contact with the young shoots and forms a protective layer of ice, which looks dangerous but acts as insulation and prevents the shoot being damaged by temperatures below freezing. Such sprinklers can be an excellent investment, doubling as a method of irrigation during dry, hot summers.

Training and Trellising

Most vineyards used to consist of innumerable individual bushes, 'head' or '*Gobelet*'-pruned back to a few buds from the short trunk after each harvest. With a few famous exceptions (among them the Moselle, parts of the Rhône, Beaujolais) most modern vineyards are 'cordoned' – that is, with the vines trained on to one, two, three or more wires parallel to the ground, supported at intervals by stakes.

Recent developments, encouraged by the need to use mechanical harvesters, have been to use higher trellising systems, often designed to spread the foliage at the top by means of a crossbar supporting two parallel wires four feet apart. The first such trellis was developed in Austria in the 1930s by Lenz Moser.

High trellises are not suitable for cool areas such as Germany, where heat radiation from the ground is essential for ripening. On the other hand they have been used immemorially in northern Portugal to produce deliberately acidic wine. Widespread 'curtains' of foliage, or 'double curtains' where the vine is made to branch on to two high supporting wires, have several advantages in warm areas. They expose a larger leaf surface for photosynthesis, at the same time shading the bunches of grapes from direct sunlight. In fertile soils which can support vigorous growth the so-called 'lyre' system, spreading the vine top into two mounds of foliage, is experimentally very successful, if not for top-quality wine, at least for good quantities of ripe grapes.

Pruning Methods

Pruning methods have been adapted to new methods of vine training where necessary. By far the most significant new development is mechanical pruning, which dispenses with skilled but laborious hand work in the depths of winter by simply treating the vine row as a hedge. Aesthetically appalling as it is, results (initially in Australia) show that a system of small circular saws straddling the vine and cutting all wood extending beyond a certain narrow compass is just as satisfactory as the practised eye and hand. Some follow-up hand pruning may be necessary, but the same method has been used in commercial apple orchards for some years with no harmful effects, and is certain to become more common in vineyards. In 1982, 40 mechanical pruners were in use in California, pruning 20,000 acres at as little as 15 per cent of the cost of hand pruning.

Growth Regulators

For many years it has been customary to trim excessively long leafy shoots from the tops and sides of vines in summer. A new development is the growth-regulating spray. Ethephon, a chemical which slowly releases ethylene gas, can be sprayed on the foliage when it has reached an ideal point of development. It inhibits further leaf growth, preventing the canopy from becoming too dense and making the plant's reserves of carbohydrates available to the fruit, instead of allowing it to waste them on useless long shoots. It apparently also encourages ripening and makes it easier for a mechanical harvester to detach the grapes from their stems.

Systemic Sprays

The traditional protection against fungus diseases such as mildew in the vineyard is 'Bordeaux mixture', a bright blue copper-sulphate solution sprayed on from a long-legged tractor (but washed off again by the next rain). New 'systemic' sprays are chemicals that are absorbed into the sap-stream of the plants and destroy their fungus (or insect) victim from inside the leaf or grape when the parasite attacks. Unfortunately fungus diseases and such pests as red-spider mites can rapidly develop resistance to specific chemicals, making it necessary for manufacturers to vary the formula (at great expense). The best-known systemic fungicide, benomyl, is now of limited use for this reason.

This glossary of modern wine techniques continues with 'From Grapes to Wine' on page 33, after the detailed treatment of grape varieties which follows.

THE VINE

A wine grower in the Clos de Vougeot has no choice about what grapes to plant. It has been a sea of Pinot Noir for centuries. Nothing else is permitted.

A wine grower in the Médoc has an important choice to make. Half a dozen varieties within the family of the Cabernets are allowed. The emphasis he places on the harsher or the smoother varieties is the basis of his house style.

A wine grower in the New World is free as air. His own taste and his view of the market are his only guide. This choice, and the debates it has started, has made all wine lovers far more grape-conscious than ever before. Not only are more and more wines named by their grape varieties, but this very fact has made the clear ascendancy of some varieties over others public knowledge.

What is a variety? It is a selection from among the infinity of forms a plant takes by natural mutation. In the basic economy of viticulture a wine grower looks first for fruitfulness, hardiness and resistance to disease in his plants. Then he looks for the ability to ripen its fruit before the end of the warm autumn weather. Lastly he looks for flavour and character.

There has been plenty of time since the discovery of wine to try out and develop different varieties. In the botanical genus *Vitis*, the vine, there are more than 20 species. The wine vine is only one, a wild woodland plant of Europe and eastern Asia, *Vitis vinifera*. It was scrambling through the treetops of France long before the idea of crushing and fermenting its grapes was imported, via Greece, from the Near East.

Nobody knows the precise origins of any of the varieties of vine that were developed locally in France, Italy, Spain, along the Danube and in the rest of wine-growing Europe. But the assumption is that they started as selections by trial from local vine varieties, possibly interbreeding with imported ones of special quality. In Germany, for instance, the Romans made the brilliant discovery of a variety with habits perfectly adapted to the cool northern climate: the Riesling, or its ancestor. Selections, adaptations or descendants from it have become all the other grapes in the German style.

There are now 4,000 or more named varieties of wine grape on earth. Perhaps 40 have really recognizable flavour and character. Of these a bare dozen have moved into international circulation, and the dozen can be narrowed again to those that have personalities so definite (and so good) that they form the basis of a whole international category of wine. They are the principal red and white grapes of Bordeaux, the same of Burgundy, the Riesling of Germany, the Gewürztraminer of Alsace and the grandfather of them all, the Muscat.

Today there is an increasing temptation to plant the champion grapes everywhere. It is a difficult argument between quality and that most precious attribute of wine – variety.

THE CLASSIC GRAPES

Riesling (Johannisberg Riesling, Rhine Riesling, White Riesling). The classic grape of Germany disputes with Chardonnay the title of the world's best white grape. The Riesling produces wines of crisp fruity acidity and transparent clarity of flavour. Even its smell is refreshing. In Germany it ranges from pale green, fragile and sharp on the Mosel to golden, exotically luscious wines, especially in the Rheinpfalz. It is remarkably versatile in warmer climates; perhaps at its most typical in Alsace, becoming more buxom in California and Australia where it ages to its unique mature bouquet of lemons and petrol more rapidly.

Chardonnay. The white Burgundy grape makes fatter, more winey and potent-feeling wine than Riesling, less aromatic when young, maturing to a rich and broad, sometimes buttery, sometimes smoky or musky smell and flavour. The finesse of Blanc de Blancs champagne, the mineral smell of Chablis, the nuttiness of Meursault, the ripe fruit smells of Napa Valley wines show its versatility. It is adapting superbly to Australia, Oregon, New Zealand, northern Italy.

Cabernet Sauvignon. The Médoc grape. Most recognizable and most versatile of red grapes, apparently able to make first-class wine in any warm soil. Small, dark, rather late-ripening berries give intense colour, strong blackcurrant and sometimes herby aroma and much tannin, which makes it the slowest wine to mature. It needs age in oak and bottle and is best of all blended with Merlot, etc., as in Bordeaux (page 48).

Pinot Noir. The red Burgundy and Champagne grape. So far apparently less adaptable to foreign vineyards, where the fine Burgundian balance is hard to achieve. Sweeter, less tannic, richer-textured than Cabernet and therefore enjoyable far younger. Never blended except in Champagne.

Gewürztraminer. The beginner's grape for its forthright spicy smell and flavour, until recently almost unique to Alsace but now spreading rapidly.

Sauvignon Blanc. The name derives from *sauvage*, wild, which could well describe its grassy or gooseberry flavour. Widespread in Bordeaux, where it is blended with Sémillon for both sweet and dry wines, but most characteristic in Sancerre. A successful transplant to the New World. It can be light and aromatic, or heavier like Chardonnay.

Muscat (de Frontignan, Muscat Blanc, Moscato Canelli). The finest of the ancient tribe of Muscats is the small white used for the sweet brown Frontignan, Asti Spumante and dry Muscats of Alsace.

Riesling

Chardonnay

Cabernet Sauvignon

Sauvignon Blanc

Pinot Noir

Gewürztraminer

Muscat

FRANCE

All of the seven classic grapes shown on pages 18 and 19 are grown to perfection in France. The Muscat, Riesling and Gewürztraminer are long-established imports, but the remaining four, the reds and whites of Burgundy and Bordeaux, appear to be France's own natives, representing an eastern and a western tradition; that of the Alps and that of the Atlantic. (They meet on the Loire.)

The map shows a selection of the other grapes that make up this great tradition. Nobody can say with confidence how many there are all told: a single variety may have four or five different names in different areas quite close together – or indeed the grape may be a local strain and not quite the same variety. Some 95 of these local characters, ranging from such common plants as the red Carignan of the Midi (there are more than 400,000 acres) to such rare ones as the white Tressallier (limited to one tiny zone), are plotted here as close to home as possible.

Gamay
The Beaujolais grape bears the name of a village in the Côte d'Or, but it has found its perfect home in the light soils of southern Burgundy, where it makes the world's most gaily flowing mealtime wine.

RED GRAPE VARIETIES

Abouriou grown in Cahors; also known as 'Gamay du Rhône'.
Aléatico muscat var. of Corsica, makes a wine of the same name.
Alicante syn. of Grenache.
Alicante-Bouschet prolific var. of southern table-wine vineyards.
Aramon high-yielding southern table-wine var.
Aspiran an old var. of the Languedoc.
Auxerrois syn. of Malbec in Cahors.
Bouchet syn. of Cabernet Franc in St-Emilion.
Braquet main var. of Bellet, near Nice.
Brocol local Gaillac var.
CABERNET FRANC high-quality cousin of Cabernet Sauvignon used in Bordeaux (esp. St-Emilion) and on the Loire.
CABERNET SAUVIGNON *see* p18.
Cahors syn. of Malbec.
CARIGNAN the leading bulk-wine producer of the Midi; harmless but dull.
Carmenère archaic Bordeaux name for Cabernet.
César tannic traditional var. of Irancy (Yonne).
CINSAUT prominent southern Rhône var. that is used in Châteauneuf-du-Pape, etc.
Cot syn. of Malbec in the Loire.
Duras local Gaillac var.
Fer or **Ferservadou** used in VDQS Vins de Marcillac in the southwest.
Fuelle Noir Bellet var.
GRENACHE powerful but pale red used in Châteauneuf-du-Pape, for rosés (e.g. Tavel) and dessert wines in Roussillon.
Grolleau or **Groslot** common Loire red used in, for example, Anjou Rosé.
Grosse Vidure syn. of Cabernet Franc.
Jurançon Noir Gaillac (Tarn) grape – not used in Jurançon.
MALBEC important var. now fading from the best Bordeaux but basic to Cahors.
Malvoisie used for dessert wines (VDN) in Roussillon.
Mataro syn. of Mourvèdre.
MERLOT essential element in fine Bordeaux; the dominant grape of Pomerol.
MEUNIER or PINOT MEUNIER inferior 'dusty-leaved' version of Pinot Noir 'tolerated' in Champagne.
MONDEUSE chief red of Savoie.
MOURVEDRE tolerable Midi grape (also grown in northeast Spain).
Négrette var. of Malbec grown in Frontonnais.
Nielluccio Corsican var.
Noirien syn. of Pinot Noir.
PETIT VERDOT high-quality subsidiary grape of Bordeaux.
Pineau d'Aunis local to the Loire valley, esp. Anjou.
PINOT NOIR *see* p18.
Portugais Bleu widespread in the southwest, especially Gaillac.
Poulsard Jura var. blended with Trousseau.
Pressac St-Emilion syn. for Malbec.
Sciacarello Corsican var.
SYRAH widespread and the great grape of Hermitage (Rhône), blended in Châteauneuf-du-Pape.
Tannat tannic var. of the southwest, esp. Madiran.
Tempranillo Spanish (Rioja) var. grown in the Midi.
Trousseau majority grape in Jura reds but inferior to Poulsard.
Valteliner or **Velteliner** pink Savoie var., alias Malvoisie.
Vidure, Petit, syn. of Cabernet Sauvignon.

For white grape varieties, see page 22.

Reims
Marne
Seine
CHARDONNAY
MEUNIER
CHAMPAGNE
PARIS
PINOT NOIR
Moselle
Strasbourg
RIESLING
MUSCAT
ALSACE
CHASSELAS
GEWURZTRAMINER
Seine
YONNE
César
Chablis
CHARDONNAY
Loire
Angers
Tours
CHENIN BLANC
LOIRE
FOLLE BLANCHE
GAMAY
MUSCADET
Nantes
Gros Plant
Grolleau
CAB.FRANC
Cot
Pouilly
PINOT NOIR
CHASSELAS
Cher
PINOT NOIR
JURA
Savagnin
Poulsard
Trousseau
BURGUNDY
ALIGOTE
Vienne
GAMAY
CHARDONNAY
SAUV.BLANC
Allier
Loire
GAMAY
Tresallier
PINOT NOIR
Lyon
SAVOIE
MONDEUSE
Jaquère
Rhône
Isère
Tannat
Charente
Colombard
Cognac
FOLLE BLANCHE
St-Emilion
MERLOT
Frontignan
Blaye
St-Emilion
Dordogne
CAB.SAUV.
MERLOT
Bordeaux
CAB.FRANC
SAUV.BLANC
UGNI BLANC
MALBEC
PETIT VERDOT
MUSCADELLE
SEMILLON
SAUVIGNON BLANC
Garonne
Auxerrois
Lot
MALBEC
Cahors
Fer
Tarn
Duras
Port.Bleu
GAMAY
Gaillac
Brocol
Négrette
Mauzac
CAB.SAUV.
SYRAH
Baïse
Garonne
Picpoul
Tannat
Béarn
Jurançon
Adour
CAB.FRANC
CAB.SAUV.
SYRAH
GAMAY
SYRAH
GRENACHE
CINSAUT
MUSCAT
Durance
Alicante-Bouschet
Aramon
CAB.SAUV.
Aspiran
LANGUEDOC
CINSAUT
MOURVEDRE
CARIGNAN
MERLOT
GRENACHE
CINSAUT
MOURVEDRE
PROVENCE
UGNI BLANC
Rolle
GRENACHE
Braquet
Fuelle Noir
Nice
Alicante-Bouschet
Tempranillo
Aramon
CHARDONNAY
UGNI BLANC
MACABEU
Malvoisie
CARIGNAN
GRENACHE
ROUSSILLON
Aude
CHARDONNAY
CAB.SAUV.
GAMAY MAIN RED GRAPE VARIETIES
Tannat Other red grape varieties
ALIGOTE MAIN WHITE GRAPE VARIETIES
Arbois Other white grape varieties
Vineyard areas
AOC and VDQS areas
Km. 0
80
160
240
Miles 0
80
160

Chenin Blanc
Almost neutral in flavour, Chenin Blanc of the Loire possesses an inbuilt balance of strength and acidity that makes it capable of many styles from fresh and appley to old, brown and buttery.

Sémillon
The one grape that makes only truly great wine when it rots. Sémillon is grown and blended with Sauvignon in Bordeaux because of its proclivity to rot nobly in a misty autumn.

ALIGOTE secondary Burgundy grape of high acidity. Wines for drinking young.
ALTESSE Savoie var. Wines are sold as 'Roussette'.
Arbois main white or tinted var. of Touraine.
Arruffiac Béarnais var. (Pacherenc du Vic Bilh).
Auvergnat or **Auvernat** Loire term for the Pinot family.
Baroque used in Béarn for Pacherenc du Vic Bilh.
Beaunois syn. of Chardonnay at Chablis.
Beurot syn. in Burgundy of Pinot Gris.
Blanc Fumé syn. of Sauvignon at Pouilly-sur-Loire.
Blanquette syn. of Mauzac.
Bourboulenc Midi (Minervois, La Clape) var., also goes into (red) Châteauneuf-du-Pape.
Camaralet Jurançon var.
CHARDONNAY *see* p18.
CHASSELAS neutral var. used in Pouilly-sur-Loire and Alsace.
CLAIRETTE common neutral-flavoured Midi grape, also makes sparkling Rhône Clairette de Die.
Colombard minor Bordelais grape.
Courbu Madiran var. (alias Sarrat).
FOLLE BLANCHE formerly the chief Cognac grape, also grown in Bordeaux and Britanny.
Frontignan syn. of Ugni Blanc in Blaye, Bordeaux.
Gamay Blanc syn. of Chardonnay in the Jura.
GEWÜRZTRAMINER *see* p18.
Gros Manseng one of the main grapes of Jurançon.
Gros Plant syn. of Folle Blanche in the western Loire.
Jaquère the grape of Apremont and Chignin in Savoie.
Jurançon Blanc minor Cognac var. (not in Jurançon).
Klevner name used for Pinot Blanc in Alsace.
Loin de l'Oeil south-western var. used in Gaillac.
MACABEU or MACCABEO Catalan var. used in Roussillon for dessert 'VDN'. A sort of Malvoisie.
Malvoisie syn. of Bourboulenc in the Midi.
MARSANNE with Roussanne the white grape of Hermitage (northern Rhône).
Mauzac used in Blanquette de Limoux and Gaillac.
Morillon syn. of Chardonnay.
MUSCADELLE minor, slightly muscat-flavoured var. used in Sauternes.
MUSCADET gives its name to the wine of the western Loire.
MUSCAT *see* p18.
Nature syn. of Savagnin at Arbois.
Ondenc Gaillac var.
Petit Manseng southwestern var. used in Jurançon, etc.
Petite Sainte Marie syn. of Chardonnay in Savoie.
Picpoul syn. of Folle Blanche in Armagnac, the southern Rhône and the Midi (Picpoul de Pinet).
Pineau de la Loire syn. in the Loire of Chenin Blanc (not a Pinot).
Pinot Blanc closely related to Pinot Noir; grown in Burgundy, Champagne and Alsace.
Pinot Gris (Tokay d'Alsace) a mutation of the Pinot Noir, widespread in Alsace.
Piquepoul *see* Picpoul.
RIESLING *see* p18.
Rolle Italian Vermentino in Provence.
Romorantin grown only at Cheverny on the Loire; makes dry, often sharp wine.
Roussanne (with Marsanne) makes white Hermitage.
Roussette syn. of Altesse in Savoie.
Sacy minor var. of Champagne and the Yonne.
St-Emilion syn. of Ugni Blanc in Cognac.
SAUVIGNON BLANC *see* p18.
SAVAGNIN the 'yellow wine' grape of Château-Chalon (Jura); related to Gewürztraminer.
Sylvaner the workhorse light-wine grape of Alsace.
Traminer *see* Gewürztraminer.
Tresallier var. of the extreme upper Loire (St-Pourçain-sur-Sioule), now fading.
UGNI BLANC common Midi grape; Italy's Trebbiano; 'St-Emilion' in Cognac.
Vermentino Italian grape known in Provence as Rolle; possibly the Malvoisie of Corsica.
Viognier rare aromatic grape of Condrieu in the northern Rhône.

ITALY

Italy's grape catalogue is probably the longest of all. With wine-growing so universal a factor of Italian life, uninterrupted for millennia before the phylloxera, local selection has blurred the origins and relationships of many varieties beyond recall. Is the fish caught off Tunisia and called by an Arab name the same as a similar one caught in the Adriatic and called by a name peculiar to the Romagna? Italian grapes are scarcely less slippery a subject.

In general their selection has been on the grounds of productivity and good health, along with adaptability to the soil and reliable ripening, rather than great qualities of flavour or ability to age. The mass of Italian grapes are therefore sound rather than inspiring; their flavours muted or neutral. The only international classic to (maybe) come from Italy is the (Gewürz)traminer, from the South Tyrol.

But once you start to list the exceptions, the Italian grapes with personality and potentially excellent quality, it does seem strange that more of them have not yet made a real name for themselves in the world. The Nebbiolo, the Barbera, the Teroldego, the Brunello, the Montepulciano, the Aglianico are reds with much to offer. There are fewer first-class whites, but Cortese, Greco, Tocai, Verdicchio and Vernaccia all make original contributions, and the Moscato of Piedmont, while not exclusively Italian, is a very Italian interpretation of the most ancient of grapes.

More and more is being heard of Cabernet, Merlot, Pinot Bianco and even Chardonnay and Rhine Riesling. The northeast is now almost as international in its ampelography as any of the wine areas of the New World. The appearance of Cabernet and Chardonnay in Chianti in recent years is an important sign of changes in the wind.

The central question over the future of Italian wine is how far she will defend her traditions (which is the purpose of the DOC legislation) in sticking to her indigenous grapes, and how far she will bow to the international trend – as she is tending to do in wine-making techniques.

For the moment, while the world is still only beginning to learn what variety Italy offers, she will do well to develop her native flavours to the full. They include as wide a range as the wines of any country – France included.

As the map on the following page shows, there is little of agricultural Italy where no grapes at all are grown. On the map, areas of intensive viticulture are distinguished from areas where wine-growing may be important but wines are anonymous, and the

Nebbiolo
The greatest grape of Piedmont, the base of Barolo, Barbaresco, Gattinara, etc., is named for the fog, 'nebbia', of the northwestern autumn. Its wine varies from smoothly fruity to biting black, ageing superbly.

Trebbiano Toscano
The common white grape of central Italy, known in France as Ugni Blanc; a component of (red) Chianti. Its wine is low in acidity and aroma, pleasantly soft but easily oxidized.

grape varieties listed on page 25 are located in the regions where they play a dominant role – although a dozen or so varieties are found as major performers or supporting actors in many different regions. Barbera, Trebbiano, Sangiovese, for example, appear on the map in capitals where they are most prominent and in small letters elsewhere.

There is no general rule on the mention of grape varieties on labels: local custom dictates whether the wine is labelled by place, grape or a name unrelated to either. With the current increase in variety consciousness, it seems likely that producers will make more of the grape varieties in future – at least on wines destined for export.

RED GRAPE VARIETIES

Aglianico source of full-bodied Taurasi in Campania and Aglianico del Vulture in Basilicata.
Aleatico muscat-flavoured grape used for dark dessert wines in Latium, Apulia and elsewhere.
Barbera dark, acidic Piedmont var. widely grown in the NW.
Bombino Nero used in Apulia's Castel del Monte *rosato*.
Bonarda minor var. widespread in Lombardy and Piedmont.
Brachetto makes pleasant, fizzy Piedmont wines.
Brunello di Montalcino a noble strain of Tuscany's Sangiovese.
Cabernet widespread in the NE; increasing elsewhere.
Calabrese source of Sicilian DOC Cerasuolo light reds.
Cannonau leading dark var. of Sardinia for DOC wines.
Carignano (French Carignan), prominent in Sardinia.
Cesanese good Latium red.
Chiavennasca Nebbiolo in Valtellina, N Lombardy.
Corvina Veronese main grape of Valpolicella, Recioto, Bardolino.
Croatina much used in Lombardy's Oltrepò Pavese.
Dolcetto low-acid Piedmont var., source of several DOCs.
Freisa Piedmont var., makes sweet, often fizzy wines.
Gaglioppo source of most Calabrian reds, inc. Cirò.
Grignolino makes light, pleasant wines around Asti in Piedmont.
Guarnaccia red var. of Campania, esp. Ischia.
Lagrein grown in Alto Adige for faintly bitter reds and dark rosés.
Lambrusco prolific source of Emilia's effervescent wines.
Malbec seen occasionally in Apulia and Venezia.
Malvasia Nera makes sweet, fragrant, sometimes sparkling DOC reds in Piedmont; also a fine dessert wine in Apulia.
Marzemino dark grape grown in Trentino and Lombardy.
Merlot Bordeaux native widely grown in Italy, esp. in the NE.
Monica makes Sardinian DOC reds.
Montepulciano dominant dark var. of Abruzzi; Molise.
Negroamaro potent Apulian var. of the Salento peninsula.
Nerello Mascalese Sicilian grape, source of Etna reds and rosés.
Petit Rouge used in some Valle d'Aosta reds.
Piedirosso or **Per'e Palummo** features in Campanian reds.
Pinot Nero Burgundy's Pinot Noir, grown in much of NE Italy.
Primitivo Apulian grape, said to be Zinfandel.
Raboso worthy Veneto native.
Refosco source of dry, full-bodied Friuli DOC reds. Known as Mondeuse in France.
Rossese fine Ligurian var., makes DOC at Dolceacqua.
Sangiovese mainstay of Chianti and one of Italy's most widely planted vines.
Schiava widespread in Alto Adige.
Spanna syn. for Nebbiolo.
Teroldego unique to Trentino, makes Teroldego Rotaliano.
Tocai Rosso or **Tocai Nero** makes DOC red in Veneto's Colli Berici.
Uva di Troia main grape of several DOC wines in N Apulia.
Vespolina often blended with Nebbiolo in E Piedmont.

WHITE GRAPE VARIETIES

Albana Romagna grape, makes dry and semi-sweet wines.
Arneis Piedmont var. that is enjoying a revival.
Biancolella native of Ischia.
Blanc de Valdigne source in Valle d'Aosta of Blanc de Morgex, Blanc de La Salle.
Bombino Bianco main grape of Apulia's San Severo *bianco*; in Abruzzi, known as Trebbiano d'Abruzzo.
Bosco in Liguria the main ingredient of Cinqueterre.
Carricante main Etna white.
Catarratto widely grown in W Sicily; used in Marsala, Bianco d'Alcamo, etc.
Chardonnay grown in Trentino-Alto Adige, Veneto and Friuli.
Cortese used in S Piedmont's finest whites; found also in Lombardy's Oltrepò Pavese.
Fiano in Campania makes Fiano di Avellino.
Forastera partners Biancolella in Ischia *bianco*.
Garganega main grape of Soave.
Greco Campania's best white.
Grillo figures, usually with Catarratto, in Marsala.
Inzolia used in Sicilian whites, inc. Marsala and Corvo *bianco*.
Malvasia common for both dry and sweet wines, esp. in Latium (for Frascati, etc.).
Moscato widespread in sparkling wines (e.g. Asti Spumante) and dessert wines (e.g. the Moscatos of Sicily).
Müller-Thurgau increasing in Friuli, Trentino-Alto Adige.
Nuragus ancient Sardinian grape.
Picolit Friuli source of Italy's most expensive dessert wine.
Pigato grown only in SW Liguria; makes good table wines.
Pinot Bianco Burgundy's Pinot Blanc, grown all over N Italy. Weissburgunder in Alto Adige.
Prosecco prominent in Veneto, mainly for sparkling wines.
Rheinriesling *see* Riesling Renano.
Riesling Italico not a true Riesling, probably native to NE Italy. Used in DOCs.
Riesling Renano the Rhine Riesling, superior to Riesling Italico.
Sauvignon grown in parts of NE Italy for DOC varietals.
Tocai Friulano used for DOC whites in Lombardy and Veneto as well as in its native Friuli.
Traminer native of Alto Adige.
Trebbiano d'Abruzzo *see* Bombino Bianco.
Verdeca Apulian grape used in southern DOC whites.
Verdicchio main light grape of the Marches.
Verduzzo Friulian var. used also in the Veneto for both dry and dessert wines.
Vermentino source of DOC white in Sardinia and good table wines in Liguria.
Vernaccia di Oristano in Sardinia makes a sherry-like dessert wine.
Vernaccia di San Gimignano ancient Tuscany var., wine of the same name.

Pinot Grigio
France's Pinot Gris (Ruländer in Germany) is one of the successes of northeast Italy, where it can make first-class full-bodied fruity wine.

GERMANY

The international reputation of German wine for a unique effect of flowery elegance is based on one grape alone: the Riesling. But the widespread use of the Riesling as we know it is probably no more than two or three hundred years old. Germany has several old varieties of local importance which continue to hold their own. More significantly, her vine breeders have been struggling for a century to produce a new vine that offers Riesling quality without its inherent disadvantage – ripening so late in the autumn that every vintage is a cliffhanger. The centenary of the first important Riesling cross (with Silvaner) was celebrated in 1982. The past 100 years have seen its fruit, the Müller-Thurgau,

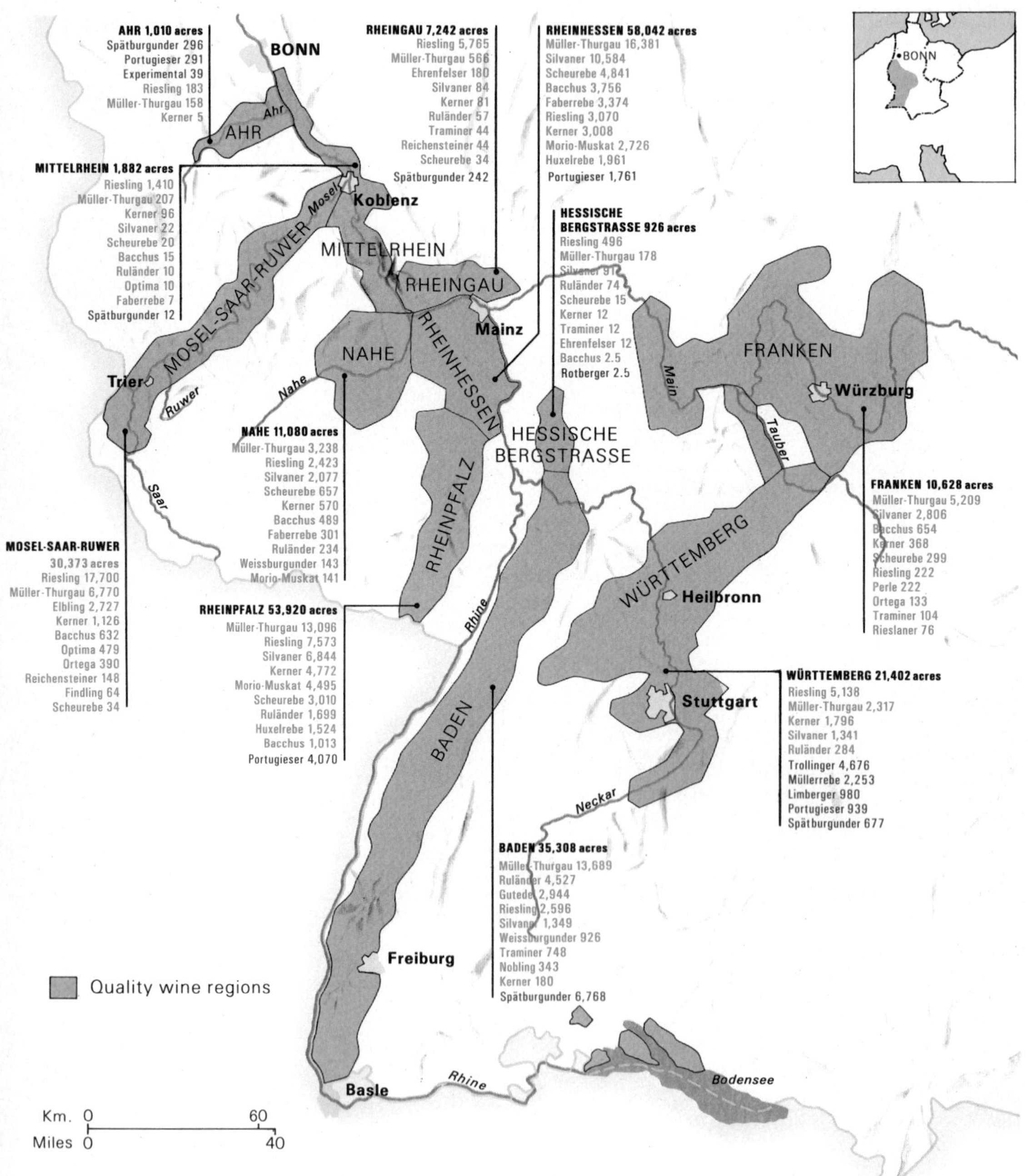

become Germany's most popular grape, with 61,000 acres planted. (Riesling is an easy second, with 45,400 acres.)

Yet none of the new varieties, not even the Müller-Thurgau, has supplanted Riesling in the best and warmest vineyards. None has achieved more than either a sketch or a caricature of its brilliant balance and finesse. Nor have any survived such ultimate tests of hardiness as January 1979, when the temperature dropped by 40 degrees, to −20°F (−29°C), in 24 hours. Thousands of vines were killed. Riesling survived.

Eighty per cent of the German vineyard is white. Of the 12 per cent that is red, Spätburgunder (Pinot Noir) is marginally more widely planted than the inferior Portugieser, and twice as common as Trollinger. The map shows the acreages of the most widely planted varieties, white and red, region by region, together with the total vineyard area under cultivation for each region.

GRAPE VARIETIES

Bacchus a new early-ripening cross of (Silvaner × Riesling) × Müller-Thurgau. Spicy but rather soft wines, best as Ausleses, frequently used as *Süssreserve*.
Ehrenfelser (Riesling × Silvaner). A good new cross, between Müller-Thurgau and Riesling in quality.
Elbling once the chief grape of the Mosel, now only grown high upriver. Neutral and acidic but clean and good in sparkling wine.
Faber Weissburgunder × Müller-Thurgau, with a certain following in Rheinhessen and the Nahe.
Gewürztraminer *see* p18.
Gutedel south Baden name for the Chasselas, or Swiss Fendant. Light, refreshing but short-lived wine.
Huxelrebe (Gutedel × Courtillier musqué). A prolific new variety, very aromatic, with good sugar and acidity. Popular in Rheinhessen.
Morio-Muskat 7,000 acres. It is hard to believe that this early-ripening cross of Silvaner and Weissburgunder has no Muscat blood. The wine it makes in Rheinpfalz and Rheinhessen is good but often too blatant and best blended with something more neutral (e.g. Müller-Thurgau).
Optima (Silvaner × Riesling × Müller-Thurgau). An improvement on Bacchus, particularly in Rheinpfalz. Delicately spicy.
Ortega (Müller-Thurgau × Siegerrebe). Very early ripening, aromatic and spicy with good balance. On trial on the Mosel and in Franken.
Perle (Gewürztraminer × Müller-Thurgau). A very aromatic new cross under trial in Franken.
Reichensteiner Müller-Thurgau × (Madeleine angevine × Calabreser Fröhlich). A Euro-cross, slightly better for both sugar and acid than Müller-Thurgau.
Riesling *see* p18.
Scheurebe the second cross (Riesling × Silvaner) to become celebrated, now well established (Rheinhessen, Rheinpfalz) for highly aromatic, often unsubtle wine. At its best when sweet.
Silvaner a late ripener like the Riesling, also badly affected by drought in light or thin soils, steadily giving ground to Müller-Thurgau and others. Scarcely noble, but at its best (in Franken and Rheinhessen) the true yeoman; blunt, trustworthy, with unsuspected depths.
Weissburgunder (Pinot Blanc) makes good fresh full-bodied wine in Baden.

Kerner
The most successful of the new crosses (Riesling × Trollinger), an early-ripening understudy for Riesling, which it superficially resembles in liveliness and balance. A Muscat aroma betrays it.

Müller-Thurgau
Germany's most widely grown grape is the elder brother of many compromises between the ultimate quality of Riesling and such mundane matters as early ripening and heavy crops.

SPAIN AND PORTUGAL

Spain and Portugal have been net exporters, rather than importers, of grape varieties. A few of the international varieties have been planted, but they have certainly not yet taken hold in a way that radically alters the wine, whereas their grapes exported to the world include the Palomino (to California, South Africa and Australia), the Verdelho (to Australia) and, probably, the Carignan, much the most widespread red grape of the South of France.

There are few 'varietals' in Spain and Portugal. Most wines contain proportions of at least three grapes, balanced for their qualities. The most notable exceptions are the four varietals of Madeira: Sercial, Verdelho, Bual and Malmsey.

Tempranillo
The basis of Rioja, especially Rioja Alavesa. Grown in most parts of Spain as, for example, Ull de Llebra in Catalonia, Cencibel in La Mancha and Valdepeñas.

RED GRAPE VARIETIES

Agua Santa early-ripening red of Bairrada, giving stronger wine than the Baga.
Alvarelhão Dão variety, also grown for port.
Azal red grape with high tartaric acid, used for *vinho verde.*
Bastardo a rather pale and low-acid but aromatic and well-balanced grape used for port and in Dão.
Baga dark, tannic, potentially noble grape of Bairrada.
Borraçal red *vinho verde* grape providing high malic acidity.
Cabernet Sauvignon slowly being planted in Spain, e.g. Penedés for Torres' Gran Coronas, in Navarra by Sarria at Vega Sicilia and by Riscal in Rioja.
Cariñena Carignan in France, originated in Cariñena (Aragón) but now more grown in Catalonia.
Castelão a minor Bairrada red, soft and neutral.
Cencibel syn. in La Mancha and Valdepeñas for Tempranillo.
Garnacha Tinta used in Rioja Baja for powerful, if pale Riojas, also Penedés, and Navarra where it dominates. Syn. French Grenache Noir.
Graciano the most 'elegant' and aromatic of Rioja grapes, gives quick-maturing wine.
Jaen a constituent of red Dão.
Mazuelo a Riojan red grape, possibly syn. for Cariñena.
Mencía used in León and Galicia for light reds.
Monastrell a widely grown red of good colour and texture, especially in Penedés, the Levante and Valdepeñas.
Mourisco Semente a minor grape of port and the north of Portugal.

Madeira

Officially regulated wine regions

Other wine-producing regions

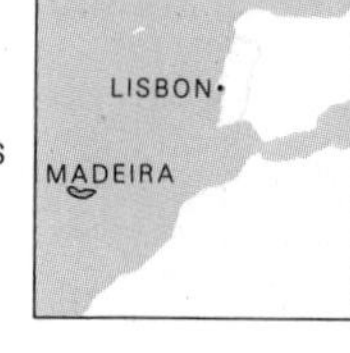

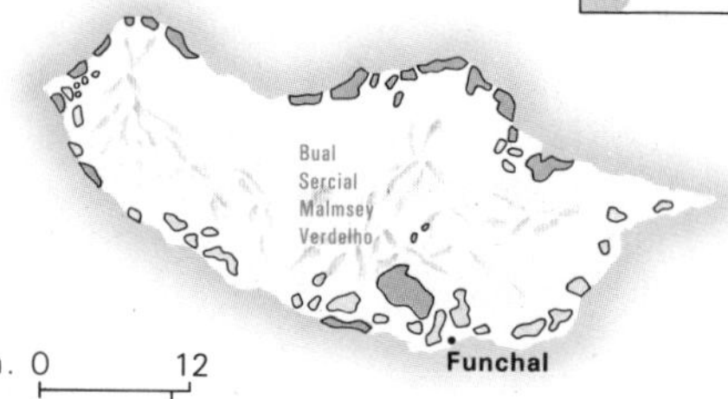

Km. 0 12
Miles 0 6

Palomino
Palomino Bianco is the great sherry grape, in two subvarieties: Basto and (more common) Fino. It is also grown in León, Huelva and elsewhere.

Pinot Noir Torres grows Pinot for his red Santa Digna. Also found in Navarra.
Ramisco the tannic, blue-black secret of Colares. Needs very long ageing.
Samsó Penedés variety.
Souzão deeply coloured and excellent port grape.
Tinto Aragonés a form of Garnacha Tinta; one of the grapes of Vega Sicilia.
Tinta Pinheira minor Bairrada variety; pale, low acid but alcoholic.
Tintorera one of the Valdepeñas grapes.
Touriga Nacional big-yielding port variety, also used in Dão.
Ull de Llebre Penedés synonym for Tempranillo.
Vinhão *vinho verde* red grown for its relatively high alcohol.

WHITE GRAPE VARIETIES

Airén *see* Lairén.
Albariño the best Galician variety for clean, dry, often *pétillant* whites, also grown in Portugal for *vinho verde*.
Albillo used, with red grapes, in Vega Sicilia.
Arinto used for white Dão and Bairrada and to make the rare, dry Bucelas and sweet Carcavelos.
Barcelos recommended white Dão variety.
Bical fragrant and fine Bairrada white, complementary to the sharper Arinto.
Bual sweet Madeira grape with luscious flavours, also used in Carcavelos and Alentejo.
Chardonnay only experimentally grown in Spain, e.g. by Torres.
Gouveio minor white-port variety.
Lairén (alias Airén) the main white grape of Valdepeñas and La Mancha.
Listan syn. of Palomino.
Macabeo syn. in Catalonia of Viura. Used for sparkling wines.
Malvasía important white grape in port, Rioja, Navarra, Catalonia and the Canary Islands.
Maria Gomes the principal white grape of Bairrada.
Moscatel widespread sweet wine grape.
Pansa grown in Alella. Syn. of Xarel-lo of Penedés.
Parellada used in Penedés for delicately fruity whites and sparklers.
Pedro Ximénez grown for blending in Jerez, Málaga, and the principal in Montilla: dried, it adds intense sweetness and colour.
Traminer used (with Moscatel) by Torres for Viña Esmerelda.
Verdelho white Dão variety, better known in Madeira.
Viura the principal grape of white Rioja, also Navarra. Alias Macabeo.
Xarel-lo Catalan grape, important in Penedés.
Zalema main variety in *vino generoso* of Huelva, being replaced by Palomino.

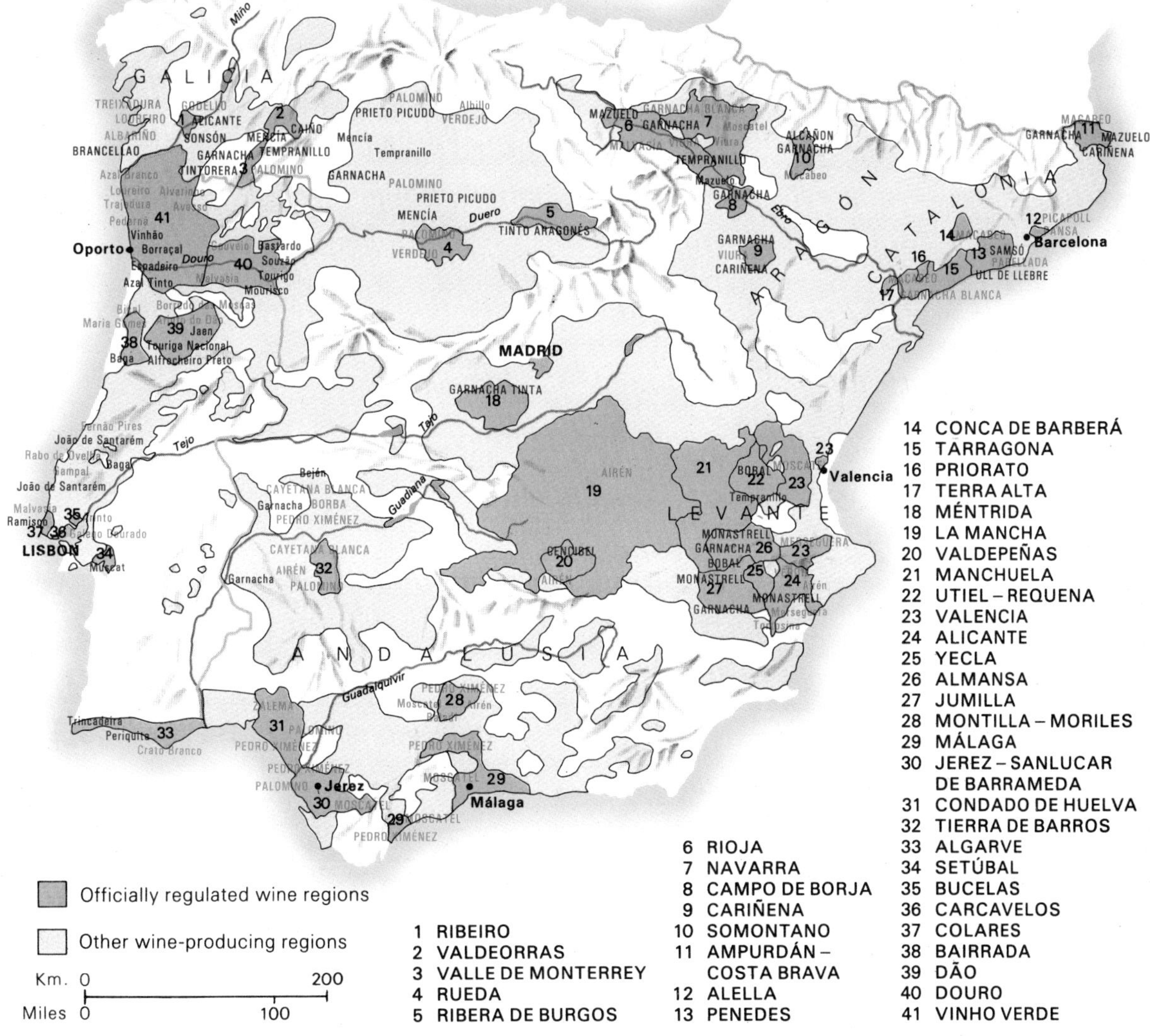

CALIFORNIA

Zinfandel
The one (good) grape that is California's own – a generous giver of versatile, fruity, sometimes spicy (but sometimes metallic) wine in any style from Beaujolais to port. It may be the Primitivo from the south of Italy.

California's vigorous and uninhibited experimentation with grape varieties in her multifarious microclimates has already proved that Cabernet Sauvignon and Chardonnay can be grown to perfection. It is now rapidly demonstrating that Riesling, Pinot Noir and Gewürztraminer can be ideally accommodated. Petite Sirah and Semillon have also made noble wine, though so far only in very small quantities.

From the 1930s on, the School of Viticulture of the University of California at Davis has insisted that varieties must be carefully matched to microclimates, and has surveyed the State thoroughly to establish its five climate regions (plotted opposite and described on page 413). The cooler climate zones where the finest varieties for table wines develop a good balance of acidity with sugar are all in the coastal counties mapped here.

The State is now in the process of matching supply and demand of the best grapes while searching for ideal vineyards, often in places where no vine has grown before. While the potential of the well-established counties of Napa, Alameda, Santa Clara and, to some extent, Santa Cruz and Sonoma is well known, recent bold plantings in Monterey, San Luis Obispo, Santa Barbara, Mendocino and elsewhere are only beginning to show their worth.

The diagrams opposite – each crate of grapes represents up to 500 acres harvested – show how dynamic this process was in the seven years 1974 to 1981, for each of the four top-quality varieties. On pages 418 and 419 the State-wide increases of other varieties are given for the whole decade.

These past trends can be plotted easily enough. It is safe to forecast an increasing acreage of white grapes, particularly Chardonnay: it fetches by far the highest price, averaging $1,097 a ton in 1981. (The average Cabernet price was $491.) To speculate about further developments is not so easy, but it is unlikely that growers will specialize as narrowly as they do in Europe. There is an insurance policy against both market changes and untimely storms in having a portfolio of varieties. It would be desirable to see trials of some of the many varieties that California has not yet planted on any worthwhile scale. The true Syrah of the Rhône, for example, is almost unknown, and there are a dozen others that should be tried.

Ultimately perhaps California will develop away from 'varietal' wines to wholly indigenous styles arrived at with blends untried in Europe. Creative wine-making like this should be right up her street.

Emerald Riesling
New California-bred varieties are designed to make refreshing wines in a hot climate. Emerald Riesling is one of the best known, with attractively lively flavours.

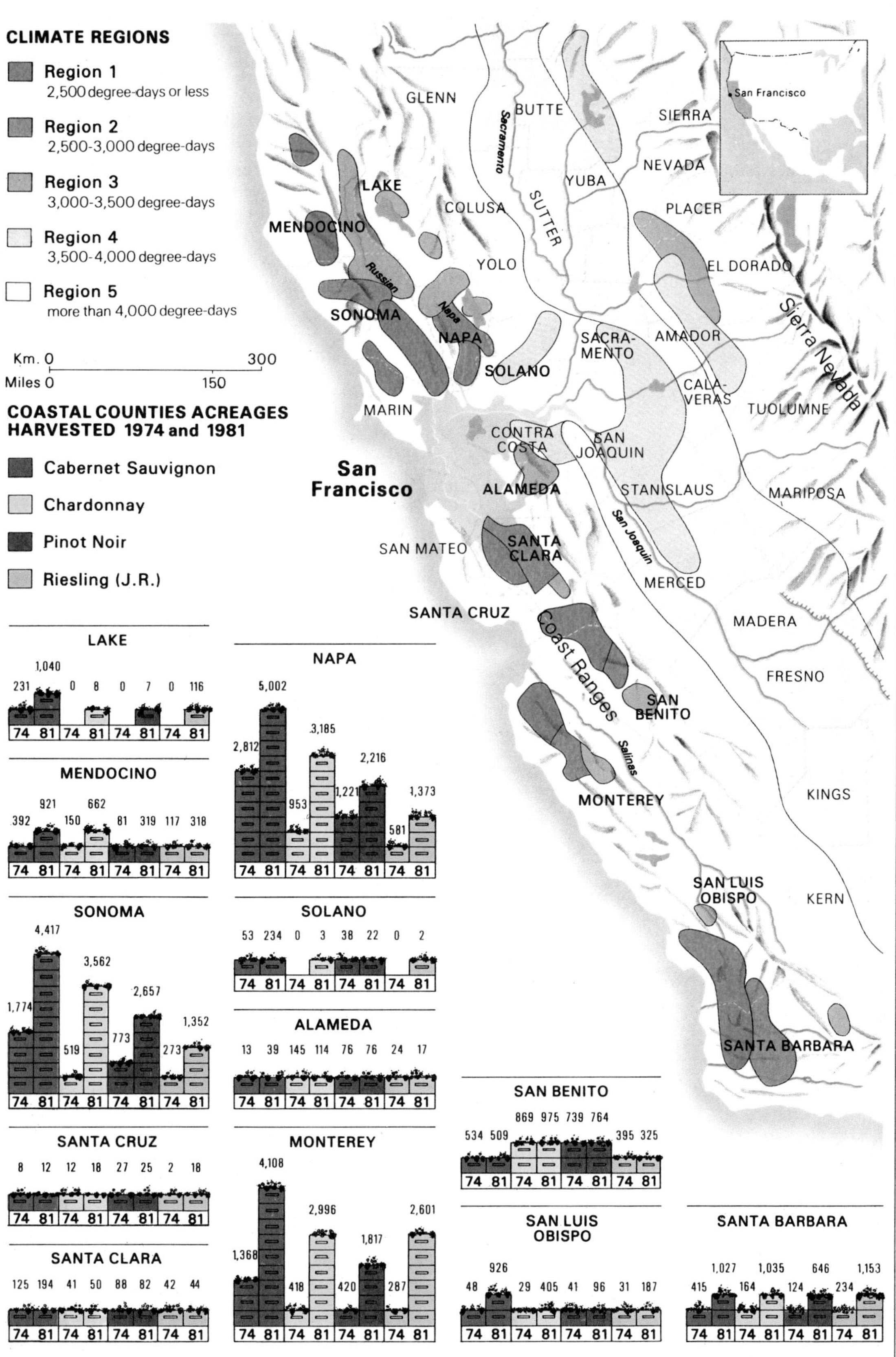
CLIMATE REGIONS
Region 1
2,500 degree-days or less
Region 2
2,500-3,000 degree-days
Region 3
3,000-3,500 degree-days
Region 4
3,500-4,000 degree-days
Region 5
more than 4,000 degree-days
Km. 0 300
Miles 0 150
COASTAL COUNTIES ACREAGES HARVESTED 1974 and 1981
Cabernet Sauvignon
Chardonnay
Pinot Noir
Riesling (J.R.)
San Francisco
GLENN
BUTTE
Sacramento
SIERRA
NEVADA
LAKE
COLUSA
SUTTER
YUBA
PLACER
MENDOCINO
Russian
YOLO
EL DORADO
Sierra Nevada
SONOMA
Napa
NAPA
SOLANO
SACRA-MENTO
AMADOR
CALA-VERAS
TUOLUMNE
MARIN
CONTRA COSTA
SAN JOAQUIN
San Francisco
ALAMEDA
STANISLAUS
MARIPOSA
SAN MATEO
SANTA CLARA
San Joaquin
MERCED
SANTA CRUZ
Coast Ranges
MADERA
FRESNO
SAN BENITO
Salinas
MONTEREY
KINGS
SAN LUIS OBISPO
KERN
SANTA BARBARA
LAKE
231 1,040 0 8 0 7 0 116
74 81 74 81 74 81 74 81
MENDOCINO
392 921 150 662 81 319 117 318
74 81 74 81 74 81 74 81
SONOMA
1,774 4,417 519 3,562 773 2,657 273 1,352
74 81 74 81 74 81 74 81
SANTA CRUZ
8 12 12 18 27 25 2 18
74 81 74 81 74 81 74 81
SANTA CLARA
125 194 41 50 88 82 42 44
74 81 74 81 74 81 74 81
NAPA
2,812 5,002 953 3,185 1,221 2,216 581 1,373
74 81 74 81 74 81 74 81
SOLANO
53 234 0 3 38 22 0 2
74 81 74 81 74 81 74 81
ALAMEDA
13 39 145 114 76 76 24 17
74 81 74 81 74 81 74 81
MONTEREY
1,368 4,108 418 2,996 420 1,817 287 2,601
74 81 74 81 74 81 74 81
SAN BENITO
534 509 869 975 739 764 395 325
74 81 74 81 74 81 74 81
SAN LUIS OBISPO
48 926 29 405 41 96 31 187
74 81 74 81 74 81 74 81
SANTA BARBARA
415 1,027 164 1,035 124 646 234 1,153
74 81 74 81 74 81 74 81

SOUTHEAST EUROPE

The grape varieties of southeast Europe are as old as those of the west. The Romans colonized the Danube at the same time as the Rhine. Under the Austro–Hungarian Empire the only wines to reach international fame were those of Hungary, led by Tokay. The local grapes, therefore, evolved slowly on their own course making their own sort of spicy, often sweetish whites and dry tannic reds.

The eastern fringes of the Alps in Slovenia, Austria and north into Bohemia (Czechoslovakia) are essentially white wine country, dominated by their local low-key form of the Riesling (variously known as Italian, Welsch, Olasz or Laski), and Austria by its sappy, vigorous Grüner Veltliner. Hungary is most prolific in native white grapes of strength and style, led by the Furmint of Tokay. Its red, the Kadarka, is widespread in the Balkans, more recently joined by the Pinot Noir (Nágyburgundi) and Gamay (Kékfrankos). Warmer climates near the Adriatic and Black Seas have favoured reds and sweet whites. The last 20 years, however, have seen an invasion of classics from the west.

FROM GRAPES TO WINE

Controlling Yield
Higher quantity means lower quality. Acceptance of this golden rule is built into the appellation regulations of France, Italy and most other wine-producing nations. In France the highest-quality areas limit the *rendement*, or yield, to 35 hectolitres a hectare (about two tons an acre) or even less. *Vins de pays* are allowed to produce up to 80 hectolitres or even more. In Italy the limits are expressed in a similar way, as so many quintals (100 kg) of grapes a hectare, with a limit on the amount of juice that may be extracted from each quintal.

California as yet has no regulations in this regard – which, in view of its *laissez-faire* philosophy, is not surprising. It is surprising, however, that Germany permits enormous crops. In 1900 the average yield there was 25 hectolitres a hectare; 100 hectolitres a hectare is now normal in the Federal Republic. Modern German wine-making deliberately concentrates on lightness and transparency of flavour. It lays all the emphasis on 'balance' between sweetness and fruity acidity. As a result most of its wines lack concentration and the ability to improve for more than a few years in bottle. Today it is more realistic to rewrite the golden rule to read 'higher quantity means lighter, more rapidly maturing wine' – the style which is most in demand.

Mechanical Harvesting
A machine for picking grapes, saving the stiff backs (and high wages) of the tens of thousands who turn out to the harvest each year, only became a reality in the 1960s (in New York State, picking Concord grapes). In 1981, 400 machines harvested one third of all America's wine grapes. The mechanical harvester is an inevitable advance. In France it is rapidly graduating from trials to complete acceptance in big vineyards.

The machine works by straddling the vine row and violently shaking the trunks, while slapping at the extremities of the vine with flexible paddles or striker bars. The grapes fall on to a conveyor belt, which carries them from near ground level to a chute above the vine tops. Here they pass in front of a fan which blows away any loose leaves and are shot into a hopper towed by a tractor in the next alley between the vines. In many cases the hopper leads straight to a crusher and the crusher to a closed tank, so that the grapes leave the vineyard already crushed, sheltered from sunlight and insects and dosed with sulphur dioxide to prevent oxidation.

The harvester has many advantages. It can operate at night, when the grapes are cool. It needs only two operators. Whereas a traditional team may have to start while some grapes are still unripe, and finish when some are overripe, the machine works fast enough to pick a whole vineyard at ideal maturity. The harvesting rate in California is up to 150 tons (or up to about 40 acres) a day.

Disadvantages include the need for especially robust trellising, the loss of perhaps ten per cent of the crop and the slight risk of including leaves in the crush. The machines may not yet be fully reliable, and there is a shortage of skilled operators.

Botrytis Infection
The benevolent aspect of the fungus mould *Botrytis cinerea* as the 'noble rot' which produces great sweet wines receives so much publicity that its malevolent appearance in the vineyard at the wrong time can be forgotten. In some regions (particularly in Germany) its prevalence has made it the most serious and widespread disease the grower has to deal with. The more fertile the vineyard and luxuriant the vine, the more likely it is to strike at the unripe or (most vulnerable) semi-ripe grapes and rot the bunch. It starts by attacking grapes punctured by insects or 'grape worm'; controlling the bugs is therefore the most effective protection. Only when the sugar content in the grapes has reached about 70° Oechsle or 17° Brix (enough to make wine of about 9° natural alcohol) does evil rot become noble rot. For a description of noble rot *see* page 78 (Château d'Yquem).

The occurrence and exploitation of noble rot in the vineyards of California has been one of the most noteworthy innovations of recent years. California has coined the inelegant word 'botrytized' (with the stress on the 'bot') to mean infected with *Botrytis cinerea* – of the noble variety.

Sugar and Acid Levels
The crucial decision of when to pick the grapes depends on the measurement of their sugar and acid contents. As they ripen sugar content increases and acid decreases. For each type of wine there is an ideal moment when the ratio is just right.

Ripening starts at the moment called *véraison*, when the grape, which has been growing slowly by cell division, still hard and bright green, begins to grow rapidly by the enlargement of each cell. This is when red grapes begin to change colour.

Sugar content is usually measured with a hand-held 'refractometer'. A drop of juice is held between two prisms. Light passing through it bends at a different angle according to its sugar content: the angle is read off on a scale calibrated as degrees Brix, Oechsle or Baumé (for a table comparing the confusingly different ways of measuring ripeness *see* page 497).

In warm weather sugar content may increase by up to 0.4° Brix (to use the California measure) a day, while acidity drops by as much as 0.15°. 'Ripe' grapes vary between about 18° and 26° Brix (i.e. with a potential alcohol level of 9.3 to 14 per cent by volume). Different levels of acidity are considered ideal for different styles of wine. In Germany acid levels as high as 0.9 per cent would be commendable for a wine of 11.3 per cent potential alcohol (90° Oechsle). In France or California the recommended acid level for grapes with the same sugar content would be approximately 0.7 per cent for white wine and slightly lower for red.

The third variable taken into account is the pH of the juice. This is a measure of the strength, rather than volume, of its acidity. The lower the figure, the sharper the juice. Normal pH in wine is in the range 2.8 to 3.8. Low pH readings are desirable for stability and (in red wines) good colour.

A leading California wine maker, Walter Schug, uses the pH reading as his signal to pick. 'A sharp rise in pH, usually upon reaching 3.25 or over, means that the fruit should be picked regardless of the degree Brix.'

MAKING WINE

Handling the Fruit

A good wine maker will not accept grapes that have been badly damaged on the way from the vineyard, or with a high proportion of mouldy bunches or what the Californians call MOG (matter other than grapes, e.g. leaves, stones and soil). For wine-making at the highest standard the bunches are picked over by hand – '*triage*' – and rotten grapes thrown out. Where large quantities are involved a degree of imperfection has to be accepted.

Several regions of Europe specify the size and design of container that must be used for bringing in the grapes. The object here is to prevent the weight of large quantities from crushing the grapes at the bottom before they reach the cellar. The huge 'gondolas' often used for transporting grapes in California, often under a hot sun, have the distinct drawback that many of the grapes at the bottom will be broken, and macerating in juice, long before they even reach the carefully controlled hygienic conditions of the winery.

SO_2

The first step in all wine-making procedures is the addition of a small dose of sulphur dioxide to the crushed grapes, or must. Nothing has supplanted this universal antiseptic of the wine maker in protecting the must from premature or wild fermentation, and both must and wine from oxidation, though some advanced wine makers use very little and strive to use none – putting instead physical barriers (e.g. inert gases) between the juice or wine and the oxygen in the atmosphere.

The amount of SO_2 allowed is regulated by law. Wine with too much has a sharp brimstone smell and leaves a burning feeling in the throat – a common occurrence in the past, particularly in semi-sweet wines where the sulphur was used to prevent refermentation in the bottle. Sterile filters have now eliminated the need for this and the consumer should be unaware that wine's old preservative is still used at all.

White Wine – Immediate Pressing or 'Skin-contact'

Fashionably light, fresh and fruity white wines are made by pressing the grapes as soon as possible after picking. The object is to prevent the juice from picking up any flavours or 'extract' from the skin. The grapes are gently crushed (*foulé*) just hard enough to break their skins. This 'pomace' is then loaded directly into the press. In some wineries looking for the greatest freshness, the juice or even the grapes may be chilled.

Many bigger wineries now use a 'dejuicer' between the crusher and the press. This may consist of a mesh screen, sometimes in the form of a conveyor belt, through which the 'free' juice falls. A dejuicer reduces the number of times the press has to be laboriously filled and emptied, but it also increases the chance of oxidation of the juice. A form of dejuicer that avoids oxidation is a stainless steel tank with a central cylinder formed of a mesh screen. The crushed pomace is loaded into the space around this cylinder and carbon dioxide is pumped under pressure into the headspace. The free juice is gently forced to drain out via the central cylinder, leaving relatively little pomace to go into the press. Up to 70 per cent can be free-run juice, leaving only 30 per cent to be extracted by pressing.

Fuller and more robust wines with more flavour, and tannins to preserve them while they age, are made by holding the skins in contact with the juice in a tank for up to 24 hours after crushing. This maceration (at a low temperature, before fermentation starts) extracts some of the elements that are present in the skins but not the juice. The pomace is then dejuiced and pressed as usual. Some old-fashioned wine makers might go even further and ferment white wines with their skins, like red wines – but the resulting wine would be too 'heavy' for today's taste.

White Wine: Stems or No Stems

White grapes are usually pressed complete with their stems. The reason is that unfermented grape flesh and juice is full of pectins and sugar, slippery and sticky. The stems make the operation of the press easier, particularly when it comes to breaking up the 'cake', to press a second time. The press should not be used at a high enough pressure to squeeze any bitter juice out of stems or pips.

Types of Press

There is a wide choice of types of press, ranging from the old-fashioned vertical model, in which a plate is forced down on to the pomace contained in a cylindrical cage of vertical slots, to the mass-production continuous 'Coq' press. The first is the most labour intensive but still produces the clearest juice; the second is very cheap and easy to run but cannot make better than medium-grade wine. Most good wineries choose either a Vaslin horizontal basket press, which works on a principle similar to the old vertical press, squeezing the pomace by means of plates which are brought together by a central screw, or a Willmes 'bladder' or 'membrane' press. A bladder press contains a sausage-shaped rubber balloon which when inflated squeezes the pomace against the surrounding fine grille. Both are 'batch' presses, meaning that they have to be filled and emptied anew for each batch of pomace, whereas the continuous press spews forth an unending stream of juice below and 'cake' at the far end.

White Wine – Cold Fermentation

The most revolutionary invention in modern wine-making is controlled-temperature fermentation, particularly for white wines, which in warm climates used to be flat, low in acid and lack-lustre. What used to be achieved naturally by using small barrels in the cold cellars of Europe is now practised industrially in California, Australia and elsewhere by chilling the contents of often colossal stainless steel vats. Most of such vats are double-skinned or 'jacketed' with a layer of glycol or ammonia as the cooling agent between the skins. Another cooling technique is to dribble cold water continuously down the outside surface. A second-best method is to circulate the wine through a heat exchanger (or a coil submerged in cold water) outside the vat.

Each wine maker has his own idea about the ideal temperature for fermentation. Long, cool fermentation is reputedly good for fruity flavours, though when practised to extremes on certain grapes, particularly nonaromatic sorts, it seems to leave its mark on the wine as a 'pear-drop' or acetaldehyde smell. A number of modern Italian white wines, and even occasionally red ones, are spoilt by over-enthusiastic refrigeration. In Germany, to the contrary, very cold fermentation has gone out of fashion. The normal temperatures for white-wine fermentation in California are between 8° and 15°C (46°–59°F). In France 18°C (64°F) is considered cold. If the temperature is forced down too far the fermentation will 'stick' and the yeasts cease to function. It can be difficult to start again and the wine will almost certainly suffer in the process.

A completely different approach is used to make 'big', richer, smoother and more heavy-bodied wines from Chardonnay and sometimes Sauvignon Blanc. They are fermented at between 15° and 20°C (59°–68°F), or in barrels even as high as 25°C (77°F). California Chardonnay in this style is made in exactly the same way as white burgundy (*see* page 107).

White Wine – Clarifying the Juice

Modern presses are more efficient than old models but they tend to produce juice with a higher proportion of suspended solids (pieces of grape skins, flesh, pips or dirt). Fermentation of white wine with these solids tends to produce bitterness, so the juice must be cleaned first. This can be done by holding it for a day or more in a 'settling' tank, allowing particles to sink to the bottom, by filtering through a powerful 'vacuum' filter, or (the fastest method) by use of a centrifuge pump, which uses centrifugal force to throw out all foreign bodies. Over-centrifuged wine can be stripped of desirable as well as undesirable constituents: great care is needed.

White Wine – Adjusting Acidity

Either de- or re-acidification of white-wine must may be necessary, depending on the ripeness of the crop. Overacid juice is de-acidified by adding calcium carbonate (chalk) to remove tartaric acid, or a substance called Acidex, which removes malic acid as well by 'double-salt precipitation'. In Germany the addition of sugar and (up to 15 per cent) water to wines of Qualitätswein level and below naturally lowers the proportion of acidity. In France chaptalization with dry sugar (permitted in the centre and north) has the same effect to a lesser degree. In the south of France, on the other hand, only concentrated must, not sugar, is allowed for raising the alcoholic degree: it naturally raises the acid level at the same time.

In California and other warm countries where the usual problem is too little acid it is permitted to add one of the acids that naturally occur in grapes. Malic, citric and tartaric acid are all used. Tartaric is to be preferred since it has no detectable flavour and also helps towards tartrate stability (*see* Cold Stabilization). But it is more expensive.

Tanks and Vats

The unquestioned grandeur and nobility of traditional fermenting vats of oak (or sometimes such woods as chestnut, acacia or redwood) is accompanied by many disadvantages. Most important are the problems of disinfecting them and keeping them watertight between vintages.

Early in this century concrete began to replace them in newer and bigger wineries. It is strong, permanent and easy to clean. Moreover it can be made in any shape to fit odd corners and save space. Like wood, however, it is a bad conductor of heat. The only way to cool wine in a concrete vat is to pump it out through a cooling plant.

In modern wineries stainless steel is king. It is strong, inert, very easy to clean and simple to cool (conducting heat perfectly). A steel vat can even be moved with relative ease. Moreover it is versatile: the same tank can be used for fermentation and, later in the year, for storage, ageing or blending. Its high initial cost is thus quite quickly recouped.

To make good wine a winery must have ample capacity. It often happens that in an abundant vintage there is a shortage of space. Grapes cannot be stored so the only answer is to cut short the fermenting time of the early batches. With red wines this will mean shorter maceration on the skins and thus lighter wine. Well-designed modern wineries not only have plenty of tank space, they have tanks in a variety of sizes to avoid leaving small lots of wine in half-full containers or being obliged to mix them.

Yeasts

There are yeasts naturally present in every vineyard which will cause fermentation if they are allowed to. Some consider them part of the stamp, or personality, of their property and believe they help to give their wine its individuality. Many modern wineries, wanting to keep total control, take care to remove the natural yeast (by filtering or centrifuging), or at least to render it helpless with a strong dose of SO_2. Some even 'flash-pasteurize' the juice by heating it to 55°C (131°F) to kill off bacteria and inhibit the wild yeasts. Then they proceed to inoculate the must with a cultured yeast of their choice which is known to multiply actively at the temperature they choose for fermentation. Some of the most popular wines in California go by the promising names of 'Montrachet', 'Champagne' and 'Steinberg'.

The secret is to start the fermentation with a generous amount of active yeast; once the whole vat is fermenting such problems as oxidation can temporarily be forgotten. The activity of yeast increases rapidly with rising temperature. For each additional degree Celsius, yeast tranforms ten per cent more sugar into alcohol in a given time. The ceiling to this frantic activity occurs at about 30° to 35°C (86°–95°F) when the yeasts are overcome by heat. A 'run-away' fermentation can 'stick' at this temperature, just as most yeasts will not function below about 10°C (50°F).

Specialized use of flor yeast for producing sherry has greatly advanced in recent years. New methods have been found of producing the sherry effect much faster and more certainly than with the traditional naturally occurring layer of flor floating on the wine.

White Wines – Malolactic Fermentation

Secondary or malolactic fermentation (*see* Red Wine – Malolactic Fermentation) is less common with white wine than with red. It is sometimes encouraged, to reduce excess acidity in wines from cool climates (e.g. Chablis and other parts of Burgundy, the Loire, Switzerland, but less commonly in Germany). Its complex biological nature may help to add complexity to flavours. In regions where acidity tends to be low, such as California, malolactic fermentation in white wines is generally avoided.

White Wines – Residual Sugar

A completed natural fermentation makes a totally dry wine, all its sugar converted to alcohol. The only exceptions are wines made of grapes so sweet that either the alcohol level or the sugar, or both, prevents the yeasts from functioning.

To make light sweet wines, either the fermentation has to be artificially interrupted or sweet juice has to be blended with dry wine. The former was the old way. It needed a strong dose of SO_2 to stop the fermentation, and more in the bottle to prevent it starting again. The invention of filters fine enough to remove all yeasts, and means of bottling in conditions of complete sterility, now solve the sulphur problem. But wine makers today generally prefer the second method: blending with 'sweet reserve'. This is the standard procedure for producing the sweet and semi-sweet wines of Germany up to Auslese level and is increasingly used elsewhere.

The method used is to sterilize a portion of the juice instead of fermenting it. (It can be stored in a deepfreeze as a block of ice.) The majority of the wine is made in the normal way, fermented until no sugar is left. The 'sweet reserve' (in German *Süssreserve*) is then added to taste and the blend bottled under sterile conditions. The addition of unfermented juice naturally lowers the alcohol content of the wine.

Some of the best wine makers prefer to maintain a small degree of unfermented ('residual') sugar in certain wines (California Rieslings and Gewürztraminers, for example) by cooling the vat to stop fermentation at the appropriate moment, then using a centrifuge and/or fine filtering to remove the yeasts and sterilize the wine.

White Wine – After Fermentation

After white wine has fermented it must be clarified. The traditional method was to allow it to settle and then rack it off its lees (largely of dead yeast cells). When Muscadet is bottled *sur lie* this is exactly what is happening. Modern wineries, however, tend to use a centrifuge or a filter for this clarification, too, if necessary with the additional precaution of fining with a powdery clay (from Wyoming) called bentonite, which removes excess proteins, potential causes of later trouble in the form of cloudy wine. Bentonite fining is also sometimes used on the must before fermentation.

White wines not intended for ageing (i.e. most light commercial wines) then need only to be stabilized and filtered before they can be bottled and distributed.

White Wine – Cold Stabilization

The tartaric acid which is a vital ingredient in the balance and flavour of all wines has an unfortunate habit of forming crystals in combination with either potassium (quite big sugary grains) or calcium (finer and whiter powdery crystals). In former times wine was kept for several years in cool cellars and these crystals formed a hard deposit on the walls of their casks, known in Germany as '*Weinstein*' – 'wine stone'. With faster modern methods, most wineries consider it essential to prevent the crystals forming after the wine is bottled – which they will unless something is done about it. Although the crystals have no flavour at all and are totally natural and harmless, there are always ignorant and querulous customers who will send back a bottle with any sign of deposit.

Unfortunately it is a costly business to remove the risk of tartrate crystals. The simplest way is to chill the wine to just above freezing point in a tank for several days. The process is accelerated by 'seeding' with added tartrate crystals to act as nuclei for more crystals to form. More efficient ways of achieving this strictly unnecessary object will keep research chemists busy for years to come.

Red Wine – Stems or No Stems

Each red-wine maker has his own view about whether the grape stems should be included, wholly or in part – and it changes with the vintage. In Beaujolais and the Rhône the stems are always included, in Burgundy usually a proportion, in Bordeaux few or none, in Chinon on the Loire the stems are left on the vine. Opinions are equally divided in other countries, but in California stems are usually excluded.

The argument for leaving the stems out is that they add astringency, lower the alcohol content, reduce the colour and take up valuable space in the vat. The argument for keeping some of them in is that they help the process of fermentation by aerating the mass, they lower the acidity and they make pressing easier.

Red Wine – Pumping Over

When a vat of red wine ferments the skins float to the surface, buoyed up by bubbles of carbon dioxide, which attach themselves to solid matter. The 'cap' (French, '*chapeau*', Spanish '*sombrero*') that they form contains all the essential colouring matter – and is prone to overheat and be attacked by bacteria. It is therefore essential to keep mixing the cap back into the liquid below. There are several methods.

In Bordeaux the cap is often pushed under by men with long poles. In Burgundy, with smaller vats, it is trodden under ('*pigeage*') by men, formerly naked, who jump into the vat. Another widespread method is to fit a grille below the filling level which holds the cap immersed ('*chapeau immergé*'). But the most widespread modern method is 'pumping over', taking wine by a hose from the bottom of the vat and spraying it over the cap, usually several times a day.

Several ingenious alternatives have been invented. The 'Rototank' is a closed horizontal cylinder which slowly rotates, continually mixing the liquids and solids inside. An automatic system developed in Portugal, where the traditional way of extracting the colour was night-long stomping by all the village lads to the sound of accordions, involves an ingenious gusher device activated by the build-up of carbon dioxide pressure in a sealed tank.

Red Wine – Heating the Must

One of the modern ways of achieving the goal of deep-coloured red wine without the astringency of tannins arising from long vatting is to boil the must before fermentation. It was a method apparently used centuries ago to darken the 'black' wine of Cahors. It is only recommended, however, for wines with a limited potential life span.

Red Wine – Pressing

By the time fermentation is finished, or nearly finished and merely simmering slightly, most (up to 85 per cent) of the red wine is separated from the solid matter and will run freely from the vat. This 'free run' or *vin de goutte* is siphoned out of the vat into either barrels or another tank. The remaining 'marc' is pressed.

Red wine is pressed in the same types of presses as white, but after fermentation the pulp and skins have partly disintegrated and offer less resistance.

Relatively gentle pressure will release very good quality *vin de presse*, which is richer in desirable extracts and flavours than the *vin de goutte*. It may need such treatment as fining to reduce astringency and remove solids, but in most cases it will be a positive addition and make better wine for longer keeping. Wine from a second, more vigorous, pressing will almost always be too astringent and be sold separately, or used in a cheap blend.

The Value of Barrels

Developments in California have drawn attention to what has long been known, but taken for granted, in France and elsewhere: that new barrels have a profound effect on the flavour of wine stored in them – and even more on wine fermented in them. California Chardonnays fermented in the same French oak as white burgundy can have an uncanny resemblance to its flavour.

Barrels were invented (probably by the Romans) of necessity as the most durable and transportable of containers, supplanting the amphora and the goatskin in regions that could afford them. They have developed to their standard sizes and shapes over centuries of experience. The 200-odd-litre barrels of Bordeaux, Burgundy and Rioja are the most that one man can easily roll or two men carry – but they also happen to present the largest surface area of wood to wine of any practicable size.

The advantages of this contact lie partly in the very slow transfer of oxygen through the planks of the barrel, but mainly through the tannin and other substances that the wine dissolves from the wood itself. The most easily identified (by taste or smell) of these is vanillin, which has the flavour of vanilla. Oak tannin is useful in augmenting, and slightly varying, the tannins naturally present in wine as preservatives. Other scents and flavours are harder to define, but can be well enough expressed as the 'smell of a carpenter's shop'.

Which wines benefit from this addition of extraneous flavours? Only those with strong characters and constitutions of their own. It would be disastrous to a fragile Moselle or a Beaujolais Nouveau. The 'bigger' the wine and the longer it is to be matured, the more oak it can take.

New barrels are extremely expensive. $250 is a typical 1982 price. The full impact of their oak flavour diminishes rapidly after the first two or three years' use, but there is a lively trade in second-hand barrels, particularly those that have contained great wines. Barrels can also be renewed to full pungency by shaving the wine-leached interior down to fresh wood.

Another way of achieving the complexity of oak flavour in wine is by blending in a fraction in which oak chips or shavings have been macerated to produce an intensely oak-flavoured brew. Mention of this method is considered shocking in wine-making circles, but it is practised, is very effective and entirely harmless.

A completely different role is played by the huge permanent oak barrels, *foudres* or *demi-muids* in French, *Fuders* or *Stücks* in German, which are common in southern France, Germany, Italy, Spain and eastern Europe. Their oak flavour has been minimized or completely neutralized by constant impregnation with wine, and often by a thick layer of tartrate crystals. Their value seems to lie in offering an ideal environment, with very gradual oxidation, for the maturing and slow stabilizing of wine. Before the advent of efficient sterile bottling, a big oak vat was simply the safest place for a grower to keep his stock – sometimes for years on end, topped up with fresh wine as necessary.

In California cooperage has become something of a fetish. Comparative tastings are held between the same wine aged in oak from different French forests; even from the same forest but different barrel makers. The names of Demptos and Nadalie of Bordeaux, of Taransaud and Séguin-Moreau of Cognac and François Frères and the Tonnelleries de Bourgogne Burgundy are more familiar in the Napa Valley than in France. Current opinion seems to be that Limousin oak, faster growing with wider growth rings, has less flavour and is better for Chardonnay and Pinot Noir (which in California are only kept in oak one year or less); Nevers and Tronçais oak, slower-grown and offering more extract, is better for Cabernet, which spends two or even three years in barrel. American white-oak uncharred Bourbon barrels are also used. They offer less flavour and tannin (but a higher tannin/flavour ratio) – good for Cabernet and Zinfandel, less so for white wines. Baltic, Balkan and other oaks are also used and much has been written about their relative merits. Since there is no visual difference and a cooper's shop contains oak from many sources, one may well be sceptical about such fine distinctions in any case. Other factors such as the thickness of the staves, whether they have been split or sawn, air dried or kiln dried, steamed or 'toasted', even whether the barrel is washed in hot water or cold can all start arguments among the initiated.

Red Wine – Carbonic Maceration
The technique of fermenting uncrushed grapes known as *macération carbonique* has been developed in France since 1935 by Professor Michel Flanzy and others. The method is described on page 146. It began to make a real impact in the early 1970s in dramatically improving the quality of the better Midi wines. It is now well established in France as the best way to produce fruity, 'supple', richly coloured reds for drinking young, but its acceptance has been surprisingly slow in other countries. It is particularly surprising that California has paid so little attention to it. Low acidity tends to make pure maceration wines short lived, which is inappropriate for the finest growths. But a proportion can be a valuable element in a blend with a tannic and/or acidic red.

Fining
The ancient technique of pouring whipped egg-whites, gelatin, isinglass (fish glue), blood or other coagulants into wine is still widely used both on must and finished wine, despite modern filters and centrifuges. Its object is to clean the liquid of the finest suspended solids, which are too light to sink. The 'fining', poured on to the surface, slowly sinks like a superfine screen, carrying any solids to the bottom. Certain finings such as bentonite (*see* White Wine – After Fermentation) are specific to certain undesirable constituents. 'Blue' fining (potassium ferrocyanide) removes excess iron from the wine.

Racking
Once the gross lees, or sediment, in a barrel or vat have sunk to the bottom, the wine is 'racked' off them simply by pouring the clear liquid from a tap above the level of the solids. In wines that are kept over a length of time in barrels, racking is repeated every few months as more solids are precipitated. If the wine is judged to need more oxygen, racking is done via an open basin; if not, it is done by a hose linking one barrel directly to another.

Red Wine – Malolactic Fermentation
Wine growers have always been aware of a fresh activity in their barrels of new wine in the spring following the vintage. Folklore put it down to a 'natural sympathy' between the wine and the rising sap in the vineyards. It seemed to be a further fermentation, but it happened in wine that had no sugar left to ferment.

In the last 50 years the science of microbiology has found the answer. It is a form of fermentation carried on by bacteria, not yeasts, which are feeding on malic (apple) acid in the wine and converting it to lactic (milk) acid, giving off carbon dioxide bubbles in the process. It has several results: a lowering of the quantity of acidity and of its sharpness (lactic acid is milder to taste than malic); increase of stability, and a less quantifiable smoothing and complicating of the wine's flavour. For almost all red wines, therefore, it is highly desirable, and wine makers take steps to make sure that it takes place.

In most cases a gentle raising of the temperature in the cellar to about 20°C (68°F) will do. Sometimes it is necessary to import the right bacteria. Sometimes (this is considered very desirable) the malolactic fermentation can be encouraged to happen concurrently with the first (alcoholic) fermentation.

Blending for Complexity
Champagne, red and white Bordeaux, Rhône reds, Chianti, Rioja, port, are examples of wines made of a mixture of grapes. Burgundy, Barolo, sherry, German and Alsace wines are examples of one-grape wines. American 'varietal' – consciousness has tended to put a premium on the simplistic idea that '100 per cent is best'. But recent research has shown that even among wines of humble quality a mixture of two is always better than the lesser of the two and generally better than either. This is taken to prove that 'complexity' is in itself a desirable quality in wine; that one variety can 'season' another as butter and salt do eggs.

There is a general trend in California, therefore, towards Bordeaux-style blending of Merlot with Cabernet and Semillon with Sauvignon Blanc. On the other hand no other grape has been shown to improve Pinot Noir, Chardonnay or Riesling. Added complexity in their already delicious flavours either comes with the help of barrel-ageing, in Riesling with 'noble rot', or simply with years in bottle.

Filtration
The Seitz Company of Bad Kreuznach, Germany, has been the pioneer in the developing of ever finer and finer filters capable of removing almost everything, even the flavour, from wine if they are not used with discretion. Most filters consist of a series of 'pads' alternating with plates, through which the wine is forced under pressure. The degree of filtration depends on the pore size of the pads. At 0·65 microns they remove yeast, at 0·45 bacteria as well. To avoid having to change them frequently, wine is nearly always clarified by such other means as fining or centrifuging before filtration.

Some wine makers make a point of labelling their wine 'unfiltered'. They believe that it is worth running the risk of slight sediment for the sake of extra flavour. So do I.

Pasteurization

Louis Pasteur, the great French chemist of the late nineteenth century who discovered the relationship of oxygen to wine, and hence the cause of vinegar, gave his name to the process of sterilization by heating to kill off harmful organisms. In wine this means any yeast and bacteria that might start it refermenting.

A temperature of 60°C (140°F) for about 30 minutes is needed – although an alternative preferred today (for bulk wine only) is 'flash' pasteurization at a much higher temperature, 85°C (185°F), for a much shorter time (up to one minute). Normally pasteurization is only used on cheap wines not intended to mature further, although there is evidence that it does not permanently inhibit further development. Modern sterile handling and filtration is steadily phasing out pasteurization from modern wineries.

Ageing

There are two separate and distinct ways in which wine can age: 'oxidative' ageing in contact with oxygen and 'reductive' ageing when the oxygen supply is cut off. Barrel-ageing is oxidative; it encourages numerous complex reactions between the acids, sugars, tannins, pigments and multifarious polysyllabic constituents of wine.

Bottle-ageing is reductive. Once the wine is bottled the only oxygen available is the limited amount dissolved in the liquid or trapped between the liquid and the cork. (No oxygen enters through a cork.) In wines with a high carbon dioxide content (e.g. champagne) there is not even this much oxygen. Life-forms depending on oxygen are therefore very limited in their scope for activity. 'Reductive' means that the oxygen is reduced – eventually to zero. In these conditions different complex reactions between the same constituents occur at a much slower rate. The ultimate quality and complexity in most wines is only arrived at by a combination of these two forms of ageing, though the proportions of each can vary widely. Many white wines are bottled very young but improve enormously in bottle. Champagne and vintage port are matured almost entirely in bottle. Fine red wines may spend up to three years in barrel and then perhaps two or three times as long in bottle. Tawny port and sherry are matured entirely in barrel and are not normally intended for any further bottle-age.

Bottling

The question of where and by whom wine should be bottled has been much debated, but since the introduction in France of the mobile bottling unit in the 1960s it has become the rule, rather than the exception, for producers even on a small scale to bottle their own wine. The unit is simply a lorry equipped as a modern semi-automatic bottling plant. Its arrival meant that the evocative words *mis en bouteille au château* or *au domaine*, widely supposed (especially in America) to be a guarantee of authenticity and even quality, could be used by all the little properties that used to rely on merchants to bottle for them. The change rubbed both ways: some merchants' names were a guarantee of well-chosen, well-handled wine; others were not.

Modern automatic bottling lines, particularly for fragile semi-sweet wines such as Germany makes, can be like a cross between an operating theatre and a space shuttle, with airlock doors to maintain total antiseptic sterility. The wine is often 'sparged', or flushed out with carbon dioxide or an inert gas such as nitrogen, to remove any oxygen. The bottle is first filled with nitrogen and the wine filled into it through a long nozzle (a 'Mosel cock') to the bottom, pushing out the gas as the level rises. Another common precaution with standard wines is 'hot-bottling': heating the wine to about 54°C (130°F) at the moment of filling the bottle. All this is to avoid any chance of refermentation. For naturally stabilized wines that have spent a long time in barrel, such precautions should not be needed.

Carbon Dioxide for 'Spritz'

Many light white, rosé and occasionally red wines benefit from being bottled with a degree of carbon dioxide dissolved in them – just enough for a few faint bubbles to appear at the brim or the bottom of the glass. In many wines this is a natural occurrence. In others it is an easy and effective way of giving a slight prickle of refreshing sharpness to wines that would otherwise be dull, soft and/or neutral.

Cooperatives

It is arguable that the most important development for the majority of wine makers in Europe has been the rise of the cooperative movement. By pooling resources and qualifying for generous government grants and loans, the peasant wine-farmers of the past are now nearly all grape growers who deliver their whole harvest to a well-equipped central winery. Some are still fly-ridden and unpainted, 'viticultural dust-bins' as they have been called, but most are now extremely up-to-date with vats and presses far better than the district would otherwise have, and a qualified oenologist to make the wine.

A few are outright leaders in their regions: nobody else can afford such heavy investment in modern plant. Nearly all use premiums to encourage farmers to produce riper, healthier, cleaner grapes and charge fines for rot, leaves and soil in the crop.

Sparkling Wines

The *méthode champenoise* is not susceptible to many short cuts or labour-saving devices, although machines have been devised for most of the laborious hand work involved. The latest and most notable is an automatic 'riddling rack' to replace the unremitting chore of shaking and turning each bottle regularly (*see* page 175). The massive framework, which vibrates and tips automatically at intervals, is known in France as a Gyropalette, in America simply as a VLM – 'Very Large Machine'.

Other methods of making sparkling wine, none of which achieves the same degree of dissolved gas as the champagne method, include refermenting the wine in a bottle, then decanting it into a tank under pressure, filtering out the sediment (still under CO_2 pressure) and rebottling it. These wines may be labelled 'fermented in the bottle', but not 'fermented in *this* bottle' – or '*méthode champenoise*'. The *cuve close* or Charmat process avoids the first bottling by inducing the secondary fermentation in a tank, then filtering and bottling. This is the most common method for cheaper sparkling wines. Very cheap ones are sometimes simply 'carbonated' by pumping CO_2 into still wine. It does not stay there long.

Chemical Analysis

Whoever coined the phrase 'a chemical symphony' described wine perfectly. (There are, of course, string quartets too.) Good wine gets its infinitely intriguing flavour from the interweaving of innumerable organic and inorganic substances in amounts so small that they have hitherto been untraceable. But no more.

A gas chromatograph is an instrument capable of identifying and measuring up to 250 different substances in wine – so far. A single such analysis costs about $200. It (and similar instruments) can produce a graphic 'chemical profile'. Researchers at the University of California are playing the fascinating computer game of trying to match the sensory (e.g. smell and taste) perception of teams of tasters with the drawings of the chromatograph to discover which substance is responsible for which taste – the idea presumably being that once we know, vineyards and grapes will become obsolete.

At a more humdrum level it is normal to do simple laboratory checks on about 20 constituents, from alcohol and acidity to sugar and sulphur, before giving any wine a clean bill of health.

The Critical Audience

A catalogue of the influences and advances in modern wine would be one-sided without a mention of the consumer. At least as striking as the technological changes of the past 20 years has been the snowballing interest in wine as a topic as well as a drink. It began in England, spread rapidly to America, Holland, Germany, Scandinavia, and in the past few years has even stirred the great bastions of conservatism and complacency: France, Italy and Spain, the major wine-producing nations.

Books and articles about wine, comparative tastings, newsletters and reviews have turned the spotlight on the individual wine maker. The motivation is there not just to sell, but to excel. The spirit of rivalry and the friendly confrontation between producer and consumer may be the most important driving force of all. We are all the beneficiaries.

Giant propellers lessen frost dangers by causing air to circulate on spring nights

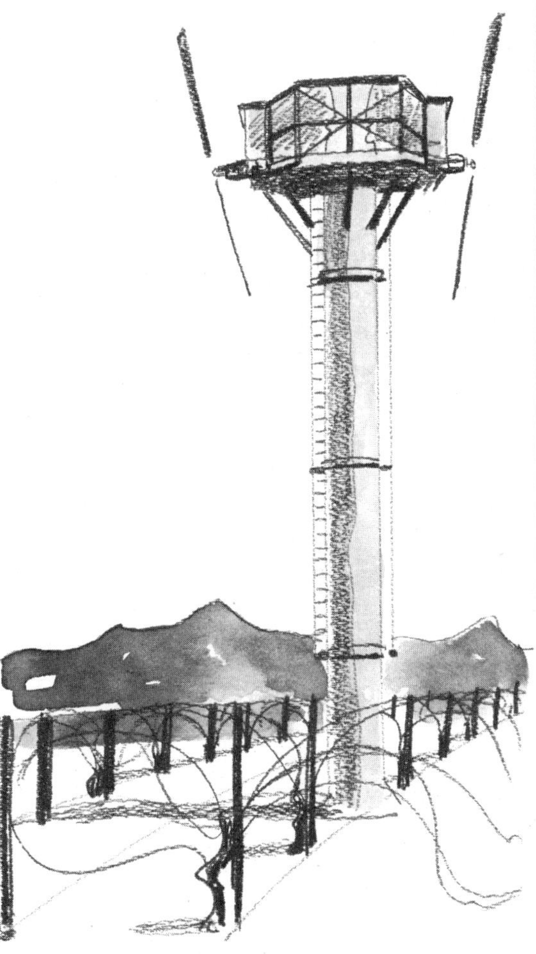

Wines Vineyards and Winemakers of the World

FRANCE

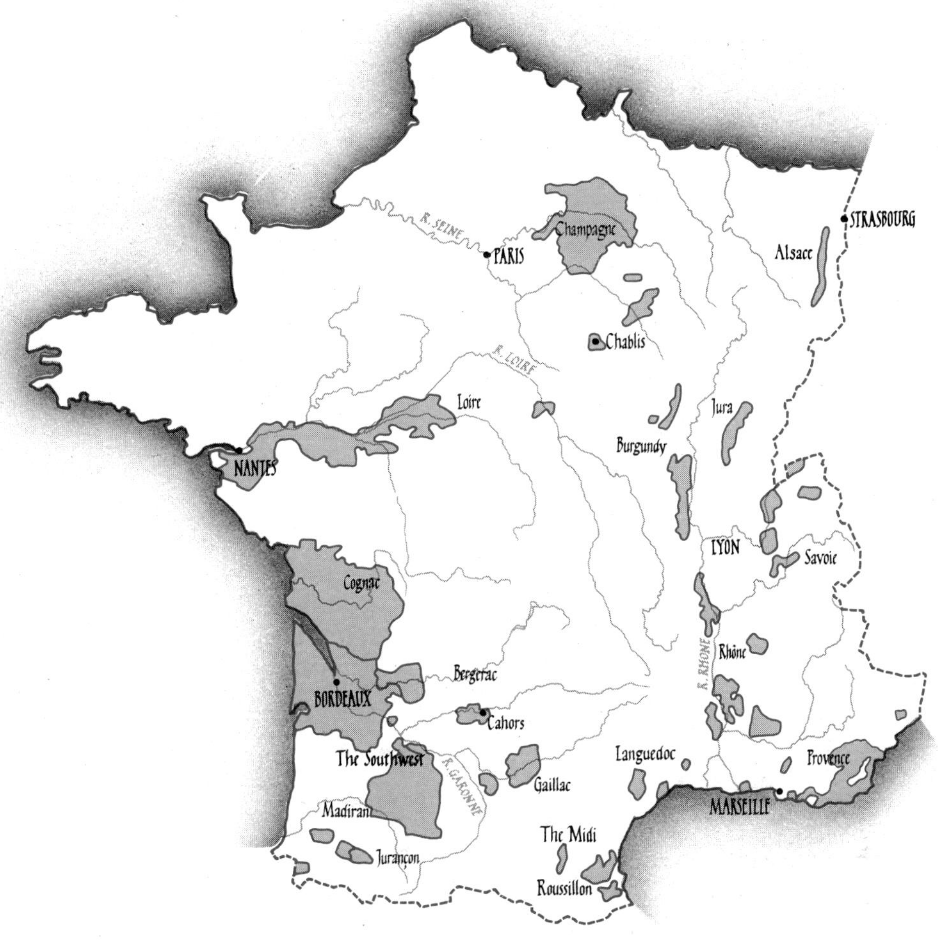

Nobody will argue with the primacy of France as the country that set the international standards by which wine is judged. Germany's Rieslings, Spain's sherry and Portugal's port are the only non-French wines to be accepted as universal models to be imitated and emulated. This is not to invalidate Chianti or Barolo or Rioja; but they remain vernacular styles, while Bordeaux, burgundy, champagne and certain wines of the Loire, the Rhône and Alsace are targets that wine makers all over the world aim at – in the first instance by planting their grapes.

It was a form of natural selection that gave France these ideas of what wine can be. Her first vineyards were planted in the Midi in the sixth or seventh centuries BC. The Romans established what are now all the highest-quality vineyard areas – Burgundy, Bordeaux, Champagne, the Loire – with the exception of Alsace. They chose them, in the first place, because they were promising-looking slopes near centres of population and with reasonable transport facilities: ideally by water, but failing water by a main trade route with good going for heavy wagons. They planted them, after trying Italian vines, with selections of the native woodland vines of Gaul and her neighbours Spain, the Rhineland and the Alps. We can be fairly certain that their descendants are the vines grown today, selected and reselected every time a vineyard was replanted.

The soils are the same; the climate and the conditions of cellarage have not changed very much. With allowances for different techniques and tastes, we can speculate that French wines have gradually defined their identities over almost 2,000 years.

Identity and fame once established, there comes the inevitable problem of fraud. For every person who actually knows what a given wine ought to taste like there are a hundred – more probably a thousand – who are ready to pay for something they will not be able to identify.

The problem is age-old. Many laws have been passed (and taxes raised) to regulate how wine is made, how much, when, where, by whom, of what grapes, and under what name and at what price it can be sold. At the turn of this century the problem became acute. The devastation of phylloxera had left Europe with a serious shortage. Such long-term customers of the best producers as the British were largely protected from the crisis, but in France it was clear that a national system of control was needed.

In 1932 the Institut National des Appellations d'Origine was founded in Paris, with offices and *ingénieurs* all over France, to regulate the whole of the quality wine industry. Another central institute, the Office National Interprofessional des Vins de Table, was founded to keep order among the peasantry producing *vins ordinaires* without the dignity of an *appellation d'origine*.

These distinctions are now central to the whole Common Market wine system. In EEC terms every wine is either a Vin de Qualité Produit dans Une Région Determinée (VQPRD) or a *vin de table* – an absurd choice of category, incidentally: Château Lafite is surely a table wine. In France the system has become more elaborate. There are now four categories of wine representing a basic classification of all the wines of France:

Appellation (d'Origine) Contrôlée (AC or AOC) A strict control of origin, grape varieties and methods used, alcoholic strength and quantity produced. Most AOC wines are limited to a basic production in the region of 40 hectolitres a hectare (445 cases an acre) but a complicated system of annual reassessment usually allows more, and sometimes very considerably more.

The nature of the AC control varies region by region. In Bordeaux the most specific and restricted appellation is a whole village, within which the individual properties ('châteaux') are given wide liberties to plant where and what (within the regional tradition) they like. By contrast, in the best sites of Burgundy each field has its own appellation. The appellation Champagne covers a whole region and its method of working. Each region is a particular case with its own logic.

The ceiling on production, or *Plafond Limite de Classement* (PLC), is always lower for Grands Crus (in regions that have them) than for humbler appellations. The differences used to provide manoeuvring space for notorious fiddles. But now stricter controls try to ensure that each appellation is treated entirely separately in the grower's cellar – an enormous task.

The AOC system was not instituted to provide quality control – only guarantees of origin and authenticity. Quality control by compulsory tasting has now been introduced in theory. In practice there are not enough qualified and impartial tasters, nor the organization nor the time to check on every wine.

Vin Délimité de Qualité Supérieure (VDQS) The second rank of appellations was instituted in 1945 for regions with worthwhile identities and traditions producing 'minor' wines. It has similar systems of control, allowing rather larger crops and (sometimes) lower strengths. In practice it has become the training ground for future AOCs. Promotion from VDQS has happened to several regions in the last decade or so – Cahors being the best known. Others, such as Corbières, are under active survey for future promotion. To be realistic, there is no sudden jump between the two.

Vin de Pays 'Country wine' is a free translation of the latest category, which came into use in 1973. *Vins de pays* are *vins de table* from specified origins, which may be as limited as a village or as wide as the whole Loire valley. Very large crops and a wide latitude of grape varieties are usually allowed. Standards vary enormously.

Many *vin de pays* labels are in practice a new way of marketing *vin ordinaire*. But an individualist who decided to grow, for example, Pinot Noir in Bordeaux, and therefore buck the appellation system, would have to call his wine *vin de pays* however good it might be (*see* page 222).

Vin de Consommation Courante Wine for current consumption. The official name for *vin ordinaire*, the daily drink of the man in the street. Its origin is not specified. Its price depends on its alcoholic degree.

Prices

The prices that are quoted for as many as possible of the appellations and many individual *crus* are intended as an indication of relative values – at least as they are perceived by the market. They are *not* the prices the consumer will pay but the 'cellar-door' wholesale price in mid-1982 for the wine of the newest vintage currently on sale, bottled and boxed. They should not be taken as representing more than the state of the market at a particular time.

BORDEAUX

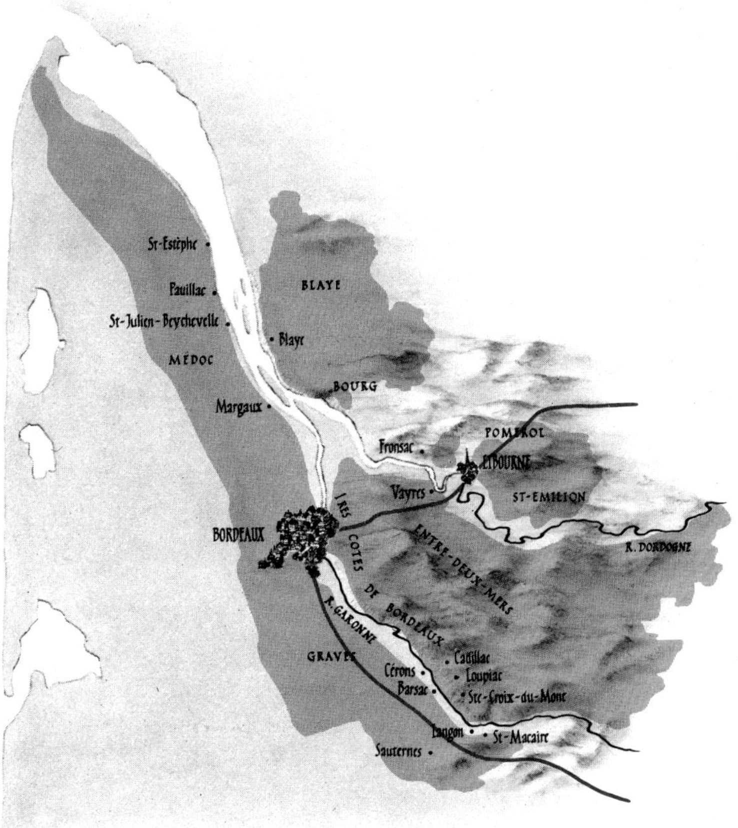

Four factors make Bordeaux the most important vineyard region of all: its quality, size, variety and unity. The last two are not contradictory but complementary. They are the reason we keep coming back for more: the range of styles and types of Bordeaux is wide enough for everybody; no two are ever identical, and yet there is an unmistakable identity among them, a clean-cut, appetizing, stimulating quality that only Bordeaux offers.

The Bordeaux character comes from the strains of grapes and the maritime climate rather than the soil (which varies from gravel to limestone to clay). And of course it comes from traditions of making, handling and enjoying wine in a certain way, an amalgam of the tastes of the French and their northern neighbours, the British, Belgians, Dutch, Germans and Scandinavians, who have paid the piper since the Middle Ages.

Today more than half Bordeaux's white wine and more than a third of its red are exported. But the proportion among the best growths (Pauillac, Margaux and Sauternes, for example) rises to two thirds or even three quarters.

Bordeaux supplies four basic styles of wine: light, everyday red, fine red, dry white and sweet, sticky, 'liquorous' white. There is not a great deal to be said about the first except that there is a vast supply, up to two million hectolitres (266 million bottles) a year, varying from the excitingly tasty to the merely passable or occasionally poor and watery. It may be offered under a brand name or as the production of a Petit Château.

There is a degree of overlap between this and 'fine' red, where the former excels itself or the latter lets the side down, but the fine red is really a distinct product, a more concentrated wine made for keeping and matured in oak. This is where the distinctions between different soils and situations produce remarkable differences of flavour and keeping qualities, more or less accurately reflected in the system of appellations and of classifications within the appellations. The total quantity available in this category is even more impressive for this class of wine: approaching two bottles for every three of the everyday red.

The dry white wines belong, with regrettably few exceptions, alongside the light reds. A very few rise to the level of fine white burgundy; most are mere refreshment – and sometimes scarcely that. There is half as much made as there is of comparable red. The sweet whites are a drop in the ocean, only about one bottle in 30, but a precious speciality capable of superlative quality, and much appreciated in Bordeaux even at a humble level as an aperitif.

Every Bordeaux vintage is subject to the most fickle of climates. Overriding all other considerations is the unpredictable seaside weather. A great vintage will give even the commonest wines an uncommon vitality, but conversely the category of fine wines can be sadly depleted by a really bad one, and the sweet whites can be eliminated altogether.

This shifting pattern of vintages against the already complicated background of appellations and properties, and the long life span of the good wines, makes the appreciation of Bordeaux a mesmerically fascinating pursuit which never ends.

BORDEAUX IN ROUND FIGURES

Over the 25 years 1955 to 1980, the total area of *appellation contrôlée* vineyards in Bordeaux fluctuated only slightly and finished exactly where it began: at 188,000 acres. But the steady total hides radical changes of structure. The number of growers at the end of the period had fallen from 56,000 to 24,000; their average holding of appellation land had therefore risen from three and a half to nearly eight acres, or ten acres if the non-AC areas are included.

With this concentration of ownership, efficiency has improved. The five years at the beginning of the period (admittedly including a disastrous frost in 1956) produced an average crop of 26 hectolitres a hectare; the last five years have produced 44. 1978 was the recent vintage nearest to the average total crop (at 41 hectolitres). The total production (figures are given in hectolitres followed by cases of a dozen bottles) in 1978 was as follows.

RED WINES

Bordeaux (the basic red appellation for minor areas; the wine need only attain 10% alcohol) 663,000 hl. 7.4m. cases

Bordeaux Supérieur (as above with an alcoholic degree of 10.5% or more) 357,000 hl. 4m. cases

The 'Côtes' (of Blaye, Bourg, Castillon, Francs and the Premières Côtes de Bordeaux; outlying areas of slightly higher quality and individuality) 326,000 hl. 3.6m. cases

The St-Emilion area, including the St-Emilion 'satellites' (Montagne, St-Georges, etc.), Pomerol and Fronsac

	440,000 hl.	5m. cases
of which St-Emilion itself produced	213,000 hl.	2.4m. ,,
and Pomerol	27,000 hl.	300,000 ,,

The whole Médoc (Médoc, Haut-Médoc, Pauillac, etc.) and **Graves**	440,000 hl.	5m. cases
of which the lower Médoc produced	108,000 hl.	1.2m. ,,
Haut-Médoc	99,000 hl.	1m. ,,
Graves	60,000 hl.	660,000 ,,
St-Estèphe	47,000 hl.	530,000 ,,
Pauillac	34,500 hl.	380,000 ,,
Margaux	34,500 hl.	380,000 ,,
Moulis and Listrac	30,000 hl.	330,000 ,,
St-Julien	26,000 hl.	290,000 ,,

WHITE WINES

Total production of dry whites	873,000 hl.	9.7m. cases
of which plain Bordeaux was	540,000 hl.	6m. ,,
Entre-Deux-Mers	194,000 hl.	2.2m. ,,
Graves	43,000 hl.	480,000 ,,
Total production of sweet whites	120,000 hl.	1.3m. cases
of which Sauternes was	26,000 hl.	90,000 ,,
Barsac	11,000 hl.	122,000 ,,

BORDEAUX SALES IN FRANCE AND ABROAD (1980)

Total Bordeaux Reds	France	64%	export	36%
Pauillac	,,	43%	,,	57%
Margaux	,,	25%	,,	75%
St-Emilion	,,	58%	,,	42%
Pomerol	,,	58%	,,	42%
Total Bordeaux Whites	France	50%	export	50%
Graves	,,	17%	,,	83%
Sauternes	,,	36%	,,	64%

Bordeaux accounted for 16 per cent of all French wine exports and 33 per cent of all AC wine exports.

Export figures fluctuate from year to year but in 1980 the main customers were:

Belgium	220,000 hl.	2.4m. cases	(88% red)
West Germany	160,000 hl.	1.8m. ,,	(43% red)
UK	150,000 hl.	1.7m. ,,	(63% red)
Holland	150,000 hl.	1.7m. ,,	(66% red)
USA	120,000 hl.	1.3m. ,,	(58% red)
Canada	56,000 hl.	620,000 ,,	(52% red)
Switzerland	54,000 hl.	600,000 ,,	(87% red)
Denmark	50,000 hl.	555,000 ,,	(78% red)

In terms of average price paid for a bottle the order was: Switzerland, Japan, Italy, Belgium, USA, Denmark, UK and Germany.

CLASSIFICATIONS

The appellations of Bordeaux are themselves a sort of preliminary classification of its wines by quality, on the basis that the more narrowly they are defined the higher the general level of the district.

This is as far as overall grading has ever (officially) gone. More precise classifications are all local to one area without cross-referencing. They are reproduced on the pages referring to their areas. The most effective way of comparing the standing of châteaux within different areas is by price – the method used for the first and most famous of all classifications, that done for the Médoc in 1855.

In 1855 the criterion was the price each wine fetched, averaged over a long period, up to 100 years, but taking into account its recent standing and the current condition of the property. The list is still so widely used that it is essential for reference even 130 years later. A few châteaux have fallen by the wayside; the majority have profited by their notoriety to expand their vineyards, swallowing lesser neighbours. It is certain that the original classification located most of the best land in the Médoc and gave credit to the proprietors who had planted it. What they subsequently did with it has proved to be less important than the innate superiority of the gravel banks they chose to plant.

THE CONCEPT OF A CHATEAU

The unit of classification in Bordeaux is not precisely the land itself (as it is in Burgundy) but the property on the land – the estate or 'château'. It is the château that is either a first- or a fourth-growth or a Cru Bourgeois. A proprietor can buy land from a neighbour of greater or lesser standing and add it to his own and (given that it is suitable land) it will take his rank. Vineyards can therefore go up or down the scale according to who owns them.

An example. Château Gloria is an estate of great quality in St-Julien, formed since World War II by buying parcels of land from neighbouring Crus Classés. When the land changed hands it was 'classed', but because the buyer had no classed château the vines were demoted to Cru Bourgeois.

Conversely, many classed growths have added to their holdings by buying neighbouring Cru Bourgeois vines. When the Rothschilds of Château Lafite bought the adjacent Château Duhart-Milon they could theoretically have made all its wine as Lafite.

The justification for this apparent injustice is that a château is considered more as a 'marque' than a plot of ground. Its identity and continuity depend so much on the repeated choices the owner has to make, of precisely when and how to perform every operation from planting to bottling, that he has to be trusted with the final decision of what the château wine consists of. A recent sign of how seriously owners take their responsibilities is the proliferation of 'second labels' for batches of wine that fail to meet self-imposed standards.

This is the Médoc method. St-Emilion is different. Some of its châteaux, the Premiers Grands Crus, have a semi-permanent classification renewable (in theory) after ten years – and last reviewed in 1969. Others, the Grands Crus, have to submit each vintage for tasting.

Only the Médoc and the single Château Haut-Brion in Graves were classified in 1855. The list divides them into five classes, but stresses that the order within each class is not to be considered significant. Only one official change has been made since: the promotion in 1973 of Château Mouton-Rothschild from second- to first-growth.

CRUS BOURGEOIS AND PETITS CHATEAUX

Whether an unclassed château has any official rank or not is not simple either. It depends partly on whether the owner is a loner or a joiner, since membership of the Syndicate of Crus Bourgeois, the next ranking authority, is purely voluntary. A dozen estates that have been semi-officially considered 'exceptional' (but unclassed) ever since 1855 have never joined and have no official rank – which does not necessarily prevent them from printing 'Exceptionnel' on their labels.

On its latest (1978) list the Syndicate has 127 members divided into three categories described in the following paragraphs. Its members are given their official rank in the entries that follow.

Meanwhile the unofficial Crus Exceptionnels are: Ch'x Angludet (Cantenac, Margaux); Bel-Air-Marquis-d'Aligre (Soussans, Margaux); La Couronne (Pauillac); Fonbadet (Pauillac); Gloria (St-Julien); Labégorce (Margaux); Labégorce-Zédé (Margaux); Lanessan (Cussac); Maucaillou (Moulis); de Pez (St-Estèphe); Siran (Labarde, Margaux); La Tour de Mons (Soussans, Margaux); Villegeorge (Avensan, Haut-Médoc).

A **Cru Bourgeois** is a property of seven hectares (17 acres) upwards where the owner makes his own wine and has satisfied the Syndicate as to its quality. There are 68.

A **Cru Grand Bourgeois** satisfies the requirements of Cru Bourgeois and ages its wine in oak *barriques*. There are 41.

A **Cru Grand Bourgeois Exceptionnel** must be in one of the communes between Ludon and St-Estèphe, the area of the Crus Classés. It must also bottle its own wine. There are 18.

The terms Cru Artisan and Cru Paysan were formerly used for properties below Cru Bourgeois in size and/or quality. Nowadays the wine trade lumps them all together as Petits Châteaux – a relative term, since no doubt Rothschilds consider Crus Grands Bourgeois in these terms.

A great number of the thousands that used to exist are now allied to the *caves coopératives*, but many are sought out by wine merchants and given the dignity of their own labels. Many, indeed, lose their identity in the anonymity of the cooperative and then miraculously find it again later. There is no object in listing their endless names, however evocative, but to the claret lover with an open mind they are always worth exploring, offering some of the best bargains in France. In good vintages, drunk at no more than three or four years old, they can be both delicious and reasonable in price.

THE BORDEAUX CLASSIFICATION OF 1855

First-Growths (Premiers Crus)

Château Lafite-Rothschild, Pauillac
Château Latour, Pauillac
Château Margaux, Margaux
Château Haut-Brion, Pessac, Graves

Second-Growths (Deuxièmes Crus)

Château Mouton-Rothschild, Pauillac
Château Rausan-Ségla, Margaux
Château Rauzan-Gassies, Margaux
Château Léoville-Las-Cases, St-Julien
Château Léoville-Poyferré, St-Julien
Château Léoville-Barton, St-Julien
Château Durfort-Vivens, Margaux
Château Lascombes, Margaux
Château Gruaud-Larose, St-Julien
Château Brane-Cantenac, Cantenac-Margaux
Château Pichon-Longueville-Baron, Pauillac
Château Pichon-Lalande, Pauillac
Château Ducru-Beaucaillou, St-Julien
Château Cos d'Estournel, St-Estèphe
Château Montrose, St-Estèphe

Third-Growths (Troisièmes Crus)

Château Giscours, Labarde-Margaux
Château Kirwan, Cantenac-Margaux
Château d'Issan, Cantenac-Margaux
Château Lagrange, St-Julien
Château Langoa-Barton, St-Julien
Château Malescot-St-Exupéry, Margaux
Château Cantenac-Brown, Cantenac-Margaux
Château Palmer, Cantenac-Margaux
Château La Lagune, Ludon
Château Desmirail, Margaux
Château Calon-Ségur, St-Estèphe
Château Ferrière, Margaux
Château Marquis d'Alesme-Becker, Margaux
Château Boyd-Cantenac, Cantenac-Margaux

Fourth-Growths (Quatrièmes Crus)

Château St-Pierre (Bontemps et Sevaistre) St-Julien
Château Branaire-Ducru, St-Julien
Château Talbot, St-Julien
Château Duhart-Milon-Rothschild, Pauillac
Château Pouget, Cantenac-Margaux
Château La Tour-Carnet, St-Laurent
Château Lafon-Rochet, St-Estèphe
Château Beychevelle, St-Julien
Château Prieuré-Lichine, Cantenac-Margaux
Château Marquis-de-Terme, Margaux

Fifth-Growths (Cinquièmes Crus)

Château Pontet-Canet, Pauillac
Château Batailley, Pauillac
Château Grand-Puy-Lacoste, Pauillac
Château Grand-Puy-Ducasse, Pauillac
Château Haut-Batailley, Pauillac
Château Lynch-Bages, Pauillac
Château Lynch-Moussas, Pauillac
Château Dauzac, Labarde-Margaux
Château Mouton-Baronne-Philippe, Pauillac (formerly known as Mouton d'Armaihacq)
Château du Tertre, Arsac-Margaux
Château Haut-Bages-Libéral, Pauillac
Château Pédesclaux, Pauillac
Château Belgrave, St-Laurent
Château de Camensac, St-Laurent
Château Cos Labory, St-Estèphe
Château Clerc-Milon-Rothschild, Pauillac
Château Croizet-Bages, Pauillac
Château Cantemerle, Macau

The red grapes of Bordeaux

The particulars given in the following pages of each of the principal Bordeaux châteaux include the proportions of the different grape varieties in their vineyards, as far as they are known.

The classic Bordeaux varieties are all related, probably descended from the ancient *biturica*, whose name is still preserved as Vidure (a synonym for Cabernet in the Graves). Over the centuries, four main varieties have been selected for a combination of fertility, disease resistance, flavour and adaptability to the Bordeaux soils.

Cabernet Sauvignon is dominant in the Médoc. It is the most highly flavoured, with small berries making dark, tannic wine that demands ageing, but then has both depth and 'cut' of flavour. It flowers well and evenly and ripens a modest crop relatively late, resisting rot better than softer and thinner-skinned varieties. Being a late ripener it needs warm soil. Gravel suits it well, but the colder clay of Pomerol makes it unsatisfactory.

Its close cousin, the **Cabernet Franc**, is a bigger, juicier grape. Before the introduction of Cabernet Sauvignon in the eighteenth century, it was the mainstay of Bordeaux and is still widely planted, particularly in Pomerol and St-Emilion, where it is called the Bouchet. Its wine has delicious soft-fruit flavours (which are vividly seen in Chinon and Bourgueil, wines made from it on the Loire) but less tannin and 'depth'. Less regular flowering and a thinner skin are also drawbacks, at least in the Médoc.

More important today is the **Merlot**, a precocious grape that buds, flowers and ripens early, making it more vulnerable in spring but ready to pick sooner, with an extra degree of alcohol in its higher sugar. Unfortunately, at harvest time its tight bunches need only a little rain to start them rotting.

Merlot wine has good colour and an equally spicy but softer flavour than Cabernet Sauvignon, making wine that

THE LICHINE CLASSIFICATION

In 1959, Alexis Lichine proposed a totally new classification for the whole of Bordeaux to unify the system. His ranking is in five steps up from Bon Cru to Cru Hors Classe. It seems a thoroughly well-worked-out idea, even if the placings would cause arguments. Although over 20 years have passed, it may still bear fruit. Certainly Bordeaux is always rumbling with discussion about new classifications. However much the knowledgeable affect to despise them, they still have a powerful hypnotic effect.

THE WINE TRADE IN BORDEAUX

Since Roman times, when a *negotiator britannicus* was reported buying wine in Burdigala, Bordeaux's overseas trade has been one of the mainstays of the life of the city. In the Middle Ages the chief customer was England. From the seventeenth century it became the Dutch, and later the Germans, then the English again and latterly the Americans. The north of France, and above all Belgium, now absorb the biggest share, much of it by direct sales.

For two centuries up to the 1960s the trade was largely in the hands of a group of négociants, nearly all of foreign origin, with their offices and cellars on the Quai des Chartrons, on the river just north of the centre of the city. The oldest firm still in business is the Dutch Beyermann, founded in 1620. The 'Chartronnais' families, including Cruse, Calvet, Barton & Guestier, Johnston and Eschenauer, were household names and their power was considerable.

Their role has changed and their importance diminished with the modern growth of direct sales from the châteaux, of bottling at the châteaux and above all of the value of stock. A serious slump in the mid-1970s crippled several of the best-known firms. A number have been taken over by foreign interests. New ways of selling new kinds of brand-name wines have created a new class of trader.

The following entries are the 28 top Bordeaux merchants, ranked by turnover (1980 figures).

Castel Frères

Principal: Pierre Castel. Offices in Bordeaux. Turnover 737m. francs. 6% of the business is export, the great bulk of it Castelvin, 'V.C.C.' (*Vin de consommation courante*). Castel have huge properties in Arcins, Haut-Médoc, where they bought the growers' cooperative and two big châteaux, in the lower Médoc and the Côtes de Bourg.

Etablissement Cordier

Principal: Jean Cordier. Offices in Bordeaux. Turnover 236m. francs. 55% of the business is export. The Cordiers own half a dozen well-known châteaux including Gruaud-Larose, Talbot, Meyney, Lafaurie-Peyraguey, Clos des Jacobins.

Barton & Guestier

Principal: Marc Henrion. Offices in Blanquefort, near Bordeaux. Turnover 200m. francs. 77% of the business is export, mostly of appellation wines in bottle. The original firm, founded in 1725 by an Irishman whose descendants still own Ch. Langoa-Barton, is now reduced to a name belonging to Chemineau-Frères, part of Seagram's.

La Baronnie (formerly called La Bergerie)

Principal: Philippe Cottin. Offices in Pauillac. Turnover 145m. francs. 64% is export, entirely of Bordeaux wine, including the Rothschild estates and Mouton-Cadet.

C.V.B.G. (Consortium Vinicole de Bordeaux et de Gironde)

Includes Dourthe, Kressmann and several other old firms. Principal: Jean-Paul Jauffret, who as head of the C.I.V.B. introduced a successful price stabilizing system. Offices in Bordeaux, cellars at Ch. Maucaillou, Moulis. Turnover 131m. francs. 72% is export, all of appellation wines.

---

matures sooner. In the Médoc a judicious proportion – rarely above 40 per cent – is used; rather more in the Graves; more again in St-Emilion, and in Pomerol up to 95 per cent. This is the grape that gives Château Petrus its opulent texture and flavour.

A fourth red grape that is still used in small amounts in the Médoc is the **Petit Verdot**, another Cabernet cousin that ripens late with good flavour and ageing qualities, but flowers irregularly and has other quirks. A little in the vineyard is nonetheless a source of added complexity and 'backbone' in the wine.

A fifth, found more in St-Emilion and largely in the minor areas, is the **Malbec** (alias Pressac), a big, juicy, early-ripening grape which has serious flowering problems (*coulure*). It is grown in the Gironde more for quantity than quality. Paradoxically, under its synonym Auxerrois (or Cot) it is the grape of the 'black wines' of Cahors.

In the long run, a château proprietor 'designs' his wine by the choice and proportions of varieties he plants.

The white grapes

The classic white wine vineyard in Bordeaux is a mixture of two principal varieties and one or two subsidiary ones as variable in proportions as the red. **Sauvignon Blanc** and **Sémillon** make up at least 90 per cent of the best vineyards, Sauvignon for its distinct flavour and good acidity, Sémillon for its susceptibility to 'noble rot'. Thus the sweet wine vineyards of Sauternes tend to have more Sémillon, and often a small plot of the more highly flavoured **Muscadelle**. Unfortunately Sauvignon Blanc has flowering problems in Bordeaux which makes it an irregular producer, to keep a constant proportion of its grapes means having a disproportionate number of vines. Recently some excellent fresh dry white has been made entirely of Sémillon. Other white grapes include Ugni Blanc, Folle Blanche, Colombard and Riesling.

Calvet & Compagnie

Principal: Jean Calvet. Founded in Bordeaux in 1870 but originally from the Rhône, and still with connections there and in Burgundy. Turnover 123m. francs. 43% is export of many appellations. 'Caldor' is the main table-wine brand. Includes the well-known firm of Hanappier.

Maison Ginestet

Principal: Jean Merlaut. Turnover 106m. francs. A complicated company with a great history. 99% of the business is Bordeaux wine (in bottle and bulk). 25% is export.

De Rivoyre & Diprovin

Principal: Bertrand de Rivoyre. Offices at St-Loubès (Entre-Deux-Mers) for fine wines and Ambarès for Diprovin, the bulk wine division. Turnover 100m. francs. 30% is export. Owns Rayneau and Co. in the USA.

Etablissements Menjucq

Principal: Jean Menjucq. Turnover 85m. francs. A young family firm specializing in the wines of the southwest.

Lebègue & Compagnie

Principal: M. de Coninck. Turnover 84m. francs. Largely a bulk business, AC and table wines. 53% is export.

S.D.V.F. (Société de Distribution des Vins Fins)

Principal: M. Hernandez. Turnover 82m. francs. Founded in 1973 in difficult times to market fine wines bought at slump prices. 70% is export; all château wines.

Etablissements Yvon Mau & Fils

Principal: Michel Mau. Based near La Recóle. Turnover 80m. francs. 37% export, largely bulk AC and table.

Cruse & Fils Frères

The arch-Chartron family firm, founded in 1819, was sold in 1980 to the Société des Vins de France, specialists in branded table wines. Principal: François Samazeuilh. Laurent Cruse is the buyer. Turnover 75m. francs. 47% export, mainly of bottled appellation wines.

Maison Pierre Dulong

Principal: J.M. Dulong. Family firm founded in 1873. Turnover 75m. francs. 46% of business is export, mainly of AC wines in bottle and bulk to UK and the USA.

Louis Eschenauer

The old Chartronnais company was sold in 1959 to John Holt of Liverpool, now a member of the Lonrho group. Principal: Jean Rourault. Properties include Ch'x Rausan-Ségla, Olivier, Smith-Haut-Lafitte and La Garde. Turnover 70m. francs. Export 42%, appellation and table.

Les Fils de Marcel Quancard

Principal: M. Quancard. Family firm based in La Grave d'Ambarès (Entre-Deux-Mers). Turnover 70m. francs. 60% export, largely to UK, Holland and Belgium. Own several châteaux and several brands, including Bordeaux Rouge 'Le Chai des Bordes' and white 'Canter'.

Alexis Lichine & Co

Principal: Jacques Théo. Turnover in the 70m. franc range. The company was sold by Lichine to Bass Charrington with Ch. Lascombes in 1965. Largely an export business (75%) specializing in Bordeaux classed growths.

De Luze

Principal: F. Heriard Debreuil. Turnover 60m. francs. 80% export business specializing in Bordeaux wine in bottle and bulk. This traditional négociant house was bought by Rémy Martin Cognac in 1981. A large part of the business is in fine wines. Exclusive rights include Ch'x Cantenac, Beauséjour and Filhot.

Borie-Manoux

Principal: Emile Castéja. Turnover 54m. francs. 83% export, mainly appellation wines, with a growing share of the French restaurant business. Properties include Ch. Batailley. M. Castéja's brother Pierre owns Joanne & Co., specialists in fine wines (about 50% export).

Gilbey de Loudenne

Based at Ch. Loudenne in the Médoc and owned by Grand Metropolitan Ltd. Turnover 54m. francs. 82% export, mainly to UK, all Bordeaux wines including brands (La Cour Pavillon, La Bordelaise) and Ch'x Giscours, de Pez, Loudenne, Branaire, etc.

Mestrezat-Preller

Principal: Jean-Pierre Angliviel de la Beaumelle. Office in Bordeaux. Turnover 50m. francs. Merchants in Bordeaux wines from Petits Châteaux to first-growths, all in bottle. Part-owners and managers of 750 acres of vineyards, including Ch'x Grand-Puy-Ducasse, Chasse-Spleen, etc.

Maison Sichel

Principal: Peter Sichel. Office in Bordeaux. Turnover 50m. francs. 100% export business, selling Bordeaux and Midi wines in bottle and bulk, mainly to the Anglo-Saxon world. Owners of Ch. Angludet and part-owners of Palmer. Also own a winery at Verdelais in the Premières Côtes producing fruity modern claret.

Schröder & Schÿler

Founded in Bordeaux in 1739. Principal: Jean-Henri Schÿler. Owners of Château Kirwan. Turnover 40m. francs. 87% exports, particularly to Scandinavia and Holland.

Nathaniel Johnston

Principal: Nathaniel Johnston. A Bordeaux family firm founded in 1734. Turnover 25m. francs. 60% export, mostly fine wines. Exclusives include Bahans, the second wine of Haut-Brion.

Mähler-Besse

Principal: Henri Mähler-Besse. Family firm in Bordeaux with offices also in Holland and Belgium, part-owners of Ch. Palmer, specializing in branded AC Bordeaux, e.g., 'Cheval Noir' St-Emilion. Turnover 20m. francs.

Duclot

Principal: Jean-François Moueix. A subsidiary of J-P Moueix of Libourne, based in Bordeaux, specializing in top-quality wines, largely to private customers.

Dubos

Principals: 'Wum' Kaï-Nielsen and Philippe Dubos. Specialists in selling top wines to the jet set.

Mme Jean Descaves

One of the characters of Bordeaux with the biggest stock of rare old top wines at ever-increasing prices.

MEDOC

The Médoc is the whole of the wedge of land north of Bordeaux between the Atlantic and the wide estuary of the Gironde, the united rivers Garonne and Dordogne. Its vineyards all lie within a mile or two of its eastern estuarine shore on a series of low hills, or rather plateaux, of more or less stony soil separated by creeks, their bottom land filled with alluvial silt.

Dutch engineers in the seventeeth century cut these *jalles* to drain the new vineyards. Their role is vital in keeping the water table down in land which, despite its gravel content, can be very heavy two or three metres down where the vine roots go.

The proportion of *graves* (big gravel or small shingle) in the soil is highest in the Graves region, upstream of Bordeaux, and gradually declines as you go downstream along the Médoc. But such deposits are always uneven, and the soil and subsoil both have varying proportions of sand, gravel and clay. The downstream limit of the Haut-Médoc is where the clay content really begins to dominate the gravel, north of St-Estèphe.

The planting of the *croupes*, the gravel plateaux, took place in a century of great prosperity for Bordeaux under its *Parlement*, whose noble members' names are remembered in many of the estates they planted between 1650 and 1750. The Médoc was the Napa Valley of the time and the Pichons, Rauzans, Ségurs and Léovilles the periwigged Krugs, Martinis, de la Tours and Beringers.

The style and weight of wine these grandees developed has no precise parallel anywhere else. In some marvellous way the leanness of the soil, the vigour of the vines, the softness of the air and even the pearly seaside light seem to be implicated. Of course, it is a coincidence (besides being a terrible pun) that 'clarity' is so close to 'claret' – but it does sound right for the colour, smell, texture, weight and savour of the Médoc.

How they discovered which precise parts of a rather monotonous landscape would produce the best wine still remains a mystery. Somehow the names that started first have always stayed ahead. The notion of 'first-growths' is as old as the estates themselves.

Today the Médoc is divided into eight appellations: five of them limited to one commune (St-Estèphe, Pauillac, Moulis, Listrac and St-Julien), one (Margaux) to a group of five small communes, one (Haut-Médoc) a portmanteau for parts of equal merit outside the first six, and the last, Médoc, for the far north.

MARGAUX

The Margaux appellation covers a much wider area than the village: vineyards in the commune of Margaux (778 acres), plus the neighbouring communes of Cantenac (962 acres), Labarde (282 acres), Arsac (217 acres) and Soussans (340 acres) – a total of 2,579 acres, or a little more than Pauillac and a little less than St-Estèphe, with more Crus Classés than any other, and far more high-ranking ones.

Margaux is a big sleepy village, with a little *Maison du Vin* to give directions to tourists. Wine from Margaux itself comes from the lightest, most gravelly land in the Médoc and is considered potentially the finest and most fragrant of all. That of Cantenac in theory has slightly more body and that of Soussans, on marginally heavier, lower-lying land going north, less class. The châteaux of Margaux tend to huddle together in the village, with their land much divided into parcels scattered around the parish. Postcode: 33460 Margaux. Price (1981): 16.5 francs a bottle.

PREMIER CRU

Château Margaux

1er Cru Classé 1855. Owner: Mme André Mentzenopoulos.
AOC: Margaux. 182 acres red, 27 acres white; 20,000 cases.
Grape var: Cab. Sauv. 75%, Merlot 20%, Petit Verdot 5%.
Sauvignon Blanc.
Price (1980): 83 francs a bottle.

With Ch. Lafite, the most stylish and obviously aristocratic of the first-growths both in its wine and its lordly premises. The wine is never blunt or beefy, even in great years; at its best it is as fluidly muscular as a racehorse and as sweetly perfumed as any claret – the very taste and smell of elegance. Young it is not easy to appreciate, often appearing too tough and lean for its fruit.

Like Lafite, Margaux has recently emerged from 15-odd years of unworthy vintages. The late M. André Mentzenopoulos, who bought the property (for 72 million francs) in 1977, invested huge sums in a total overhaul of château, vineyards and plant. His ambition for perfection showed immediately with the excellent 1978. Professor Peynaud advised sweeping changes that put Ch. Margaux back at the very top.

The château is a porticoed mansion of the First Empire, unique in the Médoc; the *chais* and cellars, pillared and lofty, are in keeping. Magnificent avenues of plane trees lead through the estate. Some of the lowest riverside land is planted with white (Sauvignon) grapes to make a light but fittingly polished dry wine. The second label is Pavillon Rouge.

CRUS CLASSES

Château Boyd-Cantenac

3eme Cru Classé 1855. Owner: P. Guillemet.
AOC: Margaux. 44 acres; 6,500 cases. Grape var: Cab. Sauv. 67%, Cab. Franc 8%, Merlot 20%, Petit Verdot 5%.
Price (1980): 22 francs a bottle.

The strange name, like that of Cantenac-Brown, came from a 19th-century English owner. A small property not widely seen nor much acclaimed but full of stalwart old-fashioned virtues, long lasting and highly flavoured in such excellent years as 1970, '75, '78 and '79.

Château Brane-Cantenac

2eme Cru Classé 1855. Owner: Lucien Lurton.
AOC: Margaux. 211 acres; 29,000 cases. Grape var: Cab. Sauv. 70%, Cab. Franc 13%, Merlot 15%, Petit Verdot 2%.
Price (1980): 25.50 francs a bottle.

The most respected name of the Margaux second-growths; a very big and well-run property on a distinct pale gravel plateau. The wine is generally enjoyable and 'supple' at a fairly early stage but lasts well, although some critics have faulted it recently for coarseness and for developing too fast. The 1970 was disappointing for the vintage but the '75 and '78 both hold their own among the good second-growths. The second label is Ch. Notton.

Château Cantenac-Brown

3eme Cru Classé 1855. Owner: Bertrand du Vivier.
AOC: Margaux. 77 acres; 15,000 cases. Grape var: Cab. Sauv. 75%, Cab. Franc 8%, Merlot 15%, Petit Verdot 2%.

A great prim pile of a building like an English public school on the road south from Margaux. Conservative wines capable of terrific flavour (1970 is a monster) and needing 10 years' keeping in good vintages. But most Cantenac is finally a coarser wine than classic Margaux.

Château Dauzac

5eme Cru Classé 1855. Owners: Chatellier & Fils.
AOC: Margaux. 77 acres plus; 15,000 cases. Grape var: Cab. Sauv. 70%, Cab. Franc 5%, Merlot 20%, Petit Verdot 5%.

A property with no recent history to speak of, taken in hand by new owners since 1978. Await results.

Château Desmirail

3eme Cru Classé 1855. Owner: Lucien Lurton.
AOC: Margaux. 27 acres plus; 3,000 cases. Grape var: Cab. Sauv. 80%, Cab. Franc 9%, Merlot 10%, Petit Verdot 1%.

A third-growth that disappeared for many years into the vineyards and vats of Ch'x Palmer and Brane-Cantenac. M. Lurton owns the name and has recently relaunched it, with a second label, Ch. Baudry.

Château Durfort-Vivens

2eme Cru Classé 1855. Owner: Lucien Lurton.
AOC: Margaux. 49 acres plus; 6,000 cases. Grape var: Cab. Sauv. 82%, Cab. Franc 10%, Merlot 8%.
Price (1980): 25.50 francs a bottle.

It is clear that the 1855 classification overdid the second-growths in Margaux, as it did the fifth-growths in Pauillac. The name of Durfort, suggesting hardness and strength, sums up the character of this almost all-Cabernet wine – which seems to want keeping for ever. The same owner makes the much more agreeable second-growth Brane-Cantenac. Since he would be within his rights to select vats of one to sell under the name of the other, Durfort may in fact sometimes be a selection. The second label is Domaine de Curebourse!

Château Ferrière

3eme Cru Classé 1855. Owner: Mme André Durand-Feuillerat.
AOC: Margaux. 10 acres plus; 1,000 cases. Grape var: Cab. Sauv. 7%, Cab. Franc 8%, Merlot 33%, Petit Verdot 12%.

A small plot without a château. The wine is made at Ch. Lascombes and could perhaps be a selection of that growth made primarily for the restaurant trade.

Château Giscours

3eme Cru Classé 1855. Owner: Pierre Tari.
AOC: Margaux (at Labarde). 182 acres; 25,000 cases. Grape var: Cab. Sauv. 66%, Merlot 34%.
Price (1980): 32 francs a bottle.

One of the great success stories of modern Bordeaux and a popular candidate for promotion. The vast Victorian property has been virtually remade since the 1950s by the Tari family, formerly Algerian wine farmers. Their new broom has even included making a 20-acre lake to alter the microclimate: by creating turbulence between the vines and the neighbouring woodland it helps to ward off spring frosts. The wines are tannic, robustly fruity, often dry but full of the pent-up energy that marks first-class Bordeaux – not the suavely delicate style of Margaux.

Château d'Issan

3eme Cru Classé 1855. Owners: The Cruse family.
AOC: Margaux. 75 acres; 11,000 cases. Grape var: Cab. Sauv. 80%, Merlot 20%

One of the (few) magic spots of the Médoc: a moated 17th-century mansion down among the poplars where the slope of the vineyards meets the riverside meadows (once highly productive of wine). Issan is never a 'big' wine, but old vintages have been wonderfully, smoothly persistent. Recent ones appear rather too light to last as well.

Château Kirwan

3eme Cru Classé 1855. Owners: Schröder & Schÿler.
AOC: Margaux. 86 acres; 7,000–12,000 cases. Grape var: Cab. Sauv. 31%, Cab. Franc 31%, Merlot 33%, Petit Verdot 5%.

The third-growth neighbour to Brane-Cantenac. It seems to have few friends among the critics, although it is carefully and lovingly family run and at its best (1961, '70, '75, '79) is as long-lived and classic as any of the second-growths of Margaux.

Château Lascombes

2eme Cru Classé 1855. Owners: Bass Charrington.
AOC: Margaux. 240 acres; 35,000–40,000 cases. Grape var: Cab. Sauv. 46%, Cab. Franc 8%, Merlot 34%, Petit Verdot 12%.

A superb great property (one of the biggest in the Médoc) restored by the energy of Alexis Lichine in the 1950s to making delectable, smooth and flavoury claret. Such poor vintages as '72 and '74 have turned out well, 'great' ones sometimes disappointingly – although not the '61. The second label is Ch. La Gombaude.

Château Malescot St-Exupéry

3eme Cru Classé 1855. Owner: Roger Zuger.
AOC: Margaux. 74 acres; 12,000 cases. Grape var: Cab. Sauv. 55%, Cab. Franc 10%, Merlot 30%, Petit Verdot 5%.

A handsome house in the main street of Margaux with vineyards scattered north of the town. For many years it was run in tandem with Marquis d'Alesme-Becker, but since 1979 has taken flight on its own, showing signs of becoming even finer – although it has already been compared with Mouton-Rothschild for depth of fruity flavour hidden by the tannic hardness of youth. Lighter years (for example '71 and '73) can be delicate and more typical Margaux.

Château Marquis d'Alesme-Becker

3eme Cru Classé 1855. Owner: Jean-Claude Zuger.
AOC: Margaux. 17 acres plus; 3,500–4,000 cases. Grape var: Cab. Sauv. 29%, Cab. Franc 29%, Merlot 29%, Petit Verdot 13%.

A small vineyard in Soussans, run by the brother of the owner of Ch. Malescot. Its wines are known for old-fashioned toughness, the flavour of the heavier soil of Soussans, giving them long life. The wine-making is modern, but the Zuger zeal is perennial.

Château Marquis-de-Terme

4eme Cru Classé 1855. Owner: Pierre Sénéclauze.
AOC: Margaux. 77 acres; 11,500 cases. Grape var: Cab. Sauv. 45%, Cab. Franc 15%, Merlot 35%, Petit Verdot 5%.

A respected old name not enough seen in commerce; the greater part is sold direct to French consumers. It is made notably tannic for very long life – or, more realistically perhaps, for the taste of the French, who like really tough, 'grippy' wine. An original, and none the worse for that.

Château Palmer

3eme Cru Classé 1855. Owners: Société Civile du Château Palmer.
AOC: Margaux. 86 acres; 11,000 cases. Grape var: Cab. Sauv. 45%, Cab. Franc 5%, Merlot 40%, Petit Verdot 10%.

A candidate for promotion to first-growth, whose best vintages (1961, '66, '70, '75, '78) set the running for the whole Médoc. They combine finesse with most voluptuous ripeness, the result of a superb situation on the gravel rise just above Ch. Margaux and old-fashioned long fermentation with not too many new barrels, but, probably most of all, the very skilful selection by the three owners, French, Dutch and English, whose flags fly along the romantic roofline of the château.

Château Pouget

4eme Cru Classé 1855. Owner: P. Guillemet.
AOC: Margaux. 20 acres; 3,500 cases. Grape var: Cab. Sauv. 85%, Merlot 10%, Petit Verdot 5%.

The same property as, and in practice an alternative label for, Boyd-Cantenac.

Château Prieuré-Lichine

4eme Cru Classé 1855. Owner: Alexis Lichine.
AOC: Margaux. 143 acres; 28,000 cases. Grape var: Cab. Sauv. 52%, Cab. Franc 12%, Merlot 31%, Petit Verdot 5%.
Price (1981): 30 francs a bottle.

The personal achievement of Alexis Lichine, who assembled a wide scattering of little plots around Margaux in the 1950s and created one of the most reliable and satisfying modern Margaux, harmonious and even rich at times, needing 10 years to show its real class. The second label is Ch. Clairefort and the third is Haut-Prieuré.

Château Rausan-Ségla

2eme Cru Classé 1855. Owners: MM. Holt (Lonrho group).
AOC: Margaux. 94 acres; 14,000 cases. Grape var: Cab. Sauv. 51%, Cab. Franc 11%, Merlot 36%, Petit Verdot 2%.
Price (1981): 42.50 francs a bottle.

The larger of the two parts of the estate that used to be second only to Ch. Margaux, but has fallen far behind in recent times. At its best ('61, '66, '75) exceedingly fragrant in the Margaux manner, but not the echoing symphony a second-growth should be. The most interesting thing Edmund Penning-Rowsell can find to say about it is the fact that it was (in 1956) the last of the great Bordeaux properties where the grapes were trodden. The former Cru Bourgeois Ch. Lamouroux has been absorbed into the vineyard.

Château Rauzan-Gassies

2eme Cru Classé 1855. Owners: Paul Quié & Fils.
AOC: Margaux. 74 acres; 10,000 cases. Grape var: Cab. Sauv. 40%, Cab. Franc 23%, Merlot 35%, Petit Verdot 2%.
Price (1980): 25 francs a bottle.

No more remarkable than its twin over the last 2 decades. Its 1970 was fading at only 10 years old. A new generation took over in the late 1970s; the 1979 is reputed to be outstanding.

Château du Tertre

5eme Cru Classé 1855. Owner: Philippe Capbern Gasqueton.
AOC: Margaux. 110 acres; 14,000 cases. Grape var: Cab. Sauv. 80%, Cab. Franc 10%, Merlot 10%.
Price (1980): 25 francs a bottle.

Over the last decade there has been better and better wine (starting with a superb 1970) from this formerly obscure vineyard in the backwoods at Arsac. The owner of Calon-Ségur has taken it in hand and given it a strong, robustly fruity character. A wine of the future.

Enjoying claret

There are four important variables among the red wines of Bordeaux. The most important is the vintage, the next the class or quality of the wine, the third its age and the fourth the region.

Ripe vintages upgrade all qualities and districts, intensify their characters, make them slower to mature and give them a longer life span.

The Bordeaux habit is to drink young wines rather cooler than mature ones, and Médocs cooler than St-Emilions and Pomerols. Wines still in the firmness of their youth are served with such strongly flavoured or rich dishes as game or duck (and especially young St-Emilion with Dordogne lampreys cooked in red wine). Mature wines are served with plain roasts of lamb or beef and very old wines with all kinds of white meat or fowl.

It is worth noting that lamb is the almost inevitable choice at banquets in the Médoc.

Enjoying Sauternes

Sauternes and the other sweet white wines of Bordeaux (Barsac, Ste-Croix du Mont) are served locally with such rich first courses as foie gras or smooth pâtés, melon, fish or sweetbreads in creamy sauces, or to bring out the sweetness in lobster. They are popular as apéritifs and also survive the onslaught of a salty Roquefort much better than red wines. They go excellently with simple fruit tarts, or fruit, or alone after a meal. 'Very cool, but not iced,' is the regular formula for describing the right temperature.

Enjoying dry white Bordeaux

Dry white Bordeaux is served in the region with almost any fish dish, especially with oysters (which are often served iced, accompanied by hot and peppery little sausages – an exciting combination). It cuts the richness of pâtés and terrines, but is generally not served as an apéritif without food.

OTHER CHATEAUX

Château L'Abbé-Gorsse-de-Gorsse
Margaux. 25 acres; 4,000 cases. One of a group playing with the name Labégorce north of Margaux. Has not made the reputation of its bigger neighbours.

Château d'Angludet
Cantenac. Owner: Peter Sichel. 72 acres; 7,750 cases. Home of the English partner of Ch. Palmer and, like it, badly undervalued in the official classification. Firm, foursquare wines which take time to show their class.

Château Bel-Air-Marquis d'Aligre
Soussans. Owner: Pierre Boyer. 42 acres; 2,500 cases plus. Despite its grand name, one of the more basic and backward Margaux. It usually rewards patience.

Château Canuet
Margaux. Owner: Jean Rooryck. 20 acres; 3,750 cases. Little-known property with a house in Margaux and scattered vineyards reconstituted since 1967 by the former owner of Ch. Labégorce. Price (1981): 20 francs a bottle.

Château Deyrem-Valentin
Soussans. Owner: Jean Soye. 18 acres; 3,000 cases.

Château La Gurgue
Margaux. Owners: Les Grands Vignobles. 22 acres; 2,000 cases. A run-down château in the centre of Margaux. Since 1978 under the same energetic direction as Ch. Chasse-Spleen and due to re-emerge.

Château Haut-Breton-Larigaudière
Soussans. Owner: Ghislaine de Moor. 10 acres; 1,600 cases. A tiny property better known as one of the few good restaurants in the Médoc.

Domaine de l'Ile Margaux
Margaux. Owner: Mme L. D. Sichère. 33 acres; 3,000 cases. On an island on the river and therefore outside the Margaux appellation, but a fascinating place and rather good wine.

Château Labégorce
Margaux. Owner: Jean Condom. 69 acres; 10,000 cases. A potential frontrunner, grand mansion and all, considered unofficially a Cru Exceptionnel. At present making wine with less than real Margaux elegance.

Château Labégorce-Zédé
Soussans. Owner: Luc Thienpont. 43 acres; 9,500 cases plus. Among the best minor Margaux, in the same Flemish family as the famous Vieux-Château-Certan in Pomerol. One of nature's Crus Exceptionnels.
Price (1980): 13 francs a bottle.

Château Marsac-Séguineau
Soussans. Owners: Les Grands Vignobles. 18 acres; 4,400 cases. Part of the same group as Ch. Grand-Puy-Ducasse (Pauillac).

Château Martinens
Grand Bourgeois, Cantenac-Margaux. Owners: Mme Dulos and J. P. Seynat-Dulos. 55 acres; 4,000 cases. A good property getting better with the adoption of barrel-ageing in the late 1970s. The 18th-century château was built, they say, by three English sisters, the Whites (the subjects of the limerick?).

Château Montbrun
Cantenac. Owner: Lebègue. 20 acres; 3,400 cases.

Château Paveil de Luze
Grand Bourgeois, Soussans: Owner: Baron Geoffrey de Luze. 26 acres plus; 3,000 cases. A gentlemanly estate with smooth, well-mannered wine to match. The small vineyard is being gradually enlarged.

Château Pontac-Lynch
Cantenac. Owner: René Bondon. 17 acres; 1,700 cases. A little place between Ch. Palmer and the river, chiefly remarkable for bearing two of Bordeaux's most illustrious names.

Château Siran
Labarde. Owner: William-Alain Miaihle. 72 acres; 8,000 cases. A fine estate run by a fanatic, regularly making most attractive wine and determined to win classed-growth status (which 40% of his vineyard formerly had, before changes of ownership). Miaihle has commissioned a historical map to put the cat among the pigeons by proving that many classed-growths have a lower proportion of '1855' land than Siran. His heliport and his antinuclear cellar seem to point to a man who means business.

Château Tayac
Cru Bourgeois, Soussans-Margaux. Owner: André Favin. 61 acres; 12,000 cases. Estate with modern ideas, supplies the 'Savour-Club de France'.

Château La Tour-de-Mons
Soussans. Owner: Bertrand Clauzel. 46 acres plus; 6,000 cases. A romantic, old-fashioned little property owned for many years by the family who recently sold Ch. Cantemerle. Generally considered a natural Cru Exceptionnel with round, well-structured wines (40% Merlot).

Château Margaux: the avenue

MOULIS AND LISTRAC

Moulis and Listrac are two communes of the central Haut-Médoc with their own appellations but without the flair of the famous names. Between Margaux and St-Julien the main gravel banks lie farther back from the river with heavier soil. No château here was classified in 1855 but a dozen Crus Bourgeois make admirable wine of the tougher kind. The best soil is on a great dune of gravel stretching from Grand Poujeaux in Moulis (where Châteaux Chasse-Spleen and Maucaillou are candidates for promotion) inland through Listrac.

The total area of vines is 860 acres in Moulis, 1,324 in Listrac (which has seen some of the biggest expansion in the last few years). Closer to the river the villages of Arcins, Lamarque and Cussac have only the appellation Haut-Médoc (q.v.). Postcode: 33480 Castelnau de Médoc.
Price (1981): 12 francs a bottle.

MOULIS AND LISTRAC CHATEAUX

Château La Bécade
Cru Bourgeois, Listrac. *See* Ch. Lafon.

Château Biston-Brillette
Moulis. Owner: Michel Barbarin. 30 acres; 5,500 cases.

Château Brillette
Grand Bourgeois, Moulis. Owner: Raymond Berthault. 70 acres; 9,500 cases. A rising reputation among the good bourgeois wines of Moulis, on the next plateau to the various Poujeaux.

Château Cap Léon Veyrin
Cru Bourgeois, Listrac. Owners: A. and J. Meyre. 20 acres; 3,500 cases.

Château Chasse-Spleen
Grand Bourgeois Exceptionnel, Moulis. Dir: Mme B. Villars. 127 acres; 20,000 cases. Regularly compared with Crus Classés for style and durability. Expertly made with classic methods. Belongs to the owners of Ch. Grand-Puy-Ducasse.

Château Clarke
Cru Bourgeois, Listrac. Owner: Baron Edmond de Rothschild. 185 acres plus; 25,000 cases. A new (since 1973) Rothschild project with every advantage. Second labels Ch. Malmaison and Ch. Peyrelebade.

Château La Closerie
Cru Bourgeois, Moulis. Owner: Mlle Marguerite Douat. 17 acres; 2,100 cases. Small but one of the best.

Château Duplessis-Fabre
Cru Bourgeois, Moulis, Owner: Guy Pagès. 30 acres; 7,500 cases. Run jointly with Ch. Fourcas-Dupré in neighbouring Listrac.
Price (1981): 15 francs a bottle.

Château Duplessis (-Hauchecorne)
Grand Bourgeois, Moulis. Owners: Les Grands Crus Réunis. 40 acres; 3,000 cases. Lighter, more easy-going wine than most in this parish. Part of the same group as Ch. Grand-Puy-Ducasse (Pauillac).

Château Dutruch-Grand Poujeaux
Grand Bourgeois Exceptionnel, Moulis. Owner: François Cordonnier. 59 acres plus; 10,000 cases. Old family property, now one of the leaders of the parish. Tannic wine for long maturing.

Château Fonréaud
Cru Bourgeois, Listrac. Owners: L. and M. Chanfreau. 96 acres; 11,500 cases. Well known with its sister-château Lestage for pleasant, rather light wines.

Château Fourcas-Dupré
Grand Bourgeois Exceptionnel, Listrac. Dir: Guy Pagès. 103 acres; 20,000 cases. (Part of the vineyard is in Moulis.) One of the best in an area of excellent Crus Bourgeois.
Price (1980): 13.50 francs a bottle.

Château Fourcas-Hosten
Grand Bourgeois Exceptionnel, Listrac. Dir: Robert de Crèvecoeur. 96 acres; 8,500 cases. The outstanding property of Listrac today; perfectionist wine-making. 40% Merlot suits the relatively heavy soil, making stylish, concentrated wine to lay down.

Château Gressier Grand-Poujeaux
Moulis. Owners: The Ste-Affrique family. 37 acres; 5,000 cases. Formerly owners of Fourcas-Hosten, hence the confusingly similar label.
Price (1981): 21 francs a bottle.

Château Lafon
Grand Bourgeois, Listrac. Owner: J-P. Théron. 82 acres; 11,000 cases. Also known as Ch. La Bécade.

Château Lestage
Cru Bourgeois, Listrac. Owners: L. and M. Chanfreau. 130 acres; 15,000 cases. *See* Ch. Fonréaud.

Château Lestage-Darquier-Grand Poujeaux
Moulis. Owner: Michel Bernard. 20 acres; 1,000 cases plus.

Château Maucaillou
Moulis. Owner: Dourthe Frères. 100 acres; 20,000 cases. Important property of at least Grand Bourgeois standing, with vineyards partly in Listrac and Lamarque. Good deep wine, tannic but fruity.

Château Mauvezin
Moulis. Owners: Société Viticole de France. 148 acres; 21,000 cases. A big new estate, like nearby Ch. Clarke a sign of the growing importance of the Moulis-Listrac area.

Château Moulin à Vent
Grand Bourgeois, Moulis. Owner: Dominique Hessel. 54 acres plus; 6,000 cases. Run with energy and competence by a young owner since 1978.

Château Moulis
Moulis. Owner: M. J. Darricarrère. 30 acres; 2,500 cases.

Château Pomeys
Moulis. Owner: Xavier Barenne. 18 acres; 1,250 cases.

Château Poujeaux
Grand Bourgeois Exceptionnel, Moulis. Owner: Jean Theil. 108 acres; 16,000 cases. Sometimes known as Poujeaux-Theil. The principal property of the Poujeaux plateau, known for wines of firm underlying structure, fine but daunting when young. Second label: La Salle de Poujeaux.

Château Renouil-Franquet
Moulis. Owner: Jeanne Bacquey. 30 acres; 3,300 cases.

Château Ruat-Petit-Poujeaux
Moulis. Owner: Pierre Goffre-Viaud. 18 acres; 2,800 cases.

Château Saransot-Dupré
Listrac. Owner: Yves Raymond. 20 acres; 3,300 cases.

Château Semeillan
Listrac. Owner: Balleu-Faulat. 28 acres; 3,750 cases.

Cave Coopérative Grand Listrac
Listrac. 320 acres; 38,000 cases plus. One of the biggest Médoc cooperatives with a good reputation.

ST-JULIEN

St-Julien is the smallest of the top-level appellations of the Médoc, with only 1,820 acres, but most of this is classed second-, third- or fourth-growth (no first and no fifth, and very little Cru Bourgeois). Its prominent gravel plateau by the river announces itself as obviously one of the prime sites of Bordeaux. St-Julien harmonizes force and fragrance with singular suavity to make the benchmark for all red Bordeaux, if not the pinnacle. Farther inland, towards the next village, St-Laurent, the wine is less finely tuned. The two villages of St-Julien and Beychevelle are scarcely enough to make you slow your car. Postcode: 39320 St-Julien.
Price (1981): 16 francs a bottle.

CRUS CLASSES

Château Beychevelle

4eme Cru Classé 1855. Owners: The Achille-Fould family.
AOC: St-Julien. 170 acres; 30,000 cases. Grape var: Cab. Sauv. 72%, Cab. Franc 3%, Merlot 24%, Petit Verdot 1%.
Price (1980): 29 francs a bottle.

A regal 17th-century château with riverside vineyards and dazzling roadside flowerbeds on the hill up to St-Julien from the south. Its silky, supple, aristocratic wine is the one I most associate with the better class of English country house. Blandings must have bulged with it. It can be difficult when young but finds a blue-blooded elegance after 10 years or so. 1964, '66, '67, '70, '71 and '75 are all good examples. 1976 and '78 appear disappointing so far. The curious boat on the label commemorates its admiral founder, to whose rank passing boats on the Gironde used to *baisse les voiles* – hence, they say, the name. The second label is Réserve de l'Amiral.

Château Branaire-Ducru

4eme Cru Classé 1855. Owners: Mme N. Tari and Jean-Michel Tapie.
AOC: St-Julien. 118 acres; 20,000 cases. Grape var: Cab. Sauv. 60%, Cab. Franc 10%, Merlot 25%, Petit Verdot 5%.
Price (1980): 28 francs a bottle.

One of the most reliable Bordeaux estates. Vineyards in several parts of the commune; the château opposite Beychevelle. Model St-Julien, relying more on flavour than force; notably fragrant and attractive wine, a favourite of mine in 1966, '70, '74, '75 and '76.

Château Ducru-Beaucaillou

2eme Cru Classé 1855. Owner: Jean-Eugène Borie.
AOC: St-Julien. 110 acres; 12,000–19,000 cases. Grape var: Cab. Sauv. 65%, Cab. Franc 5%, Merlot 25%, Petit Verdot 5%.
Price (1980): 30 francs a bottle.

Riverside neighbour of Ch. Beychevelle with a château almost rivalling it in grandeur, if not in beauty, built over its barrel cellars. One of the few great châteaux permanently lived in by the owner, who also owns Ch'x Grand-Puy-Lacoste and Haut-Batailley in Pauillac. Always among the top Médocs with the firm but seductive flavour of the best St-Juliens. The Cru Bourgeois Lalande-Borie (q.v.) is also made here.

Château Gruaud-Larose

2eme Cru Classé 1855. Owners: Etab. Cordier.
AOC: St-Julien. 189 acres; 32,000 cases. Grape var: Cab. Sauv. 63%, Cab. Franc 9%, Merlot 24%, Petit Verdot 3%.

Second-growth with a magnificent vineyard on the south slope of St-Julien, the pride of the powerful merchant house of Cordier (*see also* Talbot, Meyney, Cantemerle, Lafaurie-Peyraguey, etc). Consistently one of the fruitiest, smoothest, easiest to enjoy of the great Bordeaux, although as long-lived as most. A good bet in an off vintage. Cordier wines come in long-necked bottles. Second wine: Sarget de Gruaud-Larose.

Château Lagrange

3eme Cru Classé 1855. Owners: The Cendoya family.
AOC: St-Julien. 123 acres; 20,000 cases. Grape var: Cab. Sauv. 58%, Merlot 40%, Petit Verdot 2%.
Price (1980): 20 francs a bottle.

A magnificent wooded estate inland from St-Julien but unfashionable in recent years (1962 was excellent) and certainly below its third-growth rank. Professor Peynaud has been called in to advise and recent vintages have regained momentum.

Château Langoa-Barton

3eme Cru Classé 1855. Owners: The Barton family.
AOC: St-Julien. 49 acres; 8,000 cases. Grape var: Cab. Sauv. 70%, Cab. Franc 7%, Merlot 15%, Petit Verdot 8%.

The noble château where Léoville-Barton is made and home of the Bartons. Similar excellent wine, although by repute always a short head behind the Léoville.

Château Léoville-Barton

2eme Cru Classé 1855. Owners: The Barton family.
AOC: St-Julien. 85 acres; 16,000 cases. Grape var: Cab. Sauv. 70%, Cab. Franc 7%, Merlot 15%, Petit Verdot 8%.
Price (1980): 28 francs a bottle.

The southern and smallest third of the Léoville estate, the property of the Irish Barton family since 1821. One of the finest and most typical St-Juliens, often richer than Léoville-Las Cases, made with very conservative methods in old oak vats at the splendid 18th-century Ch. Langoa, built over its barrel cellars. Ronald Barton has been a lion of the Médoc for decades.

Château Léoville-Las Cases

2eme Cru Classé 1855. Owners: Société du Château Léoville-Las Cases.
AOC: St-Julien. 198 acres; 30,000 cases. Grape var: Cab. Sauv. 65%, Cab. Franc 13%, Merlot 17%, Petit Verdot 5%.
Price (1980): 29 francs a bottle.

The largest third of the ancient Léoville estate on the boundary of Pauillac, adjacent to Ch. Latour. Still owned by descendants of the Léoville family; run by Paul Delon, one of the Médoc's best wine makers. A top-flight second-growth and a favourite of the critics, consistently producing connoisseur's claret, extremely high-flavoured and dry for a St-Julien, needing long maturing and leaning towards austerity. The stone gateway of the vineyard is a landmark but the *chais* are in the centre of St-Julien beside the château, which belongs to Léoville-Poyferré.

The second wine is Clos du Marquis. *See also* Château Potensac (Médoc).

Château Léoville-Poyferré

2eme Cru Classé 1855. Owners: Société Civile du Domaine de St-Julien.
AOC: St-Julien. 131 acres; 23,000 cases. Grape var: Cab. Sauv. 65%, Cab. Franc 5%, Merlot 30%.
Price (1980): 29 francs a bottle.

The central portion of the Léoville estate, including the château. Potentially as great a wine as Léoville-Las Cases, although not the same critical success in the last 20 years. A new director, one of the Cuvelier family, is set on rivalling his neighbour. The second wine takes the name of a Cru Bourgeois, Ch. Moulin-Riche.

Château St-Pierre (-Sevaistre)

4eme Cru Classé 1855. Owners: MM. Castelein and Van den Bussche.
AOC: St-Julien. 44 acres; 8,000 cases. Grape var: Cab. Sauv. 63%, Cab. Franc 15%, Merlot 20%, Petit Verdot 2%.

The smallest and least-known St-Julien classed growth but superbly situated and excellently managed by its Belgian owners. No glamour, but fruity, deep-coloured wine from old vines at a reasonable price.

Château Talbot

4eme Cru Classé 1855. Owners: Etab. Cordier.
AOC: St-Julien. 210 acres; 38,000 cases. Grape var: Cab. Sauv. 70%, Cab. Franc 5%, Merlot 20%, Petit Verdot 5%.

One of the biggest and most productive Bordeaux vineyards, just inland from the Léovilles, sister château to Gruaud-Larose and home of its owner. Marshal Talbot was the last English commander of Aquitaine. Like Gruaud-Larose, a rich, fruity, smooth wine but without quite the same plumpness or structure. Also a small quantity of dry white 'Caillou Blanc'. The second label is Connétable Talbot.

OTHER CHATEAUX

Château Beauregard
St-Julien. Owner: H. Palomo. 5 acres. 600 cases.

Château La Bridane
Cru Bourgeois, St-Julien. Owner: R. Saintout. 38 acres; 6,000 cases.

Château du Glana
Grand Bourgeois Exceptionnel, St-Julien. Owner: Gabriel Meffre. 109 acres; 14,000 cases. Oddly unrenowned as one of St-Julien's only two big unclassed growths. The owner is a wine merchant with several properties who has built a giant *chai* more like a warehouse just north of St-Julien. His splendidly sited vineyards produce respectable wine.

Château Gloria
St-Julien. Owner: Henri Martin. 110 acres; 20,000 cases. The classic example of the unranked château of exceptional quality, the creation of the illustrious mayor of St-Julien (and Grand Maître of the Commanderie du Bontemps, the ceremonial order of the Médoc). He assembled the vineyard in the 1940s with parcels of land from neighbouring Crus Classés, particularly Ch. St-Pierre. The wine is rich and long-lasting with less oak flavour than most fine Médocs, being matured in 7,000-litre casks instead of 225-litre *barriques*. Ch. Haut-Beychevelle-Gloria and Ch. Peymartin are names for selections made for certain markets.
Price (1980): 25 francs a bottle.

Château Lalande Borie
St-Julien. Owner: J. E. Borie. 45 acres; 4,500 cases. A vineyard bought in 1970 by the owner of Ch. Ducru-Beaucaillou, where the wine is made. In effect, a second label for Ducru.

Château Moulin de la Rose
St-Julien. Owner: G. Delon. 10 acres; 1,100 cases.

Château Terrey-Gros-Caillou and Château Hortevie
St-Julien. Owners: MM. Fort and Pradère. 44 acres; 5,000 cases. A union of two small properties producing very creditable St-Julien.
Price (1981): 19.50 francs a bottle.

Château Teynac
St-Julien. Owner: P. Gauthier. 14 acres; 1,600 cases.

Commanderie du Bontemps de Médoc et des Graves

The Médoc unites with the Graves in its ceremonial and promotional body, the Commanderie du Bontemps de Médoc et des Graves. In its modern manifestation it dates from 1950, when a group of energetic château proprietors, on the initiative of the regional deputy, M. Emile Liquard, donned splendid red velvet robes and started to 'enthronize' dignitaries and celebrities, wine merchants and journalists at a series of protracted and very jolly banquets held in the *chais* of the bigger châteaux.

The Commanderie claims descent from an organization of the Knights-Templar of the Order of Malta at St-Laurent in the Médoc in 1155 – a somewhat tenuous link. Its three annual banquets are the festivals of Saint Vincent (the patron saint of wine) in January, the Fête de la Fleur (when the vines flower) in June and the Ban des Vendanges, the official proclamation of the opening of the vintage, in September. Male recruits to the Commanderie are usually entitled Commandeur d'Honneur, and females Gourmettes – a pun meaning both a woman gourmet and the little silver chain used for hanging a cork around the neck of a decanter.

The sculpted lion at Château Léoville-Las Cases

PAUILLAC

Pauillac is the only town in the vineyard area of the Médoc, and a pretty quiet one at that. Within the last generation it has been enlivened (if that is the word) by a huge Shell oil refinery on the river immediately north and a marina (although the word sounds more animated than the fact) along its tree-lined quay. Disappointingly there is no old hotel, no restaurant haunted by wine growers. Only the *Maison du Vin* (worth a visit) on the quay gives a hint of its world renown. That, and the famous names on signs everywhere you look in the open steppe of the vineyards.

The wine of Pauillac epitomizes the qualities of all red Bordeaux. It is the virile aesthete; a hypnotizing concurrence of force and finesse. It can lean to an extreme either way (Latour and Lafite representing the poles) but at its best strikes such a perfect balance that no evening is long enough to do it justice. There are 2,336 acres of vineyards with more Crus Classés than any other commune, surprisingly weighted towards fifth-growths – several of which are worth much better than that. Postcode: 33250 Pauillac.
Price (1981): 16 francs a bottle.

PREMIERS CRUS

Château Lafite-Rothschild

1er Cru Classé 1855. Owners: The Rothschild family.
AOC: Pauillac. 225 acres; 20,000–30,000 cases. Grape var: Cab. Sauv. 70%, Cab. Franc 5%, Merlot 20%, Petit Verdot 5%.
Price 1980: 83 francs a bottle.

See The Making of a Great Claret page 60.

Château Latour

1er Cru Classé 1855. Owners: Société Civile de Château Latour.
AOC: Pauillac. 123 acres; 20,000 cases. Grape var: Cab. Sauv. 75%, Cab. Franc 10%, Merlot 10%, Petit Verdot 5%.
Price 1980: 80 francs a bottle.

Ch. Latour is in every way complementary to Ch. Lafite. They make their wines on different soils in different ways; the quality of each is set in relief by the very different qualities of the other. Lafite is a tenor; Latour a bass. Lafite is a lyric; Latour an epic. Lafite is a dance; Latour a parade.

Baron Philippe de Rothschild, proprietor of Mouton, achieved a lifetime's ambition in 1973 when the property joined the first-growths

Lafite lies on Pauillac's northern boundary with St-Estèphe, Latour on the southern, St-Julien, limit of the commune four miles away on the last low hill of river-deposited gravel before the flood plain and the stream that divides the two parishes. The ancient vineyard, taking its name from a riverside fortress of the Middle Ages, surrounds the modest mansion, its famous domed stone tower and the big square stable-like block of its *chais*. Two other small patches of vineyard lie half a mile inland near Ch. Batailley.

For nearly three centuries the estate was in the same family (and up to 1760 connected with Lafite). Its modern history began in 1963, when the de Beaumonts sold the majority share to an English group headed by the banker Lord Cowdray and including the wine merchants Harveys of Bristol. They set in hand a total modernization, starting with temperature-controlled stainless steel fermenting vats in place of the ancient oak. Combined English and French talent has since rationalized and perfected every inch of the property, setting such standards that Latour has, rather unfairly, become almost more famous for the quality of its lesser vintages than for the splendour of such years as 1961, '64, '66, '70, '71, '75, '76, '78 and '79. Its consistency and deep, resonant style extends into its second label, Les Forts de Latour, which fetches a price comparable to a second-growth château and is unusual in not being offered until it is at least halfway to bottle maturity (e.g. 1974 released 1982). Les Forts comes partly from vats of less than the Grand Vin standard, but mainly from two small vineyards, formerly Latour, farther inland towards Batailley. These were replanted in 1966 and their wine first used in the blend in the early 1970s. There is also a third wine, modestly labelled Pauillac, which by no means disgraces its big brothers. Alas, it is sold only in France.

Château Mouton-Rothschild

1er Cru Classé 1855. Owner: Baron Philippe de Rothschild.
AOC: Pauillac. 175 acres; 22,500 cases. Grape var: Cab. Sauv. 85%, Cab. Franc 10%, Merlot 5%.
Price (1980): 83 francs a bottle.

Mouton is geographically neighbour to Lafite, but gastronomically closer to Latour. Its hallmark is a deep concentration of the flavour of Cabernet Sauvignon, often described as resembling blackcurrants, held as though between the poles of a magnet in the tension of its tannin – a balancing act that can go on for decades, increasing in fascination and grace all the time. In 1976 I noted of the 1949 Mouton: 'Deep unfaded red; huge, almost California-style nose; resin and spice; still taut with tannin, but overwhelming in its succulence and sweetness. In every way magnificent.'

More than any other château, Mouton-Rothschild is identified with one man, Baron Philippe de Rothschild, who came to take it over as a neglected property of his (the English) branch of the Rothschild family in 1922. This remarkable man of many talents (poet, dramatist, racing-driver among them) determined to raise Mouton from being first in the 1855 list of second-growths to parity with Lafite. It took him 51 years of effort, argument, publicity, and above all perfectionist wine-making. He gained official promotion in 1973, the only change ever made to the 1855 classification.

What modest house there was at Mouton is no longer inhabited. Baron Philippe and his American wife Pauline created a completely new house in the stone stable block opposite and collected in the same building the world's greatest museum of works of art relating to wine, displayed with unique flair (and open to the public by appointment).

The baron's love of the arts (and knack for publicity) led him to commission a different famous artist to design the top panel of the Mouton label every year from 1945 on. Of these vintages the most famous are the 1949 (the owner's favourite), '53, '59, '61, '66, '70 and '75.

Other properties of the baron's in Pauillac are the Châteaux Mouton-Baronne-Philippe and Clerc-Milon, and La Baronnie, his company that produces and markets Mouton-Cadet, the best-selling branded Bordeaux. Mouton itself has no second label; wine not up to Grand Vin standard is blended (along with much else) into Mouton-Cadet, which maintains a consistently high level of value for money.

CRUS CLASSES

Château Batailley

5eme Cru Classé 1855. Owners: The Nonie-Borie family, Dir: Emile Castéja.
AOC: Pauillac. 110 acres; 20,000 cases. Grape var: Cab. Sauv. 70%, Cab. Franc 5%, Merlot 22%, Petit Verdot 3%.

The name of the estate, another of those divided into easily confusable parts, comes from an Anglo-French disagreement in the 15th century. Charles II's favourite wine merchant was called Joseph Batailhé – I like to think he was a son of this soil, the wooded inland part of Pauillac. Batailley is the larger property and retains the lovely little mid-nineteenth-century château in its 'English' park. Its wine is tannic, muscle-bound for years, never exactly graceful but eventually balancing its austerity with sweetness: old (20-year) bottles keep great nerve and vigour. These are the Pauillacs that approach St-Estèphe in style.

Château Clerc-Milon

5eme Cru Classé 1855. Owner: Baron Philippe de Rothschild.
AOC: Pauillac. 68 acres; 9,500 cases. Grape var: Cab. Sauv. 70%, Cab. Franc 10%, Merlot 20%.
Price 1980: 27 francs a bottle.

An obscure little estate known as Clerc-Milon-Mondon until 1970, when it was bought by Baron Philippe de Rothschild. The vineyard (there is no château) is promisingly positioned between Château Lafite, Château Mouton-Rothschild and Pauillac's notorious riverside oil refinery. Typical Rothschild perfectionism, energy and money have made a series of good vintages, starting with a remarkably fine 1970.

Château Croizet-Bages

5eme Cru Classé 1855. Owners: Paul Quié & fils.
AOC: Pauillac. 52 acres; 8,000 cases. Grape var: Cab. Sauv. 37%, Cab. Franc 30%, Merlot 30%, Petit Verdot and Malbec 3%.

A property respected for round and sound, not exactly glamorous Pauillac, belonging to the owners of Ch. Rauzan-Gassies, Margaux. No château, but vineyards on the Bages plateau between Lynch-Bages and Grand-Puy-Lacoste. Compared with the firmness and vigour of the Lynch-Bages of the same year, the 1961 at 20 years old was rather old-ladyish, sweet but fragile. Recent vintages have a name for consistency. The second label is Enclos de Moncabon.

Château Duhart-Milon-Rothshild

4eme Cru Classé 1855. Owners: The Rothschild family.
AOC: Pauillac. 98 acres; 10,000–15,000 cases. Grape var: Cab. Sauv. 70%, Cab. Franc 5%, Merlot 20%, Petit Verdot 5%.
Price (1980): 29 francs a bottle.

The little sister (or baby brother) of Ch. Lafite, on the next hillock inland, known as Carruades, bought by the Rothschilds in 1964 and since then completely replanted and enlarged. Its track record was for hard wine of no great subtlety, but the resolve (seen at Lafite recently) to make the best possible extends to Duhart-Milon. The '75 was surprisingly light, honeyed but without the depth of the vintage. The '76 is delicious and the '79 will be excellent. As the young vines age this will be a great château again. The second label is Moulin de Duhart.

Château Grand-Puy-Ducasse

5eme Cru Classé 1855. Owners: Société Civile de Grand-Puy-Ducasse.
AOC: Pauillac. 80 acres; 14,000 cases. Grape var: Cab. Sauv. 70%, Merlot 25%, Petit Verdot 5%.

Three widely separated plots of vineyard, one next to Grand-Puy-Lacoste, one by Pontet-Canet, the third nearer Batailley, and *chais* on the Pauillac waterfront next to the *Maison du Vin* (the former château). Much replanted and renovated by the same company that owns Ch. Chasse-Spleen (Moulis) since 1971 but already known for big, well-built and long-lived wine (e.g. 1961, '64, '66, '67, '70). Can only be expected to improve as new plantations age.

Château Grand-Puy-Lacoste

5eme Cru Classé 1855. Owner: Jean-Eugène Borie.
AOC: Pauillac. 86 acres; 8,000–14,000 cases. Grape var: Cab. Sauv. 75%, Merlot 25%.
Price (1980): 21.50 francs a bottle.

For a long time, in the words of the 'Bordeaux bible', '*très supérieur à son classement*'. Sold in 1978 by the Médoc's greatest gastronome, Raymond Dupin, to one of its most dedicated proprietors, Jean-Eugène Borie (of Ducru-Beaucaillou, Haut-Batailley, etc.), whose son Xavier runs it. A rather remote but attractive property with an extraordinary romantic garden, a thousand miles from the Médoc in spirit, on the next 'hill' inland from the Bages plateau. The wine has tremendous 'attack', colour, structure and sheer class. The 1978 is a wonder.

continued on page 62

CHATEAU LAFITE-ROTHSCHILD

The Making of a Great Claret

This is the place to study the author's control of his superlatives. Wine for intelligent millionaires has been made by this estate for well over 200 years, and when a random selection of 36 vintages, going back to 1799, was drunk and compared recently the company was awed by the consistency of the performance. Underlying the differences in quality, style and maturity of the vintages, there was an uncanny resemblance between wines made even a century and a half apart.

It is easy to doubt, because it is difficult to understand the concept of a Bordeaux 'cru'. As an amalgam of soil and situation with tradition and professionalism, its stability depends heavily on the human factor. Sometimes even Homer nods. Lafite had its bad patch in the 1960s and early 1970s. Since 1976 it has once again epitomized the traditional Bordeaux château at its best.

As a mansion, Lafite is impeccably chic rather than grand; a substantial but unclassical eighteenth-century villa, elevated on a terrace above the most businesslike and best vegetable garden in Médoc, and sheltered from the north by a titanic cedar of Lebanon. There are no great rooms; the red drawing-room, the pale blue dining-room and the dark green library are comfortably cluttered and personal in the style of 100 years ago. The Rothschild family of the Paris bank bought the estate in 1868. It has been the apple of their corporate eye ever since. In 1980 the 40-year-old Baron Eric de Rothschild took over responsibility from his uncle Elie, who had been in charge since 1946.

Grandeur starts in the *cuvier*, the vat house, and the vast low barns of the *chais*, where the barrels make marvellous perspectives of dwindling hoops seemingly for ever. History is most evident in the shadowy moss-encrusted bottle cellars, where the collection stretches back to 1797 – the first Bordeaux ever to be château-bottled, still in its original bin.

Quality starts with the soil: deep gravel dunes over limestone. It depends on the age of the vines: at Lafite an average of 40 years. It depends even more on restricting their production: the low figure of 20 hectolitres a hectare (1.25 tons or 972 bottles an acre) is achieved by modest manuring and stern pruning.

Vintage in the Médoc starts at any time between early September and late October, depending on the season, when the grapes reach an optimum ripeness, judged above all by the sugar content (although allowance may have to be made for the threat of rainy weather or an attack of rot). In a big vineyard (Lafite has 225 acres) it is impossible to pick every grape at precisely the ideal moment. Picking teams start on the Merlot, which ripens first, and move as quickly as they can. Lafite employs 250 people to shorten the harvest as far as possible.

The vital work of selection starts in the vineyard, with bunches that are unevenly ripe or infected with rot being left on the ground. It continues at the *cuvier*, where the grapes arriving in *douilles*, which hold enough for one barrel of wine, are inspected before being tipped in the *égrappoir-fouloir*, a simple mill that first strips the grapes off the stalks, then half crushes them. (A subtle difference here; most estates use a *fouloir-égrappoir* that crushes and destems at the same time: perfectionists remove the stalks first. By controlling the speed of the rollers it is possible to prevent green grapes being crushed at all.)

The crushed grapes, each variety separately, are pumped into splendid upright oak vats, gleaming with varnish on the outside, each holding between 15,750 and 20,250 litres. If the natural sugar in the grapes would produce less than 11.5 per cent of alcohol in the wine, enough pure sugar is added to make up the difference. In mild weather the juice and pulp start to ferment spontaneously within a day. In cold weather the whole *cuvier* is heated.

The temperature of fermentation is controlled to rise no higher than 30°C (85°F) – enough to extract the maximum colour from the skins; not enough to inhibit the yeasts and stop a steady fermentation. If it threatens to go higher, the must wine is pumped from the bottom of the vat to the top through a serpentine cooling system. Pumping it over the floating 'cap' of skins also helps to extract their colour.

Fermentation may take anything from one week to three depending on the yeasts, the ripeness of the grapes and the weather. The wine may be left on the skins for up to a total of 30 days if necessary to leach the maximum colour and flavour from them. By this time, with luck, the malolactic fermentation will be under way or even finished. The juice is now run off into new 225-litre *barriques* made at the château of Limousin oak from the forest of Tronçais, north of the Massif Central. The remaining 'marc' of skins and pips is pressed in a hydraulic press. Some of the 'press' wine, exaggeratedly tannic, can be blended in if necessary. At Lafite the proportion varies between ten per cent and none at all.

The *barriques*, up to 1,100 of them in a plentiful year, stand in rows in the *chai*, loosely bunged at the top while the malolactic fermentation finishes. Early in the New Year the proprietor, his manager, the *maître de chai* and the consultant oenologist, Professor Peynaud, taste the inky, biting new wine to make the essential selection: which barrels are good enough for the château's Grand Vin, which are fit for the second wine, Moulin des Carruades, and which will be rejected as mere Bordeaux Rouge. This is the moment for the '*assemblage*' of the wines of the four different varieties, up to now still separate. The barrels are emptied into vats to be blended, the barrels washed and slightly sulphured and the assembled wine put back.

For a further year they stand with loose bungs, being topped up weekly to make good any 'ullage', or loss by evaporation. During this year they will be 'racked' into clean casks two or three times and 'fined' with beaten egg whites. The white froth poured on to the top coagulates and sinks, taking any floating particles with it to the bottom. When the year is up the bungs are tapped tight with a mallet and the casks turned '*bondes de côté*' – with their bungs to the side. From now on the only way to sample them is through a tiny spiggot hole plugged with wood at the end of the cask.

At Lafite the wine is kept in cask for a further 18 months, until the third spring after the vintage, then it is given a final racking, six casks at a time, into a vat which feeds the bottling machine. If it were bottled straight from individual casks there would be too much variation.

Complicated as it is to relate, there is no simpler or more natural way of making wine. The factors that distinguish first-growth wine-making from more modest enterprises are the time it takes, the number of manoeuvres and the rigorous selection.

Baron Eric de Rothschild

Château Haut-Bages-Libéral

5eme Cru Classé 1855. Owners: The Cruse family.
AOC: Pauillac. 54 acres; 8,000 cases. Grape var: Cab. Sauv. 78%, Merlot 17%, Petit Verdot 5%.

A vineyard bordering Ch. Latour to the north. The property of the Cruse family for 20 years and probably making better wine than its rather limited reputation suggests. While many of Pauillac's seemingly endless fifth-growths should go higher, this one is about where it should be.

Château Haut-Batailley

5eme Cru Classé 1855. Owner: Jean-Eugène Borie.
AOC: Pauillac. 49 acres; 6,000 cases. Grape var: Cab. Sauv. 65%, Cab. Franc 10%, Merlot 25%.
Price (1980): 20.50 francs a bottle.

Another property of the man whose gifts have established Ducru-Beaucaillou among the leaders. He makes similar but rather less rustic and more gentlemanly wine than his Batailley neighbour. The neighbouring Cru Bourgeois Ch. La Couronne is effectively a selection of Haut-Batailley of a certain style. The second label of Haut-Batailley is La Tour 'Aspic. For reliability and sheer tastiness there are few wines you can choose with more confidence than any of these.

Château Lynch-Bages

5eme Cru Classé 1855. Owners: The Cazes family.
AOC: Pauillac. 170 acres; 25,000 cases. Grape var: Cab. Sauv. 70%, Cab. Franc 10%, Merlot 15%, Malbec and Petit Verdot 5%.
Price (1980): 29 francs a bottle.

An important estate fondly known to its many English friends as 'lunch-bags'; a perennial favourite for sweet and meaty, strongly Cabernet-flavoured wine, epitomizing Pauillac at its most hearty. The Bages plateau, south of the town, has relatively 'strong' soil over clay subsoil. The best vintages (1961, '70, '75) are very long-lived; the '61s are still developing in 1982. The director, Jean-Michel Cazes, Pauillac's leading insurance broker and son of its very popular mayor, has rebuilt the crumbling château beside the great cavernous, gloomy *chais*. His other property is Les Ormes-de-Pez in St-Estèphe. The second label is Haut-Bages-Averous. There is also a tiny supply of soft, fruity Sémillon white.

Château Lynch-Moussas

5eme Cru Classé 1855. Owner: Emile Castéja.
AOC: Pauillac. 54 acres plus; 8,500 cases. Grape var: Cab. Sauv. 70%, Cab. Franc 5%, Merlot 25%.
Price 1980: 17.75 francs a bottle.

Stablemate since 1969 of its neighbour Ch. Batailley. M. Castéja is busily replanting the large but almost derelict estate. 1971 is the first vintage of note. 1975, '76, '78 are good. This must be a good investment.

Château Mouton-Baronne-Philippe

5eme Cru Classé 1855. Owner: Baron Philippe de Rothschild.
AOC: Pauillac. 123 acres plus; 15,000 cases. Grape var: Cab. Sauv. 65%, Cab. Franc 5%, Merlot 30%.

Originally Mouton-d'Armailacq, bought in 1933 by Baron Philippe de Rothschild and renamed in 1956, the name altered again from Baron to Baronne for the Baroness Pauline (d. 1976) in 1974. The vineyard is south of Mouton, next to Pontet-Canet, on lighter, even sandy soil which with a higher proportion of Merlot gives a lighter, quicker-maturing wine, but made to the customary Mouton standards.

Château Pédesclaux

5eme Cru Classé 1855. Owner: Bernard Jugla.
AOC: Pauillac. 49 acres; 8,000 cases. Grape var: Cab. Sauv. 70%, Cab. Franc 7%, Merlot 20%, Petit Verdot 3%.

The least renowned classed growth of Pauillac, scattered around the commune like Grand-Puy-Ducasse, enthusiastically making solid wines much to the taste of its principal customers, the Belgians. M. Jugla (*see also* Ch. Colombier Monpelou) uses the names of two of his Crus Bourgeois, Grand-Duroc-Milon and Bellerose, as second labels.

Château Pichon-Longueville au Baron de Pichon-Longueville

2eme Cru Classé 1855. Owners: The Bouteiller family.
AOC: Pauillac. 77 acres; 11,000 cases. Grape var: Cab. Sauv. 75%, Merlot 23%, Malbec 2%.
Price (1980): 37 francs a bottle.

The next entry gives the background to the unwieldy name. The present owners (also of Lanessan in Cussac) bought the property with its jauntily turreted and spired château in 1935. Current critical opinion favours the wines of the other Pichon. Baron wines are perhaps more full-bloodedly Pauillac, tougher to taste when young, slower developing, but finally extremely satisfying. The '78 is among the 10 best Médocs of the year.

Château Pichon-Longueville, Comtesse de Lalande

2eme Cru Classé 1855. Owners: The Miaihle family. Dir: Mme de Lencquesaing.
AOC: Pauillac. 148 acres; 17,500 cases. Grape var: Cab. Sauv. 45%, Cab. Franc 12%, Merlot 35%, Petit Verdot 8%.

Two châteaux share the splendid 225-acre Pauillac estate that was planted in the 17th century by the same pioneer who planted the Rauzan estate in Margaux. The châteaux are still owned by his descendants, the various sons and daughters of the Barons de Pichon-Longueville. Two thirds of the estate eventually devolved on a daughter who was Comtesse de Lalande – hence the lengthy name, which is often shortened to Pichon Lalande or Pichon Comtesse. The present owners bought it in 1926.

The mansion lies in the vineyards of Ch. Latour, but its vineyard is across the road, behind the other Pichon château, stretching back into the country towards Batailley, where the subsoil grows heavier with a higher clay content. The southern portion of the vineyard is actually in St-Julien. This fertile soil gives a relatively big crop, especially of Merlot; the wine lacks the concentration of Latour but adds a persuasive perfumed smoothness which makes it one of the most fashionable second-growths.

Big investment in the 1960s and new administration and expert advice since 1978 are now making fabulously good wine of the kind everyone wants – stylish Pauillac of the St-Julien persuasion; not so rigid with tannin and extract that it takes decades to mature. The '66 is good, the '70 better, and each vintage since 1975, but particularly the '78, are among the best of their years. The second label is Réserve de la Comtesse.

Château Pontet-Canet

5eme Cru Classé 1855. Owner: Guy Tesseron.
AOC: Pauillac. 182 acres; 20,000–45,000 cases. Grape var: Cab. Sauv. 70%, Cab. Franc 8%, Merlot 20%, Malbec 2%.
Price (1980): 17 francs a bottle.

Sheer size has helped Pontet-Canet to become one of Bordeaux's most familiar names. That, and over a century of ownership by the shippers Cruse & Fils Frères. Its situation near Mouton promises top quality; the 1929 was considered better than the Mouton of that great year. But 1961 was the last great vintage Pontet-Canet has made, and that, like all its wines of that epoch, was very variable from bottle to bottle. The Cruse family did not believe in château bottling. In 1975 the estate was sold to M. Tesseron of Cognac (and Ch. Lafon-Rochet, St-Estèphe), son-in-law of Emmanuel Cruse. The '75 is impressive, the '76 pleasant, the '78 sternly tannic and the '79 very good – things are looking up. The double-decker *cuvier, chais* and bottle cellars are on an enormous scale even by Médoc standards. Seeing the importance of selection on such a vast estate, perhaps we shall see a Pontet-Cadet.

OTHER CHATEAUX

Château Anseillan
Owners: Soc. Lafite-Rothschild. No vines at present.

Château Bellerose
Cru Bourgeois. Second wine of Ch. Pedesclaux.

Château Colombier Monpelou
Grand Cru Bourgeois. Owner: Bernard Jugla. 40 acres; 6,000 cases. Usually attractive stablemate of the Cru Classé Ch. Pedesclaux.

Château La Couronne
Owner: Jean-Eugène Borie. A selection of Ch. Haut-Batailley's wine 'in a certain style', in certain years. Always good; an unofficial Cru Exceptionnel.

Château La Fleur Milon
Grand Cru Bourgeois. Owner: André Gimenez. 30 acres; 4,600 cases.

Château Fonbadet
Owner: Pierre Peyronie. 38 acres; 5,700 cases. A good growth in the category considering itself 'exceptionnel', not officially recognized as such. Part of the vineyard is now Ch. Le Plantey (q.v.). M. Peyronie also owns Ch'x La Tour du Roc-Milon, Haut-Pauillac, Padarnac and Mont-Grand Milon, all in Pauillac.

Les Forts de Latour
See Ch. Latour.

Château Gaudin
Owner: Pierre Bibian. 21 acres; 3,000 cases.

Château Grand Duroc Milon
Cru Bourgeois. A second label of Ch. Pedesclaux.

Château Haut Bages Monpelou
Cru Bourgeois. Owners: Hérit. Borie-Manoux (Emile Castéja). 25 acres; 4,500 cases. Part of the former vineyard of Ch. Duhart-Milon, now in the same hands as Ch. Batailley and better than its rank.

Château Haut-Padarnac
Cru Bourgeois. Owner: Bernard Jugla. Another wine from the Ch. Pedesclaux estate.

Moulin des Carruades
The second wine of Ch. Lafite-Rothschild.

Château Pibran
Cru Bourgeois. Owner: M. Billa. 25 acres; 4,500 cases.
Price (1981): 17 francs a bottle.

Château Le Plantey
Owner: Gabriel Meffre. 40 acres. Formerly part of Ch. Fonbadet, M. Meffre, a merchant, also owns Ch. Glana (St-Julien).

Château Roland
Owners: Soc. Lafite-Rothschild. No vines at present. The manager of Ch. Lafite lives in the house

La Tour d'Aspic
Owner: Jean-Eugene Borie. Second label of Ch. Haut-Batailley.

Château La Tour Pibran
Owner: Jacques Gounel. 20 acres; 3,400 cases.

Château La Tour du Roc-Milon
Owner: Pierre Peyronie. 37 acres; 5,700 cases. *See* Ch. Fonbadet.

Cave Coopérative La Rose Pauillac
Growers' cooperative with an average production of 52,000 cases a year of well-made Pauillac. Labels include Château La Rose.

Caves Coopératives of the Médoc
Annual production in cases

Bégadan	226,400
St-Estèphe	175,500
Prignac	141,650
St-Yzans	106,500
Queyrac	71,700
Ordonnac	70,250
St-Seurin-de-Cadourne	66,250
Vertheuil	63,500
Listrac	62,700
St-Sauveur	55,500
Pauillac	52,250
Cissac	22,500

Using a hand press to crush a sample of grapes

ST-ESTEPHE

St-Estèphe is more pleasantly rural than Pauillac; a scattering of six hamlets with some steepish slopes and (at Marbuzet) wooded parks. It has 2,660 acres of vineyards, mainly Crus Bourgeois, on heavier soil planted with, as a rule, a higher proportion of Merlot to Cabernet than the communes to the south. Typical St-Estèphe keeps a strong colour for a long time, is slow to show its virtues, has less perfume and a coarser, more hearty flavour than Pauillac with less of the tingling vitality that marks the best Médocs. With a few brilliant exceptions the St-Estèphes are the foot soldiers of this aristocratic army. Postcode: 33250 Pauillac.
Price (1981): 15 francs a bottle.

CRUS CLASSES

Château Calon-Ségur

3eme Cru Classé 1855. Owner: Philippe Capbern Gasqueton.
AOC: St-Estèphe. 123 acres; 20,000 cases. Grape var: Cab. Sauv. 50%, Cab. Franc 25%, Merlot 25%.
Price (1980): 30 francs a bottle.

The northernmost classed growth of the Médoc, named after the 18th-century Comte de Ségur who also owned Lafite and Latour but whose 'heart was at Calon' – and is remembered by a red one on the label. A relatively 'easy' wine compared with Montrose, sometimes with more flesh than excitement, but impressively full of flavour as befits its class. The walled vineyard surrounds the fine château. Other Capbern-Gasqueton properties are du Tertre (Margaux) and d'Agassac (qq.v.).

The eccentric Chinese pagoda-style architecture of Château Cos d'Estournel makes it a landmark in St-Estèphe

Château Cos d'Estournel

2eme Cru Classé 1855. Owners: The Ginestet and Prats families.
AOC: St-Estèphe. 140 acres; 20,000 cases. Grape var: Cab. Sauv. 50%, Cab. Franc 10%. Merlot 40%.
Price (1980): 32.50 francs a bottle.

Superbly sited vineyard sloping south towards Ch. Lafite. No house but a bizarre chinoiserie *chai*. The most (perhaps the only) glamorous St-Estèphe, one of the top second-growths with both the flesh and the bone of great claret and a good record for consistency. The director, Bruno Prats, uses modern methods to make wine with old-fashioned virtues, including very long life. The second label is Ch. (de) Marbuzet; Ch. Petit-Village in Pomerol also belongs to him. The 's' of Cos is sounded, like most final consonants in southwest France.

Château Cos Labory

5eme Cru Classé 1855. Owner: François Audoy.
AOC: St-Estèphe. 37 acres; 6,000 cases. Grape var: Cab. Sauv. 35%, Cab. Franc 25%, Merlot 35%, Petit Verdot 5%.

A business-like little classed growth next door to Cos d'Estournel, but only geographically. The rather scattered vineyards with a high proportion of Merlot vines make a blunt, honest St-Estèphe, relatively soft and fruity for drinking in 4 or 5 years.

Château Lafon-Rochet

4eme Cru Classé 1855. Owner: Guy Tesseron.
AOC: St-Estèphe. 110 acres; 8,000-15,000 cases. Grape var: Cab. Sauv. 70%, Cab. Franc 8%, Merlot 20%, Malbec 2%.
Price (1981): 22 francs a bottle.

A single block of vineyard sloping south towards the back of Ch. Lafite on the south bank of St-Estèphe. The château was rebuilt in the 1960s by the cognac merchant Guy Tesseron, who spares no expense to make good wine and has steadily improved the property. He makes full-bodied, warm, satisfying wine which is worth keeping for smoothness, but does not seem to find great finesse.

Château Montrose

2eme Cru Classé 1855. Owner: Jean-Louis Charmolue.
AOC: St-Estèphe. 158 acres; 23,500 cases. Grape var: Cab. Sauv. 65%, Cab. Franc 5%, Merlot 30%.
Price (1980): 29.50 francs a bottle.

Isolated, seemingly remote property overlooking the Gironde north of St-Estèphe with a style of its own; one of the 'firmest' of all Bordeaux, hard and forbidding for a long time, notably powerful in flavour even when mature. The deep colour and flavour of the wine probably come from the clay subsoil under reddish, iron-rich gravel. Being right on the river also helps the grapes to early ripeness. The second label is Ch. Demereaulemont.

OTHER CHATEAUX

Château Andron-Blanquet
Grand Bourgeois Exceptionnel. Owner: François Audoy. 39 acres; 5,500 cases. Made at Cos Labory (Cru Classé *see* Cos Labory). Second label: Ch. Saint-Roch (Bourgeois).
Château Beau Site
Grand Bourgeois Exceptionnel. Owners: The Castéja-Borie family (*see* Ch. Batailley, Pauillac). 55 acres; 6,400 cases. A fine situation in the hamlet of St-Corbian. Distributed by Borie-Manoux.
Château Le Boscq
Owner: Lucien Durand. 34 acres; 4,700 cases.
Château Capbern-Gasqueton
Grand Bourgeois Exceptionnel. Owner: same family as Calon-Ségur (Cru Classé *see* Calon-Ségur). 85 acres; 20,000 cases. Ch'x Grand-Village-Capbern, La Rose-Capbern, Moulin-de-Calon all refer to the same property. Distributors: Dourthe Frères.
Château Coutelin-Merville
Grande Bourgeois. Owner: Guy Estager. 36 acres; 6,000 cases.
Château Le Crock
Grand Bourgeois Exceptionnel. Owners: Cuvelier & Fils. 74 acres; 14,000 cases. A classical mansion in a fine park, home of the owners of Léoville-Poyferré (Cru Classé, St-Julien). Second label: Cru St-Estèphe-La Croix.
Château Haut-Marbuzet
Grand Bourgeois Exceptionnel. Owners: H. Dubosq & Fils. 100 acres; 18,000 cases. Ch. Chambert and Ch. MacCarthy-Moula are Crus Bourgeois with the same owners. Each about 17 acres; 2,000 cases.
Château Houissant
Owners: Jean Ardouin & Fils. 49 acres; 10,000 cases.
Price (1981): 12 francs a bottle.
Château Lafitte-Carcasset
Owner: Vicomte de Padirac. 71 acres; 14,000 cases. Ch. Brame Les Tours is on the same estate.
Price (1981): 13 francs a bottle.
Château MacCarthy
Grand Bourgeois. Owner: André Raymond. 14 acres; 2,500 cases.
Château MacCarthy-Moula
Cru Bourgeois (*see* Ch. Haut-Marbuzet).
Château (de) Marbuzet
Grand Bourgeois Exceptionnel. The second label of Cos d'Estournel (Cru Classé *see* Cos d'Estournel).
Château Meyney
Grand Bourgeois Exceptionnel. Owners: Cordier (the négociants; *see also* Ch. Gruaud-Larose, St-Julien). 125 acres; 25,000 cases. Known for reliability rather than brilliance.
Château Morin
Cru Bourgeois. Owners: The Sidaine family. 24 acres; 4,000 cases.
Château Les-Ormes-de-Pez
Grand Bourgeois. Owners: The Cazes family (*see* Ch. Lynch-Bages, Pauillac). 70 acres; 14,000 cases. Extremely popular and highly regarded property. Second labels: La Tour-Haut-Vignoble, Ch. Moulin Joli.
Price (1980): 19 francs a bottle.
Château de Pez
Owners: The Bernard family. Dir: Robert Dousson. 60 acres; 10,000 cases. The best Cru Bourgeois in St-Estèphe, although not a member of the Syndicate. Noble long-lived wine of classed-growth standard. (Cab. Sauv. 70%, Merlot 15%, Cab. Franc 15%.) Distributors: Gilbeys of Loudenne.
Price (1980): 22 francs a bottle.
Château Phélan-Ségur
Grand Bourgeois Exceptionnel. Owners: The Delon family. 125 acres; 22,000 cases. Important property including also Ch'x Fonpetite and La Croix.
Price (1980): 13.75 francs a bottle.
Château Tronquoy-Lalande
Grand Bourgeois. Owner: Mme Castéja. 40 acres; 4,600 cases. Well distributed by Dourthe Frères.

OTHER GROWTHS

Château Beauséjour
42 acres; 4,000 cases (also Ch. Picard).
Château Beau-Site-Haut-Vignoble
50 acres; 6,400 cases.
Château Canteloup
41 acres; 3,500 cases (also Ch. la Commanderie; property of G. Meffre, *see* Ch. Glana, St-Julien).
Château Clauzet
9 acres; 1,750 cases.
Château Lartigue
17 acres; 1,500 cases.
Château St-Estèphe and Château Pomys
50 acres; 7,000 cases.
Château La Tour-de-Marbuzet
18 acres; 2,000 cases.
Château La Tour-des-Termes
50 acres; 7,000 cases.

Visiting châteaux

Visitors to the Médoc will have no difficulty in finding châteaux willing to show them how they make their wine, and to let them taste it from the barrel. One simple way of arranging a château visit is to call at one of the little offices called *Maison du Vin*. The principal one is in the heart of Bordeaux near the Grand Théâtre. Margaux, Pauillac, St-Estèphe and several other villages have local ones. They will suggest an itinerary and if necessary make contacts.

An even simpler method, but only really practicable for those who speak some French, is to stop at any of the many châteaux that advertise *vente directe* – direct sales – on roadside signs. They include some important châteaux as well as many modest ones. At any reasonable time (i.e. not during the harvest or any period of frantic activity, and not at lunch time, from noon to two o'clock) you can expect a more or less friendly welcome from the *maître de chai*, the cellar master.

In big châteaux he is a man of considerable dignity and responsibility, whatever he is wearing. He has seen many visitors pass and will make up his own mind, rightly or wrongly, about how much to show you. He will expect moderate praise for the chilly, tannic and (to the non-expert) almost untastable sample he draws from the barrel and hands you in a glass. Unless an obvious receptacle (often a tub of sawdust) is provided you may – indeed must – spit it out on the floor. I tend to wander off ruminating to the doorway and spit into the outside world. It gives me a chance to compose my thoughts – and recover from my grimace.

Clearly the idea of *vente directe* is that you should buy a bottle or two, but you need not feel obliged. The *maître de chai* would often just as soon accept a 5 or 10 franc tip.

Advanced students will have to judge for themselves how far into detailed discussion of techniques, weather conditions and earlier vintages the *maître de chai* is prepared to go. It is not unknown for young and even not-so-young bottles to be opened in the enthusiasm of explanation. But it is scarcely reasonable to expect such treatment.

HAUT-MEDOC

Haut-Médoc is the catch-all appellation for the fringes of the area that includes the most famous communes. It varies in quality from equal to some of the best in the very south, where Château La Lagune in Ludon and Château Cantemerle are out on a limb, to a level only notionally higher than the best of the lower, northerly end of the Médoc. Some of this land lies along the river in the middle of the appellation, in the low-lying communes of Arcins, Lamarque and Cussac – which also, it must be said, have some very good gravel. Some lies back inland along the edge of the pine forest.

With a total of 6,523 acres, the Haut-Médoc appellation is only an indication, not a guarantee, of high quality.

Price (1981): 11.50 francs a bottle.

CRUS CLASSES

Château Belgrave

5eme Cru Classé 1855. Owners: Société d'Exploitation. Dir: M. Gugés.

AOC: Haut-Médoc. 107 acres; 25,000 cases. Grape var: Cab. Sauv. 40%, Cab. Franc 20%, Merlot 35%, Petit Verdot 5%.

A lost property until 1980, now ultra-modernized with the advice of Professor Peynaud. Hold your breath.

Château de Camensac

5eme Cru Classé 1855. Owners: The Forner family.

AOC: Haut-Médoc. 149 acres; 20,000 cases. Grape var: Cab. Sauv. 60%, Cab. Franc 20%, Merlot 20%.

Neighbour of Ch'x Belgrave, La Tour-Carnet and Lagrange in the St-Laurent group, inland from St-Julien and out of the serious running for many years. Largely replanted since 1965 by M. Forner, the energetic Spanish owner of the neighbouring huge Cru Bourgeois la Rose-Trintaudon. The result is good, full bodied, forthright wine with plenty of vigour, needing much longer maturing than the 'easy' Cru Bourgeois.

Château Cantemerle

5eme Cru Classé 1855. Owners Etab. Cordier.

AOC: Haut-Médoc. 61 acres; 6,000–8,000 cases. Grape var: Cab. Sauv. 45%, Cab. Franc 10%, Merlot 40%, Petit Verdot 5%.

Price (1980): 30 francs a bottle.

The next château north from La Lagune, hidden behind a wooded 'park' of mysterious beauty with canals reflecting graceful white bridges and immense trees. The tree beside the house on the pretty engraved label is a plane that now dominates the house completely – a monster.

The old-fashioned estate with dwindling vineyards (half their former size) and totally traditional methods was sold in 1981 to the shipper Cordier (*see* Ch. Gruaud-Larose, St-Julien), who will doubtless extend and modernize it. The old peculiarities included de-stalking the grapes by rubbing the bunches through a wooden grille, fermentation at a high temperature and the use of well-aged barrels for as long as two and a half years. The result, with light soil and a good deal of Merlot, was wine of incredible charm yet formidable stability. Vintages of the '50s and '60s were marvellous; those of the '70s not quite so good.

Château La Lagune

3eme Cru Classé 1855. Owners: Maison Champagne Ayala. Manager: Mme Boyrie.

AOC: Haut-Médoc. 137 acres; 25,000 cases. Grape var: Cab. Sauv. 55%, Cab. Franc 20%, Merlot 20%, Petit Verdot 5%.

Price (1980): 26 francs a bottle.

The nearest important Médoc château to Bordeaux and a charming 18th-century villa. The vineyard had almost disappeared in the 1950s, when it was totally replanted and equipped with the latest steel vats and pipes. In 1961 the owners of Ayala champagne bought it and have been making better and better wine as the vines have rooted deeper in the light, sandy gravel. Sweetness, spiciness, fleshiness and concentration are all qualities found in it by critics. In poor vintages it can almost caricature itself with a rather jammy effect; in great ones it is now on a par with such second-growths as Léoville-Las Cases and Ducru-Beaucaillou. Like a first-growth, La Lagune uses new barrels for all the wine every year.

Château La Tour-Carnet

4eme Cru Classé 1855. Owner: Marie-Claire Lipschitz.

AOC: Haut-Médoc. 79 acres; 16,000 cases. Grape var: Cab. Sauv. 53%, Cab. Franc 10%, Merlot 33%, Petit Verdot 4%.

Price (1980): 21 francs a bottle.

A moated medieval castle in the relatively rolling, wooded back country of St-Laurent, restored in the 1960s and still perhaps suffering from the youth of its vines. The wine is light in colour and pretty in style, maturing quickly. I find it enjoyable, but this is scarcely a fourth-growth if Cantemerle is a fifth.

The châteaux – how the list was compiled

'The only complete list of wine growers in any serious part of France is the telephone directory.' The remark was made to me in Burgundy but it is equally true for much of Bordeaux. Everybody is a wine grower. So who do you put in and who do you leave out?

The answer is a long sifting process, starting with published lists of classified properties at various levels of importance, going through members of syndicates, reviewing wine lists, books and articles, re-reading tasting notes and finally, most of all, relying on people on the spot – merchants, mayors of villages, brokers who specialize in one corner of the country. I am acutely aware of the subjectivity of everything short of the telephone book – but this is the nature of the subject matter.

Some growers have reputations exceeding their worth; others are worthy workers and reliable suppliers but have never known how, or felt the need, to build a reputation.

In some areas where vineyards are very small I have simply had to employ the guillotine – which has been abolished for its original purpose. Otherwise I would not have dared. (*See* index pages 102–103.)

OTHER CHATEAUX

Château d'Agassac
Grand Bourgeois Exceptionnel, Ludon. Dir: P. Capbern-Gasqueton. 86 acres plus; 6,500 cases. The Médoc's most romantic château, medieval, moated and deep in the woods. The owner (also of Ch'x Calon-Ségur and du Tertre) is making increasingly good wine. The Cru Classé La Lagune is nearby.
Château Aney
Cru Bourgeois, Cussac. Owners: Raimond Père & Fils. 54 acres; 11,000 cases. Cussac is the nearly flat parish south of St-Julien.
Château d'Arche
Ludon. Owner: F. Duchesne. 25 acres; 2,500 cases.
Château d'Arcins
Arcins. Owners: Castel. 185 acres; 35,000 cases. The two biggest Arcins properties have recently been restored by the important wine-merchant family of Castel, famous for their Castelvin brand. Their huge new stone-clad warehouse seems to fill the village. Their presence here is bound to make the neglected name of Arcins familiar. Its wine should be of Cussac standard, which can be high.
Château d'Arnauld
Arcins. Owner: Jean Theil. 27 acres; 3,000 cases. (*See* Ch. Poujeaux, Listrac.) A good conservative wine maker.
Château Balac
Cru Bourgeois, St-Laurent. Owner: M. Touchais. 30 acres; 8,000 cases. The Touchais family are better known for their Anjou wines. They make a little white at Balac.
Château Barreyres
Arcins. Owners: Castel. 160 acres; 34,000 cases. An imposing property near the river, now linked with Ch. d'Arcins (q.v.).
Château Beaumont
Grand Bourgeois, Cussac. Owner: B. Soulas. 100 acres plus; 12,600 cases plus. Grand but dormant château in the woods north of Poujeaux, awakened by a new owner in 1979. Second label: Moulin d'Arolgny.
Price (1981): 12 francs a bottle.
Château Bel-Orme-Tronquoy-de-Lalande
Grand Bourgeois, St-Seurin. Owner: Paul Quié. 60 acres; 10,000 cases. Well-regarded property of the family that owns Ch'x Rauzan-Gassies and Croizet-Bages. Tannic wines for keeping. Easily confused with Ch. Tronquoy-Lalande, St-Estèphe.
Château Bonneau
Cru Bourgeois, St-Seurin. Owner: M. Micalaudy. 12 acres; 3,300 cases.
Château Le Bourdieu
Vertheuil. Owner: Mlle Barbe. 134 acres; 12,000 cases plus. Vertheuil lies just inland from St-Estèphe on similar clayey gravel. This big property (which includes the château with the promising name of Victoria) can make good St-Estèphe-style wine.
Château Le (du) Breuil
Cru Bourgeois, Cissac. Owner: Gerard Germain. 57 acres; 13,000 cases. On the edge of the parish just behind the Carruades plateau of Pauillac and Ch. Duhart-Milon. Stylish wines.
Château Caronne-Ste-Gemme
Grand Bourgeois Exceptionnel, St-Laurent. Owner: A. Nony-Borie. 101 acres; 15,000 cases. A substantial property whose label is a mass of medals, but all of long ago. I have found the wine well made but tannic, needing long storage.
Château Charmail
St-Seurin. Owner: M. Sèze. 19 acres; 3,000 cases.
Château Cissac
Grand Bourgeois Exceptionnel, Cissac. Owner: Louis Vialard. 80 acres; 14,000 cases. A pillar of the bourgeoisie; reliable, robust, mainstream Médoc at its best after 10 years or so. M. Vialard is a man of authority and style. Second label: Ch. de Martiny.
Château Citran
Grand Bourgois Exceptionnel, Avensan. Owner: Jean Cesselin. 178 acres; 23,500 cases. A pace-setting Cru Exceptionnel with a wide following and a long record of good vintages. Round, full wine (40% Merlot) with ageing potential. Directed until 1979 by Jean Miaihle (*see* Ch. Coufran, St-Seurin), since then by his brother-in-law.
Château Coufran
Grand Bourgeois, St-Seurin. Owner: Jean Miaihle. 148 acres; 27,000 cases. The northernmost estate of the Haut-Médoc, unusual in being 80% Merlot to make softer, more 'fleshy' wine than its neighbouring sister – Ch. Verdignan (q.v.). Jean Miaihle is president and spokesman for the league of Crus Bourgeois (*see also* Ch. Citran, Avensan).
Château La Dame Blanche
Le Taillan. Owners: MM. Jean and Henri-François Cruse. 11 acres; 1,000 cases plus. The other side of the house at Ch. du Taillan: the name given to the pleasant white of Sémillon and Colombard.
Château Dillon
Blanquefort. Owner: Ecole d'Agriculture. 73 acres; 12,000 cases. The local agricultural college. Some good wines, particularly in '78 and '79.
Château Fonpiqueyre
Cru Bourgeois, St-Sauveur. Included in Ch. Liversan.
Château Fontesteau
Grand Bourgeois, St-Sauveur. Owner: René Léglise. 50 acres; 4,000 cases. Good conservative wine in the classic Médoc style for maturing.
Château Fort Vauban
Cru Bourgeois, Cussac. Owner: A. Noleau. 100 acres; 12,500 cases. Vauban was the military architect who built the Fort-Médoc on the river at Cussac.
Château Le Fournas
St-Sauveur. 34 acres; 6,300 cases.
Château Grandis
St-Seurin-de-Cadourne. Owner: M. Figeron. 14 acres; 1,700 cases.
Château Grand Moulin
Grand Bourgeois, St-Seurin. Owner: R. Gonzalvez. 75 acres; 20,000 cases. Also appears under the name Ch. Lamothe.
Château Hanteillan
Grand Bourgeois, Cissac. Dir: P. Brion. 96 acres; 12,000 cases. Old property lavishly restored and replanted since 1973, now making exciting wine. Since 1979 Ch. Larrivaux-Hanteillan has been part of the same estate. The second wine is Ch. La Tour du Vatican.
Château Hourtin-Ducasse
Cru Bourgeois, St-Sauveur. Owner: Maurice Marengo. 40 acres; 6,000 cases.
Château Lamarque
Grand Bourgeois, Lamarque. Owner: M. Gromand d'Evry. 112 acres; 25,000 cases. The finest remaining medieval fortress in the Médoc, in the village where the ferry leaves for Blaye. Developed by the present owners up to Cru Exceptionnel standards, proving the potential of the central Médoc.
Château Lamothe-de-Bergeron
Cru Bourgeois, Cussac. Owners: Les Grands Vignobles. 104 acres; 16,000 cases. The same owners as Ch. Grand-Puy-Ducasse.
Château Lamothe-Cissac
Grand Bourgeois, Cissac. Owner: G. Fabre. 72 acres; 16,500 cases. Up-to-date property related (by marriage) to Ch. Cissac.
Château Le Landat
Cru Bourgeois, Cissac. Owner: G. Fabre (*see* Lamothe-Cissac). 17 acres; 2,500 cases.
Château Lanessan
Cussac. Owners: The Bouteiller family. 106 acres; 17,000 cases. Includes Ch. La Chesnaye-Ste-Gemme. An extravagant Victorian mansion and park with a popular carriage museum. The best-known estate in Cussac with the standards of a Cru Exceptionnel, if not a Cru Classé. Polished rather than exciting wine.
Price (1980): 22 francs a bottle.
Château Larrivaux
Cissac. 24 acres; 3,600 cases. Now mostly swallowed up by Ch. Hanteillan.
Château Lartigue de Brochon
Cru Bourgeois, St-Seurin. Owner: M. Gautreau. 30 acres; 8,000 cases. M.

Gautreau is also proprietor of the admirable Sociando-Mallet.
Château Lestage
St-Seurin. Owner: M. Simon. 28 acres; 5,700 cases.
Château Lieujean
St-Sauveur. Owner: André Baron. 30 acres; 6,700 cases.
Château Liversan
Grand Bourgeois, St-Sauveur. Owner: A. von Campe. 100 acres; 7,800 cases. Charming German-owned property including Ch. Fonpiqueyre. Conscientious wine-making. Second labels Ch'x des Moulinets and Les Hormes.
Price (1981): 11.50 francs a bottle.
Château Ludon-Pomiés-Agassac
Ludon. A name belonging to Ch. La Lagune, Cru Classé.
Château Malescasse
Lamarque. Owner: Alfred Tesseron. 70 acres; 12,000 cases plus. Estate replanted in the 1970s by American owners, bought in 1981 by the Tesserons of Ch. Pontet-Canet. Promises good wine as the vines mature.
Château Malleret
Grand Bourgeois, Le Pian. Owner: Comte Bertrand du Vivier. 50 acres plus; 11,000 cases plus. The handsome country house of the head of the shipping firm de Luze, on the doorstep of Bordeaux.
Château Le Meynieu
Grand Bourgeois, Vertheuil. Owner: J. Pedro. 22 acres; 4,000 cases. A recent addition to the number of serious and competent bourgeois châteaux.
Château Moulin Rouge
Cru Bourgeois, Cussac. Owner: J. Veyries. 24 acres; 2,750 cases.
Château Peyrabon
Grand Bourgeois, St-Sauveur. Owner: Jacques Babeau. 82 acres; 12,750 cases. Well-structured, tannic wine from a 90% Cabernet vineyard, sold more to appreciative private clients than through merchants. The château had the rare distinction of a visit by Queen Victoria. Second labels include Ch. Pierbone.
Château Pichon
Parempuyre. Owners: Delor & Co. 23 acres; 2,400 cases.
Château Plantey de la Croix
Cru Bourgeois, St-Seurin. Second label of Ch. Verdignan.
Château Pontoise-Cabarrus
Grand Bourgeois, St-Seurin. Owner: M. Terreygeol. 48 acres; 13,500 cases. A serious, well-run property.
Château La Providence
Bordeaux Supérieur, Ludon. 16 acres; 700 cases. The vineyard is just outside the appellation Haut-Médoc. Rather good wine.
Château Puy Castéra
Cru Bourgeois, Cissac. Owner: M. Marès. 60 acres; 13,000 cases. A recent creation, apparently in good hands.
Château Ramage La Batisse
Cru Bourgeois, St-Sauveur. Owner: M. Monnoyeur. 118 acres; 22,000 cases. A creation of the last 20 years. Now one of the bigger Cru Bourgeois with modern methods but traditional oak-aged style, winning medals for quality.
Château du Retou
Cussac. Owner: R. Kopp. 51 acres; 6,500 cases.
Château Reysson
Grand Bourgeois, Vertheuil. Owners: Grand Vignobles de Bordeaux. 99 acres. 15,000 cases. A member of the same group as Ch. Grand-Puy-Ducasse with the same competent management. Its former owner also had a property with the odd name of L'Abbaye Skinner.
Château Romefort
Cru Bourgeois, Cussac. Owner: Laurent Poitou. *See* Ch. La Tour du Haut Moulin.
Château de la Rose Maréchal
Cru Bourgeois, St-Seurin. A second label of Ch. Verdignan.
Château La Rose-Trintaudon
Grand Bourgeois, St-Laurent. Owners: The Forner family. 388 acres; 68,000 cases. The biggest estate in the Médoc, planted since 1965, owned and managed by the same family as the admirable Rioja Marques de Caceres (and the neighbouring Cru Classé Ch. Camensac). Modern methods include mechanical harvesting. Quantity does not seem to impede steady, enjoyable quality.
Château de St-Paul
St-Seurin. Owner: M. Bouchet. 47 acres; 12,000 cases.
Château Ségur
Grand Bourgeois, Parempuyre (alias Ch. Ségur-Fillon). Owner: Jean-Pierre Grazioli. 81 acres; 19,000 cases. One of the finer Crus Bourgeois, on good, deep gravel in the extreme south of the Médoc. Popular in Holland.
Château Sénéjac
Le Pian. Owner: Charles de Guigné. 44 acres; 6,000 cases plus. Old family property with American connections, now carefully run and worth following.
Château Senilhac
St-Seurin. Owner: M. Grassin. 28 acres; 5,700 cases.
Château Sociando-Mallet
Grand Bourgeois, St-Seurin. Owner: J. Gautreau. 35 acres; 10,000 cases. Wine with an increasing reputation, made for maturing. *See also* Ch. Lartigue.
Château Soudars
St-Seurin. Owner: Eric Miaihle (son of Jean, Ch. Coufran). 24 acres; 5,900 cases.
Château du Taillan
Grand Bourgeois, Le Taillan. Owners: MM. Jean and Henri-François Cruse. 40 acres; 5,000 cases. Pleasant red, 60% Merlot, from a charming estate just north of Bordeaux. Ch. La Dame Blanche is the same property.
Château La Tour du Haut Moulin
Grand Bourgeois, Cussac. Owner: Laurent Poitou. 70 acres; 11,000 cases. Full-flavoured wine (45% Merlot) with a wide following. Until his retirement in 1982, M. Poitou managed several other estates for Les Grandes Vignobles (e.g. Ch. Reysson).
Château La Tour du Mirail
Cru Bourgeois, Cissac. Owner: H. Vialard (*see* Ch. Cissac). 24 acres; 7,200 cases.
Château La Tour du Roc
Arcins. Owner: M. Robert. 27 acres; 5,500 cases.
Château La Tour St-Joseph
Cru Bourgeois, Cissac. Owner: Vve. Milineau. 47 acres; 10,000 cases.
Château Tourteran
St-Sauveur. 24 acres; 7,200 cases. Same owner as Ch. Ramage-La-Batisse.
Château Verdignan
Grand Bourgeois, St-Seurin. Owner: Jean Miaihle. 114 acres; 26,000 cases. In contrast to its sister-château Coufran, Verdignan has the classic Médoc proportion of Cabernet and needs keeping 2 or 3 years longer.
Château Villegeorge
Avensan. Owner: Lucien Lurton. 24 acres; 2,300 cases. A minor property of the owner of Ch. Brane-Cantenac and many others, a Cru Exceptionnel in all but name. Deep, rich-flavoured wine from a 50% Merlot vineyard.

Caves Coopératives
Château Chevalier d'Ars
Arcins. 125 acres; 12,000 cases plus. Arcins, in the 'hollow middle' of the Haut-Médoc, had hardly any properties making their own wine until recently. The coop was supposed to be popular among less scrupulous neighbours with grander names for topping-up wines.
'Cru La Paroisse St-Seurin de Cadourne'
St-Seurin de Cadourne. 325 acres; 40,000 cases. The coop of the next parish north from St-Estèphe.
Fort Médoc
Cussac. 100 acres; 12,000 cases. Sound cooperative cellar at the impressive riverside fort built by Vauban to command the Gironde.

APPELLATION MEDOC

The lower Médoc (in the sense of being farther down the Gironde) was formerly called Bas-Médoc, which made it clear that it was this area and not the whole peninsula under discussion. The soil and therefore the wines are considered inferior here. The last of the big-calibre gravel has been deposited by glaciers higher up between Graves and St-Estèphe. Although the ground continues to heave gently the humps become more scattered and their soil much heavier with a high proportion of pale, cold clay, suited to Merlot rather than Cabernet (although patches of sandier soil persist here and there). The wine has distinctly less finesse and perfume, but good body and 'structure' with some of the tannic 'cut' that makes all Médocs such good wines at table. Good vintages last well in bottle without developing the sweet complexities of the Haut-Médoc at its best.

The last decade has seen a great revival of interest in this productive area. Half a dozen big properties have made the running and now offer a good deal, if not a bargain. The 1981 basic price was about 10.5 francs a bottle compared with 11 francs for the appellation Haut-Médoc. The best properties fetch about 100 per cent more than this, whereas in the Haut-Médoc the range runs up to about 500 per cent of a base price.

In 1980 there were 6,585 acres in production in the appellation (out of 25,000 in the whole of Médoc). The legally permitted yield here is slightly higher than in the Haut-Médoc: 45 hectolitres compared with 42 a hectare.

Much the most important commune is Bégadan, with several of the most prominent estates and a very big growers' cooperative. Nearly a third of the whole appellation comes from the one parish. Next in order of production comes St-Yzans, Prignac, Ordonnac, Blaignan, St-Christoly and St-Germain.

The principal producers are given here in alphabetical order, followed by the names of their communes. The central town for the whole area is Lesparre (postcode for all the communes mentioned is 33340 Lesparre).

Price (1982): 10.5 francs a bottle.

LOWER MEDOC CHATEAUX

Château Bellerive
Cru Bourgeois, Valeyrac. Owner: G. Perrin. 27 acres; 4,700 cases.

Château Bellevue
Valeyrac. 27 acres; 6,400 cases.

Château Les Bertins
Cru Bourgeois, Valeyrac. Owner: Dom. Codem (*see* Ch. Greyssac). 49 acres; 6,000 cases.

Château Le Bosq
Cru Bourgeois, St-Christoly. Owner: C. Lapalu (*see also* Ch. Patache d'Aux). 24 acres; 7,000 cases.

Château Carcannieux
Cru Bourgeois, Queyrac. Dir: M. Paul. 22 acres; 5,700 cases.

Château La Cardonne
Grand Bourgeois, Blaignan. Owners: Groupe Lafite-Rothschild. 156 acres; 36,000 cases. A Rothschild development since 1973, a great boost to the lower Médoc with its prestige and predictably well-made wine.

Château du Castéra
Cru Bourgeois, St-Germain. 106 acres; 12,500 cases. A lovely old place with a drawbridge, relic of more exciting times (it was besieged by the English in the 14th century) belonging to the owners of Ch. Lascombes, Margaux.

Château La Clare
Cru Bourgeois, Bégadan. Owner: Paul de Rozières. 50 acres; 10,000 cases. Also owns Ch. Grivière, Blaignan.

Château La France
Cru Bourgeois, Blaignan. Owner: M. Feuvrier. 18 acres; 4,200 cases.

Château Gallais-Bellevue
See Ch. Potensac, Ordonnac.

Château Greyssac
Bégadan. Owner: Dom. Codem. Dir: François de Gunzburg. 140 acres; 16,500 cases. Big, efficient property making sound, light wine, popular in the United States. Second label: Ch. Les Bertins.

Château Haut-Canteloup
Grand Bourgeois, Couquèques. Owners: MM. Sarrazy and Vilas. 73 acres; 20,000 cases.

Château Hauterive
St-Germain d'Esteuil. Owner: M. Lafage. 168 acres; 32,000 cases plus.

Château Haut Garin
Cru Bourgeois, Bégadan. Owner: M. Hue. 16 acres; 4,900 cases.

Château Houbanon
Cru Bourgeois, Prignac. Owner: M. Delayet. 24 acres; 4,000 cases.

Cru Lassalle
See Château Potensac, Ordonnac.

Château Laujac
Bégadan. Owner: M. Bernard Cruse. 62 acres; 14,500 cases. A home of the famous family of shippers, hence well known abroad long before most of the other châteaux in the district.

Château Lavalière
Cru Bourgeois, St-Christoly. Owner: M. Cailloux. 38 acres; 11,000 cases.

Château Lestruelle
St-Yzans
See Cave Coop.

Château Livran
St-Germain (includes La Rose Garomey). Owner: Robert Godfrin. 109 acres; 12,000 cases. A lovely old country house with old vines (50% Merlot). Says M. Godfrin: 'We have the pleasures we deserve.'

Château Loudenne
Grand Bourgeois, St-Yzans. Owner: Gilbey. 96 acres (80 red, 16 white); 14,000 cases. The showplace of the area; a low, pale pink château on a hill of gravelly clay overlooking the river. In English hands for over a century. Great care in wine-making produces well-balanced and long-lived red and one of Bordeaux's best dry whites. The brands La Cour Pavillon and La Bordelaise are bottled here. Price (1980): 17 francs a bottle.

Château Monthil
Cru Bourgeois, Bégadan. Owner: M. Gabas. 41 acres; 8,800 cases.

Château Les Ormes-Sorbet
Grand Bourgeois, Couquèques. Owner: M. Boisvert. 45 acres; 11,000 cases. A conscientious wine maker to be watched.

Château Panigon
Cru Bourgeois, Cibrac. Owner: M. Lamolière. 55 acres; 14,000 cases.

Château Patache d'Aux
Grand Bourgeois, Bégadan. Owner: Claude Lapalu. 90 acres; 26,000 cases. Popular full-flavoured Médoc with wide distribution.

Château Pontet
Cru Bourgeois, Blaignan. Owner: M. Courrian. 20 acres; 4,800 cases.

Château Potensac
Grand Bourgeois, Ordonnac (includes Ch. Gallais-Bellevue, Cru Lassalle and Ch. Goudy La Cardonne). Owner: Paul Delon. 116 acres; 30,000 cases. A very successful enterprise of the owners of Ch. Léoville-Lascases. Well-made, fruity, enjoyable claret (by whatever name) with a stylish flavour of oak – no doubt barrels retired from Léoville.

Château St-Bonnet
Cru Bourgeois, St-Christoly. Owner: M. Solivères. 82 acres; 23,000 cases. Price (1981): 9 francs a bottle.

Château Sigognac
Grand Bourgeois, St-Christoly. Owner: Mme Bonny-Grasset. 104 acres; 12,000 cases.

Château La Tour-Blanche
Cru Bourgeois, St-Christoly. Owner: D. Hessel (*see also* Ch. Moulin à Vent, Moulis). 62 acres; 11,000 cases.

Château La Tour de By
Grand Bourgeois, Bégadan (includes Ch'x La Roque de By, Moulin de la Roque, Caillou de By). Dir: Marc Pagés. 150 acres; 30,000 cases. Extremely successful estate with a growing reputation for enjoyable and durable, if not literally fine, wine.
Price (1980): 13.50 francs a bottle.

Château La Tour du Haut-Caussan
Cru Bourgeois, Blaignan (alias Ch. Pontet). Owner: M. Courrain. 20 acres; 4,800 cases.

Château des Tourelles
Cru Bourgeois, Blaignan. Owner: M. Migneau. 50 acres; 13,000 cases.

Château La Tour Prignac
Prignac. Owner: Philippe Castel. 324 acres; 77,000 cases. Vast new enterprise of the Castelvin family, whose Haut-Médoc headquarters is at Arcins (*see* Ch. d'Arcins).

Château La Tour St-Bonnet
Cru Bourgeois, St-Christoly. Owner: A. Lafon. 100 acres; 15,000 cases plus. One of the pioneers of the lower Médoc renaissance. Produces consistently good wine.

Château Vernoux
Cru Bourgeois, Lesparre. Owner: M. Ducout. 50 acres; 4,600 cases plus. A new recruit: just planted, and the only property at the local market town.

Château Vieux Robin
Cru Bourgeois, Bégadan. Owner: M. Dufau. 30 acres; 6,500 cases.

Vieux-Château Beaujus
Pontiac. Owner: Thea Uther. 40 acres; 5,000 cases.

Vieux-Château Landon
Cru Bourgeois, Bégadan. Owner: Philippe Gillet. 49 acres; 14,000 cases. An energetic proprietor with ambitions. Sound, lively wine.

Caves Coopératives
Bégadan – the largest in the area, with grapes from about 1,400 acres. Labels include Ch. Bégadanais.
Prignac – about 250 acres.
St-Yzans – about 250 acres. Ch. Lestruelle is a label for their better wine. As an example of cooperative quality, the 1970 was excellent at 12 years old.

Racking the wine in the Victorian chai at Château Loudenne

GRAVES

Wine was first made at Bordeaux in what is now the city and the suburbs immediately across the river and to the south. Graves was the name given to the whole of the left (city) bank of the Garonne for as far as 40 miles upstream, beyond the little town of Langon, and back away from the river into the pine forests of the Landes – an area not much different in size from the wine-growing Médoc, but more cut up with woodland and farms and containing few extensive vineyards or big châteaux. Graves' distinguishing feature (hence its name) is its open, gravelly soil, the relic of Pyrenean glaciers in the Ice Ages. In fact, the soil varies within the region just as much as that of the Médoc. Sand is common. Pale clay and red clay are both present. But as in the Médoc, it is pretty certain that by now most of the potentially good vineyard land is being put to good use. In all there are some 3,735 acres of vineyards.

But Graves is too diffuse to grasp easily. It would be helpful (and accurate) if the authorities established an appellation Haut-Graves to distinguish the few communes of the northern section where all the Crus Classés are situated. An enclave in the south of the region has quite different style – of landscape, ownership and wine. This is Sauternes.

Although Graves is almost equally divided between red wine and white, the great majority of the top-quality wine is red. The words commonly used to explain how red Graves differs from Médoc all make it sound less fine: 'earthy', 'soft', 'maturing sooner' sound more homely than inspiring. The late Maurice Healey got it in one when he said that Médoc and Graves were like glossy and matt prints of the same photograph. The matt picture can be equally beautiful, but less crisp and sharp-edged, with less glittering colours.

White Graves at its best is a rare experience – and an expensive one. Very few estates even aim for the unique combination of fullness and drive that comes to white Graves with time. The best is equal in quality to the great white burgundies. Opinion is divided even on the grapes to make it with. Some favour all Sémillon, some all Sauvignon and some a mixture, in various proportions. Some make it in stainless steel and bottle it in the early spring. Others (including the best) make it and mature it, at least briefly, in new oak barrels. The tendency among the lesser growths making dry wine has been to pick too early for full ripeness. Sauvignon Blanc in any case ripens unevenly here. The best makers now concentrate on full ripeness and complete fermentation to give clean, dry wine with plenty of flavour.

The communes of what I shall call 'Haut-Graves' are as follows, starting in the north on the doorstep of Bordeaux: Pessac and Talence (in the suburbs); Gradignan and Villenave-d'Ornon (with very little wine today); Léognan, the most extensive, with six classed growths; Cadaujac and Martillac. South of this district, but increasingly important for similar wine, is Portets. Cérons, on the threshold of Barsac and Sauternes, makes both sweet and dry white wine, the dry now gaining in quality and popularity. Price (1982): 9.5 francs a bottle.

The châteaux of Graves were classified in 1953 and 1959 in a blunt yes-or-no fashion which gives little guidance. Château Haut-Brion having been included in the Médoc classification 100 years earlier, 12 other châteaux were designated Crus Classés for their red wine, in alphabetical order. In 1959, six of them and two additional châteaux were designated Crus Classés for white wine. There is no other official ranking in Graves so all the rest can call themselves Crus Bourgeois (or presumably, come to that, Crus Exceptionnels) as they like. Lichine's classification usefully includes Graves (and St-Emilion and Pomerol) as well as the Médoc. He recognizes 14 Graves châteaux.

PREMIER CRU

Château Haut-Brion

1er Cru Classé 1855, Pessac. Owner: Domaine Clarence Dillon. AOC: Graves. 108 acres; 12,000 cases. Grape var: Cab. Sauv. 55%, Cab. Franc 20%, Merlot 25%.
Price (1980): 80 francs a bottle.

The first wine château to be known by name, late in the 17th century, and although now surrounded by the suburbs of Bordeaux still one of the best of all, regularly earning its official place beside the four first-growths of the Médoc. The '76 and '78 have both been judged the best of their years.

The situation of the 16th-century manor house of the Pontacs is no longer particularly impressive, but its 10 metres deep gravel soil gives deep-flavoured wine that holds a remarkable balance of fruity and earthy flavours for decades. Mouton has resonance, Margaux has coloratura; Haut-Brion just has harmony – between strength and finesse, firmness and sweetness. I shall never forget the taste of an Impériale of the 1899 – the most spell-binding claret I have ever drunk. The present owners, the family of an American banker, Clarence Dillon, bought the estate in a near-derelict condition in 1935. The present president is Dillon's granddaughter. Haut-Brion was the first of the first-growths to install stainless steel vats for the quite quick and relatively warm fermentation which is its policy. Rather than select the 'best' strain of each vine, M. Delmas, the administrator, believes in diversity. He reckons to have nearly 400 different clones in the vineyard. This, and the fairly high proportion of Cabernet Franc, contribute complexity and harmony. As for age, Haut-Brion demands it. The good vintages of the 1960s – '61, '62, '64, '66 – are still developing; the apogee of the 1970s is still many years away. A tiny quantity of very good white Graves (50-50 Sauvignon-Sémillon) is also made and sold at an extravagant price.

The second wine of the château, Bahans-Haut-Brion, is unusual in being a non-vintage blend.

CRUS CLASSES

Château Bouscaut

Cru Classé de Graves (red and white), Cadaujac. Owners: Société Anonyme du Château Bouscaut. (Jean-Bernard Delmas and Lucien Lurton.)
AOC: Graves. 75 acres; 10,000 cases. Grape var: Merlot 60%, Cab. Franc 5%, Cab. Sauv. 35%.

The object of vast expense by American owners from 1969; a handsome 18th-century house with rather low-lying vineyards which have badly needed draining. The Merlot suits this soil better and dominates the vineyard, giving solid wine without, it must be said, overwhelming charm.

The 15 acres of white grapes are predominantly Sémillon; their wine is also more sound than thrilling. In 1980 Lucien Lurton of Ch. Brane-Cantenac bought the estate in collaboration with its former administrator, the man who runs Ch. Haut-Brion.

Château Carbonnieux

Cru Classé de Graves (red and white), Léognan.
Owner: Marc Perrin.
AOC: Graves. 86 acres red, 86 acres white; 15,000 cases. Grape var. red: Cab. Sauv. 50%, Cab. Franc 10%, Merlot 30%, Malbec and Petit Verdot 10%; white: Sauv. 65%, Sém. 35%.
Price (1981): Red and white, 26 francs a bottle.

An old embattled monastery built around a courtyard, restored and run by a family who left Algeria in the 1950s. Bigger and hence better known than most Graves properties, particularly for its white wine, one of the flag-carriers for white Graves. The white is aged briefly in new oak *barriques*, then bottled young, thus keeping freshness while getting some of the proper oak flavour. Three or four years in bottle perfect it. The red faces more competition but is well-made typical Graves, dry and persistent.

Anthony Perrin has also recently restored a small red vineyard, Ch. Le Sartre, and a white one, Ch. La Tour-Léognan, in the same commune.

Domaine de Chevalier

Cru Classé de Graves (red and white), Léognan.
Owner: Jean Ricard.
AOC: Graves. 37 acres; 5,000 cases. Grape var. red: Cab. Sauv. 65%, Cab. Franc 5%, Merlot 30%; white: Sauv. 70%, Sém. 30%.

A strange place to find a vineyard, in the middle of a wood and accompanied by no memorable château; just a plain house. Tree lover that I am, I always wonder why M. Ricard does not chop down a few to add to one of the best but smallest Graves vineyards. The soil and the style of the red wine are similar to the nearby Haut-Bailly; starting stern, maturing dense and savoury. 1961, '64 and '66 were all magnificent in 1981 and the good work continues.

The white wine is second only to Laville Haut-Brion in quality, designed for astonishingly long life. It is made with the care of a great Sauternes, fermented and matured in barrels. To drink it before 5 years is a waste, and the flavours of a 15-year-old bottle can be breathtaking.

Château Couhins

Cru Classé de Graves (white), Villenave-d'Ornon. Owners: Institut National de la Récherche Agronomique. 17 acres. Grape var: Sauv. 50%, Sém. 50%.

The property of the National Institute for Agricultural Research and a Cru Classé without either château or identity at present. It was managed throughout the 1970s by André Lurton, who made both the Grand Vin and a rosé at his Ch. La Louvière, down the road at Léognan. Another part of the property has been run separately at Cantebau-Couhins. Now apparently they are reunited and run by I.N.R.A. The white, when last sighted, was a very high-quality modern, vibrant, grapey wine, good for cutting rich food; not intended for laying down.

Bordeaux glossary

Barrique the standard Bordeaux barrel for ageing and sometimes shipping the wine; holds 225 litres.
Cépage, encépagement grape variety; choice of grape varieties in a vineyard.
Chai, maître de chai the storage place for wine in barrels, in the Médoc usually a barn above ground or slightly sunk in the earth for coolness; in St-Emilion frequently a cellar. The cellar master in charge of all wine-making operations.
Chef de culture in larger properties, the outdoors equivalent of the *maître de chai*; the foreman of the vineyard.
Collage fining; clarification of the wine, usually with beaten egg white.
Cru 'growth' – any wine-making property, as in Cru Classé, Cru Bourgeois, etc.
Cuve, cuvier, cuvaison vat, vat-house, vatting (i.e. time the wine spends fermenting in the vat).
Engrais (chimique, organique) fertilizer (chemical, organic).
Fouloir-égrappoir (foulage, éraflage) rotary machine for tearing the grapes off their stalks and crushing them. *Foulage* is crushing, *éraflage* removing the stalks.
Gérant general manager of a property, the man in charge.
Grand Vin not a recognized or regulated term, but generally used to mean the first or selected wines of a property, in contrast to the second or other wines.
Millésime the vintage year (e.g. 1982).
Monopole a contract between a grower and shipper for the monopoly in handling his wine.
Négociant a merchant or 'shipper'.
Oenologue oenologist or technical wine-making consultant.
Porte-greffe root-stock of phylloxera-resistant vine on to which the desired variety is grafted.
Propriétaire owner.
Récolte harvest.
Régisseur manager or bailiff of an estate.
Rendement (à l'hectare) crop (measured in hectolitres per hectare).
Taille pruning.
Tonneau the measure in which Bordeaux is still bought and sold from the château (900 litres, or from *barriques*) although such big barrels are no longer in use.
Viticulteur a wine grower.

PROFESSOR EMILE PEYNAUD

No single man has had such a direct influence over the style and standards of wine-making in Bordeaux over the last 40 years as Emile Peynaud. A former director of the Station Oenologique of the University of Bordeaux, he is France's most celebrated consultant oenologist, with an astonishing list of clients among the châteaux and the growers' cooperatives of Bordeaux. His great book *Le Goût du Vin* is a recent exposition of his philosophy of wine. To his clients his preliminary advice has sometimes been brutal: he has declined to advise a château unless the owner is prepared to be more selective in choosing his 'Grand Vin', and to sell substandard vats under a second label – or in bulk.

Peynaud has looked for better balance and keeping qualities with less harshness in claret by encouraging harvesting of the grapes as ripe as possible, then adding to the 'free-run' wine at least some of the more tannic pressed wine to give a firm tannic structure. But above all he emphasizes selection at every stage. His clients include, or have included: Châteaux Lafite, Margaux, Cheval Blanc, Rauzan-Gassies, Brane-Cantenac, Giscours, Boyd-Cantenac, Malescot, Prieuré-Lichine, Léoville-Lascases, Léoville-Poyferré, Ducru-Beaucaillou, Lagrange, Beychevelle, Branaire-Ducru, Pichon-Lalande, Duhart-Milon, Batailley, Haut-Batailley, Grand-Puy-Lacoste, La Lagune, Pape-Clément, La Mission-Haut-Brion, Malarctic-Lagravière, Haut-Bailly, Pavie . . .

Château Couhins-Lurton

A 4-acre fraction of Ch. Couhins run by André Lurton, making 800 cases of white.

Château de Fieuzal

Cru Classé de Graves (red), Léognan. Owner: Georges Negrevergne.
AOC: Graves. 42 acres; 6,600 cases. Grape var. red: Cab. Sauv. 65%, Merlot 30%, Petit Verdot and Malbec 5%; white: Sauv. 60%, Sém. 40%.

Perhaps the least known (and one of the smallest) classed Graves châteaux, in no way spectacular but capable of tuning the masculine, tannic, earthy style of the region to fine harmony (e.g. 1970, '75, '78). A new proprietor in 1973 gave it a fresh push. The small production (900 cases) of white is not technically 'classé' although it is as good as some that are (particularly 1970, '71, '78).

Château Haut-Bailly

Cru Classé de Graves (red), Léognan. Owner: Jean Sanders.
AOC: Graves. 57 acres; 8,500 cases. Grape var: Cab. Sauv. 34%, Cab. Franc 16%, Merlot 26%, old vines (a mixture, mainly Petit Verdot) 24%.
Price (1981): 38 francs a bottle.

A modest-looking place with a farmyard air, the property of a devoted Belgian, generally considered one of the top four châteaux of (red) Graves. It makes no white wine. One quarter of the vineyard is a mixed plantation of very old vines. Relatively shallow stony soil over hard clay is an unusual site for a great vineyard and the result can be problems during drought (1976 Haut-Bailly has a raisiny flavour). 1975 was also unlucky. The great years (1966, '70, '78, '79) I can best describe as nourishing, like long-simmered stock, deep, earthy and round. I love them.

Château Laville-Haut-Brion

Cru Classé de Graves (white), Talence. Owners: Société Civile des Domaines Woltner.
AOC: Graves. 12 acres; 1,200 cases.
Grape var: Sém. 60%, Sauv. 40%.
Price (1980): 100 francs a bottle.

The white wine of La Mission-Haut-Brion, first made in 1928 on a patch where M. Woltner decided the soil was too heavy for his red. Bordeaux's best dry white wine. Drunk young its quality may go unnoticed – and its price will certainly seem excessive. The wine is fermented in oak *barriques* and bottled from them the following spring. Its qualities – apart from an increasingly haunting flavour as the years go by – are concentration and the same sort of rich-yet-dry character as Ygrec, the dry wine of Ch. d'Yquem, but with more grace.

Château Malartic-Lagravière

Cru Classé de Graves (red and white), Léognan. Owner: Jacques Marly-Ridoret.
AOC: Graves. 34 acres; 7,500 cases red, 900 cases white.
Grape var. red: Cab. Sauv. 55%, Cab. Franc 20%, Merlot 25%; white: Sauv. Blanc 100%.
Price (1980): 20.50 francs a bottle.

A generally underrated château of notable quality for both red and white wine. A square stone house in a typical Graves landscape, patched with woods and gently tilted vineyards. M. Marly (with Professor Peynaud's advice) succeeds in making traditional wine by modern methods (and with unusually high yields for such quality). The red is a firm, austere, dark-coloured *vin de garde*, finishing fine rather than fleshy. The white (unusual in being all Sauvignon) is dazzling when young but becomes even better – and more typical of Graves – with 5 or 10 years in bottle.

Château La Mission-Haut-Brion

Cru Classé de Graves (red). Talence. Owners: Société Civile des Domaines Woltner.
AOC: Graves. 30 acres; 48,000 cases. Grape var: Cab. Sauv. 60%, Cab. Franc 5%, Merlot 35%.
Price (1980): 64 francs a bottle.

The immediate neighbour and rival to Haut-Brion, equally in the Bordeaux suburbs of Pessac and Talence with the Paris-Madrid railway running in a cutting (good for the drainage) through the vineyard. The Woltners claim that the urban surroundings give them the advantage of one degree centigrade (1.8°F) higher temperature than the open country, and also a large harvesting force at short notice.

The wines show the effect of warm and dry conditions: concentration and force. Beside Haut-Brion, which is no weakling, they can appear almost butch. Michael Broadbent makes use of the words iron, earth, beef and pepper in his notes on various vintages. After due time (often 20 years) they combine warmth with sweetness in organ-like tones. Château La Tour-Haut-Brion is the second wine; a greater character than Haut-Brion's 'Bahans', distinctly tough and tannic (press wine is used). For those – there are many in Bordeaux – who like their wine with 'grip'. The extraordinary white wine, Laville-Haut-Brion, is discussed separately. The Woltners are energetic and devoted proprietors with interests also in the Conn Creek winery in Napa, California.

Château Olivier

Cru Classé de Graves (red and white), Léognan. Owner: P. de Bethmann.
AOC: Graves. 37 acres; 9,000 cases. Grape var. red: Cab. Sauv. 65%, Cab. Franc 15%, Merlot 20% white: Sém. 65%, Sauv. 33%, Muscadelle 2%.

A moated fortress with vineyards operated for the owner by the shippers Eschenauer & Co. (part of the Lonrho group). Its red wine has never enjoyed the fame of its white, which is of the modern school of easy-come, easy-go Graves; a good, light meal-opener. The red vineyards were replaced not long ago and promise serious wine. Ch. Smith-Haut-Lafitte is under the same management.

Château Pape-Clément

Cru Classé de Graves (red), Pessac. Owners: The Montagne family.
AOC: Graves. 66 acres; 10,000 cases. Grape var: Cab. Sauv. 66.5%, Merlot 33.5%.
Price (1980): 41 francs a bottle.

One-time property of Bertrand de Goth, the 14th-century Bishop of Bordeaux who, as Clement V, brought the papacy to Avignon, in fact the Pape du Châteauneuf. The vineyard is in scattered plots and one large block at the extreme edge of Pessac, where it is quasi-rural and the gravel soil finer but no less deep. There is no Cabernet Franc in the vineyard but a high proportion of Merlot. New barrels are used for the whole crop and M. Mussyt, the manager, works closely with Professor Peynaud. The result is a sort of St-Julien among the Graves: wine with plenty of punch but no exaggerated tannin; easier, more 'supple', ready to drink sooner than the Haut-Brions. The '70 is superb at 12 years old; the '75 and '78 need to wait until they are 10.

Château Smith-Haut-Lafitte

Cru Classé de Graves (red), Martillac. Owner: Louis Eschenauer.
AOC: Graves. 111 acres; 20,000 cases. Grape var. red: Cab. Sauv. 73%, Cab. Franc 11%, Merlot 16%, white: Sauv. 100%.

A famous old estate now separated from its original château (which reminded me of an English country rectory) to be reborn and rebuilt, with an almost Californian air of good times ahead. An Eschenauer enterprise which has had a good reputation for many years and looks set to increase and improve on it. The red is round, satisfying Graves; the white (14 acres, not a classed growth) a modern-style grapey Sauvignon.

Château La Tour-Haut-Brion

Cru Classé de Graves (red), Talence. Owners: Société Civile des Domaines Woltner.
AOC: Graves. 20 acres; 3,200 cases. Grape var: Cab. Sauv. 60%, Cab. Franc 5%, Merlot 35%.
Price (1981): 42 francs a bottle.

See Château La Mission-Haut-Brion.

Château La Tour-Martillac

Cru Classé de Graves (red and white), Martillac. Owner: Jean Kressmann.
AOC: Graves. 47 acres; 7,500 cases. Grape var: Cab. Sauv. 65%, Cab. Franc 6%, Merlot 25%, Malbec and Petit Verdot 4%.

The home of the retired shipper Jean Kressmann, a remote little property once in the Montesquieu family (who owned the magnificent moated La Brède nearby). The owner is an enthusiast who patiently cultivates old vines for quality. The white wine, now made in tiny quantities, is classic Graves, best with bottle-age; the red is a good example of the robust, savoury style of the region.

OTHER CHATEAUX

Château Arricaud
Landiras. Owner: A. J. Bouyx. 70 acres; 8,000 cases white: Sém. 70%, Sauv. 25%, Muscadelle 5%; 3,000 cases red: Cab. Sauv. 65%, Merlot 30%, Malbec 5%. Substantial property overlooking the Garonne valley from the south of Barsac, recently making medal-winning wines.

Château Baret
Villenave-d'Ornon. Owners: The Ballande family. 33 acres; 2,000 cases white, 1,800 cases red. Property in the heart of 'Haut-Graves', formerly famous for white wine, unremarkable now.

Château Les Carmes Haut-Brion
Pessac. Owners: Chantecaille & Co. 9 acres; 1,800 cases red: Cab. Sauv. 10%, Cab. Franc 40%, Merlot 50%. A miniature neighbour of Haut-Brion with good Cru Bourgeois standards.

Château Cazebonne
St-Pierre-de-Mons. Owner: Marc Bridet. 15 acres red; 20 acres white.

Château de Chantegrive
Podensac. Owners: Henri and Françoise Lévêque. 54 acres; 14,500 cases red: Cab. Sauv. 60%, Merlot 40%. 57 acres; 12,000 cases white: Sém. 50%, Sauv. 30%, Muscadelle 20%. One of the most substantial properties of the central Graves, using modern methods. The wines are sold under several names, including Ch. Bon Dieu des Vignes, Mayne-Lévêque and Mayne d'Anice.

Château Cheret-Pitres
Portets. Owner: J. Boulanger. 30 acres; 4,000 cases red: Merlot 50%, Cab. 50%.

Château Chicane
Toulenne. Dir: Pierre Coste. 16 acres; 3,000 cases red: two thirds Cab. Sauv. M. Coste, the leading wine merchant of Langon, makes some of the best wines of the district: ripe, vigorous reds and fresh but ripe, grapey whites.

Château de Courbon
Toulenne. Owner: Jean Sanders (*see* Ch. Haut-Bailly). 16 acres; 2,500 cases white: Sauv. 40%, Sém. 60%.

Château Crabitey
Portets. Owners: an orphanage. Minor property making some 3,000 cases of useful red wine.
Château du Cruzeau
St-Médard-d'Eyrans. Owner: André Lurton. 86 acres; 18,000 cases red. 35 acres; 3,000 cases white: Sauv. 85%, Sém. 15%. A Lurton property bought and replanted in 1973. St-Médard, on the southern fringe of 'Haut-Graves', has deep, pebbly soil which should mean good wine.
Château de Doms
Portets. Dir: L. Parage. 55 acres; 3,500 cases white, 3,000 cases red. Second label: Clos du Monastère.
Château Ferrande
Castres. Dir: Marc Teisseire. 80 acres; 14,000 cases red: Cab. Sauv. 40%, Merlot 40%, Cab. Franc 20%. 22 acres; 4,500 cases white: Sauv. 60%, Sém. 40%. The principal property of Castres, just north of Portets, with a good reputation.
Ch. Lognac is the second label.
Château de France
Léognan. Owner: Bernard Thomassin. 37 acres; 6,000 cases red: Merlot 50%, Cab. Sauv. 25%, Cab. Franc 25%. A minor property among some of the best of the district, recently modernized and enlarged. The second wine is Ch. Coquilles (Bordeaux Supérieur).
Domaine de Gaillat
Langon. Dir: Pierre Coste (*see* Ch. Chicane). 20 acres; 4,000 cases red.
Château La Garde
Martillac. Owners: Louis Eschenauer & Co. 100 acres; 20,000 cases red: Cab. Sauv. 70%, Merlot 30%. 16 acres; 2,000 cases white: Sauv. Bl. 94%, Sém. 6%. One of the biggest and best Graves bourgeois estates. The red in good vintages is robust and meaty. I have never encountered the white.
Château Gazin
Léognan. Manager: Jacques Fourés. 25 acres; 4,000 cases red: Cab. Sauv. 90%, Merlot 10%.
Château Grand-Abord
Portets. Owner: M. Dugoua. 30 acres; 4,000 cases red, 2,000 cases white. Recently a well-made red.
Domaine La Grave
Portets. Manager: Peter Vinding-Diers. 2,500 cases red: Merlot 60%, Cab. Sauv. 40%; 600 cases white: Sém. 100%. Very promising new property run by the Danish wine maker of Ch. Rahoul.
Château des Jaubertes
St-Pierre-de-Mons. Owner: Marquis de Pontac. 15 acres red, 20 acres white.
Château Jean-Gervais
Portets. Owners: M. F. Counilh & Fils. 74 acres; 10,000 cases white.
Château Larrivet-Haut-Brion
Léognan. Owner: Mme Jacques Guillemaud. 40 acres; 6,000 cases red: Cab. Sauv. 60%, Merlot 40%; 500 cases white. One of the better second-rank Graves, although a long way from Haut-Brion in every sense.
Château La Louvière
Léognan. Owner: André Lurton. 86 acres; 16,000 cases red: Cab. Sauv. 80%, Merlot 20%. 27 acres; 7,500 cases white: Sauv. 85%, Sém. 15%. The show place of M. Lurton's considerable estates, a noble 18th-century house where he makes avant-garde dry white of Loire-like freshness and typically masculine, earthy red of Cru Classé standard.
Château Magence
St-Pierre-de-Mons. Owner: Dominique Guillot de Suduiraut. 38 acres; 7,000 cases white: Sém. 50%. Sauv. 50%. 22 acres; 5,000 cases red: One third each Cab. Sauv., Cab. Franc and Merlot. Prominent over the last decade as one of the most modern properties; a leader in fresh, dry white wine and fruity red for drinking young. The owner is president of a group of like-minded proprietors.
Château Millet
Portets. Owners: The de la Mette family. 140 acres; 25,000 cases. The biggest property in Portets, with the most imposing château. The vineyard was formerly half red and half white, but the emphasis is increasingly on red wine. Second label: Ch. du Clos Renon.
Château Montalivet
Pujols-sur-Ciron. Dir: Pierre Coste (*see* Ch. Chicane). 27 acres; 5,500 cases red. 9 acres; 2,000 cases white.
Château St-Pierre
See Ch. Les Queyrats.
Château Piron
St-Morillon. Owner: André Boyreau. 32 acres; 5,000 cases white; 1,000 cases red. An old family property in the hinterland of Graves on gravel slopes with a chalk content that favours white wine.
Château de Portets
Portets. Owner: Jean-Pierre Théron. 80 acres; 5,000 cases red: one third Cab. Sauv. two thirds Merlot; 6,000 cases white: Sém. 64%, Sauv. 36%. The reputation of Portets is growing, particularly for red wine. A good workmanlike example.
Château Les Queyrats
St-Pierre-de-Mons. Owners: The Dulac family. 64 acres white; 32 acres red. A traditional Graves estate with mixed farming and mixed wines: whites both dry and sweet and a sturdy red. Clos d'Uza (once a Lur Saluces farm) is attached. Some of the wine is sold abroad as Ch. St-Pierre; good, tasty, conservative Graves.
Château Rahoul
Portets. Owners: Les Vignobles Len Evans. Wine maker: Peter Vinding-Diers. 37 acres; 5,000 cases red: Merlot 80%, Cab. Sauv. 20%; 250 cases white: Sém. 100%. Australian-owned estate rapidly making a reputation for stylish wood-aged reds and crisp whites. The leader in the commune.
Château Respide
St-Pierre-de-Mons and Langon. Owner: Pierre Bonnet. 38 acres in St-Pierre; 5,000 cases white and 70 acres of red, on the sandy soil of Langon, have been known longer than most in this up-and-coming area. A 20-year-old bottle of white Respide at the old Café de Bordeaux was nearly great, soft but sappy Graves.
Château de Rochemorin
Martillac. Owner: André Lurton. 113 acres; 20,000 cases red. 15 acres; 3,000 cases white: Sauv. Bl. 80%, Sém. 20%. A major old estate abandoned to the woods in the 1930s, replanted since 1973 by M. Lurton. A name to look out for in the future.
Château Le Sartre
Léognan. Owners: Soc. Civile. Manager: Antony Perrin. Cab. Sauv. 60%, Merlot 30%, others 10%. (*See* Ch. Carbonnieux.)
Château Toumilon
St-Pierre-de-Mons. Owner: Jean Sevenet. 30 acres. A minor Graves producing some 2,500 cases of pleasant red and the same of dry white. Second label: Ch. Cabanes.
Château La Tour-Léognan
Léognan. Owners: Soc. Civile. Manager: Antony Perrin. Sauv. 60%, Sém. 40%. (*See* Ch. Carbonnieux.)
Château La Tour-Bicheau
Portets. Owners: Y. Daubas & Fils. 50-acre property among the good red producers of Portets. About 7,000 cases.
Château Tourteau-Chollet
Arbannats. Owners: Les Grands Vignobles. 70-acre property of the important Mestrezat-Preller group. Red and white wines.
Château Le Tuquet
Beautiran. Owner: Paul Ragon. 45 acres; 8,000 cases white: Sauv. and Sém. 45 acres; 8,000 cases red: Cab., Merlot, Malbec. The principal property of Beautiran, on the main road from Bordeaux to Langon.
Château La Vieille France
Portets. Owner: Michel Dugoua. 10 acres; 2,000 cases red. 10 acres; 2,500 cases white. 17 acres; 4,000 cases Bordeaux Supérieur Rouge. A sound and enterprising proprietor who also owns Ch. Grand-Abord.

SAUTERNES

Towards the south of the Bordeaux region, red wine-making dwindles to insignificance compared with white. A slightly warmer and drier climate and very limey soil are ideal for white grapes; the wine naturally has what the French call great '*sève*' – sap – a combination of body and vitality.

The best of the region is the relatively hilly enclave of Sauternes, an appellation that applies to five villages just south of a little tributary of the Gironde called the Ciron. On the other side of the Ciron (on flatter land) lies Barsac, which also has the right to the appellation. The Ciron is said to be responsible for misty autumn conditions that give rise to the famous 'noble rot', and the possibility of *vin liquoreux*. For the last 150 years Sauternes has specialized in this extraordinarily concentrated golden dessert wine – unfortunately against increasing economic odds.

Unlike most of the Graves region, Sauternes has big estates in the manner of the Médoc. Historically its position on the inland route up the Garonne gave it military importance. Later, its fine climate and its good wine made it a desirable spot to replace castles with mansions. A score of these were already famous for their 'sappy' white wine when the 1855 classification was made for the Paris Exhibition. They were classified in three ranks, with Château d'Yquem alone in the first, nine classed as Premiers Crus and another nine as Deuxièmes Crus – which is, broadly speaking, still a fair classification, except that divisions of property have increased the Premiers Crus to 11 and the Deuxièmes to 12. They are surrounded by a host of unofficial Crus Bourgeois, some of comparable quality. The combined vineyard area of the six communes is 4,700 acres. There is no *cave coopérative*.

The laborious procedure for making great Sauternes is described on pages 78 and 79. Sadly, it is unrealistic for most proprietors, who cannot afford the labour needed to pick single grapes at a time, or the new barrels, or the years of waiting.

The ultimate short cut, used by many of the humbler growers, is simply to wait for fully ripe grapes (hoping that at least a few are 'nobly rotten'), pick them all together, add sugar to bring the potential alcohol up to about 18 per cent, then stop the fermentation with sulphur dioxide when the fermentation has produced 13 or 14 degrees, leaving the wine sweet. It is a bastard approach to wine-making, with predictably mediocre results. The wine has none of the classic Sauternes flavour and should, in fairness, be called something else.

What is the classic flavour? It depends on the vintage. In some it is forceful, hot and treacly. In others it is rich and stiff with flavour, but almost literally sappy and not very sweet. In the best, with all the grapes 'nobly rotten', it is thick with sugar yet gentle, creamy, nutty, honeyed. Barsacs tend to be a little less rich than Sauternes, but can produce their own spellbinding equilibrium of the rich and the brisk. Bottles can be better than ever after as much as 40 or 50 years.

The postal address for the whole of Sauternes is 33210 Langon. Price (1981): 9 francs a bottle.

PREMIER GRAND CRU

Château d'Yquem

1er Cru Supérieur 1855. Owner: Comte Alexandre de Lur Saluces.
AOC: Sauternes. 250 acres; 5,500 cases (plus up to 2,000 dry white Bordeaux). Grape var: Sém. 80%, Sauv. 20%.
Price (1978): 225 francs a bottle.

Indisputably the greatest sweet wine of France, but recognized as the best white wine of Bordeaux long before the fashion for sweet wine was initiated in the 19th century. The same family has controlled its destiny throughout. The extreme pains that go into its making are described in detail on pages 78 and 79. Yquem also makes 'Y' (pronounced Ygrec), a dry wine, made from half Sauvignon, half Sémillon. It has some of the concentration of Yquem, and the same alcohol content, but only a trace of sweetness for balance.

PREMIERS CRUS

Château Climens

1er Cru Classé 1855. Owner: Lucien Lurton.
AOC: Barsac. 74 acres; 4,200 cases. Grape var: Sém. 80%, Sauv. 20%.

Barsac's sweetest and richest wine, made by the old methods with a crop nearly as derisory as that at Yquem, giving it almost caramel concentration as it ages. The property was bought in 1971 (a superb vintage) by the owner of Ch. Brane-Cantenac (Margaux). The locals pronounce the final 'ns' emphatically, with a sort of honking effect.

Château Coutet

1er Cru Classé 1855. Owner: Marcel Baly.
AOC: Barsac. 90 acres; 8,000 cases. Grape var: Sém 80%, Sauv. 15%, Muscadelle 5%.

With Ch. Climens, the leading growth of Barsac, using traditional methods of barrel fermentation to make exceptionally fine and stylish wine (although strangely failing in the great '67 vintage). The old manor house dates back to the English rule of Aquitaine. In the best years (1971, '75, '76) a selection of the '*crême de tête*', the richest wine, is labelled 'Cuvée Madame'.

Château Guiraud

1er Cru Classé 1855. Owners: Société Civile. Dir: Hamilton Narby.
AOC: Sauternes. 134 acres, plus 37 acres of red grapes (Bordeaux Supérieur); 7,000 cases plus 8,000 cases red plus 1,000 cases dry white. Grape var: white: Sém. 54%, Sauv. 42%, Muscadelle 4%; red: Cab. Sauv. 55%, Merlot 45%.
Price (1980): 26.50 francs a bottle.

The southern neighbour of Yquem which has been coasting recently, looking for a buyer. A Canadian company took up the challenge in 1981 and intends to employ Yquem-like methods, picking individual grapes and fermenting in new barrels. Meanwhile, existing vintages scarcely show the potential. The quantity of red wine, 'Pavillon Rouge de Château Guiraud', is surprising.

Clos Haut-Peyraguey

1er Cru Classé 1855, Bommes. Owner: Jacques Pauly.
AOC: Sauternes. 37 acres; 3,000 cases. Grape var: Sém 85%, Sauv. 15%.

Formerly the upper part of the same estate as Ch. Lafaurie-Peyraguey, separated in 1879 and in the Pauly family since 1914. A modest estate making relatively light wine with care. The Cru Bourgeois Ch. Haut-Bommes has the same owners.

Château Lafaurie-Peyraguey

1er Cru Classé 1855, Bommes. Owner: Jean Cordier.
AOC: Sauternes. 49 acres; 4,500 cases. Grape var: Sém. 98.5%, Sauv. 1.5%.
Price (1980): 33 francs a bottle.

A fortress to challenge Yquem – militarily, that is – with a fine reputation for beautifully structured, long-lived Sauternes. Despite fermentation and ageing in barrels, recent vintages seem less tenacious.

Château Rabaud-Promis

1er Cru Classé 1855, Bommes. Owner: Paul Lanneluc.
AOC: Sauternes. 74 acres; 3,750 cases. Grape var: Sém. 80%, Sauv. 18%, Muscadelle 2%.
Price (1980): 25 francs a bottle.

The larger part of the formerly important Rabaud estate, now no longer in the front rank.

Château Rayne-Vigneau

1er Cru Classé 1855, Bommes. Owners: MM. de la Beaumelle, Merlaut and Dumarc.
AOC: Sauternes. 164 acres; 16,500 cases. Grape var: Sém. 65%, Sauv. 30%, Muscadelle 5%.
Price (1979): 38 francs a bottle.

A big estate now detached from its château but celebrated in history for its soil being – literally – full of precious stones. The fortunate Vicomte de Roton (a Pontac, whose descendants still have the château) found himself picking up sapphires, topaz, amethysts and opals by the thousand. (The rest of the soil is gravel.) Modern methods produce rich and good, but not the most ambitious, Sauternes and a little Rayne-Vigneau Sec.

Château Rieussec

1er Cru Classé 1855, Fargues. owner: Albert Vuillier.
AOC: Sauternes. 136 acres; 6,500 cases plus. Grape var: Sém 80%, Sauv. 19%, Muscadelle 1%.
Price (1980): 32.75 francs a bottle.

The eastern neighbours of Yquem, perched even higher on the same line of hills, with a strange gazebo a little too like a gun emplacement to be considered an ornament. Particularly arid gravel soil contributes to a very low yield of relatively light, less-sweet wine sometimes compared with Barsac. The wine is fermented in stainless steel and kept in cellars in mature barrels, which seem to keep it particularly fresh and lively. The '62 has been favourite of mine for years. 1971, '75 and '79 are all first class. A dry white, inspired by Yquem's 'Y', is called 'R'. A second label for sweet wine is Clos Labère.

Château Sigalas Rabaud

1er Cru Classé 1855, Bommes. Owner: Marquise de Lambert des Granges.
AOC: Sauternes. 34 acres; 2,000–2,500 cases. Grape var: Sém. 75%, Sauv. 25%.
Price (1980): 30 francs a bottle.

One third of the former Rabaud estate, descended for over a century in the Sigalas family. The wine is made and aged in tanks to avoid oak flavours and concentrate on richness and finesse, which it has in abundance.

Château Suduiraut

1er Cru Classé 1855, Preignac. Owner: L. Fonquernie's heir (Mme Frouin).
AOC: Sauternes. 173 acres; 11,600 cases. Grape var: Sém. 85%, Sauv. 15%.
Price (1980): 34 francs a bottle.

A château of great splendour with a park of great beauty and the next vineyard to Yquem, going north. One of the most respected names, despite a period of relative neglect in the early 1970s. The new manager, Pierre Pascaud, is forthright and determined. Suduiraut at its best ('67 and '76) is plump and unctuous, truly *liquoreux*; the poor man's Yquem.

Château La Tour Blanche

1er Cru Classé 1855, Bommes. Owners: Ministère d'Agriculture, Dir: M. Roger Serra.
AOC: Sauternes. 67 acres; 6,000 cases. Grape var: Sém. 75%, Sauv. 23%, Musc. 2%.
Price (1980): 24 francs a bottle.

Probably the first estate on which sweet Sauternes was made (*see* Ch. d'Yquem, The Making of a Great Sauternes) and placed first after Yquem in the 1855 classification. Bequeathed to the French state in 1912 by M. Osiris, whose name still appears on the label. The vineyard slopes steeply westwards towards the River Ciron, the Bommes–Barsac boundary. It is now a college of viticulture, and students help in the nursery and bottling. Fermentation is temperature controlled in steel tanks, stopped by chilling and filtration at about 14% alcohol, then 2 years in barrels. Not great wine, but businesslike. 1975 is the best recent vintage. The second label is Cru St-Marc. A little red wine is also made.

DEUXIEMES CRUS

Château d'Arche

2eme Cru Classé 1855. Owners: The Bastit-St-Martin family.
AOC: Sauternes. 88 acres; 4,500 cases. Grape var: Sém. 80%, Sauv. 15%, Muscadelle 5%.

Respectable rather than inspired Sauternes, at its best typically luscious. *See also* Ch. d'Arche-Lafaurie. A part of Ch. Lamothe also belongs to the Bastit-St-Martins.

Château d'Arche-Lafaurie

2eme Cru Classé 1855. Owners: The Bastit-St-Martin family.
AOC: Sauternes. 30 acres; 2,000 cases.

The junior partner of Ch. d'Arche.

CHATEAU D'YQUEM

The Making of a Great Sauternes

Wine has no legend more imposing than the hilltop fortress of Yquem and its golden nectar. Only France could produce such a monument to aristocratic craftsmanship. Others talk about quality; the Lur Saluces family has made quality its dynastic vocation for 200 years.

In 1785 Josephine Sauvage d'Yquem, whose family had already held the estate for 200 years, married the Comte de Lur Saluces. Two years later Thomas Jefferson paid a famous visit to the château and rated the wines so highly that he ordered a consignment for America. But if you want to taste the wine that impressed him you must seek out the rare 'Y', the dry wine of the château, because the modern concept of Sauternes as a *vin liquoreux*, an intensely sweet, concentrated and unctuous dessert wine, dates from 50 or 60 years after his visit. It was introduced in 1836 by the German proprietor of Château La Tour-Blanche, Monsieur Focke, who experimented with the method used to make the great sweet wines of the Rhine. It was apparently first used at Yquem in 1847.

Today, the painstaking care at Yquem is hard to exaggerate. A description of its methods is a description of the ideal – to which other châteaux only approximate to a greater or lesser degree.

The principle must first be understood. Under certain autumnal conditions of misty mornings and sunny afternoons, one of the forms of mould common in vineyards reverses its role; instead of ruining the grapes, it is entirely beneficial. Given a healthy, ripe and undamaged crop without other fungus infections, it begins to feed on the sugar and the tartaric acid in each grape, probing with roots so fine that they penetrate the microscopic pores of the grape-skin. The grapes rapidly shrivel, turning first grey with fungus spores, then warm violet-brown, their skins mere pulp. By this time they have lost more than half their weight, but less than half their sugar. Their juice is concentrated, extremely sweet and rich in glycerine. If conditions are perfect (as they were in 1967 and 1976) the process is sudden and complete; not a grape in the bunch is recognizable. They are a repulsive sight.

Unfortunately in most years the process is gradual; the berries rot patchily – even one by one. At Yquem the pickers, in four gangs 40 strong, move through the vines at a snail's pace gathering the grapes, if necessary, one at a time, then going back over the same vines again and again, up to ten, once up to eleven, times. The final crop amounts to about one glass of wine per vine.

In the *cuvier* the grapes are slightly sulphured, put through a gentle wooden *fouloir* (crusher), then immediately pressed in old-fashioned vertical presses three times, the 'cake' being cut up with shovels and thrown into a strange mill to remove the stalks between pressings. The whole day's picking – up to 40 barrels – is assembled together in one vat, then poured straight into new oak *barriques*, filling them three quarters full, to ferment. The day's crop, the '*journée*', is the critical unit to be tasted again and again to see whether it has the qualities of the Grand Vin. If it does not have those qualities it will be sold to the trade as anonymous Sauternes. There is no

court of appeal, no second wine, at Yquem.

The *chai* is heated to 20°C (68°F) to encourage a steady fermentation, which lasts between two and six weeks. When it reaches between 13 and 14 degrees of alcohol a miraculous natural control, an antibiotic produced by the botrytis, stops the yeasts working, leaving up to 120 grammes of sugar to a litre (12 per cent of the wine). Without this antibiotic the alcohol would reach 17 degrees, throwing the wine right out of balance. The sums are critical here. Twenty per cent total sugar ('potential alcohol') in the juice is ideal. With 25 per cent, the fermentation would stop at nine or ten degrees – as in Trockenbeerenauslese. (The extreme example is Tokay Essence, with so much sugar that the potential alcohol content is 35 degrees but fermentation never starts at all.)

Château d'Yquem is kept for no less than three and a half years in cask, racked every three months and never bunged tight – which means twice-weekly topping up over the whole period, and a loss by evaporation of 20 per cent. The wine is so thick that it never 'falls bright', or clears itself fully by gravity. The sediment, at the same density as the liquid, remains in suspension. So it must be '*fined*' – but never with egg whites, says Alexandre de Lur Saluces; one of the eggs might be bad.

The Comte Alexandre de Lur Saluces, the present proprietor, is nephew of the famous Marquis Bertrand, whose last vintage before his death was the great 1967. He also owns the exceptional Cru Bourgeois Château de Fargues. Pierre Meslier, his manager, is owner of Château Raymond-Lafon.

Château Broustet

2eme Cru Classé 1855. Owner: Eric Fournier.
AOC: Barsac. 39 acres; 3,000 cases. Grape var: Sém. 63%, Sauv. 25%, Muscadelle 12%.

Remembered as the property of the cooper who standardized the now-universal Bordeaux *barrique*. His descendants (who also run the great Ch. Canon, St-Emilion) make a distinguished wine, rich but not *liquoreux*. 1976, surprisingly, was a failure. Also a dry white, Camperos. Their second label is Ch. de Ségur.

Château Caillou

2eme Cru Classé 1855. Owner: J. Bravo.
AOC: Barsac. 37 acres. 4,000 cases. Grape var: Sém. 90%, Sauv. 10%.

A businesslike property on the higher ground of 'Haut' Barsac, near Ch. Climens (although not recently in good form). With the owner's other Barsac property, Ch. Petit-Mayne, it also produces a dry white, Domaine Sarraute, which I have found rather clumsy.

Château Doisy-Daëne

2eme Cru Classé 1855. Owners: Pierre Dubourdieu.
AOC: Barsac. 34 acres; 3,500 cases. Grape var: Sém. 100%, for Barsac, plus Sauv., Muscadelle and Riesling for dry wine.

In the forefront of modern wine-making with sophisticated use of steel and new oak to make fresh, lively sweet wines and a trend-setting dry one, a model for growers who want to restore the old prestige of Graves. The same estate contains Ch. Cantegril, making both sweet white and a good red.

Château Doisy-Dubroca

2eme Cru Classé 1855. Owner: Lucien Lurton.
AOC: Barsac. 8 acres; 500 cases. Grape var: Sém. 75%, Sauv. 25%.

A small property linked for a century to the neighbouring Ch. Climens and now made with the same traditional techniques of intense care (and Professor Peynaud's advice).

Château Doisy-Védrines

2eme Cru Classé 1855. Owners: Pierre Castéja.
AOC: Barsac. 52 acres; 3,000 cases. Grape var: Sém. 85%, Sauv. 15%.

I always assumed from its quality that this was a first- rather than a second-classed growth. It is one of the rich Barsacs, fermented in barrels and built for long life. It is much liked in the UK.

Château Filhot

2eme Cru Classé 1855. Owner: Comte Henri de Vaucelles.
AOC: Sauternes. 148 acres; 8,000–11,000 cases. Grape var: Sém. 65%, Sauv. 33%, Muscadelle 2%.

A palace, or nearly, built by the Lur Saluces family in the early 19th century on the edge of the woods south of Sauternes. The big vineyard on sandy soil produces distinctively light wines by classical Sauternes standards. They are all the more appetizing and savoury for it; excellent for rich fish dishes and such shellfish as lobster, crawfish and crab cooked with cream. The 1975 had a slightly salty tang that I found delicious.

Château Lamothe

2eme Cru Classé 1855. Owner: Jean Despujols.
AOC: Sauternes. 20 acres; 2,000 cases. Grape var: Sém. 70%, Sauv. 15%, Muscadelle 15%.

Minor Sauternes bottled within a year for early drinking.

Château de Malle

2eme Cru Classé 1855, Preignac. Owner: Comte Pierre de Bournazel.

AOC: Sauternes (and Graves). 55 acres; 5,000 cases Sauternes, 6,000 cases red Graves, 3,000 cases white Graves. Grape var. white: Sém. 75%, Sauv. 22%, Muscadelle 3%; red: Cab. Sauv. 80%, Merlot 20%.

The most beautiful house and garden in Sauternes – possibly in Bordeaux – and much appreciated by tourists. Built for the owner's family (related to the Lur Saluces) about 1600. 'Italian' gardens were added 100 years later. The vineyard is in Sauternes and Graves and produces roughly equal quantities of sweet white and red. The red (made by carbonic maceration) is called Ch. du Cardaillan, the dry white, Chevalier de Malle.

The vineyard, on light sandy soil, was entirely replanted in 1956. The owner is a trained oenologist who 'designs' his wine, using both stainless steel and new oak to produce fruitiness with undertones – excellent Sauternes.

Château de Myrat

2eme Cru Classé 1855, Barsac.

A beautiful property, but the owner, one of the Pontac family, rooted up his vines in 1976.

Château Nairac

2eme Cru Classé 1855, Barsac. Owners: M. and Mme Heeter-Tari.

AOC: Sauternes. 37 acres; 1,800–2,000 cases. Grape var: Sém. 90%, Sauv. 6%, Muscadelle 4%.

One of the most positive signs of a renaissance in Sauternes. A young American, Tom Heeter, married the daughter of the dynamic M. Tari of Ch. Giscours (Margaux). Since 1971, they have made this formerly run-down estate one of the leaders of the district, with wines of the racy, less sticky Barsac style that bear keeping 10 years or more. Professor Peynaud was called in for his invaluable advice. The dignified mansion lies on the low ground near the village of Barsac and the Garonne. The new owners are renovating the house, which was not lived in for many years. Sadly, floods did terrible damage to the property in 1982.

Château Romer du Hayot

2eme Cru Classé 1855, Fargues. Owner: André du Hayot.

AOC: Sauternes. 37 acres; 4,000 cases. Grape var: Sém. 67%, Sauv. 33%.

The château was demolished for the new autoroute and the wine is made at the owner's Cru Bourgeois Ch. Guiteronde in Barsac. A modern Sauternes, aged 2 years in tanks.

Château Suau

2eme Cru Classé 1855. Owner: M. Roger Biarnés.

AOC: Barsac. 16 acres; 1,450 cases. Grape var: Sém. 80%, Sauv. 10%, Muscadelle 10%.

The relic of a more important property, near the Garonne on heavier soil than the best growths. The wine is made at the owner's home, Château de Navarro, Illats, Graves, together with his Sauternes Cru Bourgeois, Domaine du Coy.

OTHER CHATEAUX

Château Bastor-Lamontagne
Cru Bourgeois, Preignac. Owners: Crédit Foncier de France. 90 acres; 7,500 cases. A substantial and well-kept property with a history of good vintages to substantiate its claim to be 'as good as a second-growth'.

Château Cantegril
Cru Bourgeois, Barsac. Owner: A. Masencal. 50 acres; 4,500 cases. Part of the former Ch. Myrat vineyard, beautifully kept but rather unambitious in its wine: clean, fresh, sweet – not much more.

Château de Fargues
Cru Bourgeois, Fargues. Owners: The Lur Saluces family. 25 acres; 1,000 cases. Grape var: Sém. 80%, Sauv. 20%. A proud castle in ruins, with a diminutive vineyard but the perfectionist standards of Yquem. Lighter wine, but impeccable and sometimes brilliant (e.g. '67, '75).

Château Haut Bommes
Cru Bourgeois, Bommes. Owner: Jacques Pauly (*see* Clos Haut-Peyraguey). Well-sited, potentially excellent little property. The 1929 was perfection of cream and toffee in 1981.

Château Liot
Cru Bourgeois, Barsac. Owners: David & Fils. 94 acres; 8,300 cases. Grape var: Sém. 60%, Musc. 35%, Sauv. 15%. Large property on the best slopes in Barsac. The unusual proportion of Muscadelle makes certain years very flavoury; the general level is 'good commercial', sometimes over-sulphured.

Château du Mayne
Cru Bourgeois, Barsac. Owner: Jean Sanders. 32 acres; 2,000 cases. Grape var: Sauv. 30–35%, Sém. 65–70%. A pretty cream house among ancient vines (many 80 years old) cultivated for small amounts of very good wine. The same owner as Ch. Haut-Bailly (Graves).

Château de Ménota
Cru Bourgeois, Barsac. Owner: Robert de Labat. 40 acres; 4,500 cases.

Château Padouen
Cru Bourgeois, Barsac. Manager: Peter Vinding-Diers. 25 acres; 2,000 cases. Newly restored little vineyard on sandy soil at the northern edge of Barsac, going to great lengths to make classic wines and some very delicate dry ones.

Château Pernaud
Cru Bourgeois, Barsac. Owner: Dr. Regnensperger. 50 acres; 4,500 cases. An old property down by the Ciron, replanted and now run by the dynamic manager of Ch. Suduiraut. Worth watching.

Château Piada
Cru Bourgeois, Barsac. Owner: Jean Lalande. 30 acres; 2,500 cases. Grape var: Sauv. 70%, Ries. 30%. One of the better-known lesser Barsacs, unconventional in methods but successful with both its sweet wine and dry 'Clos du Roy'.

Château Raymond-Lafon
Cru Bourgeois, Sauternes. Owner: Pierre Meslier. 30 acres; 1,000 cases. Grape var: Sém. 75%, Sauv. 20%, Musc. 5%. Owned by the manager of Ch. d'Yquem, neighbour to the great château, made with similar care and potentially first-class (e.g. '75, '78).

Château de Rolland
Cru Bourgeois, Barsac. 50 acres; 5,000 cases. An attractive little hotel and restaurant (the only one in Barsac) with worthwhile wine of its own.

Château Roumieu
Cru Bourgeois, Barsac. A 50-acre vineyard next to Ch. Climens, divided between the Goyaud and Bernadet families. The wines I have tasted have been respectable.

Ch. Roumieu-Lacoste
Cru Bourgeois, Barsac. Owner: A. Dubourdieu. 30 acres; 2,500 cases. The sister-in-law of the owner of the excellent Doisy-Daëne makes good wine here.

Château Simon
Cru Bourgeois, Barsac. Owner: J. Dufour. 25 acres; 2,000 cases. A well-run property, in the same hands as the little Ch. Grand-Mayne (Barsac).

ST-EMILION

As a town, every wine lover's idea of heaven; as an appellation, much the biggest for high-quality wine in France, producing not much less than the whole of the Côte d'Or of Burgundy. Nowhere is the civic and even the spiritual life of a little city so deeply imbued with the passion for making good wine.

St-Emilion, curled into its sheltered corner of the hill, cannot expand. Where other such towns have spread nondescript streets over the countryside, around St-Emilion there are priceless vineyards, most of its very best, lapping up to its walls. It burrows into its yielding limestone to find building blocks and store its wine – even to solemnize its rites. Its old church is a vast vaulted cave, now used for the meeting of the Jurade (*see below*).

The vineyards envelop several distinct soils and aspects while maintaining a certain common character. St-Emilion wines are a degree stronger than Médocs, with less tannin. Accessible, solid tastiness is their stamp, maturing to warm, gratifying sweetness. They are less of a puzzle than Médocs when young and mature faster, but are no less capable of asking unsolvable questions as they age.

The best come from the relatively steep *côtes*, the hillside vineyards and the cap of the escarpment around the town, and from an isolated patch of gravel soil on the plateau two miles northwest, almost in Pomerol. The *côtes* wines are the more smiling, in degrees from enigmatic to beaming; the wines of the *graves* more earnest and searching. Michael Broadbent defines the difference as 'open' (*côtes*) and 'firm' (*graves*). But they can easily be confused with each other, with Médocs, with Graves and even with burgundy. And some of the same qualities are found in vineyards on substantially different soils, both down in the sandy *sables* region in the Dordogne valley below the town and in the five 'satellite' villages to the north and east.

The classification of St-Emilion follows a pattern of its own. It was settled in 1954 and is the only one planned to be regularly revised; even, for the top category, to be revised every year.

It names two châteaux (Cheval Blanc and Ausone) as Premiers Grands Crus Classés 'A' and ten as 'B'. The Bs are the approximate equivalent in value to Médoc second- and third-growths. Then come 72 Grands Crus Classés, elected for (about) ten years. They were last listed in 1969. The next list is due in 1983 – probably with very little change.

The third category is simply Grand Cru, for which proprietors have to reapply every year by submitting their wines for tasting. In 1982, the six villages with the right to apply mustered 172 hopeful Grands Crus, nearly all of which qualified.

Obviously St-Emilion is not an area of big estates. The average size of holding is about 20 acres, the biggest not much more than 100 and many as small as five or six, making a mere few hundred cases. Of the 172 Grands Crus applicants 94 were over seven hectares (17 acres), the qualifying size for a Médoc Cru Bourgeois. In fact 'Grand Cru' in St-Emilion, unqualified, is the same broad category as the three levels of the bourgeoisie in the Médoc.

The present system is widely recognized to be unsatisfactory. As Alain Querre, one of the leading figures of the district and owner of Château Monbousquet, says, 'Grands Crus are not as grand as they sound. Their wine can be; but sometimes just as you discover a good one something changes and the next vintage is no good.' The resources and stability of a big establishment are usually lacking. Querre is the leading proponent of a revision to the classification by the Jurade which will take effect soon. The object is to simplify the ranking to Grands Crus and the rest. Any château will be able to apply for Grand Cru rank every year. If it fails the tasting tests it will be plain St-Emilion – for that year. In addition an annual tasting by a panel of consumers will award honours to the 12 best wines of the vintage. Whether this amount of testing is practicable, and whether the growers will accept the new system, remains to be seen. Postcode: 33330 St-Emilion.

Price (1982): 12 francs a bottle.

The Jurade de St-Emilion

The ceremonial and promotional organization of St-Emilion is probably the oldest in France. The Jurade de St-Emilion was formally instituted by King John of England and France in 1199 as the body of elders to govern the little city and its district – a dignity granted to few regions at the time. Nobody seriously pretends that the modern institution is a linear descendant, but its impressive processions to Mass in the great parish church and to its own candle-lit solemnities in the monolithic former church, cut out of the solid limestone in the centre of the town, are full of dignity as well as good humour.

The Jurade also plays an increasing role in the control of quality and administration of the various categories of châteaux. Its newly initiated annual tastings are likely to give a boost to St-Emilion quality in a similar way to the *tastevinage* undertaken by the Chevaliers de Tastevin in Burgundy.

On a memorable autumn weekend in 1981 the Jurade visited the great medieval city of York, arriving by river in a state barge, to process to the Minster for a service conducted by the Archbishop, and to dine in the splendour of Castle Howard. They do these things with style.

PREMIERS GRANDS CRUS

Château Ausone

1er Grand Cru Classé 1969. Owner: Mme J. Dubois-Challon. AOC: St-Emilion. 17 acres; 2,000 cases. Grape var: Merlot 50%, Cab. Franc 50%.
Price (1980): 90 francs a bottle.

If you were looking for the most promising vineyard site in the whole Bordeaux area this would be first choice. No wonder its name is associated with the Roman poet Ausonius (connoisseur also of the Moselle). It slopes south and east from the rim of the St-Emilion escarpment, whose limestone cap has been quarried for building and provides perfect cool, commodious cellars. The soil is pale alkaline clay, in a shallow layer over permeable limestone (which vine roots love). The château (where the owner lives) is a dainty building perched above and among the vines, where an old white mare shambles around doing the cultivating, hull-down in the green leaves.

Ausone went through a long eclipse when its wine was good, but not good enough. Its neighbours seemed to dim their lamps at the same time. Matters have been put right since 1975 by a new manager, Pascal Delbeck, and each good vintage now takes its proper place among the first-growths. 1976, '78 and '79 are all confirmed excellent. Wine-making here is exactly the same in principle as in the Médoc. New barrels are used for the whole, pathetically small crop. (I was present by chance at a cellar tasting of Ausone '78 from barrels washed before filling with steam, hot water and cold water. The differences were astonishing. Hot water won.) The wine is bottled slightly sooner than Médoc first-growths and its whole evolution to drinkability is slightly quicker, yet its potential life span, judging by very rare old bottles, is no shorter. The final result is the pure magic of claret, sweet lively harmony with unfathomable depths.

Château Cheval Blanc

1er Grand Cru Classé 1969. Owner: Jacques Hébrard (Société Civile Fourcaud-Laussac).
AOC: St-Emilion. 86 acres; 11,500 cases. Grape var: Cab. Franc 66%, Merlot 33%, Malbec 1%.
Price (1980): 83.50 francs a bottle.

Although it shares the first place in St-Emilion with Ausone, the soil and situation (and tradition) of Cheval Blanc are totally different. It lies back on the plateau near the boundary of Pomerol on much deeper soil, an irregular mixture of gravel, sand and clay with clay subsoil. The main grape is Cabernet Franc (known in these parts as Bouchet). There is no white horse here, and the château is an unfanciful cream-painted residence that for some

A horse still works the steep vineyards set close to the town of St-Emilion

reason always reminds me of Virginia. The new *chais* are a more imposing building. The same family (now represented by a son-in-law, Jacques Hébrard) have always owned the property since its 19th-century beginning.

Cheval Blanc is the Mouton of St-Emilion: the blockbuster. The 1947 is a legend, a wine of heroic style and proportions, with the combined qualities of claret, port, sculpture and Hermés or Gucci – or is this lèse-majesté? Thc '61 is still not ready; a tough piece of beef that seems to need to marinate for years. Not all vintages are so awe-inspiring: '66, '71, '76 are very rich but quite approachable. 1975 is the one for the 21st century.

Château Beau Séjour

1er Grand Cru Classé 1969. Owner: Michel Bécot.
AOC: St-Emilion. 16 acres; 9,000 cases. Grape var: Cab. Sauv. 20%, Cab. Franc 20%, Merlot 60%.

Two thirds of an estate that was divided in 1869 (the smaller part got the house). The vineyard slopes west from the crest behind Ch. Ausone. Michel Bécot, helped by his two sons, Gérard and Dominique, since 1969 has modernized the property with a complete new *cuvier* and restored its dimmed reputation to that of a leader in the tight circle of the St-Emilion *côtes*, making the sort of rich wine for the medium term (say 10 years) that makes St-Emilion so popular.

Château Beauséjour

1er Grand Cru Classé 1969. Owners: Duffau-Lagarosse heirs. Dir: Jean-Michel Fernandez.
AOC: St-Emilion. 11 acres; 3,300 cases. Grape var: Cab. Sauv. 25%, Cab. Franc 25%, Merlot 50%.

The smaller part of Beauséjour but with the charming house and garden. Run in the traditional small family château style with the care fitting to a splendid site. The wine is powerful and concentrated but tannic, made in the tree-planting spirit for the next generation. For them, buy '78 and '79.

Château Belair

1er Grand Cru Classé 1969. Owner: Mme J. Dubois-Challon.
AOC: St-Emilion. 28 acres; 4,000 cases. Grape var: Merlot 60%, Cab. Franc 40%.

The bigger but junior brother of Ch. Ausone with the same owner and manager. Part of the same sloping vineyard, plus a patch on the flat top of the hill behind. It has its own quarry caves and, like many St-Emilion châteaux, its own chapel (full of lumber). The wine is now excellent (e.g. the 1979), close to Ch. Ausone but perhaps, to split hairs, a shade clumsier (or less deft).

Château Canon

1er Grand Cru Classé 1969. Owner: Eric Fournier.
AOC: St-Emilion. 44 acres; 8,000 cases. Grape var: Merlot 55%, Cab. Franc 40%, Cab. Sauv. 2.5%, Pressac 2.5%.
Price (1980): 32 francs a bottle.

My instinct is to spell the name with two 'n's: a great bronze gun-barrel (rather than a genteel cleric) expresses the style of Canon nicely. If it were only bigger this would be one of the most famous Bordeaux; generous, masculine, not too aggressive young, but magnificent with 20 years in bottle. The 1970 is a joy and the '75, '78 and '79 will be no less. A totally traditional family operation with nothing but oak to be seen.

Château Figeac

1er Grand Cru Classé 1969. Owner: Thierry de Manoncourt.
AOC: St-Emilion. 85 acres; 12,500 cases. Grape var: Cab. Sauv. 35%, Cab. Franc 35%, Merlot 30%.
Price (1980): 36 francs a bottle.

Ch. Figeac has the aristocratic air of a Médoc Cru Classé and once had an estate on the grand Médoc scale, including what is now Ch'x Cheval Blanc, Beauséjour and two others which still bear the name of Figeac. The house could be called a mansion and the park has a seigneurial feeling absent in most of the Libournais. The owner even has the features of an old-school aristocrat. The present vineyard, still among the biggest in St-Emilion, has stonier ground and a higher proportion of Cabernet Sauvignon than the others – which may account for its different style from Cheval Blanc. Figeac is more welcoming, less dense and compact; closer to a Médoc (again) in its structure of sweet flesh around a firm spine. It is big but not strapping, maturing relatively early and beautifully sweet in maturity. The 1970 was deceptively easy drinking even at 5 years old. Recent vintages have been notably successful.

Clos Fourtet

1er Grand Cru Classé 1969. Owner: André Lurton.
AOC: St-Emilion. 42 acres; 5,500 cases. Grape var: Merlot 60%, Cab. Franc 20%, Cab. Sauv. 20%.

The first Cru Classé that visitors stumble on as they walk out of the lovely old walled town into the vineyards. A modest-looking place, but with a warren of limestone cellars. (The old quarry-cellars are said to run for miles under the plateau, one château's cellars connecting with another. Paradise for an oenospelaeologist-burglar.) Old vintages of Clos Fourtet were tough going for many years. The 1966 was still immature in 1982. More recently (with Professor Peynaud's advice) the wine has been made a bit kindlier; a 10-year wine in the top flight. The owner is the brother of Lucien Lurton, the proprietor of Ch. Climens (Sauternes), who also owns Ch. Brane-Cantenac (Margaux).

Château La Gaffelière

1er Grand Cru Classé 1969. Owner: Count de Malet-Roquefort.

AOC: St-Emilion. 40 acres; 8,000 cases. Grape var: Cab. Sauv. 10%, Cab. Franc 25%, Merlot 65%.

The tall Gothic building at the foot of the hill up to St-Emilion, with vineyards at the foot of Ausone and Pavie. Three centuries in the Malet-Roquefort family, a history of noble vintages ('55 was a favourite), although recent experience has been less consistent. The young count unaccountably served a truly terrible 1969 at a Jurade banquet at Castle Howard in 1981. The '79 is rich and well balanced, the '80 (a difficult year) lean and stringy.

Château Magdelaine

1er Cru Classé 1969. Owners: Etablissements Jean-Pierre Moueix.

AOC: St-Emilion. 21 acres; 5,000 cases. Grape var: Cab. Franc 20%, Merlot 80%.

Impeccably conducted little property next to Ch. Belair, with a vineyard on the plateau and another on the south slope. The wine is made like a first-growth by Christian Moueix and Jean-Claude Berrouet, the brilliant resident oenologist of the house of Moueix at Libourne. Its high proportion of Merlot makes it almost a Pomerol, but less plummy, with the 'meat' of St-Emilion and great finesse. There can scarcely be a more reliable or fascinating St-Emilion to watch vintage by vintage.

Château Pavie

1er Grand Cru Classé 1969. Owners: Jean-Paul Valette.

AOC: St-Emilion. 86 acres plus; 16,000 cases. Grape var: Cab. Sauv. 20%, Cab. Franc 25%, Merlot 55%.

A priceless site, the whole south-by-west slope of the central St-Emilion *côtes*; the biggest vineyard on the hill with the advantage of both top and bottom as well; some good should come out of almost every vintage. The spacious cellars are dug under the top part of the vineyard, whose vine roots can be seen rejoicing in their fragrant humidity. The house lies in the middle of the vines. Pavie is known for warm, round claret of medium weight, more delicious than deeply serious: 'supple' is the technical term. The '64 and '71 were famous successes; '76 has matured remarkably quickly; '79 is a longer runner. The Valettes also own Ch. Pavie-Décesse on the not-quite-so-good slopes next door.

Château Trottevieille

1er Grand Cru Classé 1969. Owners: Héritiers Castéja-Borie.

AOC: St-Emilion. 18 acres; 4,000–5,000 cases. Grape var: Cab. Sauv. 25%, Cab. Franc 25%, Merlot 50%.

Detached from the solid block of Crus Classés along the *côtes*, on the plateau east of the town, on richer-looking but still shallow clay with pebbles over limestone. The owners are the Médocain Castéja family of Ch. Batailley (Pauillac). Full-flavoured wine with plenty of character, not intended for very long maturing.

GRANDS CRUS CLASSES

Château L'Angélus

Owners: The Bouard family. 60 acres; 12,000 cases. Grape var: Cab. Franc 60%, Merlot 40%.

Price (1980): 32 francs a bottle.

On the slope below Ch. Beauséjour where the soil is heavy. Very up-to-date techniques produce good, if rather bland commercial wine.

Château L'Arrosée

Owner: François Rodhain. 21 acres; 4,000 cases. Grape var: Merlot 50%, Cab. Sauv. 35%, Cab. Franc 15%.

The name means 'watered' (by springs). The wine, on the contrary, has been concentrated and serious. At the bottom of the *côtes* near the town.

Château Baleau

See Ch. Grandes-Murailles

Château Balestard-La-Tonnelle

Owner: Jacques Capdemourlin. 21 acres; 3,500 cases. Grape var: Merlot 65%, Cab. Franc 20%, Cab. Sauv. 10%, Malbec 5%.

The same family has held this property since the 15th-century poet Villon described its wine as '*ce divin nectar*'. I have been more prosaically satisfied with this full-bodied, meaty wine.

Château Bellevue

Dir: L. Horeau. 14 acres; 2,000 cases.

Well named for its situation high on the west slope of the *côtes*. I have not tasted the wine.

Château Bergat

Dir: Emile Castéja (*see* Ch. Batailley, Pauillac). 7 acres; 1,100 cases. Grape var: Merlot 50%, Cab. Sauv. 25%, Cab. Franc 25%.

Tiny vineyard in the sheltered gully east of the town.

Château Cadet-Bon

Owner: François Gratadour. 9 acres: 1,000 cases. Grape var: Merlot 60%, Cab. Sauv. 20%, Cab. Franc 20%.

Just north of the town where thin clay over rock gives solid dark wines.

Château Cadet-Piola

Owners: M. Jabiol & Fils. 17 acres; 3,000 cases. Grape var: Merlot 51%, Cab. Sauv. 28%, Cab. Franc 18%, Malbec 3%.

Memorable for the only Bordeaux label to portray (and very prettily) the female bosom. A reliable sturdy wine, neighbour to Cadet-Bon.

Château Canon-La-Gaffelière

Owner: Comte de Neipperg. 45 acres; 10,500 cases. Grape var: Merlot 65%, Cab. Franc 30%, Cab. Sauv. 5%.

German-owned property on sandy soil by the railway under the *côtes*. No great 'stuffing', but good easy wine.

Château Cap de Mourlin

Owner: Madeleine, widow of Jean Capdemourlin (*see* Ch. Balestard). 23 acres; 4,000 cases.

One mile north of St-Emilion on clay soil. Half of the same property as the next entry with appropriately more feminine, less meaty and tannic wine.

Château Cap de Mourlin

Owner: Jacques Capdemourlin. 20 acres; 2,600 cases. Grape var: Merlot 59%, Cab. Franc 30%, Cab. Sauv. 8%, Malbec 3%.

The other half of the old family property.

Château La Carte et Le Châtelet

Owner: Pierre Berjal. 11 acres; 2,000 cases. Grape var: Merlot 34%, Cab. Sauv. 33%, Cab. Franc 33%.

Immediate neighbour of the best *côtes* vineyards, jointly owned by M. Bécot of Ch. Beau Séjour and M. Berjal. It must be worth investigating.

Château Chapelle-Madeleine

Owner: Mme Dubois-Challon. Half acre; 45 cases.

A diminutive plot next to Ch. Ausone (q.v.).

Château Chauvin

Owner: Henri Ondet. 28 acres; 4,200 cases. Grape var: Merlot 70%, Cab. Franc 20%, Cab. Sauv. 10%.

An unexceptional *graves* vineyard.

Château La Clotte

Owners: Héritiers Chaileau. 12 acres; 2,000 cases (av.). Grape var: Merlot 70%, Cab. Franc 20%, Cab. Sauv. 10%.

Beautifully situated in the fold of the hill east of the town. Run in partnership with J-P. Moueix of Libourne to make seductively soft wine.

Château La Clusière

Owner: Consorte Valette. 7 acres; 900 cases. Grape var: Merlot 65%, Cab. Sauv. 15%, Cab. Franc 20%.

Part of the vineyard of Ch. Pavie (q.v.) not up to Premier Grand Cru standard.

Château Corbin

Owner: Geneviève Blanchard-Giraud. 28 acres; 5,800 cases. Grape var: Merlot 60%, Cab. Sauv. 40%.

Corbin is the northern hamlet of *graves* St-Emilion, near the Pomerol boundary and sloping gently northeast. Some flesh, some tannin but not very distinctive wine.

Château Corbin-Michotte

Owner: Noël Boidron. 17 acres; 3,000 cases.
Price (1981): 25.50 francs a bottle.

See the previous entry; but this seems to me more delicate and 'supple'.

Château La Couspaude

Owner: Aubert. 17 acres; 4,000 cases.

A low-profile *côtes* property. Nothing to report.

Château Coutet

Owner: J. David Beaulieu. 23 acres; 2,500 cases. Grape var: Merlot 60%, Cab. Sauv. 20%, Cab. Franc 10%, Malbec 10%.

Minor *graves* château not to be confused with the great Barsac of the same name.

Château Le Couvent

Owner: Jean Moucheboeuf. One acre; 100 cases.

The tiny vineyard at the foot of the medieval Tour du Roy in the middle of the town. It looks immaculate. I long to taste the wine.

Château Couvent-des-Jacobins

Owner: Mme Joinaud. 17 acres; 3,000 cases. Grape var: Merlot 60%, Cab. Franc 25%, Cab. Sauv. 15%.

Excellent *côtes* vineyard right under the town walls to the east, with cellars in the town centre.

Château Croque-Michotte

Owner: Mme Géoffrion-Rigal. 30 acres; 6,700 cases. Grape var: Merlot 90%, Cab. 10%.
Price (1980): 25.50 francs a bottle.

Graves property on the Pomerol border near Corbin; wine with the plumpness of a minor Pomerol but nonetheless worthwhile.

Château Curé-Bon-La-Madeleine

Owner: Maurice Lande. 11 acres; 1,600 cases. Grape var: Merlot 80%, Cab. Franc 20%.

Bon was the curé who owned this little patch among the great *côtes* vineyards of Canon, Belair, etc. Concentrated and powerful wine, the '79 jammy but tannic – most impressive.

Château Dassault

Owners: Société Civile. 48 acres; 9,000 cases.

One of the biggest *graves* vineyards, northeast of the town. Moderate wine, but new planting and equipment promise improvements.

Château La Dominique

Owner: Clement Fayat. 40 acres; 6,500 cases. Grape var: Cab. Sauv. 16.5%, Cab. Franc 16.5%, Merlot 67%.

Neighbour to Cheval Blanc and producer of some of the most attractive rich fruity wine in good vintages.

Château Faurie-de-Souchard

Owners: Jabiol & Fils. 18 acres; 3,400 cases. Grape var: Merlot 65%, Cab. Franc 26.5%, Cab. Sauv. 8.5%.

Confusingly the neighbour of Petit-Faurie-de-Soutard. The same owners as of Ch. Cadet-Piola; not quite such good wine.

Caves Coopératives of the Libournais
Annual production in cases

Lugon	412,500
Maransin	363,500
Guîtres	210,500
Périssac	188,500
Lapouyade	171,000
Aubie et Espessas	120,500
St-Christophe-de-Double	89,500

Caves Coopératives of St-Emilion
Annual production in cases

St-Emilion	565,250
Gardegan	297,200
Puisseguin-Lussac	277,150
Francs	138,500
Montagne	89,000
Sales Union (SICA) at Puisseguin	

Château Fonplégade

Owner: Armand Moueix. 42 acres; 9,000 cases. Grape var: Merlot 67%, Cab. Sauv. and Cab. Franc 16.5% each.

One of the grander châteaux, on the *côtes* among the very best, yet never one of the great names. Delicious meaty wine that seems persistently underrated.

Château Fonroque

Owner: J-P. Moueix. 42 acres; 9,000 cases. Grape var: Merlot 70%, Cab. Franc 25%, Cab. Sauv. 5%.

A relatively modest member of the impeccable Moueix stable. Dark, firm wine of definite character.

Château Franc-Mayne

Grand Cru Classé 1969. Owner: The Theillassoubre family. 17 acres; 2,000 cases. Grape var: Merlot 70%, Cab. Franc 30%.

A serious little property on the western *côtes*, managed by the same man who manages the well-known Ch. Trottevielle.

Château Grand-Barrail-Lamarzelle-Figeac

Grand Cru Classé 1969. Owners: Carrère & Fils. 86 acres; 17,000 cases. Grape var: Merlot 90%, Cab. Franc 10%. Price (1981): 20 francs a bottle.

The biggest of the Grands Crus Classés, the same size as Ch. Cheval Blanc, near Figeac on the *graves* plateau. Widely seen: not otherwise outstanding.

Château Grand-Corbin

Owner: Alain Giraud. 28 acres; 4,500 cases. Grape var: Merlot 60%, Cab. Sauv. 40%.

Property with old vines, very near to Pomerol. Produces standard-quality wine.

Château Grand-Corbin-Despagne

Grand Cru Classé 1969. Owners: The Despagne family. 62 acres; 11,000 cases. Grape var: Merlot 65%, Cab. Franc 30%, Cab. Sauv. 5%.

One of the northernmost St-Emilions in the Pomerol corner of the *graves* plateau. Dark, well-made, manly wine.

Château Grand-Mayne

Owner: Jean-Pierre Nony. 39 acres; 7,000 cases. Grape var: Merlot 50%, Cab. Sauv. 10%, Cab. Franc 40%.

Smooth, 'supple' wine from the western *côtes*.

Château Grand-Pontet

Owners: The Bécot and Pouroquet families. 35 acres; 6,500 cases. Grape var: Merlot 65%, Cab. Franc 25%, Cab. Sauv. 10%.

Owned by the shippers Barton & Guestier from 1965 to 1980 and made smooth, attractive and easy drinking wine. Michel Bécot (of Beau Séjour, next door) calls it 'Gironde Burgundy' – surely a two-edged compliment.

Château Grandes-Murailles

Owners: The Reiffers family. 49 acres; 11,400 cases.

The tiny 5 acres around the towering ruined church walls by the north gate of the town provide the *nom de guerre* for two other Grands Crus Classés in the same ownership: Château Baleau and Clos St-Martin. The wine is not normally remarkable.

Château Guadet-St-Julien

Owner: Robert Lignac. 11 acres; 1,600 cases. Grape var: Merlot 80%, Cab. Franc 10%, Cab. Sauv. 10%.

Vineyard just out of town to the north; cellars in the rue Guadet. I have not encountered the wine.

Château Haut-Corbin

Owner: Edward Guinaudie. 11 acres; 2,500 cases. Grape var: Merlot 67%, Cab. Sauv. 33%.

The least of the Corbins up near the Pomerol border.

Château Haut-Sarpe

Owner: Jean-François Janoueix. 26 acres; 6,000 cases. Grape var: Merlot 60%, Cab. Franc 30%, Cab. Sauv. 10%.

The Janoueix family are merchants in Libourne with 6 small properties in Pomerol. Haut-Sarpe straddles the border of St-Christophe des Bardes, east of St-Emilion, among good properties making firm, earthy wine.

Clos des Jacobins

Owners: Etab. Cordier. 18 acres; 3,500 cases. Grape var: Merlot 85%, Cab. Franc 10%, Cab. Sauv. 5%.

The house of Cordier makes characteristically attractive wine here; in the centre of the commune where *côtes* begin to shade to *graves*. This is in the 'open' *côtes* style.

Château Jean-Faure

Owner: Michel Amart. 40 acres; 5,600 cases. Grape var: Cab. Franc 60%, Merlot 30%, Malbec 10%.

A central *graves* vineyard between the Corbins and Ch. Cheval Blanc.

Château Laniote

Owners: The Freymond-Rouja family. 11 acres; 2,500 cases.

One of the many little properties so appreciated in Belgium that they are unknown elsewhere. The cave in the hillside where Saint Emilion himself lived in the 7th century is on the property.

Château Larcis-Ducasse

Owner: Mme H. Gratiot-Alphandery. 24 acres; 4,500 cases. Grape var: Merlot 60%, Cab. Franc 20%, Cab. Sauv. 10%, Malbec 10%.

The best vineyard of St-Laurent-des-Combes, splendidly sited on the *côtes* just east of Ch. Pavie (q.v.). A good bet, but oddly much beefier and less elegant than its Premier Grand Cru neighbour.

Château Larmande

Owners: The Meneret-Capdemourlin family. 36 acres; 5,500 cases. Grape var: Merlot 60%, Cab. Franc 25%, Cab. Sauv. 15%.

Next door to Ch. Cap de Mourlin. Recent investment and replanting should make this a wine to watch.

Château Laroze

Owner: Georges Meslin. 70 acres; 12,000 cases. Grape var: Merlot 50%, Cab. Franc 40%, Cab. Sauv. 10%.

Low on the western *côtes* on sandy soil. Not one of the outstanding vineyards, but modern and well managed, capable of very good wine (e.g. 1975).

Clos La Madeleine

Owner: Herbert Pistouley. 5 acres; 800 cases. Grape var: Merlot 50%, Cab. Sauv. and Cab. Franc 25% each.

Tiny *côtes* plot belonging to the owner of Ch. Magnan-La-Gaffelière (Grand Cru). Apparently all sold in Belgium.

Château Matras

Owner: Veronique Gaboriaud. 23 acres; 3,500 cases. Grape var: Cab. Franc 55%, Merlot 30%, Cab. Sauv. 10%, Malbec 5%.

Beautifully sited château at the foot of the western *côtes* next to Ch. L'Angélus. Wine said to be light but good.

Château Mauvezin

Owner: Pierre Cassat. 10 acres; 1,000 cases. Grape var: Merlot 40%, Cab. Franc 50%, Cab. Sauv. 10%.

A *côtes* property I have never been able to find; not to be confused with the Moulis (Médoc) château.

Château Moulin-du-Cadet

Owners: Ets. J-P. Moueix. 12 acres; 2,000 cases. Grape var: Merlot 70%, Cab. Sauv. 30%.

Impeccably made wine typical of the Moueix establishment. A combination of clay soil and a *côtes* situation gives solidity and sweetness.

Château L'Oratoire

Owners: Soc. Civile Peyreau. 20 acres; 3,700 cases. Grape var: Merlot 75%, Cab. Franc 20%, Cab. Sauv. 5%.

A *côtes* property that has grown recently, but not yet in reputation.

Château Pavie-Decesse

Owners: The Valette family. 20 acres; 2,600 cases. Grape var: Cab. Sauv. 20%, Cab. Franc 20%, Merlot 60%.

The junior partner of Ch. Pavie, from the flatter land at the top of the *côtes*. The wine is considered a shade harder, less supple and 'giving' than Pavie.

Château Pavie-Macquin

Owner: Antoine Corre. 25 acres; 2,300 cases.

A worthy neighbour of Ch. Pavie.

Château Pavillon-Cadet

Owner: Anne Llammas. 4 acres; 750 cases. Grape var: Cab. Franc 50%, Merlot 50%.

A little *côtes* property with Breton connections.

Château Petit-Faurie-de-Soutard

Owner: Mme Aberlen. 17 acres; 2,500 cases. Grape var: Merlot 60%, Cab. Franc 31%, Cab. Sauv. 6%, Malbec 3%.

Neighbour of the Cap de Mourlins, now managed by Jacques C. Readily confused with next-door Faurie-de-Souchard. Technically *côtes* wines, but like Ch. Soutard (of which it was once a part) harder to penetrate.

Château Le Prieuré

Owner: Baronne Guichard. 12 acres; 1,500 cases. Grape var: Merlot 70%, Cab. Franc 30%.

On the eastern *côtes* in an ideal situation but apparently ticking over at present.

Château Ripeau

Owner: Michel Janoueix. 36 acres; 4,700 cases. Grape var: Merlot 40%, Cab. Franc 40%, Cab. Sauv. 20%.

A well-known *graves* château in the past, considered on a par with La Dominique. Less prominent today.

Château St-Georges-Côte-Pavie

Owner: Jacques Masson. 12 acres; 2,000 cases.

An enviable spot between Pavie and Ch. La Gaffelière by the road up to the town.

Clos St-Martin

See Ch. (Les) Grandes-Murailles.

Château Sansonnet

Owner: Francis Robin. 7 acres; 3,000 cases. Grape var: Merlot 40%, Cab. Franc 40%, Cab. Sauv. 20%.

Potentially fine neighbour to Ch.Trottevieille on the eastern *côtes*. On 'hold' recently.

Château La Serre

Owner: Bernard d'Arfeuille. 12 acres; 1,500–3,500 cases. Grape var: Merlot 80%, Cab. Franc 20%.

Just outside the town on the *côtes* to the east. Despite its surprising proportion of Merlot, this seems a tougher wine than its neighbour La Clotte.

Château Soutard

Owner: Jacques de Ligneris. 48 acres; 7,000 cases. Grape var: Merlot 65%, Cab. Franc 30%, Cab. Sauv. 5%.

An important property on a rocky outcrop north-by-east of the town. Well-made, warm and welcoming wine. The great vintages are classics.

Château Tertre-Daugay

Owner: Léo de Malet-Roquefort. 20 acres plus; 2,000 cases. Grape var: Merlot 70%, Cab. Franc 30%.

A spectacularly well-sited château on the final promontory of the *côtes* west of Ch. Ausone, apparently in disarray for some years, but since 1978 in new hands and replanting. Full production should be about 3,000 cases.

Château La Tour-Figeac

Owners: Soc. Civile. 34 acres; 6,000 cases. Grape var: Merlot 60%, Cab. Franc 40%.

Formerly part of Ch. Figeac, now owned by Franco-German interests and managed by the same man who manages Ch. Canon-La-Gafelière. Very worthy wine.

Château La Tour-du-Pin-Figeac

Owner: Micheline Giraud. 24 acres; 3,500 cases

A predominantly Merlot vineyard north of Figeac, beside Cheval Blanc, but not above average in quality.

Château La Tour-du-Pin-Figeac

Owners: Armand Moueix & Co. 21 acres; 4,400 cases. Grape var: Merlot 50%, Cab. Franc 50%.

A good steady *graves* wine from a situation that suggests something better, among the great plateau vineyards.

Château Trimoulet

Owner: Michel Jean. 43 acres; 8,000 cases. Grape var: Merlot 67%, Cab. Sauv. and Cab. Franc 16.5% each.

A *côtes* vineyard in name, but on deep soil on the slope northwards down to the boundary of St-Georges.

Château Troplong-Mondot

Owner: Claude Valette. 70 acres; 13,500 cases. Grape var: Merlot 65%, Cab. Sauv. 15%, Cab. Franc 10%, Malbec 10%.

A famous vineyard on the crest of the *côtes* east of the town, above Ch. Pavie and 100 metres above the valley floor. Reliably good wine, deserving much better in the classification than many of its so-called peers.

Château Villemaurine

Owner: Robert Giraud. 17 acres; 4,000 cases. Grape var: Cab. Sauv. 50%, Merlot 50%.
Price (1980): 30 francs a bottle.

At the gates of the town, a *côtes* vineyard with far more Cabernet Sauvignon than most, consequently less easy wine but worth waiting for. There are splendid cellars.

Château Yon-Figeac

Owners: Lussiez Frères. 52 acres; 7,500 cases. Grape var: Merlot 50%, Cab. Sauv. 25%, Cab. Franc 25%.
Price (1980): 20.50 francs a bottle.

A former part of the Figeac domaine in the *graves*; one of the better reputed of its class.

GRANDS CRUS

* The quality of such a number of châteaux obviously varies very widely. Those marked with an asterisk are known to me to have particularly high and consistent standards.

Château Badette
St-Emilion. Owner: Daniel Arraud. 11 acres; 4,000 cases.
Château Barde-Haut
St-Christophe des Bardes. Owner: Jean-Claude Gasparous. 38 acres; 4,500 cases.
Château Beau Mayne
St-Emilion. Owners: Soc. Joinaud Borde. 22 acres.
Château Bellefont Belcier
St-Laurent des Combes. Owners: Soc. du Château. 32 acres; 3,850 cases.
Château Bellefont-Belcier-Guillier
St-Laurent des Combes. Owner: Philippe Guillier. 21 acres; 2,750 cases.
Château Bellegrave
Vignonet. Owner: Pierre Dangin. 26 acres; 6,250 cases.
Château Bellisle-Mondotte
St-Laurent des Combes. Owners: Escure. 69 acres; 8,650 cases.
Château Bigaroux
St-Sulpice de Faleyrens.. Owner: Didier Dizier. 38 acres; 7,000 cases.
Château Bonnet
St-Pey d'Armens. Owner: Roger Bonnet. 46 acres; 10,700 cases.
Château Cadet Pontet
St-Emilion. Owner: Michel Merias. 18 acres; 3,350 cases.
Château du Calvaire
St-Etienne de Lisse. Owner: J-P. Cisterne. 24 acres; 4,800 cases.
Château Cantenac
St-Emilion. Owner: Albert Brunot. 35 acres; 6,250 cases.
Château Canteranne
St-Etienne de Lisse. Owner: Trabut-Cussac. 24 acres; 4,150 cases.
Château Capet Guillier
St-Hippolyte. Owners: Soc. du Château. 34 acres; 8,050 cases.
Château Carboneyre
Vignonet. Owner: Raby-Saugeon. 52 acres; 11,000 cases.
Château Cardinal Villemaurine
St-Emilion. Owner: Pierre Carille. 24 acres; 4,450 cases.
Château Carteau Côtes Daugay
St-Emilion. Owners: Paul Berrand & Fils. 30 acres; 5,850 cases.
Château Carteau Matras
St-Emilion. Owner: Claude Bion. 31 acres; 5,700 cases.
Château du Cauze
St-Christophe des Bardes. Owners: Soc. du Château. 49 acres; 10,750 cases.
Château La Chapelle Lescours
St-Sulpice de Faleyrens. Owner: Pierre Quenten. 18 acres; 4,200 cases.
Château Cormey-Figeac
St-Emilion. Owner: Robert Moreaud. 44 acres; 3,950 cases.
Château Côtes Bernateau
St-Etienne de Lisse. Owner: Régis Lavau. 26 acres; 6,300 cases.
Château Côtes de la Mouleyre
St-Etienne de Lisse. Owner: Pierre Roques. 22 acres; 4,150 cases.
Château Côtes Puyblanquet
St-Etienne de Lisse. Owner: Daniel Bertoni. 19 acres; 4,650 cases.
Château Couvent des Templiers
St-Emilion. Owners: Hérit. Meneret. 41 acres; 6,750 cases.
Château Croix de Bertinat
St-Sulpice de Faleyrens. Owner: Christian Lafaye. 19 acres; 4,750 cases.
Château La Fagnousse
St-Etienne de Lisse. Owner: Anne-Marie Coutant. 18 acres; 2,150 cases.
Château de Faleyrens
St-Sulpice de Faleyrens. Owner: Jacques Brisson. 26 acres; 3,650 cases.
Château Ferrand
St-Hippolyte. Owner: Baron Bich. 64 acres; 13,600 cases.
Château La Fleur*
St-Emilion. Owners: Ets. J-P. Moueix. 2,500 cases.
Château La Fleur Pipeau
St-Laurent des Combes. Owner: Pierre Mestreguilhem. 55 acres; 13,150 cases.
Château Fombrauge*
St-Christophe des Bardes. Owner: Ch. Bygodt. 103 acres; 21,150 cases.
Château Fonrazade
St-Emilion. Owner: Guy Balotte. 22 acres; 4,500 cases.
Château Fourney
St-Pey d'Armens. Owners: Vignobles Rollet. 37 acres; 2,310 cases.
Château Franc Bigaroux
St-Sulpice de Faleyrens. Owner: Yves Blanc. 22 acres; 5,350 cases.
Château Gaillard
St-Hippolyte. Owner: Jean-Jacques Nouvel. 41 acres; 9,900 cases.
Château Gaubert
St-Christophe des Bardes. Owner: Honoré Menager. 20 acres; 2,350 cases.
Château La Grâce Dieu
St-Emilion. Owner: Maurice Pauty. 28 acres; 7,000 cases.
Château La Grâce Dieu Les Menuts
St-Emilion. Owner: Max Pilotte. 28 acres; 5,450 cases.
Château Gravet
St-Sulpice de Faleyrens. Owner: Jean Faure. 18 acres; 4,300 cases.
Château Guadet Le Franc Grâce Dieu
St-Emilion. Owner: Germain Siloret. 20 acres; 2,950 cases.
Château Gueyrot
St-Emilion. Owners: Tour du Fayet Frères. 21 acres; 5,000 cases.
Château Guillemin La Gaffelière
St-Emilion. Owner: Paul Fomperier. 21 acres; 4,750 cases.
Château Guinot
St-Etienne de Lisse. Owner: Simone Tauziac. 18 acres; 4,000 cases.
Château Haut Brisson
Bignonet. Owner: Yves Blanc. 23 acres; 5,600 cases.
Château Haut Lavallade
St-Christophe des Bardes. Owner: Jean-Pierre Chagneau. 25 acres; 5,400 cases
Château Haut Plantey
St-Emilion. Owner: Michel Boutet. 18 acres; 3,350 cases.
Château Haut Pontet*
St-Emilion. Owners: Limouzin Frères. 2,500 cases.
Château Haut Ségottes
St-Emilion. Owner: Danielle André. 17 acres; 2,650 cases.
Château L'Hermitage
St-Emilion. Owner: Brunot. 35 acres.
Château Jacques Blanc
St-Etienne de Lisse. Owners: Soc. du Château. 52 acres; 7,200 cases.
Château Jean Voisin
St-Emilion. Owners: Soc. Chassagnoux. 29 acres; 3,700 cases.
Château Le Jura
St-Emilion. Owner: Edward Guinaudie. 20 acres; 4,700 cases.
Château Lapelletrie
St-Christophe des Bardes. Owners: Soc. des Vignobles P. Jean. 30 acres; 4,850 cases.
Château Lapeyre
St-Etienne de Lisse. Owner: Simone Tauziac. 18 acres; 4,000 cases.
Château Laroque*
St-Christophe des Bardes. Owners: J-P. Moueix. 108 acres; 16,200 cases.
Château Lassèque
St-Hippolyte. Owner: Eliane Freylon. 53 acres; 13,000 cases.
Château Legrange de Lescure
St-Sulpice de Faleyrens. Owner: Jacqueline Pesquier. 42 acres; 9,700 cases.
Château Lescours
St-Sulpice de Faleyrens. Owners: Soc. du Château. 74 acres; 11,200 cases.
Château Marquis de Mons
St-Hippolyte. Owner: Micheau Maillou Palatin. 29 acres; 5,500 cases.
Château Mazerat
St-Emilion. Owner: Gouteyron & Fils. 28 acres; 5,800 cases.
Clos des Menuts
St-Emilion. Owner: Pierre Rivière. 50 acres; 9,150 cases.
Château Milon
St-Christophe des Bardes. Owner: Christian Bouyer. 47 acres; 9,850 cases.
Château Monbousquet*
St-Sulpice de Faleyrens. Owners: The Querre family. 69 acres; 14,550 cases.

Château Montlabert
St-Emilion. Owners: Soc. du Château. 28 acres; 6,000 cases.
Château Moulin Bellegrave
Vignonet. Owner: Max Perier. 20 acres; 4,000 cases.
Château Palais Cardinal La Fuie
St-Sulpice de Faleyrens. Owner: Gérard Frétier. 34 acres; 7,300 cases.
Château Panet
St-Christophe des Bardes. Owner: Jean-Claude Carles. 60 acres; 10,350 cases.
Château Patris
St-Emilion. Owner: Michel Querre. 18 acres; 3,000 cases.
Château Peyreau
St-Emilion. Owner: Michel Boutet. 33 acres; 6,200 cases.
Domaine de Peyrelongue
St-Emilion. Owner: Pierre Cassat. 19 acres; 2,350 cases.
Château Pindefleurs*
St-Emilion. Owner: Micheline Dior. 19 acres; 2,300 cases.
Château Pipeau
St-Laurent des Combes. Owner: Pierre Mestreguilhem. 55 acres; 13,000 cases.
Château Pontet Clauzure
St-Emilion. Owners: Soc. du Château. 25 acres; 4,000 cases.
Château Pourret
St-Emilion. Owner: François Ouzoulias. 42 acres; 3,900 cases.
Château de Pressac
St-Etienne de Lisse. Owner: André Pouey. 71 acres; 12,000 cases.
Château Puy-Blanquet*
St-Etienne de Lisse. Owner: Jacquet. 50 acres; 4,450 cases.
Château Puyblanquet
St-Etienne de Lisse. Owner: Jean-François Carrille. 43 acres; 7,400 cases.
Château Quentin
St-Christophe des Bardes. Owners: Soc. du Château. 63 acres; 11,600 cases.
Château du Rocher
St-Etienne de Lisse. Owners: G.F.A. du Château. 32 acres; 4,500 cases.
Château de Rol
St-Emilion. Owner: Jean Sautereau. 18 acres; 3,000 cases.
Château La Rose Côte Rol
St-Emilion. Owner: Yves Mirande. 21 acres; 5,000 cases.
Château La Rose Pourret
St-Emilion. Owner: Bernard Warion. 18 acres; 2,500 cases.
Château Rozier
St-Laurent des Combes. Owner: Jean Bernard Saby. 43 acres; 7,000 cases.
Château La Sablière
St-Emilion. Owner: Robert Avezou. 22 acres; 5,300 cases.
Château St-Christophe
St-Christophe des Bardes. Owner: Gilbert Richard. 21 acres; 4,000 cases.
Château St-Pey
St-Pey d'Armens. Owner: Maurice Musset. 23 acres; 4,400 cases.
Château de St-Pey
St-Pey d'Armens. Owners: Ph. and J-P. Musset. 46 acres; 9,000 cases.
Château Tour des Combes
St-Laurent des Combes. Owner: Jean Darribehaude. 28 acres; 6,450 cases.
Château Tour St-Pierre
St-Emilion. Owner: Jacques Goudineau. 23 acres; 4,750 cases.
Château Touzinat
St-Pey d'Armens. Owner: Yves Nérac. 19 acres.
Château Trapaud
St-Etienne de Lisse. Owner: André Larribière. 30 acres; 6,000 cases.
Clos Trimoulet
St-Emilion. Owner: Guy Appollot. 18 acres; 3,350 cases.
Château Val d'Or
Vignonet. Owner: Roger Bardet. 24 acres; 6,000 cases.
Vieux Château Chauvin
St-Emilion. Owner: Pierre Manuel. 28 acres; 4,800 cases.
Château Vieux Rivallon
St-Emilion. Owner: Charles Bouquey. 21 acres; 2,550 cases.
Château Vieux Sarpe
St-Christophe des Bardes. Owner: Jean-François Janoueix. 19 acres; 4,400 cases.

Cave Coopérative 'Royal St-Emilion'
Union du Producteurs. 795 acres; 158,000 cases.

MERCHANTS IN LIBOURNE

Most of the thriving trade of St-Emilion, Pomerol and their neighbours is handled by a group of négociants clustered on the quai du Priourat, by the rustic riverside of the Dordogne. A peculiarity of Libourne business is the number of independent salesmen known as *Les Corrèziens* (they hail from the Corrèze, up-country along the Dordogne and scarcely a land of opportunity). *Les Corrèziens* spend a winter season in the north of France and Belgium collecting private orders, which they pass to the quai du Priourat. Other houses are based in St-Emilion and the villages around.

Principal Libourne négociants in approximate order of importance are:

Etablissements Jean-Pierre Moueix, Libourne.
Principal: Jean-Pierre Moueix. The family firm that makes the running in Libourne, owning or managing a score of the best châteaux (see the château entries). Duclot in Bordeaux is related.
Maison Lebègue, Libourne.
Dealers in a wide range of wines in bottle and bulk.
Armand Moueix, Pomerol.
Merchants and proprietors based at Château Taillefer, Pomerol.
Etablissements Pierre Jean, St-Christophe-des-Bardes.
Specialists in St-Emilion in bottle and bulk.
Maison Grenouilleau, Ste-Foy-La-Grande.
Maison Horeau-Beylot, Libourne.
A family firm of proprietors and shippers founded in 1740.
Maison Jean Milhade, Galgon.
Merchants based in the Fronsac area.
Maison d'Arfeuille, Libourne.
Merchants and proprietors.
Maison Audy, Libourne.
Etablissements Marcel Bonneau, Branne (Entre-Deux-Mers).
Maison Daniel Querre, Libourne.
Merchants and proprietors of Château Monbousquet, St-Emilion.
Maison Pierre Rivière, St-Emilion.
Maison Joseph Janoueix, Libourne.
Maison Michel Querre, Libourne.
Etablissements Jean-René Feytit, St-Emilion.
Maison René Vedrenne, Libourne.
Maison François-Bernard Janoueix, Libourne.

Bordeaux trade measures

For official and statistical purposes, all French wine production is measured in hectolitres, but each region has its traditional measures for maturing and selling its wine. In Bordeaux the measure is the *tonneau*, a notional container since such big barrels are no longer made. A *tonneau* consists of 4 *barriques* – the barrels used at the châteaux, and still sometimes for shipping. A *barrique bordelaise* must by law contain 225 litres, which makes 25 cases of a dozen 75 cl. bottles each. The *tonneau* is therefore a simple and memorable measure: 100 cases of wine.

University research

The standard of wine-making and the understanding of problems that beset both grapes and wine have been immeasurably enhanced over the last century, but especially the last 40 years, by the Station Oenologique of the University of Bordeaux. A succession of famous directors has included Professor Ulysse Gayon, a pupil of Louis Pasteur, who introduced the science of microbiology to wine-making. His grandson, Jean Ribereau-Gayon, succeeded him and was in turn succeeded in guiding the wine makers of Bordeaux along scientific lines by his pupil, Emile Peynaud, and his own son, Pascal Ribereau-Gayon.

THE 'SATELLITES' OF ST-EMILION

Apart from the five saintly villages (SS Emilion, Laurent, Christophe, Etienne and Hippolyte) that are considered part of the appellation St-Emilion, five more to the north and east are granted the privilege of adding St-Emilion to their names. They are known as the satellites. They lie just north of the little river Barbanne, which forms the northern boundary of glory and renown. Their citizens argue that the formation of the valley gives two of them, St-Georges and Montagne, a better situation than some of St-Emilion. Be that as it may, those two, plus Puisseguin, Lussac and Parsac, are honoured. Proprietors in St-Georges and Parsac may call their wine Montagne-St-Emilion if they wish. Those in Parsac do, but St-Georges has a splendid château that gives it pride in its own name. Their wine is indeed like St-Emilion and can be made almost equally meaty and long lived. More growers, however, prefer using a good deal of Merlot and making softer (still strong) wine that can be delicious in two or three years. Postcode: 33570 Lussac. Price (1981): 10.6 francs a bottle.

PUISSEGUIN-ST-EMILION LEADING CHATEAUX

Château Beauséjour
Owner: Annick Dupuy. 46 acres; 7,600 cases.
Château Bel Air
Owner: Robert Adoue. 28 acres; 5,000 cases.
Château Guibeau-La Fourvieille
Owner: Jean Bourlon. 86 acres; 15,500 cases.
Château des Laurets
Owner: Mme Bécheau-Lafonta. 66 acres; 12,000 cases.
Château de Puisseguin
Owner: Jean Robin. 47 acres; 8,500 cases.
Château Roc de Boissac
Owner: Jean Sublett. 72 acres; 13,000 cases.
Château de Roques
Owner: Michel Sublett. 36 acres; 6,600 cases.
Château Soleil
Owner: Jean Soleil. 28 acres; 5,200 cases.
Château Teyssier
Owners: Soc. Civ. 35 acres; 6,500 cases.
Roc de Puisseguin
Owners: Union des Producteurs Réunis, Cave Coopérative de Puisseguin. 315 acres; 60,000 cases.

PUISSEGUIN-ST-EMILION OTHER CHATEAUX

Château Cassat 64 acres.
Château Le Chay 32 acres.
Château Chêne-Vieux 27 acres.
Château Durand Laplaigne 30 acres.
Château Gontet 29 acres.
Château Haut Bernon 24 acres.
Château Hermitage la Garenne 18 acres.
Château Le Mayne 20 acres.
Château de Mole 28 acres.
Château du Moulin 29 acres.
Château Moulin des Laurets 24 acres.
Château Moulins Listrac 23 acres.
Château La Tour Guillotin 37 acres.
Château Vaisinerie 26 acres.

LUSSAC-ST-EMILION LEADING CHATEAUX

Château de Barbe-Blanche
Owner: A. Bouvier. 27 acres; 3,000 cases.
Château Bel-Air
Owner: Gabriel Roi. 25 acres red, 4,000 cases; 23 acres white, 3,000 cases.
Château Lucas
Owner: M. Vauthier. 8,000 cases red, 2,000 white.
Château de Lussac
Owner: Marquis de Sercey. 7,500 cases.
Château du Lyonnat
Owner: Jean Milhade. 25,000 cases.
Château Petit-Refuge
Owner: Georges Turbet-Belos. 17 acres; 3,000 cases red, 500 white.
Château La Tour de Grenet
Owner: M. Brunot. 62 acres; 12,500 cases.
Château La Tour de Ségur
Owner: Maître Boncheau (monopoly of Dourthe Frères). 6,000 cases red, 1,000 white.
Château des Vieux Chênes
Owner: M. Debès. 10,000 cases.

MONTAGNE–ST-EMILION CHATEAUX

Château Barraud
Owner: Robert Laydis. 34 acres; 7,000 cases.
Château Bayard
Owner: Christian Bruno Laporte. 61 acres; 12,000 cases.
Château Bayard
Owner: Philippe Gouze & Fils. 34 acres; 7,000 cases.
Château Beauséjour
Owner: Lucien Laporte. 31 acres; 6,000 cases.
Château Biquette
Owner: Yvette Bertin. 23 acres; 4,500 cases.
Château Bonneau
Owner: Alain Despagne. 25 acres; 5,000 cases.
Château Calon
Owner: Jean-Noël Boidron. 54 acres; 10,000 cases.
Château Corbin
Owner: François Rambeaud. 50 acres; 10,000 cases.
Château Coucy
Owners: The Maurèze family. 43 acres; 8,000 cases.
Château Fontmuret
Owners: Simonnet Père & Fils. 25 acres; 5,000 cases.
Château Gilet
Owner: G. Cally. 22.5 acres; 4,500 cases.
Château Gilet Bayard
Owner: Michel Darnajou. 25 acres; 4,600 cases.
Château Haute Faucherie
Owner: Yvette Audinet. 22.5 acres; 4,500 cases.
Château des Moines
Owner: Raymond Edgard Tapon. 26 acres; 5,000 cases.
Château Montaiguillon
Owner: M. Amart. 62 acres; 13,000 cases.
Château Mouchet
Owner: Primo Grando. 29 acres; 5,500 cases.
Château St-André-Corbin
Owner: Robert Carré. 54 acres; 10,000 cases.
Château Teyssier
Owner: Durand Teyssier. 48 acres; 9,000 cases.
Château des Tours
Owner: Louis Yerlès. 166 acres; 30,000 cases.
Vieux-Château-St-André (Corbin)
Owner: Jean-Claude Berrouet. 12 acres; 2,500 cases.

MONTAGNE–ST-EMILION: OTHER CHATEAUX

Château Bertinau 22.5 acres.
Château Bonde 14.5 acres.
Château Colas Nouet 20.5 acres.
Château Goujon 15 acres.
Château Négrit 28.5 acres.
Château Plaisance 48.5 acres.

ST-GEORGES–ST-EMILION CHATEAUX

Château Macquin
Owner: Denis Corre. 45 acres; 9,000 cases.
Château Maison Neuve
Owner: Michel Coudroy. 37 acres; 7,000 cases.
Château St-Georges
Owner: M. Pétrus Desbois. 125 acres; 25,000 cases.

PARSAC–ST-EMILION CHATEAUX

Château Parsac
27 acres.
Château Plaisance
Owner: Robert René Erésue. 26 acres; 5,000 cases.
Château du Puy
18.5 acres.

COTES DE CASTILLON CHATEAUX

Château Blanzac
St-Magne-de-Castillon. Owners: Michel Depons & Fils. 39 acres; 6,500 cases.
Château Cafol
St-Magne-de-Castillon. Owner: M. G. Castéra. 50 acres; 8,500 cases.
Château Chinchon-La-Bataille
Castillon-La-Bataille. Owners: The Larmazelle family. 42 acres; 8,000 cases.
Château de Clotte
St-Philippe-d'Aiguille. Owner: Veuve Guéret. 37 acres; 6,500 cases.
Château Les Demoiselles
St-Magne-de-Castillon. Owner: Rémy Daut. 62 acres; 11,000 cases.
Château Faugères
Ste-Colombe. Owner: Esquissaud de Faugères. 62 acres; 10,000 cases.
Château Gerbay
Gardegan. Owner: Alix Yerlès. 32 acres; 6,000 cases.
Château Lartigue
Belvès-de-Castillon. Owner: Veuve Larroque. 25 acres; 3,500 cases.
Clos Maison Rouge
St-Magne-de-Castillon. Owner: M. Goumaud. 37 acres; 6,500 cases.
Château Mansy
St-Magne-de-Castillon. Owner: M. de Lestang. 25 acres; 4,500 cases.
Château de Monbadon
Monbadon. Owner: Le Baron José de Montfort. 124 acres; 6,000 acres.
Château Moulin Rouge
St-Magne-de-Castillon. Owner: M. Bassilieaux. 50 acres; 10,000 cases.
Château Paret
St-Genès-de-Castillon. Owner: Jean Fauché. 34 acres; 5,000 cases.
Château la Pierrière
Tourtirac. Owner: Robert de Marcillac. 37 acres; 6,500 cases.
Château de Pitray
Gardegan. Owner: Vicomte de Pitray. 62 acres; 12,000 cases.

POMEROL

If there are doubters (and there are) about the differences that different soils make to wine, they should study Pomerol. In this little area, flanked by the huge spread of St-Emilion, like a market-garden to Libourne on the north bank of the Dordogne, there are wines as potent and majestic as any in France cheek by jowl with wines of wispy, fleeting fruitiness and charm – and dull ones, too.

The soil grades from shingly sand around the town of Libourne through increasingly heavy stages to a climactic plateau where the clay subsoil is very near the surface. A yard down, the clay is near-solid and packed with nuggets of iron. This, at the giddy height of 50 feet above its surroundings, is in every sense the summit of Pomerol.

Pomerol will always be an abstruse, recherché corner of the wine world. Its whole vineyard area is no larger than St-Julien, the smallest of the great communes of the Médoc. Perhaps half of this (as against two thirds of St-Julien) is of truly distinctive, classed-growth standard. The size of the properties is correspondingly small. There are 180 members of the growers' syndicate, sharing 1,850 acres: ten acres each on average. The biggest estate is 120 acres. Many growers have a mere acre or two – enough for 200 or 300 of the annual total of about 300,000 cases entitled to the appellation. There is no cooperative: small growers tend to make their wine and sell it direct to consumers all over France, and particularly to Belgium.

It is only 100 years since the name of Pomerol was first heard outside its immediate area, yet tradition has already provided it with a clear identity. Its best soil is clay; therefore cold. The early-ripening Merlot does better than the later Cabernet, and of the Cabernets the Franc (alias Bouchet) rather than the Sauvignon. The mellow, brambly Merlot and the lively, raspberryish Bouchet pick up the iron from the clay, are matured in fragrant oak – and *voilà*, you have a greatly over-simplified recipe for Pomerol. Where does it get its singular texture of velvet, its chewy flesh, its smell of ripe plums and even cream, and even honey? Wherever, it was more than an edict from the bureaucracy that fixes appellations.

Authorities put Pomerol between St-Emilion and the Médoc in style. To me it is closer to St-Emilion; broader, more savoury and with less 'nerve' than Médocs of similar value, maturing in five years as much as Médocs do in ten – hence tending to overlay them at tastings, as California wines do French. Great Pomerols, however, show no sign of being short lived. No official classification of Pomerol has ever been made. Professor Roger published a personal one in 1960, in *The Wines of Bordeaux*, dividing 63 châteaux into four ranks, with Château Pétrus on its own, Yquem-like, at the head. I have taken the advice of the most influential voice in the district, the merchants and proprietors Etablissement Jean-Pierre Moueix of Libourne, in listing 40 properties as the best in the district. Below these I list only others with more than the average (ten acres) of vineyard. Postcode: 33500 Libourne.
Price (1981): 18 francs a bottle.

FIRST-GROWTH

Château Pétrus

Owners: Mme Lacoste and Jean-Pierre Moueix.
AOC: Pomerol. Area: 27 acres; 3,750 cases. Grape var: Merlot 95%, Cab. Franc 5%.
See Pétrus, Pomerol's First-Growth page 95.

The statue of St Peter at Pétrus; the saint appears on the label, too

LEADING CHATEAUX

Château Beauregard

Pomerol. Owner: Paul Clauzel. 32 acres; 4,100 cases. Grape var: Merlot 48%, Cab. Franc 44%, Cab. Sauv. 5%, Malbec 3%.
Price (1980): 26 francs a bottle.

In contrast to most of the modest 'châteaux' of Pomerol, the 17th-century Château Beauregard is so desirable that Mrs Daniel Guggenheim had it copied stone for stone on Long Island. Relatively light gravel and lots of 'Bouchet' make this a delicate, round and 'charming' wine.

Château Bourgneuf-Vayron

Pomerol. Owner: Xavier Vayron. 21 acres; 4,200 cases. Grape var: Merlot 80%, Cab. Sauv. 20%.

In the heart of Pomerol between Trotanoy and Latour. Potent, plummy wine; not the most stylish.

Château La Cabanne

Pomerol. Owner: Jean-Pierre Estager. 22 acres; 3,000 cases. Grape var: Merlot 60%, Cab. Franc 30%, Malbec 10%.

The name means 'the hut' or the 'shanty', which seems excessively modest for an estate in the heart of Pomerol with Trotanoy as a neighbour. I have never seen the wine in England but the best local judges rate it well. The soil is middling between gravel and clay.

Château Certan de May

Pomerol. Owner: Mme Barreau. 11.5 acres; 1,600 cases. Grape var: Merlot 70%, Cab. Franc 30%.

Formerly called Ch. Certan. Perfectly sited between Vieux Château Certan and Pétrus. Not in this class but steady, well-made wine needing time to soften (especially the excellent 1975).

Château Certan-Giraud

Pomerol. Owner: Philippe Giraud. 17 acres; 1,850 cases. Grape var: Merlot 70%, Cab. Franc 30%.

Includes the former Ch. Certan-Marzelle. Considering its situation next to Pétrus, this seems a lean wine.

Château Clinet

Pomerol. Owner: Georges Audy. 15 acres; 2,800 cases. Grape var: Merlot 50%, Cab. Sauv. 35%, Cab. Franc 15%.

A central but second-rank vineyard. M. Audy thinks of his wine as being like Pauillac; harder and less round than Pomerol.

Clos du Clocher

Pomerol. Owner: Jean Audy. 14 acres; 1,500 cases.

Central vineyard next to the Certans making well-balanced, middle-weight wine with plenty of flavour.

Château La Conseillante

Pomerol. Owner: Louis Nicolas. 29 acres; 4,000 cases. Grape var: Merlot 45%, Cab. Franc 45%, Malbec 10%.
Price (1980): 38 francs a bottle.

The splendid silver-on-white label is designed around an 'N' for the family that has owned the château for more than a century. Coincidentally, London's Café Royal has the same motif for the same reason.

La Conseillante lies between Pétrus and Cheval Blanc, but makes a more delicate, as it were high-pitched wine. sometimes as fine and fragrant as any Pomerol but less plummy and fat. Fermentation is now in stainless steel. Professor Peynaud has been consulted and recent vintages are first class.

Château La Croix

Pomerol. Owner: J-F. Janoueix. 32 acres; 5,750 cases. Grape var: Merlot 60%, Cab. Sauv. 20%, Cab. Franc 20%.

Includes Ch. La Croix-St-Georges. Another 6 acres is La Croix-Toulifaut. These crosses are in the south of the commune on relatively light soil with a high iron content, not to be confused with Croix de Gay on the northern edge. Sturdy wine not noted for finesse but repaying bottle age.

Château La Croix de Gay

Pomerol. Owners: The Raynaud-Ardurat family. 28 acres; 5,000 cases. Grape var: Merlot 80%, Cab. Sauv. 15%, Cab. Franc 5%.

A well-run, second-rank vineyard on the gravelly clay sloping north down to the river Barbanne. The '76 is a splendid concentrated wine.

Clos L'Eglise

Pomerol. Owners: Michel and François Moreau. 14.5 acres; 2,200 cases. Grape var: Merlot 60%, Cab. Franc 20%, Cab. Sauv. 10%, Malbec 10%.

A superb little vineyard on the north rim of the plateau, bought in the 1970s by the owners of the bigger but less distinguished Ch. Plince on the outskirts of Libourne. Old vintages were backward, long-lived wines. The '78 seems more anxious to be loved.

Château L'Eglise-Clinet

Pomerol. Owner: Mme G. Durantou. 11 acres; 1,500 cases (but usually more). Grape var: Merlot 60%, Cab. Franc 30%, Malbec 10%.

Generally rated above Clinet; a stouter production with tannin and even brawn.

Château L'Enclos

Pomerol. Owner: Mme Marc. 23 acres; 2,500 cases. Grape var: Merlot 80%, Cab. Franc 20%.

With Clos René, one of the most respected châteaux of the western half of Pomerol, with the sort of deeply fruity and rewarding wine that impresses you young but needs at least 7 or 8 years in bottle to do it justice.

Château L'Evangile

Pomerol. Owner: Louis Ducasse. 33 acres; 2,500 cases (usually considerably more). Grape var: Merlot 67%, Cab. Franc 33%. Price (1979): 38 francs a bottle.

In the top 10 of Pomerol for both quality and size. At its best (e.g. 1975) a voluptuous, concentrated wine for a long life, but accused of being facile in lesser vintages. Its situation between Pétrus and Cheval Blanc is propitious, to say the least.

Château Feytit-Clinet

Pomerol. Owners: The Domergue family. 15 acres; 1,600 cases. Grape var: Merlot 85%, Cab. Franc 15%.

I have had some wonderful old wines from this little château, across the road from the illustrious Latour à Pomerol. Under Moueix management since the mid-1970s. Largely replanted in 1975 and 1976, so the young vines need time to give their best.

Château La Fleur Gazin

Pomerol. Owner: Maurice Borderie. 12 acres; 1,250 cases. Grape var: Merlot 80%, Cab. Franc 20%.

Northern neighbour of Ch. Gazin, makes marvellously elegant, smooth, well-bred wine. I found myself noting the 'noble flavour' of the '79.

Château La Fleur Pétrus

Pomerol. Owner: Jean-Pierre Moueix. 18 acres; 2,100 cases. Grape Var: Merlot 75%, Cab. Franc 5%

The third best Moueix Pomerol – which is high praise. The vineyard is more gravelly than Pétrus and Trotanoy, the wine less fat and fleshy with more obvious tannin at first, poised, taut, asking to be aged. The '75 is exceptionally ripe and plummy; '76 typically fine but considerably lighter; '78 impressively concentrated and '79 even better. Somehow the jaunty label with a waving flag fails to give the right impression.

Château Le Gay (*see* Château Lafleur)

Château Gazin

Pomerol. Owner: Etienne de Baillieucourt. 56 acres; 8,000 cases. Grape var: Merlot 50%, Cab. Franc 25%, Cab. Sauv. 25%. Price (1980): 25 francs a bottle.

One of the biggest properties, despite selling a section to its neighbour, Ch. Pétrus, in 1970. The record is uneven; at best a fittingly fruity, concentrated wine but usually a shade dull.

Château Gombaude-Guillot

Pomerol. Owners: S. H. Laval & Filles. 17 acres; 1,700 cases.

A well-regarded property (listed by Prof. Roger as a 'first-growth') right in the centre near the church, but a wine I have never tasted.

Château la Grave Trigant de Boisset

Pomerol. Owner: Christian Moueix. 20 acres; 2,150 cases. Grape var: Merlot 85%, Cab. Franc 15%.

Not the most full-bodied Pomerol. but particularly well balanced and stylish with tannin to encourage long development. The pretty château near the *route nationale* to Lalande and Perigueux was restored in the 1970s by the man who runs Ch. Pétrus. The soil here is *graves*, not clay – hence finesse rather than flesh.

Château Lafleur

Pomerol. Owners: Mlles Marie and Thérèse Robin. 33 acres; 2,400 cases. Grape var: Merlot 50%, Cab. Franc 50%.

The two adjacent properties of the Robin sisters are united in the statistics, but distinct in quality. Lafleur (next to La Fleur Pétrus) is a model of balance, body with finesse and considerable style. Le Gay (across the road to the north) is a shade plainer and perhaps less potent. Both are nursed by their elderly owners like children and must be among the most consistently good Pomerols.

Château Lafleur du Roy

Pomerol. Owner: Yvon Dubost. 6.5 acres; 1,350 cases.

Little property on the outskirts of Libourne, near Ch. Plince. A minor wine with a good name.

Château Lagrange

Pomerol. Owner: Jean-Pierre Moueix. 20 acres; 2,000 cases. Grape var: Merlot 90%, Cab. Sauv. 10%.

Another Moueix property in the Pétrus group on the plateau. Less spectacularly flavoury than some of its neighbous, probably on account of younger vines. But the '78 has plenty of power.

Château Latour à Pomerol

Pomerol. Owner: Mme L.P. Lacoste-Loubat. 18 acres; 1,500 cases. Grape var: Merlot 80%, Cab. Sauv. 20%.

The property is run by the house of Moueix for one of the

family who own a share of Pétrus (and run the best restaurant in Libourne). They regard it as their number four Pomerol, with a fuller, fruitier style than La Fleur Pétrus: more fat, less sinew – words can be very misleading. Paradoxically, it is a *graves* wine, from westwards of the fat band of clay.

Château Moulinet

Pomerol. Owner: Armand Moueix. 43 acres; 5,000 cases. Grape var: Merlot 70%, Cab. Franc 30%.

An isolated estate on the northern edge of Pomerol where both the soil and the wine are lighter; the wine is stylish notwithstanding.

Château Nenin

Pomerol. Owner: M. Despujol. 61 acres; 7,400 cases. Grape var: Merlot 50%, Cab. Franc 30%, Cab. Sauv. 20%. Price (1980): 28 francs a bottle.

One of the biggest properties, lying between the great Trotanoy and La Pointe, but raising two cheers rather than three from most critics. In my experience a good safe bet.

Château Petit-Village

Pomerol. Owner: Bruno Prats. 27 acres; 3,750 cases. Grape var: Merlot 66%, Cab. Sauv. 28%, Cab. Franc 6%.

Uppermost Pomerol from the Cheval-Blanc zone. Impressive wine, but whereas the Prats' St-Estèphe château, Cos d'Estournel, is universally praised, the word most often used about Petit-Village is 'expensive'. My experience is of new vintages. I note that Michael Broadbent has had several disappointments with older ones, though he approved of a 1920 tasted at 60 years old.

Château La Pointe

Pomerol. Owner: Bernard d'Arfeuille. 52 acres; 6,750 cases. Grape var: Merlot 55%, Cab. Franc 40%, Malbec 5%.

Sister château of La Serre, St-Emilion, and big enough to be widely known. The vineyard is on the doorstep of Libourne, in gravel and sand over the famous iron-bearing clay. The wine is powerful and can be memorable. The '76 was exciting to smell, like honey and cream, slightly marred by a trace of bitterness in the finish. Very ripe years like '75 and '70 seem to need a long time to settle down.

Château La Providence

Pomerol. Owner: Jean Dupuy. 7 acres; 250 cases.

A recommended little property I have not visited.

Clos René

Pomerol. Owner: Pierre Lasserre. 38 acres; 6,800 cases. Grape var: Merlot 60%, Cab. Sauv. 30%, Malbec 10%.

Unpretentious and on the unfashionable (western) side of the commune, yet unmistakably serious Pomerol. Not so agreeable young as many others, but a great bottle to store away and forget for 10 years. The vintages of the late 1970s promise well.

Château Rouget

Pomerol. Owner: François-Jean Brochet. 31 acres; 3,000 cases. Grape var: Merlot 34%, Cab. Franc 33%, Cab. Sauv. 33%. Price (1980): 19.50 francs a bottle.

I cast envious eyes on Ch. Rouget each time I pass; it has the prettiest situation in Pomerol in a grove of trees leading down to the river Barbanne. New management since 1974 is improving what was an old-fashioned, slow-moving wine. No 1977 was bottled at all.

Château de Sales

Pomerol. Owner: Henri de Lambert. 116 acres; 16,000 cases. Grape var: Merlot 66%, Cab. Franc 17%, Cab. Sauv. 17%.

The only noble château of Pomerol, remote down long avenues to the northwest, then rather disconcertingly having the railway line running right through the garden. The big vineyard is beautifully run and the wine increasingly well made, yet without the concentration and sheer personality of the great Pomerols. The second label is Château Chantalouette.

Château du Tailhas

Pomerol. Owners: P. Nebout & Fils. 26 acres; 5,200 cases.

The southernmost Pomerol vineyard, a stone's throw from the edge of the sandy riverside area of St-Emilion. The authorities say it still has Pomerol's iron-rich clay subsoil, hence its special character, but I have never drunk it – it all goes to Belgium.

Château Trotanoy

Pomerol. Owner: Jean-Pierre Moueix. 27 acres; 3,300 cases. Grape var: Merlot 85%, Cab. Franc 15%.

Now generally allowed to be the runner-up to Ch. Pétrus, made by the same hands to the same Rolls-Royce standards. The little vineyard is on the western slope (such as it is) of the central plateau. The vines are old, the yield low, the darkly concentrated wine matured in new *barriques* (which lend it a near-Médoc smell in youth). For 10 years or more the best vintages have a thick, almost California-Cabernet texture in your mouth. Tannin and iron shows through the velvet glove. The 1979, '76 and '71 are considered the best recent vintages; the debate is whether the '71 was at its peak after a decade. To me its fleshy richness, however seductive, still promises more than it gives. I shall be thoroughly English and hang it until it drops off the hook.

Château Vraye-Croix-de-Gay

Pomerol. Owner: La Baronne Guichard. 9 acres; 900 cases. Grape var: Merlot 50%, Cab. Franc 40%, Cab. Sauv. 10%.

The name means 'the real Croix-de-Gay', implying that the neighbours pinched the name. Jockeying for position seems appropriate here on the northern rim of the precious plateau. Good Pomerol, but I have no record of very notable bottles.

Vieux Château Certan

Pomerol: Owner: M. Thienpont. 34 acres; 6,300 cases. Grape var: Merlot 50%, Cab. Franc 25%, Cab. Sauv. 20%, Malbec 5%. Price (1980): 32 francs a bottle.

The first great name of Pomerol, though overtaken at a canter by Pétrus in the last 30 or 40 years. The style is quite different; drier and less fleshy but balanced in a Médoc or Graves manner. At early tastings substance can seem to be lacking, to emerge triumphantly later. The 1945 was unforgettable in 1980. The Belgian owner lives in the handsome old château halfway between Pétrus and Cheval Blanc.

Château La Violette

Pomerol. Owner: Mme Servant. 8 acres; 1,550 cases.

A little neighbour of the big Ch. Nenin, as modest as its name, but recommended by those who know it.

CHATEAU PETRUS

Pomerol's First-Growth

As Château Yquem is to Sauternes, so Château Pétrus is to Pomerol; the perfect model of the region and its aspirations. Like its region, Pétrus is a miniature; there are 4,000 cases in a good year, and often less. Among first-growths it is unique in that it has never been officially classified, and that its emergence as a wine worth as much or more than any other red Bordeaux only started in 1945. The Loubat family were the promoters of its quality and status. Since 1961 it has been owned jointly by Madame Loubat's niece, Madame Lacoste, and Jean-Pierre Moueix.

The house of Moueix, directed by Jean-Pierre with his son Christian and his nephew Jean-Jacques, holds centre stage in Pomerol. Its modest offices and vast *chais* on the Libourne waterfront have a position of prestige without an exact equivalent anywhere in France. The resident oenologist, Jean-Claude Berrouet, has technical control of a score of the best properties both in St-Emilion and Pomerol.

Pétrus is the flagship. Outwardly it is a modest little place. The *cuvier* is a cramped space between batteries of narrow concrete vats. The *chais*, recently rebuilt, are more spacious, but by no means grand.

The magic lies in the soil. No golf course or wicket is more meticulously tended. When one section of ancient vines (the average age is 40 years) was being replaced I was astonished to see the shallow topsoil bulldozed aside from the whole two-acre patch and the subsoil being carefully graded to an almost imperceptible slope to give a shade more drainage. It was a remarkable opportunity to see how uninviting this famous clay is.

The principle of wine-making at Pétrus is perfect ripeness, then ruthless selection. If the October sun is kind, the Merlot is left to cook in it. It is never picked before lunch, to avoid diluting the juice with dew. The crop is small, the new wine so dark and concentrated that fresh-sawn oak, for all its powerful smell, seems to make no impression on it. At a year old the wine smells of blackcurrants. At two a note of tobacco edges in. But any such exact reference is a misleading simplification. Why Pétrus (or any great wine) commands attention is by its almost architectural sense of structure; of counterpoised weights and matched stresses. How can there be such tannin and yet such tenderness?

Because Pétrus is fat, fleshy, not rigorous and penetrating like a Médoc but dense in texture like a Napa Cabernet, it appears to be 'ready' in ten years or less. Cigar smokers probably should (and anyway do) drink it while it is in full vigour. To my mind it takes longer to become claret. In a sense the great vintages never do.

OTHER CHATEAUX

Château Bel-Air
Owners: Sudrat & Fils. 32 acres; 2,000 cases.

Château Bellevue
Owner: R. Brieux. 12 acres; 1,300 cases.

Château de Bourgueneuf
Owner: P. Larthoma. 12 acres; 1,900 cases.

Château Le Caillou
Owner: L. Giraud. 17 acres; 1,700 cases.

Château Cloquet
Owner: Maurice Vigier. 16.5 acres; 1,300 cases.

Château la Commanderie
Owner: Soc. Ch. La Commanderie. 14 acres; 2,500 cases.

Château La Croix-du-Casse
Owners: Soc. du Ch. La Croix du Casse. 21 acres; 3,500 cases.

Domaine de l'Eglise
Owner: P. Castéja. 13 acres; 1,900 cases.

Château Ferrand
Owners: Soc. Civ. du Ch. Ferrand. 38 acres; 4,850 cases.

Château Franc-Mallet
Owner: G. Arpin. 13 acres; 1,500 cases.

Château Grand-Moulinet
Owner: Jean-Marie Garde. 39 acres; 6,900 cases.

Domaine de Grangeneuve
Owners: Veuve Gos & Fils. 15 acres; 3,050 cases.

Château Grate-Cap
Owner: A. Janoueix. 25 acres; 2,900 cases.

Château Haut-Maillet
Owner: P. Delteil. 12 acres; 1,120 cases.

Château Maison Blanche
Owner: Gérard Despagne. 10 acres; 1,500 cases.

Château Mazeyres
Owner: S. A. Guerre. 21 acres; 3,700 cases.

Clos Mazeyres
Owners: Laymarie & Fils. 23 acres; 3,500 cases.

Château La Patâche
Owner: Mme Forton. 13 acres; 2,250 cases.

Château Plince
Owner: M. Moreau. 20 acres; 1,500 cases.

LALANDE-DE-POMEROL

The northern boundary of Pomerol is the little river Barbanne. The two communes on its other bank, Lalande and Néac, share the right to the name Lalande-de-Pomerol for red wine which at its best is certainly of junior Pomerol class. Traditionally, they have grown more of the Malbec (or Pressac), a difficult grape which is now going out of fashion. But the gravel-over-clay in parts is good and two châteaux, Bel-Air and Tournefeuille, have high reputations. Altogether there are 2,100 acres of vines; 250 more than Pomerol. Some 170 growers (without a cooperative) make an average total of 320,000 cases. The price is generally a shade higher than for a plain St-Emilion, though a third less than for Pomerol. Postcode: 33500 Libourne. Price (1982): 9 francs a bottle.

LALANDE-DE-POMEROL CHATEAUX

Château des Annereaux
Lalande-de-Pomerol. Owners: MM. Hessel and Milhade. 54 acres; 10,000 cases.

Château de Bel-Air
Lalande-de-Pomerol. Owner: Jean-Pierre Musset. 25 acres; 4,000 cases.

Château La Commanderie
Lalande-de-Pomerol. Owner: Mme Lafon. 5,000 cases.

Château La-Croix-St-André
Néac. Owner: M. Carayon. 37 acres; 6,000 cases.

Château La Gravière
Lalande-de-Pomerol. Owner: Mme Cascarret-Salesse. 3,000 cases.

Château Laborde
Lalande-de-Pomerol. Owner: J-M. Trocard. 4,000 cases.

Château des Moines
Owner: M. W. Darnajou. 2,000 cases.

Château Moncet
Néac. Owner: La Baronne de Jerphanion. 8,000 cases.

Château Moulin-à-Vent
Néac. Owner: P. Couffin. 5,000 cases.

Château Perron
Lalande-de-Pomerol. Owners: The Massonié family. 25 acres; 6,000 cases.

Château Sergant
Lalande-de-Pomerol. Owner: Jean Milhade. 6,000 cases.

Château Siaurac
Néac. Owner: La Baronne de Guichard. 50 acres; 10,000 cases.

Château Teysson
Lalande-de-Pomerol. Owner: Mme Servant-Dumas. 32 acres; 6,000 cases.

Château Tournefeuille
Néac. Owners: The Sautarel family. 6,000 cases.

BORDEAUX'S MINOR REGIONS

The vast extent of the Gironde vineyards begins to sink in when you look at the number and size of growers' cooperative cellars dotted over the *département*. Most of the areas covered by this section are cooperative-dominated. Most communes have one or two well-established châteaux–their old manor houses, whose wine has been made in the manner of a not-very-ambitious family business time out of mind.

In many cases the small grower has sold his vineyard to the bigger grower as an alternative to joining the cooperative. A number of well-run larger châteaux are thereby adding to their acreage, revising their methods and starting to specialize in either red or white instead of dabbling in both. In some cases they have switched from third-rate sweet wines to second-rate (occasionally even first-rate) dry ones. A large number are beginning to figure on wine-lists.

They cover a wide spectrum of styles and qualities, which are discussed in the head-note to each area. In each area I list the châteaux, their proprietors and production, which I have tasted or which have been recommended to me by local brokers and friends.

A note on their appellations: to many commercial growers with no great aspirations to quality, the dignity of the local appellation is not worth the trouble and restrictions it entails. If the vines are capable of producing 100 hectolitres a hectare (which they are) and the maximum crop allowed to be called Entre-Deux-Mers or Premières Côtes de Bordeaux is 50 hectolitres, the grower wants at least twice the price to restrict his crop and go through the formalities of claiming the appellation. But there is no such premium. He can get virtually the same price for non-appellation table wine – and twice as much of it.

FRONSAC AND CANON-FRONSAC

The town of Libourne lies on the Dordogne at the mouth of its little northern tributary, the Isle. In its enviable situation it has Pomerol as its back garden, St-Emilion as its eastern neighbour, and only one mile to the west another, surprisingly different, little wine area.

Fronsac is a village on the Dordogne at the foot of a jumble of steep bumps and hollows, a miniature range of hills (up to 300 feet) where vines and woods make pictures as pretty as any in Bordeaux. Several of the châteaux were obviously built as country villas rather than as plain farms. Under it all there is limestone. The vines are nearly all red, the usual Bordeaux varieties, traditionally with more stress on the soft and juicy Malbec than elsewhere. Having plenty of colour and alcohol, Fronsac wine has been much used in the past as *vin de médecin* for weaklings from more famous places.

There are 2,400 acres of vineyards divided into two appellations. Two thirds of the hills (the lower parts) are Fronsac; the top third, where the soil is thinner with more lime, is Canon-Fronsac. It is the fate of Fronsac to live in the shadow of its famous neighbours. Its wines can be delectable, full of vigour and spice, hard enough to resemble Graves or St-Emilion more than Pomerol, and worth a good five years' ageing. In the last 20 years they have claimed their place at the head of Bordeaux's 'minor' red appellations. Postcode: 33500 Libourne.
Price (1981): Fronsac 9.6 francs a bottle, Canon-Fronsac 12 francs.

CANON-FRONSAC CHATEAUX

Château Bodet
Fronsac. Owner: M. Leymarie. 37 acres; 5,000 cases.
Château Canon
St-Michel-de-Fronsac. Owner: Christian Moueix. 25 acres; 4,000 cases.
Château Canon de Brem
Fronsac. Owner: Mme de Brem (Mme Barre). 25 acres; 3,000 cases. The second label is Château Pichelèvre.
Château Coustolle
Fronsac. Owner: Alain Roux. 50 acres; 7,000 cases.
Château Dalem
Saillans, Fronsac. Owner: Michel Rullier. 37 acres; 6,000 cases.
Château du Gaby
Fronsac. Owner: M. de Kermoal. 37 acres; 5,000 cases.
Château du Gazin
St-Michel-de-Fronsac. Owner: M. Robert. 62 acres; 11,000 cases.
Château Junayme
Fronsac. Owner: R. de Coninck-Horeau. 50 acres; 7,000 cases.
Château Mausse
St-Michel-de-Fronsac. Owner: Guy Janoueix. 25 acres; 4,000 cases.
Château Mazeris
St-Michel-de-Fronsac. Owner: M. de Cournuaud. 35 acres; 3,900 cases.
Château Mazeris-Bellevue
St-Michel-de-Fronsac. Owner: Jacques Bussier. 37 acres; 5,000 cases.
Château Moulin-Pey-Labrie
Fronsac. Owner: Jacques Seurt. 17 acres; 3,000 cases.
Château du Pavillon and Château Grand-Renouil
Fronsac and St-Michel-de-France. Owners: Jean Ponty & Fils. 25 acres; 5,000 cases.
Château Toumalin
Fronsac. Owner: M. d'Arfeuille. 20 acres; 4,000 cases.
Château Vincent
St-Aignan. Owner: Bernard Oulié. 25 acres; 3,500 cases.
Château Vray-Canon-Boyer
St-Michel-de-Fronsac. Owners: R. de Coninck (Horeau-Beylaut). 20 acres; 2,500 cases.
Château Vrai-Canon-Bouché
St-Michel-de-Fronsac. Owners: The Roux-Oulié family. 32 acres; 3,000 cases.

FRONSAC CHATEAUX

Château de Carles
Saillans, Fronsac. Owner: Mme Jacques Chastenet. 62 acres; 8,000 cases.
Château La Dauphine
Fronsac. Owner: Mme de Brem (run by Mme Barre). 50 acres; 8,000 cases.
Château de Fronsac
Fronsac. Owners: The Seurin family. 17 acres; 2,200 cases.
Château Lagüe
Fronsac. Owners: The family Roux-Oulié. 25 acres; 4,000 cases.
Château Mayne-Vieil
Galgon, Fronsac. Owner: Roger Sèze. 173 acres; 18,000 cases.
Château Puyguilhem
Saillans, Fronsac. Owner: Mlle Mothes. 25 acres; 5,000 cases.
Château Richelieu
Fronsac. Owners: M. Viaud Père & Fils. 50 acres; 6,000 cases.
Château La Rivière
La Rivière, Fronsac. Owner: Jacques Borie. 124 acres; 20,000 cases.
Château Villars
Saillans, Fronsac. Owner: G. C. Gaudrie. 50 acres; 8,000 cases.

COTES DE BOURG

The right bank of the Gironde was a thriving vineyard long before the Médoc across the water was planted. Bourg, lying to the north of the Dordogne where it joins the Garonne (the two form the Gironde), is like another and bigger Fronsac: hills rising steep from the water to 200 feet or more, but unlike the hills of Fronsac almost solidly vine covered. The Côtes de Bourg makes as much wine as the lower Médoc – and so does its immediate neighbour to the north, the Côtes de Blaye. Bourg specializes in red wine of a very respectable standard, made largely of Merlot and Cabernet Franc, round and full-bodied and ready to drink at 4 or 5 years – but certainly not in a hurry. The châteaux that line the river bank have to all appearances a perfect situation. Farther back from the water is largely cooperative country with an increasing proportion of white wine of no special note. Postcode: 33710 Bourg sur Gironde.
Price (1981): 8.5 francs a bottle.

COTES DE BOURG CHATEAUX

Château de Barbe
Villeneuve. Owner: M. Savary de Beauregard. 148 acres; 28,000 cases.
Château La Barde
Tauriac. Owner: Alain Darricarrère. 74 acres; 10,000 cases.
Château du Bousquet
Bourg. Owners: Castel Frères. 148 acres; 44,000 cases.
Château Brûle-Sécaille
Tauriac. Owner: Jean Rodet. 44 acres; 10,000 cases.
Château de Civrac
Lansac. Owner: Jean-Paul Jaubert. 35 acres; 5,500 cases.
Château La Croix de Millorit
Bayon. Owner: M. Jaubert. 43 acres; 7,500 cases.
Château Falfas and Château La Goncarde
Bayon. Owner: Mme M. Jauvert. 44.5 acres; 7,000 cases. 30 acres; 7,000 cases.
Château de La Grave
Bourg. Owner: Robert Bassereau. 100 acres; 10,000 cases red, 4,000 white.
Château Grand-Jour
Prignac-et-Marcamps. Owner: Mme Gaignerot. 64 acres; 12,500 cases red, 1,500 white.
Château Gros-Moulin
Bourg. Owner: M. Eymas. 86 acres; 10,000 cases.
Château Guionne
Lansac. Owner: Richard Porcher. 62 acres; 9,000 cases.
Château Haut Macau
Tauriac. Owners: Bernard and Jean Mallet. 50 acres; 8,000 cases.
Château Les Heaumes
St-Ciers-de-Canesse. Owner: Max Robin. 37 acres; 8,500 cases.
Château Lalibarde
Bourg. Owner: Roland Dumas. 86 acres; 20,000 cases red, 2,000 white.
Château Lamothe
Lansac. Owner: Pierre Pessonier. 50 acres; 7,000 cases.
Château Laurensanne
St-Seurin-de-Bourg. Owner: Jean-François Levraud. 50 acres; 10,000 cases red, 2,000 white.
Château Mendoce
Villeneuve. Owner: Philippe Darricarrère. 30 acres; 3,000 cases.
Château Mille-Secousses
Bourg. Owner: Jacques Darricarrère. 185 acres; 45,000 cases (red and white).
Château Peychaud
Teuillac. Owners: Jean and Bernard Germain. 79 acres; 15,000 cases.
Château Rousset
Samonac. Owner: Mme Teisseire. 44 acres; 10,000 cases.
Château Tayac
Bayon. Owner: Pierre Saturny. 44 acres; 7,000 cases.
Château de Thau
Gauriac. Owner: Léopold Schweitzer. 111 acres; 15,000 cases.

PREMIERES COTES DE BLAYE

Two miles of water, the widening Gironde, separates Blaye from the heart of the Médoc. Blaye is the northernmost vineyard of the 'right bank'; the last place, going up this coast, where good red wine is made. North of this is white-wine country; the fringes of Cognac. Blaye already makes about one third white wine, a rather nondescript, full-bodied, sometimes semi-sweet style which no doubt could be improved.

Premières Côtes de Blaye is the appellation reserved for the better vineyards, nearly all red, whose wine is to all intents like that of Bourg – although generally considered not quite as good or full-bodied. Cooperatives handle about two thirds of the total production. Nonetheless the following châteaux are worth noting. Postcode: 33390 Blaye.
Price (1981): 8.1 francs a bottle.

PREMIERES COTES DE BLAYE CHATEAUX

Château Barbé
Cars. Owner: Claude Carreau. 62 acres; 10,000 cases red, 2,500 white.
Château de Beaumont
Plassac. Owner: Léopold Schweitzer. 22 acres; 4,000 cases.
Château Belair
St-Paul-de-Blaye. Owner: Pierre Mourlot. 37 acres; 4,000 cases red, 4,000 white.
Château Bellevue
Plassac. Owner: M. de la Garcie. 44 acres; 8,000 cases.
Château Bourdieu
Berson. Owner: Jean-Kléber Michaud. 82 acres; 20,000 cases (red and white).
Château Les Carrelles
St-Paul-de-Blaye. Owner: Claude Carreau. 74 acres; 10,000 cases red, 3,500 white.
Château Charron
St-Martin-Lacaussade. Owners: M. Doudet-Beaudry. 74 acres; 15,000 cases (red and white).
Château Les Chaumes
Fours. Owner: Robert Parmentier. 62 acres; 4,000 cases red, 2,000 white.
Château L'Escadre
Cars. Owners: Georges and J-M. Carreau. 74 acres; 15,000 cases (red and white).
Domaine de Florimond
La-Brède. Owner: Louis Marinier. 110 acres; 7,000 cases red, 8,000 white.
Château Gontier
Blaye. Owner: M. F. Levraud. 74 acres; 12,500 cases.
Château Grolet
Plassac. Owner: J. B. Mallambic. 86.5 acres; 20,000 cases (red and white).
Château de Jussas
St-Christoly-de-Blaye. Owners: R. and B. Bourdillas. 74 acres; 1,000 cases red, 15,000 white.
Château Le Menotat
St-Androny. Owner: Edouard Cruse. 25 acres; 6,000 cases red, 1,000 white.
Château Monconseil-Gazin
Plassac. Owner: Michel Baudet. 37 acres; 5,000 cases.
Château Pardaillan
Cars. Owner: Claude Carreau. 37 acres; 4,000 cases red, 2,000 white.
Château Perenne
St-Genés-de-Blaye. Owner: Veuve Morin. 99 acres; 20,000 cases.
Château Peyredoulle
Berson. Owners: Jacques and Bernard Germain. 50 acres; 9,000 cases.
Château La Rivalerie
St-Paul-de-Blaye. Owner: M. Bauchet. (Reg. Michel Elie.) 20,000 cases.
Château Segonzac
St-Genés-de-Blaye. Owner: Mme Pierre Dupuy. 74 acres; 4,500 cases red, 3,000 white.
Château Les Tuileries
Berson. Owner: Christian Alins. 62 acres; 10,000 cases red.
Château Valrone
On the island of Patiras, Bordeaux Supérieur. Owners: MM. Bertolus and Poullet. 74 acres; 12,000 cases red, 8,000 white.
Château Virou
St-Girons. Owner: Mme François Monier. 10,000 cases red, 10,000 white.

PREMIERES COTES DE BORDEAUX

A long, narrow strip of the east bank of the Garonne facing Graves across the river enjoys the doubtful prestige of this appellation. Its hinterland is Entre-Deux-Mers. The wooded and often very beautiful riverside bluffs have no such clear identity. At their northern end they were some of Bordeaux's original Roman and medieval vineyards – now buried under houses. At their southern end, at Cadillac and into Sainte-Croix-du-Mont, they are known for sweet wines, at their best up to Sauternes standards.

Along the way the mix is about half red and half white, the white largely sweet but without convincing stickiness – the sort that is going rapidly out of style. Some growers are learning to make it dry, others are planting red instead. Red Premières Côtes is potentially much better than plain Bordeaux Supérieur from less well-placed vineyards, but only fetches the same price or a few sous more. Lack of incentive to try harder is a real problem. Nonetheless there are those who do, and some very grand and prosperous names appear among the owners who are improving this part of Bordeaux. It has the combination of remoteness and accessibility that attracts businessmen.

A notable example of a pioneer in the region is Peter Sichel, who has a New World-style winery at Verdelais where he vinifies the grapes he buys in the district to make very fruity and attractive claret for drinking young. Oddly, the practice of buying grapes, common elsewhere, is almost unknown in Bordeaux except in the cooperative, profit-sharing, system.
Price (1981): 8 francs a bottle.

LEADING CHATEAUX OF THE PREMIERES COTES

Château Arnaud-Jouan
Cadillac. Owner: Albert Darriet. 3,000 cases red, 18,000 white.
Château Beau-Rivage
Baurech. Owner: M. Languens. 86 acres; 15,000 cases red, 1,000 white.
Château Beau-Site
Monprimblanc. Owner: M. Desmerie. 49 acres.
Château du Biac
Langoiran. Owner: Mme Bonnard. 32 acres; 1,000 cases red, 5,000 white.
Château Birot
Béguey. Owner: Jacques Boireau. 86 acres; 5,000 cases red, 15,000 white.
Domaine de Bouteilley
Yvrac. Owner: Jean Guillot. 50 acres; 10,000 cases red.
Château Bréthous
Camblanes. Owner: François Verdier. 50 acres; 10,000 cases red.
Château de Caillavet
Capian. Owners: Soc. Civ. 16,000 cases red, 3,000 white.
Château de l'Espinglet
Rions. Owner: M. Raynaud. 74 acres; 4,000 cases red, 8,000 white.
Château Fayau
Cadillac. Owner: Jean Mèdeville. 10,000 cases red, 30,000 white.
Château du Grand Moueys
Capian. Owners: MM. N. Lacour and A. Icard. 197.5 acres; 10,000 cases red, 10,000 white.
Château du Grava
Haux. Owner: Jean-Luc-Duale. 247 acres; 40,000 cases red.
Château Gravelines
Semens. Owner: M. Dubourg. 74 acres; 6,000 cases red, 8,000 white.
Château Grimond
Quinsac-Camblane. Owner: Pierre Young. 197.5 acres; 33,000 cases red.
Château Haut-Brignon
Cenac. Owner: René Fourès. 148 acres; 25,000 cases red.
Château Jourdan
Rions. Owner: A. Guillot de Suduiraut. 111 acres; 4,000 cases red, 8,000 white.
Château du Juge
Cadillac. Owner: M. Bessault. 99 acres; 3,000 cases red, 18,000 white.
Château du Juge
Haux. Owner: Jean Mèdeville. 62 acres; 4,000 cases red, 5,000 white.
Château Justa
Cadillac. Owner: Yves Mas. 10,000 cases red, 10,000 white.
Château Lafaurie
Semens. Owner: P. Sauvestre. 62 acres; 5,000 cases red, 5,000 white.

Château Lafitte
Camblanes. Owner: M. Rouzaud. 4,500 cases red, 700 white.
Château Le Gardéra (white) and Château Laurétan (red)
Langoiran. Owners: Ets. Cordier. 247 acres; 10,000 cases red, 30,000 white.
Château Lamothe
Haux. Owner: M. Néel. 62 acres; 3,000 cases red, 6,000 white.
Château Léon and Domaine de Camélon
Carignan. Owner: M. F. Mähler-Besse. 3,000 cases red, 2,000 white.
Château Maillard
Yvrac. Owner: Francis Germe. 50 acres; 4,000 cases red, 4,000 white.
Château Malagar
St-Maixant. Owner: M. Dubourg. 34 acres; 2,000 cases red, 4,500 white.
Château Mony
Rions. Owner: Marquis de Barbentane. 62 acres; 3,000 cases red, 10,000 white.
Château Péconnet
Quinsac. Owner: M. Amiel. 123.5 acres; 15,000 cases red, 5,000 white.
Château Peyrat
Beguey. Owner: Mme David. 99 acres; 5,000 cases red, 20,000 white.
Château du Peyrat
Capian. Owner: M. Lambert. 158 acres; 6,000 cases red, 15,000 white.
Domaine de Poncet
Omet. Owner: Gérard David. 123 acres; 10,000 cases red, 20,000 white.
Château de Ramondon
Capian. Owners: M. Sangers and Mme Van Pé. 198 acres; 7,000 cases red, 6,000 white.
Château Reynon
Béguey. Owners: Pierre Dubourdieu and Jacques David. 'Vieilles Vignes de Sauvignon'. 2,500 cases.
Château La Roche
Baurech. Owner: Julien Palau. 50 acres; 4,000 cases red, 4,000 white.
Château Suau
Capian. Owner: M. Raoux. 111 acres; 20,000 cases (replanting vines from white to red).
Château du Tasta
Camblanes. 5,000 cases red, 500 white.
Château Videau
Cardan. 74 acres; 5,000 cases red, 10,000 cases white.

ENTRE-DEUX-MERS

The two 'seas' in question are the rivers Dordogne and Garonne, whose converging courses more or less define the limits of this big wedge-shaped region; the most diffuse and territorially the most important in Bordeaux. The appellation is now for dry white wine only. The red made here is Bordeaux or Bordeaux Supérieur (or just *vin de consommation courante*).

The south of the region is relaxed patchwork countryside with as much woodland and pasture as vineyard. The north is almost a monoculture of the vine. Its biggest cooperative, at Rauzan, makes over one million cases a year.

Entre-Deux-Mers is the one wine Bordeaux has succeeded in redesigning in modern marketing terms. The region was bogged down with cheap sweet wine nobody wanted any more. Some bright spark thought of the catch-phrase '*Entre deux huitres, Entre-Deux-Mers*' ('Between two oysters,' etc . . .) and a rosy future opened up for dry white: the Muscadet of the southwest.

I have yet to taste an Entre-Deux-Mers of the sort of quality that would win medals in California – but the world needs its staples too. It varies from the briskly appetizing to the thoroughly boring, but in ways that are hard to predict. A good cooperative is just as likely to produce a clean and bracing example as a property with a long name. La Gamage, a blend of the best wines from the union of cooperatives, sets a standard that others emulate.

Within the appellation an area limited to the southern communes with theoretically superior wine can use the appellation 'Haut-Benauge' in addition to 'Entre-Deux-Mers' or 'Bordeaux'. Price (1981): 9 francs a bottle.

ENTRE-DEUX-MERS CHATEAUX

Château Bonnet
Grézillac. Owner: André Lurton. 60,000 cases, red and white.
Château Canet
Guillac. Owner: Jacques Large. 62 acres; 4,500 cases red, 8,000 white.
Château de Camarsac
Camarsac. Owner: Lucien Lurton.
Château de Courteillac
Ruch. Owner: Baron du Foussat. 74 acres; 6,000 cases red, 8,000 white.
Château de Cugat
Blasimon. Owner: Mme F. Meyer. 74 acres; 3,000 cases red, 5,000 white.
Château Fonchereau
Montussan. Owner: Mme Georges Vinot-Postry. 67 acres; 5,000 cases red, 5,000 white.
Château La France
Beychac-et-Cailleau. Owners: Soc. Civ. du Château. 148 acres; 8,000 cases red, 26,000 white.
Château Le Gay
St-Sulpice-et-Cameyrac. Owner: Romain Maison. 99 acres; 12,000 cases red, 4,000 white.
Château de Goélane
St-Léon. Owner: Angel Castel. 123 acres; 20,000 cases red, 5,000 white.

Caves Coopératives of Blaye, Bourg and Cubzac
Annual production in cases

St-Savin-de-Blaye	537,750
Pugnac	281,750
Tauriac	241,750
Générac	228,100
St-Gervais	223,750
Anglade	218,000
Lansac	151,500
Cars	134,000
St-Vivien-de-Blaye	92,000
Gauriac	77,000
Bourg-s/Gironde	76,500

Caves Coopératives of Entre-Deux-Mers
Annual production in cases

Rauzan	1,105,000
Sauveterre-de-Guyenne	442,000
Ste-Radegonde	396,000
Espiet	395,750
Romagne	379,000
St-Pey-de-Castets	321,500
Créon	315,000
Nerigean	301,500
Gironde	299,000
Ruch	288,750
Monségur	285,250
Blasimon	257,750
Génissac	248,000
Mesterrieux	238,500
Flaujagues	188,500
Cazaugitat	175,250
Vayres	166,500

Château du Grand-Puch
St-Germain-du-Puch. (Ch. Moulin Blanc for white.) 444 acres; 60,000 cases, red and white.
Château Guibon
Daignac. Owner: André Lurton. 62 acres; 5,000 cases red, 5,000 white.
Château Launay
Soussac. Owner: M. Greffier. 85 acres; 1,000 cases red, 30,000 cases white.
Château Martinon
Gornac. Owner: M. Trollier. 86 acres; 5,000 cases red, 15,000 white.
Château de Martour
Nérigean. Owner: Dominique Lurton. 49.5 acres; 1,000 cases red.
Château Puymiran
Montussan. Owner: The Degueil family. 111 acres; 23,000 cases red, 13,000 white.
Château de Quinsac
Quinsac. Owners: Soc. Civ. du Château. 5,000 cases red.
Château Raymond & Ch. Ramonet
Owner: Baron R. de Montesquieu. (Excl. Dourthe.) 20,000 cases red, 5,000 white.
Château Reynier
Grézillac. Owner: Dominique Lurton. 198 acres; 35,000 cases, red and white.
Château La Sablière & Dom. de Fongrave
Gornac. Owner; Pierre Perromat. 111 acres; 10,000 cases red, 15,000 white.
Château Senailhac
Tresses. Owners: The Magnat family. 148 acres; 15,000 cases red, 8,000 white.
Château La Tour-Puymiraud
Montussan. Owner: Emile Fazilleau. 148 acres; 10,000 cases red, 7,500 white.
Domaine de Toutigeac
Targon. Owner: René Mazeau. 494 acres; 70,000 cases red, 2,000 white.
Château de Tustal
Sadirac. Owner: Comte d'Armaillé. 111 acres; 6,000 cases red, 14,000 white.

STE-CROIX-DU-MONT AND LOUPIAC

The southern end of the Premières Côtes de Bordeaux faces Barsac and Sauternes across the Garonne. From Cadillac southwards the speciality is sweet white wine, growing more 'liquorous' the nearer it gets to Sauternes. Ste-Croix-du-Mont gazes across at the hills of Sauternes from its higher river bank and often shares the same autumnal conditions that lead to noble rot and sticky wines. Without quite the same perfection of soil or pride of tradition it cannot afford the enormous investment in labour needed to make the greatest wines, but it succeeds remarkably often in producing wine at least as good as run-of-the-mill Sauternes, and often better.

To my surprise I have been given Ste-Croix-du-Mont in the German Palatinate by a grower famous for his Beerenausleses, who told me he thought it compared well with his wines. (I must admit the Riesling said more to me.)

The only differences in the regulations between Sauternes and these right-bank wines is the quantity allowed. The same grapes and alcohol content are required but the grower is allowed 40 hectolitres per hectare as against only 25 for Sauternes. This is not to say that perfectionist growers make their full quota. They also make dry wines of potentially fine quality and a little light red. There are 980 acres of vineyards with some 140 proprietors and a *cave coopérative*, producing an average total of some 450,000 cases, which is rather more than Barsac. It sells for 8.5 francs, a mere half of the Sauternes prices.

Loupiac is not quite so well placed and makes slightly less liquorous wines on 700 acres. Half the proprietors take their grapes to the cooperative.
Postcode: 33410 Cadillac.
Price (1981): 8.5 francs a bottle.

STE-CROIX-DU-MONT CHATEAUX

Château Bel-Air
Owner: Michel Méric. 8,000 cases white.
Château Bertranon
Owner: M. Remeau. 1,000 cases red, 2,500 white.
Château Bouchoc
Owner: M. Ballade. 2,000 cases white.
Château Coullac
Owner: Gérard Despujols. 3,500 cases white.
Château Lagrave
Owner: M. Trinon. 3,000 cases white.
Château Lafüe
Owner: Jean Sicres. 2,000 cases red, 2,000 white.
Château Lamarque
Owner: Roger Bernard. 4,000 cases red, 5,000 white.
Château Laurette
Owner: François Pons. 1,000 cases red, 7,000 white.
Château Loubens
Owner: M. de Sèze. ('Fleuron Blanc' is dry white.) 1,000 cases red, 6,000 white.
Château Morange
Owner: M. Durr. 6,000 cases white.
Château L'Oustau-Vieil
Owner: M. Sessac. 2,000 cases white.
Château du Pavillon
Owner: M. d'Arfeuille. 5,000 cases white.
Château La Rame
Owner: C. Armand. 2,000 cases red, 2,000 white.
Château de Tastes
Owners: The Prats family. 300 cases white.

LOUPIAC CHATEAUX

Château du Cros
Owner: Michel Boyer. 20,000 cases white.
Château Dauphiné-Rondillon
Owner: J. Darriet. 10,000 cases white.
Château de Loupiac, Domaine de Gaudiet and Château Pontac
(also called **Ch. Loupiac-Gaudiet**)
Owner: Marc Ducau. 10,000 cases white.
Château Mazarin
Owner: M. Courbin-Meyssan. 15,000 cases white.
Château de Ricaud
Owners: The Wells family. 12,000 cases white.
Château du Vieux-Moulin
Owner: Mme J. Perromat. 1,500 cases red, 3,500 white.

GRAVES DE VAYRE AND STE-FOY-BORDEAUX

Within the same block of vineyard two smaller zones have separate appellations defined with Gallic precision, one on the basis of its soil and potential for something out of the rut, the other, I suspect, for political reasons.

Graves de Vayres, across the river from Libourne, has more gravel than its surroundings. Unfortunately its name invites comparison with Graves, which it cannot sustain. The whites are made sweeter than Entre-Deux-Mers. The quickly maturing reds have been compared in a charitable moment to minor Pomerols.

The other appellation, Ste-Foy-Bordeaux, looks like a natural part of the Bergerac region cobbled on to Bordeaux. Its wines are not notably different from the Dordogne wines of Bergerac, and its history is identical. For centuries it was where the Dutch went for the two commodities most in demand in the Low Countries and the Baltic: sweet wine and wine for distilling.

CÔTES-DE-BORDEAUX-ST-MACAIRE

Ten villages beyond Ste-Croix-du-Mont rejoice in this appellation for their 45,000 cases of semi-sweet wine, a trickle of which finds its way to Belgium. Otherwise the district would be of purely local interest were it not for the Château Malromé at St-André-du-Bois, the '*délicieux nid de douceur et de poésie*' where Toulouse-Lautrec's mother lived and where, in 1901, the painter died. Postcode: 33490 St-Macaire.

CERONS

The appellation Cérons applies to the three Graves villages (Podensac and Illats are the other two) that abut on to Barsac on the north and have a natural tendency to make sweet wines. Their wines are classified according to their natural degree of alcohol as either Graves or Graves Supérieures (at 11 or 12 degrees and naturally dry), or at half a degree more as Cérons, which inclines to be *moelleux*, the grey area which is sweet but not *liquoreux*. Occasionally it attains *liquoreux* stickiness. All depends on the autumn and the vinification, which in the past used sulphur as its crutch and left much to be desired. Modern methods can mean much cleaner and better wine, as the growing reputations of some of the properties indicate.

460 acres with 140 growers produce some 70,000 cases of Cérons (and more Graves), but sweet or dry it only fetches about 8.5 francs a bottle. France consumes nearly all of it; the only export is a trickle to Belgium and Germany. Postcode: 33720 Podensac.

CERONS CHATEAUX

Château Archambeau
Illats. Owner: Jean Dubourdieu. 2,500 cases white.

Château du Barrail
Cérons. Owner: Guy Uteau. 8,000 cases white.

Château de Cérons and Château de Culvimont
Cérons. Owner: Jean Perromat. 6,500 cases.

Château Chantegrive
Podensac (*see* Graves).

Château Le Grand-Enclos
Cérons. Owners: Lataste Frères. 13,000 cases white.

Château de Ferbos and Lalannette-Pardiac
Cérons. Owner: Jean Perromat. 3,000 cases white.

Château Mayne-Binet
Cérons. Owner: Jean Perromat. 2,000 cases.

BORDEAUX AND BORDEAUX SUPERIEUR

The basic appellations underlying all the more specific and grander names of Bordeaux are available to anyone using the approved grape varieties, achieving a certain degree of alcohol and limiting the harvest to a statutory maximum (which varies from year to year). The standing definitions for red wines are:

Bordeaux must have 10 degrees at a maximum of 50 hectolitres a hectare.

Bordeaux Supérieur needs 10.5 degrees at a maximum of 40 hectolitres a hectare – hence more concentration and flavour.

For white wines:

Bordeaux must have 10.5 degrees at 50 hectolitres.

Bordeaux Supérieur needs 11.5 degrees at 40 hectolitres a hectare.

CUBZAC

The districts that regularly carry the simple appellation, having no other, include St-André-de-Cubzac and the nearby Cubzac-Les-Ponts, and Guitres and Coutras. Cubzac is where the great iron bridge built by Eiffel (of the tower) crosses the Dordogne on the way from Bordeaux to Paris. It lies between the hills of Fronsac and those of Bourg, on flat land which can nonetheless make respectable wine. Postcode: 33240 St-André-de-Cubzac.
Price (1982): 3.80 and 4 francs a bottle.

CUBZAC CHATEAUX

Château Timberlay
St-André-de-Cubzac. Owner: R. Giraud. 185 acres; 50,000 cases red, 6,000 cases white.

Château du Bouilh
St-André-de-Cubzac. Owner: Le Comte de Feulhade de Chauvin. 124 acres; 22,500 cases red, 4,000 cases white.

Château de Terrefort-Quancard
Cubzac-les-Ponts. Owners: The Quancard family. 150 acres; 33,000 cases red.

GUITRES AND COUTRAS

Guitres and Coutras are very much on the fringe, to the north of Cubzac where wine-growing used to be directed towards Cognac. One property in the area uses a typically Pomerol mix with 75% Merlot on clay soil with encouraging results. Postcode: 33230 Coutras.

Château de Méaume
Maransin. Owner: Alan Johnson-Hill. 70 acres; 10,000 cases red.

Caves Coopératives of the Premières Côtes de Bordeaux, Loupiac-Ste-Croix-du-Mont and Côtes de Bordeaux St-Macaire
Annual production in cases

Langoiran	165,000
Quinsac	159,500
St-Pierre-d'Aurillac	112,500

Caves Coopératives of the Côtes de Ste-Foy
Annual production in cases

Les Lèves	520,000
Landerrouat	441,500
Gensac	344,000
La Roquille	149,000

Sales Union (SICA) at de Landerrouat and at des Leves

Sovicop-Producta

This unfortunately named organization is not a productivity drive by the K.G.B. but a union of *caves coopératives* which has been highly influential over the last 20 years in improving the standards of cooperative-made wines and finding them markets.

It has some 40 members, all cooperatives, in Bordeaux and the neighbouring Dordogne and Lot-et-Garonne (including, therefore, Bergerac and the Côtes de Duras). Its recent experiments with inducing malolactic fermentation to lower the acidity of low-price white wines are one example of how it has helped coops and their customers. Another is carbonic maceration of red wines to give a Beaujolais effect to cheap red Bordeaux.

Bordeaux wine prices

Individual prices are given for the majority of the *Crus Classés* of Bordeaux and for each appellation. They are bottle prices, calculated on the basis of the ex-cellars price quoted in early 1982 for the 1980 vintage unless otherwise stated, with an allowance of 50 francs a case (the approximate going rate) for bottling, labelling and packing. Thus a wine offered at 20,000 francs a *tonneau* (100 cases) is quoted at 20,000 plus 5,000 francs divided by 1,200, which equals approximately 21 francs a bottle.

These prices are only useful for comparisons between châteaux and appellations. They bear no direct and quantifiable relationship with the final price after shipping costs, profits and taxes have been added. They are also, of course, likely to rise quite steeply, especially if prospects for the next vintage look doubtful.

BORDEAUX CHATEAUX INDEX

BURGUNDY

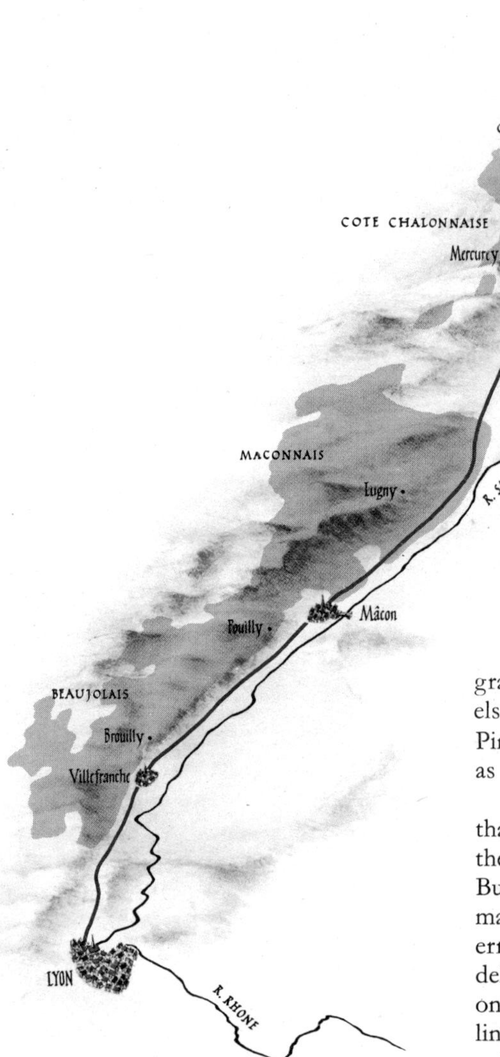

Burgundy has the best-situated shop window in France, if not in Europe. The powerful, the influential, the enterprising and the curious have been filing by for two millennia along the central highway of France, from Paris to Lyon and the south, from the Rhine and the Low Countries to Italy. Every prince, merchant, soldier or scholar has seen the Côte d'Or, rested at Beaune or Dijon, tasted and been told tall tales about the fabulous wine of this narrow, scrubby hillside.

Whether any other hillside could do what the Côte d'Or can is a fascinating speculation – without an answer. What it does is to provide scraps of land and scattered episodes of weather that bring two grape varieties to a perfection not found anywhere else. In certain sites and in certain years only, the Pinot Noir and Chardonnay achieve flavours valued as highly as any flavour on earth.

So specific are the sites and the conditions needed that the odds are stacked quite strongly against them. It is an uncertain way to make a living. So Burgundy has organized itself into a system that makes allowances – for crop failures, for human errors, for frailties of all kinds. Its legislation is a delicate structure that tries to keep the Burgundian one jump ahead of his clients without them tumbling to the fact.

If this is not a history book, it is not an exposé either. It is intended to be a portrait. And the painter is in love with the sitter.

The Burgundy of wine falls into five distinct parts. What is true of the Côte d'Or is equally true of Chablis, its northern outpost, but much less so of the region of Mercurey and the regions of Mâcon and Beaujolais to the south. The chapters on these areas summarize the local issues and conditions.

There is no simple or straight answer to the conundrum of Burgundy. The essential information is presented here in the form of geographical lists of the vineyards, their appellations and official ranking, and alphabetical lists of growers and merchants, showing who owns what and giving some idea of his standing.

THE CLASSIFICATION OF BURGUNDY

Bordeaux has a random series of local classifications of quality. Burgundy has a central system by which every vineyard in the Côte d'Or and Chablis (although not in Beaujolais and the Mâconnais) is precisely ranked by its appellation. Starting at the top, there are some 30 Grands Crus which have their own individual appellations. They do not (except in Chablis) use the names of their communes. They are simply and grandly Le Corton, Le Musigny, Le Montrachet. In the nineteenth century the villages that were the proud possessors of this land added the Grand Cru name to their own: Aloxe became Aloxe-Corton; Chambolle, Chambolle-Musigny; Puligny and Chassagne both added Montrachet to their names. Hence the apparent anomaly that the shorter name in general means the better wine.

In parentheses it must be said that the decisions about which sites are Grands Crus are old and in some cases unfair. They were taken on observations of performance over many years. Their soil is ideal. They are generally the places that suffer least from spring frost, summer hail and autumn rot. But they can be well or badly farmed. There are certainly some of the next rank, Premier Cru, which reach or exceed the level of several Grands Crus. The rank of Premier Cru is given with much deliberation over detail to certain plots of land in the best non-Grand Cru vineyards of all the best communes. For several years a review has been in progress that entails nit-picking over minute parcels of vines. For some communes it is complete – for others not. The upshot is, for example, that in the Pommard vineyard (or *climat*) of Les Petits Epenots plots 2 to 8 and 13 to 29 are classed as Premier Cru, while plots 9 to 12 are not. I give this instance not to confuse the issue but to show how extremely seriously the authorities take the matter.

The biggest and best Premiers Crus have reputations of their own, particularly in the Côte de Beaune (where Le Corton is the only red Grand Cru). Such vineyards as Volnay Caillerets and Pommard Rugiens can be expected to produce fabulously good wine under good conditions. In such cases the producer proudly uses the name of the vineyard. The law allows the vineyard name to be printed on the label in characters the same size as the commune name. There are smaller Premiers Crus, however, without the means to acquire a great reputation, whose wine is often just sold as, for example, Volnay Premier Cru. Often a grower's holdings in some vineyards are so small that he is obliged to mix the grapes of several holdings in order to have a vatful to ferment. This wine will have to settle for an unspecific name.

The Grands Crus and Premiers Crus form an almost unbroken band of vineyard occupying most of the Côte d'Or slope. The villages with their evocative names – Gevrey-Chambertin, Aloxe-Corton, Pommard – generally sit at the foot of the slope, encompassing in their parish boundaries both the best (upper) land and some, less good or even distinctly inferior, either on the flat at the bottom or in angles of the hills that face the 'wrong' way. This also is classed. The best of it, but not up to Premier Cru standard, is entitled to use the name of the village and the vineyard. In practice not many vineyards below Premier Cru rank are cited on labels. The law in this case demands that a vineyard name be printed in characters only half the size of the commune name. The *appellation contrôlée* here applies to the village name, not the vineyard. In the descriptions of properties that follow, I refer to these as 'Village' wines.

Inferior land within a village is not even allowed the village name. It falls under the rubric of *appellations régionales*: the most specific name it can have is Bourgogne (when it is made from the classic grapes, red and white, of the region), Bourgogne Passe-tout-grains, Bourgogne Aligoté or Bourgogne Grand Ordinaire. For an explanation of these terms see page 108.

GRAPES AND WINE

Burgundy is easier wine to taste, judge and understand than Bordeaux. The Pinot Noir, which gives all the good reds of the Côte d'Or, has a singular and memorable smell and taste, sometimes described as 'pepperminty', sometimes as 'floral' or 'fleshy'; certainly beyond the reach of my vocabulary.

Singular as it is, it varies in 'pitch' more than most grapes from one site to another and one vintage to another. In unripe years it smells mean, pinched and watery (German red wines give a good idea of the effect). At the other extreme it roasts to a raisiny character (many California Pinot Noirs are out of key in this way).

The ideal young red burgundy has the ripe-grape smell with neither of these defects, recognizably but lightly overlain with the smell of oak. And it tastes very much as it smells; a little too astringent for pleasure but with none of the wither-wringing, impenetrable tannin of a great young Bordeaux. Good burgundy tastes good from birth.

The object of keeping it in barrels is to add the flavour of oak and some tannin and to allow the wine to stabilize naturally. The object of maturing it in bottle is to achieve softness of texture and a complex alliance of flavours that arise from the grape, yet seem to have little to do with it. Fine old red burgundy arrives at an intense, regal red with a note of orange (the decorator's 'burgundy' is that of young wine). It caresses the mouth with a velvet touch which loses nothing of vigour by being soft. And it smells and tastes of a moment of spring or autumn just beyond the grasp of your memory.

Strange to say, white burgundy can have a distinct resemblance to red – not exactly in smell or taste but in its texture and 'weight' and the way that it evolves.

Chardonnay wine is not markedly perfumed when it is new: just brisk and, if anything, appley. The traditional burgundy method of fermenting it in small barrels immediately adds the smell of oak. Thereafter, the way it develops in barrel and bottle depends very much on which district it comes from, and on the acid/alcohol ratio of the particular vintage. An ideally balanced vintage such as 1978 keeps a tension between the increasingly rich flavours of maturity and a central steeliness, year after year. A sharp, barely ripe vintage such as 1977 leans too far towards the steel – and not very springy steel at that. A very ripe vintage such as 1976 produced many wines that were too fat and lacked 'cut'. All in all, however, the success rate of white burgundy vintages is very much higher than that of red.

HOW BURGUNDY IS MADE

Red burgundy is normally made in an open-topped cylindrical wooden *cuve* filled to about two thirds of its capacity with grapes crushed in a mill (*fouloir/égrappoir*) which removes some or all of the stalks. Every grower has his own theory of how much or little of the stems should be included, depending on the ripeness of the grapes (and of their stalks), the colour and concentration of the vintage, and whether he wants to make a tannic *vin de garde* or a softer wine to mature more quickly. Ultra-conservative growers still tend to include all the stalks. Among the arguments in favour are that it makes the pressing easier – to the contrary that it robs the wine of colour and can add bitter tannin.

To start the pulpy mass fermenting it is sometimes necessary to add a measure of actively fermenting wine from another vat, with a teeming yeast population – known as a *pied de cuve*. In cold weather it may also be necessary to warm the must with heating coils. The ancient way to get things moving was for all (male) hands to strip naked and jump in, lending their body heat to encourage the yeast. In an account of the Côte d'Or in 1862 by Agoston Haraszthy, reporting to the government of California, 'Five days is generally sufficient for the fermenting of wine in this part, unless it is cold weather, when the overseer sends his men in a couple of times more in their costume *à l'Adam* to create the necessary warmth.' He adds that 'This, in my eyes, rather dirty procedure could be avoided by throwing in heated stones or using pipes filled with steam or hot water.' And indeed it is. Pinot Noir needs a warm fermentation to extract all the colour and flavour from the skins.

The operation of *pigeage*, or mixing the floating cap of skins with the fermenting juice, is still sometimes performed in small cellars by the vigneron or his sons, scrupulously hosed down, in bathing shorts, but more up-to-date establishments either pump the juice from the bottom of the vat over the '*chapeau*' ('*remontage*') or use a grille which prevents the cap from floating to the top ('*chapeau immergé*'). I am told by practitioners that it is the positively physical rubbing of the 'marc' by *pigeage* that is important. It liberates elements that *remontage* or *chapeau immergé* cannot possibly obtain.

Individual ideas on the right duration of this '*macération*' of the skins in the *cuve* vary from a very few days to up to almost three weeks, by those who are determined to get deep-dyed wine with maximum 'extract' – hence flavour. The 'free-run' wine is then drawn off and the *marc* pressed in presses of every shape and form. The wine of the first pressing is usually added to the free-run juice and the ensemble filled into barrels, old or new according to the means and motives of the proprietor, to settle down and undergo its quiet secondary, malolactic, fermentation as soon as may be. The malolactic fermentation is often encouraged by raising the temperature of the cellar. Once they have finished this infantile fretting they are moved ('racked bright') into clean barrels.

Fine red burgundies are usually kept in barrel for up to two years – not quite as long as the best Bordeaux. Unlike Bordeaux, they are racked from one barrel to another as little as possible to avoid contact with the air. They are simply topped up and left alone until it is time for bottling. Two months before bottling they may need to be 'fined' to remove the very faintest haze. Some cellars use filters to clarify the wine, but other producers avoid this. Others – and this is the subject of heated debate – prefer to pasteurize their red wines before bottling to eliminate micro-organisms.

MAKING WHITE BURGUNDY

The procedure for making all dry white wines, white burgundy included, is virtually standardized today. The object is maximum freshness, achieved by minimum contact with the air. Careful, clean and cool handling of the grapes is followed by a quick pressing and slow, cool fermentation.

In big modern plants in Chablis, and the best of the big cooperative cellars of the Mâconnais, this clinical procedure is carried out and the flavours of the resulting wines owe everything to grape and soil. Chablis, having more acidity and a more distinctive flavour, can benefit from maturing in a steel or concrete vat and then in bottle for a considerable time. The simpler, rounder taste of Mâcon wines has little to gain by keeping.

But the classic white burgundies of the Côte d'Or are another matter. They are pressed in the same speedy way but are fermented in small oak barrels, filled to allow a little airspace on top. The finest and most concentrated wines are given new barrels for at least half of the crop every year. The pungent, almost acrid smell of new oak becomes part of the personality of the wine from the start. The majority of growers, those with good but not the finest land, settle for barrels that have been used several times before, perhaps replacing a few each year. In this case the oak has less of the obvious carpenter's-shop effect on the wine; the barrel is simply the ideal size and shape of container for maintaining fermentation at an even, low temperature, cooled by the humid ambience of the cellar. A greater volume of wine would generate too much heat as fermentation progresses.

Fermentation over, the wine stays in the barrel, on its yeasty sediment, until it becomes clear, which may take a good six months. It is then racked into clean barrels and kept until the maker judges it is ripe for bottling. What he is doing is allowing a gentle and controlled oxidation of the wine to introduce nuances and breadth of flavour that would otherwise not develop. It is then ready for drinking – unless the buyer wants to continue the ageing process in the bottle. To me the possibility of this 'reductive' ageing is the whole point of buying the great white burgundies. No other white wines reward patience so well.

The ancient way of warming the must to start burgundy fermenting

ADDING SUGAR

It is regular practice to add sugar to the must, the unfermented grape juice, in Burgundy, as it is in most of France. According to growers, long experience has shown that slightly more than the natural degree of sugar produces a better fermentation and a more satisfactory final wine. It is not purely the extra one or two degrees of alcohol but the evolution and final balance of the wine that is affected (they say).

All 'chaptalization' is strictly controlled by law. Until 1979 there was a statutory allowance for each Burgundy appellation. Since 1979, each year has been treated *ad hoc*, the minimum natural degree and the maximum degree after chaptalization being decided in view of the vintage as a whole. Nobody in any appellation is permitted to add more than two per cent alcohol to any wine by adding sugar. (There is a temptation to add the maximum: sugar not only increases the total volume of wine, it makes it easier to sell. The extra alcohol makes it taste more impressive and 'flattering' in its youth when buyers come to the cellar to taste.)

In 1981 the regulations in Burgundy stipulated that to use the humblest appellation for red wine, Bourgogne, the wine must have a natural alcoholic degree of 10. The maximum degree allowable, after chaptalization, was 13 degrees. So a 10-degree wine was permitted to be raised to 12 degrees, 10.5 to 12.5, and 11 and upwards to 13.

The equivalent figures for white wine are always 0.5 degree higher: e.g. Bourgogne Blanc must be naturally 10.5 degrees and may be pushed up to 13.5 degrees.

As the dignity of the appellation increases, so does the degree. The minimum and maximum figures set for 1981 in higher appellations were as follows:

Appellation communale or 'Village'; e.g. Aloxe-Corton:

red	minimum 10.5°	maximum 13.5°
white	,, 11°	,, 14°
Premier Cru, e.g. Aloxe-Corton Les Fournières:		
red	minimum 11°	maximum 14°
white	,, 11.5°	,, 14.5°
Grand Cru, e.g. Corton:		
red	minimum 11.5°	maximum 14.5°
white	,, 12°	,, 14.5°

The best producers, using their judgement, usually chaptalize between 1 and 1.5 degrees – rarely to the maximum, but rarely not at all (except for white wines, which in good vintages often reach 13° naturally). Maximum degrees are limits rather than goals.

GENERAL APPELLATIONS

There are four appellations that are available to growers in the whole of Burgundy with certain provisos:

Bourgogne

Red, white or rosé wines. The whites must be Chardonnay and/or Pinot Blanc. The reds must be Pinot Noir, with the exception of the Yonne, where the César and the Tressot are traditional and are admitted, and the 'crus' of Beaujolais, whose Gamay may be sold as 'Bourgogne'. No other Beaujolais wine or other Gamay is allowed.

The maximum crop is 50 hectolitres a hectare. Strength: 10 degrees for red and rosé, 10.5 degrees for white. It is worth ageing Bourgogne Rouge at least two years.
Price (1981): 12 francs a bottle (red), 14–15 francs (white).

Bourgogne Passe-tout-grains

Red or rosé wines from any area made of two thirds Gamay and at least one third Pinot Noir fermented together. Maximum crop 50 hectolitres a hectare. Minimum strength 9.5 degrees. Passe-tout-grains can be delicious after at least one year's ageing, and is not as heady as Beaujolais.
Price (1981): 10.80 francs a bottle.

Bourgogne Aligoté

White wine of Aligoté grapes, with or without a mixture of Chardonnay, from anywhere in Burgundy. Maximum crop 50 hectolitres a hectare. Minimum strength 9.5 degrees. One commune, Bouzeron in the Côte Châlonnaise, has gained its own appellation for Aligoté. Aligoté often makes a sharp wine with considerable local character when young.
Price (1981): 12.5–14 francs a bottle.

Bourgogne Grand Ordinaire (or Bourgogne Ordinaire)

Red, white or rosé from any of the permitted Burgundy grape varieties. Maximum crop 50 hectolitres a hectare. Minimum strength 9 degrees for red and rosé, 9.5 degrees for white. This appellation is now not often used.

The slatted wooden press and cylindrical vats typical of Beaujolais

BURGUNDY IN ROUND FIGURES

'Greater Burgundy', the region including not only the Côte d'Or but Beaujolais, the Mâconnais, Mercurey and the Yonne (Chablis), now produces 15 per cent of all *appellation contrôlée* wines.

In the past 25 years the area under vines has increased by nearly one half from 66,700 acres to 94,000 acres. The increase has been uniform in all districts except the Yonne, where the Chablis vineyards have expanded by more than 200 per cent. At the same time vineyards producing non-appellation *'vins de consommation courante'* have decreased sharply.

The trend, as in Bordeaux and elsewhere in France, has been towards more specialization and fewer but bigger holdings of vines. For example, in the Côte d'Or in 1955, 16,500 farmers had vineyards of less than 2.5 acres. The figure today is less than 2,000. In contrast the number of 'exploitations' of between 12.5 and 25 acres has more than doubled, of those between 25 and 50 almost trebled, and of those of 50 acres and upwards quadrupled. Similar trends, if anything more marked, apply to the other areas of Burgundy. Today approximately 10,000 growers own 94,000 acres and produce a total of about 2 million hectolitres (22.25 million cases).

The average production for the three years 1979–81 is given below for the principal brackets of Burgundy appellations.

White wines	**hl.**	**cases**
Côte d'Or Grand and Premier Crus	2,400	27,000
Côte d'Or other ('Village') wines	35,000	389,100
Chablis	80,000	893,000
Côte Chalonnaise	7,000	77,000
Mâcon 'Crus' (e.g. Pouilly Fuissé)	49,000	544,000
Mâcon Blanc (other)	88,000	976,000
Beaujolais	5,300	59,000
Regional appellations (simple Bourgogne, etc.)	60,000	666,000
Total production of white wines	326,700	3,631,100

Red wines	**hl.**	**cases**
Côte d'Or Grand and Premier Crus	9,250	103,000
Côte d'Or other ('Village') wines	125,000	1,385,000
Côte Chalonnaise	27,500	305,000
Mâcon	51,000	570,000
Beaujolais and Beajolais-Villages	812,000	9m.
Beaujolais 'Crus' (e.g. Fleurie)	284,000	3,153,000
Regional appellations (simple Bourgogne, etc.	166,000	1,842,000
Total production of red wines	1,474,750	16,358,000

Total 1,801,450 hl. 19,989,100 cases (cf. Bordeaux: 3.9m. hl. 43.3m. cases)

Exports total approximately 55 per cent of production. The principal export markets for Burgundy in 1981 were:

Switzerland	28% by volume	24% by value	(mainly white)
USA	15% ,, ,,	21% ,, ,,	(mainly white)
UK	13% ,, ,,	13% ,, ,,	(equally red and white)
West Germany	13% ,, ,,	11% ,, ,,	(mainly red)
Belgium/Luxembourg	9% ,, ,,	10% ,, ,,	(mainly red)

CHABLIS

Chablis and the few other scattered vineyards of the *département* of the Yonne are a tiny remnant of what was once the biggest vineyard area in France. It was the 100,000 acres of the Yonne, centred around the city of Auxerre, that supplied the population of Paris with its daily wine before the building of the railways brought them unbeatable competition from the Midi. Whether one is to draw any conclusion from the fact that its best vineyard was called La Migraine is hard to say.

Any vineyard so far north is a high-risk enterprise. When falling sales were followed by the phylloxera disaster, Auxerre turned to other forms of agriculture. Chablis dwindled but held on, encouraged by the merchants of Beaune, who provided its chief outlet. When it was first delineated as an appellation in the 1930s there was not much more than 1,000 acres, but they included the hillside of the seven Grands Crus. Nobody could ignore the quality of their wine. I remember a 45-year-old half-bottle of Les Clos 1923 as being one of the best white wines I ever drank.

It was the merchants of Beaune who made Chablis famous. In the simple old days when Beaune, being a nice easy name to remember, meant red burgundy, Chablis meant white. The name was picked up and echoed around the wine-growing world as a synonym for dry white wine. In California it still is.

But the real thing remained a rarity. Year after year, spring frosts devastated vineyards and discouraged replanting. Only in the 1960s did new methods of frost control turn the scales. The introduction of sprinkler systems to replace stoves among the vines on cold spring nights made Chablis profitable. Advances in chemical weed and rot control made it very attractive to invest in a name that was already world famous. Within a decade the acreage doubled, with each acre yielding far more wine, more reliably, than ever before. It continues to grow. Today there are 4,000 acres, and an average crop approaches one quarter of all white burgundy.

There is inevitably an old guard that strongly resists the granting of the appellation to so much new land. As in the rest of Burgundy, however, the Grands Crus and Premiers Crus are more or less sacrosanct: it is in Chablis '*simple*' or 'Village', without a vineyard name, that there is room for more expansion.

Straight unqualified 'Village' Chablis, as it is generally made today, competes in the marketplace with Mâcon-Villages. In style it is lighter, sharper, drier and cleaner, with more of a 'lift' in your mouth. A good example is distinctly fruity with a quality that only Chardonnay gives. A poor one, on the other hand, is simply neutral and more or less sharp. A small amount of wine from inferior plots is only allowed the appellation Petit Chablis. Many say it should not be called Chablis at all.

Premier Cru and Grand Cru Chablis are different wines; distinct steps upward in body, flavour and individuality. Some people find the best Premiers Crus the most satisfyingly typical, with plenty of flavour and a distinctive 'cut' of acidity. The Grands Crus add a richness and strength which rounds them out; occasionally too much so. To be seen at their best they need at least three and sometimes up to ten years ageing in bottle. Those made in barrels (the minority) keep longest and best.

The scent and flavour that develop are the quintessence of an elusive character you can miss if you only ever drink Chablis young. I can only define it as combining the fragrances of apples and hay with a taste of boiled sweets and an underlying mineral note that seems to have been mined from the bowels of the earth.

Chablis' price has not kept pace with its value. Grand Cru Chablis is happily in much better supply than Bâtard-Montrachet, otherwise it could well fetch as high a price. Premier Cru Chablis from a good grower is the best value in white burgundy.

The Vineyards of Chablis

Chablis comes in 4 grades: Chablis AC, (also known as '*simple*' or '*Village*'), Petit Chablis, Premier Cru and Grand Cru. The superior Premier Cru covers 1,084 acres with a further 770 authorized. Vineyard names (listed here) are sometimes used in conjunction with Premier Cru names. Grand Cru occupies an authorized area of 250 acres.

Premiers Crus

Fourchaume, divides into Fourchaume, Vaupulent, Côte de Fontenay, Vaulorent, L'Homme Mort.
Montée de Tonnerre, divides into Montée de Tonnerre, Chapelot, Pied d'Aloup.
Monts de Milieu
Vaucoupin
Les Fourneaux, divides into Les Fourneaux, Morein, Côte des Prés-Girots.
Beauroy, divides into Beauroy and Troesmes.
Côte de Léchet
Vaillons, divides into Vaillons, Châtains, Séché, Beugnons, Les Lys.
Mélinots, divides into Mélinots, Roncières, Les Epinottes.
Montmains, divides into Montmains, Forêts and Butteaux.
Vosgros, divides into Vosgros and Vaugiraut.
Vaudevey, a new Premier Cru, coming into production in 1983.

Grands Crus

Blanchots, Bougros, Les Clos, Grenouilles, Preuses, Valmur and Vaudésir. La Moutonne is a vineyard of 5.75 acres in Vaudésir and Les Preuses.

CHABLIS GROWERS

René Dauvissat

8 rue Emile Zola, 89800 Chablis.

Monsieur Dauvissat's great-grandfather was a cooper, so it is no surprise that his cellars, unlike most in Chablis today, are still full of barrels. He ages the wine from his 23 acres at least 12 months in wood in the old style. His best wines are the Grands Crus Les Clos and Les Preuses – 7 acres in all. His remaining 16 acres are all Premier Cru.

Paul Droin

3 rue Montmain, 89800 Chablis.

Droin's great-grandfather presented his wines to Napoleon III when he visited Auxerre in 1866. His cellars have not changed overmuch. But he keeps the wines from his 17 acres of Premiers Crus (mainly Vaillons) in barrels for 6 months, and his Grands Crus for 12 months, whereas his great-grandfather would have kept them for several years. The Grands Crus are Vaudésir, Les Clos, Valmur and Grenouilles – 9 acres in all. They are some of the finest Chablis made today.

Joseph Drouhin

7 rue d'Enfer, 21200 Beaune.

The famous Beaune négociant has since 1979 added 67 acres of Chablis to his domaine and makes immaculate, beautifully tender and aristocratic wine from the Grands Crus Vaudésir, Les Clos, Preuses and vividly typical Premier Cru from his holdings in Vaillons, Côte de Lechet, Mont de Milieu, etc.

Jean Durup

9 Grande Rue, Maligny, 89800 Chablis.

The large and growing estate of Jean Durup, President of the lobby that favours expanding the appellation Chablis. He has a total of 140 acres, of which 32 are in Premiers Crus (principally Fourchaume). An impeccable stainless steel winery whose wines appear under the names Durup, Domaine de l'Eglantière, Château de Maligny, Domaine de la Paulière and Domaine de Valéry.

William Fèvre

Rue Jules Ratier, 89800 Chablis.

The largest owner of Chablis Grands Crus and a traditionalist in his wine-making – one of the very few in Chablis to age his wine in new oak barrels. His 40 acres of Grands Crus include 10 of Les Clos, 15 of Bougros and 7 of Les Preuses, with 3 each of Valmur and Vaudésir and 1.5 of Grenouilles. He has a similar amount of Premiers Crus, split into 7 vineyards of which the biggest are 6.5 acres in Vaulorent and 6 in Montmains-Forêt. He also owns 18 acres of Chablis '*simple*'. William Févre heads the *Syndicat de Défense de l'Appellation Chablis*, the body which is in favour of restricting the appellation to well-proven sites.

Lamblin & Fils

Maligny, 89800 Chablis.

A négociant and grower, whose 26 acres account for only 10% of his wine: the rest is bought as grapes or juice from others. 'Domaine' wines include small parcels of Grands Crus Valmur (2 acres) and Les Clos (2.5 acres), and 12 acres of Premiers Crus. Chablis is 70% of his business; the rest is white Bourgogne Blanc, Aligoté, white table wine and sparkling. The Lamblin style is light and fresh; the wines are for drinking young and not for ageing. Other labels include Jacques Arnouls, Jacques de la Ferté, Paul Javry, Bernard Miele.

Henri Laroche

16 rue Auxerroise, 89800 Chablis.

A Chablis family in its fourth and fifth generations with Henri and his son, Michel, and in full vigour with two separate estates: Domaine Laroche of 62 acres and Domaine La Jouchère of 73. La Jouchère has 17 acres of the Premier Cru Vaillons, and Dom. Laroche 17 of Grand Cru, the biggest part (12 acres) being in Blanchots. Much of their wine is seen abroad under the name Bacheroy-Josselin. (Other names are Alain Combard, Henri Josset, Ferdinand Bacheroy, Jacques Millar, Jean Baulat, Roland Foucard.) The Laroche style is austere, vigorous, very typical of Chablis at its modern best. Their Grands Crus should be kept for 3 to 6 years.

Long-Depaquit

45 rue Auxerroise, 89800 Chablis.

A first-class old family company now merged with the négociants Bichot of Beaune but run autonomously. Of their 100-odd acres 48 are Chablis '*simple*', 30 Premiers Crus and 20 Grands Crus, including 6.4 of Vaudésir. Their most famous property is the 6-acre Moutonne vineyard, a part of the Grands Crus Vaudésir and Les Preuses, whose history goes back to the Abbey of Pontigny and its monks, who apparently skipped like young sheep under its inspiration. Long-Depaquit wines are very thoughtfully and professionally made with modern methods, but not for instant drinking.

Louis Michel

11 boulevard Ferrières, 89800 Chablis.

The son and grandson of small growers who has tripled his acreage by dedicated wine-making. He now has 30 acres of Premiers Crus (mainly in Montmains and Montée de Tonnerre) and 6 acres of Grands Crus (Vaudésir 3; Grenouilles and Les Clos 1.3 each). Michel believes in letting the wine make itself as far as possible. He uses no barrels, but by modest yields and careful handling makes concentrated wines that repay years of bottle-age. He also has a second label recently launched: Domaine de Vaubourg. 80% of his wine is exported.

J. Moreau & Fils

Route d'Auxerre, 89800 Chablis.

The largest proprietor in Chablis, and now a big business in non-Chablis white wines from the north of France, skilfully made and marketed. Total sales are some 375,000 cases a year. The Moreaus have been in business since 1814 and built up an estate of 175 acres. 125 acres of this is the Domaine de Biéville, appellation Chablis '*simple*', and 25 is Premier Cru Vaillons. Of their 25 acres of Grands Crus, 17 are Les Clos and include the Clos des Hospices, bought by the Moreaus from the local hospital in 1850. All the wine is made to be drunk young and fruity – very fruity in the case of Les Clos.

François Raveneau

Rue de Chichée, 89800 Chablis.

A little domaine (18 acres) in Grands Crus (Valmur, Les Clos, Blanchots) and Premiers Crus. Very traditional wines aged in barrels for at least 12 months and sold mainly to restaurants in France (including the Hôtel de l'Etoile in Chablis which has a fine selection of some of his earlier vintages). His wines age admirably.

A. Regnard & Fils

89800 Chablis

A family firm of négociants, founded in 1860, handling wine of all qualities with appropriate use of barrels for ageing some of the best. Their specialities are Premier Cru Fourchaume and Grands Crus Vaudésir and Valmur. As well as Chablis they sell Aligoté and Sauvignon de St-Bris. Other labels used are Michel Rémon and Albert Pic.

Gérard Rottiers

Rue Auxerroise, 89800 Chablis.

A new and growing property with 35 acres producing and 25 more planted. 22 acres are giving stylish Premiers Crus (mainly Fourchaume and Montmain) intended to be drunk young. 2.5 acres of Grand Cru Vaudésir makes the *vin de garde* of the house.

Simmonet-Febvre & Fils

9 avenue Oberwessel, 89800 Chablis.

A small domaine of 10 acres but a well-known négociant going back five generations. The present head is Jean-Claude Simmonet. The company makes wine from bought-in juice as well as its own, particularly from the Premiers Crus Mont de Milieu, Montée de Tonnerre, Fourchaume and Vaillons. Their best wine is the Grand Cru Preuses. Other wines they offer are Aligoté, Irancy, Sauvignon de St-Bris, and Crémant de Bourgogne. Other labels are Jean-Claude Simmonet, André Vannier, Georges Martin, Jean Deligny, Alexandre Goulard and Gilles Blanchard.

Jacques Tremblay

La-Chapelle-Vaupelteigne, 89800 Chablis.

A century-old domaine of 18 acres, but Tremblay likes young wine and has cast out barrels. He has 5 acres of Premier Cru Fourchaume but mainly makes drink-me-quick Chablis.

Robert Vocoret

Rue d'Avallon, 89800 Chablis.

A century-old family domaine of 76 acres, 10 in Grands Crus (Les Clos, Valmur, Blanchots), 33 in Premiers Crus and 33 in Chablis '*simple*'. Vocoret is one of the very few Chablis growers left who ferment as well as age their wine in barrels. The result is wine with less of the immediately appealing 'fruit' but a firm grip that rewards keeping.

Cave Coopérative 'La Chablisienne'

89800 Chablis

One quarter of the whole production of Chablis comes from this growers' cooperative, founded in 1923 and now handling the grapes from 1,240 acres, of which 837 are Chablis '*simple*', 240 Premiers Crus, 125 Petit Chablis and 37 Grands Crus. Of the Grands Crus vineyards, 17 acres of Grenouilles and 12.5 acres of Les Preuses are significant holdings. Fourchaume, with 86 acres, is much their most important Premier Cru. All their methods are modern and their wine well made, clean and honest. Most of it is exported, under about 50 different labels, usually the names of grower-members. 'La Chablisienne' is sometimes seen.

THE COTE D'OR

The heart of Burgundy is the 30-mile line of hills running south from Marsannay on the southern outskirts of Dijon, inclining westwards as it goes and presenting a broadening band of southeast-facing slopes until it stops at Santenay. The eight villages of the northern sector, ending at Prémeaux, are the Côte de Nuits. The 20 villages running south from Aloxe-Corton are the Côte de Beaune.

The Côte de Nuits is almost exclusively devoted to red wine – almost all Pinot Noir. On these steep, sharp slopes the most potently flavoured, concentrated, eventually smooth and perfumed wines are made.

The villages are listed here from north to south. Each is briefly described with an appreciation of its wine and a list of its Grands Crus (if any) and Premiers Crus, their acreages and the vineyard acreage of the whole commune. In several cases the official limits are still under discussion and acreages are provisional or unknown. An average 1981 price is given for each of the majority of the appellations. The growers listed under each village entry are those whose particulars will be found in the list of Côte d'Or growers starting on page 124. It is by no means an exhaustive list – only the telephone directory is that.

The details of growers' holdings, in almost every case supplied by themselves, give a vivid picture of the infinitely complex structure of the world's most highly prized vineyards.

Marsannay-la-Côte

Average production 21,000 cases of red and rosé. Famous for its superlative Pinot Noir rosé with its own appellation. One of the biggest domaines of the Côte d'Or, Clair-Daü, has its cellars here.

Fixin

The Premiers Crus are splendidly situated and capable of wines as good as those of Gevrey-Chambertin. Even the 'village' wines are stouthearted and long-lived. Between Fixin and Gevrey-Chambertin the village of Brochon has no appellation of its own. Its better vineyards are included in Gevrey-Chambertin. The lesser ones are plain Côte de Nuits-Villages. This appellation is also available to growers in Fixin.

PREMIERS CRUS

Total area 316 acres:
Premiers Crus 51 acres:
Arvelets (8)
Clos du Chapitre (11.8)
Cheusots (4.5)
Hervelets (9.5)
Meix-Bas (5)
Perrière (12)
Queue de Hareng*
En Suchot*
Le Village*
*Name is in use but no acreage specified in the latest official documents.

Appellation Communale 265 acres.
Appellations Regionales 234 acres.

GROWERS

André Bart
Bouchard Ainé & Fils
Clemencey Frères
Dom. Pierre Gelin
Dom. de la Perrière
Charles Quillardet

Gevrey-Chambertin

There is a very wide range of quality in the production of Gevrey – the biggest of any of the townships of the Côte d'Or. Some of its flat vineyards beyond the valley road are of middling quality only. But there is no questioning the potential of its constellation of Grands Crus. Chambertin and the Clos de Bèze are acknowledged to lead them; an extra charge of fiery concentration gives them the edge. The seven others must always keep the 'Chambertin' after their names; Clos de Bèze may put it before, or indeed simply label itself Chambertin. They are all stern, essentially male (since everything in France has a gender) wines that I cannot imagine even Astérix himself tossing back in bumpers. Obélix, perhaps. French critics claim for Chambertin the delicacy of Musigny allied to the strength of a Corton, the velvet of a Romanée and the perfume of the Clos Vougeot. I have certainly tasted fabulous complexity, but delicacy is not the word I would choose. Great age is probably the key. Two of the Premiers Crus of Gevrey on the hill behind the village, Les Varoilles and Clos St-Jacques, are widely thought to be on the same level of quality as the bevy of hyphenated Chambertins. Prices (1981): Village wines 32.50–36 francs a bottle, Charmes, Chapelles, Mazis, etc., 54–57.5 francs, Chambertin and Clos de Bèze 81–87.5 francs.

GRANDS CRUS

(No specified acreage in latest official documents.)
Chambertin (69.8)
Chambertin Clos de Bèze (37.5)
Chapelle-Chambertin (13.5)
Charmes- (or Mazoyères-) Chambertin (76)
Griotte-Chambertin (5)
Latricières-Chambertin (15)
Mazis-Chambertin (20)
Ruchottes-Chambertin (7.5)

PREMIERS CRUS

Total area 211 acres:
Bel Air (6.5)
La Boissière*
Cazetiers (25)
Champeaux (16.5)
Champitonnois (also called Petite Chapelle) (10)
Champonnets (8)
Clos du Chapitre (2.5)
Cherbaudes (5)
Closeau (1.3)
Combe-aux-Moines (11.78)
Combottes (11.3)
Corbeaux (7.5)
Craipillot (6.8)
Ergots (3)
Estournelles (5)
Fonteny (9)
Gémeaux*
Goulots (4.5)
Issarts (1.5)
Lavaut (23.5)
Perrière (6)
Poissenot (5.5)
Clos Prieur (5)
La Romanée*
Clos St-Jacques (16.5)
Véroilles (15)
*No acreage specified in the latest official documents.
Appellation Communale 760 acres.
Appellations Regionales in the commune: 234 acres.

GROWERS

Thomas Bassot
Albert Bichot
J.C. Boisset
Bouchard Père & Fils
Dom. Camus Père & Fils
Dom. Damoy
Joseph Drouhin
Dom. Dujac
Faiveley
Dom. Pierre Gelin
Dom. Antonin Guyon
Moillard
Charles Quillardet
Joseph Roty
Dom. Armand Rousseau
Dom. F. Tortochot
Dom. Louis Trapet
Dom. des Varoilles

Morey St-Denis

The least known of the villages of the Côte de Nuits despite having three Grands Crus to its name and part of a fourth. Clos de la Roche is capable of making wine with the martial tread of a Chambertin; Clos St-Denis marginally less so; Clos de Tart (at least as its sole owner interprets it) is considerably lighter. All the wines of Morey are worth study, for authenticity and a chance of a bargain. Prices (1981): Village wines 31–32.50 francs a bottle, Clos de la Roche and Clos St-Denis 54–57.50 francs.

GRANDS CRUS

Bonnes Mares (a small part) (2.5)
Clos des Lambrays (22)
Clos de la Roche (41.75)
Clos St-Denis (16.35)
Clos de Tart (17.5)

PREMIERS CRUS

Total area 68 acres:
Clos Baulet (5)
Les Blanchards*
Maison Brûlée (2.5)
Clos Bussière (7.5)
Chaffots (2.5)
Charmes (2.5)
Charrières (5)
Chénevery (7.5)
Aux Cheseaux*
Façonnières (2.5)
Genevrières (7.5)
Gruenchers (7.5)
Millandes (10)
Monts Luisants (white) (7.5)
Clos des Ormes (10)
Riotte (5)
Côte Rôtie (5)
Ruchots (6.5)
Sorbés (7.5)
Clos Sorbés (7.3)
*Name in use but no acreage specified in the latest official documents.
Appellation Communale 200 acres.
Appellations Regionales 305 acres.

GROWERS

Ets. Bertagna
Dom. Clair-Daü
Dom. Dujac
Dom. Georges Lignier
Dom. Mommessin
Dom. Ponsot

Chambolle-Musigny

The lilt of the name is perfectly appropriate for the wines of this parish – and so is the apparent evocation of the muse. It is hard to restrain oneself from competing in similes with the much-quoted sages of Burgundy, but here it seems to me Gaston Roupnel has it precisely right. Musigny, he says, 'has the scent of a dewy garden . . . of the rose and the violet at dawn.' Le Musigny is my favourite red burgundy, closely followed by the Premiers Crus Les Amoureuses and Les Charmes and the other Grand Cru, Les Bonnes Mares. A contributory reason is that some particularly good wine makers own this land. Prices (1981): Village wines 37.50 francs a bottle, Amoureuses 57.50–64 francs, Bonnes Mares 57.50–64 francs, Musigny 87.50 francs.

GRANDS CRUS

Bonnes Mares (also in Morey St-Denis) (33.5)
Musigny (28)

PREMIERS CRUS

Total area 152.5 acres:
Amoureuses (12.5)
Baudes (7.5)
Beaux Bruns (5)
Borniques (2.5)
Charmes (12.5)
Châtelots (5)
Combottes (5)
Aux Combottes (5)
Cras (10)
Derrière la Grange (10)
Fousselottes (10)
Fuées (15)
Groseilles (2.5)
Gruenchers (5)
Hauts Doix (2.5)
Lavrottes (2.5)
Noirots (5)
Plantes (5)
Sentiers (10)
Appellation Communale 315 acres.
Appellations Regionales 83.5 acres.

GROWERS

Bouchard Père & Fils
Dom. Clair-Daü
Georges Clerget
Joseph Drouhin
Dom. Drouhin-Laroze
Dufouleur
Dom. Dujac
Faiveley
Jean Grivot
Dom. Antonin Guyon
Leroy
Dom. Machard de Gramont
Pierre Ponnelle
Dom. G. Roumier
Dom. des Varoilles
Henri de Villamont
Dom. Comte de Vogüe

Vougeot

Historically the great vineyard of the Clos (de) Vougeot has the most resounding reputation in Burgundy. One hundred and twenty-five acres within a single wall built by the fourteenth-century monks of Cîteaux had a certain presence. Unquestionably the land at the top of the slope, next to Musigny and Grands Echézeaux, is equal to the best in Burgundy. But with its present fragmented ownership (some 80 growers have parcels) it is rare to meet a bottle that answers this description. Or perhaps I do not try often enough. Classical references to it always stress its perfume. My impression is generally of a more meaty, extremely satisfying but less exotic wine than those of its great neighbours.
Price (1981): 57.50–61 francs a bottle.

GRAND CRU

Clos de Vougeot (125)

PREMIERS CRUS RED

Total area 24.25 acres:
Cras
Clos de la Perrière
Petits Vougeots

PREMIER CRU WHITE

Vigne Blanche or Clos Blanc de Vougeot (4.5)
Appellation Communale 17 acres.
Appellations Regionales 10.5 acres.

GROWERS

Pierre A. André
Ets. Bertagna
Champy Père & Fils
Dom. Clair-Daü
Georges Clerget
Joseph Drouhin
Dufouleur Frères
Dom. René Engel
Faiveley
Jean Grivot
Dom. Henri Lamarche
Leroy
Dom. Machard de Gramont
Mugneret-Gibourg
Charles Noëllat
Pierre Ponnelle
Dom. Jacques Prieur
Dom. G. Roumier
Dom. des Varoilles

Flagey-Echézeaux

Exists as a village but not as an appellation, despite the fact that it has two Grands Crus in the parish. They are effectively treated as being in Vosne-Romanée, having the right to 'declassify' their wine under the Vosne name. In reality Grands Echézeaux is at Grand Cru level – an ideal site adjacent to the best part of the Clos Vougeot. Its wines can have all the flair and the persuasive depths of the greatest burgundy. But the huge 75-acre Les Echézeaux would be more realistically classified as one or several Premiers Crus. Its lack of any readily spotted identity joined with its apparently unmanageable name means that it sells for a reasonable price. There is a lightness of touch, a gentle sweetness and airy fragrance about a good Echézeaux which make it less of a challenge than the biggest burgundies.

Vosne-Romanée

If Chambertin has the dignity, the name of Romanée has the glamour. Only the very rich and their guests have ever even tasted La Romanée-Conti. The Domaine de la Romanée-Conti, sole owner of that vineyard and the next greatest, La Tâche, casts its exotic aura equally over Richebourg, Romanée-St-Vivant and Grands Echézeaux, where it also owns or manages property. The Domaine's wines are marked with a character that seems to be their own, rather than that of Vosne-Romanée as a whole. The Premier Cru La Grande Rue, for example, is marvellous wine in a different style, despite being sandwiched between La Tâche and La Romanée-Conti. Out of the torrent of words that has poured around Vosne and

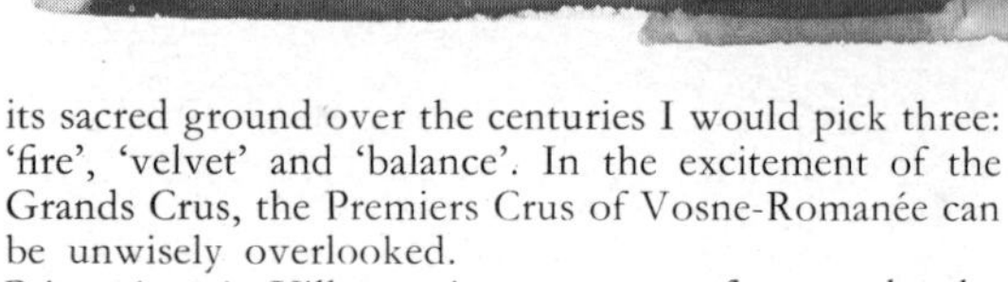

its sacred ground over the centuries I would pick three: 'fire', 'velvet' and 'balance'. In the excitement of the Grands Crus, the Premiers Crus of Vosne-Romanée can be unwisely overlooked.
Prices (1981): Village wines 32.50–34 francs a bottle, Suchots and Echézeaux 37.50–47.50 francs, Grands Echézeaux 71 francs, Richebourg 104 francs.

GRANDS CRUS

Total area 163.5 acres:
Echézeaux (75)
Grands Echézeaux (22.5)
Richebourg (20)
La Romanée (2)
Romanée-Conti (4.5)
Romanée-St-Vivant (23)
La Tâche (15)

PREMIERS CRUS

Total area 120.5 acres:
Beaux-Monts (6)
Brulées (10)
Chaumes (17.5)
Les Gaudichots (14.5)
Grande-Rue (2.5)
Malconsorts (14)
Petits Monts (9)
Clos des Réas (5)
Reignots (4.5)
Suchots (33.5)
Appellation Communale 227 acres. Appellations Regionales 198 acres.

GROWERS

Albert Bichot
Dom. Clair-Daü
Georges Clerget
Dom. Réne Engel
Jean Grivot
Dom. Jean Gros
Dom. Henri Lamarche
Dom. Machard de Gramont
Moillard
Mongeard-Mugneret
Mugneret-Gibourg
Dom. Mugneret-Gouachon
Charles Noëllat
Dom. de la Romanée-Conti
Charles Viénot

The walled city of Beaune is honeycombed with magnificent vaulted cellars dating back to the Middle Ages

Enjoying burgundy

White burgundy is incomparable as the white wine to accompany the first course of a formal meal and pave the way for a fine red wine – of either Burgundy or Bordeaux. Lighter and more acid wines are excellent with charcuterie; mature full-bodied ones are as satisfying as red wines with poultry or veal.

Red burgundy can be so delicate that it begs to be appreciated alone, without food. In contrast, it can be so massive in flavour and vinosity that the pungency of well-hung game is not too much for it. Lighter wines benefit by being served relatively cool. Only full-scale well-matured burgundies should be served at the 'room temperature' of Bordeaux. In Burgundy red wine is seldom, if ever, decanted.

Nuits St-Georges

As a town, Nuits does not bear comparison with the alluring city of Beaune; its walls have gone and it has no great public monuments. But it is the trading centre of the Côte de Nuits, seat of a dozen négociants, its endless silent cellars maturing countless big-bellied *pièces*. In another way, too, it echoes Beaune: its long hill of vines produces highly prized and famous wine without a single peak. If Nuits had a Grand Cru it would be Les St-Georges, and possibly Les Vaucrains, Les Cailles and Les Porrets on the slope above and beside it. But none of these vineyards has convinced the world that its wine alone rises consistently above the Premier Cru level.

Compared with the wines of Beaune, which they sometimes are, those of Nuits are tougher, less fruity and giving in their youth, and often for many years. It is hard to understand why they should be the popular favourite of Anglo-Saxon countries, as they are, since ten years is often needed to turn toughness to warmth of flavour. The best Nuits has marvellous reserves of elusive character that demand leisurely investigation.

Prémeaux, the village to the south (whose name recalls the spring waters which are its other product) is part of the appellation Nuits St-Georges and itself has a run of Premiers Crus of equal merit, squeezed on to a steep and narrow slope between the road and the woods.

Prices (1981): Village wines 36–37.50 francs a bottle, Les St-Georges, Vaucrains 44–47.50 francs.

PREMIERS CRUS

Total area 355 acres:
Aux Argillats (4.5)
Les Argillats (11)
Clos des Argillières, Prémeaux (11)
Clos Arlots, Prémeaux (16.5)
Boudots (15)
Bouselots (10.5)
Cailles (8.5)
Chaboeufs (7.5)
Chaignots (14.5)
Chaîne-Carteau (6)
Champs Perdrix (1.8)
Clos des Corvées, Prémeaux (19)
Corvées-Paget*, Prémeaux
Cras (7.5)
Crots (10)
Damodes (21)
Didiers (6)
Clos des Forêts, Prémeaux (17.5)
Clos des Grandes Vignes, Prémeaux (5)
Hauts Pruliers (0.5)
Clos de la Maréchale, Prémeaux (25)
Murgers (12.5)
Aux Perdrix, Prémeaux (8.5)
Perrière (7.5)
Perrière-Noblet (0.75)
Porets (17.5)
Poulettes (5)
Procès (5)
Pruliers (17.5)
Richemone (5.5)
Roncières (5)
Rousselots (10)
Rue de Chaux (5)
Les St-Georges (18.5)
Clos St-Marc*, Prémeaux
Thorey (12.5)
Vallerots (2)
Vaucrains (15)
Vignes Rondes (9.5)
*Name is in use but no acreage specified in the latest official documents.
Appellation Communale 42 acres.
Appellations Régionales 735 acres.

GROWERS

Jules Belin
J.C. Boisset
F. Chauvenet
Robert Chevillon
Robert Dubois & Fils
Dufouleur
Faiveley
Henri Gouges
Jean Grivot
Dom. Jean Gros
Dom. de la Juvinière
Lupé-Cholet
Dom. Machard de Gramont
Moillard
Mugneret-Gibourg
Dom. Mugneret-Gouachon
Hospices de Nuits St-Georges
Dom. de la Poulette
Henri Remoriquet & Fils
Charles Viénot

Côte de Nuits-Villages

This appellation is a consolation prize for the parishes at either end of the main Côtes: Prissey, Comblanchien and Corgoloin next to Prémeaux on the road south, and Fixin, Brochon and Marsannay on the Dijon road beyond Gevrey-Chambertin. Fixin and Marsannay have appellations of their own. For the others this is the highest aspiration. Stone quarries are more in evidence than vineyards on the road to Beaune. The marble sawn from the hill here is some of France's best. Only one important vineyard stands out as a Premier Cru *manqué*; the Clos des Langres, property of La Reine Pédauque, the extreme southern tip of the Côte de Nuits.

Price (1981): 21–22.50 francs a bottle.

Ladoix-Serrigny

The Côte de Beaune starts with its most famous landmark, the oval dome (if you can have such a thing) of the hill of Corton. The dome wears a beret of woods but its south, east and west flanks are all vines, forming parts of three different parishes: in order of approach from the north Ladoix-Serrigny, Aloxe-Corton and – tucked round the corner out of sight – Pernand-Vergelesses. The best vineyards of all three are those on the mid- and upper slopes of the hill, which share the appellation Corton Grand Cru (the only red Grand Cru of the Côte de Beaune) and in parts, for white wine, Corton-Charlemagne.

Ladoix-Serrigny has the smallest part of 'Corton', and not the best, in its vineyards of Rognet-Corton and Les Vergennes, names which are not used but subsumed in the general title of Corton, as all the Grand Cru territory can be. Similarly the 'village' wines of Ladoix, which few people have heard of, tend to take advantage of the appellation Côte de Beaune-Villages.

GRANDS CRUS

Total area 55 acres:
AOC Corton-Charlemagne white wines only
Basses Mourettes (2.5)
Hautes Mourettes (4.5)
Le Rognet et Corton (7.85)
AOC Corton red and white wines
Les Carrières (1)
Les Grandes Lolières (7.5)
Les Moutottes (2)
Le Rognet et Corton (20.75)
La Toppe au Vert (0.25)
Les Vergennes (8.5)
Parts of Ladoix-Serrigny may be sold under the appellation Aloxe-Corton, the rest may be sold as Côte de Beaune-Villages. Total area 845 acres.

PREMIERS CRUS

Total area 56.5 acres:
Basses Mourettes (2)
Bois Roussot (4.5)
Le Clou d'Orge (4)
La Corvée (17.5)
Hautes Mourettes (1.5)
Les Joyeuses (2)
La Micaude (4)
Appellation Communale Ladoix-Serrigny: 298 acres.
Appellations Regionales 421 acres.

GROWERS

Bouchard Père & Fils

Aloxe-Corton

The major part of the Grands Crus Corton and Corton-Charlemagne dominates this parish, but leaves a substantial amount of lower land with the appellation Aloxe-Corton, both Premier Cru and 'Village'. It is important to remember that Corton is always a superior appellation to Aloxe-Corton.

It is almost impossible (and in any case not really essential) to grasp the legalities of the Grands Crus here. 'Corton' embraces a dozen different adjacent vineyards, the top one of which is actually called Le Corton. The others may be labelled either Corton, or, for example, Corton-Clos du Roi, Corton-Bressandes. On such a big hillside there is inevitably a wide range of style and quality. Bressandes, lowest of the Grands Crus, is considered to produce richer wine (from richer soil) than Clos du Roi above it . . . and so on.

Corton-Charlemagne is a white Grand Cru from some of the same vineyards as red Corton – those on the south slope and the top ones where the soil is paler and more impregnated with lime. Perversely enough there is also a (rarely seen) appellation for white Grand Cru Corton.

True to their national inclinations, the French rate (red) Corton the best wine of the hill, comparing it for sheer force of personality with Chambertin, whereas the British speak of Corton-Charlemagne in the same breath as Le Montrachet. I have certainly been surprised to see French authors mildly liken it to Meursault. It expresses great driving vigour of a kind closer to Montrachet, though with more spice, even earth, and correspondingly less of the simple magic of ripe fruit. It is in the nature of Corton-Charlemagne to hide its qualities and show only its power, as red wines do, for as many as seven or eight years. Red Corton needs keeping as long as the Grands Crus of the Côte de Nuits. The dominant name among Corton growers, both red and white, is Louis Latour, whose press-house and cellars are cut into the foot of the hill and who gives the name of his château, Grancey, to a selection of Corton of even greater than usual power.
Prices (1981): Village wines 32.50–34 francs a bottle, Le Corton and Les Bressandes 41–44 francs, Corton Charlemagne 54 francs.

GRANDS CRUS

Total area 120.5 acres:
AOC Corton red wines only
Le Charlemagne (41.85)
Le Corton (28.85)
Les Languettes (17.85)
Les Pougets (24.25)
Les Renardes (7)
AOC Corton-Charlemagne for white wines only (in same parcels as reds above)
Le Charlemagne (41.85)
Le Corton (28.85)
Les Languettes (17.85)
Les Pougets (24.25)
AOC Corton for red and white wines (i.e., *not* Corton-Charlemagne) (177.5 acres):
Les Bressandes (43)
Les Maréchaudes (11)
Les Perrières (23.5)
Les Renardes (28)
Le Clos du Roi (26.5)
Parts (smaller than 10 acres) of Les Chaumes and Voirosses, Les Combes, Les Fiètres, Les Grèves, Les Meix, Les Meix Lallemand, Les Paulands, Le Village and La Vigne au Saint in Aloxe-Corton.

PREMIERS CRUS

Appellation Aloxe-Corton Premiers Crus, 72 acres:
Les Chaillots (11.5)
Les Fournières (13.75)
Les Guèrets (6.5)
Les Valozières (16)
Les Vercots (10.5)
and parts (smaller than 10 acres) of La Coutière, Les Maréchaudes, Les Meix, Les Moutottes, Les Paulands, La Toppe au Vert
Appellation Communale 222 acres.
Appellations Regionales 13.25 acres.

GROWERS

Pierre A. André
Dom. Bonneau du Martray
Bouchard Père & Fils
Louis Chapuis
Doudet-Naudin
Joseph Drouhin
Dom. F. Dubreuil-Fontaine
Faiveley
Dom. Goud de Beaupuis
Dom. Antonin Guyon
Louis Jadot
Dom. de la Juvinière
Louis Latour
Dom. Lequin-Roussot
Dom. Lucien Jacob Leroy
Dom. Machard de Gramont
Dom. Prince de Mérode
Moillard
Pierre Ponnelle
Dom. Daniel Senard
Dom. Tollot-Beaut & Fils
Dom. Tollot-Voarick
Charles Viénot
Dom. Michel Voarick

Pernand-Vergelesses

The Grand Cru of Pernand-Vergelesses is Corton-Charlemagne; there is no red Corton on the western slope of the hill (the only western slope in the whole of the Côte d'Or). But its Premiers Crus are in a completely different situation, directly facing Corton-Charlemagne across the narrow valley that leads up to this hidden village. The Premiers Crus are red; they continue the best vineyards of neighbouring Savigny, and in a sense those of Beaune.

GRAND CRU

Total area 42.62 acres:
AOC Charlemagne (white only) and AOC Corton (red only) are both in same parcel:
En Charlemagne (42.5)

PREMIERS CRUS

Total area 140 acres:
Basses Vergelesses (45)
Caradeux (35)
Creux de la Net (7.5)
Fichots (27.5)
Ile des Vergelesses (23)
Total area 828 acres.
Appellation Communale
Pernand-Vergelesses: 338 acres.
Appellations Regionales 350 acres.

GROWERS

Dom. Bonneau du Martray
Chanson Père & Fils
Doudet-Naudin
Dom. Germain au Château
Dom. Antonin Guyon
Dom. Laleure Piot
Louis Latour
Dom. Lucien Jacob Leroy
Rapet Père & Fils
Dom. Tollot-Voarick
Dom. Michel Voarick

Savigny-Les-Beaune

Savigny, like Pernand-Vergelesses, stops the head of a little valley cut back into the Côte and grows vines on both sides of it. On the Pernand side they face south, on the Beaune side northeast. The best are at the extremities of the parish, where both incline most to the east; respectively Les Vergelesses and Lavières, and La Dominode and Marconnets. The valley is drained by the little river Rhoin. Savigny has a substantial château, a great number of good growers, and best of all a tendency to more moderate prices than its neighbours. Its wines are in every way classic, apt to age, yet never ultra-chic. They need a good vintage to bring them up to their full strength – but whose do not?
Price (1981): 21–22·50 francs a bottle.

PREMIERS CRUS

Total area approx. 530 acres:
Basses Vergelesses (4.5)
Bataillère (also called Aux Vergelesses) (42.5)
Charnières (5)
Clous (38)
Dominodes (22.5)
Fourneaux*
Grands Liards (25)
Gravains (16.5)
Guettes (53.5)
Hauts Jarrons (15)
Hauts Marconnets (23)
Lavières (45)
Marconnets (23)
Narbantons (25)
Petits Godeau (19)
Petits Liards*
Peuillets (53)
Redrescues (2.5)
Rouvrettes (14.5)
Serpentières (33.5)
Talmettes (7.5)
Aux Vergelesses (42.5)

*Name is in use but no acreage specified in the latest official documents.

GROWERS

Pierre A. André
G.A.E.C. Simon Bize & Fils
Bouchard Père & Fils
Chandon de Briailles
Chanson Père & Fils
Dom. Clair-Daü
Doudet-Naudin
Dom. P. Dubreuil-Fontain
Dom. Goud de Beaupuis
Dom. Antonin Guyon
Dom. de la Juvinière
Dom. Lucien Jacob Leroy
Dom. Machard de Gramont
Ch. de Meursault
Dom. Pavelot Père & Fils
Seguin-Manuel
Dom. Tollot-Beaut & Fils
Dom. Tollot-Voarick
Henri de Villamont

Beaune

Beaune offers more temptation than any town to turn an encyclopaedia into a guide book. It begs to be visited. Walking its wobbly streets between its soothing cellars is one of the great joys. The oldest, biggest, grandest and most of the best négociants have their warrens here. They also own the greater part of its wide spread of vineyards. Do not look to Beaune for the most stately or the most flighty wines. '*Franc de goût*' is the classic description, which is almost impossible to translate, 'Franc' signifies straight, candid, open, real, downright, forthright and upright. Not dull, though. Young Beaune is already good to drink; as it ages it softens and broadens its bouquet. If there is a pecking order among the Premiers Crus the following are near the top of it: Les Grèves, Fèves, Cras, Champimonts and Clos des Mouches (which also produces a rare and excellent white wine). But nobody would claim to be able to distinguish them all, and more depends on the maker than the site. For this reason the various 'monopoles' of the négociants are usually worth their premium. Their names are prefixed with the word 'Clos'. The three biggest landowners are Bouchard Père & Fils, Chanson and the Hospices de Beaune. Prices (1981): Village wines 24 francs a bottle, Bressandes, Cent Vignes, Grèves, etc., 27.50–31 francs.

PREMIERS CRUS

Total area 854 acres:
Aigrots (37)
Avaux (33.5)
Bas des Teurons (17.9)
Blanches Fleurs (23)
Boucherottes (22)
Bressandes (44)
Cent Vignes (58)
Champs Piments (41)
Chouacheux (12.5)
Coucherias (57)
Cras (12.5)
Ecu (7.5)
Epenottes (35)
Fèves (10.5)
En Genêt (12.5)
Grèves (79.5)
Sur les Grèves (10)
Marconnets (25.2)
Mignotte (5)
Montée Rouge (41)
Montrevenots (20)
Clos des Mouches (61.4)
Clos de la Mousse (8)
En l'Orme (5)
Perrières (8)
Pertuisots (14)
Reversées (13)
Clos du Roi (34)
Seurey (3)
Sisies (21)
Teurons (38)
Tiélandry (4)
Toussaints (15)
Vignes Franches (25)

Acreages in Beaune are not officially confirmed.

GROWERS

Robert Ampeau & Fils
Besancenot-Mathouillet
Bouchard Aîné & Fils
Bouchard Père & Fils
Louis Carillon & Fils
Chanson Père & Fils
Coron Père & Fils
Doudet-Naudin
Joseph Drouhin
Dom. Michel Gaunoux
Dom. Germain au Château
Dom. Goud de Beaupuis
Hospices de Beaune
Louis Jadot
Dom. Michel Lafarge
Louis Latour
Lycée Agricole & Viticole
Dom. Machard de Gramont
Mazilly Père & Fils
Ch. de Meursault
Moillard
Jean Monnier & Fils
Dom. René Monnier
Maison Albert Morot
Patriarche
Dom. Jacques Prieur
Guy Roulot & Fils
Dom. Daniel Senard
René Thévenin-Monthélie & Fils
Dom. Tollot-Beaut & Fils
Dom. Tollot-Voarick

Chorey-Les-Beaune

The little appellation of Chorey-Les-Beaune slips off the map down into the plain. Its wine is generally commercialized as Côte de Beaune-Villages.

ROMANEE – CONTI

A Great Burgundy Estate

All the conundrums of wine come to a head at this extraordinary property. It has been accepted for at least three centuries that wine of inimitable style and fascination comes from one four-and-a-half-acre patch of hill, and different wine, marginally but consistently less fascinating, from the sites around it. Romanée-Conti sound like a supersuccessful public relations exercise. In some ways it is even organized as one. But there is no trick.

On such a small scale, and with millionaires eager for every drop, it is possible to practise total perfectionism. Without the soil and the site the opportunity would not be there: without the laborious pursuit of perfection it would be lost. A great vineyard like this is largely man-made. The practice in the days of the eighteenth-century Prince de Conti, who gave it his name, was to bring fresh loam up from the pastures of the Saône valley in wagonloads to give new life to the soil. Ironically, today the authorities would forbid so much as a bucketful from outside the appellation. Does this condemn the great vineyard to a gradual decline?

The coproprietors of the Domaine today are Mme Bize-Leroy and M. Aubert de Villaine, whose home is at Bouzeron near Chagny (where he makes

particularly good Aligoté). Their policy is to delay picking until the grapes are consummately ripe, running the gauntlet of the autumn storms and the risk of rot, simply rejecting all the grapes that have succumbed. The proportion of stems put in the vat depends on the season. Fermentation is exceptionally long: from three weeks to even a full month. All the wine is matured in new barrels every year. There is a minimum of racking and filtration. It is indeed, as Mme Bize-Leroy says, the grapes that do it.

As the prices of the Domaine's wines are so spectacularly high, one expects to find them not only exceptional in character but in perfect condition. They are essentially wines for very long bottle-ageing. What is surprising is that they often show signs of instability. It is almost the hallmark of 'D.R.C.' wines that they are instantly recognizable by their exotic opulence, yet rarely identical from bottle to bottle. Too often bottles are in frankly poor condition.

The same elusive quality applies to the wine in your glass. Of a bottle of La Tâche 1962, which has been one of the very best burgundies for years (at least in my view), I noted in 1982: 'Overwhelming high-toned smell of violets to start with, changing within 20 minutes to a more deep and fruity bouquet which seemed at first like oranges, then more like blackcurrants. The flavour was best about half an hour after opening – exotically rich and warm – then seemed to become a bit too alcoholic and lose some of its softness. Very exciting wine – not least for the speed and range of its metamorphoses.'

The precise holdings of the Domaine are as follows:

La Romanée-Conti, 4.45 acres, average production 7,000 bottles.
La Tâche, 14.8 acres, 24,000 bottles.
Richebourg, 8.6 acres, 14,000 bottles.
Grands-Echézeaux, 8.7 acres, 14,000 bottles
Echézeaux, 11.5 acres, 18,500 bottles
Romanée-St-Vivant is rented '*en fermage*' from the Domaine Marey-Monge, whose name appears on the label.
Le Montrachet, 1.66 acres, 2,500 bottles.

M. de Villaine conducts the distribution in the United States, which buys 50 per cent of the crop, and Britain, which buys 10 per cent. The house of Leroy takes care of the rest of the world: 5 per cent each goes to Germany, Switzerland and Japan, 5 per cent to other countries, and 20 per cent is sold in France. (*See also* Leroy, page 134.)

Château Meursault

Côte de Beaune

This appellation was instituted, as it seems, to discover who was dozing during the complexities of Côte de Beaune-villages (*see* page 123). It applies only to wine from Beaune (which has no reason to use it) or from another 22 acres adjoining, which appear to be just as deserving. La Grande Châtelaine and the Clos des Topes are the only vineyards I know that use it, for an admirable white as well as red.

Pommard

In the war of words that continually tries to distinguish one village from another, the wines of Pommard seem to have been labelled '*loyaux et marchands*': 'loyal and commercial'. 'Loyal' is awkward. Reliable might be a fair translation. In any case the suggestion is not of poetic flights. Pommard makes solid, close-grained wines of strong colour, aggressive at first, bending little even with age. Les Rugiens with its iron-red soil is the vineyard with most of these qualities, considered the best of the village. Les Epenots, on the edge of Beaune, gives rather easier wine. But there are some proud and decidedly loyal growers in the parish.

Prices (1981): Village wines 32.50–36 francs a bottle, Epenots, Rugiens, etc., 36–41 francs.

PREMIERS CRUS

Total area 309 acres:
Argillières (37)
Arvelets (20)
Bertins (8.5)
Clos Blanc (11)
Boucherottes (4.5)
Chanière (25)
Chanlins Bas (17.5)
Chaponnières (8)
Les Charmots (7)
Combes Dessus (7)
Clos de la Commaraine (10)
Croix Noires (10.5)
Derrière St-Jean (3)
Epenots (25)
Fremiers (12.5)
Les Jarollères (8)
Clos Micot (7)
Petits Epenots (51)
Pézerolles (15)
Platière (14)
Poutures (11)
Refène (6)
Rugiens-Bas (15)
Rugiens-Haut (14)
Sausilles (9)
Clos du Verger (6)
Appellations Communale 522 acres.
Appellations Regionales 823 acres.

GROWERS

Robert Ampeau & Fils
Dom. Marquis d'Angerville
Bouchard Père & Fils
Dom. Jean Clerget
Dom. Mme B. de Courcel
Dom. Clos des Epenaux
Dom. F. Gaunoux
Dom. Michel Gaunoux
Dom. Goud de Baupuis
Dom. Bernard & Louis Glantenay
Dom. Lequin-Roussot
Leroy
Dom. Machard de Gramont
Mazilly Père & Fils
Ch. de Meursault
Dom. Michelot-Buisson
Dom. Jean Monnier & Fils
Dom. René Monnier
Dom. de Montille
Dom. Parent
Dom. Jean Pascal & Fils
Ch. de Pommard
Henri Potinet-Ampeau
Dom. de la Pousse d'Or
Dom. Ropiteau-Mignon
Joseph Voillot

Volnay

Corton and Volnay are the extremes of style of the Côte de Beaune. The first regal, robust, deep-coloured and destined to dominate; the second tender, 'lacy', a lighter red with a soft-fruit scent, all harmony and delight. The dictum goes that Volnay is the Chambolle-Musigny of the Côte de Beaune. Personally I find it exact: each is my favourite from its area. To shift the ground a little, Château Latour answers to Corton; Lafite lovers will want Volnay.

The lovely little village hangs higher in the hills than its neighbours, its Premiers Crus on the mid-slopes below. The long ramp of vines that leads down to Meursault contains Les Caillerets, in now-obsolete terms the *tête de cuvée*; something between a Premier Cru and a Grand Cru. Champans, beside it under the village, reaches the same class. There is no clear division between Volnay and its southern neighbours, Meursault in the valley and

Monthélie on the hill. The same style of wine, even the same vineyard names continue. Meursault is allowed to use the name of Volnay for red wine grown in its part of Caillerets, Santenots, Petures and Cras. To taste them beside the white Premiers Crus of Meursault is to discover that red and white wine are by no means chalk and cheese. Prices (1981): Village wines 29 francs a bottle, Caillerets, Champans, Clos de Chênes, etc., 34–36 francs.

PREMIERS CRUS

Total area 284 acres:
Angles (8)
Aussy (4)
Barre (3)
Brouillards (14)
Caillerets (36)
Caillerets Dessus*
Carelle sous la Chapelle (9.5)
Carelle Dessous (3.5)
Champans (28)
Chanlin (7)
Clos des Chênes (38)
Chevret (15)
Clos des Ducs (6)
Durets*
Fremiets (18.25)
Lurets (5)
Mitans (10)
Ormeau (11)
Petures*
Pitures Dessus (9)
Pointe d'Angles (3)
Pousse d'Or (5)
Robardelle (7.5)
Ronceret (5)
Santenots (20)
Taille Pieds (22)
En Verseuil (1.5)
Village de Volnay (16)
*Name in use but no acreage specified.
Appellation Communale 241 acres
Appellations Regionales 378 acres.

GROWERS

Robert Ampeau & Fils
Dom. Marquis d'Angerville
Bouchard Père & Fils
Dom. Jean Clerget
Joseph Drouhin, Beaune
Jacques Gagnard-Delagrange, Chassagne-Montrachet
Dom. F. Gaunoux
Dom. Bernard & Louis Glantenay
Dom. Antonin Guyon
Dom. Michel Lafarge
Dom. Joseph Matrot & Pierre Matrot
Ch. de Meursault, Meursault
Dom. René Monnier
Dom. de Montille
Dom. Jean Pascal & Fils
Henri Potinet-Ampeau, Meursault
Dom. de la Pousse d'Or
Dom. Jacques Prieur, Meursault
Dom. Ropiteau-Mignon
Joseph Voillot

Monthélie

Just as Corton-Charlemagne goes on round the corner into Pernand-Vergelesses, so the best Volnay vineyard flows into the lesser-known Monthélie. It changes its name to Les Champs-Fulliots. The centre of interest in the village of Monthélie is its château, the property of its most distinguished grower, Robert de Suremain.
Price (1981): 21–24 francs a bottle.

PREMIERS CRUS

77 acres:
Cas Rougeot (1.5)
Champs Fulliot (20)
Duresses (16.5)
Château Gaillard (1.2)
Clos Gauthey (4.5)
Lavelle (15)
Meix-Bataille (6.5)
Riottes (1.85)
Taupine (4)
Vignes Rondes (7)
Total area 305 acres:
Appellation Communale Monthélie: 261.5 acres,
Regionales: 103.5 acres

GROWERS

Dom. Ropiteau-Mignon
Dom. René Thévenin-Monthélie & Fils
Robert de Suremain

Meursault

If Meursault has convinced itself that it is a town, it fails to convince visitors looking for amenities – still less action. Its streets are a bewildering forest of hoardings to cajole the tourist into the cellars that are its whole *raison d'être*. Levels of commercialism vary. In one property half-hidden with invitations to enter I was told, and curtly, that I could not taste unless I was going to buy. There seemed to be no answer to my mild protest that I could not tell if I was going to buy until I had tasted.

There is a mass of Meursault, and it is mixed. Its model is a drink that makes me thirsty even to think of it; a meeting of softness and succulence with thirst-quenching clarity and 'cut'. A 'Village' Meursault will be mild; the higher up the ladder you go the more authority and 'cut' the wine will have. I am thinking of a '78 Premier Cru Charmes from Joseph Matrot, which at three years old was almost painful to hold in your mouth: this is the authority and concentration of a first-class wine of a great vintage. With age comes rounding out, the onset of flavours people have described with words like oatmeal and hazelnuts and butter; things that are rich but bland.

The white wine vineyards of Meursault are those that continue unbroken into Puligny-Montrachet to the south, and the best those that are nearest to the parish line: Les Perrières, Les Charmes, Les Genevrières. The hamlet of Blagny, higher on the same hill, also contains Meursault Premiers Crus of the top quality: Sous le Dos d'Ane and La Pièce sous le Bois – names that seem to express a rustic crudity which is far from being the case. Village wines from high on the hill (Les Tillets, Les Narvaux) are excellent. Like Blagny they are slow to develop.

The red wines of Meursault go to market as Volnay. Prices (1981): Village wines 24–26 francs a bottle, Premiers Crus 34–36 francs.

PREMIERS CRUS

Total area 1,257 acres:
Red and white: 215 acres;
white only: 110 acres;
red only (Volnay): 72 acres.
Divided as follows
Red and white:
Bouchères (10.5)
Caillerets (2.5)
Charmes Dessous (41.6)
Charmes Dessus (32.25)
Cras (8.75)
Genevrières Dessous and Genevrières Dessus (26)
Goutte d'Or (13)
Jennelotte (13)
Perrières Dessous and Perrières Dessus (34)
Petures (26)
La Pièce sous le Bois (28)
Poruzots (10.75)
Poruzots Dessus (17.5)
Santenots Blancs (7.5)
Santenots du Milieu (20)
Sous le Dos d'Ane (7.5)
Red (Volnay) only:
Les Plures (26)
Les Santenots Blancs (7)
Les Santenots Dessous (19)
Les Santenots du Milieu (20)
Total acreage: 1,257 acres.
Appellation Communale Mersault: 735 acres.
Appellations Regionales 103.5 acres.

GROWERS

Robert Ampeau & Fils
Dom. Marquis d'Angerville
Bouchard Père & Fils
Dom. Clerget
Dom. Darnat
Dom. F. Gaunoux
Dom. Antonin Guyon
Dom. Jean Joliot & Fils
Dom. Michel Lafarge
Dom. de Comtes Lafon
Dom. Leflaive
Leroy
Dom. du Duc de Magenta
Dom. Joseph Matrot & Pierre Matrot
Mazilly Père & Fils
Ch. de Meursault
Dom. Michelot-Buisson
Dom. Jean Monnier & Fils
Dom. René Monnier
Henri Potinet-Ampeau
Dom. Jacques Prieur
Ropiteau Frères
Guy Roulot & Fils
Dom. Etienne Sauzet
René Thévenin-Monthélie
Joseph Voillot

Blagny

Blagny has no appellation of its own, but possesses excellent vineyeards in both Meursault and Puligny-Montrachet. Total area 134 acres.

PULIGNY-MONTRACHET PREMIERS CRUS

51 acres:
La Garenne (24.5)
Hameau de Blagny (10.5)
Sous le Puits (16.75)
Appellations Communales
Blagny: 19.5 acres.

MEURSAULT PREMIERS CRUS

58 acres:
La Jeunelotte (12.5)
La Piece sous le Bois (29)
Sous Blagny (5.5)
Sous le Dos d'Ane (12.5)
Appellations Communales
Blagny: 4.5 acres.

GROWERS

Robert Ampeau & Fils
Dom. Leflaive
Dom. Joseph Matrot & Pierre Matrot
Dom. Jean Pascal & Fils

Auxey-Duresses

The village above and behind Meursault where a valley at right angles to the Côte provides a south slope at the right mid-point of the hill for a limited patch of Premier Cru vineyard, mostly planted in Pinot Noir. Among other growers, the Duc de Magenta produces white wine like very crisp Meursault which I find more exciting than Auxey red. Much of the red, I gather, is sold as Côte de Beaune-Villages. The village also shelters the fabulous stocks of Leroy, the *'Gardien des Grands Millésimes'*.
Price (1981): 21–24 francs a bottle.

PREMIERS CRUS

78 acres:
Bas des Duresses (20)
Bretterins (5)
Duresses (20)
Ecusseaux (8)
Grands Champs (10)
Reugne (8)
Climat or Clos du Val (23)
Total acreage: 1,235 acres.
Appellation Communale
Auxey-Duresses: 341 acres.
Appellations Regionales
815 acres.

GROWERS

Robert Ampeau & Fils
Leroy
Domaine du Duc de Magenta
Henri Potinet-Ampeau
Guy Roulot & Fils
Roland Thévenin

St-Romain

A pretty little village lurking in the second wave of hills, behind Auxey-Duresses, and only recently promoted to Côte de Beaune-Villages status. It has no Premier Cru land, being too high on the hills, and makes more and better white wine than red. Roland Thévenin is the most important proprietor based here.

Puligny-Montrachet

Puligny and Chassagne appear at first sight like Siamese twins linked by their shared Grand Cru, Le Montrachet. But the impression is false. Puligny is a dedicated white-wine parish. Chassagne, despite the Montrachet of its name, earns most of its living from red.

There is no magic by which white wine from Meursault Charmes must taste different from the Puligny Premier Cru Les Combettes, which meets it at the boundary. I can only repeat that I would expect the Puligny-Montrachet to have a slightly more lively taste of fruit, a bit more bite and perhaps a floweriness which is not a Meursault characteristic. Sheaves of old tasting notes tend to contradict each other, so my description is pure Impressionism – all that airy metaphor in dabs of paint representing orchards does seem to have something to do with the taste I cannot describe.

What is more tangible is the superiority of the Premiers Crus. Those of Combettes and Champs Canet at the Mersault end of Puligny, and the part of Blagny that lies in this parish with the appellation Blagny Premier Cru, can be expected to be closer to Meursault in style. A slightly higher premium is normally put on the ones that border the Grands Crus: Le Cailleret and Les Pucelles.

Two of the Grands Crus that are the white-wine climax of Burgundy lie entirely in Puligny-Montrachet; Chevalier-Montrachet, the strip of hill above Montrachet, and Bienvenues-Bâtard-Montrachet, half the shallower slope below. The accepted appreciation of 'Chevalier' is that it has the fine flavour of Montrachet but in less concentrated form (concentration being the hallmark of this grandest of all white wines). The critics do not normally distinguish between Bienvenues and Bâtard (to shorten their unwieldy names). Any such generalization is inevitably overturned by the next tasting of a different vintage or a different grower's wine.

As for Puligny-Montrachet 'Village' without frills – it is still expensive. Is it worth more than Meursault? It is probably more consistent, and a shade more aggressive in flavour. In 1982 Meursault came about midway among the prices of premium California Chardonnays; Puligny-Montrachet near the top.
Prices (1981): Village wines 31–32.50 francs a bottle, Premiers Crus 36 francs, Bâtard-Montrachet 64–71 francs, Montrachet 87.50–104 francs.

GRANDS CRUS

Total area 56.5 acres:
Bâtard-Montrachet (25)
Bienvenues-Bâtard-Montrachet (6)
Chevalier-Montrachet (15.5)
Montrachet (10)

PREMIERS CRUS

Caillerets (9.75)
Chalumeaux (14.25)
Champs Canet (8)
Clavoillons (13.5)
Combettes (16.5)
Folatières (43)
Garenne (28)
Hameau de Blagny (11)
Pucelles (16.5)
Referts (34)
Sous le Puits (16.75)
Appellation Communale
Puligny-Montrachet: 282 acres.
Appellations Regionales
606 acres.

GROWERS

Robert Ampeau & Fils
Bouchard Père & Fils
Carillon Père & Fils
Joseph Drouhin
Louis Jadot
Dom. Leflaive
Leroy
Lycée Agricole & Viticole
Dom. du Duc de Magenta
Dom. Jean Monnier & Fils
Dom. René Monnier
Dom. Jean Pascal & Fils
Dom. Jacques Prieur
Dom. de la Romanée-Conti
Ropiteau Frères
Dom. St-Michel
Dom. Etienne Sauzet
Roland Thévenin

Chassagne-Montrachet

Almost half of the Grands Crus Le Montrachet and Bâtard-Montrachet and the whole of Criots-Bâtard-Montrachet occupy the hill corner that ends the parish to the north. Unfortunately, the steep south-facing slope that runs at right angles to them, along the road to St-Aubin in the hills, has not enough soil for vines. If this were the Douro there would be terraces. Between here and the village there is some Premier Cru land, but the famous wines begin again where the Côte picks up its momentum and its tilt in the Clos St-Jean above the little township. Caillerets, Ruchottes and Morgeot are names seen on expensive and memorable white bottles. Clos St-Jean, La Boudriotte ... in fact all the rest stress red.

Any association of ideas that suggests that red

Chassagne should be a light wine is quite wrong. Far from being a gentle fade-out from Volnay, Chassagne returns to the meat and muscle of Corton or the Côte de Nuits. The best example I know of the brilliant duality of this land is the Duc de Magenta's Clos de la Chapelle, part of the Premier Cru Abbaye de Morgeot, which is half red and half white, and (at least in the early 1970s) was brilliant on both counts. Red Chassagne, moreover, sells at the price of the lesser-known villages – much cheaper than the grand names of the Côte de Nuits and every bit as satisfying.

Prices (1981): Village wines 29–31 francs a bottle, Premiers Crus 32.50 francs, red wines 21–24 francs.

GRANDS CRUS

Total area 43 acres (all white):
Bâtard-Montrachet (30)
Criots-Bâtard-Montrachet (4)
Montrachet (9)

PREMIERS CRUS

(Both red and white, except that En Cailleret produces red only and Cailleret, also known as Chassagne, produces white only):
Abbaye de Morgeot*
Boudriotte (45)
Brussolles (45)
Cailleret (15)
En Cailleret (15)
Champs Gain (71)
Chenevottes (28)
Grands Ruchottes (7.5)
Macherelles (10)
Maltroie (23)
Morgeot (9.75)
Romanée*
Clos St-Jean (36)
Vergers (23)
*No acreage specified in the latest official documents.

GROWERS

Dom. Bachelet-Ramonet Père & Fils
Soc. Louis Carillon Fils
Jacques Gagnard-Delagrange
J.N. Gagnard Dupont
Dom. Lequin-Roussot
Dom. du Duc de Magenta
Ch. de la Maltroye
Albert Morey
Dom. Jacques Prieur
Ramonet-Prudhon
Dom. Etienne Sauzet

Le Montrachet

All critics agree that the best Montrachet is the best white burgundy. In it all the properties that make the mouth water in memory and anticipation are brought to a resounding climax.

The first quality that proclaims it at a tasting with its neighbours is a concentration of flavour. I have wondered how much this is due to its singular site and its soil and how much to the regulations (and common sense) that keep its crop to a minimum. There is little doubt that other good vineyards could pack more punch if their keepers kept them more meanly pruned and fertilized, picked late and used only the best bunches. Such economics only work for a vineyard whose wine is as good as sold before it is made, at almost any price.

The principal owners of Le Montrachet are the Marquis de Laguiche (whose wine is handled by Drouhin of Beaune), Baron Thénard of Givry, Bouchard Père & Fils, Fleurot-Larose of Santenay, Roland Thévenin and the Domaine de la Romanée-Conti.

Price (1981): 87.50–104 francs a bottle.

St-Aubin

St-Aubin is a twin to St-Romain, a village tucked into the first valley behind the Côte but with a slight advantage of situation that gives it some Premiers Crus, mainly exploited for red wine. The village of Gamay (presumed source of the grape that makes Beaujolais but is a taint to the Côte d'Or) contributes about half the land in this appellation. Raoul Clerget and Hubert Lamy make a speciality of it, but the greater part is sold as Côte de Beaune-Villages.

Santenay

It is a conceit, I know, but I have always found the names of the villages of Burgundy a useful clue to the nature of their wines. Chambertin has a drum-roll sound, Chambolle-Musigny a lyrical note, Pommard sounds precisely right for its tough red wine and so does Volnay for its more silky produce. Santenay sounds like good health. (Funnily enough it has a far-from-fashionable spa that treats rheumatism and gout.) Healthiness is the right sort of image to attach to its wines. They are rather plain, even-flavoured with no great perfume or thrills but good solid drinking. At their best, in Les Gravières, La Comme and Le Clos de Tavannes, they are in the same class as Chassagne-Montrachet, weighty and long-lived. Other parts of the parish with stonier, more limey soil have paler reds and a little white wine.

Price (1981): Village wines 21–24 francs a bottle.

PREMIERS CRUS

Total area 1,018 acres (red and white):
Beauregard (82)
Beaurepaire (42.5)
Comme (80)
Gravières (72.5)
Maladière (33)
Passe Temps (31)
Clos des Tavannes (66)

GROWERS

André Bart
Dom. Fleurot-Larose
Dom. Lequin-Roussot
Mestre, Père & Fils
Dom. René Monnier
Dom. de la Pousse d'Or
Dom. St-Michel

Côte de Beaune-Villages

All the villages of the Côte de Beaune, with the exception of Beaune, Pommard, Volnay and Aloxe-Corton, have this as a fallback appellation in red wine (only). This includes three rather forlorn little villages which share the vineyard Les Maranges, along the hill just west of Santenay and to their regret just over the *département* line of the Côte d'Or, in the outer darkness of Saône-et-Loire. Their names are Sampigny, Dézize and Cheilly – but Côte de Beaune-Villages is more likely to appear on their labels. The wines are well structured with deep colour, generally quite tannic. They age well and make splendid drinking when 8 years old, as the local clientele buying direct have proved time and again. In an average year some 130,000 cases make use of this appellation.

Price (1981): 19 francs a bottle.

CHEILLY-LES-MARANGES

Premiers Crus (red and white):
Boutières, Maranges and Plantes de Maranges (together 108 acres)

DEZIZE-LES-MARANGES

Premier Cru (red and white):
Maranges (150)

SAMPIGNY-LES-MARANGES

Premiers Crus (red and white):
Clos des Rois (36)
Maranges (35)

André Gagey of Maison Louis Jadot

GROWERS AND MERCHANTS

The almost literally priceless land of the Côte d'Or is broken up into innumerable small units of ownership, variously expressed as ares (a hundredth of a hectare) and centiares (a hundredth of an are) or as *ouvrées* (an old measure which is one twenty-fourth of a hectare, or about a tenth of an acre). These little plots come about by the French system of inheritance, by the size of the capital needed to buy more, and by the dread of local disasters, which make it inadvisable to put all your eggs in one basket.

They mean that a grower who has, say, 20 acres may well have them in 30 different places – in many cases just a few rows of vines separated from his others in the same vineyard.

Meanwhile, the precious land is also divided by ancient custom into a jigsaw of '*climats*', or fields, sometimes with natural and obvious boundaries, sometimes apparently at random. Each '*climat*' is a known local character with a meaning and value to the farmers that is hard for an outsider to grasp.

Overlay the one pattern on the other and you have the fragmentation of ownership which bedevils buyers of burgundy. Whereas in Bordeaux a château is a consistent unit doing one (or at most two) things on a reasonably large scale, a Burgundy domaine is often a man and his family coping with a dozen or more different wines with different needs and problems. If he is a good husbandman of vines his talent does not necessarily extend to the craftsmanship of the cellar – or vice versa. For any number of reasons, inconsistency is almost inevitable.

There are important exceptions in the form of bigger vineyards with richer owners. But the concept of the little man trying to do everything is fundamental. It explains the importance of the négociants or 'shippers', whose traditional role is to buy the grower's new wine, mature it and blend it with others of the same vineyard or village or district to make marketable quantities of something consistent.

It does not need much imagination to see that an unscrupulous merchant could get away with almost anything under these conditions. Consumers have probably always, since Roman times, had grounds for complaint. Now the old and profitable game of 'stretching' the limited supplies with imports from the south is made very much harder by the application of the strict appellation laws. But there is still plenty of room for manoeuvre in the area of quality. There are government inspectors, but nobody pretends there is real and effective inspection.

When most consumers hear that merchants are venal their reaction is to look for authenticity from the growers, direct. Bottling at the domaine has been presented as the answer. It brings us back, though, to the basic question: who is more competent and more conscientious? Ownership of a corner of a fine and famous field does not carry with it a technical degree in wine-making or '*élévage*' – the 'bringing up' of wine in the cellar – or bottling.

It can be a depressing experience to taste a set of broker's samples submitted to a négociant from good vineyards even after a good vintage. A considerable proportion of the wines are likely to be either oversugared or in poor condition, or both.

By the time the négociant has selected, blended and perhaps treated the wines for faults, there may be a question over their precise 'authenticity' – but they should at least be good to drink and give the customer what he expects for his money.

Lycée Agricole & Viticole

16 avenue Ch. Jaffelin, 21200 Beaune.

The young farmers' college of Beaune, founded in 1884, has 18 acres of Beaune Premier Cru in Les Perrières, Les Bressandes, Les Montées Rouges, Les Aigrôts, Les Teurons and Les Champimonts, 8 acres of Beaune-Village, 10.5 of Côte de Beaune and Bourgogne Rouge, 6.5 of Beaune Blanc and Bourgogne Blanc and 2.5 acres of Puligny-Montrachet (white), making some 2,500 cases of first-rate, long-lived wine sold direct to private clients.

Robert Ampeau & Fils

6 rue du Cromin, 21190 Meursault.

An outstanding domaine of nearly 30 acres whose white wines are particularly respected. The best known are the whites from Meursault Perrières, Charmes and La Pièce sous le Bois (partly in Blagny), 11 acres in all, and 2 acres in Puligny Les Combettes; wines with a good 10-year life span. Reds include 1 acre of Beaune Clos du Roi, 4 of Savigny Premier Cru (Lavières and Fourneaux) and 4 of Pommard. 'It is always difficult,' says M. Ampeau, 'to talk objectively about your own wine.'

Pierre A. André

Château de Corton-André, 21420 Aloxe-Corton.

Négociants and growers on the largest scale. Pierre André founded La Reine Pédauque. His 'château' at Corton is the centre for the 105-acre estate, which includes parts of Clos Vougeot (2.6 acres), Corton (Clos du Roi, Renardes, Combes and Charlemagne), Savigny Premier Cru Clos des Guettes (7.5 acres) and also the 'monopole' Clos des Langres. Products also include Bourgogne Réserve Pierre André, Mâcon-Villages and Supérieur 'Domaine du Prieuré de Jocelyn'; Fleurie 'Domaine de la Treille', Beaujolais-Villages, Coteaux du Tricastin from the Rhône, etc. Sales are largely to restaurants and private clients in France, with only 15% exports.

Domaine Marquis d'Angerville

Clos des Ducs, Volnay, 21190 Meursault.

The impeccable domaine of a totally dedicated nobleman: 25 acres of Volnay Premier Cru, 1 of Pommard and 2.5 of Meursault Santenots – a rare appellation and a singularly succulent white. The Clos des Ducs is an unusual steep and chalky 5.3-acre vineyard whose wine is noticeably alcoholic, tends to be pale and to my mind misses the velvet of the best Volnay. I prefer the domaine's more sumptuous Champans (from 10 acres). All its wines are beautifully made. I believe the greater part is exported to Switzerland and America.

Domaine Bachelet-Ramonet Père & Fils

Chassagne-Montrachet, 21190 Meursault.

A domaine founded in 1979 by fourth-generation growers in Chassagne with 25 acres, including parcels of Bâtard-Montrachet, Chassagne Les Caillerets, Ruchottes and La Romanée, La Grande Montagne on the highest land and Morgeot, Clos St-Jean and Clos de la Boudriotte (the last two red) at the foot of the slopes. The Bâtard is extremely fine wine.

André Bart

24 rue de Mazy, 21160 Marsannay-La-Côte.

A domaine of 24 acres, 13.5 of them in Bourgogne red, white and rosé at Marsannay and the neighbouring Couchey, 4.5 at Fixin, 4 at Santenay and 2 in the Grands Crus Bonnes Mares and Clos de Bèze. Rosé de Marsannay and Fixin Premier Cru Les Hervelets are the specialities.

Thomas Bassot

21220 Gevrey-Chambertin

Old-established (1850) négociants at Gevrey-Chambertin now belonging to the Swiss firm of Ziltener. A source of very good wines, but a picture clouded in 1982 by financial complications.

Jules Belin

Prémeaux-Prissey, 21700 Nuits St-Georges.

Domaine of 30 acres in Prémeaux (Nuits Premier Cru Clos Arlots, red and white wines) and Comblanchien (Côte de Nuits-Villages), best known as the first house to make and market Marc de Bourgogne commercially (in about 1900). Formerly it was only distilled by growers for their own comfort. The Belin brand is 'Vieux à la Cloche'.

Etablissements Bertagna

21640 Vougeot

Owners of some of the limited area of Vougeot Premier Cru outside the Clos Vougeot, including the 'monopole' Clos de la Perrière (6 acres), the hill just below Le Musigny. I have found this wine brilliantly vivid and much better than other growers' Clos Vougeot. Bertagna have a total of 30 acres, with 3.7 each in Echézeaux and Gevrey-Chambertin and 1 each in (Morey) Clos de la Roche and Clos St-Denis.

Domaine Besancenot-Mathouillet

19 rue de Chorey, 21200 Beaune.

A small (19-acre) domaine with high standards created not long ago by a Beaune citizen of great repute and scholarship, M. Besancenot, whose help I gratefully acknowledge. He died, alas, in 1981. 16 acres are in Beaune Premiers Crus (Bressandes, Clos du Roi, Toussaints, etc.), of which half is a parcel of Cent-Vignes with venerable vines, some 50 years old, which can give one of the best wines of Beaune. A part of the domaine which is rented includes a little Aloxe-Corton Premier Cru and 2.5 acres of Pernand-Vergelesses, where there are some vines of Pinot Blanc.

Maison Albert Bichot

6 bis boulevard Jacques Copeau, B.P. 49, 21200 Beaune.

The biggest exporter of burgundy, with 80% of its 100-million-franc turnover in exports. The firm was founded in Beaune in 1831 and in 1927 opened an office in Bordeaux (where it owns the firm of Chantecaille). As a négociant Bichot also trades under the names of several of the companies it has taken over: Paul Bouchard, Charles Drapier, Rémy Gauthier, Bouchot-Ludot, Léon Rigault, Maurice Dard, etc. As a grower, Bichot owns 2 domaines: Clos Frantin in the Côte d'Or and Long-Depaquit in Chablis. The Domaine du Clos Frantin, based at Vosne-Romanée, has 42 acres, scattered through Gevrey-Chambertin (including Chambertin), Richebourg, Clos Vougeot, Grands-Echézeaux, Echézeaux, Vosne-Romanée Les Malconsorts, Nuits St-Georges and Corton. *See also* Lupé-Cholet. Their own wines are first-rate; as négociants they sell all sorts.

Simon Bize & Fils

21420 Savigny-Les-Beaune

A domaine of 28 acres entirely in Savigny, with 10.5 acres in the Premiers Crus Vergelesses (7.5 acres), Guettes and Marconnets. Father and son go to the length of buying new barrels for a third of the crop, which argues ambition for quality. Vergelesses is their speciality. They also make 100 cases of a Bourgogne Blanc called Les Perrières.

Domaine Henri Boillot

Volnay, 21190 Meursault.

A total of 54 acres makes this a major domaine in Volnay (10 acres), Puligny-Montrachet (10 acres, including the 'monopole' Clos de la Mouchère) and Pommard Premier Cru (5.5 acres).

Jean Claude Boisset

2 rue des Frères Montgolfier,
21700 Nuits St-Georges.

A recent (1961) foundation with ultramodern methods and equipment and huge stocks, including fine Côte d'Or wines as well as Côte du Rhône, Beaujolais, etc. A small domaine ('Boisset Deschamps') of 27 acres is in Nuits Premier Cru Les Damodes, Gevrey-Chambertin, Côte de Nuits-Villages and appellation Bourgogne. The house also buys grapes, and has made some important purchases of wine at the Hospices de Beaune. Secondary labels include Honoré Lavigne, Blanchard de Cordambles, Georges Meurgey and Louis Deschamps.

Domaine Bonneau du Martray

Pernand-Vergelesses, 21420 Savigny-les-Beaune.

One of the biggest producers of the inimitable Corton-Charlemagne, with a solid block of 22 acres making some 3,000 cases a year, and an adjacent 5 acres giving red Corton Grand Cru. The famous Cuvée François de Salins, the costliest wine of the Hospices de Beaune, comes from the same prime hill-corner site. The domaine's wine is made in an unpretentious cellar in Pernand by the owner, Comte Jean Le Bault de la Morinière, using a modern press but otherwise strictly traditional methods, including new barrels for fermentation. The Corton-Charlemagne behaves more like a red, ageing majestically. Three-star restaurants, alas, offer it at 3 years old when it should be 10. 80% is exported – I hope to people with cellars.

Bouchard Aîné & Fils

36 rue Ste-Marguerite, 21200 Beaune.

The smaller Bouchard, although almost as old as the giant. A domaine with 62 acres of (all red) vines in Mercurey (Clos La Marche and Vignes du Chapitre) and Beaune, which also makes (in Beaune) the wines of the Domaine Marion at Fixin (Clos du Chapitre, La Mazière and a little Chambertin-Clos de Bèze). Their wines are generally considered correct rather than exciting. A second trade name is H. Audiffred.

Bouchard Père & Fils

Au Château, 21200 Beaune.

The biggest domaine in Burgundy and one of the best négociants, run by Bouchards from father to son since 1731. No less than 180 of their 209 acres (Domaines du Château de Beaune) are Grands Crus and Premiers Crus; their magnificent cellars in the old fortress of Beaune itself hold stocks of 20,000 *pièces* (barrels) or 6 million bottles.

Their biggest holdings are in Beaune, where their 48 acres of Premiers Crus include the 'monopoles' of the famous 10-acre Grèves Vigne de l'Enfant Jésus, the 8-acre Clos de la Mousse and the 5-acre Clos St-Landry. Other large plots are 20 acres of Les Aigrots, 11 of Les Avaux and about 6 each of Marconnets and Les Cent Vignes. Wine from smaller parcels is made and sold as Beaune du Château Premier Cru. Beyond Beaune their principal parcels are 18 acres in Corton (some 10 of red Corton and 8 of Corton-Charlemagne), nearly 10 in Savigny Les Lavières, 14 in Volnay (of which over 9 is Caillerets), a little Pommard, Chambolle-Musigny and Chambertin, and important plots of 2.6 acres in Le Montrachet and over 5 – the biggest part – in Chevalier-Montrachet. Among their more notable wines are Volnay Caillerets labelled as 'Ancienne Cuvée Carnot', untypically foursquare and long-lived Volnay from very old vines. They also have exclusive distribution rights over the Grand Cru La Romanée and Premier Cru Aux Reignots from the Château de Vosne-Romanée, an excellent Premier Cru Nuits St-Georges, 'Clos St-Marc', and two thirds of the production of Bourgogne Aligoté Bouzeron (a new appellation, since 1979). From the Hautes Côtes de Beaune they distribute the Château de Mandelot, and from Brouilly in Beaujolais the Domaine de Saburin.

All Bouchard's domaine reds are aged in new barrels, for a relatively short period to keep them fruity while adding the scent of the oak. Their domaine wines have never shown the slightest sign of quantity chasing out quality. While such important houses as this, Jadot, Latour and Drouhin maintain their standards, there is no danger of burgundy declining in its influence and appeal. 60% of Bouchard's wines are exported.

Lionel J. Bruck

6 quai Dumorey, 21700 Nuits St-Georges.

A flourishing merchant house which has contracts with growers totalling 110 acres in the Côte d'Or, including the 15-acre Domaine of the Château de Vosne-Romanée, a parcel of Corton Clos du Roi and 17 acres of the Savigny Premier Cru Clos des Guettes. The same firm uses the name F. Hasenklever.

Domaine Georges Bryczek

Morey St-Denis, 21220 Gevrey-Chambertin.

A Pole, and a sculptor as well as a grower, with the 8-acre Premier Cru Clos-Sorbés and a parcel of Morey 'Village' where he makes strapping wines from old vines. Bryczek caused a stir by dedicating a 'Cuvée du Pape'.

Domaine Camus Père & Fils

21220 Gevrey-Chambertin

A family property built up between 1860 and 1934 to a total of 37 acres, including 4 of Chambertin and over 16 of Charmes-Chambertin, with parcels of Latricières and Mazis. M. Camus uses a long maceration of the skins under a blanket of carbon dioxide to extract maximum colour and flavour. His 1976, his favourite vintage of recent years, will need a decade to develop.

Louis Carillon & Fils

Puligny-Montrachet, 21190 Meursault.

A proud little family domaine, going back 350 years, with 3 generations, Robert, Louis and Jacques, all working together on their 27 acres. They include a little patch of Bienvenues-Bâtard-Montrachet, 5 acres of Puligny Premier Cru and 12 of Puligny 'Village', with smaller parcels of Chassagne, Mercurey and St-Aubin. Half the crop is sold in barrels to négociants, half in bottles to clients. Carillon's Puligny Les Combettes is particularly respected.

Yves Chaley

Curtil-Vergy, 21220 Gevrey-Chambertin.

A skilful grower of the lighter wines of the Hautes Côtes de Nuits with 16 acres of Pinot Noir and 5 of Aligoté. The red is vatted for 12 days in stainless steel and aged 18 months in oak barrels. Five years is a good age for it. The fruity white is bottled at 1 year for immediate drinking.

Champy Père & Cie

5 rue du Grenier à Sel, 21200 Beaune.

A small proprietor and négociant, founded in 1720 and still in the same family (the name is now Boudet). In their Beaune *cuverie* they make 'traditional' wines from 6 acres of Clos Vougeot, 5 of Savigny Premier Cru La Dominode and 7 of Beaune Premiers Crus Les Avaux, and a little Clos des Mouches. As négociants they handle wines from all parts of Burgundy, exporting 50%.

Emile Chandesais

Fontaine, 71150 Chagny.

A négociant with a reputation for wines from the Région de Mercurey.

Domaine Chandon de Briailles

21420 Savigny-Les-Beaune

An important 45-acre property, largely in the best red-wine vineyards of Savigny (Les Lavières) and the neighbouring Ile des Vergelesses in Pernand. Also considerable owners in Corton with 7.5 acres in Bressandes, 2.5 in Clos du Roi and a little Corton Blanc.

Chanson Père & Fils

10 rue Paul Chanson, 21200 Beaune.

Négociants and growers (founded 1750) with a fine domaine of 110 acres, 74 of them in Beaune Premiers Crus, 15 in Savigny and 17 in Pernand-Vergelesses (which include 2 acres of Chardonnay). Their best wines are perhaps their Beaune Clos des Fèves (9.3 acres), Teurons (15 acres) and Bressandes (5.2 acres), but they have parts of all the best Beaune '*climats*' and make excellent Savigny Premier Cru La Dominode. The taste of the company is for wine aged in wood until it seems to lack fruit and colour, but will mature, as they assure us, '*sans surprise*'. It is an old-fashioned way of producing stable wines for long keeping. A question mark hangs over their '76s, which lacked 'fruit' in the first place.

Louis Chapuis

21420 Aloxe-Corton

Farms 23.5 acres, of which he owns 12.5 and rents the rest. They include 1.63 acres of Corton-Charlemagne, producing 220 cases a year. Nearly 10 acres of Corton produce 1,500 cases of red. 5.5 acres of Corton Premier Cru and 7 of Aloxe-Corton more than double this quantity. White wine fermented in barrels; red in open vats to be *vins de garde*. His 1976 Corton was outstanding.

F. Chauvenet

6 route de Chaux, 21700 Nuits St-Georges.

One of the larger merchant houses, founded in 1853, currently connected with Margnat, the table-wine company. It owns 108 acres at the Domaine de Pérignon in the Yonne (near Chablis) making Passe-tout-grains, and large estates in the Côtes du Rhône and Corsica. Also 2 acres in Nuits St-Georges. Its most famous product is Red Cap sparkling red burgundy, which has a big Canadian market. It has the biggest share of the Burgundy direct-sales business in France and Belgium. Other names include Chevillot (selection of the Hôtel de la Poste at Beaune) and a 50% share (with the Max family) in the brand Louis Max.

Robert Chevillon

68 rue Felix-Tisserand, 21700 Nuits St-Georges.

A typical little 20-acre estate, part owned and part rented, producing some good Premier Cru Nuits St-Georges from (especially) Les Cailles, Les St-Georges, Les Vaucrains, etc. Also a little Passe-tout-grains to use a plot of Gamay.

Domaine Clair-Daü

21160 Marsannay-la-Côte

Probably the biggest family-owned domaine in the Côte d'Or, founded in 1818 by François Daü with properties in the northern Côtes. In 1919, a Daü daughter married Joseph Clair of Santenay. The bulk of their vineyards (67 acres) are at Marsannay, where they make particularly good Bourgogne Rouge and Blanc, Passe-tout-grains and Aligoté, and where Joseph Clair created a Pinot Noir Rosé de Marsannay which now has its own appellation. To many it is the best rosé in France outside Champagne; a lilting lyric in the key of Pinot Noir.

The Domaine's Grands Vins cover 37 acres: in Gevrey-Chambertin it has a parcel in the Premier Cru Clos St-Jacques (6 acres), the 'monopole' of the 2-acre Clos du Fonteny, 5 acres of the Grand Cru Clos de Bèze and part of Chapelle-Chambertin. It owns 3.7 acres of Bonnes Mares, including the whole block in Morey St-Denis. In Chambolle-Musigny it owns part of Les Amoureuses and several plots of the highest 'Village' land above Bonnes Mares on the hill.

In Vosne-Romanée, too, the Clair-Daü vines are above the Grands Crus of Romanée: 2.5 acres called Champs-Perdrix. 'Although this vineyard will never reach the fame of its neighbours,' they say, 'we are very proud of it.' Their only Côte de Beaune vineyard is 5 acres of Savigny Premier Cru La Dominode. Clair-Daü's red wines are not intended to be flatteringly fruity when young. The plain Bourgogne Rouge needs 3 years in bottle, the Grands Crus 10-15.

Domaine Clerget

Volnay, 21190 Meursault.

A little domaine of 13 acres with an incredibly long history: the Clergets made wine in Volnay in 1268, the time of the Crusades. The pride of the house is their resounding Volnay Caillerets. Other parcels are in the Premier Cru Carelle sous la Chapelle and Volnay 'Village' Clos du Verseuil, in Pommard Rugiens and Meursault 'Village'. Madame Clerget only bottles good vintages.

Georges Clerget

21640 Vougeot

Owner of 7.5 acres and farmer of another 2.5: a very small domaine divided with equal (1.25-acre) plots in Chambolle-Musigny Premier Cru Charmes, Chambolle 'Village', Vougeot Premier Cru, Morey St-Denis and Vosne-Romanée. The rented parts are 2.5 acres in Echézeaux and a bare third of an acre in Bonnes Mares. The 'Charmes' is M. Clerget's own favourite; he does not like his wines too 'hard'. He removes three quarters of the stems and ferments for 8-10 days to achieve his gentle style.

Raoul Clerget

St-Aubin, 21190 Meursault.

For sheer antiquity the Clergets have no competitors. This house was apparently founded in 1270. They are now growers in a small way and négociants in quite a big one with a range of Côte d'Or wines of a high standard, and Beaujolais, table wines, and one of Burgundy's best Crèmes de Cassis. Their St-Aubin (red and white) is a house speciality. 1979 was the first vintage of their own replanted St-Aubin Domaine de Pimont.

Coron Père & Fils

B.P. 117, 21200 Beaune.

Three generations of Corons ran their house until 1970, when it was inherited by Bernard Dufouleur. A small domaine of 10 acres is spread among 5 Beaune Premiers Crus. Apart from Côte d'Or wines, the house sells Beaujolais and Mâcon. Amsler-Lecouvreur is another trade name.

Domaine de Madame Bernard de Courcel

21630 Pommard

The Courcels have made Pommard here for 400 years. Their 25-acre domaine includes the 12-acre 'Grand Clos des Epenots' within the Premier Cru Epenots, and 2.5 acres of Rugiens. The vats, vertical press and cellars are strictly traditional. I opened a 16-year-old bottle of 1966 Courcel Rugiens to find out where I should be pitching my enthusiasm. Pommard is not normally my favourite burgundy. This wine was astonishingly dark and pure 'burgundy' red. The smell and taste were stubborn and inaccessible on first opening. After 2 hours in a decanter it began to give off a seductive creamy smell of nuts and damsons, which developed into what Michael Broadbent describes as fish-glue – in any case the smell of very fine old burgundy. Yet curiously the flavour remained austere and straight backed. Good but not great.

Domaine Damoy

Rue de Lattre de Tassigny, 21220 Gevrey-Chambertin.

The biggest single share of Chambertin and Clos de Bèze (14.25 acres) belongs to the Damoy family. (Their other interests include the Château du Moulin à Vent in Beaujolais and Château La Tour de By in the Médoc.) Apart from 170 cases of Chambertin and 1,800 of Clos de Bèze of high quality, they make 900 of Chapelle-Chambertin and 600 of a Gevrey-Chambertin 'Monopole' Clos du Tamisot.

Domaine Darnat

20 rue des Forges, 21190 Meursault.

The owner of the tiny 'Clos Richemont', 1.5 acres in the Premier Cru Meursault Les Cras which produces a mere 400 cases, but of model Meursault, stiff with flavour. Old bottles have a tarry tang overlying rich depths. Darnat also has another acre of Meursault 'Village' and a little Bourgogne Blanc.

Domaine Darviot

21200 Beaune

Owners of 40 acres, 11 in Beaune Premiers Crus, 4 in Meursault and land in Monthélie and Savigny-Les-Beaune. They sell most of their wine in bulk.

Domaine Delagrange-Bachelet

Chassagne-Montrachet, 21190 Meursault.

One of the best-known domaines in Chassagne, of 25 acres which include 1.25 acres each of Bâtard- and Criots-Bâtard-Montrachet, 2.5 of Premier Cru Caillerets, 5 of Morgeot (red and white) and small plots of Volnay and Pommard Premiers Crus. I have had impeccable white wines, both the grand Bâtard and 'Village' Chassagne-Montrachet, from this domaine.

Maison Doudet-Naudin

1 rue Henri Cyrot, 21420 Savigny-Les-Beaune.

A house associated with 'old-fashioned', very dark-coloured, concentrated, almost 'jammy' wines which have had a great following in Britain in the past. Berry Bros. & Rudd of St. James's bottled many of them. To today's taste, looking for fresh grapey flavours, they seem 'cooked'. But they last, and 20-year-old bottles can be richly velvety and full of character. Their own domaine of 12.5 acres is in Savigny (Les Guettes, red, and Le Redrescul, a not-very-graceful white), in Beaune Clos du Roy, Corton, Aloxe-Corton and Pernand-Vergelesses. Other names are Albert Brenot and Georges Germain.

Joseph Drouhin

7 rue d'Enfer, 21200 Beaune.

A leading family-owned (founded in 1880) négociant with one of the biggest domaines in Burgundy, recently augmented by 67 acres in Chablis. Now a total of 131 acres comprises Chablis, Chablis Grand Cru Les Clos and Vaudésir, Beaune Clos des Mouches, Corton-Charlemagne, Bâtard-Montrachet, Volnay Clos des Chênes, Corton Bressandes, Chambolle Musigny Amoureuses, Clos de Vougeot, Echézeaux, Grands-Echézeaux, Bonnes Mares, Griotte Chambertin, Chambertin and Musigny. The head of the house is Robert Drouhin.

The whole gamut of wines is very conscientiously made, rising to the appropriate peaks of quality in the Grands Crus. The speciality of the house is the excellent Beaune Clos des Mouches: long-lived, full-bodied wine, both red and white. After a serious fire in 1972 things did not go well for a while, but from 1976 on standards are first class. Red wines are fermented in oak at a fairly high temperature with at least half of their stems, and macerated for up to 2 weeks. New barrels are used for half the red and a quarter of the white. The best vintages (e.g. '76 red, '78 red and white, '81 white) are designed for long maturing. Drouhin also has sole rights on the superb Montrachet of the Marquis de Laguiche. As a négociant, he handles a wide range of well-chosen wines from all over Burgundy.

Crémant – a new term of quality

Three high-quality French white-wine regions are successfully establishing a new appellation for their best-quality sparkling wine. The term '*crémant*', originally used in Champagne for wines produced at about half the full sparkling-wine pressure, thus gently fizzing instead of frothing in the glass, has been borrowed (with the consent of Champagne) as a controlled term for these full-sparklers of high quality. A new term was needed because the old one, '*mousseux*', had acquired a pejorative ring: any old fizz made by industrial methods could (and can) use it. Burgundy and the Loire in 1975, and Alsace in 1976, joined in agreeing that *crémant* had to be made with champagne-type controls. Specifically, they concern the grape varieties used, the size of the crop, the way it is delivered to the press-house with the bunches undamaged and the pressure that should be applied (with a limit of two thirds of the weight of the grapes being extracted as juice). Thereafter, the champagne-method rules apply, with the minimum time in bottle with the yeast being specified as 9 months in Burgundy and Alsace and 12 in the Loire. (An influential lobby wants to increase the 9 months to 12.)

The result of these controls is a category of sparkling wine of excellent quality, though so far in very small supply. Heavy initial investment deters cellars from upgrading from *mousseux* to *crémant*. But in 1982 for the first time the overall total passed 5 million bottles and there is no doubt that appreciation for the new idea will rapidly increase

Robert Dubois & Fils

Prémeaux, 21700 Nuits St-Georges.

An up-to-date family estate with 34 acres, of which 9 in Nuits include 1.3 in the Premiers Crus Les Porets and Les Argillières. They use 'thermovinification', heating the must to get plenty of colour, followed by the usual methods. Three quarters of their production of 7,500 cases is exported.

Domaine P. Dubreuil-Fontaine Père & Fils

Pernand-Vergelesses, 21420 Savigny-Les-Beaune.

Bernard Dubreuil, the present manager, is the grandson of the founder of this 34-acre domaine, with 7.5 acres of Grand Cru Corton (principally Bressandes) and 2.7 of Corton-Charlemagne, as well as 7.5 of Savigny Premier Cru Vergelesses and 14 of Pernand (red and white). His father Pierre has been mayor of Pernand for years and does the honours of the village for visitors with a perfect range of the wines of this privileged corner. His Grands Crus need keeping for a good 10 years.

Dufouleur Frères

B.P. 5, rue de Dijon, 21700 Nuits St-Georges.

An old family firm of négociants (4 brothers and their father) with a small domaine in Nuits St-Georges, Clos Vougeot and Musigny and also vineyards at Mercurey in the Côte Chalonnaise. Their wines are powerful and full of flavour.

Domaine Dujac

Morey St-Denis, 21220 Gevrey-Chambertin.

Jacques Seysses is the 'Jac' of the name. He is widely regarded as the most serious wine maker in Morey St-Denis, with natural, patient (necessarily expensive) methods: fermenting stems and all for as long as possible, using new barrels, never filtering. The result is freshness with depth, as red burgundy should be. At 10 years his '72s are splendid. Clos de la Roche, where he has 4.5 acres, is his own favourite of his 25-acre domaine, which includes nearly 4 acres of Clos St-Denis, 7.5 of Morey 'Village', 3 of Gevrey-Chambertin Premier Cru 'Combottes', and small parcels of Charmes-Chambertin, Chambolle-Musigny Premier Cru, Echézeaux and of Bonnes Mares. Domaine Dujac wines are listed by most of France's three-star restaurants and have been served at the Elysée.

Domaine René Engel

Vosne-Romanée, 21700 Nuits St-Georges.

A well-known name in Burgundy as raconteur as well as vigneron. *Propos sur l'Art de Bien Boire* is his philosophy in print. The domaine of 17 acres includes 3.4 acres on the upper slope of the Clos Vougeot and plots in Grands-Echézeaux, Echézeaux and Vosne-Romanée (both Premier Cru and 'Village'). Despite the familiar name I have seen few bottles of his wine; much is sold in cask, but his own bottlings are said to be excellent.

Domaine du Clos des Epenaux

Place de l'Eglise, 21630 Pommard.

The 13-acre section of the Pommard Premier Cru Epenots belonging to the Comte Armand has different spelling to signify its identity. Part of the plot has 60-year-old vines. It makes undramatic burgundy that demands the word 'serious' and lasts for many years.

Bourgogne Faiveley

21700 Nuits St-Georges

The Faiveleys, an unbroken family succession since 1830, have the biggest domaine in Burgundy: 282 acres. 178 acres are in Mercurey, where their 18-acre 'monopole' Clos des Myglands is their best-known wine. 12 are in the neighbouring Rully. In Nuits they have 13 acres (8 are Premiers Crus) of their own and rent the entire Clos de la Maréchale, a 24-acre Premier Cru 'monopole' in Prémeaux. 20 acres in Gevrey-Chambertin includes 3 each of the Grands Crus Mazis, Latricières and Clos de Bèze and 8.5 of Premiers Crus. They own 3.7 acres of Clos Vougeot, 2 of Echézeaux, 1.25 of Chambolle-Musigny, including a parcel of Le Musigny, and in the Côte de Beaune they have a 7-acre 'monopole' Corton Clos des Cortons at Ladoix and a little Corton Blanc. In addition they have 20 acres of Bourgogne Rouge scattered about, and in communes where they own no vines they buy grapes and make the wine themselves at Nuits.

As if all this were not activity enough, Guy Faiveley, father of the present president of the company, François, has been the most active and entertaining protagonist of the Chevaliers de Tastevin for many years.

Faiveley wines are solidly structured, built-to-last burgundies. It is only the price that anyone finds to question.

Domaine Fleurot-Larose

21590 Santenay

This domaine of 42 acres also has vineyards at Pouilly-sur-Loire and is linked with the Santenay négociant Prosper Maufoux. Its main holding is 17 acres of Chassagne-Montrachet Premier Cru Abbaye de Morgeot (red and white) and 12.5 of Santenay Premier Cru, but it also owns three quarters of an acre of Le Montrachet and half as much Bâtard-Montrachet.

---

once the term *crémant*, in its new meaning, is well understood.

Members of the Union of Producers of Crémant de Bourgogne are:

R. Chevillard, La Rochepot
Caves Delorme-Meulien, Rully
Cave de Lugny-St-Gengoux, Lugny
Labouré-Gontard, Nuits St-Georges
Moingeon-Gueneau Frères, Nuits St-Georges
Parigot-Richard, Savigny-les-Beaune
SICA du Vignoble Auxerrois, Bailly, St-Bris-le-Vineaux

Marc de Bourgogne and Cassis

The pulpy residue of skins, pips and stalks left in the press after the juice has been run off is often distilled to produce a spirit known as marc. The clear spirit is matured in oak to give it colour and, with luck, a little finesse.

Most marc is made by growers for private consumption. Some of the larger houses, such as Bouchard Père & Fils and Louis Latour, make carefully aged commercial versions which have a following.

Cassis is an alcoholic blackcurrant liqueur which serves to soften the sharpness of white wine – in Burgundy usually Aligoté – in a proportion of 1 of cassis to 3 or 4 of wine. The resulting drink is often called Kir after a brand of cassis which was developed by Canon Félix Kir, one-time mayor of Dijon.

Jacques Gagnard-Delagrange

Chassagne-Montrachet, 21190 Meursault.

A seventh-generation family of growers whose 13-acre domaine includes 2 acres of Le Montrachet, 4.5 of Chassagne Premier Cru (Morgeot and Boudriotte), half an acre of Bâtard-Montrachet and 5 acres of red Chassagne. Also 1 acre of Volnay-Champans.

Abel Garnier

21190 Meursault

A small négociant specializing in Meursault (where he also has 10 acres of vines). His wines that have been shipped to the UK have been admirable.

Domaine F. Gaunoux

21190 Meursault

François Gaunoux is the President of the Comité de Viticulture of the Côte d'Or and brother of Michel Gaunoux of Pommard. His 28-acre domaine, started in 1955, has 11 acres in Meursault (5 in the Premiers Crus Perrières and Goutte d'Or), 3 in Volnay Clos des Chênes, 2 each in the Premiers Crus Beaune Clos des Mouches and Pommard (Rugiens and Epenots). Also 7 more of Pommard 'Village'.

M. Gaunoux's tasting notes (I have not tasted his wines) show his candid evaluation and appreciation of *vins de garde*. The '76 whites, he says, are too strong and tend to oxidize; the '73 reds are too diluted – but the '78s! His own favourites are his Beaune and Volnay.

Domaine Michel Gaunoux

21630 Pommard

Brother of François of Meursault, considered by Hubrecht Duijker to contest the crown of best grower in Pommard with Jacques Parent. Gaunoux has 26 acres, about 12 of them in Pommard Premier Cru with the biggest part in Epenots and the best (2 acres) in Rugiens. There are also 3 acres of Corton Bressandes and 2.5 of Beaune Epenottes.

The wine is made with a fairly cool, slow fermentation which seems to extract all the lasting power of Pommard, staying firm and robust for a good decade.

Geisweiler

1 rue de la Berchère, 21700 Nuits St-Georges.

The biggest growers in the Hautes Côtes de Nuits, with two large properties: the Domaine de Bévy of 173 acres (of which 50 are Chardonnay for white wine) and the Domaine des Dames Hautes of 42 acres just above Nuits St-Georges. The latter makes a bigger, more impressive red wine. The house policy is clearly to cut the cost of drinking honest burgundy. The family which started the company in 1804 is now a majority shareholder, with Grand Metropolitan Hotels and Sopromec. The firm's other interests are dealing in table wines (under the name Colcombet), appellation burgundies, Côte du Rhône (Larbalestier), Loire (Goubard), Beaujolais (Duret) and in Château Lézin, a 125-acre Bordeaux Supérieur. Another brand is A. Rossigneux. Scandinavia and Holland are important markets.

Domaine Pierre Gelin

62 route des Grands Crus, Fixin, 21220 Gevrey-Chambertin.

Stephen Gelin and André Molin run this well-known estate at the very northern end of the Côte de Nuits. They have 7.5 acres in Gevrey-Chambertin (including 1 acre of Mazis and 2 of Clos de Bèze) and 35 in Fixin, with important parts of the best-known Premiers Crus; Clos du Chapitre (12 acres), Clos Napoléon (5 acres) and Les Hervelets (1.5 acres). They destem all their grapes before a long fermentation in traditional oak *cuves*; age in some old barrels and some new. Critical opinion seems to favour their Clos du Chapitre first, Napoléon second. Their Clos de Bèze is on a heroic scale.

Domaine Germain au Château

Chorey-Les-Beaune, 21200 Beaune.

François Germain's turreted medieval Château de Chorey, below the *côtes* north of Beaune, has 10 acres of red in Chorey, 15 in Beaune Premier Cru and 5 (white) Pernand-Vergelesses. His Beaune includes Teurons (5 acres), Cent Vignes and Vignes Franches, and the 'Domaine de Saux' (Beaune Crus and Boucherottes – 6 acres). Total production is about 3,500 cases. Germain's philosophy is gentle and natural wine-making from old vines. The grapes are fermented with stems and aged in new barrels for some time before racking, letting fermentation finish slowly and naturally. The result is real finesse in full-bodied wines needing age.

Jean Germain

21190 Meursault

A committed cellar-craftsman who sets very high standards in the small quantities (about 3,000 cases in total) of white burgundies from his own small property in Meursault (La Barre, Meix Chavaux) and Puligny-Montrachet. He also makes the wine of the little Domaine Darnat in Meursault, whose Clos Richemont is outstanding. 'Selections Jean Germain' is run in conjunction with Tim Marshall of Nuits St-Georges.

Soc. des Domaines Bernard & Louis Glantenay

Volnay, 21190 Meursault.

The 18-acre domaine of the mayor of Volnay and his brother; largely Volnay (7.5 acres) and Pommard (3 acres) 'Village', with 3 acres of Volnay Premier Cru and a little Bourgogne, Passe-tout-grains and Aligoté. A wholly traditional establishment selling partly in cask to the négociants but increasingly bottling at the domaine.

Domaine Elmerich Gouachon

21700 Nuits St-Georges

Their 12-acre 'monopole' Nuits Premier Cru Clos des Corvées is held up by some as the outstanding vineyard of the commune.

Domaine Goud de Beaupuis

Château des Moutots, 21200 Chorey-Les-Beaune.

A family domaine founded in 1787 with 25 acres, principally red wines in the Premiers Crus of Pommard (Epenots), Beaune (Grèves, Vignes Franches, Theurons), Savigny (Vergelesses) and Aloxe-Corton. Also some white Aligoté. Sales are largely to restaurants in France.

Domaine Henri Gouges

7 rue du Moulin, B.P. 70, 21700 Nuits St-Georges.

In many minds the top grower of Nuits; a complete specialist with all his 20 acres in the Premiers Crus, including the whole 9 acres of the Clos des Porrets. His other main plots are in Les St-Georges (2.7 acres), Les Pruliers (4.6) and Les Vaucrains (2.4). In Les Perrières he makes a minute amount of rich and fragrant white wine from a mutant albino clone of Pinot Noir. Gouges' reds reach Grand Cru class: powerful, slow to develop and long in the finish.

Jean Grivot

Vosne-Romanée, 21700 Nuits St-Georges.

A deeply dedicated grower with a number of small parcels of exceptionally good land – 25 acres in all. He has 4.5 acres of Clos Vougeot and nearly 10 of Vosne-Romanée, including 2.3 in the excellent Premier Cru Beaumonts and bits of Suchots and Brûlées, which are sandwiched between the Grands Crus Richebourg and Echézeaux. Five acres of Nuits Premiers Crus and 1.5 of Chambolle-Musigny give a wide range of top-class wines. Grivot believes in dense planting for small crops. He likes ripe wines without acidity or 'brutality' but with bouquet. His family, he says, left him no family tree: just vines, a cellar and experience.

Domaine Jean Gros

Vosne-Romanée, 21700 Nuits St-Georges.

A grower well known for his Vosne-Romanée who has expanded with a plantation of 11 acres up in the Hautes Côtes at Arcenant, some 7 miles west of Vosne. In Vosne he has the 'monopole' of the 5.25-acre Clos des Réas, a Premier Cru down by the road, as well as 7.5 acres of 'Village' land. Two acres are in a frost-prone gully where he has ingeniously doubled the spacing between the vines to allow free movement of air on spring nights. His total is 30 acres. 50% is sold to private clients in France, the other half exported.

Domaine Antonin Guyon

21420 Savigny-Les-Beaune

A very substantial domaine of 116 acres, half of it at Meuilley in the Hautes Côtes de Nuits, where vineyards abandoned after the phylloxera have been replanted in the last 20 years. Otherwise the biggest holdings are 8 acres each in Pernand-Vergelesses Premier Cru and Chambolle-Musigny; 6 each in Gevrey-Chambertin 'Village' and Aloxe-Corton Premier Cru, 5.5 in Corton Grand Cru and Corton-Charlemagne (1.4 acres), 5.5 in Savigny and 2 each of Meursault-Charmes and Volnay Clos des Chênes. Also a tiny parcel of Charmes-Chambertin. Altogether a remarkable spread of good sites, considering which it is strange that the name is not better known. Being a recent creation the firm uses modern methods (e.g. keeping white wines under a blanket of inert nitrogen to preserve freshness). Their Cortons are their particular pride.

Jaboulet-Vercherre

5 rue Colbert, 21200 Beaune.

A family firm of negóciants originally from the Rhône, with notable wines from their own 35-acre domaine. The 10-acre Premier Cru Clos de la Commaraine around the old château of the same name in Pommard is their particular pride. They also have some excellent Corton-Bressandes and a Beaune Premier Cru Clos de l'Ecu. Their wines are made at a modern plant visible from the autoroute.

Maison Louis Jadot

5 rue Samuel Legay, 21200 Beaune.

A family firm based in the medieval Couvent des Jacobins since the early 19th century, when they were growers on the slopes of Beaune. The Domaine Louis Jadot now covers 61 acres, including their original holding, the 6-acre Clos des Ursules in Les Vignes Franches. In Beaune they also own 2.5 acres of the Premier Cru Theurons, the same of Vignes Franches and 6 of Boucherottes on the edge of Pommard, with Pommard-like sturdy wine. In Corton they own 5 acres of Pougets (Grand Cru) and the same of Corton-Charlemagne. In Puligny-Montrachet they own a little over 1 acre each of Les Folatières and Chevalier-Montrachet (a plot they call Les Demoiselles, after the spinster sisters Adèle and Julie Voillot who sold it to them in 1846). Their brilliant white wines are probably their greatest pride: nobody makes better Corton-Charlemagne or Chevalier-Montrachet. But Jadot reds are equally reliable: their domaine wines lead a first-class list of classic burgundies. A shining example of a grower-cum-négociant.

Maison Jaffelin

Caves du Chapitre, 2 rue Paradis, 21200 Beaune.

An old company of négociants, originally distillers, occupying the magnificent 13th-century cellar of the canons of Notre Dame in the centre of Beaune. The company was bought by Joseph Drouhin (q.v.) in 1969 but still acts as an independent négociant.

Domaine Jean Joliot & Fils

Nantoux, 21190 Meursault.

Nantoux is a village in the hills only 3 miles west of Pommard, the northernmost of the Hautes Côtes de Beaune. Jean Joliot has 17 acres in the Hautes Côtes, where he makes some 2,000 cases of good red wine, which is austere for burgundy but highly popular with private clients, half of them abroad. He uses traditional methods, ages his wine in barrels and bottles it himself with his sons Jean-Baptiste and Roland. On the Côte d'Or he has a parcel of Beaune Premier Cru Boucherottes, 2.5 acres of Pommard, and 5 acres of Meursault and a little Aligoté.

Domaine de la Juvinière

Clos de Langres, Corgoloin, 21700 Nuits St-Georges.

The Clos de Langres is the southernmost limit of the Côte de Nuits on the way to Beaune, a walled vineyard still equipped with the ancient *pressoir* of the Bishop of Langres. The domaine centred here is the property of La Reine Pédauque, négociants in Beaune. Apart from the 8-acre Clos, the substantial 60-acre estate has 10 in Savigny, 13 in Corton and Aloxe-Corton, 2.7 of Clos Vougeot and 1.5 of Corton-Charlemagne. Their wines tend to be written off as commercial and lacking individuality, but those visiting Beaune may try them for themselves in the domaine's hospitable exhibition cellars.

Domaine Michel Lafarge

Volnay, 21190 Meursault.

An old family estate which survived the doldrums of Burgundy in the mid-1930s by the initiative of M. Lafarge's grandfather, who bottled his wine and attacked the Paris market with it in person. There are still bottles of 1904 in the cellar. Of the 18.5 acres, 10.5 are in Volnay (4.5 Premier Cru), 2.5 in Meursault, 1 in Beaune Grèves and the rest in rather good Bourgogne vineyards (including Passe-tout-grains and Aligoté). Painstaking vinification, throwing out rotten grapes, fermenting for 10-plus days and using about one third new barrels.

Domaine des Comtes Lafon

Clos de la Barre, 21190 Meursault.

The most famous part of the 31-acre Lafon domaine is their three-quarter-acre parcel of Le Montrachet, which year by year makes one of the finest of all white wines. The biggest part (16 acres) is in Meursault and includes 2 acres of Premier Cru Perrières, more than 4 of Charmes, parts of Genevrières and Goutte d'Or and 7.4 of Meursault 'Village', the best of which is the Domaine's 'Clos de la Barre'. For red wines the Lafons have 11 acres in Volnay (Santenots 8.6, Champans 1.2, Clos des Chênes 1). René Lafon, who runs them for the family, is an innovative wine maker. To get the maximum colour in Volnay he starts the wine in an open *cuve*, then moves it to a closed one, under strictly controlled temperature, where its cap is submerged. For white wine he encourages immensely long fermentation – until the following March or April. It gives, he says, 'long' wines.

Domaine Laleure Piot

Pernand-Vergelesses, 21420 Savigny-Les-Beaune.

A 20-acre domaine producing reputable Pernand-Vergelesses, particularly 1,000 cases of white, with some Grand Cru Corton Bressandes and Premier Cru Vergelesses from Savigny and Pernand.

Domaine Henri Lamarche

Vosne-Romanée, 21700 Nuits St-Georges.

A fourth-generation little family domaine with the good fortune to own the 'monopole' of La Grande Rue, a narrow strip of 3.5 acres running up the hill between Romanée-Conti and La Tâche, the two greatest Grands Crus. Why it is not also a Grand Cru nobody seems to know. A bottle of the 1961 at 21 years old was a miracle of subtle sensuality; understated beside La Tâche, but in its quieter way among the great bottles of my experience. The rest of the 25-acre property includes 2.5 acres of Clos de Vougeot, and parcels of Grands-Echézeaux and the Vosne-Romanée Premiers Crus Malconsorts and Suchots.

Jean Lamy & Fils

St-Aubin, 21190 Meursault.

A much-respected family with 54 acres in Chassagne and Puligny-Montrachet, Santenay and St-Aubin, and a little Bâtard-Montrachet, divided between the Lamy sons Hubert and René.

Louis Latour

18 rue des Tonneliers, 21204 Beaune.

One of Burgundy's names to conjure with, founded in the 18th century and since 1867 owned and directed, father-to-son, by Latours called Louis. The centre of their domaine is the 'Château' de Grancey at Aloxe-Corton, one of the first large-scale, purpose-built 'wineries' in France: 3 stories above ground and 2 below. The domaine totals 125 acres, of which some 103 are in Corton and Aloxe-Corton, including 25 of Corton-Charlemagne, 47 of red Corton Grand Cru, a 6-acre 'monopole' of Grand Cru Clos de la Vigne au Saint and 11 of Premier Cru Les Chaillots. Some 12 acres in Beaune Premier Cru include 7 of Vignes Franches. There are 2 acres of Chambertin and similar parcels of Romanée-St-Vivant and Pernand-Vergelesses Ile des Vergelesses. Latour has a famous 1.3 acres of Chevalier-Montrachet Les Demoiselles.

Latour is most celebrated for his white wines, above all Corton-Charlemagne, which he almost literally put on the map at the end of the 19th century. They are powerful and must be kept. I was surprised to learn that he pasteurizes his reds, which in theory should mean there is no point in keeping them – which is certainly not the case.

Domaine wines account for one quarter of their turnover. Their selections of other wines, particularly whites, are reliable. Montagny is a speciality to look out for. Three quarters of the firm's business is in export.

Domaine Leflaive

Puligny-Montrachet, 21190 Meursault.

Perhaps the most highly regarded white-wine specialist of the Côte d'Or, a family property dating back to 1745, now totalling 50 acres in superb sites. They include 5 acres each in Bâtard- and Chevalier-Montrachet, 2.5 (which is half) of Bienvenues-Bâtard, 7.5 of the Puligny Premier Cru Les Pucelles, 10 of Clavoillon next door and 2 of Combettes. He also has 9 acres of Puligny 'Village' and a patch of (red) Blagny. Vincent Leflaive proceeds by caution and good taste to make exceptional white burgundy. This combination of power and finesse is the benchmark of Puligny – the sublimation of Chardonnay.

Domaine Lequin-Roussot

21590 Santenay

A well-known domaine founded by the Lequin family in 1734. Each generation since, say the brothers René and Louis, has contributed its stone to the edifice. They now have 37 acres, of which 22 are in Santenay (7 Premier

France's most historic and beautiful charitable hospital; the medieval Hospices de Beaune

The Hospices de Beaune

The Hospices de Beaune has a unique role as a symbol of the continuity, the wealth and the general benevolence of Burgundy. It was founded as a hospital for the sick, poor and aged of Beaune in 1443 by the Chancellor to the Duke of Burgundy, Nicolas Rolin, and his wife Guigone de Salins. They endowed it with land in the Côte de Beaune for its income; a practice that has been followed ever since by rich growers, merchants and other citizens. The Hospices now owns about 138 acres of vineyards and much more farmland.

The wine from its scattered vineyard plots is made in *cuvées*, not necessarily consisting of the wine of a single *climat* but designed to be practicable to make and agreeable to drink. Each *cuvée* is named after an important benefactor of the Hospices. There are 34 *cuvées*, all but one in the Côte de Beaune.

The wine is sold, *cuvée* by *cuvée* and cask by cask, at a public auction on the third Sunday of November in the market hall across the road from the Hospices. The profits are spent on running the hospital, which now has every sort of modern equipment. Its original wards, chapel and works of art are open to the public.

Buyers include merchants, restaurants, individuals and syndicates from all over the world, who are attracted by the idea of supporting this ancient charity, and the publicity that accompanies it. The wine-making of the Hospices has been much criticized recently, and it is certainly not easy to judge the wines so soon after the harvest, when buyers have to make their choice. Both excellent and second-rate bottles are produced, but the cachet of a Hospices label means a great deal.

The third weekend in November is the most important date in the Burgundy calendar, known as *Les Trois Glorieuses* from the three feasts which make it a stiff endurance test. On Saturday the Chevaliers de 'Tastevin hold a gala dinner at the Clos de Vougeot. On Sunday after the auction the dinner is at the Hospices and Monday lunch is a wine-growers' feast known as the *Paulée* at Meursault: this last a gigantic bottle party.

Cru). In Chassagne they have 2.5 acres of red Premier Cru Morgeot and 1 of white Premier Cru (Morgeot and Caillerets); also three quarters of an acre of Bâtard-Montrachet producing 1,100 bottles in an average year. The rest of the domaine is scattered in small parcels in Corton (Les Languettes), Pommard and Nuits St-Georges. The policy is to destem the bunches and aim for big but not hard wines, then to sell them as they mature.

Leroy

Auxey-Duresses, 21190 Meursault.

A company known to the world as much for the personality (and reputed wealth) of its owner, Mme Lalou Bize-Leroy, as for its wines. She is both grower and négociant as well as coproprietor and distributor of the Domaine de la Romanée-Conti (of which she inherited half from her father). She is also a well-known mountaineer and a formidable wine taster. Leroy's total of 12 acres is small but choice, including white vines in Meursault and Auxey-Duresses and small parcels of red in Chambertin, Musigny, Clos de Vougeot, Pommard and Auxey-Duresses. The style of the house is very firmly aimed at *vins de garde*. The reds are unstemmed and stay in the vat for 3 weeks, are racked only once, fined with egg whites and never filtered. Strength comes from fully ripe grapes – never more than 1 degree of chaptalization. At 10 years the wines taste young; at 20 in full bloom. Other growers' wines passing through Leroy's hands seem to acquire (or are chosen for) the same qualities. They need patience, and they cost a fortune. The '*Gardien des Grands Millésimes*', as she styles herself, has a stock of 2.5 million bottles.

Domaine Lucien Jacob Leroy

Echevronne, 21420 Savigny-Les-Beaune.

A fifth-generation domaine based at Echevronne in the hills behind Corton. Half of the 45-acre domaine is in the Savigny–Pernand–Aloxe-Corton triangle, the other half is in the Hautes Côtes de Beaune. M. Jacob uses closed fermenting vats instead of the traditional open-topped ones but ages his wine in barrels.

Lupé-Cholet

Clos de Lupé, 21700 Nuits St-Georges.

Two amusingly aristocratic sisters, the Comtesses Inès and Liliane de Mayol de Lupé, run this old family business, best known for its Nuits Premier Cru 'Chateau Gris', a 10-acre parcel of Les Crots above the town which has produced some memorable *vins de garde*. Their elegant house in Nuits also has the 8-acre Clos de Lupé (appellation Bourgogne) beyond the garden. Some years ago the company merged with Bichot of Beaune.

Domaine Machard de Gramont

34 rue Thurot, 21700 Nuits St-Georges.

A 25-acre domaine created over the last 15 years by 2 young brothers with amazing energy and professionalism. Much of their best land was abandoned '*friches*', the stony edges of good vineyards, until they planted it. A family problem sadly reduced their holdings from 75 acres in 1983. Their biggest plots now are in Nuits (6.5 acres of Premier Cru, especially Hauts-Pruliers, 7.5 of 'Village'), Pommard (10 acres of the excellent Clos Blanc, a 'Village' site of Premier Cru quality), and Savigny-les-Beaune (5 acres, mostly Premier Cru Les Guettes). They also have 2.5 acres of Beaune Premier Cru Epenottes and small parcels in Chambolle-Musigny and Aloxe-Corton (very tasty, this). They ferment at a high temperature (35°C/95°F) with most of the stems, age in barrels in cellars and rack their wine as little as possible. Their policy is only to bottle selections from good vintages and old vines, and to sell the rest in bulk. The brothers are modest about their achievement, but they make some of the best red burgundy of its class today.

Domaine du Duc de Magenta

Abbaye de Morgeot, Chassagne-Montrachet, 21190 Meursault.

The descendant of the French victor of the battle of Magenta (1859, with Piedmont against the Austrians) owns 30 acres, of which 11 – half red and half white – are the Clos de la Chapelle of former Cistercians of the Abbaye de Morgeot, a dependency of Cluny. 5 acres are the Premier Cru 'Clos de la Garenne' in Puligny, 8 (red and white) in Auxey-Duresses and 2 in Meursault 'Meix Chavaux'. All his wines are firm, vigorous and full of character, keeping well. His red 'Morgeot' has been outstanding. The 1969 in 1982 had a beautiful flavour of cherries and almonds. But recent vintages have been less impressive.

Château de la Maltroye

Chassagne-Montrachet, 21190 Meursault.

The source of some outstanding bottles of white Chassagne under the 'monopole' label of the château. The 32-acre estate also has a small piece of Bâtard-Montrachet and red-wine vineyards in Chassagne Clos St-Jean and Santenay La Comme.

Domaine Tim Marshall

21700 Nuits St-Georges

A tiny property of only 1 acre in the Nuits Premiers Crus Les Perrières and Les Argillats, the work of a Yorkshireman who has carved out a unique place for himself as a broker, guide, philosopher and friend to Anglo-Saxons (and Burgundians too) in Burgundy.

Domaine Joseph Matrot & Pierre Matrot

21190 Meursault

A family domaine of the usual size (it is remarkable how many have between 30 and 40 acres). 4 acres are in the Puligny Premiers Crus Combettes and Chalumeaux, 4 in Meursault Charmes and Perrières and another 4 of white in the Meursault section of Blagny. There are 3.5 acres of red Volnay-Santenots and an unusual red Blagny, the 6-acre La Pièce sous le Bois, which makes a vivid, rather harsh wine as a change from the gentler Volnay. I have found his Meursault (particularly his Charmes) beautifully made. The '78 has real class and authority.

Prosper Maufoux

21590 Santenay

One of the most respected of family firms in the traditional business of buying, 'bringing-up' and selling burgundy from small growers. The present principal, Pierre Maufoux, is grandson of the founder. Maufoux red wines are reliably *vins de garde*; on many occasions I have found even his 'Village' wines have been in perfect condition at 20 years and his Premiers and Grands Crus exceptional. For Santenay has a share in the Domaine St-Michel (q.v.), which also supplies him with Pouilly Fumé. I have found his Chablis Mont de Milieu and Vaudésir reliable, typical and good value; his Santenay Blanc, Meursault Charmes and (particularly) Puligny-Montrachet Les Folatières first class. This house is the answer to anyone who thinks that all good burgundy is domaine bottled. Marcel Amance is another trade name.

Mazilly Père & Fils

Meloisey, 21190 Meursault.

Growers in the Côte de Beaune since 1600, largely in the Hautes Côtes (8.5 acres) with 2.5 acres of Pommard, 2 of Meursault and 1 of Beaune Premier Cru. Sound, strong wines aimed for body more than finesse.

Domaine Prince Florent de Mérode

21550 Ladoix-Serrigny

A domaine of high standing in Corton and Pommard. Of the 26 acres, some 9 are in Corton Grand Cru and the same in the 'monopole' Pommard Clos de la Platière.

Mestre Père & Fils

21590 Santenay

One of the bigger domaines of Santenay, in the fifth generation, with 17.5 acres of Premiers Crus in all the best vineyards, and smaller holdings in Aloxe-Corton (7.5 acres, of which 1.5 is Corton Grand Cru), Chassagne-Montrachet, and Ladoix and Cheilly (Appellation Côte de Beaune). Careful wine-making, but surprisingly only 20% is bottled at the domaine. The Swiss (who love Santenay) buy the greater part in cask. In 1971, incidentally, the whole crop was destroyed by hail.

Château de Meursault

21190 Meursault

A 100-acre domaine with the signature of the Comte de Moucheron, the former owner, bought in 1973 by the négociants Patriarche of Beaune and turned into a showplace for visitors, with a permanent help-yourself tasting in the spectacular medieval cellars. The vineyards include substantial parcels of the Meursault Premiers Crus Charmes and Perrières – which are sold as Ch. de Meursault – and the former gardens of the château, replanted with vines as the 'Clos du Château'. Red vineyards include part of the Premiers Crus of Volnay (Clos des Chênes), Pommard (Clos des Epenots), Beaune (Fèves, Grèves, Cent Vignes, Clos du Roi) and Savigny. The total production averages 17,000 cases. My impression is that the whole range, but particularly the Meursaults, are extremely well made – and expensive.

Domaine Michelot-Buisson

31 rue de la Velle, 21190 Meursault.

A family property of 50 acres in the best sites in Meursault (Genevrières, Charmes, Perrières), in Puligny, Pommard and lesser appellations. M. Michelot says he is inclined to pull up his lesser vineyards and reduce his stocks, having no stomach for the threatened bureaucratization of the wine trade by the present government.

Moillard

21700 Nuits St-Georges

A family firm in the fifth generation (the name is now Thomas) with a 45-acre domaine, but also making wine from purchased grapes from a much larger area and playing the traditional role of négociants with stocks of no less than 8 million bottles – certainly the biggest in Nuits. They are known for the efficiency and modernity of their techniques, and still respected for their domaine wines, which are made 'supple' and round for relatively early drinking. The domaine includes little parcels of 8 different Nuits Premiers Crus (Clos de Thorey and Clos des Grandes Vignes are 'monopoles'), Chambertin and Clos de Bèze, Bonnes Mares, Clos Vougeot, Romanée St-Vivant and Vosne-Romanée Beaumonts and Malconsorts, Corton Clos du Roi and Corton-Charlemagne.

Domaine Mommessin

La Grange St-Pierre, B.P. 504, 71009 Mâcon.

The famous Beaujolais growers have owned the whole of the 18.5-acre Grand Cru Clos de Tart in Morey St-Denis since 1932. They use the unusual technique of keeping the 'cap' of skins immersed throughout the fermentation. The wine is fine but still on the light side, surprisingly for a Grand Cru, neighbour to Bonnes Mares.

Mongeard-Mugneret

21670 Vosne-Romanée

37-acre estate making long-lived Vosne Les Suchots, Echézeaux, Grands-Echézeaux, Vougeot, etc.

Domaine Jean Monnier & Fils

20 rue du 11 Novembre, 21190 Meursault.

The Monniers have been growers in Meursault since 1720. Their 37 acres comprise 12 acres of Meursault (including Charmes and Genevrières), 2.5 acres of Puligny-Montrachet, 1.25 acres of Beaune, 10 acres of Pommard, 10 acres of Bourgogne Rouge and 1.75 acres of Bourgogne Aligoté. 7 acres of Pommard is their 'monopole' Clos des Cîteaux in Les Epenots.

Domaine René Monnier

6 rue Docteur Rolland, 21190 Meursault.

The Monnier family has built up one of the biggest private domaines in the Côte de Beaune – 45 acres – over 150 years. The biggest plots are in Meursault Chevalières and the Premier Cru Charmes, Beaune Cent Vignes and Toussaints and Puligny Folatières. Other plots are in Pommard, Volnay and Santenay. The reds are fermented for as long as possible at a high temperature (for plenty of colour) and aged in one third of new barrels a year. The whites are balanced between half new oak and half stainless steel; a typical balance of old and new aimed at wine with plenty of flavour not needing long ageing. The name is well known in three-star restaurants.

Domaine de Montille

Volnay, 21190 Meursault.

The 18-acre property of a Dijon lawyer, scattered among the Premiers Crus of Volnay (Champans, Taillepieds, Mitans) and Pommard (Epenots, Rugiens, Pézerolles). Christopher Fielden reports that his wines are particularly flavoursome, well made and durable.

Albert Morey & Fils

Chassagne-Montrachet, 21190 Meursault.

An old family domaine of some 30 acres, largely in Chassagne and almost equally divided between white and red wines. 'The French drink the red', says M. Morey. His best-known white wine is the Premier Cru Les Embrasées (2.5 acres), though his 2 acres of Caillerets, 1 each of Morgeot and Les Champs-Gains and a tiny plot in Bâtard-Montrachet are all excellent. He also owns 2 acres of Santenay for red and rents 2 of Beaune Grèves. By replacing a quarter of his barrels with new ones each year, he keeps a desirable moderate flavour of oak in the wine.

Maison Albert Morot

Château de la Creusotte, 21200 Beaune.

15 acres of Beaune Cru in Teurons, Grèves, Cent Vignes, Toussaints, Bressandes and Marconnets. 5 acres of Savigny-Vergelesses 'Clos la Bataillère'. Guy Chopin makes well-judged red wines, especially Beaune Marconnets (e.g. '76) and Cent Vignes, and one of the best wines of Vergelesses.

Mugneret-Gibourg

Vosne-Romanée, 21700 Nuits St-Georges.

There are 7 growers called Mugneret in Vosne. This domaine, run by Georges Mugneret, distinguishes itself by adding his mother's maiden name. Of the 17 Mugneret-Gibourg acres, Georges reasonably describes the Grands Crus part (in Echézeaux, Clos Vougeot and Ruchottes-Chambertin) as 'modest'. It amounts to less than an acre. They have 2.7 acres of Nuits Premier Cru; the rest is Vosne-Romanée 'Village'. The yield is low and the wine serious. 'Each vigneron,' says Mugneret, 'has his own methods. We are empirical first; scientific second. Nobody could fully explain the peculiarities of his wine, even if he wanted to.'

Domaine Mugneret-Gouachon

Prémeaux-Prissey, 21700 Nuits St-Georges.

Bernard Mugneret runs his father's property in Vosne-Romanée and his father-in-law's in Nuits – a total of 26 acres, of which 8.5 are his 'monopole' Premier Cru Les Perdrix in Prémeaux. He has 3 acres each of Echézeaux and Vosne-Romanée and over 8, producing 750 cases, of Bourgogne Rouge. Les Perdrix is a splendid wine regularly bought and shipped to the USA since 1959 by the late Frank Schoonmaker and his successors.

Charles Noëllat

Vosne-Romanée, 21700 Nuits St-Georges.

Well known as a substantial grower in the Grands Crus, with 4 acres of Clos Vougeot and 5.5 in Romanée St-Vivant (3.7 acres) and Richebourg. The rest of the 35-acre domaine is in Vosne and Nuits, Premiers Crus and 'Villages', with the addition of 2 acres of Savigny-Les-Narbantons in 1980. Christopher Fielden has found his style 'heavy'; others have felt disappointed with some recent wines. My experience with his Richebourg left me richly satisfied.

Hospices de Nuits St-Georges

Rue Henri Challand, 21700 Nuits St-Georges.

The lesser-known and smaller Nuits counterpart of the great Hospices de Beaune, founded in 1634 and now endowed with 31 acres. They include 14 of Nuits Premier Cru and 5.5 of Nuits 'Village'. The rest is Bourgogne and Bourgogne Grand Ordinaire, which is sold in bulk. The best *cuvées* are sold by auction in March. The Cuvée des Soeurs Hospitalières is Nuits (Village) Les Fleurières; the Cuvée Les Sires de Vergy is Les St-Georges; the Cuvées Fagon, Duret and Cabet are Les Didiers. All are serious *vins de garde*.

Domaine Parent

21630 Pommard

A 37-acre domaine founded in 1750, best known for its Pommard; Epenots, Epenottes and Clos Micault, but also with vineyards in Volnay and Beaune. A 5-year-old bottle of his Clos Micault 1977 showed what a good grower can make of a bad year. A '78 at the same tasting was many years from maturity.

Domaine Jean Pascal & Fils

Puligny-Montrachet, 21190 Meursault.

A family domaine of 19 acres which developed in the 1960s and now bottles and exports most of its wine, particularly to America. Holdings include 2 acres of Pommard and one of Volnay (with some good Premier Cru Caillerets), but the house speciality is Puligny-Montrachet, where it owns over 10 acres, including 4.4 of Premiers Crus. Les Chalumeaux is the best wine. Fermentation for the reds is rather short; classic for the whites.

Patriarche Père & Fils

Couvent des Visitandines, 21200 Beaune.

Possibly the biggest firm in Burgundy (it claims to have the biggest cellars) with a history going back to 1780. Patriarche has a paradoxical image: on one hand proprietor of the excellent Ch. de Meursault and Beaune Premiers Crus totalling 100 acres, regularly the biggest buyer at the Hospices de Beaune auctions and a house of great prestige; on the other a brand which the snob in me would describe as definitely down-market. Perhaps it is the dismal design of their labels. Their greatest success must be Kriter Brut de Brut, created in the early 1960s as a high-quality, non-appellation sparkling wine. The Kriter factory on the road south of Beaune boasts a vast celebratory fountain. Appellation wines account for 60% of turnover. Brand names include Père Patriarche, Cuvée Jean Baptiste, Noëmie Vernaux.

Pavelot Père & Fils

21420 Savigny-Les-Beaune

The Pavelots have been growers in Savigny since 1640. Their domaine comprises 25 acres, about half of it in the Premier Cru vineyards of the slopes. Their wines are made in modern conditions. They bottle the best, notably Savigny 'Dominode' and 'Guettes', and sell the rest in cask to négociants.

Domaine de la Perrière

Fixin, 21220 Gevrey-Chambertin.

An unusually simple property making only one wine: the famous Fixin Clos de la Perrière, established by the Cistercian monks of Cîteaux in the 12th century. The original manor, its cellars and their great press, 700 years old, are still here. The 13 acres produce some 2,000 cases of bold, uncompromising wine, made by long fermentation (up to 3 weeks) in covered vats with most of the stems included. Then long barrel-ageing and no filtration – very much what the monks must have done. The wine has been compared with Chambertin for power, if not for finesse.

Château de Pommard

21630 Pommard

The château is very much in evidence from the main road, with a label and a sales approach which might lead one to think it is strictly for tourists. In fact it is extremely serious; with 50 acres said to be the biggest single vineyard with one proprietor in Burgundy, and acknowledged to make excellent wine from a high proportion of old vines. Despite being a 'Village' wine, it is made like a good Premier Cru. The owner, Jean-Louis Laplanche, uses new barrels every year, keeps the wine 2 years in wood and does not filter. The tourists are important too: all his sales are direct to private clients.

Maison Pierre Ponnelle

Abbaye St-Martin, 53 avenue de l'Aigue, 21200 Beaune.

One of the smaller négociants, evidently thriving, with new premises outside Beaune and a new shop in the town. The present director, Bruno Ponnelle, is the great-grandson of the founder. Their domaine is only 12 acres, but includes parcels of Musigny, Bonnes Mares, Charmes-Chambertin, Clos Vougeot, Corton Clos du Roi and Beaune Grèves. Their wine list is remarkable in quality and diversity and in the old stocks they offer. In my experience Ponnelle wines are absolutely true to type and very long-lived: a 1950 Clos Vougeot (not a famous year) was in good condition in 1980.

Domaine Ponsot

Morey St-Denis, 21220 Gevrey-Chambertin.

A 20-acre domaine over a century old, all in Morey St-Denis except for a small parcel of Latricières-Chambertin. Half of the total is in the splendid Clos de la Roche, making wine difficult to distinguish from Chambertin. White Premier Cru Morey 'Monts Luisants' is Ponsot's other speciality; some 250 cases of one of the few whites of the Côte de Nuits, grown on high trellising 'Swiss-style' on the steep upper slopes.

Henri Potinet-Ampeau

Monthélie, 21190 Meursault.

A grower who prides himself on making wines to keep 20 years or more. His 27 acres include red wines from the Volnay Premiers Crus Santenots and Clos des Chênes, and Pommard Les Pézerolles, and whites from Meursault Charmes and Perrières and Auxey-Duresses 'Les Duresses'. 1976 is the year of the century, he says – and so is 1978!

Poulet Père & Fils

12 rue Chaumergy, 21200 Beaune.

A firm of négociants with a long history, known for sturdy wines rather than finesse.

Domaine de la Poulette

Grande rue à Corgoloin, 21700 Nuits St-Georges.

A family domaine of 37 acres dating back to the 18th century. Half the production is Côte de Nuits-Villages (red and a little white), but the domaine makes some 1,100 cases of the Nuits St-Georges Premiers Crus Les St-Georges, Vaucrains and Poulettes; also a little Vosne-Romanée Les Suchots and Corton Renardes. 'Traditional' vinification at relatively cool temperatures.

Domaine de la Pousse d'Or

Volnay, 21190 Meursault.

A domaine of 32 acres entirely in the Premiers Crus of Volnay, Pommard and Santenay. Its reputation is as high as any in the Côte de Beaune. Almost every three-star restaurant offers its wines. The domaine has 3 'monopoles' in Volnay: Clos de la Bousse [*sic*] d'Or, Clos des Soixante Ouvrées and Clos d'Audignac. The first and last are typically gentle and sociable Volnay, delicacy and elegance that reaches its peak in the 'Bousse d'Or'; the '60 Ouvrées', however, is a prime piece of the Caillerets, more forceful wine demanding maturity. (An *ouvrée* is one twenty-fourth of a hectare: 60 = 2.5 hectares = just over 7 acres.) Another parcel of Caillerets of the same size produces lighter wines. Two similar plots in Santenay's best Premiers Crus (Tavannes and Gravières) and 2.5 acres of Pommard Jarollières complete the domaine. Gérard Potel, the director, ferments his wine for 12 to 14 days, looking, he says, 'for long life but finesse, with subtle and delicate perfumes. Ideally wine with the maximum freshness and maximum *nervosité*.' The 1966 Jarollières was sublime in 1982.

Domaine Jacques Prieur

Rue des Santenots, 21190 Meursault.

One of Burgundy's most remarkable properties, including parts of both Chambertin and Montrachet, with all its 35 acres in great vineyards. Its architect was Jacques Prieur, one of the prime movers of the Chevaliers de Tastevin, whose son Jean now runs it with the help of his brother-in-law Pierre Poupon, author of several standard books on Burgundy. The vines include 2.4 acres in Chambertin and Clos de Bèze, 2 in Musigny, 3 in Clos de Vougeot, 4.5 in Beaune (Clos de la Féguine), 6 in the Volnay Premiers Crus Santenots, Clos des Santenots and Champans, 8 in Meursault Clos de Mazeray (red and white), 4 in Puligny Les Combettes and Chevalier-Montrachet and 1.4 (making 2,000 bottles) of Le Montrachet. All the wines (some 5,000 cases a year) are made in Meursault in modern conditions. The domaine has a faultless reputation for both red and white wines. Asked to choose one remarkable success from the last decade, Pierre Poupon named the 1973 Volnay Clos des Santenots.

Charles Quillardet

21220 Gevrey-Chambertin

An enterprising grower of the northern *côtes* with 40 acres of vines between Gevrey and Dijon, including a parcel of Chambertin, vines in Fixin and Marsannay (where he makes a Bourgogne Rosé) and in the suburbs of Dijon itself, at Larrey, where he has restored an ancient vineyard with the Rabelaisian name of Montre Cul, 'Show your backside' – from the posture of the workers on the steep slope.

Ramonet-Prudhon

Chassagne-Montrachet, 21190 Meursault.

One of the great names of white burgundy. Half of the 34-acre domaine is white, including immaculately made Bâtard- and Bienvenues-Bâtard-Montrachet, delicate and racy Chassagne Premier Cru Les Ruchottes, and excellent Chassagne 'Village'. Their red wines are less famous but remarkably fine: Clos de la Boudriotte, Clos St-Jean and red Chassagne 'Village' are as good as any red wines of the southern Côte de Beaune. Father and son, Pierre and André, share the domaine. Pierre labels his wine Ramonet-Prudhon; André uses his own name.

Rapet Père & Fils

Pernand-Vergelesses, 21420 Savigny-Les-Beaune.

A highly reputed 30-acre domaine including parcels of Corton-Charlemagne and (red) Corton Grand Cru, Pernand-Vergelesses Premier Cru and Bourgogne (red and white). The enigmatic Monsieur Rapet's motto is '*Le moins on en dit, le mieux on se porte*' – in other words, 'My wine speaks for itself.'

La Reine Pédauque

21200 Beaune

A well-known commercial house owned by Pierre André.

Remoissenet Père & Fils

21200 Beaune

A small domaine of 6 acres in Beaune Premier Cru (where Grèves and Toussaints make their own best wines) but an important broker and négociant who supplies the burgundies of the French firm of Nicolas and the Bristol one of Avery's. Through the latter I have had many good bottles, particularly of white wines.

Henri Remoriquet & Fils

25 rue de Charmois, 21700 Nuits St-Georges.

An established family of growers in Nuits with 2.3 acres in Premiers Crus Les St-Georges, Rue de Chaux and Les Damodes and 7 Nuits 'Villages', including 2 acres in Les

Allots, a good '*climat*' on the road to Vosne-Romanée, which is domaine-bottled and the house speciality. M. Remoriquet was a pioneer of the Hautes Côtes de Nuits with 2.5 acres at Chaux, 2 miles west on top of the hill.

Domaine de la Romanée-Conti

Vosne Romanée, 21700 Nuits St-Georges.

See Romanée-Conti – A Great Burgundy Estate, pages 118 and 119.

Ropiteau Frères

21190 Meursault

The firm are négociants handling the output of their own Domaine Ropiteau-Mignon and other wines. The domaine is the biggest in Meursault with 12 acres of Premiers Crus in Genevrières, Perrières and 4 other '*climats*', and 32 in the 'Village' vineyards. Four acres each of Premier Cru Puligny and Monthélie make them strong in fine white wines. Their red holdings are small parcels in Volnay, Monthélie, Pommard, Beaune (Grèves), Clos Vougeot, Echézeaux and Chambolle-Musigny. The top Ropiteau whites are ideal white burgundy, balancing oak and grape flavours and needing time to develop.

Joseph Roty

21220 Gevrey-Chambertin

A small but impeccable grower in Charmes-Chambertin, Gevrey Premier Cru and Villages.

Guy Roulot & Fils

1 rue Charles Giraud, 21190 Meursault.

A family domaine of 35 acres, 15 in Meursault (including Perrières and Charmes), 6 in Auxey-Duresses red, with a quantity of Beaune, of Passe-tout-grains, Bourgogne and Aligoté. Also a still making Fine de Bourgogne (brandy) and Marc de Bourgogne. For white wines Roulot waits for maximum ripeness and ferments in barrels renewed by one third a year, bottling just before the next harvest. For both whites and reds he uses the unusual phrase '*garde garantie 10 ans*'. Serious, well-judged wines.

Domaine G. Roumier

Chambolle-Musigny, 21220 Gevrey-Chambertin.

Jean-Marie Roumier directs the family property, started in 1924, with 35 acres; 18 in Chambolle-Musigny, 6 in Morey St-Denis, 6 of very old vines in Bonnes Mares, 2.5 in Clos de Vougeot and about 1 each in Le Musigny and Les Amoureuses. His brother Alain is cellar master at the Domaine de Vogüé. The family's wines are classics of depth and harmony. Their Bonnes Mares 1976 is their first choice.

Domaine Armand Rousseau

21220 Gevrey-Chambertin

One of the most respected growers of Chambertin. The founder's son, Charles Rousseau, now owns 19 acres, including 4 of Chambertin, 2 of Clos de Bèze, and parcels in Mazis and Charmes-Chambertin as well as in the Clos de la Roche in Morey and (his particular pride) 5.5 acres of Gevrey Clos St-Jacques on the hill above the village. His wine is vatted for 2 weeks. No one makes bigger, more gutsy burgundies.

Domaine Roux Père & Fils

St-Aubin, 21190 Meursault.

A competent small proprietor whose 9 acres in St-Aubin, 4.5 in Santenay Premiers Crus and 1 in Puligny-Montrachet can be relied on for the true taste of their respective villages. He is also known for good Passe-tout-grains.

Domaine St-Michel

21590 Santenay

An estate jointly run by Michel Gutrin and the Santenay négociant Pierre Maufoux (q.v.). They own 64 acres, mainly in Santenay 'Village', Premier Cru Comme and Clos Rousseau, and in Puligny-Montrachet for white wines. Also a 20-acre vineyard at Pouilly-sur-Loire. Their Bourgogne Rouge St-Michel is good value. Most sales are to private clients in France.

Domaine Etienne Sauzet

Puligny-Montrachet, 21190 Meursault.

Etienne Sauzet (who died in 1975) was the third of the 5 generations who have built up a reputation for richly flavoured white burgundies. The house style is to keep the wines on their lees for a year to develop flavour and 'fat'. Their main holding is 13 acres in Puligny Premiers Crus, with 4 each of Combettes (their best-known wine) and Champ-Canet. They have a further 8 acres in Puligny, 2 in Chassagne and small parcels of Bâtard- and Bienvenues-Bâtard-Montrachet.

Maison Séguin-Manuel

Rue de Bourgogne, 2142c Savigny-Les-Beaune.

The date of foundation, 1720, gives this a claim to being the oldest merchant in Burgundy. The small domaine is all in Savigny; most of the business is in other appellations, including Beaujolais, Côtes du Rhône, spirits and Oeil de Perdrix sparkling rosé.

Domaine Daniel Senard

21420 Aloxe-Corton

Farms 21 acres of his own land, 12 of them in the Grands Crus of Corton, Clos du Roi and Bressandes, and the entire 5-acre 'Clos Meix'; 6.5 in (red) Aloxe-Corton and small parcels of Beaune Les Coucherias and Chorey-Les-Beaune. Also two thirds of an acre of Aloxe-Corton making 900 bottles of white Pinot Gris, or 'Beurot' – powerful wine for long maturing. A total of 2,300 cases a year. The eighth generation of Senards operate in 14th-century cellars (and a tower). Exceptionally long-lived and well-balanced reds are made by controlling fermentation temperatures. Exports are 80% of sales.

Robert de Suremain

Château de Monthélie, 21190 Meursault.

A small but famous estate whose 20 acres of old vines in Monthélie produce a red wine comparable with one of the best Volnays. He also has a white-wine vineyard in Rully.

Roland Thévenin

Château de Puligny-Montrachet, 21190 Meursault.

The dynamic proprietor (and restorer) of both the Château de Puligny-Montrachet and the ancient Moulin aux Moines at Auxey-Duresses: mayor of St-Romain (where he also has 20 acres), a passionate writer, collector and white-wine maker. Although he is also a négociant, it is his own Puligny-Montrachet, especially Les Folatières, that keeps his name in the forefront.

Domaine René Thévenin-Monthélie & Fils

St-Romain, 21190 Meursault.

A reputable family domaine since 1868 with 34 acres, half of them white St-Romain and the remainder equally divided between Monthélie and Beaune.

Thévenot-Le-Brun & Fils

Marey-Les-Fussey, 21700 Nuits St-Georges

Maurice Thévenot's father bought an abandoned monastic walled vineyard, the Clos du Vignon, in the Hautes Côtes de Nuits in 1933. Maurice and his sons replanted in 1967 and now have 50 acres making some of the best wine of the Hautes Côtes from Pinot Noir (27 acres), which is mixed with Gamay for his Passe-tout-grains, and Aligoté, which is bottled without racking to be drunk very young and faintly fizzy. In the Clos du Vignon he also grows Chardonnay and Pinot Gris ('Beurot') for *vin de garde*.

Domaine Tollot-Beaut & Fils

Chorey-Les-Beaune, 21200 Beaune.

A family property since 1880 with impeccable standards, sometimes cited as a model for Burgundy. Of a total of 47 acres, about half is at Chorey and half divided among the Premiers Crus of Beaune (Grèves and Clos du Roi, 4.5 acres), Savigny and Aloxe-Corton, with some 300 cases a year of Corton-Bressandes, 200 of Le Corton and 100 of Corton-Charlemagne (white). No secrets but careful traditional wine-making, plunging the 'cap' twice a day and controlling the temperature. The special pride of the house is in Corton-Bressandes and Beaune Clos du Roi.

Domaine Tollot-Voarick

Chorey-Les-Beaune, 21200 Beaune.

A 42-acre domaine based at Chorey, just north of Beaune, where it also owns a restaurant, Le Bareuzai. The bulk of its vineyards are outside the grander areas of the Côte, growing Pinot Noir, Gamay and Aligoté at Chorey, Ladoix-Serrigny and Comblanchien. Nearly 9 acres, however, are in Aloxe-Corton and 2 in Pernand Premier Cru Les Vergelesses. Two are in Savigny and 2 in Beaune Clos du Roy. A well-equipped property which takes intelligent pains and every opportunity of making *vins de garde*, in new barrels where the wine warrants the expense.

Domaine F. Tortochot & Fils

21220 Gevrey-Chambertin

A 25-acre family property highly respected for the firm, long-lived style of Gevrey-Chambertin. They own parcels of between 1 and 2 acres in the Grands Crus Charmes- and Mazis-Chambertin, a similar piece of Lavaux St-Jacques on the hill above the village and considered worthy of Grand Cru standing, some good land in Morey St-Denis and a half acre in Clos Vougeot.

Domaine Louis Trapet

53 route de Beaune, 21220 Gevrey-Chambertin.

Five generations of Trapets have worked to build up a domaine of 42 acres, including nearly 9 of Chambertin, over 5 in Latricières and Chapelle-Chambertin, the same in Gevrey Premiers Crus and 17 in the Gevrey 'Village' vineyards. Jean Trapet's great-grandfather started his success by being one of the first in the Côte d'Or to graft vines during the phylloxera epidemic of the 1870s. The pride of the house is its Chambertin, made in the traditional way but not as massive as Rousseau's (q.v.).

Domaine des Varoilles

11 rue de l'Ancien Hôpital, 21220 Gevrey-Chambertin.

A 30-acre domaine with one of the highest reputations in Burgundy for serious *vins de garde* that really must be matured. It takes its name from its 15-acre Clos des Varoilles, planted on the south-facing hill above Gevrey by monks from Langres in the 12th and 13th centuries. The Clos du Couvent, Clos du Meix des Ouches and La Romanée are other 'monopoles' in Gevrey, besides 2 acres of Charmes- and Mazoyères-Chambertin, 1.3 of Bonnes Mares and 3.3 of Clos de Vougeot. The director, Jean-Pierre Naigeon, makes some of Burgundy's firmest, best-structured wines, selecting from old vines and constantly mixing in the skins during fermentation. He quotes the gourmet-critic Gaston Roupnel on Varoilles wines: 'Only age can tame its almost savage force . . . and give it at last the scents of violets and spring.' Amen.

Henri de Villamont

Rue du Docteur Guyot, 21420 Savigny-Les-Beaune.

Negóciants and growers founded by the huge Swiss firm of Schenk in 1964, when they bought the 15-acre Domaine Marthenot at Savigny and the 10-acre Domaine Modot in Chambolle-Musigny and Grands-Echézeaux. In 1969 they bought the business of Arthur Barolet in Beaune. The name Barolet figures largely in their annals since they found and marketed the extraordinary hoard of fine old burgundies of the late Dr. Barolet in 1968.

Domaine Michel Voarick

21420 Aloxe-Corton

A 36-acre family 'exploitation' which includes farming the famous 6-acre Corton Cuvée Dr. Peste for the Hospices de Beaune. Voarick owns 6 acres of Corton Grand Cru (Clos du Roi, Bressandes, Languettes, Renardes) and 3.5 of Corton-Charlemagne, besides 8 acres in Pernand-Vergelesses, 10 in Aloxe-Corton and 2 along the Côte in Romanée St-Vivant. A total of some 2,500 cases of red and 400 of white. Old-fashioned methods include fermenting stalks-and-all in oak *cuves* to make *vins de garde*. Voarick's own favourite is his Corton Languettes 1978.

Domaine Comte Georges de Vogüé

Chambolle-Musigny, 21220 Gevrey-Chambertin.

Considered by many the finest domaine in Burgundy, descended by inheritance since 1450. The name de Vogüé appears in 1766. Splendid vaulted cellars under the 15th-century house hold the production of 30 acres. 18 are in Le Musigny, 6.6 in Bonnes Mares, 1.5 in the Premier Cru Les Amoureuses and 4.5 in the appellation Chambolle-Musigny. 3,000 Chardonnay vines in Musigny produce some 100 cases a year of a unique Musigny Blanc. The name Vieilles Vignes is given to the best wine, which is burgundy at its grandest and yet most subtle – beyond description. The years 1969 and 1978 are the proprietor's favourites.

Joseph Voillot

Volnay, 21190 Meursault.

An unpretentious property built up by inheritance and marriages from father to son to a total of 25 acres. 10 in Volnay are half in the Premiers Crus; 7.5 in Pommard include 2.5 of the Premier Cru Pézerolles, on the border of Beaune above Les Epenots, giving Voillot's favourite wine. His philosophy is a good warm fermentation to extract all possible colour and flavour from the skins. He also has 1 acre of Meursault Premier Cru.

Cave Coopérative des Grands Vins Rosés

21 rue de Mazy, 21160 Marsannay-La-Côte.

One of the few growers' cooperatives of the Côte d'Or, founded in 1929 and now counting 19 members whose properties vary between 2 and 35 acres. The very big harvest of 1979 produced 9,000 cases of Bourgogne Rouge and their speciality, Rosé de Marsannay, which is largely sold to passing tourists in summer.

THE COTE CHALONNAISE

Santenay brings the Côte d'Or to a close at its southern end. There is scarcely time for lunch at the luxurious Lameloise at Chagny before the wine scout has to be alert again for the five villages that make up the Côte Chalonnaise. In fact, Chalon-sur-Saône has little to do with the district today and the tendency is to refer to the Région de Mercurey, the biggest and best known of the wine parishes. But in antiquity Chalon was one of the great wine ports of the Empire. It was the point where wine coming or going north to or from Paris or the Moselle had to be transshipped from river to road – 25,000 amphoras were found in one dredging operation in the Saône at Chalon.

The Côte from Chagny southwards is less distinct and consistent than from Santenay northwards. So is its wine. Rising demand and prices have only recently made wine-growing profitable rather than marginal, and encouraged replanting of land abandoned after phylloxera, or whose owners were killed in World War I.

Although its best wines are up to minor Côte de Beaune standards, it is hard to pin them down with a regional character. They vary remarkably from village to village.

Mercurey and Givry are dedicated 90 per cent to red wine, which should be firm and tasty Pinot Noir at least on a level with, say, a good Côte de Beaune-Villages; if anything harder and leaner, with Givry, traditionally the bigger wine, demanding longer keeping.

Rully is split equally between red wine and white. Here the white at its best is marvellously brisk with a touch of real class. The red, at least as most growers make it today, can be rather thin compared with Mercurey. High acidity in Rully whites makes them ideal for sparkling wines.

Montagny is entirely a white-wine appellation, with the peculiarity that all its wines of 11.5 degrees alcohol or more are entitled to be labelled Premier Cru – which seems scarcely fair to the carefully limited Premiers Crus of the other villages. Montagny whites tend to have a little more body and less finesse than those of Rully. The one most often seen abroad, a selection by the Beaune négociant Louis Latour, is quite a fat dry wine.

The fifth appellation of the Côte Chalonnaise is the only specific one for the Aligoté grape in Burgundy. The village of Bouzeron, between Rully and Chagny, has made a speciality of what is normally a plain, sharp café wine. In 1979 it was granted the appellation Bourgogne Aligoté de Bouzeron.

Besides these specific appellations the Région de Mercurey makes a considerable quantity of honourable Bourgogne Rouge, most of which is sold in bulk. But a few growers in Bouzeron and St-Désert take pride in bottling it. Like all red burgundy, it should be kept a minimum of two years in bottle.

The other regional speciality is Crémant de Bourgogne, sparkling wine whose quality will amaze those who think that champagne is first and the rest nowhere. (*See* note on page 128.)

Three sizeable producers account for most of the annual total of some 170,000 cases of Crémant. They are Delorme-Meulien at Rully, R. Chevillard at La Rochepot on the road to Paris, and Parigot-Richard at Savigny-Les-Beaune.

To summarize the region:

Mercurey	average crop		180,000 cases, 90% red, 10% white
Givry	,,	,,	44,000 cases, 90% red, 10% white
Rully	,,	,,	66,000 cases, 50% red, 50% white
Montagny	,,	,,	40,000 cases 100% white
Bourgogne Aligoté de Bouzeron	,,	,,	11,000 cases 100% white

Tasting from the cask

MAJOR PRODUCERS

Château de Chamirey
See Antonin Rodet

Chanzy Frères
Domaine L'Hermitage, Bouzeron, 71150 Chagny.

One of the two considerable domaines in Bouzeron with some 20 acres in that village, 30 in Rully and 5 in Mercurey. Over half of the Bouzeron vineyard is planted in Aligoté, which is considered Burgundy's best. Chanzy's Bourgogne (i.e. Pinot Noir and Chardonnay) vineyards in Bouzeron are called Clos de la Fortune. His biggest production is of Rully Rouge (2,500 cases from 19 acres). His Mercurey vineyards are called Clos du Roy. Daniel Chanzy is insistent that red burgundy must be kept 3 or 4 years in bottle to show its personality.

Jean-François Delorme
Domaine de la Renarde, Rully, 71150 Chagny.

The most remarkable enterprise in the region; an estate of 140 acres built up from scratch in 20 years, largely by reclaiming former vineyards abandoned long ago and turned to scrub. Delorme is equally well known as one of Burgundy's best specialists in sparkling wine, for which the very clean, slightly austere whites of Rully are excellent. 50 acres of the domaine in Rully are Chardonnay; 60 are Pinot Noir. Varot is the 44-acre vineyard that gives Delorme's best white, which is notable for freshness and finesse. Its austerity brings it closer in character to Chablis than, say, a Mâcon white. Domaine de la Renarde red is also delicate, 'nervous' and without surplus flesh. A comparison with his Mercurey (he has 9 acres) shows the Mercurey to be plumper and to have more substance. He also has 11 acres of Givry, 4 of Bouzeron Aligoté and 12 at La Rochepot growing Pinot Noir for Crémant de Bourgogne. The last, made in an impressive new cellar, is a real alternative to champagne – a *cuvée* that is tasty without being coarse; delicate without being timid.

Michel Derain
St-Désert, 71390 Buxy.

A small-scale producer of 'serious' Bourgogne Rouge and Givry Blanc from 14 acres.

Du Gardin
71640 Givry

Owners of the 15-acre 'monopole' Clos Saloman in Givry for over 300 years.

Michel Goubard
St-Désert, 71390 Buxy.

An example of how good Bourgogne Rouge without a specific appellation can be in this part of the Côtes. Goubard bottles some 2,000 cases of pure Pinot Noir and a little Chardonnay and Aligoté from his 21 acres. The rest he sells in bulk.

Henri and Paul Jacqueson
Place Ste-Marie, Rully, 71150 Chagny.

Father and son together take great pride in this small domaine of 16 acres making wine in the old way. The reds are trodden by foot, stems and all, fermented for up to 18 days and raised in new barrels every year. 6 acres of Rully Premier Cru are called 'Les Clouds' (red) and 'Grésigny' (white). The other wines are (red) Mercurey and Rully, and some Aligoté and Passe-tout-grains. Their label is seen in some very smart restaurants.

Domaine Michel Juillot
Mercurey, 71640 Givry.

One of the best Mercurey makers, regularly carrying off gold medals for the red Clos des Barraults from his 42 acres (of which 5 are Chardonnay). He destems all his grapes, ferments in open vats and buys one third of his barrels new each year. His '78 is an example of Mercurey at its best.

Paul and Yves de Launay
Clos du Château de Montaign, Mercurey, 71640 Givry.

A traditional small property around the ruins of the Château de Montaign, making Mercurey red and some Aligoté.

Jean Maréchal
Mercurey, 71640 Givry.

Maréchals have made Mercurey for 300 years. 17 of their 22 acres are in the Premiers Crus, almost all red. The aim is to produce long-lived wines. Jean Maréchal's 1971, his favourite of the decade, was excellent in 1981.

Armand Monassier
Domaine du Prieuré, Rully, 71150 Chagny.

The property of a Paris restaurateur (Chez Les Anges, one-star, Boulevard Latour-Maubourg), born in Rully, who since 1958 has assembled a total of 18 acres, 11 of Rully Rouge (5 are Premier Cru) and 5 of Rully Blanc (half Premier Cru). With a little red Mercurey, he also makes Crémant de Bourgogne, Passe-tout-grains, *marc* and *fine*.

E. and X. Noël-Bouton
Domaine de la Folie, Rully, 71150 Chagny.

A substantial property with 1,000 years of history, in the parish of Chagny but in the appellation of Rully. The 44 acres are in one block around the house, with Chardonnay in a majority, producing some 3,300 cases a year of Rully Blanc Clos St-Jacques; Pinot Noir making 2,500 cases of Rully Rouge Clos de Bellecroix; and a smaller patch of Aligoté. Xavier Noël-Bouton buys as much as 40% of his barrels new each year to make aromatic wines with the potential to develop.

François Protheau & Fils
Mercurey, 71640 Givry.

A major Mercurey domaine of 62 acres, including 18 in Clos L'Evèque, 12 in La Fauconnière and 10 in the Clos des Corvées.

Domaine Ragot
Poncey, 71640 Givry.

A small domaine in its fourth generation, with 10 acres of Givry Rouge and 5 of Givry Blanc out of a total of 18. The proportion of white is unusually high for Givry and the keeping qualities of the wine are remarkable – particularly in years of high acidity. Ripe vintages such as '78, '76 and '71, says M. Ragot, are best drunk sooner. His red and white are both regular gold-medal winners.

Antonin Rodet
Mercurey, 71640 Givry.

An important négociant as well as proprietor in Mercurey. The fourth generation of the Rodet family is represented by the Marquis de Jouennes d'Herville, the present head of the firm, whose name appears on the domaine's label, Château de Chamirey. The 66-acre vineyard consists of nearly the whole of the Mercurey Premier Cru Clos du Roi and produces some 8,500 cases of red and 1,500 of white. To many, the red Château de Chamirey is the archetypal Mercurey.

Antonin Rodet deals in wines from all parts of Burgundy, taking special pride in its Bourgogne Rodet (red and white), Mercurey, Meursault and Gevrey-Chambertin.

Domaine Roy-Thévenin

Château de la Saule, Montagny-Les-Buxy, 71390 Buxy.

A 23-acre property almost entirely devoted to making fresh, vigorous, white Montagny. The grapes are pressed as quickly as possible after picking, the juice fined and fermented in big oak barrels, to be bottled the following June. While freshness is the main aim, the 'big' vintages have been known to improve for 8 or 10 years.

Domaine Saier

Mercurey, 71640 Givry.

Purchasers, in 1979, of the 22-acre Grand Cru Clos des Lambrays in Morey St-Denis, which has been missing from the ranks of great burgundies for some years. They are replanting.

Hugues de Suremain

Mercurey, 71640 Givry.

A leading proprietor and President of the growers' syndicate of Mercurey, whose own 30 acres are known for concentrated and age-worthy wines.

Société Civile du Domaine Thénard

71640 Givry

Much the grandest estate of Givry, with 50 acres in the village (almost all red Premiers Crus) but better known to the world as the owner of the second-biggest single plot of Le Montrachet, 4.5 acres, as well as 2 acres each of Corton Clos du Roi, Iles des Vergelesses and Grands-Echézeaux. The property has been in the family for 200 years (the present proprietor is called Jacques Bordeaux Montrieux). All the wine is made in the atmospheric oak-beamed *cuverie* and cellars at Givry. Three Givry Premiers Crus, all robust *vins de garde*, are sold under their vineyard names: Boischevaux, Cellier aux Moines and Clos St-Pierre.

A. and P. de Villaine

Bouzeron, 71150 Chagny.

A grower better known as coproprietor of the Domaine de la Romanée-Conti, but equally proud to have helped bring Bouzeron from obscurity to having its own appellation in 5 years (1973–78) of impeccable wine-making. He treats Aligoté as a noble grape, using half barrels (for finesse) and half tanks (for fruit). His Bourgogne Rouge is similarly made, with selective pickings, long fermentation with the stems, and no rackings. His 13.5 acres of Aligoté produce about 2,000 cases a year. 9 acres of Chardonnay are called Bourgogne Blanc Les Clous and 16 acres of Pinot Noir are called by their vineyard names, La Digoine and La Fortune.

Cave des Vignerons de Buxy

Les Vignes de la Croix, St-Gengoux Le Nuit, 71390 Buxy.

The important and very modern growers' cooperative for Buxy and Montagny, founded in 1931 but re-equipped recently. Its members own 1,360 acres of vines, mainly with generic appellations (Bourgogne Rouge, Passe-tout-grains. Aligoté and Bourgogne Grand Ordinaire are its principal productions). The one exception is white Montagny, of which they produce 20,000 cases a year.

MACON

Say 'Mâcon' to most wine drinkers today and their knee-jerk response will be 'Blanc'. The region is riding high on the reliability and uncomplicated pleasantness of its Chardonnay whites. They have the advantage of being recognizably white burgundy but half the price of Côte d'Or wines, and marvellously easy to choose – since most of them are made by skilful cooperatives and marketed by their efficient central Union des Coopératives Vinicoles de Bourgogne de Saône-et-Loire.

The Mâconnais is a widespread and disjointed region, taking its name from the important commercial city on the Saône just outside its limits to the east. It has little of the monoculture of Beaujolais; its mixed farming land is more attractive, and in places geologically spectacular. Poully-Fuissé is its only appellation with Grand Vin aspirations.

Most Mâcon wine used to be red, made of Gamay but grown on heavy chalky soil which prevents it from ripening to Beaujolais softness and vitality. Mâcon Rouge was indeed merely *vin ordinaire* with an appellation until Beaujolais methods of fermentation were introduced. Recently there have been some much better wines up to Beaujolais-Villages standards.

Pinot Noir from the Mâconnais can aspire no higher than the appellation Bourgogne Rouge or (mixed with Gamay) Passe-tout-grains.

Chardonnay now occupies two thirds of the vineyards, including (in the more northerly communes in particular) a strain of Chardonnay known as the 'Musqué' for its decidedly richer, melony-musky flavour. Used to excess it can produce a blowsy, unsubtle wine. In due proportion it adds a hint of richness to otherwise rather straight dry white; undoubtedly an element in the popularity of Mâcon Blanc. All the best Mâcon Blanc is labelled either Mâcon-Villages or with the name of a particular village.

Pouilly-Fuissé rises higher in the quality league, for local reasons of soil and situation – but not as much higher as its price infers. The four villages in the appellation area have been prominent over the centuries, partly for their proximity to Mâcon, partly as a tourist attraction for the mighty limestone bluffs that dominate them and the prehistoric traces that litter the district, partly for the chalky clay and sunny slopes that make their wine at least as good as any south Burgundy white.

Pierre Bréjoux describes it as 'masculine and long-lived', but variable according to the precise location of the vineyard in a country that is all bumps and dips. Such variations are not easy to follow where there are very few domaines of more than a few acres. The best I have tasted have been full-bodied and dry but rather half-hearted in flavour compared with, say, Meursault or a good Chablis. The growers' cooperative of Chaintré is much the biggest source of Pouilly-Fuissé.

The fact that wines of more or less equal value are produced in the surrounding area has given rise to two other appellations. The smaller Pouilly-Vinzelles (which includes Pouilly-Loché) has somehow failed to catch the public's eye. The much larger St-Véran, which scoops in eight villages, including the northern fringe of the Beaujolais country, was added as recently as 1971 and now offers extremely good value.

THE APPELLATIONS OF MACON

The Mâconnais has 5 appellations of its own and shares the right to 5 more with the rest of Burgundy. Its own appellations are:

FOR WHITE WINES

Mâcon Blanc. Chardonnay wine from delimited areas with a minimum 10 degrees of natural alcohol. This wine can also be labelled Pinot Chardonnay de Mâcon. Price (1982): 15 francs a bottle.

Mâcon Supérieur. The same with one more degree of alcohol.

Mâcon-Villages (or Mâcon- followed by the name of one of 43 villages in the eastern half of the region). The best known of these are Clessé, Prissé, Lugny, Viré and Chardonnay – the village with the credit for finding the noblest white grape of France. The minimum degree is 11, as for Mâcon Supérieur. Price (1982): 15 francs a bottle.

St-Véran. The same as for Mâcon-Villages but from 8 of the southernmost communes, overlapping into Beaujolais at St-Amour. The 8 are Chânes, Chasselas, Davayé, Leynes, Prissé, St-Amour, St-Vérand [*sic*] and part of Solutré, which is not in the appellation Pouilly-Fuissé. Davayé and Prissé lie to the north, the rest are to the south of Pouilly-Fuissé but offer very similar wines, which can also be sold as Beaujolais Blanc, Mâcon-Villages or Bourgogne Blanc if the customer prefers one of these names. If a particular vineyard is named on the label the minimum degree is 12, with the implication that the wine is better and more concentrated.

Pouilly-Fuissé. Chardonnay wine of 11 degrees from specified parts of the villages of Pouilly, Fuissé, Solutré, Vergisson and Chaintré. If a vineyard name is used it must have 12 degrees. Price (1982): 21 francs a bottle.

Pouilly-Vinzelles. The same rules as for Pouilly-Fuissé, but wine from the 2 villages of Vinzelles and Loché to the east – marginally less good but more than marginally cheaper.

FOR RED WINES

Mâcon Rouge. Gamay red wine of at least 9 degrees. It can also be made pink and offered as Mâcon Rosé. Price (1982): 10.50 francs a bottle.

Mâcon Supérieur. The same with an extra degree of alcohol and from certain specified zones. It can also be labelled as Mâcon- (followed by a village name), but *not* Mâcon-Villages.

GENERAL APPELLATIONS

Aligoté. As in the rest of Burgundy.

Bourgogne. For Chardonnay whites and Pinot Noir reds.

Bourgogne Grand Ordinaire. For whites.

Crémant de Bourgogne. As in the rest of Burgundy.

Passe-tout-grains. For Gamay and Pinot Noir (2:1) reds.

The Chante-Flûte

The region of Mercurey has its own equivalent of the Confrèrie des Chevaliers de Tastevin which sits in judgement on wines submitted for their special approval. Approved wines, which are always among the best of the region, wear a special label to signify that they have been 'Chante-Flûte.

Enjoying Mâcon and Beaujolais

White Mâcon is as adaptable as any French white wine for all-purpose use. Well chilled it is a good apéritif. Slightly less cold it serves the same purposes as more prestigious white burgundies. Beaujolais Nouveau, though often served alone, slightly chilled, as a party wine, can be very fatiguing and thirst-making – especially when (as often happens) its alcoholic degree is particularly high. Its cheerful properties are better appreciated with terrines or cheeses, picnic or kitchen food. Beaujolais crus of good vintages aged 3 or 4 years in bottle often begin to resemble fine Rhône wines – more rarely Côte d'Or wines. They are best served at the same temperature as red burgundy and with similar food.

MACON PRODUCERS

The great bulk of Mâcon, both white and red, is produced by the 18 growers' cooperatives of the area. The best known are those of Chaintré (for Pouilly-Fuissé), Lugny (for Mâcon-Lugny and Mâcon Rouge Supérieur), Prissé (Mâcon-Prissé and St-Véran) and Viré (Mâcon-Viré).

All except those marked with an asterisk are distributed by the Union des Coopératives Vinicoles de Bourgogne de Saône-et-Loire, Charnay-Les-Mâcon, 71008 Mâcon, which also offers a good Crémant de Bourgogne under various labels, among them Prince de Chardonne.

The following are the few individual producers with more than a local reputation. The average holding is about 10 acres, producing 2,000–3,000 cases a year.

Pouilly-Fuissé
Château de Beauregard, Fuissé, owner Georges Burrier
Clos de Bourg, Fuissé, owner Maurice Luquet
Joseph Corsin, Fuissé
Roger Duboeuf, Chaintré
Château de Fuissé, owner Marcel Vincent. The outstanding grower of the area.
Claude Guérin, Vergisson

Pouilly-Vinzelles
Jean Mathias, Chaintré

Mâcon-Clessé
Jean Thevenet, Quintaine-Clessé, Lugny

St-Véran
Lycée Agricole, Davayé
Georges Chagny, Leynes
Andre Chavet, Davayé
R. Duperron, Leynes

Mâcon-Viré
Clos du Chapitre, Viré, owner Jacques Depagneux
Château de Viré, Viré, owner Hubert Desbois

In addition very good wines are offered by several of the négociants well known for their Beaujolais; notably Georges Duboeuf, Thorin and Piat, and by Louis Latour, Robert Drouhin and Louis Jadot of Beaune.

CAVES COOPERATIVES

Production figures are for AOC wines only. Most of these coops also make a limited amount of *vin de table*, which is mostly sold in bulk.

Aze*
71260 Lugny. 447 acres; 150 members; 84,300 cases.

Bissey-sous-Cruchaud
71390 Buxy. 168 acres; 94 members; 26,700 cases.

Buxy*
71390 Buxy, 1,200 acres; 203,600 cases.

Chaintré
71570 La Chapelle de Guinchay. 412 acres; 163 members; 11,500 cases.

Chardonnay*
71700 Tournus. 363 acres; 150 members; 72,700 cases.

Charnay-Les-Mâcon
71000 Mâcon. 135 acres; 64 members; 27,650 cases.

Genouilly
71460 St-Gengoux Le National. 168 acres; 182 members; 16,600 cases.

Igé*
71960 Pierreclos. 543 acres; 109 members; 130,400 cases.

Lugny*
71260 Lugny. 2,084 acres; 469 members; 491,500 cases.

Mancey
71240 Sennecey-Le-Grand. 264 acres; 175 members; 39,000 cases.

Prissé
71960 Pierreclos. 741 acres; 237 members; 175,000 cases.

Sennece-Les-Mâcon*
71000 Mâcon. 93 acres; 108 members; 19,200 cases.

Sologny
71960 Pierreclos. 414 acres; 148 members; 87,400 cases.

Verzé
71960 Pierreclos. 415 acres; 100 members; 108,500 cases.

'La Vigne Blanche'
Clessé, 71260 Lugny. 259 acres; 83 members; 71,700 cases.

Vinzelles
71145 Vinzelles. 298 acres; 131 members; 61,300 cases.

Vire*
71260 Lugny. 629 acres; 237 members; 165,600 cases.

The hills of Beaujolais rise from the plain of the Saône to a height of more than 1,500 feet.

BEAUJOLAIS

The Beaujolais region is no more complex than its lighthearted wine. Twelve appellations take care of the whole 55,000 acres and the 12 or 13 million cases of wine they make every year. They could really be reduced to half a dozen without greatly grieving anyone but the gastronomes of Lyon. What is needed is a grasp of the essential grades of quality and a good address list – which need not be long.

The great majority of Beaujolais is made either by a growers' cooperative or by tiny properties. Two thousand five hundred Beaujolais makers have between two and ten acres – enough to make, say, up to 3,000 cases each. Another 1,400 have between 10 and 18 acres – which will keep their clients supplied, but scarcely make a reputation.

The details given here are therefore a guide to the major sources of Beaujolais, the merchants and cooperatives of the region, and a very short selection of some standard-setting properties.

The world's perception of Beaujolais today is very different from what it was 15 years ago. Beyond its own region and Paris, where it was *the* café wine, it used to be traded as a cut-price burgundy, imitating the weight of the Pinot Noirs of the Côte d'Or; by dint of picking as ripe as possible and adding plenty of sugar, achieving strength without grace. I have always been mystified by mid-nineteenth-century figures showing Beaujolais crus with 15 degrees of alcohol (while Médocs had 9 or 10 degrees). Very few red wines need anything like that strength, and least of all Gamay, which lacks the flavour to countenance it. The Gamay of Beaujolais has no great fruity flavour; well made and in the modern manner it lures you in with its sappy smell and a combination of soft juiciness and a slight nip – the perfect recipe for quenching thirst.

HOW BEAUJOLAIS IS MADE

The secret of the fresh grape fruitiness of Beaujolais lies in the way the Gamay – a grape of modest pretentions to quality – is handled and fermented. Wine-making in the Beaujolais combines the classic method of burgundy with *macération carbonique* – the activity of enzymes inside an uncrushed grape which, provided it is surrounded by carbon dioxide, causes an internal fermentation and the extraction of colour and flavour from the inner skin.

The trick is to fill the fermenting vat with grapes in their whole bunches, on their stalks, as little crushed and damaged as possible. In a modern Beaujolais *cuverie* a common way is to load the vat with a belt-elevator carrying the bunches to an opening in the top. The weight of the upper grapes crushes the lower ones, which start a normal fermentation with their natural yeasts. The carbon dioxide given off by this (helped along with gas from a bottle, if necessary) blankets off the air from the uncrushed upper layers. Here the grapes quietly feed on themselves, many of them splitting in the process. After six or seven days the vat is about one third full of wine. The liquid is then run off, the solid pressed and the two products blended together. In normal red-wine making the *vin de presse* is in a minority (and may not be used at all). In the Beaujolais method it accounts for between two thirds and three quarters of the total. At this stage the juice still has unfermented sugar in it. Fermentation has to finish before it is stable enough to be called wine. The law says that this will happen by 15 November, but in years when the harvest is late some fairly brutal methods of stabilization are needed to 'finish' the wine in time.

THE APPELLATIONS OF BEAUJOLAIS

Most basic is plain Beaujolais, from the southern half of the region, south of Villefranche, where the Gamay is encouraged to produce large quantities on heavy soil. (Although there is nothing to stop growers anywhere in Beaujolais using the appellation.) This is essentially now-or-never wine, originally destined to be sold on draught in local cafés and by the carafe in restaurants. It is best drunk as young as possible. The date after which it can be sold *en primeur* is 15 November. The term *nouveau*, while often used with the same intention, really only means the wine of the last harvest, until the next. The minimum alcoholic degree is 9, but this is regularly exceeded either naturally or by adding sugar. For this reason the appellation Beaujolais Supérieur, only different in requiring 10 degrees, is little used. 'Beaujolais' applies to red, white or rosé, but the great majority is red.

Total area is 22,035 acres; average production 5,679,077 cases a year.

Price (1982): 11.40 francs.

GROWERS

Alain Bidon
Chessy-Les-Mines, 69380 Lozanne, with 30 acres.

Robert Doat
Domaine de Bois Franc, Jarnioux, 69640 Denice, with 53 acres.

Jean Garlon
Beauvallon, Theizé, 69620 Le Bois d'Oingt, with 7.5 acres.

Régis Manus
'La Paisible', 69480 Anse, with 16 acres.

Jean Pagnon
Morance, 69480 Anse, with 15 acres.

Antoine Pein
Theizé, 69620 Le Bois d'Oingt, with 30 acres.

COOPERATIVES

Beau Vallon
Theizé, 69620 Le Bois d'Oingt, with 813 acres.

Bois d'Oingt
69620 Bois d'Oingt, with 144 members, 529 acres and 97,000 cases.

Soc. Viticole Beaujolaise
Liergues, 69400 Villefranche, with 1,100 acres and 239 members.

Member of the Eventail de Vignerons Producteurs is **Tissier-Depardon** near Chânes.

BEAUJOLAIS-VILLAGES

The northern half of the region, or Haut-Beaujolais, has steeper hills, warmer (because lighter and more sandy) soil, and makes better wine. Beaujolais-Villages is the appellation that covers the whole of this area, 30 villages in all, but 9 small zones in the north, identified by combinations of slopes and soils that are peculiar to themselves, are singled out as the Beaujolais 'crus' – the aristocrats.

Beaujolais-Villages makes a better *vin de primeur* than plain Beaujolais, except in untypically hot vintages. It has a minimum of 10 degrees alcohol and more backing of fruit and body – more flavour, in fact – to complement the rasp of new fruit juice. It is almost always worth its fairly modest premium, both *en primeur* and even more when it has been or will be kept. Good Villages is at its best in the summer after the vintage, and can hold for another year. Besides the 'crus', the region as a whole has some producers whose wines are regularly up to 'cru' standards.

Total area is 15,193 acres; average production 3,784,477 cases a year.

Price (1982): 12.25 francs.

GROWERS

Etienne Jambon
Château Thulon, Lantigné, 69430 Beaujeu, with 30 acres.

Claude & Michelle Joubert
Lantigné, 69430 Beaujeu, with 20 acres.

Durieu de Lacarelle
Dom. de Lacarelle, St-Etienne-des-Oullières, 69830 St-Georges de Reneins, with 345 acres.

René Miolane
Le Cellier, Salles, 69830 St-Georges de Reneins, with 34 acres.

Monternot
'Les Places', Blace, 69830 St-George de Reneins, with 20 acres.

Gilles Perroud
'Le Basty', Lantigné, 69430 Beaujeu, with 30 acres.

André Vernus
'Le Pouzet', St-Etienne-La-Varenne, 69830 St-Georges de Reneins, 20 acres.

Cave Coopérative (Soc. Viticole Beaujolaise)
Liergues, 69400 Villefranche (Appellation Beaujolais), with 239 members and 1,111 acres.

Members of the Eventail de Vignerons Producteurs include **Tissier-Depardon** and **Henri Fontaine** at Leynes.

THE 'CRUS' OF BEAUJOLAIS

The map shows that between the railway along the Saône valley and the 450-metre contour line in the Beaujolais mountains to the west, from just south of Belleville to the boundary with the Mâconnais, the vine has the landscape to itself. Sandy, stony or schistous granite-based soils without lime give the Gamay a roundness and depth of flavour it lacks elsewhere. Here it is pruned hard and trimmed plant by plant as an individual. The minimum strength of the wine is the same as for all the Villages, but when it is sold with a vineyard name the required minimum is a degree higher.

Cru Beaujolais can be offered *en primeur*, but not until a month after Beaujolais and Villages, from 15 December. It would be a pity to prevent it being poured for Christmas. The best crus are never treated in this way; they are kept in barrel or vat until at least the March after the vintage. Their full individuality and sweet juicy smoothness take anything from six months to six years in bottle to develop. Three of the crus, Morgon, Chénas and above all Moulin-à-Vent, are looked on as *vins de garde*, at least by Beaujolais standards.

BROUILLY

The southernmost and the largest of the crus, enveloping areas in 5 villages (Odenas, St-Lager, Cercié, Charentay, St-Etienne-La-Varenne and Quincié) grouped around the isolated Mont de Brouilly (*see* Côtes de Brouilly). The word 'typical' is most often used for Brouilly – not surprisingly for the biggest producer lying in the very heart of the region. This means the wine is full of grapey flavour and vigour but not aggressive in its first year.

Total area is 2,917 acres; average production 745,222 cases a year. Price (1982): 19.50 francs.

Château de Briante
Mme de Buttet, St-Lager, 69220 Belleville.

Château de la Chaize
M. de Roussy de Salles, Odenas, 69830 St-Georges de Reneins. The biggest estate in Beaujolais with 360 acres.

Philippe Dutraive
Dom. des Combes, Charentay, 69220 Belleville.

Claude Geoffray
Le Grand Vernay, Charentay, 69220 Belleville.

Château de Nervers
M. de Chabannes, Odenas, 69830 St-Georges de Reneins.

Château de Pierreux
Marquise de Toulzouet, Odenas, 69830 St-Georges de Reneins.

Cave Coopérative de Bel-Air
St-Jean d'Ardières, 69220 Belleville, with 276 members and 1,080 acres (*see also* Côtes de Brouilly).

Members of the Eventail de Vignerons Producteurs are **André Ronzière** at Bonnège, Charentay; **André Large** at Odenas; **Lucien** and **Robert Verger**.

CHENAS

The smallest cru, sheltered from the west by a wooded hill (Chénas is derived from *chêne*, an oak) and including part of the commune of La Chapelle-de-Guinchay. Certain Chénas wines achieve formidable strengths, but its vineyard sites are too varied for the appellation to be readily identifiable or its style reliable.

Total area is 625 acres; average production 138,677 cases a year.

Price (1982): 21 francs.

Domaine Champagnon
Les Brureaux, Chénas, 69840 Juliénas.

Fernand Charvet
Le Bourg, Chénas, 69840 Juliénas:

Château de Jean Loron
Gabriel Desvignes, 71570 La Chapelle-de-Guinchay.

Emile Robin
Le Bois Retour, Chénas, 69840 Juliénas.

Cave du Château de Chénas (Coopérative)
Chénas, 69840 Juliénas, with 286 members and a total of 664 acres (not all in Chénas).

COTES DE BROUILLY

The slopes of the Mont de Brouilly give a stronger, more concentrated wine than the surrounding appellation Brouilly, but in much smaller quantities. The minimum degree here is 10.5 – the highest in Beaujolais. These wines are said to develop the high-toned scent of violets after 2 or 3 years in bottle. Certainly after warm vintages they benefit from keeping that long.

Total area is 707 acres; average production 169,144 cases a year.

Price (1982): 19.51 francs.

Château Delachanal
M. Leffert, Odenas, 69830 St-Georges de Reneins.

Château Thivin
Mme Geoffray, Odenas, 69830 St-Georges de Reneins.

Mme Veuve Joubert
La Poyebade, Odenas, 69830 St-Georges de Reneins.

Cave Coopérative de Bel-Air
St-Jean d'Ardières, 69220 Belleville, with 276 members and 1,080 acres (appellation Brouilly, Côte de Brouilly, Morgon, Beaujolais and Villages).

FLEURIE

The pretty name, a substantial supply and a singular freshness of flavour all contribute to making this the most memorable and popular Beaujolais cru. Fleurie is often irresistible in its first year, with the result that the full, sweet silkiness of its maturity at 3 or 4 years is little known.

Total area is 1,930 acres; average production 464,144 cases a year.

Price (1982): 21 francs.

M. Darroze
Clos des quatre vents, 69820 Fleurie.

Château de Fleurie
Mme Roclore, Mâcon 71000.

Logis du Vivier
Mlle Yvonne Couibes, 69820 Fleurie.

Société Civile du Château de Poncié
69820 Fleurie.

Marcel Rollet
69820 Fleurie.

Cave Coopérative des Grands Vins de Fleurie
69820 Fleurie, with 309 members and 891 acres.

The member of the Eventail de Vignerons Producteurs is **Maurice Bruone** at Montgenas, who produces about 1,000 cases a year.

CHIROUBLES

All southeast facing on the higher slopes, making some of the best-balanced and most-prized Beaujolais in limited quantities. This is the first cru to be 'supple and tender' for the eager Paris restaurateurs.

Total area is 790 acres; average production 196,388 cases a year.

Price (1982): 19.5 francs.

Domaine Emile Cheysson
Les Farges, 69115 Chiroubles, with 54 acres.

Château Javernand
M. Fourneau, 69115 Chiroubles, with 47 acres.

Domaine du Moulin
Mlle Dory, Le Bourg, 69115 Chiroubles, with 42 acres.

Château Les Pres
Héritiers de Raousset, 69115 Chiroubles, with 25 acres.
Cave Coopérative (Maison des Chiroubles)
69115 Chiroubles, with 66 members and 212 acres.
Cave Coopérative Vinicole
69115 Chiroubles.
Members of the Eventail de Vignerons Producteurs are **Christian Lafay, René Savoye, Georges Passot** at Grosse Pierre, **Philippe Govet**.

JULIENAS

With St-Amour, the northernmost cru (the *département* boundary between Rhône and Saône-et-Loire runs between them). Substance, strong colour and vigour, even tannin, mean that Juliénas needs 2 years or more to age. It is considered mealtime Beaujolais rather than a thirst quencher.

Total area is 1,350 acres; average production 336,800 cases a year.

Price (1982): 21 francs.

Ernest Aujas
69840 Juliénas.
Château des Capitans
Bernard Sarrau, 69840 Juliénas.
M. Foillard
Dom. de la Dime, 69830 St-Georges de Reneins.
Château Juliénas
M. Condemine, 69840 Juliénas.
M. J. Perrachon
Dom. Bottière, 69840 Juliénas.
M. P. Poulachon
71000 Mâcon.
Domaine de la Vieille Eglise
Héritiers Paul Loron, Pontanevaux, 71570 La Chapelle-de-Guinchay.
Cave Coopérative des Grands Vins de Juliénas
69840 Juliénas.
Members of the Eventail de Vignerons Producteurs are the **Château de Juliénas'** Monnet vineyard and **André Pelleier**.

MORGON

The wide spread of vineyards around Villié-Morgon, between Brouilly and Fleurie, are credited with a character so peculiar that '*morgonner*' has become a verb for a way that other wines sometimes (when they are lucky) behave. The soil here is schistous, and the peculiarity is described as a flavour of wild cherries. I have not found them so identifiable as this suggests, but they are among the bigger and longest-lasting wines of Beaujolais.

Total area is 2,530 acres; average production 617,344 cases a year.

Price (1982): 19.5 francs

Paul Collonge
Domaine de Ruyère, 69910 Villié-Morgon.
Jean Ernest Demont
Javernière, 69910 Villié-Morgon, with 10 acres.
Louis Desvignes
Le Bourg, 69910 Villié-Morgon, with 20 acres.
G.F.A. Domaine Lièven, Château de Bellevue
69910 Villié-Morgon, with 29 acres.
Pierre Piron
Morgon, 69910 Villié-Morgon, with 30 acres.
Domaine du Py
Pierre Savoye, Les Micouds, 69910 Villié-Morgon, with 33 acres.
Général Jacques de Zelicourt
Le Bourg, 69910 Villié-Morgon.
Members of the Eventail de Vignerons Producteurs are **Georges Brun, Louis Genillon** and **Louis Desvignes**.

MOULIN-A-VENT

There is no village of Moulin-à-Vent, but a sailless windmill among the hamlets between Romanèche-Thorins and Chénas gives its name to the most 'serious' and expensive Beaujolais appellation. Moulin-à-Vent *en primeur* is almost a contradiction in terms. It should be firm, meaty and savoury wine that has less of the surging scent of Beaujolais in its first year but builds up a bouquet resembling burgundy in bottle. Some growers age it briefly in small oak barrels to add to the structure that will preserve it. Moulin-à-Vent is always served last in a Beaujolais meal, often with the cheeses, which will dominate the lighter wines (and it, too, as often as not).

Total area is 1,490 acres; average production 374,000 cases a year.

Price (1982): 26 francs.

Propriété Bourisset
Fermier des Hospices de Romanèche, Romanèche-Thorins, 71570 La Chapelle-de-Guinchay.
Château des Jacques
Dom. J. Thorin, Romanèche-Thorins, 71570 La Chapelle-de-Guinchay.
Propriété Labruyère
Romanèche-Thorins, 71570 La Chapelle-de-Guinchay.
Domaine Monrozier
Les Moriers, 69820 Fleurie.
Château du Moulin-à-Vent
Mme Bloud, Romanèche-Thorins, 71570 La Chapelle-de-Guinchay.
Domaine de la Tour du Bief
Chénas, 69840 Juliénas.
Cave du Château de Chénas
Chénas, 69840 Juliénas.
(Appellation Chénas and Moulin à Vent), with 286 members and 685 acres.
Members of the Eventail de Vignerons Producteurs are **Raymond Degrange** at Romanèche; **Raymond Degrange** and the **Héritiers Devillaine; Alphonse Mortet** and **Jean Brugne** at Vivier and Fleurie.

ST-AMOUR

The one Beaujolais appellation in the Mâconnais – its white wine is entitled to the appellation St-Véran. The power of suggestion is strong, so its promising name may have some bearing on my predilection for this wine. I find it next to Fleurie and Chiroubles in delicacy and sweetness – pleading to be drunk young, yet tasting even better after 2 or 3 years in bottle. As one of the smallest areas it is, alas, not often seen.

Price (1982): 20 francs.

Total area is 650 acres; average production 154,000 cases a year.

Domaine des Billards
Mme Jean Teissier, Les Charmilles, 71000 Mâcon; and Mme Jean Barbet, Pontanevaux, 71570 La Chapelle-de-Guinchay.
M. Perrichon
Dom. de la Pirolette, St-Amour-Bellevue, 71570 La Chapelle-de-Guinchay.
Château de St-Amour
M. Siraudin, St-Amour-Bellevue, 71570 La Chapelle-de-Guinchay.
Paul Spay
Au Bourg, St-Amour-Bellevue 71570 La Chapelle-de-Guinchay.
Cave Coopérative du Bois de la Salle
69840 Juliénas (Appellation Juliénas and St-Amour), with 272 members and 770 acres.
Members of the Eventail de Vignerons Producteurs are **Patissier** and **Finaz Devillaine.**

MERCHANTS OF BEAUJOLAIS AND MACON

Aujoux & Cie
St-Georges de Reneins
A Swiss-owned company which supplies a great deal of Beaujolais in bulk to Switzerland. Their own vineyards surround their cellars. The Aujoux label is seen particularly in Scandinavia.

Paul Beaudet
Pontanaveux, 71570 La Chapelle-de-Guinchay.
Fourth-generation family firm run by Paul's son Jean, well known in top restaurants and in the USA for its own Domaine Chénas and other good wines.

Bouchacourt
Le Fief, Chénas, 69840 Juliénas.
A small merchant with a good reputation. His wines are often seen in Paris restaurants.

Caves de Champclos
route de Beaujeu, 69220 Belleville.
A small firm dealing in quality wines.

Chanut Frères
Romanèche-Thorins, 71570 La Chapelle-de-Guinchay.
A family company of moderate size, recently expanding into the supermarket business.

Chevalier Fils
Charnay Les Mâcon, 71000 Mâcon,
An old-established family company dealing in above-average quality wines in both bottle and bulk; also make sparkling wine under their own label.

David & Foillard
69830 St-Georges de Reneins
Reputedly the biggest firm of négociants in the Rhône, with wide international trade.

Georges Duboeuf
Romanèche-Thorins, 71570 La Chapelle-de-Guinchay.
A young, dynamic and skilful company, leader in the café, hotel and restaurant (not supermarket) business. Duboeuf is widely regarded as 'Mr. Beaujolais'.

Pierre Ferraud
31 rue Marechal Foch, 69220 Belleville.
A small company with one of the highest reputations for quality.

Jacquemont Père & Fils
Romanèche-Thorins, 71570 La Chapelle-de-Guinchay.
Not a label you will see, but the biggest *commissionaires* or middlemen in Beaujolais.

Loron & Fils
Pontanevaux, 71570 La Chapelle-de-Guinchay.
A large, high-quality family business, formerly mainly dealing in bulk but now selling more and more in bottle, under several brand names. Offers some good domaine wines and good-value, non-appellation *vins de marque*.

Mommessin
La Grange St-Pierre, 71009 Mâcon.
Until recently a very traditional family business, now diversifying into *vins de marque* as well as Beaujolais, where it has exclusive arrangements with several good domaines. The house also owns the Grand Cru Clos de Tart in the Côte de Nuits.

Ph. Moreau
4 rue G. Lecomte, 71000 Mâcon.
A small family company of good repute.

François Paquet
St-Lager, 69840 St-Georges de Reneins.
A family firm which started with simple *vins de café*, now stronger in Beaujolais and Mâconnais appellation wines.

Pasquier-Desvignes
St-Lager, 69220 Belleville.
A company with a long history but modern ideas, diversified into *vins de pays* and VDQS wines as well as Beaujolais, particularly in supermarkets. Their Beaujolais brand is Le Marquisat.

Pellerin
A subsidiary of Rivat, a major Lyon *vin de table* specialist. Owners of Château des Capitans, Juliénas, where they also make their own Fleurie and Morgon.

Piat
71570 La Chapelle-de-Guinchay
Founded in Mâcon in 1849. Now one of the biggest firms, especially in export, belonging to International Distillers and Vintners. Moved to very modern premises in 1980. Uses a special 'Piat' bottle, based on the traditional 'pot' of Beaujolais, for a classic range of Beaujolais and Mâcon wines, including a good standard Beaujolais and Mâcon-Viré. Also red and white branded table wines 'Piat d'Or'.

Sarrau
St-Jean d'Ardières, 69220 Belleville.
A dynamic and imaginative young company, both growers and merchants. They have a branch on La Réunion!

Louis Tête
St-Didier sur Beaujeu, 69430 Beaujeu.
A specialist in the high-class restaurant trade, particularly well known in Switzerland.

Thorin
Pontanevaux, 71570 La Chapelle-de-Guinchay.
A traditional family company, owners of the superb Château des Jacques in Moulin-à-Vent and Ch. de Loyses, Beaujolais Blanc. Trade is largely in bottled wines. Their supermarket brand is Faye.

Trenel Fils
Le Voisinet, Charney Les Mâcons, 71000 Mâcon.
A small family affair with a very good local reputation, particularly in Mâcon restaurants. They also produce delectable crème de cassis and framboise.

Valette
77 route de Lyon, 71000 Mâcon.
A subsidiary of the Société des Vins de France, the same company as Lionel J. Bruck in Nuits St-Georges.

The Eventail de Vignerons Producteurs

This establishment at Corcelles-en-Beaujolais is a group of conscientious small producers from all parts of the region and the southern Mâconnais who make their own wine but collaborate in bottling and marketing it. Their average holdings are between 12 and 25 acres. Their central cellars offer a fascinating range of the products of the region. The names of members of the Eventail (the word means 'fan') are given below those of other recommended producers under each appellation.

JURA

Connoisseurs of the French countryside each have their favourite corner. I hope never to be forced to make a final choice, but I have a shortlist ready, and the Jura is on it.

These limestone mountains (they give their name to a whole epoch of geology – the Jurassic) roll up towards Switzerland from the plain of the Saône in Burgundy. Halfway in a straight line from Beaune to Geneva you come to the delicious timbered and tiled little town of Arbois, where Pasteur lived, then Poligny, then Château-Chalon, the heart of a completely original wine country. The Jura vineyards are small (much smaller than they once were; currently 2,800 acres and growing). But their origins are as old as Burgundy's, their climate and soil singular and their grapes their own.

Jura producers are fond of making a wide range of wines, from *méthode champenoise* sparkling to *vin jaune*. The overall appellation, for everything except *vin jaune*, is Côtes du Jura. This appellation covers a long strip of country from north of Arbois to south of Cousance. Arbois is another general AC with higher alcohol stipulated. L'Etoile covers whites and *vins de paille* from the valley around L'Etoile to the south of the region.

The vineyard sits on a band of heavy clay, rich in lime, exposed along the mountain slopes between 900 and 1,350 feet high. Woods, bovine pastures and limestone cliffs constantly interrupt the continuity of the vines. Unlike Alsace to the north, which lies in the rain shadow of the Vosges, the west-facing Jura is often deluged by summer rain. Hail is a frequent problem here. But September and October are usually sunny. Jura grapes have been selected because they thrive in deep damp soil, given a good sun-warmed slope. The most widespread is the Poulsard – a pale red which is the nearest thing to a rosé grape. Another obscure red, the Trousseau, is grown with it to stiffen its too 'supple' wine. Pinot Noir is increasingly added to give more colour and backbone to red wine – but red is in a minority: most of the wine is rosé, fermen-

Arbois

ted on its pale skins as though intended to be red.

Nowadays the Chardonnay is the standard grape for light white wines; it performs well here (under the alias of Melon d'Arbois or Gamay Blanc) but certainly not spectacularly. Much of it is made into sparkling wine. But the real speciality is a local variant of the Traminer called the Savagnin or Nature. Savagnin is a late ripener and a small cropper, but its wine is powerful in alcohol and flavour. Used merely for topping up barrels of Chardonnay it gives them, as they age, a marvellously rustic style. Used alone it behaves in a most peculiar way that makes it comparable with fino sherry. The young wine is left in old barrels with a history of making *vin jaune*, not filled to the top but in the normally perilous state of 'ullage'. A flor yeast, presumably residing in the barrel wood, rapidly grows as a film on the surface of the wine, excluding direct contact with oxygen. The wine is left thus, for a statutory minimum of six years, without being topped up. At the end of six years, a miraculous stability has (or should have) come over it. A finished *vin jaune* is an impressive apéritif, intense in flavour, obviously slightly oxidized but long and fine and altogether worthwhile. The commune (not château) of Château-Chalon is famous for the best, although good *vins jaunes* are made all over the area. Wine produced in such restricted quantities (and by no means every year), then aged for six years, is inevitably expensive. Like Tokay it comes in smaller than standard bottles that help to disguise the price. (The *clavelin* of the Jura, long-necked and hunch-shouldered, holds 64 centilitres.) I cannot pretend it is anything like as good value, as reliable, or even as delicious, as a first-class fino sherry. But it exists – and as wine lovers we should be grateful for variety and support it, especially in such time-honoured forms as this.

Another time-honoured regional speciality, *vin de paille*, has virtually disappeared – at least in its authentic form. It was made by hanging bunches of grapes in the rafters (or laying them on straw – *paille* – mats) to dry and concentrate their sweetness in the manner of Italian Vin Santo.

The Jura vineyard was decimated by phylloxera and took many years to recover. Today it thrives – largely on the tourist trade and faithful private customers in France. There are 1,000 growers, but only 200 who make more than 330 cases a year, and only about a dozen with more than 30 acres.

JURA PRODUCERS

Château d'Arlay

Arlay, 39140 Bletterans.

The Jura's one lordly estate, descended in the same family since the 12th century, when it was a Hapsburg stronghold, and at various times in the hands of the Prince of Orange, William the Silent, the English King William III and almost but not quite Frederick the Great of Prussia. The present owners, the Count and Countess Renaud de Laguiche, can claim indirect descent not only from this galaxy of monarchs but also have family ties with the Marquis de Laguiche of Montrachet, the de Vogüés of Champagne and Chambolle-Musigny, and the Ladoucettes of Pouilly-Fumé. As for their vines, some 160 acres are being progressively reconstituted with the help of a well-known *vigneron* from Champagne, Georges Vesselle of Bouzy. At present they produce a pale Pinot Noir red, the usual Jura rosé, white wine of Chardonnay topped up with Savagnin, and *vin jaune*.

Caves Jean Bourdy

Arlay, 39140 Bletterans.

A cornerstone of the Jura wine industry, dating back to the 16th century, with bottles of such famous vintages as 1820 and 1784 still in the cellars. Jean Bourdy retired in 1979 after 52 years to be succeeded by his son Christian. Their model Jura wines come from 1 acre in Château-Chalon (all Savagnin) and 12 in Arlay, where they make red, rosé and Chardonnay white as well as *vin juane*. Sales of 2,500 cases are 85% in France – like most Jura *vignerons,* mainly to private clients.

Hubert Clavelin

Le Vernois, 39210 Voiteur.

The proprietor of 38 acres between Château-Chalon and L'Etoile, highly regarded by his neighbours for his Côtes du Jura red, white and 'yellow', and his *méthode champenoise* Brut. His name recalls the unique long-necked pint bottle used uniquely for *vin jaune*.

Château Gréa

Rotalier, 39190 Beaufort.

A mere 14 acres, but the pride of the Gréa family for nearly 300 years. Their descendants the de Boissieus have owned it since 1962 and made it the quality leader of the southern Côtes du Jura.

Their specialities are Le Clos, a light Chardonnay white, Le Chanet, a blend of Chardonnay with Savagnin which gives a much more forceful *vin de garde*, a rosé called Sur La Roche and a *vin jaune* of pure Savagnin, En Cury.

Henri Maire

Château-Montfort, 39600 Arbois.

Very much the biggest producer and marketer of Jura wines and a principal force behind the reestablishment of what was a dwindling wine region. Imaginative and aggressive sales strategy has made Maire a household name. The very modern Maire domaines, with wide-spaced vines, cover some 750 acres, of which the chief are Montfort (150 acres), Grange Grillard (125), Sorbief (150) and La Croix d'Argis (200). They produce a vast range of wines under all the Jura appellations, plus many brand names. Sparkling Vin Fou is perhaps the best known; its name is on street corners all over France. One of my favourites is the pale dry rosé, or *vin gris*, called Cendré de Novembre. Some of the reds are distinctly sweet – not to my taste. Up to 90% of annual sales of over 400,000 cases is by mail order and door-to-door salesmen in France. Henri Maire has also been a regular buyer of fine burgundies at the Hospices de Beaune auction, and ships Souverain wines from California to France.

Désiré Petit & Fils

Pupillin, 39600 Arbois.

Gérard and Marcel are the two Petit '*fils*' who own and operate this old family property of nearly 30 acres, divided into 16 little parcels in the sheltered coomb of Pupillin, and neighbouring Arbois and Grozon. The property was modernized in 1979: stainless steel and old casks stand side by side. The vines are 40% Poulsard, 30% Chardonnay, 15% Pinot Noir, 13% Savagnin and 2% Trousseau.

Domaine de la Pinte

39600 Arbois

A modern estate created by Roger Martin in 1955 on abandoned vineyard land of the chalky clay loved by the Savagnin. 30 of his 62.5 acres are white grapes, 27 Poulsard for rosé and the rest Trousseau and Pinot Noir for red. All is appellation Arbois if it reaches the necessary alcoholic degree (11.5° for rosé, 12° for white and 14° for *vin jaune*). 20% of 8,300 cases is exported.

J. Reverchon & Fils

GAEC de Chantemerle, 39800 Poligny.

A third-generation family of growers with only 15 acres (appellation Côtes du Jura) but a typically wide range of hand-made wines in small quantities – including *vin jaune*, *méthode champenoise* and Macvin, as well as many small lots of red, white and rosé, in a grand total of 2,000 cases. Dispatch is no problem: tourists take it all away with them.

Jacques Tissot

39600 Arbois

A 30-acre property of no great age but recommended by discerning judges for its Arbois wines of all colours.

Vandelle Père & Fils

Château de l'Etoile, GAEC, 39570 Lons le Saunier.

The Château de l'Etoile exists no more, but the Vandelle family have 40 acres of its land in production and 17 more planted. Their specialities are Vin Blanc de l'Etoile of Chardonnay, *vin jaune*, Macvin, the local 'ratafia' of grape juice and brandy, and *méthode champenoise* Brut. Rosé is made from Poulsard alone and red from a mixture of Trousseau, Gamay and Pinot Noir, both in wooden vats. Very few of their annual 80,000 bottles leaves France.

CAVES COOPERATIVES

Arbois

39600 Arbois

Founded 1906. 130 members; 370 acres; 60,000 cases AOC wines: Arbois red, white and rosé. The oldest and biggest of the Jura coops.

Château-Chalon et Côtes du Jura

39120 Voiteur

Founded 1958. 68 members; 158 acres; 20,000 cases AOC wines: Côtes du Jura white and rosé, Château-Chalon Jaune, Côtes du Jura Jaune. The only cooperative producing Château-Chalon.

L'Etoile

L'Etoile, 39570 Lons-Le-Saunier.

Founded 1912. 18 members; 25 acres; 2,500 cases AOC wine: L'Etoile. A little white-wine-only cellar.

Poligny, Caveau des Jacobins

39800 Poligny

Founded 1907. 12 members; 61.7 acres; 9,000 cases AOC wine: Côtes du Jura red, rosé and white. Perhaps the prettiest cooperative in France, occupying a splendid old deconsecrated church in the centre of the lovely little town. Huge barrels stand under the soaring vaulted pillars. By modern standards, however, the wine barely passes muster.

Pupillin

39600 Arbois

Founded 1909. 25 members; 79 acres; 10,500 cases AOC wines: Arbois-Pupillin white, red, rosé; Côtes du Jura white and rosé. Pupillin is a perfect little example of a Jura country village, with only 192 inhabitants, all living by and for the vine.

SAVOIE

The wine country of Savoie follows the river Rhône south from the Lake of Geneva, then lines the Lac du Bourget around Aix-Les-Bains, then hugs the sides of the valley south of Chambéry and turns the corner eastwards into the Val d'Isère. It exists more as opportunistic outbreaks than as a cohesive vineyard. Its appellations are consequently complicated: more so than its simple, fresh and invigorating wine.

Three quarters of Savoie wine is white, based on half a dozen different grapes. Along the south shore of the Lake of Geneva (Haute Savoie) it is the Chasselas, the grape the Swiss know as Fendant. Crépy is the best-known cru, with Marignan, Ripaille and Marin, all light and often sharp wines. Ayze has a name for its sharpish *pétillant*.

Seyssel is your opportunity to win a bet. Few people realize or remember that it is France's northernmost Rhône wine. The grapes here are Roussette (alias Altesse) and Molette: Roussette, the aristocrat of Savoie, reaches a relatively high degree of sugar, body and flavour; Molette is a mild little thing. Seyssel has built an international reputation by developing its naturally fizzy tendency into fully fledged *méthode champenoise* sparkling. The firm of Varichon & Clerc, who are the specialists, produce a singularly delicate and delicious *cuvée* – quite one of France's best – but demand seems to have outrun supply; they have been forced to buy grapes outside the area and relabel it Blanc de Blancs Mousseux.

Still or *pétillant*, dry or sometimes slightly sweet Roussette wines with local reputations are made along the Rhône valley and the Lac du Bourget at Frangy, Marestel and Monthoux. Occasional super-vintages put them on a level with Vouvray.

The third principal white grape, and the commonest of the region, is the Jacquère. South of Seyssel, still on the Rhône, the district of Chautagne, centred on its cooperative at Ruffieux, makes Jacquère white and the grape dominates the vineyards south of Chambéry: Chignin, Apremont, Abymes and Montmélian. Chignin has the best southern hillside exposure. Its Jacquère fetches a franc more a bottle than its neighbours, Apremont and Les Abymes.

Suburbia is invading these lovely vineyards fast. Montmélian, a little alpine village a few years ago, is now hideous with housing estates. So far the red-wine vineyards on the slopes of the Val d'Isère are almost intact, but I suspect not for long. Their centre is the *cave coopérative* at Cruet, serving Cruet, Arbin, Montmélian and St-Jean de la Porte. Much its best wine, to my mind, is its Mondeuse (especially that of Arbin). Gamay is ten centimes more, and Pinot Noir another two francs, but Mondeuse is the character: a dark, slightly tannic, smooth but intensely lively wine that reminds me a little of Chinon, the 'raspberry' red of the Loire.

There are other local specialities too: Roussette is the highest priced white of the Cruet cooperative; a yellow, full-bodied, slightly bitter wine you might take for an Italian. And Chignin grows the Bergeron, either a rare local grape or (say some) the Roussanne of the (lower) Rhône. This is the only Savoyard white wine that ages with distinction.

Savoie's AOCs are shadowed by the VDQS Bugey to the west on the way to Lyon, with an even more complex set of names, hard to justify in reality. The white VDQS is Roussette de Bugey, although the rules only demand Roussette grapes if a village name is used (the 'crus' are Anglefort, Arbignieu, Chanay, Langieu, Montagnieu and Virieu-Le-Grand). Plain Roussette de Bugey can contain Chardonnay. VDQS Vin de Bugey is red, rosé or white and also has its crus: Virieu-Le-Grand, Montagnieu, Manicle, Machuraz and Cerdon. Cerdon, in turn, is also an individual VDQS for sparkling *mousseux* and merely fizzy *pétillant*.

SAVOIE PRODUCERS

ABYMES
Cave Coopérative 'Le Vigneron Savoyard', 73190 Apremont (also for Apremont, Gamay, Mondeuse, Vin de Pays de Grésivaudan).

APREMONT
Cave Coopérative 'Le Vigneron Savoyard' (as above),
Pierre Boniface, 73800 Les Marches.
Jean-Claude Perret, 73800 Les Marches, and many others.

AYZE
Marcel Fert, 74130 Marignier.

CHIGNIN
J-F Girard-Madoux, 73800 Chignin.

CHIGNIN AND CHIGNIN-BERGERON
The Quénard family (5 separate branches: André, Claude, Jean-Pierre, Raymond, René) 73800 Chignin.

CHAUTAGNE
Cave Coopérative de Chautagne, 73310 Ruffieux.

CRÉPY
L. Mercier & Fils, 74140 Douvaine.

CRUET
Cave Coopérative de Vente des Vins Fins, 73800 Cruet (also for Chignin, Roussette de Savoie, Gamay, Mondeuse, Pinot, Arbin, *mousseux* and *pétillant*).

FRANGY
Jean Neyroud & Fils, 74270 Designy.

MARESTEL
Henri Jeandet, 73170 Jongieux.

MARIGNAN
Canelli-Suchet, La Tour de Marignan, 74140 Sciez.

MARIN
Claude Delalex, 74200 Marin.

MONTERMINOD
Château de Monterminod, 73190 Challes-Les-Eaux.

MONTHOUX
Michel Million Rousseau, 73170 St-Jean-de-Chevelu.

MONTMELIAN
Cave Coopérative de Vente des Vins Fins, 73800 Montmélian (also Abymes, Apremont, Chignin, Marestel, Chignin-Bergeron, Gamay, Mondeuse, Arbin, Chautagne).
Louis Magnin, 73800 Arbin (also red Arbin).

RIPAILLE
Fichard (négociant), Grands Chais Léman/Mont-Blanc, 74170 Chens-sur-Léman.
Château de Ripaille

SEYSSEL
Etablissements Donati (J. Quénard), 73000 Barberaz.
Georges Mollex, 01420 Corbonod.
Domaine de la Taconnière, 01420 Seyssel.
J. Perrier & Fils, 73800 Les Marches.
Varichon & Clerc (négociants: sparkling specialists). 014120 Seyssel. General negociants for Savoie wines.

Weighing grapes at a cave coopérative

LOIRE

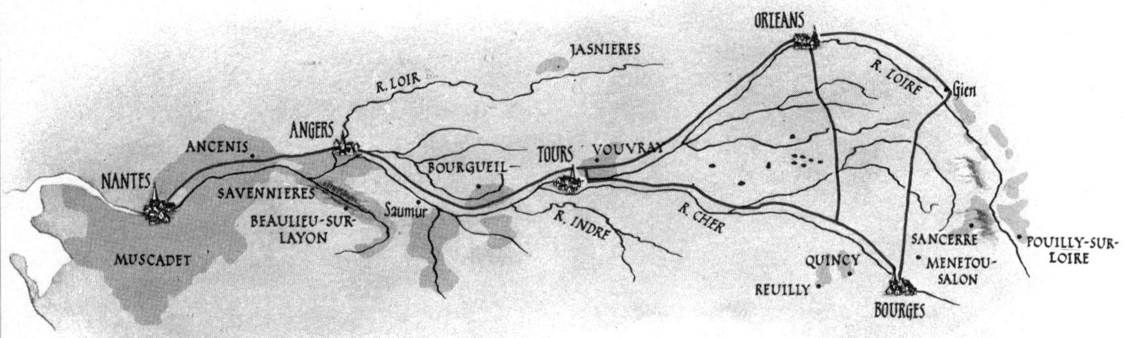

It is marvellous with what felicity, what gastronomic *savoir-vivre*, the rivers Rhône and Loire counterbalance one another on their passage through France. For 100 miles or so they even run parallel, flowing in opposite directions 30 miles apart.

They decline the notion of rivalry: in every way they are complementary. The Rhône gives France its soothing, warming, satisfying, winter-weight wines. The Loire provides the summer drinking.

The Loire rises within 100 miles of the Mediterranean. Wine is made in earnest along some 250 miles of its course and on the banks of its lower tributaries. It is a big stretch of country, and one might expect a wide variety of wines. The long list of the appellations encourages the idea, but it is not difficult to simplify into half a dozen dominant styles based on the grape varieties.

The Loire has three principal white grapes and two red (but only one that gives fine wine). Among the whites, the centre stage is held by the Chenin Blanc (alias Pineau de la Loire). It dominates in Touraine and even more so in Anjou, its produce ranging from neutral/acidic base material for sparkling Saumur to toffee-rich, apparently immortal, dessert wines. It is so versatile because it has little identifiable flavour: its qualities lie more in balance and vitality. It keeps a high acid content even when it ripens (which it can do) to extremely high levels of sugar. Aromatically it is noncommittal – until it matures. Even then it has fruit salad and *crème brûlée* both within its repertoire.

Downstream from Anjou the dominant white grape is the Muscadet – again a low-profile variety. Early ripening and (in contrast) low acidity, rather than any great aroma, makes it ideal for instant drinking with *fruits de mer*.

Upstream in Touraine and beyond to Pouilly and Sancerre is the country of the Sauvignon Blanc, in this climate one of the most intensely aromatic grapes in France.

The Cabernet Franc is the quality red grape of the Loire, at its very best at Chinon in Touraine and almost equally successful in parts of Anjou. It is shadowed everywhere by the Gamay, which can make a fresh one-year wine but no more in this climate. Both are responsible for very large quantities of more or less amiable rosé, one of the region's great money-spinners.

Two or three other grapes are to be found named on Loire labels: the white Gros Plant of the Muscadet region (a sharp grape which might be described as its Aligoté); the Pinot Noir, grown to make red wine in Sancerre; Chardonnay in Haut-Poitou. One or two are traditional and accepted: a white variety called Romorantin gives the thin wine of Cheverny; the red Groslot gives café rosé everywhere. The peasants of the region used to grow a great number of ignoble plants, but in the last 30 years they have been slowly ousted from the vineyards in favour of the principal types and an understudy cast of Cabernet Sauvignon, Malbec (here called Cot), Pinot Meunier, and such local characters as Arbois and Pineau d'Aunis and even Furmint from Hungary and Verdelho from Madeira.

As with grapes, so with regions, the Loire is simply divisible into its upper waters, above Orleans, which with their hinterland near Bourges produce Sauvignon Blanc whites, its famous slow-moving centre, where it passes in infinite procession among the châteaux of Touraine and Anjou, and its broad maritime reaches, where the wind carries the hint of shrimps far inland.

LOIRE WINES

All Loire AOC and VDQS wines are listed below. The production figures for each wine are given in cases. Most of these figures are an average of four crops, but in some cases only one year's total is available and this is indicated. Prices are those prevailing in late 1982. They are for a bottle (ex-cellar), of basic appellation or VDQS wine.

Coteaux d'Ancenis
(red) VDQS. Lower Loire. 98,000 cases. Light Gamay, occasionally Cabernet, reds from the north bank opposite Muscadet.

Coteaux d'Ancenis
(white) VDQS Lower Loire. 1,350 cases. A tiny quantity of Malvoisie (Pinot Gris), Verdelho, Chardonnay, etc.

Anjou
(red) AC. West central. 658,000 cases. Light, mainly Cabernet Franc reds from a wide area (an alternative to Saumur). 10–12 francs.

Anjou
(white) AC. West central. 731,000 cases. Mainly Chenin Blanc and often slightly sweet – no special quality. 8–9 francs.

Anjou Coteaux de la Loire
(white) AC. West central. 15,000 cases. A limited area along both banks of the river west of Angers, including the superior Savennières. Chenin Blanc of variable quality, normally dry. 8-16 francs.

Anjou Gamay
(red) AC. West central. 74,000 cases. Light reds for first-year drinking. 10–12 francs.

Cabernet d'Anjou
(rosé) AC. West central. 1.5m. cases. The best-quality rosé, normally rather sweet; at its best from Martigné, Tigné and La Fosse-Tigné in the Coteaux du Layon. 7–9 francs.

Rosé d'Anjou
(rosé) AC. West central. 2m. cases. The biggest production of the Loire; pale sweet rosé from Gamay, Groslot, Cabernet, Cot, Pineau d'Aunis. 8–9 francs.

Coteaux de l'Aubance
(white) AC. West central. 21,000 cases. Chenin Blanc, often semi-sweet or nearly dry, from the south bank opposite Angers, north of the (superior) Coteaux du Layon. 8–12 francs.

Côtes d'Auvergne
(red) VDQS. The extreme upper Loire. 36,000 cases. Near Clermont-Ferrand, formerly famous as Chanturgues, Châteaugay, Corent. Made principally from Gamay.

Côtes d'Auvergne
(white) VDQS. The extreme upper Loire. Very little made. Very light Chardonnay, superseding the red.

Bonnezeaux
(white) AC. West central. 7,950 cases. 250-acre Grand Cru of Chenin Blanc in the Coteaux du Layon, Anjou. In fine years with noble rot a great sweet wine; otherwise 'nervy' and fine. 15–20 francs.

Bourgueil
(red) AC. Central. 293,000 cases. Excellent red of Cabernet Franc from the north bank opposite Chinon, Touraine. For drinking young and cool or maturing like Bordeaux. 13–16 francs.

Châteaumeillant
(red) VDQS. Upper Loire. 5,950 cases (1981). Minor area of Gamay and Pinot Noir south of Bourges. Light reds or very pale *gris* rosés.

Cheverny
(red) VDQS. East central. 41,000 cases (1981). Small but growing supply of light Gamay red and rosé from south of Blois.

Cheverny
(white) VDQS. East central. 42,000 cases (1981). Sharp white from the local Romorantin, south of Blois, giving way to the better-known Loire grapes. 8–10 francs.

Chinon
(red) AC. Central. 334,000 cases. Fine Cabernet Franc red, sometimes superb and capable of ageing many years, but generally drunk young and cool. The most important Loire red. 13–17 francs.

Chinon
(white) AC. Central. 880 cases. Practically extinct Chenin Blanc, Rabelais' *vin de taffeta*.

Côtes du Forez
(red) VDQS. Extreme upper Loire. 19,700 cases (1981). The southernmost Loire vineyards, south of Lyon: good Gamay, Beaujolais-style.

Coteaux du Giennois
(red) VDQS. Upper Loire. 15,100 cases (1981). Very light reds, Pinot Noir and Gamay, from just downstream of Pouilly/Sancerre towards Gien.

Coteaux du Giennois
(white) VDQS. Upper Loire. 1,200 cases (1981). Chenin Blanc and Sauvignon from the same area; a dying breed.

Haut-Poitou (vin du)
(red) VDQS. South central. 92,500 cases (1981). Flourishing largely Gamay vineyard south of Anjou.

Haut-Poitou (vin du)
(white) VDQS. South central. 62,500 cases (1981). Expanding production of Sauvignon and Chardonnay.

Jasnières
(white) AC. North central. 2,600 cases. Small Chenin Blanc area north of Tours. Wine like Vouvray, if less rich. Ages very well.

Coteaux du Layon
(white) AC. West central. 412,000 cases. The biggest area of quality Chenin Blanc, south of Angers, generally semi-dry or -sweet; it includes the Grands Crus Quarts de Chaume and Bonnezeaux. 10–16 francs.

Coteaux du Layon Chaume
(white) AC. West central. 15,600 cases. A superior appellation for Coteaux du Layon with an extra degree of ripeness, comparable to a 'Villages' AC in the Rhône. 15–20 francs.

Coteaux du Loir
(red) AC. North central. 3,000 cases. Dwindling area of Pinot Noir and Gamay north of Tours on the Loir, a tributary of the Loire.

Coteaux du Loir
(white) AC. North central. 1,700 cases. Chenin Blanc from the Loir. The best is Jasnières.

Crémant de Loire
(red) AC. General. 2,650 cases. Recent appellation for high-quality sparkling wine – little used for red. 15–20 francs.

Crémant de Loire
(white) AC. General. 135,600 cases. Recent appellation for high-quality sparkling wine. 15–20 francs.

Rosé de Loire
(rosé) AC. General. 176,000 cases. A newish (1974) appellation for dry rosés with 30% Cabernet – not widely used. 7–9 francs.

Ménétou-Salon
(red) AC. Upper Loire. 12,000 cases. A minor rival to Sancerre with similar light Pinot Noir.

Ménétou-Salon
(white) AC. Upper Loire. 18,400 cases. Like the red, a rival to Sancerre with Sauvignon Blanc. 18–25 francs.

Montlouis
(white) AC. East central. 56,300 cases. The reflected image of Vouvray across the Loire: dry, semi-sweet and occasionally sweet wines. 10–12 francs.

Montlouis Mousseux
(white) AC. East central. 39,700 cases. The sparkling version of Montlouis Blanc. 12–15 francs.

Muscadet
(white) AC. Lower Loire. 322,000 cases. A large area but a small part of Muscadet production. (*see* Muscadet de Sèvre et Maine). 9–12 francs.

Muscadet des Coteaux de la Loire
(white) AC. Lower Loire. 141,500 cases. The smallest section of Muscadet, on the Loire upstream of Muscadet de Sèvre et Maine. 8–11 francs.

Muscadet de Sèvre et Maine
(white) AC Lower Loire. 3.2m. cases. Much the biggest Loire AC: the best part of Muscadet, east of Nantes. 10–12 francs.
Gros Plant du Pays Nantais
(white) VDQS. Lower Loire. 1.5m. cases. Sharp white of Gros Plant (or Folle Blanche) from the Muscadet area. 7–9 francs.
Orléannais (vin de l')
(red) VDQS. Upper Loire. 33,150 cases (1981). Light reds of Pinot Meunier, popular in Paris, particularly as vinegar.
Orléannais (vin de l')
(white) VDQS. Upper Loire. 1,350 cases (1981). Very minor whites, largely of Chardonnay.
Pouilly Fumé
(white) AC. Upper Loire. 178,000 cases. Powerful aromatic Sauvignon Blanc from opposite Sancerre. 20–25 francs.
Pouilly sur Loire
(white) AC. Upper Loire. 17,000 cases. Adequate white of Chasselas from the same vineyards as Pouilly Fumé – *must* be drunk young. 18–23 francs.
Quarts de Chaume
(white) AC. West central. 6,900 cases. 112-acre Grand Cru of the Coteaux du Layon. In certain years, glorious rich wines of Chenin Blanc. 19–25 francs.
Quincy
(white) AC. Upper Loire. 19,000 cases. Small source of attractive Sauvignon Blanc west of Bourges, 12–18 francs.
Reuilly
(red) AC. Upper Loire. 23,600 cases. Neighbour to Quincy with light pinot Noir reds.
Reuilly
(white) AC. Upper Loire. 83,500 cases. Sauvignon Blanc.

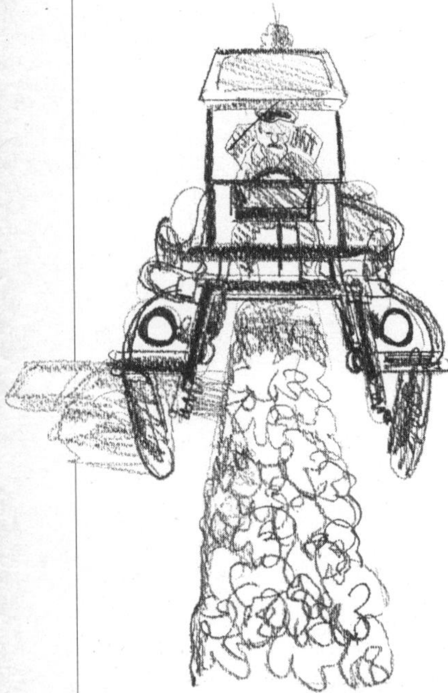

Côtes Roannaises
(red) VDQS. The extreme upper Loire. 15,750 cases (1981). Minor Gamay region not far from Beaujolais, in distance or style.
St-Nicolas de Bourgueil
(red) AC. Central. 180,500 cases. Neighbour to Bourgueil with similar excellent Cabernet Franc. 14–18 francs.
St-Pourçain-sur-Sioule
(red) VDQS. The extreme upper Loire. 80,000 cases. The famous local wine of Vichy: largely Gamay from chalk soil – good café wine.
St-Pourçain-sur-Sioule
(white) VDQS. The extreme upper Loire. 50,000 cases. Vichy's equally famous white of Tresallier and other Loire grapes – generally rather sharp.
Sancerre
(red) AC. Upper Loire. 115,000 cases. Light Pinot Noir red and rosé from chalky soil better known for white. 20–25 francs.
Sancerre
(white) AC. Upper Loire. 475,000 cases. Fresh, eminently fruity and aromatic Sauvignon Blanc. 20–25 francs.
Saumur
(red) AC. West central. 95,250 cases. Light Cabernet reds from south of Saumur – can also be sold as Anjou. 10–12 francs.
Saumur
(white) AC. West central. 304,000 cases. Crisp Chenin Blanc – often even sour. Most is made into sparkling wine. 9–11 francs.
Cabernet de Saumur
(rosé) AC. West central. 17,000 cases. The local Saumur appellation for pure Cabernet rosé. 8–10 francs.
Saumur-Champigny
(red) AC. West central. 243,000 cases. The best Cabernet reds of Anjou, from the northern part of the Saumur area just east of the city. 12–16 francs.
Coteaux de Saumur
(white) AC. West central. 870 cases. Chenin Blanc, often dry, from a similar but larger area than Saumur-Champigny. 9–12 francs.
Saumur Mousseux
(red) AC. West central. 37,825 cases. *Méthode champenoise* red of Cabernet and Gamay.
Saumur Mousseux
(white) AC. West central. 862,000 cases. *Méthode champenoise* Chenin Blanc; increasingly popular and sometimes excellent. 15–20 francs.
Savennières
(white) AC. West central. 11,500 cases. Sometimes splendid, powerful, long-lived, dry Chenin Blanc from west of Angers. It includes the Grands Crus Roche aux Moines and Coulée de Serrant. 16–22 francs.

Thouarsais (vin de)
(red) VDQS. South central. 2,100 cases. A tiny enclave of Gamay south of Saumur.
Thouarsais (vin de)
(white) VDQS. South central. 3,650 cases. The Chenin Blanc of Thouars, often rather sweet.
Touraine
(red) AC. East central. 872,000 cases. The label will name the grape, normally Gamay, here made into a passable substitute for Beaujolais – at least in warm years. 9–11 francs.
Touraine
(white) AC. East central. 821,000 cases. The label names the grape, usually Sauvignon Blanc in a tolerable imitation of Sancerre – but it can be painfully unripe. 9-12 francs.
Touraine-Amboise
(red) AC. East central. 49,000 cases. Light reds of Gamay, Cabernet and Cot from just east of Vouvray. 9–11 francs.
Touraine-Amboise
(white) AC. East central. 25,000 cases. Chenin Blanc, sometimes capable of Vouvray-like quality. 9–12 francs.
Touraine-Azay-Le-Rideau
(red) AC. East central. 9,900 cases. A minor outpost of Groslot for rosé between Tours and Chinon.
Touraine-Azay-Le-Rideau
(white) AC. East central. 11,300 cases. Tiny Chenin Blanc vineyard renowned for its Saché, occasionally as rich as Vouvray.
Touraine-Mesland
(white) AC. East central. 9,750 cases. Less important dry white of Chenin Blanc and Sauvignon.
Touraine-Mesland
(red) AC. East central. 69,700 cases. Rather good Gamay from the north bank of the Loire opposite Chaumont.
Valençay
(white) VDQS. Upper Loire. 5,400 cases. An outpost of Gamay on the eastern border of Touraine.
Valençay
(red) VDQS. Upper Loire. 24,000 cases (1981). Dry white of Chenin Blanc, Sauvignon and others.
Coteaux du Vendômois
(red) VDQS. North central. 25,800 cases (1981).
Coteaux du Vendômois
(white) VDQS. North central. 5,350 cases (1981).
Vouvray
(white) AC. East central. 369,000 cases. Dry, semi-sweet or sweet Chenin Blanc of potentially superb quality, according to the vintage. 10–13 francs.
Vouvray Mousseux
AC. East central. 247,000 cases. The sparkling version of Vouvray. 12–16 francs.

MUSCADET

It is hard to resist the notion of Muscadet as Neptune's own vineyard: nowhere is the gastronomic equation quite so simple and clear cut – or appetizing. Britanny provides the *fruits de mer*; the vineyards clustering south and east of Nantes provide oceans of the ideal white wine.

Muscadet is both the grape and the wine – and the zone. The grape came from Burgundy (where it is still sometimes found as the Melon de Bourgogne) as an early ripener that was satisfied with thin stony soil. Early ripening (about 15 September) gets it in before the autumn rain in this often cloudy and windswept vineyard. The Muscadet (or Melon) has low natural acidity that makes it particularly vulnerable in contact with air. To avoid oxidation and to bottle the wine as fresh and tasty as possible, the local tradition is to leave the new wine in its barrel at the end of fermentation, lying on its own yeasty sediment (*sur lie*) and to bottle it in March or April directly from the barrel – racking it, as it were, straight into bottles without fining or filtering. A certain amount of carbon dioxide is still dissolved in the wine and helps to make it fresh and sometimes faintly prickly to the tongue. With modern quantities and economics such careful bottling barrel by barrel is becoming rare, but the aim is still the same – except among certain growers who look for a more fully developed wine for further ageing.

Thus there are different styles of Muscadet, but it is hard to pin them down except by tasting each producer's wares. The extremes are a very light, fruity but essentially rather mild wine or, by contrast, one with a pungently vegetable and somehow 'wild' flavour, which can be very exciting with oysters or clams. the latter style can mature surprisingly well: I have had a five-year-old bottle (of 1976) which had achieved a sort of quintessential soft dryness I found delectable with turbot.

Much the greatest concentration of Muscadet vineyards is just east of Nantes and south of the Loire, in the area named for the rivers Sèvre and Maine. Eighty per cent of the 24,000 acres of vineyards are Sèvre et Maine; the rest is divided between the Coteaux de la Loire with 1,100 acres scattered eastwards towards Anjou, and plain Muscadet with 2,000 acres dotted over a wide area south of Nantes.

All three appellations are interspersed with plantations (6,500 acres in all) of the secondary white grape of the area, the Gros Plant or Folle Blanche, which stands in relation to Muscadet as Aligoté does to Chardonnay: an acknowledged poor relation, but with a faithful following of its own. Gros Plant du Pays Nantais is a VDQS, not an appellation wine like Aligoté. It is always sharp, often 'green', sometimes coarse, but can be made by a sensitive hand into a very fresh if fragile wine. It would be a natural Breton progression to drink a bottle of Gros Plant with oysters, then Muscadet with a sole. Gros Plant has a minimum alcoholic degree of 11; Muscadet a maximum of 12. Controling the maximum degree is unusual, but particularly necessary in a region where chaptalization is normal and natural acidity low. Oversugared Muscadet would be a graceless brute.

For red wine the region has very little to offer. Five hundred acres among the Muscadet vineyards of the Coteaux de la Loire around the town of Ancenis grow Gamay and a little Cabernet for light red and rosé which is sold as VDQS Coteaux d'Ancenis.

MUSCADET PRODUCERS

Gautier Audas

44115 Basse-Goulaine

A moderate-size négociant, selling 83,000 cases a year, with his own domaine of 45 acres. He believes in bottling and drinking Muscadet as young as possible, but says the time to buy it is in either April/May or October/November; not at the height of summer.

Domaine du Bois Bruley

44690 St-Fiacre-sur-Maine

A 30-acre farm belonging to one of the Chéreau family, producing Muscadet de Sèvre et Maine *sur lie* and Gros Plant du Pays Nantais, distributed by Chéreau-Carré.

Léon Boullault & Fils

Domaine des Dorices, 44330 Vallet.

A fine sloping vineyard run with great care to produce Muscadet in 2 styles, both bottled *sur lie* but one for drinking young, the other for 2 or 3 years' ageing. The Boullaults have 68 acres of Muscadet and 8 of Gros Plant, from which they also make a little *méthode champenoise* sparkling wine called Leconte.

Domaine de Chasseloir

44690 St-Fiacre-sur-Maine

A 42-acre estate on the banks of the river Maine belonging to the Chéreau family, making about 7,500 cases of Muscadet de Sèvre et Maine bottled *sur lie* at the property, distributed by Chéreau-Carré whose HQ is at Chasseloir.

Château du Coing de St-Fiacre

44690 St-Fiacre-sur-Maine

A 65-acre estate at the confluence of the rivers Sèvre and Maine, belonging to one of the Chéreau family. Its Muscadet de Sèvre et Maine, bottled at the Château *sur lie*, is distributed by Chéreau-Carré.

Donatien-Bahuaud & Cie

Château de la Cassemichère, 44330 Vallet.

High-quality négociants for wines from the whole Loire who use an original house-style of bottle. Their Château de la Cassemichère is a modern vineyard of 55 acres. The wine is fresh and very attractive. Another 12-acre plot is planted with Chardonnay, which is officially only a *vin de table*, but a very good one, called Le Chouan. Other Donatien brands include a Muscadet Cuvée des Aigles and a Muscadet *sur lie* called Fringant.

Joseph Drouard

Domaine des Hauts Pémions, Monnières, 44690 La Haye-Fouassière.

A 32-acre property making full-bodied Muscadet de Sèvre et Maine of great character. Although it is bottled *sur lie* it benefits by a year in bottle.

R.E. Dugast

Domaine des Moulins, Monnières, 44690 La Haye-Fouassière

A small (22-acre) family estate with a high reputation for very fresh and clear Muscadet de Sèvre et Maine *sur lie*. The second label is Cuvée des Grands Quarterons. Also small amounts of *méthode champenoise* brut from Gros Plant, which M. Dugast says should be drunk at 3°–5°C.

B. Fleurance & Fils

Les Gautronnières, 44330 La Chapelle-Heulin.

The Fleurance family cultivate 50 acres, three quarters of it producing an excellent Muscadet de Sèvre et Maine *sur lie*, the rest Gros Plant and a red *vin de pays* of Gamay and Cabernet. The distinct character of their Muscadet is best seen, they say, at Christmas of the year following the harvest.

Marquis de Goulaine

Château de Goulaine, Haute-Goulaine, 44120 Verton.

The showplace of Muscadet; westernmost of the great Renaissance châteaux of the Loire, still in the family which has held it for 1,000 years. It is now an efficient example of the stately home trade, with rooms available for functions, and its own wine as the inevitable choice. Grapes from 80 estate acres plus bought-in grapes from another 100 produce very good examples of the modern style. 30% of the Muscadet is bottled *sur lie*. Most of this '*Cuvée du Millénaire*' wine is from a vineyard of old vines called Montys near the château. The Marquis quotes the old proverb 'two months, two years' which means do not drink Muscadet earlier than 2 months, nor later than 2 years, after bottling.

Grand Fief de la Cormeraie

Monnières, 44690 La Haye-Fouassière.

A little 10-acre property of one of the Carré family. Its Muscadet de Sèvre et Maine *sur lie* is a frequent gold-medal winner, distributed by Chéreau-Carré.

Jacques Guindon

La Couleverdière, St-Géréon, 44150 Ancenis.

A family firm of growers who offer soft, exceptionally fine Muscadet des Coteaux de la Loire and the VDQS Coteaux d'Ancenis (Gamay red and rosé) and Malvoisie (Pinot Gris). Production of 20,000 cases is sold 88% in France, 10% in Britain.

Pierre Lusseaud

Château de la Galissonnière, 44330 Vallet.

One of the outstanding estates for full-flavoured Muscadet, comprising 2 properties – La Galissonnière and Château de la Jannière. The 74 acres are picked with mechanical harvesters and every modern method is used to make the liveliest wine without losing the *goût de terroir* of Muscadet.

Marcel Martin

La Sablette de Mouzillon, 44330 Vallet.

A family firm of growers and négociants a century old. Their 60 acres of Muscadet and 30 of Gros Plant are in Vallet and Mouzillon. They bottle a part of both *sur lie*. Altogether, with bought-in grapes, they produce 200,000 cases (40% export).

Martin-Jarry

Domaine du Champ aux Moines, 44450 La Chapelle Basse Mer.

A long-established family firm of négociants handling some 80,000 cases (but much of it in bulk) largely on the export market. Their Muscadet de Sèvre et Maine is bottled *sur lie*. Other wines are Gros Plant and a white *vin de table*, Crustacés.

Bringing in the harvest at Domaine de Chasseloir

Gilbert Métaireau

44140 Aigrefeuille-sur-Maine

A 47-acre farm, three quarters Muscadet, one quarter Gros Plant. Traditionalist in method and style, bottling appropriate wines *sur lie*.

Louis Métaireau

St-Fiacre-sur-Maine, 44690 La Haye-Foussière.

A unique enterprise formed by 9 producers, led by Louis Métaireau, who all sell their wine under his label. They act as a selection panel, all tasting all their wines together, 'blind', and only accepting those they all mark higher than 15 out of 20. Then each grower bottles his own wine, *sur lie*, without filtering and brands the cork with his initials. Together they own 188 acres. 7 of the 9 have also bought the 68-acre 'Grand Mouton' estate, which they operate together. All Métaireau wines are classic fresh Muscadets without exaggerated flavour. He insists on 'finesse'. Grand Mouton wines are made deliberately slightly underripe, *très sauvage* for the first 1 or 2 years (when they go well with shellfish). At 3 or 4 years they mellow enough to partner sole.

Moulin de la Gravelle

Gorges, 44190 Clisson.

A 21-acre vineyard in the Chéreau family stable making Muscadet de Sèvre et Maine bottled *sur lie*.

Château La Noë

44330 Vallet

A lordly domaine, unusual in Muscadet, with a stately neoclassical mansion and the biggest single vineyard in the area, covering 162 acres. The family of the Comte de Malestroit de Bruc have owned it since 1740. The present count (who is equally well known as an author) makes an unusual full-bodied Muscadet with small crops, not bottled *sur lie* but intended for 2 or 3 years bottle-ageing. He compares his wine with Chablis.

Château de l'Oiselinière

44120 Vertou

A 20-acre property of the Carré family, on the Sèvre. The wine is bottled *sur lie* and distributed by Chéreau-Carré.

Robert Pichaud

Domaine du Pisseraide, Les Laures, 44330 Vallet.

A 32-acre property which wins medals for Muscadet de Sèvre et Maine *sur lie*, best drunk in its first year.

Henri Poiron

Les Quatres Routes, Maisdon-sur-Sèvre, 44690 La Haye-Fouassière.

A nurseryman with 30 acres of Muscadet vines producing wine in the 'wilder', more earthy and solid style; less finesse and more meat than many modern makers.

Enjoying Loire wines

The wide range of Loire wines covers almost every gastronomic eventuality. For apéritifs there are the excellent sparkling wines (and even better *crémants*) of Saumur and Vouvray, or the pungent dry Chenin Blanc wines of Savennières.

For seafood there is the incomparable match of Muscadet; for charcuterie Gros Plant du Pays Nantais or a young Pouilly Fumé; for richer fish dishes with sauces either more and better Muscadet or a Sancerre or Pouilly Fumé 2 or 3 years old.

For entrées Chinon, Bourgueil and Saumur-Champigny provide either Beaujolais-style young wines, freshly fruity, or the weight of riper vintages with 5 or 6 years' maturity. Mature Savennières or Vouvray sec or demi-sec can make an interesting alternative to white burgundy for certain richly sauced creamy dishes.

Sancerre is the inevitable local choice with strong cheeses, with milder ones the sweet wines of the Coteaux du Layon can be excellent.

Light young Coteaux du Layon, appley sweet and very cold, can be a remarkable picnic wine. The nobly rotten sweet wines of Bonnezeaux and Quarts de Chaume are some of France's finest dessert wines. Like the great German sweet wines they are complete in themselves – perhaps better alone than with any food.

Marcel Sautejeau

Domaine de l'Hyvernière, 44330 Vallet.

One of the larger Muscadet négociants, family-run, with 2 properties at Le Pallet (l'Hyvernière and Clos des Orfeuilles) and the Domaine de la Botinière at Vallet. His Muscadet is mechanically harvested and bottled *sur lie* to be drunk within 2 years. Total turnover of wine from the whole Loire valley is more than 800,000 cases a year (30% exports).

Sauvion & Fils

Château du Cléray, 44330 Vallet.

A flourishing family firm of growers and négociants. Their estate is the historic Château du Cléray, with 62 acres of Muscadet and 12 of Gros Plant. The domaine wine *sur lie* is light and attractive. A special prestige *cuvée* chosen by a committee of restaurateurs and others is called Cardinal Richard. La Nobleraie is a brand name for wine made from purchased grapes.

Jean Nicholas Schaeffer

Domaine de la Haute Maison, 44860 St-Aignan.

Growers with 3 properties totalling 50 acres: Le Rafou-Tillières, La Bourdelière, Les Chaboissières. The traditional methods are carried out with very modern equipment. Good Muscadet de Sèvre et Maine *sur lie* and Gros Plant for drinking in the first year.

Gabriel Thébaud

La Hautière, St-Fiacre-sur-Maine, 44690 La Haye-Fouassière.

A long-established family estate and négociant business with a high reputation for its domaine wine, La Hautière, and its branded Muscadet de Sèvre et Maine *sur lie*, Les Doyennes. They describe their Muscadet as 'light, lively and gay', and their Gros Plant as 'dry, fruity and slightly sharp'. Production is about 20,000 cases (40% exports).

André Vinet

44330 Vallet

One of the big négociants of the region, with a turnover of more than 400,000 cases, 80% sold in France. His brands include Scintillant, Château La Touche, Château de la Cormerais Cheneau and Domaine de la Croix.

Cave Coopérative La Noëlle

44150 Ancenis

Founded 1955; 377 members with 1,100 acres producing 231,000 cases (54% AOC). Wines are Anjou, Crémant, Cabernet; VDQS Gros Plant and Gamay (rosé); plus Vin de Pays des Marches de Bretagne (red and white).

ANJOU-SAUMUR

Muscadet is the most single-minded of all French vineyards. Anjou, its neighbour to the east, has a gamut of wines as complete as any region of France. Its biggest turnover is in rosé, but its sparkling wine industry at Saumur is second only to Champagne in size, its best reds are considerable Cabernets, and its finest wines of all, sweet and dry Chenin Blanc whites, rank among the great apéritif and dessert wines of France.

Rosé is the great money-spinner. Rosé d'Anjou is a sweetish light pink from which nobody expects very much – a blend of Cabernet, Cot and Gamay with the local Groslot and Pineau d'Aunis. Cabernet d'Anjou is also rosé (not red) but an appellation to treat with more respect: the Cabernet Franc (here often called the Breton) is the best red-wine grape of the Loire; its rosé can be full of its raspberry-evoking flavour, too. The best examples come from Martigné-Briand, Tigné, and La Fosse de Tigné in the heart of the Coteaux du Layon – which is also the most important district for Chenin Blanc white wines with an inclination to sweetness.

With one exception all the considerable vineyards of Anjou lie along the south bank of the Loire and astride its tributaries the Layon, the Aubance and the Thouet. The exception is Savennières, the local vineyard of the city of Angers, which interprets the Chenin Blanc in its own way: as a forceful and intense dry wine. Savennières contains two small Grands Crus, La Roche aux Moines and La Coulée de Serrant. The wines of these, or of any of the top-quality Savennières growers, are awkward and angular at first with high acidity and biting concentration of flavour. They need age, sometimes up to 15 years, to develop their honey-scented potential. When they reach it they are excellent apéritifs. Drunk younger, they need accompanying food.

Savennières faces Rochefort-sur-Loire across the broad river, complicated with islands. Rochefort is the gateway to the long valley of the Layon, where the Chenin Blanc may be dry (and acid and pernicious) but where all the fine wines are at least crisply sweet like an apple, and the best deeply and creamily sweet with the succulence of Sauternes. The district contains two substantial Grands Crus, Quarts de Chaume and Bonnezeaux, where noble rot is a fairly frequent occurrence and sheer concentration pushes the strength of the wine up to 13 or 14 degrees. Yet curiously these sweet wines are never aged in barrels. They are in a sense the vintage port of white wines: like vintage port bottled young (in their case in their first spring) to undergo all their development with minimum possible access to oxygen. The eventual bouquet is consequently as clean, flowery and fresh-fruity as the grape itself, with the resonance and honeyed warmth of age. Great old Vouvray is so similar that it would be a brave man (or a native) who could claim to know them apart. Like German wines of fine vintages they perform a balancing-act between sweetness and sustaining acidity. But no German wine of modern times can hold its balance for half as long.

The neighbouring Coteaux de l'Aubance and Coteaux de la Loire follow in the wake of the Coteaux du Layon.

Saumur's sparkling wine industry is built upon Chenin Blanc, which has the acidity to produce successful *méthode champenoise* wines. The main producers, many of which are also négociants dealing in a range of Loire wines, are listed on page 163.

Saumur is the centre of eastern Anjou, with a set of appellations of its own, for dry or medium-dry white wines of Chenin Blanc (usually blended with some Sauvignon and/or Chardonnay), for sparkling and *crémant* versions of the same, and for red and rosé wines of Cabernet Franc and Pineau d'Aunis. The red-wine vineyards are scattered to the south of the city. The appellation Saumur-Champigny (which covers three quarters of them) has enjoyed a recent leap to fame and fashion, with its light, savoury, herby reds. The exceptional vintage of 1976, when such wines as the Château de Chaintre took on deeper tones of real richness, was a great boost to their popularity. In normal years such concentration is hard to attain.

To the south of Saumur, the Thouet valley has its own VDQS for Gamay red and Chenin white, called Vins de Thouarsais after their country town.

ANJOU-SAUMUR PRODUCERS

Maison Aubert Frères

La Varenne, 49270 St-Laurent des Autels.

A grower (in Muscadet and Anjou) and négociant bought in 1979 by Louis Eschenauer of Bordeaux. 2 domaines, Mirleau and Les Hardières, contribute to a production of more than 400,000 cases, most of which is sold in France.

Domaine des Baumard

Logis de la Giraudière, 49190 Rochefort-sur-Loire.

Jean Baumard is a senior figure of the Loire, from a family going back 250 years at Rochefort, former Professor of viticulture at Angers and now president of the Union of Syndicats AOC de la Loire. 50 acres of the 70-acre domaine is Chenin Blanc in Quarts de Chaume, Savennières (including part of the Clos du Papillon) and Coteaux du Layon (Clos de Ste-Catherine). 10 acres of Cabernet Franc and 5 of Cabernet Sauvignon produce Anjou Rouge Logis de la Giraudière. 5 acres of Chardonnay make an all-Chardonnay Crémant de Loire. Baumard uses no wood 'to avoid oxidation'. He calls Savennières 'the Meursault of the Loire' and Quarts de Chaume its 'Yquem', preferring Savennières young and Chaume either before 3 years or after 8. Between 3 and 8, he says, it goes through an eclipse. Clos de Ste-Catherine is hard to classify: neither sweet nor dry but very lively – recommended with summer fruit or as an apéritif.

Albert Besombes 'Moc-Baril'

St-Hilaire-St-Florent, 49404 Saumur.

The fourth generation of a family company of négociants in all the main Loire appellations, especially red wines of Anjou and Touraine and white and rosé *pétillant naturel*, slightly fizzy wine developed by M. Besombes. An expanding firm, exporting an impressive three quarters of a 10,000-case production.

Armand Bizard

Château d'Epiré, 49170 St-Georges-sur-Loire.

The Bizards have owned the property, with 25 acres of vines, since 1749. Armand Bizard was a meat packer before he succeeded his father 25 years ago. He uses barrels, and keeps them in the 12th-century church beside the château. 17 acres are Chenin Blanc for Savennières; full-bodied, dry and made slowly for long ageing – and eventually a long flavour. In 1982 his current drinking was 1969. He also grows a little Cabernet for Rosé d'Anjou and Gamay and Groslot for Rosé de la Loire.

Jacques Boivin

Château de Fesles, 49380 Thouarcé.

Jacques Boivin is the fourth generation to make remarkable Bonnezeaux. He owns 32 acres of the Grand Cru and another 45 of Cabernet, Groslot and Gamay for red and rosé, with an unusual 6 acres of Chardonnay – which here is a mere *vin de pays*. His Bonnezeaux is selected (when possible) for noble rot and fermented in small (220-litre) barrels. Many consider it the best of the appellation.

Etablissements Bouvet-Ladubay

St-Hilaire-St-Florent, 49416 Saumur.

A major producer of sparkling Saumur (see page 163) and also a producer of non-appellation wine from Anjou and Touraine. The firm are also négociants for all Loire wines. Bouvet-Ladubay became part of the Taittinger group in 1974. Over half the production is exported.

Château de Chaintre

Dampierre-sur-Loire, 49400 Saumur.

Owner: Bernard de Tigny. A charming old country house and notable producer of Saumur-Champigny from 42 of its 50 acres. The low underground barrel-cellars were used up to the 1978 vintage, but I have the impression that barrels are no longer used. The '76 was a splendid wine and the '78, though much lighter, firm and attractive.

Jean-Pierre Chéné

Impasse de Jardins, Beaulieu-sur-Layon, 49190 Rochefort-sur-Loire.

52 acres of vines belonging to an old Beaulieu family, recently taken over by a new generation. 25 are Chenin Blanc, 20 Cabernet. The best sweet Côteau du Layon-Beaulieu comes from 3 vineyards: Clos du Paradis Terrestre, Clos des Mulonnières and Clos des Ontinières. Up to 3 months slow, cool fermentation in barrels preserves aromas (and results in alcohol as high as 15° plus 3° remaining in the wine as sugar). Even the Cabernet d'Anjou (rosé) is 12° plus 2° of sugar. Chéné intends to make more red Cabernet and brave the tannin to get a *vin de garde*.

Claude Daheuiller

Les Varinelles, Varrains, 49400 Saumur.

A long-established family of predominantly red-wine makers with 35 acres of Cabernet in Saumur-Champigny, now made with modern methods and winning medals in Paris. The Daheuillers also make a little Saumur *méthode champenoise* from Chenin Blanc grown on very chalky soil.

Paul Filliatreau

Chaintres, 71570 La Chapelle de Guichay.

One of the growers who has brought Saumur-Champigny to prominence recently. His 61 acres of Cabernet include some century-old vines; vinified separately as '*Vieilles Vignes*'. His vats are stainless steel and his technique up to date, but his wine is designed for bottle-age. 5 more acres make dry white.

Guy Gousset

Clos de l'Aiglerie, 49190 Rochefort-sur-Loire.

A typical Layon family property of 38 acres, half Chenin Blanc and half Cabernet with a little Groslot for red and rosé. The red is kept 1 year in wood.

Mme J. de Jessey

Domaine du Closel, Savennières, 49170 St-Georges-sur-Loire.

A 38-acre estate producing classic white Savennières, concentrated wine fermented in wood, and a little (8 acres) Cabernet (appellation Anjou Coteaux de la Loire) also fermented in barrels. Mme de Jessey is the great grand-daughter of Napoleon's *aide-de-camp* Emmanuel de Las Cases, who returned here in 1820 from St-Helena to write his famous memoirs.

Mme A. Joly

Château de la Roche-aux-Moines, Savennières, 49170 St-Georges-sur-Loire.

A beautiful little estate in an outstanding situation, chosen by monks in the 12th century. The main vineyard is the 17-acre Coulée de Serrant. Madame Joly also owns 5 acres of La Roche aux Moines called the Clos de la Bergerie. Chenin Blanc here makes some of its most intense dry (or off-dry) wines of extraordinary savour and longevity. With a yield of only about 1,700 cases the wine is on allocation, at a suitably high price.

A. Laffourcade

Château de Suronde, 49190 Rochefort-sur-Loire.

The principal proprietor of Quarts de Chaume with 50 of the 112 acres of the Grand Cru, and another 25 acres of Coteaux du Layon. The great sweet wine is made Sauternes-style with a crop of between 20 and 25 hectolitres a hectare picked as the grapes shrivel with noble rot. Fermentation is in 4,000-litre *foudres*, or great barrels.

Jacques Lalanne

Château de Belle Rive, 49190 Rochefort-sur-Loire.

A major proprietor of the Grand Cru Quarts de Chaume with 42 acres surrounding the château. Almost Yquem-like methods are used, accepting a tiny crop from old vines pruned hard (12 hectolitres a hectare) and picking only nobly rotten grapes in successive *triers* around the vineyard. Fermentation in barrels takes most of the winter. The great difference between this and Sauternes (apart from the grapes) is that bottling is done at the end of April 'when the moon is waxing' and all maturation takes place in bottle rather than barrel. The wine can scarcely be appreciated for 5, sometimes 10, years – and lasts for 50.

Sylvain Mainfray

rue Jean Jaurès, 49400 Saumur.

A small family firm (founded 1901) of quality négociants, handling some 30,000 cases of appellation wines of Anjou, Saumur and Touraine, mostly bottled at the growers. Mme Mainfray also owns the 25-acre Château d'Aubigné.

Domaine de la Motte

49190 Rochefort-sur-Loire

A 40-acre family property run by a son, André Sorin, whose total involvement shows in the quality of his wines (and whose sense of humour in the name of his Anjou Sec: Clos des Belles Mères – Mothers-in-law). Coteaux du Layon Rochefort is the appellation of his sweetest and best white. He grows a little Chardonnay as well as the usual local grapes for white, red and rosé.

Vins Mottron

rue d'Anjou, 49540 Martigné-Briand.

A family of négociants and growers with a long history but a very modern outlook; originators of a PVC-packed single-glass portion of table wine. They own 50 acres of Grolleau, Cabernet, Chenin Blanc and Sauvignon and use cold fermentation for a range that includes 40% appellation wines, the rest *vins de table* in the fresh Loire style. Production is about 80,000 cases.

De Neuville

St-Hilaire-St-Florent, 49400 Saumur.

Négociants and sparkling wine producers in the chalk caves of Saumur, with 100 acres principally in Chenin Blanc for their high-quality *mousseux*, a regular medal winner. Their total sales of all Loire appellations average about 130,000 cases.

Rémy Pannier

St-Hilaire-St-Florent, 49400 Saumur.

The 'maison leader de la Loire' as general négociants, with a big turnover in all Loire wines and a good reputation for quality. The director, Philippe Treutenaere, is a member of the family that started the house in 1885. As growers they own 100 acres of Cabernet for Cabernet d'Anjou and Chenin for Anjou Blanc. Their methods are modern, blends well-made and marketing imaginative.

M. Pisani-Ferry

Château de Targy, Parnay, 49400 Saumur.

A four-towered *manoir*, in the family since 1655, with 12 acres of Cabernet Franc (and a little Chenin Blanc). The red is Saumur-Champigny, fermented in stainless steel and aged from February to September in oak.

René Renou (fils)

49380 Thouarcé

The sixth generation to bear the same name has 45 acres, one third in the Grand Cru Bonnezeaux and a third each of Cabernet and Groslot for red and rosé respectively. Renou is President of the Bonnezeaux growers.

Domaine des Rochettes

Mozé-sur-Louet, 49190 Rochefort-sur-Loire.

Proprietor Gérard Chauvin. 49 acres of Cabernet Sauvignon, Cabernet Franc and Chenin Blanc; also land in Coteaux de l'Aubance.

Yves Soulez

Château de Chamboureau
Savennières, 49170 St-Georges-sur-Loire.

One of the most successful Anjou growers, fully modernized and using steel and temperature control in a way which seems quite alarming on the Loire. He recently acquired the Château de la Bizolière to enlarge his property to 59 acres, 37 in Savennières, 10 in AOC Anjou Rouge (half-and-half Cabernet Franc and Cabernet Sauvignon) and the rest in Anjou Blanc (Sauvignon Blanc and Chenin

Blanc). Bottling is done as early as the beginning of January in an effort to capture the maximum fruit flavours. The Savennières is very dry and often rather prickly with carbon dioxide. Young it is not very appealing: a few years in bottle give it dimensions it lacks as young wine.

Pierre Yves Tijou

Domaine de la Soucherie, 49190 Rochefort-sur-Loire.

Tijou's parents bought this 75-acre domaine in 1952. It includes some of the Grand Cru Quarts de Chaume; most is in Coteaux du Layon in Chenin Blanc, with Cabernet for red and rosé. No wood is used for the white. An Anjou Blanc has 5% Sauvignon added to Chenin Blanc for aroma.

Les Vins Touchais and Les Vignobles Touchais

49700 Doué La Fontaine

One of the biggest growers and négociants of the Loire and recently one of the most celebrated. Les Vignobles Touchais own 400 acres, of which 120 are Chenin Blanc in Coteaux du Layon and Anjou Blanc. 180 are Cabernet and 100 Groslot for red and rosé. The Touchais family have been growers for centuries and have amassed astonishing stocks of fine old sweet Layon wines – the best, sold as Moulin Touchais, maturing almost indefinitely. Wines in stock include 1978, '77, '75, '71, '69, '64, '59, '55, '49, '45, '43, '42, '37, '33, '28, etc. At 20 years the '59 was full of vigour and deep honeyed flavour – a very great dessert wine. The bulk of the business of Les Vins Touchais (founded 1947) is in rosé and other popular regional wines. Cuisse de Bergère – Shepherdess's Thigh – is appropriately sweet and blushing.

Union Vinicole du Val de Loire

St-Hilaire-St-Florent, 49400 Saumur.

Formerly the house of Goblet (founded 1877; Jacques Goblet is president). An associate of the SPAR grocery group selling 80% of over 500,000 cases – growing fast – through their shops. Négociants in all Loire wines and table wines under the names Goblet and Le Caveau.

Compagnie de la Vallée de la Loire

49260 Montreuil-Bellay

A recent (founded 1965) big-scale general négociant for the Loire with many wines and brands, in bulk and bottle, mostly using the name of the founder, Henri Verdier, or one of his family. Total sales approach 1.25m. cases, one third to England.

CAVES COOPERATIVES

Les Caves de la Loire

49320 Brissac

A union of 3 cooperative cellars, at Brissac, Beaulieu-sur-Layon and Tigné, producing some 25,000 cases of the general Anjou appellations with modern equipment. As much as half of their production is exported.

Les Vignobles de la Cour de Pierre

49190 Rochefort-sur-Loire

A sales cooperative with 10 members, all small growers in Rochefort, who make their wine personally but band together to sell it on the export market. There are only up to 4,000 cases but it is well received; especially the *moelleux* Coteaux du Layon Rochefort.

SPARKLING SAUMUR

The in-built acidity of Chenin Blanc is the cause and justification of the Saumur sparkling-wine industry, which is based in the chalk caves of St-Hilaire-St-Florent, just west of Saumur. It uses the champagne method to produce cleanly fruity, usually very dry wines at half champagne prices, less characterful and complex but just as stimulating.

Remuage in Saumur

Major producers

Ackerman-Laurance

St-Hilaire-St-Florent, 49416 Saumur. The original and probably still the biggest firm, founded in 1811 when Ackerman, a Belgian, introduced the *méthode champenoise* to the Loire. Still a leader with the new extra-quality Crémant de Loire. 330,000 cases.

Maison Veuve Amiot

49400 Saumur. Founded 1884, now owned by Martini & Rossi. 250,000 cases of sparkling Saumur, Anjou and Crémant du Roi (Crémant de Loire).

Bouvet-Ladubay

St-Hilaire-St-Florent, 49416 Saumur. The second oldest (1851) of the sparkling-wine houses. Excellent sparkling Saumurs include Brut de Blanc, Extra Dry Blanc and Carte Blanche demi-sec. Also vintage Crémant de Loire and Crémant Rosé. See also page 161.

Etablissements Gratien, Meyer & Seydoux

Ch. de Beaulieu 49400 Saumur. A twin company to the Champagne house of Alfred Gratien. 40 acres of vineyards (Chenin Blanc and Cabernet) over the cellars. Products are sparkling Saumur, Crémant de Loire Brut, Anjou Rosé and Rouge Dry (also sparkling). Gratien and Meyer is a touch more full-bodied than most Saumurs. Other brands are Rosset and Henri d'Alran, and an apéritif G & M Royal.

Langlois-Château

St-Hilaire-St-Florent, 49416 Saumur. This old house merged with Bollinger in 1973. Principally producers of fine sparkling Saumur but also négociants in the major Loire wines.

De Neuville

St-Hilaire-St-Florent, 49416 Saumur. Producer of quality sparkling Saumur from 100 acres.

Vignerons de Saumur à St-Cyr en Bourg

49260 Montreuil Bellay. The Saumur growers' cooperative for sparkling (and other) wines, uniting some 1,750 acres, half Chenin Blanc and half red grapes. Their Saumur Brut Cuvée de la Chevalerie and Crémant de Loire Prince Alexandre are particularly well thought of. Other wines in a total of 200,000 cases include Saumur-Champigny, Anjou Rosé, etc., under the name of Bonnamy.

TOURAINE

It is hard to define Touraine more precisely than as the eastern half of the central Loire, with the city of Tours at its heart and a trio of goodly rivers, the Cher, the Indre and the Vienne, joining the majestic mainstream from the south.

Almost on its border with Anjou it produces the best red wines of the Loire. Chinon and Bourgueil lie on the latitude of the Côte de Beaune and the longitude of St-Emilion – a situation that produces a kind of claret capable of stunning vitality and charm. The Cabernet Franc, with very little if any Cabernet Sauvignon, achieves a sort of pastel sketch of a great Médoc, smelling sweetly of raspberries, begging to be drunk cellar-cool in its first summer, light and sometimes astringent, yet surprisingly solid in its construction: ripe vintages behave almost like Bordeaux in ageing, at least to seven or eight years.

Much depends on the soil: sand and gravel near the river produce lighter, faster-maturing wine than clay over *tuffeau* limestone on the slopes (*coteaux*). These differences seem greater than those between Chinon and Bourgueil; certainly than any between Bourgueil and its immediate neighbour on the north bank, St-Nicolas de Bourgueil, although this has a separate appellation of its own.

Touraine's other famous wine is Vouvray, potentially the most luscious and longest lived of all the sweet Chenin Blanc whites, though, like German wines, depending more on the vintage than the site for the decisive degree of sugar that determines its character. The best vineyards are on the warm chalky *tuffeau* slopes near the river and in sheltered corners of side valleys. A warm dry autumn can overripen the grapes here by sheer heat, or a warm misty one can bring on noble rot to shrivel them. In either case great sweet Vouvray will be possible, with or without the peculiar smell and taste of *botrytis cinerea*. Cool years make wines of indeterminate (though often very smooth and pleasant) semi-sweetness, or dry wines – all with the built-in acidity that always keeps Chenin Blanc lively (if not always very easy to drink). The solution to overacid wines here, as in Saumur, is to make them sparkle by the *méthode champenoise*.

It is an odd coincidence that each of the great Loire wines comes with a pair across the river: Savennières with Coteaux du Layon, Bourgueil with Chinon, Sancerre with Pouilly and Vouvray with Montlouis. Montlouis, squeezed between the south bank of the Loire and the north bank of the converging tributary Cher, is not regarded, except by those who make it, as having quite the authority and attack of great Vouvray. Its sites are slightly less favoured and its wines softer and more tentative. They can sparkle just as briskly, though, and ripen almost as sweet.

Outside these four appellations Touraine has only a modest reputation; no county-wide appellation for a popular drink such as Anjou Rosé. I suggest that the future lies with the general (and self-explanatory) Sauvignon and Gamay de Touraine; reasonably priced substitutes for – respectively – Sancerre and Beaujolais, two of France's most fashionable and overpriced appellations. They are not as fine as either, but an awful lot cheaper.

TOURAINE PRODUCERS

Claude Amirault

Clos des Quarterons, St-Nicolas de Bourgueil, 37140 Bourgueil.

A property of 37 acres well distributed on the lighter soils of St-Nicolas. 2,500 cases of lightly fruity wine sold to restaurants and private clients.

Claude Ammeux

Clos de la Contrie, St-Nicolas de Bourgueil, 37410 Bourgueil.

A charming 20-acre property at the foot of the coteaux, almost in Bourgueil. M. Ammeux feeds his very old vines on seaweed and looks for flavour and alcohol at the expense of big crops.

Audebert & Fils

37140 Bourgueil

One of the biggest producers of Bourgueil and St-Nicolas de Bourgueil with 67 acres and modern equipment. His production of over 40,000 cases is sold under 2 labels: Domaine du Grand Clos and Vignobles Les Marquises – easy wines for drinking cool in their youthful prime.

Marcel Audebert

Caves St-Martin, Restigné, 37140 Bourgueil.

A long-established family with 25 acres in Restigné, appellation Bourgueil. Their wine is fermented and aged in wood and M. Audebert also keeps stocks for ageing in bottle.

M. Berger

Caves des Liards, 37270 Montlouis-sur-Loire.

A third-generation property of 50 acres, 80% in Chenin Blanc for still, sparkling and *pétillant* Montlouis, the rest in Sauvignon for Touraine Blanc and Cabernet Franc for Touraine Rouge. The wine is all bottled in spring and aged in bottle – about 8,300 cases a year.

Aimé Boucher

Huisseau-sur-Cosson, 41350 Vineul.

A family firm of négociants founded in 1900, widely regarded as setting the highest standards in Touraine and the upper Loire. The director, Claude Kistner, chooses wines from growers and moves them to the firm's own cellars in each area. Specialities include Vouvray (still and sparkling), Sancerre and Crémant de Loire. Chinon and Bourgueil spend 1 year in wood. Production 42,000 cases.

Bougrier

St-Georges-sur-Cher, 41400 Montrichard.

A century-old family firm of growers (with 37 acres, the Domaine Guenault) and négociants. The domaine produces Sauvignon, Cabernet Franc, Gamay and Chenin Blanc, all AOC Touraine. 60% of the total turnover of 375,000 cases in all Loire wines is exported.

Caslot-Galbrun

La Hurolaie, Benais, 37140 Bourgueil.

One of the oldest established families of growers in Bourgueil, whose 27 acres seem to produce some of the juiciest, deepest coloured, most age-worthy wine. Fermentation is in stainless steel, but methods and standards are unchanged. Production at most is 2,500 cases.

Caslot-Jamet

Domaine de la Chevalerie, Restigné, 37140 Bourgueil.

Paul Caslot, married to a Jamet daughter, farms 25 acres of old Cabernet on the hill and makes firm deep-toned Bourgueil, aged up to 18 months in wood and intended to age a further 3, 4, or more years.

Etablissement Pierre Chainier

La Boitardière, 37400 Amboise.

A flourishing young négociant business, started in 1970 and already selling some 330,000 cases of a full range of Loire wines, specializing in Touraine. Pierre Chainier also owns the Château de Pocé, with 50 acres of Gamay, on a south slope facing the Château of Amboise across the Loire (Appellation Touraine-Amboise).

Couly-Dutheil

12 rue Diderot, 37500 Chinon.

A grower of Chinon and négociant for other Loire wines, founded in 1910 by B. Dutheil, developed by René Couly and now run by his sons Pierre and Jacques. Their 100 acres of Chinon are divided between wines of plain and plateau, sold as Domaine de Turpenay and Domaine René Couly, and the (better) wines of the *coteaux*, the Clos de l'Echo and Clos de l'Olive. Equipment is modern, with temperature control and automatic turning of the skins in the stainless steel vats. The object is wine drinkable by the following Easter but able, as Chinon is, to age in bottle for several years. Total turnover is 46,000 cases.

Dutertre Père & Fils

Limeray, 37400 Amboise.

A 66-acre family property run by father (Gabriel) and son (Jacques). 50-odd acres are Cabernet, Malbec, Gamay and Pinot Noir for red and rosé Touraine-Amboise. They also make sparkling and still dry whites in their rock-cut cellar.

A. Foreau

Clos Naudin, 37210 Vouvray.

The Foreau family own 30 acres of prime vineyards and aim to age their wine for as long as possible before selling it – an expensive procedure but essential to let its character develop. 10 years is a good age for a 'new' Vouvray. Their output is about 3,300 bottles of sweet, dry, demi-sec and sparkling.

André Freslier

'La Caillerie', 37210 Vouvray.

M. Freslier and his son Jean-Pierre make serious dry Vouvray from 20 acres, fermenting the wine in old 600-litre casks (*'demi-muids'*). He recommends 4–5 years ageing in bottle. Also dry fizzy Vouvray *pétillant*.

Girault-Artois & Fils

Domaine d'Artois, 37400 Amboise.

A thoroughly modern property of 50 acres of Touraine-Mesland, specializing in softly fruity reds under the names Domaine d'Artois and Château Gaillard. Also Sauvignon and Chenin Blanc whites, rosé and Crémant de Loire. François Girault uses mechanical harvesting and stainless steel tanks, with *macération carbonique* for his red wine.

René Gouron & Fils

37500 Chinon

The Gouron family have 43 acres at Cravant Les Coteaux, producing some 5,000 cases of outstanding Chinon and a little Touraine rosé *pétillant*.

Gaston Huet

Domaine du Haut-Lieu, 37210 Vouvray.

Perhaps the most respected name in Vouvray, a family of growers for 3 generations making wine of the highest quality from 3 vineyards, Le Haut-Lieu, Le Mont and Le Clos du Bourg, sweet or dry, still or sparkling according to the season. M. Huet is mayor of Vouvray.

Charles Joguet

Sazilly, 37220 L'Ile Bouchard.

An artist-*vigneron*, painter and sculptor as well as farmer of 30 acres of Chinon and one of its best wine makers. His best old vines are in the Clos de la Dioterie. His up-to-date cellar has automated *pigeage* of juice and skins in stainless steel vats followed by ageing for up to 18 months in *barriques* bought from Château Latour in 1970.

Lamé-Delille-Boucard

Ingrandes de Touraine, 37140 Bourgueil.

A considerable property of 65 acres, divided almost equally between 4 communes with the appellation Bourgueil: Ingrandes, St-Patrice, Restigné and Benais. The grouping is recent, although M. Lamé comes from an old *vigneron* family. He uses wooden vats and describes his wines as ranging from succulent to fragile, depending on the vintage.

Jean-Claude Mabilot

St-Nicolas de Bourgueil, 37140 Bourgueil.

A grower with 17 acres, all beside his house. He makes as much as 4,000 cases of light red with the typical raspberry aroma, which he claims will keep for 7 years even in 'medium' vintages, and up to 30 in great ones.

Paul Maître

SCEA Domaine Raguenières, Benais, 37140 Bourgueil.

A 30-acre Bourgueil property making a little rosé as well as nearly 5,000 cases of clean, fairly tannic, marvellously scented red compared by M. Maître with Bordeaux – especially in its keeping properties.

Henri Marionet

Domaine de la Charmoise, Soings, 41230 Mur de Sologne.

A modern-minded grower with a new 50-acre vineyard of Gamay and Sauvignon Blanc. He uses *macération carbonique* to get a Beaujolais effect in his Gamay de Touraine, and strives for round and fruity Sauvignon.

J.M. Monmousseau
41400 Montrichard

The Taittinger group of Champagne owns this century-old sparkling-wine house, but the director is still Armand Monmousseau. Their own 150 acres of vines at Azay-Le-Rideau, Montlouis and St-Georges-sur-Cher provide a quarter of the grapes for a fine light *méthode champenoise* sparkler. Production is about 100,000 cases, plus 40,000 of still wines of other Loire regions.

Claude Moreau
La Taille, St-Nicolas de Bourgueil, 37140 Bourgueil.

Moreaus abound in St-Nicolas. They go back 5 generations, and Claude Moreau has 5 *vigneron* sons. His own vineyard is 15 acres; his aim, by keeping the wine in barrels for 1 year, is to make it durable as well as fragrant. But he has no old stocks – the customers take it fresh from the bottling line.

E. & D. Moyer
37270 Montlouis-sur-Loire

A respected old family of growers (since 1825) with 33 acres of very old vines. The Moyers go to the length of successive pickings to crush nothing but ripe grapes, making both their sec and demi-sec as ripe and round as possible.

Gaston Pavy
Saché, 37190 Azay-Le-Rideau.

The best-regarded name in this little appellation, with 5 acres of Chenin Blanc making notably intense semi-sweet Chenin Blanc and 2.5 acres of Groslot and Malbec for a surprisingly durable dry rosé.

J.B. Pinon
Caves aux Tuffières, Lhomme, 72340 La Chartre-sur-le-Loir.

An old family of growers from Vouvray, now leading producers of dry Jasnières (as well as Vouvray *pétillant*). They also grow Pineau d'Aunis and Gamay for red and rosé Coteaux du Vendômois (VDQS). Jasnières needs bottle-age to soften its bite.

Prince Poniatowsky
Le Clos Baudoin, 37210 Vouvray.

Maker of some immortal Vouvray from 2 Grand Cru vineyards, Clos Baudoin and Aigle Blanc. The fine vintages have what the Prince calls '*race*' – breeding – that takes 25 or 30 years to reach its full flowering. The 1854 in the cellar is apparently excellent. The estate is 54 acres, 52 of Vouvray and 2 of Touraine, used for *méthode champenoise* Brut de Brut. Half of some 5,000–7,000 cases a year is exported.

Jean Maurice Raffault
La Croix, Savigny-en-Véron, 37420 Avoine.

In 10 years M. Raffault, whose family have been *vignerons* since 1700, has expanded his vineyards from 12 to 70 acres with parcels scattered over 6 communes, all in the appellation Chinon. He makes the wines of different soils separately. His Clos des Lutinières comes from gravel, Les Galluches from sandier soil, Les Picasses and Isore from the local *tuffeau* and Clos de Galon from chalky clay. All the grapes are destalked, then fermented for up to 40 days before being aged for 1 year in *barriques*. He is one of the very few Chinon growers still using *barriques*, aiming for stable, tannic wine which will keep 10 years. His current production is 5,800 cases, rising steadily. Only 10% is exported.

Olga Raffault
Savigny-en-Véron, 37500 Chinon.

One of several Raffaults in and around this village at the western end of the Chinon appellation. (Another, Raymond, owns Château Raifault [*sic.*]). The estate is 37 acres, with fermentation in steel vats, then ageing in wooden ones, keeping the wine of different sites separate. Clients (who include the famous restaurant Barrier at Tours) can choose from a range of generally fruity and fairly full-bodied wines.

Joel Taluau
Chevrette, St-Nicolas de Bourgueil, 37140 Bourgueil.

22 acres of St-Nicolas and 3 of Bourgueil producing 1,500 cases of fragrant light red. It needs an exceptional year like 1976 to give it deeper colour and body.

Jean-Paul Trotignan
10 rue des Bruyères, 41140 Noyers sur Cher.

A small supplier of the Paris market with carefully made Sauvignon, Gamay and Cabernet (which he considers a *vin de garde*), all AOC Touraine. About 3,000 cases.

Jean Vrillon
Faverolles-sur-Cher, 41400 Montrichard.

A long-established grower with a small business in *méthode champenoise* AOC Touraine and red and white Vin de Pays du Jardin de la France. 1,250 cases, sold in Brittany and Paris.

CAVES COOPERATIVES

Haut-Poitou
86170 Neuville de Poitou

Director: Gérard Raffarin. The VDQS zone of Haut-Poitou is well south of the Loire on the road to Poitiers, where 47 communes on the chalky soil of a plateau used to supply distilling wine to Cognac. In 1948, a coop was founded and succeeded in raising standards to the point where in 1970 the region was promoted to VDQS. Full AOC status now cannot be far away.

Today the coop has 1,200 members farming 2,250 acres, growing by 125 acres a year. Sauvignon Blanc yields a highly characteristic and aromatic dry white, Gamay a light red and Cabernet Franc a dry rosé. New plantings of Chardonnay have been a great success, producing something like featherweight Chablis. All wines are bottled and should be drunk very young. Production 850,000 cases, including *vins de table* and Vin de Pays du Jardin de la France.

La Confrèrie des Vignerons de Oisly et Thesée
Oisly, 41700 Contres

A young (1961) cooperative with 60 members, which is making great efforts to create a new style and image for the valley of the Cher in eastern Touraine. Their aim is to design a well-balanced light red and white using a blend of grapes. The white is Sauvignon, Chenin Blanc and Chardonnay, the red Cabernet Franc, Cot (Malbec) and Gamay. The cooperative's brand for their selection of each is Baronnie d'Aignan. Production is 160,000 cases (and rising), all AOC wines. President: Claude Boucher.

Château du Nozet

THE UPPER LOIRE

It might well surprise the *vignerons* of Sancerre and Pouilly, the uppermost of the mainstream Loire vineyards, to learn what a profound influence their produce has had on forming modern tastes in white wine. It is an area of generally small and unsophisticated properties – with one or two well-organized exceptions. But it has an easily recognizable style of wine, pungent and cutting, with the smell and acidity of Sauvignon Blanc grown in a cool climate.

Although Sauvignon is planted on a far larger scale in Bordeaux its wine never smelt and tasted so powerfully characteristic there as it does on the Loire. The Bordeaux tradition is to blend it with the smoother and more neutral Sémillon. But now Bordeaux has seen the world paying white burgundy prices for the assertive (some say obvious) Loire style, it is paying it the sincerest form of flattery. Californians, with vastly different growing conditions, have adopted the term Fumé to indicate that their Sauvignon Blanc aims at the Loire flavour (rather than the broader, riper, to some *passé*, style of Graves). One might say that the world discovered the Sauvignon Blanc and its singular flavour through the little vineyard of Sancerre and the even smaller one of Pouilly-sur-Loire.

What is the flavour? It starts with the powerful aroma, which needs no second sniff. 'Gunflint,' suggesting the smell of the sparks when flint strikes metal, is a traditional way of characterizing it. In unripe vintages tasters talk of cats, and I have been reminded of wet wool. Successful Sancerres and Pouilly Fumés have an attractive smell and taste of fresh blackcurrants, leaves and all, and a natural high acidity which makes them distinctly bracing. Sancerre normally has more body and 'drive' (and higher acidity) than Pouilly Fumé; consequently it can benefit from two or three years' ageing, where Pouilly needs only a year or so.

For reasons of tradition the Pouilly vineyards also contain a proportion of the neutral Chasselas grape, which cannot be sold as 'Fumé' but only as Pouilly-sur-Loire – a pale, adequate, rather pointless wine, which must be drunk very young.

Sancerre, on the other hand, is almost as proud of its Pinot Noir red and rosé as its Sauvignon white. They never achieve the flavour and texture of burgundy. In fact, they frequently have the faintly watery style of German Spätburgunder (the same grape). Nor do they age satisfactorily. But they are highly appreciated at source.

SANCERRE PRODUCERS

Pierre Archambault

Caves du Clos la Perrière, Verdigny, 18300 Sancerre.

A family firm of growers (62 acres) and négociants producing 37,500 cases of Sancerre a year (white, red and rosé) and Pouilly Fumé, and a white *vin de table* Les Roches Blanches. They use modern equipment in spacious natural rock cellars, exporting 35% of production. M. Archambault particulary recommends his Sancerre with the local goats'-milk cheese: Crottin de Chavignol.

Bernard Bailly-Reverdy & Fils

Bué, 18300 Sancerre.

M. Bailly is a distinguished traditional grower with 25 acres in no less than 15 different sites including the famous Clos du Chêne Marchand. 8 acres are Pinot Noir. His white from other vineyards is called Domaine de la Mercy Dieu. He looks for (and finds) a balance of fruit and finesse, particularly in his white wine.

Bernard Balland & Fils

Bué, 18300 Sancerre.

An enthusiastic young descendant of a long line of growers with about 20 acres. He sells 2 excellent whites, Grand Chemarin and Clos d'Ervocs, and a red and rosé, Les Marnes. His style of white is very fresh, sweet-smelling and long on the palate.

Philippe de Benoist

Domaine du Nozay, 18300 Sancerre.

A small high-quality domaine started in 1970 by the brother-in-law of Aubert de Villaine, co-owner of the Domaine de la Romanée-Conti. He is increasing his acreage, now about 10 acres, and making Sancerre as delicately rounded as possible.

Etablissements Cordier

Bué, 18300 Sancerre.

The great Bordeaux house of Cordier has a well-known Sancerre estate of 70 acres, producing white Clos de la Poussie, red Guche Pigeon and rosé Orme aux Loups. All 3 are fresh and fragrant wines of low acidity designed to be drunk very young (even the red).

Francis & Paul Cotat

Chavignol, 18300 Sancerre.

A very small, totally traditional and most prestigious grower making only about 1,000–1,500 cases. The Cotat brothers do everything themselves, use an old wooden press, ferment in casks and never fine or filter: instead they bottle at the full moon in May when the wine is clear and still. Bottles from the 1930s in their cellar are still in good condition.

Lucien Crochet

Bué, 18300 Sancerre.

A family holding of 37 acres of the famous Clos du Chêne Marchand; 30 in Sauvignon, the rest Pinot Noir. Classic methods produce excellent wine.

André Dezat

Chaudoux, Verdigny, 18300 Sancerre.

An old-school grower, mayor of the village, who works in clogs and a beret and loves his red wines as they age – though I prefer them young. One third of his 30 acres is Pinot Noir. His whites are extremely fine and even elegant.

Gitton Père & Fils

Ménétréol-sous-Sancerre, 18300 Sancerre.

A family estate of 50 acres, almost entirely Sauvignon, developed since 1945. Gitton makes his wine in many different batches according to different soils – no less than 11 Sancerre *cuvées* with different labels, and 2 Pouilly Fumés. The whites are fermented in barrels and aged 8 months in *cuves*, the reds fermented in *cuves*, then aged 2 winters in barrels. Altogether an original house with a style of its own.

Paul & Fils

Domaine Prieur, Verdigny, 18300 Sancerre.

A prominent family of growers for generations with 25 acres in several good sites, including Les Monts-Damnés (which is chalky clay) and the stonier Pichon, where an unusually high proportion (10 acres) of their property is Pinot Noir. Their white is made to age 2 or 3 years; the rosé of Pinot Noir mysteriously seems to share its quality – even its Sauvignon flavour. The red is made like very light burgundy. They make some 4,200 cases, half of which is exported.

Lucien Picard

Bué, 18300 Sancerre.

Picard's Clos du Chêne Marchand is one of the most solid Sancerres, with style and vigour to keep it going 3 or 4 years. His Clos du Roy is scarcely less remarkable. The two account for 8 of his 17.5 acres; 4.5 of the balance are Pinot Noir.

Jean Reverdy

Domaine des Villots, Verdigny, 18300 Sancerre.

A succession of Reverdys since 1646 have farmed about 15 acres, now 12 Sauvignon and 3 Pinot Noir. They have installed modern equipment in the cellar but make classic wines, particularly their white, which can mature for 3 or 4 years.

Lucien Thomas

Clos de la Crêle, 18300 Sancerre.

A 15-acre property making crisp white Sancerre by slow fermentation in stainless steel, and red aged for 12 months in oak and 6 in bottle.

Jean Vacheron & Fils

18300 Sancerre

A particularly welcoming family of growers whose wines can be tasted in summer in the centre of Sancerre at Le Grenier à Sel. They own 45 acres, two thirds of it Sauvignon, and offer 3 whites: Les Romains, Le Clos des Roches and Le Paradis; red Les Cailleries and rosé Les Guignes Chèvres. Their equipment and ideas are modern, but the red ferments for as long as 5 weeks before ageing a year in Burgundian casks. Half their 6,600-case production is exported.

Jean Vatan

Chaudoux, 18300 Sancerre.

A respected old family of growers with 12 acres, 8 Sauvignon and 4 Pinot Noir for red and rosé.

Cave Coopérative des Vins de Sancerre

18300 Sancerre

Founded 1963. 166 members; 412 acres; 75,000 cases, 98% AOC. A serious producer of typical Sancerre.

POUILLY PRODUCERS

Monsieur Blanchet

Les Berthiers, St-Andelain, 58150 Pouilly-sur-Loire.

The third generation of Blanchets has 10 acres of Sauvignon and 2.5 of Chasselas. M. Blanchet racks his wine once in January and bottles it early, scorning any treatment to prevent the formation of tartrate crystals, which he says his clients understand.

Gérard Coulbois

58150 Pouilly-sur-Loire

Old family property with 13 acres of Pouilly-Fumé, 3 of Chasselas. Classic methods but cement vats, no barrels.

Serge Dagueneau

Les Berthiers, 58150 Pouilly-sur-Loire.

A 25-acre family vineyard with a sound reputation for typically fruity and full-flavoured Pouilly-Fumé. Dageneau uses no fining but filters before bottling early in spring.

Paul Figeat

Les Loges, 58150 Pouilly-sur-Loire.

A *vigneron* family for 200 years, respected for fresh Pouilly-Fumé, which is made to be drunk young. Of their 20 acres a small and decreasing fraction is Chasselas for plain Pouilly-sur-Loire.

Jean Claude Guyot

58150 Pouilly-sur-Loire

A third-generation small producer from 20 acres of Sauvignon for Pouilly-Fumé and a little Chasselas. He uses tanks of steel and cement and some 600-litre casks.

J.M. Masson-Blondelet

58150 Pouilly-sur-Loire

The Masson and Blondelet families (united by marriage in 1974) work 11 acres of Sauvignon and 3 of Chasselas with great skill to produce 1,700 cases of Pouilly-Fumé and a little Pouilly-sur-Loire. Their best vines, in the Bascoins vineyard, are vinified separately. In 1979 and 1980 they won gold medals at Mâcon and Paris.

Château du Nozet

58150 Pouilly-sur-Loire

The major producer and promoter of the fine wines of Pouilly with a production of over 85,000 cases, largely from company-owned vineyards of 150 acres. The young Baron Patrick de Ladoucette is the head of the family firm, which has 3 labels: Pouilly-Fumé de Ladoucette, Sancerre Comte Lafond and a prestige *cuvée* Pouilly-Fumé Baron de L. Half the total production is exported, the other half is sold in France exclusively to the grander restaurants.

Michel Redde

58150 Pouilly-sur-Loire

One of the best-known producers of Pouilly-Fumé, from 45 acres in the heart of the appellation with 17 more planted. A modern installation with stainless steel vats, operated by the fifth and sixth generations of Reddes in succession. They bottle as early as possible for maximum fruity freshness.

Caves St-Vincent

Domaine Saget, 58150 Pouilly sur-Loire.

A fifth-generation growers' family affair run by the brothers Saget, expanded since 1976 into a négociant business with a production of 58,000 cases, but still based on 38 acres of family vines, with 25 more planned. Their technique is long cool fermentation with minimum disturbance of the wine and no malolactic fermentation to reduce the high natural fruity acidity. They sell 3 brands of Pouilly-Fumé: Les Loges, Les Chaumes and Château de la Roche, and 2 Sancerres: Clos du Roy and Château de Thauvenay.

Château de Tracy

58150 Pouilly-sur-Loire

The family of the Comte d'Estutt d'Assay has owned the Château, on the Loire just downstream from Pouilly, since the 16th century. 46 acres produce some 6,500 cases of superb Pouilly-Fumé by traditional methods.

OTHER SANCERRE PRODUCERS

Cave des Chanvières
Verdigny, 18300 Sancerre. Paul and Claude Fournier. 30 acres.

Vincent Delaporte
Chavignol, 18300 Sancerre. 25 acres.

Pierre & Alain Dezat
Maimbray, 18300 Sancerre. Brothers with a growing reputation for impressively full-bodied Sancerre from some 20 acres.

Domaine des Garmes
Chaudoux, Verdigny, 18300 Sancerre. Michel and Jacques Fleuriet. 25 acres. Also uses the name Clos du Carroy Maréchaux.

Michel Girard
Verdigny, 18300 Sancerre. 2,000 cases of respected red, white and rosé.

Pierre Girault
Bué, 18300 Sancerre. 10 acres in Le Grand Chemarin.

Château de Maimbray
Sury-en-Vaux, 18300 Sancerre. George Roblin. 27 acres, Sancerre white, red and rosé.

Paul Millérioux
Champtin, Crazancy-en-Sancerre, 18300 Sancerre. 27 acres.

Roger Neveu
Verdigny, 18300 Sancerre. 25 acres (5 Pinot Noir) in Clos des Bouffants.

Pierre & Etienne Riffault
Verdigny, 18300 Sancerre. 12 acres.

Jean-Max Roger
Bué, 18300 Sancerre. 17 acres (4 Pinot Noir) in Clos du Chêne Marchand and Le Grand Chemarin.

Château de Sancerre
18300 Sancerre, Marnier-Lapostolle family. 35 acres.

OTHER POUILLY PRODUCERS

Robert Minet & M. Seguin
Le Bouchet, 58150 Pouilly-sur-Loire. 11 acres of Sauvignon, 2.5 of Chasselas.

Didier Pabiot
58150 Pouilly-sur-Loire. A keen young man with 9 acres of Sauvignon producing, more planted.

Cave Coopérative Pouilly-sur-Loire
Les Moulins à Vent, 58150 Pouilly-sur-Loire. Founded 1948. 108 members; 198 acres, 25,000 cases, of which 88% are AOC Pouilly Fumé and Pouilly-sur-Loire, and the balance Coteaux du Giennois VDQS red.

MINOR REGIONS

The success of Sancerre and Pouilly has encouraged what were dwindling outposts of vineyards in less favoured situations to the west of the Loire to expand their plantings. The names of Ménétou-Salon, Quincy and Reuilly are now accepted as Sancerre substitutes at slightly lower prices (but longer odds against a fine ripe bottle).

Much higher up the river where it cuts through the Massif Central several scattered vineyard areas relate less to the Loire than to southern Burgundy and the Rhône. The most famous is St-Pourçain-sur-Sioule, once a monastic vineyard. Its wine is almost all consumed today to mitigate the effects of treatment at the spa of Vichy – but it is hard to see how it could ever have had more than a local following. Price is so far the main thing in favour of the remaining VDQS areas of the heights of the Loire. The Côtes Roannaise and de Forez and the Côtes d'Auvergne grow the right grapes for quality – Gamay, Chardonnay, some Pinot Noir and Syrah.

REUILLY PRODUCERS

Robert Cordier & Fils
36260 Reuilly. A family with 15 acres, 10 of Sauvignon for Reuilly and 5 of Pinot Noir and Gamay. Pinot Noir makes a Reuilly rosé.

Olivier Cromwell
36260 Reuilly. This grower's remarkable name descends, he thinks, from Scottish guards of Charles VII and Louis XI. His reputation rests on Reuilly rosé of Pinot Noir (5 acres) and Sauvignon (8 acres).

Claude Lafond
Bois St-Denis, 36260 Reuilly. A 17-acre estate divided into Sauvignon Blanc for very dry white, Pinot Noir for pale red and some Pinot Gris, which goes into a rather sweet rosé, which M. Lafond likes to age up to 5 years.

MENETOU-SALON PRODUCERS

Domaine de Chatenoy
18110 St-Martin d'Auxigny. The ancestors of Bernard Clément have owned this estate since 1560. 42 acres produce 6,500 cases of red, white and rosé Ménétou-Salon. Despite their freshness, his wines sometimes reach 13° of alcohol. He recommends them as apéritifs as well as table wines.

Georges Chavet
Les Brangers, 18110 St-Martin d'Auxigny. A 35-acre property which regularly wins gold medals, particularly for its rosé of Pinot Noir, which has been described as the best dry rosé in France. 18 months in bottle round out its flavour.

Jean-Paul Gilbert
18110 St-Martin d'Auxigny. A leading family of growers of Ménétou-Salon since the 18th century. From some 40 acres they produce Sauvignon white and Pinot Noir red and pale rosé – the red made with *chapeau immergé* and up to 3 weeks in the vat. Since 1976 a series of natural catastrophes – drought, frost, rot, poor flowering and hail – has halved their previous production of about 8,000 cases.

Jean Teiller
Ménétou-Salon, 18110 St-Martin d'Auxigny. A small but growing property with 18 acres divided equally between Sauvignon and Pinot Noir. The proprietor ferments in cement tanks and 600-litre wooden casks, bottles the white in spring, the red the following September.

Bringing in the harvest in the Loire

QUINCY PRODUCERS

Claude Houssier
Domaine du Pressoir, 18120 Quincy. *Vigneron* with 20 acres all in Quincy, producing Sauvignon only. Houssier avoids chaptalization if possible and aims for long-lived serious dry wines. His production of 2,500 cases is almost all sold in France.

Maison Meunier-Lapha
18120 Quincy. An old family of growers with 28 acres, half in Quincy planted with Sauvignon for its racy white, half of Vin de Pays du Cher of Pinot and Gamay. Their 3,500 cases are snapped up locally and by Parisians.

Raymond Pipet
Quincy, 18120 Lury-sur-Arnon. Carefully made Quincy from 32 acres. M. Pipet de-stems his Sauvignon and looks for finesse and moderate acidity.

COTES DU FOREZ

Cave Coopérative
Trelins, 42130 Boen. Founded 1962. 257 members; 988 acres; 113,000 cases, 55% VDQS Côtes du Forez and 25% Vins de Pays d'Urfe. The grape is the Gamay, this coop the dominant producer.

ST-POURÇAIN

Union des Vignerons
03500 St-Pourçain-sur-Sioule. The cooperative (founded 1952) dominates this once famous 'central' vineyard, formerly a monastic stronghold. 350 members farm 750 acres of Sauvignon, Sacy, Aligoté, Chardonnay and Tressalier whites and Pinot Noir and Gamay reds. Modern methods make 50,000 cases of white, 28,000 of rosé (decreasing) and 80,000 of red (increasing). The red is made either *en primeur* or aged in vats for 8 months. *Cuvée speciale* white is 40% Sauvignon, 60% Chardonnay, cold-shouldering the once dominant local Tressalier.

CHAMPAGNE

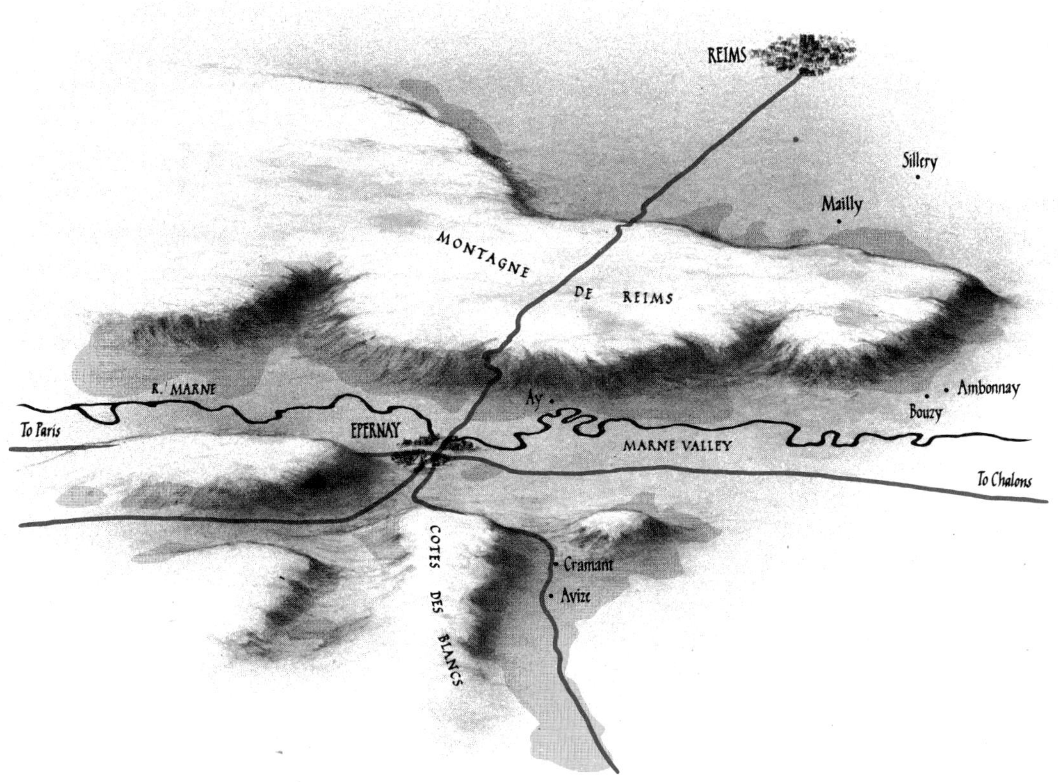

Champagne is the wine grown in the northernmost vineyards of France. The champagne method is something that is done to the wine to make it sparkling – and can be done to any wine. Other sparkling-wine makers would like us to believe that the method is all that matters. What really matters is the wine. It was one of the best in France long before the method was invented. The difference between the best champagne and the merely good (bad is hard to find) is almost entirely a matter of the choice and treatment of grapes, their variety, their ripeness, their handling and the soil that bears them. The difference between champagne and other sparkling wines is the same, only more so.

Most of the grapes of Champagne are grown by small farmers or even part-timers with other jobs. Some sell their grapes to big houses, some to cooperatives and some make wine themselves. Some buy back wine from cooperatives to label and sell as their own. Any merchant buying champagne can think up a name (a 'Buyer's Own Brand') and print a label. So there is no limit to the number of brands. In itself this lends strength to the score or so of houses with the best-known names and the widest distribution; they are often bought simply as safe bets. But size and wealth also allow them to buy the best materials, employ the best staff and stock their wine longest. (Time is vital to develop the flavours.) The great houses push to the limit the polishing and perfecting of an agricultural product.

The 'method' began 200 years ago with the genius of a Benedictine monk, Dom Pérignon of Hautvillers, apparently the first man to 'design' a wine by blending the qualities of grapes from different varieties and vineyards to make a whole greater, more subtle, more satisfying than any of its parts. This blend, the *cuvée*, is the secret patent of each maker. The best are astonishingly complex, with as many as 30 or 40 ingredient wines of different origins and ages, selected and balanced by nose and palate alone. Houses with their own vineyards tend to stress the character of the grapes they grow themselves: the heavier Pinot Noir of the Montagne de Reims or the lighter Chardonnay of the Côte des Blancs – each village is subtly different. Very few have enough to supply all their needs; in years of shortage competition for the best grapes is intense. Prices are fixed by a percentage system explained on page 180.

Pérignon (or a contemporary) discovered how to make his wine sparkling by a second fermentation in a tightly corked bottle – a process with dangers and complications that took another century to master completely. The principle is outlined on pages 174 and 175.

The sparkle is caused by large amounts of carbon dioxide dissolved in the wine. The '*mousse*' or froth in the glass is only part of it – you swallow the greater part. Carbon dioxide is instantly absorbed by the stomach wall. In the bloodstream it accelerates the circulation, and with it the movement of the alcohol to the brain. This is where champagne gets its reputation as the wine of wit and the natural choice for celebration. Other sparkling wines made by the same method can justifiably claim to have the same effect. But not the same taste.

THE PRINCIPAL CHAMPAGNE HOUSES

Besserat de Bellefon

Murigny. Founded 1843. Owned by Pernod-Ricard since 1976. Visits: appt. only.

NV: Brut Réserve, Demi-Sec, Crémant Blanc, Crémant des Moines Rosé, Brut Intégral. Vintage: Brut.

An outstanding success of the last 2 decades, rebuilt with the most modern plant to produce very fine light wines much appreciated in top French restaurants.

Brut Intégral is a totally dry wine in the latest fashion. France takes 80% of the total sales of 1.8m. bottles a year. Switzerland and West Germany are chief export markets.

J. Bollinger

5 1160 Ay. Founded 1829. Privately owned. Visits: appt. only.

NV: Brut, Spécial Cuvée. Vintage: Brut, Rosé, Tradition R.D., Vieilles Vignes Françaises. Still wines: Red Ay, Côte aux Enfants, made for domestic use.

A top-quality traditionalist house making full-bodied masculine champagne with body, length, depth and every other dimension. Wines are kept on their yeast as long as possible; in the case of R.D. about 10 years, giving extra breadth of flavour. A tiny patch of ungrafted prephylloxera Pinot Noir in Ay gives Vieilles Vignes Françaises; very rare, expensive and powerfully flavoured.

70% of grapes from Bollinger's own 346 acres, mainly Mt de Reims, average rating 99%. Remainder bought from Côte des Blancs and Verteuil, Marne valley. Production: approx. 1.2m. bottles a year. Stock: 5.7m. bottles (end of 1980). Exports, often by restricted quota, make up 75% of sales. UK is largest market.

Madame Bollinger (d. 1977) directed the company for 30 years. *See* page 174.

Canard-Duchêne

1 rue Edmond Canard, 51500 Ludes. Founded 1868. Public company, controlled by Veuve Clicquot-Ponsardin. Visits: at regular hours, appt. only in July or August.

NV and Vintage Charles VII. Coteaux Champenois is made in limited quantities in prolific years.

The non-vintage is a good lively party wine, finely frothy, not notably impressive in scent but with a definite fragrance of flavour.

Vineyards at Ludes supply a small proportion of needs. Production: 2.3m. bottles a year. Stock is 7m. bottles. 75% of production is sold within France.

Deutz & Geldermann

51160 Ay. Founded 1838. Family owned. Subsidiary companies: Delas (Rhône), L'Aulée (Loire). Visits: appt. only.

NV: Brut, Demi-Sec, Crémant. Vintage: Brut, Blanc de Blancs, Rosé, Réserve George Mathieu, Cuvée William Deutz.

The house style is 'traditional' and full-bodied, reflecting the high percentage of Ay wines in the *cuvées* and long ageing on the yeast. Exceptionally good vintage wines.

Grapes come from 99 acres of own vineyards in Marne valley (mostly Ay) and other areas, averaging 96.5%. Grapes (never wine) are bought in from best crus of the same areas. Production: 700,000 bottles a year. Deutz aim to have $3\frac{1}{2}$-4 years' stock, but two small harvests have reduced this to 3.2 years (2.3m. bottles). Sales in France 48%; Italy is the largest export market with 12%.

A deliberately small house, a founder member of the 'Grandes Marques' of Champagne.

George Goulet

2/4 avenue du General Giraud, 51100 Reims. Founded 1867. Owned by Les Grands Champagnes de Reims (which includes Abel Lepitre [q.v.] and St-Marceaux). Visits: appt. only.

NV: Demi-Sec, Dry Goût Americaine, Extra Quality Brut, 'G' (Blanc de Blancs). Vintage: Extra Quality Brut, Crémant Blanc de Blancs, Rosé Brut, Cuvée du Centenaire. Still wines: Bouzy Rouge, Blanc de Blancs.

Outstanding full-flavoured NV with a high proportion of Pinot Noir and deliciously smooth and drinkable Crémant, recommended by the firm for 'les lunchs'.

No vineyards. Production: 1m. bottles a year, with stocks of 3.5-4m. Exports to many countries, especially South America and Africa.

Charles Heidsieck & Henriot

51100 Reims. Founded 1808, family controlled. Visits: appt. only.

Heidsieck. NV: Brut. Vintage: Brut, Rosé, Blanc de Blancs, La Royale.

Henriot. NV: Souverain. Vintage: Souverain, Blanc de Blancs, Brut, Rosé, Le Premier, Réserve Baron Philippe de Rothschild.

Charles Heidsieck has long been known particularly for its long-lived classic vintage wines. Henriot is notably dry, even austere.

The two houses, originally one until 1875, were reunited in 1976. In 1980 they took over Trouillard and de Venoge (qq.v.) of Epernay. Henriot has 272 acres of vines, mainly in white grapes, and stresses Chardonnay in its *cuvées*, while Heidsieck stresses Pinot Noir. The policy is to adapt wines to individual markets. Total annual sales approach 5m. bottles. Stocks vary from 15-18m. bottles.

The original Charles Heidsieck was the 'Champagne Charlie' of the song, who made a fortune in America but almost lost it in the Civil War.

Heidsieck Monopole

83 rue Coquebert, 51100 Reims. Founded 1785. Public company linked with Mumm (owned by Seagram) since 1972. Visits: at regular hours.

NV: Dry Monopole, Red Top Sec, Green Top Demi-Sec. Vintage: Dry Monopole, Monopole Brut Rosé, Diamant Bleu.

A fairly small house famous for powerful, full-bodied, long-lived wine in the 'grand noir' style, i.e. with more black than white grapes. Diamant Bleu is the luxury *cuvée* and bears long keeping.

Sales are about 2m. bottles a year, largely supplied by the firm's own 277 acres (average rating 97%) plus leased vineyards. Stocks are about 6m. bottles. Exports go to 139 countries, with West Germany and Switzerland taking more than half.

The firm owns the historic Moulin de Verzenay, a windmill used as a field HQ in World War I, now used for receptions.

Henriot *see* Heidsieck, Charles

Krug

5 rue Coquebert, 51100 Reims. Founded 1843. Privately owned, linked with Rémy Martin, Cognac. Visits: appt. only.

Krug market only 2 champagnes, both of luxury quality and price: Grande Cuvée NV and Vintage. Grande Cuvée is a blend of 7 to 10 vintages and 20 to 25 different growths. The Vintage is made rarely and then in very small quantities.

Grande Cuvée has a high proportion of Chardonnay brilliantly blended for great finesse, very dry, elusively fruity, gentle yet authoritative at the same time. The Vintage tends to be more powerful, with great ageing qualities. Both are among the finest of all champagnes, but the Krugs make a point of preferring 'Grande Cuvée'.

Grapes come from 37 acres of Krug vineyards in Ay (100%) and Le Mesnil (99%) and by long-term contract from 37 acres in Avize (100%) owned by a Krug board member. The other 65-70% of grapes needed come from Leuvrigny (Pinot Meunier), Ay, Ambonnay and Rilly (Pinot Noir), and Le Mesnil, Oger, Avize and Villers Marmery (Chardonnay). All 3 grapes go into each blend.

All fermentation is still carried out in traditional 205-litre oak casks. Ageing is long and the whole cellar process is supervised by Henri Krug, a fifth-generation member of the family.

Sales of 500,000 bottles are based on stock of 3m., giving an exceptionally high ratio of 1:6. 70% is exported, Italy and UK being the largest markets. Krug's wines are sold only by specialist outlets and supplies are limited.

Lanson

12 boulevard Lundy, 51100 Reims. Founded 1760. Public company controlled by the Lanson and Gardinier families. Visits: at regular hours.

NV: Black Label Brut, Demi-Sec, Rosé. Vintage: Brut. Small quantities of Coteaux Champenois blanc and rouge, also ratafia and marc de Champagne.

Black Label is extremely popular for its full and fruity, though dry, style. Lanson vintage is distinctly delicate in contrast, released in exceptional years only (e.g. '69, '71, '75).

Production: 5-6m. bottles a year, almost half from the firm's own 568 acres in 12 scattered prime sites (average 97%), including Bouzy, Ambonnay, Dizy, Cramant, Avize and Oger, with the balance from neighbouring growers. Stocks are about 22m. bottles.

Sales are 50% in France, with UK the largest export market with 10%. The company is directed by a fifth-generation Lanson, but the emphasis today is on modernity in techniques and marketing.

Laurent-Perrier

Avenue de Champagne, 51150 Tours-sur-Marne. Founded 1812. Privately owned. Close links with Cordier in Bordeaux. Visits: appt. only.

NV: Brut, Cuvée Grand Siècle, Ultra Brut, Rosé Brut. Vintage: Brut Millésime. Still wines: white Blanc de Blancs de Chardonnay, red Pinot Franc.

The house style is full and mature but clean-flavoured and long on the palate. Ultra Brut is a completely dry, totally sugarless wine. The policy is to use most of the best wines in the non-vintage blend rather than reserving them for vintage and prestige *cuvées*.

Grapes come from 1,420 acres either owned or under long-term contract. Supplies come from the Mt de Reims (45%), Côte des Blancs (40%) and Marne valley (15%);

Choosing champagne

The knowledge essential for buying champagne to your own taste is the style and standing of the house and the range of its wines. Other relevant points included in the entries on these pages are the ownership and date of foundation, whether you may visit the cellars, where most of the grapes come from, the annual sales and size of stock and the principal markets of the house. To some extent you may deduce style and quality from the sources of grapes and their standing in the percentage table on page 180, in conjunction with the average age of the wine (the stocks divided by the annual sales. N.B. the current figures reflect a shortage of stocks). Most houses offer wines in the following categories:

Non-vintage (NV). A *cuvée* maintained, as near as possible, to exactly the same standard year after year: usually fairly young. The standard gauge of the 'house style'.

Vintage. Best-quality wine of a vintage whose intrinsic quality is considered too good to be hidden in a non-vintage *cuvée*. Normally aged longer on the yeast than non-vintage; more full-bodied and tasty, with the potential to improve for several more years.

Rosé. A blend of a small quantity of still red wine from one of the Pinot Noir villages (often Ay or Bouzy) with white sparkling champagne. In many cases entrancingly fruity and fine and one of the house's best *cuvées*.

Blanc de Blancs. A *cuvée* of white (Chardonnay) grapes only, with great grace and less 'weight' than traditional champagne.

Blanc de Noirs. A *cuvée* of black grapes only, sometimes faintly pink or '*gris*' and invariably rich and flavoury.

Cuvée de Prestige (under many names). A super-champagne on the hang-the-expense principle. Moët's Dom Pérignon was the first; now most houses have one. Fabulously good though most of them are there is a strong argument for two bottles of non-vintage for the price of one *cuvée de prestige*.

Crémant. A half-pressure champagne, preferred by some people who find a normal one too gassy – particularly with food.

Coteaux Champenois. Still white or red wine of the Champagne vineyards, made in limited quantities when supplies of grapes allow. Naturally high in acidity but can be exquisitely fine.

Brut, Extra Dry, etc. What little consistency there is about these indications of sweetness or otherwise is shown on page 176.

BOLLINGER

The Making of a Great Champagne

Although champagne was invented in the seventeenth century the industry as we know it is pre-eminently a product of the nineteenth. Most of the great houses were founded between 1780 and 1880. Architecturally and technologically champagne is high Victorian in concept and style.

The Bollinger establishment at Ay is typical in its impressive but compact plan; its buildings and cellars grouped around and under the original owner's house.

As in a Bordeaux château, the agricultural operations are based here, the grapes are brought in and crushed, the wines are fermented and racked and bottled. But the same premises are also a factory for the elaboration of the bottled wine into sparkling champagne, requiring a considerable labour force and huge cellars. The Bollinger house employs 60 people in its 350 acres of vineyards (which produce about three quarters of the wine processed), and 60 in the cellars (apart from an office staff of 20).

Bollinger champagne, in brief, is made like this: harvesting is done with great care to reject split grapes and avoid breaking whole ones. Prematurely crushed grapes give colour to the juice. If necessary the crop is sorted by hand before pressing.

The grapes are pressed, black and white separately, in very large, square, vertical presses taking four tons at a time – the best way to extract the juice gently. They are pressed three or four times, the cake of skins and stalks being cut up and redistributed each time. Only the first and sometimes part of the second pressings are kept for the house *cuvées*.

The greater part of the must is fermented in well-aged 205-litre oak barrels. Overacid must is fermented in large steel tanks that encourage a secondary, malolactic, fermentation that reduces acidity. The wine is racked two or three times during the winter to clean it. In March it is tasted and sorted into lots for blending to make the *cuvées*. At this stage in making, the non-vintage blend wine from previous vintages, stored in the cellars in magnums under slight pressure, barely *crémant*, is added in a proportion of up to one third. The *cuvée* is then bottled with a little fresh yeast and a precisely measured addition of sugar that, when fermented, will add one per cent to the alcoholic content and produce a gas pressure of six atmospheres. (In times past a high proportion of bottles used to burst in the cellars.) Non-vintage wine is sealed with a metal cap, vintage with a cork held in place by a metal clamp. The bottles are well shaken, then stacked in the cold (40°F/4°C) limestone cellars; the non-vintage for two years, the vintage for four or five and the house speciality, Tradition Récemment Dégorgé, for as long as ten years.

The fermentation of the added sugar, although slow at the low temperature, is finished within one and a half to three months. The object of leaving the wine long beyond that time is to mature it in contact with the yeast, which adds another dimension to the flavour.

When the wine is aged enough there comes the problem of removing the yeast. The bottles are moved to racks, where they stand cork downwards at an angle of 45 degrees. Every day for up to three months each bottle is slightly shaken, slightly twisted and tipped slightly nearer the vertical by skilled '*remueurs*' who each handle some 30,000 bottles a day. At each *remuage* the sediment of yeast cells slips closer to the cork.

When all the sediment is resting on the cork the bottles are moved upside down to an icy brine bath, where the ends of their necks containing the sediment are frozen solid. The skilled process of 'disgorging' consists of removing the cork (or cap), letting the pressure in the bottle blow out the plug of frozen sediment, then topping up the bottle and immediately recorking it, with a wire 'muzzle' to hold the cork in. The bottles are then cellared again for at least several months before being washed, labelled, and boxed for dispatch.

Most of these stages have been ingeniously mechanized by the big champagne houses, the latest development being the 'very large machine', a tilting palette, that performs the *remuage* mechanically. Bollinger's director Christian Bizot is not averse to efficiency, but he considers that a house with a firm grasp of the very top of the market, selling only one million bottles a year, has too much to lose to risk any short cuts.

the average rating is 96%. Production: 6m. bottles a year planned to rise to 8m. in 1983 and 10m. in the late 1980s. Stocks (1981) are 1.8m. bottles. Sales are 45% in France, with Belgium the leading export market (20%).

Laurent-Perrier has risen from ninety-eighth position in the champagne sales league in 1945 to fourth in 1981. It is now the biggest privately owned house.

Mercier

75 avenue de Champagne, 51200 Epernay. Founded 1858, now owned by Moët & Chandon.
Visits: at regular hours.
NV: Extra Rich (for UK only), Demi-Sec, Demi-Sec Réserve, Brut, Brut Réserve. Vintage: Brut Réserve, Brut Réserve Rosé, Réserve de l'Empereur.

Mercier, like the rest of the Moët group, has the virtue of size: consistency of supply means reliability. The stress is on dry, brut champagne, with blends tailored for individual markets.

Source of grapes: *see* Moët & Chandon. Sales average 5.5m. bottles a year, the major market being France.

Always known for their clever publicity, the firm's best stunt was unplanned: in 1900 a tethered balloon, in which the public could taste the wines, broke loose and carried a waiter and 9 involuntary passengers across the German border where customs fined them 20 crowns for failing to declare the champagne.

Moët & Chandon

20 avenue de Champagne, 51200 Epernay. Founded 1743. Public company with large family shareholdings. They are owners of Mercier and Ruinart (qq.v.), Domaine Chandon in California, and Christian Dior perfume, and wine producers in Brazil, Argentina and Portugal. They are also partners with Hennessey Cognac in the Moët-Hennessey holding company.
Visits: at regular hours.
NV: White Star Demi-Sec, White Star Extra-Dry, Première Cuvée (for UK only), Brut Imperial, Crémant Demi-Sec. Vintage: Brut Imperial and Rosé, Dry Imperial and Rosé (UK), Dom Pérignon and Dom Pérignon Rosé. Still wines: Saran (still white Chardonnay), Bouzy Rouge, for domestic use only, produced only 5 times in the last 35 years.

Moët's various *cuvées* maintain a light, dry style which rounds out nicely with age. Very wide sources of supply ensure consistency of the huge quantities of NV, which often scores high in comparative tastings for polish and balance. Dom Pérignon is almost as fine as its reputation, with a distinguished almost almond-like flavour, crisp and very long-lived.

The group owns vineyards in 10 out of the 12 Grand Cru communes. Total holding is 2,124 acres (nearly 2% of the total Champagne vineyard), with 1,712 acres in production. Grapes from these vineyards supply Ruinart and Mercier as well as Moët.

Sales average 17.5m. bottles a year. Exports are to 154 countries, the biggest markets being UK and USA, in both of which Moët have a third of the champagne market. 25% of all champagne exported comes from Moët and its associated companies.

Moët was the favourite of Napoleon, hence the Brut Imperial brand. The firm owns the Abbey of Hautvillers, where Dom Pérignon discovered the principles of champagne making in the 17th century.

Mumm

29 rue du Champ de Mars, 51100 Reims. Founded 1827. Public company. Majority shareholder Seagram, Canada. Mumm owns Perrier-Jouët and Heidsieck Monopole (qq.v.).

Visits: at regular hours.
NV: Cordon Vert (demi-sec), Double Cordon (sec), Extra-Dry (mainly for N. American market), Cordon Rouge. Vintage: Cordon Rouge, René Lalou, Cordon Rosé. Also Crémant de Cramant Blanc de Blancs (brut).

Very dry, light and well-balanced wines from a preponderance of Chardonnay. Cordon Rouge is very correct but has been almost too light, perhaps lacking a little character, recently. The vintage Rosé and lightly sparkling Crémant, made from Chardonnay grapes from the village of Cramant, are both excellent.

Grapes come from 556 acres of owned vineyards, producing 20% of the firm's needs, and on contract from 35-45 different vineyards according to the year. Mumm's own holdings are spread across the region, with the biggest concentrations in Mailly, Ambonnay, Bouzy, Vaudemanges, Avenay, Ay, Avize and Cramant. The average rating of the Mumm vineyards is 95%.

Annual production is over 8m. bottles, and stocks are 25m. bottles. This ratio is slightly better than for other large houses and reflects Mumm's caution about a possible supply shortage. North America takes 36% of exports, with Italy the next-biggest customer at 20%.

Joseph Perrier

51000 Châlons-sur-Marne. Founded 1825. Family owned.
Visits: appt. only.
NV: Cuvée Royale Brut, Brut Blanc de Blancs, Demi-Sec, Crémant, Rosé. Vintage: Brut, Cuvée du Cent-Cinquantenaire. Still red: Cumières Rouge, in decreasing production. Still whites: Chardonnay (blend of Grands Crus) and Coteaux Champenois Blanc de Blancs.

The house style is known for lightness and freshness (the non-vintage is particularly pretty) but the wines age admirably.

One third of the grapes comes from their vineyards at Cumières, Damery, Hautvillers and Verneuil, rated on average at 90%. Sales around 600,000 bottles a year with 3 years' stock in reserve for the NV and 5 years' for the vintage wines.

Exports concentrate on Europe (75%), split between Belgium, Italy, UK and Luxembourg. The house supplied Queen Victoria and Edward VII and today concentrates on restricted quantities, high quality, and a traditional approach.

Perrier-Jouët

26 avenue de Champagne, 51200 Epernay. Founded 1811.
Owned by Mumm (q.v.).
Visits: at regular hours.
NV: Grand Brut. Vintage: Brut, Rosé. Luxury cuvées: Blason de France and Belle Epoque.

Respected for first-class, very fresh and crisp but by no means light NV and luxury *cuvées* with plenty of flavour. Belle Epoque comes in an Art Nouveau, flower-painted bottle. Well-aged, unusual rosé.

Perrier-Jouët owns 267 acres of vineyards, 96 in Cramant. Grapes also come from some 30 other crus. Sales average 2m. bottles a year from stocks of at least 8m. Half the production is exported, 20% of it to the USA.

Piper Heidsieck

51 boulevard Henri-Vasnier, 51100 Reims. Founded 1785.
(Same foundation as Heidsieck Monopole.) Privately owned.
Visits: at regular hours.
NV: Brut, Demi-Sec. Vintage: Brut Extra, Rosé, Florens Louis, Brut Sauvage.

Well-regarded, relatively delicate wines. Florens Louis is the luxury *cuvée*, produced only in the best vintages and only from the 12 top communes. Brut Sauvage is totally dry with no dosage but extra age in the blend.

A medium-sized Grande Marque selling about 5m. bottles a year with UK, Italy and USA the main export markets. The firm owns no vineyards and buys mainly in the Mt de Reims and Côte des Blancs. Stocks are about 3 years' shipments.

Florens Louis is named after the founder of the house, who travelled to the Petit Trianon in 1785 to present his champagne to Marie Antoinette.

Pol Roger

1 rue Henri-Lelarge, 51200 Epernay. Founded 1849, still family-owned and run. Visits: appt. only.
NV: White Foil, Brut. Vintage: Brut, Rosé, Blanc de Chardonnay. Luxury cuvée: P.R.
(vintage, not available in all countries).

Fairly small house consistently regarded among the best half-dozen and a personal favourite of mine for 20 years. Outstandingly clean and crisp NV; stylish long-lived vintage, one of the best rosés and soft, 'tender' Chardonnay.

One third of grapes comes from the firm's 136 acres,

Serving and enjoying champagne

When. For celebrations any time, as an apéritif, very occasionally with light meals, with dessert (sweet 'demi-sec' only), in emergencies, as a tonic.
How. At 45°-50°F/7°-10°C, colder for inexpensive champagne, up to 54°F/13°C for very fine mature ones. In a tall, clear glass, not a broad, shallow one. To preserve the bubbles, pour slowly into a slightly tilted glass.
How much. Allow half a bottle (three glasses) per head for an all-champagne party. Half as much when it is served as an apéritif before another wine.
What to look for. Plenty of pressure behind the cork, total clarity, abundance of fine bubbles lasting indefinitely, powerful but clean flavour and finish, and balance – not mouth-puckeringly dry or acid, not cloyingly sweet. Above all moreish. House styles will become apparent with experience.

Who makes champagne?

In 1970 there were 2,900 growers making their own champagne. By 1980 the figure was over 5,000. The proportion of sales represented by grower-producers and cooperatives rose from a quarter in 1970 to over a half in 1980. Most of this growth was within France and represents direct sales and mail order. The *maisons* continue to dominate the export trade.

Dosage, dryness and sweetness

When champagne is disgorged the loss of the frozen plug of sediment needs making good to fill the bottle. At this stage the sweetness of the finished wine is adjusted by topping up (*dosage*) with a '*liqueur d'expédition*' of wine mixed with sugar and sometimes brandy. A few firms make a totally dry wine, topped up with wine only and known by names such as Brut Nature or Brut Intégral. The great majority have some sugar added. The following are the usual percentages of sugar in the *dosage* for each style (although they vary from house to house):

Brut: 0.5-1.5%. Very dry.
Extra Dry: 1.5-2.5%. Dry.
Sec: 2-4%. Slightly sweet.
Demi-sec: 4-6%. Distinctly sweet.
Doux: Over 6%. Very sweet.

The landscape of Champagne: vines on the Montagne de Reims at Villedommange

average 93% (30 more being planted), mainly in the Côte des Blancs. Production about 1.4m. bottles; stock about 5m. bottles. Sales 55% France, then UK, Italy, USA, Belgium, Switzerland, etc. The brand is particularly associated with Sir Winston Churchill. On his death the label was given a black border.

Pommery & Greno

5 place General Gouraud, 51100 Reims. Founded 1836. Family controlled. Visits: at regular hours.

NV: Brut, Carte Blanche (demi-sec), Drapeau Sec. Vintage: Brut, Rosé Special.

After several years of genteel coasting under old family management, a takeover by the dynamic Gardinier family in 1980 heralds new ideas and an expansion to double the production. The firm's tradition is for very fine and notably dry champagnes, complex and yeasty rather than fruity. The rosé is almost excessively dry.

Grapes from 741 acres of vineyards in the Côte des Blancs and the Montagne de Reims, average over 99%. Further supplies from small growers. Production: 3.8m. bottles, with stocks of 3 years' supply. Exports take 67%, with West Germany and Italy the largest markets.

Pommery's cellars comprise 9 miles of Roman chalk-pits, some decorated with bas-reliefs. Madame Pommery, who took over the running of the firm in 1858, invented a special *cuvée* for Britain which is still sold there. The marque was represented in Britain by André Simon. Madame Pommery built the company's famous offices to a plan concocted from those of several British castles.

Louis Roederer

21 boulevard Lundy, 51100 Reims. Founded 1819. Privately owned. Visits: appt. only.

NV: Brut, Extra Dry, Grand Vin Sec (medium), Carte Blanche (sweet). Vintage: Brut, limited quantities of Cristal Brut (in clear bottles), Brut Rosé and Cristal Rosé.

The house style is notably smooth and mature, epitomized by the excellent full-bodied non-vintage and the fabulous Cristal, one of the most luscious champagnes, racy but deeply flavoured. Recent vintages have aged more rapidly than earlier ones particularly the 1975.

80% of grapes come from the house's own 370 acres of vines (Mt de Reims 98, Marne valley 124, Côte des Blancs 148: all rated over 95%). Production is dictated by these supplies: 1.5–1.8m. bottles a year. Stock: 6m. bottles. Sales in France 40%, with USA the leading export market with 15.5%. Up to 1916 half of the sales were in Russia, where Czar Alexander II demanded crystal bottles.

Ruinart Père & Fils

4 rue Crayères, 51100 Reims. Founded 1729 – one of the older Champagne firms. Now owned by Moët & Chandon. Visits: at regular hours.

NV: La Maréchale, Brut Tradition, Brut Réserve, Dom Ruinart Blanc de Blancs, Dom Ruinart Rosé. Vintage: Brut, Rosé. Still wine: Chardonnay (white).

Extremely stylish among the lighter champagnes both in non-vintage and vintage. The luxury Dom Ruinart is among the most notable blancs de blancs. See comments under Mercier.

Source of grapes: *see* Moët & Chandon. Sales average 1m. bottles a year. France is the major market.

Napoleon's Josephine enjoyed Ruinart – but unfortunately refused, after her divorce, to honour the bills she ran up as Empress.

Salon le Mesnil

Le Mesnil-sur-Oger. Founded 1911. Public company. Visits: appt. only.

The sole house to produce only vintage blanc de blancs champagne. They have declared just 17 vintages in the last 52 years.

Salon pioneered blanc de blancs wines and still leads in quality if not quantity, with light, extremely delicate and totally dry wine; really for connoisseurs. 15 years is a good age for them.

All grapes come from Côte des Blancs commune of Le Mesnil, rating 98%. The house owns vines and buys from a few growers, the same ones since early this century.

Production is only 60,000 bottles a year, yet stock is nearly 500,000 bottles: 8 years' supply – one of the biggest sales/stock ratios in Champagne. Sales to European and USA markets are rationed. Techniques are described as 'artisan' – everything done by hand. Marketing is entirely by personal recommendation.

Taittinger

9 place St-Niçaise, 51100 Reims. Founded 1734 as Forest Fourneaux, name changed to Taittinger in 1931. Public company controlled by Taittinger family.
Visits: appt. only.
NV: Brut Réserve. Vintage: Brut, Comtes de Champagne (blanc de blancs), Comtes de Champagne Rosé. Still white: La Marquetterie Coteaux Champenois (all Chardonnay).

The style of the Brut wines derives from the dominance of white grapes in the blend. Comtes de Champagne is one of the most delicate, exquisitely luxurious prestige *cuvées*.

Taittinger own 600 acres and also buy from other growers, mostly on the Côte des Blancs. Main sources of grapes are Avize, Chouilly, Cramant, Mesnil and Oger. Sales around 3.8m. bottles; stock: 12m. bottles. France drinks about 45%; Italy leads the export market with 13% followed by the USA, Belgium, Switzerland and UK.

Taittinger's cellars, parts of which date from Roman times, belonged in the 13th century to the monks of St-Niçaise, who traded in Champagne wines.

Veuve Clicquot-Ponsardin

12 rue de Temple, 51100 Reims. Founded 1772. A public company, family-controlled; also own Champagne Canard-Duchêne. Visits: at regular hours.
NV: Yellow Label, White Label Rich. Vintage: Gold Label, Rosé, La Grande Dame. Still wines: Coteaux Champenois, Bouzy Rouge.

Large, prestigious and influential house making classic 'big' champagne in a firm, full-flavoured style, and an outstanding rosé that ages superbly.

650 acres of vineyards are widespread, average 97%. Production: about 6.5m. bottles; stock about 4 years' supply. Exports dominate, especially to Italy, UK, Venezuela, Scandinavia, Australia.

The company's success was founded by 'The Widow' Clicquot, who took over the business in 1805 at the age of 27, when her husband died. She invented the now universal '*remuage*' for clarifying the wine and produced the first rosé champagne. The descendants of her partner Edouard Werlé now run the firm.

OTHER PRODUCERS

Ayala, Ay
Traditionalist house with 60 acres of vines making nearly 1m. bottles of weighty, old-style wines. Also a lighter blanc de blancs. Once highly fashionable and still respected. Montebello is another label.

Barancourt, Bouzy
Small house with some 120 acres specializing in a rather heavy vintage blanc de noirs, rosé and still red Bouzy.

Billecart-Salmon, Mareuil-sur-Ay
NV: Brut. Vintage: Brut. Cuvée N.F. Billecart. Family-owned house, founded 1818. Concentrates on Brut NV and on French market (80% of sales). The blend contains a high proportion of Pinot Noir to Chardonnay (60:30). All grapes are bought in. Slow, cool fermentation produces a light, fresh style. Sales: 420,000 bottles a year.

Boizel, Epernay
Family business, also uses the names Louis Kramer and Camuset. The prestige *cuvée* is Joyau de France. No vineyards. Production: 500,000 bottles a year, half of which is exported.

Bonnet, Oger
Small family firm with 25 acres specializing in blanc de blancs.

De Castellane, Epernay
NV: Brut Blanc de Blancs, Brut Croix de St André. Vintage: Brut, Brut Blanc de Blancs, Rosé Brut, Commodore Cuvée. Still white and red wines in prolific years. An independent family firm. Production: 1.5m. bottles a year, of which 70% is sold in France. First fermentation in oak and stress on Pinot Noir gives the wines structure and solidity.

A. Charbaut & Fils, Epernay
NV and Vintage Blanc de Blancs. Family-owned house in partnership with de Courcy (q.v.). Specializes in blanc de blancs. Owns 128 acres of 90-100% vineyards supplying half its needs. Sales are 2.5m. bottles a year, 40% exported. Stockists include many great restaurants of N. France, Pan-Am and TWA.

De Courcy Père & Fils, Epernay
NV: Brut Crémant Blanc de Blancs, Rosé. Vintage: Brut; also Coteaux Champenois. Family-owned house linked with Charbaut (q.v.). Pioneers in export markets of the *crémant* (lightly sparkling) style.

Giesler, Avize
Now owned by the giant Marne & Champagne concern (q.v.). The brand is popular in the south of France, but little is exported. Wines made are NV: Extra Superior Brut. Vintage: Giesler, Rosé, Blanc de Blancs, Cuvée Grande Origin. Despite their origin within the Marne company, these wines show individuality of style.

Gosset, Ay
Gosset has good claim to being the oldest champagne house: the firm is now run by the 15th and 16th generations in descent from the founder, Pierre, who was mayor of Ay in 1584. Since 1980 it has been linked with Philipponat (q.v.). Three wines are produced: NV: Spécial Réserve, Brut Rosé, Grand Millésime; all showing the Ay 'grands noirs' style. Production: 200,000 bottles a year.

Gratien, Alfred, Epernay
Small traditionalist house linked with Gratien & Meyer at Saumur. Makes excellent dry wines fermented in small barrels. Supplies the I.E.C. Wine Society in England.

Jacquesson & Fils, Dizy, Epernay
NV: Perfection Brut, Blanc de Blancs, Rosé Brut. Vintage: Perfection Brut. Founded 1798, one of the 9 oldest Champagne firms. Sole proprietor: Jean Chiquet. Their 54 acres of vineyards at Dizy, Ay, Hautvillers and Avize supply more than half their requirements. Characterized by a high proportion of Chardonnay – the blanc de blancs is made entirely from their 27 acres at Avize. Sales: 500,000 bottles a year, 80% in France.

Abel Lepitre, Reims
Family firm well known in French restaurants for its Crémant Blanc de Blancs. Its prestige *cuvée* is Prince A. de Bourbon Parme. No vineyards. Linked with George Goulet (q.v.) and St-Marceaux, a group with total sales of nearly 700,000 bottles a year.

Mailly-Champagne, Mailly
Major cooperative, founded in 1929, now with 70 members owning 173 acres in highly rated, chiefly Pinot Noir, vineyards. Top wine: Cuvée des Echansons. Sales approx. 700,000 bottles a year, including exports in Europe.

Marne & Champagne, Epernay
One of the giants of the industry with 16km of cellars and a stock of 74m. bottles. The name is hidden behind many brands and BOBs. The best known is A. Rothschild with its prestige Réserve Grand Trianon.

Massé Père & Fils, Reims
Owned by Lanson and bottled at their premises. Massé is sold only in France.

Montebello *see* Ayala

Oudinot, Avize
Family firm with some 90 acres selling 800,000 bottles, the best labelled Cuvée du Marechal. Also owns the brand A. G. Jeanmaire.

Philipponat, Mareuil-sur-Ay
Small family house best known for its full-bodied vintage Clos des Goisses. 500,000 bottles a year. Now linked with Gosset (q.v.).

St-Gall *see* Union Champagne

St-Marceaux *see* Abel Lepitre
St-Michel *see* Union Champagne
Trouillard, Epernay
The other half of De Venoge (q.v.) similarly specializing in BOBs and since 1980 a part of the Heidsieck/Henriot group.
Union Champagne, Avize
Giant modern cooperative representing 1,000 growers through 10 smaller coops. Stock of 10-12m. bottles, annual production 5m. Supplies many BOBs, also wines under St-Michel and St-Gall labels. Four fifths of the wine are returned to growers for sale under their own labels.
De Venoge, Epernay
Important house specializing in BOBs, now (with Trouillard) part of the Heidsieck/Henriot group.

MINOR PRODUCERS

The number of champagne houses is growing and has now passed 150. Many produce 'Buyer's Own Brands' for overseas shippers and hotel chains, others only export to one or two markets, or may only sell within France. However, such companies are not necessarily small.

Bauget-Jouette, Epernay
Beaumet Chaurey, Epernay
Paul Berthelot, Dizy
Bichat, Reims
Billiard, Gaétan, Epernay
Bouché Père & Fils, Pierry
Château de Boursault, Boursault
Bricout, A., & Co, Avize
Brun, Edouard, & Co, Ay
Brun, René, Ay
Bur, Vve Paul, Reims
Burtin, Epernay

De Castelnau, Epernay
De Cazanove & Co, Avize
Chanoine Frères, Rilly-la Montagne
Collery, Ay
Compagnie Française des Grands Vins, Reims
Comptoir Vinicole de Champagne, Reims

Defond, Marcel, Reims
Delamotte Père & Fils, Avize
Desmoulins, A., & Co, Epernay
Doré, Noël, Rilly-la-Montagne
Driant, Emile, Ay
Driant, Robert, Ay
Dubois, Michel, Epernay
Dueil, Reims
Duval-Leroy, Vertus

Eliniaux, Roland, Ay

Fournier & Co, Reims
France Champagne, Epernay

Gardet & Co, Rilly-la-Montagne
Gentils, Lucien, Dizy
Gentils, René, Epernay
Germain, H., & Fils, Rilly-la-Montagne
Gobillard, Paul, Epernay
Guy, Roger, Reims

Hamm, Emile, & Fils, Ay

Iverne, Bernard, Ay

Jacquinot & Fils, Epernay
Jamart & Co, Saint-Martin-d'Ablois
Jardin & Co, Le Mesuil-sur-Oger

Kruger, Louis, Epernay

Legras, R. & L., Chouilly
Lemoine, J., Rilly-la-Montagne
Lenoble, Damery, Epernay

Mansard Baillet, Epernay
Martel, G.H., & Co, Epernay
Medot & Co, Reims
Michel, Emile, Verzenay
Montvillers, Ay
Morel, G., Fils, Reims

Paillard, E.M., Reims
Pierlot, Jules, Epernay
Pierre, Marcel, Reims
Ployez-Jacquemart, Rilly-la-Montagne

Ralle, Eugène, Verzenay
Rapeneau, Ernest, Epernay
Roederer, Théophile, Reims
Rohrbacher, Jean, Epernay

Sacotte, Epernay
Sacy, Verzy
S.A.M.E., Epernay
Société Générale de Champagne, Ay
Société Vinicole Golden Roy, Epernay

Tarin, Le Mesnil-sur-Oger
Tassin, Bernard, Celles-sur-Ource
Telmont J. de, & Co, Damery

Valentin, Epernay
Vaudon, Pierre, Avize
Vazart, Lucien, Chouilly

Waris, Jean, Avize

The politics of scarcity

Champagne suffers from a chronic shortage of wine that has pushed the price of grapes up in 10 years from 4.9 francs to 23 francs a kilo in 1980 – a price that means that the grapes for each bottle cost 31.25 francs.

There are 60,688 acres of vineyard within the appellation Champagne (which was determined in 1927). Pressure for permission to extend this is intense. Another 12,350 acres are considered suitable, but since the lucky owner of farmland who has been granted the appellation may see its value rise by 2,500 per cent or more, there are complicated jealousies involved.

Total sales in 1980 were 176 million bottles, of which 115 million were sold by the merchant houses and 61 million by growers. Growers have greatly increased their share of the market in recent years (in 1949 it was only 11 per cent). They operate mainly in France at 'direct' prices, unfortunately reducing the stocks available for export by the merchants (who maintain the highest standards and the international prestige of champagne).

Of the 176 million bottles in 1980, 121 million were drunk in France and only 55 million were exported. France's amazing thirst for champagne, and the growers' willingness to supply it rather than sell to merchants, means that the exporters are having to retrench in foreign markets for lack of stock. Where they retreat, other sparkling wines step in. For all the present prosperity of Champagne there is a feeling of impending crisis.

Mixing in the dosage

The percentage system

Each harvest, the price a grower gets for his grapes is determined by a committee made up of C.I.V.C. officials, growers, producers and a government representative. The C.I.V.C. – Comité Interprofessionel du Vin de Champagne – is the official body that controls, promotes and defends the industry. The vineyards of the region are rated on a quality scale ranging downwards from 100 to 80 per cent. The average percentage rating of a champagne house's grape supplies is a key figure, for it establishes the quality of the firm's raw materials. Where this figure is available it is given in the entries. While each vineyard has a percentage rating, this is based on a notional good-quality harvest and the prices may be lowered across the board if the quality of grapes in a particular year is low. Or they may be increased in times of shortage, as they were in 1980 by no less than 10 francs a kilo.

Producers of grapes from 100 per cent vineyards can ask the full price, others *pro rata*.

The harvest

The leading vineyards, with their percentage ratings, are as follows:

Marne Valley

Ay	100%	black grapes
Mareuil-sur-Ay	98%	,,
Dizy-Magenta	95%	,,
Avenay	93%	,,
Bisseuil	93%	,,
Champillon	93%	,,
Mutigny	93%	,,
Cumières	90%	,,
Hautvillers	90%	,,

Côte d'Ambonnay

Ambonnay	100%	black grapes
Bouzy	100%	,,
Louvois	100%	,,
Tauxièrres-Mutry	100%	,,
Tours-sur-Marne	100%	,,
Tours-sur-Marne	90%	white grapes

Côte d'Epernay

Choilly	95%	white grapes
Choilly	90%	black grapes
Pierry	90%	,,

Côte des Blancs

Avize	100%	white grapes
Cramant	100%	,,
Le Mesnil-sur-Oger	99%	white grapes
Oger	99%	,,
Oiry	99%	,,
Cuis	95%	,,
Grauves	95%	,,
Cuis	90%	black grapes
Grauves	90%	,,

Côte de Vertus

Vertus	95%	black grapes
Bergères-Les-Vertus	95%	white grapes
Bergères-Les-Vertus	90%	black grapes

Montagne de Reims

Beaumond-sur-Vesle	100%	black grapes
Mailly	100%	,,
Puisieulx	100%	white grapes
Sillery	100%	black grapes
Verzenay	100%	,,
Verzy	99%	,,
Trépail	95%	white grapes
Villers-Marmery	95%	,,
Chigny-Les-Roses	94%	black grapes
Ludes	94%	,,
Montbré	94%	white grapes
Rilly-La-Montagne	94%	black grapes
Villers-Allerand	90%	white grapes

Champagne and food

There is no single classic dish for accompanying champagne, but champagne makers like to encourage the idea that their wine goes with almost any dish. Vintage champagne certainly has the fullness of flavour to go with most, but many people find sparkling wine indigestible with food. Champagne is the apéritif wine *par excellence*, and marvellously refreshing after a rich meal. Meanwhile there is the less fizzy Crémant, the still Coteaux Champenois, white or red (notably Bouzy Rouge) – and of course Bordeaux and burgundy.

Prices

The price of a bottle of champagne from the producer varies in a range from 40 francs for the wine of a small *récoltant-manipulant* (grower and maker) with no reputation to 80 francs for a classic merchant's non-vintage wine, and 160 francs for the most expensive *cuvée de prestige*.

Rosé des Riceys

Within the borders of Champagne lies one of France's most esoteric little appellations, specifically for a Pinot Noir rosé. Les Riceys is in the extreme south of Champagne. Most of its production is champagne, but in good ripe vintages the best Pinot Noir grapes, with a minimum natural 10°, are selected. The floor of an open wooden vat is first covered with grapes trodden by foot. Then the vat is filled with whole unbroken bunches. Fermentation starts at the bottom and the fermenting juice is pumped over the whole grapes. At a skilfully judged moment the juice is run off, the grapes pressed and the results 'assembled' to make a dark rosé of a unique sunset tint and, as its makers describe it, a flavour of gooseberries. The principal practitioner is Alexandre Bonnet, who has recently made it only in 1976, '80 and a little in '81. The postcode is 10340 Les Riceys.
Price (1981): about 54 francs a bottle.

ALSACE

After all the regions of France whose appellation systems seem to have been devised by medieval theologians, Alsace is a simple fairy tale.

A single appellation, Alsace, takes care of the whole region. Alsace Grand Cru is the same, with higher standards.

Nor are there Germanic complications of degrees of ripeness to worry about. Alsace labelling is as simple as Californian: maker's name and grape variety are the nub. The difference is that in Alsace a host of strictly enforced laws mean that there are no surprises. The grapes must be 100 per cent of the variety named, properly ripened and fermented dry with no sweetening added. The wines are correspondingly predictable and reliable. Their makers would like them to be considered more glamorous. In order to have their wines named among the 'greats' they are laying increasing emphasis on late picking, on wines from selected sites – on 'Cuvées de Prestige' of various kinds. What matters more to most drinkers is that Alsace guarantees a certain quality and a certain style more surely than any other wine region. It makes brilliantly appetizing, clean-cut and aromatic wine to go with food, and at a reasonable price.

The region is 70 miles long by one or two miles wide: the eastern flank of the Vosges mountains in the *départements* of the Haut-Rhin and the Bas-Rhin where the foothills, between 600 and about 1,200 feet, provide well-drained southeast- and south-facing slopes under the protection of the peaks and forests of the Vosges. The whole region is in their rain-shadow, which gives it some of France's lowest rainfall and most sustained sunshine.

On the principle that watersheds are natural boundaries, Alsace should be in Germany. It has been, but since the Rhine became the frontier it has been French. Its language and architecture remain Germanic. Its grape varieties are Germanic, too – but handled in the French manner they produce a different drink.

What is the difference? The ideal German wine has a certain thrilling balance of fruity sweetness and acidity. It has relatively little alcohol and resulting 'vinosity', which allows the tension of this balance to stand out in sharp relief. The components in all their complexity (or lack of it) can clearly be tasted.

Less than ideal (i.e. most) German wines are ingeniously, often excellently, made to reproduce this state of affairs by artificial means. After fermentation the missing element is the sweet fruitiness. So it is supplied by adding grape juice. The wine is sterilized to prevent further fermentation and the balance holds up in the bottle.

By contrast, an Alsace wine is given its extra or artificial ripeness in the form of sugar before fermentation. The natural ripeness must reach a level that in most parts of Germany would give it 'Qualitätswein' status. It can then be chaptalized with dry (not dissolved) sugar to produce an extra 2.5 degrees of alcohol. The minimum permitted natural alcohol being 8.5 degrees, the resulting wine has 11 degrees, which is the strength that the French are accustomed to in most of their white wines. All the added sugar being totally fermented, the wine is completely dry. The aromatic (or otherwise) character of its grapes stands out cleanly and clearly.

Although most of the best Alsace wines are still fermented in oak the barrels are antiques, thickly lined with tartrate crystals that prevent any flavours of wood or oxidation. So the wines start very simple and straight. They are bottled as soon as possible in the spring (or latest in the autumn) after the vintage. Most are drunk young – which is a pity. Bottle ageing introduces the elements of complexity which are otherwise lacking. A good Riesling or Gewürztraminer or Pinot Gris is worth at least four years in bottle and often up to ten.

Late picking, Vendange Tardive, is the means by which Alsace growers are scaling the heights of prestige which Burgundy and Bordeaux have so far monopolized. A hot summer (1976 was the latest famous example) provides such high sugar readings in the grapes that fermentations stop with considerable natural sweetness still remaining in the wine. They reach an alcohol level that would be uncharacteristic of a modern German Auslese. The resulting combination of strength, sweetness and concentrated fruity flavour is still peculiar to Alsace. When (as in 1976) the autumn also brings the noble rot it adds another welcome dimension of flavour. The Hugel family, who have been pioneers with these luscious wines, have got over the problem of terminology for late-picked wines by coining the expression *Sélection des Grains Nobles*. If the individual 'grains' or grapes are selected it is what the Germans call a Beerenauslese.

The 70-mile length of the Alsace vineyards falls into two *départements*, the Haut-Rhin and the Bas-Rhin. The centre of the finest area lies in the Haut-Rhin, in the group of villages north and south of Colmar with the extravagantly half-timbered and flower-decked little town of Riquewihr as its natural wine capital; a sort of St-Emilion of the Vosges.

The climate is warmest and driest in the south, but scarcely different enough to justify the popular inference that Haut-Rhin is parallel to, let us say, Haut-Médoc. There is no suggestion of lower quality in the name Bas-Rhin; it is simply lower down the river Rhine. Even farther down, going directly north, are the German Palatinate vineyards, producing the richest and some of the greatest of all German Rieslings.

Human nature being what it is many truckloads of Bas-Rhin grapes are taken south at harvest time to go into blends with Haut-Rhin labels.

More important are the individual vineyard sites with the best soils and microclimates. Thirty or 40 Vosges hillsides have individual reputations, which in Burgundy would long ago have been enshrined in law. Alsace has been on the point of listing certain vineyards as 'Grands Crus' for many years.

A few of these names are used often enough on labels to be familiar already. Kaefferkopf at Ammerschwihr is particularly noted for its Gewürztraminer; Schoenenberg at Riquewihr for its Riesling; Kaysersberg's Schlossberg, Guebwiller's Kitterlé, Turckheim's Eichberg and Brand, Béblenheim's Sonnenglanz are other examples.

Ownership of these vineyards is noted in the following list of producers.

It is probable that 1983 will be the year when the first two dozen site-names will be officially delimited and recognized for the first time. They are expected to be followed by another dozen or so in due course. Almost every village in Alsace wants to have its best hillside recognized as a Grand Cru.

The wine from these Grands Crus '*Lieux-dits*' (or sites) will only have to fulfil the same standards as a Grand Cru does today without a site-name. The wine will not necessarily be better – but it will have to come from the slope in question – and in due course such slopes will no doubt come to be known as characters with a certain style.

GROWERS AND COOPERATIVES

The vineyards of Alsace are even more fragmented in ownership than those of the rest of France. With 9,200 growers sharing the total of 29,000 acres the average individual holding is just over three acres.

The chances of history established a score or more leading families with larger estates – still rarely as much as 100 acres. With what seems improbable regularity they trace their roots back to the seventeenth century, when the Thirty Years War tore the province apart. In the restructuring of the industry after the wars of this century these families have grouped smaller growers around them in a peculiar pattern consisting of their own domaine plus a wine-making and merchanting business. They contract to buy the small growers' grapes and make their wine – very often using their own domaine wines as their top-quality range. As the following details of these larger houses show, the pattern is repeated all over Alsace.

The small grower's alternative to a contract with a grower/négociant (or just a négociant) is the local cooperative. Alsace established the first in France, in 1895, and now has one of the strongest cooperative movements. Their standards are extremely high and they often provide the best bargains in the region.

Alsace grapes

Chasselas (In German Gutedel, in Swiss Fendant.) Formerly one of the commonest grapes, rarely if ever named on a label, but used for its mildness in everyday blends, including the so-called 'noble' Edelzwicker.

Clevner or Klevner A local name for the Pinot Blanc (q.v.).

Knipperlé Like the Chasselas, a common blending grape not named on labels.

Gewürztraminer Much the most easily recognized of all fine-wine grapes, whose special spicy aroma and bite epitomizes Alsace wine. Most Alsace Gewürztraminer is made completely dry but intensely fruity, even to the point of slight fierceness when it is young. With age remarkable citrus fruit smells and flavours, suggesting grapefruit, intensify. Gewürztraminer of a fine vintage, whether made dry or in the sweet Vendange Tardive style, is worth maturing almost as long as Riesling. The fault of a poor Gewürztraminer is sometimes softness and lack of definition, or alternatively a heady heaviness without elegance. In a range of Alsace wines Gewürztraminer should be served last, after Rieslings and Pinots.

Pinot Blanc An increasingly popular grape, giving the lightest of the 'noble' wines; simply fresh and appetizing without great complexity. This is the base wine for most Crémant d'Alsace.

Pinot Gris or Tokay d'Alsace After Riesling and Gewürztraminer the third potentially great-wine grape of the region. First-class Tokay has a dense, stiff and intriguing smell and taste which is the very opposite of the fresh and fruity Pinot Blanc. It is almost frustrating to taste, as though it were concealing a secret flavour you will never quite identify. Tokays mature magnificently with broad, rich deep-bosomed wines whose only fault is that they are not refreshing.

Pinot Noir A grape that is made into both red and rosé in Alsace, but it is sometimes necessary to read the label to know which is which. The must is often heated to extract colour, but the result is never more than a light wine, without the classic Pinot flavour found in, for example, Bouzy Rouge from Champagne.

Riesling The finest wine grape of Alsace, as it is of Germany, but here interpreted in a totally different way. Alsace Rieslings are fully ripened and fully fermented, their sugar all turned to

LEADING ALSACE PRODUCERS

Caves J. Becker

Zellenberg, 68340 Riquewihr.

The Beckers have been growers at Riquewihr since 1610. Their 23 acres are in the Zellenberg vineyard halfway to Ribeauvillé, planted with 44% Gewürztraminer, 33% Riesling, 8% Pinot Noir, 6% Pinot Blanc, 4% Muscat, 2% each of Chasselas and Sylvaner, 1% Pinot Gris. Oak barrels but modern controls make them a typical small firm of grower/merchants, buying grapes to make up a total of 40,000 cases a year (8% exports). They also own the brand Gaston Beck.

Léon Beyer

68420 Eguisheim

A family firm founded in 1880, now directed by Léon Beyer and his son Marc. Their 75 acres of vines are in Eguisheim (28 Gewürztraminer, 23 Riesling, 7 each of Pinots Blanc, Gris and Noir and 3 of Muscat). Beyer's best wines are full-bodied and dry, clearly designed to go with food and often seen in top restaurants in France. I have seen some remarkably preserved 10- and even 20-year-old examples. Riesling Cuvée des Ecaillers and Gewürztraminer Cuvée des Comtes are their principal brands.

E. Boeckel

67140 Mittelbergheim

Grower and négociant (founded 1853) with 50 acres in and around Mittelbergheim, regarded as a steady producer of traditional wines. His standard Sylvaner, Riesling and Gewürztraminer are labelled Zotzenberg; Brandluft and Wibelsberg are selected Rieslings; Château d'Isembourg his best Gewürztraminer. Exports are 55% of a total of 35,000 cases.

Dopff 'Au Moulin'

68340 Riquewihr

Another family firm of 17th-century origins, with the largest vineyard holdings of central Alsace. A total of 185 acres, principally in the Schoenenberg at Riquewihr for Riesling and Eichberg at Turckheim for Gewürztraminer, with Pinot Blanc in the Hardt vineyards near Colmar grown specifically for Crémant d'Alsace, which Dopff pioneered at the turn of the century. *Crémant* is an increasing part of their business, which is known for delicate and individual wines. Special Fruits de Mer is a good blend. Total sales 200,000 cases, 30% exported.

Dopff & Irion

'Château de Riquewihr', 68340 Riquewihr.

One of the biggest grower/merchants of Alsace, still run by members of the Dopff and Irion families whose forebears have made wine at Riquewihr for 3 centuries, combining in 1945. They own 87 acres in Riquewihr, producing some 17,000 cases of their own Riesling Les Murailles (from the Schoenenberg), Gewürztraminer Les Sorcières, the very attractive Muscat Les Amandiers and Pinot Gris Les Maquisards. In addition they produce 270,000 cases from the grapes of 500 small growers under contract, representing 1,100 acres. Their main brands are very dry Crustaces and the fuller Crystal; also a Crémant d'Alsace. 45% of sales are exports.

Théo Faller

Domaine Weinbach, 68240 Kaysersberg.

A distinguished domaine of 62 acres of former monastic land, the Clos des Capucins, now run by the widow and son of the late Théo Faller, who is buried amongst his vines. The family policy is to harvest as late as possible and use full maturity to give the wines maximum character, structure, length on the palate and the potential to age. Cuvée Théo is the standard label for Riesling and Gewürztraminer, with Vendanges Tardives in certain vintages (e.g. 1981). The Domaine Weinbach label is a superb piece of calligraphy: the best Alsace label. Total production is about 13,000 cases (14% exported).

Maison Louis Gisselbrecht

67650 Dambach-La-Ville

The Gisselbrecht family formed two separate businesses in 1936. This is the smaller one, proprietors of 12 acres at Dambach-La-Ville planted with Riesling, Gewürztraminer and Pinots Blanc and Noir. Riesling is the real speciality of the house; very clean, dry and balanced. Grapes are also bought to make a total of 58,000 cases.

---

alcohol, which gives them a firmer and more definite structure than German Wines. Dryness and the intensity of their fruit flavour together make them seem rather harsh to some people. I have found a prejudice against Alsace Riesling in California. In fact, they range from light refreshment in certain years to some of the most aromatic, authoritative and longest-lasting of all white wines.

Muscat Until recently Alsace was the only wine region where Muscat grapes were made into dry wine. The aroma is still hothouse sweet but the flavour is crisp and very clean, sometimes with a suggestion of nut kernels. It is light enough to make an excellent apéritif.

Alsace appellations

One of the 'noble' grape names, or the term Edelzwicker, which means a blend of grapes, is usually the most prominent word on Alsace labels.

Appellation Alsace Wine from any permitted grape variety with a maximum crop of 100 hectolitres a hectare and a minimum natural degree of 8.5 alcohol.

Appellation Alsace Grand Cru Wine from one of the 'noble' grape varieties with a maximum crop of 70 hectolitres a hectare and a minimum natural degree of 10 for Riesling and Muscat, 11 for Gewürztraminer and Pinot Gris (Tokay).

Appellation Alsace Grand Cru (with a vineyard name). The same standards as Grand Cru with proviso that the grapes come from the delimited site named.

Alsace prices

Hugel & Fils quoted the following ex-cellar prices, a bottle, in late 1982: Sylvaner 1979: 16.10 francs, Pinot Blanc 1981: 16.80 francs, Gewürztraminer 1981: 25.80 francs, Riesling 1980: 17.40 francs, Riesling 1981: 20.50 francs, Pinot Noir 1981: 22.60 francs, Tokay Cuvée Tradition 1979: 25 francs, Gewürztraminer Cuvée Tradition 1979: 28 francs, Riesling Cuvée Tradition 1981: 25.30 francs, Gewürztraminer Réserve Personnelle 1979: 32.60 francs, Riesling Réserve Personnelle 1979: 32.80 francs, Tokay Réserve Personnelle Vendange Tardive 1976: 111.30 francs, Riesling Réserve Personnelle Vendange Tardive 1976: 105.10 francs, Riesling Sélection de Grains Nobles 1976: 179.10 francs.

Willy Gisselbrecht & Fils

67650 Dambach-La-Ville

The larger of the two Gisselbrecht houses, owning 37 acres in and near Dambach-La-Ville and buying grapes to make a total of 125,000 cases a year (35% exported). Regular exhibitors and medal winners at the Paris and Mâcon fairs, particularly with Gewürztraminer.

Heim

68111 Westhalten

A substantial wine maker using the grapes of a group of growers with 222 acres in total. The vineyards include parts of 3 particularly good sites: Strangenberg for Pinot, Zinnkoepflé for Gewürztraminer and Bollenberg for Riesling (sold as Les Eglantiers). Top wines are fermented in oak; other methods are modern. Products include Imperial Brut, a good Crémant d'Alsace, and a range of wines under the names Heim, Meyer, Anne Koehler, Anne d'Alsace and Mittnacht. Total production is about 125,000 cases, 40% exported.

Hugel & Fils

68340 Riquewihr

The best-known Alsace label in the Anglo-Saxon world. A typical combination of grower and négociant, in the family since 1637, with 62 acres in Riquewihr producing their top wines. Of these 11 are in the Schoenenberg and 19 in the Sporen vineyards. 47% is Gewürztraminer, 46% Riesling, 4% Pinot Gris and 3% Muscat. The house style is full, round and 'supple', fermented dry but less apparently so than some houses. The speciality that Hugels have pioneered is late-gathered wines to the level of German Beerenausleses (though German terms are not used). The quality ladder for Riesling, Gewürztraminer, etc., goes Regular, Cuvée Tradition, Réserve Personnelle, Vendange Tardive (big wines with definite sweetness) and in certain years Sélection de Grains Nobles (very sweet). Hugel wines mature particularly well: Cuvées Tradition and Réserves Personnelle need at least 3 years. In 1981, the 1970 Riesling Réserve and 1967 Gewürztraminer Réserve were both at the top of their form. Other brands made of purchased grapes are Flambeau d'Alsace, Fleur d'Alsace, Couronne d'Alsace, Cuvée les Amours and (Pinot Blanc) Les Vignards. Total sales are about 100,000 cases a year, 80% exported.

Domaine Klipfel

67140 Barr

A leading family domaine combined with a négociant business (André Lorentz). 82 acres planted with 40% Gewürztraminer, 30% Riesling, 15% Pinot Gris, the rest Pinot Blanc, Muscat and Sylvaner, produce the Domaine wines: Gewürztraminer Clos Zisser and Freiberg, Riesling Kirchberg and Kastelberg and Tokay Freiberg – all traditionally oak-fermented and matured, with occasional Vendanges Tardives. Bought-in grapes are vinified in tanks for the Lorentz label. Total sales of 80,000 cases are largely to French restaurants and private customers. 30% is exported, largely to Germany.

Vins d'Alsace Kuehn

68770 Ammerschwihr

Growers and négociants founded in 1675. Their 20 acres of vines are in Ammerschwihr, partly in the famous Kaefferkopf vineyard, with all the usual varieties. The wines are made in wood in the 17th-century cellars, much as they have been for 300 years. Other brand names are Albert Schoech and Kuehn-Schiele. 45% is exported.

Kuentz-Bas

Husseren-Les-Châteaux, 68420 Herrlisheim près Colmar.

A family firm of growers and négociants, owning 30 acres of Riesling, Muscat and Gewürztraminer, Pinots Blanc, Gris and Noir in Husseren, Eguisheim and Obermorschwihr. Regular prize winners with firm and dry, well-balanced and elegant wines. Their Pinot Noir is made by *macération carbonique* to achieve colour, but is still a light wine to drink cool. There are plans to go in for super-selection of late-gathered sweet wines when conditions allow (as they did in 1981). A very pleasant Edelzwicker is called La Mariette. One third of sales is exported.

Maison Michel Laugel

67520 Marlenheim

Perhaps the biggest of Alsace wine makers, with annual sales of 330,000 cases. Their popular brand is Pichet d'Alsace, a blend of 85% Pinot Blanc, 10% Riesling and 5% Gewürztraminer – an excellent Edelzwicker at a reasonable price. Their main varieties are well-made, quite light wines for drinking fresh. The Laugel family owns a 12-acre vineyard of Pinot Noir in Marlenheim from which they make a well-known rosé.

Gustave Lorentz

68570 Bergheim

150-year-old family firm of growers and négociants, among the biggest producers and exporters with 250,000 cases a year, half exported. They own 75 acres with their best vines in the Altenberg and Kanzlerberg.

Muré

68250 Rouffach

A family of growers dating back to 1630, owners since 1928 of a historic vineyard at Rouffach, the old monastic Clos St-Landelin of 45 acres. All the usual vines are planted in the Clos, which has warm, stony and limey soil and notably low rainfall. Its wines are intense in character and round in style, intended (except the Sylvaner and Pinot Noir) as *vins de garde*. Muré also has a négociant business with a different label, selling some 50,000 cases a year.

Preiss Henny

68630 Mittelwihr

One of the larger growers as well as négociants with 79 acres distributed in 7 communes between Riquewihr and Colmar. The Preiss family use modern wine-making methods. Their top wines are Riesling Cuvée Marcel Preiss and Gewürztraminer Cuvée Camille Preiss. 45% of sales are exported.

Jean Preiss-Zimmer

68340 Riquewihr

Consistently fine wines, particularly Gerwürztraminer, from vineyards around Riquewihr.

Domaines Viticoles Schlumberger

68500 Guebwiller

The biggest domaine in Alsace, family owned, with 320 acres at Guebwiller at the southern end of the region. Guebwiller's warm climate, sandy soil and sheltered sites allied with old-style methods, relatively small crops and ageing in wood make Schlumberger wines some of the richest and roundest of Alsace, with sweet and earthy flavours of their own. Their best wines come from the Kitterlé vineyard and repay several years' bottle-ageing.

Total production is about 80,000 cases, 45% exported. Nearly half of exports go to Belgium.

Pierre Sparr & ses Fils

68240 Sigolsheim

Another family firm of growers and merchants dating back to the 17th century. Their own vines cover 75 acres in 6 communes between Turkheim and Bennwihr, including Riesling in the Schlossberg (Kaysersberg) and Altenberg vineyards, and Gewürztraminer in Brand at Turckheim and Mambourg at Sigolsheim. These are the company's top wines. Total sales are 233,000 cases, 30% of which is exported.

F.E. Trimbach

68150 Ribeauvillé

A historic (1626) family domaine and négociant house with a reputation for particularly fine and delicate dry wines. They own 30 acres in Ribeauvillé, Hunawihr and Bergheim and lease 37 in Riquewihr and Mittelwihr. 40% is Riesling; 35% Gewürztraminer. Their special pride is the Hunawihr Riesling Clos Ste-Hune, one of the most stylish Alsace wines. A fascinating tasting of old vintages showed it at its best after about 7 years. Each variety is made at 3 quality levels: standard (vintage), Réserve and Réserve Personnelle. Two prestige Rieslings are Clos Ste-Hune and Cuvée Frédéric Emile, Gewürztraminer Cuvée des Seigneurs de Ribeaupierre is equally fine. 60% of a total production of 63,000 cases is exported.

Alsace Willm

67140 Barr

A very traditional firm with a high reputation, taken over in 1980 by Roger Bahl. It is best known for its Gewürztraminer vineyard of 18 acres, Clos Gaensbroennel, and its 10 acres of Riesling in the Kirchberg. The Gewürztraminer is well ripened and fermented completely dry, making it a firm and impressive *vin de garde*. Its delicate Riesling and very clean, fresh Sylvaner (also Clos Gaensbroennel) are both very attractive. Total sales are about 40,000 cases, two thirds exported.

Domaine Zind-Humbrecht

Wintzenheim, 68000 Colmar.

The domaines of the Humbrechts of Gueberschwihr (since 1620) and the Zinds of Wintzenheim united in 1959 and are now run by Léonard Humbrecht. Humbrecht is a fanatic for the individuality of each vineyard's soil and microclimate, and a pioneer believer in low-temperature (15°C/60°F) fermentation. He makes highly individual wines from 4 vineyards: Brand at Turckheim (which makes light and fruity wines, especially Riesling), Herrenweg at Turckheim (fruity and aromatic Gewürztraminer), Hengst at Wintzenheim (more full-bodied *vins de garde*) and Rangen at Thann, where his 10-acre Clos St-Urbain gives top-quality Rieslings. The whole domaine is 64 acres of Gewürztraminer, Riesling and other usual varieties. 63% of his 17,000-case (average) production is exported.

André and Jean ('Johnny') Hugel, two of the trio of brothers at the head of this ancient house.

ALSACE COOPERATIVES

Andlau-Barr
67140 Barr. 197 members with a total area of 321 acres in 9 communes. Specialities are Zotzenberg and Klevner de Heiligenstein.

Bennwihr
68630 Bennwhir-Mittelwihr. 250 members with a total area of 662 acres in 8 communes. Specialities are Riesling, Rebgarten and Gewürztraminer Côtes de Bennwihr. Brands are Poème d'Alsace and Rève d'Alsace.

Dambach-La-Ville
67650 Dambach-La-Ville. 160 members with a total area of 358 acres in 7 communes.

Union Vinicole Divinal
67210 Obernai. A union of 7 cooperatives using the brand name Divinal on the usual range of wines, drawn from all over Alsace. Its total production amounts to 1 bottle in 20 of all Alsace wine. Total 500,000 cases (20-25% exports).

Eguisheim
68420 Eguisheim. Cooperative Vinicole with 470 members and a total area of 1,425 acres in 10 communes. Specialities are Gewürztraminer Cuvée St-Léon IX, Riesling Cuvée des Seigneurs, Pinot Noir Prince Hugo, Blanc de Blancs brut (*méthode champenoise*). Total production is 460,000 cases (15% exports)

Caves de Hoen
68980 Béblenheim. 617 acres in 8 communes. Top wines come from the Grand Cru Sonnenglanz. Brands used include Cave de Béblenheim, Eugène Deybach, Baron de Hoen. Total production 200,000 cases (20% exports).

Ingersheim et Environs
68000 Colmar. 156 members, 504 acres, in 7 communes. Top wines are labelled Florimont. Production 170,000 cases (20% exports).

Kientzheim-Kaysersberg
68240 Kayserberg. 124 members with a total area of 333 acres in 3 communes. Specialities include Riesling Schlossberg and Gewürztraminer Kaefferkopf.

Orschwiller
67600 Selestat. 137 members with a total of 250 acres in 5 communes. Production is about 80,000 cases, sold mainly in France.

Pfaffenheim-Gueberschwihr
68250 Rouffach. Has 200 members, with a total area of 395 acres in 7 communes. Specialities include a Crémant d'Alsace, Hartenberger, and Gewürztraminer from the Grand Cru Goldert. Total production 125,000 cases (25% exports).

Ribeauvillé et Environs
68150 Ribeauvillé. The oldest growers cooperative in France (founded 1895) now has 90 members with 385 acres in 5 communes. The speciality is Le Clos du Zahnacker. Total 150,000 cases (30% exports).

Sigolsheim et Environs
68240 Kayersberg. 617 acres, all in the commune of Sigolsheim. Specialities include a Crémant d'Alsace. Comte de Sigold, and a Pinot Blanc made without the use of any sulphur dioxide, Walthari Wine. Total 250,000 cases (50% exports).

Traenheim et Environs
67310 Wasselonne. 263 members, 543 acres in 14 communes. Brands used include Le Roi Dagobert and Cuvée St-Eloi.

Turckheim
68230 Turckheim. 261 members with a total area of 470 acres in 7 comunes. Specialities are Gewürztraminer Baron de Turckheim, Pinot Côtes du Val St-Grégoire.

Vieil-Armand
68360 Soultz-Wuenheim. 120 members, 296 acres in 6 communes. Brands include Château Ollwiller (Riesling and Pinot Noir).

Westhalten et Environs
68111 Westhalten. 168 members, 617 acres in 3 communes and also Gundolsheim, Orschwihr, Steinbach-près-Cérnay. Specialities are Gewürztraminer and Sylvaner Zinnkoepfle and Vorberg, Muscat, Pinot Blanc Bollenberg. Production about 200,000 cases (20% exports).

The harvest at Hunawihr, Alsace

RHONE

After many years of virtually ignoring the Rhône valley and its wines the wine trade has recently begun to find in it all sorts of virtues. More perhaps than stand up to dispassionate examination.

While its finest wines, Côte Rôtie and Hermitage, are still oddly undervalued, great quantities of what is scarcely more than high-strength *vin ordinaire* have climbed to the price of Bordeaux. It would be wrong to discount my personal taste in this. I admit to not liking, except on very rare occasions, wines of the strength of Châteauneuf-du-Pape. But strength aside, it seems to me that common grapes can never make better than common wine. Most of the grapes of the Rhône are either coarse or neutral in flavour. At their best they are grown in soil that exalts their qualities by men of taste who are aware of the flavours they are producing. More often, I feel, the well-worn eulogies of scents of truffles and woodlands, violets and raspberries are pure wishful thinking. Or (more charitably) that they only apply to wines far older than we are now accustomed to drinking. It is hard not to contrast the Rhône with California and the progress that has been made there in the last ten years.

You will find that I wax more enthusiastic when talking about particular wines.

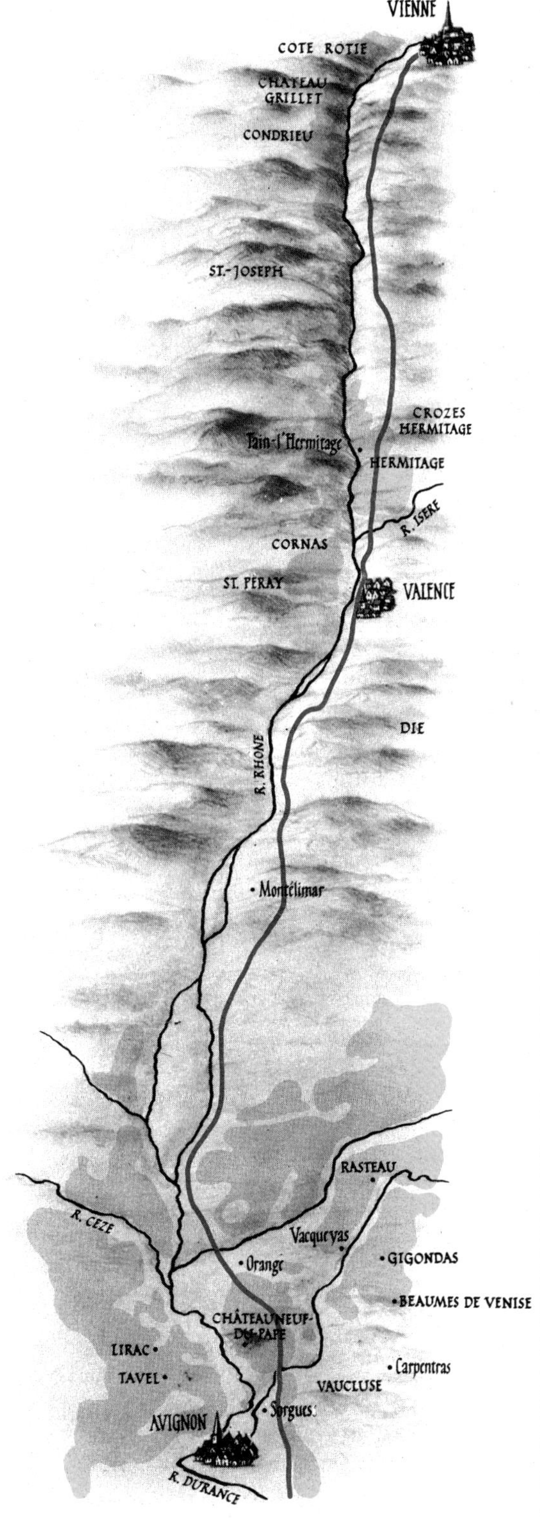

NORTHERN RHONE

The characteristic of the northern Rhône is dogged single-mindedness: one grape, the Syrah, grown on rocky slopes that need terracing to hold the soil. The red wines are all Syrah (alias Sérine), a grape with concentrated fruity flavour but so darkly tannic that the custom is to add between 2 and 20 per cent of white grapes to leaven it.

The northernmost appellation, Côte Rôtie, used to be a mere 250 acres of terraced hill above the village of Ampuis. Recently the appellation has been enlarged to include up to 750 acres of plateau land behind the Côte proper. Côte Rôtie means 'roasted hill'; two sections of the hill, with paler (more chalky) and darker soil, are known respectively as the Côte Blonde and the Côte Brune. Their wines are normally blended by growers who have only a few acres in total. The Syrah here is grown and mixed with up to 20 per cent (but usually less) of Viognier. Partly from this aromatic component, but probably more from the singular soils of the hill, it draws a delicacy that makes Côte Rôtie eventually the finest, if not the most powerful, of all

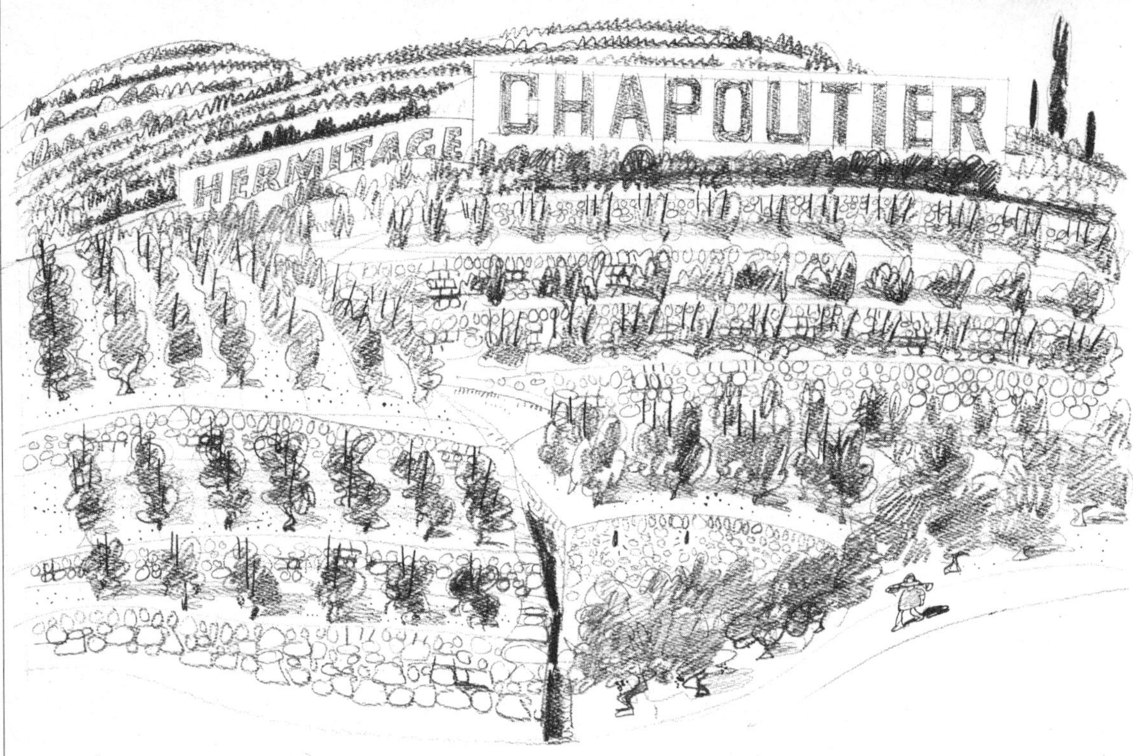

The Chapoutier domaine at Hermitage

Rhône wines. Between 10 and 20 years of age it moves closer to great Bordeaux than any other French wine, with an open, soft-fruity, perhaps raspberry bouquet that recalls the Médoc, yet with a warmer texture.

Condrieu, where the rare Viognier makes white wine, is only three miles downstream from Ampuis on the same south-facing right bank. St-Joseph covers a 30-mile stretch of the same river bank and its immediate hinterland with some very good sites but no consistency. A good example (such as Jaboulet's Grand Pompée) is clean, dark and sufficiently fruity Syrah without the grip or depth of Hermitage; wine to drink at four or five years.

The same in general is true of Crozes-Hermitage, the appellation for the east bank around Tain-L'Hermitage, without the advantage of the great upstanding mass of granite to help grill its grapes. Again, it is uneven in quality, ranging from near-Hermitage to an uninspiring commercial wine.

Few famous vineyards are as consistent as Hermitage. Its whole 320-acre surface faces full south at an angle that maximizes the warmth of the sun. Four fifths are planted with Syrah, the rest with two white grapes, Roussanne and Marsanne, that produce a wine as splendid in its way as the red. A century ago white Hermitage (then all Roussanne) was reckoned the best white wine in France, keeping 'much longer than the red, even to the extent of a century'. It is surprising to find white wine of apparently low acidity keeping well at all. Yet at ten years (a good age for it today) it has a haunting combination of foursquare breadth and depth with some delicate, intriguing, lemony zest.

St-Joseph and Crozes-Hermitage, incidentally, also make white wines of the same grapes which can be excellent. When they are aged they are best served cool, not chilled.

Red Hermitage has the frankest, most forthright, unfumbling 'attack' of any of the Rhône wines. Young, it is massively purple-black, uncomplicated by smells of new oak, powerfully fruity, almost sweet beneath a cloak of tannin and takes years to lose its opacity. Many people enjoy it in this state, or so it seems, because mature bottles are rare.

Cornas concludes the red-wine appellations of the northern Rhône with a sort of country cousin to Hermitage – another dark Syrah wine which only becomes a drink for fastidious palates after years in bottle. The area under vines is expanding and now stands at almost as much as Hermitage.

South of Cornas the appellation St-Péray is a surprising one – for a *méthode champenoise* sparkling wine of Marsanne and Roussanne grapes which, providing you forget the finesse of champagne or the *crémants* of northern France, has much to be said for it. It is a heavy-duty sparkler of almost sticky texture, even when it is dry. With age it develops a very pleasant nutty flavour.

Rhône prices are on page 194.

NORTHERN RHONE PRODUCERS

Guy de Barjac
07130 Cornas

A 5-acre family vineyard going back to the 14th century. Old-fashioned 100% Syrah wine needs 18 months in wood and several years in bottle. The label is La Barjasse.

Albert Bégot
26600 Tain L'Hermitage

An interesting small grower with 10 acres of red and white Crozes-Hermitage who uses only 'biological' methods – no chemicals in the vineyards. His red is aged up to 4 years in wood.

J.F. Chaboud
07130 St-Péray

The fourth generation of the Chaboud family has 25 acres of Marsanne and Roussanne. 80% of production is champagne-method St-Péray. The *sec* is pure Marsanne.

Emile Champet
Le Port, 69420 Ampuis.

The Champet family has an international reputation on the strength of a mere 4 acres of Côte Rôtie: 450 cases a year of sternly tannic red.

M. Chapoutier
26600 Tain L'Hermitage

Founded in 1808, this is one of the most distinguished names of the Rhône both as growers and négociants. Their 176-acre domaine consists of 75 acres of Hermitage (red and white), 6.25 of Côte Rôtie, 12 of Crozes-Hermitages Les Meysonniers, 14 of St-Joseph Deschants red and white and 70 of Châteauneuf-du-Pape (red and white) La Bernardine. Methods are wholly traditional, even to treading the grapes. Their domaine wines are aged in small barrels of either oak or sweet chestnut. Everyone should taste their white Hermitage Chante Alouette at 10 or more years old – a revelation after most modern whites. Total sales 83,800 cases; 60% exported.

J.L. Chave
Mauves, 07300 Tournon-sur-Rhône.

Gérard Chave has just celebrated 500 years of direct succession in his 18 acres of Hermitage. His red and white are both among the best and longest-lived wines of France.

Auguste Clape
07130 St-Péray, 07130 Cornas.

A grower with 10 acres of Cornas and 2.5 of St-Péray. His Cornas is dark purple, almost black, intensely tannic – the perfect wine for Roquefort, he says.

Pierre Coursodon
Mauves, 07300 Tournon-sur-Rhône.

Family property of 17 acres on the better slopes of St-Joseph. Red and white wines both improve with age.

Delas Frères
07300 Tournon-sur-Rhône

Long-established growers and négociants now owned by Champagne Deutz and recently moved to modern premises. They have 50 acres of vineyards, half in Hermitage (red and white), 12 in Cornas, 6 in Côte Rôtie and 5 in Condrieu. Wines from the southern Rhône are bought in. Delas wines are marginally cheaper than their rivals but seem to lack nothing in character and staying power. A 1973 Hermitage Blanc Marquise de la Tourette was superbly round and deep-flavoured in 1982. The red was still young.

Albert Dervieux
69420 Ampuis

One of the small growers of Côte Rôtie with 7.5 acres in 3 parcels, making 3 different wines: La Garde in the Côte Blonde, the Côte Brune and a patch he calls Viaillère. The bouquet of the wine, he says, varies from violets to raspberries depending on the soil. It needs at least 5 or 6 years and lasts for 20.

Desmeure Père & Fils
26600 Tain L'Hermitage

Family property of about 40 acres in Hermitage and Crozes-Hermitage, making red and white wines in bulk by traditional methods. Three quarters of their annual 2,700 cases go to private clients.

Pierre Dumazet
07340 Serrières

A tiny trickle of Condrieu and St-Joseph to very smart restaurants and private clients. His Condrieu is kept in barrels on the lees until secondary fermentation ends.

Jules Fayolle & ses Fils
Gervans, 26600 Tain L'Hermitage.

A family property of 17.5 acres in Crozes-Hermitage and 2.5 red Hermitage, founded in 1786. The reds are old-fashioned, 3 years aged in wood; the Marsanne white (from 6 acres) is bottled young and fresh.

Château Grillet
42410 Pelussin

The smallest property in France with its own Appellation Contrôlée, owned by the Neyret-Gachet family since 1830. The vineyard is just over 6 acres of perilous terraces forming a suntrap 500 feet above the bank of the Rhône. 20,000 Viognier vines yield no more than 320 cases a year of highly aromatic wine which is aged 18 months in oak. It is obviously a very expensive speciality, but opinions are divided about whether any sort of ageing improves Viognier wine.

Bernard Gripa
Mauves, 07300 Tournon-sur-Rhône.

Perhaps the best grower in St-Joseph. His 10 acres is two thirds red, fermented with stems and aged a year in wood. His whites are 90% Marsanne, made crisp and deliciously refreshing.

Jean-Louis Grippat
07300 Tournon-sur-Rhône

The eighth generation of Grippats struggles with the terraces of St-Joseph (8 acres, mainly red) and Hermitage (4 acres, mainly white) to produce a total of less than 2,000 cases a year. Their St-Joseph red is a good 5-year wine, but their Hermitage white is worth 10 years.

E. Guigal
69420 Ampuis

A family of growers and négociants specializing in Côte Rôtie, which they grow themselves on 7.5 acres and buy as grapes from 40 other small growers. They ferment the whole bunches in a closed vat for up to 3 weeks, then age it in barrels for 3 years, avoiding both fining and filtration if possible. The object is extremely long-lived wines (but fresh Condrieu). Their 2 labels are La Moulieu and La Landonne. Total production is 12,000 cases.

Paul Jaboulet Ainé

26600 Tain L'Hermitage

Growers and négociants since 1834, now run by 3 members of the founding family with Gérard Jaboulet in charge. The house is a pacesetter for the whole Rhône both as grower and merchant. Their domaine of 160 acres is in Hermitage (50 acres red, 12.5 white) and Crozes-Hermitage (80 red, 15 white). All 4 are among the best each year; the red Hermitage La Chapelle in great vintages (1961, 1978) is one of France's greatest wines, maturing over 25 years or more. Each Jaboulet wine has a name as well as an appellation, as follows: Hermitage (red) La Chapelle; (white) Le Chevalier de Sterimbourg. Crozes-Hermitage (red) Domaine de Thalabert; (white) Mule Blanche. St-Joseph Le Grand Pompée. Côte Rôtie Les Jumelles. Tavel L'Espiègle. Châteauneuf-du-Pape Les Cedres and a very full and fruity Côtes du Rhône Parallèle 45 (also rosé and white). Another label is Jaboulet-Isnard. Total sales are about 83,000 cases, 55% exported.

Robert Jasmin

69420 Ampuis

A famous name, though a small property, with 6 acres of Côte Rôtie (increasing to 7.5). Traditional vinification, adding 5–10% of white Viognier to the black Syrah and ageing in barrel for 18–24 months. The yearly production of his La Chevalière d'Ampuis is about 1,100 cases.

Marcel Juge

07130 Cornas

A small grower of hearty red Cornas and sparkling St-Péray. Most of his wines are sold in bulk, though the proportion in bottle is increasing.

Robert Michel

07130 Cornas

A simple old-fashioned family holding of 10 acres, partly on the hills giving the typically tough red, partly lighter wine from the foot of the slope. Neither is fined nor filtered before bottling. The former is at least a 10-year wine.

Paul Multier

Château du Rozay, 69420 Condrieu.

Among the few producers of Condrieu, with a reputation as high as any. He is slowly adding to his 3.75 acres of precipitous terraces. Fermentation is in barrels, where the wine stays until its second fermentation is finished. Maximum production at present is 416 cases a year.

Paul-Etienne Père & Fils

07130 St-Péray

A family firm of négociants and producers of sparkling St-Péray for 160 years. Wines of traditional style from all parts of the Rhône. Sales 42,000 cases, 80% in France.

Georges Vernay

69420 Condrieu

The leading figure in Condrieu today with 15 acres of Viognier, mostly planted on reclaimed abandoned terraces. His wine is bottled in its first spring (or even winter) for freshness – and because demand outruns supply. He also has 4.5 acres of Côte Rôtie and small vineyards in St-Joseph and Côtes du Rhône.

J. Vidal-Fleury

69420 Ampuis

The oldest and biggest domaine of Côte Rôtie terraces with a princely 20 acres. They make wines from the 2 Côtes, Brune and Blonde, separately and also together. The principal label is La Rolande. Total annual production is 2,500 cases. It takes 10 years for the real finesse of these wines to emerge.

Alain Voge

07130 Cornas

The Voge family, in its fourth generation here, makes Cornas from 12 acres by old methods (including treading) and sparkling St-Péray, from 4 acres of Marsanne, by the champagne method.

Condrieu

Condrieu had almost died out 20 years ago. Its unique vine, the white Viognier (spelt by some of its growers Vionnier), was biologically degenerate, low yielding and short lived. Its cliff-hanging vineyards could not be worked profitably and the acreage was reduced to 18, plus the 6 acres of the separate appellation Château Grillet, using the same grape. Thanks to modern methods of revivifying degenerate plants the Viognier is now more or less back on its feet, fallen terraces have been reclaimed and the total acreage has doubled to 35. The famous restaurants of the Rhône have made the world very aware of this rare wine, and its price is now equal to Corton-Charlemagne, while Château Grillet costs as much as Le Montrachet.

To me Condrieu is unquestionably worth it. Its scent and flavour have no parallel. Some critics evoke May-blossom. I am left groping, with the idea in the back of my mind that Germany provides a precedent. I have also been reminded of it by certain California Chardonnays. It begins with flowers, hints of spices and lingers for minutes as perfume in your throat. It is breath-taking *en primeur* – before it has even finished fermenting, in fact, and before the law allows it to wear its appellation. A 100-franc bottle of *vin de table* in a restaurant in Condrieu in November was still half sweet, faintly *pétillant* and one of the loveliest things I have ever swallowed. As healthy stocks of Viognier vines build up it must become a priority for other regions to attempt – particularly California, Australia and South Africa. Condrieu's one fault, in my experience, is that it does not improve in bottle. I have had only disappointments when I have tried cellaring it.

Vivarais and Ardèche

Up in the hills to the west of the Rhône the vineyards of the Vivarais and the Coteaux de l'Ardèche are another region in the course of development. The Côtes du Vivarais has VDQS status, which the best of the Coteaux de l'Ardèche (still *vins de pays*) probably deserve. The most promising grapes are Syrah and Cabernet Sauvignon. The normal custom is to mix them with Grenache, Cinsaut and the like. A pure Syrah from the Ardèche made by *macération carbonique* was a remarkably fruity and forthcoming wine.

SOUTHERN RHONE

The catch-all appellation for the huge spread of southern Rhône vineyards is Côtes du Rhône. It is not a very exigent title: big crops of up to 52 hectolitres a hectare are eligible so long as they reach 11 degrees of alcohol. The area covers a total of 82,750 acres in more than 100 communes north of Avignon, describing a rough circle among the low hills surrounding the widening Rhône. It leaves out only the alluvial bottom land around the river itself. In 1981, it made more than three times as much wine as the appellation Beaujolais – indeed considerably more than the whole of Burgundy and not very much less than the Bordeaux crop. Ninety-nine per cent of it is red or rosé. In such an ocean of wine there are several estates that set standards of their own, and good négociants choose and blend well. The thing to bear in mind is that Côtes du Rhône is for drinking young, while it is reasonably fruity.

There is a tradition in the area of making a very light café wine known as *vin d'une nuit* – vatted for one night only. It has been more or less superseded by the adoption of Beaujolais tactics to make a Rhône *primeur* with some of the qualities of new Beaujolais – but not with the exciting smell of the new Gamay. Regular red Côtes du Rhône is unpredictable, but compared with basic Bordeaux as a daily drink it is more warm and winey, less fresh and stimulating.

Côtes du Rhône-Villages is the inner circle. Thirty years ago growers in two communes east of the valley, Gigondas and Cairanne, and two to the west, Chusclan and Laudun, raised their sights to making stronger, more concentrated *vin de garde*. Limiting their crop to 35–42 hectolitres a hectare (according to the vintage) and ripening their grapes to give 12.5 degrees alcohol they made better wine and got better prices. A number of their neighbours followed suit. In 1967, the appellation Côtes du Rhône-Villages was decreed for a group of what has now risen to 17 communes totalling 7,900 acres. Gigondas has been promoted to an appellation of its own, and this seems likely to happen to others in the group as they establish their identity and build their markets. The full list is given on page 194.

Certainly Vacqueyras could promote such a claim. As an example of the style of the area it might be compared with Gigondas. Tasted together (the 1976, a good vintage for both from Paul Jaboulet) the Gigondas is fuller and rounder, with more 'stuffing'; the Vacqueyras is more 'nervous', harsh at first but developing a very pleasant dusty, slightly spicy, bouquet. (The Gigondas has very little.) Both are emphatically *vins de garde*: at five or six years they still need decanting a good 12 hours ahead – or keeping another three years.

Of the communes which are not -Villages, Uchaux and Châteauneuf-de-Gadagne are areas of apparent promise. On about the same quality level as Côtes du Rhône comes the appellation Coteaux du Tricastin, inaugurated in 1974, for vineyards higher up the east bank of the river.

Notes on Tavel and Lirac are given on page 197.

SOUTHERN RHONE PRODUCERS

Pierre Amadieu

Gigondas, 84190 Beaumes de Venise.

Growers and négociants with 300 acres on the hills of Gigondas and 87 in the Côtes du Ventoux (where they make red, white and rosé). They also handle Châteauneuf-du-Pape, Côtes du Rhône and -Villages. Brand names Font Gelado, Bois de Candale, Le Goutail and Romane Machotte – a total of 83,000 cases a year.

Domaine des Anges

84570 Mormoiron

Malcolm Swan, an English ex-advertising man, has 20 acres of Grenache, Syrah, Cinsaut and Carignan and makes 2,300 cases of full-flavoured 'Beaujolais-type' Côtes du Ventoux for drinking young.

Arnoux & Fils

84190 Beaumes de Venise

Use bought-in grapes (mainly Grenache, Cinsaut, Syrah) to make a total of 29,000 cases of Côtes du Rhône and -Villages, Gigondas, Vacqueyras, Côtes du Ventoux and Vin de Pays du Vaucluse. At the 1981 wine fair at Orange they were chosen as 'wine makers of the year' for the Côtes du Rhône, particularly for their Vacqueyras.

Château d'Aqueria

30126 Tavel

A 17th-century property owned by the Olivier family since 1919. 112 acres are in Tavel, 6 in Lirac. By ageing the Tavel in big casks for a few months they aim to stiffen it a little to survive longer in bottle.

J.A. Assémat

30150 Roquemaure

The achievement, since 1963, of a young oenologist with modern ideas. He has created two properties: Domaine Les Garrigues of 40 acres (all Lirac) and Domaine des Causses et St-Eymes (85 acres in Lirac, 15 in Laudun). His wines range from Rouge d'Eté *en primeur* to a Syrah made by adding fresh Syrah to the pulp left after macerating his rosé – a double dose of skins, giving wine which will stand up, he says, 'even to thyme and rosemary'. They are lively wines made with flair and gastronomic awareness.

Bellicard d'Avignon

Château de Piot, 84000 Avignon.

A century-old négociant with a good solid reputation for wines from the whole Rhône, now owned by Piat of Mâcon and part of the Grand Metropolitan empire.

Domaines Bernard

30126 Tavel

The Bernards have two properties totalling 125 acres; Domaine de la Genestière in Tavel and Lirac and Domaine de Longval in Tavel. The Tavel is made with a short maceration (12–24 hours) on the skins followed by fining the must (not the wine). Also some Lirac Blanc.

Domaine des Bernardins

84190 Beaumes de Venise

Madame Maurin runs a third-generation family domaine of 40 acres producing some 2,200 cases of fresh and luscious Muscat de Beaumes de Venise and twice as much red wine, largely Côtes du Rhône but about 700 cases of Côtes du Rhône-Villages Beaume. The red is Grenache and Syrah with a little Carignan, aged 6 months in wood.

Château Boucarut

30150 Roquemaure

The son-in-law of M. Valat of Ch. St-Maurice-L'Ardoise makes a popular Lirac from 50 acres.

Romain Bouchard

84600 Valréas

The Bouchards have a family tree as tall as that of the Bouchards of Beaune – and curiously enough they compare their wine to Beaune. They are growers with 38 acres of Valréas (Côtes du Rhône-Villages), where they aim to achieve brilliance and harmony rather than rude rustic wine. Despite its relative lightness and no barrel-ageing, they say it will live 15 years (and 'evoke the Côte de Beaune'). Bottling is done in a plant shared by neighbours in the Enclave des Papes. The label is Domaine du Val des Rois. They are also négociants with 3 brands: Cuvée de la 8eme Génération, Roseroy and Coronne.

Edmond Burle

La Beaumette, Gigondas, 84190 Beaumes de Venise.

The fourth generation of the Burles still have 60-year-old Grenache vines in their vineyards in Gigondas and Vacqueyras – about 40 acres in scattered parcels. Vinification is 'modernized traditional' with concrete vats and a hydraulic press. Gigondas Les Pallierondes is their *vin noble*, which M. Burle likes to deliver to clients personally.

Domaine de Castel Oualou

30150 Roquemaure

An important Lirac property of 126 acres developed over the past 20 years by the Pons-Mure family. Madame Pons-Mure carried off the top gold medal in the 1982 Paris Fair for her splendid 1981 Lirac Rouge, which contains Syrah and Mourvèdre. She also makes a little pleasant white of Ugni Blanc, Clairette and Picpoul, and rosé containing Clairette on a basis of Cinsaut and Grenache.

Chambovet & Fils

Château de l'Estagnol, 26130 St-Paul Trois Châteaux.

The Chambovet family have built up a vineyard of 200 acres, 16 miles north of Orange on sandy slopes that give Côtes du Rhône of warm piney and herbal character. The vines are Syrah, Grenache, Cinsaut and Mourvèdre in approximately equal proportions; the Syrah is fermented by *macération carbonique*. A special *cuvée* with extra Syrah, more colour and body is called La Serre Du Prieur.

Maurice Charavin

Domaine du Char-à-Vin [*sic.*], 84110 Rasteau.

A family property going back to the years of the French Revolution; 37 acres making the classic sweet Rasteau, entirely from Grenache, and an old-style red from Grenache, Syrah and Carignan aged 1 year in oak barrels and bottled without filtering. Some of the barrels are 100 years old. Only his rosé is given modern treatment.

Domaine du Devoy

30126 St-Laurent-des-Arbes

Owners the Lombardo brothers. An excellent property of 87 acres on various soils, planted in Grenache, with Cinsaut, Mourvèdre and Syrah. Full-coloured, distinguished, even elegant reds with no wood-ageing. Also a little rosé.

Domaine Durban

84190 Beaumes de Venise

Jacques Leydier is a reticent but excellent producer of both Muscat de Beaumes de Venise and red Côtes du Rhône-Villages.

Domaine du Grand Montmirail

Gigondas, 84109 Beaumes de Venise.

A 68-acre Gigondas estate recently bought by Denis Cheron *see* Pascal). Low production from old Grenache vines is being adapted with more Syrah to make more assertive wines for longer life in a new winery. The 5,500-case production has 3 names: Domaine du Roucas de St Pierre, Domaine de St Gens and Domaine du Pradas.

Domaine de Grangeneuve/Domaine des Lones

Roussas, 26230 Grignan.

The Bour family were pioneers of the new appellation Coteaux du Tricastin in the 1970s, when they planted 250 acres with Grenache, Syrah and Cinsaut. Their first wine under the domaine label was in 1974. Red (and a very little rosé) are made in stainless steel and aged up to 2 years before bottling.

Pierre Labeye

Domaine de la Tour d'Elyssas, 26290 Donzère.

Dynamic pioneer of the Coteaux du Tricastin who arrived from the north of France in 1965, bulldozed 2 barren hilltops and planted 360 acres of Grenache (150 acres), Cinsaut (100), Syrah (75) and Carignan. The varieties are vinified separately in an ultramodern gravity-fed system. Production is 100,000 cases a year of 3 main types: Syrah (unblended) aged 2 years in vats, Cru de Meynas, one third Syrah, a *vin de garde*, and Cru de Devoy, largely Grenache but no Syrah, for drinking young.

Domaine Maby

30126 Tavel

A family property of 225 acres, half in Tavel, where they make the wine as fresh as possible by the old method, a quarter in Lirac for 'big' reds and a quarter Côtes du Rhône for light red.

Château de Manissy

30126 Tavel

A Tavel property run by the missionary fathers of the Sainte-Famille. They make a deep-coloured rosé aged in wood for up to 18 months.

Domaine Martin

Plan de Dieu, 84150 Travaillan.

The Martin family have 75 acres on the plateau of Plan de Dieu near Gigondas. Unusually, they age their Côtes du Rhône red for 3 years in big oak casks. Part of their production is Rasteau Vin Doux Naturel.

Etablissement Gabriel Meffre

Gigondas, 84190 Beaumes de Venise.

A major modern domaine of over 550 acres in Châteauneuf, Gigondas and the Côtes du Rhône. The Meffre family have 5 Rhône and Provence properties: the Château du Vaudieu, 80 acres of Châteauneuf-du-Pape making a *vin de garde*; the Domaine des Bosquets and Château Raspail, each about 45 acres in Gigondas (Bosquet fruitier, Raspail more powerful); the Domaine du Bois des Dames of 165 acres at Violes and the huge and historic Château de Ruth with 220 acres at Ste-Cecile des Vignes. The last two make good fruity Côtes du Rhône red, and the Château de Ruth a light fresh white as well.

A. Ogier & Fils

84700 Sorgues

The great-grandsons of the founder run this Avignon firm of négociants, dealing in most southern Rhône appellations. They have exclusive rights in 2 Côtes du Rhône estates, Domaine Romarin at Domazan and Château St-Pierre d'Escarvaillac at Caumont, and with Domaine de la Gavotte at Puyloubier, Côtes de Provence. They also market several brands of table wine. Total sales exceed 150,000 cases a year.

Pascal SA

Vacqueyras, 84190 Beaumes de Venise.

A 60-year-old merchant house revitalized by its recent owner and wine maker, Denis Cheron. Pascal own 8 acres of Vacqueyras and buy grapes for a total of 85,000 cases of Vacqueyras, Gigondas, Côtes du Rhône and -Villages, Côtes du Ventoux and Vins de Pays de Vaucluse. Cheron looks for roundly fruity wines with depth and vitality, removing all stalks and fermenting 5-8 days. Good selection and technique make him a quality leader. 50% of production is exported, some under the name Augustin Peyrouse. Cheron also owns the Domaine du Grand Montmirail (q.v.).

Domaine Pelaquie

30290 Laudun

The grandsons of Joseph Pelaquie, one of the *vignerons* who first promoted the Côtes du Rhône, run a small estate, principally in Laudun with a little Lirac. Very old vines make it a good example of the region.

Gabriel Roudil & Fils

Le Vieux Moulin, 30126 Tavel.

A family property since 1870 with 150 acres, 112 of them in Tavel with some in Lirac and some in Côtes du Rhône. Some 190,000 cases of Tavel Domaine du Vieux Moulin are their main product. The formula is 60% Grenache, 25% Cinsaut, 10% Picpoul, and 5% Carignan, macerated on the skins for between 12 and 24 hours, fermented dry and bottled at 6 months. Red Lirac has Syrah and Mourvèdre in addition for colour, macerates for 8 – 10 days and spends 1 year in wood. The same traditional method is used for red Côtes du Rhône. Another label for Roudil's Tavel is Réserve de Carvaillons. Roudil's wines are among the regular winners at the Paris and Mâcon Fairs.

Domaine Louis Rousseau

30290 Laudun

The Rousseaus have 60 acres in Lirac for red and 10 in Laudun for Côtes du Rhône-Villages red and rosé. Like many growers in the area they settled from Algeria in the early 1960s. Their wine-making is 'traditional', but without barrels.

Les Fils de Hilarion Roux

Domaine Les Gallières, Gigondas, 84190 Beaumes de Venise.

The family wine in the manner of Châteauneuf-du-Pape since the year of Waterloo. Low yields, long macerating of the bunches, 3 years oak-ageing make tannic wine for patient clients – 80% in France. 60 acres produce 6,500 cases.

Château St-Estève

Uchaux, 84100 Orange.

The Français-Monier family have owned the 130-acre estate for 200 years. Uchaux lies on a sandy ridge north of Orange which gives ripe, warm wines with body and character. From 40% Grenache, 20% each Syrah and Cinsaut and a little Mourvèdre, Roussanne and even Viognier. The property produces 5 wines: St-Estève Grande Reserve red *vin de garde*, St-Estève Tradition, a light Friand de St-Estève *en primeur*, a rosé and a white.

Domaine St-Gayan

Gigondas, 84190 Beaumes de Venise.

The Meffre family (Roger, father, and Jean-Pierre, son) claim to have 600 years of Gigondas *vigneron* forebears. They produce much-appreciated tannic Gigondas up to 14.5 degrees alcohol, reeking (they say) of truffles and crushed fruit, from ancient vines yielding only 28 hectolitres a hectare. Also big-scale Côtes du Rhône and -Villages in Sablet and Rasteau.

Château St Maurice-L'Ardoise

30290 Laudun

An ancient estate on the site of a Roman temple of Jupiter, owned by André Valat. 250 acres, principally Côtes du Rhône-Villages with some *vins de pays* and a little Lirac. 15% Syrah gives the wine some body and style.

Château St-Roch

30150 Roquemaure

The 100-acre Lirac property of Antoine Verda, making good warming red Lirac intended to age in bottle, some 'supple' rosé and a trace of soft white. The same proprietor has started the new Domaine Cantegril-Verda, also at Roquemaure, with 45 acres of Côtes du Rhône red. The crop is 25% higher than in Lirac and the wine correspondingly lighter, for drinking young.

Domaine Ste-Anne

30200 Bagnols sur Cèze

A 50-acre estate (15 more planted) making Côtes du Rhône and -Villages red and white; the reds by *macération carbonique*.

Château de Ségriès

30126 Lirac

The 50-acre estate is owned by Comte de Regis de Gatimel, whose family inherited it in 1804. He makes a tannic red *vin de garde*, fermenting stalks and all and ageing 2 years in concrete tanks. His rosé is also aged but his white, picked just before ripeness, is bottled as young as possible. Notwithstanding the whites apparently age well in bottle for up to 5 years.

Domaine de la Tour de Lirac

30150 Roquemaure

An 80-acre estate developed over the last 20 years, specializing in red Lirac, aged 1 year in tanks and intended to be drunk young and lively. They also produce some light rosé.

Château du Trignon

Gigondas, 84190 Beaumes de Venise.

An old (1898) family estate with modern ideas making excellent wine. Charles Roux uses *macération carbonique* to make rich and savoury Gigondas, more fruity and less tannic in youth than the old style, maturing up to, say, 8 years. His 120 acres are divided between Gigondas and Sablet and Rasteau.

Château de Trinquevedel

30126 Tavel

François Demoulin is one of the leading growers of Tavel, with interesting ideas on adapting his methods to the state of the crop, using partly old techniques and partly new (chilling and *macération carbonique*). He believes a little bottle-age improves his Tavel.

Domaine de Verquière

84110 Sablet

A staunchly traditionalist family property of 120 acres in three 'Villages' – Sablet, Vacqueyras and Rasteau. 70% is Grenache, for both reds and Rasteau VDN. Louis Chamfort still keeps his best Villages reds in oak until he judges them ready. The '76 was bottled in 1982.

La Vieille Ferme

84100 Orange

A négociant's brand for 2 wines: a red Côtes du Ventoux made as a *vin de garde* and a delicate white from high vineyards on the Montagne de Luberon.

SOUTHERN RHONE COOPERATIVES

There are more than 60 coops producing Côtes du Rhône and the other wines of the region. A few have gained a reputation equal to that of the best private growers and négociants. These include:

Chusclan
30200 Bagnols-sur-Cèze. Founded 1939 (by Joseph Rivier, who is still at its head). 127 members; 1,600 acres producing 440,000 cases, 200,000 Côtes du Rhône and -Village (Chusclan). Painstaking methods include vinifying each variety (there are 9) separately by both traditional vatting and *macération carbonique*. M. Rivier is very specific about the attributes of his wines: reds 'scented with ripe plums and bay leaves', rosé 'perfumed with acacia and wild strawberries'. The white, merely described as 'young and fruity', is in fact a technical achievement; a well-balanced wine with plenty of flavour. Brand names are Seigneurie de Gicon, Cuvée des Monticaud, Prieuré St-Julien.

La Courtoise
St-Didier, 84210 Pernes-Les-Fontaines. Founded 1924. 350 members; 2,500 acres producing 280,000 cases, of which 95,000 are AC Côtes de Ventoux. More Syrah is being grown to stiffen the previously pale and light reds.

Gigondas
Gigondas, 84190 Beaumes de Venise. Founded 1955. 124 members; 350 acres producing 79,000 cases, 67,000 of Gigondas. Three quarters of the grapes are Grenache; Syrah and Mourvèdre add colour and grip. The wine is bottled after 18 months in wood.

De Orgnac-L'Aven
07150 Vallon-Pont-d'Arc. Founded 1924. 83 members; 1,000 acres producing 230,000 cases, of which half is VDQS Côtes du Vivarais. Syrah, Cinsaut, Grenache and Clairette make light but firm reds, rosés and whites, 'which perfectly reflect our wild and arid hills'. A year in bottle is enough.

Rasteau
84110 Vaison-La-Romaine. Founded 1925. 200 members; 2,500 acres producing sweet *vin doux naturel* (red and white), Côtes du Rhône-Villages, plain Côtes du Rhône and *Vin de Table* Festival du Crutat.

Tavel
30126 Tavel. Founded 1937. 140 members; 890 acres producing 280,000 cases. They use the traditional local method of macerating the skin, cold fermentation to avoid tannins, then sell (and drink) as soon as possible.

Union des Vignerons de l'Enclave des Papes
84600 Valreas. Union of 1,800 growers marketing Côtes du Rhône under the Enclave des Papes label.

CLAIRETTE DE DIE

Clairette de Die is like a sorbet between the substantial main dishes of the northern and southern Rhône. The energy of the local cooperative has revived a fading appellation. Clairette de Die is at its best when made sparkling, but one or two traditional growers make a satisfying nutty still wine.

Albert Andrieux
26340 Saillans. Small grower of still Clairette de Die, of which his Domaine du Plot is a good example.

Buffardel Frères
26150 Die. An old family firm making an annual 17,000 cases of Clairette de Die, but by the *méthode champenoise*.

Cave Coopérative de Clairette de Die
26150 Die. Three quarters of the appellation is handled by this 529-member coop producing 273,000 cases of Brut, Tradition and still wines from 2,000 acres. The Brut is a dry sparkling wine of Clairette grapes 'with an aroma of lilac and lavender'. Tradition is a sweet fizz of Muscat de Frontignan. The method involves fermentation in bottle (but, unlike champagne, of the original grape-sugar), then filtering and decanting to another bottle under pressure. Other wines are Gamay red and Aligoté/Chardonnay white, for which they have their own AOC Châtillon en Diois.

Côtes du Rhône-Villages
The 17 communes entitled to this appellation are: Drôme: Rochegude, Rousset-Les-Vignes, St-Maurice-sur-Eygues, St Panteléon-Les-Vignes, Vinsobres. Vaucluse: Cairanne, Rasteau, Roaix, Sablet, Séguret, Vacqueyras, Valréas, Visan, Beaumes-de-Venise. Gard: Chusclan, Laudun, St-Gervais.

Rhône prices
Négociants Paul Jaboulet Ainé quoted the following ex-cellar prices, a bottle, in late 1982: Côtes du Rhône: red, white and rosé 12.90 francs, Villages 14.40 francs, Vacqueyras 14.80 francs. Côtes du Ventoux 9.70 francs. Crozes Hermitage: 1980, 14.20 francs; Mule Blanche white 1980, 18.50 francs; Domaine de Thalabert 1980, 15.60 francs. Hermitage: 1980, 30.70 francs; La Chapelle 1980, 38.70 francs. Côte Rôtie Les Jumelles red 1980, 39.00 francs. Condrieu 52 francs. Cornas 1980, 24.00 francs. Gigondas red 1980, 21.70 francs. Châteauneuf-du-Pape Les Cèdres 1980, 27.00 francs, white 31.50 francs. Lirac rosé 14 francs. Muscat de Beaumes de Venise 30 francs. St-Joseph 1980, 17 francs.

Château des Fines Roches

CHATEAUNEUF-DU-PAPE

Châteauneuf-du-Pape is much the biggest and most important specific Rhône appellation. If its 7,400 acres of vines produced as plentifully as those of its neighbours there would be more Châteauneuf-du-Pape than Côtes du Rhône-Villages. But small crops are mandatory. Concentration is the very essence of this wine. Its vines grow in what looks like a shingle beach of big, smooth, oval stones that often cover the whole surface of the vineyard. Each vine is an individual low bush.

Where all other French appellations specify one or two, at most four, grape varieties of similar character, the tradition in Châteauneuf-du-Pape is to grow a dozen with widely different characteristics. It is not clear whether this is primarily an insurance policy, or simply accumulated tradition. Some growers assert that each of them, even the coarse or simply neutral ones, adds to the complexity of the wine. New plantations, however, are tending to cut down the number to four or five. The base, always in the majority and sometimes as much as 80 per cent, is Grenache. The other essentials are Cinsaut, Syrah, Mourvèdre, and the white Clairette or Picpoul, or both. Varieties that could be described as optional are (red) Cournoise, Muscardin, Vaccarèse and (white) Piccardan, Roussanne, Terret Noir and Bourboulenc. The white varieties are used in the red wine as well as made into white Châteauneuf-du-Pape on their own.

Grenache and Cinsaut are described as providing strength, 'warmth' and softness; Mourvèdre, Syrah, Muscardin and Vaccarèse as adding structure, colour, 'cut' and refreshment to the flavour, and the ability to live for long enough to develop a bouquet. The white grapes are there for mildness and (optimistically) finesse. Although the legal minimum is 12.5 degrees of alcohol, 13.5 degrees is considered the lowest acceptable by the best growers, who are happy to see 14.5 degrees.

And the result? We have all had great, dull, headachy wines called Châteauneuf-du-Pape. There is no distinct 'varietal' handle by which to grasp either the aroma or the flavour. Commercial examples are usually made to be very warm and 'giving' and slightly fruity. The best estates, however, make *vins de garde* that are quite impenetrable at under five years and difficult under ten. When a bouquet does start to develop it is still elusive. It is rather part of a glowing roast-chestnut warmth about the whole wine. Eventually, in the best examples, latent finesse and the essential sweetness of a great wine will emerge. Much the best I have ever drunk was a 1937 in perfect condition in 1981.

White Châteauneuf-du-Pape, formerly a long-lived wine, rich and elusive, is today more often made for drinking within three years at most.

CHATEAUNEUF-DU-PAPE PRODUCERS

A. Amouroux

Clos de l'Oratoire, 84230 Châteauneuf-du-Pape.

A well-reputed grower making a total of 8,000 cases, including red and a little white Châteauneuf-du-Pape and a Vin de Pays de Vaucluse with some Cabernet Sauvignon.

Père Anselme

84230 Châteauneuf-du-Pape

The name recalls a wise old ancestor of the founder of this firm of négociants and wine makers, producing most of the Rhône appellations with a total sale of 170,000 cases a year. Apart from AC wines they have 3 brands, La Fiole du Pape, Marescal and Petit Duc; they also own the Mule du Pape restaurant at Châteauneuf and a famous old nougat factory, Arnaud-Soubeyran, at Montelimar. Négociants Jean-Pierre Brotte are part of the same concern. Brotte, once independent, pioneered local bottling rather than shipping in cask.

Château de Beaucastel

84350 Courthézon

The fourth generation of the Perrin family makes one of the best wines of the region on this big property dating back to the 17th century. Their Châteauneuf vineyard is 173 acres, plus 75 of Côtes du Rhône. All 13 authorized grapes, with relatively high proportions of Syrah and Mourvèdre, a 25 hectolitre a hectare crop, 15-day fermentation in the traditional square stone vats and 2 years' ageing in oak give the wine depth and durability. A little white Châteauneuf is made of 80% Roussanne and 20% Grenache Blanc. The Côtes du Rhône is called Cru de Coudoulet. One of the Perrin brothers is making a good Côtes du Ventoux, La Vieille Ferme.

Domaine de Beaurenard

84230 Châteauneuf-du-Pape

Paul Coulon represents the seventh generation on this family property of 75 acres. He also owns the 110-acre Ferme Pisan (AC Côtes du Rhône) at Rasteau. Both are planted with the same mixture of 70% Grenache and 10% each of Syrah, Cinsaut and Mourvèdre. He produces richly aromatic wine with a technique related to the Beaujolais method: two thirds of his crop are crushed, the other third undergoes *macération carbonique*. His wine is slightly less tannic as a result, but rich and deep.

Caves Bessac

84230 Châteauneuf-du-Pape

A century-old firm of négociants with a good name for traditional Châteauneuf-du-Pape, Tavel, Côtes du Rhône and -Villages. Also Côte Rôtie and Hermitage. Sales are 200,000 cases a year. Huge stocks of Châteauneuf-du-Pape are still kept in barrels.

Jean Deydier

Les Clefs d'Or, 84230 Châteauneuf-du-Pape.

One of the smaller of the leading estates with 50 acres; a low yield and 2 years wood-ageing giving *vins de garde*. Also a very successful white in small quantities.

Félicien Diffonty

84230 Châteauneuf-du-Pape

A 42-acre Châteauneuf family property making strong old-style wine, Cuvée du Vatican, fermented on the skins for up to 25 days. Also white and 'cerise' Vins de Pays du Gard, Mas de Bres, from 36 acres.

Château Fortia

84230 Châteauneuf-du-Pape

The family estate of the instigator of the system of Appellations Contrôlées, Baron Le Roy de Boiseaumarié, who in 1923 first defined the best vineyard land of the region in terms of the wild plants, thyme and lavender, growing together, an early ecologist. Today the best 7,000 cases from the 70 acres are château bottled; the rest sold in bulk. Methods are traditional, using 75% Grenache and as many old vines as possible. The present owner favours the local Counoise in preference to Syrah. The wine is aged in wood and sold at 3 years, intended for maturing up to 15 years. 10% of the production is white Châteauneuf-du-Pape.

Château de la Gardine

84230 Châteauneuf-du-Pape

A family property of 250 acres, half of them in Châteauneuf-du-Pape, the remainder in Côtes du Rhône and Villages at Rasteau, Roaix and Buisson. Both the Châteauneuf (red and white) and Côtes du Rhône-Villages carry the château name. The Brunels aim for a reasonably 'supple and elegant' wine rather than a pugilist, ageing their Châteauneuf 3 years in wood.

Domaine de Mont-Redon

84230 Châteauneuf-du-Pape

The biggest single vineyard (235 acres) in Châteauneuf, with a long history, bought in 1921 by Henri Plantin and now run by his grandsons M. Abeille and M. Fabre. From its immensely stony ground comes some of the toughest Châteauneuf, macerated for 3 weeks to stiffen its spine, and aged for between 2 and 3 years in 10,000-litre oak barrels. The only change with the times, says Jean Abeille, is in not being able to age the wine for clients in bottle as well – a necessary process they must do themselves. Exactly the same wine is sold in some markets under the following names: Cuvée des Felibres, Vignoble Abeille, Vignoble Fabre and Les Busquières. 40 acres of Côtes du Rhône at Roquemaure have recently been added to the estate. Mont-Redon is the largest producer of white Châteauneuf.

Société Louis Mousset

84230 Châteauneuf-du-Pape

One of the biggest Rhône estates, built up by 5 generations of the Mousset family to a total of over 600 acres, 260 in Châteauneuf-du-Pape including the Ch. des Fines Roches (112 acres), Dom. de la Font du Roi (62), Dom. du Clos St-Michel (25) and Dom. du Clos du Roi (62). Four Côtes du Rhône estates are called Ch. du Bois de la Garde, Ch. du Prieuré, Dom. de Tout-Vent and Dom. du Grand Vaucroze. They also have 3 brand names: Cigalière, Les Trois Couronnes and Tourbillon. The headquarters is the Ch. des Fines Roches, one of the great names of the area.

Société du Domaine de Nalys

84230 Châteauneuf-du-Pape

Estate of 120 acres growing the classic 13 grapes to make one of the fresher examples of Châteauneuf, aged only up to a year in wood before bottling. Also small amounts of white.

Domaine de la Nerte

84230 Châteauneuf-du-Pape

One of the great names of Châteauneuf, quoted in the

19th century as a separate and slightly better wine than Châteauneuf itself. The estate today has 145 acres (5 for white wines) with a rather simplified planting (Grenache, Mourvèdre, Cinsaut, Syrah and Clairette). Vinification is traditional; the wine is aged 2 or 3 years in wood.

Clos des Papes

84230 Châteauneuf-du-Pape

A property in direct descent from father to son for more than 300 years. Paul Avril has 80 acres, 80% Grenache with Syrah, Muscardin and Vaccarèse. His aim is power and structure. He is not afraid of tannin and believes Châteauneuf needs years in bottle. 20% of his 9,000-case total is white.

Domaine Pierre Quiot

Château Maucoil, 84100 Orange.

Possibly the oldest named estate of Châteauneuf-du-Pape, producing the traditional style of wine on 75 acres (with a second label, Quiot St-Pierre). Also 35 acres of Gigondas under the name of Pradets and 15 of Côtes du Rhône Patriciens.

Château Rayas

84230 Châteauneuf-du-Pape

A small but outstanding property often cited as the best of Châteauneuf. The Reynaud family have 38 acres (5 are white grapes), planted with 90% Grenache, the balance Cinsaut and Syrah. They age the red for 2 or 3 years in wood depending on the vintage. The white is outstanding for long ageing. Ch. Fonsalette (Côtes du Rhône) is also made at Rayas.

Les Fils de Joseph Sabon

Clos Mont Olivet, 84230 Châteauneuf-du-Pape.

The 3 sons of Joseph Sabon are the fourth generation to make wine they describe as 'well-structured, highly aromatic and long in the mouth' – traditional Châteauneuf – from 52 acres. It is a graphic indication of the concentration of Châteauneuf that their average yield is 2,000 cases, whereas from another 15 acres at Boltère (Vaucluse) they crop 4,750 cases of Côtes du Rhône.

Noël Sabon

Chante Cigale, 84230 Châteauneuf-du-Pape

The name means 'the song of the cicada' – if song is the right word. Noël Sabon is the third generation to own this 100-acre property, now considered among the 10 best of Châteauneuf. The vineyards are 80% Grenache, 10% Syrah and 5% each of Mourvèdre and Cinsaut – no white grapes and no white wine. Old-style vinification and at least 18 months in cask make serious *vin de garde*.

Caves St-Pierre-Sefivin

84230 Châteauneuf-du-Pape

A very large family company of proprietors and négociants with a stable of well-known names, including 4 Châteauneufs: St-Pierre, Ch. St-André, Dom. des Pontifs and Dom. Condorcet and the Lirac Ch. de Ségriès. Their bottling company, the Société des Vins Fins de la Vallée du Rhône, handles an annual 500,000 cases.

Domaine de la Solitude

84230 Châteauneuf-du-Pape

The Lançon family make their wine by *macération carbonique* – a style of Châteauneuf ready to drink much younger than the traditional tough wine. Their 75 acres are planted in a simplified mixture of Grenache, Cinsaut and Syrah.

Domaine du Vieux Télégraphe

84370 Bedarrides.

A long-established 120-acre estate taking its name from the old signal tower on the hill. The third and fourth generations of the Brunier family make 5,800 cases of a really conservative Châteauneuf; dark, tannic and unyielding for years. The vines are 80% Grenache, 10% Cinsaut and 5% each of Syrah and Mourvèdre. The stony soil, a yield of only 34 hectolitres a hectare and long fermentation of the whole bunches account for the concentration of the wine.

Caves Reflets de Châteauneuf-du-Pape

84230 Châteauneuf-du-Pape

A collaboration between growers for bottling and distribution. The chief members are: Lucien Brunel, Les Cailloux, Pierre Lancon, La Solitude, Guy Nicolet, Chante Perdrix, Joseph Sabon, Clos du Mont-Olivet.

Tavel and Lirac

A similar area to Châteauneuf-du-Pape a few miles west, on the other side of the Rhône, has traditionally been famous for its rosé, made with the same grapes. Tavel has a unique reputation for full-bodied dry rosé, made not by fermenting the wine briefly on its (red) grape skins, as most other rosés are made, but by a period of up to 2 days of maceration before fermentation starts. (The yeasts have to be inhibited by sulphur dioxide, or in modern cellars by cooling.) The wine is then pressed and fermented like white wine. I have never been attracted by this powerful, dry, rather orange-pink wine, any more than by similar rosés from Provence. It is regarded, though, as one of the classics. Like Racine, it should be re-read from time to time.

Lirac, the northern neighbour to Tavel, has been specializing more recently in red wines, which at their best are very pleasantly fruity and lively, and in other cases strong and dull.

Ventoux and Lubéron

Where the Rhône valley merges with Provence to the east, the 10-year-old appellation Côtes du Ventoux has forged ahead in volume, now far out-producing the united Côtes du Rhône-Villages. Among some very reasonable reds the outstanding wine is that of Jean-Pierre Perrin, brother of the owner of Ch. de Beaucastel. He is also experimenting with a Chardonnay from Lubéron. The Côtes du Lubéron, the hills along the north of the Durance valley (famous throughout France for its asparagus), also makes a substantial contribution to this great source of red wine. Lubéron is still only a VDQS, but its reds (and whites) may appeal more for their relative lightness than some of the more pedestrian efforts of the Rhône. These is some very adequate sparkling white Lubéron.

North of the Lubéron near Manosque, the VDQS Coteaux de Pierrevert is a further extension of these Rhône-style vineyards, making light wine.

OTHER PRODUCERS

Bérard & Fils
84370 Bédarrides. Merchants and proprietors with 300 acres, including the Domaine Terre Ferme. Locally highly regarded, especially for their fresh white.

La Bernardine
The 70-acre property of the négociants Chapoutier (*see* northern Rhône). Big old-style wine.

Théophile Boisson & Fils
Domaine du Père Caboche, 84230 Châteauneuf-du-Pape. An old family of growers including the current president of the Châteauneuf *syndicat*. Their 75 acres are 80% Grenache. The wine is made in stainless steel in the lighter style.

Les Cèdres
The excellent brand-name Châteauneuf of Paul Jaboulet (*see* northern Rhône).

Domaine Chante-Perdrix
84230 Châteauneuf-du-Pape. A 45-acre property to the south of Châteauneuf, not far from the Rhône. Very concentrated high-strength wine.

Remy Diffonty
Domaine du Haut des Terres Blanches, 84230 Châteauneuf-du-Pape. Owner of some 80 acres, producing fine *vins de garde* by old methods, including 3 years in oak.

Château de la Font du Loup
84350 Courthézon. Owner: J. R. Melia. A small (40-acre) estate with old vines and methods making fine aromatic wine.

Domaine du Grand Tinel
84230 Châteauneuf-du-Pape. A traditionalist estate of 180 acres, the property of M. Elie Jeune, the former mayor of the commune.

Château La Grande Gardiole
84350 Courthézon. The property of André Rey of Gigondas, distributed by Mommessin of Beaujolais.

René Jouffron & Fils
Réserve des Cardinaux, 84230 Châteauneuf-du-Pape. A 40-acre property making wines distinguished for long ageing and eventual complexity.

Domaine Jean Trintignant
85 acres of Châteauneuf, plus Côtes du Rhône. Good red wine in the lighter style and sometimes admirable white.

Château de Vaudieu
84230 Châteauneuf-du-Pape. 180 acres, part of the large Gabriel Meffre properties based at Gigondas. Sound wines from an admirably situated vineyard near Ch. Rayas.

Université du Vin
The crenellated towers of the ancient château of Suze-La-Rousse house the Rhône's Université du Vin, founded in 1978. The first institution of its kind in the world, it is open to professionals – growers, négociants, restaurateurs – and amateurs.

From October to April, courses are run for growers; for the rest of the year others in the wine business and amateurs study tasting, the whole spectrum of viticulture and wine-making and 'the art and civilization of wine'.

Highly sophisticated laboratories and tasting rooms ('with the calm ambience that allows the necessary concentration') serve the University and the official bodies of the Rhône. The laboratories have the latest electronic equipment for wine, vine and soil analysis. Other amenities are an *oeothèque* and a museum.

Université du Vin, Château de Suze-La-Rousse, 26130 Suze-La-Rousse.

A négociant assesses the crop

PROVENCE

Until recently it was just as well to approach Provence, as most people do, in an indolent frame of mind with serious judgement suspended. Most of its wine was passable at best; sun-glass rosé with too much alcohol and too little taste. There were a few reds of character, and careful wine makers even made white wine that was almost refreshing, but the quality rarely justified the price. Wines as good could be found in the Rhône, and even in the hills of the Midi, for less money.

Provence depended for too long on its captive audience of holiday makers. It still makes nearly twice as much rosé as red, and only a trickle of white. I have tried, but always failed, to enjoy strong dry rosé made from the non-aromatic grapes of the region, the same Carignan, Cinsaut and Grenache as the Rhône, with an even smaller proportion of Syrah and Mourvèdre to give flavour. There are sometimes aromas of herbs and pines – the heady sunbaked smell of the land. But only recently have better grapes been planted and modern controls implemented. 1977 was the year when Côtes de Provence was promoted from a VDQS to an AOC. For a few estates it was a recognition of their real quality. For the majority it was more in anticipation and encouragement of progress to come.

Côtes de Provence is an alarmingly wide area for an appellation, including the coast from St-Tropez to beyond Toulon to the west, and a great stretch of country inland, north of the Massif des Maures back to Draguignan and the first foothills of the Alps.

Before all this became an AOC, however, there were already four little local appellations where the wine was considered consistently above average.

The biggest and unquestionably the best is Bandol, a ten-mile stretch of coast and its hinterland just west of Toulon. The production is some 200,000 cases, and Bandol red can have a quality that has traditionally been rare in Provence: tannic firmness that makes it a two-year wine at least, lasting without problems up to six or seven years. The law requires it to spend 18 months in cask. The reason is a high proportion of the 'aromatic' Mourvèdre, which apparently appreciates the heat of rocky terraces. There is also Bandol rosé and white.

Farther west along the coast, almost in the outskirts of Marseille, the fishing port of Cassis is known for its (relatively) lively and aromatic white, for which the bouillabaisse restaurants of Marseille see fit to charge Grand Vin prices.

The authorities apparently feel that the wines of the district of Aix-en-Provence, north of Marseille, are inferior to the mixed bag of the Côtes de Provence. They remain VDQS, all but the microscopic enclave of Palette, an appellation area just east of Aix dominated by Château Simone (q.v.). Despite this official snub they include what is probably the best red-wine estate in Provence, and the best VDQS property in France – Château Vignelaure (q.v.). Others, such as the Château de Fonscolombe (q.v.), are probably behind only by the length of time it takes their newly planted Cabernet vines to reach maturity.

Behind Nice in the hills at the extreme other end of Provence the 100-acre appellation of Bellet is justified by wine that is considerably better than the generally dismal prevailing standard of its neighbours. The Côte d'Azur seems to disprove the theory that a sophisticated clientele spurs wine makers to make fine wine.

PROVENCE PRODUCERS

Jean Bagnis & Fils

83390 Cuers

A family company of growers and négociants with 32 acres (making 6,600 cases) at Château de Crémat in the tiny appellation Bellet above Nice in the hills. Expensive wine but distinctly tastier than their standard Côtes de Provence, the brand L'Estandon, 290,000 cases of which seem to appear everywhere in this part of the world.

Domaine de la Bernarde

83340 Le Luc

M. and Mme Meulnart did a California-style switch from industry to wine-making *par amour du vin* and took over this old 210-acre farm 1,000 feet up north of the Maures. Results include Cuvée St-Germain red – best vintages only, long fermentation, wood-aged then matured in bottle – which has won a run of medals at Mâcon. Drink at 8–12 years old, advises Mme Meulnart. Also good rosé; La Bernarde, a lighter red, and a white. 16,500 cases.

Commanderie de Peyrassol

83340 Le Luc

The Commanderie was founded by the Templars in 1204 and acquired by the Rigord family in 1890. 148 acres produce 33,000 cases of Côtes de Provence and Vin de Pays des Maures of all 3 colours, produced by modern methods and well up to modern standards.

Domaine de la Croix

83420 La Croix-Valmer

Century-old Cru Classé of 285 acres near Cavalaire-sur-Mer, stressing red *vins de garde* and vinifying special unblended *cuvées* of Cabernet Sauvignon and Mourvèdre sold as such. Production 45,000 cases, 15% exported.

Domaine des Féraud
83550 Vidauban

Owned by the Laudon-Rival family for 3 generations. Paul Rival, the former owner of Château Guiraud, Sauternes, ran the property for 25 years until 1955 then handed over to his nephew Bernard Laudon, who is still in charge. 86 acres of AOC Côtes de Provence. Médoc-inspired Cabernet Sauvignon, Syrah and Mourvèdre; whites from Sémillon, also rosé. Production 13,600 cases. Second label: Pisse-Margot.

Château de Fonscolombe
13610 Le-Puy-Ste-Reparade

The Marquis de Saporta has two properties north of Aix – this (235 acres) and the Domaine de la Crémade (160 acres). Both have been in his family since 1720. A noble Renaissance château now notable as a principal collaborator with SICAREX Méditerranée in upgrading local wine quality. Modern techniques for whites and rosés and traditional oak vinification for reds. Total production 90,000 cases.

Bernard Gavoty
83340 Le Luc

A grouping of 3 domaines – Domaine du Grand Campdumy, proprietor P. Gavoty (136 acres), Domaine du Petit Campdumy, proprietor B. Gavoty (136 acres), and Domaine des Pomples, proprietor J. Brusse (49 acres). Half the reds are *macération carbonique*, the rest traditional.

Charles-Marie Gruey
Château Grand'Boise, 13530 Trets.

A handsome and ambitious estate of 106 acres around a 17th-century château. The oak-aged red has won gold medals at the Mâcon fair. Production of red, rosé and a *méthode champenoise* sparkling rosé totals 19,000 cases.

Château Minuty
Gassin, 83990 St-Tropez.

M. Gabriel Farnet's 100-acre property near St-Tropez has a fine house and a serious reputation for its oak-aged Cuvée de l'Orotaire. Production 22,000 cases. Second label: Domaines Farnet.

Clos Mireille
83250 La Londe-Les-Maures

A 123-acre coastal vineyard, owned by Ott (q.v.) of Cru Classé status producing 16,500 cases of full-flavoured blanc de blancs from Sémillon and Ugni Blanc.

Moulin des Costes
83740 La Cadière d'Azur

The brothers Bunan, Paul and Pierre, have 74 acres of steep vineyards at La Cadière and at nearby Le Castellet (Mas de la Rouvière). Most is rosé AOC Bandol, but some excellent long-lived red is made. Production 10,000 cases.

Domaines Ott
06600 Antibes

Founded 1896 by a native of Alsace, now the owner of 3 properties producing top-quality Provence wines by traditional methods: limited yield, no sulphur, oak ageing. 25% of production exported to 50 countries. *See* Clos Mireille, Château Romasson, Château de Selle.

Domaine des Planes
83520 Roquebrune-sur-Argens

Christopher Rieder, who with his wife Ilse farms 62 Côtes de Provence acres in the Argens valley, is a graduate of both Geisenheim and Montpellier and owns vineyards in Germany and Switzerland. 12,500 cases include unblended Muscat, Grenache and Cabernet Sauvignon wines, plus AOC Côtes de Provence red, white and rosé.

Les Maitres Vignerons de la Presqu'ile de St-Tropez
Gassin, 83990 St-Tropez.

This semicoop chooses *cuvées* made by member producers, bottles the wine and markets it. Production 133,000 cases. Uses brands Ch. de Pampelonne and Cave St-Roch.

Château Romasson
Le Castellet, 83150 Bandol.

Old property of 123 acres now belonging to Ott (q.v.) producing 16,500 cases of white, red and 3 rosés.

Domaine de St-André de Figuière
83250 La Londe-Les-Maures

Father and son André and André-Daniel Connesson farm 40 acres between St-Tropez and Toulon. New underground cellars produce 5,000 cases, soon to rise to 8,500 of red and rosé. Biological cultivation and careful vinification have earned a run of gold medals at Mâcon.

Château de Selle
Taradeau, 83460 Les Arcs.

Owners: Domaines Ott (q.v.) 100 acres planted with Sémillon, Ugni Blanc, Cabernet Sauvignon, Cinsaut and Grenache. 13,500 cases of Côtes de Provence red, white and rosé, rated Cru Classé.

Château Simone
Palette, 13100 Aix-en-Provence.

One of two properties in the tiny AOC Palette. 37 acres provide local restaurants with a very satisfactory speciality: wines that really taste of the herbs and pines of the countryside. The red ages well; the white could be considered an acquired taste.

Domaine Tempier
83150 Bandol

Lucien Beyraud and his 2 sons are the staunchest champions of Bandol, making remarkably flavoury and long-lived red and rosé from 62 acres. The red (two thirds of production) is 60% Mourvèdre, the rest Grenache, Cinsaut and a little Carignan from very old vines. It is aged 2 years in oak.

Château Vannières
83740 La Cadière d'Azur

A leading Bandol producer on an estate of 130 acres dating back to 1532. Besides excellent Bandol, the total production of 14,000 cases includes Côtes de Provence red, rosé and white. 40% is exported.

Château Vignelaure
83560 Rians

The first estate to demonstrate to the world that Provence could produce very good wines of more than local interest. Georges Brunet had already restored Château La Lagune in the Médoc when he came here in the 1960s and planted Cabernet Sauvignon with the local vines. The 111 acres are only VDQS Coteaux d'Aix en Provence, but in a class above most appellation wines of Provence or farther afield. Wines from the early 1970s are still in good condition. Production is about 20,000 cases.

OTHER PRODUCERS

Domaine de La Bastide Neuve
Le Cannet des Maures, 83340 Le Luc. René Brochier makes his reds the old-fashioned way – *pas de ciment* – and ages them in small acacia casks. 4,100 cases from 32 acres near Le Luc, including a pure Grenache red Pavillon Rouge.
Château de Beaulieu
13840 Rognes. A large (740-acre) estate in the Coteaux d'Aix en Provence VDQS region. Reds contain 20% Cabernet Sauvignon, whites are half Sauvignon Blanc. Vinification is traditional. The proprietors, R. Touzet & Fils, produce 125,000 cases.
Château de Bellet
St-Romain de Bellet, 06200 Nice. Mme Rose de Charmace's property is one of only two sizeable ones in the tiny AOC Bellet. The other is Ch. de Crémat (see Bagnis).
Les Borrels
Domaine Les Fouques, 83400 Hyères. Newly revived seaside property linked with Domaine de Clastron (q.v.).
Mas Calendal
13260 Cassis. Jean-Jacques Bodin-Bontoux's property produces AOC Cassis rosé and white. A local pioneer of domaine bottling.
Château Clarettes
83460 Les Arcs. Old property with 30 acres in production and more, including Cabernet Sauvignon, being planted. Red *vin de garde*, also AOC white and rosé and Dom. de Fantroussière *vin de table*.
Domaine de Clastron
83920 La Motte. A new (1980) start for a large old farm in the Argens valley making Côtes de Provence of all 3 colours and red and rosé Vin de Pays du Var. Traditional varieties plus Cabernet Sauvignon. Cool fermentation whites and rosés, traditional reds.
Domaine de Curebeasse
83600 Fréjus. Jean Paquette's 42 acres produce 6,600 cases of Côtes de Provence, half rosé. M. Paquette, a partisan for his region's wines, stresses the contribution of volcanic soil.
Le Domaine des Embiez
Ile des Embiez, Le Brusc, 83140 Six Fours Les Plages. 4,000 cases of traditionally made Côtes de Provence from 22 acres on an island between Bandol and Toulon. The island harbours Paul Ricard's powerboat centre, and the Domaine calls a *cuvée* after him.
Château de Gairoird
83390 Cuers. Philippe Deydier de Pierrefeu makes 13,000 cases, mostly red, some rosé, from 64 acres northeast of Toulon, using modern methods. Other label: Domaine St-Jean. The rosé leads his exports, especially to the US.
Château La Gordonne
Pierrefeu du Var, 83390 Cuers. A 284-acre estate owned by Domaines Viticoles des Salins du Midi (q.v. Bouches du Rhône) producing red, white and rosé Côtes de Provence from shale soil on the Maures foothills. 77,000 cases.
Domaine de la Grande Lauzade
13400 Aubagne. Jean-François Brando makes 9,000 cases of traditional-style red (stressing Syrah) and rosé from 52 acres near Le Luc.
Château de Mentonne
83510 Lorgues. Traditional property west of Draguignan, 200 years in Mme Perrot de Gasquet's family. 13,000 cases of Côtes de Provence from 59 acres.
Domaine de Nestuby
Cotignac, 83570 Carces. Jean Roubaud's 100 acres in the upper Argens valley yield up to 33,000 cases of Côtes de Provence.
Pradel
06270 Villeneuve Loubet. Merchant dealing in Côtes de Provence, Bellet and Bandol wines. Annual production 110,000 cases, 75% exported.
Domaine Christiane Rabiega
83300 Draguignan. 45-acre property. Traditional methods produce medal-winning Côtes de Provence.
Vignobles François Ravel
Château Montaud, Pierrefeu du Var, 83390 Cuers. Family company with 680 acres AOC Côtes de Provence and 150 Vin de Pays des Maures inland from Hyères. Wines include an unblended Cabernet Sauvignon. Production 160,000 cases AOC, 40,000 *vin de pays*. Other labels: Ch. de Guiranne, Ch. Garamache.
Domaine Richeaume
13114 Puyloubier. The German proprietor, M. Hoesch, ages his reds in oak for 2 years. 3,300 cases from 54 acres on the slopes of Mt. St-Victoire, east of Aix-en-Provence.
Domaine de Rimauresq
83790 Pignans. A family property in the Maures of 64 acres, rated Cru Classé. Hubert Isnard began bottling the wine in 1981 after a 20-year gap. Production in bottle, 2,500 cases, planned to double.
Etablissements Bernard Camp Romain
83550 Vidauban. Leading négociant founded in 1910, today doing world-wide business in Provence wines. Sales 290,000 cases.
Domaine du Château du Rouet
83490 Le Muy. Bernard Savatien's 30,000-case production from 148 acres in the Argens valley comprises Côtes de Provence of all colours and Vin Mousseux Le Rouet made by both *cuve close* and *méthode champenoise*.
Domaine de St-Antoine
83990 St-Tropez. 3,000 cases of red and rosé from 17 acres of very old vines.
Clos Ste-Magdelaine
13260 Cassis. Proprietor François Sack has 16 acres of vines right on the Mediterranean producing 2,500 cases of classic white Cassis and 830 of rosé.
Château St-Martin
Taradeau, 83460 Les Arcs. A handsome old house with deep cellars, in the Rohan Chabot family since the 17th century. The proprietor, Comtesse de Gasquet, makes 13,000 cases of Côtes de Provence Cru Classé from 99 acres.
Domaine de la Tour
13600 La Ciotat. Traditional 37-acre property making 8,300 cases of Côtes de Provence red, rosé and blanc de blancs.
Domaine de la Tour Campanets
13610 Le Puy Ste-Reparade. A newly created 65-acre vineyard in the VDQS region north of Aix. Marcel Laffourges has built a gravity-fed tower *cuverie* that does away with pumps, which he feels injure the wine. 11,500 cases.
Les Vins Breban
83170 Brignoles. Négociants and large-scale makers of *cuve close* sparkling wine, also Côtes de Provence, Domaine de Paris; and Coteaux Varois, Domaine de Fontlade and Domaine de Merlançon.

Caves Coopératives
Vinicole L'Ancienne
83490 Le Muy. Côtes du Provence and Vin de Pays du Var, all colours, from a coop founded in 1913. 25,000 cases.
Vins de Bandol Caves du Moulin de la Roque
83740 La Cadière-d'Azur. Founded 1950. 150 members with 425 acres of AOC Bandol red, white and rosé. Production 55,000 cases. This 'serious' coop competes with Bandol's private estates, producing quality wines at sensible prices.
De Pierrefeu
83390 Cuers. Founded 1922, 310 members farming 2,148 acres, production of AOC wines: 301,000 cases, producing AOC Côtes de Provence and *vins de pays*.
Les Vignerons Provençaux
Château de Beaulieu, 13840 Rognes. A 'SICA' uniting a growers' coop, the Union des Coopératives Vinicoles des Bouches du Rhône, the Château de Beaulieu (q.v.), and a distributor, Touzet. Produces Côtes de Provence, Coteaux d'Aix-en-Provence VDQS, *vins de pays* Bouches-du-Rhône and 'Perlaire' *vin de table*.
La Vidaubanaise
83550 Vidauban. 480 members farm 2,700 acres of AOC Côtes de Provence and 617 of *vins de pays* in the Argens valley. Production 142,000 cases.

THE MIDI

The arc of country from the Spanish border to the mouth of the Rhône may well be France's oldest vineyard. It is certainly its biggest. Uncountable quantities of unwanted wine are pumped from its plains to the despair of politicians all over Europe. Until the last decade there was not a great deal more to say. Traditions of better wine-growing persisted in the hills, but at such economic disadvantage that there seemed little future for them.

There was no demand and no premium for extra effort until the 1960s, when educated wine makers and merchants began to realize that it was only the grapes that were wrong: the soils and climates of hundreds of hill villages have enormous potential. The penny dropped at the same time as California rose from its slumber. In the Midi, low morale, bureaucracy, peasant conservatism, typically complicated land ownership have all been brakes on progress. Otherwise there would by now be famous Cabernets from the Corbières. If California can do it, why not the South of France? But the French way is to move cautiously along established lines. To improve wines, not to change them.

Upgrading started with the wine-making process. The introduction of *macération carbonique* was the vital first step. It extracted from dull grapes juicy flavours that nobody knew were there. The process is now a long way down the road, and a handsome list has begun to emerge of properties and cooperatives with good wine to offer, and better on the way as they hasten to replant with the 'aromatic' grapes that the public want.

The Midi of quality wine divides into four distinct regions. Following the right-hand curve of the coast north from the Spanish border, they are the Roussillon in the Pyrenean foothills, most famous for sweet apéritif and dessert wines; the Corbières, red-wine country; the smaller Minervois in the southernmost foothills of the Cevennes, also best known for red wine; and the scattered Coteaux du Languedoc, producing decent red, white and rosé as islands in an ocean of *vin ordinaire*.

Precisely what constitutes a quality area and which are the 'right' grapes for it is studied here with as much Gallic precision as on the slopes of Beaune. It is not long since VDQS was the senior rank in these parts. Now several areas have been promoted to AOC and others are about to matriculate. More detailed gradings will be needed, by which some areas will be '*villages*' or '*supérieurs*'. Layer upon layer of legislation is the French way.

This is also the country of the *vins de pays*. Pages 222–226 give details of the innumerable 'country wine' districts. But to sell your wine as a *vin de pays* is also an interesting alternative to growers who find the panoply of appellation too oppressive. There is a danger of the situation arising which Italy already knows, where the bright pioneer believes (and rightly) that his wine is more important than its label. Some of the best wines of the Midi are sold as *vins de pays* because Cabernet or Merlot is not cricket under the existing rules.

In most areas, cooperative cellars dominate. They vary widely in size, sophistication and quality. The best produce wine as good as the best growers. The coop ranking system is explained on page 204.

ROUSSILLON

Of all the endless vineyards of the Midi, the Roussillon is most firmly planted in Frenchmen's minds as a place of promise. It has the prestige of an ancient and unique product, its *vin doux naturel*, practically unknown outside France but so proud of its origins that it looks on port (an approximate equivalent) as an imposter.

Its sheltered seaside hills around Perpignan and inland up the valleys of the Agly and the Tet also make some formidable red wines; the biggest and most highly coloured of the many based on the Carignan around the coast. The 'Côtes du Roussillon' and their superior 'Villages' were promoted to full *appellation contrôlée* status in 1977. The best examples, stiffened with superior 'aromatic' grapes, have some of the structure of, for example, Châteuneuf-du-Pape, though with more roundness and a softer texture. Many are best young when their fruit flavour is at its peak, but more and more growers are deliberately ageing in oak and sometimes in bottle too, to add complexity to sheer beef.

One small red-wine area at the seaside resort of Collioure on the Spanish border has had its own appellation since 1949 for a singular concentrated wine in which Carignan plays little part, a blend principally of Mourvèdre and Grenache Noir with intense flavours unlike anything else north of the Spanish border. Two other villages 20 miles inland from Perpignan, Caramany and Latour-de-France, acquired their own appellations in 1977. The activities of the extremely modern cooperative at Montalba-Le-Château in the same 'Villages' zone between the Agly and Tet valleys are creating more and more interest in this area.

The *vins doux naturels* apparently owe their origin to the revered figure of Arnaldo da Villanova, the thirteenth-century sage and doctor of Montpellier, who introduced the still from Moorish Spain. It was he who first added *eau de vie* to naturally very strong wine to stop the fermentation and maintain a high degree of natural sugar – hence the term '*doux naturel*'. But whereas in port the *eau de vie* represents a quarter of the volume and more than half the alcoholic strength, in *vins doux naturels* it is limited to ten per cent of the volume, while the natural strength of the wine has by law to reach no less than 15 degrees. It is not for a foreigner, with the privilege of an education in port, to hold forth on the qualities of VDNs. Aged, they acquire an oxidized flavour known by the Spanish term *rancio*. A few producers age them in 30-litre pear-shaped glass jars known as *bonbonnes* (from the Spanish *bombonas*).

ROUSSILLON PRODUCERS

Mas Amiel
66460 Maury. Owner: M. Dupuy. Produces vintage VDN for sale at 5 or 10 years old. 345 acres; 35,000 cases of Maury from Grenache Noir.

Paul Baillo
66300 Thuir. Major replanting and *macération carbonique* have improved this property. 123 acres; 20,000 cases of Muscat de Rivesaltes, Rivesaltes and Côtes du Roussillon.

Domaine de Caladroy
Belesta, 66720 Latour-de-France. Owner: Arnold Bobo. 296 acres; 30,000 cases of Muscat de Rivesaltes, Rivesaltes and Côtes du Roussillon.

Domaine de Canterrane
Trouillas, 66300 Thuir. Owner: Maurice Conté. One of the finest estates in Roussillon, with stock of more than 1m. bottles. Vintages back to 1974 are very impressive. 370 acres; 80,000 cases of Rivesaltes, Muscat de Rivesaltes and Côtes du Roussillon.

Château Cap de Fouste
Villeneuve de la Raho, 66200 Elne. Bought in 1979 by the local growers' *mutualité agricole* and now in full swing with new planting. Its wine already shows great promise. 148 acres; 20,000 cases of Côtes du Roussillon.

Cazès Frères
66600 Rivesaltes. Modernized and replanted with Grenache, Syrah and Mourvèdre and Malvoisie. *Macération carbonique*, oak-ageing and bottle-ageing in air-conditioned cellars. 200 acres; 27,500 cases of Rivesaltes, Muscat de Rivesaltes, Côtes du Roussillon, Côtes du Roussillon Villages and *vin nouveau*.

Mas Chichet
Chemin de Charlemagne, 66200 Elne. Owner: Paul Chichet. A pioneer with Cabernet and Merlot in association with Grenache and Syrah – and also remarkable pure Cabernet aged in oak. 62 acres; 15,500 cases of Vin de Pays Catalan red and rosé.

Château de Corneilla
66200 Elne. Owner: M. Philippe Jonqueres d'Oriola. 60 acres producing AOC red. Grape varieties are Carignan, Grenache Noir, Cinsaut and Syrah. The property was built in 1150 and restored in the 17th century.

Mas de la Dona
66310 Estagel. Owner: Jacques Baissas. 62 acres; 8,500 cases of Côtes du Roussillon Villages from a splendid schist vineyard.

Château de l'Esparrou
Canet-Plage, St-Nazaire, 66140 Canet. Owner: Jean-Louis Rendu. Replanted with stress on Mourvèdre and Syrah, making excellent Côtes du Roussillon by *macération carbonique* and barrel-ageing. 247 acres; 60,000 cases of Rivesaltes, Muscat de Rivesaltes, Côtes du Roussillon and *vins de pays*.

Château de Jau
Cases de Péné, 66600 Rivesaltes. Improving vines and *macération carbonique* make some of the best Côtes du Roussillon. Also outstanding Muscat and good whites of Malvoisie and Macabeu.

M. Jaubert-Noury
St-Jean Lasseille, 66300 Thuir. Replanting with Syrah and Mourvèdre, and Malvoisie for whites. Good Côtes du Roussillon, also light *vin nouveau*, by *macération carbonique*. 247 acres; 38,500 cases of Rivesaltes, Muscat de Rivesaltes, Côtes du Roussillon.

Domaine du Mas Blanc
66650 Banyuls-sur-Mer. Owner: Dr. Parse. The leading producer of AOC Collioure. 10 acres of schist: 50% Mourvèdre, 30% Syrah, 20% Grenache Noir and Carignan. Long fermentation and 2 years in wood give remarkable wine. 25 acres of Banyuls VDN (90% Grenache Noir, 10% Carignan) aged either in wood or in bottle.

Le Moulin
66330 Cabestany. Owner: Vidal Rossines. An old estate with a fine reputation, particularly for aged Banyuls. 118 acres; 26,500 cases of Rivesaltes, Muscat de Rivesaltes, Banyuls and Côtes du Roussillon.

Mas Péchot; Mas Balande
66600 Rivesaltes; 66000 Perpignan. Owner: Henri Lacassagne. Mas Péchot is one of the best vineyards of Muscat '*petits grains*' in the region. 370 acres; 66,500 cases of Muscat de Rivesaltes and Côtes du Roussillon Villages.

Château de Rey
St-Nazaire, 66140 Canet. Owner: Mme Georges Sisqueille. 247 acres; 30,000 cases of Muscat de Rivesaltes, Rivesaltes and Côtes du Roussillon.

Domaine de Roquebrune
St-Nazaire, 66140 Canet. Owner Marcellin Casenobe cherishes his old Carignan vines. Very sound *macération carbonique* reds. 64 acres; 16,500 cases of Rivesaltes and Côtes du Roussillon.

Domaine St-Luc
Passa Llauro Torderes, 66300 Thuir. Owner: M. Talut. 100 acres; 16,500 cases of Rivesaltes and Côtes du Roussillon.

Domaine de Sau
66300 Thuir. Owner: Albert Passama. 222 acres; 50,000 cases of Côtes du Roussillon and *vins de pays*.

Tresserre
66300 Thuir. Owner: M. Vaquer. Well-made red, rosé and white are fermented long and cold; reds are aged in bottle up to 6 years before being released. 86 acres; 12,000 cases of Rivesaltes and *vin de table* rosé, red and white.

Château de Villeclare
Palau del Vidre, 66700 Argeles-sur-Mer. Owners: Héritiers Jonquères d'Oriola. 173 acres; 40,000 cases of Côtes du Roussillon.

CAVES COOPÉRATIVES

Agly
66600 Rivesaltes. Rating: 13. Founded 1942. 120 members; 750 acres producing 61,000 cases of AOC Côtes du Roussillon and Villages red; Rivesaltes Tuilé; Muscat; 24,000 cases *vins de table*.

Baixas
66390 Baixas. Rating: 13. Founded 1923. 475 members; 4,400 acres producing 400,000 cases of AOC Rivesaltes VDN white and red; Muscat de Rivesaltes white; Côtes du Roussillon white and red; Côtes du Roussillon Villages red; plus 114,000 cases Vin de Pays Côtes Catalanes and *vins de table*.

Banyuls 'La Banyulencque'
66650 Banyuls-sur-Mer. Rating: 13. Founded 1926. 546 members; 1,953 acres producing 135,000 cases of Banyuls VDN; Banyuls Grand Cru VDN; Collioure red.

Banyuls 'L'Etoile'
66650 Banyuls-sur-Mer. Rating: 12. Founded 1921. 58 members; 310 acres producing 24,000 cases of Banyuls VDN.

Banyuls 'Les Vignerons'
66650 Banyuls-sur-Mer. Rating: 13. Founded 1963. 166 members; 758 acres producing 45,000 cases of AOC Banyuls VDN.

Banyuls 'L'Union de Producteurs'
66650 Banyuls-sur-Mer. Rating: 13. Founded 1963. 166 members; 758 acres producing 57,000 cases of AOC Banyuls VDN; Banyuls Grand Cru VDN; Collioure red.

Caramany
66720 Latour-de-France. Rating: 13. Founded 1925. 101 members; 820 acres producing 88,000 cases of AOC Côtes du Roussillon Villages Caramany red and Côtes du Roussillon red and rosé, plus 50,000 cases *vins de pays* and *vins de table*.

Cassagnes
Cassagnes, 66720 Latour-de-France. Rating: 12. Founded 1924. 94 members; 807 acres producing 70,000 cases of AOC Côtes du Roussillon Villages red, Rivesaltes VDN and Muscat, plus 55,000 cases Vin de Pays Val d'Agly and *vins de table*.

Lesquerde
66220 Lesquerde. Rating: 13. Founded 1923. 70 members; 963 acres producing 64,000 cases of AOC Rivesaltes VDN, Côtes du Roussillon, white and red and Villages red, plus 100,000 cases Vin de Pays Val d'Agly and *vins de table*.

Maury
66460 Maury. Rating: 14. Founded 1910. 344 members; 4,199 acres producing 434,000 cases of VDN Maury red, and Côtes du Roussillon and Villages red, plus 110,000 cases *vins de pays* and *vins de table*.

Montalba-Le-Château
66130 L'Ile-sur-Tet. Rating: 10. Founded 1920. 85 members; 840 acres producing 40,000 cases of Côtes du Roussillon red and rosé plus *vins de pays*.

Montner
66720 Latour-de-France. Rating: 14. Founded 1919. 119 members; 1,086 acres producing 76,000 cases of Côtes du Roussillon Villages, Rivesaltes VDN red and white, Muscat de Rivesaltes white, plus 100,000 cases Vin de Pays Val d'Agly and *vins de table*.

Planèzes
66720 Latour-de-France. Rating: 12. Founded 1923. 45 members; 427 acres producing 31,000 cases of AOC Côtes du Roussillon Villages red and Rivesaltes, plus *vins de table*.

Rasiguères
66720 Rasiguères. Rating: 13 Founded 1919. 90 members; 706 acres producing 60,000 cases of AOC VDN Rivesaltes; Muscat de Rivesaltes; Côtes du Roussillon Villages red; Côtes du Roussillon rosé.

St-Vincent
66310 Estagel. Rating: 12. Founded 1979. 160 members; 1,800 acres producing 169,000 cases of AOC Rivesaltes VDN red and white; Côtes du Roussillon red and rosé; Côtes du Roussillon Villages red and rosé; plus 238,000 cases Vin de Pays Côtes Catalanes and Pyrénées-Orientales, and *vins de table*.

Tarerach
Tarerach, 66320 Vinca. Rating: 12. Founded 1923. 20 members; 355 acres producing 8,000 cases of AOC Côtes du Roussillon red plus 53,000 cases Vin de Pays Coteaux du Fenouillèdes and *vins de table*.

Tautavel 'Les Maîtres Vignerons'
66720 Tautavel. Rating: 13. Founded 1927. 225 members producing 170,000 cases of AOC Rivesaltes; Muscat de Rivesaltes; Côtes du Roussillon and Villages red; plus 62,000 cases Vin de Pays Côtes Catalanes and *vins de table*.

Terrats
66300 Terrats. Rating: 13. Founded 1932. 145 members; 1,750 acres producing 210,000 cases of AOC Muscat de Rivesaltes, Rivesaltes and Côtes du Roussillon red, white and rosé, plus 100,000 cases Vin de Pays Catalan and *vins de table*.

Terroir de Cerbère
66290 Cerbère. Rating: 12. Founded 1931. 105 members; 244 acres producing 13,500 cases of AOC Banyuls.

OTHER COOPERATIVES

'Aglya', 66310 Estagel
Bages, 66670 Bages
Banyuls-dels-Aspres, 66300 Thuir
Belesta, 66720 Latour-de-France
Le Boulou, 66160 Le Boulou
'La Cabestanyenca', 66330 Cabestany
Collioure, 66190 Collioure
Elne, 66200 Elne
Espira de l'Agly, 66600 Espira de l'Agly
Feilluns, 66220 St-Paul-de-Fenouillet
Fourques, 66300 Fourques
Lamsac, 66720 Latour-de-France
Latour-de-France, 66720 Latour-de-France
Perpignan 'Mas Llaro', 66000 Perpignan
Pezilla-de-Conflent, 66730 Sournia
Pezilla-La-Rivière, 66370 Pezilla-La-Rivière
St-Jean-Lasseille, 66300 Thuir
'La Tautavelloise', Tautavel, 66720 Latour-de-France
Thuir, 66300 Thuir
Trouillas, 66300 Thuir
Vingrau, 66600 Vingrau

Cooperatives

In most cases, the cooperative cellars listed have been selected on a system rating them with up to 15 points; five each for quality of terrain, grape varieties planted and wine-making technique. Comparison of the ratings of different areas shows that coops in some zones, such as Roussillon, get consistently higher scores than others, indicating environmental advantages.

As the foundation dates show, most of the cooperatives were started between the wars as a response to depressed wine prices.

Midi prices

Typical prices a bottle, ex-cellar, in late 1982:
Banyuls 17 francs
Corbières 6-7 francs
Côtes du Roussillon 6 francs
Côtes du Roussillon-Villages 7.5 francs
Côtes du Languedoc 6 francs
Fitou 7.5 francs
Maury VDN 15.5 francs
Minervois 6.5 francs
Muscat de Rivesaltes 16.5 francs
Rivesaltes 13.5 francs

CORBIERES

Justice has been slow in coming to the Corbières, the biggest VDQS area in France, long overdue (at least in parts) for its own *appellation contrôlée*. It is a huge region, stretching from Narbonne inland almost to Carcassonne and the same distance south to the borders of the Roussillon. It rises and rolls in parched hills of pale limestone suddenly embroidered in bold patterns with the green stitches of vines. The neutral red Carignan has long been dominant.

A good site, restraint in cropping and careful wine-making made solid enough wines, but with little flavour and no future. Improvements are taking the form of wine-making with *macération carbonique*, to coax at least an illusion of fruitiness from the grapes, and more radically replanting with 'aromatic' (i.e. not neutral) varieties.

There are some big properties as well as the thousands of growers who contribute to the cooperatives. Two areas in the southeast corner of Corbières, largely coop country, have long enjoyed the appellation Fitou for their reds, on the grounds that they are more age-worthy than the rest. The following list describes the best properties, district by district, together with some of the promising ones: names to look out for in the future.

The total production of the Corbières averages 7.5m. cases.

CORBIERES DISTRICTS AND PRODUCERS

BIZANET

Important commune in the central Corbières near Narbonne.

J. B. Benet
Château de Bouquignan. Harsh, strong soil gives concentrated and aromatic wines even from the commoner grapes. 66.5 acres; 16,500 cases.

Simone Mirouse
Château de Beauregard. High-quality Syrah rosé – one of the top Corbières properties. 107 acres; 28,500 cases.

Prieuré de St-Amans
One of the best red Corbières, made by *macération carbonique* followed by ageing in oak barrels. 27.5 acres; 7,000 cases.

Marie Terral
Château de Quilhanet. A Grenache and Carignan vineyard, sensibly undercropped. *Macération carbonique* and barrel-ageing. 270 acres; 41,500 cases.

Cave Coopérative 'La Corbière Bizanetoise'
Bizanet, 11200 Lézignan Corbières. Rating: 9. Founded 1935. 308 members; 1,543 acres producing 101,000 cases of Corbières plus 342,000 cases Vin de Pays Val d'Orbieu red and *vins de table*.

BOUTENAC

In the hills of central Corbières, west of Bizanet.

Berges & Reverdy
Domaine de la Voulte Gasparet. Ideal soil and first-class techniques of *macération carbonique* and wood-ageing. 125 acres; 27,000 cases.

Georges Bertrand
Domaine de Villemajou. One of the best technicians of the region with a fine vineyard. Reds (maceration and wood-ageing) and dry rosés are full of character. 124 acres; 32,000 cases.

Yves Laboucarie
Domaine de Fontsainte. Some of the best land in the Corbières and very good wine-making. Maceration and wood-ageing for splendid reds, and a very pale rosé *gris de gris*. 104 acres; 41,000 cases.

CAMPLONG

A little commune at the foot of the Montagne d'Alaric, the highest ground of the northern Corbières.

Bouffet
Château de Vaugelas. A substantial estate with good wine, though techniques could be improved. 258 acres; 41,000 cases.

COUSTOUGE

Remote village of the Hautes Corbières.

Bringuier
A small property on excellent soil that makes good wine even of the dominant Carignan. 39.5 acres; 13,500 cases.

FABREZAN

A well-known commune in the north-central Corbières near the autoroute.

Mlle Huc
A big well-situated estate with a high proportion of 'aromatic' varieties, capable of making very good wines. 197 acres; 16,500 cases.

GRUISSAN

A pretty seaside village full of tourists at the foot of La Clape.

Pierre Clement
Château Le Bouis. Well-made medal-winning rosés and white wine. 89 acres; 17,500 cases.

LAGRASSE

A centre of the northern Hautes Corbières.

Antoine André
Château de Pech Lat. A fine property with a wide range of red, rosé, white and VDNs. 250 acres; 43,000 cases.

Cave Coopérative Lagrasse
11220 Lagrasse. Rating: 10. Founded 1952. 100 members; 360 acres producing 23,000 cases of Corbières red and Montagne d'Alaric rosé, plus 52,000 cases Vin de Pays Val d'Orbieu red and *vins de table*.

MONTSERET

Central Corbières village. Accessible from Narbonne.

Surbezy Cartier
Château des Ollieux. A very good vineyard being replanted with 'aromatic' varieties. Up-to-date maceration methods are making good wine. 106 acres; 26,500 cases.

Cave Coopérative Montseret
11200 Lézignan Corbières. Rating: 9. Founded 1949. 164 members; 1,486 acres producing 181,000 cases of Corbières red plus 180,000 cases Vin de Pays l'Aude red and *vins de table*.

RIBAUTE

A little village near Fabrezan under the Montagne d'Alaric.

Peresse
Campagne de Ciceron. Small and modern with 'aromatic' varieties producing white, red and pale *gris de gris*. 54 acres; 11,000 cases.

ST-ANDRÉ DE CABRERISSE

Deep in the central Corbières.

Guiraud
Domaine de Montjoie. Replanting and modern methods; stylish, full-flavoured wine. 83 acres.

Château Les Palais
The best-known Corbières estate, a pioneer with *macération carbonique* in the 1960s. Excellent and reliable quality. 252 acres; 54,000 cases.

TUCHAN
In the mountainous south of the Hautes Corbières.
Château de Nouvelles
One of the finest estates in the region. Part has the appellation Fitou. Also Rivesaltes VDN. 200 acres.
Cave Coopérative Mont Tauch
11350 Tuchan. Rating: 11. Founded 1931. 416 members; 2,366 acres producing 326,000 cases of AOC Fitou red; Rivesaltes red and white; Muscat de Rivesaltes red and white; VDQS Corbières red, white and rosé; Corbières Supérieures red, white and rosé; plus 100,500 cases Vin de Pays Coteaux Cathares red and *vins de table*.

VILLENEUVE LES CORBIERES
Between Tuchan and Durban in the heart of the Hautes Corbières.
Cassignol
One of the few private producers of AOC Fitou. Recent replanting. 112 acres; 16,500 cases.
Cave Coopérative 'Pilote de Villeneuve Les Corbières'
Villeneuve Les Corbières, 11360 Durban Corbières. Rating: 10. Founded 1948. 72 members; 788 acres producing 123,700 cases of AOC Fitou red and white; Muscat de Rivesaltes red and white; Rivesaltes red and white; VDQS Corbières white, red and rosé; plus 18,000 cases *vins de pays* and *vins de table*.

Other Caves Coopératives
'L'Avenir'
Villeseque des Corbières, 11360 Durban Corbières. Rating: 9. Founded 1931. 162 members; 995 acres producing 106,000 cases of VDQS Corbières red and rosé, plus 112,500 cases Vin de Pays Vallée du Paradis red and *vins de table*.
'Cap Leucate'
11370 Leucate. Rating: 9. Founded 1921. 356 members; 1,336 acres producing 117,000 cases of AOC Fitou red; Muscat de Rivesaltes white; Rivesaltes white; VDQS Corbières red, white and rosé; plus 44,000 cases *vins de table*.
Cascastel
11360 Durban Corbières. Rating: 12. Founded 1921. 77 members; 998 acres producing 139,000 cases of AOC Fitou red; VDN Muscat de Rivesaltes; VDN Rivesaltes Grenache white; VDQS Corbières red and white; plus 21,000 cases Vin de Pays Vallée du Paradis red and *vins de table*.
Corbières
Conilhac-Corbières, 11200 Lézignan Corbières. Rating: 9. Founded 1933. 173 members; 950 acres producing 84,000 cases of VDQS Corbières red, white and rosé, plus 138,000 cases Vin de Pays Coteaux du Lézignanais red and white, and *vins de table*.
Durban
11360 Durban Corbières. Rating: 9. Founded 1913. 279 members; 1,850 acres producing 230,000 cases of VDQS Corbières red, plus 164,500 cases Vin de Pays Vallée du Paradis red and white, and *vins de table*.
Embres & Castelmaure
11360 Durban Corbières. Rating: 13. Founded 1921. 113 members; 704 acres producing 81,500 cases of VDQS Corbières red, white and rosé, plus 97,000 cases Vin de Pays Vallée du Paradis red and *vins de table*.
Fitou
11510 Fitou. Rating: 9. Founded 1933. 200 members; 1,257 acres producing 107,000 cases of AOC Fitou red; Muscat de Rivesaltes white; VDN Rivesaltes; VDQS Corbières red and white; plus 32,000 cases *vins de pays* and *vins de table*.
Fraisse Les Corbières
11360 Durban Corbières. Rating: 9. Founded 1920. 115 members; 713 acres producing 94,500 cases of VDQS Corbières red and rosé, plus 55,500 cases Vin de Pays Vallée du Paradis red and *vins de table*.
Paziols
11530 Paziols. Rating: 10. Founded 1913. 237 members; 7,400 acres producing 224,500 cases of AOC Fitou red; Rivesaltes white; VDQS Corbières red and white; plus 166,000 cases Vin de Pays Coteaux Cathares red and *vins de table*.
'Portel'
11490 Portel des Corbières. Rating: 9. Founded 1924. 280 members; 1,875 acres producing 168,000 cases of VDQS Corbières red, plus 218,000 cases Vin de Pays Coteaux du Littoral Audois red and *vins de table*.
'Chateau de Queribus'
Cucugnan, 11350 Tuchan. Rating: 11. Founded 1928. 56 members; 484 acres producing 36,000 cases of VDQS Corbières red, plus 60,000 cases Vin de Pays Cucugnan red, white and rosé, and *vins de table*.
'St-Martin'
11540 Roqueforte des Corbières. Rating: 9. Founded 1949. 234 members; 1,447 acres producing 183,000 cases of VDQS Corbières red, white and rosé, plus 119,000 cases Vin de Pays l'Aude red and *vins de table*.

BLANQUETTE DE LIMOUX

The most unexpected and original of all the wines of the Midi is the high-quality sparkling wine of Limoux, tucked away behind the Corbières on the upper reaches of the river Aude above Carcassonne. There is substantial evidence that this lonely area of hilly farms produced France's first sparkling wine, at least a century before Champagne.

It uses the Mauzac (alias Blanquette), the white grape 'with a slight smell of cider' which is the base for the rustic bubbly of Gaillac. (Gaillac was a Roman wine town; its antiquity may be immense.) Whatever its origins, the traditional Limoux formula is Mauzac for sprightliness plus Clairette for mildness, originally just *pétillant*, but now made by the *méthode champenoise* to full pressure and extremely high standards of delicate blending. Chenin Blanc now also plays a part. The latest development is the addition of a little Chardonnay in the best *cuvées* for fuller flavour; if Blanquette has a fault, it is a slightly pinched, lemony finesse which can benefit by plumping out.

Eighty per cent of the entire production of the 4,000 acres under vines is in the hands of the vast, ultra-modern cooperative. Founded in 1946, the coop now has 650 members and in 1981 produced 540,000 cases of Blanquette. Rating: 14. In 1976 it linked with the predominantly red-wine coop at Tuchan, in the Hautes Corbières, which produces 200,000 cases a year of AC Fitou and Corbières VDQS.

A few Coopérateurs take back their wine to 'finish' it themselves, but the remarkably high standards of the cooperative make it hard to improve on their product – and certainly not in value for money.

Recently the coop has added to its repertoire a selection of the best red wine from its members' vineyards, which include a surprising proportion of Cabernet and Merlot. It offers a very pleasant full-bodied and soft brand called Sieur d'Arques, an excellent Vin de Pays de la Haute Vallée de l'Aude under the name Fécos, and an astonishingly Bordeaux-like *cuvée* called Anne des Joyeuses – one of the best non-appellation coop wines in France.

Another coop, at Gardie, near St-Hilaire, makes small quantities of Blanquette de Limoux from 250 acres. Rating: 10.

MINERVOIS

The river Aude parts the last wrinkles of the Pyrenees from the first of the Massif Central, and the Corbières from the Minervois. The Minervois is a 40-mile stretch of its north bank, encompassing both the gravelly flats along the river and the very different hills behind, topped by a plateau at 600 feet. Rivers have cut deep ravines in its soft brown rock, in one place leaving a mid-river island for the tiny town of Minerve. The plateau is dry, treeless *garrigue* where the vine struggles and even the Carignan makes wine with nerves and sinews. Modern wine-making in the high Minervois has produced some deliciously vital, well-engineered wines with a structure not of old oak beams, as the word *charpente* seems to imply, but more like an airframe; delicately robust.

The commercial centre of the region is below on the plain. A SICA, a group of ten cooperatives, produces large quantities of Vin de Pays de Peyriac to the specification of Chantovent, one of the biggest table-wine companies. But Chantovent is also the owner of an estate at La Livinière in the foothills which produces some of the best Minervois, going to the length of ageing it in retired Médoc *barriques*, and the cooperative in the same village has followed suit. Two cooperatives in fact have started selecting and ageing their best wine to sell as 'Jean d'Alibert'.

Area: 85,000 acres (half is potential VDQS but only 10,000 is fully qualified with the right grape varieties). Production: 2.6m. cases of Minervois, 14,000 of St-Jean-de-Minervois VDN.

The Minervois is semi-officially divided into five zones, distinguished by topography and weather conditions, listed below with their best producers.

MINERVOIS ZONES AND PRODUCERS

ZONE 1

Around Ginestas in the east, on the plain with relatively high rainfall. Its light reds are for drinking young. There are also some clean modern white wines.

Mme Dominique de Bertier
Château de Paraza, 11200 Lézignan Corbières. The reds are classic and the rosés fine and fruity. 173 acres; 37,000 cases of red and rosé VDQS.

Christian Bonnel
Domaine de la Lecugne, Bize Minervois, 11120 Ginestas. 22.5 acres; 4,500 cases of red VDQS.

Bernard Mazard
Château du Vergel, 11120 Ginestas. 34 acres; 9,000 cases of red and white VDQS.

Jacques Meyzonnier
Pouzols Minervois, 11120 Ginestas. Very good medal-winning *macération carbonique* wine with the label 'Domaine Meyzonnier'. 13 acres; 3,000 cases of red VDQS Minervois.

Guy Rancoule
Domaine de l'Herbe Sainte, Mirepasset, 11120 Ginestas. A good varied vineyard; the rosé and whites are fine and fruity. 22 acres; 4,000 cases of red, white and rosé.

Caves Coopératives

'Les Coteaux de Pouzols Minervois'
Pouzols Minervois, 11120 Ginestas. Rating: 10. Founded 1936. 142 members; 953 acres producing 275,000 cases, of which 71,000 are VDQS red, white and rosé.

'Les Crus de Montouliers'
Montouliers, 34310 Capestang. Rating: 8. Founded 1937. 106 members; 763 acres producing 252,000 cases, of which 44,700 are VDQS red.

ZONE 2

The south-central area on the plain of the Aude is hottest and driest with richer reds, also for drinking young.

Jean Barthes
Château de St-Julia, 11800 Trebes. 33 acres; 7,500 cases of red and white.

Jean Baptiste Bonnet
Domaine de Gibalaux, Laure Minervois, 11800 Trebes. 59 acres; 13,500 cases of red.

Bernard de Crozals
Domaine de Homs, Rieux, Minervois, 11160 Caunes, Minervois.

Christian Ferret
Château de Badens, Badens, 11800 Trebes. 35 acres; 10,000 cases of red.

Alfred Keim
Domaine de Prat Majou, Laure Minervois, 11800 Trebes. 25 acres; 5,500 cases of red.

Soc. Mesnard Bellissen
Domaine de Millegrand, 11800 Trebes. 101 acres; 22,500 cases of red.

Jean-Pierre Ormières
Château de Fabas, Laure Minervois, 11800 Trebes. 84 acres; 22,000 cases of red.

Guy Panis
Château du Donjon, Bagnoles, 11600 Conques-sur-Orbiel. 42 acres; 10,500 cases of red.

Aymard de Soos
Château de Russol, Laure Minervois, 11800 Trebes. 74 acres; 20,000 cases of red.

Jean de Thelin
Château de Blomac, Blomac, 11700 Capendu. 80 acres; 18,000 cases of Minervois, traditional red wine, well made with 10% Syrah. Also 175 acres of *vins de table* vineyard where experiments are being made with Cabernet, Merlot and the Spanish Tempranillo. One of the grandest cellars of the region.

Caves Coopératives

'Les Coteaux de Minervois'
Pépieux, 11700 Capendu. Rating: 7. Founded 1951. 265 members; 2,376 acres producing 800,000 cases, of which 40,600 are VDQS red and rosé.

Laure Minervois
11800 Trebes. Rating: 7. Founded 1929. 270 members; 2,640 acres producing 721,000 cases, of which 106,000 are VDQS red, white and rosé.

Peyriac Minervois
11160 Caunes Minervois. Rating: 7. Founded 1930. 252 members; 1,358 acres producing 307,000 cases, of which 30,700 are VDQS red, white and rosé. Peyriac and its district have given their name to France's biggest-selling *vins de pays*, produced for Chantovent by a group of cooperatives.

ZONE 3

The north-central area in the foothills; makes the best-structured reds for keeping.

Gérard Blanc
Domaine de Ste-Eulalie, La Livinière, 34210 Olonzac. 30 acres; 7,000 cases red.

Mme Suzanne de Faucompret
Domaine de la Senche, La Livinière, 34210 Olonzac. 39 acres; 8,750 cases red.

Soc. Gourgazaud
Château de Gourgazaud, La Livinière, 34210 Olonzac. The extremely influential pioneering property of Chantovent, the huge table-wine company. Success with *macération carbonique* encouraged investment in the area, including the SICA Coteaux de Peyriac for *vins de pays* and the Domaine de Gourgazaud for experimental Vin de Pays de l'Hérault. 74 acres; 20,000 cases of red.

Marcel Julien
Château de Villeranbert, 11160 Caunes Minervois. 24,000 cases of red.

Paul Mandeville
Domaine de Vaissière, Azille, 11700 Capendu. A pioneering property with modern vineyards including Cabernet Sauvignon, Merlot and even Bleu Portugais. Its Vin de Pays de l'Aude (or de l'Oc) is sold by Chantovent.

Jacques Maris
La Livinière, 34210 Olonzac. 25 acres; 5,500 cases of red and white.

Mme Moureau & Fils
Château de Villerambert, Château de Villegly, 11160 Caunes Minervois. 84 acres; 2,700 cases of red and rosé.

Marc Remaury
Domaine du Pech d'André, Azillanet, 34210 Olonzac. 30 acres; 7,750 cases of red, rosé and white.

J. A. Tallavignes
Château de Paulignan, Trausse Minervois, 11160 Caunes Minervois. Recognized locally as a highly original and competent wine maker. 34.5 acres; 5,700 cases of red and white.

Caves Coopératives d'Azillanet
Azillanet, 34210 Olonzac. Rating: 8. Founded 1922. 250 members; 1,682 acres producing 424,000 cases, of which 70,000 are VDQS red and rosé.

'Les Costos Roussos'
Trausse, 11160 Caunes Minervois. Rating: 8. Founded 1937. 217 members; 1,511 acres producing 359,000 cases, of which 84,900 are VDQS red, white and rosé.

'Coteaux du Haut Minervois'
La Livinière, 34210 Olonzac. Rating: 8. Founded 1923. 196 members; 1,358 acres producing 309,800 cases, of which 48,000 are VDQS red and rosé. The best red, Jean d'Alibert, is made by *macération carbonique* and aged in Bordeaux barrels.

'Felines Minervois'
34210 Olonzac. Rating: 7. Founded 1929. 178 members; 1,383 acres producing 277,000 cases, of which 15,100 are VDQS red and rosé.

'La Vigneronne'
11160 Caunes Minervois. Rating: 10. Founded 1922. 430 members; 1,832 acres producing 361,000 cases, of which 48,700 are VDQS red, including Selection 'Jean d'Alibert'.

ZONE 4
The high plateau around Minerve, has the harshest climate and makes the strongest and biggest wine. St-Jean-de-Minervois in this zone has its own appellation for Muscat *vin doux naturel*.

Mme Jacqueline Le Calvez
La Caunette, 34210 Olonzac. Well situated on the sunny hillsides of La Caunette. Replanting is making a first-class vineyard. Very good vinification. 30 acres; 5,750 cases of red.

Caves Coopératives de Vinification d'Aigne
Aigne, 34210 Olonzac. Rating: 8. Founded 1948. 130 members; 1,531 acres producing 186,500 cases, of which 31,600 are VDQS red, white and rosé.

St-Jean-de-Minervois
34360 St-Chinian. Rating: 12. Founded 1955. 65 members; 518 acres producing 80,000 cases, of which 34,600 are VDQS Minervois and 10,000 are AOC white Muscat de St-Jean-de-Minervois. The main cellar for this little sweet-wine appellation.

ZONE 5
The western zone, has the highest rainfall and least distinguished wines.

Caves Coopératives 'La Grappe'
Villeneuve Minervois, 11160 Caunes Minervois. Rating: 7. Founded 1925. 364 members; 2,297 acres producing 558,000 cases, of which 79,800 are VDQS red, white and rosé.

'Malves Bagnoles'
Malves-en-Minervois, 11600 Conques-sur-Orbiel. Rating: 7. Founded 1948. 119 members; 908 acres producing 233,000 cases, of which 23,400 are VDQS red and rosé.

Villalier
11600 Conques-sur-Orbiel. Rating: 8. Founded 1934. 178 members; 968 acres producing 232,000 cases, of which 180,000 are VDQS red, white and rosé.

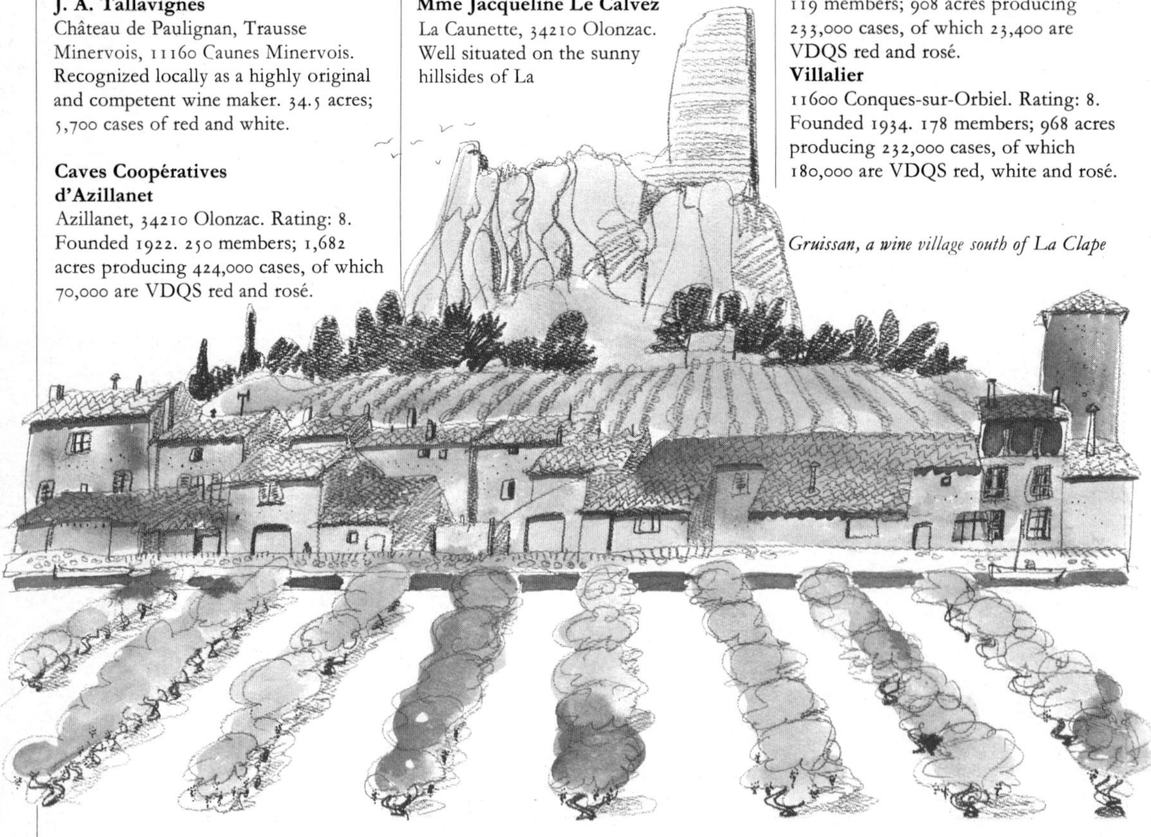

Gruissan, a wine village south of La Clape

COTEAUX DU LANGUEDOC

The stress in this name is on the Coteaux. The plains of the Languedoc between Narbonne and Montpellier are the notorious source of calamitous quantities of low-strength blending wine. But certain of its hillsides have VDQS status and hardly less potential for quality than Corbières and Roussillon. In general their wines are lighter and harsher – but not necessarily so. A dozen separate areas, confusingly scattered across the map, produce named and worthwhile wines.

The concentration is to the north of Béziers, in the first foothills of the Cevennes where the river Hérault leaves its torrents to become placid and poplar-lined. Cabrières, Faugères, St-Saturnin are such foothill vineyards. The best known of them, the only ones with an international reputation of their own, are Faugères and St-Chinian, in the hills to the west towards the Minervois. Their reds can be full-bodied, distinctly savoury wines, admirably suited to vinification by *macération carbonique*. St-Chinian, partly on chalky clay and partly on dark purple schist full of manganese, is worth careful study. The variety of soils in these hills gives character to their wine. The Berlou valley, on the purple schist, is outstanding for riper, rounder reds than the rest of the region.

The most individual, and an area with exciting potential, is La Clape, the isolated limestone massif like a beached island at the mouth of the river Aude, between Narbonne and the sea. Soil and climate conditions on La Clape have shown that they can produce highly distinctive white wines. Cool sea breezes give the hills a microclimate of their own. Blanc de la Clape, made of standard southern grapes, or better from Malvoisie (alias Bourboulenc), is clean if unexciting when young. But real character comes with ageing: at five or six years it can have some of the style of a good Rhône white. Better grape varieties may make magnificent wines. One domaine at least has already planted Chardonnay.

COTEAUX DU LANGUEDOC DISTRICTS AND PRODUCERS

CABRIERES
In the Cevennes foothills. Best known for light *rosé de goutte*, made without pressing.

Cave Coopérative 'Les Coteaux de Cabrières'
34800 Clermont-l'Hérault. Rating: 10. Founded 1938. 150 members; 988 acres producing 219,500 cases, of which 49,000 are VDQS Coteaux du Languedoc Cabrières and 13,000 AOC Clairette du Languedoc.

COTEAUX DE VERARGUES
Near Lunel, between Montpellier and Nimes. *See* Muscat de Lunel page 212.

FAUGERES
Westernmost of the Cevennes foothill districts with some very competent producers of red and instant rosé.

Bernard Vidal
La Liquière, Cabrerolles, 34480 Magalas. Ideally situated with the best grape varieties for red, rosé and white with real finesse. Uses *macération carbonique*.

Vidal-Gaillard
Château de la Liquière, Cabrerolles, 34480 Magalas. Good grape varieties on excellent schist soil. Well-managed wine-making by *macération carbonique*.

Caves Coopératives 'Les Crus Faugères'
34600 Bedarieux. Rating: 11. Founded 1961. 201 members; 1,304 acres producing 271,000 cases, of which 101,000 are VDQS Faugères.

Laurens
34480 Magalas. Rating: 10. Founded 1938. 382 members; 3,309 acres producing 744,400 cases, of which 165,000 are VDQS Faugères.

LA CLAPE
Seaside limestone hills near Narbonne, best for white and rosé.

Soc. Aupècle
Domaine des Monges-Schaefer, Château de Capitoul, 11100 Narbonne. A substantial estate in the centre of La Clape, using traditional methods capable of improvement.

J. Boscary
Château de Rouquette-sur-Mer, 11100 Narbonne. A remarkable site on the rocky slopes of La Clape near the sea. The most modern wine-making for high-quality red, white and rosé; perhaps the best of the area. The reds are aged in oak barrels.

Robert Bottero
11560 Fleury d'Aude. Small but high-quality white-wine grower.

Combastet
Château de Ricardelle de la Clape, 11100 Narbonne. Part of the estate is up on the limestone of La Clape and makes good traditional wines from a variety of grapes.

Egretier
Château de Complazens, Armissan, 11110 Coursan. Good grapes and situation on La Clape. Well-made wines.

Philippe Hue
Château de Salles, Salles d'Aude, 11110 Coursan. Classic 'Clape' red of Carignan, Grenache and Syrah come from part of the estate. M. Hue also makes an interesting *vin de pays* of Merlot and a dry rosé of Cinsaut.

J. B. Jousseaume
Domaine de Ricardelle de la Clape, 11100 Narbonne.

Yves Lignères
Domaine de Vires, 11100 Narbonne. A steadily improving property, both in grape varieties and wine-making. At present the best wines are *macération* reds.

Domaine de Pech Redon
11100 Narbonne. A restored old estate in a lovely situation high on La Clape but near the sea. A wide variety of vines make good *macération* red, white and excellent dry rosé.

de St-Exupery
Château de Pech Celeyran, Salles d'Aude, 11110 Coursan. A largely Cabernet and Merlot vineyard producing some good wine.

Jean Ségura
Domaine de Rivière La Haut, 11560 Fleury d'Aude. A leading protagonist in the area of high-quality white wine based on Bourboulenc grapes – the long-lived speciality of La Clape.

Vaille
Des Ruffes, Salleles du Bosc, 11110 Coursan.

LA MEJANELLE
Obscure little region near the sea, east of Montpellier.

SICAREX Méditerranée
The principal influence in improving the wines of the central south has been the advanced research station of SICAREX Méditerranée known as the Domaine de l'Espiguette. The Cape Canaveral of French viticulture is the remote promontory between the Camargue and the Mediterranean, beyond the new resort of Le Grau-du-Roi. The architecture of the Domaine expresses its approach to wine; California itself has nothing more unblinkingly futuristic.

SICAREX – the initials stand for Société d'Intérêt Collectif Agricole de Recherches Expérimentales (*pour l'Amélioration des Produits de la Vigne*) – is a cooperative with some 60 members scattered as far apart as Aix-en-Provence and the Ardèche (far up the Rhône), the Var at the far side of Provence, the Vins de Pays des Sables of its immediate neighbourhood and, over to the west, the Coteaux du Languedoc.

Its chief role is to prove to its members and other growers that investment in better grape varieties will pay. It stands for Cabernet, Merlot, Syrah and Mourvèdre, the 'aromatic' varieties, to be blended with the standard Carignan, Grenache and their like. It stands against the bulk-producing junk varieties of Alicante and, worst of all, Aramon, which still exist in large numbers.

Suiting the better varieties to different soils, making test-lots of their wine, test-marketing them to the tourists at Grau-du-Roi are all facets of its research. Cabernet and Merlot appear very adaptable to soils and site conditions; Syrah less so and Mourvèdre extremely demanding. The Spanish Tempranillo is another promising early-ripener for poor sites.

Much of the wine-making is by *macération carbonique* or a modified version made necessary by machine-harvesting the grapes.

Temperature control is basic, both cooling for fruity light wines and warming to extract colour and tannins for *vins de garde*.

By French standards some of the SICAREX ideas are revolutionary. They will 'design' a wine of (say) 95 per cent tasteless Ugni Blanc with 5 per cent Muscat, or Carignan with Cabernet. The aromatic variety dominates and makes neutral wine highly palatable.

These experiments have important and exciting implications for *vins de pays*. But where they leave some of the duller of the regulated traditional appellations of the Midi is a good question. The brand-name of a number of the Domaine wines is Espigou.

De Colbert
Château de Flaugergues, 34000 Montpellier.
Delbez
Mas de Calage, St-Aunès, 34130 Mauguio.
Teissier
Domaine de la Costière, 34000 Montpellier.

MONTPEYROUX
Northern district for reds near the famous Gorges de l'Hérault.
Cave Coopérative Les Coteaux du Castellas
34150 Gignac. Rating: 10. Founded 1950. 245 members; 1,655 acres producing 418,000 cases, of which 79,000 are VDQS Coteaux du Languedoc and Montpeyroux.

PIC ST-LOUP
2,000-foot peak due north of Montpellier. Red *vins de café*.
Arles
Domaine de Lascours, Sauteyrargues, 34270 St-Mathieu-de-Tréviers.
Lauriol
Domaine de la Roque, Fontanes, 34270 St-Mathieu-de-Tréviers.
Recouly
Domaine de Cantaussels, Les Matelles, 34270 St-Mathieu-de-Tréviers.
Domaine de Villeneuve
Claret, 34270 St-Mathieu-de-Tréviers.

Caves Coopératives
Les Coteaux de Montferrand
34270 St-Mathieu-de-Tréviers. Rating: 9. Founded 1950. 164 members; 1,603 acres producing 535,800 cases, of which 69,800 are VDQS Coteaux du Languedoc Pic St-Loup.
Les Coteaux de St-Gely-du-Fesc
34980 St-Gely-du-Fesc. Rating: 9. Founded 1939. 179 members; 795 acres producing 261,600 cases, of which 16,000 are VDQS Pic St-Loup.
Les Coteaux de Valflaunes
34270 St-Mathieu-de-Tréviers. Rating: 9. Founded 1939. 140 members; 1,580 acres producing 441,000 cases, of which 52,700 are VDQS Coteaux du Languedoc and Pic St-Loup.

PINET (PICPOUL DE)
Pleasant dry white with 12° of alcohol and a touch of freshness.
C. Gaujal
Château de Pinet, 34850 Pinet. Extremely carefully made Picpoul white and *vins de pays* from Merlot.

QUATOURZE
A neglected little zone near Narbonne.
Yvon Ortola
Notre Dame du Quatourze, 11100 Narbonne.

ST-CHINIAN
The biggest and most important zone, soon to be an *appellation contrôlée*, in the Cevennes foothills to the west. Potentially excellent solid and smooth reds.
Calmette
Cazedarnes, 34460 Cessenon.
F. Guy & S. Peyre
Château de Goujan, 34490 Murviel Les Béziers. A substantial property making 3 excellent wines: Coteaux de Murviel from Merlot and Cabernet, classic St-Chinian (Carignan, Grenache and Syrah) by *macération carbonique*, and Cabernet rosé.
Libes-Cavaille
St-Nazaire de Ladarez, 34490 Murviel Les Béziers.
Miquel
Cazal-Viel, 34460 Cessenon.
Pierre Petit
Villespassans, 34360 St-Chinian. A first-class St-Chinian property using *macération carbonique*.

Caves Coopératives
Causses & Veyran
34490 Murviel-Les-Beziers. Rating: 10. Founded 1946. 203 members; 1,516 acres producing 378,500 cases, of which 56,000 are VDQS and Coteaux du Languedoc Lou Coulinadou and St-Chinian.
Les Coteaux de Cebazan
34360 St-Chinian. Rating: 10. Founded 1965. 166 members; 1,457 acres producing 336,300 cases, of which 92,000 are VDQS Coteaux du Languedoc and St-Chinian.
Coteaux de Creissan
34370 Cazouls-Les-Beziers. Rating: 9. Founded 1951. 158 members; 802 acres producing 293,000 cases, of which 27,000 are VDQS St-Chinian.
Les Coteaux du Rieu Berlou
34360 St-Chinian. Rating: 13. Founded 1965. 90 members; 1,094 acres producing 264,800 cases, of which 140,000 are VDQS St-Chinian.

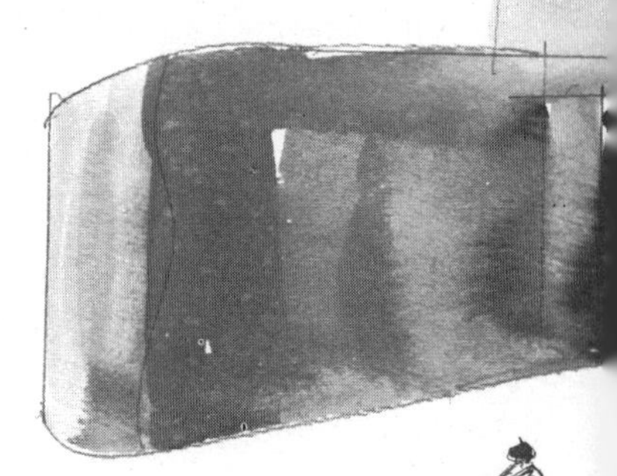

Les Crus Cazedarnais
34460 Cessenon. Rating: 9. Founded 1954. 143 members; 1,099 acres producing 311,400 cases, of which 64,000 are VDQS Coteaux du Languedoc and St-Chinian.
Quarante
34310 Capestang. Rating: 9. Founded 1934. 415 members; 2,756 acres producing 1m. cases, of which 214,000 are VDQS Coteaux du Languedoc and St-Chinian.
Les Vins de Roquebrun
34460 Cessenon. Rating: 13. Founded 1967. 140 members; 864 acres; 165,600 cases, of which 112,600 are VDQS Coteaux du Languedoc and St-Chinian.

ST-CHRISTOL
In a group with Verargues and St-Drézery north of Lunel. No notable activity.
Gabriel Martin
St-Christol, 34400 Lunel.
Cave Coopérative Les Coteaux de St-Christol
34400 Lunel. Rating: 9. Founded 1941. 189 members; 1,630 acres producing 514,900 cases, of which 70,300 are VDQS Les Coteaux de St-Christol.

ST-DREZERY
See St-Christol
Spitaleri
Mas de Carrat, St-Drézery, 34160 Castries.

Cave Coopérative de les Coteaux de St-Drézery
34160 Castries. Rating: 9. Founded 1939. 207 members; 1,289 acres producing 460,000 cases, of which 29,000 are VDQS St-Drézery and Coteaux du Languedoc.

ST-GEORGES-D'ORQUES
On the western outskirts of Montpellier, once fashionable with English tourists interned by Napoleon. Red wine, largely of Cinsaut.
Grill
Château de l'Engarran, Laverune, 34430 St-Jean-de-Vedas.
Cave Coopérative de St-Georges-d'Orques
34680 St-Georges-d'Orques. Rating: 9. Founded 1947. 262 members; 1,346 acres producing 304,800 cases, of which 89,500 are VDQS St-Georges-d'Orques and Coteaux du Languedoc.

ST-SATURNIN
Active vineyards in the *garrigue* of the Cevennes foothills with rather good lively reds and a very light 'Vin d'une Nuit'. Neighbour to Montpeyroux.
Cave Coopérative de St-Saturnin
34150 Gignac. Rating: 11. Founded 1951. 178 members; 1,600 acres producing 404,000 cases, of which 147,000 are VDQS St-Saturnin and Coteaux du Languedoc red and rosé.

OTHER PRODUCERS
J. M. Bonnevialle
St-Jean de la Blaquière, 34700 Lodève.
Château de la Condamine Bertrand
34230 Paulhan. Particularly well-made and successful white wine from Clairette grapes.

Daniel Delclaud
Domaine de St-Jean d'Aumières, 34150 Gignac.
B. Gaujal
Château de Nizas, Nizas, 34320 Roujan.
André Heulz
St-André-de-Sangonis, 34150 Gignac.

Domaine du Parc
34120 Bézenas. Owner: M. Henri L'Epine. a 105-acre vineyard bounded by a 17th-century wall, producing Vin de Pays de l'Hérault from Carignan, Merlot and Cabernet Sauvignon.

Caves Coopératives
St-Felix de Lodez
34150 Gignac. Rating: 9. Founded 1942. 249 members; 1,852 acres producing 473,800 cases, of which 81,200 are VDQS Coteaux du Languedoc and 3,900 are AOC Clairette du Languedoc.
St-Jean-de-la-Blaquière
34700 Lodève. Rating. 10. Founded 1947. 268 members; 2,062 acres producing 48,700 cases, of which 113,800 are VDQS Coteaux du Languedoc.

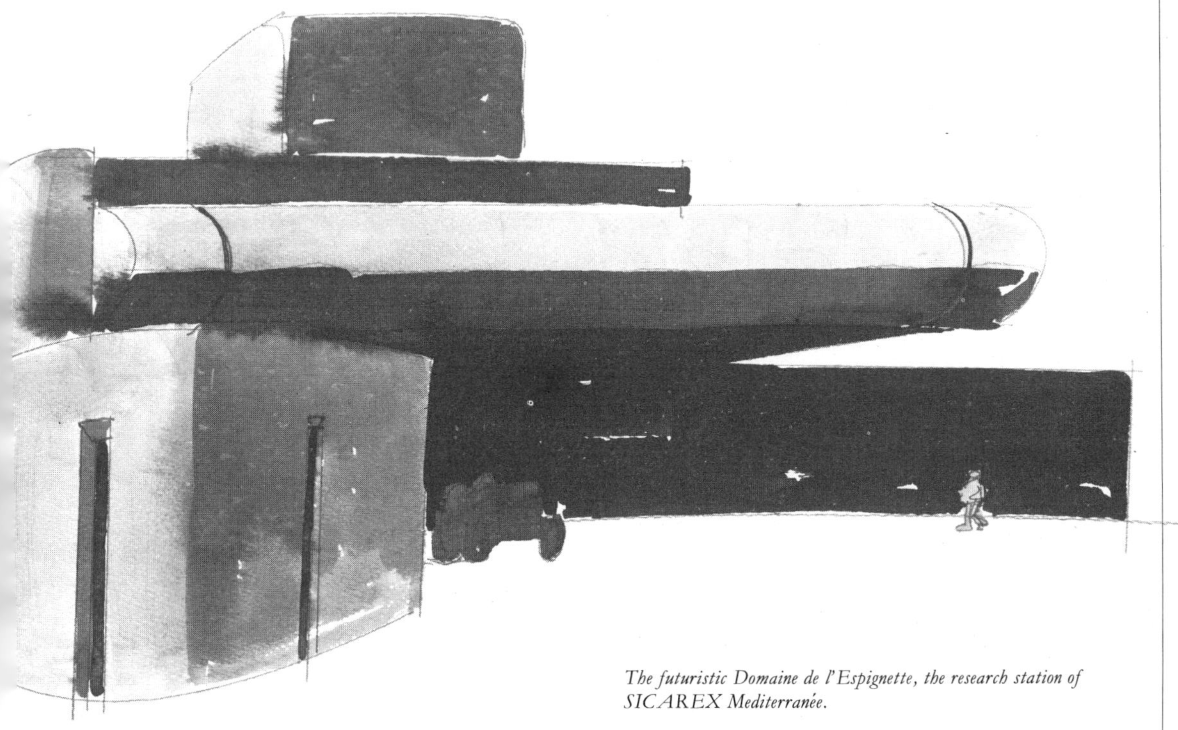

The futuristic Domaine de l'Espignette, the research station of SICAREX Mediterranée.

THE MUSCATS OF LANGUEDOC

Three small zones along the central south coast, between the wine port of Sète and the marshes of the Camargue, have appellations (and an antique reputation) for sweet brown Muscat *vins doux naturels*.

Frontignan is the biggest and best known. The Muscat vineyards stretch along the coast through Mireval (the second appellation) towards Montpellier. The grape is the '*muscat à petits grains ronds*'; its wine powerfully aromatic, brown and sticky, but lacking (at least as it is made today) the freshness and finesse of Muscat de Beaumes de Venise. The third area is Lunel, halfway between Montpellier and Nîmes, just inland from the Camargue.

The cooperatives of Frontignan and Lunel are the major producers. One other big grower of Frontignan and Mireval is M. Robiscau, who created Le Mas Neuf des Aresquiers at Vic La Gardiole (34110 Frontignan) 20 years ago, ripping up 200 acres of rocky terrain where desultory vines were growing to make a modern vineyard.

Caves Coopératives

Muscat de Frontignan

34110 Frontignan. Rating: 13. Founded 1910. 380 members; 1,358 acres producing 121,000 cases.

Muscat de Lunel

Verargues, 34400 Lunel. Rating: 12. Founded 1956, 72 members; 437 acres; 50,000 cases of AOC Muscat de Lunel.

Muscat de Mireval – Cave de Rabelais

34840 Mireval. Rating: 12. Founded 1961. 78 members; 237 acres producing 22,000 cases.

CLAIRETTE DU LANGUEDOC

A scarcely merited AOC for a generally dull and dispiriting dry white from Clairette grapes grown in several communes along the Hérault. Much of it is fortified as a cheap apéritif and sold under such names as 'Amber Dry'.

Domaine de la Condemine

34230 Paulhan. M. Jany runs a very new property which has 14 acres of Clairette of unusually good quality.

Caves Coopératives

Adissan

34230 Paulhan. Rating: 8. Founded 1929. 280 members; 1,808 acres; 579,100 cases, of which 8,266 are VDQS Coteaux du Languedoc red and rosé and 7,600 are AOC Clairette du Languedoc.

La Clairette d'Aspiran

34800 Clermont-l'Hérault. Rating: 9. Founded 1932. 322 members; 2,297 acres producing 625,000 cases, of which 39,000 are VDQS Coteaux du Languedoc and 34,000 are AOC Clairette du Languedoc.

La Fontesole

34320 Roujan. Rating: 9. Founded 1930. 309 members; 1,482 acres; 515,000 cases, of which 31,000 are VDQS Coteaux du Languedoc and 13,300 are AOC Clairette du Languedoc.

Peret

34800 Clermont-l'Hérault. Rating: 6. Founded 1932. 198 members; 1,296 acres producing 347,500 cases, of which 3,750 are VDQS Coteaux du Languedoc red and rosé. Also AOC Clairette du Languedoc.

BOUCHES-DU-RHONE

This *département* of the Rhône delta was almost a vinous blank, a pause between the mass production of the Languedoc and the scattered vineyards of Provence, until modern technology stepped in. Only in one area south of Nîmes, the Costières du Gard, a deep deposit of pebbles from the former river bed provides good ripening conditions, officially recognized by a VDQS for Rhône-style reds and rosé. For some strange reason a corner of this area even has an AOC for its white Clairette de Bellegarde.

Technology took an unexpected form. The massively wealthy Compagnie des Salins du Midi, the producer of a large proportion of France's salt from the seawater lagoons of this coast, began experimenting with vines in the sand flats along the shore. Their original wines were made with inferior varieties, but today the Vins des Sables du Golfe du Lion (under the trademark Listel) include such '*améliorateurs*' as Cabernet and Sauvignon Blanc.

COSTIERES DU GARD PRODUCERS

Château Roubaud

Gallician, 30600 Vauvert. Owner: Mme Annie Molinier. Founded 1902. This château (in name only) comprises 173 acres producing 44,500 cases of Costières du Gard. Only 5% is exported.

Mas St-Louis La Perdrix

30127 Bellegarde. Owner: Mme Lamour. Founded 1812 but run by the Lamour family for only the past 30 years. 348 acres planted with Carignan, Cinsaut, Grenache, Cabernet, Syrah and Clairette de Bellegarde produce 44,500 cases. 80% of production is Costières du Gard. The rest is *vins de table*.

Cave Coopérative de Bellegarde

30127 Bellegarde. President: M. Darboux. 280 members; 2,025 acres producing 184,000 cases a year, of which 24,000 are Clairette de Bellegarde and the rest Costières du Gard.

OTHER PRODUCERS

Domaine de l'Amarine

30127 Bellegarde. Nicolas Godepski.

Domaine de St-Benezey

30800 St-Giles du Gard. M. Pohe, makes 44,000 cases.

Château St-Vincent

Jonquiers St-Vincent, 30300 Beaucaire. M. de Mandol makes very good-quality Costières du Gard.

VINS DES SABLES DU GOLFE DU LION

Domaines Viticoles des Salins du Midi (Listel)

34063 Montpellier. Founded 1856 (vineyards from 1875). Wine Director: Pierre Julian. Sales 1.6m. cases. The biggest wine estate in France, with no less than 4,200 acres, largely in the unlikely environment of the sand dunes of the Gulf of Lions. Salins du Midi is a vast salt company. In the 19th century it started ploughing its profits into pioneering vineyards in the phylloxera-free sand. It has maintained the highest standards and made the Vins de Pays des Sables du Golfe du Lion a sort of appellation of its own, led by its Domaines de Villeroy, de Jarras and du Bosquet.

It uses sand as an almost neutral growing medium, excludes seawater with dykes of fresh water, fertilizes and fixes the sand with winter cereals and produces wines of remarkable clarity, simplicity and charm of flavour at moderate prices. As well as the sand vineyards 600 acres in the Var at Pierrefeu and Ollières produce Côtes de Provence and Vins de Pays de Maures and des Coteaux Varois.

CORSICA: L'ILE DE BEAUTE

The importance of France's dramatically mountainous island of Corsica is almost entirely as a producer of bulk material for table-wine blends. When France lost Algeria, its wine growers flooded into the island to plant the plains of the east coast with the basic grapes of Algeria and the Midi – Carignan, Grenache and Cinsaut. In the period 1960-1973 the island's vineyards expanded from 20,000 to 77,000 acres. Then came a period of retrenchment, with 9,000 acres being pulled up again. So the vast majority of Corsica's vineyards are young, in common grapes and on relatively big properties formed for quantity rather than quality – with an average yield over the island of 76 hl/ha.

The appellation Vin de Corse was instituted in 1976 as an encouragement to limit crops. The specific interest of Corsican wine, such as it is, lies in seven more limited appellations relating to the best vineyards, which retain traditional grape varieties. These include the red Nielluccio and Sciacarello, and the white Vermentino, Malvoisie and Trebbiano (Ugni Blanc).

One appellation, Patrimonio in La Conca d'Oro in the north of the island, is relatively long-established for rosé and red made primarily of Nielluccio, with one degree higher minimum alcohol (12.5) than the rest of the island's wines.

Ajaccio, the capital, has Sciacarello red and rosé and Vermentino white. Calvi and the region of Balagne in the northwest have a relatively high proportion of AOC wine. Cap Corse specializes in dessert wines, including sweet Muscat.

Porto-Vecchio and Figari and the flat southeast have more modern vineyards, but using a good proportion of Nielluccio. Sartène, around Propriano in the southwest, is the area with the highest proportion of appellation wines (75 per cent), of Corsican grapes – mainly Sciacarello – and of traditional-style small growers working on good hill slopes. On the whole, the south is the place to look for the most interesting wine.

Much the greatest concentration of table-wine vineyards is on the central east coast in the region of Ghisonaccia-Aleria.

PRINCIPAL CORSICAN PRODUCERS

Albertini Frères, Clos d'Alzeto, 20151 Carri-d'Orcino
Couvent d'Alzipratu, Zilia
Clos Capitoro, 20166 Porticcio
Dominique Gentile, 20217 St-Florent
Clos Nicrosi, 20247 Rogliano
Domaine de Paviglia, 2000 Ajaccio
Comte Peraldi, 20167 Mezzavia
Domaine La Ruche Foncière, 20215 Arena-Vescovato
Domaine de Torraccia, 20210 Porto-Vecchio

Caves Coopératives
Aghione, 20255 Aghione
Aleria, 20270 Aleria
Calenzana, Coteaux de Balaone Suare, 20214 Calenzana
La Marana Rusignani, 20290 Lucciana
Patrimonio, 20253 Patrimonio
Sartène, 20100 Sartène
SICA de Figari, 20131 Pianottoli

Corsica is entitled to the Vin de Pays name L'Ile de Beauté

THE SOUTHWEST

The southwest corner of France exists in calm self-sufficiency. Its rich food and notable wines seem, like its beauty and tranquillity, to be its private business. To the east lie the great vineyards of the Languedoc; to the north Bordeaux; Spain lies beyond the towering Pyrenees. In their foothills and the river valleys of the Tarn, the Garonne, the Lot, the Gers, the Adour and the Gave, a different race of wines is grown, bearing no relation to the Midi and remarkably distinct from Bordeaux. Historically some of these wines, notably Cahors and Gaillac, were exported via Bordeaux and known as the wines of the *Haut-Pays*, the high country. Some use the Bordeaux grapes. But all except those closest to the Gironde (Côtes de Buzet, Côtes de Marmande) have real character of their own to offer. A variety of grapes with extraordinary local names, some of them Basque, give a range of flavours found nowhere else. The world is beginning to discover them and encourage the expansion of a depleted vineyard. Fashion is swinging towards the regional idiosyncrasies the southwest has to offer.

BERGERAC

The wily law-givers of the seventeenth century were never short of dodges for discouraging rivals to their main interests. Bergerac is a happily situated region with fine slopes and soil as far inland as shipping can easily penetrate up the river Dordogne. To prevent it competing on equal terms with Bordeaux it was compelled to use smaller barrels, which carried a higher tax. Apparently the Dutch were the only nation partial enough to its wines to ignore the tax and keep buying. Hence a virtual monopoly of the region's trade, which inclined it towards Dutch taste: sweet white wines and thin dry ones for distilling. The sweet ones became and remained the pride of the region. Monbazillac is its most famous name. But in this century medium-sweet and thin dry wines have been hard to sell. So the Bergeraçois tried red. Demand has switched to and fro between red and white with Bergerac tending to be a step behind. Recent plantings have been largely in the Bordeaux red grapes, which perform excellently here, with Merlot in the majority. Now there is a shortage of dry white in Bordeaux. With a current near-equilibrium between red and white grapes, Bergerac should at last be well placed for the campaign it is waging to become better known.

Château de Panisseau, Thénac

It is not one simple appellation, but like Bordeaux an all-embracing one with subsections determined by slopes, soil and microclimates. Bergerac unqualified is light (minimum 10 degrees) red, unmistakably claret-like by nature; an indistinguishable substitute for many light Bordeaux reds, at a slightly lower price. It need not be so light, as some 12-degree wines from the chalky northern part of the region with the appellation Pécharmant bear witness. Young vines may account for the picnic style of much of the red at present. Côtes de Bergerac is a little weightier with 11 degrees.

The dry white is sold as Bergerac Sec. Several skilful and enterprising growers, not least at the cooperatives, have introduced a firm flavour of Sauvignon into wine that is still predominantly Sémillon and the lesser Bordeaux varieties. With cool, clean fermentation in stainless steel, they are making a Sancerre-style wine with more substance than its imitators in Touraine.

No less than five little appellations apply to sweet

and semi-sweet whites (which rely on Sémillon and hope for a degree of 'noble rot'). Just south of the town of Bergerac, Monbazillac, with its operatic château (the property of the local cooperative), is capable of truly luscious and powerful (15-degree) wines, obviously related to Sauternes. They only lack the miraculous harmony of fruity acidity that makes a great Sauternes – but this does not shorten their lives. I have lingered long over 40-year-old Monbazillac that had turned a fine tobacco colour.

Côtes de Saussignac is a scarcely used appellation for similar, slightly less rich wine from the slopes to the west of Monbazillac.

To the north of the Dordogne, Montravel is a slightly superior Bergerac Sec, but the distinctions between the appellations Côtes de Montravel, Haut-Montravel and Rosette, all for dry to semi-sweet wine with a certain body, seem to complicate matters unnecessarily. Total production: 3.7m. cases. Price 9.5 francs a bottle.

BERGERAC PRODUCERS

Châteaux Belingard, du Chayne, Boudigand

Pomport, 24240 Sigoulès.

Owner: Comte de Bosredon. 260 acres. 3 properties in Monbazillac run together to produce 2 red Côtes de Bergerac, Châteaux du Chayne and Boudigand, dry white Château du Chayne and sweet Château Belingard Monbazillac.

Reds are made by *macération carbonique* for drinking unaged; the dry white is a sharpish Sauvignon. Monbazillac ages 2 years in wood. A *méthode champenoise* Brut is also named Belingard. The property contains traces of druidical doings which the Count is pleased to discuss.

Château du Bloy

Bonneville, 24230 Vélines.

Owners: The Guillermier brothers. 87 acres: 62 red, one quarter each Merlot, the 2 Cabernets and Malbec; 25 white, Sauvignon, Sémillon, Muscadelle and Muscadet.

A recent (1967) appellation Montravel property making a full, rather rich red with no wood-ageing, a dry white of pure Sauvignon, another an unusual blend of Muscadet, a little Sémillon and Muscadelle. Dry whites are not aged; red and sweet whites are kept 2 years in cement vats.

Château La Borderie

Monbazillac, 24240 Sigoulès.

Owner: Dominique Vidal. 165 acres. The Monbazillac grapes are one third each Muscadelle, Sauvignon and Sémillon. Red grapes are one third each Merlot and the 2 Cabernets.

The Vidals have 2 properties in Monbazillac. La Borderie, bought in 1968, has 87 acres of Monbazillac, aged in large oak vats for up to 4 years. Red from 42 acres is kept 1 year in stainless steel, 1 in cask. Dry white from 17 acres is pure Sauvignon, bottled in spring. Château Treuil de Nailhac, their older, smaller estate, is being replanted to produce red and Sauvignon white as well as Monbazillac.

Château Le Caillou

Rouffignac, 24240 Sigoulès.

Owner: Pierre Eymery. 62 acres: 37 white, mainly Monbazillac (Sémillon 70%, Sauvignon and Muscadelle 15% each); 25 red (Merlot 50%, Cabernet Franc and Sauvignon 25% each).

Half the red is over the Gironde border and therefore appellation Bordeaux. Apart from some Bergerac Sec made of almost pure Sauvignon, M. Eymery uses very traditional methods, ageing reds and sweet Monbazillac up to 3 years in mature barrels.

Domaine Constant

Castang, Lamonzie St-Martin, 24130 La Force.

Owner: Jean-Louis Constant. 50 acres of Monbazillac (Château Lavaud), 30 of Bergerac red, rosé and white.

Usual grape varieties, but rosé is pure Cabernet Sauvignon, dry white pure Sauvignon Blanc. About 850 cases of red Bergerac made in a tannic style, without destemming, bottled in its first summer, needs keeping. 400 cases each of rosé and white are for drinking young. 600 cases of Monbazillac are aged 2 years in wood and in a good year age well in bottle.

Château Court-Les-Mûts

Razac de Saussignac, 24240 Sigoulès.

Owner: Pierre-Jean Sadoux. 58 acres of white (Sémillon 75%, Sauvignon 25%) and red (Merlot 42%, Cabernet Sauvignon 33%, Cabernet Franc 26%).

The young oenologist Sadoux has established a modern winery with a good reputation, one of the few producing sweet Côtes de Saussignac *moelleux* as well as dry white Bergerac, semi-sweet Côtes de Bergerac and a soft fruity red (no barrels), all winning medals. 'Vin de Fête' is a *méthode champenoise* Brut.

Château Le Fage

Pomport, 24240 Sigoulès.

Owner: Maurice Gérardin. 100 acres: 25 red producing 6,500 cases, largely Merlot; 75 white producing 2,000 cases dry Sauvignon, 6,000-9,000 Monbazillac, largely Sémillon with Sauvignon and Muscadelle.

Family-owned estate for 200 years. Wine-making without barrels is traditional for the region: ageing is in enamelled vats – Monbazillac for 3-4 years. Red, like dry white, is bottled in spring unaged.

Domaine du Haut Pécharmant

24100 Bergerac.

Owner: Mme Reine Roches. 45 acres (plus 5 newly planted); Merlot 50% Cabernet Franc and Sauvignon 40%, Malbec 10%. 9,000 cases.

Pécharmant is made with modern materials but very traditional ideas: fermenting with stems and no filtration. The result is aggressively full-flavoured wine to age 7 or 8 years in bottle.

Domaine de la Jaubertie

Colombier, 24560 Issigeac.

Owner: Henry Ryman. 93 acres, half red (Merlot 45%, Cabernet Sauvignon 45%, Cabernet Franc and Malbec 5% each); half white (Sauvignon 55%, Sémillon 45%).

Ryman, well known in Britain for his stationery shops, bought the property in 1973. He uses cold fermentation in stainless steel to make crisply fruity white, bottled as soon as possible. Reds are bottled after about 18 months, including 3-4 months in barrels. 2 or 3 years in bottle brings out their character. When conditions are right (e.g. 1981) Ryman makes a little Monbazillac. Domaine du Grand Champ is a second label.

Château de Monbazillac

Monbazillac, 24240 Sigoulès.

The showplace of the region, owned by the local cooperative association. *See* UNIDOR.

Château de Michel Montaigne

24230 Vélines

Owners: The Mähler-Besse family.

The home of the great 16th-century philosopher (his study tower can be visited) and the country retreat of a distinguished Bordeaux négociant and part-owner of Château Palmer.

Château de Panisseau

Thénac, 24240 Sigoulès.

Owners: The Becker family. 125 acres. 250,000 cases. Red: one third each Cabernet Sauvignon, Cabernet Franc, Merlot. White: Sauvignon, Sémillon and Chenin Blanc in varying proportions.

A stunning little 11th-century fortress, developed since 1958 as a modern wine estate, offering a pure Sauvignon dry white of great finesse and an original, more full-flavoured dry blend of Sémillon and Chenin with 10% Sauvignon. The red is less exciting.

Château Poulvère

Monbazillac, 24240 Sigoulès.

Owner: Jean Borderie. 212 acres.

One of the biggest properties in the area, producing 17,000 cases of Monbazillac, 11,000 of red Bergerac and a very small quantity of rosé and dry white. Barrels are used only for Monbazillac, and only for 8-12 months.

Château Thénac

Le Bourg, Thénac, 24240 Sigoulès.

Owner: M. Cazalis. 23 acres. White: all Sauvignon. Red: Merlot and Cabernet Franc.

An old château bought in 1976, restored and showing promise.

Domaine Theylet Marsalet

St-Laurent-des-Vignes, 24100 Bergerac.

Owner: Marcel Monbouché. 80 acres producing 10,000 cases of Monbazillac (one third each Sauvignon, Sémillon, Muscadelle), 6,000 cases red Bergerac and about 5,000 Bergerac Sec.

M. Monbouché at his 17th-century property is unusual in his all-organic methods, ageing for up to 3 years in wood and not filtering. He is also unusual in selling 'varietal' Merlot and Cabernet Sauvignon unblended.

Château Tiregand

24100 Creysse

Owner: Comtesse de St-Exupéry. 82 acres: 75 red (Merlot 45%, Cabernet Sauvignon 30%, Cabernet Franc 15%, Malbec 10%); 7 white (Sauvignon 65%, Sémillon 35%). 8,000 cases.

The biggest property in Pécharmant, dating from the 13th century and in the same family since 1831. A south slope on chalky soil gives the wine body for up to 2 years' barrel-ageing and sometimes up to 10 in bottle. The 1978 was splendid, like good-quality Bordeaux. The small white vineyard makes a Bergerac Sec, Les Galinoux. Creysse is in the Dordogne valley just upstream from the town of Bergerac.

UNIDOR (Union des Coopératives Vinicole de la Dordogne)

24100 St-Laurent-des-Vignes

The Union of 9 Bergerac cooperatives and 4 in Lot-et-Garonne is much the biggest factor in the local scene, making and marketing 41% of all the wines of the appellation up to a very tolerable standard. Its reds, like its grapey dry whites, are made to drink young. One member, the Monbazillac cooperative, also operates Château Monbazillac, making a good standard of sweet wine but without the expensive refinements of wine-making that could make it very fine. The Union is based at St-Laurent-des-Vignes in the Monbazillac region just south of the town of Bergerac.

CAHORS

Cahors is certainly the most celebrated red wine of the scattered regions of the southwest. The ancient town on the river Lot with its famous fortified bridge is linked in the public mind with dramatic-sounding 'black wine'. The Lot took its produce down to the Garonne and the Garonne to Bordeaux, where it was either used to colour claret or shipped abroad under its own sombre colours. The legendary blackness of Cahors came from the Malbec, a grape grown in Bordeaux more for big crops than quality. But in its Cahors manifestation (where it is known as the Auxerrois) it is a horse of quite a different colour. On the rocky limestone *causses* above the winding Lot its crops are small and its skin thick. The old method of long fermentation (and often boiling some of the must to concentrate it) produced wine much darker than Bordeaux claret.

Cahors was destroyed by phylloxera in 1880 and struggled back very slowly, with little to raise it above the second class of VDQS until the 1960s and 1970s, when a businesslike cooperative and a handful of estates pulled the region together. It was promoted to appellation status in 1971, not for wines of any extraordinary colour or concentration but for well-balanced, vigorous and agreeable reds. The Auxerrois is now 70 per cent of the vineyard, blended with Merlot and Tannat (as in Madiran), supported by Dame Noire (alias Jurançon Noir) and a little Syrah and Gamay.

Most of the vineyard is now on the alluvial valley land, which is very gravelly in places. Some say that a blend of valley and *causse* wine has more qualities than either alone. That of the *causse* is naturally harder and longer lived, but the trend today is to keep the wine relatively light and drink it much younger, even after two years, making a point of its appetizing 'cut'. Most growers advise drinking it cool.

Total production: 800,000 cases.

Price: 12-20 francs a bottle.

Cahors: the bridge

CAHORS PRODUCERS

M. Baldès
Clos Triguedina, 46700 Puy-L'Evêque.

The eighth generation of the Baldès family own 100 acres and produce Cahors of 2 qualities – Clos de Triguedina is made to drink young; Prince Probus is aged for 3 years in new oak casks and needs another 2 or 3 years in bottle. The vineyard is 70% Auxerrois, 20% Merlot and 10% Tannat.

Château de Chambert
Floressas, 46700 Puy-L'Evèque.

Marc Delgoulet of the Caves St-Antoine has rebuilt and replanted this property of 126 acres. The first harvest was 1978, but the wine is already among the more concentrated, fruity and balanced of the area, promising well.

Durou & Fils
Gaudou, Vire-sur-Lot, 46700 Puy-L'Evêque.

A fifth-generation family estate that survived the lean years and now makes spicy and stylish wine from 50 acres aged in wood 2 years.

Jean Jouffreau
Château de Cayrou, 46700 Puy-L'Evêque.

The Jouffreau family has owned the famous 25-acre Clos de Gamot at Prayssac for 300 years. The vines are all Auxerrois, many of them the original post-phylloxera replantation. In 1972 Jean Jouffreau bought the 75-acre Château de Cayrou, now planted with 70% Auxerrois, 20% Merlot, 7% Tannat and 3% Gamay. He ferments for up to 4 weeks in stainless steel and ages in big and small barrels for up to 5, 8 or more years – an individualist whose wines, always worth tasting, can last 20 years.

L. E. Reutenauer
Pech d'Angely and Château Peyrat, 46002 Cahors.

Luc Reutenauer is president of the syndicate of Cahors growers and one of the most dynamic promoters of their wine. He himself owns 28 acres but his principal role is as négociant, with a turnover of 80,000 cases of wines designed for specific markets. Recently he has added an estate wine, Domaine des Vignals 1980. All, he insists, should be served at cellar, not room, temperature.

Rigal & Fils
Château de St-Didier, Parnac, 46140 Luzech.

A family firm of négociants and owners of the Château de St-Didier with 173 acres planted. Rigal also distributes a number of other domaine wines (incl. Le Castelas, Soullaillou, du Park), his own brands of Tradition and Carte Noire (vintage) and other wines of the southwest.

Caves St-Antoine
19102 Brive La Gaillard

Major producers and négociants of both Cahors and Gaillac, founded in 1963 by Marc Delgoulet. His Cahors properties are Château de Chambert (q.v.), Domaine du Single and Clos des Batuts, which are distributed by Menjucq. In Gaillac they own the Domaine de la Martine. They also deal in *vins de pays* of the Cité de Carcassone, Coteaux de Peyriac (Hérault) and Coteaux de Quercy (Lot) and AC Bergerac – a total of 420,000 cases.

Georges Vigouroux
Château de Haute Serre, Cieurac, 46003 Cahors.

Both as grower and négociant, M. Vigouroux has invested enormous energy in Cahors. The Château de Haute Serre is the culmination of his work; a stony hilltop site of 150 acres, 4 miles south of Cahors, reclaimed from scrub since 1970 with a new winery big enough to ferment and age its wine as slowly as necessary. The varieties are 70% Auxerrois, 15% Tannat and 15% Merlot. Fermentation is in stainless steel for up to 3 weeks and ageing in barrels for 18 months. In 1982 the 1976 vintage was showing great promise. The name Caves du Roc is also used.

OTHER PRODUCERS

Jean Bernède
Clos la Coutale, Vire-sur-Lot, 46700 Puy-L'Evêque.
Henri Bessières
Peyebos, 46220 Prayssac.
André Bouloumié
Les Cambous, 46220 Preyssac.
Charles Burc
'Courbenac', 46700 Puy-L'Evêque.
Burc & Fils
Roques, Leygues, 46700 Puy-L'Evêque.
Colette Delfour
Gaillac, 46140 Luzech.
Dumeaux & Fils
Vire-sur-Lot, 46700 Puy-L'Evêque.
Durou & Fils
'Gaudou', Vire-sur-Lot, 46700 Puy-L'Evêque.
Jacques Jouves
'Cournou', St-Vincent-Rive-d'Olt, 46140 Luzech.
Roger Labruyère
'Garrigues', Vire-sur-Lot, 46700 Puy-L'Evêque.
Mathieu Lescombes
Domaine de Paillas, Floressas, 46700 Puy-L'Evêque.
M J-C Valière
Domaine de Boliva, 46001 Cahors.
Charles Verhaegue
Domaine du Cedre, Vire-sur-Lot, 46700 Puy-L'Evêque.
SCEA de Quattre et Treilles
Domaine de Quattre, Bagat en Quercy, 46800 Montcuq.

GAILLAC

Gaillac is one of the most productive and economically important of the scattered vineyards of the southwest. Historically it has supplied not only Albi, the capital of its *département*, the Tarn, but places much farther away – its reds having a name for amazing transportability and longevity. Some believe that it was established as a vineyard area before Bordeaux, when the Romans were still based on the Midi. It lies at the highest navigable point on the river Tarn, which flows to the sea through the Garonne, past Bordeaux. Its unheard-of indigenous grape varieties encourage the idea of extreme antiquity. Its reds are the Duras, the Brocol, the Ferservadou and its white the Mauzac, the Ondenc and the Loin de l'Oeil (or l'En de l'El).

A century ago it was considered necessary to keep Gaillac reds 8 years in barrel and 12 years in bottle. The Mauzac was favoured because it makes sweet, or fairly sweet, wine with a 'faint smell of cider'. The modern reconstruction of the industry, based on enormous cooperatives, has opted for less exotic ideas. A tradition of bottling white wine before its original fermentation was over, to make a sort of rustic champagne, has been modified. Sauvignon, Merlot, Syrah and Gamay have been brought in. All the wines are now lighter and more neutral than they used to be; the whites today are either plain and dry, or dry with a fizzy freshness induced by keeping them on their lees and bottling under pressure to make Gaillac Perlé, or *moelleux* (semi-sweet with 2 degrees of sugar unfermented). The reds are fairly firm and well-structured but otherwise unremarkable. Total production: 625,000 cases. Average price: 10.5 francs a bottle.

GAILLAC PRODUCERS

Jean Albert
Domaine de Labarthe, 81150 Marsac-sur-Tarn.
One can hardly say typical when there are so few private producers on any scale in the region, but M. Albert makes a representative range: a full-weight red of local grapes, Duras, Brocol and the Ferservadou, a very light Gamay *vin de primeur*, sweet white of Mauzac and dry white of Sauvignon blended with Loin de l'Oeil – no sparkling wine.

Jacques Auque
Mars Pignou, 81600 Gaillac.
A family estate of 45 acres specializing in traditional dry white Gaillac (no sweet, no sparkling); a blend of Mauzac, Sauvignon and Loin de l'Oeil, and its red opposite number, made of Duras, Brocol, Merlot and Cabernet Franc, aged for 1 year in big wooden casks and best bottle-aged for 5 years.

Boissel-Rhodes
Château de Rhodes, 81600 Gaillac.
A century-old estate of 75 acres now mainly concerned with *méthode champenoise* (1,800 cases under the name René Rieux) and red, both Gamay *primeur* and *vin de garde* of the area, brewed from Duras, Syrah, Ferservadou or Brocol and Gamay. Some sparkling wine is also made by the '*méthode gaillaçoise*' – bottled before the first fermentation is finished, then treated as in the champagne method.

CAVES COOPERATIVES

Gaillac et du Pays Cordais
Labastide de Lévis, 81150 Marsac-sur-Tarn.
The major producer of Gaillac, founded in 1949, with 680 members farming some 5,000 acres, half of it Gaillac AOC and half Vin de Pays du Tarn. Its wines have gained some character and charm – qualities they used to lack. A considerable amount is sparkling, but their Gaillac Perlé, a very fresh half-fizzy dry white, is more original and better value. The red *vin de pays* made by carbonic maceration is another good buy. Of the 600,000-case production 20% is now exported, by the GIVISO group.

Rabastens
81800 Rabastens
Rabastens is southwest of Gaillac, making similar wine. This 1956 coop has 540 members farming 4,500 acres of Gaillac AOC and Vin de Pays du Tarn.

Tecon
81600 Gaillac
A smaller rival to the coop at Labastide de Lévis, founded in 1953, with 450 members farming 2,250 acres.

Union Vinicole Coopérative
81600 Gaillac
The original coop of the region, founded in 1926, with 880 members but only a small amount of AOC Gaillac. Most of its wine is *vin de table*.

COTES DE BUZET

When Bordeaux was firmly limited to the *département* of the Gironde, one of the upcountry sources of claret to be hardest hit was the hills south of Garonne in the north of the Armagnac country: the Côtes de Buzet. Happily, white wine for distillation was an alternative crop, but the gravel and chalky clay on good southeast slopes had long produced very satisfactory red wine. In the last 30 years they have been reconstituted and are doing better than ever. The cooperative at Damazan dominates the area, making red wine to good Bordeaux standards. Average price: 9.5 francs a bottle.

COTES DE BUZET PRODUCERS

Domaine de Janicot

A 20-acre estate contracted to the négociants Menjucq.

Domaine Padère

Ambrus, 47160 Damazan.

The unexpected enterprise of a distinguished citizen of Beaujolais, M. Bloud of the Château de Moulin-à-Vent, who wanted to try his hand at something new and since 1973 has planted more than 100 acres of Côtes de Buzet, with 58 more projected. The château is 150 years old but only had a scrap of vineyard. At present M. Bloud uses no barrels, preferring the flavour of fruit uncomplicated, but he will be experimenting with 3 months in barrels and 12 in vats before bottling.

Château Pierron

47160 Damazan

One of the few old-established estates of Buzet, owned by M. Hérail since 1932. 66 acres, half red grapes (50% Merlot, 25% each of the Cabernets) and half white for Armagnac. He ages his Côtes de Buzet 12-18 months in Bordeaux *barriques*.

Caves Réunis des Côtes de Buzet

Buzet-sur-Baize, 47160 Damazan.

The overwhelming majority of Côtes de Buzet comes from this model cooperative, which has steadily expanded and improved the vineyards of the area since 1954 and can claim the credit for its promotion to appellation status in 1973. The man responsible, Jean Mermillo, was a former manager of Château Lafite. 520 members farm 2,900 acres, 98% in the Bordeaux red grapes: 40% Merlot and 30% each of the Cabernets. The wine must be described as a light but round and satisfying claret. A splendidly tasty special selection from older vines on the best soils (some gravel, some chalky clay) is labelled Cuvée Napoléon. A little dry white wine is made, also of the classic Bordeaux grapes.

MADIRAN

Madiran is the wine that came back from the dead. Thirty years ago the vineyard in the Vic Bilh hills on the southern edge of the Armagnac country, 25 miles north of Pau, had dwindled to a dozen acres. Today there are 2,000, and some would claim that Madiran is the best red of the southwest, Cahors included. If it lacked the advantages of Cahors, fame and accessibility, it also avoided the identity crisis which still bothers the better-known wine. The name of 'black wine' lingers, while the reality is merely a healthy red.

The peculiar quality of Madiran is to start life with a disconcerting bite, then to mellow quite rapidly into claret with a most singular style and texture. The bouquet has the teasing qualities of a good Médoc or Graves. When I was looking for the right word for a nine-year-old 1973 from the main cooperative of the region, I was so struck by its silkiness on the tongue that I hesitated over the rather lame 'liquid', then tried 'limpid'. Later I looked Madiran up in Paul de Cassagnac's *French Wines*, a little-known but extremely rewarding work of 1936. 'An infinitely fluid savour' were the first words that struck my eye. So Madiran is consistent, despite its near demise; across 45 years it still caresses the palate in a seductively swallowable way.

This is the more odd in that de Cassagnac fulminates against 'the inferior Tannat', a 'common grape' being introduced to replace the Cabernet in the region for the sake of its bigger crop. All real Madiran, he says, is Cabernet. Yet today its producers tell us the secret of its character is the grape that sounds like tannin, and gives all the harshness its name implies; a smaller-berried cousin of the Malbec, Cot or (in Cahors) Auxerrois. A high proportion of Tannat, they say, is essential. I should like to taste a wholly Cabernet Madiran to judge for myself.

The Vic Bilh hills, a sort of very *piano* rehearsal for the soaring Pyrenees, parallel to the south, give their name to the produce of the Pacherenc, a local white grape. Pacherenc du Vic Bilh is grown by the same growers as Madiran and consists of a complicated blend with Mansengs, Sémillon, Sauvignon and Courbu (alias Sarrat). Traditionally it is as sweet a wine as the autumn permits, but some growers make it dry, and some bottle it straight from its lees in spring like Muscadet.

The same growers also produce red, rosé and white wines for the appellation Béarn, which meet their fate in the excellent local restaurants. Prices: Madiran 9.7-11.5 francs, Béarn 7.5-8.5 francs a bottle.

MADIRAN PRODUCERS

Domaine Barréjat
Maumusson, 32400 Riscle. An old Capmartin family estate of 37 acres, planted in half Tannat and half Cabernet Franc. The wine is kept in oak for 8 months and needs 4 or 5 years in bottle to soften. Moderately priced at about 14 francs a bottle.

Alain Erumont
Domaine Bouschasse, Maumusson, 32400 Riscle. An important and expanding estate, whose 54 acres have recently been almost tripled by the purchase of Ch. Montus (62 acres) and a part share in another 37 acres. The grapes are half Tannat and one quarter each of the Cabernets. 8–10 years is a good age. Also Pacherenc white.

Domaine Laplace
Aydie, 64330 Garlin. The Madiran of M. Laplace is said to be 100% Tannat, and some of his huge old vines to have survived the phylloxera. His 75-acre vineyards also produce a fresh Pacherenc and an Eau de Vie.

Château de Peyros
Corbères Abères, 64350 Lembeye. Denis de Robillard has 57 acres planted in this very old vineyard, with 45% Tannat and 55% Cabernet Franc. His friends call his wine 'Le Bordelais du Madiran'; the relatively high proportion of Cabernet makes it rounder and more 'elegant', with a more pronounced bouquet than its neighbours. At about 24 francs a bottle it is also the dearest.

Domaine de Sitère
A 40-acre vineyard of very old vines, mostly Tannat. Distributed by Menjucq.

August Vignau
Domaine Pichard, Soublecause, 65700 Maubourguet. A 25-acre estate, half Tannat and half Cabernets, locally considered one of the best of Madiran.

Caves Coopératives

Union des Producteurs Plaimont
St-Mont, 32400 Riscle. A union of 3 cooperatives, at St-Mont, Aignan and Plaisance, founded in 1974. 1,350 members; 265 acres in the appellation area produce fine Madiran; 1,000 acres of VDQS Côtes de St-Mont and 2,000 of Vin de Pays Côtes de Gascogne.

Tursan
40320 Geaune. Tursan is a VDQS neighbour of Madiran. The cooperative (founded 1937, with 420 members and 1,000 acres) is the biggest producer of these interesting country wines.

Vic Bilh-Madiran
Crouseilles, 64350 Lembeye. The principal producer of Madiran, making nearly half the total. Founded 1950. 350 members have 870 acres, 60% Tannat, 40% Cabernets which will rise to 1,750 by 1984. Half the current production of 125,000 cases is AOC Madiran, the rest white Pacherenc, Béarn red and rosé and *vin de pays*, Vin des Fleurs. Certain old bottles are very fine indeed.

Vinicole de Bellocq
64270 Salies-de-Bearn. Salies takes its name from its salty spring, provider of the necessary preservative for curing the famous jambon de Bayonne. Its cooperative of 245 members, 500 acres, is the chief source of Béarn appellation red, rosé and white, 50,000 cases a year.

des Vins d'Irouléguy et du Pays Basque
64430 St-Etienne de Baigorry. The sole source today of the Basque wine, Irouléguy, which is made to a recipe almost identical with Madiran: half and half Tannat and Cabernet. Founded 1954. 220 members; 460 acres producing some 33,000 cases of AOC Irouléguy.

JURANCON

All references to Jurançon start with the story of the infant King Henri IV, whose lips at birth, in Pau in 1553, were brushed with a clove of garlic and moistened with Jurançon wine – a custom said still to be followed in the Bourbon family, though without such spectacular results. The point is that Jurançon is strong, not just in alcohol but in character. Its highly aromatic grapes ripen on the Pyrenean foothills south of Pau in autumns warmed by south winds from Spain. Its flavour is enhanced by small crops (36 hectolitres a hectare for dry wine and 28 for sweet). The sweet *moelleux* is, or should be, made by harvesting very late, in November, when hot days and freezing nights have shrivelled the grapes (*passerillage*) and concentrated their juice.

The two principal grapes are the Gros and Petit Manseng, the latter not only smaller but tastier. Both give wines of high degree with a remarkably 'stiff' and positive structure in your mouth, almost fierce when young but maturing to scents and flavours variously described as like such exotic fruits and spices as mangoes, guavas and cinnamon. Colette provided tasting notes I will not presume to rival: 'I was a girl when I met this prince; aroused, imperious, treacherous as all great seducers are – Jurançon.'

JURANCON PRODUCERS

Alfred Barrère
Clos Camcaillau, Lahourcade, 64150 Mourenx. The Barrère property of 38 acres goes back to 1580 – its name is Basque for *champs de cailloux*, the stony field. 42% is planted in Gros Manseng, 33% in Petit Manseng and Courbu, bottled in spring. *Moelleux* is made in 2 qualities, *crème de tête*, picked in successive selections of the most shrivelled Petit Manseng, sometimes with noble rot, and a standard quality, both aged 2 winters in oak.

Jean Chigé
64110 Jurançon. The Chigés have owned their 12-acre Cru Lamouroux for 250 years. They grow the Gros Manseng for dry Jurançon and the Petit for sweet, which they control with sulphur when the fermentation has left 60 grams a litre (6%) of the natural sugar. Both wines are aged for 18 months in oak or chestnut casks. Private customers buy almost all of it.

Alexis Guirouilh
Domaine Guirouilh, Lasseube, 64290 Gan. The 20-acre Clos Guirouilh has been in the family since 1670. 60% is planted with Gros Manseng for dry wine, which is bottled in its first spring, the rest in Petit Manseng, which is picked very late, partly dried on the vine and freezing cold, to ferment very slowly into *moelleux*, either alone or with a proportion of Gros Manseng. The sweet wine is kept in oak for up to 2 years before bottling and will keep up to 20 in bottle.

Cave Coopérative de Gan-Jurançon
64290 Gan. The Gan cooperative (founded in 1950) dominates the increasing production of this famous old white wine. 350 members farm 875 acres, and another 250 are planned.

COTES DE DURAS

The Côtes de Duras has the misfortune, like Bergerac, to lie just over the departmental boundary from Bordeaux – more particularly from Entre-Deux-Mers. Its wine is in every way comparable: most of it fresh, sometimes rather thin dry white made to taste as far as possible of Sauvignon, though the greater proportion of the grapes are Sémillon, Ugni Blanc, Colombard and Mauzac. One third is red, with as much as 60 per cent Cabernet Sauvignon, 30 per cent Merlot and a little Cabernet Franc and Malbec. The red, however, does not seem to have the potential of the more recently recognized appellation Côtes de Buzet. Much of it is made by *macération carbonique* to produce a fleetingly fruity effect. The majority of growers belong to cooperatives over the border in Entre-Deux-Mers. Duras itself has only had a coop since 1960.

Cave Coopérative des Vignerons des Coteaux de Duras
47120 Duras. Competent but relatively small cooperative, founded in 1960. 102 members farm 870 of the 5,000-odd acres of the appellation to produce 100,000 cases of Côtes de Duras, two thirds of it white, which is marketed by UNIDOR (q.v.).

COTES DU FRONTON

The slopes around Fronton, 15 miles north of Toulouse and only 20 west of Gaillac, achieved appellation status in 1975 for their ripely fruity red, which up to then had been a secret kept by the people of Toulouse. The local red grape is called the Négrette, a relation of the Tannat of Madiran, the Auxerrois of Cahors and the Malbec of Bordeaux. For those who cannot resist the infinite complications of ampelography I should add that the Négrette turns up in the Charente (of all places) as Ragoutant.

Château Bellevue-La-Forêt
31620 Fronton. The outstanding new property of a hitherto obscure region. Since 1974 Patrick Germain has planted 215 acres with the traditional grapes of the area: 50% Négrette, 25% Cabernets and 25% Syrah and Gamay. The different varieties are fermented separately, then blended to make a roundly fruity wine of immediate appeal, which will presumably get even better as the vines mature. Already half his 55,000-case production is exported.

Caves Coopératives 'Les Côtes du Fronton'
31620 Fronton. The biggest coop of the Côtes du Frontonnais, founded 1947. 600 members now producing nearly 250,000 cases of red and rosé appellation wine and 800,000 of *vin de table.*

Villaudric
Villaudric, 31620 Fronton. The smaller and younger (1949) but more highly regarded coop. 326 members; 2,120 acres producing 60,000 cases of red and rosé Côtes du Frontonnais and 5 times as much Villaudric *vin de table.*

COTES DU MARMANDAIS

The Côtes du Marmandais lies right on the fringes of Bordeaux and must be considered unlucky still to rank only as a VDQS rather than AOC. Its light red (its major product) certainly comes under the general heading of 'claret', and its Sauvignon/Sémillon white is comparable to everyday Bordeaux. Two cooperatives make nearly all the wine, marketed through UNIDOR at Monbazillac, and are inspiring more and better planting by the multitude of small growers. Average production: 289,000 cases.

Cave Coopérative Intercommunale de Cocumont
47250 Bouglon. Younger (1957) and smaller but more progressive than its brother-cooperative, also producing Vin de Pays de l'Agenais and *vins de table*, and even a little Bordeaux Rouge. Members are replanting with good advice; wine-making is very modern. 83,000 cases a year.

Société Coopérative Vinicole des Côtes du Marmandais
47200 Marmande. The older (1948) and bigger of the two considerable cooperatives that make 42,000 cases of VDQS Côtes du Marmandais and about 4 times as much Vin de Pays de l'Argenais and *vins de table.* There are 510 members with 800 acres, now mainly planted with Merlot and Cabernet for the reds, but where such obscure local varieties as Abourion and Bouchalés may still be found. The Marmandais red is like soft lightweight claret, ageing well up to about 4 years.

GIVISO
47000 Agen. The initials stand for Groupement d'Intérêt Economique de Vignerons du Sud Ouest. The organization was started in 1975 to represent 7 leading cooperatives of southwestern areas with increasing production and rising standards. The members are the cooperatives of Côtes du Buzet, Côtes d'Olt at Parnac (Cahors), Gaillac et Pays Cordais at Labastide, Gran-Jurançon, Vic Bilh-Madiran and Busca-Maniban (Armagnac).

VINS DE PAYS

Throughout 1981 and 1982 a stream of decrees flowed from Paris, signed by the Minister of Agriculture, setting out the regulations for newly coined *vins de pays*. The object has been to give pride to local production that has hitherto had no identity. Wines that have been used until now entirely for blending, or at best to go labelless to the local bars, are now to be made to minimum standards and in regulated quantities.

Hence the significance of this list of *vins de pays*, which has never been generally published before and is still, of necessity, incomplete. It sets out the ground rules for wines that will build reputations, for some that have already started – and no doubt also for others that nobody will ever hear of again.

The first essential information is the area delimited. Some are as local as three or four parishes; some as sweeping as the whole of the Loire valley (Vins de Pays du Jardin de la France). One may assume that a small area represents a positive local tradition which is worth nurturing.

The second important control is over the grape varieties to be grown. In some cases one or more classic grapes are prescribed as obligatory, while a number of others are tolerated up to a percentage. Some areas do not specify varieties at all.

The last two indicators are the minimum natural alcoholic strength required (of which you can broadly say the higher the strength the better the wine is likely to be) and the maximum crop allowed (the lower the better). Most *vins de pays* are allowed 80 hectolitres a hectare, which would be very high in an *appellation contrôlée* area but very low in the *vin de table* vineyards of Languedoc.

The entries are organized in the following way. The name of the *vin de pays* is followed by the *département* or region, whichever is most familiar. Next comes the date of establishment. Then the area delineated with, where possible, a central town and some indication of the type of terrain.

Maximum crop is only given when it differs from 80hl/ha, and minimum alcohol when it differs from the almost universal 10.5 to 11 degrees. Grape varieties are listed where specified.

Where the rules do not specify the grape varieties no varieties are mentioned; it can be assumed that the standard grapes of the region are used. The colour of wine is only given when all three colours are not made. Occasionally technical details such as planting density, pruning and training methods, sugar levels and minimum acidity are regulated, and this is noted in the entries. The producers whose names are given have been recommended by local experts. Most *vins de pays* production comes from *caves coopératives*. Production figures refer to the 1981 crop.

Modern caves cooperatives dominate many of the vins de pays districts

RHONE AND PROVENCE

Most of the wine-growing areas of the Rhône and Provence are entitled to the wide-ranging Côtes du Rhone or Provence AOCs. The *vins de pays* cover outlying, often interesting, districts and one or two zones within the AOC areas. Bouches-du-Rhône has its own *vin de pays*.

Coteaux de l'Ardèche
Ardèche. 1981. 14 communes in the Ardèche and Chassezac valleys in the southern Ardèche, in the foothills of the Cevennes. 10°. Grapes, red: 70% minimum of one or more of Cabernet Franc, Cabernet Sauvignon, Carignan, Cinsaut, Counoise, Gamay, Grenache, Merlot, Pinot Noir, Picpoul, Syrah. White: 70% minimum of one or more of Aligoté, Bourboulenc, Chardonnay, Marsanne, Roussanne, Sauvignon, Viognier, Picpoul Gris. Producers: M. Dupre, Lagorce, 07150 Vallon Pont d'Arc; GAEC Brunel, St-Remèze, 07700 Bourg St-Andeol. 6 coops including Ruoms, 07120 Ruoms. Production 775,000 cases.

d'Argens
Provence. 1980. 17 communes around Draguignan in the Argens valley, mostly land also entitled to the AOC Provence. 100hl/ha.

Coteaux des Baronnies
Rhône. 1981. Area around Rémuzat and Rosans, north of Mont Ventoux in the Alpine foothills. Grapes, red and rosé: Cinsaut, Grenache, Gamay, Syrah, Pinot Noir plus up to 30% others. White: Rhône varieties plus Aligoté and Chardonnay. 3 coops including Nyons (26110) and Puymeras (84110). Production 130,000 cases.

Comté de Grignan
Rhône. 1981. 9 cantons around Vinsobres and Grignan in the lower Rhône. 10°. Grapes, red and rosé: Grenache, Syrah, Cinsaut, Mourvèdre, Gamay, Pinot Noir plus up to 30% others. White: normal Rhône varieties. 2 coops at Suze La Rousse, 26130 and St-Maurice-sur-Eygues, 26110 Nyons.

Mont-Caume
Provence. 1982. 12 communes around Bandol. Producers: Vincent Racine, Hubert Jouve, La Cadière d'Azur (83740). Coop at St-Cyr-sur-Mer (83270). Production 220,000 cases.

Principauté d'Orange
Rhône. 1980. Cantons of Bolléne, Orange, Vaison-La-Romaine and Valréas, east of the Rhône in the Côtes-du-Rhône Villages country: Min. alch: 10.8, max 11.8. Pruning methods specified. 100hl/ha.

Petite Crau
Bouches-du-Rhône. 1982. 4 communes in the Petite Crau hills south of Avignon. Min. alch: 11°, no more than 12·5° for white and 13° for red and rosé. Pruning systems regulated. 1 coop at Noves (13550). Production 55,000 cases.

Collines Rhodaniennes
Central Rhône. 1981. Parts of 4 *départements* on both banks. 10°. Grapes, red and rosé: Syrah, Gamay, plus Pinot Noir, Merlot and Cabernet Franc in some districts, plus secondary grapes up to 30%. White: traditional Rhône varieties plus Chardonnay in some districts. 4 coops including St-Désirat, 07340 Serrières.

Coteaux Varois
Provence. 1981. 46 communes to the west of the Var. Producers: M. Gassier, Dom. St-Estève, Brue-Auriac; Claude Courtois, Le Val; Bruno Latil, Brignoles (83170); Jean Louis Vial, Brignoles (83170) Dom. des Chabert, Garéoult; Dom. St-Jean, Villecroze; Compagnie des Salins du Midi, Ollières. 32 coops. 2·2m. cases.

THE GARD

The *département* of the Gard stretches from the Rhône at Avignon west into the hills of the Cevennes. The chief town is Nîmes. Most of the *département* is wine-growing country, and there is a *vin de pays* for the whole area: Vin de Pays du Gard. 10 other *vins de pays*, covering areas of varying size, are listed below. None specifies grape varieties.

Mont Bouquet
Gard. 1982. 19 communes around Vézenobres, northwest of Nîmes. 2 coops at Brouzet Les Alès, 30580 Lussan, and St-Maurice-de-Cazevieille, 30190 St-Chaptes. Production 160,000 cases.

Coteaux Cévenols
Gard. 1981. 24 communes northeast of Alès in the Cevennes foothills. Producers: M. Silhol, St-Victor de Malcap, 30500 St-Ambroix. 4 coops including Rochegude, 30430 Barjac.

Coteaux de Cèze
Gard. 1981. 46 communes on the west bank of the Rhône around Bagnols-sur-Cèze and Roquemaure. 4 coops including Pont St-Esprit (30130) and Roquemaure (30150). Production 225,000 cases.

Serre de Coiran
Gard. 1982. 23 communes south of Alès in the Cevennes foothills. 6 coops including Cardet, 30350 Ledignan. Production 165,000 cases.

Coteaux Flaviens
Gard. 1981. 9 communes to the southwest of Nîmes. Producers: Domaine de Campuget, 30129 Manduel. Domaine de Cassagnes, 30800 St-Gilles. Coops at Beauvoisin (30640) and Bouillargues (30230). Production 330,000 cases.

Coteaux du Pont du Gard
Gard. 1981. 19 communes around Remoulins, between Nîmes and Avignon. 8 coops including Vers-Pont-du-Gard, 30210 Remoulins. Production 550,000 cases.

Coteaux de Salavès
Gard. 1981. 28 communes around St-Hippolyte-du-Fort in the west of the *département*. Producers: M. Pieyre, Mandiargues, 30170. 4 coops including Moulezan, 30350 Ledignan. Production 330,000 cases.

Uzege
Gard. 1981. 26 communes around Uzès, north of Nîmes. Producers: M. Reboul, Sagues, 30700 Uzès. 5 coops including St-Quentin-La-Poterie, 30700.

Vaunage
Gard. 1981. 14 communes to the west of Nîmes. 3 coops including Clarensac (30870). Production 110,000 cases.

Côtes du Vidourle
Gard. 1981. 15 communes around Sommières, west of Nîmes. Producers: Marcel Granie, Aspères (30860). 3 coops including Villevieille, 30250 Sommières. Production 111,000 cases.

HERAULT

The Hérault is the biggest wine-producing *département* in France. Vin de Pays de l'Hérault covers the whole area. 27 local districts have individual sets of regulations. Some of the areas cover land which is in the St-Chinian and Minervois VDQS zones, and others include communes entitled to the Coteaux du Languedoc AOC. *See* the chapter on the Midi (pages 202–213) for more details.

Vicomté d'Aumelas
Hérault. 1982. 14 communes south of Gignac in the Hérault valley. Technical restrictions. 6 coops, including Vendémian and Puilacher, 34230 Paulhan. Production 28,000 cases.

Bénovic
Hérault. 1982. 15 communes in the extreme east of the *département*. Coop at Beaulieu, 34160 Castries. Production 100,000 cases.

Berange
Hérault. 1982. 7 communes around Castries and Lunel in the southeast of the *département*. Producers: M. de Forton, Baillargues (34670). 2 coops at Baillargues and Montaud, 34160 Montaud Castries. Production 110,000 cases.

Bessan
Hérault. 1981. Commune of Bessan, inland from Agde. Producers: René Fulcrand; Clarou L'Epine, both at Bessan (34550). Coop at Bessan. Production 110,000 cases.

Côtes du Brian
Hérault. 1982. 13 communes around

Minerve and Olonzac in the Minervois. Producers: Robert Caffort, Minerve; Aimé Fraisse, St-Jean de Minervois; Laurent Mari, Aignes; Luc Mondie, Aigues-Vives; M. Marcon, St-Jean de Minervois. 9 coops including 'La Vigneronne Minervoise', 34210 Olonzac.

Cassan
Hérault. 1982. 4 communes around Roujan in the central Hérault. 75hl/ha. Coop at Roujan (34320). Production 55,000 cases.

Caux
Hérault. 1981. Commune of Caux, north of Pézenas. Producers: Henri Collet, Dom. de Daurion. Coop at Caux, 34720. Production 275,000 cases.

Côtes du Ceressou
Hérault. 1981. 15 communes near Clermont L'Hérault. 70hl/ha. Producers: M. Servent, Dom. de Fabregues, Aspiran; GFA Pages Renouvier, Nizas; Bernard Jany, Dom. de la Condamine, Paulhan (34230); SCA St-Pierre de Granonpiac, St-André de Sangonis. 8 coops including Aspiran, 34230 Paulhan.

Cessenon
Hérault. 1982. Commune of Cessenon, east of St-Chinian. Coop at Cessenon (34460). Production 20,000 cases.

Coteaux d'Enserune
Hérault. 1981. 11 communes west of Béziers. Producers: Dom. d'Auveille et Montels, Capestang; Dom. de la Garrigue, Nissan Les Enserune; Dom. de la Grande Camargue, Montady. 6 coops including Nissan Les Enserune (34440).

Coteaux de Fontcaude
Hérault. 1982. 6 communes south of St-Chinian. Producers: Pierre Comps, Puisserguier, B. Farret d'Asties, Dom. de Cariètes, Quarante, 34310 Capestang. Production 500,000 cases.

Sables du Golfe du Lion
Hérault and Gard. 1982. Sand dunes and coastal strips in parts of 12 communes to the west of the mouth of the Rhône. Grapes, red and rosé: Cabernet Sauvignon, Cabernet Franc, Carignan, Cinsaut, Grenache, Lledoner Pelut, Merlot, Syrah and up to 30% others. White: Ugni, Clairette, Carignan, Muscats, Sauvignon and up to 30% others. Producers: Cave Coopérative d'Aigues Mortes, 30220 Aigues Mortes; Compagnie des Salins du Midi, 34000 Montpellier; SICAREX Mediterranée, 30240 Le Grau du Roi. (*See* page 212.)

Monts de la Grage
Hérault. 1982. 6 communes in the hills around St-Chinian. 1 coop at St-Chinian (34360). Production 220,000 cases.

Gorges de l'Hérault
Hérault. 1982. 3 communes in the upper Hérault valley around Gignac. Wine-making restrictions. White and rosé 11°, red 10·5°. 2 coops including Gignac (34150).

Coteaux de Laurens
Hérault. 1982. 10·5°. Min. acidity specified. 7 communes around Laurens and Faugères. 1 coop: Laurens, 34480 Magalas.

Coteaux du Libron
Hérault. 1981. 6 communes around Béziers. Technical specifications. Producers: G. Vidal, Béziers; Norbert Alker, Dom. Les Bergeries, Béziers; Georges Gaujal, Dom. de Libouriac, Béziers. 5 coops including Béziers (34500).

Val de Montferrand
Hérault. 1982. Parts of 5 cantons north of Montpellier. Technical specifications. Producers: M. Pagevy, Dom. du Viviers, 34170 Jacou; GAEC de Brunet, Causse de la Selle (34380). 9 coops including Assas, 34160 Castries. Production 550,000 cases.

Collines de la Moure
Hérault. 1982. 27 communes around Frontignan and Mireval. Producers: P. Leenhard, Dom. de Lunac, Fabregues; H. Artignan, Vic La Gardiole; M. de Gaulard d'Allaines, Abbaye de Valmagne, Villevayrac. 10 coops including Montarnaud, 34570 Pignan. Production 1.6m. cases.

Coteaux de Murviel
Hérault. 1982. 9 communes in the Orb valley. 6 coops including Murviel, 34490 Murviel des Béziers.

Haute Vallée de l'Orb
Hérault. 1982. 31 communes in the northwest of the *département*. 70hl/ha. 10·5°. 2 coops including Bousquet d'Orb (34260). Production 220,000 cases.

Littoral Orb-Hérault
Hérault. 1982. 7 communes southeast of Béziers. Grapes, red: up to 10% Alicante-Bouchet, up to 40% Carignan, up to 50% Cinsaut, at least 10% Grenache. Rosé: up to 40% Carignan, up to 60% Cinsaut, at least 10% Grenache. White: up to 80% Terret Gris, minimum 20% other quality varieties. Coop at Portiragnes (34420).

Pézenas
Hérault. 1982. Commune of Pézenas. Coop at Pézenas (34210). Production 65,000 cases.

Coteaux de Salagou
Hérault. 1981. 20 communes around Lodève in the hills. 70hl/ha. Technical specifications. 3 coops including Octon, 34800 Clermont-l'Hérault. Production 200,000 cases.

Côtes de Thau
Hérault. 1981. 5 communes around Florensac, near the coast at Agde. Technical specifications.
5 coops including Pomérols (34810). Production 275,000 cases.

Côtes de Thongue
Hérault. 1982. Red and white. 14 communes around Sevrain, north of Béziers. 8 coops, including Montblanc, 34290 Servian.

AUDE

The entire *département* of the Aude, which stretches inland from Narbonne, is entitled to Vin de Pays de l'Aude.

Haute Vallée de l'Aude
Aude. 1981. 55 communes around Limoux. Min. 11°. Max. 12°, 70hl/ha. Grapes, red and rosé: Cabernet Sauvignon, Cabernet Franc, Cot, Merlot. White: Chenin, Chardonnay, Sémillon, Terret Blanc, Terret Gris. Pruning systems regulated. 2 coops at Couiza (11190) and Rouffiac-d'Aude, 11250 St-Hilaire. Production 11,000 cases.

Hauterive en Pays d'Aude
Aude. 1982. 8 communes in the Corbières and the Orbieu valley. Grapes: wide range. 6 coops.

Coteaux du Littoral Audois
Aude. 1980. Communes of Gruissan, Bages, Fitou, Lapalme, Leucate, Peyriac-de-Mer, Port-La-Nouvelle, Sigean, Caves, Feuilla, Portel and Treilles, on the coast east of the Corbières hills. 100hl/ha. 4 coops including Gruissan, 11430 Gruissan.

Hauts de Baden
Aude. 1982. Commune of Baden, south of the Minervois. Producers: Jean Poudou, Jacques Hortola, Gérald Branca, all at Baden, 11300 Trèbes.

Coteaux de la Cabrerisse
Aude. 1981. 3 communes around Thézan in the Corbières. Grapes: only Carignan, Cinsaut, Grenache, Syrah, Mourvèdre, Terret, Clairette, Cabernet Franc, Cabernet Sauvignon, Merlot, Lladoner Pelut, Alicante-Bouschet. 2 coops at Thézan and St-Laurent, 11200 Lezignan. 445,000 cases.

Coteaux de la Cité de Carcassonne
Aude. 1982. 11 communes around Carcassonne. 10·5°. 70hl/ha. Grapes, red and rosé: Carignan, Alicante-Bouschet, Cinsaut and Grenache with minimum of 10% Cabernet Sauvignon, Cabernet Franc or Merlot. White: wide range. Planting density and acidity controlled. Producers: Pierre Castel, Pennautier; Louis Gobin, Cavanac; André Castel, Rustiques; Yves Barthez, Pennautier. 5 coops.

Coteaux Cathares
Aude. 1981. 10 communes around Tuchan. Grapes: wide range, red and rosé. 8 coops.

Cucugnan
Aude. 1982. Commune of Cucugnan in the Corbières. Grapes: any. 1 coop at Cucugnan, 11350 Tuchan. Production 44,000 cases.

Val de Cesse
Aude. 1981. Canton of Ginestas, Minervois, northwest of Narbonne. Producers: Jean Gleizes, Ouveillan; Pierre Calvet, Ouveillan; Pierre Fil, Mailhac; Jacques Meyzonnier, Pouzols. 4 coops including St-Nazaire d'Aude, 11120 Ginestas.

Val de Dagne
Aude. 1981. 13 communes in the northern Corbières. 70hl/ha. Grapes: usual local varieties. 3 coops at Montlaur, Monze and Servies-en-Val (11220).

Côtes de Lastours
Aude. 1981. 21 communes in the Cabardès and the Fresquel valley on the slopes of the Montagne Noir north of Carcassonne. Grapes: wide range. Producers: Mme Vve Cazaux, Villemoustaussou; M. Gianesini, Dom. Jouclary, Conques-sur-Orbiel; Antoine Maurel, Conques-sur-Orbiel. Coop at Salsigne, 11600 Conques-sur-Orbiel. Production 165,000 cases.

Coteaux de Lézignanais
Aude. 1981. 10 communes around Lézignan north of the Corbières. Red. Grapes: wide range. 4 coops.

Côtes de la Malepère
Aude. 1980. 30 communes. Red and rosé. Principal grape varieties: Merlot, Cot, Cinsaut – any one of which must represent 60%. Rest any combination of Cabernet Franc, Cabernet Sauvignon, Grenache Noir, Llandoner Pelut and Syrah. Rosé: principal grapes Cinsaut, Grenache Noir, Lladoner Pelut. Others (max. 30%) Merlot, Cot, Cabernet Sauvignon, Cabernet Franc and Syrah. Vines must be grown at minimum density of 3,000 root stocks per hectare, other technical restrictions. 100hl/ha.

Coteaux de Miramont
Aude. 1981. 9 communes around Capendu in the valley east of Carcassonne. Producers: M. Lemaire, Capendu; Mme Vve Achille Marty, Douzens; Mme Alice Loyer, Fonties; Mme Hélène Gau, Barbaira. 5 coops including Capendu (11700).

Coteaux de Narbonne
Aude. 1982. 4 communes near Narbonne. 3 coops. 45,000 cases.

Val d'Orbieu
Aude. 1982. 13 communes in the Orbieu valley west of Narbonne. Grapes, red and rosé: Carignan, Cinsaut, Grenache, Alicante-Bouschet, Picpoul, Terret Noir. White: Clairette, Macabeu, Bourboulenc, Carignan Blanc, Grenache Blanc. Producers: Jacques Berges, Boutenac; M. Baille, Fabrezan; Armand Sournies, Camplong d'Aude; Honoré Deu, St-André Roquelonge; Mme Marie Rouanet, St-André Roquelonge; Mme Marie Huc, Fabrezan. 4 coops. 1·1m. cases.

Côtes de Perignan
Aude. 1981. 5 communes in the area around La Clape at the mouth of the Aude. 3 coops including Fleury d'Aude (11560). Production 220,000 cases.

Coteaux de Peyriac
Aude and Hérault. 1981. 19 communes in the Minervois. 9 coops. 2·2m. cases, mostly sold by Chantovent.

Côtes de Prouillé
Aude. 1982. 39 communes around Razès, southwest of Carcassonne. Grapes: wide range. Producers: Château de Malviès, 11240 Belvèze du Razès. 2 coops at Arzens (11290) and Routier, 11240 Belvèze du Razès.

Coteaux de Termènes
Aude. 1982. 9 communes in the Corbières around Termènes. Grapes, red and rosé: Carignan, Cinsaut, Grenache, Syrah, Merlot, Cabernet, Cot, Terret, Alicante-Bouschet, Gamay. White: usual varieties. 1 coop at Villerouge Termènes, 11330 Mouthoumet. Production 110,000 cases.

Vallée du Paradis
Aude. 1981. 11 communes in the southern Corbières. Producers: M. Amiel, M Mique, M. Bringuier and M. Navarro all at Coustouge; M. Caziniol at Fraisse-Corbières. 7 coops including Cascatel, 11360 Durban Corbières. Production 330,000 cases.

ROUSILLON AND THE CORBIERES

The Corbières hills, which the Pyrénées-Orientale *département* shares with the Aude to the north, have several interesting *vins de pays* that are listed here and under the Aude. The county to the south, consisting of plains and the foothills of the Pyrenees, uses the Catalan name for its 2 defined districts.

Val d'Agly
Corbières. 1982. 15 communes around St-Paul de Fenouillet. 8 coops including Belesta, 66720 La Tour de France. Production 165,000 cases.

Catalan
Roussillon. 1981. Area stretching inland from Perpignan and Argelès. Producers: Michel Cases, Ste-Colombe (66300); Dom. de Casinobe, Trouillas (66300). 20 coops, SICA at Perpignan. 750,000 cases.

Côtes Catalanes
Roussillon. 1981. Area north and west of Perpignan. Producers: Cazes Frères, Rivesaltes (66600); Maurice Puig, Claira (66530). 10 coops. 275,000 cases.

Coteaux des Fenouillèdes
Corbières. 1982. 17 communes in the Corbières north of Prades. 11 coops including Arboussols (66320).

Vins de Pays in practice

The Vins de Pays system has given adventurous proprietors in previously backward areas the chance to progress. An example is Pierre Besinet, who with his neighbours formed the Vignerons de Cante-Cigale to exploit the name Vin de Pays de l'Hérault. Three properties close to Agde on the coast well away from the 'Coteaux', Domaine des Amourettes, M. Besinet's Domaine du Bosq and Domaine de la Grange Rouge, market their wines together under the Cante-Cigale label. They have planted Syrah and Cabernet Sauvignon to spice the traditional Carignan, Cinsaut, Grenache and Alicante, and have adopted modern techniques to get aroma and freshness from local white varieties.

The most adventurous Cante-Cigale wine is the Cinsaut-Syrah, a blend of half of each variety made by *macération carbonique*. The aim is the maximum bouquet and the minimum of tannin, with a balance of taste 'between the resilience of the Syrah and the suppleness of the Cinsaut'. M. Besinet feels the wine could age 2 to 3 years, but at 1 year it is dark, aromatic and intensely fruity, attractive when chilled. The wine has only 11° of alcohol, a moderate strength for its degree of flavour, making it very inviting to drink young.

We can expect modern wine-making ideas to transform other unknown *vins de pays* in a similar fashion.

THE SOUTHWEST

The *départements* of the Landes and Pyrénées-Atlantique have their own *vins de pays*. Local zones range from the Lot southwestwards and cover some interesting areas also holding AOC or VDQS rank. The name Comté Tolosan covers the entire Southwest.

Agenais
Southwest. 1982. Most of the *département* of Lot-et-Garonne. 70hl/ha. Grapes: wide range including Cabernets, Gamay and Sauvignon. 4 coops, including Côtes du Marmandais, Beaupuy, 47200 Marmande. Production 135,000 cases.

Côtes de Brulhois
Southwest. 1981. Parts of 8 cantons south of the Garonne around Agen. 70hl/ha. Grapes, red and rosé: at least 70% Abouriou, Cabernets, Cot, Fer, Gamay, Merlot, Tannat. White: Sémillon, Mauzac, Muscadelle, Sauvignon, Ugni Blanc. 2 coops at Goulens Layrac (47390) and Danzac (82340).

Côtes de Gascogne
Southwest. 1981. Almost the entire *département* of the Gers (the Armagnac country). Grapes: wide range of traditional and quality varieties. Producers: M. Esquiro, Dom. de la Higuère, Mirepoix (32540); M. Ribel, Pitre à Montestruc (32390). 7 coops including Lagraulet Gondrin, 32330 Gondrin. Production 275,000 cases.

Coteaux de Glanes
Southwest. 1981. 7 communes in the upper Dordogne valley, département of the Lot. 70hl/ha. 10°. Red and rosé. Grapes: at least 70% Gamay or Merlot. Coop at Glanes, 46130 Bretenoux.

Coteaux et terrasses de Montauban
Southwest. 1980. 14 communes between Cahors and Montauban in the cantons of Montauban, Monclar-de-Quercy Negrepelisse and Villebrumier, Lot-et-Garonne. 10°. Main varieties: Gamay, Merlot, Syrah, Cabernet Franc, Cabernet Sauvignon and Tannat. Secondary varieties: up to 30% of Gamay teinturier de Bouze and Gamay teinturier de Chaudenay. Abouriou, Jurançon, Alicante-Bouschet and Cot are only permitted until 1995. Minimum density of vines: 3,000 per hectare. 100hl/ha.

Coteaux du Quercy
Southwest. 1982. The southern part of the Lot and the north of Tarn-et-Garonne, between Cahors and Lafrançaise. 10°. Grapes: at least 70% Cot, Gamay, Cabernets, Merlot or Tannat. Producer: Ariès Belon, Puylaroque 82240. Production 65,000 cases.

Côtes du Tarn
Southwest. 1981. Wide area of the Tarn around Gaillac and Cordes. Grapes: wide range. Producers: Jean Labert, Castanet; M. de Faramard, Ch. Lastours, L'Ile-sur-Tarn. 4 coops including Gaillac (81600). Production 1·3m. cases.

Comté Tolosan
11 *départements* in southwest France. 1982.

LOIRE

The entire Loire valley, including areas where few vines grow, is entitled to make wine under the Vins de Pays du Jardin de la France rules. Each Loire *département* has its own denomination.

Marches de Bretagne
Lower Loire. 1981. Area to the south of the Loire east of Nantes. Producers: Marcel Chiron, 'La Moranderie', Mouzillon, 44430 Vallet; Joseph Chiron, La Chapelle St-Florent, 44410 St-Florent Le Vieil; Georges Fleurance, 'L'Anière', La Chapelle Heulin, 44330 Vallet; Mme Vve Odette Barre, 'Bonne Fontaine', 44430 Vallet; Gabriel Perraud, 'La Vérignonière', 44190 Clisson. Coop at Ancenis. Production 160,000 cases.

Pays Charentais
Charente and Charente-Maritime. 1981. Entire *départements*. 70hl/ha. 11° red, 11·5° white. Grapes, red; Cabernet Franc, Cabernet Sauvignon, Merlot, Tannat (on the Ile de Ré only) plus up to 20% others. White: Chenin Blanc, Colombard, Folle Blanche, Muscadelle, Sauvignon, Sémillon, Ugni Blanc. Sugar and acidity regulated.

Coteaux du Cher et de l'Arnon
Upper Loire. 1981. 10 communes around Quincy and Reuilly. Grapes, red and rosé: Gamay, Pinot Noir, Pinot Gris, plus 30% others. White: Chardonnay, Sauvignon, plus 30% others. Production 90,000 cases.

Jardin de la France
Loire. 1981. Most of the Loire basin. Producers: Jean Motheron, 49450 Martigue-Briand; Georges Lalanne, Ch. de Tigné, 49770 Tigne; Bore Frères, 49620 La Pommeraye; Pierre Moreau, La Vernelle, 36600 Valençay; Jean-Claude Barbellion, Marcé à Oisly, 41700 Contres: Jacky Preys, Meusnes, 41130 Selles-sur-Cher. Négociants. SA Bougrier, St-Georges-sur-Cher, 41400 Montrichand; Société Vinicole de Touraine, Cour-Cheverny, 41700 Contres. 7 coops.

Retz
Lower Loire. 1982. Area to the south of the Loire west of Nantes. Producers: André Choblet, 44830 Bouaye; Adolphe Richer, St-Cyr en Retz, 44580 Bourgneuf-en-Retz; Pierre Gout, St-Pierre Château de la Tour, 44710 Port St-Père. Coop at Ancenis (44150). Production 165,000 cases.

Urfé
Loire. 1982. A wide area in the *département* of Loire, in the upper Loire valley. Grapes, red and rosé: at least 70% Gamay and Pinot Noir. White: Chardonnay, Aligoté, Pinot Gris, Viognier, Gamay.

Fiefs Vendéens
Lower Loire. 1981. 6 small areas in the Vendée. 70hl/ha. Producers: Pierre Richard, Brem-sur-Mer; Jean Mourat, Sables d'Olonne; Christian Jard, Rosnay; Bernard Babin, Brem-sur-Mer; Rachel Davies, St-Florent des Bois; Mercier Frères, La Chargnée, Vix; André Reverseau, Rosnay; P. & X. Coirier, Pissotte. Production 165,000 cases.

CENTRAL FRANCE

Gorges & Côtes de Millau
Aveyron. 1981. 25 communes in the Tarn valley. 60hl/ha. 4 types of wine made: 2 reds based on Gamay and Syrah, rosé 50% Gamay, white from Chenin and Mauzac. Coop at Agnessac (12520). Production 22,000 cases.

SOUTHERN FRANCE

L'Ile de Beauté
Corsica. 1981. Entire island. Min. 10·5°. Max. 12°. Grapes: many, with Carignan and Cinsaut not to exceed 25% and 50% respectively of planted area. Producers: M. René Touboul, Domaine de Pojale, 20270 Aléria. Domaine de San Giovanni, 20270 Aléria. Mme Jeanne Salvat, Linguizetta, 20230 San Nicoloa. Mme Raymond Guidicelli, Domaine de Liccetto, 20270 Aléria. 7 coops. Production 1·6m. cases.

Pays d'Oc
Midi and Provence. 1981. Ardèche, Aude, Bouches-du-Rhône, Gard, Hérault, Pyrénées-Orientales, Var and Vaucluse. Detailed technical specifications, but no yield restrictions.

JURA AND SAVOIE

Balmes Dauphinoises
Savoie. 1982. Northern part of the *département* of the Isère, around Morestel and Crémieu. Min. alch: 9·5°. Grapes, red and rosé: at least 70% Gamay, Pinot Noir, Syrah, Merlot or Mondeuse. White: at least 70% Chardonnay or Jacquère.

Franche-Comté
Jura. 1982. *Départements* of Jura and Haute Saône. 9° for red and rosé, 9·5° for white. Grapes: only Chardonnay, Auxerrois, Pinot Noir, Pinot Gris and Gamay. 70hl/ha. Coop at Champlitte.

Coteaux du Grésivaudan
Savoie. The Isère valley around Grenoble. 9·5°. Grapes, red and rosé: at least 70% Gamay, Pinot Noir or Etraire de la Dui. White: at least 70% Jacquère, Chardonnay or Verdesse. 2 coops.

GERMANY

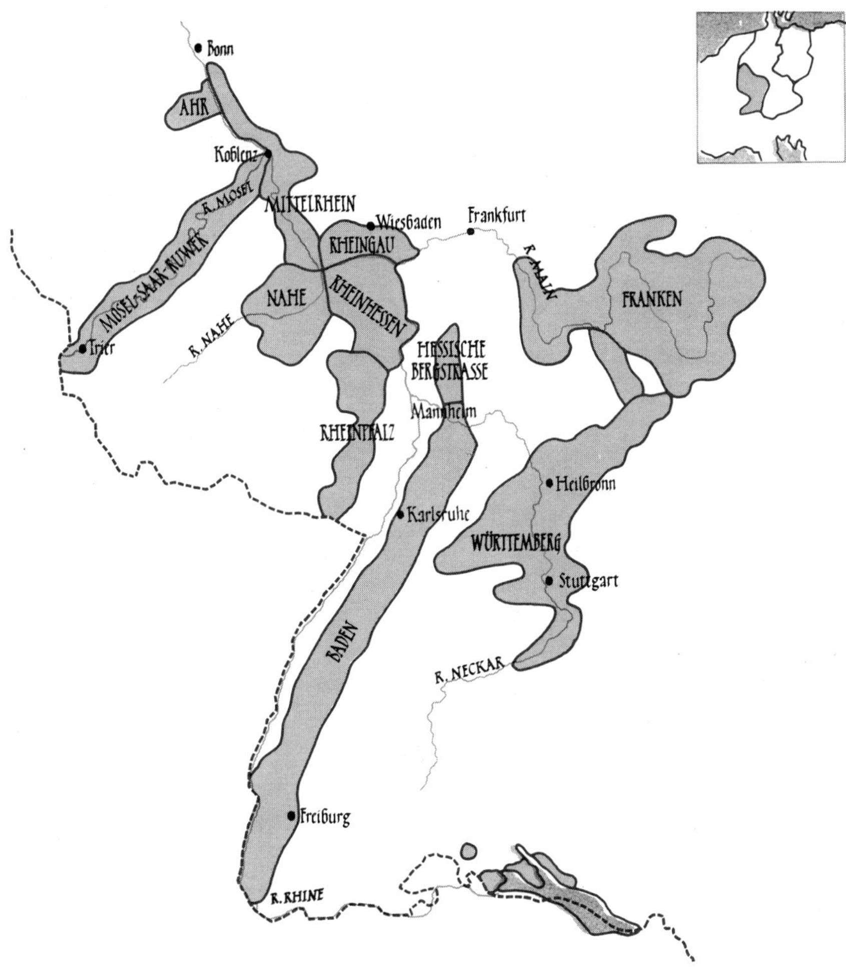

I have sometimes wondered why there is no Chair of German Wine Studies at any of our universities. The subject has just the right mixture of the disciplined, the recondite and the judgemental to appeal to academic minds.

It can be approached as geographical, historical, meteorological, legislational, chemical-pastoral, pastoral-gastronomical, chemical-comical . . . there are enough departments to fill a college.

The German way with wine has a different logic from the French, the Italian or that of any other country. It is highly structured and methodical, making its full explanation a daunting task, but it has a unity of purpose which makes the principle, if not the practice, easy to grasp.

In Germany ripeness is all. All German quality criteria are based on the accumulated sugar in the grapes at harvest time. There is no ranking of vineyards as in France; no specific recipes for varieties of grapes as in Italy. All German (quality) labels tell the same details of the wine in the same order. Despite the difficulties of Gothic type they are the world's most consistent and informative labels – up to a carefully calculated point. Beyond that point you need either an elephantine memory or a good clear reference book to delve further.

The wine laws of Germany were radically reformed in 1971 and since then have been subject to further revision. But their strategy remains unaltered. They divide all German wine into three strata. The lowest, Tafelwein, of tolerable quality, low strength, subject to relatively few controls, is correspondingly barred from claiming any specific vineyard origin. It is assumed to be a blend of wines that have required additional sugar. The only important, potentially confusing, point to remember is the difference between Deutsche Tafelwein, which must be German in origin, and Tafelwein without the qualification, which contains wine from other European countries (normally Italy). A low-strength neutral base wine is easily cleaned up and given some superficial German characteristics by using very aromatic 'sweet reserve'. The use of heavily Gothic labels has obviously been intended to encourage the innocent to believe that the wine is indeed German. A new category of Tafelwein, called Landwein, with stricter rules (*see* pages 232 and 273) was introduced in 1982 as a sort of German *vin de pays*.

The second category of German wine was christened Qualitätswein bestimmter Anbaugebiete: QbA for short. The term means 'quality wine from a designated region'. To a German the difference between this and the top category of wine, Qualitätswein mit Prädikat, is doubtless clear and simple. Unfortunately the legislators did not take non-Germans into account. It must be stressed to them continually that the two classes of Qualitätswein are far apart, distinguished by a basic difference. The first is made with added sugar; the second is what used (before 1971) to be called, much more directly and succinctly, *natur* or *naturrein*. In other words the grapes had enough natural sugar to make wine. 'Mit Prädikat' is hard to translate. 'With special attributes' is the stilted official version. It certainly does not reflect the status of QmP wines as the top category in which, without exception, all the best wines of Germany are included.

Qualitätswein mit Prädikat all carry a designation of maturity of their grapes as part of their full names, in the following order: simply ripe grapes of the normal harvest are Kabinett; late-gathered (therefore riper) are Spätlese; selected late-gathered are Auslese. The precise sugar content (or 'must weight') and therefore potential alcohol required for each category in each region is stipulated in the regulations (*see* opposite).

At this point most wines begin to retain distinct natural sweetness. If an Auslese is fermented fully dry it will be noticeably high in alcohol by German standards. Two degrees of ripeness and selectivity beyond Auslese remain: Beerenauslese, in which the individual berries are selected for extreme ripeness and concentration, and Trockenbeerenauslese, in which only berries dried and shrivelled by noble rot (occasionally by unseasonal heat) are selected. Sugar levels in such wines are commonly so high that fermentation is seriously hampered and may be reluctant to take place at all. 'TBAs' (to use the current California abbreviation) are usually a stable conjunction of very modest alcohol level (as low as 5.5%) and startlingly high sugar. They are less than half as strong as Château Yquem, which is made in much the same way, and correspondingly twice as sweet.

One further category remains separate because of the way it is made: Eiswein is made by crushing grapes that have frozen solid on the vine. Crushing before they thaw means that the almost pure water which constitutes the ice is separated from the sugar, acids and other constituents, which have a lower freezing point. The result, like a TBA, is intensely concentrated, but much less ripe and more acidic. It can be simply extraordinary, its high acid giving it the potential for almost limitless ageing.

The name and ranking of a QmP wine is always set forth on its label in the same order. First comes the town or village (Gemeinde) name; then the vineyard; then the grape (in some classic Riesling areas this is inferred and omitted); then the category of ripeness – Kabinett, Spätlese, Auslese, Beerenauslese.

Only one complicating factor, and the major fault in the 1971 German law, prevents this formula from being crystal clear. It is the concept of the Grosslage, or extended vineyard. Unfortunately labels do not, and are not allowed to, distinguish between a precise vineyard site, known as an Einzellage, and a group of such sites with very much less specificity: a Grosslage. Grosslage groupings were made with the idea of simplifying the sales of wines from lesser-known Einzellagen. Notoriety comes more easily to bigger units. But their names are in no way distinguishable from Einzellage names and I have never met a person who claims to have memorized them. The consumer is therefore deprived of a piece of information to which he has a right. As a further confusing factor, in some areas Einzellagen are also groups of separate vineyards deemed to have a common personality. There is thus no truly clearcut distinction between the categories. In the pages that follow some regions are described in terms of their villages (Gemeinden) and some on the basis of their Grosslagen, according to the ruling local practice. The names of the Einzellagen producing the finest wines will be found in the entries for each region's Producers.

One exceptional use of the Grosslage name must, however, be mentioned. In the making of Trockenbeerenausleses, picking tiny quantities of dried berries, a single Einzellage often fails to produce enough to fill even a small cask. Trockenbeerenausleses are therefore often the sum of grapes from several sites and use the Grosslage name.

The often-quoted rule of thumb, based on the Kabinett-Spätlese-Auslese scale, is 'the sweeter the wine the higher the quality'. While it is still true to say that quality is directly related to ripeness, the question of sweetness is now very much at the discretion of the wine maker (and the consumer). Sweetness in most modern German wines is adjusted to suit the market, by adding unfermented grape juice to fully fermented, fully dry wine just before bottling. The grower looks for a harmonious balance between acidity, alcohol and fruity sweetness in his wine. In the past he achieved it by stopping the fermentation while some natural sweetness remained (not difficult in a cold cellar, using sulphur dioxide). Today he ferments his wine to full dryness and natural stability, but keeps some of the must in its fresh, sweet, unfermented state for later blending.

In some areas there is an apparently growing demand for fully dry, unsweetened wines. To be so described, as '*trocken*', on the label, they must contain less than 9 grams of sugar a litre. In tasting *trocken* wines it soon becomes clear how much a little 'sweet reserve' adds to the charm, balance and drinkability of most German wines: they have to have unusually good figures to survive such naked scrutiny. A halfway category, *halbtrocken*, with up to 18 grams of sugar a litre, more often achieves the right balance of fullness and bite to make satisfactory mealtime wine. Wines with less than 4 grams of sugar a litre are safe for diabetics and can be labelled *diabetiker*.

German growers produce astonishing quantities. France, Italy and other countries make low yields a precondition for their appellations. In Germany only 'must weight' counts. A big crop is simply taken as evidence of a healthy vineyard. Average crops have grown from 25 hectolitres a hectare in 1900 to 40 (about the French AOC level) in 1939, and in the 1970s were averaging well over 100. 1982 hit a record: 171 hl/ha average, with a maximum close to 200.

Without this high productivity German wines would have priced themselves out of the market. Their remarkable achievement is to have quadrupled their yield while maintaining, and probably in most cases improving, their quality. A typical crop on one of the finest sites today is about 70 hl/ha (about twice that of a top Bordeaux château). If anything has been lost it is the concentration of flavours that gave the best of the old low-yield wines the ability to mature for decades. Yet nobody can complain at the condition of the great 1971 vintage (average yield 79.8 hl/ha) a decade later. The almost equally splendid 1976 produced an average of 100 hl/ha throughout Germany.

A more arguable point is that the current law, in setting simple minimum ripeness standards for Ausleses and the other top categories, simply invites growers to achieve that minimum and no more. The old rules allowed eager wine makers to differentiate between their standard and better-than-standard Ausleses, such terms as 'Feine' or 'Feinste Auslese' carrying considerable premiums. If the terms were open to abuse, they also rewarded the patient and ambitious perfectionist. Today he will still signal to his clients which are his best casks of wine, but often in an obscure semaphore of coloured capsules, no less open to abuse because it is closed to the uninitiated.

The official answer to any doubts about the standards or authenticity of German wines is that each wine is both analysed and tasted officially before being issued with a unique Prüfungsnummer, which appears on every label. All official tastings employ a standard 20-point scheme, which is also used for the awarding of the gold, silver and bronze medals at both national (D.L.G.) and regional levels.

In the lists of producers on the pages that follow, prices, unless otherwise stated, refer to the current vintage on sale in 1982 'at the cellar door'.

Statutory sugar levels

Regions	**Table wine**	**Quality wine**	**Kabinett**	**Spätlese**	**Auslese**	**Beerenauslese**	**Trockenbeeren-auslese**
The first figure is potential percentage alcohol; the second figure is degrees Oechsle							
Ahr	5°/44	7°/57	9.1°/70	10°/76	11.1°/83	15.3°/110	21.5°/150
Hessische Bergstrasse	5°/44	7.5°/60	9.5°/73	11.4°/85	13°/95	17.7°/125	21.5°/150
Rheingau	5°/44	7.5°/60	9.5°/73	11.4°/85	13°/95	17.7°/125	21.5°/150
Central Rhine	5°/44	7.5°/57	9.1°/70	10°/76	11.1°/83	15.3°110	21.5°/150
Mosel-Saar-Ruwer	5°/44	7°/57	9.1°/70	10°/76	11.1°/83	15.3°/110	21.5°/150
Nahe	5°/44	7°/57	9.1°/70	10.3°/78	11.4°/85	16.5°/120	21.5°/150

THE REGIONS

Germany's finest wines come from hillside vineyards facing the southern half of the compass. In this northern climate the extra radiation on land tilted towards the sun is often essential for ripeness. Other factors also come into account: the climate-moderating presence of water; shelter from wind; fast-draining and heat-retentive soil.

Fine German wines, in fact, come from almost every type of soil from slate to limestone, clay to sand – given other optimal conditions. The effects of different soils on the character of wines from one grape, the Riesling, is a fascinating subplot of German oenology. But climate and microclimate, orientation and angle of hill come first.

Germany has 11 broadly designated wine regions (bestimmte Anbaugebiete) divided into 32 more narrowly defined Bereichs. The Bereichs are in turn divided into Gemeinden (villages) and the villages into Einzellagen (single sites, or vineyards). The latter are also grouped, several sites and often several villages at a time, as Grosslagen. In most cases a Grosslage name remains more or less permanently attached to the name of a single village, the best known within its radius, which is known as its Leitgemeinde. To confuse matters, at present, growers usually have the option of choosing which village name to prefix their Grosslage name. Grosslage names will become more familiar and easier to identify when they are eventually attached officially and unchangeably to a single Gemeinde. Niersteiner Gutes Domtal is the perfect example of a highly successful Leitgemeinde/Grosslage in the public eye and memory.

Top-quality wines are almost always pinpointed as narrowly as possible by their makers, and therefore come to market under their Einzellage names. There are some 2,600 Einzellagen (since the 1971 law abolished a figure close to ten times this number).

The 11 principal wine areas fall into five broad divisions. The most important is the Rhine valley, including its lesser tributaries, from Rheinpfalz (the Palatinate) in the south, past Rheinhessen, the Rheingau and the Nahe, the Mittelrhein and finally to the little tributary Ahr near Bonn in the north. Second comes the Mosel, flowing north with its tributaries the Saar and the Ruwer to meet the Rhine at Koblenz. Third comes the vast but scattered region of Baden in the south, from Heidelberg all the way to the Swiss border. Fourth comes Franken (or Franconia), the vineyards of the Main valley in northern Bavaria. Fifth, and rarely spoken of outside Germany, comes the disjointed and diverse region of Württemberg.

On the export market the first two are far and away the most important. The picture in Germany is rather different, with great loyalty (and high prices) for the wines of the last three. Foreigners tend to meet German wine either as a commercial blend ('Liebfraumilch') or as the produce of one of the many great historic estates of the Rhine or Mosel. Only rarely have the wines of the smaller local grower been offered abroad. Yet very often this small farmer-cum-innkeeper (for most of them sell their wine 'open' by the glass in their own cheerful little Weinstube) epitomizes the style and vitality of his region. His wines are generally less fine than those of sophisticated noble estates. But they have character, often charm, and sometimes brilliant dash and fire.

Germany in round figures

The total vineyard area of Germany is 228,376 acres, farmed by 89,471 growers. In 1964 there were 122,000 growers, but both the acreage and the number of vintners have declined steadily, while modern methods have greatly increased productivity. The total harvest fluctuates widely with weather conditions. 1982, the biggest to date, produced nearly double the modern (10-year) annual average of 8,500,000 hectolitres (94,440,000 cases).

Production in recent years, with yield per hectare:

1979	8,180,000 hl 93.4 hl/ha	(90,890,000 cases)
1980	4,630,000 hl 51.8 hl/ha	(51,440,000 cases)
1981	7,300,000 hl 78.95 hl/ha	(81,100,000 cases)
1982	15,776,000 hl 170.62 hl/ha	(175,289,000 cases)

The regional acreage figures below indicate the percentage of the 1982 crop yielded by the four biggest regions:

Rheinhessen	58,042 acres	(23.9%)
Rheinpfalz	53,920 acres	(24.4%)
Baden	35,308 acres	(12.4%)
Mosel-Saar-Ruwer	30,373 acres	(15%)
Württemberg	21,402 acres	
Nahe	11,080 acres	
Franken	10,628 acres	
Rheingau	7,242 acres	
Mittelrhein	1,882 acres	
Ahr	1,010 acres	
Hessische Bergstrasse	926 acres	

The principal export markets for German wine in 1982, both in volume and value, were:

	Volume hl	1,000 DM
UK	297,186	106,405
USA	229,870	105,736
Netherlands	112,152	37,180
Canada	66,857	30,950
Denmark	58,257	16,477

LEADING EXPORT HOUSES

Deinhard & Co.
Koblenz/Rhein. Family controlled. Principals: Rolf Wegeler-Deinhard, Hanns Christof Wegeler-Deinhard. Turnover DM260m. in 1981. Estates in Mosel, Rheingau and Rheinpfalz producing quality wines and sparkling wine. Exports to 84 countries.

Weingut Louis Guntrum
Nierstein/Rhein. Family company. Principals: Lorenz and Hanns Joachim Guntrum. Annual turnover DM14m. Merchants with their own estates in Rheinhessen producing mostly Riesling.

Arthur Hallgarten GmbH
London and Geisenheim. Established in the Rheingau in 1898, and in London (by Fritz Hallgarten) in 1933. Now run by his son Peter. Annual turnover £5m. Specialities: individually selected estate wines and regional wines of all regions, especially Mosel-Saar-Ruwer.

Hermann Kendermann OHG
Bingen. Owners: Herr Hans-Walter Kendermann and Jürgen Kendermann. Specialities are Black Tower Liebfraumilch, Green Gold Moselle, German generic and estate-bottled wines.

Langenbach & Co.
Worms. Owner: Whitbread Breweries, London. Annual turnover DM25–40m. Wines from estates in Liebfrauenstift-Kirchenstück Worms and Waldrach, Ruwer. Also of other districts and foreign countries. Sparkling wines; speciality 'Kalte Ente'. Large exports.

Sigmund Loeb GmbH
Trier. Principals: Anthony Goldthorp, London; Josef Steinlein, Trier. Wines of Mosel-Saar-Ruwer, Rheinhessen, Rheinpfalz; particularly fine qualities. 100% export.

Rudolf Müller KG
Reil an der Mosel. Principals: Walter Müller, Dr. Richard Müller, Margit Müller-Burggraef. Annual turnover DM42m. Own estates in Mosel and wines from other estates. Also sparkling wines. Exports 65%.

Weingut Ferdinand Pieroth GmbH
Burg Layen. Owners: The Pieroth family. Turnover DM583m. in 1981. Specialists in direct sales of wines of all German wine districts.

Carl Reh
Leiwen. Owner: Deinhard & Co. (q.v.). Annual turnover DM50m. Complete German range. Exports 33%.

Franz Reh & Sohn KG
Leiwen. Owners: The Reh family. Principal: Herbert Reh. Annual turnover nearly DM50m.

St. Ursula Weinkellerei
Bingen. Own estates in Rheinhessen. Producers of Goldener Oktober and other brands. (*See* Weingut Villa Sachsen, Rheinhessen producers.)

H. Sichel Söhne
Alzey. Owners: Moët-Hennessy Corporation USA, Peter MF Sichel, Walter A. Sichel, Friedrich Weidmann, Henri-Louis Hess. Exports approx. 2.2m. cases of German wine annually (about 14% of total German exports), best known for Blue Nun Liebfraumilch.

Walter S. Siegel GmbH
Wachenheim an der Weinstrasse. Owner: Walter Siegel Ltd., London. Rhine and Mosel wines; also Schloss Reinhartshausen (Rheingau).

Weingut Zimmermann-Graef
Zell. Principals: Fritz and Paul Hübinger. Speciality is 'Zeller Schwarze Katz'. Typical Mosel Riesling of all qualities. Exports more than 50%.

Serious wine tasting takes place in the cellars around a 'Karossel'. The owner, his wine maker and cellarmen appraise the vintage.

GLOSSARY OF GERMAN WINE TERMS

For details of the main German white and red grape varieties, see pages 18–19 and 26–27.

Abfüllung (or ***Abzug***) bottling (e.g. Schlossabzug: 'bottled at the castle').
Amtliche Prüfung certification of standard quality by chemical analysis and tasting. Compulsory since 1971 for all QbA and QmP wines (qq.v.). Each wine is given an A.P. number which must be displayed on the label.
Anbaugebiet a wine region in the broad sense, of which (for 'quality' wines) there are 11 (e.g. Mosel-Saar-Ruwer, Baden).
Anreichern 'enriching' – adding sugar to the must to increase the alcohol; the equivalent of the French chaptalization. In Germany no sugar may be added to wines in the QmP categories (q.v.) but all Tafelwein and QbA wine may be assumed to have been 'enriched'.
Auslese literally 'selected': the third category of QmP wines, made only in ripe vintages and usually naturally sweet. Ausleses often have a slight degree of 'noble rot' which adds subtlety to their fruity sweetness. Good Ausleses deserve ageing in bottle for several years to allow their primary sweetness to mellow to more adult flavours.
Beerenauslese literally 'selected grapes': the category of QmP wine beyond Auslese in sweetness and price, and theoretically in quality. Only very overripe or 'nobly rotten' grapes are used to make intensely sweet, often deep-coloured wines which age admirably.
Blau 'blue'; when used of grapes, means 'red' or 'black'.
Bereich one of 32 districts or subregions (e.g. Bereich Bernkastel) within the 11 Gebiets. Bereich names are commonly used for middling to lower quality wines (they are legal for Tafelwein and QbA as well as QmP) blended from the less-distinguished vineyards of the district.
Bundesweinprämierung a national wine award presented by the D.L.G. (q.v.) to wines selected from regional prize winners. The tastings are held at Heilbronn in Württemberg. 17.5 points out of 20 wins a bronze medal, 18.5 a silver medal and 19.5 a 'Grosser Preis'. Winners normally display their achievement on a neck label on bottles of the wine in question.
Deutsche(r) 'German'; distinguishes Tafelwein from German grapes from inferior mixtures of the wines of 'various E.E.C. countries', often sold with pseudo-German labels.
Deutsches Weinsiegel a red seal of quality available to producers whose wines exceed the minimum required standards for their categories (see Amtliche Prüfung) by set figures (e.g. 2 points out of 20). The gold Export Weinsiegel has similar standards. A yellow Weinsiegel is available for *trocken* (q.v.) wines only.
Diabetiker-Wein the driest category of German wines, with less than 4 grams of unfermented sugar a litre and thus safe for use by diabetics.
D.L.G. The German Agricultural Society (Deutsche Landwirtschafts Gesellschaft), the body that judges and presents the national wine awards. *See* Bundesweinprämierung.
Domäne 'domain' – in Germany a term used for State-owned properties, or 'Staatsweingüter'. There are six, all with high standards; the biggest in the Rheingau and Franken and the best on the Nahe.
Edelfäule 'noble rot'. For a full explanation see Château d'Yquem, page 78.
Eigenem 'own'. 'Aus eigenem Lesegut' means 'from his own harvest'.
Einzellage an individual vineyard site recognized by the law. There are some 2,600 Einzellagen in Germany. Before 1971 there were 10 times as many. In 1971 the minimum size was increased to 12.5 acres. Not all Einzellagen are therefore in contiguous parcels, particularly in Baden and Württemberg. A Grosslage (q.v.) is a unit of several Einzellagen supposedly of the same quality and character. The Einzellage or Grosslage name follows the village (Gemeinde) name on the label.
Eiswein wine made by pressing grapes that have been left hanging on the vine into mid-winter (sometimes January) and are gathered and pressed in early morning, while frozen solid. Since it is the water content of the grape that freezes, the juice, separated from the ice, is concentrated sugar, acidity and flavour. The result is extraordinarily sweet and piquant wines with almost limitless ageing capacity, less rich but more penetrating than Beeren- or Trockenbeerenausleses, often fetching spectacular prices.
Erzeugerabfüllung 'own bottling'; the equivalent of the French *mis au domaine* or *mis au château*.
Erzeugergemeinschaft a producers' association, usually for sales purposes, as distinct from a cooperative for making wine.
Fass a barrel. 'Holz-fasse' are oak barrels, the traditional containers in German cellars.
Flasche bottle – the same word as the English 'flask'.
Flurbereinigung the term for the Government-sponsored 'consolidation' of vineyard holdings by remodelling the landscape, a process that has revolutionized the old system of terracing in most parts of Germany, making the land workable by tractors and rationalizing scattered holdings.
Füder the Mosel barrel, an oak oval holding 1,000 litres or about 111 cases.
Gebiet region.
Gemeinde village, parish or commune. The village name always comes before the vineyard on German labels.
Grosslage a 'collective vineyard', consisting of a number of Einzellagen (q.v.) of similar character and quality. The 33 German Bereichs contain 150 Grosslagen divided into 2,600 Einzellagen – although a few Einzellagen are not attached in this way. Unfortunately the wine law does not permit the label to distinguish between a Grosslage and an Einzellage name. Grosslage names are normally used for wines below the top quality, but also sometimes for such wines as Trockenbeerenausleses when a single Einzellage cannot produce enough grapes to fill even a small barrel.
Jahrgang vintage (year).
Halbtrocken 'half-dry' – wine with no more than 18 grams of unfermented sugar a litre, therefore drier than most modern German wines but sweeter than a *trocken* wine (q.v.).
Kabinett the first category of natural, unsugared, Qualitätswein mit Prädikat (see page 229 for formal ripeness requirements). Fine Kabinett wines have qualities of lightness and delicacy which make them ideal refreshment, not inferior in the right context to heavier (and more expensive) Spätlese or Auslese wines.
Kellerei wine cellar; by inference a merchant's rather than a grower's establishment (which would be called a Weingut).
Landespreismünze regional wine prizes, which act as the 'heats' for the National Bundesweinprämierung (q.v.).
Landwein a new (1982) category for Tafelwein from one of 20 designated areas, of not more than 18 grams a litre residual sugar and therefore *trocken* or *halbtrocken*.
Lesegut crop.
Liebfraumilch a much-abused name for a mild 'wine of pleasant character' officially originating in Rheinpfalz, Rheinhessen, Rheingau or Nahe. It must be in the QbA category and should be of Riesling, Silvaner or Müller-Thurgau grapes. Since neither its

character nor quality is remotely consistent, varying widely from shipper to shipper, its popularity can only be ascribed to its simple and memorable name.

Mostgewicht 'must weight'. The density or specific gravity of the grape juice, ascertained with a hydrometer, is the way of measuring its sugar content. The unit of measurement is the 'degree Oechsle' (q.v.).

Natur, naturrein terms for natural, unsugared wines, obsolete since 1971 when the present QmP categories came into being.

Neuzuchtung new (grape) variety. German breeders have produced a score of new varieties which are slowly being accepted or rejected by growers.

Oechsle the specific gravity, therefore sweetness, of German must is measured by the method invented by Ferdinand Oechsle (1774–1852). Each gram by which a litre of grape juice is heavier than a litre of water is one degree Oechsle. The number of degrees Oechsle ÷ 8 is the potential alcoholic content of the wine if all the sugar is fermented. *See* page 229.

Ortsteil a place-name with a standing independent from its Gemeinde or village. Certain famous estates (e.g. Schloss Vollrads) are allowed to omit the names of their villages from their labels.

Perlwein slightly fizzy Tafelwein, often artificially carbonated under pressure. A small measure of acidic carbon dioxide freshens up dull wines.

Pokalwein wine served 'open' in a large glass (Pokal) in a café or Weinstube.

Prädikat *see* QmP.

Prüfungsnummer the individual A.P. number given to each 'quality' wine after testing. *See* Amtliche Prüfung.

QbA Qualitätswein bestimmter Anbaugebiete: 'quality wine of a designated region'. The category of wine above Tafelwein and Landwein but below QmP (q.v.). QbA wine has had its alcohol enhanced with added sugar. It must be from one of the 11 Anbaugebiete (unblended), from approved grapes, reach a certain level of ripeness before sugaring and pass an analytical and tasting test to gain an A.P. number. In certain underripe vintages a high proportion of German wine comes into this category and can be very satisfactory, although never reaching the delicacy and distinction of QmP wine.

QmP Qualitätswein mit Prädikat. 'Quality wine with special attributes' is the awkward official description of all the finest German wines, beginning with the Kabinett category and rising in sweetness, body and value to Trockenbeerenauslese. The ripeness requirements for each region are listed on page 229. QmP wines must originate in a single Bereich (q.v.) and are certificated at each stage of their career from the vineyard on.

Rebe grape (Rebsorte: grape variety).

Restsüsse 'residual sugar': the sugar remaining unfermented in a wine at bottling, whether fermentation has stopped naturally or been stopped artificially. The minimum, in a wine for diabetics, is about 4 grams a litre. In a Trockenbeerenauslese it may reach astonishing figures of more than 300 grams a litre, with very little of the sugar converted to alcohol.

Roseewein, Roséwein pale pink wine from red grapes.

Rotling pale red wine from mixed red and white grapes.

Rotwein red wine.

Säure acidity (measured in units per 1,000 of tartaric acid). The essential balancing agent to the sweetness in German (or any) wine. As a rule of thumb a well-balanced wine has approximately one unit per 1,000 (ml.) of acid for each 10 degrees Oechsle (q.v.). Thus an 80° Oechsle wine needs an acidity of approximately 0.8.

Schaumwein sparkling wine – a general term for low-priced fizz. Quality sparkling wines are called Sekt.

Schillerwein a pale red (Rotling) of QbA or QmP status, produced only in Württemberg.

Schloss castle.

Schoppenwein another term for Pokalwein – wine served 'open' in a large glass.

Sekt Germany's quality sparkling wine, subject to similar controls to QbA wines.

Spätlese literally 'late-gathered'. The QmP category above Kabinett and below Auslese, with wines of a higher alcoholic degree and greater body and 'vinosity' than Kabinetts. Also often considerably sweeter but not necessarily so. A grower must notify the authorities of his intention to pick a Spätlese crop, and tasting panels establish a consensus of what constitutes proper Spätlese style in each vintage and region. Spätleses, particularly dry ones, are often the best German wines to drink with a meal and have greater potential for long bottle-ageing than most Kabinetts.

Spitzen 'top', a favourite German term, whether applied to a vineyard, a grower or a vintage.

Stück the standard traditional oak cask of the Rhine, holding 1,200 litres or about 133 cases. There are also Doppelstücks, Halbstücks and Viertel(quarter)stücks, holding the logical quantities.

Süssreserve unfermented grape juice with all its natural sweetness, held in reserve for 'back-blending' with dry, fully fermented wines to arrive at the wine maker's ideal of a balanced wine. This sweetening (which also lowers the alcoholic content) is often overdone, but a judicious hint of extra sweetness can enhance fruity flavours and make an average wine considerably more attractive.

Tafelwein 'table wine', the humblest category of German wine. (Without the prefix Deutsche it is not German, however Gothic the label.) The origin, alcohol content and grape varieties are all controlled but Tafelwein is never more than a light wine for quenching thirst, and frequently fails even in this.

TBA *see* Trockenbeerenauslese.

Trocken 'dry' – the official category for wines with less than 9 grams of unfermented sugar a litre. Trocken wines have recently been much in fashion for use with meals, but frequently taste arid, hollow and unbalanced compared with *halbtrocken* (q.v.) versions of the same wines, adjusted with Süssreserve (q.v.).

Trockenbeerenauslese 'selected dried grapes' (frequently shortened to TBA). Ironically the precise opposite of the last entry, the 'dry' here referring to the state of the overripe grapes when picked in a shrivelled state from 'noble rot' and desiccation on the vine. Such is the concentration of sugar, acid and flavours that Oechsle readings of TBA must (never in more than minute quantities) can reach more than 300°. TBA wines are reluctant to ferment and rarely exceed 6% alcohol, the remaining intense sweetness acting as a natural preservative and slowing down maturation for many years. Only Eisweins (q.v.) mature more slowly.

Weinberg vineyard, even when it is not a 'berg' (hill) but flat.

Weingut wine estate. The term may only be used by growers who grow all their own grapes.

Weinprobe wine tasting.

Weinstein the thick deposit of potassium tartrate crystals forming a glittering rock-like lining to old barrels.

Weissherbst a rosé wine of QbA status made from red grapes of a single variety, the speciality of Baden and Württemberg, but also the fate of some sweet reds of other regions which fail to achieve a full red colour. ('Noble rot' attacks the pigments and often makes red Ausleses excessively pale.)

Winzer wine grower.

Winzergenossenschaft, Winzerverein growers' cooperative.

Zuckerrest the same as Restsüsse (q.v.).

MOSEL-SAAR-RUWER

One regional (Gebiet) name covers the long and tortuous route of the Mosel from Luxembourg to the Rhine and both its wine-growing tributaries. It is justified by the wine. To a surprising degree the wines of the Mosel (Upper, Middle and Lower), of the Saar and the Ruwer are homogeneous in style, however widely they vary in quality. They are the brightest, briskest, most aromatic and yet most hauntingly subtle of all the fruit of the Riesling. This is essentially Riesling country, and no soil or situation brings out the thrilling harmony of the finest of all white grapes to better effect.

Low-priced Mosels, sold under such popular labels as Moselblümchen (the regional equivalent of Liebfraumilch), Zeller Schwarze Katz or Kröver Nacktarsch, or under the generously wide Bereich name of Bernkastel, can be mean and watery wines. They are not Riesling but Müller-Thurgau. The finer sites all grow Riesling, and all go to great pains to identify themselves precisely (*see* Producers' entries). The complications of nomenclature can become excruciating, but the rewards are sublime.

The Mosel wears its first few tentative vineyards in France, flows through Luxembourg festooned with them, then enters Germany near the old Roman capital of Trier to be joined by the rivers Saar and Ruwer. It is their side valleys, rather than the main stream, that have the first great Mosel vineyards. Upper Mosel ('Obermosel') wines at their best are gentle. A good deal of the pleasantly neutral, rather sharp Elbling grape is grown on sites where Riesling fails to ripen. Riesling also has difficulty ripening on the Saar and Ruwer. But when it does, on their best slopes, the results are unsurpassed anywhere on earth: quintessential Riesling, clean as steel, haunting with the qualities of remembered scents or distant music.

One Bereich name, Saar-Ruwer, covers the Saar and Ruwer, with two Grosslagen: Scharzberg for the Saar, Römerlay for the Ruwer. The Upper Mosel has its own Bereich name, Obermosel, divided into two Grosslagen: Gipfel and Königsberg. Below it the Saar valley begins the catechism of Germany's great vineyards.

SAAR

Serrig

The uppermost wine village of the Saar (still higher up are steelworks). Steel is also the appropriate metaphor; Serrig has problems ripening Riesling and makes much excellent acid base-wine for Sekt. The State Domain is its principal estate. In exceptionally warm autumns its wines become fables. 233 acres.

Irsch, in a side valley to the north of Serrig, is a minor wine village with the same problems as Serrig.

Growers Schloss Saarstein. Bert Simon. Staatlichen and Weinbaudomänen. Verienigte Hospitien.

Saarburg

The principal town of the area, with several good growers on slopes that are capable of great finesse in good years. 185 acres.

Growers Fischer. Forstmeister Geltz. Rudolf Müller. Freiherr von Solemacher.

Ockfen

The first of the noble Saar vineyards is the great hump of the Bockstein in Ockfen, owned by the State Domain and many others. Again, a dry autumn is needed for balanced wines. 190 acres.

Growers Duhr. Fischer. Friedrich-Wilhelm-Gymnasium. Forstmeister Geltz. Milz Laurentiushof. Rudolf Müller. Reverchon. Rheinart. Hermann Freiherr von Schorlemer. Freiherr von Solemacher. Staatlichen Weinbaudomänen.

Ayl

The village faces the whale-like ridge of its Kupp vineyard across a flat valley. Thrillingly sweet-and-sour wines at their best. 270 acres.

Growers Bischöflichen Weingüter. Rheinart.

Wawern

A small village with no site name to conjure with, but excellent wines in the true Saar style. 103 acres.

Grower Fischer.

Wiltingen

The hub of the Saar region, surrounded by major vineyards and giving its name to most Saar Grosslage wines ('Wiltinger Scharzberg'). Its best estate, Scharzhofberg – remember the essential 'hof' – is considered so important that it dispenses with the name of Wiltingen on its label. A galaxy of the top producers own land in the dozen first-rate vineyards, which often produce some of Germany's most delectably elegant, balanced, ageworthy wine. 790 acres.

Growers Bischöflichen Weingüter. Duhr. Le Gallais. Graf zu Hoensbroech. Apollinar Joseph Koch. Felix Müller. Egon Müller-Scharzhof. Reverchon. Rheinart. Schlangengraben. Hermann Freiherr von Schorlemer. Vereinigte Hospitien. Bernd van Volxem.

Kanzem

Just downstream from Wiltingen, Kanzem evokes only slightly less superlatives for its much smaller area of steep vineyards dropping to the river. Wines with teasing hints of earth and perhaps spice. 185 acres.

Growers Bischöflichen Weingüter. Rudolf Müller. Reverchon. Schlangengraben. Vereinigte Hospitien.

Oberemmel

In a side valley east of Wiltingen, Oberemmel has some superb sites, including Hütte and Rosenberg, and considerable land of rather less distinction. 625 acres.

Growers Bischöflichen Weingüter. Friedrich-Wilhelm-

Gymnasium. von Hövel. Oberemmeler Abteihof. Bernd van Volxem. Otto van Volxem.

Filzen

Towards the mouth of the Saar, Filzen has a smaller reputation but some good growers. 145 acres.
Growers Max-G. Piedmont. Reverchon.

Konz

The town at the meeting place of Saar and Mosel includes in its boundaries the place names Falkenstein (known for its 45-acre Hofberg), Filzen and Mennig.
Grower Friedrich-Wilhelm-Gymnasium.

RUWER

Trier

Trier's own vineyards and those of the tiny river Ruwer (pronounced Roover) together make up only a drop in the ocean, yet one of the most precious drops of all. Ruwer wines are feather-light, often *spritzig*; on the face of it scarcely more serious than *vinho verde*. Yet if quintessential Riesling is made anywhere it is here; frail but tenacious, even dry wines poised in balance for years and sweet ones growing subtly harmonious for decades.

The boundaries of Trier now include the vineyards of Avelsbach, brilliantly exploited by the State Domain and the Cathedral estates (Hohe Domkirche) to make the most of their perfume, despite a tartness that dogs them in all but the ripest years.
Growers Bischöflichen Weingüter. Staatlichen Weinbaudomänen. Thiergarten. Vereinigte Hospitien.

Waldrach

The first Ruwer wine village coming downstream, Waldrach is the least celebrated, though its wines have almost the potential of the next, Kasel. Growers include Bischöflichen Weingüter and the shippers Langenbach of Worms. 300 acres.

Kasel

The 'capital', tiny as it is, of the Ruwer. Its best site, Nies'chen, performs wonders of delicacy, charm and perfume. 220 acres.
Growers Bischöflichen Weingüter. Patheiger. St. Irminenhof. Bert Simon.

Mertesdorf

Known entirely for the one magnificent estate, Maximin Grünhaus, that faces it across the little valley.
Grower von Schubert.

Eitelsbach

Almost equally identified with one estate, the Karthäuserhofberg. These last two in their different styles are the 'first-growths' of the Ruwer, and hold that rank in comparison with any properties in Germany.
Grower Karthaüserhof.

MIDDLE MOSEL

Bereich Bernkastel

The Bereich Bernkastel, still known to old-timers by its pre-1971 name of Mittelmosel, contains all the best vineyard sites of the main stream, now slowed and broadened by locks to make it a noble river, winding in matchless beauty through alternating cliffs of vineyard to right and left. Whichever side confronts the river with a high hill and makes it bend, offers vines the inclination they need towards the sun.

Bernkastel is the natural centre of the region; a major crossing point (to the town of Kues opposite), an irresistible architectural museum in its huddle of tall timbered houses, and the producer of its most celebrated wine.

Authors differ on where the villages of noteworthy quality upstream and downstream begin and end. The conservative view limits the classic Mittelmosel to the stretch from Trittenheim to Ürzig. But excellent estates extend much farther upstream and downstream in the best sites. Those on the extremities are more dependent, like the Saar and Ruwer, on exceptional seasons. But lovely, lively, classic Riesling is within their grasp and their names should be remembered along with the more obvious Piesport, Bernkastel and Wehlen.

The first villages below Trier to present good south-facing slopes to the Mosel are Longuich and (across its bridge) Schweich, then the hamlets of Longen and Lörsch, all in the Grosslage (Longuicher) Probstberg. No particularly distinguished growers have illuminated their names, but in first-class vintages they can make notable wine. The majority of the vines here are Riesling, the first essential for fine Mosel.

Mehring

Mehring is somewhat better known, partly because of its size, no doubt partly because the famous Friedrich-Wilhelm-Gymnasium is among the owners of its south slope. Here the Grosslage St. Michael applies to the better sites. Those facing northeast round the river bend have the Grosslage name Probstberg again, making a more modest commodity. 1,000 acres.
Grower Friedrich-Wilhelm-Gymnasium.

The little village of Pölich, with its best vineyard the 255-acre Held, marks the next sharp kink in the river. The Grosslage St. Michael continues here all round the next sweeping right-hand bend through the villages of Detzem, Schleich, Ensch, Thörnich, Bekond and Rivenich (these two lying back in western side valleys) to the relatively celebrated little town of Klüsserath.

Klüsserath

The Einzellage Bruderschaft (brotherhood) not only has a pleasant name; its 600-odd acres are planted with 90% Riesling. This can be taken as a starting point for the Middle Mosel. The Grosslage is St. Michael.
Grower Franz Reh.

Köwerich

Köwerich lies on the south bank of the river, facing the steep and narrow Einzellage Laurentiuslay (100% Riesling) across the water. Its other vineyards are not in the same class. Grosslage St. Michael.

Leiwen

Leiwen also lies on the south bank and shares the name of Laurentiuslay with Köwerich, but for a detached fragment of vineyard on the opposite side of the river with a different exposure. Leiwen's other vineyards are not so privileged. 1,125 acres in Grosslage St. Michael.
Growers Domklausenhof. Loewen. Rey.

Trittenheim

Trittenheim occupies the centre of a splendid oxbow bend, with equally fine sites on both sides of the river. Although its vines seldom if ever produce wine of great body, they achieve classic Riesling finesse in a more delicate style. Poor vintages find them thin. From Trittenheim north the Grosslage is (Piesporter) Michelsberg. 750 acres.
Growers Bischöflichen Weingüter. Dünweg. Milz Laurentiushof. Reh.

Neumagen-Dhron

Neumagen lies on a straight south–north stretch of the river; Dhron in the valley of the tributary Dhron behind the hill. There are good but not outstanding sites in both villages, on both sides of the river, the best being the Hofberger, steep and sheltered in the Dhron valley. Rosengärtchen and the tiny Sonnenuhr are the best-placed sites in Neumagen. 875 acres in Grosslage Michelsberg.
Growers Bischöflichen Weingüter (Dhron). Domklausenhof (Neumagen). Dünweg (Neumagen and Dhron). Friedrich-Wilhelm-Gymnasium (Neumagen and Dhron). Hain (Neumagen and Dhron). Matheus-Lehnert (Dhron). Milz Laurentiushof (Neumagen and Dhron).

Piesport

The village lies in the middle of the biggest south-facing horseshoe of the steepest vineyards on the river. All the north-bank vineyards are fine, although Goldtröpfchen is much the most famous. These Piesporters are the most succulently pleasing of all Mosels, uniting ripeness and a touch of spice with the underlying 'nerve' that gives lasting power and style. They are seldom very full-bodied, even by Mosel standards, yet they leave a glowing, golden impression. The number of top-class growers with property here is both cause and effect. Piesport's flat land on the south bank is the Einzellage Treppchen. It is not in the same class. 1,250 acres in Grosslage Michelsberg.
Growers Bischöflichen Weingüter. Domklausenhof. Dünweg. Haart. Hain. Matheus-Lehnert. Reh. Reuscher-Erben. Tobias. Vereinigte Hospitien.

Minheim

Minheim lies on an oxbow bend, a replica of Trittenheim but without its good fortune in the steepness or orientation of its slopes. 475 acres in Grosslage Michelsberg.

Wintrich

Wintrich echoes the geography of Neumagen, its best site, Ohligsberg, lying by the river to the south of the village. Here the Bernkastel Grosslage Kurfürstlay takes over from (Piesporter) Michelsberg. 675 acres.

Kesten

Kesten has vineyards on both sides of the Mosel as it turns again to flow east, but only one outstanding site, Paulinshofberger, facing south across the river. 313 acres in Grosslage Kurfürstlay.
Growers Deinhard. Kees-Kieren.

The landscape of the Mosel

Monzel and Osann

These two villages lie behind Kesten in the hills with no remarkable sites but some fair ones. Their wine is as likely to be sold as Bernkasteler Kurfürstlay as by their own little-known names.

Brauneberg

Brauneberg, on the south bank, faces its proudest possession, the Juffer, across the water. Before the Doktorberg in Bernkastel rose to fame, this was the highest-priced Mosel; robust wine of body and full of fruit which aged admirably, in the style of the time, to amber pungency. The name of Brauneberg's hamlet, Filzen, is sometimes seen on good-value bottles. 758 acres in Grosslage Kurfürstlay.

Growers Zach. Bergweiler-Prüm. Fritz Haag. Karp-Schreiber. Licht-Bergweiler. St. Nikolaus Hospital. Thanisch.

Maring-Noviand

Lying in a side valley north of the river opposite Brauneberg, Maring-Noviand has some well-sheltered if not ideally exposed sites, the Honigberg forming a southwest-facing arc in imitation of a river bend but unfortunately one hill back from the all-important river.

Veldenz and Mulheim

These villages carry the vineyards back from the Mosel up a southern side valley; again useful sources of fair-quality wines, rising to heights only in great vintages.

Lieser

Lieser has a position as prime as Brauneberg's Juffer, without its great reputation. The soil seems to mark it with a stony tang of its own. Confusingly, most of Lieser, although next door to Bernkastel, has the Grosslage name of Beerenlay, peculiar to itself. 520 acres.

Growers Deinhard. Hermann Freiherr von Schorlemer. Schloss Lieser Freiherr von Schorlemer. Thanisch.

Bernkastel-Kues

This is the hub of the Middle Mosel: Kues, the larger town, on flat land on the left bank; Bernkastel across the bridge, crammed up against its precipitous vineyards, with the most famous of them, the Doktor, apparently on the point of sliding straight into its streets. Bernkastel's best wines bring together all the qualities of the Mosel: delicacy and drive, force and grace, honey and earth. Riesling, in other words, and pure grey slate. A suggestion of a flinty edge often distinguishes them from their neighbours.

The vineyards are divided into two Grosslagen: Kurfürstlay for the herd (which includes many vineyards upstream from the town boundaries) and Badstube for the select few Einzellagen that share the best hill with the Doktor. 425 acres.

Growers Zach. Bergweiler-Prüm. Deinhard. Friedrich-Wilhelm-Gymnasium. Josephshof. Lauerberg. Licht-Bergweiler. Meyerhof. Pfarrkirche. J. J. Prüm. S. A. Prüm Erben, S. A. Prüm. St. Johannishof. St. Nikolaus Hospital. Clemens Freiherr von Schorlemer. Hermann Freiherr von Schorlemer. Selbach-Oster. Maximinhof Studert-Prüm. Thanisch. Thaprich. Thiergarten. Vereinigte Hospitien. Zentralkellerei Mosel-Saar-Ruwer.

Graach

Bernkastel melts into Graach, Graach into Wehlen and Wehlen into Zeltingen along the five-mile hill of uninterrupted vines that starts with the Doktorberg. It rises over 700 feet above the river, hardly deviating from its ideal vertiginous tilt or its steady orientation south-southwest. It may well be the single largest vineyard of sustained superlative quality in the world.

Graach has a major share of this treasure: all its vines are sandwiched between Bernkastel and Wehlen's greatest site, the Sonnenuhr. Its wines can achieve similar intensity and richness; they belong firmly in the top flight of the Mosel. 300 acres in Grosslage Münzlay.

Growers Abteihof. Zach. Bergweiler-Prüm. Christoffel. Deinhard. Friedrich-Wilhelm-Gymnasium. Fritz Haag. Josephshof. Kees-Kieren. Lauerberg. Licht-Bergweiler. Meyerhof. Otto Pauly. Pfarrkirche. J. J. Prüm. S. A. Prüm Erben, S. A. Prüm. St. Johannishof. St. Nikolaus Hospital. Clemens Freiherr von Schorlemer. Hermann Freiherr von Schorlemer. Selbach-Oster. Maximinhof Studert-Prüm. Thanisch. Vereinigte Hospitien. Weins-Prüm. Zentralkellerei Mosel-Saar-Ruwer.

Wehlen

Another of the villages whose growers have the pleasure of admiring their best vineyard across the river. The Sonnenuhr, with the sundial that gives the vineyard its name conspicuous among the vines, lies directly opposite the village centre. The other Wehlen vineyards are on the south bank and have less to offer. (Klosterberg is the best.) The fame of Wehlen hangs entirely on its one great site and the honeyed quintessence of Riesling it can produce. 398 acres in Grosslage Münzlay.

Growers Zach. Bergweiler-Prüm. Christoffel. Deinhard. Lauerberg. Licht-Bergweiler. Meyerhof. Nicolay. J. J. Prüm. S. A. Prüm Erben, S. A. Prüm. St. Johannishof. St. Nikolaus Hospital. Michel Schneider. Hermann Freiherr von Schorlemer. Selbach-Oster. Maximinhof Studert-Prüm. Weins-Prüm Erben.

Zeltingen

The village is called Zeltingen-Rachtig, being a union of two small settlements, again with land on both sides of the river. This is the biggest wine-growing commune on the Mosel, and consequently often met with. It is also one of the best, with a Sonnenuhr vineyard only slightly less renowned than Wehlen's, and the excellent Schlossberg above it giving powerful, beautifully balanced, rather earthy wines. The famous name of Himmelreich is one of those which has been extended to embrace sites of very uneven quality, facing several points of the compass. On the opposite shore, Deutschherrenberg tends to less ripeness but foreshadows the famous spicy flavour of its neighbour, Ürzig. 625 acres in Grosslage Münzlay.

Growers Zach. Bergweiler-Prüm. Ehses-Geller-Erben. Friedrich-Wilhelm-Gymnasium. Josephshof. Nicolay. J. J. Prüm. S. A. Prüm Erben, S. A. Prüm. Clemens Freiherr von Schorlemer. Hermann Freiherr von Schorlemer. Selbach-Oster. Vereinigte Hospitien.

Ürzig

Ürzig tucks all its modest parcel of vineyards into a sheltered bend of the river facing southeast, on deep slaty soil mixed with red clay in snug crannies where the Riesling ripens to a high level of spicy intensity. Würzgarten means 'spice garden'. Its wines have strong character and should be among the most identifiable of the great Middle Mosels. From Ürzig downstream to Kröv the Grosslage is Schwarzlay. 150 acres.

Growers Bischöflichen Weingüter. Christoffel. Benedict Loosen-Erben. Rudolf Müller. Nicolay. St. Johannishof. Weins-Prüm Erben.

Erden

The village lies opposite Ürzig, surrounded by the broad, gentle slopes of its Einzellage Busslay, a Müller-Thurgau rather than a Riesling site, comparable to Piesport's Treppchen. Erden's fine vineyards lie on the opposite bank next to Ürzig. The tiny Prälat is the best, and the last of the truly great vineyards of the Mosel on this downstream route – although Erdener Treppchen, alongside, and Herrenberg, above, are also excellent Riesling sites. 300 acres in Grosslage Schwarzlay.
Growers Zach. Bergweiler-Prüm. Bischöflichen Weingüter. Christoffel. Nicolay. Weins-Prüm Erben.

Kinheim

Kinheim, on the north bank, has one fine site, Hubertuslay, but here the soil is beginning to change to a less outrageously slaty mixture and the chance of superlative wine-making to diminish. 300 acres in Grosslage Schwarzlay.
Growers Kees-Kieren. Nicolay.

Kröv

Kröv makes its reputation and its fortune more on its Grosslage name Nacktarsch (and the accompanying label showing a little boy being spanked with his pants down) than on its Einzellagen, good though their wine can be in a freshly fruity style that foreshadows the lower reaches of the Mosel. 875 acres.

Traben-Trarbach

The next across-the-river pair of settlements, these share yet another mighty oxbow bend. But here the riverside slopes have moderated and the best steep sites are back in the folds of the hills in the side valley behind Trarbach. 790 acres in Grosslage Schwarzlay.

Enkirch

As the river recovers its northward course, Enkirch has a site that recalls Neumagen and Dhron, with the steep riverfront facing west and a side valley (Steffensberg) facing south. Riesling here makes wines of balanced, deft lightness and spiciness which deserve a higher reputation. 525 acres in Grosslage Schwarzlay.
Grower Carl Aug. Immich-Batterieberg.

Reil

The next major left-bank centre, Reil has good sheltered slopes for Riesling. The best are Goldlay, across the river, and Sorentberg, tucked into a side valley. These produce light wines, capable of gulpable fruitiness in good vintages. The Grosslage is Vom Heissen Stein.
Grower Rudolf Müller.

Pünderich

Both sides of the river at the next right-hand bend are in Pünderich. The steep slopes are dying away here, and Riesling sites are limited. Nonnengarten makes softly fruity Rieslings; the huge Marienburg lighter and more flowery wine. Grosslage Vom Heissen Stein.

LOWER MOSEL

Zell

The best-known wine community (and the Bereich name) of the Lower Mosel, due in some measure to its memorable Grosslage name Schwarze Katz and the inevitable black cat on the label. Zell and Zell-Merl, immediately downstream, both have steep slopes with slaty soil, planted largely in Riesling and capable of very tempting, light but aromatic and flowery wines. 1,800 acres.
Grower Michel Schneider.

Bullay

A small community, little known to the outside world, with limited but very worthwhile steep slaty slopes producing fine light Riesling. Kronenberg, sheltered in a side valley, gives particularly satisfying wine. 130 acres in Grosslage Grafschaft.
Grower Ewald Theod. Drathen.

Neef

Little Neef, on the right bank at the next bend below Bullay, rejoices in one very fine steep slope in the classic Mosel style: the 98-acre Frauenberg. The Grosslage is Grafschaft.
Grower Ewald Theod. Drathen.

Similar favoured sites occur less and less frequently as the Mosel flows tortuously on past Senheim, Mesenich, Elenz and Cochem, then takes a straighter course north towards Koblenz, vines still hugging its immediate banks. The Grosslage names for this lower section are Grafschaft, Rosenhang, Goldbaumchen and finally Weinhex. The best-known village of the final reaches is Winningen, with its Einzellagen Uhlen, Hamm and Domgarten growing fine Rieslings almost within sound of the bells of Koblenz.

LEADING MOSEL-SAAR-RUWER PRODUCERS

Weingut Zach. Bergweiler-Prüm Erben

Gestade 15, 5550 Bernkastel-Kues. Owner: Dr. Peter Pauly. 23.5 acres. Einzellagen: Bernkasteler – Doktor, Badstube, Graben, Lay, Bratenhöfchen, Matheisbildchen, Schlossberg and Johannisbrünnchen; Graacher – Himmelreich and Domprobst; Wehlener – Sonnenuhr and Rosenberg; Zeltinger Himmelreich; Erdener Busslay; Brauneberger – Juffer Sonnenuhr and Juffer.

Inheritors of a fine part of the famous Prüm properties. 50% of the estate is on the steepest slopes, 25% on moderate slopes and 25% on level ground. 95% is Riesling. The wide range of wines is made in both stainless steel and oak, emphasizing vineyard character as far as possible. The owner's wife belongs to the Berres family who own Nicolay of Ürzig. Prices: from DM 5.00.

Der Bischöflichen Weingüter Trier

Postfach 1326, Gervasiusstrasse 1 (Ecke Rahnenstrasse), 5500 Trier. Director: Wolfgang Richter. 259 acres in the Middle Mosel, Saar and Ruwer.

The biggest estate under one management in the Mosel-Saar-Ruwer was formed by the union in 1966 of 3 independent charitable properties: the Bishop's Seminary (Priesterseminar), the Trier cathedral (Domkirche) estates and the Bishop's Hostel (Konvikt). It has now also leased 4 other small church estates. The vineyard management and the pressing are carried on independently at the 3 main charities' press houses; all the juice is then brought to the 400-year-old central cellar in Trier for fermentation and cask-ageing. 95% of the whole estate is Riesling.

The Priesterseminar originates from a gift in 1773 by

the Prince-Bishop Clemens Wenceslaus (a great promotor of Riesling over lesser vines). Its 85 acres are in 7 villages. In the Middle Mosel: Erdener Treppchen (7.5); Ürziger Würzgarten (1); Dhroner Hofberger (6); Trittenheimer Apotheke (4.2) and Altärchen (4). On the Ruwer: Kaseler Nies'chen (16). On the Saar: Kanzemer Altenberg (21); Scharzberg (planted 1.25 acres with Spätburgunder for red wine); Wiltinger Kupp (12.8); Ayler Kupp (10).

The Hohe Domkirche has only 2 holdings: 25 acres at Wiltingen on the Saar (20 in the Scharzhofberg, 5 in the Rosenberg) and 34 at Avelsbach on the outskirts of Trier (sole ownership of the 24-acre Altenberg and 10 acres of Herrenberg).

The Bischöfliches Konvikt is the biggest of the three, dating back to 1653, with 97 acres. On the Ruwer 47 acres of Eitelsbacher Marienholz and 10 of Kaseler Kehrnagel; on the Saar 15.5 acres of Ayler Kupp and 11.5 (solely owned) of Ayler Herrenberger; 6 acres at Avelsbach by Trier and far down the Mosel at Piesport 7 acres of Goldtröpfchen.

The leased church properties are at Oberemmel on the Saar, Waldrach and Eitelsbach on the Ruwer, and in Trier – a total of 20 acres.

All this wine is superbly well-made, emphasizing lightness and finesse, with a high proportion of dry and medium-dry wines. If anything the Priesterseminar properties have the highest reputation of all.

Gutsverwaltung Deinhard

Martertal 2, 5550 Bernkastel-Kues. Manager: Norbert Kreuzberger. 68 acres in the villages of Bernkastel, Graach, Wehlen, Kesten, Lieser and Kasel. Einzellagen: Bernkasteler – Doktor (3.7), Graben (7), Lay (2.5), Bratenhöfchen (8.5), Mattheisbildchen (1.25), Johannisbrünnchen (3.7) and Schlossberg (0.25); Graacher – Himmelreich (1.75) and Domprobst (1); Wehlener – Sonnenuhr (9), Klosterberg (5.5) and Rosenberg (1.25); Kestner Paulinshofberger (3); Lieserer Schlossberg (2.5); Kaseler – Nies'chen (6), Hitzlay (8), Kehrnagel (1.25) and Herrenberg (1.75).

The Mosel estate of the famous Koblenz wine merchants started in 1900 with the sensational purchase of part of the Doktor vineyard for 100 gold marks a square metre. Further acquisitions totalled some 30 acres in 1981, when a long lease of vineyards in Wehlen from the Dr. Zach. Bergweiler-Prüm estate more than doubled their Mosel holdings. 89% is on steep slopes and 88% is Riesling. The average crop is between 75 and 80 hl/ha. The cellars, press house and a villa now occupied by the manager are in Kues near the railway station.

Deinhard's Mosels are perfectly true to type with little sweetening: classic wines to show the subtle differences of the terrain. Bernkasteler Doktor concentrates all the qualities, but all their Middle Mosel Kabinetts and better are serious wines for bottle-ageing, and the Kasel wines from the Ruwer are distinctly brisk and piquant.

Weinkellerei & Weingut Ewald Theodor Drathen KG

Auf der Hill, 5584 Alf. Owners: Ewald Theod. Drathen KG. 15 acres. Einzellagen: Alfer Hölle (5.5 solely owned); Neefer Frauenberg (7); Bullayer Sonneck (3).

A family merchant house founded in 1860 with a small estate that includes part of the remarkable Frauenberg, which is 100% Riesling. Their Alf vines are 50% Riesling, 40% Müller-Thurgau, 10% Optima; Bullay is all Müller-Thurgau. Drathen's Frauenberg is not quite a great wine, but has overwhelming simple charm. Prices: DM 5.50 – 45.00.

Weingüter Dr. Fischer

Bocksteinhof, 5511 Ockfen-Wawern. Owner: Dr. med. Hanns-Heinz Fischer. 59 acres. Einzellagen: Ockfener – Bockstein (21), Herrenberg (4.5) and Geisberg (4); Saarburger Kupp (6); Wawerner Herrenberger (25 acres, solely owned).

A principal Saar estate with 2 centres: the Bocksteinhof in the vines at the foot of the great towering Bockstein and an 18th-century former monastic property in a meadow below the Herrenberg, the best site in Wawern. 98% is Riesling. Dr. Fischer's wines are admirable examples of the freshness and drive of good Saar Rieslings. Price: DM 5.40.

Stiftung Staatliches Friedrich-Wilhelm-Gymnasium

Weberbachstrasse 75, 5500 Trier. Director: Benedikt Engel. 111 acres. Saar Einzellagen: Falkensteiner Hofberg; Pellingener Jesuitengarten (solely owned); Oberemmeler Scharzberg; Ockfener Geisberg. Mosel Einzellagen: Mehringer – Blattenberg, Goldkupp and Zellerberg; Trittenheimer – Altärchen and Apotheke; Neumagener Rosengärtchen; Dhroner Hofberger; Graacher – Domprobst and Himmelreich; Zeltingen – Sonnenuhr and Schlossberg; Bernkasteler – Bratenhöfchen and Graben.

Another of the great institutions of Trier, the (formerly Jesuit) school, founded 1563, which boasts Karl Marx as an old boy. The vineyards (87% Riesling) are beautifully maintained and in prime condition; cellar techniques are excellent and the wines generally among the Mosel's best. Prices: from DM 5.70.

Weingut Le Gallais

5511 Kanzem. Owner: Mme Rochon de Pons. 6 acres. Einzellage: Wiltinger Braune Kupp.

Herr Egon Müller of Scharzhof, with his immensely high standards, runs this little property for the French owner. Only QmP wines are sold as Braune Kupp; the Grosslage name Scharzberg is for QbA wine, some of which comes from Müller's own estate. The Kabinett wines are light; higher qualities are aromatic and spicy. All are 100% Riesling. Prices: from DM 4.00.

Weingut Forstmeister Geltz Erben

Heckingstrasse 20, 5510 Saarburg. Director: Hans-Joachim Zilliken. 21 acres. Einzellagen: Saarburger – Rausch (9), Antoniusbrunnen (4) and Bergschlösschen (5); Ockfener – Bockstein (2.5) and Geisberg (1.25).

The family estate of the much-respected Master Forester of the King of Prussia, Ferdinand Geltz (1851–1925), now run by his great-grandson Hans-Joachim Zilliken. The wines are made very traditionally, in casks, and designed for long age in bottle. A 1979 fully dry Spätlese is outstanding. Beerenausleses from the estate have broken auction price records. Prices: from about DM 7.00.

Weingut von Hövel

Agritiusstrasse 5–6, 5503 Konz-Oberemmel. Owner: Eberhard von Kunow. 29.5 acres. Einzellagen: Oberemmeler Hütte (solely owned) and Scharzhofberg.

A former part of the monastic St. Maximin estate with Romanesque cellars and a beautiful old farmhouse. Von Hövel's Hütte is exceptionally fine and elegant even by Saar standards; a light but lovely wine. Prices: from DM 5.80.

Chr. Karp-Schreiber

5551 Brauneberg. Owner: Günter Karp. 7.5 acres. Einzellagen: Brauneberger – Hasenläufer, Juffer, Juffer Sonnenuhr and Mandelgraben.

A family property since 1664. Gunter Karp and his son Alwin make prize-winning Rieslings and (in Mandelgraben) Müller-Thurgau and Kerner, mostly sold to private customers. Prices: from DM 5.00.

Karthäuserhof Gutsverwaltung Werner Tyrell

(Formerly H. W. Rautenstrauch), Karthäuserhof 1, 5500 Trier-Eitelsbach. Owners: Maria and Werner Tyrell. 50 acres. Einzellage: Eitelsbacher Karthäuserhofberg.

A beautiful old manor of the Carthusian monks in a side valley of the Ruwer, bought by the ancestor of the present owner when Napoleon secularized church land. The long hill of Karthäuserhofberg is divided into Kronenberg (one half), Burgberg, Sang and the tiny Orthsberg and Stirn; all belong to the estate, which also breeds Prussian Trakehner horses. The wines can be fabulous in great vintages, but tend to have harsher acidity (and are usually made drier) than the only comparable Ruwer estate, Maximin Grünhaus (*see* von Schubert). The bottle is unmistakable, with only a narrow label on the neck, none on the body. Prices: from DM 7.80.

Reichsgraf von Kesselstatt

Postfach 3240, 5500 Trier. Owners: Günther and Käthi Reh. 200 acres in most of the best villages.

This was the greatest private estate of the Mosel-Saar-Ruwer, with 150 acres, when it was bought in 1978 by Günther Reh, son of Carl Reh of Leiwen. Since then the empire has expanded with the addition of several more high-quality estates (listed below), either bought, leased or part owned. Each has its own character but the general standard is very high and almost the entire estate is planted with Riesling.

The splendid baroque Kesselstatt palace in Trier, from which the Counts promulgated the planting of Riesling in the 18th century, is the headquarters. The estate is in 4 parts, each with its own press house and cellars. The most famous is the Josephshof at Graach, which owns the whole Josephshöfer Einzellage of 15 acres high on the hill between the greatest vineyards of Bernkastel and Wehlen. DM 6.00 – 12.50.

Weingut Domklausenhof Piesport/Mosel. Einzellagen: Piesporter – Domherr (4.5), Goldtröpfchen (13.5) and Treppchen (7.5); Neumagener Rosengärtchen (8); Leiwener Laurentiuslay (10).

Weingut Geschwister Ehses-Berres Zeltingen/Mosel. 2 acres including Zeltinger – Sonnenuhr and Schlossberg.

Weingut Dr. J. B. Hain Neumagen-Dhron/Mosel. 7.25 acres including Einzellagen: Dhroner Häschen; Piesporter Goldtröpfchen; Neumagener Rosengärtchen.

Weingut Der Josephshof Graach/Mosel. Einzellagen: Josephshöfer (15); Graacher Himmelreich (2.7); Bernkastler – Doktor (0.37) and Stephanus-Rosengärtchen (5); Zeltinger Sonnenuhr (0.4).

Apollinar Joseph Koch Wiltingen/Saar. Einzellagen: Scharzhofberg (5); Wiltinger Gottessfuss (5). One of the great names of the Saar.

Felix Müller Wiltingen/Saar. Einzellagen: Scharzhofberg (2.5); Wiltinger Rosenberg (3). Classic Saar production makes wines of elegance and ripeness.

Weingut Oberemmeler Abteihof Oberemmel/Saar. Einzellagen: Menniger – Herrenberg (11.8) and Euchariusberg (6.5); Scharzhofberg (7.5); Oberemmeler – Karlsberg (20.5), Rosenberg (9) and Agritiusberg (6).

Weingut Kaseler St. Irminenhof Kasel/Ruwer. Einzellagen: Kaseler – Nies'chen (9), Herrenberg (5) and Hitzlay (6.5); Waldracher Heiligenhäuschen (14.8).

Staatsminister a.D. Otto van Volxem Oberemmel/Saar. 7 acres including Scharzhofberg (4.5).

Weingut J. Lauerburg

5550 Bernkastel. Owner: Karl-Heinz Lauerburg. 10 acres. Einzellagen: Bernkasteler – Schlossberg, Johannisbrünnchen, Badstube, Matheisbildchen, Lay, Bratenhöfchen and Doktor; Wehlener Sonnenuhr; Graacher Himmelreich.

A small but very prestigious family estate founded in 1700 (when the cellars were dug under the vineyards). 100% Riesling, making wines intended for considerable bottle-ageing. Prices: from DM 5.00.

Rudolf Müller GmbH & Co. KG

Postfach 20, 5586 Reil. Managing Directors: Walter Müller and Dr. Richard Müller. 32.5 acres. Einzellagen: Reiler – Moullay-Hofberg, Sorentberg, Goldlay and Falklay; Ockfener – Bockstein, Herrenberg and Geisberg; Scharzhofberg; Saarburger Antoniusbrunnen; Kanzemer Sonnenberg; Ürziger Würzgarten.

Best known for its brand of Bereich Bernkastel, 'The Bishop of Riesling'. Frau Müller's mother was a Thanisch and left her half of the famous Bernkastel estate. The company's base is now a new cellar and 'Splendid-Sektkellerei' at Kinheim.

Weingut Egon Müller-Scharzhof

5511 Wiltingen. Owner: Egon Müller.

See facing page.

Nicolay'sche Weingutsverwaltung

Würzgartenstrasse 41, Postfach 130, 5564 Ürzig. Owners: Helga Pauly-Berres, Alfred Berres and Dr. Peter Pauly. 37 acres. Einzellagen: Ürziger – Würzgarten and Goldwingert (solely owned); Erdener – Treppchen, Herrenberg and Prälat; Zeltinger – Himmelreich and Deutschherrenberg; Wehlener Klosterberg; Kinheimer Hubertuslay.

Peter Nicolay was a famous innkeeper of a century ago. The Berres family are his descendants, now connected by marriage to the Paulys who own Zach. Bergweiler-Prüm Erben of Bernkastel. The Chairman is Dr. Karl Christoffel, a senior wine-book author. 60% of the estate is on steep slopes; 92% is Riesling. The wines are matured as individuals in oak and offer the full spectrum of styles that come from the bend in the Mosel from Wehlen to Kinheim. Prices: DM 5.00–11.00.

Weingut der Pfarrkirche

Bernkastel, 5559 Longuich. Owner: Kath. Kirchengemeinde. About 26 acres. Einzellagen: Bernkasteler – Graben, Lay, Bratenhöfchen, Schlossberg and Johannisbrünnchen; Graacher Himmelreich.

The old estate of the parish church, now run by Schmitt Söhne of Longuich. The vines are on the steep slaty slopes which give a particular smack of the soil to good Bernkastel. Price: DM 4.00.

EGON MÜLLER

A great Saar estate

German wine-making at its highest level can best be described as wine for wine's sake. In a fine vintage the producer is almost passive, like a painter before a sunset. Rather than try to mould the vintage to his preconceived ideal he is dedicated to interpreting what nature provides. If one man embodies this approach to wine it is Egon Müller, the owner of the Scharzhof Manor at Wiltingen on the Saar and 27.5 acres of the steep Scharzhofberg above it. His late-picked wines regularly fetch the highest prices at the annual auction of 'The Ring' of the best Mosel growers at Trier. Egon Müller's great-great-grandfather bought the estate, formerly church land like so much of Germany's best, when it was secularized under Napoleon. It is very much the old family house, its hall lined with trophies of the chase and its library with leather-bound books. A tasting of the new vintage with Egon Müller takes place in the half-light of the hall, standing at a round table with a ring of green bottles and little tumblers.

The Riesling he grows on the steep grey schist of the Scharzhofberg is Riesling in its naked purity. Only Kabinett and better wines are made with the estate name, and each is fermented apart in its own cask. The samples at the tasting are of different casks. As the late part of the harvest approaches the differences between casks increase. The Kabinetts will probably all be bottled as one wine, but Spätleses may be kept in separate lots, and there may be five or six different Ausleses as each day's ripening intensifies the honeyed sweetness of the latest wines. It is very rare in the cold Saar vineyards to have grapes ripe enough for a Beerenauslese; Trockenbeerenausleses are rarer still. But a gold-topped Auslese (once called a feinste Auslese) from Egon Müller has as much penetrating perfume, vitality and 'breeding' as any wine in Germany. Its measured sweetness is matched with such racy acidity that the young wine may almost make you wince. Yet time harmonizes the extremes into a perfectly pitched unity, a teasing, tingling lusciousness that only Riesling, only the Saar, only the Scharzhofberg can achieve.

Weingut J. J. Prüm

5554 Wehlen. 34 acres. Owner: Dr. Manfred Prüm. Einzellagen: Wehlener – Sonnenuhr (11), Klosterberg and Nonnenberg; Graacher – Himmelreich and Domprobst; Zeltinger Sonnenuhr; Bernkasteler – Bratenhöfchen and Lay.

The most famous family of growers of the Middle Mosel, with records going back to the 12th century. Johann Josef Prüm developed the present estate, dying in 1944; his son Sebastian (d. 1969) was an equally renowned grower. Sebastian's son Manfred is now in charge. The estate house, down by the river, looks up to the great Sonnenuhr vineyard, of which it has one of the largest holdings, across the water. The huge sundials among the vines here and in Zeltingen were built by an earlier Prüm. The estate's signature is wine of glorious honeyed ripeness, setting off the raciness of Riesling grown on slate with deep notes of spice and honey. Its reputation was at its zenith in the 1950s and 1960s.

Weingut S.A. Prüm Erben, S.A. Prüm

Uferallee 25–36, 5550 Bernkastel-Wehlen. Owner: Raimund Prüm. 12.5 acres. Einzellagen: Wehlener – Sonnenuhr, Klosterberg and Nonnenberg; Bernkasteler – Badstube and Johannisbrünnchen; Graacher – Himmelreich and Domprobst; Zeltinger Schlossberg.

Part of the great Prüm estate which became separate in 1911, was divided into 6 parts in 1964 but has since been partially reconstituted and recently enlarged. The third generation since 1911 took over in 1981. The wines are made with great emphasis on the character of each cask. The biggest holding (5 acres) is Wehlener Sonnenuhr – a dry Spätlese of 1979 was outstanding.

Franz Reh & Söhn GmbH & Co. KG

Römerstrasse 27, 5559 Leiwen. President: Herbert Reh. Two estates with about 32 acres. Einzellagen: Leiwener – Laurentiuslay and Klostergarten; Trittenheimer – Apotheke and Altärchen; Piesporter – Goldtröpfchen and Gärtchen (solely owned); Dhroner Hofberger; Klüsserather Bruderschaft; Piesporter – Günterslay and Treppchen.

A highly successful and fast-growing merchant house with the brands Kellerprinz, Klosterprinz and Hockprinz, shipping 1m. cases a year. Also the owners of 2 estates, Josefinengrund at Leiwen and Marienhof at Piesport. Prices: from DM. 3.00.

Weingut Edmund Reverchon

Saartalstrasse 3, 5503 Konz. Owner: Eddie Reverchon. 62 acres. Einzellagen: Filzener – Steinberger, Urbelt and Herrenberg (solely owned); Wiltinger – Gottesfuss and Klosterberg; Okfener – Bockstein and Geisberg; Kanzemer Altenberg; Karthäuser Klosterberg.

The friendly family estate of the Reverchons, based at Konz near the confluence of the Saar and the Mosel. Light, *spritzig* wines with high acidity, 50% Riesling, others Müller-Thurgau and Scheurebe. Filzener Herrenberg is the pride of the house – from Sekt to Gold-capsuled Ausleses. Prices (1981): DM 3.50 – 23.00.

Weingut Adolf Rheinart Erben

Weinstrasse 25, 5559 Longuich. Director: Heinzgünter Schmitt. 26 acres. Einzellagen: Schodener–Saarfeilser-Marienberg; Ockfener – Bockstein and Herrenberg; Ayler Kupp; Wiltinger Schlangengraben.

A well-known name on the Saar with some 26 acres, all on good sloping sites, now owned by Schmitt Söhne of Longuich. 80% is Riesling; 20% new varieties. Ockfener Bockstein produces the estate's best wine.

Weinkellerei H. Schmitt Söhne

Weinstrasse 8, 5559 Longuich. Director: Gerd Schmitt.

Big-scale wine merchants with a turnover of 2.5m. cases a year. They own 3 properties: G. Schmitt-Schenk'sches at 5559 Longuich, Weingut Petershof at 5501 Waldrach on the Ruwer and Adolf Rheinart Erben on the Saar, and have contracts with 1,000 small growers who deliver grapes to 6 press houses. They also manage the parish church (Pfarrkirche) properties at Bernkastel. Their brand-names include Kurprinz and Jägerschoppen.

Michel Schneider Nachf.

Merlerstrasse 28, 5583 Zell. Owner: Franz Schneider. 150 acres. Einzellagen: Wehlener – Abtei, Klosterhofgut and Hofberg (74 acres solely owned); Zeller Marienburger (42); Merler – Königslay-Terrassen, Adler, Sonneck and Klosterberg; Zeller – Nussberg and Petersborn.

Half the property is in Wehlen and half divided between Zell and Merl on the Lower Mosel. The Schneider family, growers in Zell since 1869, bought and painstakingly restored an old Cistercian property, Kloster Machern at Wehlen, in 1969. The Wehlen estate is 100% Riesling and the entire property 75% Riesling, 10% Müller-Thurgau and 15% new varieties. Most of the wines are made in the popular medium-sweet style.

Hermann Freiherr von Schorlemer GmbH

5550 Bernkastel-Kues. Owners: The Meyer family. Manager: Herbert Longen. 116 acres in the Mosel and Saar with 5 estates in Lieser, Zeltingen and Graach, Wehlen and Bernkastel, Wiltingen and Ockfen.

One of the largest old family estates on the Mosel, with 5 separate properties (listed below) bought from the von Schorlemers in 1969 and 1974 by Peter Meyer, the present President of Meyer-Horne, wine merchants in Bernkastel. 90% is Riesling; all the wines are made in oak. Schloss Lieser, the vast Victorian mansion of the von Schorlemers in their glory, has its best sites in the steep Niederberg-Heldenberg. The firm also produces Riesling Sekt from individual vineyards. Prices: from DM 4.20.

Weingut Clemens Freiherr von Schorlemer Zeltingen and Graach. Einzellagen: Bernkasteler – Schlossberg, Badstube, Kueser Kardinalsberg; Graacher – Himmelreich, Domprobst, Abtsberg; Zeltinger Sonnenuhr.

Weingut Schloss Lieser, Freiherr von Schorlemer Lieser. Einzellagen: Lieserer – Schlossberg, Niederberg-Helden and Süssenberg.

Weingut Meyerhof Graach, Wehlen and Bernkastel.

Weingut Franz Duhr Nachf. Ockfen. Einzellagen: Ockfener Bockstein; Wiltinger Sandberg (solely owned).

Weingut Schlangengraben Wiltingen. Einzellagen: Wiltinger Schlangengraben; Kanzemer Altenberg.

C. von Schubert, Maximin Grünhaus

5501 Grünhaus/Trier. Directors: Andreas and Carl von Schubert (father and son). 80 acres. Einzellagen: Maximin Grünhäuser Bruderberg (10), Herrenberg (42), Abtsberg (28).

The outstanding estate of the Ruwer and one of Germany's greatest, with a unique undivided hill of vines dominating the beautiful, formerly Benedictine-owned manor house, whose cellars go back to Roman times and whose records start in AD 966. It was bought by the von Schubert family in 1882. The bottom 10 acres are called

Bruderberg (for the brothers); the middle to upper 42 Herrenberg (for gentlemen); the finest and steepest middle part of 28 acres Abtsberg (for the Abbot). The estate does not use the local Grosslage name Römerlay but offers all its wines under its own singularly beautiful label. Ausleses and sweeter wines of good vintages are sublime: infinitely subtle but surprisingly spicy and powerful, ageing 20 years or more. Even the lesser wines are a revelation. The average crop is only 50 hl/ha.

Prices of the 1980 vintage for QbA wines reflect the scale: Bruderberg DM 6.40 a bottle, Herrenberg DM 6.80, Abstberg DM 7.20.

Bert Simon, Weingut Herrenberg

5512 Serrig-Saar. Owner: Bert Simon. 80 acres. Einzellagen: Serriger – Herrenberg, Würtzberg and König Johann Berg (each 16 acres solely owned) and Antoniusberg (3); Staadt Maximiner Prälat (12 solely owned); Niedermenniger Sonnenberg (3); Eitelsbacher Marienholz (2.5); Mertesdorfer Herrenberg (2.5); Kaseler – Kehrnagel (10), Nies'chen (0.5) and Herrenberg (0.5).

A dynamic young estate started in 1968 with the purchase of the old von Schorlemer vineyards in Serrig, and enlarged since with 4 more small estates in excellent sites. 85% is Riesling, 8% Müller-Thurgau and 7% Weissburgunder, unusual on the Saar but, Simon finds, good for adding substance to his 'racy' Rieslings.

Weingut Freiherr von Solemacher

551 Saarburg Bez. Trier. Owner: Baron Raitz von Frentz. 13.5 acres. Einzellagen: Saarburger – Bergschlösschen, Antoniusbrunnen and Rausch (12.35); Ockfener – Bockstein and Herrenberg (1.25).

The Baron lives in a castle in the Eifel mountains shown on his label. The Weingut, which was destroyed in World War II, had been in the family for 100 years. 80% is Riesling, 20% Müller-Thurgau. The wines are lively and *spritzig* with natural carbon dioxide, changing character completely in great keeping years such as 1976.

Verwaltung der Staatlichen Weinbaudomänen

Deworastrasse 1, 5500 Trier. Director: Dr. Bruno Sambale. 212 acres. Einzellagen: Avelsbacher – Hammerstein, Rotlay and Kupp (78); Ockfener – Bockstein, Heppenstein and Herrenberg (25); Serriger – Vogelsang, Heiligenborn and Hoeppslei (84); Trierer – St. Maximiner Kreuzberg, Deutschherrenberg and Deutschherrenköpfchen (25).

The immensely impressive estate founded by the King of Prussia in 1896, and bearing his eagle on the label, was largely carved out of oak woods in the Saar valley. 80% of the vineyards are on steep slopes of up to 70° gradient, 85% of the vines are Riesling. Visitors can see the precipitous Serrig estate from a narrow-gauge railway.

The wine is still made in 1,000-litre casks: the splendid vaulted cellars contain 600 of different sizes, as well as bottles going back to the great 1921 vintage, and a dank, mossy chamber where the Director conducts tastings. The range of qualities is wide (it includes Sekt made of Serriger Riesling). There are great stylish steely wines and some rather ordinary ones. Prices: Qualitätswein DM 5.00 – 6.00; Auslese from DM 10.00.

Weingut Wwe. Dr. H. Thanisch

5550 Bernkastel-Kues. Owners: The Dr. H. Thanisch family. 32.5 acres. Einzellagen: Bernkasteler – Doktor, Badstube and Lay; Brauneberger Juffer Sonnenuhr; Graacher Himmelreich; Lieserer Schlossberg.

The family estate (with roots going back to 1650) that made the worldwide reputation of the famous Doktor vineyard at the turn of the century when King Edward VII, visiting Bad Homburg, took a fancy to the name. The grandfather's stately villa of 1880 is still the Gutshaus. 80% of the vines are Riesling, with new varieties only in Lieser, where a new vineyard was bought recently. The cellars are dark dripping caves 100 feet under the slate of the vineyards that produce the most famous Mosel. The standard of wine-making remains impeccable. *See* Rudolf Müller of Reil for the family connection.

Weingut Thiergarten

5500 Trier. Owners: Georg-Fritz and Hildegard von Nell. 40 acres chiefly in Trier. Einzellagen: Trierer-Benediktinerberg (12), Kurfürstenhofberg (13.5), Thiergarten unterm Kreuz (8.5) and Thiergarten Felsköpfchen (3.75); also 2.5 acres in the Saar and 0.6 in Bernkastel.

A former Benedictine manor, bought in 1803 by the von Nells, whose descendants run the small estate personally. Enthusiastic producers of excellent and individual, light and potentially long-lived wines, almost all Riesling except Benediktinerberg, which is 25% Müller-Thurgau. Half the wines are dry or medium-dry.

Güterverwaltung Vereinigte Hospitien

Krahnenufer 19, 5500 Trier. Director: Dr. Hans Pilgram. 111 acres. Vineyards in Serrig, Wiltingen, Scharzhofberg and Kanzem on the Saar; and in Trier, Piesport, Bernkastel, Graach and Zeltingen on the Mosel. Sole ownership of Trierer Augenscheiner, Serriger Schloss Saarfelser Schlossberg, Wiltinger Hölle and Piesporter Schubertslay.

One of the great charitable institutions of Trier, occupying Germany's oldest cellars, built as a Roman warehouse. Napoleon united ('Vereinigte') the numerous charities of Trier in the Benedictine abbey of St. Irminen, which continues to be a free (600-bed) hospital like the Hospices de Beaune, financed by its vineyards and other considerable estates. It takes its label, a gold figure of Sanctus Jacobus (St. James of Compostela) from the medieval hospital incorporated by Napoleon. 84% of the vines are Riesling. The wines are made and matured in cask and include some fine and typical Mosels and Saars, though recently they have tended to be made too sweet for purist taste.

Weingut Bernd van Volxem

5511 Wiltingen a.d. Saar. Owner: Bernd van Volxem. 25 acres. Einzellagen: Wiltinger – Scharzhofberg, Gottesfuss, Klosterberg, Braunfels, Schlangengraben and Schlossberg; Oberemmeler Rosenberg.

A fourth-generation family estate planted with 70% Riesling, 15% Müller-Thurgau and some Kerner, Weissburgunder and Ruländer. Peter van Volxem's finest wines are his Scharzhofbergers and Wiltinger Gottesfuss. He offers a range of ***trocken*** and ***halbtrocken*** wines up to Spätlese level, generally light, crisp and true to Saar style. Prices (1981): DM 5.00 – 9.80.

Zentralkellerei Mosel-Saar-Ruwer

5550 Bernkastel-Kues. Director: Dr. Rudolf Rinck.

The central cooperative for the Mosel-Saar-Ruwer handles daunting quantities, 1.7m. cases, but maintains remarkably high standards. A total of 4,100 growers all over the region deliver their grapes from 5,000 acres: 60% Riesling, 20% Müller-Thurgau and 20% Elbling. Most of the wines are QbA of fresh character, dry or sweet to taste, but some very fine Ausleses have been made. Prices: from DM 3.80.

OTHER PRODUCERS

Weingut Otto Dünweg
Moselstrasse 5-7, 5559 Neumagen-Dhron. 16 acres. Einzellagen: Neumagener – Rosengärtchen, Laudamusberg and Engelgrube; Dhroner Hofberger, Grosser Hengelberg (solely owned) and Roterd; Trittenheimer Apotheke; Piesporter – Goldtröpfchen, Kreuzwingert (solely owned) and Treppchen. The great-grandson of the founder runs this top-quality little estate, which also owns a merchant's business (run by the son and grandson of the owner). The estate is 99% Riesling, the cellars damp, with oak casks, regularly producing medal-winning wines.

Weingut Johann Haart
Trevererstrasse 12, 5555 Piesport. Director: Alfons Haart. 15 acres. Einzellagen: Piesporter– Goldtröpfchen (5), Falkenberg (1.5), Günterslay (2), Treppchen (8). One of the larger Piesport family estates, going back to 1337. Half the property (Treppchen) is on gentle slopes planted with Müller-Thurgau and new varieties. The other half is 100% Riesling and makes classic ripe and honeyed Goldtröpfchen, Falkenberg and Günterslay. From DM 3.80.

Weingut Graf zu Hoensbroech
Klosterbergstrasse 108, 5511 Wiltingen. Owner: Hubert Schmitz. 6 acres. Einzellagen: Wiltinger – Kupp, Braunfels and Klosterberg. The Schmitz family has farmed the old Hoensbroech land since 1948 and bought it in 1968. 80% is Riesling; the best Auslese comes from the Kupp. From DM 4.50.

Carl Aug. Immich-Batterieberg
5585 Enkirch. Owner: Georg Immich. About 11 acres. Einzellagen: Enkircher – Ellergrub, Zeppwingert, Steffensberg and Batterieberg (solely owned). The Immichs have been growers in Enkirch since 1425. Georg Immich qualified at the Geisenheim Wine School and stoutly defends the Mosel traditions of Riesling and oak. From DM 4.60.

Weingut Schlosskellerei Freiherr von Landenberg
Moseluferstrasse, am Kriegerdenkmal, 5591 Ediger-Eller. Owners: Nelly von Landenberg and family. 22 acres. Einzellagen: Ellerer – Bienenlay, Engelströpfchen, Höll, Kapplay, Pfirsichgarten and Calmont; Ediger – Osterlämmchen, Elzhofberg, Stubener Klostersegen; Senheimer – Rosenberg and Lay; Mesenicher Deuslay. The old family of Landenberg keeps 2 hotels in Cochem as well as this popular estate with a wine museum in the old manor house. Vines are 99% Riesling, making full-bodied, positively fruity wine.

Weingut P. Licht-Bergweiler Erben
Bernkastelerstrasse 33, 5551 Brauneberg. Owners: Leo and Ria Licht (father and daughter). About 30 acres. Einzellagen: Brauneberger – Juffer, Hasenläufer, Mandelgraben and Klostergarten; Wehlener Sonnenuhr; Graacher Domprobst; Bernkasteler Johannisbrünnchen. The Licht family inherited this 200-year-old property with traditional methods and cellars. Their finest wines are from the Juffer.

Weingut Karl Loewen
Matthiasstrasse 30, 5559 Leiwen. Owner: Karl Loewen. 12 acres. Einzellagen: Leiwener – Laurentiuslay and Klostergarten; Detzemer Würzgarten and Maximiner Klosterlay; Pölicher Held. The Loewens bought the once monastic land when it was secularized by Napoleon. It includes a very steep slope in the Laurentiuslay where Riesling ripens magnificently. The house speciality is really full, dry Riesling made in the style of centuries ago. From DM 4.00.

Weingüter Benedict Loosen-Erben
Würzgartenstrasse 1, 5564 Ürzig. Owners: Hanni and Hugo Müller. Small growers with 8.5 acres in the best sites of Erden and Ürzig (they own Ürzig's sundial, set in the Würzgarten) and a Weinstube, the Klosterhof, in Ürzig. From DM 4.50.

Weingut J. Matheus-Lehnert
In der Zeill, 5559 Neumagen-Dhron. Owner: Ferdinand Krebs-Matheus. 6 acres. Einzellagen: Piesporter – Goldtröpfchen, Michelsberg and Treppchen; Dhroner Hofberger and Roterd. A fine small property: 90% Riesling and 90% steep slopes. Wood-aged Ausleses from his old vaulted cellar win gold medals locally and nationally. From DM 4.00.

Weingut Milz Laurentiushof
5559 Trittenheim. Owner: Karl Josef Milz. About 25 acres. Einzellagen: Neumagener – Laudamusberg, Rosengärtchen and Nusswingert; Dhroner Hofberger; Trittenheimer – Altärchen, Apotheke, Felsenkopf and Leiterchen (last two solely owned); Ockfener Geisberg. A family house by the church, Milz property since the 17th century. The vines are all Riesling and the wines well-balanced towards dryness. From DM 4.80.

Ökonomierat Max-G. Piedmont
Saarstalstrasse 1, 5503 Konz-Filzen. Owner: Max-G. Piedmont. 15 acres. Einzellagen: Filzener – Pulchen, Urbelt and Steinberger. A fourth-generation family estate in the narrow valley of the lower Saar. 95% is Riesling; stylish dry wines matured in oak. From DM 4.50.

Weingut Schloss Saarstein
5512 Serrig. Owner: Dieter Ebert. 23 acres. Einzellagen: Serriger – Antoniusberg and Schloss Saarsteiner. Ebert is a refugee from East Germany who acquired the property in 1952. 92% is Riesling; typically light and racy Saar wine. From DM 4.60.

Weingut St. Johannishof
Zach. Bergweiler-Prüm Erben and Pet. Loosen Erben. 5550 Bernkastel. Owner: Dr. Peter Loosen. About 25 acres. Einzellagen: Bernkasteler – Doktor, Badstube, Graben and Lay; Graacher Himmelreich; Wehlener – Sonnenuhr and Klosterberg, Ürziger Würzgarten; Erdener – Prälat and Treppchen. This combination of two small properties is planted with 90% Riesling, 90% of which is on the steepest slopes. Some of the best wines come from the little Erdener Prälat right by the river. From DM 5.00.

St. Nikolaus Hospital
Cusanusstift, Cusanusstrasse 2, 5550 Bernkastel-Kues. 20 acres. Einzellagen: Wehlener Sonnenuhr; Graacher Himmelreich; Bernkasteler – Badstube, Bratenhöfchen and Lay; Kueser – Kardinalsberg and Weissenstein (solely owned); Lieserer – Süssenberg and Helden; Brauneberger Juffer. The foundation of the 15th-century theologian and philanthropist Cardinal Nikolaus Cusanus of Kues, whose library is still in the old hospital by the bridge. Purist Rieslings from some superb sites. From DM 5.50.

Weingut Geschwister Selbach-Oster
Uferallee 23, 5553 Zeltingen. Owner: Hans Selbach. 7.5 acres. Einzellagen: Zeltinger – Himmelreich, Schlossberg and Sonnenuhr; Wehlener Klosterberg; Graacher Domprobst; Bernkasteler – Badstube and Schlossberg. The Selbach family, growers since 1661, have leased some excellent old church land in Zeltingen. The wines are oak-matured, generally dry and lively.

Oskar Tobias
5555 Piesport. An outstanding specialist in Piesporter Goldtröpfchen, of which he has some of the finest plots, planted entirely with Riesling.

Weingut Dr. F. Weins-Prüm Erben
Uferallee 20, Bernkastel/Wehlen. Owner: Herr Selbach-Weins. About 17 acres. Einzellagen: Graacher – Himmelreich and Domprobst; Wehlener – Sonnenuhr and Klosterberg; Ürziger Würzgarten; Erdener – Treppchen and Prälat. The cellars of this old property date back to 1560. Its Sonnenuhr and Prälat Rieslings are in particular demand. From DM 5.00.

AHR AND MITTELRHEIN

Perverse as it seems, Germany's northernmost wine region specializes in red wine. The Ahr is a western tributary of the Mittelrhein, not far south of Bonn, whose steep sides are clothed almost continuously in vines for ten miles: 1,000 acres, of which 30% is Spätburgunder, 30% Portugieser and other red grapes, and 40% Riesling and Müller-Thurgau.

The white wines, when ripe, have a distinct aromatic lilt which is very attractive. Real ripeness for red grapes is almost impossible here. The wine is pale and thin, often made distinctly sweet, and would probably be extinct were it not for the beauty of the valley, the nearness of large rich centres of population, and the German fondness of a walk in the vineyard followed by an evening in a snug little restaurant drinking the proprietor's wine.

No less than 900 small growers till the soil, most of them banded into seven cooperatives, but a hundred or so making and selling their own wine. There is only one Grosslage name: Klosterberg, covering the 11 villages and 43 Einzellagen.

Mittelrhein

A more logical name for this spectacular but dwindling wine region would be the Lower Rhine. It is exactly analogous to the Lower Mosel – the part of the river downstream from the classic sites, where custom (and extraordinary effort) maintain a narrow necklace of vineyards on the immediate riverside slopes – and sometimes cliffs. There are 1,900 acres of vines along some 60 miles of river, starting near Oberdiebach on the left bank, almost opposite Assmannshausen, the last of the Rheingau, and wriggling north on either or both sides of the river as far as Königswinter.

Riesling is the principal grape of the morsels of vineyard that cling to the hills. It makes good, usually austere and even sharp wine, used in good vintages in the Weinstuben of its growers and in poor ones for processing as Sekt.

The Mittelrhein has 11 Grosslagen, in order following the river: Schloss Reichenstein (villages: Trechtingshausen, Niederheimbach, Oberheimbach); Schloss Stahleck (villages: Oberdiebach, Manubach, Bacharach, Bacharach-Steeg); Herrenberg (villages: Kaub, Dörscheid); Schloss Schönburg (villages: Perscheid, Langscheid, Dellhofen, Oberwesel, Damscheid, Niederburg, Urbar); Loreleyfelsen (villages: Bornich, St. Goarshausen, Patersberg, Nochern, Kestert, Kamp-Bornhofen); Burg Rheinfels (villages: St. Goar, St. Goar-Werlau); Gedeonseck (villages: Boppard, Spay, Brey, Rhens); Marksburg (villages: Filsen, Osterspai, Braubach, Lahnstein, Koblenz, Koblenz-Ehrenbreitstein, Urbar, Vallendar); Lahntal (villages: Obernhof, Weinähr, Nassau, Dausenau, Bad Ems, Fachbach); Hammerstein (villages: Leutesdorf, Hammerstein, Rheinbrohl, Bad Hönningen, Leubsdorf, Dattenberg, Linz, Kasbach, Unkel); Petersberg (villages: Rhöndorf, Königswinter, Niederdollendorf, Oberdollendorf).

AHR AND MITTELRHEIN PRODUCERS

Weingut-Weinkellerei Adeneuer
5483 Ahrweiler. Owner: Marianne Adeneuer. 12 acres. Einzellage: Walporzheimer Gärkammer (solely owned). A complete red-wine specialist with 500 years of tradition in the family. 60% Spätburgunder, 40% Portugieser, producing wines as stylish as any on the Ahr.

August Perll
Oberstrasse 81, 5407 Boppard. Mittelrhein. 9 acres. Einzellage: Bopparder Hamm. A small grower of Riesling on the vertiginous slopes of the Boppard bend of the Rhine. Dry wines of character.

Jakob Sebastian Nachf.
Brückenstrasse 111, 5481 Rech/Ahr. 12 acres. Einzellagen: Heppinger Berg; Neuenahrer Sonnenberg; Ahrweiler Daubhaus; Walporzheimer Kräuterberg; Dernauer Burggarten; Recher – Hardtberg, Blume and Herrenberg; Mayschosser – Silberberg, Mönchberg, Burgberg and Schieferlay. An old wine-growing family with a complicated little red-wine estate (of which it owns 70%). The Mayschoss vines are rented from Fürst von Arenberg. Heppingen, with heavier soil, produces the 'biggest' wines; most are Kabinetts ranging from very light to quite firm and dry. The Sebastians are also wholesale merchants.

Staatliche Weinbaudomän Kloster Marienthal
5483 Bad Neuenahr-Ahrweiler. 50 acres. Einzellagen: Marienthaler – Klostergarten and Stiftsberg; Walporzheimer – Pfaffenberg, Himmelchen, Alte Lay and Kräuterberg; Ahrweiler – Rosenthal and Silberberg. Grosslage: Klosterberg. Vines are 58% Spätburgunder, 15% Portugieser, 22% experimental red-wine varieties. An Augustinian convent from the 12th to the 19th century; now the model Ahr estate producing the most prestigious reds, including many Ausleses – a taste which has no equivalent abroad.

Weingut Jean Stodden
5481 Rech/Ahr. 10 acres. Einzellagen: Mayschosser Mönchberg; Dernauer Burggarten; Recher – Blume, Hardtberg and Herrenberg. A little estate, merchant-house and distillery for four generations; 35% Portugieser, 25% Spätburgunder, 30% Riesling, 10% Müller-Thurgau. Its Portugieser is very light, Spätburgunder in good years warm and 'fiery', Riesling quite sharp and Müller-Thurgau mild. Steep slopes and slate are the secret of the best sites.

Weingut Heinrich Weiler
Mainzerstrasse 2-3, 6532 Oberwesel am Rhein. Mittelrhein. 12 acres. Einzellagen: Oberweseler – Römerkrug and St. Martinsberg; Engeholler Goldemund; Kauber – Backofen and Rosstein (solely owned). Perhaps the best-known property of this lovely part of the Rhine valley, 80% Riesling, 8% Müller-Thurgau, with steeply terraced slaty vineyards capable of full-flavoured, even fruity Riesling.

RHEINGAU

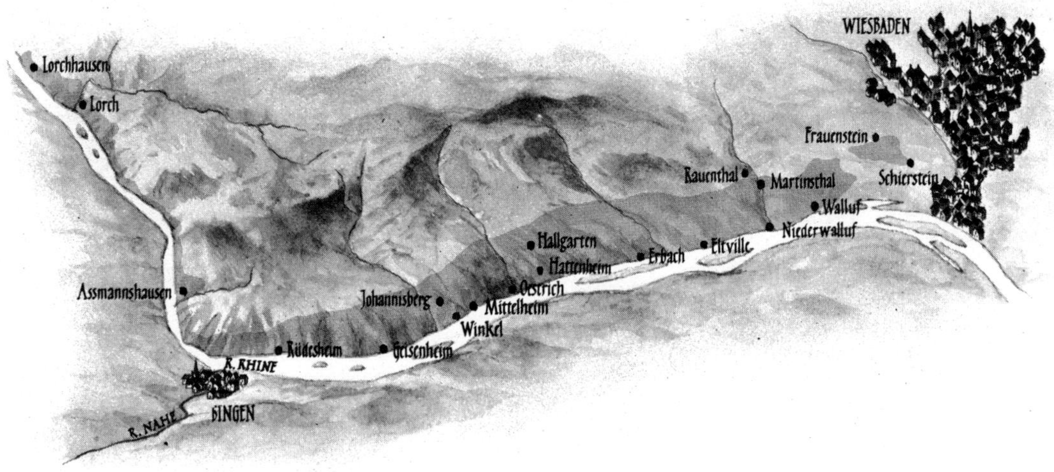

The Rheingau can add to the inherent quality of its wines the merits of consistency and coherence. It is the tidiest major German wine region; 20 miles of monoculture along the north bank of the Rhine, the whole of the short stretch where it flows southwest instead of north, deflected by the tall and sheltering Taunus mountains.

The extremities of the area are Hochheim at the upstream end, overlooking not the Rhine but the tributary Main joining from the east, and Lorch downstream. The heart of it, where vines and urbanization battle it out along the river's busiest shore, is the 20-mile stretch from Walluf to the Rüdesheimer Berg, a towering prow of hill that churns the river into rapids as it fights to turn north once more. The entire region has the Bereich name Johannisberg with Grosslagen: Daubhaus, Steinmächer, Deutelsberg, Erntebringer and Burgweg.

In the minds of its purists (and promoters) Rheingau and Riesling are inextricably linked. Although, in fact, 25 per cent of its vineyards are planted with lesser grapes, the Rheingau owes entirely to the Riesling the force, the cut, the drive and follow-through that make its fine wines the best of the Rhine.

The purest magic is when all this vitality is captured in the relative delicacy and miniature scale of a Kabinett wine. It is not so difficult to be impressive with forceful late-gathered Spätleses or Ausleses. It is when the region is judged on what it can pack into its lightest category of wine that the Rheingau, along with parts of the Mosel, the Nahe and the Rheinpfalz (Palatinate), stands out as one of the world's greatest vineyards.

Hochheim

The vineyards are separated from the main Rheingau by Wiesbaden and many an autobahn. The isolated hillside owes its survival to the strength of character of the wines: full-bodied to the point of coarseness (and immensely long lived) in hot years, but generally combining Riesling finesse with a soft earthiness of their own. The English term 'hock', meaning any Rhine wine, is a contraction of 'hockamore' – an early attempt at pronouncing Hochheimer. 597 acres in Grosslage Daubhaus.

Growers Allendorf. Aschrott. Staatsweingut Eltville. Stadt Frankfurt. Königin Victoria Berg. Schloss Schönborn. Werner.

Wiesbaden

Wiesbaden is not normally seen as a wine name except on the labels of its 11-acre Neroberg. The wines of the rest of its 371 acres are normally bottled under the Grosslage name: Rauenthaler Steinmächer.

Walluf

The little-known village stretches back from the river front up the valley of its stream. Most of its wines, which can be full-flavoured and keep excellently, take advantage of the Grosslage name Rauenthaler Steinmächer.

Growers Arnet. J. B. Becker. Frankensteiner Hof, Espenschied. Richter-Boltendahl.

Martinsthal

The altitude, soil, shelter and orientation of Martinsthal, 600 feet up and a good mile from the river, facing south, are very similar to those of its more famous neighbour Rauenthal. Rauenthal's best sites are steeper, but Martinsthal also makes wines of full, spicy flavour in good vintages. The Grosslage name Steinmächer has not overwhelmed its identity. 193 acres.

Growers Diefenhardt. Frankensteiner Hof, Espenschied. Strigens.

Rauenthal

The Leitgemeinde of the Grosslage Steinmächer lies high on the hill above its skirt of highly prized vineyards. From Baiken and Gehrn the State Domain and others coax bottles of smoothly measured, spicy, notably firm yet almost low-key Ausleses. Drier wines, including Kabinetts, are less distinctive than a Rauenthaler of a very ripe vintage. 242 acres.

Growers J. B. Becker. Diefenhardt. Staatsweingut Eltville. Eser. Frankensteiner Hof, Espenschied. Jonas. Freiherr zu Knyphausen. Langehof. Schloss Rheinhartshausen. Richter-Boltendahl. Schloss Schönborn. Freiherrlich Langwerth von Simmern. Strigens. Sturm.

Eltville

The most substantial town of the Rheingau waterfront, the headquarters of the State Domain and several other important estates, with ample gently sloping vineyards just below the first class in soil and situation, and correspondingly often a better bargain than more exclusive names. 595 acres in Grosslage Steinmächer.

Growers Allendorf. Arnet. J. B. Becker. Belz Erben. Diefenhardt. Staatsweingut Eltville. Schloss Eltz. Landgräflich Hessisches. Jonas. Freiherr zu Knyphausen. Richter-Boltendahl. Freiherrlich Langwerth von Simmern. Strigens.

Kiedrich

The atmospheric old village lies 2 miles up a little valley from Eltville and the river. Thanks to a Victorian English benefactor, its Gothic church of rosy stone is still resplendent with Gregorian sounds. Vinously, Kiedrich occupies a place just behind Rauenthal, also needing the ripeness of a good vintage to give the ultimate vitality to its flavour. 425 acres in Grosslagen Heiligenstock and Steinmächer.

Growers Belz Erben. Schloss Groenesteyn. Jonas. Freiherr zu Knyphausen. Landgräflich Hessisches. Lamm-Jung. Hans Lang. Nikolai. Robert von Oetinger. Schloss Reinhartshausen. Richter-Boltendahl. Georg Sohlbach. Steinmacher-Prinz. Strigens. Tillmanns Erben. Wagner-Weritz. Dr. R. Weil.

Erbach

The town is like a western continuation of Eltville, but lapped round with vineyards on every side. Strangely, here it is not the apparently best-sited vineyards tilting up behind the town that produce the best wine but a low-lying strip by the river (and the railway) with deep, fat, marly soil, suggesting by its position that it is both a frost trap and a swamp after rain. It is neither, but bears the name of Marcobrunn; for centuries a synonym for luxuriously full and high-flavoured hock. In fact, the drainage is excellent, the 5-degree slope sufficient and the whole of this stretch of riverbank a suntrap. Erbach used to share the vineyard, then simply known as Marcobrunner, with its neighbour Hattenheim. They now share the Grosslage name Deutelsberg. 666 acres.

Growers Freiherr zu Knyphausen. Lamm-Jung. Nikolai. Robert von Oetinger. Schloss Reinhartshausen. Richter-Boltendahl. Schloss Schönborn. Freiherrlich Langwerth von Simmern. Tillmanns Erben. Wagner-Weritz.

Hattenheim

The name of Hattenheim is not as celebrated as its great vineyards deserve. Down by the river, round the lovely little timbered town, Mannberg, Wisselbrunnen and Nussbrunnen share the suntrap qualities of Marcobrunn. High on the hill behind is perhaps the most famous vineyard in Germany, the Steinberg. (As an Ortsteil it omits the Gemeinde name.) Behind the Steinberg, up the wooded coomb of the purling Erbach, lies Kloster Eberbach, the great Cistercian monastery belonging to the State Domain, now effectively the ceremonial headquarters of the German wine industry.

The wines of Hattenheim thus range from the sensuous, smooth and subtly spicy products of the riverside to the martial harmonies of the Steinberg. The great walled vineyard was chosen 700 years ago by the monks for its exposure high on the flank of the hill on stony ground. They were looking for power and concentration, which with Riesling means steel as well as scent. The State Domain has recently been testing some of the new grape varieties in the Steinberg, producing wines of almost outrageous perfume. Steinberger Riesling needs time. Its harshness sometimes fights with sweetness for years before the harmonies emerge. 568 acres in Grosslage Deutelsberg.

Growers Staatsweingut Eltville. Engelmann. August Eser. Vereinigte Weingutsbesitzer Hallgarten. Freiherr zu Knyphausen. Hans Lang. Schloss Reinhartshausen. Balthasar Ress. Richter-Boltendahl. Schloss Schönborn. Freiherrlich Langwerth von Simmern. Tillmans Erben. Wagner-Weritz.

Hallgarten

Hallgarten continues the succession of upland villages from Rauenthal and Kiedrich, here rising to the Rheingau's highest point: vines in the Hendelberg are more than 700 feet above the river. With less mist and less frost than below, cooler nights, more sunshine and wind, combined with alkaline clay in the soil, Hallgarten wines are big-bodied and slow to develop – certainly below the first rank in charm but with some of the attack of Steinbergers. The Grosslage name for these 516 acres of vineyards is Mehrhölzchen.

Growers Allendorf. Deinhard. Engelmann. August Eser. Vereinigte Weingutsbesitzer Hallgarten. Nikolai. Riedel. Oswald Rühl Erben. Schloss Schönborn.

Oestrich

Nestling snugly along its wharves, Oestrich is the biggest vineyard commune and one of the most reliable names of the middle rank, rising to star quality in Ausleses from the best growers in the Lenchen; wines of sinful, almost oily lusciousness. 1,094 acres in Grosslagen Gottesthal and Mehrhölzchen.

Growers Allendorf. Altenkirch. Basting-Gimbel. Deinhard. August Eser. Vereinigte Weingutsbesitzer Hallgarten. Hupfeld Erben. Kühn. Balthasar Ress. Schloss Schönborn.

Mittelheim

Mittelheim is squeezed between Oestrich and Winkel, while its wines are half in the Winkel Grosslage of Honigberg and half in Erntebringer, going to market as Johannisbergers. Its reputation thus dispersed, wines that proudly bear the name Mittelheim are likely to have character at a reasonable price. 413 acres in Grosslagen Erntebringer and Honigberg.

Growers Allendorf. Deinhard. August Eser. Vereinigte Weingutsbesitzer Hallgarten. Hupfeld Erben. Kühn. Schloss Schönborn.

Winkel

Winkel continues to line the river road with a hugger-mugger blend of buildings and vineyards at the foot of the slopes that lead up to two of the greatest sites on the Rhine: Schloss Johannisberg, obvious on the skyline, and Schloss Vollrads, sheltering discreetly in a fold of the hill at the back of the parish. Schloss Vollrads is the great name of Winkel, but an Ortsteil which sheds no reflected glory on its neighbours. The flag-carrying vineyard for Winkel is its Hasensprung (Hare leap), the eastern flank of the hill of Schloss Johannisberg. It gives very lovely, perfumed and almost delicate wines of infinite nuance and distinction. 650 acres in Grosslagen Erntebringer and Honigberg.

Growers Allendorf. Basting-Gimbel. Baron von Brentano. Deinhard. August Eser. Landgräflich Hessisches. Johannisberger Rosenhof. Johannishof. G. H. von Mumm. Schloss Schönborn. Freiherr von Zwierlein.

Johannisberg

Johannisberg is the village behind the famous Schloss. It is also the Bereich name for the entire Rheingau. California vintners call their Rieslings after it. In fact, it must be the most borrowed name in Germany. What is its special quality? The situation of Schloss Johannisberg, dominating the river from a sort of saluting base of its own, explains itself.

The wines of Schloss Johannisberg inevitably have a hard time living up to their reputation. The competition from the neighbours, moreover, could hardly be fiercer in this area where ancient and noble estates are the rule rather than the exception. There is considerable justice in looking on Johannisberg as the epitome of the Rheingau; the place where all its qualities of vitality, spice, delicacy and grace come together. 291 acres in Grosslage Erntebringer.

Growers Fritz Allendorf. Deinhard. Landgräflich Hessisches. Hupfeld Erben. Schloss Johannisberg. Johannisberger Rosenhof. Johannishof. G. H. von Mumm. Balthasar Ress. Schloss Schönborn. Hof Sonneck.

Geisenheim

The riverside town below Johannisberg is known by name as much for its research and teaching institute, the H.Q. of German viticulture, grape breeding and oenology, as for its excellent vineyards, only a little, if at all, below the best in potential. The Rothenberg, a modest mountain above the centre of the town, has produced Rieslings whose perfume has driven me almost to ecstasy. Fuchsberg (where the experimental plots of the Institute are) and Mäuerchen, higher on the hill on the way to Rüdesheim, have almost ideal situations and soil – though Fuchsberg can be struck by untimely frosts. 1,057 acres in Grosslagen Burgweg and Erntebringer.

Growers Allendorf. Basting-Gimbel. Deinhard. Institut für Kellerwirtschaft der Forschungsanstalt Geisenheim. Hessische Forschungsanstalt. Landgräflich Hessisches. Holschier. Johannishof. G. H. von Mumm. Balthasar Ress. Schloss Schönborn. Vollmer. von Zwierlein.

Rüdesheim

Rüdesheim brings the main block of the Rheingau to a triumphant close. Here the crest of the Taunus mountains closes in on the river and squeezes the vineyards into steeper and steeper formation. The town is the tourist centre of the Rheingau, with a summer population it is pleasanter to avoid (but with a very useful car ferry to Bingen).

The vineyards west of the town, becoming steeper and narrower as they approach the river bend, carry the distinctive name of Berg after Rüdesheimer and before their individual names. Until recently they were terraced in tortuous steps and ramps, impossible to work except by hand. An astonishingly bold Flurbereinigung relandscaped the whole hillside. For a while bulldozers looked as if they would roll into the river. Now all is orderly again and the Berg wines once more the ripest, strongest, most concentrated (if not the subtlest) of the Rhine. 724 acres in Grosslage Burgweg.

Growers Allendorf. Altenkirch. Basting-Gimbel. Breuer. Deinhard. Staatsweingut Eltville. August Eser. Frankensteiner Hof, Espenschied. Hessische Forschungsanstalt. Schloss Groenesteyn. Landgräflich Hessisches. Holschier. Carl Jung. Jacob Lill IV. G. H. von Mumm. Nägler. Schloss Reinhartshausen. Balthasar Ress. Schlotter. Schloss Schönborn.

Assmannshausen

Everything changes at the Rüdesheim bend – even the colour of the wine. The village of Assmannshausen, with its sheltered valley of vines giving west on to the river, is two thirds planted with Spätburgunder to produce a red which at best is pallid and at worst pink. It has little appeal to foreigners, but the German cognoscenti dote on it.

The State Domain (at Eltville) is the principal producer, obtaining remarkable prices for sweet Ausleses of a disconcerting colour. The sweetness helps to mask the lack of a kernel of real Pinot Noir flavour which is common to all German reds. 430 acres in Groslagen Steil and Burgweg.

Growers Allendorf. Staatsweingut Eltville. König. G. H. von Mumm. Schlotter.

Lorch and Lorchhausen

These villages are the transition from Rheingau to Mittelrhein – though still within the Rüdesheim Grosslage, Burgweg. The best growers produce very creditable Riesling even without the natural advantages of the Rheingau. 449 acres.

Growers Lorch: Altenkirch. Graf von Kanitz. Schloss Schönborn. Lorchhausen: Schloss Schönborn.

Sekt

Germany has found a way of turning her awkward excesses of under-ripe wine, the inevitable result of her northerly situation, into pleasure and profit. They make the ideal base material for her national sparkling wine, Sekt. Sekt may be either champagne-method (*flaschengarüng*) or tank fermented, may be made of any grapes from any region and may even include imported wines.

All the better Sekts, however, fall within the German wine laws as either Qualitätswein or Qualitätswein mit Prädikat (which means of course that the wine must be entirely German). Many of the best specify that they are entirely Riesling wines and some specify their exact origins. There is, in fact, a huge range of qualities from the banal to the extremely fine. The best examples have nothing in common with champagne except bubbles: their flavour is essentially flowery and fruity with the inimitable Riesling aroma in place of champagne's mingled fruits and yeast and age. The principal producers are: Deinhard & Co., Koblenz. Faber Sektkellerei Faber, Trier. Fürst von Metternich, Johannisberg. Henkell & Co., Wiesbaden. Peter Herres, Trier. Christian Adalbert Kupferberg, Mainz. Matheus Müller, Eltville. Schloss Böchingen, Böchingen. Schloss Saarfels Sektkellerei Spicka, Serrig/Saar. Söhnlein Rheingold, Wiesbaden.

RHEINGAU PRODUCERS

Geheimrat Aschrott'sche Erben Weingutsverwaltung

Kirchstrasse 38, 6203 Hochheim am Main. Director: Holger Schwab. 39.2 acres. Einzellagen: Hochheimer – Kirchenstück, Domdechaney, Hölle, Stielweg and Reichstal.

Along with Domdechant Werner (q.v.), the other major all-Hochheim property. 90% is Riesling, 10% Reichensteiner, Ruländer and Müller-Thurgau. The wines are typical Hochheimers: powerful and succulent from their fertile soil and southern slopes. The Aschrott family established itself in 1823 but the 6 owners now live in England and Australia. Prices: from DM 4.40.

Baron von Brentano'sche Gutsverwaltung Winkel

Am Lindenplatz 2, 6227 Oestrich-Winkel. Owner: Udo, Baron von Brentano. 25 acres. Einzellagen: Winkeler – Hasensprung, Jesuitengarten, Gutenberg and Dachsberg.

A relatively small family estate since 1804, entirely in Winkel, proud of its historic associations with Goethe, Beethoven and the romantic literary and artistic life of the Rhine in Imperial times. Goethe's profile appears in blue on the label of selected 'Goethewein' from the Hasensprung and Jesuitengarten. The estate is 97% Riesling and maintains old-fashioned high standards in a museum-like atmosphere. Prices: from DM 5.00.

Weingut des Hauses Deinhard (Gutsverwaltung J. Wegeler Erben)

Friedensplatz 9, 6227 Oestrich-Winkel. 138 acres. Einzellagen: Oestricher – Lenchen, Doosberg and Klosterberg (42 acres); Hallgartener Schönhell (2.5); Mittelheimer – Edelmann and St. Nikolaus (22); Winkeler – Hasensprung and Jesuitengarten (10); Johannisberger Hölle (1.5); Geisenheimer – Rothenberg, Kläuserweg and Schlossgarten (37); Rüdesheimer – Magdalenenkreuz, Bischofsberg, Berg Rottland, Berg Schlossberg and Berg Roseneck (23).

The very substantial Rheingau estate of the Koblenz merchant house of Deinhard, assembled by Geheimer Rat (Counsellor) Wegeler, a Deinhard partner and cousin, a century ago. 88% is Riesling, 6% Müller-Thurgau, 6% Scheurebe, Ruländer, Gewürztraminer and others. 30% of the estate is on steep slopes. With an average crop of 70–75 hl/ha the average production is 35,000 cases.

Deinhards are known for their old-fashioned devotion to quality. Karl-Felix Wegeler is in charge. The Wegeler wines are true individuals; the best (especially from Oestricher Lenchen, Winkeler Hasensprung, Geisenheimer Rothenberg and the vineyards on the Rüdesheimer Berg) are often long-lived classics. Since 1970 Eisweins have been a house speciality.

Altogether one of the biggest and most reliable Rheingau producers. On the export market the wines are sold as 'estate-bottled' Deinhard.

Verwaltung der Staatsweingüter Eltville

Schwalbacherstrasse 56-62, 6228 Eltville. Director: Dr. Hans Ambrosi. 480 acres in Assmannshausen (principally for red wine), Rüdesheim, Hattenheim, the Steinberg, Rauenthal, Hochheim and Bensheim/Heppenheim (the last outside the Rheingau on the Hessische Bergstrasse between Darmstadt and Heidelberg). Einzellagen: Assmannshäuser Höllenberg (51 acres); Rüdesheimer – Berg Schlossberg, Berg Rottland, Berg Roseneck and Bischofsberg (total 51); Hattenheimer – Engelmannsberg and Mannberg, and Erbacher Marcobrunn (33); Steinberger (79); Rauenthaler – Baiken, Gehrn, Wülfen and Langenstück; Kiedricher Gräfenberg; Eltviller – Sonnenberg and Taubenberg (99); Hochheimer – Domdechaney, Kirchenstück, Stein and Berg (17); Bensheimer – Streichling, Kalkgasse and Schönberger Herrnwingert, and Heppenheimer Steinkopf (77).

The Rheingau State Domain at Eltville is the biggest and perhaps the most prestigious domain in Germany, based on monastic vineyards which were ceded to the Duke of Nassau under Napoleon, thence to the Kingdom of Prussia and now to the State of Hessen, whose capital is nearby Wiesbaden. The 7 estates are administered from an unromantic headquarters at Eltville by Dr. Ambrosi, himself of Romanian origin and one of Germany's best-known wine authors and enthusiasts.

For its ceremonial H.Q. the Domain has the magnificent and perfectly preserved Cistercian abbey of Kloster Eberbach (1135), in a wooded valley behind Hattenheim, and the most famous of its vineyards, the 79-acre Steinberg, a walled 'clos' comparable to the Clos Vougeot (but unlike Vougeot still in one ownership). Kloster Eberbach is the scene of annual auctions of the wines of the Domain and certain of its distinguished neighbours; also of the 10-year-old German Wine Academy, which runs regular courses for amateurs and professionals. It was here that the word 'Cabinet' was first used (for the vintage of 1712) to designate reserve-quality wine – a meaning totally altered by modern laws.

The estates are planted with 75% Riesling, 10% Spätburgunder, 8.5% Müller-Thurgau and 6.5% new varieties. Wine-making methods are extremely modern; there is more stainless steel than oak and wines are bottled very young.

The Domain is immensely impressive and impeccably run, and must be counted as one of the greatest wine estates on earth. Its wines fetch high prices at auction, particularly the Eisweins, which it has made a speciality, and the sweet Assmannshausen reds – although these are rarely seen outside Germany.

The sheer size and complexity of the enterprise may have something to do with the fact that critics no longer find its wines as inspiring as they were. Steinberger should be the Rheingau's greatest wine: a model of Riesling at its most elegant, elusive, thought-provoking. . . . Could it be that modern controls give the cellar-master too many decisions to make?

Schloss Groenesteyn

Postfach 1180, 6229 Kiedrich. Owner: Baron von Ritter zu Groenesteyn. The estate is in 2 parts, 38 acres in Kiedrich and 48 in Rüdesheim. Einzellagen: Kiedricher – Gräfenberg, Wasseros and Sandgrub (Grosslage: Heiligenstock); Rüdesheimer – Berg Rottland, Berg Roseneck, Berg Schlossberg, Bischofsberg, Klosterlay and Magdalenenkreuz (Grosslage: Burgweg).

Another of the lordly estates of the Rheingau, dating from 1400, held by the Barons von Ritter zu Groenesteyn since 1640 and based at their great baroque mansion (the schloss) in Kiedrich, with its cellars in Rüdesheim. Vines are 90% Riesling, 10% Müller-Thurgau. The wines are kept in the old way in individual barrels to encourage variety and nuance, the Kiedrichers delicate and scented; the Rüdesheimers (especially from the Berg sites) fruity and spicy. A wide variety of wines is available from the cellars. Prices from DM 5.00.

Landgräflich Hessisches Weingut

6225 Johannisberg. The estate now consists of 75 acres in Einzellagen Rüdesheimer – Bischofsberg, Berg Rottland and Berg Roseneck; Geisenheimer – Fuchsberg, Mäuerchen and Kläuserweg; Johannisberger – Goldatzel, Hölle, Klaus and Vogelsang; Winkeler – Gutenberg, Jesuitengarten, Dachsberg and Hasensprung; Eltviller – Langenstück, Taubenberg and Sonnenberg; Kiedricher Sandgrub and Rauenthal (where the Grosslage name, Steinmächer, is used).

The Count (Landgraf) of Hessen bought this estate in 1958 from the family of Kommerzienrat Krayer. 85% of the vines are Riesling, with a little Spätburgunder and an unusual (for the Rheingau) speciality, a plot of the spicy Scheurebe in Winkeler Dachsberg, planted by the former manager, Heinz Scheu, son of the famous breeder who introduced the grape in the Rheinpfalz. The present manager is Karl-Heinz Glock. 'Kurhessen' is the brand name for Sekt. The range of wines is wide for a medium-sized estate but the quality is high. Prices: from DM 5.00.

Schloss Johannisberg

Fürst von Metternich-Winneburg'sche Domäne Rentamt, 6222 Geisenheim-Johannisberg. 86.5 acres.

The most famous estate of the Rhine, whose name is often used to designate the true Riesling vine. Its first planting is credited to Charlemagne; the first monastery was built on its hilltop commanding the Rhine in 1100; full flowering came in the 18th century under the Prince-Abbot of Fulda. Its vintage of 1775 was the first to be gathered overripe (the Abbot's messenger having arrived late with permission to pick): the term Spätlese and the appreciation of noble rot are said to have started with this incident.

The estate was secularized under Napoleon and presented in 1816, after the Treaty of Vienna, by the Austrian Emperor to his Chancellor, Prince Metternich, for his diplomatic services. His descendant Prince Paul Alfons von Metternich-Winneburg is still nominally the owner, although the estate is now part of a group controlled by the food tycoon Rudolf August Oetker of Bielefeld, together with the neighbouring von Mumm estate.

In 1942 the monastery-castle (but not its cellar) was destroyed in an air raid. It is now totally rebuilt. The vineyard, in one block on the ideally sloping skirts of the castle hill, is planted entirely in Riesling. Technically it is an Ortsteil – a local entity which needs no Einzellage name. Average production is 70 hl/ha, a potential total of some 27,000 cases. The varying qualities within this mass of wine are designated by two different labels and 10 coloured capsules as well as the usual terminology. Standard wines are labelled with the Metternich coat of arms with capsules ranging from yellow (for QbA) to red (Kabinett), green (Spätlese), pink (Auslese) and pink-gold (Beerenauslese). The other label, with a picture of the estate, has an orange capsule for Kabinett, white for Spätlese, sky-blue for Auslese, blue-gold for Beerenauslese and gold for Trockenbeerenauslese. A third label (in Germany only) carries a landscape and a portrait of the great Prince Metternich. The capsules were originally wax – in German, *Lack*; thus Rotlack equals red seal, Grünlack, green seal, etc. (Coincidentally, the characteristic bouquet of mature Johannisberg is said to be a smell of burning sealing wax.)

At their best Schloss Johannisberg's wines are extraordinarily firm in structure, concentrated and long-lived, with every quality of classic Riesling grown on an exceptional site. I have drunk an 1870 which at a century old was still vigorous and bore traces of its original flavour. Recent wines, like those of several of the great lordly estates, have shown signs of commercialization: lightness and lack of 'grip'. The defence is that few people intend to keep them for maturing.

The majority of Schloss Johannisberg is now drunk abroad and, I fear, by people who have no yardstick to judge it by. Ausleses of 1971 and 1976 were quite properly superb, but this is only as it should be.

Weingut Graf von Kanitz

Rheinstrasse 49, 6223 Lorch. Owner: Count Carl Albrecht von Kanitz. 48 acres. Einzellagen: Lorcher – Schlossberg, Kapellenberg, Krone, Pfaffenwies and Bodental-Steinberg.

An ancient family property on steep slopes of varying soils, from slaty to sandy loam, giving fine but milder, softer wines than the main Rheingau. 90% is Riesling, 4.5% Müller-Thurgau, 2.5% Gewürztraminer and the rest new varieties (Kanzler, Kerner, Ehrenfelser). The inheritance, dating from the 13th century, includes the earliest Renaissance building of the area, the Hilchenhaus in Lorch, now a Weinstube.

Weingut Freiherr zu Knyphausen

Klosterhof Drais, 6228 Eltville. Owner: Gerko, Baron zu Knyphausen. 43 acres. Einzellagen: Erbacher – Marcobrunn, Siegelsberg, Hohenrain, Steinmorgen and Michelmark; Hattenheimer Wisselbrunnen; Kiedricher Sandgrub; Eltviller Taubenberg; Rauenthaler Steinmächer.

A former monastic estate of the Cistercians of Kloster Eberbach, bought in 1818 by the Baron's forebears. 80% is Riesling, 10% Spätburgunder and 10% various white varieties, including Gewürztraminer. The property is run on traditional and personal lines, making full-flavoured wines.

Weingut Königin Victoria Berg

Rheinstrasse 2, 6203 Hochheim. Owner: Irmgard Hupfeld. 12.3 acres. Einzellage: Hochheimer Königin Victoria Berg (solely owned).

Queen Victoria stopped to watch the vintage in this fortunate vineyard on the lower slopes of Hochheim in 1850. The then owners, the Pabstmann family, were not slow to commemorate the visit, getting the Queen's permission to rename the vineyard after her, erecting a Gothic monument and designing the most tinselly (now quite irresistible) label. Deinhards, who sell the wine abroad, go to great lengths to maximize its quality. It is not Hochheim's finest, but full, soft, flowery and just what Queen Victoria might well have enjoyed. The label is printed in black and white for QbA wines, yellow and gold for Trocken wines and glorious Technicolor for QmP wines. Prices: from DM 6.50.

G. H. von Mumm'sches Weingut

Schulstrasse 32, 6225 Johannisberg. Owner: Rudolf August Oetker. 173 acres. The Weingut is sole owner of Johannisberger – Hansenberg (10 acres) and Schwarzenstein (10). Other Einzellagen: Johannisberger – Vogelsang (14), Hölle (9), Mittelhölle (15) and Klaus (3.7); Rüdesheimer – Berg Rottland (3.7), Berg Schlossberg (1.2) and Berg Roseneck (8.6); Assmannshäuser – Höllenberg, Hinterkirch and Frankenthal; Geisenheimer – Mönchspfad, Kilzberg and Kläuserweg; Winkeler – Dachsberg and Hasensprung.

An estate founded on the profits of the legendary 1811 'Comet' vintage, when the banker Peter Mumm of Frankfurt bought the whole crop of Schloss Johannisberg (which was temporarily in the hands of one of Napoleon's marshals, Kellermann). Mumm bought land in Johannisberg and the neighbourhood. In 1957 Rudolf August

Oetker of Bielefeld, famous for his grocery products, bought the property and has much enlarged it to its present 173 acres. 20 acres are planted in Spätburgunder in Assmannshausen; the balance of vines is 100% Riesling.

Oetker also controls Schloss Johannisberg. The technical wine-making side of both properties is now handled at the Mumm cellars; the administration at Schloss Johannisberg.

The Mumm wines have evolved in a modern style with the emphasis on dry and semi-dry categories. The better qualities are still wood-matured and well balanced to age moderately. The estate owns a restaurant at Burg Schwarzenstein, high above Johannisberg, where its wide range of wines is on offer.

Schloss Reinhartshausen

6229 Erbach. Owners: The Princes of Prussia. 165 acres between Erbach and Hattenheim. Einzellagen: Erbacher – Marcobrunn, Schlossberg (solely owned), Siegelsberg, Rheinhell (solely owned), Hohenrain, Steinmorgen, Michelmark and Honigberg; Hattenheimer – Wisselbrunnen and Nussbrunnen; Kiedricher Sandgrub; Rauenthaler – Wülfen; Rüdesheimer Bischofsberg.

The riverside estate of the Prussian royal family; the mansion is now a luxury hotel facing the tranquil green island of Mariannenaue (Rheinhell) across the busy waters of the Rhine. 80% of the estate is Riesling; the rest is divided between Weissburgunder for full-bodied dry wine, Spätburgunder for light red and Weissherbst (rosé), and Gewürztraminer and Kerner (aromatic wines for the table).

The rich loam of Erbach, especially Marcobrunn, gives notably full-bodied wines. The island's wine is also soft and rich. The estate uses traditional casks and maintains a balance between top-quality wines (recently particularly good) and commercial lines, some sold under the subsidiary name 'Prinz von Preussen'. Prices: from DM 5.80.

Balthasar Ress

Rheinallee 7-11, 6229 Hattenheim. Director: Stefan B. Ress. Some 50 acres scattered among good sites. Einzellagen: Rüdesheimer – Berg Rottland, Berg Schlossberg, Bischofsberg, Kirchenpfad, Klosterlay and Magdalenenkreuz (5); Geisenheimer Kläuserweg (9); Hattenheimer – Wisselbrunnen, Nussbrunnen, Hassel, Heiligenberg, Schützenhaus, Engelmannsberg and Rheingarten (16); and small sites in Johannisberg, Hallgarten, Winkel, Oestrich, Erbach, Kiedrich and Hochheim.

A century-old family firm of growers and merchants (under the name Stefan B. Ress). Vines are 83% Riesling, 5% Spätburgunder. In 1978 Ress rented the 10-acre Schloss Reichartshausen, originally Cistercian property but latterly neglected. Ress wines are cleanly made, bottled very early for freshness, balanced in sweetness for modern taste. Each year a modern artist is commissioned to paint a label for a selected Auslese of top quality (e.g. Hattenheimer Wisselbrunnen, Oestricher Doosberg). Prices: from DM 5.00.

Domänenweingut Schloss Schönborn

Hauptstrasse 53, Hattenheim, 6228 Eltville. Owner: Count Dr. Karl von Schönborn-Wiesentheid. 160 acres. Einzellagen: Hattenheimer – Pfaffenberg (15, sole owner), Nussbrunnen (5), Wisselbrunnen (2.5), Engelmannsberg (3.7), Schützenhaus (5); Erbacher Marcobrunn (5); Rauenthaler – Baiken (5), Rothenberg (2) and Wülfen (0.5); Hallgartener Schönhell (1.25); Oestricher Doosberg (32); Mittelheimer St. Nikolaus (3); Winkeler – Dachsberg and Gutenberg (10), Jesuitengarten (2.5) and Hasensprung (7.5); Johannisberger Klaus (10); Geisenheimer – Schlossgarten (8.5), Mäuerchen (2.5), Rothenberg (1.25), Mönchspfad (3.5) and Kläuserweg (2.5); Rüdesheimer – Berg Schlossberg (2.5), Berg Rottland (3.5) and Bischofsberg (2); Lorcher – Krone (2.5), Schlossberg (1.25) and Kapellenberg; Lorchhäuser Seligmacher (0.5); Hochheimer – Domdechaney (3.7), Kirchenstück (6), Hölle (7.5), Stielweg, Reichestal and Sommerheil.

The biggest privately owned estate in the Rheingau, since 1349 in the hands of a family of great political and cultural influence. The present owner lives in his Franconian castles of Pommersfelden and Wiesentheid. The same Director, Domänenrat Robert Englert, has run the wine estates for more than 20 years and his signature appears on the labels.

Critics are divided over the recent performance of Schönborn wines. Some find them beautifully balanced – the ultimate in finesse. Others have described them as the 'Rubens of the Rheingau', while others have found them heavy and oversweetened. They come in vast variety from the central Marcobrunn to Lorch at the extreme west of the region and Hochheim at the extreme east. 91% of the estate is Riesling, 3% Müller-Thurgau, 2.8% Spätburgunder, 2% Weissburgunder (made into a fully dry wine) and 1.2% experimental varieties. All the wines are stored in small casks and should repay keeping in bottle.

Commercialism may have affected parts of the range, but the best Schönborn wines are undoubted Rheingau classics. Prices: from about DM 6.50.

Freiherrlich Langwerth von Simmern'sches Rentamt

Langwerther Hof, Postfach 15, 6228 Eltville. The present Baron Friedrich owns a property held by his family since 1464, now amounting to 100 acres (98% Riesling) in the best sites of Erbach, Hattenheim, Rauenthal and Eltville, including Erbacher Marcobrunn (4); Hattenheimer – Nussbrunnen (16), Mannberg (15) and Rheingarten; Rauenthaler – Baiken (4) and Rothenberg; Eltviller Sonnenberg (26).

The Gutshaus is the beautiful Renaissance Langwerther Hof in the ancient riverside centre of Eltville – one of the loveliest spots in the Rheingau. The richly heraldic (if scarcely legible) red label is one of the most reliable in Germany for classic Riesling, whether dry or sweet, balanced to age for years. Prices: from DM 7.50.

Schloss Vollrads

6227 Oestrich-Winkel.
Owner: Graf Matuschka-Greiffenclau.

Erwein Matuschka-Greiffenclau, an impressively involved young man who presides over this magnificent old estate in the hills a mile above Winkel, is the 29th in a line of Greiffenclaus who have owned estates in Winkel since at least 1100. Their original 'Grey House' in Winkel, one of the oldest in Germany, is now a wine-restaurant. In about 1300 the family built the castle, whose great stone tower symbolizes their estate, accepted as an Ortsteil, a separate entity which uses no commune or Einzellage name. The 116 acres are entirely Riesling, of the old Rheingau strain that gives the 'raciest', relatively light but very long-lived wines. Schloss Vollrads specializes in dry wines with as little residual sugar as possible. On average about half the production of some 20,000 cases is QmP wine, Kabinett or better (34% Kabinett, 10% Spätlese, 2% Auslese and very sweet wines).

Since 1979 the estate has rented the Weingut Fürst Löwenstein, a 42-acre neighbouring princely estate in

Hallgarten (Einzellagen Jungfer, Schönhell and Hendelberg), which produces relatively riper, mellower and more aromatic wines than the austere Vollrads style. Georg Senft, the cellar-master at Vollrads, makes both. The Löwenstein wines are more immediately pleasing: the Vollrads need several years' bottle-age.

The estate has technical and commercial connections with the excellent Bürklin-Wolf and Paul Anheuser estates in Rheinpfalz and Nahe; also an informal link with the Suntory winery in Japan, where Vollrads is well known. Visitors to Vollrads can taste a wide range and by booking can take part in sumptuous 'Lukullische' tastings with appropriate meals from a well-known Mainz restaurant. Count Matuschka leads this gastronomic match-making personally.

Different qualities of the estate's wines are distinguished by an elaborate system of coloured capsules: green for QbA, blue for Kabinett, pink for Spätlese, white for Auslese, gold for Beerenauslese and Trockenbeernauslese, with a code of silver bands for dry wines and gold for sweeter wines.

Weingut Dr. R. Weil

Mühlberg 5, 6229 Kiedrich. Owner: Dr. Robert Weil. 46 acres. Einzellagen: Kiedricher – Sandgrub (13), Wasseros (19), Klosterberg (5) and Gräfenberg (9).

The leading estate of Kiedrich with a fine old reputation for Kiedrich's characteristically spicy delicacy of flavour. The Weils bought the property in 1868, partly from an Englishman, Sir John Sutton, still remembered as a benefactor by the village where he restored the splendid Gothic church and its famous organ. The vintages of the late 1970s have not shown this estate at its best. Prices: from DM 6.00.

Domdechant Werner'sches Weingut

Rathausstrasse 30, 6203 Hochheim. 33 acres Einzellagen: Hochheimer – Domdechaney, Kirchenstück, Hölle, Stielweg, Stein, Sommerheil, Reichestal and Hofmeister.

The Werner family bought this superbly sited manor, overlooking the junction of the Rhine and Main, from the Duke of York in 1780. The buyer's son, Dr. Franz Werner, was the famous Dean (Domdechant) of Mainz who saved the cathedral from destruction by the French. The same family (now called Werner Michel) still owns and runs the estate, making some of the most serious, full-flavoured Hochheimers from the mingled soils of the old river terraces, sloping fully south. Traditional barrel-ageing makes essentially dry but long-flavoured and long-lived wines. Prices: from DM 5.50.

COOPERATIVES

Winzergenossenschaft Hallgarten

Hattenheimerstrasse 15, 6227 Oestrich-Winkel-Hallgarten. 200 members. 250 acres in the excellent Einzellagen Hallgartener – Schönhell, Jungfer, Würzgarten and Hendelberg. The Grosslage name used is Mehrhölzchen.

The substantial local growers' cooperative of Hallgarten. Vines are 85% Riesling, 10% Müller-Thurgau. All the wine is sold in Germany.

Gebietswinzergenossenschaft Rheingau

Erbacherstrasse 31, 6228 Eltville. 310 members. 321 acres scattered through the whole region.

The major cooperative of the Rheingau. 70% of their vines are Riesling, 20% Müller-Thurgau, 7% new white varieties, 3% Spätburgunder. Total production averages 1.1m. cases, 75% sold direct and only 10% exported.

OTHER PRODUCERS

Weingut Fritz Allendorf
Winkel. Owner: Fritz Allendorf. A very old Winkel wine-growing family, more recently established as a substantial estate with 62.5 acres and 37 more rented in Assmannshausen, Rüdesheim, Johannisberg, Geisenheim, Winkel, Oestrich, Mittelheim, Hallgarten, Eltville and Hochheim, planted with 80% Riesling, 10% Spätburgunder, 6% Müller-Thurgau, 4% various others. The biggest holding is 17 acres of Winkeler Jesuitengarten. The wines are full-flavoured and generally dry or medium-dry. From DM 5.20.

Weingut Friedrich Altenkirch
Bingerweg 2, 6223 Lorch. Owner: Peter Breuer. 45.5 acres. Einzellagen: Lörcher – Schlossberg, Kappellenberg, Krone, Pfaffenwies and Bodenthal-Steinberg; Rüdesheimer – Berg Rottland, Magdalenenkreuz and Bischofsberg; Oestricher Doosberg. The former cellars of the 'Schwan' Hotel, immensely deep and long, were taken over in 1973 by Herr Breuer, who has established a successful merchant house and estate. 85% of the latter is Riesling; 6% Spätburgunder, which is increasingly popular. The commercial lines include Altenkirch Sekt. From DM 5.60.

Weingut Basting-Gimbel
Hauptstrasse 70-72, 6227 Winkel. Owner: Gerhard Hofmann. A 400-year-old family estate with about 30 acres in Winkeler – Dachsberg, Gutenberg and Hasensprung; Geisenheimer – Rothenberg, Mönchspfad and Mäuerchen; Oestricher Doosberg; Rüdesheim (Burgweg). 86% is Riesling. QbA wine is sold as (Grosslage) Johannisberger Erntebringer. A serious little commercial house with a good Weinstube.

Weingut Weinkellerei J. B. Becker
Rheinstrasse, 6229 Walluf. Owners: The Becker family (Hannelore, Hans-Josef and Maria). The Becker family of Walluf are well known as brokers as well as growers, the third generation also owning the handsome old Hotel Schwan, with a garden by the river and excellent cooking. Their vineyards now amount to 26 acres in Einzellagen: Wallufer – Walkenberg (14), Berg-Bildstock (3.75) and Oberberg (3.25); Martinsthaler Rödchen (1.5); Rauenthaler Wülfen (0.5); Eltviller Sonnenberg (3). 79.5% is Riesling, 12% Spätburgunder (made into powerful dry red wine in Wallufer Walkenberg) and 8.5% Müller-Thurgau. The Beckers' specialities are dry wines that have great character with remarkable keeping powers.

Weingut C. Belz Erben
Kiedricherstrasse 20, 6228 Eltville. Karl Ries took over his grandfather's estate in 1966 and enlarged it to 25 acres. Einzellagen: Eltviller – Sonnenberg, Taubenberg and Langenstück; Kiedricher Sandgrub; Erbacher Honigberg. 70% is Riesling, 20% Kerner. Riesling makes powerful, aromatic and sweetish wines. From DM 5.20.

Weingut G. Breuer
Grabenstrasse 8, 6220 Rüdesheim am Rhein. Owners: Heinrich and Bernhard Breuer. 20 acres in Rüdesheim: 3.25 in Berg Schlossberg, the rest divided between other Berg sites and the 'Oberfeld'. 80% is Riesling. The Breuers aim for the fine steely acidity the 'Berg' can give. They are also partners in the well-known merchant house of Scholl and Hillebrand (founded 1880) in Rüdesheim.

Diefenhardt'sches Weingut
Hauptstrasse 9-11, 6229 Martinsthal. Owner: Hans-Hermann Seyffardt. 30 acres. Einzellagen: Rauenthaler – Rothenberg and Langenstück;

Martinsthaler – Wildsau, Langenberg and Rödchen; Eltviller Taubenberg. A long-established firm (which furnished the first round-the-world Zeppelin ride in 1929) with 17th-century cellars. 85% is Riesling, 10% Spätburgunder (increasingly popular as a full dry red). Medium-dry Riesling Kabinett, made for bottle-ageing, is characteristic of the house. From DM 4.80.

Schloss Eltz

Eltville 6228. The former 100-acre estate of the Count Eltz, famous since the 17th century and with a lordly mansion on the Rhine in Eltville, fell into financial difficulties in the late 1970s and was taken over by the Hessen state. After an interim period of administration by the Langwerth von Simmern estate, its ignominious (if democratic) end is to be split up into parcels to recompense growers whose vineyards are being destroyed by a new main road.

Weingut Karl Fr. Engelmann

Hallgartenerplatz 2, 6227 Oestrich-Winkel. Owner: Adam Nass. Einzellagen: Hallgartener – Schönhell, Jungfer and Würzgarten; Hattenheimer Schützenhaus. A small estate of only about 11 acres, but producing Hallgarten wines (especially Jungfer Riesling Kabinett) of classic quality.

Weingut August Eser

Friedensplatz 19, 6227 Oestrich-Winkel. Owner: Ludwig Eser. A family estate since 1759, now consisting of 22.5 acres. Einzellagen: Oestricher – Doosberg, Lenchen and Klosterberg; Winkeler – Hasensprung and Gutenberg; Mittelheimer – St. Nikolaus and Edelmann; Rüdesheimer Bischofsberg; Hallgartener – Schönhell and Jungfer; Hattenheimer Engelmannsberg; Rauenthaler – Gehrn and Rothenberg. 90% is Riesling, 6% Ehrenfelser, 4% Müller-Thurgau. Ludwig and Joachim Eser make a full range from dry to sweet, presenting their QmP wines with an 'expertise' – a document carrying a full analysis. Their approach is modern, energetic and wins many prizes.

Frankensteiner Hof Weingut Espenschied

Marktstrasse 14, 6229 Walluf 2. Owner: Klaus Kludas. 11 acres. Einzellagen: Rüdesheimer – Berg Roseneck, Berg Rottland, Berg Schlossberg and Burgweg; Wallufer – Walkenberg, Fitusberg and Berg Bildstock; Rauenthaler – Langenstück and Steinmächer; Martinsthaler – Rödchen and Wildsau. The Espenschied family started in Rüdesheim in the 1780s and bought the Frankenstein house in Walluf at the other end of the Rheingau in 1845. The present owner bought the estate in 1975 and has enlarged it with more vines in Walluf and Rauenthal. 85% is Riesling. The wines are wood-matured, have firm acidity and regularly carry off prizes. From DM 4.40.

Weingut Ökonomierat J. Fischer Erben

6228 Eltville. Owner: Frau Fischer. A small fourth-generation property founded in 1880. Einzellagen: Eltviller – Sonnenberg, Langenstück and Taubenberg; Kiedricher Sandgrub. Vines are 90% Riesling. The Fischers' wines are outstanding models of conservative Rheingau taste, weighty and rich in flavour and made to keep a decade. Their part of the Sandgrub vineyard was formerly called Eltviller Kalbsflicht.

Weingut der Stadt Frankfurt am Main

Aichgasse 11, 6203 Hochheim. 62 acres. Einzellagen: Hochheimer – Berg (1.5), Reichestal (12), Stielweg (9), Domdechaney (2.25) Kirchenstück (6), Sommerheil (4.7), Hofmeister (7.8), Hölle (8) and Stein (7); Frankfurter Lohrberger Hang (3). The wine estates of the city of Frankfurt were taken over from a Carmelite nunnery and a Dominican monastery in 1803. They include the largest holdings in Hochheim and the only vineyard in Frankfurt. QbA and Kabinett wines are 'hearty, *spritzig* and lively'. Spätlese and upwards are dignified with 'noble' flavours. 82% is Riesling. From DM 5.10.

Institut für Kellerwirtschaft der Forschungsanstalt Geisenheim

Blaubachstrasse 19, 6222 Geisenheim. Director: Professor Haubs. About 50 acres. Einzellagen: Geisenheimer Kläuserweg, Fuchsberg, Rothenberg and Mäuerchen; Rüdesheimer Magdalenenkreuz. The Geisenheim School of Oenology produces fine Rieslings and experiments with new varieties, although still using the traditional casks.

Hessische Forschungsanstalt für Wein-, Obst- und Gartenbau

6222 Geisenheim. The horticultural and viticultural departments of the Hessen Technical School have 100 acres of vines in Geisenheimer – Rothenberg, Kläuserweg, Mäuerchen and Fuchsberg (55 acres) and Rüdesheimer – Magdalenenkreuz, Klosterberg, etc. Only 50% is Riesling and much experiment is done with miscellaneous varieties. Standards are extremely high and the wines are reliably true to type – indeed sometimes outstanding.

Weingut Hupfeld Erben

Rheingaustrasse 113, Mittelheim, 6227 Oestrich-Winkel. Owner: Arndt-Richard Hupfeld. 12.35 acres. Einzellagen: Mittelheimer Edelmann and St. Nikolaus; Oestricher – Lenchen and Klosterberg; Winkeler – Jesuitengarten and Hasensprung; Johannisberger – Hölle and Vogelsang. Planted with 85% Riesling; the rest consists of Ehrenfelser, Kerner and Gewürztraminer. Wine growers since 1907 and merchants before that, since the 1940s the Hupfelds have established themselves as a top-quality small estate, aiming for medium-dry balance, and winning regular medals. From DM 5.00.

Weingut Johannishof, Eser

6222 Johannisberg. Owners: Hans Hermann and Elfriede Eser. 44.5 acres. Einzellagen: Johannisberger – Hölle, Klaus, Vogelsang, Schwarzenstein and Goldatzel; Winkeler – Jesuitengarten, Hasensprung and Gutenberg; Geisenheimer – Kläuserweg and Kilzberg. The estate is conspicuous on the road up to Johannisberg for its huge 18th-century wine press by the door. The Esers both come from old growers' families and have made a reputation for powerful and full-flavoured wines. *Flurbereinigung* has recently remodelled the vineyards into areas that can be worked by tractor, but the deep cellars, 10 metres under the hill, are traditional; cold and damp with dark oval casks for maturing wine of character.

Weinbau Heinrich Kühn

Beinerstrasse 14, 6227 Oestrich-Winkel. Owner: Karl-Heinz Kühn. 3 acres. Einzellagen: Oestricher – Lenchen and

Tasting from the cask

Doosberg; Mittelheimer – Edelmann and St. Nikolaus. A tiny part-time business, but a maker of serious prize-winning wines (100% Riesling) specifically for long bottle-ageing.

Weingut Hans Lang
Rheinallee 6, 6228 Eltville-Hattenheim. 28 acres. Einzellagen: Hattenheimer – Schützenhaus (15), Heiligenberg (5), Wisselbrunnen (2.5), Rheingarten and Kiedricher Heiligenstock. A nurseryman, merchant and (since 1959) grower who has expanded rapidly. His style is robust with plenty of character and acidity.

Weingut Langehof
Martinsthalerstrasse 4, 6228 Eltville Rauenthal. Owner: Josef Klein. 5 acres. Einzellagen: Rauenthaler – Langenstück, Wülfen, Rothenberg and Baiken. Small but very keen grower with 90% Riesling on good slopes. Rather dry wines. His 1976 Rothenberg Beerenauslese was a considerable medal winner.

Weingut Dr. Heinrich Nägler
Friedrichstrasse 22, 6220 Rüdesheim. Owner: Dr. Heinrich Nägler. A distinguished small estate specializing in fine Rüdesheimer since the 19th century. 14.5 acres. Einzellagen: Rüdesheimer – Berg Rottland (1.75), Berg Schlossberg (2), Berg Roseneck (1.5), Bischofsberg (2), Drachenstein (5.5) and Magdalenenkreuz (1.75). 87% is Riesling, 8% Ehrenfelser, 5% Spätburgunder. Nägler goes to great lengths to achieve concentrated wines of character, thinning the grapes and nursing small individual lots. He likes rather dry wines to accompany food, but makes some luxurious polished Spätleses and Ausleses. From DM 5.50.

Weingut Heinz Nikolai
Ringstrasse 14, 6229 Erbach. About 18 acres. Einzellagen: Erbacher – Steinmorgen, Hohenrain, Michelmark and Honigberg; Kiedricher Sandgrub; Hallgartener Jungfer. A fourth-generation grower with 85% Riesling, 10% Scheurebe, 5% Ruländer. His aromatic Scheurebe and soft fat Ruländer are popular. Three quarters of his output are sweet, or at least 'mellow', wines. From DM 4.20.

Robert von Oetinger'sches Weingut
Rheinallee 1-3, 6228 Eltville-Erbach. Owner: Baron Detlev von Oetinger. 15 acres. Einzellagen: Erbacher – Hohenrain, Steinmorgen, Honigberg, Michelmark, Seigelsberg and Marcobrunn; Kiedricher Sandgrub. An old Erbach family in new premises (since 1966) by the Rhine, with Weinstube and garden. Their speciality is dry wines with pronounced acidity and powerful flavour, mainly drunk in the neighbourhood. From DM 4.50.

Weingut Richter-Boltendahl
Walluferstrasse 25, 6228 Eltville. 35.5 acres. Einzellagen: Wallufer – Langenstück and Fitusberg; Eltviller – Taubenberg, Langenstück, Sonnenberg (5.5) and Rheinberg (10.5); Rauenthaler Rothenberg; Erbacher– Honigberg, Michelmark (9), Hohenrain and Steinmorgen; Kiedricher Sandgrub; Hattenheimer Hassel. 80% is Riesling, 10% Müller-Thurgau, 4% Spätburgunder, etc. A century-old family estate. The buildings are an old barge-horse stable by the Rhine. The wines are fresh and fruity, with Eltville Rheinberg, Riesling and Scheurebe Kabinett, and Weissherbst (rosé) as specialities. From DM 4.80.

Weingut Jakob Riedel
Taunusstrasse 1, 6227 Hallgarten. Owner: Wolfgang Riedel. 8 acres. Einzellagen: Hallgartener – Jungfer, Hendelberg Schönhell and Würzgarten. A 17th-century property making full-bodied, heavy wines, bottled very young and intended for long maturing. 90% Riesling. (Ehrenfelser is used only for 'sweet reserve'.) From DM 5.00.

Weingut Valentin Schlotter
Lorcherstrasse 13, 6220 Rüdesheim. Owner: Karl-Heinz Runck. 23.5 acres. Einzellagen: Rüdesheimer – Berg Rottland, Berg Schlossberg, Berg Roseneck, Bischofsberg, Kirchenpfad, Klosterlay, Klosterberg, Drachenstein and Magdalenenkreuz (13.5); Assmannshäuser – Höllenberg and Hinterkirch (10). A well-established grower of both white and red wines. The cellars are next door to the famous inn Zur Krone in Assmannshausen. His red wines are light and flowery with a hint of almonds; his Rüdesheimer 50% *trocken* or *halbtrocken*, particularly good in 'off' vintages.

Weingut Georg Sohlbach
Oberstrasse 15, 6229 Kiedrich. Owner: Norbert Sohlbach. 11 acres. Einzellagen: Kiedricher – Sandgrub, Wasseros, Klosterberg and Gräfenberg. An old estate, originally called Bibo, with an ancient cask cellar in the centre of Kiedrich. Einzellage names are used only for Riesling – other grapes have the Grosslage name Heiligenstock. 60% is QbA wine, mainly dry or semi-dry, as fresh and flowery as possible. From DM 5.00.

Weingut Sturm & Söhn
Hauptstrasse 31, 6229 Rauenthal. Owner: Otto Sturm. 9 acres in Rauenthaler – Baiken, Wülfen, Langenstück, Gehrn and Rothenberg. Growers in Rauenthal since 1653 and much respected for their typically spicy, cask-matured wines with a long life. The largest holding is Wülfen and the best Baiken. 90% is Riesling. Sturm's 1976 TBA won the top German prize for that great vintage.

Weingutsverwaltung H. Tillmanns Erben
Hauptstrasse 2, 6228 Eltville 2 – Erbach. Owner: Wolf Jasper Musyal. 30 acres. Einzellagen: Erbacher – Hohenrain, Michelmark, Honigberg, Steinmorgen; Kiedricher Sandgrub; Hattenheimer Wisselbrunnen. Ancient cellars once owned by Kloster Eberbach. Herr Musyal believes strongly in natural methods: no herbicides, etc., and as little filtering as possible. 90% is Riesling. Half his production is dry or semi-dry. Erbacher Hohenrain is his speciality. From DM 4.40 (Ruländer); DM 5.10 (Riesling).

Weingut Wagner-Weritz
Eberbacherstrasse 86-88, 6229 Erbach. Owner: Jakob Weritz. 18.5 acres. Einzellagen: Erbacher – Michelmark, Honigberg, Hohenrain, Siegelsberg and Steinmorgen; Hattenheimer Hassel; Kidreicher Sandgrub. The old Wagner property has been enlarged by the present owner, who also bought the 'Erbacher Hof' in 1971. Substantial and firm wines, 85% Riesling, particularly from the Steinmorgen vineyard. From about DM 3.60.

Weingut Freiherr von Zwierlein
Schloss Kosakenberg, Bahnstrasse 1, 6222 Geisenheim. Owner: Frau Gisela Wegeler. The Schloss, built by the Prince-Bishop of Mainz, took its name from a Cossack regiment in Napoleon's time. The present property is about 20 acres. Einzellagen: Geisenheimer – Kläuserweg, Mäuerchen, Fuchsberg and Rothenberg; Winkeler Jesuitengarten. 100% Riesling. The finest wines are from the Kläuserweg, made rather dry, slightly tannic and intended to last a good 10 years. Otto Butsch, the manager, has firm ideas on matching Rheingau wines with food. All the estate wines are sold with a full analysis.

Cooperative
Vereinigte Weingutsbesitzer Hallgarten eG 'Die Englander'
6227 Hallgarten. Director: Rudolf Rosskopf. 150 acres, Einzellagen: Hallgartener – Jungfer, Schönhell, Würzgarten and Hendelberg; Oestricher – Lenchen and Doosberg; Hattenheimer Deutelsberg; Mittelheimer Edelmann. One of two growers' cooperatives (founded 1902) in Hallgarten, popularly dubbed 'The Englishman' because it excluded growers with less than 3 'Morgen' (i.e. about 2 acres, which made them plutocrats, like Edwardian Englishmen). 90% Riesling, 8% Müller-Thurgau, 2% new crossings. The standard of wine-making is excellent. From DM 4.90.

NAHE

The river Nahe (the 'a' is long) is a minor tributary of the Rhine, joining its broad flood from the south at Bingen, opposite the vineyards of the Rheingau. Its vineyards are thus placed centrally between the Middle Mosel, the best of Rheinhessen, the Saar and the Rheingau. Its upper reaches have some of the most perfect vineyard sites in Germany. Yet only within the last century has Riesling been planted here, and the region's full reputation as the producer of some of the world's most perfect white wines is even now scarcely established. The whole area is not large, with 11,000 acres, and its Riesling vineyards are less than a third of the total. Much of its output is unexceptional, to be compared or confused with standard Rheinhessen wine. The outstanding wines come from a mere five-mile stretch of the north bank of the upper river where it flows east, from its capital town of Bad Kreuznach, and from singular spots on southern slopes abutting the river between Kreuznach and Bingen.

The conventional way of describing Nahe wines, not surprisingly, is as being transitional between Mosel and Rhine; some say specifically between Saar and Rheingau. This is true of the weight and balance, body and structure of the fine wines of the upper Nahe: they do have the 'nerve', the backbone of the Saar with some of the meat of the weightier, more densely flavoured Rheingau. The soil, however, seems to add a certain singularity; to me the great Nahe wines often have a suggestion of ethereal Sancerre, a delicate hint of the blackcurrant leaf with a delicious mineral undertone. In their delicacy yet completeness they make hypnotic sipping, far into the night.

The whole region is divided into two Bereichs: Schlossböckelheim for the upper half, Kreuznach for the lower. Schlossböckelheim contains three Grosslagen: Burgweg (the best and most restricted, containing the core of the riverside vineyards); Paradiesgarten, and Rosengarten (almost always associated with the village of Rüdesheim – one suspects in the hope of confusion with the famous Rüdesheim of the Rhine). Kreuznach contains four Grosslagen: Kronenberg, Sonnenborn, Schlosskapelle and Pfarrgarten.

The upper (southern) Nahe region is fragmented into scattered villages with no pattern and no famous names, although reasonable wines are made at, for example, Kirschroth, Meddersheim, Mönzingen, Odernheim and Duchroth.

Schlossböckelheim

Schlossböckelheim is the first great name of the upper Nahe. It is the Bereich name, it is also a village, and its most famous vineyard, the Kupfergrube, was planted and is exploited by the impeccable State Domain at Niederhausen, the Domain buildings overlooking their prize site across a defile in the hills. Kupfergrube was a copper mine until the beginning of this century; the diggings are still discernible. Felsenberg, next door on the hill, has an almost equally ideal slope and orientation; In den Felsen and Königsfels only marginally less so. Down to Altenbamberg the Grosslage name is Burgweg.
Growers August E. Anheuser. Paul Anheuser. Crusius. Von Plettenberg. Staatlichen Weinbaudomänen. Zentralkellerei.

Niederhausen

The space between Schlossböckelheim and Niederhausen is occupied by a gentle bend in the river, offering every inclination from southwest to east to a hill of vines. The finest are in the Steinberg around the State Domain cellars, but Hermannsberg, Hermannshöhle, Klamm, Kertz and the rest are all magnificent Riesling sites.
Growers August E. Anheuser. Paul Anheuser. Crusius. Schneider. Staatlichen Weinbaudomänen.

Norheim

The much-divided vineyards of Norheim vary from steep to flat, lending themselves to a range of varieties, with fine Silvaner in Klosterberg and some well-flavoured Müller-Thurgau on the other sites. The best Riesling is found in Dellchen, Kirschheck and Kafels.
Growers August E. Anheuser. Paul Anheuser. Crusius. Landes-Lehr-und-Versuchsanstalt. Von Plettenberg. Schneider.

Traisen

Traisen is equally variable, from the sloping Nonnengarten, largely Müller-Thurgau, to the supreme Bastei, an extraordinary little ramp of Riesling at the foot of the immense red porphyry cliff of the Rotenfels. The Einzellage Rotenfels, also entirely Riesling, makes almost equally distinguished wine. The words 'race' or 'breeding' are quite unequal to its balance of finesse and fire.
Growers Hans & Peter Crusius.

Bad Münster

The Nahe turns the corner northward at the town of Bad Münster. Its vineyards, though excellent, are infinitesimal compared with those of Münster-Sarmsheim farther downstream. Münsterer Felseneck and Steigerdell, though rarely seen, produce exceptional Rieslings worth searching for. Ebernburg, with its ancient castle over the river, also has three fine steep south slopes: Schlossberg, Erzgruppe and Feuerberg.

Altenbamberg

Altenbamberg lies in a side valley two miles south of the Bad Münster bend. The hills around offer several steep and sheltered slopes, largely planted with Riesling, here lighter and tauter than on the classic riverside sites, but also some notable Müller-Thurgau and Silvaner.
Growers Paul Anheuser. Staatlichen Weinbaudomänen.

Bad Kreuznach

The hub of the Nahe is the little spa-cum-commercial city of Kreuznach. Its name is known all over the wine world for its Seitzwerke, the factory where filter technology has reached perfection. The spa section of the town is quietly pretty, made interesting (and presumably salubrious) by an ambitious system of creating ozone by pouring salt water on to vast drying frames; a bizarre feature of the road into town.

Kreuznach gives its name to the lower Nahe Bereich. It also musters the enormous total of 2,500 acres of vineyards – approaching a quarter of the entire Nahe region. They lie almost all round the town, the best of them coming close to the centre on the northwest. Kahlenberg, Steinweg, Krötenpfuhl and Brückes are considered the top sites, but several others, including Steinberg, Narrenkappe, Forst and Kauzenberg are excellent vineyards for Riesling.

On a more modest level, and with other grape varieties, the Einzellage wines of Kreuznach, in the Grosslage Kronenberg, are generally a safe bet and often a very pleasant surprise.

Growers August E. Anheuser. Paul Anheuser. Landes-Lehr-und-Versuchsanstalt. Von Plettenberg. Schlink-Herf-Gutleuthof. Winzer. Rheingräfenberg. Zentralkellerei.

Winzenheim

Winzenheim continues the left-bank vineyards of the Nahe without a break from Kreuznach. Its Einzellagen Rosenheck, Honigberg and Berg are all slopes with good potential, now included with Bad Kreuznach.

Using a refractometer to measure sugar levels of ripening grapes

Bretzenheim

The vineyards flow on from Winzenheim with increasingly loamy, fertile soil, Silvaner and Müller-Thurgau becoming more prominent than Riesling. Grosslage Kronenberg.

Growers Dr. Josef Höfer. Von Plettenberg.

Langenlonsheim

The next community of the northward-flowing Nahe has another huge vineyard area taking advantage of a south slope of sandy loam at right angles to the river. The Steinchen is largely planted with Müller-Thurgau and Silvaner, which give fairly full-bodied and aromatic wines, but a far cry from the upstream classics. The best site is the Rothenberg. Langenlonsheim is in the Grosslage Sonnenborn.

Growers Pallhuber. Schweinhardt. Erbhof Tesch. Zentralkellerei.

Laubenheim

Laubenheim, again on the river, has similar loamy slopes; none of outstanding reputation. The Grosslage here is Schlosskapelle.

Grower Erbhof Tesch.

Dorsheim

Dorsheim lies immediately west of Laubenheim, facing the community of Burg Layen and the Rümmelsheim across a little valley. Its best sites lie on the Burg Layen side, stonier and steeper than Laubenheim, with a high proportion of Riesling of real style. Goldloch and Pittermännchen are the best slopes. Grosslage Schlosskapelle.

Growers Diel auf Burg Layen. Dr. Josef Höfer. Staatlichen Weinbaudomänen.

Burg Layen and Rümmelsheim

Burg Layen and Rümmelsheim are effectively one village, with vineyard conditions similar to Dorsheim, reaching their best, for notable Silvaner and Müller-Thurgau as well as Riesling, in the Schlossberg and Hölle. Grosslage Schlosskapelle.

Growers Diel auf Burg Layen. Dr. Josef Höfer. Zentralkellerei.

Münster Sarmsheim

Münster Sarmsheim brings the Nahe vineyards to an end just before Bingen, with slopes angled southeast away from the river. The Nahe State Domain has demonstrated that these gentle inclines of stony loam are capable of ripening magnificent Riesling, more full-bodied and robust than their beautiful wines from Schlossböckelheim and Niederhausen. Dautenpflänzer is the best of the Einzellagen. Grosslage Schlosskapelle.

Growers Diel auf Burg Layen. Dr. Joseph Höfer. Staatlichen Weinbaudomänen. Zentralkellerei.

A number of villages west of the river contribute worthy wines to the Nahe contingent. Weinsheim, Sponheim, Roxheim, Wallhausen, Dalberg and Guldental all have above-average sites.

Growers Paul Anheuser. Diel auf Burg Layen. Dr. Josef Höfer. Schlink-Herf-Gutleuthof.

NAHE PRODUCERS

Weingut Ökonomierat August E. Anheuser

Brückes 53, 6550 Bad Kreuznach. Owners: August and Herbert Anheuser. 148 acres. Einzellagen: Kreuznacher – Brückes (17), Hinkelstein, Hofgarten, Kahlenberg, Krötenpfuhl, Mönchberg, St. Martin (22), Narrenkappe (30), Steinberg and Steinweg; Winzenheimer Rosenheck; Norheimer Kafels and Dellchen; Niederhäuser Hermannshöhle; Schlossböckelheimer Königsfels.

The Anheuser family dominate the best sections of the Nahe, with roots going back to the 17th century. This company (founded 1869) also owns Anheuser and Fehrs, who are merchants, not growers. Vines are 70% Riesling with Silvaner and Müller-Thurgau in approximately equal proportion and some Scheurebe, Ruländer and Kerner. The heroic rock-cut cellars are a treasure house of old vintages in vast variety. The Anheuser family is also famous in American brewing for Anheuser-Busch and Budweiser beers.

Weingut Paul Anheuser

Strombergerstrasse 15-19, 6550 Bad Kreuznach. Owner: Rudolf Peter Anheuser. The present estate consists of 136 acres. Einzellagen: Kreuznacher – Brückes, Forst, Hinkelstein (15), Kahlenberg, Kapellenpfad, Krötenpfuhl (15), Mönchberg, Mollenbrunnen, Monhard, Narrenkappe, Osterhöll, St. Martin and Tilgesbrunnen; Schlossböckelheimer – Felsenberg, Heimberg, In den Felsen (12.5 acres), Königsfels (27) and Mühlberg; Niederhäuser – Felsensteyer (12.5) and Pfingstweide; Altenbamberger – Kehrenberg, Rotenberg, Schlossberg and Treuenfels; Norheimer – Dellchen and Kafels; Roxheimer – Berg and Höllenpfad; Mönzinger Halenberg.

This house has the same origins as the previous entry, but in 1888 became a separate estate under Rudolf Anheuser, who was the first to introduce the Riesling to the Nahe. The name Rudolf still appears on some labels, adding to the general confusion. 70% is Riesling, 7% each Müller-Thurgau, Ruländer, Kerner and Weissburgunder (with some others, but not Silvaner). The speciality of the house is Riesling Kabinett *halbtrocken* with the singular Nahe character. Prices: from DM 4.80.

Weinkellereien Anheuser & Fehrs

Brückes 41, 6550 Bad Kreuznach.

Wine merchants (*see* August Anheuser).

Weingut Hans & Peter Crusius

Hauptstrasse 2, 6551 Traisen.
Owners: Hans and Peter Crusius.

See page 258.

Schlossgut Diel auf Burg Layen

6531 Burg Layen, Kreis Bad Kreuznach. Owner: Dr. Ingo Diel. 47 acres. Einzellagen: Burg Layener – Schlossberg, Rothenberg and Hölle; Dorsheimer – Goldloch, Honigberg, Pittermännchen and Klosterpfad; Münsterer Königsschloss.

The Diel family has farmed the manor surrounding the ruins of Burg Layen castle for 200 years. Dr. Diel is an enthusiast for new varieties and unusual wines: 40% of the vineyard is Riesling, 25% experimental sorts, 20% Kerner. The remaining 15% is Silvaner and Gewürztraminer. Among the new varieties is Rotberger (a red Riesling × Trollinger cross, as is the white Kerner), which makes a very popular rosé. The range is well made as well as wide: Dorsheimer Ausleses can be splendid. Prices: from DM 4.75.

Weingut Carl Finkenauer

Salinenstrasse 60, 6550 Bad Kreuznach Rhld. Owners: Carl Finkenauer Erben. 71.5 acres. Einzellagen: Kreuznacher – Brückes, St. Martin, Gutental, Narrenkappe, Forst, Krötenpfuhl and Kauzenberg; Winzenheimer Rosenheck; Roxheimer Mühlenberg.

The sixth generation of the family runs this estate in the attractive spa area of Bad Kreuznach. 46.4% is Riesling, 15.5% Müller-Thurgau, 10% Silvaner. Other varieties are Scheurebe, Kerner, and Spätburgunder for red wine. Good tasty and vigorous Nahe wines, particularly in the dry range – even extending to an unusual dry Auslese. Prices: from DM 4.40.

Weingut Dr. Josef Höfer Schlossmühle

6531 Burg Layen. Owner: Frau Maria Höfer. 86 acres. Einzellagen: Burg Layener – Johannisberg, Rothenberg, Schlossberg and Hölle; Dorsheimer – Trollberg, Klosterpfad and Honigberg; Münsterer – Trollberg and Königsschloss; Guldentaler Honigberg; Winzenheimer – Rosenheck, Honigberg, Berg and In den 17 Morgen; Bretzenheimer Hofgut and Pastorei.

A family estate since 1775, producing mellow, aromatic wines, including dry ones, from many varieties (40% Silvaner, 18% Müller-Thurgau, 15% Riesling and many of the fruity new varieties). The holdings include a ruined castle and its ancient cellars. Sales are direct to the German consumer.

Landes-Lehr-und Versuchsanstalt

Rüdesheimerstrasse 60-68, 6550 Bad Kreuznach. Director: Dr. Kadisch. 76 acres. Einzellagen: Kreuznacher – Forst, Hinkelstein (13), Hofgarten, Hungriger Wolf, Kahlenberg (14), Kapellenpfad, Mollenbrunnen, Monhard, Steinweg and Vogelsang (10); Norheimer (9) – Dellchen, Kafels and Kirschheck.

Founded in 1900 as the provincial wine school; now owned by the State of Rheinland-Pfalz and regarded as one of the best research and educational stations in Germany. Its vineyards (20% on steep sites, 40% on slopes and a small proportion on terraces, rare in the Nahe) are concentrated in Kreuznach and Norheim. Half the vines are Riesling, but much experimenting is done with new varieties, trying to catch the Nahe style. Controlled fermentation under CO_2 pressure was developed here. One of the most respected Nahe labels, regularly winning high awards.

Weingut & Weinkellerei Maximilian Pallhuber GmbH

An den Nahewiesen, 6536 Langenlonsheim. Owners: Karl-Heinz Paul and Heinz Pallhuber.

A substantial wine merchant with a small estate: 40% in Silvaner, 30% Müller-Thurgau; Kerner and Bacchus with their aromatic flavours are very popular.

Reichsgräflich von Plettenberg'sche Verwaltung

Winzenheimerstrasse, 6550 Bad Kreuznach. Owners: The Counts Wolfgang and Egbert von Plettenberg. 99 acres of own vineyards and about 20 acres leased. Einzellagen: Bretzenheimer – Vogelsang, Pastorei and Felsenköpfchen; Winzenheimer – Rosenheck and Berg; Kreuznacher – Brückes, Forst, Kapellenpfad, Hinkelstein, Narrenkappe, Mollenbrunnen, Osterhöll, Kahlenberg, St. Martin, Hofgarten and Mönchberg; Roxheimer – Höllenpfad, Berg and

Mühlenberg; Norheimer Götzenfels; Schlossböckelheimer – Kupfergrube and Felsenberg.

A family domain since the 18th century, known by this name since 1912. Now a modern winery with little romantic appeal but excellently placed vineyards and a wide selection of some of the Nahe's best wines, the most outstanding from Kreuznach. 65% of the vines are Riesling, 20% Müller-Thurgau, 15% new varieties. Prices: from DM 3.50.

Vereinigte Weingüter Schlink-Herf-Gutleuthof

6550 Bad Kreuznach. Owner: Günther Schlink. 160 acres. Einzellagen: Kreuznacher – Narrenkappe, Kronenberg, Forst, Mollenbrunnen, Hinkelstein, Osterhöll, Kahlenberg, Steinweg, Brückes, St. Martin, Kapellenpfad and Vogelsang; Roxheimer – Mühlenberg, Birkenberg and Höllenpfad.

Two 19th-century estates, Herf and Gutleuthof, united by the present owner, who added his name and whose firm, Günther Schlink KG, distributes their wines and those of a group of 35 other Nahe growers. The wines are made at Gutleuthof. Only Einzellage names are used. A 1973 Kreuznacher Forst Riesling Eiswein won a supreme award. Prices: from DM 3.00.

Weingut Jakob Schneider

Winzerstrasse 15, 6551 Niederhausen. Owner: Jakob Schneider, Jr. A mixed farm with 31 acres of vineyards on fine slopes. Einzellagen: Niederhäuser – Hermannshöhle (7.5), Rosenheck (7.5), Klamm (5), Steinwingert (4) and Rosenberg (2.5); Norheimer Kirschheck (5).

The wines are 90% Riesling and Herr Schneider uses farm manure and every natural method to produce intense wines with flavour and finesse. Prices: from DM 5.00.

HANS CRUSIUS

A great Nahe estate

Hans Crusius of Traisen in the upper Nahe is the type of German grower who quietly achieves perfection, without apparent ambition to do more than till the land that his family has owned since the 16th century.

The Crusius property is 30 acres, 22 of them in the Einzellage Traiser Rotenfels, with small parcels in Norheim, Niederhäuser Rosenberg, Schlossböckelheimer Felsenberg and a precious acre in the sandstone suntrap of Traiser Bastei. 70% is Riesling, 15% Müller-Thurgau, the rest equally Weissburgunder and Kerner.

Hans and his son Peter work in their traditional vaulted cask-cellar to produce wines of extraordinary quality and character, to my taste among the best in Germany. Each vineyard has its own character. They ascribe the remarkable delicacy of their Felsenberg and Rosenberg to the rare 'melaphyr' soil. Bastei is pungent; the steep Norheimer Kirschheck powerfully scented. Rotenfels is more scattered and variable – yet always firm with a racy clarity of flavour that is never neutral.

Weingut Bürgmeister Wilhelm Schweinhardt Nachf.

6536 Langenlonsheim. Owner: Wilhelm Schweinhardt. 40 acres. Einzellagen: Langenlonsheimer – St. Antoniusweg, Steinchen, Königsschild, Rothenberg, Bergborn, Lauerweg and Löhrer Berg.

A very old family of growers. 50% is Riesling. The grapey, light and charming wines are largely sold in West Berlin.

Verwaltung der Staatlichen Weinbaudomänen

Niederhausen-Schlossböckelheim, 6551 Oberhausen. Director: Dr. Werner Hofäcker. The vineyards total 112.5 acres. Einzellagen: Schlossböckelheimer Kupfergrube (27) and Felsenberg (5); Niederhäuser – Hermannshöhle (5), Kertz (2.5), Hermannsberg (15) (solely owned) and Steinberg (10); Traiser Bastei (2.5); Altenbamberger Rotenberg (17); Ebernburger Schlossberg (2.5); Münsterer – Dautenpflänzer (5), Pittersberg (5), Steinkopf (2.5) and Kappellenberg (2.5); Dorsheimer – Burgberg (5), Goldloch (2.5) and Honigberg (2.5).

The Nahe State Domain, which many consider the finest in Germany, was founded in 1902 by the King of Prussia and pioneered viticulture on steep slopes above the now-famous site of a former copper mine (Kupfergrube) to grow Riesling. By 1920 its wines were acknowledged superlative. In 1927 more land was added at Münster and Dorsheim in the lower Nahe and in 1953 more at Altenbamberg. The State of Rheinland-Pfalz, on its creation in 1946, took over the estate.

All the wines are Riesling with the exception of some Müller-Thurgau (100% in Münsterer Kapellenberg and Dorsheimer Honigberg; 40% in Niederhäuser Steinberg; 15% in Altenbamberger Rotenberg; 10% in Münsterer Pittersberg).

For a demonstration of the subtlety and finesse of great German wine, ranging from fine-drawn floweriness to sumptuous elegance, this estate's wines can rarely be beaten. Schlossböckelheimers are the most stylish and delicate: Niederhäusers fuller and more seductive; Traisers big, ripe and long-lived; the lower Nahe wines full-bodied and spicy. The label is the grim black eagle of Prussia. Prices: from DM 7.00.

Weingut Erbhof Tesch

Naheweinstrasse 99, 6536 Langenlonsheim/bei Bingen/Rhein. Owner: Hartmut Tesch. 99 acres. Einzellagen: Laubenheimer – Karthäuser, St. Remigiusberg, Krone; Langenlonsheimer – Löhrer Berg, Königsschild, Steinchen, St. Antoniusweg.

A principal grower of the lower Nahe valley, established since 1723; much extended and improved since 1960. The vineyards are on some of the best slopes of the region: the first 4 named, totalling 48 acres, are all Riesling. Of the others, Königsschild (8 acres) is Spätburgunder, Steinchen (17.5) Müller-Thurgau and St. Antoniusweg (9) Silvaner. Crisp, 'extrovert' Laubenheim Rieslings with considerable *spritz* are the pride of the house, which consistently wins medals with them. Sales are to private customers in Germany. Prices: from DM 5.50.

COOPERATIVES

Zentralkellerei der Nahewinzer

Winzenheimerstrasse 30, 6551 Bretzenheim. Director: Hermann Lunkenheimer. The union of 3 cooperatives, founded in 1935 and now numbering more than 2,000 members in 60 communes. A new cellar was built recently in Bretzenheim and a crushing plant in Langenlonsheim. More than 100 Einzellagen in 60 villages, with the main Grosslagen being Rüdesheimer Rosengarten, Schlossböckelheimer Burgweg, Kreuznacher Kronenberg, Burg Layener Schlosskapelle, Münsterer Schlosskapelle. The Einzellagen names used are principally in the following communes: Kreuznach, Langenlonsheim, Guldental, Wallhausen, Monzingen, Kirschroth, Odernheim.

Vines are 32% Silvaner, 30% Müller-Thurgau, 26% Riesling, 12% miscellaneous. Out of a total of 800,000 cases about 40,000 bear Grosslage names and up to 3,500 Einzellage names. The rest are Bereich, or lower-quality wines. The top quality, however, are true to type, very well made and good value. Prices: from DM 2.80.

Winzergenossenschaft & Weinkellerei Rheingräfenberg eG

Naheweinstrasse 63, 6553 Meddersheim. Director: Gerhard Held. 128 members with 378 acres in Meddersheim (237), Merxheim, Sobernheim, Nussbaum, Kirschroth, Hargesheim and Bad Kreuznach.

A top-quality cooperative with 60% Riesling, but also using much Kerner, Bacchus and Optima, based at Meddersheim, upstream from Schlossböckelheim. The best Einzellagen are Meddersheimer Rheingräfenberg and Sobernheimer Marbach. Many wines are sold under the Grosslage names Paradiesgarten and Kronenberg. Prices: from DM 3.90.

Throughout the chapter on Germany, names of the Einzellagen producing the finest wines will be found in the Producers' entries.

Luxembourg

Luxembourg has some 3,000 acres of vines along the upper Mosel, above Trier. There are 1,200 small growers, but two thirds of the country's wine is made in cooperatives. The grape varieties are Rivaner (Riesling × Silvaner) about 50 per cent, Elbling about 25 per cent, Riesling and Auxerrois about 10 per cent, with a little Gewürztraminer, Pinot Gris and Pinot Blanc. Elbling produces very weak juice and is mostly converted to sparkling wine. Rivaner is reliable, Auxerrois occasionally extremely tasty, Riesling always lean but sometimes classic.

The industry is highly organized and controlled. All vines are graded in one of five qualities: non admis (not passed), Marque Nationale, Vin Classé, Premier Cru or Grand Premier Cru.

The major producers are Caves Bernard-Massard at Grevenmacher (for sparkling wines) and Vinsmoselles S.C. at Stadtbredimus (the organization of cooperatives). Others are Caves Gales & Cie at Bech-Kleinmacher, Caves St. Martin and Caves St. Remy at Remich (which is also the H.Q. of the Government Viticultural Station), Caves Krier Frères at Remich, Feipel-Staar at Wellenstein, and Thill Frères at Schengen.

RHEINHESSEN

Anonymity behind the *nom de verre* of Leibfraumilch is the fate of most Rheinhessen wine. The heart of the wine-growing Rhineland specializes in soft, sufficiently flowery Müller-Thurgau, blunt, often rather insipid Silvaner, and (increasing rapidly) the aromatic new varieties that offer the thrills of flowery bouquet with the chance of a better balance (and a better crop) than the Müller-Thurgau. Only five per cent of its 60,000-odd acres is planted with Riesling, concentrated in its few outstanding sites. Of these by far the most important is the 'Rhein-front', the riverside communities from Dienheim to Nackenheim, with Nierstein as their centre.

Frank Schoonmaker points out in his classic book *The Wines of Germany* that of the 160-odd villages producing wine in Rheinhessen no less than 120 have names ending in 'heim' – home. They are scarcely a rarity anywhere in Germany, but this stress on domesticity seems especially fitting for Rheinhessen, an area of bland, fertile farmland whose very monotony makes it seem bigger than its mere 20 by 30 miles. The Rhine curls protectingly around its eastern and northern boundaries; the Nahe guards its western limits. The cities of Worms (in the south), Mainz, Bingen and Kreuznach mark its corners.

There are only three Bereich names which divide the whole area: Nierstein, Bingen and (for the south) Wonnegau, which means – more or less – the happy country.

Bereich Nierstein

Bereich Nierstein stretches from Mainz down the eastern half of the region to Mettenheim, including almost all the vineyards that are known by name outside Germany. The best-known Gemeinden are listed following the course of the Rhine northwards.

Alsheim

Alsheim is just north of Mettenheim, lying well back from a low-lying bend in the Rhine and subject to spring frosts. Its importance has increased recently with the spread of new vine varieties, although Riesling and Gewürztraminer both grow well here, in sandy loam. Riesling makes substantial dryish wines. Alsheim and Mettenheim are both divided between the Grosslage Krötenbrunnen (a very wide area of mixed quality) for the flat land, and Rheinblick, confined to the hilly vineyards with their view (blick) of the distant Rhine.

Growers Krebs-Grode. Rappenhof. Sittmann.

Guntersblum

Guntersblum continues the quality vineyards northward, the hills drawing nearer to the river. Like Alsheim it has two Grosslage names, Krötenbrunnen for its flat land, Vogelsgärtchen for the slopes with a chalk content in their sandy loam, which naturally makes better wine – though oddly enough in Guntersblum it seems to be the flat land which has a higher reputation. The name Krötenbrunnen itself is much used on labels – usually in conjunction with the better-known name of Oppenheim, the next Gemeinde. This is a prime example of the confusion arising from Grosslage names. Wine labelled Oppenheimer Krötenbrunnen sells well. The name is available to growers in the relatively unknown Guntersblum. They naturally tend to swallow their pride in their best Einzellagen and use the Grosslage name. Guntersblum includes the village of Ludwigshöhe, with flat vineyards.

Growers Dr. Dahlem. Krebs-Grode. Rappenhof (also in Ludwigshöhe). Schmitt-Dr. Ohnacker.

Dienheim

Dienheim is almost attached to Oppenheim, shares its Grosslage and two of its Einzellage names, and seems content to subsume its reputation in that of its more famous neighbour. The enormous Herrengarten Einzellage is on flat sandy land along the Rhine, which skirts the town of Oppenheim. This is Grosslage Krötenbrunnen. The best vineyards of both Dienheim and Oppenheim are in the Grosslage Güldenmorgen.

Growers Baumann. Braun. Dr. Dahlem. Guntrum. Freiherr Heyl zu Herrnsheim. Carl Koch Erben. Rappenhof. Gustav Adolf Schmitt. Geschwister Schuch. Heinrich Seip, Kurfürstenhof. Senfter. Sittmann. Staatsweingut Oppenheim.

Oppenheim

The first of the 'Rhein-front' wine towns going downstream, although it stands back from the river at a respectful distance on a low hill out of reach of floods. This is the end of the chalky ridge coming north from Alsheim and has its best vineyards. Roughly half the vines are Riesling, but all real Oppenheimers (recognizable by their Einzellagen names) are capable of the extra concentration and finesse that singles out 'Rhein-front' wines. The wines are always softer and broader than (for example) Rheingau wines. Their excellence lies in a vitality, a backbone that keeps them from being formless or flabby. The Oppenheimer Krötenbrunnen wines from the flat fields do not necessarily share this quality.

Growers Baumann. Braun. Dr. Dahlem. Guntrum. J. A. Harth. Carl Koch Erben. Gustav Adolf Schmitt. Geschwister Schuch. Heinrich Seip, Kurfürstenhof. Senfter. Sittmann. Staatsweingut Oppenheim.

Nierstein

The best-known name in Rheinhessen and one of the most popular in Germany and abroad, the centre of the 'Rhein-front' and an attractive little town full of wine merchants. The name of Nierstein is also a caution to those who find the fine print of vineyard names too much trouble. It can legally be used not only for its whole Bereich (one third of Rheinhessen) but also for the Grosslage name Gutes Domtal, which is available to 15 villages lying inland to the west of Nierstein, but only to one 85-acre vineyard in Nierstein, Pfaffenkappe (which in any case is in the hamlet of Nierstein-Schwabsburg and not in Nierstein itself). Thus tenuous is the link between Nierstein and its most famous product.

All the fine wines of Nierstein, and there are many, lie in three small Grosslagen hugging the town and within sight of the Rhine. The Grosslage Spiegelberg embraces all the Einzellagen on the hills above some 300 feet, just north and south of the town. Of these Hölle, Paterberg and Brückchen, south of the town, are generally considered the best. Auflangen embraces a line of steeper south-facing but lower-lying vineyards, starting at the river and running inland just north of the town along a narrow valley. Kranzberg, on the Rhine, with its subdivisions Bergkirche, Glöck and Zehnmorgen, is the best of these. Rehbach, the third Grosslage, embraces three famous steep little Einzellagen directly on the riverfront to the north, running on into the next village, Nackenheim.

The quality of the best Niersteiners is velvety softness with a kernel of fire. Dry wines are the exception; the ripeness of Ausleses happens in most vintages. In very hot years, the Spiegelberg vineyards tend to overripen and lose their 'nerve' and elegance; particularly with grapes other than Riesling.

Growers Anton Balbach Erben. Baumann. Bezirks-Winzergenossenschaft Nierstein. Braun. Guntrum. Freiherr Heyl zu Herrnsheim. Kapellenhof. Rappenhof. Gustav Adolf Schmitt. Schneider. Geschwister Schuch. Heinrich Seip, Kurfürstenhof. Senfter. Sittman. Staatsweingut Oppenheim. Strub. Wehrheim.

Nackenheim

The little village concludes the steep line of sandstone hills of the Rhein-front with its famous Rothenberg, named for the redness of its sandy loam. Rothenberg and Engelsberg, higher and on flatter land, are in the Nierstein Grosslage Spiegelberg (although to all appearances Rothenberg should be included in Rehbach). The rest of Nackenheim's small acreage, away from the river, is included in the Grosslage Gutes Domtal.

Growers Gunderloch-Lange. Gunderloch-Usinger. Guntrum. Heinrich Seip, Kurfürstenhof.

Bodenheim

Bodenheim continues the line of worthy vineyards northwards towards Mainz; good slopes but without the advantages of the riverside. Its sandy loam vineyards look eastward over the town. The Grosslage name is St. Alban.

In the interior of the Bereich Nierstein few villages are known by name. 'Gutes Domtal' has a firm grip. The other Grosslagen not mentioned above are Domherr, with no remarkable production, and Petersberg, which abuts the better part of the Bereich Wonnegau to the south. The centres with the best reputations in Petersberg are Albig and Gau-Odernheim.

Albig and Gau-Odernheim

Albig, just north of Alzey, has lately produced some fresh and pleasing wines. Gau-Odernheim lies to the northeast of Alzey.

Growers in Albig: Köster-Wolf. In Gau-Odernheim: Krebs-Grode.

Bereich Bingen

The western half of Rheinhessen (excluding its southern fringe) is all included in the Bereich Bingen. Although it abuts the excellent vineyards of the Nahe between Bingen and Kreuznach it has nothing of that quality to offer, except from the isolated Scharlachberg, the hill above Bingen itself, which looks north over the Rhine to Rüdesheim and south over an ideally sited vineyard.

Bingen

The best of Bingen's wines are Riesling, of body and firmness that recalls the Rheingau more than Rheinhessen. The Grosslage is St. Rochuskapelle.

Growers Ohler. Villa Sachsen.

Ockenheim

The southeastern neighbour of Bingen, Ockenheim (also in Grosslage St. Rochuskapelle) has a certain reputation for both white and Spätburgunder light red wines.

Grower Ohler.

Ingelheim

The city of Ingelheim, facing the Rheingau across the river a few miles east of Bingen, has an ancient reputation for its red wines – though you would probably have to go there to find an example.

The rest of Bereich Bingen is a useful source of easy-going, soft and sometimes aromatic wines (depending on the grape variety). The new crossings are widely used, along with Müller-Thurgau. The central Rheinhessen cooperative cellars at Gau-Bickelheim supply wine under the names of many of the villages, without any of them distinguishing itself above the rest.

The Grosslagen names are St. Rochuskapelle (for Bingen), Abtey, Rheingrafenstein, Adelberg, Kurfürstenstück and Kaiserpfalz. Some of the better-known towns and villages are Ockenheim, Worrstadt, Armsheim, Flonheim, Bornheim, Gau-Algesheim, Wollstein and Sprendlingen.

Flonheim

Growers Koehler-Weidmann (also at Bornheim). Köster-Wolf.

Bereich Wonnegau

The happy land of Wonnegau stretches in bucolic bliss from the city of Worms on the Rhine, the birthplace of Liebfraumilch, to the city of Alzey in the hilly country known as Hügelland where the three Bereichs of Rheinhessen meet.

Alzey

Alzey is the centre of the Grosslage Sybillenstein, and has under its wing the villages of Weinheim (promising name) and Heimersheim (which seems to carry domesticity a little too far even for Rheinhessen). This is a district of many new grape varieties and a mixture of soils, with some respectable slopes. Sandstone, slate, marl, chalk and loam are all present. Although few of its wines are widely known at present, many of them have the essential vitality and freshness to make them worth exploring.

Growers Weingut der Stadt Alzey. Köster-Wolf.

The wines tend to become heavier and less fresh as the Wonnegau spreads out south and east towards Worms. The Grosslage names here are Pilgerpfad (with a restricted inner Grosslage called Gotteshilfe), Bergkloster, Burg Rodenstein, Domblick and, around the city of Worms, Liebfrauenmorgen. The most notable towns and villages are Bechtheim and Osthofen (Grosslagen Pilgerpfad and Gotteshilfe), which form the link between Worms and Alsheim (*see* Bereich Nierstein) on a vein of chalky clay running north to the Rhein-front, and Flörsheim-Dalsheim (Grosslage Burg Rodenstein), on the same vein

just west of Worms (which is itself on sandy loam and loess: alluvial soil from the Rhine).
Growers in Bechtheim: Beyer. Brenner. Johann Geil.
In Osthofen: Ahnenhof, Hermann Müller. Glaser. May-Weissheimer.
In Flörsheim-Dalsheim: Bezirks-Winzergenossenschaft Nierstein. Müller-Dr. Becker. Schales.

Worms

Worms still maintains, in the centre of a city destroyed in World War II and rebuilt, the famous patch of vines beside the church of Our Lady, which apparently gave the name to Liebfraumilch. Their wine is well made but by no means outstanding. Grosslage Liebfrauenmorgen.
Growers Schlosskellerei Adam Hemer. Langenbach (*see* p.231).

RHEINHESSEN PRODUCERS

Bürgermeister Anton Balbach Erben

Mainzerstrasse 64, 6505 Nierstein. Owners: The Bohn family. 44.5 acres, 60% in the Grosslagen Rehbach and Auflangen, the rest in Spiegelberg. Einzellagen: Niersteiner – Hipping, Pettenthal, Ölberg, Kranzberg, Klostergarten, Rosenberg, Bildstock and Kirchplatte.

The best known of several Balbachs who were Burgermasters of Nierstein since the 17th century was Anton, who cleared woods from what is now the famous Pettenthal vineyard. The estate, down by the Rhine, with Victorian cellars now full of stainless steel, is planted with 80% Riesling, 7% Müller-Thurgau, 5% Kerner, 4% Scheurebe, 4% Silvaner. It produces some of the finest, raciest Rieslings of Rheinhessen and specializes in Ausleses, Beerenausleses and Trockenbeerenausleses. Prices: from DM 3.35.

Weinkellerei Louis Guntrum

Rheinallee 62, 6505 Nierstein. Directors: Lorenz and Hanns-Joachim Guntrum. 164 acres in the Grosslagen Rehbach, Auflangen and Spiegelberg. Einzellagen: Nackenheimer Rothenberg; Niersteiner – Pettenthal, Bergkirche, Rosenberg, Klostergarten, Findling, Hölle, Ölberg, Heiligenbaum, Orbel and Paterberg; Oppenheimer – Schloss, Herrenberg, Sackträger, Schützenhütte, Kreuz and Paterhof; Dienheimer Tafelstein.

The family business was started in 1824 in the present buildings, lying right on the Rhine. About 20% of the business is in estate-bottled wines; the vines are 30% Riesling, 25% Müller-Thurgau, 14% Silvaner, 9% Scheurebe, 7% Kerner, 4% Ruländer, 3% Gewürztraminer, 2% Bacchus and 6% new crossings under trial. The estate wines are particularly ripe and lively with a wide range of flavours, each variety and site being made individually. The 4th and 5th Guntrum generations now direct the estate and a merchant house with many bread-and-butter lines such as Liebfraumilch Seagull, Bereich Nierstein Goldgrape and a catalogue of other growers' wines from Rheinhessen. Prices: from DM 3.60.

Weingut Freiherr Heyl zu Herrnsheim

Mathildenhof, Langgasse 3, 6505 Nierstein. Owners: The von Weymarn family. 72 acres. Einzellagen: Niersteiner – Pettenthal, Hipping and Brudersberg (22 acres, Grosslage Rehbach), Bildstock, Kirchplatte and Paterberg (20, Grosslage Spiegelberg), Ölberg, Kranzberg and Heiligenbaum (18, Grosslage Auflangen); Dienheimer – Kreuz and Falkenberg (3, Grosslage Güldenmorgen); and 9 acres in the Grosslage Gutes Domtal.

A dignified manor, its gardens full of experimental vine plots, in the heart of Nierstein. The estate has been inherited for 5 generations. 55% is Riesling, particularly fine in the Rehbach and Auflangen vineyards; 18% is Silvaner, which in Ölberg makes a powerful dry wine; 18% is Müller-Thurgau, very popular from Spiegelberg. Prices: from DM 3.40.

Weingut Koehler-Weidmann

Hindenburgring 2, 6509 Bornheim. Owner: Wilhelm Weidmann. 45 acres in the Grosslage Adelberg. Einzellagen: Bornheimer – Hähnchen, Hütte-Terrassen, Schönberg and Kirchenstück; Flonheimer – Klostergarten and Uffhofener La Roche.

Müller-Thurgau and Silvaner are the main varieties in this estate, now in its 9th generation. The Riesling, however, sells out first of the dozen varieties offered. Modest cropping makes intense wines for the district with good length in the (drinker's) mouth.

Weingut Rappenhof

Bachstrasse 47-49, 6526 Alsheim. Owners: Dr. Reinhard Muth and Inge Muth. 74 acres. Einzellagen: Alsheimer – Fischerpfad, Frühmesse, Sonnenberg and Goldberg; Guntersblumer – Bornpfad, Himmelthal, Kreuzkapelle, Steinberg and Eiserne Hand; Dienheimer Siliusbrunnen; Niersteiner Rosenberg.

A very old family estate, among the best of its district, well known particularly for dry wines (two thirds of production). 35% is Riesling, 12% Weissburgunder and Blauburgunder, 10% Silvaner, 10% Müller-Thurgau, 8% Gewürztraminer. A dry Alsheimer Rheinblick (Grosslage) Spätlese is the house speciality. Prices: from DM 5.00.

Weingut Villa Sachsen

Mainzerstrasse 184, 6530 Bingen. 67 acres. Einzellagen: Bingener – Scharlachberg (29.5), Kirchberg (18.5), Schlossberg Schwätzerchen (10), Osterberg (5), Kapellenberg, Rosengarten and Bubenstück (each 1.25).

The Victorian villa starred in a bestseller of 1869, *The Country House on the Rhine*, was bought by a prince of Hessen in 1879, became a model wine estate and in 1963 was bought by St. Ursula, the big wine merchants of Bingen. 50% is Riesling, 15% Müller-Thurgau, 10% Silvaner, 10% Kerner, 5% Weissburgunder, 5% Ruländer and 5% others. The Scharlachberg is the best site, producing stylish, manly Rieslings, particularly dry and semi-dry types. Full-bodied Silvaner and mild Müller-Thurgau are also popular. Prices: from DM 3.80.

Gustav Adolf Schmitt'sches Weingut

Wilhelmstrasse 2-4, 6505 Nierstein. Owner: Georg Ottmar Schmitt. About 250 acres including Einzellagen: Niersteiner – Pettenthal, Ölberg, Hipping and Kranzberg; Dienheimer Falkenberg; Oppenheimer – Herrenberg and Kreuz; Dexheimer Doktor.

Growers since 1618, merchants since about 1920. 75% of the very big estate is planted in standard vine varieties with an emphasis on the Riesling, and about 25% in crossings such as Scheurebe, Kerner, Ehrenfelser and Bacchus. The range of wines is wide, including very fine intense and full-bodied QmP wines from the best sites. Two thirds of turnover is in such commercial lines as Liebfraumilch 'Gloria', Bereich Nierstein 'Fisherman', Bereich Bernkastel 'Silver Bell'. Prices: from DM 3.00.

Weingut Geschwister Schuch

6505 Nierstein. Owner: Diether Gunther. 39.5 acres in Grosslagen Spiegelberg, Auflangen and Rehbach. Einzellagen: Niersteiner – Ölberg, Pettenthal, Findling and Heiligenbaum; Oppenheimer Sackträger; Dienheimer Falkenberg.

One of the most respected old family estates of Nierstein, founded by the Schuchs in 1817. Planted with 50% Riesling, 20% Silvaner, 10% Scheurebe, 10% Müller-Thurgau, 10% new crossings of Bacchus, Faber and Huxelrebe. The wines are models of the gentle but distinctive 'Rhein-front' style, particularly in dry and semi-dry Riesling. Prices: from DM 3.50.

Heinrich Seip, Kurfürstenhof

Nierstein. Owner: Heinrich Seip. 87 acres in Nierstein. Einzellagen: Niersteiner – Paterberg, Bildstock, Kirchplatte, Findling, Rosenberg, Klostergarten, Pettenthal, Hipping, Kranzberg, Ölberg, Heiligenbaum, Orbel, Schloss Schwabsburg and Goldene Luft (sole owner); Oppenheimer Schloss; Dienheimer – Tafelstein, Kreuz and Falkenberg; Nackenheimer Engelsberg.

An ancient royal estate bought by the Seip family in 1950 and now regarded as a leader in wines from the new grape varieties, which occupy 15% of its vineyards. One of the specialities, a grape called Jübiläum, ripens so early that it rarely fails to make Auslese and Beerenauslese, in the rather low-acid Ruländer style. Seip's cellar techniques combine old casks with modern ideas, aiming at aromatic sweet wines of real quality and character.

Weingüter Carl Sittmann

Wormserstrasse 61, 6504 Oppenheim. Owner: Dr. Liselotte Itschner. Nearly 250 acres in Nierstein, Oppenheim, Alsheim and Dienheim, in a score of Einzellagen.

The biggest private estate in the district, inherited by the granddaughter of the founder, who also runs a big merchant house under the name Dr. Itschner. The vines are 20% Müller-Thurgau, 16% Silvaner, 14% Kerner, 12% Riesling. Wines from the best sites are matured in casks: Oppenheimer Sackträger makes splendid Ausleses. Weissherbst (rosé) under the Grosslage name Alsheimer Rheinblick is a speciality. Prices: from DM 3.00.

Staatsweingut der Landes-Lehr-und Versuchsanstalt

Zuckerberg 19, 6504 Oppenheim. Director: Dr. Finger. 100 acres. Einzellagen: Oppenheimer – Sackträger, Kreuz, Herrenberg and Zuckerberg; Niersteiner – Paterberg, Ölberg and Pettenthal; Dienheimer Tafelstein.

The regional wine school, founded in 1885 by the Duke of Hessen and now considered an exemplary college for wine makers, using the most modern methods. In 1980 the school opened a new German wine museum in the heart of Oppenheim. 40% of the estate is on steep slopes and 36% is Riesling, but only Niersteiner Pettenthal is 100% Riesling. Among the many other varieties planted, 40% are experimental vines. The school produces relatively few (20%) dry and semi-dry wines but regularly wins medals with balanced, distinctive and clean sweet ones. It formerly made some of the finest wine from the steepest sites in Nackenheim and Bodenheim as well, but has recently sold this land.

Weingut J. & H. A. Strub

Rheinstrasse 42, 6505 Nierstein. Owners: Reinhard and Walter Strub. 42 acres in Grosslagen Rehbach, Auflangen and Spiegelberg. Einzellagen: Niersteiner – Hipping, Ölberg, Heiligenbaum, Orbel, Brückchen, Paterberg, Findling and Bildstock; Dienheimer Falkenberg.

An old family estate with a good name for gentle, mellow wines from the best parts of the 'Rhein-front'. Vines are 30% Riesling, 30% Silvaner, 30% Müller-Thurgau, 10% Ruländer. Prices: from DM 4.50.

Weingut Eugen Wehrheim

Mühlgasse 30, 6505 Nierstein. Owner: Klaus Wehrheim. 22 acres in Grosslagen Auflangen, Rehbach and Spiegelberg, with most of the vines in Einzellagen Niersteiner – Orbel, Pettenthal, Klostergarten, Brückchen and Findling.

Specialists in Nierstein since 1693; 35% Riesling, 20% Silvaner, 20% Müller-Thurgau, 25% other varieties. The Rieslings are light and sprightly; more serious wines are sweet, aromatic and heavy, for example Ruländer and Huxelrebe Beerenauslese (in 1975 awarded the top German state prize). Prices: from DM 3.30.

OTHER PRODUCERS

Weingut der Stadt Alzey
Schlossgasse 14, 6508 Alzey. Director: U. Kaufmann. 45 acres. Einzellagen: Rotenfels, Kapellenberg, Kirchenstück, Mandelberg, Römerberg and Wartberg, all in the Grosslage Sybillenstein. The town of Alzey in central Rheinhessen is unusual in possessing (since 1916) its own wine estate, planted with one sixth each of Riesling, Müller-Thurgau and Silvaner; the remaining half with a score of other varieties. The wines are well made, estate bottled and among the best of their district.

Weingut Friedrich Baumann
Friedrich-Ebert-Strasse 55, 6504 Oppenheim. Owner: Friedrich Baumann. 25 acres. Einzellagen: Oppenheimer – Sackträger, Herrenberg, Kreuz, Paterhof, Daubhaus and Herrengarten; Niersteiner – Pettenthal and Findling; Dienheimer – Falkenberg and Tafelstein. A long-established family business remodelled in the 1970s but still using barrels and 40% Riesling, aiming for fresh, sprightly wines which win prizes. A quarter of the property is in the excellent Einzellage Oppenheimer Sackträger.

Brenner'sches Weingut
Pfandturmstrasse 20, 6521 Bechtheim. Owner: Bürgermeister Christian Brenner. 37 acres in Geyersberg (5), Rosengarten (5), Hasensprung (5), Heiligkreuz (6), Stein (2.5), Gotteshilfe (8.5) and Pilgerpfad (5). A family estate since 1877 and the principal grower of Bechtheim, using old methods: wooden casks in spacious cellars with an emphasis on substantial dry wines. 20% Silvaner, 30% Müller-Thurgau, 20% Riesling, 18% Weissburgunder, 12% Spätburgunder. Weissburgunder, Riesling and red wines are made absolutely dry – even Ausleses. Also dry Riesling Sekt. From DM 5.50

Dr. Dahlem Erben KG
Wormserstrasse 50, Oppenheim 6504. Owners: The Dahlem family. 67 acres. Einzellagen: Oppenheimer – Sackträger, Herrenberg (8.4), Schloss (8), Kreuz (9), Herrengarten (18) and Daubhaus; Dienheimer – Tafelstein (8.4), Paterhof and Falkenberg; Guntersblumer Kreuzkapelle. An old family estate (since 1702) among the most reliable for traditional Rheinhessen wines. The vineyards are 60% on slopes; the vines 30% Riesling, 25% each Silvaner and Müller-Thurgau, 11% new varieties. The wines are barrel-aged.

Bürgermeister Carl Koch Erben
6504 Oppenheim. Owner: Klaus Stieh-Koch. 27 acres. Einzellagen: Oppenheimer – Sackträger, Kreuz, Herrenberg, Schloss, Paterhof and Herrengarten; Dienheimer Tafelstein. In the family since 1824, concentrating on Oppenheimer Sackträger, from dry

to TBA. 35% Riesling, 15% Müller-Thurgau, 15% Silvaner, 10% Kerner, 8% Scheurebe, 6% Bacchusrebe, 5% Faberrebe, etc. The estate offers 10-year-old wines. From DM 3.80.

Weingut Köster-Wolf
6509 Albig. Owners: Werner Köster and Manfred Wolf. 54 acres. Einzellagen: Albiger – Hundskopf and Schloss Hammerstein; Flonheimer – Rotenpfad and Klostergarten; Heimersheimer Sonnenberg. Grosslagen: Petersberg, Adelberg, Sybillenstein. A 400-year-old vintner family. Their best Riesling is from 2.5 acres of steep slope in Flonheim; a particular pride is dry Silvaner, 'though most customers prefer soft, spicy wines'.

Vereinigte Weingüter Krebs-Grode
6501 Eimsheim. Owners: The Krebs family. 69 acres in Gau-Odernheim, Eimsheim, Guntersblum and Alsheim with Einzellagen: Fuchsloch, Hergottspfad, Petersberg, Ölberg, Hexelberg, Vogelgarten, Himmeltal, Römerschanze, Sonnenhang and Sonnenberg. The family estate (since 1202) has two bases: an old one in Gau-Odernheim and a new building in Eimsheim. A good source of aromatic, well-balanced wines for keeping.

Weingut Müller-Dr. Becker
6521 Flörsheim-Dalsheim. Owner: Dr. Klaus Becker. 86.5 acres. Einzellagen in Flörsheim-Dalsheim: Hubacker, Steig, Sauloch and Bürgel. Grosslage: Burg Rodenstein. Very varied and differentiated 'varietals', two thirds dry or semi-dry, made as fruity and flavoury as possible. 35% Müller-Thurgau, 30% Riesling, 10% Silvaner, 10% Burgunder, 5% Gewürztraminer, 3% Scheurebe, 2% Morio-Muskat and 5% Huxelrebe. Sauloch in particular makes good Riesling Kabinett.

Kommerzienrat P. A. Ohler'sches Weingut
Gaustrasse 10, 6530 Bingen. Owner: Bernhard Becker. 17 acres. Einzellagen: Bingener – Schlossberg-Schwätzerchen, Rosengarten and Scharlachberg; Münsterer – Kapellenberg and Dautenpflänzer; Ockenheimer – Klosterweg and St. Jakobsberg. Since the 17th century a small estate in the centre of Bingen with parcels of the best surrounding vineyards, aiming for racy, spicy, aromatic Kabinetts and Spätlese, especially from Riesling, Kerner and similar vines. From DM 4.20.

Weingut Schales
6521 Flörsheim-Dalsheim. Owners: The Schales family. 81.5 acres. Einzellagen: Flörsheimer-Dalsheimer – Hubacker, Steig, Bürgel, Sauloch and Goldberg. Grosslage: Burg Rodenstein. A sixth-generation family with a private wine museum, making the usual wide range of aromatic wines from the limestone soil of Dalsheim, which they find gives even their QbA and Kabinett wines a 5-10-year life span. 20% Müller-Thurgau, 12% Siegerrebe, 10% Riesling, 8% Huxelrebe, 7% Bacchus, 6% Kerner, 6% Gewürztraminer, 5% Faber, 5% Ruländer, etc. From DM 4.5.

Weingut Schmitt-Dr. Ohnacker
Alsheimerstrasse 41, 6524 Guntersblum. Owner: Walter Ohnacker. 21 acres in Grosslage Vogelsgärten (on slopes) with Einzellagen all in Guntersblum: Himmelthal (5), Authental (2.5), Bornpfad (1.25), Steig-Terrassen (6) and Kreuzkapelle (6); 10 acres in Grosslage Krötenbrunnen (on the flat) with Einzellagen: Eiserne Hand (7.5), St. Julianenbrunnen (1.25) and Steinberg (1.25). The vines are 26% Müller-Thurgau, 20% Riesling, 20% Silvaner, 8% Scheurebe, 6% Ruländer, 4% each of Gewürztraminer, Kerner and Bacchus, 8% Portugieser. 150 years of family ownership; now one of the best specialists in the village, with wines ranging from Himmeltal Riesling (full-bodied and slow to develop) to light-drinking Müller-Thurgau, largely aged in cask, in cellars cut into the hill out of reach of Rhine floods. From DM 4.10.

Weingut Georg Albrecht Schneider
6505 Nierstein. Owner: Albrecht Schneider. 37 acres entirely in Nierstein with holdings in all the principal Einzellagen. A modest, conscientious and candid specialist in fine Niersteiner; the seventh generation of a family of growers. 35% of his vineyard is Riesling, 25% Silvaner, 25% Müller-Thurgau, 15% various well-tried varieties (not new ones). He aims for fruity, 'nervous' wines: i.e. not too mild or sweet, bottling only the best, mainly Rieslings, under his own label.

Weingut Oberst Schultz-Werner
Bahnhofstrasse 10, 6501 Gaubischofsheim über Mainz. Owner: Hans-Christoph Schultz. About 30 acres. Einzellagen: Gau-Bischofsheimer – Herrnberg, Kellersberg, Pfaffenweg and Glockenberg. Grosslagen: Gutes Domtal and St. Alban. A family firm since 1833, with 37% Riesling, 19% Müller-Thurgau, etc. Dry and medium wines of good flavour, made with modern methods (but hand-harvested in an area of mechanical pickers).

RHEINPFALZ

Germany's most fertile, sunniest and most productive wine region takes its English name, the Palatinate, from the former Counts Palatine of the Holy Roman Empire. It stretches in a narrow 50-mile band along the eastern flank of the Haardt mountains, from the southern edge of Rheinhessen to the French frontier, where the Haardt become the Vosges. At the border, in an extraordinary sudden switch, the wines change from the flowery sweetness and lively attack of Germany to the savoury vinosity of Alsace.

With 54,000 acres of vines, Rheinpfalz is marginally second in acreage to Rheinhessen – though regularly a bigger producer. The southern half of the region, from Neustadt south, known as the Bereich Südliche Weinstrasse, is Germany's most up-to-date and intensive vineyard. The last two decades have seen formidable progress – in vine varieties, reorganization of vineyards and cellar technology.

Natural conditions are so favourable here that the city of Landau was once Germany's biggest wine market. Sadly, because it was almost entirely a Jewish enterprise, it was destroyed in 1935 by the Nazis, who then invented the Deutsche Weinstrasse and obliged each German city to adopt a wine village as its supplier of bulk wine. More than half was shipped in tanks to the Mosel for blending – a practice that continued until 1971. No wine was bottled in the region until after World War II. Judgements based on its history and reputation are therefore likely to be wide of the mark. The

Südliche Weinstrasse has no history as a producer of great wine, no great estates, yet its potential is formidable and its wines at present some of the best value in Germany – indeed in Europe.

All the prestige of Rheinpfalz is centred on the half-dozen villages at the centre of its northern half, known as the Mittelhaardt. The 1971 wine law divided the entire region into only two Bereichs: Südliche Weinstrasse for the south and Mittelhaardt-Deutsche Weinstrasse for the north, with the city of Neustadt between them. It thus gave the prestige of the Mittelhaardt to a wide range of vineyards in the north of the region which have nothing in common with it. There should be a third Bereich name for what was formerly called the Unterhaardt. (The Südliche Weinstrasse was formerly called the Oberhaardt, making a logical trio which might well have been preserved.)

Bereich Mittelhaardt-Deutsche Weinstrasse
The northernmost vineyards of Rheinpfalz, hardly separated from the southernmost of Rheinhessen, produce no wine of note or distinction.

Grosslage Schnepfenflug vom Zellertal (Zell)
This Grosslage name, often attached to the village of Zell, is as insignificant as it contrives to be ponderous. Needless to say this Zell, despite having an Einzellage called Schwarzer Herrgott, is distinct in every way from the famous Zell of the Lower Mosel with its Grosslage Schwarze Katz.

Grosslage Grafenstück (Bockenheim)
The town of Bockenheim is the centre of this productive area of some 2,000 acres. A certain amount of pale red Portugieser as well as Müller-Thurgau, Silvaner, a little Riesling and Kerner make reasonable wines on some good sloping sites.

Grosslage Höllenpfad (Grünstadt)
The city of Grünstadt marks the beginning of the Rheinpfalz vineyards in earnest. Here they fan out from the hills with good south and east slopes down on to the sandy plain towards the Rhine. Kleinkarlbach (with its little neighbour Neuleiningen) is the first of the line of Haardt villages that reaches a climax at Forst and Deidesheim. Already here the Riesling is distinctly clean and stylish, and TBA can be extraordinarily fine.
Growers Emil Hammel. Georg Fr. Spiess.

Grosslage Schwarzerde (Kirchheim)
Growers Emil Hammel. K. Neckerauer.

Grosslage Rosenbühl (Freinsheim)
Weissenheim am Sand, down on the plain five miles east, is in complete contrast. The dry sand gives a small crop of very light but clean and agreeable wine – an understatement that suits such aromatic grapes as Kerner but makes Riesling almost neutral. Phylloxera is only a recent arrival here and makes slow progress in the sandy ground. The Portugieser (30% of the vineyard) ripens well and gives a firmer, more savoury red wine than usual.
Grower K. Neckerauer.

Grosslage Kobnert (Kallstadt)
The first famous name of the Mittelhaardt is the Grosslage which was given the former name of a fine Einzellage in Kallstadt. The villages of Dackenheim, Weissenheim am Berg, Herxheim am Berg, Freinsheim, Erpolzheim, Leistadt, Ungstein and Kallstadt now all share in it – which very much lowers its tone. The best vineyards of Ungstein and Kallstadt, however, have exclusive little Grosslagen (*see* Saumagen; Honigsäckel).
Growers Koehler-Ruprecht, Kallstadt. Eduard Schuster, Kallstadt. Stauch, Kallstadt. Winkels-Herding, Dackenheim.

Annaberg
Kallstadt also boasts one of the few German vineyards to be labelled by its own name alone, the famous Annaberg. Annaberg grows Riesling and Scheurebe with a special intensity of flavour that comes from a sheltered, loamy slope and extremely disciplined wine-making. Confusingly enough, Annaberg, along with the 100-acre Kallstadter Kreidkeller, is in the Grosslage Feuerberg, which links it to Bad Dürkheim.
Grower Annaberg Stump-Fitz'sches Weingut.

Grosslage Saumagen (Kallstadt)
Kallstadt's best sites are in Saumagen, a chalky slope where both Riesling and Silvaner make remarkably ripe and intense wine.
Growers Koehler-Ruprecht. Schuster Stauch.

Grosslage Honigsäckel (Ungstein)
Ungstein's best sites (again with a chalky content) also have their own Grosslage name: Honigsäckel. The tiny 7-acre Ungsteiner Michelsberg is included in the Dürkheim Grosslage Hochmess (which just about seems to sum up the whole situation).
Growers Bassermann-Jordan. K. Fitz-Ritter. Pfeffingen. Schaefer.

Bad Dürkheim
Bad Dürkheim is the capital of the Mittelhaardt proper, the main town of the district which flows with richer, more fiery and sumptuous wine than any other in Germany. It musters more than 3,000 acres of vineyards, a busy if not precisely fashionable spa, and a famous annual Sausage Fair (at which wine is at least as much the attraction). A good deal of its wine attempts to be red, presumably for the sausages' sake.

Three Grosslage names are given to different parts of Dürkheim (and its neighbours): Feuerberg, Hochmess and Schenkenböhl.

Feuerberg (Bad Dürkheim)
Feuerberg is a long strip of mainly gentle incline which makes white wine of real character (Annaberg being the best) and reasonably well-coloured red.
Growers K. Fitz-Ritter. Johannes Karst.

Grosslage Hochmess (Bad Dürkheim)
This much smaller Grosslage is devoted mainly to Riesling and Silvaner.
Growers Bassermann-Jordan. K. Fitz-Ritter. Johannes Karst. Schaefer.

Grosslage Schenkenböhl (Wachenheim)
This is a larger area to the south, also embracing the lesser vineyards of Wachenheim.
Growers Bürklin-Wolf. K. Fitz-Ritter. Johannes Karst. Schaefer.

Grosslage Mariengarten (Forst)

The village of Wachenheim begins the real kernel of the Mittelhaardt, a large part of its vineyard devoted to Riesling by the biggest and best estates in the region. The Einzellagen Goldbächel and Gerümpel, generally considered the best, are 100% Riesling. Rheinpfalz Rieslings are all warmer in their wineyness than those farther north. Rheingaus of the Rüdesheimer Berg, perhaps Marcobrunner and Hochheim may be comparable in certain vintages. The great quality of Wachenheim and its neighbours is the elegance (in Wachenheim even the light touch) and the delicacy they deliver with all their ripeness.

In Forst the element of honeyed, velvet ripeness seems more pronounced. The tiny Jesuitengarten in Forst is probably the most famous Rheinpfalz vineyard, although its neighbours on the hill, Ungeheuer, Pechstein, Kirchenstück and Freundstück, share its qualities. The soil here is clay loam, darkened by an outcrop of black basalt, rich in potassium, which in sunny years warms and feeds the ripening grapes to sometimes astonishing concentration of flavours. The greatness of the best wine lies in elegance: however full-bodied, it seems to keep a sort of lilt or lift in your mouth.

As vineyards, Forst and Deidesheim are age-old rivals of really equal standing. As an opera-set wine town, Deidesheim is incomparable. The Rheinpfalz architectural style is dignified rather than quaint: substantial white-walled mansions dressed with rosy sandstone, monumental gateways, trim arcades and cupolas. The indoor style is heavy wainscotting, with leaded windows and mighty fireplaces. Deidesheim is lavish with the comfortable accessories for enjoyment. It is to the Rheinpfalz what Bernkastel is to the Mosel, or St-Emilion to Bordeaux.

All its best vineyards lie in the Grosslage Mariengarten. They have rather lighter, faster draining, warmer soil than those of Forst; the principal difference between the two. Black basalt from Forst is also quarried and spread on the Mariengarten vineyards to make them warmer still. The result is often perfect harmony in medium vintages when Forsters lean towards austerity.

It is almost sacrilege to plant anything but Riesling in sites which bring it to such perfection. Even Riesling with its aristocratic restraint sometimes develops flavours and scents of tropical fruit. Ausleses, Beeren- and Trockenbeerenausleses display their lusciousness in colours ranging from full gold to an almost lurid orange tint in some very sweet wines.

Growers in Wachenheim: Von Buhl. Bürklin-Wolf. Hensel. Mosbacher. Schaefer. J. L. Wolf Erben. In Forst: Bassermann-Jordan. Von Buhl. Bürklin-Wolf. Deinhard. Hahnhof. Dr. Kern. Lindenhof. Mosbacher. J. L. Wolf Erben. In Deidesheim: Bassermann-Jordan. Biffar. Von Buhl. Bürklin-Wolf. Deinhard. Hahnhof. Dr. Kern. Lindenhof. Mosbacher. J. L. Wolf Erben.

Grosslage Schnepfenflug an der Weinstrasse (Forst)

One substantial vineyard in Wachenheim, three in the little-known neighbouring Friedelsheim on the plain, three in Forst and one in Deidesheim make up this second-ranking (by the highest standards) Grosslage.

Growers Bassermann-Jordan. Von Buhl. Bürklin-Wolf. Hahnhof. Lindenhof. Mosbacher.

Grosslage Hofstück (Deidesheim)

The great name of Deidesheim is considerably extended through this area of more than 3,000 acres, 300 of them in Deidesheim, on the flat side of town where a good deal of Müller-Thurgau is grown. Few of the neighbouring villages which benefit from this big-hearted policy are ever heard of except under the umbrella name of Deidesheimer Hofstück. The very considerable exception is Ruppertsberg, the next in the north-south line of foothill villages, with magnificent sites of its own.

The best Ruppertsberg Einzellagen deserve better than to be lumped together with the vineyards of the plain. They are Reiterpfad, Spiess (all Riesling), Nussbein, Hoheburg and Gaisböhl. The larger Linsenbusch is less distinguished.

Growers Bassermann-Jordan. Biffar. Von Buhl. Bürklin-Wolf. Deinhard. Hahnhof. Dr. Kern. Lindenhof.

Grosslage Meerspinne (Neustadt, Ortsteil Gimmeldingen)

The vineyard area south of Ruppertsberg is restricted to the lower slopes of the Haardt range without spilling out into the plain. Two villages, Königsbach and Gimmeldingen, now almost connected to the substantial town of Neustadt, have good-quality vineyards at the tail end of the Mittelhaardt, certainly up to the general level of the Grosslage Hofstück. The Grosslage name Meerspinne is justifiably popular, for lighter wines than those of the central Mittelhaardt from a wider range of grape varieties (although Gimmeldingen itself has 50% Riesling). Wines of these villages sold under Einzellage names are certainly worth investigating.

Growers Von Buhl. Dr. Deinhard. Hahnhof.

Grosslagen Rebstöckel and Pfaffengrund

Growers in Grosslage Rebstöckel (Neustadt an der Weinstrasse, Ortsteil Diedesfeld): Kurt Isler. Dieter Ziegler. In Grosslage Pfaffengrund (Neustadt, Ortsteil Diedesfeld): Bergdolt. Kurt Isler.

Bereich Südliche Weinstrasse

The city of Neustadt is effectively the dividing line between the two Bereichs of Rheinpfalz where Mittelhaardt ends and Südliche Weinstrasse begins (although two Grosslagen to the south, Rebstöckel and Pfaffengrund, are officially in the Mittelhaardt).

From here south to the Alsace border the flourishing vineyard spreads out into the plain, with the city of Landau in its centre, but still, as in the Mittelhaardt, with the spine of hills along its west flank providing all the best sites.

The great majority of wines here are made and marketed by cooperatives, and Grosslage rather than Einzellage names are the rule. Even more common is a grape variety name and the simple appellation Bereich Südliche Weinstrasse.

These wines are steadily increasing in quality and are generally remarkable value for money. There is still a lively tradition of rather harsh and earthy 'Schoppenwein', or wine to be served 'open' by the quarter or half-litre glass. After a good vintage the young wine in the cafés and Weinstuben can have as much vitality and local character as any in Germany, and is very much headier than most. Strident new-variety flavours such as Morio-Muskat and Kerner are common. Ruländer and Weissburgunder are often 'thick', interesting to sip but by no means refreshing. Gewürztraminer can be close to those of Alsace – indeed Alsace now imports quantities of wine from the 'Süd-Pfalz' in bottle. Riesling is very much in the minority, but can also be good, if not precisely 'fine'. Silvaner is popular as the mildest of the wines. Müller-Thurgau is generally at its best overripened to a good sweet Auslese. Spätburgunder and Portugieser are grown for reds but without great enthusiasm or success.

The Grossläge names – Mandelhöhe, Schloss Ludwigshöhe, Ordensgut, Trappenberg, Bischofskreuz, Königsgarten, Herrlich, Kloster Liebfrauenberg, Guttenberg – are only vague guides, covering about a dozen villages each. The most notable villages lie in most cases on or near the Haardt foothills, even though their Grosslagen may extend far out into the plains to the east.

Growers Bergdolt. Kloster Heilsbruck. Marienhof. Minges. Rebholz. Schneider. Siener. Wissing. Ziegler. Gebiets-Winzergenossenschaft Deutsches Weintor.

RHEINPFALZ PRODUCERS

Weingut Dr. v. Bassermann-Jordan

6705 Deidesheim. Owner: Dr. Ludwig von Bassermann-Jordan. 117 acres in Deidesheim: Hohenmorgen (70% of the whole), Grainhübel, Kieselberg, Kalkofen, Leinhöhle, Nonnenstück; Forst: Jesuitengarten, Kirchenstück, Ungeheuer, Pechstein, Freundstück, Stift, Musenhang; Ruppertsberg: Reiterpfad, Hoheburg, Spiess, Nussbien, Linsenbusch; Dürkheim: Michelsberg and Spielberg; Ungstein: Herrenberg. Grosslagen: Hofstück, Mariengarten, Schnepfenflug and Honigsäckel.

A historic house, perhaps the first to make top-quality wines in the region, under its 18th-century founder Andreas Jordan. His grandson-in-law, Dr. Freidrich von Bassermann-Jordan, was in turn a legislator of great influence and a famous historian of wine who started an important wine museum in his medieval cellars. The present owner, his son, maintains impeccable, entirely traditional standards and methods, with Rieslings more delicate than many in the Rheinpfalz but no less long-lived. At present 92% of the estate is Riesling but the remaining 8% is being returned from other varieties to the classic.

Weingut Reichsrat von Buhl

Weinstrasse 16, 6705 Deidesheim. Owner: Georg Enoch, Reichsfreiherr von und zu Guttenberg. Director: Helmut Häussermann. 240 acres in Forst: Bischofsgarten, Ungeheuer, Pechstein, Kirchenstück, Freundstück and Jesuitengarten; Deidesheim: Nonnenstück, Paradiesgarten, Kieselberg and Leinhöhle; Ruppertsberg: Linsenbusch, Hoheburg and Reiterpfad; Wachenheim: Luginsland; Königsbach: Idig, Jesuitengarten and Ölberg. Grosslagen: Mariengarten, Schnepfenflug and Hofstück.

One of the biggest and most illustrious wine estates in Germany, founded in 1849 and still in the same family. 73% is Riesling, 14% Müller-Thurgau, 4% Gewürztraminer, 3·5% Scheurebe, all on generous flat or gently sloping fertile land. The wines are barrel-aged, powerful and full-bodied, and range from dry, even severe, café wines to TBAs. Prices: from DM 5.20.

Weingut Dr. Bürklin-Wolf

Weinstrasse 65, 6706 Wachenheim.

Owner: Bettina Bürklin. Director: Georg Raquet. 247 acres in Wachenheim: Gerümpel, Goldbächel, Altenburg, Böhlig, Luginsland, Bischofsgarten, Mandelgarten, Königswingert and Rechbächel (sole owner); Forst: Kirchenstück, Ungeheuer, Jesuitengarten, Pechstein, Bischofsgarten; Deidesheim: Hohenmorgen, Langenmorgen, Kalkofen, Herrgottsacker; Ruppertsberg: Hoheburg, Reiterpfad, Nussbien, Linsenbusch and Gaisböhl (sole owner). Grosslagen: Schnepfenflug, Mariengarten, Schenkenböhl and Hofstück.

A magnificent estate in all the best vineyards of the Mittelhaardt, generally acknowledged as the finest in the region and one of the best in Germany. It has been in the family for 400 years and the cask cellar goes back to the 16th century. Dr. Albert Bürklin, one of his country's greatest wine men, died in October 1979 and his daughter inherited the estate. The Director, formerly at the great Nahe State Domain at Niederhausen, is supremely qualified to continue the tradition.

The vines are 75% Riesling, 15% Müller-Thurgau, 4% Ehrenfelser, 2% Weissburgunder, with some Gewürztraminer, Scheurebe, Spätburgunder (for red wine) and experimental varieties. The style of wine is the most 'racy', deft and harmonious in the Rheinpfalz, from light-vintage semi-dry Riesling Kabinetts, so pure and refreshing that you could drink them for breakfast, to great orange-tinted late-picked wines of amazing spice and expressiveness. Recently some superb Eisweins (including in 1979 a very rare TBA Eiswein) have been made. Technology includes the most modern ideas; many young wine makers have learned their art here.

Gutsverwaltung Deinhard

Weinstrasse 10, 6705 Deidesheim. Director: Heinz Bauer. 46.5 acres in Deidesheim: Herrgottsacker (16) and Paradiesgarten (1.5); Ruppertsberg: Linsenbusch (20); Forst: Ungeheuer (9).

The Koblenz merchants Deinhard rented this section of the old Dr. Deinhard estate in 1973. There are said to be old family connections and the two estates are run by the same Director from the same fine sandstone Gutshaus in Deidesheim (*see* next entry), but their wines are made apart and labelled differently. Deinhard's wines, like those of their estates in the Rheingau and Mosel, are models of correct and characterful wine-making. Linsenbusch is a relatively light wine from flat land; the others are on slopes, riper and more 'Pfalzy' – Ungeheuer best of all, rarely producing less than Spätleses. 56% is Riesling, 26% Müller-Thurgau.

Weingut Dr. Deinhard

Weinstrasse 10, 6705 Deidesheim. Owners: The Renate Hoch family. Director: Heinz Bauer. 99 acres in Deidesheim: Leinhöhle, Grainhübel, Kieselberg, Kalkofen, Paradiesgarten and Nonnenstück; Ruppertsberg: Reiterpfad and Nussbien; Forst and Neustadt-Gimmeldingen.

A well-known estate built up in the 19th century by Dr. Andreas Deinhard, a founder of the German Winegrowers' Association and an influential legislator. His handsome Gutshaus (built 1848) now houses both this and the estate rented to Deinhards (*see* previous entry). Vines are 70% Riesling, 5-6% each Müller-Thurgau, Scheurebe, Gewürztraminer, Ehrenfelser, Kerner and others. The emphasis is on Kabinett wines with good acidity. Prices: from DM 6.00.

Weingut K. Fitz-Ritter

Weinstrasse Nord 51, 6702 Bad Dürkheim. Owner: Konrad Fitz. 54 acres, 17 in Grosslage Schenkenböhl: Einzellagen Dürkheimer – Abtsfronhof (sole owner) and Fronhof, and Wachenheimer Mandelgarten; 19 acres in Grosslage Hochmess: Einzellagen Dürkheimer – Michelsberg, Spielberg,

Rittergarten and Hochbenn; 9 acres in Grosslage Feuerberg: Einzellagen Dürkheimer Nonnengarten and Ellerstadter Bubeneck; 4 acres in Grosslage Honigsäckel: Einzellage Ungsteiner Herrenberg; 5 acres in Grosslage Hofstück: Einzellage Ellerstadter Kirchenstück.

A family estate with a fine classical 18th-century mansion (1785) whose park contains the largest maidenhair tree (*Ginkgo biloba*) in Germany, along with other noble trees. The Fitz family also started here (in 1828) one of the oldest Sekt businesses in Germany. 60% of their vines are Riesling, 5.5% Gewürztraminer, 6% Spätburgunder, 4% Scheurebe. Most of their wines are QmP (Kabinett or better) with a high reputation for individuality.

Weingut Hahnhof

Weinstrasse 1, 6705 Deidesheim. Owners: The Hahn family. 66 acres, in Deidesheimer – Herrgottsacker, Mäushöhle, Kalkofen, Grainhübel, Leinhöhle and Paradiesgarten; Forster – Freundstück, Jesuitengarten, Ungeheuer, Elster, Musenhang and Pechstein; Ruppertsberger – Mandelgarten, Nussbien and Königsbacher Weg. Grosslagen: Hofstück, Mariengarten and Schnepfenflug.

An unusual company (its name translates as 'hen house'), founded in 1929 to produce and market Pfalz wines, sausages and bread in its own wine bars all over Germany (there are 7 in Munich alone). It has contracts with 120 growers as well as using its own grapes (which are 57% Riesling, 25% Müller-Thurgau, 12% Silvaner) to produce a total of more than 20,000 cases a year. The company also slaughters 50-60 pigs a week and bakes countless loaves of bread (80% rye, 20% wheat flour) according to a 17th-century recipe, in an old stone oven in Deidesheim (where it owns the Hotel Deidesheimer Hof). The Hahns can claim to have popularized Pfalz wine in Germany.

Weingut Pfeffingen, Karl Fuhrmann

6702 Bad Dürkheim. Owner: Karl Fuhrmann. 25 acres in Ungsteiner – Herrenberg and Nussriegel. Grosslage: Honigsäckel.

A highly regarded little estate, formerly in the Schnell family, with buildings surrounded by vines at Ungstein on the road north from Bad Dürkheim. 40% is Riesling, 18% Müller-Thurgau, 12% Scheurebe, 15% Silvaner, 9% Ruländer, 6% Gewürztraminer and Morio-Muskat. Fuhrmann's wines have considerable finesse, the Rieslings often dry and the Scheurebes juicily rich. Even wines from 'off' vintages age long and gracefully.

Weingut Ökonomierat Rebholz

Weinstrasse 54, 6741 Seibeldingen. Owners: The Rebholz family. 22 acres. Einzellagen: Birkweiler Kastanienbusch; Siebeldinger im Sonnenschein. Grosslage: Königsgarten.

The family that pioneered quality wine-making in the area, where steep sites and varied soils give good opportunities. In 1949 Eduard Rebholz (grandfather of the present director, Hansjörg) was the first man to make a Müller-Thurgau TBA, thus making the workhorse grape respectable. The vines are 30% each Riesling and Müller-Thurgau, 15% Spätburgunder, 10% each Gewürztraminer and Ruländer. Sweet reserve is never used, so Kabinett and Spätlese wines are almost always dry, and there are no QbA wines. The resulting wines are clean, racy and exciting – outstanding in the area.

Annaberg Stumpf-Fitz'sches Weingut

6702 Bad Dürkheim-Leistadt. Owner: Frau Ingeborg Meder (née Nenninger). 12 acres, all 'Annaberg'.

Perhaps the most famous little wine property in Germany, a Roman monument, a nature reserve and an exceptional vineyard, planted with Riesling, Scheurebe and Weissburgunder. It was established as a model estate by Eugen Stumpf-Fitz a century ago. Late and small harvests give the wines concentration and a balance that preserves them for years. Scheurebes are highly aromatic, Rieslings stiff with flavour; a 1964 Auslese was perfect in 1982.

Gebiets-Winzergenossenschaft Deutsches Weintor

6741 Ilbesheim. Director: Ökonomierat Wilhelm Knecht.

The massive central cooperative of the Südliche Weinstrasse, symbolized by its great stone gateway, the 'Deutsches Weintor', which stands challengingly on the border of French Alsace at Schweigen. Its 1,255 members farm a total of 28,252 acres in 35 communes, filling its vast vat houses with a total capacity of 30m. litres – said to be the biggest in Europe.

24% is Morio-Muskat, 20% Müller-Thurgau, 16.3% Silvaner, 10% Kerner, 4% each Ruländer and Huxelrebe, 3.4% Scheurebe, only 0.2% Riesling. The resulting wines are mild and often highly aromatic (especially Morio-Muskat and its blends), mainly sweet, often with good vitality and balance which makes them excellent value. The Weintor has made several Grosslage names almost household words in Germany: e.g. Guttenberg, Kloster Liebfrauenberg, Herrlich, Bischofskreuz, Trappenberg, Königsgarten, Ordensgut and Schloss Ludwigshöhe.

OTHER PRODUCERS

Weingut Josef Biffar
Niederkirchenerstrasse 13, 6705 Deidesheim. Owner: Gerhard Biffar. 29 acres in Deidesheimer – Nonnenstück, Herrgottsacker, Mäushöhle, Kieselberg, Leinhöhle, Grainhübel and Kalkofen; Ruppertsberger – Nussbien, Linsenbusch and Reiterpfad. Grosslagen: Hofstück and Mariengarten. A well-regarded estate for traditional cask-aged wines of good balance. 70% is Riesling, 20% Müller-Thurgau.

Emil Hammel & Cie
Weinstrasse Süd 4, 6719 Kirchheim. Owners: Rudolf and Martin Hammel. 54 acres in Bissersheimer – Goldberg and Held; Kirchheimer – Kreuz, Römerstrasse, Steinacker and Geisskopf; Neuleininger Sonnenberg; Kleinkarlbacher Herrenberg; Dirmsteiner Mandelpfad. Grosslagen: Schwarzerde and Höllenpfad. Growers and merchants with a total production of some 75,000 cases – 5 times their own production, which is supplemented by buying grapes locally. The company has grown phenomenally recently as a purveyor of very good carafe wines, mainly semi-dry, with the stress on Müller-Thurgau, Riesling and (red) Portugieser (but plenty of alternatives, including the excellent St-Emilion, Château Soutard).

Kloster Heilsbruck
Klosterstrasse, 6732 Edenkoben. Owners: Ueberle & Ritzhaupt KG. Manager: Rudolf Nagel. 25 acres in Edenkobener – Klostergarten and Bergel. Old monastic buildings with the rustic atmosphere of a century ago shelter an enormous range of old oak casks with a total capacity of 450,000 litres. The oak-aged wines keep remarkably: although not particularly fine they are fascinating in representing an almost-lost tradition.

Weingut Johannes Karst & Söhne
Burgstrasse 15, 6702 Bad Dürkheim. Owner: Heinz Karst. 25 acres in Dürkheimer – Fuchsmantel, Spielberg,

Hochbenn and Michelsberg. Grosslagen: Feuerberg, Schenkenböhl and Hochmess. A family firm of growers and merchants. 80% of their own vines are Riesling, 10% Scheurebe. Scheurebe has recently become something of a speciality.

Weingut Koehler-Ruprecht
Weinstrasse 84, 6701 Kallstadt. Owners: The Philippi family. President: Otto Philippi. 21 acres in Kallstadter – Steinacker and Kronenberg. Grosslagen: Kobnert and Saumagen. A family property going back centuries, including the charming hotel 'Weincastell' – all typical antiques and local food. Vines are 65% Riesling, with red Spätburgunder as another speciality. The Kallstadt vineyards ripen grapes remarkably: Herr Philippi reports that he can always make an Auslese. Cellar methods are traditional, the wines full of flavour. From DM 5.50.

Weingut Ernst Minges
Postfach 11, 6731 Edesheim. Owner: Ernst Minges. 20 acres in Edesheimer – Forst, Mandelhang and Rosengarten; Rhodter – Rosengarten, Schlossberg and Klosterpfad; Weyherer – Michelsberg and Heide; Edenkobener – Kirchberg and Heilig Kreuz. The Grosslagen names are not used.
The Minges family gives 1285 as its date of foundation. At present it is having remarkable success with prize-winning wines, including the top state prize 4 years running. The firm is both grower and merchant, distinguishing its own wines with Einzellage names and using only grape-variety names on wines made from bought-in grapes. Its own vines are 60% Riesling (best in Edesheimer Forst, Weyherer Michelsberg, Edenkobener Kirchberg). Rhodter Rosengarten is best for Traminer (5%). Others are Kerner (6%), Silvaner (10%), etc. Restrained cropping and late picking give intense wines which are not oversweetened.

Weingut Georg Mosbacher
Weinstrasse 27, 6701 Forst. Owners: The Mosbacher family. 20 acres in Forster – Ungeheuer, Pechstein, Elster, Freundstück, Musenhang, Stift and Süsskopf; Deidesheimer Herrgottsacker; Wachenheimer Altenburg. Grosslagen: Mariengarten and Schnepfenflug.
The Mosbachers have steadily improved this small estate in the centre of Forst since they first bottled their wine in 1920. 75% is Riesling, 10% Müller-Thurgau, 5% Silvaner, 3% Traminer, 7% others. They regularly win prizes with freshly flowery wines, particularly dry Riesling Kabinett from Forster Pechstein and Stift. Wines are sold direct or at their own Weinstube. From DM 5.00.

Weingut K. Neckerauer
Ritter von Geisslerstrasse 9, 6714 Weissenheim. Owner: Klaus Neckerauer. 40 acres. Einzellagen: Hahnen, Hasenzeile, Goldberg, Altenberg, Halde and Burgweg. 16% of the property is only under the Grosslage names Rosenbühl and Schwarzerde. The third generation (sales in bottle began in 1930), Klaus is a most competent wine maker who matches varieties with soil types to produce intense dry Riesling Kabinetts, aromatic medium Kerner, fruity Müller-Thurgau and light (often 'Weissherbst') Portugieser. The sandy soil and low rainfall make crops small, particularly of Riesling. From DM 4.20.

Ludwig Schneider GmbH
Maikammerstrasse 7, 6731 St. Martin. Owners: The Schneider family. Einzellagen: St. Martiner – Baron, Kirchberg and Zitadelle. Grosslagen: Schloss Ludwigshöhe and Mandelhöhe. A merchant house (turnover 125,000 cases a year) handling the produce of the 'St. Martinus' Producers' Cooperative. It owns a beautiful old inn, one of the prettiest timbered Renaissance buildings of the Südliche Weinstrasse. The style of wines is light, extrovert, *spritzig*; good pub wines intended for people answering the same description.

Weingut Eduard Schuster
Neugasse 21, 6701 Kallstadt. Owners: Gerhard and Manfred Schuster. 47 acres in Kallstadter – Steinacker, Kronenberg and Kirchenstück. Grosslagen: Kobnert and Saumagen. The eleventh generation making wine, with a particular penchant for Silvaner, which 'blooms' on the limy marl of Kallstadt. 23% is Silvaner, 31% Riesling, with a wide variety of other vines including Muskateller. All are made in oak in vaulted sandstone cellars.

Kommerzienrat Georg Fr. Spiess
Kleinkarlbach. Owners: The Spiess family. 50 acres in Kleinkarlbacher – Herrenberg and Herrgottsacker; Neuleiningen Schlossberg. Riesling and Müller-Thurgau, about 38% each. A flourishing estate with high standards. Direct sales only. Fine Rieslings include a clean, light, vintage Sekt.

Weingut J. L. Wolf Erben
Weinstrasse 1, 6706 Wachenheim. Owners: Dieter and Ingrid Müller. 49 acres in Wachenheimer – Königswingert, Gerümpel, Altenburg and Goldbächel; Forster – Ungeheuer, Jesuitengarten and Pechstein; Deidesheimer – Herrgottsacker and Leinhöhle. Almost uniquely in the region, the vines are 100% Riesling. The wines are well made and racy, from dry to medium-sweet.

COOPERATIVES

Winzerverein Deidesheim
Prinz Rupprechtstrasse 8, 6705 Deidesheim. 428 members with 543 acres in Deidesheim, Ruppertsberg, Forst, Niederkirchen, Meckensheim and Wachenheim. Some 400 of the total acreage is Riesling; as high a proportion as in the commune as a whole. The cooperative sets standards in keeping with the wine capital of the Rheinpfalz.

Winzerverein Forst
Weinstrasse 57, 6701 Forst. Director: Heinz Lucas. Founded 1918. 117 members with 148 acres in Forst, Deidesheim and Wachenheim. Grosslagen: Schnepfenflug, Mariengarten and Hofstück. The highly regarded cooperative of Forst, with 100 acres of Riesling in fine sites. Half the sales are in bottle and half in cask to wholesalers.

Winzerverein Liebfrauenberg
Südliche Winzerstrasse 2, 6713 Freinsheim. 240 members with 691 acres in Freinsheim. Grosslagen: Kobnert and Rosenbühl. Apparently the largest coop of a single commune in Germany, well placed at the northern end of the Mittelhaardt. Two thirds of the wine is white (40% Silvaner; 30% Riesling). The red is 95% Portugieser.

Niederkirchener Winzerverein
6701 Niederkirchen bei Deidesheim. 446 members with 1,062 acres in Niederkirchen, Deidesheim, Forst and Ruppertsberg. Grosslage: Hofstück. The biggest cooperative of the Mittelhaardt, with a range of distinguished Einzellage names, 475 acres of Riesling, 350 Müller-Thurgau, 100 Portugieser and considerable Kerner, Traminer and Silvaner.

Ruppertsberger Winzerverein 'Hoheburg'
6701 Ruppertsberg. 195 members with 457 acres: 408 in Ruppertsberg and the rest in Meckenheim, Mussbach, Königsbach and Deidesheim. Grosslage: Hofstück. One third of the total is Riesling. Apart from the usual Silvaner and Müller-Thurgau, Kerner and Portugieser have an important share. The top Ruppertsberg Rieslings can be excellent.

Winzergenossenschaft Wachtenburg-Luginsland
Postfach 47, 6706 Wachenheim. Director: Rudi Burnikel, 320 members with 691 acres in Wachenheim and 123 in Gönnheim. Grosslagen: Schenkenböhl and Schnepfenflug. A largely Riesling-oriented Mittelhaardt cooperative with land in several of the best Einzellagen of Wachenheim.

HESSISCHE BERGSTRASSE

Germany's smallest separate wine region lies across the Rhine from Worms, in steep, even terraced, hills north of Heidelberg with a westerly outlook over the Rhine valley. Its fame today lies largely in the fact that the Hessen State Domain, based at Eltville in the Rheingau, has vineyards here, at Bensheim and Heppenheim.

The region is divided into two Bereichs: Umstadt, a remote minor area, away from the Rhine east of Darmstadt, principally Müller-Thurgau, and Starkenburg, a north-south hillside 10 miles long containing Bensheim, Heppenheim and five other villages with three Grosslagen and 18 Einzellagen. Starkenburg is warm enough, with its light sandy loam on its west slopes, to ripen the Riesling which dominates its vineyards, giving Rheingau-like wines without the finesse of the more famous region.

From south to north the Grosslagen are Schlossberg (for Heppenheim), Wolfsmagen (for Bensheim) and Rott (for Schönberg, Auerbach, Zwingenburg and Alsbach). Seeheim is a one-vineyard village to the north with no Grosslage name. The total area under vine is some 900 acres.

Most of the wine is made in the two cooperatives, the Bergstrasse Gebietswinzergenossenschaft at Heppenheim and the Odenwälder Winzergenossenschaft at Gross Umstadt. Both have Weinstubes, as do a score of small growers and the State Domain.

HESSISCHE BERGSTRASSE PRODUCERS

Weingut der Stadt Bensheim
6140 Bensheim. Director: Herr Blechschmitt. The town of Bensheim has a small estate of about 20 acres in the Grosslage Wolfsmagen, planted 90% with Riesling, selling most of its wine by the litre or 'open' in local cafés.

Staatsweingut Bergstrasse
Grieselstrasse 34-36, 614 Bensheim. Director: Heinrich Hillenbrand. 89.5 acres. Einzellagen: Heppenheimer – Centgericht (sole owner) and Steinkopf; Bensheimer – Steichling and Kalkgasse; Schönberger Herrnwingert (sole owner). Much the largest estate in this minor region between Frankfurt and Heidelberg, but in fact part of the old Prussian State Domain now administered from Eltville in the Rheingau (*see* page 249). Vines are 62% Riesling, 10% Müller-Thurgau, 8% Ruländer, 5% Weissburgunder, 3% Gewürztraminer. Spätburgunder and new varieties total 12%. The wines are mild, well balanced, sometimes distinctly juicy with good acidity. The best site is Centgericht in Heppenheim, especially for dry or semi-dry Kabinett.

Weingut H. Freiberger OHG
Hermannstrasse 16, 6148 Heppenheim. 30 acres. Einzellagen: Heppenheimer – Maiberg, Steinkopf, Eckweg, Guldenzoll and Stemmler. Grosslage Schlossberg. The leading private estate of the district, making a broad spectrum of powerful, uninhibited dry to medium wines of all qualities for local consumption. Vines are 44% Riesling, 17% Müller-Thurgau, 14% Ruländer, 11% Ehrenfelser and 14% Gewürztraminer, Kerner, Spätburgunder, Silvaner and Scheurebe. The late-harvest Ruländers have great character and have reached TBA sweetness.

FRANKEN

Fifty miles east of the Rheingau, beyond the city of Frankfurt, the river Main, flowing to join the Rhine at Hochheim, scribbles a huge drunken W through the irregular limestone and red marl hills of Franken (Franconia), the northern extremity of Bavaria.

The centre of the region is the baroque city of Würzburg. Its most famous vineyard, sloping down to the Main within the city itself, is Würzburger Stein. The name Stein has been traditionally borrowed by foreigners to describe Franconian wine generically (as the English shortened Hochheim to 'hock' for all Rhine wines). 'Steinwein' comes in fat flagons called Bocksbeutels, thus distinguishing itself from almost all other German wines, which come in elegant flasks. This is probably the extent of popular knowledge. It is a specialized subject, not least because its rarity value and local popularity keep the price higher than we are accustomed to pay for more famous names from the Rhine and Mosel. Most 'Frankenwein' is drunk in Bavaria, particularly in Munich, or in the wealthy cities of northern Germany. Besides, the area is exceptionally diffuse and hard to comprehend. Vineyards are only found on exceptional south slopes. The climate is harsh and serious frosts are common; the season is too short for regular success with Riesling.

Traditionally Franken has made its best wine with the Silvaner, only here and occasionally on the Rhein-front in Rheinhessen a better-than-moderate variety. Silvaner here can produce full-bodied dry wines (and occasionally sweet ones) with a noble breadth and substance; dense, even sticky in their intensity. They are regularly compared with white burgundy, not for their flavour but for their vinosity and ability to match rich food at table.

Unfortunately the Müller-Thurgau has now gained the upper hand. It works well, but rarely if ever produces the remarkable low-key stylishness of Silvaner. Scheurebe and the new Perle can do better. Bacchus tends to be aggressively aromatic; out of keeping for the region. Kerner is also too aromatic, although many people find it acceptable. In a ripe year Rieslaner is a good compromise, making excellent Ausleses with the breadth of a Silvaner and the depth of a Riesling. 1976 in the Steigerwald produced some extraordinary wines with a bouquet like salty honey.

The rambling region is divided into three Bereichs: Mainviereck for its lower reaches towards Frankfurt; Maindreieck for its heart, the district of Würzburg; and Steigerwald for its eastern extremities with the sternest climate of all. The Bereich names are frequently used, partly because a great number of the scattered vineyards are included in no Grosslage. The majority of wine, as in Rheinhessen, is made by cooperatives. Würzburg itself, however, boasts three of the oldest, biggest and best wine estates in Germany – the Bürgerspital, the Juliusspital and the Staatliche Hofkeller.

Bereich Mainviereck

Bereich Mainviereck extends across the famous Spessart forest from Aschaffenburg in the northwest down to Kreuzwertheim in the first trough of the W described by the Main. The very limited vineyard area is all close to the river with the exception of Rück, in a little eastern side valley. The soils are largely sandstone based and loamy. Two Grosslagen: Reuschberg (Hörstein) and Heiligenthal (Grossostheim) and 15 villages where no Grosslage name applies.

Growers Staatlicher Hofkeller. Juliusspital. Winzergenossenschaft Thüngersheim.

Bereich Mandreieck

Bereich Mandreieck includes Homburg and Lengfurt, next door to Kreuzwertheim, but then leaps over the central ridge of the W to an isolated area of vines on the tributary river Saale around Hammelburg. Here the soil is limestone (Muschelkalk), the soil of all the best Franconian vineyards. Nine Grosslagen: Burg (Hammelburg), Rosstal (Karlstadt), Ravensburg (Thüngersheim), Ewig Leben (Randersacker), Ölspiel (Sommerhausen), Teufelstor (Eibelstadt), Hofrat (Kitzingen), Honigberg (Dettelbach) and Kirchberg (Volkach).

The first isolated Mandreieck vineyards, grouped around Homburg and Lengfurt, have no Grosslage name. The Grosslage Hammelburger Burg, to the northeast, includes all the vineyards of the river Saale.

Growers Fürstlich Lowenstein. Schloss Saaleck. Winzergenossenschaft Hammelburg.

The western trough of the W is the centre of Franconian wine production, with Würzburg at its heart. The main concentrations of vines are in the villages north and south of Würzburg along the river, all on limestone, down to Frickenhausen, the foot of the eastern trough of the W, and in bends in the river higher up around Escherndorf and Nordheim, still on limestone but here with an overlay of marly clay. The famous hill of Escherndorfer Lump makes great Silvaners from this soil structure.

The wines of all the principal vineyards can be tasted and compared at the big, bustling Weinstuben of the three great Würzburg estates. The Juliusspital, the Bürgerspital and the Staatliche Hofkeller all maintain wonderfully comfortable and convivial cafés for the appreciation of their wines in a city which is infiltrated with vineyards to its very heart. You can look up from its famous baroque statue-lined bridge (on feast days one long café from end to end) to see the steep vine-ramp of the Leiste supporting the Marienberg Castle. The celebrated Stein vineyard covers the best parts of the south-facing hill overlooking the city – a skyline now sadly marred by ugly and intrusive new buildings. Steinwein begins to have real meaning when you have sipped a stiff Silvaner Spätlese at the Bürgerspital and gone on to marvel at Tiepolo's ceilings in the Residenz.

Growers Bürgerspital. Gebhardt. Herpfer. Juliusspital. Knoll & Reinhart. Müller. Staatlicher Hofkeller. Winzergenossenschafts Nordheim, Randersacker and Thungersheim.

Bereich Steigerwald

Wine communities to the east of the Main form this much smaller Bereich. The best known are Iphofen, Rödelsee and Castell, all on heavier marly clay soil which demands a fine summer but can deliver both full-bodied and nicely nuanced wines. Six Grosslagen: Schild (Abtswind), Herrenberg (Castell), Schlossberg (Rödelsee), Burgweg (Iphofen), Schlossstück (Frankenberg) and Kapellenberg (Zeil).

Growers Bürgerspital. Fürstlich Castell. Herpfer. Juliusspital. Knoll & Reinhart. Müller. Ernst Popp. Staatlicher Hofkeller. Wirsching. Gebietswinzergenossenschaft Franken.

FRANKEN PRODUCERS

Bürgerspital zum Heiligen Geist

Theaterstrasse 19, 8700 Würzburg. Wine Director: Rudolf Friess. 333 acres. Einzellagen: Würzburger – Stein (79), Pfaffenberg (91), Abtsleite (47) and Innere Leiste; Randersackerer – Teufelskeller (15), Marsberg and Pfülben; Veitshöchheimer Sonnenschein; Thüngersheimer Scharlachberg; Michlelauer Vollburg; Gössenheimer Homburg-Arnberg; Leinacher Himmelberg. (No Grosslage names are used.)

A splendid charity founded in 1319 for the old people of Würzburg by Johannes von Steren, and although now somewhat overshadowed by the even richer ecclesiastical upstart, the Juliusspital (q.v.), still the fourth-biggest wine estate in Germany, with the biggest share of Würzburg's famous Stein and other good south slopes. The vineyards are 20% each Riesling, Silvaner and Müller-Thurgau, the rest being Kerner, Scheurebe, Bacchus, Traminer, Ruländer, Spätburgunder, Weissburgunder and several new varieties.

Hearty, full-flavoured and dry Rieslings are the pride of the house, though a tasting at the huge 500-seater Weinstube in the venerable hospital buildings leaves an impression of powerful and flavoury wines from almost any variety.

Fürstlich Castell'sches Domänenamt

8711 Castell Unterfranken. Owners: Prince Albrecht zu Castell-Castell and Prince Michael zu Salm. 102 acres. Einzellagen: Casteller – Schlossberg (15), Kugelspiel (30), Bausch (40), Hohnart, Kirchberg, Trautberg, Reitsteig and Feuerbach (the last 2 for red wine).

A gem of an operatic princely estate with classic palace in a village on a hill, the vineyards sloping up to perfectly kept oakwoods – the princes' other pride. The Castells grow no Riesling but make fine, admirably balanced wines of Müller-Thurgau (36%), Silvaner (20%) and a catholic range of newer varieties; also admirable Sekt ('Casteller Herrenberg'). The new varieties tend to taste more or less '*schmalzig*' and trite beside the dignified soft earthiness of the classic Silvaner. Scheurebe is successfully spicy; Rieslaner excellent for Silvaner-style Ausleses. Visitors to this remote spot can taste the wines in a beautiful tasting room decorated with *trompe l'oeil*, or in the 'Weinstall', a stable-turned-restaurant. Prices: from DM 8.80.

Weinbau-Weinkellerei Christoph Hs. Herpfer

Paul-Eberstrasse 5-7, 8710 Kitzingen. Director: Peter Herpfer.

A most unusual democratically run producers' association (not a cooperative) with members in Escherndorf, Volkach, Nordheim, Sommerach, Kitzingen, Rödelsee, Würzburg, Randersacker and elsewhere. The object is individual wines made by modern methods, entirely protected from oxygen, dry in the regional style but with very distinct fruitiness. Silvaners from the limestone of Würzburg, Randersacker and Escherndorf are probably their finest wines, with Scheurebes for the richest wines in ripe vintages.

Juliusspital-Weingut

Juliuspromenade 19, 8700 Würzburg 1. Wine Director: Heinrich Selsam. 374 acres. Einzellagen: Würzburger – Stein (49), Pfaffenberg (40), Innere Leiste (10) and Abtsleite (40); Randersackerer – Teufelskeller (10) and Pfülben (12); Escherndorfer Lump; Iphöfer – Julius-Echter-Berg (20) and Kronsberg; Rödelseer Küchenmeister; Volkacher Karthäuser; Thüngersheimer Johannisberg; Bürgstädter Mainhölle. (No Grosslage names are used.)

A charitable foundation on a scale even grander than the Hospices de Beaune, founded in 1576 by the Prince-Bishop Julius Echter von Mespelbrunn and now the third-largest wine estate in Germany, supporting a magnificent hospital for the people of Würzburg. Its low-vaulted cellar, 150 metres long, was built in 1699 under the great classical 'Fürstenbau' wing by Antonio Petrini. The vineyards are 43% Silvaner, 24% Müller-Thurgau, 13% Riesling. The remaining 20% includes Gewürztraminer, Ruländer, Weissburgunder, Muskateller, Scheurebe, Spätburgunder (in Bürgstadt) and several new varieties. All are matured in oak. Aside from the classic Silvaners, the Riesling and Rieslaner are particularly fruity, extrovert and powerful. All QmP white wines have black labels (lesser white wines have green, and reds, red). The wines can be tasted in the hospital's own Weinstube. Prices: from DM 8.50.

Fürstlich Löwenstein-Wertheim-Rosenberg'sches Weingut

Kreuzwertheim. Owner: Prince Alois Konstantin zu Löwenstein-Wertheim-Rosenberg. 66 acres. Einzellagen: Homburger Kallmuth (26); Lengfurter – Alter Berg and Oberrot; Reichholzheimer Satzenberg (15; Reichholzheim is in the Bereich Badisches Frankenland in Baden); Bronnbacker – Josefsberg (12) and Kemelrain.

An isolated estate on the north bank of the Main west of the main Franken vineyards. The old Cistercian vineyards dating from the 12th century were acquired by the princely family at their secularization.

The vines are 47% Silvaner, 19.5% Müller-Thurgau, 9.2% Bacchus, 7.6% Kerner, only 4.2% Riesling, and 12.5% others. The soil is an odd mixture of sandstone and limestone, on good slopes which ripen well. The style is powerful, dry and altogether Franconian. Prices: from DM 8.30.

Staatlicher Hofkeller

Residenzplatz 3, 8700 Würzburg. Director: Dr. Eichelsbacher. 287 acres. Einzellagen: Würzburger – Stein (72) and Innere Leiste (22); Randersackerer – Teufelskeller, Pfülben and Marsberg (total 45); Hörsteiner Abtsberg (30); Grossheubacher Bischofsberg (7, red wine); Kreuzwertheimer Kaffelstein (15, red wine); Handthaler Stollberg (15); Abtswinder Altenberg (15) and Thüngersheimer Scharlachberg (66).

The superlative vineyards of the lordly Prince-Bishops of Würzburg, originating in the 12th century, are now (since 1814) the Bavarian State domain, run by the Bayerische Landesanstalt für Weinbau und Gartenbau. The great cellar under the baroque Residency at Würzburg is one of the most stirring sights in the world of wine. The vines, on many different soils, are 20% each Riesling and Müller-Thurgau, 10% each Silvaner and Rieslaner, 8% each Perle and Ortega, 6% Spätburgunder, and many others in small quantities. The object is wines of true Franconian style, balancing high acidity with powerful flavours, all either dry or semi-dry (except for Ausleses, etc.). The '76 Spätleses of Riesling and Rieslaner were the estate's ideal: highly concentrated and aromatic dry wines. The estate has a college at Veitshochheim and restaurants in Würzburg, Schloss Aschaffenburg (another cellar) and Stollberg in the Steigerwald. Prices: from DM 7.00.

Weingut Hans Wirsching

Ludwigstrasse 16, 8715 Iphofen. Owners: Hans and Dr. Heinrich Wirsching. 100 acres. Einzellagen: Iphofener – Julius-Echter-Berg, Kronsberg and Kalb; Rödelseer Küchenmeister. Grosslagen: Iphofer Burgweg, Rödelseer Schlossberg.

A family firm since 1630 with its original Gutshaus and cellars, as well as modern ones outside the village. 30% each Silvaner and Müller-Thurgau, 8% each Riesling, Kerner and Scheurebe. Half the wines are fully dry; the rest not greatly sweetened. The Wirschings take great pride in the fact that their wines (Iphofer Silvaner and Scheurebe) were recently served to the Pope. Most of their business is direct to consumers. Prices: from DM 8.00.

Throughout the chapter on Germany, names of the Einzellagen producing the finest wines will be found in the Producers' entries.

OTHER PRODUCERS

Weingut Weingrosskellerei Ernst Gebhardt
Hauptstrasse 21-23, 8701 Sommerhäusen. Owners: Karl and Ernst Hügelschäffer. 37 acres. Einzellagen: Sommerhäuser: – Reifenstein and Steinbach (21); Eibelstädter Kapellenberg; Frickenhäuser Fischer; Randersacker Teufelskeller and Marktbreiter Sonnenberg. An 18th-century family estate bought in 1888 by the Hügelschäffer family, who are also wine merchants. They make somewhat fruitier and sweeter wines than the old Franconian style with great skill, especially from their best sites: Steinbach and the famous Teufelskeller. 30% is Silvaner, 21% Müller-Thurgau, 20% Scheurebe (a favourite, distinctly blackcurranty), 7% Bacchus. They are also particularly keen on Rieslaner, Traminer and Weissburgunder. Their Weinstube in the Flemish baroque style is a well-known attraction. From DM 8.00.

Weinbau-Weinkellerei Knoll & Reinhart
8710 Kitzingen 2. Owner: Erich Knoll. 7.5 acres in the villages of Sommerach, Rödelsee and Iphofen. The second-generation firm claims to have Germany's oldest cellars (dug in AD 745). They supplement supplies with bought grapes: 35% Silvaner, 20% Kanzler, 20% Faber, 15% Müller-Thurgau, 10% Optima. An unusual emphasis on the Müller-Thurgau × Silvaner cross Kanzler, apparently very reliable here for full-flavoured wines even in mean years.

Weingut Müller
Nordheim. 15 acres in Iphofen, Nordheim, Sommerach, Frankenwinheim. A typical 300-year-old family property making fresh and charming Silvaner, pleasant Müller-Thurgau, slightly earthy Riesling and excellent crisp and spicy Scheurebe.

Weingut Ernst Popp KG
8715 Iphofen. Owner: Michael Popp. 25 acres plus 25 on contract in Iphofen and Rödelsee. A respected family firm since 1878 making dry, 'nutty' wines of character, typical of the region. 50% Silvaner, 35% Müller-Thurgau.

Schloss Saaleck-Städt, Weingut Hammelburg
Postfach 1220, 8783 Hammelburg. Director: Herr Kastner. 57 acres. Einzellagen: Saalecker Schlossberg; Hammelburger – Heroldsberg and Trautlestal; Feuerthaler Kreuz. The ancient Schloss Saaleck and its estate are the property of the town of Hammelburg, down the Main west of Würzburg. The vineyards are 50% Müller-Thurgau, 20% Silvaner, 10% Bacchus (which the director particularly favours) and other new varieties. The wines are for the most part dry with powerful fruit flavours.

COOPERATIVES

Gebietswinzergenossenschaft Franken
8710 Kitzingen-Repperndorf. Director: Bruno Landauer. The massive union (in 1959) of 7 cooperatives, drawing mainly on the Steigerwald, with 58% of the 1m. case production Müller-Thurgau; 32% Silvaner. 10 Grosslagen and 70 Einzellagen are involved. Prices seem high for mass-production wines compared with, for example, the Juliusspital. Average price DM 7.00.

Winzergenossenschaft Hammelburg
Marktplatz 11, 8783 Hammelburg. Director: Herr Baier. 62 acres in Hammelburger – Trautlestal and Heroldsberg. A tiny local cooperative offering principally Silvaner.

Winzergenossenschaft Nordheim
8711 Nordheim/Main. 199 members; 593 acres. Einzellagen: Escherndorfer – Lump and Fürstenburg; Nordheimer – Vögelein and Kreuzberg; Sommeracher – Katzenkopf and Rosenberg; etc. The principal cooperative for the upper Main wine villages: 60% Müller-Thurgau, 20% Silvaner, with 15 new varieties. Most of the members live in Nordheim and go out to tend their scattered acres. The wine is happily drunk up in Bavaria. From DM 6.80.

Winzergenossenschaft Randersacker
Maingasse 33, 8701 Randersacker. 260 members; 358 acres in Randersacker (296), Sommerhaüser (50) and Würzburg-Heidingsfeld (12). Einzellagen: Randersacker – Sonnenstuhl, Marsberg, Pfülben and Teufelskeller; Sommerhäuser Steinbach; Würzburger – Abtsleite and Kirchberg. The cooperative of one of the best areas in Franken with high standards. Müller-Thurgau and Silvaner are the two main grapes with only moderate interest in more exotic kinds. Good as the wines are, 90% is consumed locally.

Winzergenossenschaft Thüngersheim
Retzbacherstrasse 272a, 8702 Thüngersheim. Director: Georg Lutz. 235 members; 605 acres. Einzellagen: Thüngersheimer – Johannisberg and Scharlachberg; Retzbacher Benediktusberg; Veitshöchheimer Sonnenschein; Erlabrunner Weinsteig; Himmelstadter Kelter; Rück-Elsenfelder – Jesuitenberg and Schalk; Karlstadter Rosstal; Leinacher: Himmelsberg and Zellinger Sonnleite. The major cooperative of the scattered wine villages of the lower Main. More than half of its vines are Müller-Thurgau; 15% are Silvaner. Scheurebe, Kerner and Bacchus are also important, depending on the highly varied soil. Production is more than 100,000 cases of Bocksbeutels and many of the wines win gold and silver medals. From DM 7.70.

Landwein

This new (1982) category of German table wine was introduced as a response to the success of French *vins de pays* – as standard drinking but of some local character, with more style and flavour than the totally anonymous Tafelwein. 15 areas with new names but roughly corresponding to the well-known basic regions of Germany have the right to christen a Landwein if the wine in question meets certain simple requirements. The alcohol content, for example, must be 0.5% higher than that of Tafelwein. An important regulation is that the sugar content should not exceed the acidity by more than 10 grams a litre of sugar (the limit for the *halbtrocken* or halfway category). Landwein is therefore intended as a relatively dry and briskly acidic wine suitable for mealtimes. It seems certain that Rheinpfalz will produce large quantities of very satisfactory wine of this description.

The 15 Landwein areas are as follows:
Ahrtaler Landwein Ahr
Starkenburger Landwein Hessische Bergstrasse
Rheinburgen-Landwein Mittelrhein
Landwein der Mosel Mosel and Ruwer
Landwein der Saar Saar
Nahegauer Landwein Nahe
Altrheingauer Landwein Rheingau
Rheinischer Landwein Rheinhessen
Pfälzer Landwein Rheinpfalz
Fränkischer Landwein Franken
Regensburger Landwein a minuscule area on the Danube.
Bayerischer Bodensee-Landwein a small area near Lindau on Lake Constance (Bodensee), which in QbA terms is part of Württemberg, although politically it belongs to Bavaria.
Schwäbischer Landwein Württemberg
Unterbadischer Landwein northern part of Baden.
Südbadischer Landwein southern part of Baden.

WÜRTTEMBERG

The old principalities of Baden and Württemberg are united as a state, but remain separate as wine regions. Baden is much the bigger producer of the two, but it can be argued that Württemberg is the better. What is certainly true is that Württemberg cannot even satisfy its own demand. The hard-working, productive Württembergers are also some of Germany's great wine drinkers, and they prefer Württemberg wine. As a result it is scarcely ever exported and the best bottles (which are expensive) never.

The land-locked regions of Germany only take on comprehensible shapes as they are encompassed and traversed by rivers. The river Neckar is almost a Mosel in Württemberg, ambling through the hills and fed by tributaries that provide the essential south slopes for vineyards. Württemberg, like the Mosel, concentrates on Riesling for its fine white wines. But its real speciality is red and rosé made of its own indigenous grape the Trollinger, and to a lesser extent the Schwarzriesling (the Pinot Meunier in French, with the German alias of Müllerrebe), the Portugieser, the Pinot Noir (Spätburgunder) and the Limberger, which may be a form of Burgundy's Gamay. Red plantings make up half the total; if the red is not fully red it is Weissherbst, rosé, as in Baden, or mixed with white wine to make Schillerwein – a true local speciality.

As in Baden, the great majority of the production is by the cooperatives, with only a handful of relatively modest private estates. But even the cooperatives cannot simplify the complexity of a region with three Bereichs and 16 Grosslagen. The best way to understand it is to follow the northwards flow of the Neckar. On the analogy of the Mosel picture, the huge car-factory city of Stuttgart is its Trier. Here and along the tributary Rems, flowing in from the east like the Ruwer to the Mosel, are the first and some of the best Würrtemberg vineyards, the Bereich Remstal-Stuttgart.

Bereich Remstal-Stuttgart

Four thousand acres of vines are divided into five Grosslagen. Hohenneuffen is the uppermost of the river, round Neuffen, Frickenhausen and Metzingen. There is no Riesling here but light Silvaner, Müller-Thurgau and (for red) largely Schwarzriesling.

Weinsteige is the Grosslage of Stuttgart, a city where the appearance of vineyards in its midst (or at least in its suburbs Bad Cannstatt, Mühlhausen and Zuffenhausen) is particularly surprising. The vines here are mainly Trollinger and Riesling, the best-known Einzellagen (of 26) Berg, Steinhalde and Zuckerle, and in Fellbach, facing west over the Neckar towards Stuttgart, Wetzstein, Goldberg, Lämmler (entirely red wine) and Hinterer Berg.

Growers Weingärtnergenossenschaft Bad Cannstatt. Weingärtnergenossenschaft Felbach. Württembergische Hofkammer-Kellerei.

The valley of the Rems (Remstal) has three Grosslagen: Kopf (with 13 Einzellagen) centred round Schörndorf, with a good deal of Trollinger but also some fair sites for Riesling; Wartbühl (with 20 Einzellagen) round Weinstadt and Korb, with Riesling and other white grapes in the majority; and Sonnenbühl (with four Einzellagen) south of Weinstadt and the Rems, which specializes in robust Trollinger red.

Bereich Württembergisch Unterland

Much the biggest area, with 16,500 of the 21,500 acres of Württemberg's vines. The Bereich, with nine Grosslagen, spreads across the Neckar valley north of Stuttgart from Baden (where it brushes the Kraichgau) to the Bottwar valley in the east.

Grosslage Schalkstein

The first Grosslage, following the Neckar north. Its 14 Einzellagen stretch from Ludwigsburg to Hessigheim, the wine centre, with red grapes in the majority, their best wines well coloured and full-bodied.

Grower Felsengärtenkellerei, Besigheim.

Grosslage Stromberg

A widely dispersed collection of 19 Einzellagen along the tributary Enz valley to the west, with Mühlhausen and Vaihingen as centres, stretching down the Neckar valley to Kirchheim and Bönnigheim. Two thirds are red vines, with considerable Limberger.

Grower Stromberg Kellerei, Bönnigheim.

Grosslage Heuchelberg

A more intensive viniferous district with 24 Einzellagen, just north of Stromberg to the west of the Neckar. The centres are Cleebronn and Schwaigern, responsible for some of Württemberg's best Rieslings from the lime-rich soil.

Growers Weingärtnergenossenschaft Cleebronn-Güglingen-Frauenzimmern. Graf von Neipperg.

Grosslage Kirchenweinberg

This is the real kernel of Württemberg's wine region, its 12 Einzellagen including the huge 1,140-acre Katzenbeisser at Lauffen. Talheim and Flein, on the outskirts of Heilbronn, are its other centres. Schwarzriesling is the most popular grape in a predominantly red-wine area.

Growers Bentzel-Sturmfeder. Felsengärtenkellerei, Besigheim.

Grosslage Wunnenstein

A limited district east of the Neckar, including the town of Grossbottwar, with nine Einzellagen, mainly dedicated to red grapes.

Grower Weingut Graf Adelmann, 'Brüssele'.

Grosslage Schozachtal

A small area just north of Wunnenstein, with only five Einzellagen around Abstatt and Untergruppenbach.

White wines are in the majority. Some good Riesling is grown here.

Grosslage Salzberg

An important area east of Heilbronn, noted for some of Württemberg's best Rieslings. The 15 Einzellagen are spread between Eberstadt, Lehrensteinsfeld, Willsbach, Affaltrach, Eichelberg, Obersulm and Löwenstein.

Growers Schlosskellerei Affaltrach. Weingärtnergenossenschafts Eberstadt, Lehrensteinsfeld and Mittleres Weinsberger.

Grosslage Lindelberg

A more scattered region of mainly white wine, northeast of Heilbronn round the Brettach valley. Nine Einzellagen lie between Bretzfeld and Untersteinbach.

Grosslage Staufenberg

Heilbronn is an important wine centre with a first-class cooperative and the seat of the all-Germany D.L.G. annual wine championship. Its vineyards and those of the Neckar downstream are in the Grosslage Staufenberg, which has 12 Einzellagen divided almost equally between white grapes and red. The main centres are Gundelsheim, Erlenbach, Weinsberg and Heilbronn itself.

Growers Genossenshaftskellerei Heilbronn-Erlenbach-Weinsberg. Staatliche Lehr-und Versuchsanstalt Weinsberg.

Bereich Kocher-Jagst-Tauber

The northern Württemberg Bereich is much the smallest, with 1,000 acres, and the only one to specialize (90%) in white wine. It straddles the valleys of the Kocher and Jagst, Neckar tributaries from the east, and the Tauber (which flows north to the Main).

Control panel at a giant South German cooperative

Grosslage Kocherberg

The southern half of the Bereich, with 12 Einzellagen, includes Ingelfingen and Niedernhall on the Kocher.

Grower Weingärtnergenossenschaft Niedernhall.

Grosslage Tauberberg

The isolated Tauber valley vineyards (seven Einzellagen) are centred on Bad Mergentheim, Weikersheim and Niederstetten. Both the limy soil and the use of Silvaner and Müller-Thurgau recall the fact that Franken is not far away.

Grower Fürstlich Hohenlohe Lagenburg.

WÜRTTEMBERG PRODUCERS

Weingut Graf Adelmann, 'Brüssele'

Burg Schaubeck, 7141 Steinheim-Kleinbottwar. Owner: Michael, Graf Adelmann. A 37-acre estate: 30 acres in Kleinbottwar (Einzellagen Oberer Berg and Süssmund, solely owned); 7 in Hoheneck.

One of the best-known estates in Württemberg, instantly recognized by its pale-blue 'lacey' label with the name 'Brüssele' (after a former owner). Burg Schaubeck is a small but towering and venerable stronghold, apparently with Roman origins, owned by the Adelmanns since 1914. The vines are 45% red: 20% Trollinger, also Samtrot, Limberger, Muskat-Trollinger; 55% white: 20% Riesling, also Traminer, Ruländer, Müller-Thurgau, Golden Muskateller and Silvaner.

Kleinbottwar is red marl, Hoheneck limestone; both are sloping sites.

The wines are originals, with distinct characters and yet notable delicacy that makes them sometimes almost timid. Acidity tends to be low but flavours dry and complex. Specialities include Weissherbst and red wine from Muskat-Trollinger – a table grape elsewhere, making slightly raisiny wine; Samtrot (a Pinot Meunier mutation; a mature Auslese reminded me of Valpolicella); Golden Muskateller, delicate and long despite its obvious spicy character; and a soft, low-key, smoky but elegant Riesling. The quality is as high as the wines are unusual. Prices: from DM 8.50.

Weingüter und Schlosskellerei Graf von Neipperg

7103 Schwaigern Schloss. Owners: Graf and Herr Josef-Hubert von Neipperg. 71 acres. Einzellagen: Schwaigerner Ruthe (16); Neipperger Schlossberg (54); Klingenberger Schlossberg (4).

Documents prove the family to have been making wine here since 1248, shortly after the building of Burg Neipperg, the original castle. There is now a Weinstube in Schloss Schwaigern over the cellars. Vines are 58% red: 24% Limberger, 16% Schwarzriesling (Pinot Meunier), 10% Spätburgunder, 8% Trollinger; the whites are 16% Riesling, 10% Traminer, 7% each of Muskateller and Müller-Thurgau. The Neippergs introduced the Limberger (or Lemberger) to make red wine of colour and tannin; their other speciality is spicy Traminer, although their Riesling is highly thought of. Count Neipperg is also the owner of 4 properties in St-Emilion: Châteaux Canon-La-Gaffelière, La Mondotte, Clos L'Oratoire and Peyreau. Prices: from DM 7.00.

Staatliche Lehr-und Versuchsanstalt für Wein- und Obstbau Weinsberg

Hallerstrasse 6, 7102 Weinsberg. Director: Dr. Gerhard Götz. 135 acres. Einzellagen: Abstatter Burg Wildeck (solely owned); Weinsberger – Ranzenberg and Schemelsberg (solely owned); Talheimer Schlossberg; Gundelsheimer Himmelreich.

The largest wine estate in Württemberg and the oldest wine school in Germany (founded in 1866); currently being rebuilt.

Of the 110 acres in production, 14% is Riesling, 12% Müller-Thurgau, 11% each Kerner and Trollinger, 8% Limberger. A wide variety is in areas of less than 5 acres. Methods are very modern and hygienic, aiming at maximum aroma by excluding air and avoiding sulphur. The wines are generally dry and full-bodied and the reds (especially Limberger) a good colour. Visits and tastings (by arrangement) are encouraged; both the vineyards and the wine are a great advertisement for Württemberg. Prices: from DM 7.00.

Württembergische Hofkammer-Kellerei

Hölderlinstrasse 32, 7000 Stuttgart. Owner: Philipp Albrecht, Herzog von Württemberg. 58 acres in 4 scattered areas, 1 in Stuttgart (Untertürkheimer – Mönchberg and Altenberg, 19 acres) and the others to the east, north and west at Stetten (Brottwasser, 7 acres), Mundelsheim (Käsberg, 5), Hohenhaslach (6) and Maulbronn (Eilfingerberg Klosterstück, 42, solely owned).

More than half the vines are Riesling, with smaller parcels of Trollinger, Limberger, etc. The grapes are pressed locally and the must brought to the medieval ducal cellars in Stuttgart for fermentation in oak casks. The wines are classically made and the estate is generally considered to be the flagship of Württemberg wines.

OTHER PRODUCERS

Schlosskellerei Affaltrach
7104 Obersulm. Owner: Dr. Reinhold Baumann. 26.5 acres. Einzellagen: Affaltracher – Dieblesberg and Zeilberg, planted with a wide variety of red and white grapes. Originally a 13th-century foundation, bought by the present owners in 1928 and now consisting of a small estate and an associated company buying grapes from some 200 small growers to make wine and Sekt. The estate wines are mainly dry or semi-dry, intended for use at table and made to improve in bottle when possible.

Gräflich v. Bentzel-Sturmfeder'sches Weingut
7129 Ilsfeld-Schozach. Owner: Graf Hanfried von Bentzel-Sturmfeder-Horneck zu Sternau-Hohenau. 37 acres. Einzellage: Schozacher Roter Berg. An estate with 14th-century origins and 18th-century cellars. The vineyards are 25% Riesling, 21% Spätburgunder, 14% Samtrot, 10% Schwarzriesling, etc., on clay slopes which give body to the wines. The wines last well, even when the acidity is relatively low, with barrel-ageing giving them stability. Noble rot is a rare occurrence; most of the wines are dry, much appreciated in local restaurants.

Fürstlich Hohenlohe Langenburg'sche Weingüter
6992 Weikersheim im Schloss. Director: Karl-Heinz Schäfer. 65 acres. Einzellagen: Weikersheimer – Karlsberg and Schmecker (58); Tauberrettersheimer Königin (which is over the Württemberg border in Franken, 7.5). The ancient cellars of Schloss Weikersheim are used for very modern wine-making. The limestone vineyards give light, aromatic wines with a certain 'bodenton' or *gout de terroir*. This is the transition from Württemberg to Franken. Vines are 30% Müller-Thurgau, 17% Riesling, 15% Kerner, 10% Silvaner, etc. From DM 7.00.

Fürst zu Hohenlohe-Öhringen'sche Schlosskellerei
7110 Ohringen, Schloss. Owner: Prince Kraft zu Hohenlohe-Öhringen. 54 acres. Einzellage: Verrenberger Verrenberg (solely owned). A princely estate since the 14th-century, with 17th-century cellars (and even a cask dated 1702). The Verrenberg is unusual in being one sweep of vines, producing almost uniformly dry whites (85% *trocken* – the highest proportion of any German estate) and ripe reds. Half the vines are Riesling, 15% each Spätburgunder and Limberger, 8% Kerner, 7% Müller-Thurgau. From DM 6.00.

Ageing German wines

Good-quality German wines have a much longer lifespan, and benefit much more by being kept in bottle, than fashion suggests or most people suppose. The wine industry and trade have little to gain from older bottles, and have tacitly agreed that German wines are ready to drink within months of being bottled. With the enormous crops (and hence the high water content) of standard-quality modern wines there is indeed no gain from keeping bottles more than 6 months or a year. But almost all the superior-grade (QmP) wines, delectable as they may taste in their flower-and-fruity youth, have the potential to put on another dimension of flavour with maturity. When they are first offered for sale they are at their most brisk and lively, with acidity and fruitiness often tending to cancel each other out in a generally tingling and exciting effect. Some fine wines (particularly Rieslings) at this stage have remarkably little aroma.

Sometimes after a year or two in bottle the first rapture goes without maturer flavours taking its place; the wine you bought with enthusiasm seems to be letting you down. Be patient. The subtle alchemy takes longer. It may be 4 or 5 years before the mingled savours of citrus and spice and oil emerge.

Each vintage has its own timespan, but as a generalization Kabinett wines from a first-rate grower need at least 3 years in bottle and may improve for 7 or 8, Spätleses will improve for anything from 4 to 10 years, and Ausleses and upwards will benefit from 5 or 6 years up to 20 or even more.

Liebfraumilch

For most foreigners the great stumbling block to the full enjoyment of German wines is the German language. It certainly takes dogged persistence for a non-German speaker to master the polysyllabic names and categories. It is little comfort to be told that they form a logical national system by which everything can be unravelled – and still less to discover that the vaunted logic often lapses into local exceptions.

Small wonder then that most non-Germans shrug their shoulders and settle for the one name they know: Liebfraumilch – a name that guarantees nothing. The law requires only that the wines should be 'of pleasant character', and be made of certain grapes in certain regions – those which in any case produce the greatest volumes of wine. Learning the pleasures of German wine starts with abandoning Liebfraumilch.

BADEN

The Kaiserstuhl

Baden is the new force in German wine – at present only domestically, but soon no doubt on the world stage. Its vineyards have undergone no less than a revolution in recent years: they have been almost entirely rationalized and remodelled by Flurbereinigung, have doubled in size and quadrupled in output. They now lie third in yield in Germany, behind only Rheinpfalz and Rheinhessen.

Baden faces Alsace across the Rhine. It is Germany's warmest (although not necessarily its sunniest) wine region, with correspondingly ripe, high-alcohol and low-acid wines: the diametric opposite of Mosels in style and function. The best Mosel wines are for analytical sipping. Baden makes meal-time wines with a warm vinosity that approaches the French style. It is the choice of grape varieties and the taste for a trace of sweetness that distinguishes them from Alsace wines. The difference is reinforced by a slightly less favourable climate than the suntrap of the Vosges foothills.

Eighty per cent of Baden's vineyards lie in an 80-mile strip running from northeast to southwest, from Baden Baden to Basel, in the foothills of the Black Forest where it meets the Rhine valley. The balance is of purely local importance. The vineyards lie southeast on the banks of the Bodensee (alias Lake Constance), north of Baden in the minor regions of the Kraichgau and Badischer Bergstrasse, respectively south and north of Heidelberg (but now united in one Bereich with both names), and far north on the border of Franken, a little region known logically enough as Bereich Badisches Frankenland. The main thrust of Baden viticulture is thus along the Rhine from where it leaves the Bodensee to where it enters Rheinpfalz.

Baden is, even more than the southern Rheinpfalz, the land of the cooperative. More than 100 cooperatives process nearly 90 per cent of the crop, and half of all their output finds its way to the huge ZBW central cellars in Breisach on the Rhine. The ZBW bottles some 400–500 different types of wine. Baden has no powerful preference for one grape variety. The Müller-Thurgau is the workhorse, with about one third of the acreage. Spätburgunder for red and light rosé (Weissherbst) comes second with about one fifth. Then come Ruländer (Pinot Gris or Tokay d'Alsace), Gutedel, Riesling, Silvaner, Weissburgunder and Gewürztraminer. Baden's taste is clearly not for the highly aromatic new varieties: the vast majority of its white wine is made of relatively 'neutral' grapes. Its best, however, is made of Riesling and Ruländer.

Bereich Bodensee

The Bodensee and the Rhine which flows from its western end mark the German–Swiss border. The lake (Germany's biggest) counteracts the considerable altitude (about 1,500 feet above sea level) to produce a mild climate in which Spätburgunder and Müller-Thurgau both give refreshing, lightly fruity wines. The whites are often *spritzig*, the Spätburgunder either pale red or (its most attractive form) made into Weissherbst, the often very lively pale rosé which is the true local speciality. The region has less than 800 acres and only one Grosslage name: Sonnenufer. The main centres are on or near the lake shore: Bermatingen, Birnau, Kirchberg and Meersburg. Hagnau on the lake and the Erzingen farther down the Rhine also have cooperatives.

Growers Schloss Salem. Staatsweingut Meersburg.

Bereich Markgräflerland

Markgräflerland is the unexciting orchard corner of Germany between Basel and Freiburg, a district with its own taste in wine, marvellous cakes and very passable distillations of its abundant fruit. Its favourite grape is the Gutedel, the local name for what the Swiss call Fendant and the French Chasselas – in all cases a mild, not to say neutral wine maker, yet somehow very agreeable in its innocent freshness, dry and often *spritzig*. A cross between Gutedel and Silvaner called Nobling shows real promise, with surprising aroma and finesse. Otherwise the predominant grapes are Müller-Thurgau (here pleasantly aromatic) and Spätburgunder – often made as Weissherbst.

The Bereich is divided into three Grosslagen, listed here from south to north (down the Rhine).

Grosslage Vogtei Rötteln

Efringen-Kirchen is the seat of the considerable cooperative, which uses most of the 11 Einzellage names contained in the Grosslage. Weil am Rhein is another centre.

Grower Winzergenossenschaft Haltingen.

Grosslage Burg Neuenfels

Auggen, Bad Bellingen, Badenweiler, Müllheim, Laufen and Schliengen are centres of this hillier district with 18 Einzellagen.

Growers Fritz Blankenhorn. Freiburger Jesuitenschloss. Schlumberger. Erste Markgrafler Winzergenossenschaft.

Grosslage Lorettoberg

This Grosslage includes the southern outskirts of the lovely city of Freiburg. Its centres include Bad Krozingen, Ehringen, Pfaffenweiler and Ehrenkirchen, sharing 19 Einzellagen.

Growers Freiburger Jesuitenschloss. Winzergenossenschaft Pfaffenweiler.

Bereich Kaiserstuhl-Tuniberg

Northwest of Freiburg the Rhine is briefly diverted from its northward course by a volcanic outcrop from the plain, an advance guard for the Black Forest hills ranged along the eastern skyline. There are two lumps, the modest Tuniberg on the doorstep of Freiburg, then the dignified flat-topped hill of the Kaiserstuhl – 'the King's Seat'. Breisach, seat of the great central cooperative, is the Rhine port and bridge-town to France. This is the climax of the Baden wineland, with a third of all its vines and a good share of its best wine concentrated on its volcanic slopes.

The Kaiserstuhl slopes have been the subject of a spectacular relandscaping to convert them into modern vineyards. The whole broad hill now has a distinctly man-made look. The Bereich is divided into only two Grosslagen, whose Wagnerian names are therefore particularly well known. Vulkanfelsen covers the Kaiserstuhl and Atillafelsen the Tuniberg. One third of the whole region is planted with Müller-Thurgau, a quarter with Spätburgunder and another quarter with Ruländer, the Tokay d'Alsace, which performs exceptionally well on these iron-rich volcanic slopes. Low acid, always a characteristic of this grape, is compensated for by fiery concentrated flavours and density of texture, qualities that mature extremely well.

Much of the Spätburgunder is made into Weissherbst but the warmest vineyards, notably in Ihringen, Achkarren, Bickensohl and Oberrotweil on the south of the Kaiserstuhl, take pride in their red wines. Some of the best sites are also planted with Silvaner to good effect.

Growers In Grosslage Vulkanfelsen: Freiburger Jesuitenschloss. Freiherr von Gleichenstein. ZBW.

Bereich Breisgau

Breisgau is the name for the backdrop of Black Forest foothills running north behind the Kaiserstuhl-Tuniberg, from Freiburg almost to Offenburg. It has three Grosslagen: Schutterlindenberg for its northern section centred on Lahr, with only four Einzellagen; Burg Lichteneck running south to Emmendingen, with eight Einzellagen including Hecklingen with its Schlossberg; and Burg Zähringen for the hills just north of Freiburg, with seven Einzellagen, the best known of which is the steep little 15-acre Roter Bur in Glottertal, planted with 75 per cent Spätburgunder to produce a particularly lively Weissherbst.

Growers In Grosslage Schutterlindenberg: Gräflich Wolff-Metternich. In Grosslage Burg Lichteneck: Freiburger Jesuitenschloss.

Bereich Ortenau

The Black Forest foothills continue north from Offenburg to Baden Baden, the mixture of vineyard and forest with old villages and feudal castles producing unforgettable pictures. Once again there are two Grosslagen: Fürsteneck for the southern half of the Ortenau; Schloss Rodeck for the northern. Durbach, near Offenburg, is the most distinguished of its villages by reason of its lordly ownership and the Riesling (here called Klingelberger) of its steep sand and granite slopes. Durbach has all or part of 10 of the 22 Einzellagen contained in the Grosslage Fürsteneck, Ortenberg has four and Oberkirch most of the 765-acre Einzellage Renchtäler.

Schloss Rodeck is divided into 33 Einzellagen, the better known being Yburgberg and Stich den Buden at Steinbach near Baden Baden, Mauerberg at Neuweier in the same hills, farther south the Alde Gott at Sasbachwalden, Hex vom Dasenstein at Kappelrodeck and Pfarrberg at Waldulm.

Ortenau is Spätburgunder country. From somewhere in its heart (although apparently not officially recognized) comes a large supply of a popular light red called Affenthaler, distinguished only by the moulded figure of a monkey clutching the bottle. Much its best wines are its Klingelbergers and Ruländers, with some respectable Gewürztraminer and adequate Müller-Thurgau.

Growers In Grosslage Fürsteneck: Markgräflich Badis'ches Weingut. Freiburger Jesuitenschloss. Andreas Mannle. Freiherr von Neveu. Gräflich Wolff-Metternich.

Bereich Badische Bergstrasse/Kraichgau

The northernmost section of the Baden vineyards of the Rhine is so diffuse that its union in one Bereich looks like a measure of desperation. The Kraichgau is the area south of Heidelberg between the Rhine and the converging River Neckar, flowing northwest from Heilbronn in Württemberg. The Badische Bergstrasse is a southern extension of the Hessische Bergstrasse, a narrow ridge of vineyards running north–south and straddling the university city of Heidelberg.

The Kraichgau boasts three Grosslagen: Hohenberg in the south around Pforzheim, Stiftsberg to the east and Mannaberg in the northwest (and including the southern villages of the Bergstrasse: the chief of these is Wiesloch). The northern Bergstrasse has its own Grosslage: Rittersberg. Its principal town is called, simply, Weinheim.

The whole Bereich has some 4,500 acres of vineyard divided into 77 Einzellagen. Almost half its vines are Müller-Thurgau, only 10 per cent are red; the exceptional sites, such as they are, are planted with Riesling (20%) and Ruländer (13%). Neckarzimmer on the Neckar has the estate with the widest reputation.

Growers In Grosslage Stiftsberg: Burg Hornberg. Freiherrlich von Göler. Reichsgraf & Marquis zu Hoensbroech.

Bereich Badisches Frankenland

But for political boundaries this remote outpost of Baden wine-growing would be attached to its natural ally, Franken. It produces wines in the Franken style, mainly from Müller-Thurgau, and bottles them in Franconian flagons. The whole area, with some 1,300 acres of vines, is one Grosslage, Tauberklinge, and its centres are the towns of Lauda, Tauberbischofsheim and Wertheim on the Main.

The names of the Einzellagen producing the finest wines will be found in the Producers' entries

BADEN PRODUCERS

Weingut Fritz Blankenhorn KG

7846 Schliengen. Owner: Klaus Blankenhorn. 37 acres. Einzellagen: Schlienger Sonnenstück; Badenweiler Römerberg; Auggener Schäf. Grosslage: Burg Neuenfels.

A well-known producer of the light, juicy Gutedel and typical dry red of the region. Vines are 30% Gutedel, 30% Spätburgunder, 12% Müller-Thurgau, 10% Riesling and 18% different varieties of Gewürztraminer, Ruländer and Weissburgunder.

Freiburger Jesuitenschloss Staatliches Weinbauinstitut

Merzhauserstrasse 119, 7800 Freiburg. Director: Dr. Günter Staudt. 93 acres. Einzellagen: Freiburger – Schlossberg, Jesuitenschloss (14); Müllheimer Reggenhag (4); Ihringer Doktorgarten (60); Hecklinger Schlossberg (7.5); Durbacher Steinberg (7.5, solely owned).

The teaching institute of the state of Baden-Württemberg, founded in 1920 and including the 19th-century estate of the Blankenhorn brothers at Ihringen, known as Blankenhornsberg (q.v.), the most considerable on the Kaiserstuhl. The steep Durbacher Steinberg is planted with Traminer, Spätburgunder and Muskateller. The Ihringen wines are mostly dry; Durbach fruity and sweet. The wines are made with exemplary care. Prices: from DM 6.20.

Staatliches Weinbauinstitut Freiburg Blankenhornsberg

7817 Ihringen. Director: Erich Meinke. 62 acres. Einzellage: Ihringer Doktorgarten, now known as Blankenhornsberg.

See Freiburger Jesuitenschloss for ownership. The outstanding Kaiserstuhl estate, on steep volcanic slopes, planted with 18% Müller-Thurgau, 18% Spätburgunder, 13% Riesling, 10.5% Ruländer, 10% Weissburgunder, 6% Scheurebe, 24.5% other varieties and new crossings. Up to 70% of the wines are normally made dry, but with powerful acidity and flavours. 1976 was an exception, an *annus mirabilis* for sweet wines. Prices: from DM 6.60.

Staatsweingut Meersburg

Seminarstrasse 6, 7758 Meersburg. Director: Ernst Adams. 148 acres. Einzellagen: Meersburger – Lerchenberg, Bengel, Jungfernstieg, Rieschen, Chorherrenhalde and Fohrenberg. Grosslage: Meersburger Sonnenufer.

Formerly the estate of the Prince-Bishops of Meersburg. In 1802 it became Germany's first state domain, largely in Meersburg on the banks of the Bodensee. In 1956 frosts destroyed the vineyards and total reconstitution brought them up to date in varieties and methods. The vines are 40% Müller-Thurgau, 45% Spätburgunder, 10% Ruländer and 5% Weissburgunder, Traminer and Riesling. The specialities are Müller-Thurgau of the gentler kind and pinky-gold *spritzig* Spätburgunder. Prices: from DM 7.00. (Tasting tour DM 15.00.)

Markgräflich Badis'ches Weingut, Schloss Staufenberg

7601 Durbach. Owner: H.M. Max, Margrave of Baden. 69 acres, Durbacher Schloss Staufenberg (which belongs exclusively to the Weingut).

A homely old manor on a hill with skirting vineyards, 35% Riesling (alias Klingelberger), 22% Müller-Thurgau, 13% Traminer (alias Clevner), some Ruländer, Gewürztraminer, Spätburgunder and new varieties. A place of great charm, with delicate and distinguished Rieslings. Two thirds of the wines are dry; one third medium-sweet. The Margrave also owns Schloss Salem (q.v.), and Schloss Eberstein-Murgtal (28 acres), whose Spätburgunder is made at Schloss Staufenberg.

Zentralkellerei Badischer Winzergenossenschaften (ZBW)

Zum Kaiserstuhl 6, 7814 Breisach. Director: Ludwig Strub.

The mammoth central cooperative of Baden, uniting no less than 100 local cooperatives at one of the largest and most modern plants in Europe at Breisach on the Rhine. 50 cooperatives send their entire production from 12,000 acres. Altogether some 25,000 growers are involved. The vineyards, scattered all over Baden, consist of 5,000 acres of Müller-Thurgau, 2,500 of Spätburgunder, 1,700 of Ruländer, 750 of Gutedel, 500 of Riesling and 250 each of Silvaner, Weissburgunder and Gewürztraminer. Each vintage some 400–500 different wines are produced, under 50 different Einzellage and Grosslage names, with their grape varieties and qualities. It is impossible to generalize about the output of this great organization more than to say that its wines are well made and true to type and class across the whole spectrum.

OTHER PRODUCERS

Weingut Burg Hornberg
6951 Neckarzimmern. Owner: Baron Hans-Wolf von Gemmingen-Hornberg. 51 acres. Einzellagen: Neckarzimmerner – Götzhalde and Wallmauer; Michelfelder Himmelberg. An ancient steep vineyard site owned by this family since the 17th century, with 30% Riesling, 20% Müller-Thurgau, 15% Silvaner, 10% Spätburgunder, 5% Samtrot, 20% Muskateller, Traminer, Ruländer and Weissburgunder. The wines are made by traditional methods to extract the maximum from the warm site; the best are full-bodied and impressive. A restaurant provides a chance to taste a wide range.

Weingut Freiherr von Gleichenstein
Bahnhofstrasse 12, 7818 Oberrotweil. Owner: Hans-Joachim von Gleichenstein. 76.5 acres. Einzellagen: Oberrotweiler – Eichberg, Henkenberg and Käsleberg. Grosslage: Vulkanfelsen. 37% Müller-Thurgau, 30% Spätburgunder, 6% Ruländer, 5% Muskateller, 5% Silvaner, 3% Nobling and 2% each of Traminer and Riesling. An estate founded in the 17th century, in even older buildings, making conservative wines, 60% dry, the reds fermented on the skins, tannic, dry and full of character. Dry Weissherbst Spätlese, pale but full of flavour, is the unusual speciality of the house. From DM 6.00.

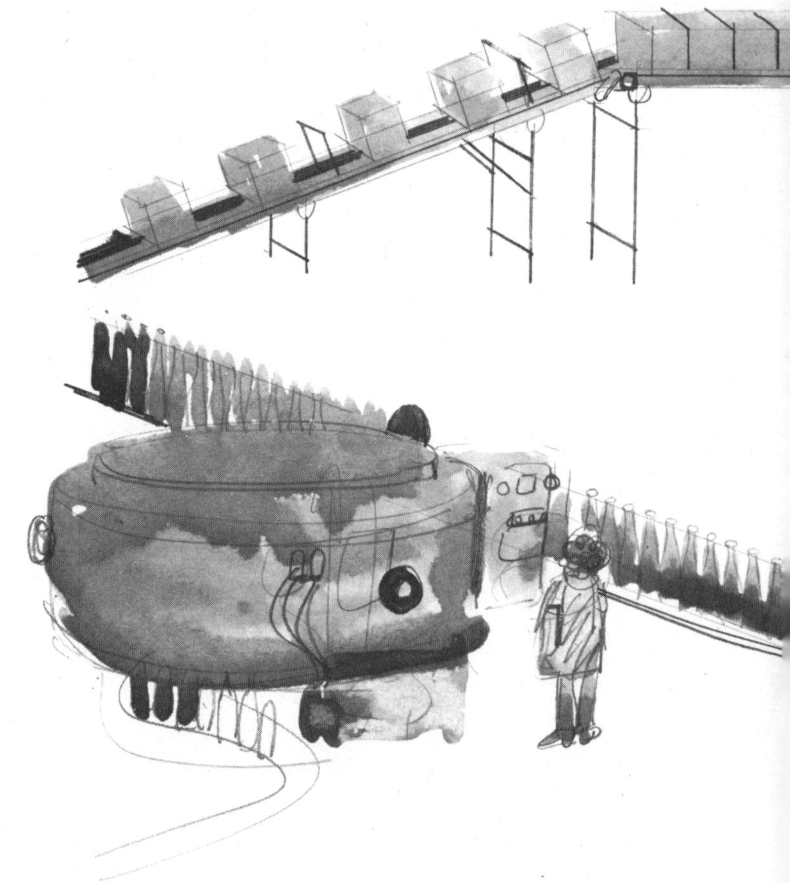

Weingut Reichsgraf & Marquis zu Hoensbroech
6921 Angelbachtal-Michelfeld. Owner: Rüdiger, Graf von and zu Hoensbroech. 29.5 acres. Einzellage: Michelfelder Himmelberg (solely owned). Grosslage: Stiftsberg. A small lordly estate of the Kraichgau,south of Heidelberg in north Baden. Powerful dry wines are made of Weissburgunder (40%), Riesling (30%), Müller-Thurgau (20%), Gewürztraminer (10%). From DM 6.35.

Weingut Andreas Männle
7601 Durbach-Heimbach 293. Director: Heinrich Männle. 43 acres. Einzellagen: Durbacher – Bienengarten (15) and Kochberg. The vines are 20% each Müller-Thurgau, Spätburgunder and Riesling, 12% each Ruländer and Clevner (Traminer), 8% Scheurebe. On the face of it a simple guesthouse wine farmer, but a specialist in fine sweet wines with some remarkable successes including extraordinary Weissherbst Eiswein. The sweet reds are a very German taste.

Weingut Freiherr von Neveu
7601 Durbach. Owner: Heinrich, Freiherr von Neveu. 30 acres. Einzellagen: Durbacher – Josephsberg and Ölberg. Grosslage: Fürsteneck. A neighbour of Schloss Staufenberg with similarly stylish wines, perhaps more full-blooded with good acidity. 41% Riesling, 22% Müller-Thurgau, 14.5% Spätburgunder, 14% Clevner, 4% Gewürztraminer, 4% Scheurebe. Müller-Thurgau is being reduced in favour of Riesling and Spätburgunder. The wines are made and matured at the estate but bottled and distributed by the ZBW cooperative at Breisach. From DM 7.00.

Weinbauversuchsgut Schloss Ortenberg des Ortenaukreises
Burgweg 19a, 7601 Ortenberg. Director: Herbert Dresel. 18.5 acres. Einzellage: Ortenberger Schlossberg. Established in 1950 as a teaching institute on former castle land, with a modern cellar and exemplary standards. 23% Müller-Thurgau, 19% Riesling, 15% Burgunder, 11% Ruländer, 8% Traminer, 8% Gewürztraminer, 8% Scheurebe, 3% Silvaner, 3% Kerner, 5% Muskateller and others. The best wines are 'Klingelbergers' (Riesling), whether 'slim' and refreshing or splendidly ripe and sweet. From DM 7.80.

St. Andreas Hospital Fonds Weingut der Stadt Offenburg
Steingrube 7, 7601 Ortenberg. Director: Alfons Decker. 81 acres. Einzellagen: Käfersberger Andreasberg; Fessenbacher Bergle; Zeller Abtsberg. A medieval almshouse taken over by the town of Offenburg in 1936 as an inn. 35% Müller-Thurgau, 17% Riesling, 16.5% Spätburgunder, 7% Kerner, 5% Gewürztraminer, 4% Scheurebe, 4% Ruländer, 4% Findling, 2% Muskat. Its standard drinking is principally Müller-Thurgau; Riesling Kabinetts are the speciality.

Schloss Salem
7777 Salem. Owner: Max, Markgraf von Baden. 190 acres in three estates: Birnau, Schloss Kirchberg and Bermatingen, all specializing in Müller-Thurgau and Spätburgunder Weissherbst. Schloss Salem is the Bodensee residence of the Margrave of Baden and the very modern central cellar of the widespread estate.

Weingut Hartmut Schlumberger
Weinstrasse 19, Laufen, 7811 Sulzburg. Owner: Hartmut Schlumberger. 10 acres. Einzellage: Laufener Altenberg.

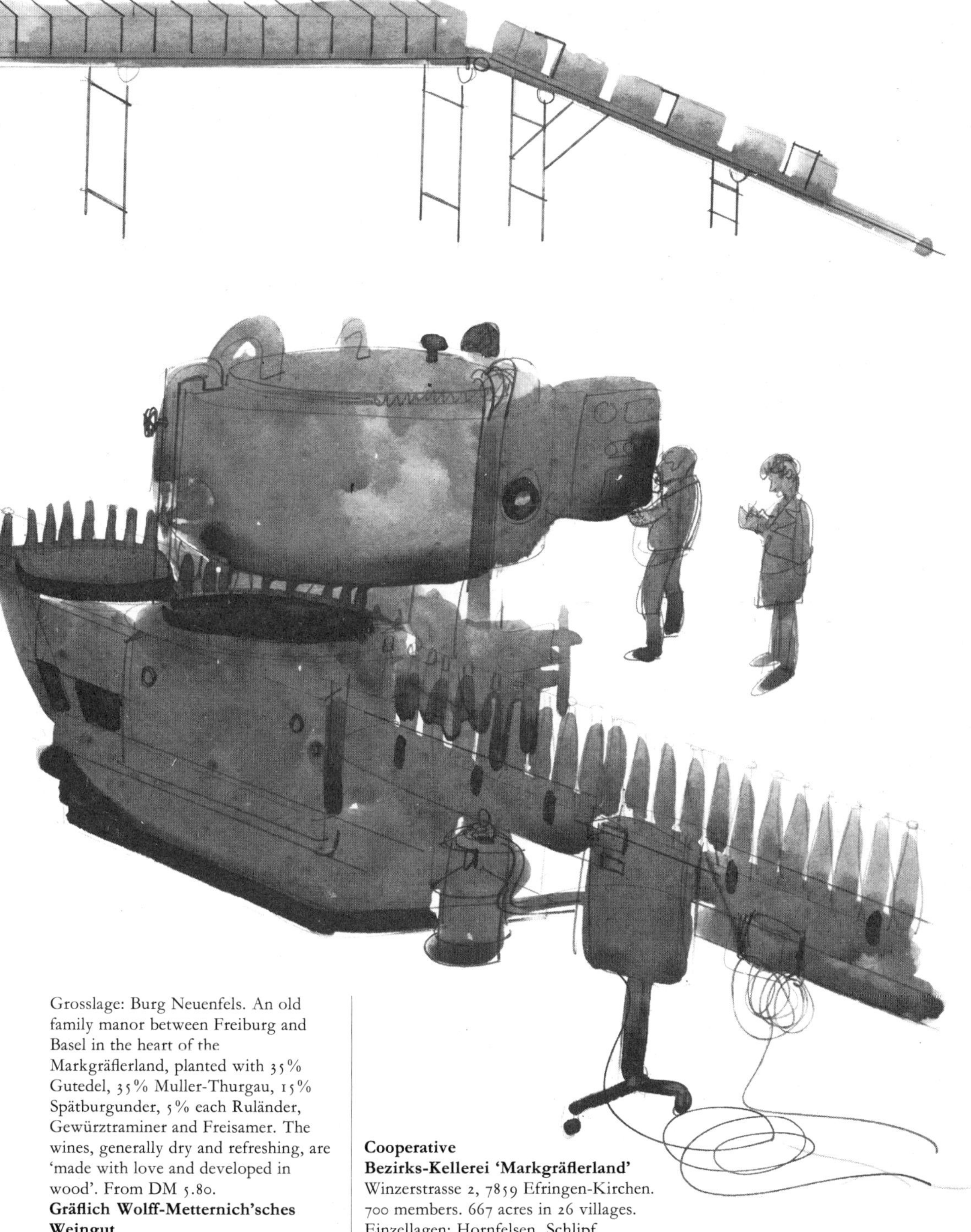

Grosslage: Burg Neuenfels. An old family manor between Freiburg and Basel in the heart of the Markgräflerland, planted with 35% Gutedel, 35% Muller-Thurgau, 15% Spätburgunder, 5% each Ruländer, Gewürztraminer and Freisamer. The wines, generally dry and refreshing, are 'made with love and developed in wood'. From DM 5.80.

Gräflich Wolff-Metternich'sches Weingut
7601 Durbach. Owner: Count Paul Josef Wolff-Metternich. A 74-acre hillside estate in Durbach and Lahr, of ancient origin, particularly proud of its late-harvest and aromatic wines. Half the vineyards are in Traminer and Riesling in almost equal proportions. Only 10% is red Spätburgunder.

Cooperative
Bezirks-Kellerei 'Markgräflerland'
Winzerstrasse 2, 7859 Efringen-Kirchen. 700 members. 667 acres in 26 villages. Einzellagen: Hornfelsen, Schlipf, Sonnhohle, Weingarten, Kapellenberg, Wolfer, Kirchberg, Ölberg, Steingässle. Grosslage: Vogtei Rötteln. Vines are 60% Gutedel, 30% Müller-Thurgau, 10% Spätburgunder. The major coop of the region, exporting significant quantities of its typical light dry wine.

The bottling hall at the ZBW cooperative's cellar at Breisach, which handles the wines of 25,000 Baden growers

ITALY

In sheer quantity of wine made, Italy now regularly surpasses even France as the vine's own country. Every one of her 20 regions is in the wine business to a greater or lesser extent. Her geography, essentially a mountain range reaching south and east from the Alps towards the subtropics, offers as wide a range of vine-worthy sites and microclimates as nature has devised.

It should come as no surprise that some of the world's best wines come from Italy. And yet it does. During the two and a half centuries when France was building the formidable structure and reputation of her quality-wine industry, and selecting and propagating her superlative vines, Italy was doing no such thing. Wine, like loyalty, remained very much a local, even a family, affair. Like bread, it was no less important for being taken for granted. But it was not measured even by national, let alone international, standards until well into this century. And when it was, Italy was inevitably judged simply as a source of low-priced wine, either for cheap and cheerful drinking or to be passed off as something else. To this day an almost incredible quantity, about half Italy's total wine exports, slinks anonymously out of the country in tankers to other parts of the E.E.C. – principally to France. High-quality wine depends entirely on demand, and nobody demanded it in Italy. It is still, to their own loss, the practice of most foreign wine merchants to list a token handful of the best-known Italian names rather than to investigate at first hand what Italy offers.

In the merchants' defence it must be said that the Italians seem to rejoice in giving their wines complicated labels. Access to them for non-Italians, even the most interested, is often blocked by a lilting litany of tuneful polysyllables in which not just the name of the wine and its maker but that of his property, and often an additional fantasy name for good measure all appear equally important. In writing tasting-notes on Italian wines it often takes me as long to identify them in my notebook as to taste and judge them.

The method of access to the essentials in the following pages tries to make the problem as simple as possible. This is how it works.

The country is divided into 20 regions. Each is treated separately, in two parts: first the names and descriptions of the wines, then a wide selection of the better and bigger wine makers, with brief accounts of their standing, methods, size and a list of the wines they offer. If you know the name of the wine or the maker but not the region, the only place to start is the index. If you know the region, go straight to the wine or the maker. Cross-referencing goes from maker to wine but not (to avoid endless repetitive lists) the other way round. The only list of producers, for example, of Chianti Classico is the list of wine makers in Tuscany, in which you will find that many Chianti makers also make other wines.

On the face of it, there is a radical division between officially controlled ('DOC') wines and others. The DOC (*Denominazione di Origine Controllata*) was instituted in 1963 as the very necessary regulatory system for Italian quality wines – an approximate equivalent to the French AOC. At present between 10 and 12 per cent of the country's total crop is thus regulated, depending on the harvest.

A DOC is a very detailed legal stipulation as to the precise character, origin, grapes, crop levels, strength, methods and ageing of a particular wine or group of wines agreed between the consortium of its producers and an expert committee in Rome. Since 1966, when the first DOC decree was signed by the President, about 200 have been declared. A summary of the DOC regulations for each of them is given in the following pages. It states the colour(s) of the wine(s), the province(s) within the region, the principal village(s) or a summary of the zone, the permitted grape varieties and their proportions, the maximum crop, the minimum alcohol level, the average total production and any regulations concerning ageing – for example, when it may be sold as a *riserva*. The maximum crop is expressed in this book in hectolitres per hectare to make it comparable with those of other countries, although the DOC regulations stipulate both the number of quintals (100 kilograms) of grapes that may be picked and also what percentage of that weight may be processed into wine – the idea being to control the maker's urge to press every last drop out of his grapes. These listings do not include the stilted official descriptions of the style of the wine or the technical data on acidity, 'extract' and the rest.

In addition, an equal number of wines are listed that are not DOC and have no official delimitation. It is the great paradox of Italian wine today that a DOC freezes a type of wine in a historical moment. A DOC is essentially the definition of a tradition – at the very moment when wine technology has reached a pitch undreamed-of before, when California (the outstanding example) is using its freedom to experiment to produce more exciting wine every year.

Not surprisingly, Italy's best wine makers are as eager to try new ideas as anyone. They therefore either ignore DOC regulations or add to their traditional wares unconsecrated products representing their aspirations for the future. However good these are – and they include almost all the great new wines of Italy – they must suffer the indignity of being officially classed as *vino da tavola* – table wine – the basic E.E.C. category for the blended wine of every day. The reader, therefore, should make no categorical distinction between DOC and other wines beyond the fact that a DOC is 'traditional' and subject to official regulation.

A further step in the regulation of certain DOCs has been instigated with a new category: DOCG. The G stands for *Garantita*; the inference being that such wines are officially guaranteed as Italy's best. The first four DOCGs are Barbaresco, Barolo, Brunello di Montalcino and Vino Nobile di Montepulciano. Albana di Romagna is to be added to the list. Anyone who tastes it may be forgiven for asking how seriously the 'G' is to be taken.

It is scarcely possible to summarize the state of Italian wine-making at present. Enormous recent investments in modern equipment and new ideas have already produced some wonderful results, but on the other hand some have stripped old friends of their character. So far the modern movement has succeeded in making both the most boring and the most brilliant of Italian wines. There is a balance to be found between tradition and technology (in grapes, in cellaring, in every aspect of wine-making). As the following pages show, Italy is very busy looking for it.

PIEDMONT

For uninhibited exploration of the varieties of grape juice and what can be made of them, no part of Europe can compare with Piedmont. The vermouth of Turin witnesses that a good brew-up is part of local tradition. For ingredients the hills of Piedmont offer such an assortment of indigenous grapes that the accepted international varieties have scarcely been planted at all.

Each of the local grapes is a character with something to offer. Each is made into wine unblended, often in several styles, and also mixed with others in brews which may be traditional or experimental, conventional or idiosyncratic. The former are frequently blessed with DOCs, the latter not – but this has no bearing on their respective qualities.

The emphasis is all on red wine. Only one Piedmont white has any history of other than local success before the last decade – and that is Asti Spumante. The Cortese is a good white grape now proving itself, but the catechism of important Piedmont wines must start with a list of the red grapes that enjoy the harsh climate of this subalpine area.

Nebbiolo comes first in quality. It takes its name from the fog (*nebbia*) that characterizes autumn here, not only closing Milan airport but creating quintessentially mellow fruitful pictures of gold-leaved vines tilting up to the grey hilltop villages.

The 1,600-foot Langhe hills south of the town of Alba on the river Tanaro provide the slopes, shelter, soil, sunshine and humidity that bring Nebbiolo to perfection in Barolo (southwest of Alba) and Barbaresco (to its east). The style of Barolo, a wine of the maximum concentration, tannin and alcohol, has no very ancient history. But it has conviction, and its growers' palates are ready for as much power as their vines will give them. The inexperienced, the timid and the claret lovers should start with Nebbiolo in its less explosive manifestations.

Barbera comes first in quantity. But it too, unlike the common grapes of the south of France, carries conviction. It can be clumsy, but good Barbera is plummy and astringent in just the right measure.

Dolcetto is quite different. No other red grape succeeds in conveying such an impression of softness while being sometimes startlingly dry. It sounds odd, but with rich food it makes a tantalizing meal opener. Dolcetto is not for ageing.

In complete contrast Freisa is inclined to be sweet and fizzy, and again in contrast Grignolino tends to the pale, mild but teasingly bitter style of wine which is common in northeast Italy. Add the lively light Bonarda and the Croatina and Vespolina and the range of possible cocktails is almost limitless.

The following list reflects the complexity of the region with more DOCs than any other – and lots of unofficial 'table' wines besides.

Would that there were space for more than a low bow towards the best fare of Italy; the truffles, the fonduta, the game and all the simple but sensuous things that give these wines their proper context.

The 14th-century castle of Cavour houses the Piedmont wine institute

DOC AND OTHER WINES

Arneis dei Roeri
Dry white table wine from the local Arneis grape grown in the Roeri hills north of Alba. Soft, richly textured and a bitter almond finish. Price: 2,000–3,500 lire.

Asti Spumante or Moscato d'Asti Spumanti
DOC. White sparkling wine. Provinces: Asti, Cuneo and Alessandria. Villages: throughout the provinces. Grape: Moscato Bianco. Max. crop: 75 hl/ha. Min. alch: 12°. Average production: 3.88m. cases.

One of Italy's true and inimitable classics: sweet, buxomly fruity but girlishly giggly with its scented froth. It is a major industry dominated by big names in the vermouth field, normally produced in tanks, not bottle-fermented, and hence moderate in price as well as alcoholic content. It tastes good very cold at any time; but not with a meal.

Barbaresco
DOC. Red wine. Province: Asti. Villages: Barbaresco, Neive, Treiso, part of Alba. Grape: Nebbiolo. Max. crop: 56 hl/ha. Min. alch: 12.5°. Average production: 167,000 cases. Aged for a minimum of 2 years, of which 1 is in wood, 3 years for *riserva*, 4 for *riserva speciale*. Price: 4,000–12,000 lire.

The immediate neighbour of Barolo, sharing most of its qualities of power and depth, youthful harshness and eventual perfumed sweetness. Great Barbaresco has a style and polish it is hard to define; it is tempting, though inaccurate, to call it the Côte Rôtie to the Hermitage of Barolo. Neither lives as long or develops so sumptuously as the Rhône wines and they remain tannicly hard even in maturity. Most growers now make all except exceptional vintages to be ready for drinking in about 4 years.

Barbera d'Alba
DOC. Red wine. Province: Cuneo. Villages: many around Alba. Grape: Barbera. Max. crop: 70 hl/ha. Min. alch: 11.5° (12° for *superiore*). Average production: 355,000 cases. *Superiore* is aged at least 2 years, of which 1 is in wood.

Barbera wines are ubiquitous in Piedmont, but the best of them fall into one of three DOCs. Alba is considered the best area for full-bodied Barbera apt for ageing – though the style is entirely at the producer's discretion.

Barbera d'Asti
DOC. Red wine. Provinces: Asti and Alessandria. Villages: from Casale Monferrato to Acqui Terme. Grape: Barbera. Max. crop: 63 hl/ha. Min. alch: 12.5° (13° for *superiore*). Average production: 1.88m. cases. Aged 2 years for *superiore*.

Critics disagree on whether this or Alba gives the best Barbera. This may be expected to be less of a 'character', with less bite. Many prefer it so.

Barbera del Monferrato
DOC. Red wine. Provinces: Alessandria and Asti. Villages: a large part of the above provinces. Grapes: Barbera 75–90%, Freisa, Grignolino and Dolcetto. Max. crop: 70 hl/ha. Min. alch: 12°. Average production: 588,000 cases. *Superiore* is aged for not less than 2 years. Price: 1,200–2,500 lire.

The optional addition of other grapes allows this to be the most frivolous of the DOC Barberas – though none of them demands to be taken too seriously.

Barengo
Red and white table wine from Barengo in the Novara hills. The red is comparable to Boca and Faro (qq.v); the white, of Greco grapes, can be dry or sweet.

Barolo
DOC. Red wine. Province: Cuneo. Villages: Barolo, Castiglione Falletto, Serralunga d'Alba, part of Cherasco, Diano d'Alba, Grinzane Cavour, La Morra, Monforte d'Alba, Novello, Roddi and Verduno. Grape: Nebbiolo. Max crop: 56 hl/ha. Min. alch: 13°. Average production: 400,000 cases. Aged in wood for at least 2 years (and in bottle for 1), 4 years for *riserva*, 5 for *riserva speciale*. Price: 4,000–14,000 lire.

If Barolo gives the palate a wrestling match it makes its eventual yielding all the more satisfying. It takes practice to understand this powerful and astringent wine. For several years all flavour and most smell is masked and inaccessible. What is hidden is an extraordinary spectrum of scents (tar, truffles, violets, faded roses, incense, plums, raspberries have all been found).

Notes on a 1974 in 1981 show how slow the process can be: 'Still a deep blackish plum colour, smelling harsh and indistinct. Strong and hard to taste, full of glow but ill-defined. More study reveals sweetness and fruit flavours, if not depth; sweetness and a genial roast-chestnut warmth grow with acquaintance (and air). Still no real development.'

I believe however that maturity comes on quite suddenly at about 10 years and little is gained by keeping bottles beyond 15.

The best vineyards are often signalled on the labels with the dialect words *sori* (a steep sheltered slope) or *bricco* (a ridge). La Morra makes the earliest developing wines, Monforte and Serralunga the slowest.

Barolo Chinato
DOC. A domestic tradition among Barolo growers is to brew apéritifs and cordials with their wine. This, the best-known 'Amaro', is made bitter with an infusion of *china* bark. Another recipe includes green walnuts, tansy, garlic, cloves and cinnamon.

Bianco dei Roeri
Arneis (q.v.) blended with rapidly pressed Nebbiolo white to make full dry wine.

Bianco dei Ronchi
Briefly barrel-aged dry white from the Novara hills.

Boca
DOC. Red wine. Province: Novara. Villages: Boca, Gattinara, part of Maggiora, Cavallirio, Prato Sesia, Grignasco. Grapes: Nebbiolo 45–70%, Vespolina 20–40%, Bonarda Novarese 20%. Max. crop: 63 hl/ha. Min. alch: 11.5°. Average production: 3,350 cases. Aged at least 2 years in wood and 1 in bottle. Price: 1,600–2,300 lire.

One of several dry reds from the hills north of Novara where Nebbiolo is called Spanna. Blending with other grapes lightens this one.

Bonarda Piemontese
Bonarda is a light red grape mostly grown in north Piedmont for blending. It can be fresh and pleasant on its own.

Brachetto d'Acqui
DOC. Red wine. Provinces: Asti, Alessandria. Villages: Acqui Terme, Nizza Monferrato and 21 others. Grape: Brachetto. Max. crop: 56 hl/ha. Min. alch: 11.5°. Average production: 10,000 cases. Price: 1,500–3,500 litre.

A light sweet fizzy red with more than a touch of Muscat in the aroma, locally appreciated with desserts.

Bramatera

DOC. Red wine. Province: Vercelli. Villages: Massarano, Brusnengo, Cruino Roasio, Villa del Bosco, Sostegno and Lozzolo. Grapes: Nebbiolo (Spanna) 50–70%, Croatina 20–30%, Bonarda and Vespolina 10–20%. Max. crop: 53 hl/ha. Min. alch: 12°. Aged for 3 years, of which 2 are in cask for *riserva*. Sold in Bordeaux-style bottles.

A 1979 DOC for a big solid blended red from the Vercelli hills, increasing in production and evidently improving with age.

Bricco del Drago

A Nebbiolo/Dolcetto blend from one grower near Alba.

Bricco Manzoni

A Nebbiolo/Barbera blend; the excellent invention of one grower at Monforte d'Alba. Price: 3,000–4,500 lire.

Campiglione

A quality Nebbiolo blend from one grower near Asti.

Campo Romano

A plummy, prickly and very pleasant blend of Freisa and Pinot Nero from one grower near Alba.

Caramino

A Spanna (Nebbiolo) blend from Caramino in Fara (q.v.). Well worth ageing up to 10 years.

Carema

DOC. Red wine. Province: Torino. Village: Carema. Grape: Nebbiolo (here called Picotener). Max. crop: 56 hl/ha. Min. alch: 12°. Average production: 11,100 cases. Aged at least 2 years in wood. Price: 3,500–6,000 lire.

A variety from the borders of Piedmont and Valle d'Aosta; a relatively lightweight Nebbiolo which can add in finesse what it loses in power. The terrain is steep and terraced, the high climate cool, and prices (especially in ski resorts) can be excessive.

Colli Tortonesi

DOC. Red and white wine. Province: Alessandria. Villages: Tortona and 29 others. Grapes: (red) Barbera 100%, or with up to 15% Freisa, Bonarda and Dolcetto; (white) Cortese. Max. crop: 63 hl/ha. Min. alch: 12° (red), 10.5° (white). Average production: 11,000 cases. Red aged at least 1 year in wood is *superiore*.

A good-quality Barbera blend with ageing potential, and a very light dry Cortese white tending to sharpness and sometimes fizzy.

Cortese dell'Alto Monferrato

DOC. White wine. Provinces: Asti and Alessandria. Villages: 33 in Asti and 51 in Alessandria. Grapes: Cortese 85%, other secondary white grapes – not aromatic ones – 15%. Max. crop: 70 hl/ha. Min. alch: 10°. Price: 1,500–2,000 lire.

An increasingly popular DOC for dry Cortese white, still or sparkling, at a humbler level than that of Gavi (q.v.).

Dolcetto d'Acqui

DOC. Red wine. Province: Alessandria (vinification is also permitted in Asti, Cuneo, Torino, Genoa and Savona). Villages: Acqui Terme and 24 others. Grape: Dolcetto. Max. crop: 66 hl/ha. Min. alch: 11.5°. Average production: 53,000 cases. Aged at least 1 year for *superiore*.

Dolcetto from here can be expected to be light everyday red of good colour and a certain character.

Dolcetto d'Alba

DOC. Red wine. Province: Cuneo. Villages: Alba, Barolo, Barbaresco, La Morra and 30 others. Grape: Dolcetto. Max crop: 63 hl/ha. Min. alch: 11.5°. Average production: 89,000 cases. Aged at least 1 year for *superiore*.

Generally considered the best DOC of Dolcetto, partly because the most skilful growers are concentrated here. The style varies from the traditional soft but dust-dry to something more fruity and refreshing. In most cases youth is a virtue.

Dolcetto d'Asti

DOC. Red wine. Province: Asti. Villages: Calamandrana, Canelli, Nizza Monferrato and 21 others. Grape: Dolcetto. Max. crop: 56 hl/ha. Min. alch: 11.5°. Average production: 18,800 cases. Aged at least 1 year for *superiore*.

Less widely seen but not consistently different from Dolcetto d'Acqui.

Dolcetto di Diano d'Alba

DOC. Red wine. Province: Cuneo. Village: Diano d'Alba. Grape: Dolcetto. Max. crop: 56 hl/ha. Min. alch: 12°. Average production: 22,200 cases. Aged at least 1 year for *superiore*.

A premium Dolcetto, generally stronger, 'thicker' and less brisk than Dolcetto d'Alba.

Dolcetto di Dogliani

DOC. Red wine. Province: Cuneo. Villages: Bastia, Belvedere, Langhe, Clavesana, Ciglie, Dogliani, Farigliano, Monchiero, Rocca di Ciglie and part of Roddino and Somano. Grape: Dolcetto. Max. crop: 56 hl/ha. Min. alch: 11.5°. Average production: 33,000 cases. Aged at least 1 year for *superiore*.

Possibly the original Dolcetto: often a good one with more 'grip' (or less soft) than some.

Dolcetto delle Langhe Monregalesi

DOC. Red wine. Province: Cuneo (vinification is also permitted in Imperia and Savona). Villages: Briaglia, Castellino Tanaro, Igliano, Marsaglia, Niella Tanaro, part of Carru, Mondovi, Murazzano, Piozzo, S.Michele Mondovi and Vicoforte. Grape: Dolcetto. Max. crop: 49 hl/ha. Min. alch: 11°. Average production: 1,100 cases. Aged at least 1 year for *superiore*.

A rarely used DOC established in 1974 for a lightweight Dolcetto said to have more aroma than most.

Dolcetto di Ovada

DOC. Red wine. Province: Alessandria (vinification is also permitted in Asti, Cuneo, Torino, Genoa and Savona). Villages: Ovada and 21 others. Grape: Dolcetto. Max. crop: 66 hl/ha. Min. alch: 11.5°. Average production: 89,000 cases. Aged at least 1 year for *superiore*. Price: 1,600–4,500 lire.

The best producers in this DOC make very lively wine, as fruity to smell as every Dolcetto and capable of developing in bottle like good Cru Beaujolais.

Erbaluce di Caluso, Caluso Passito

DOC. White wine. Provinces: Torino and Vercelli. Villages: Caluso and 35 others. Grape: Erbaluce. Max. crop: 42 hl/ha. Min. alch: 11°; 13.5° for *passito*. Average production: 16,500 cases. *Passito* is aged at least 5 years. Price (*passito*): 3,000–5,000 lire.

This is the nothern Piedmont equivalent of the Ligurian Cinqueterre and Sciacchetrà: a pleasant dry white with a tendency to sharpness and a sweet *passito* made by half-drying the same grapes. The *passito* is sometimes boosted with alcohol and then called *liquoroso*.

Fara

DOC. Red wine. Province: Novara. Villages: Fara and Briona. Grapes: Nebbiolo 30–50%, Vespolina 10–30% and Bonarda Novarese up to 40%. Max. crop: 77 hl/ha. Min. alch: 12°. Average production: 7,200 cases. Aged at least 2 years in wood and 1 in bottle. Price: 1,600–2,300 lire.

Fara, Boca and their neighbour Sizzano, similar reds of the same quality, were all early applicants for DOCs, recognized in 1969 but still limited in production.

Freisa d'Asti

DOC. Red wine. Province: Asti. Area: the hills of Asti. Grape: Freisa. Max. crop: 56 hl/ha. Min. alch: 11°. Average production: 11,000 cases. Aged at least 1 year.

A cheerful fruity sharpish red, sometimes sweet and often fizzy. It can be immensely appetizing, though the non-DOC Freisa d'Alba is often better made.

Freisa di Chieri

DOC. Red wine. Provinces: Torino, Asti and Cuneo. Villages: Chieri and 11 others. Grape: Freisa. Max. crop: 56 hl/ha. Min. alch: 11°. Production: 11,000 cases. Aged at least 1 year.

Chieri on the outskirts of Turin specializes in the sweeter style of Freisa, often fizzy, which makes good café wine.

Gabiano

DOC. Red wine.

A new local 1-commune DOC in the Monferrato Casalese hills north of Asti. A very long-lived Barbera.

Gattinara

DOC. Red wine. Province: Vercelli. Village: Gattinara. Grapes: Nebbiolo with up to 10% Bonarda. Max. crop: 63 hl/ha. Min. alch: 12°. Average production: 33,000 cases. Aged at least 2 years in wood and 2 in bottle.

The best-known Spanna (Nebbiolo) of the hills north of Novara, a quite separate enclave from Barolo and the Langhe with a broader, juicier, less austere style of wine. Few if any Gattinaras reach top Barolo standards, but they are both impressive and easy to like. The area is restricted. Prestige consequently often exceeds quality.

Gavi or Cortese di Gavi

DOC. White wine. Province: Alessandria. Villages: Gavi, Carrosio, Bosio, Parodi S. Cristoforo. Grape: Cortese. Max. crop: 70 hl/ha. Min alch: 10.5°. Average production: 86,500 cases. Price: 1,700–3,500 lire.

A recent international star, DOC'd in 1974 and led to distinction by the La Scolca estate under the name Gavi dei Gavi. No others yet quite reach the standards of mingled acidity and richness that almost says 'white burgundy'; several taste castrated by too-cold fermentation. But this area can grow this grape superbly well.

Ghemme

DOC. Red wine. Province: Novara. Villages: Ghemme and part of Romagnano Sesia. Grapes: Nebbiolo 60–85%, Vespolina and Bonarda 15–40%. Max. crop: 70 hl/ha. Min. alch: 12°. Average production: 16,650 cases. Aged for a minimum of 3 years in wood and 1 in bottle.

A very similar wine to Gattinara, generally reckoned slightly inferior, though some (like me) may prefer the rather finer, less hearty style. The best bottles at 5 or 6 years incline towards a claret-like texture.

Greco

A light dry acidic white from north Piedmont.

Grignolino d'Asti

DOC. Red wine. Province: Asti. Villages: 35 communes in Asti. Grapes: Grignolino 100%, or with up to 10% Freisa. Max crop: 56 hl/ha. Min. alch: 11°. Average production: 67,000 cases. Price: 1,800–3,500 lire.

Good Grignolino is refreshing and lively, slightly bitter, pale but not pallid.

Grignolino del Monferrato Casalese

DOC. Red wine. Province: Alessandria. Villages: 35 communes (in the Monferrato Casalese) around Casale Monferrato. Grapes: Grignolino 100%, or with up to 10% Freisa. Max crop: 45 hl/ha. Min. alch: 11°. Average production: 44,500 cases.

An additional Grignolino area to the north DOC'd a year after Grignolino d'Asti.

Lessona

DOC. Red wine. Province: Vercelli. Village: Lessona. Grapes: Nebbiolo (Spanna) and up to 25% Vespolina and Bonarda. Max. crop: 56 hl/ha. Min. alch: 12°. Average production: 2,000 cases. 2 years' ageing. Price: 5,000–7,500 lire.

This remarkably fine claret-weight Nebbiolo blend is scarce. 6 years is a good age for it.

Malvasia di Casorzo d'Asti

DOC. Red and *rosato* wine. Provinces: Asti and Alessandria. Villages: Casorzo, Grazzano Badoglio, Altavilla Monferrato, Olivola, Ottiglio and Vignale Monferrato. Grapes: Malvasia di Casorzo 100%, or with up to 10% Freisa, Grignolino and Barbera. Max. crop: 77 hl/ha. Min. alch: 10.5°. Average production: 15,500 cases.

A rare sweet sparkling light red (or *rosato*) for café work.

Malvasia di Castelnuovo Don Bosco

DOC. Red wine. Province: Asti. Villages: Castelnuovo Don Bosco, Albugnano Passerano, Marmorito, Pino d'Asti, Berzano and Moncucco. Grapes: Malvasia di Schierano 100%, or with up to 15% Freisa. Max. crop: 77 hl/ha. Min. alch: 10.5°. Average production: 3,300 cases.

Similar to Malvasia di Casorzo d'Asti, either gently bubbly or fully sparkling.

Mesolone

A good Nebbiolo/Bonarda blended dry red from the Gattinara country. For ageing at least 5 years.

Moscato d'Asti

DOC. White sparkling wine. Provinces: Asti, Cuneo and Alessandria. Villages: 49 communes. Grape: Moscato Bianco. Max. crop: 75 hl/ha. Min. alch: 10.5°. Average production: included in Asti Spumante. Price: 2,500–5,000 lire.

Effectively the base of Asti Spumante, but the regulations allow it to be slightly sweeter and lower in alcohol. Some of the best non-DOC Moscato comes from Strevi.

Moscato Naturale d'Asti

DOC. White wine. Provinces: Asti, Cuneo, Alessandria. Villages: 49 communes. Grape: Moscato Bianco. Max. crop: 75 hl/ha. Min. alch: 10.5°. Average production included in Asti Spumante.

Still or only slightly fizzy Moscato is often made with great pains to be swooningly aromatic, sweet and swallowable. It *must* be drunk as young as you can get it.

Möt Ziflon

A Nebbiolo/Bonarda/Freisa blend, lighter than most of its area in the Gattinara country.

Nebbiolo d'Alba

DOC. Red wine. Province: Cuneo. Villages: Alba and 16 others. Grape: Nebbiolo. Max. crop: 63 hl/ha. Min. alch: 12°. Average production: 66,000 cases. Price: 2,200–5,000 lire.

For those who can do without the stern majesty of Barolo but love the character of its grape this is the DOC to tie up in. 4 years is usually enough to develop a delicious bouquet of fruit ranging from plums to raspberries and, with luck, truffles.

Nebbiolo delle Langhe

A probable future DOC for declassified Barolo and Barbaresco – potentially excellent lighter wines.

Nebbiolo del Piemonte

An alternative title for any Nebbiolo wine, which can then be more specifically localized by the grower than if he used the DOC Nebbiolo d'Alba.

Pelaverga

A rare grape variety and its fizzy *rosato* grown at Saluzzo, south of Turin.

Piccone

A lighter version of Lessona (q.v.).

Pinot

Pinot Nero, Bianco and Grigio are all grown in parts of Piedmont. Fontanafredda (q.v.) makes a good dry white by blending them.

Roché or Rouchet

A rare red grape found only in the subalps above Casale Monferrato where it makes a tannic wine that ages to something perfumed and fine. Price: 5,000–6,000 lire.

Rubino di Cantavenna

DOC. Red wine. Province: Alessandria. Villages: Gabiano, Moncestino, Villamiroglio, Castel S. Pietro Monferrato. Grapes: Barbera 75–90%, Grignolino and or/ Freisa 10–25%. Max. crop: 70 hl/ha. Min. alch: 11.5°. Average production: 5,000 cases.

A minor DOC for a respectable local dry red.

Sizzano

DOC. Red wine. Province: Novara. Village: Sizzano. Grapes: Nebbiolo 40–60%, Vespolina 15–40%. Bonarda Novarese max. 25%. Max. crop: 70 hl/ha. Min. alch: 12·. Average production: 3,300 cases. Aged 2 years in wood and 1 in bottle.

Considered by many the best of the north Piedmont Spanna (Nebbiolo) blends, to be compared with Boca and Fara. Potentially a 10-year wine.

Spanna

The alias of the Nebbiolo grape in the Novara and Vercelli hills of north Piedmont, also used as a wine name for Gattinara-style wines by makers who are not enamoured of DOCs. The best-known protagonist of the name, Vallana, plans to use the DOC Boca instead, but many think a controlled use of the name 'Spanna' would help clear confusion in the area. Price: 1,000–2,500 lire.

Vinòt

The brand name of a pioneering Beaujolais-Nouveau style of instant red made of Nebbiolo with *macération carbonique* by Angelo Gaja.

PIEDMONT PRODUCERS

Duca d'Asti

Calamandrana, 14042 Asti.

Owner: M. Chiarlo & C. DOC: Barbaresco, Barbera d'Asti, Barbera del Monferrato, Cortese di Gavi, Dolcetto d'Ovada, Grignolino del Monferrato Casalese, Nebbiolo d'Alba. Other: Granduca Brut *champenoise*.

Fratelli Barale

Barolo, 12060 Cuneo.

Founded: 1870. DOC: Barbera d'Alba, Barolo, Dolcetto d'Alba. One of the most respected names in Barolo.

Produttori del Barbaresco

Barbaresco, 12050 Cuneo.

Italy's most admired cooperative, revived in 1958 by the families that founded the original winery in 1894. Director: Celestino Vacca. Wine maker: Roberto Macaluso. DOC: Barbaresco. Other: Nebbiolo. A remarkable array of *cru* Barbarescos vinified from individual plots. Potential production is about 55,000 cases from some 320 acres.

Italy glossary

The keys to deciphering Italian labels and wine lists are given below. For grape names, see the notes in the colour section on Italian grape varieties on page 25. For DOC regulations see the introduction on pages 282–283.

Abboccato slightly sweet.
Amabile a little sweeter than *abboccato*.
Amaro bitter.
Annata the year of the vintage.
Asciutto totally dry.
Azienda (on a wine label) a wine estate.
Bianco white.
Botte cask or barrel.
Bottiglia bottle.
Cantina wine cellar.
Cantina sociale or ***cooperativa*** a growers' cooperative cellar.
Casa vinicola a wine firm, usually making wine from grapes it has not grown on its own estate.
Cascina northern term for a farm or estate.
Chiaretto 'claret' – meaning very light red or even rosé.
Classico the 'classic' heart of a DOC zone, by implication (and usually) the best part.
Consorzio a consortium of producers of a certain wine, who join forces to control and promote it.
Dolce fully sweet (technically, with between 5% and 10% residual sugar).
Enoteca 'wine library' – Italy has many establishments with wide national or regional reference collections of wine.
Etichetta label.
Fattoria Tuscan term for a farm or wine estate.
Fiasco (plural ***fiaschi***) flask; the traditional straw-cased Chianti bottle.
Frizzante slightly fizzy, but with much less pressure than sparkling wine.
Gradazione alcoolica (grad. alc.) alcoholic degree in % by volume.
Imbottigliato (or ***messo in bottiglia***) ***nel'origine*** (or ***del produttore all'origine***) estate bottled.
Liquoroso strong, often but not necessarily fortified, wine, whether sweet or not.
Marchio depositato registered brand.
Metodo champenois the champagne method.
Nero black or very dark red.
Passito wine made from grapes half-dried to concentrate them; strong and usually sweet.

Terre del Barolo

Castiglione Falletto, 12060 Cuneo.

A big cooperative with high standards. DOC: Barbera d'Alba, Barolo, Dolcetto d'Alba, Dolcetto di Diano d'Alba, Nebbiolo d'Alba. Members have holdings in some of Alba's best vineyards; the wines are reliable and often tasty, if lighter than the best growers' wines.

Marchesi di Barolo

Barolo, 12060 Cuneo.

One of the larger Barolo houses, founded in 1861, formerly owned by Marchesa Giulia Falletti, whose family originated Barolo wine. Now a corporation. DOC: Asti Spumante, Barbaresco, Barbera d'Alba, Cortese di Gavi, Dolcetto d'Alba, Freisa d'Asti, Nebbiolo d'Alba. The house owns 100 acres and buys from 400 more. Its collection of old vintages is probably unique.

La Battistina

Novi Ligure, 15067 Alessandria.

DOC: Gavi. A new estate with 54 acres of Cortese vines. A Gavi to watch: already a prize winner.

Bersano (Antica Podere Conti della Cremosina)

Nizza Monferrato, 14049 Asti.

Founded in 1896 by the Bersano family. The firm was bought by Seagrams in 1967. DOC: Barbaresco, Barbera d'Alba, Barolo, Cortese di Gavi, Dolcetto d'Alba, Moscato d'Asti, Oltrepò Pavese Pinot Spumante.

A large and solidly established firm, its 100,000 cases come from 290 acres of its own land and other grapes bought in DOC zones. The wine museum created by the late Arturo Bersano is open 5 days a week.

Lorenzo Bertolo

10122 Torino

A merchant house that selects, ages and bottles many wines from Piedmont and other regions.

Giacomo Borgogno & Figli

Barolo, 12060 Cuneo.

Owners: The Boschis family. DOC: Barbera d'Alba, Barolo, Dolcetto d'Alba. Already a major Barolo firm, Borgogno recently acquired the small and prestigious house of E. Pira & Figli.

Luigi Bosca & Figli

Canelli, 14053 Asti.

Founded: 1831. Owners: The Bosca family. DOC: Asti Spumante, Barbaresco, Barbera d'Asti, Barbera del Monferrato, Dolcetto d'Alba, Gavi, Grignolino d'Asti. Other: Canei, Chardonnay and *champenoise* Brut Nature and Riserva del Nonno. 700 acres of vineyards.

Enoteca Braida

Rocchetta Tanaro, 14030 Asti.

Owner: Giacomo Bologna. DOC: Barbaresco, Barbera d'Asti, Barolo, Brachetto d'Acqui, Dolcetto d'Alba, Grignolino d'Asti, Moscato Naturale d'Asti. More than a talented wine maker, Bologna is a prominent figure in Italian wine. I must single out his Moscato as one of Italy's most ravishing throatfuls.

Carlo Brema & Figlio

Incisa Scapaccino, 14045 Asti.

DOC: Barbera d'Asti, Grignolino d'Asti. Carlo Brema's Barbera is outstanding.

V. B. Bruzzone

Strevi, 15019 Alessandria.

Founded: 1860. The firm is linked with Villa Banfi. President: Giuseppina Viglierchio. Wine makers: Joseph Reiterer and Ezio Rivella. DOC: Asti Spumante, Brachetto d'Acqui, Dolcetto d'Acqui, Gavi. Other: Moscato di Strevi, *spumante champenoise* and others. More than 4,000 cases of *champenoise* and about 8,000 cases each of other major types come from 100 acres of Bruzzone vines and purchases from another 250 acres. The Gavi is a particularly good example of a cold-fermentation modern white.

Luigi Calissano & Figli

Alba, 12051 Cuneo.

Founded in 1872, now part of the Swiss Winefood group. Calissano produces and sells 500,000 cases of Piedmont DOC and other wines and vermouth. The *champenoise* Duca d'Alba Brut and Realbrut are the most notable.

Mario Capuzzo

Castagnole Monferrato, 14030 Asti.

DOC: Barbera d'Asti. Other: Grignolino, Roché, Saraprino. The red Roché is an exceptional rarity.

Pastoso medium (not very) dry.
Podere a farm or wine estate.
Produttore producer.
Riserva, riserva speciale DOC wines that have been matured for a statutory number of years (the *speciale* is older). *See* DOC entries.
Rosato rosé.
rosso red.
Secco dry.
Semisecco semi-dry (in reality, medium-sweet).
Spumante sparkling.
Stabilimento the company's premises.
Stravecchio very old (a term regulated under DOC rules, not permitted elsewhere).
Superiore superior in any one of a number of ways specifically designated by DOC rules. *See* DOC entries.
Tenementi or ***tenuta*** holding or estate.
Uva grape.
Vecchio old. *See* DOC entries for regulations.
Vendemmia the vintage, also used in place of *annata* on labels.
Vigna, vigneto vineyard.
Vignaiolo, viticoltore grape grower.
Vin or ***vino santo*** wine made from grapes dried indoors over winter.
Vino da arrosto 'wine for a roast' – implying a red of full body and maturity – 'Sunday best'.
Vino cotto cooked (concentrated) wine.
Vino novello the wine of the current year, now used in the same sense as Beaujolais 'Nouveau'.
Vino da pasto everyday wine.
Vino da taglio blending or 'cutting' wine, of high degree and concentration.
Vino da tavola the regulation term for non-DOC wines, the equivalent of French *vin de table* but not (such is the E.E.C.) of German *Tafelwein*.
Vite vine.
Vitigno grape variety.

Giorgio Carnevale

Rocchetta Tanaro-Cerro, 14030 Asti.

A distinguished family firm founded in 1880. Owner and wine maker: Giorgio Carnevale. DOC: Barbaresco, Barbera d'Asti, Barolo, Brachetto d'Acqui, Freisa d'Asti, Grignolino d'Asti, Moscato d'Asti. Other: Cortese, Dolcetto, Nebbiolo. Carnevale selects, ages and bottles 30,000 cases of some of Asti's most impressive wines.

Tenuta Carretta

Piobesi d'Alba, 12040 Cuneo.

Owners: The Veglia family. DOC: Barbera d'Alba, Barolo, Dolcetto d'Alba. Nebbiolo d'Alba. Other: Bianco dei Roeri, Bonarda, Brachetto, Freisa. An interesting range of wines from 4 vineyards.

Fratelli Cavallotto

Castiglione Falletto, 12060 Cuneo.

Owners: Olivio and Gildo Cavallotto. DOC: Barbera d'Alba, Barolo, Dolcetto d'Alba. Other: Favorita, Grignolino, Nebbiolo. The Cavallottos' 40 acres of vines include the excellent slope of Bricco Boschis.

Ceretto

Alba, 12051 Cuneo.

Founded: 1935. Owners: Bruno and Marcello Ceretto. DOC: Barbaresco, Barbera d'Alba, Barolo, Dolcetto d'Alba, Nebbiolo d'Alba. The Ceretto brothers have expanded the family firm (which produces 12,500–15,000 cases from concessions of some 60 acres) to include model estate wineries of Bricco Asili in Barbaresco (5 acres, 650 cases) and Bricco Rocche in Barolo (26 acres, 4,500 cases). They are also part owners of I Vignaioli di Santo Stefano (for Asti and Moscato d'Asti) and the new Cornarea estate for Arneis (q.v.) in the Roeri hills.

Pio Cesare

Alba, 12051 Cuneo.

A pillar of tradition in the Alba area, founded in 1881 by Cesare Pio, grandfather of Luigi Boffa, who runs the winery with his son Pio. DOC: Barbaresco, Barbera d'Alba, Barolo, Dolcetto d'Alba, Nebbiolo d'Alba. Other: Grignolino. Pio Cesare owns 20 acres in Barolo, 15 in Barbaresco and selects grapes from regular suppliers for 21,000 cases of some of the best Piedmont wines.

Francesco Cinzano

10121 Torino

Founded in the 18th century, Cinzano became a corporation in 1922. Chief wine maker: Ezio Mignone. DOC: Asti Spumante. Other: Cinzano Brut and Principe di Piemonte Blanc de Blancs *champenoise*. The renowned vermouth firm, with affiliate bottling plants in other countries, also produces sparkling wines, table wines, spirits and soft drinks. Cinzano controls the wine houses of Florio in Marsala, Spalletti for Chianti and Col d'Orcia in Montalcino.

Tenute Cisa Asinara dei Marchesi di Gresy

Barbaresco, 12050 Cuneo.

Founded in the last century on the site of a Roman villa. Owner: Alberto di Gresy. Wine maker: Paolo Torchio. DOC: Barbaresco, Dolcetto d'Alba. Other: Nebbiolo della Martinenga. From 80 acres of the prized Martinenga and Palazzina vineyards, di Gresy makes 3,000–4,000 cases of big, angular Barbaresco or lighter Nebbiolo and 4,000 cases of austere Dolcetto. Some grapes from those vineyards and 45 acres in the Monferrato hills are sold.

Elvio Cogno (Poderi Marcarini)

La Morra, 12064 Cuneo.

Founded: 1961. Elvio Cogno, the wine maker, also runs the Marcarini estate owned by Anna Marcarini. DOC: Barbera d'Alba, Barolo, Dolcetto d'Alba. Other: Freisa delle Langhe. Cogno's masterful Barolo Brunate and La Serra (3,000 cases from 21 acres of Marcarini land) and Dolcetto (2,000 cases from 3 plots) are consistently ranked with the best wines of those DOCs.

Le Colline (Monsecco)

Gattinara, 13045 Vercelli.

Founded in the early 1950s by Don Ugo Ravizza, who formed a corporation in 1974. DOC: Barbaresco, Ghemme. Other: Monsecco. From 45 acres in Gattinara, Ghemme and Treiso (for Barbaresco), 1,250 cases of each type. The long-lived Monsecco, though not registered as DOC, demonstrates just how good Gattinara could be.

Aldo Conterno

Monforte d'Alba, 12065 Cuneo.

DOC: Barbera d'Alba, Barolo, Dolcetto d'Alba. Other: Freisa, Grignolino. Conterno's skills as grower and wine maker stem from 5 generations of forebears. He served in the US army before taking up the family tradition of making wine with passion and humour. His Dolcetto is soft, his Freisa brisk and his Barolo notably harmonious, despite its massive chassis of tannin. 37 acres at Bussia Soprana produce some 8,000 cases.

Giacomo Conterno

Monforte d'Alba, 12065 Cuneo.

Founded: 1770. Owner: Giovanni Conterno. DOC: Barbera d'Alba, Barolo, Dolcetto d'Alba. Conterno is most noted for his Barolo Monfortino, chosen from the best vintages and aged 8 years in casks.

Giuseppe Contratto

Canelli, 14053 Asti.

Founded in 1867, the firm is headed by Alberto Contratto. Wine maker: Remo Cattaneo, DOC: Asti Spumante, Barbaresco, Barbera d'Asti, Barolo, Cortese dell'Alto Monferrato, Dolcetto d'Alba, Freisa d'Asti, Grignolino d'Asti, Nebbiolo d'Alba. Other: *méthode champenoise* sparkling wines. Though the firm makes still wines, some from family vineyards, it is most noted for champagne-method Asti Spumante, Contratto Brut, Reserve for England, Riserva Bacco d'Oro and semi-sweet Imperial Riserva Sabauda.

Paolo Cordero di Montezemolo

La Morra, 12064 Cuneo.

DOC: Barolo, Dolcetto d'Alba. A small producer with a high reputation. Cordero's 2,000 cases of Barolo from Monfalletto and Enrico VI vineyards (32 acres total) are made for relatively young drinking (they are not *riservas*) without losing depth and intensity.

Luigi Dessilani & Figlio

Fara, 28073 Novara.

Founded: 1924. Wine maker: Enzio Lucca. DOC: Fara, Gattinara. Other: Barbera, Bonarda, Caramino, Cornaggina, House Wine, Spanna. Of the 10,000–15,000 cases from 50 acres, the Caramino and Gattinara are most admirable.

Dogliani 7 Cascine
La Morra, 12064 Cuneo.

A cooperative making lively modern-style wines. DOC: Barbaresco, Barbera d'Alba, Barbera d'Asti, Dolcetto d'Alba, Moscato d'Asti. Other: Cortese, Grignolino, Nebbiolo, Pinot Spumante.

Cascina Drago
San Rocco Seno d'Elvio, 12051 Cuneo.

Founded: 1721. Owner: Luciano de Giacomi. DOC: Dolcetto d'Alba. Other: Bricco del Drago (Dolcetto-Nebbiolo), Campo Romano (Freisa-Pinot Nero), Pinot Nero. De Giacomi is a virtuoso red-wine maker.

Luigi Einaudi
Dogliani, 12063 Cuneo.

Founded in 1907 by Luigi Einaudi, who later became president of Italy. Owners: Mario, Roberto and Giulio Einaudi. DOC: Barolo, Dolcetto di Dogliani. Other: Barbera, Nebbiolo. From 60 acres, 12,750 cases with emphasis on Dolcetto and traditional-style Barolo.

Fontanafredda (Tenimenti di Barolo e di Fontanafredda)
Serralunga d'Alba, 12050 Cuneo.

The most impressive wine estate of Piedmont, founded in 1878 by Conte Emanuele Guerrieri, son of King Victor Emmanuel II, and Contessa Rosa di Mirafiori; now owned by the Monte dei Paschi di Siena bank. Wine maker: Livio Testa. DOC: Asti Spumante, Barbaresco, Barbera d'Alba, Barolo, Dolcetto d'Alba. Other: Contessa Rosa Spumante *champenoise*, Noble Sec Spumante, Pinot Bianco. A major producer of Barolo (50,000 cases) and Asti (135,000 cases). The winery has been perfecting production of about 300,000 cases from 250 acres of estate and bought-in grapes. Price (Pinot): 2,300 lire.

Franco-Fiorina
Alba, 12051 Cuneo.

Founded: 1925. Owner: Elsa Franco. DOC: Barbaresco, Barbera d'Alba, Barolo, Dolcetto d'Alba, Nebbiolo d'Alba. Other: Bianco Fiorina, Freisa, Grignolino, Favorita del Roeri, Moscato Naturale, Primaticcio Vino Novello. A respected house that buys all the grapes it needs for 25,000 cases of DOC wines and limited amounts of others.

Gaja
Barbaresco, 12050 Cuneo.

Founded: 1859. Owner: Angelo Gaja. Barbaresco, Barbera d'Alba (Vignarey), Dolcetto d'Alba (Vignabajla), Nebbiolo d'Alba (Vignaveja). Other: Nebbiolo del Piemonte, Vinòt. Price: (Vinòt): 4,500 lire. *See* below.

Fratelli Gancia
Canelli, 14053 Asti.

A family firm that pioneered the champagne method in Italy. Founded in 1850 by Carlo Gancia, now headed by Piero and Vittorio Vallarino Gancia. Wine maker: Giancarlo Scaglione. DOC: Asti Spumante, Oltrepò Pavese Pinot and Riesling della Rocca. Other: Gran Riserva Carlo Gancia Brut *champenoise*, Il Brut, Pinot di Pinot. Now also a producer of vermouth and spirits, Gancia remains a leader in sparkling wine with 1.25m. cases a year.

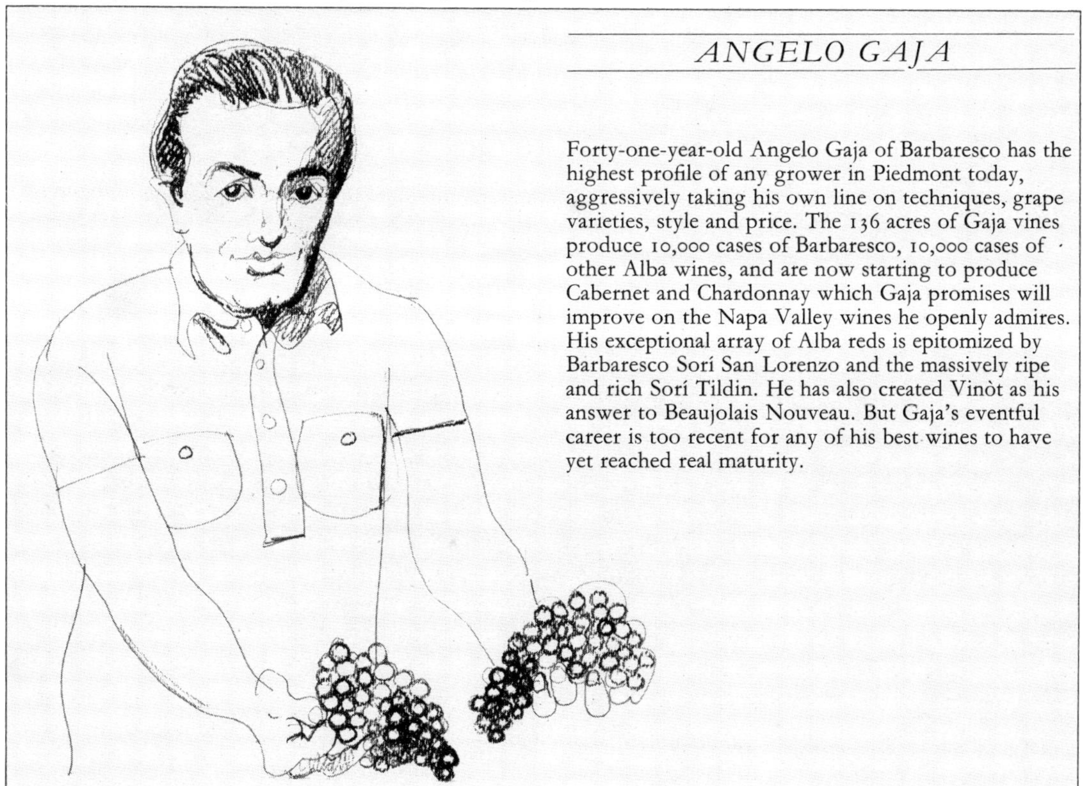

ANGELO GAJA

Forty-one-year-old Angelo Gaja of Barbaresco has the highest profile of any grower in Piedmont today, aggressively taking his own line on techniques, grape varieties, style and price. The 136 acres of Gaja vines produce 10,000 cases of Barbaresco, 10,000 cases of other Alba wines, and are now starting to produce Cabernet and Chardonnay which Gaja promises will improve on the Napa Valley wines he openly admires. His exceptional array of Alba reds is epitomized by Barbaresco Sorí San Lorenzo and the massively ripe and rich Sorí Tildin. He has also created Vinòt as his answer to Beaujolais Nouveau. But Gaja's eventful career is too recent for any of his best wines to have yet reached real maturity.

Amilcare Gaudio

Vignale Monferrato, 15049 Alessandria.

DOC: Barbera d'Asti, Barbera del Monferrato, Grignolino del Monferrato. A winery with high standards.

Bruno Giacosa

Neive, 12057 Cuneo.

Founded: 1890. DOC: Barbaresco, Barbera d'Alba, Dolcetto d'Alba, Grignolino d'Asti, Nebbiolo d'Alba. Other: Arneis, Freisa. Bruno Giacosa is one of Piedmont's best wine makers, admired for powerful Alba reds that age with grace. He buys all the grapes he needs for some 10,000 cases from his pick of well-sited vineyards.

Cantina del Glicine

Neive, 12057 Cuneo.

Owner: Roberto Bruno. DOC: Barbaresco, Barbera d'Alba, Dolcetto d'Alba. A minuscule wine house of growing reputation.

Istituto Professionale di Stato per l'Agricoltura Carlo Ubertini

Caluso, 10014 Torino.

Founded: 1867. DOC: Erbaluce di Caluso. An agricultural college that has upgraded standards of Erbaluce white. It sells a part of its small production.

Martini & Rossi

10123 Torino

Founded in 1863. Martini & Rossi IVLAS is now part of the General Beverages holding of Luxembourg. Wine maker: Giovanni Cavagnero. DOC: Asti Spumante. Other: Riserva Montelera Brut *champenoise*. The world-famous vermouth firm is a major producer (about 1m. cases) of sparkling wines.

Harvesting in Piedmont.

Cantina Mascarello

Barolo, 12060 Cuneo.

Founded in 1919 by Giulio Mascarello. The owner and wine maker is Bartolo Mascarello. DOC: Barolo. A tiny but remarkable Barolo maker.

Giuseppe Mascarello & Figlio

Monchiero, 12060 Cuneo.

Founded: 1881. Owner-wine maker: Mauro Mascarello. DOC: Barbaresco, Barbera d'Alba, Barolo, Dolcetto d'Alba, Nebbiolo d'Alba. About 800 cases of each type. The excellent Barolo Monprivato comes from a 6.8-acre family vineyard. A magnum of the '67 was just past its best in 1981. Other grapes are bought from choice plots.

Enrico Giovannini Moresco

Treiso, 12050 Cuneo.

DOC: Barbaresco. Wine from his Barbaresco 'Grand Cru' vineyard, Pajoré, is now made by Angelo Gaja.

Castello di Neive

Neive, 12057 Cuneo.

Owner: Italo Stupino. DOC: Barbaresco, Barbera d'Alba, Dolcetto d'Alba, Moscato d'Asti. A small winery first made famous in 1862 when the French oenologist Louis Oudart won a gold medal for his Neive wine at the London Exposition. It still produces some of the best Barbaresco.

Parroco di Neive

Neive, 12057 Cuneo.

Owner: Church of SS. Pietro and Paolo. The wine maker is Achille Cogno, the priest's brother. DOC: Barbaresco, Barbera d'Alba, Dolcetto d'Alba, Moscato d'Asti. Divine wines, all from church properties.

Nuova Cappelletta

Vignale Monferrato, 15049 Alessandria.

Owners: The Arzani family. DOC: Grignolino del Monferrato Casalese. Giacomo Bologna (*see* Enoteca Braida) produces this excellent Grignolino for the Arzanis.

Fratelli Oddero

La Morra, 12064 Cuneo.

Founded: 1878. Owners: Giacomo and Luigi Oddero. DOC: Barbaresco, Barbera d'Alba, Barolo, Dolcetto d'Alba, Nebbiolo d'Alba. Other: Freisa. Respected family winery making about 16,000 cases from 50 acres of their own vines. Their wines are slighter and develop sooner than the most massive from, for example, Monforte.

Pasquero-Elia Secondo

Bricco di Neive, 12057 Cuneo.

DOC: Barbaresco, Dolcetto d'Alba. The Barbaresco of the Sorì d'Paytin vineyard has Barolo depth and structure. The '78 had an extraordinary praline flavour under early sharpness and tannin: an impressive wine.

Cantina della Porta Rossa

Diano d'Alba, 12055 Cuneo.

Owners. Berzia and Rizzi. DOC: Barbaresco, Barbera d'Alba, Barolo, Dolcetto di Diano d'Alba, Moscato d'Asti. Other: Nebbiolo. A noteworthy new house.

Alfredo Prunotto

Alba, 12051 Cuneo.

Founded in 1904 as a cooperative, acquired by Alfredo Prunotto in 1920 and, recently, by oenologists Giuseppe

Colla and Carlo Filiberti, who have moved to a handsome new establishment on the edge of Alba. DOC: Barbaresco, Barbera d'Alba, Barolo, Dolcetto d'Alba, Nebbiolo d'Alba. Very careful traditional wine-making produces 13,000 cases of benchmark Alba wines: gentle, plummy Nebbiolo and complex Barolo are first class. All wines are bottle-aged for a year before sale.

Renato Ratti (Abbazia dell'Annunziata)
La Morra, 12064 Cuneo.
Founded in 1962 in the cellars of the ancient abbey, which date from 1479. DOC: Barbaresco, Barbera d'Alba, Barolo, Dolcetto d'Alba, Nebbiolo d'Alba. The owner, Renato Ratti, is president of the consortiums of Barolo, Barbaresco and Asti Spumante, member of the national DOC committee, author, lecturer and curator of the wine museum in the abbey. He makes 7,500 cases of beautifully clear and deep, typically astringent wines from 12 acres of his own and grapes from committed friends.

Giuseppe Ratto
San Lorenzo di Ovada, 15076 Alessandria.
DOC: Dolcetto d'Ovada. A fanatical maker of lively Dolcetto, which he claims will keep for 10 years.

Ottavio Riccadonna
Canelli, 14053 Asti.
Founded in 1921, now headed by Ottavio Riccadonna. DOC: Asti Spumante. Other: President Brut Riserva Privata and President Extra Brut (both *champenoise*), President Reserve Crystal Extra Secco, President Reserve Rosé. The large vermouth and marsala firm also markets the Valfieri line of Piedmont and Alto Adige wines.

Alfredo & Giovanni Roagna (I Paglieri)
Barbaresco, 12050 Cuneo.
DOC: Barbaresco, Dolcetto d'Alba. Alfredo Roagna makes fine, tannic, tight and not heavy Barbaresco from his steep Pajè vineyard.

Podere Rocche di Manzoni
Monforte d'Alba, 12065 Cuneo.
Founded: 1974. Owner: Valentino Migliorini. DOC: Barbera d'Alba, Barolo, Dolcetto d'Alba. Other: Bricco Manzoni, Trabense, Valentino Brut *champenoise*. Migliorini (a restaurateur in Emilia-Romagna) and his oenologist, Sergio Galletti, make 8,500 cases of Alba reds from 37 acres, including his original and excellent Bricco Manzoni of Nebbiolo blended with Barbera and aged in *barriques*. His sparkling dry Trabense and Valentino Brut come from the Colli Piacentini and Oltrepò Pavese in Lombardy. Prices (1982): Dolcetto 2,300 lire; Manzoni 3,500 lire a bottle.

Antica Casa Vinicola Scarpa
Nizza Monferrato, 14049 Asti.
One of the outstanding Piedmont firms founded in the mid-19th century; now directed by Mario Pesce. DOC: Barbaresco, Barbera d'Asti, Barolo, Grignolino d'Asti, Nebbiolo d'Alba. Other: Brachetto, Dolcetto, Freisa, Rouchet. Scarpa's wines are all models of their genre, from Barolo to Barbera to his unique soft, rich red Rouchet or (a bargain) his smooth Nebbiolo.

Paolo Scavino
Castiglione Falletto, 12060 Cuneo.
DOC: Barbera d'Alba, Barolo, Dolcetto d'Alba. An outstanding small grower.

La Scolca
Rovereto di Gavi, 15066 Alessandria.
Owners: Vittorio and Federica Soldati. DOC: Gavi. A 12-acre estate whose Gavi dei Gavi has recently made the world take the Cortese grape seriously. It has the body and balance of good white burgundy. Price: 7,000 lire.

Sella Bramaterra
Roasio, 13060 Vercelli.
Owners: The Sella family. DOC: Bramaterra. Other: Orbello. The Bramaterra branch of the Sella holdings, managed by Fabrizio Sella, makes 3,750 cases from 22 acres. Bramaterra is a medium-weight blended Nebbiolo; Orbello a lighter version.

Sella Lessona
Lessona Castello, 13060 Vercelli.
Founded: 1671. Owners: The Sella family. DOC: Lessona. Other: Piccone. The Lessona branch of the Sella holdings is managed by Venanzio and Fabrizio Sella, making 2,000–2,500 cases from 20 acres. The style of the wine has been lightened recently for quicker consumption. Piccone is its younger brother.

Filippo Sobrero & Figli
Castiglione Falletto, 12060 Cuneo.
Owner-wine maker: Violante Sobrero. DOC: Barolo, Dolcetto d'Alba. Mini-production of exceptional Barolo.

Castello di Tassarolo
Castello di Tassarolo, 15060 Alessandria.
Owner: Marchesi Spinola. DOC: Gavi. The first quality is smooth, soft and excellent. A second pressing (in Bordeaux bottles) was rougher but full of character. Price (1980): 4,800 lire a bottle.

Antonio Vallana & Figlio
Maggiora, 28014 Novara.
Owner-wine maker: Bernardo Vallana. DOC: Boca. Other: Barbera, Bianco, Bonarda, Grignolino, Spanna. The best-known producers of Spanna. Their wines, from their own and other vineyards with a motley collection of labels, have much of the Nebbiolo's virtues without excess tannin. You can smell the truffles at 5 years. The Vallana collection of old vintages (for sale) goes back decades. In future more of their wine will be DOC Boca.

Castello di Verduno
Verduno, 12060 Cuneo.
Owners: The Burlotto family. The former property of the Italian royal house. DOC: Barolo. Other: Pelaverga.

Vietti
Castiglione Falletto, 12060 Cuneo.
Owner-wine maker: Alfredo Currado, son-in-law of founder Mario Vietti. DOC: Barbaresco, Barbera d'Alba, Barolo, Dolcetto d'Alba, Nebbiolo d'Alba. Other: Arneis, Freisa, Grignolino, Moscato. Young Currado wines are intensely vital and even fragrant; old vintages mellow and luxurious. He makes 8,000 cases from purchased grapes. For carefree zing his Freisa is hard to beat.

Voerzio
La Morra, 12064 Cuneo.
Owners: Roberto and Giovanni Voerzio. DOC: Barbaresco, Barbera d'Alba, Barolo, Dolcetto d'Alba, Nebbiolo d'Alba. Other: Favorita, Freisa di La Morra. A small winery emerging with uninhibited style.

OTHER PRODUCERS

Giovanni Accomasso & Figlio
La Morra, 12064 Cuneo. DOC: Barolo, Dolcetto d'Alba.

Antica Contea di Castelvetro
Castel Boglione, 14040 Asti. Cooperative. DOC: Barbera d'Asti, Barbera del Monferrato, Dolcetto d'Asti, Freisa d'Asti.

Antoniolo
Gattinara, 13045 Vercelli. Owner: Mario Antoniolo. DOC: Gattinara. Other: Spanna. A leading name in Gattinara.

Bera
Neviglie, 12050 Cuneo. Owners: Fratelli Bera. DOC: Barbera d'Alba, Dolcetto d'Alba.

Nicola Bergaglio & Figlio
Rovereto di Gavi, 15066 Alessandria. DOC: Gavi. A widely admired maker of Gavi.

Fratelli L. & M. Bianco
Barbaresco, 12050 Cuneo. Owner: Alfredo Bianco. DOC: Barbaresco.

Cascina Biggio
Migliandolo di Portacamaro, 14037 Asti. Owner: Paolo Biggio. 400 cases of Grignolino at its finest.

Fratelli Biletta
Casorzo, 14032 Asti. DOC: Barbera d'Asti, Freisa d'Asti, Grignolino d'Asti. Other: Malvasia Nera.

Serio & Battista Borgogno
Barolo, 12060 Cuneo. DOC: Barolo.

Agostino Brugo
Romagnano Sesia, 28078 Novara. Founded: 1894. DOC: Gattinara, Ghemme. Other: Spanna.

Cantina Sociale di Canelli
Canelli, 14053 Asti. Cooperative. DOC: Asti Spumante, Moscato d'Asti.

Tenuta Cannona
Carpeneto, 15071 Alessandria. DOC: Barbera del Monferrato, Dolcetto di Ovada.

Colué
Diano d'Alba, 12055 Cuneo. Owner: Massimo Oddero. DOC: Barbaresco, Barbera d'Alba, Barolo, Dolcetto d'Alba, Nebbiolo d'Alba.

G. & L. Fratelli Cora
10129 Torino. DOC: Asti Spumante. Other: Pinot del Poggio Spumante, Royal Ambassador Brut *champenoise*.

Redento Dogliotti & Figli
Castiglione Tinella, 12053 Cuneo. DOC: Barbera d'Alba, Dolcetto d'Alba, Moscato d'Asti.

Luigi Ferrando
Ivrea, 10015 Torino. DOC: Carema, Erbaluce di Caluso. Other: Gamay-Pinot Nero della Valle d'Aosta.

Castello di Gabiano
Gabiano Monferrato, 15020 Alessandria. Owner: Cattaneo Giustiniani. DOC: Barbera d'Asti, Gabiano, Grignolino d'Asti.

Gemma
Barbaresco, 12050 Cuneo. Owner: Alfredo Roagna & C. DOC: Barbaresco, Barbera d'Alba, Barolo, Dolcetto d'Alba.

Fratelli Giacosa
Neive, 12057 Cuneo. Owners. Leone, Renzo and Valerio Giacosa. DOC: Barbaresco, Barbera d'Alba, Barolo.

La Giustiniana
Rovereto di Gavi, 15066 Alessandria. DOC: Gavi.

Corrado Gnavi
Caluso, 10014 Torino. DOC: Erbaluce di Caluso.

Kiola
La Morra, 12064 Cuneo. DOC: Asti Spumante, Barbaresco, Barbera d'Alba, Barolo, Dolcetto d'Alba. Other: Pinot Spumante.

Ermenegildo Leporati
Casale Monferrato, 15040 Alessandria. DOC: Barbera del Monferrato, Grignolino del Monferrato.

Castello di Lignano
Frassinello Monferrato, 15035 Alessandria. Owner: Lorenzina Fusier Sassone. DOC: Barbera del Monferrato, Grignolino del Monferrato.

Luigi Nervi & Figlio
Gattinara, 13045 Vercelli. DOC: Gattinara. Other: Spanna.

Cantina Sociale dei Colli Novaresi
Fara, 28073 Novara. Cooperative. DOC: Fara. Other: Barengo Bianco, Bonarda, Caramino.

Ormezzano
Lessona, 13060 Vercelli. Owner: Maurizio Ormezzano. DOC: Lessona.

Livio Pavese
Treville Monferrato, 15030 Alessandria. DOC: Barbera d'Asti, Barbera del Monferrato, Grignolino del Monferrato.

Luigi Perazzi.
Roasio, 13060 Vercelli. DOC: Bramaterra.

Cantina Vignaioli Elvio Pertinace
Treiso, 12050 Cuneo. Cooperative. DOC: Barbaresco. An impressive grouping of Barbaresco growers.

Vignaioli Piemontesi
14100 Asti. Cooperative. DOC: Asti Spumante, Barbera d'Asti, Barbera del Monferrato, Cortese dell'Alto Monferrato, Dolcetto d'Acqui, Moscato d'Asti.

Ponti
Ghemme, 28074 Novara. DOC: Boca, Ghemme, Sizzano. Other: Spanna.

Cantina Produttori Nebbiolo di Carema
Carema, 10010 Torino. An admirable small cooperative founded in 1959. DOC: Carema.

Renato Rabezzana
San Desiderio di Calliano, 14031 Asti. DOC: Barbera d'Asti, Dolcetto d'Alba, Grignolino d'Asti, Nebbiolo d'Alba. Other: Arneis dei Roeri, Favorita, Fromentin.

Tenuta dei Re
Castagnole Monferrato, 14030 Asti. Owners: The Re family. DOC: Barbera d'Asti, Grignolino d'Asti. Grapes are selected for less than 6,000 cases from 250 acres.

Francesco Rinaldi & Figli
Barolo, 12060 Cuneo. Owners: Luciano and Michele Rinaldi. DOC: Barbaresco, Barbera d'Alba, Barolo, Dolcetto d'Alba.

Rizzi
Treiso, 12050 Cuneo. Owner: Ernesto Dellapiana. DOC: Barbaresco, Barbera d'Alba, Dolcetto d'Alba.

Roche
Alba, 12051 Cuneo. Owners: A. and C. Ferrero. Wine maker: Carlo Brovia. DOC: Barbaresco, Barbera d'Alba, Barolo, Dolcetto d'Alba, Dolcetto di Diano d'Alba.

Gigi Rosso
Castiglione Falletto, 12060 Cuneo. Owners: Rosso and Saglietti. DOC: Barolo, Dolcetto d'Alba, Dolcetto di Diano d'Alba.

Castello di Salabue
Ponzano Monferrato, 15020 Alessandria. Owner: Carlo Cassinis. DOC: Barbera del Monferrato.

Cantina Sociale di Sizzano e Ghemme
Sizzano, 28070 Novara. Cooperative. DOC: Ghemme, Sizzano.

Marchesi Spinola
Acqui Terme, 15011 Alessandria. DOC: Asti Spumante, Brachetto d'Acqui, Dolcetto d'Asti, Moscato d'Asti.

La Spinona
Barbaresco, 12050 Cuneo. Owner-wine maker: Pietro Berutti. DOC: Barbaresco, Barbera d'Alba, Dolcetto d'Alba. Other: Freisa, Grignolino, Nebbiolo.

Terre del Dolcetto
Prasco, 15010 Alessandria. Cooperative. DOC: Dolcetto di Ovada.

Cantina Sociale di Tortona
Tortona, 15057 Alessandria. Cooperative. DOC: Colli Tortonesi Barbera, Cortese.

Valmosé
Ovada, 15076 Alessandria. Owner-wine maker: E. Colla. DOC: Barbera del Monferrato, Brachetto d'Acqui, Dolcetto di Ovada, Moscato d'Asti.

G. L. Viarengo & Figlio
Castello di Annone, 14043 Asti. DOC: Barbera d'Asti, Grignolino d'Asti.

Marchese Villadoria (CE.DI.VI.)
Rivoli, 10098 Torino. Trademark of CE.DI.VI., a bottler and shipper of numerous Piedmontese wines.

VALLE D'AOSTA

The Valle d'Aosta is France's umbilical cord to Italy (and vice versa). Its narrow confines lead to the Mont Blanc Tunnel and the Saint Bernard Pass, bringing it a devastating toll of trucks. Small vineyards perched in south-facing crannies along the valley manfully carry wine-making almost all the way from Piedmont to Savoie, with a corresponding meeting of their respective grapes: Nebbiolo and Barbera from the south join Gamay and Petit Rouge (which tastes suspiciously like Mondeuse) from the north, with Swiss Petit Arvine, some Moscato and Malvasia (Pinot Gris) and two indigenous grapes, Blanc de Valdigne and red Vien de Nus.

Quantities are very small: the skiers of Courmayeur help the townsfolk of Aosta prevent exports from the region. Donnaz is the better known of two minor DOCs: a Nebbiolo comparable with Carema. Aostan wines are interesting *sur place* but do not represent good value for money.

VALLE D'AOSTA PRODUCERS

Ecole d'Agriculture Aoste
11100 Aosta. Experimental cellars of the regional agriculture school founded in 1969. Malvoisie de Cossan, Petit Rouge, Riesling-Sylvaner, Sang des Salasses (Pinot Noir), Vin des Chanoines (Gamay), Vin du Conseil (Petite Arvine). Joseph Vaudan, a priest, directs wine-making at the school, producing some of the best wines of Aosta. 2,250 cases from 12 acres.

Antoine Charrère
Aymaville, 11010 Aosta. Aymaville La Sabla. A fine red made from Petit Rouge.

Clos Gerbore
11100 Aosta. Owner: Giovanni Gerbore. Gamay, Petit Rouge. About 1,000 cases from 5 acres.

Celestino David
La Salle, 11015 Aosta. Blanc de La Salle.

Caves Coopératives de Donnaz
Donnaz, 11025 Aosta. Cooperative. DOC: Donnaz.

Filippo Garin
St. Pierre, 11010 Aosta. Torrette. An outstanding red from Petit Rouge enjoyed by skiers at Garin's restaurant, Maison de Filippo, at Entrèves de Courmayeur.

Association des Viticulteurs de La Salle
La Salle, 11015 Aosta. Cooperative. Blanc de La Salle, Blanc du Blanc de La Salle Spumante.

Association Viticulteurs Morgex
Morgex, 11017 Aosta. Blanc de Morgex. Albert Vevey directs this cooperative of growers who work Europe's second-highest vineyards – up to 3,400 feet. The wine has rarity value, but is light and can be sharp.

Augusto Pramotton
Parrocchia Sant'Ilario, Nus, 11020 Aosta. Crème du Vien de Nus, Malvoisie de Nus. Pramotton is a priest who makes an exalted, lightly sweet Malvoisie (probably a Pinot) from a few vines on church property.

Octave Vallet
Sarre, 11010 Aosta. La Colline de Sarre et Chesallet (Gamay-Petit Rouge).

Ezio Voyat
Chambave, 11023 Aosta. Chambave Rouge, Moscato di Chambave, Passito di Chambave. Voyat's wines have an élite following in Italy.

Professional tasting panels are an important part of the DOC system

LIGURIA

The crescent of the Ligurian coast, linking France and Tuscany, is scarcely regarded as a wine region and has never been an exporter. But in the centre of the crescent lies Italy's greatest port, and one of its most cosmopolitan cities, Genoa. Genoa demands, and gets, much better than ordinary whites for its fish and reds for its meat from the scattered vineyards of the hilly coast.

There are only two DOC zones in Liguria: white Cinqueterre in the seaside vineyards to the east towards Tuscany, and red Rossese di Dolceacqua on the borders of France. Cinqueterre might be regarded as just the local name for a sort of white which is found right down the coast; Rossese has more originality – indeed real style. Other local whites are Coronata and Polcevera.

Liguria's wine list is a much longer one than its list of DOCs, but if the officially ranked wines are rarely exported, much less are the individualistic productions of its many small wine makers.

DOC AND OTHER WINES

Buzzetto di Quiliano

A very light, often scarcely ripe, dry white (Buzzetto is the grape) from west of Genoa. *See also* Granaccia.

Cinqueterre

DOC: White wine. Province: La Spezia. Villages: Riomaggiore, Vernazza, Monterosso, La Spezia. Grapes: Bosco 60%, Albarola and/or Vermentino 40%. Max. crop: 63 hl/ha. Min. alch: 11° for Cinqueterre, 13.5° for Cinqueterre Sciacchetrà. Average production: Cinqueterre 44,500 cases; Sciacchetrà 220 cases. Price: 1,300–2,000 lire.

The largely legendary dry white of the beautiful Ligurian coast southeast of Genoa. It should be cleanly fruity. Sciacchetrà is made with the same grapes shrivelled in the sun to achieve concentration and sweetness. It is worth a detour, but not a journey.

Granaccia di Quiliano

A singular fresh pale red as crisp as a cherry with a very dry finish. Singularity extends to the label, which is a sheet of music. From west of Genoa.

Linero

Red and white table wines from near the coast at La Spezia. The red is a blend including Nebbiolo and Sangiovese – fresh firm wine. The white blends Vermentino, Malvasia and Trebbiano to give a more soft and solid wine than Cinqueterre. There is also an above-average Barbera di Linero with ageing potential.

Pigato

Another local white grape responsible for a full-bodied and alcoholically strong, usually dry, aromatic white along the coast west of Genoa. Price: 1,400–2,500 lire.

Rossese di Albenga

Rossese is the notable regional red grape with potential for both light and dark wines of fine flavour and balance. Albenga is on the coast between Dolceacqua (in the hills behind Ventimiglia and San Remo) and Genoa.

Rossese di Dolceacqua or Dolceacqua

DOC: Red wine. Province: Imperia. Villages: Dolceacqua, Ventimiglia and 13 others. Grape: Rossese. Max. crop: 63 hl/ha. Min. alch: 12°. 27,700 cases. Price: 1,500–2,200 lire.

The claret of the coast near the French frontier – a country wine with a good balance of fruit and bite, best at about 3 years, when it can develop a real bouquet to linger over.

Torre

Red and white table wines from Arcola at the eastern end of the Ligurian coast.

Vermentino

The commonest white grape of the coast, grown particularly to the west of Savona (west of Genoa). Standards vary, but an example from Giuncheo was slightly green, yet with an almost oily softness. It should be faintly aromatic and dry: in fact a good fish wine.

LIGURIA PRODUCERS

Silvio Anfosso
Dolceacqua, 18035 Imperia. DOC: Rossese di Dolceacqua.

Rubino Balestra & Tornatore
Dolceacqua, 18035 Imperia. DOC: Rossese di Dolceacqua.

Cantine Calleri
Salea di Albenga, 17031 Savona. Pigato di Albenga, Rosa di Albenga, Rossese di Albenga, Vermentino.

Silvano Cozzani
Manarola, 19010 La Spezia. DOC: Cinqueterre.

Crespi
Dolceacqua, 18035 Imperia. DOC: Rossese di Dolceacqua. Other: Vermentino.

Emilio Croesi
Perinaldo, 18030 Imperia. DOC: Rossese di Dolceacqua. From Vigneto Curli, the critics' choice for Rossese.

Enzo Guglielmi
Soldano, 18030 Imperia. DOC: Rossese di Dolceacqua.

Michele Guglielmi
Soldano, 18030 Imperia. DOC: Rossese di Dolceacqua. At 3 years 'Colli di Soldano' has a claret-like 'cut' and real style.

Fratelli Pozzo
Piamboschi di Cisano sul Neva, 17035 Savona. Pigato.

Cantina G. Tognoni
Castelnuovo Magra, 19030 La Spezia. Owner: Maria Elisa Tognoni. Barbera di Linero, Linero Bianco, Linero Rosso. The late General Tognoni 'invented' these original and highly successful blended dry reds and smooth whites.

Vairo
Pietra Ligure, 17027 Savona. Pigato di Albenga. Rossese di Albenga, Vermentino di Pietra Ligure.

Eno Val d'Arroscia
Pieve di Teco, 18026 Imperia. Owner: Fratelli Lupi. Pigato, Pornassio Ormeasco, Vermentino. The Pornassio Ormeasco from mountain vineyards shows uncommon finesse for a Dolcetto and ages well, up to 6 years or so.

LOMBARDY

Lombardy has always kept a low profile in the world of wine. It has no world-famous name. Oltrepò Pavese, its productive and profitable viticultural heart, is scarcely a name to conjure with. Valtellina, the last alpine valley before Switzerland, commands more respect with its hard Nebbiolo reds. The lakeside wines of Garda have romantic associations. But a region needs a flag carrier which embodies its special qualities, and this Lombardy has not yet provided.

Efforts to create a memorable name, particularly in the Oltrepò Pavese, have resulted in a confusion of faintly comic-sounding brands (Red Arrow, Spitfire, Judas' Blood). In contrast to Piedmont, with its proliferation of DOCs, Lombardy has a mere dozen, but those of Oltrepò Pavese in particular, and Valtellina to a lesser degree, are umbrellas for a number of regulated brands or types of wine.

The grapes of Piedmont and the grapes of the northeast are all grown here, and frequently blended. It is inescapably a zone of transition with rich possibilities but no clear identity to bank on.

DOC AND OTHER WINES

Barbacarlo

An enclave of the Oltrepò Pavese (q.v.) near Broni well known for its unusual full-bodied *frizzante* red, which can be dry or semi-sweet but always finishes faintly bitter. Unlike other fizzy reds Barbacarlo is often aged in bottle.

Barbera

One of the commonest red grapes of Lombardy, used both blended and alone. In Oltrepò Pavese it can be DOC.

Bonarda

Another red grape with DOC rights in the Oltrepò Pavese. Dark, soft and bitter in the finish.

Botticino

DOC. Red wine. Province: Brescia. Villages: Botticino, Brescia, Rezzato. Grapes: Barbera 30–40%, Schiava Gentile 20–30%, Marzemino 15–25%, Sangiovese 10–20%. Max. crop: 91 hl/ha. Min. alch: 12°. Production: 9,400 cases.

A fairly powerful and sweetish red; the local red-meat wine, preferred with 4 years or so of maturity.

Buttafuoco

A forceful concentrated red of blended Barbera, Uva Rara and Croatina produced near Castana (under the umbrella DOC Oltrepò Pavese). 2 years' barrel-age does not prevent it fizzing when it is poured.

Canneto

A lightish dry (sometimes sweet) blended red of the Oltrepò Pavese with the bitter aftertaste of the district.

Capriano del Colle

DOC. Red wine. Province: Brescia. Villages: Capriano del Colle and Poncarale. Grapes: Sangiovese 40–50%, Marzemino 35–45%, Barbera 3–10%. Max. crop: 87 hl/ha. Min. alch: 11°. Production: limited cases. Capriano del Colle-Trebbiano is a white from Trebbiano di Soave grapes.

A recent DOC for light local wines, unknown before.

Cellatica

DOC. Red wine. Province: Brescia. Villages: Brescia, Gussago Cellatica, Collebeato, Rodengo-Saiano. Grapes: Schiava Gentile 35–45%, Barbera 25–30%, Marzemino 20–30%, Incrocio Terzi n.l. (Barbera × Cabernet Franc) 10–15%. Max. crop: 84 hl/ha. Min. alch: 11.5°. Average production: 23,300 cases.

A respectable mild red, at its liveliest young and cool.

Clastidio

Red, white and *rosato* table wines from within the Oltrepò Pavese DOC zone. Price: 1,700–2,500 lire.

Clastidium

A highly unusual barrel-aged white of Pinot Nero and Grigio made only by Angelo Ballabio at Casteggio. Burton Anderson describes it as 'dry but mouth-filling and silky, maintaining light colour, gorgeous fruity flavour and flowery bouquet for 8–10 years or more.' The very antithesis of most modern Italian whites. Price: 10,000 lire.

Colle del Calvario

Potentially good Merlot/Cabernet red and Pinot white from Grumello, a town in the hills east of Bergamo.

Colli Morenici Mantovani del Garda

DOC. Red, white and *rosato* wine. Province: Mantova. Villages: Castiglione delle Stiviere, Cavriana, Monzambano, Ponti sul Mincio, Solferino and Volta Mantovana. Grapes: (white) Garganega 20–25%, Trebbiano Giallo 20–25%, Trebbiano Nostrano 10–40%; (red and *rosato*) Rossanella 30–60%, Rondinella 20–50%, Negrara Trentina 10–30%. Max. crop: 65 hl/ha. Min. alch: 11°. Average production: 27,500 cases. Price: 1,200–1,700 lire.

Lightweight local wines, though with a long history. Virgil mentioned them. The white could pass for Soave.

Franciacorta Rosso and Pinot

DOC. Red and white wine. Province: Brescia. Villages: 21 communes south of Lake Iseo. Grapes: (red) Cabernet Franc 40–50%, Barbera 20–30%, Nebbiolo 15–25%, Merlot 10–15%; (white) Pinot Bianco. Max. crop: 81 hl/ha. Min. alch: 11° for Rosso, 11.5° for Pinot. Production: 166,500 cases.

Red Franciacorta is very pleasant light wine of some character. The Pinot is used to make *spumante* of splendid potential: Brut, Crémant or a rosé. Ca' del Bosco Franciacorta is one of Italy's best sparkling wines. Price: (*spumante*): 6,500–13,000 lire.

Frecciarossa

A well-known estate near Casteggio (*see* Producers).

Gaggiarone Amaro

An aged Bonarda red from the Oltrepò Pavese.

Groppello

A local red grape of southwest Garda.

Grumello
A subregion of Valtellina Superiore (q.v.).

Inferno
Another subregion of Valtellina Superiore (q.v.).

Lugana
DOC. White wine. Provinces: Brescia and Verona. Region: the south end of Lake Garda between Desenzano and Peschiera. Grapes: Trebbiano di Lugano 100%, or with other light grapes up to 10% (but not aromatic types). Max. crop: 87 hl/ha. Min. alch: 11.5°. Average production: 100,000 cases.

Formerly a glamorous rarity to be sought out in such lovely spots as 'olive-silvery' Sirmione. Now a very pleasant light dry white, scarcely distinguishable from an upper-class Soave.

Merlot
Increasingly grown as a 'varietal' wine in Lombardy. Very satisfactory, though not included in a DOC.

Montevecchia
Red and white table wines from Brianza near Milan.

Moscato di Scanzo
A great rarity from Bergamo: an excellent tawny dessert Muscat.

Müller-Thurgau
The German grape is successfully grown in the Oltrepò Pavese, though not admitted in its DOC.

Oltrepò Pavese
DOC. Red and white wine. Province: Pavia. Area: Oltrepò Pavese. Grapes: (red) Barbera up to 65%, Croatina minimum 25%, Uva Rara up to 45%, and/or Ughetta. Max. crop: 71 hl/ha. Min. alch: 11.5°. Average production (total): 1.27m. cases.

The DOC for general reds from the Oltrepò Pavese. Most of the more distinctive wines of the area are either specifically named (e.g. Barbacarlo, Buttafuoco) or have a specified grape variety dominant (e.g. Barbera, Pinot).

Pinot
Pinot Nero, Grigio and Bianco are all widely grown in Lombardy. The Oltrepò Pavese is a major supplier of base wines of Pinot for *spumante* made in Piedmont and elsewhere.

Riesling
The Oltrepò DOC includes both Italian and Rhine Rieslings without distinguishing them. Both grow well here.

Riviera del Garda Bresciano
DOC. Red and *rosato* wine. Province: Brescia. Villages: 30 communes on western and southwestern shore of Lake Garda. Grapes: Groppello 50–60%, Sangiovese 10–25%, Barbera 10–20%, Marzemino 5–15%. Max. crop: 85 hl/ha. Min. alch: 11°. Average production: 194,500 cases. Aged for a least 1 year for *superiore*. Price: 1,200–2,000 lire.

The mirror image of Valpolicella and Bardolino from the other side of the lake. Commercial qualities at least are similar, although classic Valpolicella is far deeper in flavour. The village of Moniga del Garda makes a pale Chiaretto which is lively and good when very young.

Rosso di Bellagio
A good non-DOC blend including Cabernet, Merlot and Pinot Nero. Bellagio is on Lake Como.

Rosso dei Frati
Pleasant fizzy red from Lugana (q.v.), better known for its white.

San Colombano al Lambro
An area southeast of Milan producing pleasant light blended reds and whites.

Sangue di Giuda
A fizzy, often sweet red called 'Judas' Blood' is the sort of wine that makes 'serious' wine lovers turn their eyes to heaven. It should be tried without prejudice. There are good ones.

Sassella
A subregion of Valtellina Superiore (q.v.).

Sfursat or Sfurzat or Sforzato
Valtellina's equivalent of the Recioto of Valpolicella; a strong (14.5°) red made of semi-dried grapes, in this case Nebbiolo. The bottles are sometimes labelled Castel Chiuro. Age certainly improves it as it turns tawny, but whether the final result pleases you is a personal matter.

Tocai di San Martino della Battaglia
DOC. White wine. Provinces: Brescia and Verona. Villages: Sirmione, Desanzano, Lonato, Pozzolengo, Peschiera. Grape: Tocai Friulano. Max. crop: 81 hl/ha. Min. alch: 12°. Average production: 33,300 cases. Price: 1,500–2,200 lire.

A distinctive character among Garda wines; dry, yellow and tasty with something of the typical local bitterness in the finish. It is best drunk as young as possible.

Valcalepio
DOC. Red and white wine. Province: Bergamo. Villages: 15 in the Calepio valley. Grapes: (white) Pinot Bianco 55–75%, Pinot Grigio 25–45%; (red) Merlot 55–75%, Cabernet Sauvignon 25–45%. Max. crop: 58 hl/ha. Min. alch: 11.5°. Average production: 16,600 cases.

A small production, principally red, of light wines with an ancient name but modern grape varieties. The red is aged 2 years in wood, the white not at all.

Valgella
A subregion of Valtellina Superiore (q.v.).

Valtellina and Valtellina Superiore
DOC. Red wine. Province: Sondrio. Subdistricts: Sassella, Grumello, Inferno and Valgella for *superiore*, 19 communes for Valtellina. Grapes: Nebbiolo (called Chiavennasca) 70%, plus Pinot Nero, Merlot, Rossola, Brugnola or Pignola Valtellinese. *Superiore* is 100% Nebbiolo. Max. crop: 84 hl/ha. Min. alch: 11° for Valtellina, 12° for Valtellina Superiore. Aged for not less than 2 years, of which 1 is in wood, 4 years for *riserva*. Total average production: 678,000 cases. Price: 1,600–2,500 lire, *superiore* and Sfursat: 2,500–6,500 lire.

The most successful excursion of Nebbiolo outside its home region of Piedmont. Plain Valtellina can be expected to be a fairly 'hard' light red. The named *superiores* develop considerable character as dry, claret-weight wines with hints of autumnal mellowness. It is hard to discern consistent differences between Sassella, Inferno, etc., but the first is generally considered the best. Switzerland (St-Moritz is just over the mountain) is a principal consumer. *See also* Sfursat.

LOMBARDY PRODUCERS

Guido Berlucchi

Borgonato di Cortefranca, 25040 Brescia.

President: Guido Berlucchi. Wine maker: Franco Ziliani. Cuvée Imperiale Berlucchi Brut, Grand Crémant, Max Rosé, Pas Dosé, all *champenoise*. This relatively new firm may be Italy's largest producer of champagne-method wines – some 170,000 cases from their own 173 acres in the Franciacorta DOC zone plus bought in grapes.

Ca' del Bosco

Erbusco, 25030 Brescia.

Founded: 1968. Owners: The Zanella family. Wine maker: André Dubois. DOC: Franciacorta Pinot, Rosso. Other: Rosa Ca' del Bosco, Rosé Ca' del Bosco *champenoise*, Vino Novello di Erbusco. One of Italy's best sparkling-wine makers. Their production of 25,000 cases from 94 acres is dominated by Brut, Crémant and remarkably fine Dosage Zèro from Pinot and Chardonnay. Dubois (from Epernay) works in ideal oenological conditions.

Il Casale

Santa Maria della Versa, 27047 Pavia.

Owner: Antonio Duca Denari. DOC: Oltrepò Pavese. The best grapes from 60 acres are selected for 3,000 cases. Rosso del Roccolo is the best wine.

Folonari (Fratelli Folonari Antica Casa Vinicola)

25100 Brescia

Founded: 1825. Now part of the Swiss Winefood group. Folonari has grown to become one of Italy's largest producers of table wines, bottling more than 4m. cases of wine a year, none of it exactly remarkable, partly from its own vineyards in Apulia and elsewhere.

Frecciarossa

Casteggio, 27045 Pavia.

A 50-acre estate founded in the early 1920s 'in imitation of Château Lafite' by the late Giorgio Odero, and now owned by his daughters, Anna and Margherita. DOC: Oltrepò Pavese. Odero had great influence in improving wine in Lombardy and his estate continues to produce good red, white and *rosato*, although any resemblance to Bordeaux is imaginary.

Lino Maga

Broni, 27043 Pavia.

Owner: Lino Maga. DOC: Oltrepò Pavese. Other: Montebuono. The estate originated Barbacarlo (1,700 cases), one of Italy's most praised and most durable bubbly reds.

Monsupello

Torricella Verzate, 27050 Pavia.

Founded: 1893. Carlo Boatti continues the family tradition. DOC: Oltrepò Pavese. Other: Barbera Magenga, Croatina, Great Ruby. The red Monsupello Podere La Borla is the pride of this estate, which bottles 7,500 cases from 20 acres.

Nera

Chiuro, 23030 Sondrio.

Founded: 1936; headed by Pietro Nera. DOC: Valtellina, Valtellina Superiore. 110,000 cases from 370 acres. The Valtellina Superiore Signorie is outstanding.

Tenuta Pegazzera

Casteggio, 27045 Pavia.

Owners: Jimmy and Giorgio Fassio. Wine maker: Giuseppe Bossi. DOC: Oltrepò Pavese. This newly restored estate, one of the Oltrepò's handsomest and oldest, emerged in 1981 with the zone's most exciting wines, including *barrique*-aged Pinots and Riesling. 13,000 cases from 55 acres.

Cantina Sociale di Santa Maria della Versa

Santa Maria della Versa, 27047 Pavia.

A respected cooperative, founded in 1905, directed by Antonio Duca Denari. Its 700 members own nearly 5,000 acres of vines. DOC: Oltrepò Pavese. It sells a fraction of the production under its own label, most notably Gran Spumante Brut *champenoise*.

Enologica Valtellinese

23100 Sondrio

Founded: 1873. DOC: Valtellina, Valtellina Superiore. One of the oldest and largest Valtellina wineries maintains admirable standards in 150,000 cases from 60 acres of its own vines and purchases from small growers. Antica Rhaetia Riserva and deeply concentrated Sfursat deserve special note.

Visconti

Desenzano del Garda, 25015 Brescia.

A family firm founded in 1908; now headed by Franco Visconti. DOC: Bardolino, Lugana, Oltrepò Pavese Moscato, Riviera del Garda Bresciano. Other: Merlot, Pinot Grigio, Riesling, Verduzzo. Visconti's skilled use of modern techniques makes him the quality leader in Lugana.

Spumante

Italy is not only the second-largest export market for champagne but also an increasing producer of good sparkling wines by the champagne method – which many Italian producers prefer to call the *metodo classico*. Producers in many parts of Italy now buy Pinot and Chardonnay grapes from the Oltrepò Pavese in central Lombardy to elaborate with their own *cuvées* as far apart as Piedmont and Tuscany. The following is a list of the top-quality brands.

Fontanafredda Contessa Rosa, Piedmont
Contratto Brut, Piedmont
Cinzano Principe di Piemonte, Piedmont
Calissano Duca d'Alba, Piedmont
Riccadonna President Brut, Piedmont
Càvit Pinot Brut Spumante, Trentino
Equipe 5, Trentino
Ferrari Gran Spumante Reserva, Trentino
Marchesi Antinori (Oltrepò grapes), Tuscany
Ca' del Bosco Franciacorta, Lombardy
Santa Maria della Versa, Oltrepò Pavese, Lombardy
Guido Berlucchi Pinot di Franciacorta, Cortefrancâ, Lombardy
Venegazzù, Veneto
Valentino (Migliorini) Brut, Cuneo, Piedmont
Garofoli Gran Spumante Nature, Loreto Marches
Attilio Fabrini Verdicchio Nature, Marches

OTHER PRODUCERS

Pietro Achilli
Santa Maria della Versa, 27047 Pavia. Owner: Francesco Achilli. DOC: Oltrepò Pavese. Other: Pinot Spumante Santa Maria Brut.
Giacomo Agnes
Rovescala, 27040 Pavia. Gaggiarone Amaro.
Giovanni Agnes (Poggiopelato)
Rovescala, 27040 Pavia. DOC: Oltrepò Pavese.
Bianchina Alberici
Castana, 27040 Pavia. DOC: Oltrepò Pavese. The premier producer of Buttafuoco, making some 3,000 cases of vivid, concentrated wine from terraced vineyards.
Marco Bellani
Casteggio, 27045 Pavia. DOC: Oltrepò Pavese. Other: Cravello Rosato, Marco Bellani Brut *champenoise*, Rairon.
Tullio Bellani (Il Frater)
Casteggio, 27045 Pavia. DOC: Oltrepò Pavese.
Cantina Sociale Bergamasca
San Paolo d'Argon, 24060 Bergamo. Cooperative. DOC: Valcalepio Bianco, Rosso. Other: Merlot, Schiava.
Fratelli Berlucchi
Borgonato di Cortefranca, 25040 Brescia. DOC: Franciacorta Pinot, Rosso. Other: Pinot Grigio.
Pietro Bracchi
Botticino, 25080 Brescia. DOC: Botticino.

Cantina Sociale di Casteggio
Casteggio, 27045 Pavia. Cooperative. DOC: Oltrepò Pavese.
La Castellina
23030 Sondrio. Owner: Fondazione Fojanini. DOC: Valtellina Superiore. Sassella only.
Cooperative Vitivinicola Cellatica-Gussago
Cellatica, 25060 Brescia. Cooperative. DOC: Cellatica, Franciacorta.
Pietro dal Cero
25019 Lugana di Sirmione. DOC: Lugana. Other: Merlot Rosato, Rosso dei Frati.
Clastidio-Angelo Ballabio
Casteggio, 27045 Pavia. DOC: Oltrepò Pavese. Other: Ballabio Spumante Brut and Rosato *champenoise*, Clastidio Bianco, Rosato, Clastidium, Narbusto. The cellar master, Aldo Piaggi, is particularly proud of his Clastidium, a singular, long-lived white from Pinot.
Tenuta Le Fracce-Mairano
Mairano di Casteggio, 27045 Pavia. Owner: Fernando Bussolera. DOC: Oltrepò Pavese.
Longhi-de Carli
Erbusco, 25030 Brescia. DOC: Franciacorta.
Cascina Madonna Isabella
Casteggio, 27045 Pavia. Owner: Giulio Venco. DOC: Oltrepò Pavese. Rosso della Madonna Isabella (800 cases) is a gem of the Oltrepò.
Maggi
Stradella, 27049 Pavia. Owner: Angelo Maggi. Wine makers: Giuseppe Bassi and Marco Maggi. Cristal Pinot *champenoise*. There are some 4,000 cases of this exciting new *brut* from Pinot Nero and Chardonnay.
Cella di Montalto
Montalto, 27040 Pavia. Owner: Giampero Canegallo. DOC: Oltrepò Pavese. Notable Riesling.
Montelio
Codevilla, 27050 Pavia. Founded: 1848. Owner: A. Mazza Sesia. DOC: Oltrepò Pavese. Other Merlot, Müller-Thurgau.
Monte Rossa
Bornato, 25040 Brescia. Owner: Paola Rovetta. DOC: Franciacorta. Admirable Brut and Brut Non Dosato *champenoise*.
Tenuta di Nazzano
Rivanazzano, 27055 Pavia. Owner: Maria Cecilia di San Pietro Rati Opizzoni, whose family has made wine there since 1840. DOC: Oltrepò Pavese. Grapes are selected from the property for 5,000 cases.
Nino Negri
Chiuro, 23030 Sondrio. Founded: 1897. Now part of the Swiss Winefood group. DOC: Valtellina, Valtellina Superiore. Other: Castel Chiuro (Sfursat) Bianco, Rosso. 125,000 cases from company vineyards and purchases.
M. Pasolini
Mompiano, 25060 Brescia. Owner: Mario Pasolini. Ronco di Mompiano red.
Arturo Pelizzati
23100 Sondrio. Founded: 1860. The firm is now part of the Swiss Winefood group. DOC: Valtellina, Valtellina Superiore. 125,000 cases based on vineyards in the upper Valtellina.
Prandell
San Martino della Battaglia, 25010 Brescia. DOC: Lugana, Riviera del Garda Bresciano, Tocai di San Martino della Battaglia. Other: Pinot Grigio, Prandell Brut *champenoise*, Rosé Prandell Brut *champenoise*.
Premiovini
25100 Brescia. Founded: 1825. The firm bottles or distributes numerous DOC wines from several regions under the trade or company names Anforio, Contessa Matilde, Della Staffa, Nozzole, Pegaso, Plauto, Poggetto, San Grato, Torre Sveva.
Quattro Castagni
Cadelazzi di Torrazza Coste, 27050 Pavia. Owners: The Girani family. DOC: Oltrepò Pavese.
Rainoldi
Chiuro, 23030 Sondrio. Owner: Giuseppe Rainoldi. DOC: Valtellina, Valtellina Superiore.
Ercole Romano
San Martino della Battaglia, 25015 Brescia. DOC: Tocai di San Martino della Battaglia.
Salvalai Vini
Bagnolo Mella, 25021 Brescia. Producers and bottlers of DOC wines of Lugana, Riviera del Garda Bresciano, Verona and others.
San Carlo
Chiuro, 23030 Sondrio. DOC: Valtellina Superiore.
Tona
Villa di Tirano, 23030 Sondrio. Founded in 1892 by Giovanni Tona, now owned by his grandson Gianluigi Bonisolo. DOC: Valtellina, Valtellina Superiore. Other: Pignolino Spumante. From 50 acres, 13,500 cases of consistently fine Valtellina.
Edmondo Tronconi
Rovescala, 27040 Pavia. Owner: Alberto Tronconi. DOC: Oltrepò Pavese. 4,500 cases from 25 acres mostly in fine Oltrepò Bonarda.
Luigi Valenti
Cigognola, 27045 Pavia. DOC: Oltrepò Pavese. The house specializes in *frizzante* Sangue di Giuda.

TRENTINO-ALTO ADIGE

The valley of the river Adige is Italy's corridor to the Germanic world; a narrow, rock-walled but surprisingly flat-bottomed and untortuous trench among high peaks which has carried all the traffic of millennia over the Brenner Pass from the land of olives to the land of firs.

So Germanic is its northern half, the Alto Adige, that at least half its inhabitants know it as the Südtirol and think of Italy as a foreign country. Much of its wine goes north to market labelled in German.

The Trentino has a more southern culture, but even Trento feels only halfway to Italy. The region's wines are correspondingly cosmopolitan, using most of the international grape varieties.

The Alto Adige has made more, and more successful, interpretations of the white classics. The shelter and warmth of its best slopes counterpoised by its altitude give excellent balance of ripeness and acidity.

Farther south in the Trentino the emphasis is more on red, with Bordeaux-style blends gaining ground. But happily local taste still maintains the ascendancy of the native reds. The Schiava, Lagrein and Teroldego all seem to be mountain-bred versions of the grapes of Valpolicella. In slightly different ways they all share the smooth inviting start and the lingering bitter finish which you could call the *goût de terroir* of northeast Italy.

DOC AND OTHER WINES

Alto Adige (Südtirol)

DOC. Red and white wine. Province: Bolzano. Villages: 33 communes with vineyards above 700 metres for red grapes and 900 metres for white. Grapes: 95% of any of the following: Moscato Giallo (Goldenmuskateller), Pinot Bianco (Weissburgunder), Pinot Grigio (Ruländer), Riesling Italico (Welschriesling), Riesling × Sylvaner (Müller-Thurgau), Riesling Renano (Rheinriesling), Sylvaner, Sauvignon, Traminer Aromatico (Gewürztraminer), Cabernet, Lagrein Rosato (L. Kretzer), Lagrein Scuro (L. Dunkel), Malvasia (Malvasier), Merlot, Moscato Rosa (Rosenmuskateller), Pinot Nero (Blauburgunder), Schiava (Vernatsch), plus 5% of any other; 85% Schiava and 15% of any other.

Max. crop ranges from 98 hl/ha (for Schiava and Lagrein) down to 56 hl/ha (for Moscato Giallo). Min. alch: 11° for Moscato Giallo and Bianco, Riesling Italico, Riesling Renano, Riesling × Sylvaner, Sylvaner, Merlot: 11.5° for Pinot Grigio, Traminer Aromatico, Cabernet, Lagrein Rosato, Lagrein Scuro, Malvasia, Pinot Nero; 12.5° for Moscato Rosa; 10.5° for Schiava. Alto Adige Lagrein Scuro, Merlot, Pinot Nero aged for 1 year is *riserva*; Cabernet aged for 2 years is *riserva*. Total average production: 1.41m. cases.

The general DOC for a large Y-shaped zone following the Adige and Isarco valleys through the mountains, with Bolzano at their fork. Of the 17 varieties allowed, the classic international grapes form the majority, several of them doing as well here as anywhere in Italy. Cabernet, Gewürztraminer, Pinot Bianco and Rheinriesling can all be outstanding. The local characters are the Lagrein, red or rosé, which makes a fruity, rich, smooth and flowing wine with a bitter twist, and the Schiava, which could be described as a jolly junior version of the same thing. The Traminer is also very much a local character, having its birthplace at Tramin (Termeno) just south of Bolzano.

The same geographic area has several more restrictive DOCs (Santa Maddalena, for example) but they are not necessarily superior in quality. Alto Adige is one of Italy's biggest suppliers of export-quality wine.

Caldaro or Lago di Caldaro or Kalterersee

DOC. Red wine. Provinces: Bolzano and Trento. Villages: 19 communes south of Bolzano. Grapes: Schiava 85–100%, Pinot Nero and Lagrein 15%. Max. crop: 98 hl/ha. Min. alch: 10.5° (11° for Auslese or 'Scelto'). Production: 2.77m. cases.

The German name Kalterersee is more common than the Italian on this light and often sweetish red, originally grown around the lake southwest of Bolzano (now designated on labels as 'Classico'). Like all Schiava it has a bitter finish which helps to make it refreshing, though some of the bottles shipped to Germany are so revoltingly sweet and mawkish that the freezer is the only way of making them drinkable.

Castel San Michele

One of the most highly regarded reds of the region, a Cabernet-Merlot blend from the regional agricultural college at San Michele, north of Trento. It needs 4–5 years' bottle-age.

Casteller

DOC. Red wine. Province: Trento. Villages: 26 communes from Trento south. Grapes: Schiava at least 30%, Lambrusco up to 40% and Merlot 20%. Max. crop: 94 hl/ha. Min. alch: 11°. Average production: 1m. cases.

The light dry everyday red of the southern half of the region from Trento to Lake Garda.

Colli di Bolzano or Bozner Leiten

DOC. Red wine. Province: Bolzano. Villages: Laives, Terlano, S. Genesio, Bolzano, Renon, Fie, Cornedo. Grapes: Schiava 90%, Lagrein and Pinot Nero 10%. Max. crop: 91 hl/ha. Min. alch: 11°. Average production: 55,500 cases.

A similar light wine to Caldaro (q.v.) but more often dry.

Foianeghe

A successful Cabernet-Merlot red for ageing, made by Fedrigotti (*see* Producers) south of Trento.

Kolbenhofer

A superior Schiava red made at Tramin by Hofstätter.

Meranese di Collina or Meraner Hügel

DOC. Red wine. Province: Bolzano. Villages: around Merano, on both sides of the Adige river. Grapes: Schiava and Tschaggeler. Max. crop. 87 hl/ha. Min. alch: 10.5°. Average production: 133,000 cases.

The local light red of Merano, for the young and hot to drink young and cool.

Nosiola

A Trentino white grape not found (at least under this name) elsewhere. The wine is aromatic, fruity, dry and (surprise!) finishes with a bitter note.

San Leonardo

One of the successful Cabernet-Merlot reds of the Trentino. *See* San Leonardo (Gonzaga) under Producers.

Santa Maddalena or St. Magdalener

DOC. Red wine. Province: Bolzano. Villages: the hills to the north, above Bolzano (Classico is from Santa Maddalena itself). Grapes: Schiava and Tschaggeler. Max. crop: 87 hl/ha. Min. alch: 11.5°. Average production: 445,000 cases.

An obvious relation to Caldaro but from better vineyards, more concentrated and stronger. Under Mussolini it was absurdly pronounced one of Italy's 3 greatest wines (Barolo and Barbaresco were the others). This and Lagrein Dunkel must be considered the first choice among typical reds of Bolzano.

Sorni

DOC. Red and white wine. Province: Trento. Villages: Lavis, Giovo and S. Michele all'Adige, north of Trento. Grapes: Schiava 70%, Teroldego 20–30% and Lagrein up to 10% for red; Nosiola 70% and others 30% for white. Max. crop: 98 hl/ha. Min. alch: 10° white; 10.5° red; 11° is 'Scelto' or Auslese. Average production: 67,000 cases.

A 1979 DOC for reds and whites from around the village of Sorni. Both are light dry wines for summer drinking.

Terlano or Terlaner

DOC. White wine. Province: Bolzano. Villages: Terlano, Meltina, Tesimo, Nalles, Andriano, Appiano, Caldaro (Terlano and Nalles are 'Classico'). Grapes: Pinot Bianco plus Riesling Italico, Riesling Renano, Sauvignon and Sylvaner 50%. Max. crop: 91 hl/ha. Min. alch: 11.5° for Terlano, Riesling Renano and Sylvaner; 10.5° for Riesling Italico; 11° for Pinot Bianco and 12° for Sauvignon. Average production: 139,000 cases.

The best whites of the Alto Adige are grown in this part of the valley, particularly just west of Bolzano where Terlano has excellent southwest slopes. Pinot Bianco, Riesling Renano, Sauvignon and sometimes Sylvaner can all make wines of real body and balance, occasionally in the international class. Terlano without a grape name is a Pinot Bianco blend and often a good buy.

Teroldego Rotaliano

DOC. Red wine. Province: Trento. Villages: Mezzocorona, Mezzolombardo, S. Michel all'Adige (all on the Campo Rotaliano). Grapes: Teroldego, with Lagrein or Pinot Nero up to 10%. Max. crop: 91 hl/ha. Min. alch: 11.5° (12° aged 2 years is *superiore*). Average production: 175,000 cases.

Pergola-trained Teroldego vines on the alluvial gravel of the Campo Rotaliano give the best of the typical (smooth, well-fleshed, finally bitter) reds of the region.

Trentino

DOC. Red and white wine. Province: Trento. Villages: a long zone from Mezzocorona north of Trento to 15 miles north of Verona. Grapes: Cabernet, Lagrein, Marzemino, Merlot, Pinot Nero, Pinot, Riesling, Traminer Aromatico and Moscato. Max. crop varies from 63 to 87 hl/ha. Min. alch: 11° for Cabernet, Lagrein, Marzemino, Merlot, Pinot, Riesling; 11.5° for Pinot Nero; 12° for Traminer Aromatico; 13° for Moscato. Average production: 613,000 cases. Age: at least 1 year for Lagrein, Marzemino, Merlot, Moscato, Pinot Nero; 2 years for Cabernet; 4 for Vino Santo.

The southern counterpart of the DOC Alto Adige, with almost as great a range of wines but more emphasis on reds. Cabernet is well established here with excellent results; Lagrein gives some of the best examples of the regional style. Merlot is common – best in its blends with Cabernet (which are not DOC). Pinot Bianco and Traminer are the best of the dry whites, Moscato is potentially excellent dessert wine.

Valdadige or Etschtaler

DOC. Red and white wine. Provinces: Trento, Bolzano and Verona. Villages: 73 communes. Grapes (red) Schiava and/or Lambrusco 30% and the rest Merlot, Pinot Nero, Lagrein, Teroldego and/or Negrara; (white) Pinot Bianco, Pinot Grigio, Riesling Italico or Müller-Thurgau 20%; the rest Bianchetta Trevigiana, Trebbiano Toscano, Nosiola, Vernaccia, Sylvaner and/or Veltliner Bianco. Max. crop: 98 hl/ha. Min. alch: white 10.5°, red 11°. Average production: 1.1m. cases.

The catch-all DOC for most of the Adige valley from Merano to Verona. No high standards are imposed, but producers who add 'varietal' names self-impose them.

Valle Isarco or Eisacktaler

DOC. White wine. Province: Bolzano. Villages: parts of 12 communes in the Isarco valley northeast of Bolzano to Bressanone (Brixen). Grapes: Traminer Aromatico, Pinot Grigio, Veltliner, Sylvaner or Müller-Thurgau. Max. crop ranges from 70 to 91 hl/ha. Min. alch: 11° for Traminer Aromatico, Pinot Grigio; 10.5° for Veltliner, Sylvaner, Müller-Thurgau. Average production: 47,500 cases.

The white wines of this alpine valley are all light and need drinking young, in contrast to the 'stiffer' wines of Terlano to the west.

de Vite

An original fine dry white from a Riesling hybrid made by Hofstätter (*see* Producers).

TRENTINO-ALTO ADIGE PRODUCERS

Càvit (Cantina Viticoltori Trento)

38100 Trento

Founded: 1957. A consortium of 15 cooperatives with no less than 4,500 growers, who produce 70–75m. litres a year from 17,300 acres, about 75% of the wine of Trento province. Only a select part is issued under the Càvit label. Chief wine maker: Giacinto Giacomini. DOC: Casteller, Teroldego Rotaliano, Trentino, Valdadige. Other: Chardonnay, Pinot Grigio, 4 Vicariati, table wines. This immense but effective cooperative is unbeatable for quality at a reasonable price. Notable are Gran Spumante Càvit Brut Brut (*charmat*) and 4 Vicariati (Cabernet-Merlot).

Barone de Cles

Mezzolombardo, 38017 Trento.

Owners: Leonardo and Michele de Cles, whose family has made wine since the 12th century and in the current vineyards since the 16th century. DOC: Teroldego Rotaliano, Trentino. Other: Chardonnay, Dama delle Rose, Pinot Grigio. 23,000 cases from 75 acres. Teroldego is the family tradition, but Barone de Cles also excels with Chardonnay and Lagrein.

von Elzenbaum

Tramin, 39040 Bolzano.

Wine has been made on the estate since at least 1533. Owner: Anton von Elzenbaum. DOC: Alto Adige. Other: Edelweisser. 3,000–3,500 cases of Blauburgunder (Pinot Nero) and Gewürztraminer, and 300 cases of Rheinriesling from 37 acres. The Gewürztraminer is Italy's most highly regarded – appropriately, since Tramin gave its name to the grape.

Conti Bossi Fedrigotti

Rovereto, 38068 Trento.

A family firm founded about 1860. DOC: Trentino. Other: Foianeghe Bianco, Rosso, Schiava Rosato, Teroldego della Vallagarina. 30,000 cases from 75 acres. Best known for Foianeghe Rosso (Cabernet-Merlot).

Ferrari

38040 Trento

A family firm founded in 1902 in the heart of Trento; long the leading name in Italian champagne-method wines. The firm is now run by Franco, Gino and wine maker Mauro Lunelli. Ferrari Brut, Brut de Brut Millesimato, Brut Rosé, Extra Dry, Riserva Giulio Ferrari. Ferrari wines have great finesse, to the point of austerity.

Giorgio Gray

Appiano, 39100 Bolzano.

Owner-wine maker: Giorgio Gray. DOC: Alto Adige. The elusive Giorgio Gray (who designed Lamborghini's wines) now demonstrates his gifts in some of Italy's most convincing wines – red and white – under the names Bellendorf, Herrnhofer and Kehlburg.

J. Hofstätter

Tramin, 39040 Bolzano.

Founded: 1907. Now owned by Konrad Oberhofer and family and son-in-law Paolo Foradori. DOC: Alto Adige, Caldaro. Other: de Vite, Kolbenhofer. An outstanding assortment of South Tyrolean wines from 86 acres of family vines and purchases from growers with 400 acres.

Istituto Agrario Provinciale San Michele all'Adige

San Michele all'Adige, 38010 Trento.

The agricultural college built around Castel San Michele is a national leader in viticultural research. From 100 acres of vines, the college makes several wines both for experiment and commerce, including the excellent Castel San Michele (a Cabernet-Merlot blend).

Kettmeir

Caldaro, 39052 Bolzano.

One of the biggest firms of the region, founded in 1908. Owner: Franco Kettmeir. DOC: Alto Adige, Caldaro, Santa Maddalena, Terlano. Other: Chardonnay, Grande Cuvée Brut, Gran Spumante Rosé, Merlot Siebeneich, Moscato Atesino. From family vineyards and 200 growers with a total of some 3,700 acres, Kettmeir produces about 280,000 cases of very honourable wines.

Lagariavini

Volano, 38060 Trento.

Founded in 1972, a union of 2 older wineries. DOC: Teroldego Rotaliano, Trentino. Other: Chardonnay, Mori Vecio (Cabernet-Merlot), Moscato, Müller-Thurgau. A considerable establishment making 8,500 cases of each major type, plus some Brut di Concilio *champenoise*.

Alois Lageder

39100 Bolzano

Founded: 1855. Owner: Alois Lageder. DOC: Alto Adige, Caldaro, Santa Maddalena, Terlano. This well-known family winery owns 50 acres and buys from growers with another 1,000 acres for about 450,000 cases.

Conti Martini

Mezzocorona, 38016 Trento.

Founded: 1977. Owners: The Martini family. Wine maker: Christina Martini. DOC: Teroldego Rotaliano, Trentino. Other: Müller-Thurgau, Pinot Grigio. A new 25-acre estate producing wines of exceptional class.

Cantina Sociale Cooperativa di Mezzocorona

Mezzocorona, 38016 Trento.

Cooperative. DOC: Teroldego Rotaliano, Trentino, Valdadige. Other: Chardonnay, Pinot Grigio, Rotari Brut *champenoise*. This ultramodern cooperative is a pacesetter with Chardonnay, much sold under the Bollini label.

Klosterkellerei Muri-Gries

39100 Bolzano

DOC: Alto Adige, Santa Maddalena, Terlano. Other: Malvasier di Gries. The ancient cellars of the Benedictine monastery of Gries, now in the heart of Bolzano, continue to produce marvellously typical wines.

Pojer & Sandri

Faedo, 38010 Trento.

Founded: 1975. Owners: Pojer (oenologist) and Fiorentino Sandri (viticulturist). Chardonnay, Müller-Thurgau, Nosiola, Pinot Nero, Schiava, Vin dei Molini. The youthful producers, with 15 acres, use what they call 'technologically advanced artisan methods' to make about 2,000 cases each of Müller-Thurgau and Schiava, less of the others – all remarkable for a delicately floral scent and fruity crispness. The Schiava is pale and pretty.

Tenuta San Leonardo

Borghetto all'Adige 38060 Trento.

A wine estate from at least the 13th century, it has belonged to the Guerrieri Gonzaga family since early in this century. Owner: Anselmo Guerrieri Gonzaga. DOC: Trentino. Other: San Leonardo (Cabernet-Merlot). 5,500 cases of Cabernet, 3,300 each of Merlot and San Leonardo – classic Trentino reds – from 37 acres.

Cesarini Sforza

38100 Trento

Founded in 1974 with Lamberto Cesarini Sforza as a partner. Wine maker: Bruno Trentini. The house makes only sparkling wines from Pinot and Chardonnay, by both *champenoise* and *charmat* methods.

de Tarczal

Marano d'Isera, 38060 Trento.

Owners: Ruggero and Geza dell' Adami de Tarczal. Red wines from the Isera valley include fine Cabernet, Merlot, Schiava, Teroldego and an outstanding Marzemino.

Zeni

Grumo di San Michele all'Adige, 38010 Trento.

Founded: 1882. Run by Roberto Zeni. DOC: Teroldego Rotaliano, Trentino. Other: Chardonnay, Rosé di Pinot. 800–1,200 cases of each type from 10 acres. Zeni is an excellent wine maker; his Chardonnay is perfumed, his Teroldego harmonious and rounded.

After DOC?

A monumental effort of organization and definition produced, within 20 years from 1962, 200-odd DOCs covering some 450 styles of wine. It was precisely the discipline that Italy needed both to concentrate her producers' minds on quality and to convince the rest of the world that she was in earnest; that her labels were to be trusted.

The DOCs are accurate records of the regional practice of the time when they were promulgated. Whatever a consensus of growers agreed as normal and satisfactory within the traditions of their area was, after consultation with Rome, engraved on the tablets.

What is not often clearly understood is that the practices being followed and approved were in many, if not most, cases far from optimal. In the matter of grape varieties the DOC enshrined what the farmers had planted in their vineyards, not what they should, or might, have planted to produce the best wine. It allows, for example, a proportion of white grapes in Chianti which can almost make it a *rosato*.

The growers in most cases allowed themselves crops far larger than could be consistent with fine wine. Since surplus is a perpetual headache in Italy this was short-sighted. They also set high minimum alcohol levels based on their old fear of unstable wine – whereas with modern techniques lower alcohol is both practicable and desirable.

Again, in their search for stability (and with their inherited taste for wines aged almost to exhaustion in oak) they set minimum ageing limits which run clean counter to the modern trends for clearly fruity and fragrant, or else bottle-aged and complex, wines. For the time being the only alternative, for producers who are reluctant to be bound by ideas they reject, is to label their wine *vino de tavola*.

It may well be that DOC has served its purpose, and that a new generation of wine laws will be based on quality rather than 'tradition'.

OTHER PRODUCERS

Abbazia di Novacella (Stiftskellerei Neustift)
Bressanone, 39042 Bolzano. DOC: Valle Isarco. A lovely 12th-century monastery with 120 acres.

La Vinicola Sociale Aldeno
Aldeno, 38060 Trento. Cooperative. Founded: 1910. DOC: Casteller, Trentino. Other: San Zeno, Sgreben.

Josef Brigl
Cornaiano, 39050 Bolzano. DOC: Alto Adige, Caldaro, Terlano.

Remo Calovi
Faedo, 38010 Trento. DOC: Trentino. A miniscule production of particularly good Müller-Thurgau.

Dolzan
Mezzolombardo, 38016 Trento. DOC: Teroldego Rotaliano, Trentino. Other: Pinot Grigio, Saltner (Cabernet-Merlot).

Donati
Mezzocorona, 38016 Trento. Owner: Pierfranco Donati. DOC: Teroldego Rotaliano, Trentino.

Fratelli Dorigati
Mezzocorona, 38016 Trento. Owners: The Dorigati family. Cabernet, Grener, Lagrein, Pinot Bianco, Rebo (Marzemino-Merlot hybrid), Teroldego – all table wines.

Eisacktaler Kellereigenossenschaft (Cantina Sociale della Valle d'Isarco)
Chiusa, 39043 Bolzano. DOC: Valle Isarco. A respected cooperative making fine Isarco whites.

Fratelli Endrizzi
San Michele all'Adige, 38010 Trento. Founded: 1885. Owners: Franco and Paolo Endrizzi. DOC: Trentino, Valdadige. Other: Teroldego di San Michele.

Equipe Trentina Spumanti
Mezzolombardo, 38017 Trento. Owner: Letrari & C. Wine maker: Pietro Turra. This respected specialist in *champenoise* uses the trademark Equipe 5 on Brut, Brut Riserva, Extra Dry, Rosé Brut and Sec. 17,000 cases.

Giuseppe Fanti
Pressano di Lavis, 38015 Trento. Lagrein, Nosiola di Pressiano.

V. Foradori & Figli
Mezzolombardo, 38017 Trento. DOC: Teroldego Rotaliano, Trentino.

Gaierhof
Roverè della Luna, 38030 Trento. Founded: 1976. Owner: Luigi Togn. DOC: Caldaro, Sorni, Teroldego Rotaliano, Trentino, Valdadige. About 20,000 cases from 32 acres at Sorni.

Haderburg
Salorno, 39040 Bolzano. Owner: A. Ochsenreiter. Haderburg *champenoise*.

Hirschprunn
Magré, 39040 Bolzano. DOC: Alto Adige, Caldaro.

Cantina Sociale di Isera
Isera, 38060 Trento. Cooperative. DOC: Trentino. Other: Marzemino di Isera.

Kellereigenossenschaft Kaltern (Cantina Sociale Caldaro)
Caldaro, 39052 Bolzano. DOC: Alto Adige, Caldaro.

Cantina Sociale Lavis-Sorni-Salorno
Lavis, 38015 Trento. Cooperative. DOC: Caldaro, Sorni, Trentino.

Letrari
Nogaredo, 38060 Trento. Founded: 1976. Owner: Maria Vittoria Aste Letrari. DOC: Trentino. Other: Maso Lodron (Cabernet-Merlot). 18,000 cases.

H. Lun
39100 Bolzano. Founded: 1840. Owners: The Lun family. DOC: Alto Adige, Santa Maddalena. Wine from certain plots carries the trade name Sandbichler.

Fratelli Pedrotti
Nomi, 38060 Trento. DOC: Casteller, Trentino, Teroldego Rotaliano, Valdadige. Other: Morlacco, Pinot Spumante Brut *champenoise*.

Fratelli Pisoni
Pergolese Sarche, 38070 Trento. DOC: Trentino. Other: Gran Spumante Pisoni Brut *champenoise*, San Siro Bianco, Rosso.

Castel Rametz
Merano, 39012 Bolzano. DOC: Alto Adige, Meranese di Collina, Santa Maddalena.

Cantina Sociale di Roverè della Luna
Roverè della Luna, 38030 Trento. Cooperative. DOC: Caldaro, Trentino.

Schloss Sallegg
39100 Bolzano. Owner: Eberhard Kuenburg. DOC: Alto Adige, Caldaro. Kuenburg's lightly sweet Moscato Rosa ('Rosenmuskateller') is exquisite.

Schloss Schwanburg (Rudolf Carli Eredi)
Nalles, 39010 Bolzano. Founded: 1884. DOC: Alto Adige, Caldaro, Santa Maddalena, Terlano. Other: Schwanburger Geierberg, Schlosswein, Sonnenberg.

Kellereigenossenschaft Terlan (Cantina Sociale Terlano)
Terlano, 39018 Bolzano. DOC: Alto Adige, Terlano. Other: Blume von Keller.

Kellereigenossenschaft Tramin (Cantina Sociale di Termeno)
Tramin, 39040 Bolzano. DOC: Alto Adige, Caldaro. Other: Hexenbichler.

Vaja
39100 Bolzano. The corporation is owned by the Swiss Winefood group. DOC: Alto Adige, Caldaro, Santa Maddalena. 115,000 cases.

W. Walch
Tramin, 39040 Bolzano. Owners: The Walch family. DOC: Alto Adige, Caldaro, Santa Maddalena, Terlano.

VENETO

The hinterland of Venice is one third mountain, two thirds plain. Its northernmost boundary is with Austria, high in the Dolomites; in the south it is the flat valley of the Po. All the important wines of the Veneto are grown in the faltering alpine foothills and occasional hilly outcrops in a line eastwards from Lake Garda to Conegliano. Verona, near Lake Garda, is the wine capital, with a greater production of DOC wine from its vineyards of Soave, Valpolicella and Bardolino than any other Italian region. So important are these three in the export market that Verona has a claim to being the international wine capital of the whole of Italy. The nation's biggest wine fair, Vinitaly, takes place in Verona in April.

To the east Conegliano has another claim: to be the nation's centre of viticultural technology and research.

The Verona and Conegliano areas have strong traditions of using grape varieties peculiar to themselves: Garganega, the Soave grape, the Corvina of Valpolicella and the Prosecco, which makes admirable sparkling wine at Conegliano, are unknown elsewhere. But less established and self-confident areas, such as the Berici and Euganean hills and the Piave, prolific flatland vineyards on the borders of Friuli-Venezia Giulia to the east, try their luck with a range of international varieties: Pinots, Cabernets and their kin. Merlot is the standby red of the region and rapidly improving from acceptable to delicious.

DOC AND OTHER WINES

Amarone

See Valpolicella.

Bardolino

DOC. Red and rosé wine. Province: Verona. Villages: Bardolino and 15 others. Grapes: Corvina Veronese 50–65%, Rondinella 10–30%, Molinara 10–20%, Negrara, Rossignola, Barbera and Sangiovese 10%. Max. crop: 91 hl/ha. Min. alch: 10.5° (11.5° aged 1 year for *superiore*). Average production: 2.25m. cases.

A pale red and an even paler Chiaretto; a lighter version of Valpolicella with the same quality (in a good example) of liveliness. Bardolino is on glacial deposits which do not warm up as well as the limestone of Valpolicella. Like Valpolicella it is briskest and best in the year after the vintage. Guerrieri Rizzardi (*see* Producers) makes a sort of Bardolino Recioto called Rosso San Pietro.

Bianco di Custoza

DOC. White wine. Province: Verona. Villages: Pescantina, Sommacampagna and Villafranca, and 9 other communes. Grapes: Trebbiano Toscano 5–15%, Garganega 20–30%, Tocai Friulano 5–15%, Cortese 20–30%. Max crop: 91 hl/ha. Min alch: 11°. Average production: 220,000 cases.

The southern neighbour of Soave, with no differences of character consistent enough to record.

Breganze

DOC. Red and white wine. Province: Vicenza. Villages: Breganze, Fara, Mason and Molvena, and parts of 9 others. Grapes, Breganze Bianco: Tocai, plus Pinot Bianco, Pinot Grigio, Reisling Italico, Sauvignon and Vespaiolo, max. 15%. Breganze Rosso: Merlot, plus Marzomina, Groppelo, Cabernet Franc, Cabernet Sauvignon, Pinot Nero and Freisa, max. 15%. Breganze-Cabernet: Sauvignon or Franc. Breganze-Pinot Nero: Pinot Nero. Breganze-Pinot Bianco: Pinot Bianco and Pinot Grigio. Breganze-Vespaiolo: Vespaiolo. Max. crop: 91 hl/ha. Min. alch: 11° for white, red; 11.5° for Cabernet, Pinot Nero, Pinot Bianco and Vespaiolo. Average production: 309,000 cases.

Light and agreeable 'varietal' wines from the birthplace of the great architect Palladio. Pinot Bianco and Cabernet are the best (*see* Maculan under Producers).

Cabernet di Pramaggiore

DOC. Red wine. Provinces: Venice, Pordenone, Treviso. Area: between the Livenza and Tagliamento rivers – 19 communes. Grapes: Cabernet Franc and/or Cabernet Sauvignon 90% and Merlot 10%. Max. crop: 77 hl/ha. Min. alch: 11.5° (12° aged 3 years for *riserva*). Average production: 44,500 cases.

Both Cabernet and Merlot thrive on the coastal plain. The Cabernet needs age and has distinct character.

Campo Fiorin

An unusually serious interpretation of Valpolicella by Masi (*see* Producers). The wine is macerated with the skins of Recioto (q.v.) after pressing.

Capitel San Rocco

A similar serious red to Campo Fiorin from Tedeschi (*see* Producers). Also a clean, fairly pale-bodied dry white.

Colli Berici

DOC. Red and white wine. Province: Vicenza. Villages: 28 communes south of Vicenza. Grapes: 7 varieties, with limited (10–15%) admixture of other local grapes. The range is Garganega (comparable with Soave), Tocai Bianco, Sauvignon, Pinot Bianco, Merlot, Tocai Rosso (sharp fruity young red), Cabernet. Cabernet of 12.5° aged for 3 years is *riserva*. Max. crop: 98 hl/ha. Min. alch: 10.5° for Garganega. Average production: 306,000 cases.

These hills between Verona and Padua have clear potential for quality, best demonstrated by their Cabernet.

Colli Euganei

DOC. Red and white wine. Province: Padua. Villages: Este and 17 others south of Padua. Grapes: (red) Merlot 60–80%, Cabernet Franc, Cabernet Sauvignon, Barbera and Raboso Veronese 40–20%; (white) Garganega 30–50%, Serprina 20–40%, Tocai and/or Sauvignon 20–30%, Pinella, Pinot Bianco and Riesling Italico max. 30%; (Moscato) Moscato Bianco. Max. crop: 75 hl/ha. Min. alch: 10.5° for white and Moscato, 11° for red. Average production: 166,500 cases.

Euganean wine, despite its long history, is generally rather dull. The best at present is the non-DOC Cabernet and a branded red, Sant'Elmo.

Costozza

A leading estate in the Colli Berici, making good Cabernet, Pinot Nero and Riesling but not using the DOC.

Durello

A local white grape used in blends and solo for a fresh, emphatic wine to be drunk young.

Gambellara

DOC. White wine. Provinces: Verona and Vicenza. Villages: Gambellara, Montebello Vicentino, Montorso and Zermeghedo. Grapes: Garganega 80–90%, Trebbiano di Soave 5–20%. Max. crop: 98 hl/ha. Min. alch: 11° for Gambellara (11.5° for *superiore*); 12° for Recioto di Gambellara; 14° for Vin Santo di Gambellara. Vin Santo di Gambellara must be aged for at least 2 years. Average production: 561,000 cases.

Soave's eastern neighbour, worth trying as an alternative. Its Recioto version is sweet (and sometimes fizzy). Vin Santo is sweet and strong.

Merlot

The major red grape of the eastern Veneto, included in the major DOC zones but often found as a 'table wine' which may be the sign of an individualist product of quality. (*See* Villa dal Ferro-Lazzarini under Producers.) Its best wines are dark and nicely fruity, often ending with an astringent note.

Merlot di Pramaggiore

DOC. Red wine. Province: Venice. Villages: 19 communes between the Livenza and Tagliamento rivers. Grapes: Merlot, Cabernet up to 10%. Max. crop: 77 hl/ha. Min. alch: 11.5° (12° aged at least 3 years for *riserva*). Production: 277,500 cases.

See under Cabernet di Pramaggiore.

Montello and Colli Asolani

DOC. Red and white wine. Province: Treviso. Villages: Monfumo, Montello and others. Grapes: Prosecco for white, Cabernet or Merlot for red (up to 15% blending allowed). Max. crop: 70 hl/ha. Min. alch: 10.5° for white; 11° for Merlot (11.5° with 2 years' ageing for *superiore*); 11.5° for Cabernet (12° with 2 years' ageing for *superiore*). One of the 2 years must be in barrel. Average production: 66,500 cases.

A new DOC with a small supply of Cabernet and more of Merlot and Prosecco, which is usually fizzy and often sweet. The hills around Asolo were a resort during the Renaissance, famous for Palladio's villas. The most famous wine estate of the area is Venegazzù (*see* Venegazzù-Conte Loredan-Gasparini under Producers).

Piave

DOC. Red and white wine. Provinces: Venice, Treviso. Villages: from Conegliano to the Adriatic sea. Grapes: Merlot, Pinot Grigio, Pinot Nero, Raboso, Cabernet, Tocai or Verduzzo. Max. crop: 91 hl/ha. Min. alch: 11° for Merlot, Tocai, Verduzzo; 11.5° for Cabernet. 12° Merlot aged 2 years is *vecchio*, 12.5° Cabernet aged 3 years is *riserva*. Average production: 1.85m. cases.

The river Piave flows through flat country to the sea north of Venice (at Jesolo). Cabernet and Merlot both thrive here, making rather dry wines that benefit from ageing. The whites need drinking young.

Pinot Bianco, Grigio, Nero

All three Pinots are found in the Veneto; none achieves the quality found farther east in Friuli-Venezia Giulia. Some good Pinot Spumante is made by Maculan and Chardonnay Spumante by Venegazzù-Conte Loredan-Gasparini (*see* Producers).

Pramaggiore

See Cabernet and Merlot di Pramaggiore.

Prosecco di Conegliano-Valdobbiadene

DOC. White wine. Province: Treviso. Villages: much of Treviso, but only S. Pietro di Barbozza, Valdobbiadene, for Superiore di Cartizze. Grapes: Prosecco, Verdiso up to 10%. Max. crop: 84 hl/ha. Min. alch: 10° (10.5° for Superiore di Cartizze). Average production: 666,500 cases.

The native Prosecco grape gives a rather austere and charmless yellowish dry wine but responds well to being made fizzy, whether *frizzante* or *spumante*, particularly in its semi-sweet and sweet forms. Valdobbiadene is a restricted zone where the wines have a finer texture, greater length on the palate and the right to the title Superiore di Cartizze.

Raboso del Piave

The local Raboso grape makes an astringent red wine which is worth meeting, especially with 4 or 5 years' bottle-age.

Recioto

See Valpolicella.

Soave and Recioto di Soave

DOC. White wine. Province: Verona. Villages: Soave and 12 others. Grapes: Garganega 70–90%, Trebbiano di Soave 10–30%. Max. crop: 98 hl/ha. Min. alch: 10.5° for Soave; 11.5° for Soave Superiore (not before July following the vintage). Average production: 4.65m. cases.

The most popular of all Italian white wines. Its simple name seems to express its simple nature: it is smooth, light and easy to drink. When it is well made and above all fresh it is hugely tempting. The zone is immediately east of Valpolicella, making Verona a singularly well-watered city. A central zone of Soave is entitled to the term Classico, which in this case is worth an extra hundred lire or two. To taste the wine at its best, look for Pieropan (*see* Producers), though Bolla and the colossal cooperative are reliable. Recioto di Soave is a concentrated, semi-sweet and rich-textured version made of semi-dried grapes.

Tocai di Lison

DOC. White wine. Provinces: Venice, Pordenone, Treviso. Villages: 19 communes on the border of Friuli-Venezia Giulia. 'Classico' is around the town of Lison. Grapes: Tocai Friulano 95%, other white grapes 5%. Max. crop: 70 hl/ha. Min. alch: 11.5°. Average production: 222,000 cases.

An attractive light wine of faintly smoky aroma and typically bitter 'almond' finish, perhaps the best of the Tocais of the region.

Valpolicella and Recioto della Valpolicella

DOC. Red wine. Province: Verona. Villages: 19 communes in the hills north of Verona, the westernmost 5 of which are the 'Classico' zone. Grapes: Corvina Veronese 55–70%, Rondinella 25–30%, Molinara 5–15%, Rossignola, Negrara, Barbera, Sangiovese up to 10%. Max. crop: 84 hl/ha. Min. alch: 11° (12° aged at least 1 year for *superiore*). Recioto must have 14° potential alcohol of which at least 12° is actual. Average production: 3.66m. cases.

Valpolicella, like Chianti, has too wide a range of qualities to be easily summed up. At its best it is one of Italy's most tempting light reds, always reminding one of cherries, combining the smooth and the lively and ending with the bitter-almond hallmark of almost all northeast Italian reds. In commerce it can be a poor, pale, listless sort of wine. Part of the secret lies in its age and condition: the youngest is always best, no matter what its makers or the DOC regulations may say. 'Classico' is also better; the pick of the villa-dotted vineyards are in the hills skirted to the south and west by the river Adige, divided by the river from Bardolino. Soave lies at the opposite, eastern, end of the zone.

At any Veronese gathering the last bottle to be served is Recioto, either in its sweet form or its powerful, dry, velvety but astringent and bitter Amarone. Recioto is made by half drying selected grapes to concentrate their sugars, then giving them a long fermentation in the New Year. If the fermentation is allowed to go on to the bitter end the result is Amarone. Many critics find it one of Italy's greatest red wines. My advice is to keep a glass of young Valpolicella at hand to quench your thirst. Recioto is also made in a fizzy form.

Venegazzù

The estate of Conte Loredan (*see* Producers) in the DOC Montello-Colli Asolani, but most famous for its non-DOC Cabernet-Merlot blend in the Bordeaux style, comparable perhaps to a powerful rustic St-Emilion, and its *méthode champenoise spumante*.

VENETO PRODUCERS

Allegrini

Fumane di Valpolicella, 37022 Verona.

Owners: The Allegrini family for 3 generations. Wine maker: Giovanni Allegrini. DOC: Valpolicella-Recioto-Amarone. Other: Pelara. 17,500 cases from 75 acres, including some of the most persuasive Valpolicella Classico Superiore and Amarone.

Bertani

37121 Verona

Founded: 1857; now headed by Gaetano Bertani. DOC: Bardolino, Soave, Valpolicella-Valpantena, Valpolicella-Recioto-Amarone. Other: Bertarosé. From 500 acres of family vines and 500–600 acres belonging to suppliers, this venerable house makes 185,000 cases, notably Secco-Bertani Valpolicella and aged Amarone.

Bolla

37100 Verona

Founded in Soave in 1883, the firm – FRABO S.p.A. – is now run by the Bolla brothers. DOC: Bardolino, Soave, Valpolicella-Recioto-Amarone. Grapes acquired from more than 3,500 acres of vines are processed in 4 ultra-modern plants in the Verona area to make nearly 1.5m. cases. Bolla, synonymous with Soave in the United States, is a leader in viticultural research through the Sergio Bolla Foundation.

Carpenè Malvolti

Conegliano, 31015 Treviso.

A family firm, founded in 1868 by Antonio Carpenè. His descendant Antonio Carpenè still directs and makes the wine. DOC: Prosecco di Conegliano. Other: Carpenè Malvolti Brut *champenoise*. With production of 285,000 cases, a leading name in Italian sparkling wine.

Col Sandago

Pieve di Soligo, 31053 Treviso.

Founded: 1960. A modern winery run by the oenologist Orlandi. DOC: Prosecco di Conegliano. Other: Cabernet, Coste delle Pergole, Merlot, Pinot Grigio, Val de Brun, Wildbacher. Potential for 50,000 cases from 197 acres of vines.

Costozza

Costozza di Longare, 36023 Vicenza.

An ancient estate acquired by the da Schio family in 1832. Owner: Alvise da Schio. Costozza Cabernet, Picolit, Pinot Rosato, Riesling. Italian judges see the Cabernet as a good match for Bordeaux. Wine is aged in caves quarried for stone by the sculptor Orazio Marinalli.

Villa dal Ferro-Lazzarini

San Germano dei Berici, 36040 Vicenza.

The vineyards and cellars of his 16th-century villa have been renewed in the last 20 years by Alfredo Lazzarini. DOC: Colli Berici. 5,700 cases with individual names – Cabernet (Le Rive Rosse). Merlot (Campo del Lago), Pinot Bianco (Bianco del Rocolo), Pinot Nero (Rosso del Rocolo), Tocai (Costiera Granda), Riesling (Busa Calcara) – from 20 acres. The Merlot and Pinot Nero are models of their kind and must be ranked with Italy's best.

Villa Girardi (Tenuta Bure Alto)

San Pietro Incariano, 37029 Verona.

DOC: Bardolino, Soave, Valpolicella-Recioto-Amarone. Notable wines from 86 acres under both the Villa Girardi and Tenuta Bure Alto labels.

Lamberti

37017 Lazise sul Garda

Part of the Swiss Winefood group. DOC: Bardolino. Lugana, Riviera del Garda Bresciano, Soave, Valpolicella-Recioto-Amarone. Other: Spumante Brut Rosato. From extensive company vineyards in Bardolino and purchases elsewhere, Lamberti produces 1.5m. cases of good commercial quality.

Loredan

See Venegazzù-Conte Loredan-Gasparini.

Luxardo de' Franchi

Castelnuovo di Teolo, 35037 Padova.

The estate, which includes a monastery where wine was made in the 13th century, is owned by the Luxardo de' Franchi family, who invented Maraschino cherry liqueur. DOC: Colli Euganei. The red is called Sant' Elmo, the white, Monte Venda.

Maculan

Breganze, 36042 Vicenza.

Founded: 1937. Owners: Fausto and Franca Maculan. DOC: Breganze. Other: Costa d'Olio Rosato Torcolato. From 75 acres, including family property, 400–1,000 cases of each of 12 types of wine. The Breganze Cabernet Fratta and sweet white Torcolato have given this small winery a great reputation.

Masi

Gargagnago, 37020 Verona.

The firm is run by the Boscaini family, producers of wine for 6 generations. Wine maker: Nino Franceschetti. DOC: Bardolino, Soave, Valpolicella-Recioto-Amarone.

Other: Campofiorin, Masianco, Rosa Masi. Unerring selection (partly from their own vineyards) and ingenious techniques have made this medium-large winery a touchstone for Verona wines. But best of all is the youngest vintage of Valpolicella.

Pieropan

Soave, 37038 Verona.

Owner: Leonildo Pieropan (whose grandfather won a prize for Soave in 1906). DOC: Soave-Recioto. Other: Riesling Italico. Pieropan produces 10,000 cases of what is generally rated the best Soave Classico from 20 acres of his own vines and 17 rented acres.

Ponte (Cantina Sociale Cooperative di Ponte di Piave)

Ponte di Piave, 31047 Treviso.

The cooperative (founded 1948) has 965 members with 5,650 acres of vines and a plant capacity of 25m. litres. DOC: Piave. Other: Pinot Bianco, Pinot Grigio, Riesling Italico, Raboso, Rosato, Sauvignon. A major supplier of Veneto wines. The best are sold under the Ponte label.

Giuseppe Quintarelli

Negrar di Valpolicella, 37024 Verona.

Founded in 1924 by the owner's father. DOC: Valpolicella-Recioto-Amarone. 6,000 cases processed under traditional methods with unsurpassed devotion from 25 acres. Some consider this Amarone the finest.

Le Ragose

Arbizzano, 37020 Verona.

Founded: 1969. Owners-wine makers: Maria Marta Galli with her husband Arnaldo. DOC: Valpolicella-Recioto-Amarone. Other: Montericco. The Gallis meticulously select grapes from their 26 acres for some of Valpolicella's very best wines.

Guerrieri Rizzardi

Bardolino, 37011 Verona.

A family estate going back to the 18th century, with a small but interesting museum. Owner: Antonio Rizzardi. DOC: Bardolino, Soave, Valpolicella-Amarone. Other: Bianco and Rosso San Pietro. From vineyards in Bardolino, Valpolicella and Soave, 60,000 cases of splendid Verona wines. The Bardolino is admirably lively – one of the best of the pale breed.

Castello di Roncade

Roncade, 31056 Treviso.

Owner: Vincenzo Ciani Bassetti. DOC: Piave. Other: Castello di Roncade, Pinot Grigio, Tocai. An impressive fortress with a worthy Cabernet/Merlot blend.

Santa Margherita

Fossalta di Portogruaro, 30025 Venezia.

Owners: The Marzotto family. Director: Arrigo Marcer. Wine maker: Giorgio Mascarin. DOC: Alto Adige, Grave del Friuli, Piave, Pramaggiore, Prosecco di Conegliano, Tocai di Lison. Other: Chardonnay Atesino, Pinot Brut, Rosé Brut. An *avant-garde* winery: Italy's undisputed leader in the Pinot Grigio field.

Cantina Sociale di Soave

Soave, 37038 Verona.

Among several claimants to be the largest cooperative in Europe, but certainly the biggest producer of Soave. Founded in 1930, it has 603 members with more than 6,000 acres of vines, 80% in the Soave DOC zone. DOC: Bardolino, Soave, Valpolicella. Production is more than 1.5m. cases of Soave, some under the Cantina's label, some to bottlers and shippers. It also makes more than 100,000 cases of Valpolicella and more than 50,000 cases of Bardolino.

Venegazzù-Conte Loredan-Gasparini

Venegazzù del Montello, 31040 Treviso.

The estate was founded in 1940 by Piero Loredan, descendant of Venetian doges, and bought by Giancarlo Palla in 1974. DOC: Prosecco del Montello e dei Colli Asolani. Other: Brut *champenoise*, Pinot Bianco, Pinot Grigio, Venegazzù Della Casa, Venegazzù Etichetta Nera, Venegazzù Rosso. From 123 acres, 33,000 cases of white and 17,000 of red, including the famous reserve Della Casa, a Bordeaux-style blend of great character and class, like a big, not exactly genteel, St-Emilion.

Zardetto

Conegliano, 31015 Treviso.

Founded in 1969 by oenologist Pino Zardetto. DOC: Cartizze, Prosecco di Conegliano. Other: Zardetto Brut. 7,500 cases of sparkling wines. Zardetto Brut, made by a modified *charmat* process, which prolongs the yeast fermentation, tastes like a good *champenoise*.

Zonin

Gambellara, 36053 Vicenza.

The Zonin family firm, founded in 1921, claims to be Italy's largest private winery with production of nearly 4.5m. cases. DOC: Bardolino, Gambellara, Recioto di Gambellara, Valpolicella. Other: *spumante* and table wines. The firm bases its production on nearly 750 acres of vines. It also has vineyards in Virginia, USA.

Prices

The prices quoted in this book are all in local currency and are what the grower receives per bottle at his own cellar. They do not normally include taxes, shipping costs, or merchants' profits. They therefore do not relate directly to what you will pay in a shop. (California prices are an exception; they are the same in a store or at the cellar door). The object is to show what prices prevailed at one particular time (late 1982) for the purposes of comparison between region and region, and between growers and wines within a region or a country. It is wrong to draw too many conclusions from such bold comparisons. Prevailing conditions often cause local distortions. The price of Beaujolais, for example, soars in the summer after a good vintage, and Bordeaux opening prices are sometimes doubled within weeks. Yet price is the final measure of esteem, and much can be learned by taking it into account.

OTHER PRODUCERS

Cantine Aldegheri
Sant'Ambrogio di Valpolicella, 37010 Verona. DOC: Bardolino, Soave, Valpolicella-Recioto-Amarone.
Anselmi
Monteforte d'Alpone, 37032 Verona. DOC: Bardolino, Soave, Valpolicella. Among the best of Soave.
Antica Quercia (Riello)
Scomigo di Conegliano, 31020 Treviso. Owner: Luisa Mazzarocchi Riello. DOC: Prosecco di Conegliano. Other: Merlot, Pinot Bianco, Riesling, Spumante Brut *champenoise*, Tocai.
Bianchi Kunkler
Mogliano Veneto, 31020 Treviso. DOC: Piave. Other: Riesling.
Biscardo
Bussolengo, 37012 Verona. DOC: Bardolino, Soave, Valpolicella-Recioto-Amarone. The firm owns 270 acres of vines near Verona and also markets DOC wines from Piedmont, Tuscany and Latium.
Desiderio Bisol & Figli
Santo Stefano di Valdobbiadene, 31040 Treviso. DOC: Cartizze, Prosecco di Valdobbiadene. Other: Spumante Classico Brut *champenoise*, Rosé Brut *champenoise*.
Ca' Furia
Calmasino di Bardolino, 37011 Verona. Owner: Luigi Planzi. DOC: Bardolino, Lugana. Other: Pinot Bianco.
Adamo Canel & Figli
Col San Martino, 31010 Treviso. DOC: Cartizze, Prosecco di Valdobbiadene.
Canella
San Donà di Piave, 30027 Venezia. DOC: Grave del Friuli, Piave, Prosecco di Conegliano, Tocai di Lison.
Cavalchina
Custoza, 37066 Verona. Owner: Giulietto Piona. DOC: Bianco di Custoza. Other: Pinot Bianco. Among the better whites of Verona.
Cantina Club
33100 Treviso. DOC: Cartizze, Prosecco. Other: Pinot Grigio, Spumante Brut Rust, Rosé Rust.
Colle de' Cipressi
Calmasino di Bardolino, 37010 Verona. DOC: Bardolino.
Cantina Colli del Soligo
Solighetto, 31053 Treviso. Cooperative. DOC: Cartizze, Piave, Prosecco di Conegliano-Valdobbiadene.
Deroà
San Polo di Piave, 31020 Treviso. DOC: Piave. Other: Malbec, Pinot Grigio, Raboso, Sauvignon.
Fratelli Fabiano
Sona, 37060 Verona. DOC: Bardolino, Bianco di Custoza, Soave, Valpolicella-Recioto-Amarone.
Fratelli Fraccaroli
Peschiera del Garda, 37019 Verona. Owners-wine makers: Francesco and Giuseppe Fraccaroli. DOC: Lugana. About 8,000 cases of first-rate Lugana.
Cantine Nino Franco
Valdobbiadene, 31049 Treviso. Founded: 1919. Owner: Giovanni Franco. DOC: Cartizze, Prosecco di Valdobbiadene.
Cantina Sociale di Gambellara
Gambellara, 36053 Vicenza. Cooperative. DOC: Gambellara.
Cantina Sociale La Montelliana e dei Colli Asolani
Montebelluna, 31040 Treviso. Cooperative. DOC: Montello e Colli Asolani.
Montresor
37100 Verona. DOC: Bardolino, Bianco di Custoza, Soave, Valpolicella-Recioto-Amarone.
Fratelli Pasqua
37100 Verona. DOC: Bardolino, Soave, Valpolicella-Recioto-Amarone, Valdadige.
A. & G. Pergreffi
Cisano di Bardolino, 37010 Verona. DOC: Bardolino, Soave, Tocai di San Martino della Battaglia, Valpolicella-Recioto-Amarone.
Silvio Piona
Custoza, 37066 Verona. DOC: Bianco di Custoza.
Fratelli Poggi
Affi, 37010 Verona. DOC: Bardolino.
Quarto Vecchio-Petternella
Legnago, 37045 Verona. Owner: Giovanni Petternella. DOC: Bardolino, Soave, Valpolicella. Other: Merlot, Quarto Vecchio (Cabernet-Merlot).
Mario Rossi
31100 Treviso. Fol Blanc de Blancs Spumante.
L. Ruggeri & C.
Valdobbiadene, 31049 Treviso. DOC: Alto Adige, Cartizze, Prosecco di Valdobbiadene, Pramaggiore, Tocai di Lison. Other: Pinot Grigio, Ruggeri Brut *champenoise*.
Russolo
Pramaggiore, 30020 Venezia. Owner: I. Russolo & C. DOC: Alto Adige, Grave del Friuli, Pramaggiore, Tocai di Lison. Other: table wines of Alto Adige, Friuli, Veneto.
Tenuta Sant'Anna
Loncon di Annone Veneto, 30020 Venezia. Owner: Agricola Rus S.p.A. DOC: Grave del Friuli, Pramaggiore, Tocai di Lison. Other: Pinot Grigio, Prosecco, *spumante*. The firm owns more than 600 acres of vines in the Veneto and some 250 acres in Grave del Friuli.
Santa Sofia
Pedemonte, 37020 Verona. Owner: Giancarlo Begnoni & C. DOC: Bardolino, Bianco di Custoza, Soave, Valpolicella-Recioto-Amarone.
A. G. Santi
Illasi, 37031 Verona. Founded in 1843, the winery became part of the Swiss Winefood group in 1974. DOC: Bardolino, Soave, Valpolicella-Recioto-Amarone. Other: Durello, Durello Spumante Brut *champenoise*. Durello and Castello d'Illasi Valpolicella are the best of a production of 90,000 cases.
Sant'Osvaldo
Loncon di Annone Veneto, 30020 Venezia. DOC: Pramaggiore, Tocai di Lison. Other: Pinot Bianco, Pinot Grigio, Raboso, Refosco, Sauvignon.
Sartori
Negrar, 37024 Verona. DOC: Bardolino, Soave, Valpolicella-Recioto-Amarone.
Fratelli Speri
Pedemonte, 37020 Verona. DOC: Soave, Valpolicella-Recioto-Amarone.
Fratelli Sterzi
San Martino Buon Albergo, 37036 Verona. DOC: Bardolino, Soave, Valpolicella. Other: Pinot *spumante*.
Fratelli Tedeschi
Pedemonte, 37020 Verona. Founded: 1884. Owners: Silvino and Renzo Tedeschi. DOC:Valpolicella-Recioto-Amarone. Other: Capitel San Rocco Bianco, Rosso. From 20 acres of their own vines and discreet purchases the Tedeschi brothers make 11,000 cases.
Tommasi
Pedemonte, 37020 Verona. DOC: Bardolino, Bianco di Custoza, Soave, Valpolicella-Recioto-Amarone.
Valdo
Valdobbiadene, 31049 Treviso. The firm is controlled by Bolla. DOC: Aquilea, Prosecco di Valdobbiadene. Other: Valdo Brut *champenoise*. Valdo bottles a range of Aquilea wines produced by the Cantina Sociale Cooperativa del Friuli Orientale.
Cantina Sociale di Valdobbiadene
San Giovanni di Bigolino, 31030 Treviso. Cooperative. DOC: Cartizze, Prosecco di Valdobbiadene.
Verga Falzacappa
San Vendemiano di Conegliano, 31020 Treviso. DOC: Piave. Other: Pinot Nero, Sauvignon, Verduzzo.
Fratelli Zenato
Peschiera del Garda, 37019 Verona. DOC: Bardolino, Bianco di Custoza, Lugana, Riviera del Garda Bresciano, Tocai di San Martino della Battaglia, Valpolicella-Amarone.

FRIULI-VENEZIA GIULIA

There is a tidiness about the DOC arrangements in Friuli-Venezia Giulia which is due to their recent emergence as an important part of Italian viticulture. There was little folklore to get in the way of a simple carve-up into geographical zones whose wines are named for their grape varieties.

With six zones and some dozen varieties, as well as the brand names that some growers insist on adding, the combinations still reach a head-spinning number. It helps to distinguish between them if you are clear that there is one very big DOC that embraces most of the region, two superior hill zones with Colli in their names, and three smaller and newer (1975) DOCs of less significance in a row along the coastal plain.

The big zone is Grave del Friuli, DOC for the whole wine-growing hinterland from the Veneto border east to beyond Udine where the Alps reach down towards Trieste. The hills of Gorizia, right on the Yugoslav border (otherwise just known as the 'Collio'), are the oldest-established and best vineyards of the region. To their north is the separate DOC of the Colli Orientali del Friuli ('the eastern hills of Friuli') with similar growing conditions.

The coastal DOCs from west to east are Aquilea, Latisana and Isonzo; the last, adjacent to the Gorizian hills, apparently having the greatest potential for quality. The coastal vineyards tend to stress red wine, whereas the reputation of the hills is mainly based on white – whether such traditional grapes as Tocai Friulano, Malvasia, Picolit or Verduzzo, or more recent imports: the Pinots, Sauvignon Blanc and Rhine Riesling.

DOC AND OTHER WINES

Aquilea

Doc. Red and white wine. Province: Udine. Villages: Aquilea and 17 others. Grapes: Merlot, Cabernet, Refosco, Tocai Friulano, Pinot Bianco, Pinot Grigio, Riesling Renano. Max. crop: 91 hl/ha. Min. alch: 11° for Merlot, Refosco, Pinot Grigio and Riesling Renano; 11.5° for Cabernet, Tocai Friulano, Pinot Bianco. Average production: 185,000 cases.

A DOC for the varied production of the cooperative at Cervignano, named after a Roman city. The land is flat, the climate temperate and efforts at quality production only recent, but signs are that it will come, particularly with Cabernet and Merlot.

Carso

DOC. Red and white wine. Provinces: Trieste and Gorizia. Villages: 11 in the Carso hills bordering Yugoslavia. Grapes: Terrano (85%), Pinot Nero, Piccola Nera; Malvasia Istriana (85%), other authorized light grapes. Max. crop: 49 hl/ha. Min. alch: 10.5% for all 3 types: Carso or Carso Rosso, Carso Terrano and Carso Malvasia. Average production: undetermined.

Carso and Carso Terrano are virtually the same wine, both based on the Terrano (relative of Refosco) grape. Carso Malvasia is similar to other DOC Malvasia Istriana types. Terrano del Carso was historically the table wine of Trieste and supposedly builds blood because of high malic acid.

Collio Goriziano or Collio

DOC. White wine. Province: Gorizia. Villages: west of Gorizia. Grapes: Riesling Italico, Sauvignon, Tocai, Traminer, Malvasia, Merlot, Pinot Bianco, Cabernet Franc, Pinot Grigio, Pinot Nero. Max. crop: 77 hl/ha. Min. alch: Collio Goriziano or Collio 11°; Collio Malvasia 11.5°; Riesling Italico, Tocai, Pinot Bianco, Traminer, Merlot, Cabernet Franc 12°; Pinot Grigio, Sauvignon and Pinot Nero 12.5°. Average production: 458,000 cases.

A DOC of such diversity of wines and styles that California comes to mind. Fruity early-developing reds of the Bordeaux varieties are less interesting than the white specialities, particularly the aromatic Tocai Friulano and Pinot Bianco and Grigio, which at their best balance Hungarian-style 'stiffness' and strength with real delicacy. Collio without a varietal name is a light dry white of Ribolla and other local grapes. 'Pinot Bianco' sometimes includes Chardonnay and can develop burgundian richness with barrel-age. Sauvignon Blanc also promises extremely well.

Colli Orientali del Friuli

DOC. White and red wine. Province: Udine. Villages: Attimis, Buttrio, Cividale del Friuli (the centre), Faedis Manzano, Nimis, Povoletto, Tarcento, Torreano, all along the Yugoslav border north of Gorizia. Grapes: Tocai Friulano, Verduzzo, Ribolla, Pinot Bianco, Pinot Grigio, Friuli Sauvignon, Riesling Renano, Picolit, Merlot, Cabernet, Pinot Nero, Refosco, Max. crop: 77 hl/ha. Min. alch: 12° for all varieties except Picolit, which must have 15°. Average production: 350,000 cases. Merlot, Cabernet, Pinot Nero, Refosco and Picolit are *riserva* after 2 years' ageing.

The neighbouring DOC to Collio, with similar white wines, perhaps slightly less prestigious except in its native Verduzzo (q.v.) and its rare dessert white Picolit (q.v.). The splendid rustic red Refosco and Cabernet are better than Collio reds.

Grave del Friuli

DOC. Red and white wine. Provinces: Udine, Pordenone. Area: the whole of Udine and Pordenone. Grapes: Merlot, Cabernet, Refosco, Tocai, Pinot Bianco, Pinot Grigio, Verduzzo. Max. crop: 91 hl/ha. Min. alch: 11° for Merlot, Refosco, Tocai, Pinot Grigio, Verduzzo; 11.5° for Cabernet, Pinot Bianco. Production: 350,000 cases. Price: 1,200–2,900 lire.

The largest DOC of the region: biggest source of Merlot, which accounts for half of its production. Grave Merlot is soft, dark and dry with a hint of grassiness; not as good as its Cabernet (mainly Franc, not Sauvignon), which has more personality and life, nor as memorable as its fruity bitter Refosco. Grave Pinot Bianco (sometimes Chardonnay) and Tocai can be as good as Collio wines.

Isonzo

DOC: White and red wine. Province: Gorizia. Area: 21 communes around Gradisca d'Isonzo. Grapes: Tocai, Sauvignon, Malvasia Istriana, Pinot Bianco, Pinot Grigio, Verduzzo Friulano, Traminer Aromatico, Riesling Renano, Merlot, Cabernet. Max. crop: 91 hl/ha. Min. alch: 10.5° for Tocai, Malvasia Istriana, Verduzzo Friulano and Merlot; 11° for Pinot Bianco, Sauvignon, Pinot Grigio, Traminer Aromatico, Riesling Renano and Cabernet.

The DOC zone between the Collio and the Gulf of Trieste also specializes in Merlot, which can be better than that of Grave del Friuli and Cabernet for drinking young. Its white wines are light and pleasant; rarely up to Collio standards.

Latisana

DOC: Red and white wine. Province: Udine. Villages: 13 around Latisana, on the border of the Veneto (the river Tagliamento) near the lagoon of Marano. Grapes; Merlot, Cabernet, Refosco, Tocai Friulano, Pinot Bianco, Pinot Grigio and Verduzzo Friulano. Max. crop: 91 hl/ha. Min. alch: 11° for Latisana Merlot, Refosco, Tocai Friulano, Pinot Grigio and Verduzzo Friulano. Average production: 200,000 cases.

This 1975 DOC has not yet distinguished itself, although its Tocai Friulano is said to be the best of the coast. Merlot and Cabernet are light; Refosco can be more fun.

Picolit

A native grape of the Colli Orientali del Friuli and its dessert wine, one of the almost-lost legends of the 19th century along with Romania's Cotnari and the (really lost) Constantia of the Cape. It is a powerful, smooth, even dense-textured wine, not necessarily very sweet and ending in the regional style, slightly bitter. Bottles I have tasted have clearly been too young to have developed the glorious bouquet and flavour that others report. It is rare and extremely expensive (10,000–25,000 lire).

Ramandolo

A restricted name for sweet Verduzzo from vineyards in the village of Nimis in the Colli Orientali del Friuli.

Schioppettino

A native red grape of the Colli Orientali del Friuli, giving wine with some of the rasping fruitiness of a good Barbera from Piedmont.

Verduzzo

A native white grape made either into a fresh dry white 'fish' wine or a sort of Recioto, an *amabile* of partly dried grapes – *see* Ramandolo.

N.B. Verdiso is a different but similar white grape, occasionally seen as a dry wine.

FRIULI-VENEZIA GIULIA PRODUCERS

Angoris

Cormons, 34071 Gorizia.

Founded in 1648, the estate is now owned by the Locatelli family. Wine maker: Flavio Zuliani. DOC: Colli Orientali del Friuli, Isonzo. Other: Modolet Brut *champenoise*, Spirfolét *spumante*. Production is approaching 600,000 cases from 445 acres at Cormons in Isonzo and Rocca Bernarda in the Colli Orientali. Angoris also owns Fattoria Casalino in Chianti Classico.

Conti Attems

Lucinico, 34070 Gorizia

Owner: Douglas Attems Sigismondo, who carries on a centuries-old family tradition. DOC: Collio, Isonzo. Other: Rosato di Lucinico. Attems produces 17,000 cases from about 80 acres. Some favour his Pinot Grigio; others his Merlot.

Borgo Conventi

Farra d'Isonzo, 34070 Gorizia.

The former walled convent, founded in 1876, is owned by Gianni Vescovo. DOC: Collio. Other: Tocai Italico. Vescovo makes about 4,000 cases from 17 acres, including a Sauvignon Blanc which is considered one of the best in Italy. Prices: 2,800–4,000 lire.

Fratelli Buzzinelli

Cormons, 34071 Gorizia.

An excellent family winery. The Buzzinelli brothers have been bottling wine since 1955. DOC: Collio. Other: Müller-Thurgau.

Livio Felluga

Brazzano di Cormons, 34070 Gorizia.

Livio Felluga's son Maurizio represents the fifth generation of wine makers. DOC: Colli Orientali del Friuli, Collio. From 5 estates with nearly 300 acres of vines, Felluga makes about 8,500 cases of each of 8 varietals. A Pinot *spumante champenoise* is in preparation.

Marco Felluga (Russiz Superiore)

Gradisca d'Isonzo, 34072 Gorizia.

Marco (brother of Livio) Felluga founded his wine house in 1956, the Russiz Superiore estate in 1967. DOC: Collio. The Marco Felluga label consists of some 50,000 cases of the usual Collio varieties from grapes purchased from regular suppliers in Collio. Russiz Superiore, a model of its kind, consists of 170 acres from which grapes are selected from some 20,000 cases. Felluga also bottles some wine under the Villa San Giovanni label.

Conti Formentini

San Floriano del Collio, 34070 Gorizia.

The 16th-century castle and property have long belonged to the Formentini family, after whom the Furmint grape of Hungarian Tokay is said to be named. Owner: Michele Formentini. DOC: Collio. 40,000–60,000 cases from 250 acres. The castle contains an *enoteca*, restaurant and wine museum.

EnoFriulia

Capriva del Friuli, 34070 Gorizia.

Founded: 1967; directed by oenologist Vittorio Puiatti. Bianco dal Pinot Nero, Cabernet Sauvignon, Chardonnay, Merlot, Müller-Thurgau, Pinot Bianco, Pinot Grigio, Pinot Nero, Riesling Renano, Sauvignon, Tajut Rosato, Tocai, Traminer. Though Puiatti is not specific about vineyard origins, his wines are often brilliant.

Cantina Sociale Cooperative del Friuli Orientali (Molin di Ponte)

Cervignano del Friuli, 33052 Udine.

Founded: 1954. A cooperative of 120 growers expertly directed by oenologist Orfeo Salvador. DOC: Aquilea. Other: Chardonnay, Picolit, Pinot Nero, Rosato, Sauvignon, Traminer Aromatico. Some 450,000 cases are produced from 1,380 acres. Some bottles are sold under the cooperative's Molin di Ponte trademark and some by Valdo of the Veneto.

Jermann

Villanova di Farra, 34070 Gorizia.

A family estate founded in 1880; now run by Angelo and Sylvio Jermann. DOC: Collio. Other: Engel Rosé, Picolit, Vintage Tunina. Jermann makes 5,000–5,800 cases of first-rate Collio wines and the very special Vintage Tunina (from Pinot Bianco, Chardonnay, Sauvignon, Picolit, price 8,000 lire) from 22 acres of vines. Taste Tunina if you are a sceptic about Italian whites.

Fratelli Pighin

Risano, 33050 Udine.

Founded: 1963. Owners: The Pighin family. DOC: Collio, Grave del Friuli. Other: Gallorosé, Picolit, Pinot Nero. From 320 acres in Grave, production is 11,000–16,000 cases of each DOC variety. The average is 1,500 cases of each variety, less for Malvasia and Traminer, from 65 acres in Collio.

Rocca Bernarda

Ipplis, 33040 Udine.

The old Perusini family estate, which recently became the property of the Sovrano Militare Ordine di Malta (Knights of Malta). DOC: Colli Orientali del Friuli. Rocca Bernarda has long been noted for Picolit.

Villa Russiz

Capriva del Friuli, 34070 Gorizia.

A 62-acre estate founded in 1869 by a French nobleman named La Tour. It now supports the A. Cerruti orphanage. Director and wine maker: Edino Menotti. DOC: Collio. Other: Picolit. Production is 13,000–14,000 cases of some of the best wines of Collio.

Mario Schiopetto

Capriva del Friuli, 34070 Gorizia.

Founded in 1969 by Mario Schiopetto on property belonging to the Archbishopric of Gorizia since 1859. DOC: Collio. Other: Cabernet, Merlot, Müller-Thurgau, Riesling Renano. Schiopetto, one of the most skilled and courageous wine makers of Italy, makes 6,000–8,000 cases of a dozen different wines that set the standard for Friuli on 37 acres of leased land. His whites (including Rhine Riesling) are perhaps the most exceptional.

OTHER PRODUCERS

Duca Badoglio
Codroipo, 33033 Udine. DOC: Grave del Friuli. Il Blanc–Blanc *spumante*.

F. Berin
Mossa, 34070 Gorizia. Owner: Fabio Berin. DOC: Collio. Other: Chardonnay. A small winery attracting critical attention.

Cantina Sociale Casarsa-La Delizia
Casarsa della Delizia, 33072 Pordenone. Cooperative. DOC: Grave del Friuli. This large cooperative sells its bottled wines under the trademark La Delizia.

E. Collavini
Corno di Rosazzo, 33040 Udine. Manlio Collavini is the third generation of wine makers. DOC: Colli Orientali del Friuli, Collio, Grave del Friuli. 22,000 cases from about 55 acres.

Cantina Produttori Vini del Collio e dell'Isonzo
Cormons, 34071 Gorizia. Cooperative. DOC: Collio, Isonzo.

G. B. Comelli
Nimis, 33045 Udine. Owner: G. B. (Filippon) Comelli. DOC: Colli Orientali del Friuli. A tiny estate renowned for Verduzzo di Ramandolo.

Giovanni Dri
Ramandolo di Nimis, 33045 Udine. DOC: Colli Orientali del Friuli. Dri's Verduzzo di Ramandolo is a highly prized rarity; a lovely wine.

Carlo Drufovka
Oslavia, 34170 Gorizia. Wine maker: Gaspare Buscemi. DOC: Collio. Other: Dragarska, Roslavia, Runk.

Il Castello-Fantinel
Buttrio, 33042 Udine. DOC: Collio, Grave del Friuli.

Villa Frattina
Ghirano, 33080 Pordenone. DOC: Colli Orientali del Friuli, Collio, Grave del Friuli, Pramaggiore, Tocai di Lison. Other: Pinot Grigio, Refosco, *spumante*.

Gradimir Gradnik
Plessiva di Cormons, 34071 Gorizia. Gradnik maintains a century-old family tradition. DOC: Collio. A stalwart among Collio's small producers making 5,000–7,000 cases from 25 acres.

Francesco Gravner
Oslavia, 34170 Gorizia. DOC: Collio. Other: Chardonnay. A rising star in Collio.

Kechler
San Martino di Codroipo, 33033 Udine. Cabernet, Merlot, Pinot Bianco, Pinot Grigio, Tocai, Verduzzo.

Conte Gianfranco d'Attimis Maniago
Buttrio, 33042 Udine. DOC: Colli Orientali del Friuli. 50,000 cases from 185 acres.

Conti di Maniago
Soleschiano di Manzano, 33044 Udine. Owner: Filippo Martinengo. Wine maker: Gaspare Buscemi. Cabernet, Malvasia, Merlot, Picolit, Pinot Grigio, Refosco, Tocai, Verduzzo. 13,000 cases from 42 acres.

Tenuta Maseri Florio
Buttrio in Monte, 33042 Udine. Owner: Francesca Florio Maseri. DOC: Colli Orientali del Friuli. Other: Tazzelenghe.

Molino delle Streghe
Biauzzo di Codroipo, 33033 Udine. DOC: Grave del Friuli.

Morassutti
Villutta di Chions, 33089 Pordenone. Founded in 1974 by Giovanni Paolo Morassutti. DOC: Grave del Friuli, Pramaggiore, Tocai di Lison. Other: Brut Spumante, Prosecco.

Plozner
Spilimbergo, 33097 Pordenone. DOC: Grave del Friuli. Other: Chardonnay, Pinot Nero, Traminer. Plozner's Chardonnay is building an international reputation.

Castello di Porcia
33170 Pordenone. Owners: The Porcia family. DOC: Grave del Friuli, Pramaggiore, Tocai di Lison. Other: Malbeck, Sauvignon.

Pradio
Felettis di Bicinicco, 33050 Udine. Owners: Renzo and Piergiorgio Cielo. DOC: Grave del Friuli. Other: Merlot Novello. The Cielos have a smooth fruity style of their own.

Doro Princic
Pradis di Cormons, 34071 Gorizia. Owners: Doro and Sandro Princic. DOC: Collio. This tiny family winery makes gorgeous Tocai.

Ronchi di Cialla
Prepotto, 33040 Udine. Owners: Paolo and Dina Rapuzzi. DOC: Colli Orientali del Friuli. Other: Schioppettino. This small winery excels with obscure classics: Picolit, Schioppettino, Verduzzo.

Ronchi di Fornaz
Fornalis di Cividale, 33043 Udine. DOC: Colli Orientali del Friuli. An outstanding small estate.

Giovanni Scolaris
San Lorenzo Isontino, 34070 Gorizia. DOC: Collio. Scolaris acts as a négociant, selling wine under his label from some of Collio's best small properties.

Valle
Buttrio, 33042 Udine. Owner: Luigi Valle & C. DOC: Aquilea, Colli Orientali del Friuli, Collio, Grave del Friuli. Other: Franconia.

EMILIA-ROMAGNA

It is ironic that Italy's greediest culinary region, by all accounts, should put the emphasis on quantity rather than quality in its wine. Any ambition to produce better than simple thirst quenchers is recent and limited to an elect few.

Bologna, the cooks' capital, is the hub of the region and the meeting place of its two component parts. Most of the land is the flat Po valley, following it to the Adriatic between Ravenna and Venice. All the wine regions of interest lie in the foothills, however tentative, of the Apennines to the south, dividing the province from Tuscany.

Fizzy red Lambrusco leads, not just in Emilia but in the whole of Italy, for volume production of a distinct type of wine. It is an ingenious and profitable way of achieving notoriety in deep valley soils where more conventional quality is unlikely.

Romagna has nothing so exceptional. Its best-known wine is the white Albana, which has yet to distinguish itself. It is in the Colli Bolognesi and Piacentini, the hill areas nearest to Bologna and Piacenza, that progress is being made.

DOC AND OTHER WINES

Albana di Romagna

DOC. White wine. Provinces: Ravenna, Forlì and Bologna. Villages: 23 communes between Bologna and Rimini. Grape: Albana. Max. crop: 91 hl/ha. Min. alch: 12° for Albana di Romagna Secco; 12.5° for Albana di Romagna Amabile. Average production: 667,000 cases. Price: 1,000–1,700 lire.

The standard white of Bologna and east to the coast. The Albana is a mild, not to say neutral, grape whose dry wine tends to flatness, finishing bitter to satisfy local taste. It gains more character when made *amabile* and/or *spumante*.

Barbarossa di Bertinoro

A vine not found elsewhere, cultivated on a small scale at Bertinoro, the centre of the Romagna vineyards, for a good full-flavoured red with ageing potential.

Barbera

The ubiquitous red grape is popular in the area of Piacenza and in the Colli Bolognesi, where it is given DOC dignity.

Bianco della Pusterla

Scented sweetish blended white from the Colli Piacentini.

Bianco di Scandiano

DOC. White wine. Province: Emilia-Romagna. Villages: commune of Scandiano plus 5 others southwest of Reggio Emilia. Grapes: Sauvignon (locally Spergola or Spergolina) up to 85%, Malvasia di Candia and Trebbiano Romagnolo up to 15%. Max. crop: 84 hl/ha. Min. alch: 10.5°. Average production: 39,000 cases. Price: 1,400–2,000 lire.

A white alternative to Lambrusco (q.v.) made either semi-dry or distinctly sweet, sometimes fizzy and sometimes fully frothy.

Cabernet Sauvignon dei Colli Bolognesi

The Cabernet is doing well in the DOC area of Bologna and will soon be part of the DOC–very probably the best part. Price: 2,000–2,300 lire.

Chardonnay

Strictly an outlaw in the region, but grown with striking success by Enrico Vallania at Terre Rosse near Bologna.

Colli Bolognesi – Monte San Pietro-Castelli Medioevali

DOC: Red and white wine. Province: Bologna. Villages: 10 communes southwest of Bologna. Grapes: (white) Albana 60–80%, Trebbiano Romagnolo 40–20%. For named varieties: Barbera, Merlot, Riesling Italico, Pinot Bianco, Sauvignon 85%, with 15% neutral grapes allowed. Max. crop: 84 hl/ha. Min. alch: 11.5° for Barbera, Merlot; 12° for Sauvignon, Pinot Blanc, Riesling Italico; 11° for Bianco. Production: 1.13m. cases. Barbera must be 3 years old, 1 in wood, for *riserva*.

An umbrella DOC for the everyday wines of Bologna. More remarkable wines are being made in the same vineyards by growers experimenting with better grapes, including Sauvignon Blanc, Cabernet Sauvignon and Chardonnay. Growing conditions are excellent; ambition has been the missing factor.

Colli di Parma

DOC: Red and white wine. Province: Parma. Villages: 14 communes in the Apennine foothills south and west of Parma. Grapes: (red) Barbera 60–75% with Bonarda and Croatina up to 40%; (Malvasia) Malvasia di Candia 85–100%, Moscato Bianco up to 15%; Sauvignon 100%. Max. crop: red 65 hl/ha, Malvasia 71.5 hl/ha, Sauvignon 49 hl/ha. Min. alch. red 11%, Malvasia 10.5%, Sauvignon 11.5%.

In this new (1982) DOC, the red should resemble Oltrepò Pavese Rosso, the Malvasia may be either dry or *amabile*, usually *frizzante*; the Sauvignon usually still.

Colli Piacentini

This new (1983) DOC applies to 11 types of wine, including 3 former DOCs: Gutturnio dei Colli Piacentini, Monterosso Val d'Arda and Trebbianino Val Trebbia (qq.v.). The zone, adjacent to the Oltrepò Pavese of Lombardy, is very similar in range and style, covering the Apennine foothills of the province of Piacenza, a large zone with significant production. Full details have not yet been published, but grape varieties are: Barbera, Bonarda, Gutturnio dei Colli Piacentini, Malvasia, Monterosso Val d'Arda, Ortrugo, Pinot Grigio, Pinot Nero, Sauvignon, Trebbianino Val Trebbia and Val Nure.

Gutturnio dei Colli Piacentini

DOC (until 1983). Red wine. Province: Piacenza. Area: hills of Piacenza. Grapes: Barbera 60%, Bonarda 40%. Max. crop: 72 hl/ha. Min. alch: 12°. Average production: 167,000 cases.

The best-known wine of the new Colli Piacentini zone (q.v.). Strong and deep-coloured local red, once mostly sweet and fizzy, now more often finished in the modern style with potential for ageing up to 4 years or so.

Lambrusco

Lambrusco from Emilia has been the smash hit of the Italian wine industry in the last few years, selling like Coca-Cola (in more senses than one) in the United States. It is simply a sweet, semi-sweet or occasionally dry fizzy red (or pink or occasionally white) wine such as any wine maker could produce who had the foresight to see the demand. The common qualities are scarcely drinkable by a discerning wine drinker, but this misses the point. The market is elsewhere. Some see it as the training ground for future connoisseurs. Such discerning palates will choose one of the Lambruscos from a named region, of which the best is Sorbara. Prices: non-DOC 800–1,300 lire, DOC 1,000–1,700.

Lambrusco Grasparossa di Castelvetro

DOC. Red wine. Province: Modena. Villages: 14 communes south of Modena. Grapes: Lambrusco Grasparossa 85%, other Lambrusco and Uva d'Oro 15%. Max. crop: 98 hl/ha. Min. alch: 10.5°. Average production: 550,000 cases.

A lighter, more often dry, Lambrusco.

Lambrusco Reggiano

DOC. Red wine. Province: Reggio Emilia. Area: the whole province. Grapes: Lambrusco Marani, Salamino, Montericco and Maestri either singly or together. 20% Ancellotta also allowed. Max. crop: 97 hl/ha. Min. alch: 10.5°. Average production: 1.1m. cases.

The commonest, lightest and usually fizziest of DOC Lambruscos.

Lambrusco Salamino di Santa Croce

DOC. Red wine. Province: Modena. Villages: Carpi and 11 other communes north of Modena. Grapes: Lambrusco Salamino 90%, other Lambruschi and Uva d'Oro 10%. Max. crop: 105 hl/ha. Min. alch: 11°. Production: 1m. cases.

Salamino di S. Croce is a local subvariety of the Lambrusco grape with a bunch said to resemble a little salami. Its wine, frequently made dry, is popular in Modena.

Lambrusco di Sorbara

DOC. Red wine. Province: Modena. Villages: 10 communes north of Modena, including Sorbara. Grapes: Lambrusco di Sorbara 60%, Lambrusco Salamino 40%. Max. crop. 98 hl/ha. Min. alch: 11°. Average production: 1m. cases.

Good Lambrusco di Sorbara is a delight; juicy, racy, tingling and extraordinarily drinkable – a childish wine perhaps, but marvellously thirst quenching with rich food. The pink froth is a pleasure in itself. Alas, off-putting chemical flavours are all too common, even in this premium Lambrusco. Do not on any account store bottles of this; or any of them.

Marègia

A brand of dry blended white of particularly high quality. *See* Fratelli Vallunga (Producers). Price: 1,700 lire.

Merlot

Is widely grown in Emilia-Romagna mostly for blending. In the Colli Bolognesi it is DOC.

Monterosso Val d'Arda

DOC (until 1983). White wine. Province: Piacenza. Villages: Vernasca, Alseno, Lugagnano, Castell'Arquato, Gropparello Carpeneto. Grapes: Malvasia di Candia 30–50%, Moscato Bianco 10–30%, Trebbiano Romagnolo and Ortrugo 20–30%, Bervedino and/or Sauvignon 20%. Max. crop: 63 hl/ha. Min. alch: 11°. Average production: 27,750 cases.

A dry or semi-sweet, still or fizzy white of reasonable quality from the valley of a southern tributary of the Po, now in the Colli Piacentini DOC (q.v.). For drinking young.

Pagadebit

A rare white vine enjoying revival and modernization around Bestinoro in Romagna. Gentle dry wine.

Picòl Ross

An esoteric dry Lambrusco of high quality from one grower, Moro of Sant'Ilario d'Enza near Reggio.

Pinot Bianco

Widely grown in Emilia-Romagna and part of the Colli Bolognesi DOC.

Pinot Grigio

Grown on a small scale in the Colli Bolognesi but making better wine than Pinot Bianco. *See* Terre Rosse (Producers).

Rosso Armentano

According to Burton Anderson the best red of Romagna, a blend of Cabernet Franc, Sangiovese di Romagna and Pinot Nero produced by Vallunga (*see* Producers). It needs at least 6 years' ageing. Price: 2,500–3,500 lire.

Sangiovese di Romagna

DOC. Red wine. Provinces: Ravenna, Bologna, Forlì. Villages: 44 communes in Forlì, 13 in Ravenna and Bologna. Grape: Sangiovese di Romagna. Max. crop: 71 hl/ha. Min. alch: 11.5°. Aged 2 years is *riserva*. *Superiore* only from certain specified zones. Average production: 1.44m. cases.

Romagna has its own strain of the red Sangiovese, distinct from the Tuscan one which is the basis of Chianti. It makes pleasant light to medium-weight red, often with a slightly bitter aftertaste, produced in enormous quantities and enjoyed young as the Sunday wine of the region.

Sauvignon

A coming white grape in this part of Italy, possibly the best of the DOC Colli Bolognesi and the major partner in the 1977 DOC Bianco di Scandiano.

Scorza Amara

A Lambrusco-type of greater body and darker colour than most, from near Reggio Emilia.

Trebbiano di Romagna

DOC. White wine. Provinces: Bologna, Forlì, Ravenna. Villages: 56 communes in all 3 provinces. Grape: Trebbiano di Romagna. Max. crop: 98 hl/ha. Min. alch: 11.5°. Average production: nearly 1m. cases. Price: 1,000–1,700 lire.

The normally dull standard white of Romagna, produced dry and lacking the character (such as it is) of the Albana of the same region.

Trebbianino Val Trebbia

DOC (until 1983). White wine. Province: Piacenza. Villages: Goli, Gazzola, Rivergaro and Travo in the valley of the river Trebbia. Grapes: Ortrugo 35–50%, Malvasia di Candia 10–30%, Trebbiano Romagnolo 15–30%, Moscato Bianco and Sauvignon 15%. Max. crop: 63 hl/ha. Min. alch: 11°. Average production: 15,500 cases. Price: 1,000–1,500 lire.

The local dry or sweetish, still or (often) fizzy blended white of this Apennine valley south of Piacenza now in the Colli Piacentini DOC (q.v.).

EMILIA-ROMAGNA PRODUCERS

Cavacchioli

San Prospero, 41030 Modena.

Owners: Franco Cavacchiolo and brothers. DOC: Lambrusco di Sorbara, Lambrusco Grasparossa di Castelvetro, Lambrusco Salamino di Santa Croce. Other: Lambrusco Bianco. This medium-large winery is a quality leader for Lambrusco.

Chiarli-1860

41100 Modena

Founded in 1860 and still run by the Chiarli family. DOC: Lambrusco di Sorbara, Lambrusco Grasparossa di Castelvetro, Lambrusco Salamino di Santa Croce. More than 130,000 cases from 250 acres.

Corovin (Consorzio Romagnolo Vini Tipici)

47100 Forlì

A consortium of cooperatives founded in 1968. Corovin groups 12,000 growers in 23 wineries; they consign 235m. kilograms of grapes – enough for 155m. litres. DOC: Albana, Sangiovese and Trebbiano di Romagna. Other: Lambrusco and numerous table wines. Corovin bottles about 3.3m. cases, which makes it one of the world's larger wine-making complexes.

Giacobazzi

Nonantola, 41015 Modena.

DOC: Lambrusco di Sorbara, Lambrusco Grasparossa di Castelvetro, Lambrusco Salamino di Santa Croce. One of the largest producers, bottlers and shippers of Lambrusco.

Centrale del Lambrusco (Unione Cantine Sociali)

41100 Cittànova di Modena

DOC: Lambrusco di Sorbara, Lambrusco Grasparossa di Castelvetro, Lambrusco Salamino di Santa Croce. A network of cooperatives; a large and reliable supplier.

Giancarlo Molinelli

Ziano, 29010 Piacenza.

DOC: Gutturnio dei Colli Piacentini. Other: Barbera, Bonarda, Malvasia, Molinelli, Müller-Thurgau. The grower is credited with discovering the Molinelli vine, used for a sweet white.

Moro

Calerno di Sant'Illario d'Enza, 42049 Reggio Emilia.

Owner-wine maker: Rinaldo Rinaldini. DOC: Lambrusco Reggiano. Other: Amarone del Partitore, Picòl Ross, Sauvignon. Rinaldini's Picòl Ross is an aristocrat of Lambrusco.

Fattoria Paradiso

Capocolle di Bertinoro, 47032 Forlì.

A historic estate (founded in 1880) has been shaped into a viticultural paradise by Mario Pezzi and his family. DOC: Albana, Sangiovese and Trebbiano di Romagna. Other: Barbarossa, Cagnina, Pagadebit. From 60 acres, Pezzi makes 13,300 cases of exemplary wine, including the unique red Barbarossa (of a vine only he grows) and white semi-sweet Pagadebit (whose name means 'debt payer'). An *enoteca*, museum and *tavernetta* are open to the public.

Pasolini Dall'Onda

Montericco di Imola, 44026 Bologna.

Wine makers since the 16th century, the Pasolini Dall' Onda family owns properties in Romagna and Tuscany. DOC: Albana, Sangiovese and Trebbiano di Romagna, Chianti. Potential production is about 65,000 cases from nearly 200 acres of vines (on both estates).

Pusterla

Vigolo Marchese, 29010 Piacenza.

The estate once owned by the Sforza family was noted for its wines by Pope Paul II in 1543. Owner-wine maker: Giorgio Freschi. DOC: Gutturnio dei Colli Piacentini, Monterosso Val d'Arda. Other: Bianco and Rosso della Pusterla. Freschi makes about 7,700 cases from 37 acres.

Riunite

42100 Reggio Emilia

Founded in 1950, Riunite is one of the world's largest wine-making operations, grouping 26 cooperatives, including 7 outside the province of Reggio, with 2 bottling plants. Walter Sacchetti presides over the complex which includes 9,934 growers and 368 winery employees. DOC: Lambrusco Reggiano. Other: Riunite Bianco, Lambrusco, Rosato. Much of the 13.3m. cases (55% Lambrusco) is sold in the United States through the House of Banfi, by a considerable margin the biggest importer of wine into America.

Spalletti

Savignano sul Rubicone, 47039 Forlì.

The heirs of Conte G. Battista Spalletti own this winery in the 16th-century Castello di Ribano. Director-wine maker: Luigi Bonfiglioli. DOC: Sangiovese di Romagna. From about 100 acres, 12,500 cases of Sangiovese *superiore* and 670 of Rocca di Ribano *riserva*, which is commonly considered the best Sangiovese di Romagna.

Terre Rosse (Vallania)

Zola Predosa, 40069 Bologna.

Founded in 1965 by Enrico Vallania, a physician, whose genius and tenacity are charting new directions in Italian viticulture. DOC: Colli Bolognese. Other: Cabernet Sauvignon, Chardonnay, Malvasia, Pinot Grigio. 11,000 cases of splendid wines from about 50 acres.

Val Panaro

San Cesario sul Panaro, 41013 Modena.

Founded in 1951, now part of the Swiss Winefood group. DOC: Lambrusco di Sorbara, Lambrusco Grasparossa di Castelvetro, Lambrusco Salamino di Santa Croce. Other: Lambrusco Cavalli, Malvasia. About 220,000 cases.

Fratelli Vallunga

Marzeno di Brisighella, 48010 Ravenna.

A family winery founded in 1970 by oenologist Tommaso Vallunga. DOC: Albana, Sangiovese and Trebbiano di Romagna. Other: Albana Vallunga *spumante*, Marègia, Rosso Armentano, San Marten *vino novello*, Vallunga Brut *spumante*. About 30,000 cases from 86 acres of family (Moronico) vineyards and purchased grapes. Young Vallunga has given new scope to Romagnan wines, notably in the elegant Rosso Armentano of blended Sangiovese, Cabernet and Pinot Nero.

OTHER PRODUCERS

Mario Angiolini
Rami di Ravarino, 41017 Modena. Owner: Tommaso Agostinelli. DOC: Lambrusco di Sorbara. 12,500 cases of one of the most respected Lambruscos.
Gianvittorio Baldi
Modigliana, 47012 Forlì. DOC: Sangiovese di Romagna. Other: Sauvignon. An estate to watch.
Otello Burioli & Figli
Longiano, 47039 Forlì. DOC: Sangiovese di Romagna.
Cancarini-Ghisetti
Villanova di Là, 41010 Modena. DOC: Lambrusco di Sorbara.
Cantina Sociale di Carpì
Carpì, 41012 Modena. Cooperative. DOC: Lambrusco di Sorbara. Other: Carpineto *spumante*.
Cesari
Castel San Pietro, 40024 Bologna. DOC: Albana, Sangiovese and Trebbiano di Romagna. The Sangiovese *riserva* is delicious, the Rèfolo *frizzante* fun.
CIV (Consorzio Interprovinciale Vini)
41100 Modena. DOC: Lambrusco.
Aldo Conti
Monte San Pietro, 40050 Bologna. DOC: Colli Bolognesi. Other: Mezzariva Bianco, Bianco Roncandrea.
Comune di Faenza
Faenza, 48018 Ravenna. DOC: Albana, Sangiovese and Trebbiano di Romagna.

Ferrucci
Castelbolognese, 48014 Ravenna. Founded: 1931. Owner: Francesco Ferrucci. DOC: Albana, Sangiovese and Trebbiano di Romagna. A quality leader.
Fini
Solara, Bomporto 41030 Modena. DOC: Lambrusco di Sorbara. The well-known family of restaurateurs have their own Lambrusco.
Guarini (Conti Guarini Matteucci di Castelfalcino)
San Tomè, 47100 Forlì. Owner: Domenico Guarini Matteucci. DOC: Albana, Sangiovese and Trebbiano di Romagna.
Oreste Lini & Figli
Correggio, 42015 Reggio Emilia. DOC: Lambrusco Reggiano.
Marchese Malaspina
Bobbio, 29022 Piacenza. Owners: The Malaspina family. DOC: Trebbianino Val Trebbia. Other: Cabernet, Merlot.
Giuseppe Marabini
Biancanigo di Castelbolognese, 48014 Ravenna. DOC: Albana, Sangiovese and Trebbiano di Romagna.
Maschio
Rastignano di Pianoro, 40067 Bologna. DOC: Prosecco di Conegliano.

Remigio Medici & Fratelli
Villa Cadè, 42020 Reggio Emilia. DOC: Lambrusco Reggiano. Other: Terra Calda Scorza Amara, Vulcano.
Tenuta del Monsignore
San Giovanni in Marignano, 47048 Forlì. Owner: Maria Sarti Bacchini. DOC: Sangiovese and Trebbiano di Romagna.
Fattoria Montebudello (Al Pazz)
Monteveglio, 40050 Bologna. DOC: Colli Bolognese. Other: Rosso Montebudello.
Cantina Consorziale Comprensorio Monte San Pietro
Zola Predosa, 40069 Bologna. Cooperative. DOC: Colli Bolognesi.
Mossi
Ziano, 29010 Piacenza. Owner: Luigi Mossi. DOC: Gutturnio dei Colli Piacentini. Other: Müller Thurgau.
Bruno Negroni (Tenuta Bissera)
Monte San Pietro, 40050 Bologna. DOC: Colli Bolognesi. Other: Bruno Negroni Brut *champenoise*.
La Solitaria
Ziano, 29010 Piacenza. DOC: Gutturnio dei Colli Piacentini.
Tesini
Bertinoro, 37032 Forlì. Owner-wine maker: Arturo Tesini. DOC: Sangiovese di Romagna.
Trerè
Faenza, 48018 Ravenna. DOC: Albana, Sangiovese and Trebbiano di Romagna.
Tenuta Zerbina
Marzeno di Brisighella, 48010 Ravenna. Owner: Vincenzo Geminiani. DOC: Albana, Sangiovese and Trebbiano di Romagna.

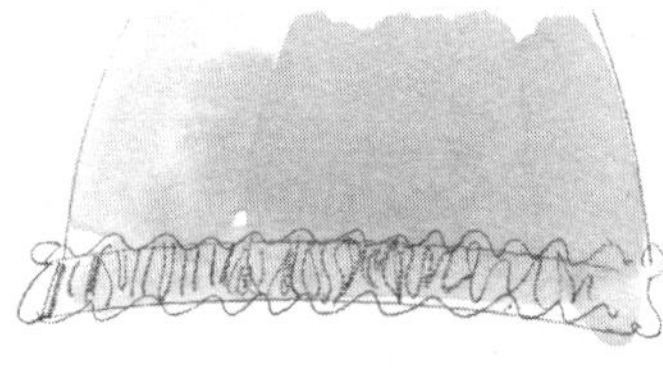

Much of Emilia-Romagna's production is typical café wine, drunk where it is made

TUSCANY

To find a national identity in such a federation of disparities as Italy is not as difficult as it sounds. The answer is Tuscany. For foreigners at least the old Tuscan countryside of villas and cypresses, woods and valleys where vine and olive mingle is Italy in a nutshell.

And so is its wine. Nine out of ten people asked to name one Italian wine would say 'Chianti'. They would have many different ideas (if they had any at all) of what it tastes like – for if ever any wine came in all styles and qualities from the sublime to the gorblimey it is Chianti – and this despite being the earliest of all regions, possibly in all Europe, to start trying to define and defend its wine. Certainly in modern times the Consorzio of its producers paved Italy's way to its DOC system.

Chianti started in the Middle Ages as a small region of constant wars and alarms between Florence and Siena. It is now the biggest and most complex DOC in Italy. There is a real unity and identity, despite its varied soils, traditions and microclimates, because they all grow the same basic red grape, or versions of it. The Sangiovese is what holds Chianti together. On the other hand, Chianti is a blended wine, and individual inclinations can show up strongly in the balance of the blend, the type of fermentation, the use or neglect of the '*governo*', the method and time of ageing.

Chianti has many departments and subregions. It also has several neighbours who claim superiority for their not-dissimilar wine: most notably Brunello di Montalcino and Vino Nobile di Montepulciano. There are enquiring spirits who are importing foreign grapes, above all Cabernet, to improve their wine and are prepared if necessary to be un-DOC'd to prove their point. More likely, however, is that Chianti, still not entirely sure of its identity, will liberalize its laws enough to keep them in.

White wine is a relative stranger here. There is no white Chianti. But several small traditional supply points have been encouraged by the world's swing to white and others have been instigated recently. Of the former, Vernaccia di San Gimignano, Montecarlo and Elba are the most important; of the latter, Galestro and Bianco della Lega – and various excellent non-DOC brands.

DOC AND OTHER WINES

Bianco della Lega

A recent innovation by the Consorzio di Chianti Classico: a dry white of surplus (white) grapes made by several producers. It has yet to establish an identity or reputation.

Bianco Pisano di S. Torpé

DOC. White wine. Provinces: Firenze and Pisa. Villages: on the borders of Chianti and Pisa. Grapes: Trebbiano Toscano 75%, plus Canaiolo, Malvasia Toscano. Max. crop: 84 hl/ha. Min. alch: 11°. No production figures yet available.

A new and apparently flourishing DOC named after a (very) early martyr – beheaded in AD 68 at Pisa. A pale dry wine with some body and a touch of bitterness.

Bianco di Pitigliano

DOC. White wine. Province: Grosseto. Villages: Pitigliano, Sorano, part of Scansano and Manciano. Grapes: Trebbiano Toscano 65–70%, Greco 30–35%, Malvasia Bianca Toscana and Verdello 15%. Max. crop: 87 hl/ha. Min. alch: 11.5°. Average production: 333,000 cases.

Pitigliano is in the extreme south of Tuscany near Lake Bolsena, the home of Est! Est!! Est!!! (*see* Latium). Its soft, dry, slightly bitter white has no particular distinction.

Bianco (and Vin Santo) della Valdinievole

DOC. White wine. Province: Pistoia. Villages: communes of Buggiano, Montecatani Terme and Uzzano. Grapes: Trebbiano plus some Malvasia, Canaiolo Bianco and Vermentino. Max. crop: 91 hl/ha. Min. alch: 11°; Vin Santo 12° for sweet, 13° for semi-sweet, 14° for dry. 3 years is required. Average production: 1,700 cases.

A small production of plain dry, sometimes slightly fizzy, white from west of Florence, made DOC in 1976. Production of Vin Santo is smaller still.

Bianco Vergine della Valdichiana

DOC. White wine. Province: Arezzo. Villages: 11 communes in Val di Chiana south of Arezzo. Grapes: Trebbiano Toscano 70–85%, Malvasia del Chianti 10–20%, others 5–10%. Max. crop: 91 hl/ha. Min alch: 11°. Production: 333,000 cases.

A satisfactory though pretty mild mid-dry white from eastern Tuscany often used as an apéritif in Chianti. A slightly bitter finish gives it some character. At least one producer (Avignonesi) makes it thoroughly crisp and tasty with additional Grecheto grapes.

Bolgheri

DOC. White and rosé wine. Province: Livorno. Villages: Bolgheri and neighbouring communes. Grapes: Trebbiano, Vermentino, Sangiovese and Canaiolo. No other details yet available.

Within this new (1983) DOC zone are vineyards for Antinori's Rosé di Bolgheri and Sassicaia. Sassicaia is not covered by the DOC.

Brunello di Montalcino

DOC. Red wine. Province: Siena. Village: Montalcino. Grape: Brunello di Montalcino. Max. crop: 70 hl/ha. Min. alch: 12.5°. Average production: 220,000 cases. Aged for at least 4 years (3.5 in wood); 5 years for *riserva*. Price: 3,500–18,000 lire.

A big dry red produced for many years by the Biondi-Santi family on 'the Pétrus principle' – that nothing is too much trouble. But sold more in the spirit of Romanée-Conti – no price is too high. The Brunello is a strain of Sangiovese which can be disciplined in this soil to give dark, deeply concentrated wines. Long (sometimes too long) barrel-ageing and – the more vital – long bottle-age are used to coax a remarkable bouquet into its rich, brawny depths. Now several dozen growers make it, with inevitably varying standards. Burton Anderson cites the following as the current leaders: Altesino, Biondi-Santi, Camigliano Costanti, Fattoria dei Barbi, Lisini, Tenuta Caparzo, Tenuta Il Poggione (*see* Producers). A younger wine from young vines is also sold as Rosso dei Vigneti di Brunello.

Candia dei Colli Apuani

DOC. White wine. Province: Massa-Carrara. Villages: communes of Carrara, Massa and Montignoso. Grapes: Vermentino Bianco 70–80%, Albarola 10–20%. Max. crop: 56 hl/ha. Min. alch: 11.5°. No production figures yet available.

A very young DOC for a dry white from the marble-quarry coast.

Carmignano

DOC. Red wine. Province: Firenze. Villages: Carmignano, Poggio a Caiano (10 miles northwest of Firenze). Grapes: Sangiovese 45–65%, Canaiolo Nero 10–20%, Cabernet 6–10%, Trebbiano Toscano, Canaiolo Bianco and Malvasia del Chianti 10–20%, Mammolo, Colorino, Occhio di Pernice 5%. Max. crop: 56 hl/ha. Min. alch: 12.5°. Average production: 14,500 cases. Aged in wood for 1 year for Carmignano, 2 years for Carmignano Riserva. Price: 3,000–7,000 lire.

Best described as Chianti with a just-tastable dollop of Cabernet, justified to the authorities by the fact that the Bonacossi family introduced it from Bordeaux generations ago. Carmignano is consistently well made and justifiably self-confident. Posterity may well thank it for the inspiration to aim all quality Chianti in this direction.

Chianti

DOC. Red wine. Provinces: Siena, Florence, Arezzo, Pistoia, Pisa. Villages: the huge zone in central Tuscany is subdivided into: Classico, Colli Aretini, Colli Fiorentini, Colli Pisane, Colli Senesi, Montalbano, Rufina. Grapes: Sangiovese 50–80%, Canaiolo Nero 10–30%, Trebbiano Toscano, Malvasia del Chianti 10–30%, max. 5% of other grapes, preferably Colorino. Max. crop: 87.5 hl/ha Chianti, 80.5 hl/ha Classico. Min. alch: 11.5° for Chianti, 12° for Classico. Average production: 1.33m. cases. Aged 2 years is *vecchio*, 3 years is *riserva*.

There are 2 basic styles of Chianti: that made as fruity and fresh as possible for local drinking in its youth (still often bottled in *fiaschi*, whether covered with straw or plastic) and drier, more tannic and serious wine aged in barrels or tanks and intended for bottle-ageing; therefore bottled in Bordeaux bottles which can be stacked. The traditional grape mixture is the same for both – basically Sangiovese but with variable additions of dark Canaiolo, white Trebbiano and Malvasia. Overuse of white grapes (which are healthy, productive and easy to grow) has made some Chiantis increasingly pale and insubstantial – many argue the DOC should not have permitted 30%. The *governo* is a local tradition of adding very sweet dried grape must (usually Colorino) to the wine after its fermentation to make it referment, boost its strength, smooth its astringency and promote an agreeable fizz which can make young *fiasco* Chianti delicious. Few producers now use the *governo* for wine that is to be aged before bottling.

Fine old Chianti Riserva has marked affinities with claret, particularly in its light texture and a definite gentle astringency which makes it feel very much alive in your mouth. Its smell and flavour are its own – sometimes reminding me faintly of mulled wine with orange and spices, faintly of chestnuts, faintly of rubber. I have also found a minty 'lift' in its flavour like young burgundy. Its mature colour is a distinct, even glowing, garnet. Some 1971 Classico Riservas compared with 1966 Médoc Crus Classés in 1982 found both these very good vintages at about the same degree of well-advanced maturity. In some cases I preferred the Chianti, which made the Médocs taste excessively dry. There was no question that the 2 were comparable – however different their flavours.

Chianti Classico

The original zone between Florence and Siena, including the towns of Castellina, Radda, Gaiole, Greve and San Casciano. Most of its best producers are members of the very active Consorzio di Chianti Classico, based in Florence, and seal their bottles with its badge, a black rooster. Many are the country residences of ancient noble families with names familiar from the Renaissance (*see* Producers). Not all the best, but most of the best Chianti is Classico.

Chianti Putto

The Consorzio grouping the 6 other Chianti zones surrounding Chianti Classico uses a pink cherub (*putto*) for its seal. The term is generally used for their wines, although not all producers belong to the Consorzio. The six zones are:

Chianti Colli Aretini
The country to the east in the province of Arezzo; a good source of fresh young wines.

Chianti Colli Fiorentini
The zone just north of Chianti Classico around Florence, especially east along the river Arno. Several estates here are at least on a level with the best Classicos.

Chianti Colli Pisane
A detached area south of Pisa making lighter, generally less considerable wine.

Chianti Colli Senesi
A fragmented and inconsistent zone including the western flank of the Classico area south from Poggibonsi, the southern fringes around Siena and the separate areas of Montepulciano and Montalcino to the south. A wide range of styles and qualities.

Chianti Montalbano
The district west of Florence that includes the separate DOC of Carmignano. Also good Chiantis, though lesser known.

Chianti Rufina
A small area 15 miles east of Florence. Rufina is a village on the river Sieve, a tributary of the Arno. The hills behind, where the magically named Vallombrosa is hidden, contain some of the best Chianti vineyards (*see* Frescobaldi under Producers).

Elba Bianco and Rosso

DOC. White and red wine. Province: Island of Elba. Grapes: (white) Trebbiano Toscano (known as Procanico) 90%; (red) Sangiovese 90%; Canaiolo, Trebbiano Toscano and Biancone 25%. Max. crop: 67 hl/ha. Min. alch: 11° for white, 12° for red. Average production: 7,800 cases.

The island off the south Tuscan coast, like a stepping stone to Corsica, has ideal dry white to wash down its fish and Chianti-style red from some highly competent producers.

Galestro

A newly invented ultramodern white produced by a group of Chianti makers using cold fermentation to instil zip and fruity freshness into Trebbiano white (which often lacks it). It is the only Italian wine to have a ceiling on its alcoholic degree: 10.5°.

Monte Antico

Chianti-style red, from the hills south of Siena, with aspirations to DOC recognition and the quality to warrant it. The Trebbiano white is less remarkable.

Montecarlo

DOC. White wine. Province: Lucca. Villages: hills of Montecarlo, Maginone, Altopascio. Grapes: Trebbiano Toscano 60–70%, Sémillon, Pinot Grigio, Pinot Bianco, Vermentino, Sauvignon and/or Roussanne 30–40%. Max. crop: 70 hl/ha. Min. alch: 11.5°. Production: 50,000 cases.

A good example of the improvements possible to Tuscan wines by allowing some more aromatic grapes to elaborate the essentially neutral Trebbiano. Montecarlo's smooth, unaggressive but interesting white can develop a very pleasant bouquet with 2 or 3 years in bottle.

Montescudaio

DOC. Red and white wine. Province: Pisa. Villages: Montescudaio and 6 other communes. Grapes: (red) Sangiovese 65–85%, Trebbiano Toscano and Malvasia up to 25%; (white) Trebbiano Toscano 70–85%, Malvasia di Chianti and Vermentino up to 30%. Max. crop: 84 hl/ha. Min. alch: 11.5° (14° for Vin Santo). Production: 44,500 cases.

Light red and white from near the coast west of Siena. The most distinguished is the strong white Vin Santo.

Morellino di Scansano

DOC. Red wine. Province: Grossetto. Villages: Scansano and 6 other communes in the very south of Tuscany. Grapes: Sangiovese plus up to 15% other red grapes. Max. crop: 84 hl/ha. Min. alch: 11.5° (12° with 2 years' ageing is *riserva*). Average production: 69,000 cases.

A recent (1978) DOC for an all-Sangiovese red. The only other one is the famous Brunello di Montalcino. The intention is clearly to build up this burly wine into something notable.

Moscadello di Montalcino

The home town of Brunello also makes a good-quality fizzy sweet Muscat white: the Asti of Tuscany.

Parrina

DOC. Red and white wine. Province: Grosseto. Villages: the commune of Orbetello. Grapes: (red) Sangiovese 80%, Canaiolo Nero, Montepulciano, Colorino 20%; (white) Trebbiano 80%, Ansonica and/or Malvasia di Chianti up to 20%. Max. crop: 84 hl/ha. Min. alch: 11.5° for white; 12° for red (which must be 1 year old). Production: 41,600 cases.

Lively wines, both red and white, from near the Argentario peninsula in south Tuscany. Parrina Bianco, caught young, can be a good glass with seafood.

Pomino

DOC. Red and white wine. Province: Firenze. Village: Pomino in the commune of Rufina. Grapes: (Pomino Bianco) Pinot Bianco and/or Chardonnay (60–80%), Trebbiano max. 30%; (Pomino Rosso) Sangiovese 60–75%, Canaiolo and/or Cabernet Sauvignon and/or Cabernet Franc 15–25%, Merlot 10–20%; (Vin Santo) Sangiovese, Trebbiano and others. Max. crop: 73 hl/ha. Min. alch. Bianco 11%, Rosso 12%, Vin Santo 15.5%. Average production: not yet established.

The move for this new (1982) DOC was led by Frescobaldis. It will apply to the already established Pomino Bianco and to what was Pomino Chianti Rufina, which will now have more Cabernet and Merlot. The zone was cited in 1716 by the Grand Duchy of Tuscany as one of the best wine areas.

Pomino Bianco

One of Tuscany's very best white wines, from a Frescobaldi property (*see* Producers) in the Chianti Rufina zone. White Pinots, Chardonnay and Sauvignon Blanc are used to demonstrate that the days of the Trebbiano are numbered.

Rosso di Cercatoia

A handmade, barrel-aged red in the style of Chianti Riserva from Montecarlo, near Lucca, best known for its white. *See* Buonamico under Producers.

Rosso delle Colline Lucchesi

DOC. Red wine. Province: Lucca. Villages: Lucca, Capannori and Porcari. Grapes: Sangiovese 45–60%, Canaiolo 8–15%, Ciliegiolo and Colorino 5–15%, Trebbiano Toscano 10–15%, Vermentino-Malvasia Toscana 5–10%. Max. crop: 84 hl/ha. Min. alch: 11.5°.

A cousin of Chianti from nearer the coast, also made in both first-year and *riserva* styles.

Rosso dei Vigneti di Brunello

The second-rank red of Montalcino, made for faster turnover than the massive Brunello (and apparently flouting the rules by using its name. It is scheduled to become Rosso di Montalcino DOC soon). It is built on a less heroic scale but shows much of the same inherent quality.

Sassicaia

An eccentric wine that may prove the most influential of all in the future shape of Tuscan wine-growing. The Marchesi Incisa della Rocchetta grows pure Cabernet Sauvignon on the coast at Bolgheri, south of Livorno – outside any recognized wine zone. What started as a whim became a sensation. He ages it in *barriques* like Bordeaux. His cousin Antinori of Florence bottles and sells it. There is very little of it, but a bottle should be surreptitiously slipped into Cabernet tastings at the top level.

Tignanello

The firm of Antinori are leading modern thinking about Chianti with this wine (and their Chiantis). It is non-DOC because it has 10% Cabernet (allowed only in Carmignano, not in Chianti). Wine-making and ageing are done Bordeaux-style with *barriques*. This is the obvious link between the eccentric Sassicaia and the traditional Chianti. It bodes well.

Val d'Arbia (formerly Bianco della Val d'Arbia)

DOC. White wine. Province: Siena. Villages: 10 along the Arbia river between Radda in Chianti and Buoconvento. Grapes: Trebbiano Toscano, Malvasia and others such as Riesling, Chardonnay, Pinot Bianco. No other information.

A 1982 DOC for a crisp, light, typically Tuscan white made in Chianti Classico country.

Vernaccia di San Gimignano

DOC. White wine. Province: Siena. Villages: the communes of San Gimignano. Grape: Vernaccia di San Gimignano. Max. crop: 70 hl/ha. Min. alch: 12° (aged 1 year for *riserva*). Average production: 22,000 cases.

Old-style Vernaccia was made as powerful as possible, fermented on its (golden) skins and aged in barrels for gently oxidized flavours to emerge. This was the wine Michelangelo loved. It can still be found like this, light amber and unfashionable, or in a modernized pale version which can be good but is hard to identify.

Vin Santo

Wine of grapes dried in the loft until Christmas (to shrivel and sweeten them) is found all over Italy, but most of all at every farm in Tuscany. It can be red or white, but white is more common. Under several DOCs it is defined and regulated, but farmers make it regardless. It should be at least 3 years old, and may be sweet or dry. A few producers age it in small barrels under the roof tiles to produce a madeira-like effect. The results can be sensational.

Vino Nobile di Montepulciano

DOC. Red wine. Province: Siena. Villages: the commune of Montepulciano. Grapes: Prugnolo Gentile (alias Sangiovese) 50–70%, Canaiolo 10–20%, Malvasia del Chianti and Trebbiano Toscano 10–20%; also (white) Pulcinculo and (red) Mammolo 8%. Max. crop: 70 hl/ha. Min. alch: 12°. Average production: 200,000 cases. Aged 2 years in wood; 3 years for *riserva*; 4 for *riserva speciale*.

Montepulciano would like to rival Montalcino, also in the south of the Chianti country. It is highly debatable whether it has anything as exceptional as Brunello to offer. This is essentially Chianti, better or worse according to its maker. The best are now following modern trends and making fine wine.

TUSCANY PRODUCERS

Antico Castello di Poppiano

Barberino Val d'Elsa, 50021 Firenze.

The castle remains in the Kunz Piast d'Asburgo Lorena family, descendants of the Hapsburgs. Wine maker: Ivo Grazi. DOC: Chianti, Chianti Classico. Other: Bois de Rose, Tegolato. The unique Tegolato is aged for 1 year in bottles on top of the castle's roof tiles, where extreme temperatures speed up the ageing process.

Marchesi L. & P. Antinori

50123 Firenze

Owners: Lodovico and Piero Antinori (succeeding Antinoris since 1385). DOC: Chianti Classico, Orvieto Classico. Other: Aleatico, Brut Nature *champenoise*, Galestro, Rosé di Bolgheri, San Giocondo, Tignanello, Villa Antinori Bianco, Vin Santo. *See* opposite.

Argiano

Montalcino, 53024 Siena.

The ancient estate of the Lovatelli family, now part of the stake of the Cinzano group in Brunello. DOC: Brunello di Montalcino. Other: Rosso Argiano. 6,500 cases of Brunnello, 5,800 of the lighter Rosso Argiano.

Artimino

Artimino, 50040 Firenze.

The 16th-century Medici villa, once surrounded by a 32-mile wall, is one of Tuscany's most impressive wine estates. DOC: Carmignano, Chianti. Other: La Ferdinanda Bianco and Rosso, Vin Ruspo, Vin Santo. About a sixth of 1,800 acres is under vine, giving excellent Chianti as well as the Cabernet-flavoured Carmignano.

Avignonesi

Montepulciano, 53045 Siena.

The 16th-century Palazzo Avignonesi, over its 13th-century cellars in the heart of Montepulciano, houses the family's barrel-aged Vino Nobile and lighter Chianti dei Colli Senesi. Experiments with Cabernet are showing great promise. A second estate near Cortona makes exceptional dry Bianco Vergine della Valdichiana.

Badia a Coltibuono

Gaiole, 53013 Siena.

DOC: Chianti Classico. Other: *bianco*, *rosato* and Vin Santo. The monks of this magical 12th-century abbey in the woods might have been the original growers of Chianti. The buildings, cellars and gardens (with an excellent restaurant) are perfectly preserved by the Stucchi-Prinetti family, owners since 1846. The hills are too high here for vines; the 95 acres of vineyards are at Monti, to the south half-way to Siena. There are few more consistently first-class Chiantis, as *riservas* back to 1958 prove.

Villa Banfi

Montalcino, 53024 Siena.

Founded in 1977 by the House of Banfi, the largest US importer of wine. DOC: Brunello di Montalcino. Other: Moscadello di Montalcino. The firm under the direction of Ezio Rivella is developing vineyards and cellars on its vast Poggio all'Oro estate at Montalcino. From some 750 acres, Banfi will soon produce 33,000 cases of Brunello and much more than 110,000 cases of Moscadello, plus Cabernet Sauvignon, Chardonnay and Rosso di Montalcino. Rivella, Italy's foremost oenologist, is using Montalcino as his base for leading Italian wine into the future. *See* page 326.

Fattoria dei Barbi

Montalcino, 53024 Siena.

Owner: Francesca Colombini Cinelli. DOC: Brunello di Montalcino. Other: Bianco del Beato, Brusco dei Barbi, Moscatello, Vin Santo. The Barbi estate has an old reputation. Its 75 acres make up to 9,000 cases of excellent Brunello, selected from good vintages.

Biondi-Santi (Il Greppo)

Montalcino, 53024 Siena.

Founded in 1840 by Clemente Santi, whose grandson, Ferruccio Biondi-Santi, is credited with originating Brunello di Montalcino. Current owners are Franco and Jacopo Biondi-Santi. DOC: Brunello di Montalcino. 2,900 cases of some of Italy's most esteemed and expensive wine come from Il Greppo and its 30 acres of old vines. Sometimes described as 'Italy's only *grand cru*'.

Poderi Boscarelli

Cervignano di Montepulciano, 53045 Siena.

Founded: 1963. Owners: Ippolito and Paola de Ferrari-Corradi. DOC: Chianti Colli Senesi, Vino Nobile di Montepulciano. Grapes are selected for 1,250 cases of Vino Nobile and 1,650 of Chianti from 22 acres. The little estate is considered the best in Montepulciano; its Vino Nobile has more depth, tone and muscle than its rivals.

Fattoria del Buonamico

Montecarlo, 55015 Lucca.

Founded: 1954. Owner: Rina Berti Grassi. DOC: Montecarlo Bianco. Other: Rosso di Cercatoia. A leading Montecarlo maker, started by the well-known Turin restaurant Al Gatto Nero. 7,000 cases from 50 acres.

Castello di Cacchiano

Monti, 53010 Siena.

A 12th-century estate near Gaiole, owned by the Ricasoli Firidolfi family and Elisabetta Balbi Valier. DOC: Chianti Classico. A steady producer of good vintages.

ANTINORI

Charting Tuscany's future

The Marchese Piero Antinori may well be to 21st-century Chianti what the Barone Ricasoli was to the Chianti of the 19th and 20th – the man who wrote the recipe. Antinori is persuasive with the eloquence of an aristocrat who does not have to raise his voice. He and his wine maker Giacomo Tachis have made this ancient Florentine house, based in the Renaissance Palazzo Antinori, Piazza Antinori, Florence, the modern pacesetter, not only for exemplary Chianti (and Orvieto) but more prophetically for Tignanello, which is Sangiovese blended with 10% Cabernet Sauvignon and aged, Bordeaux style, in new oak *barriques*. By replacing the currently obligatory 10% of white grapes in Chianti with Cabernet he has set a precedent that others are bound to follow – whether or not they are permitted to call the result Chianti.

The Antinori family has 545 acres in Tuscany (Santa Cristina, just southwest of Florence) and Umbria (Castello della Scala). Extra grapes are bought under contract. The ultramodern winery is at San Casciano (near Santa Cristina) and the Palazzo Antinori in Florence has tasting facilities. The splendid Villa Antinori, portrayed on labels of the vintage Chianti Classico (which is made by the rule book) was destroyed in World War II. Antinori and Tachis are also in the forefront of white (including sparkling) wine-making in Italy, buying Pinot and Chardonnay grapes in Lombardy for their excellent sparkling Brut. *See also* Sassicaia.

Villa Cafaggio
Panzano, 50020 Firenze.

Owner and wine maker: Stefano Farkas. DOC: Chianti Classico. A name on every 'short list' of classic Chianti; fine austere wine. 11,000 cases from 85 acres.

Villa Calcinaia
Greve, 50022 Firenze.

Founded: 1523. Owner: Neri Capponi. DOC: Chianti Classico. Other: Bianco Secco Calcinaia, Vin Santo. The Capponis are one of the great old families of Florence and Chianti. 22,000 cases of Chianti and 1,100 of the others come from 75 acres.

Capannelle
Gaiole, 53013 Siena.

Owner: Raffaele Rossetti. DOC: Chianti Classico. Other: Capannelle Bianco. A 'boutique' winery, rare in Tuscany, with 7.5 acres, 1,500 cases of prized Chianti (including bottles with silver and gold labels).

Tenuta Caparzo
Montalcino, 53024 Siena.

Wine maker: Vittorio Fiore. DOC: Brunello di Montalcino. Other: Rosso dei Vigneti di Brunello. A Brunello of growing quality and importance from a 37-acre vineyard.

Tenuta di Capezzana
Carmignano, 50042 Firenze.

Founded in the 15th century. Owned and run by Ugo Contini Bonacossi and his family. DOC: Carmignano, Chianti Montalbano. Other: Capezzana Bianco, Ghiaie della Furba, Vin Ruspo, Vin Santo. The ex-Medici villa of the Bonacossis, with its 200 acres of vines, may be the first place Cabernet Sauvignon was grown in Tuscany. The excellence of their Carmignano assured the establishment of what seemed an alien DOC in the heart of Chianti (7,000 cases are selected and sold as Villa Capezzana and Villa di Trefiano).

They also make 40,000–55,000 cases of Chianti and 12,000 cases of other wines, including a new Cabernet/Merlot blend called Ghiaie della Furba.

Castelgiocondo
Montalcino, 53024 Siena.

The estate with the largest tract of Brunello vines (437 acres) is owned by a multinational corporation, Enoviticola Senese, headed by the Marchesi de' Frescobaldi. DOC: Brunello di Montalcino. Other: Rosso di Montalcino. Production, which began with the 1975 vintage, is aimed at 20,000 cases of Brunello.

Castelgreve
Mercatale Val di Pesa, 50024 Firenze.

The Castelli del Grevepesa cooperative is the largest Chianti Classico producer: 5m. litres from 193 growers with nearly 2,000 acres. DOC: Chianti Classico. Other: Valgreve Bianco, Vin Santo. 135,000–170,000 cases are bottled under the Castelgreve or Castelpesa labels.

Castell'in Villa
Castelnuovo Berardenga, 53033 Siena.

Founded in 1968 by Riccardo and Coralia Pignatelli della Leonessa (the wine maker). DOC: Chianti Classico. Other: Bianco della Val d'Arbia, Vin Santo. Some 400,000 litres of excellent Chianti and 75,000 litres of white, of which about 25,000 cases are sold in bottle, from 150 acres.

Luigi Cecchi & Figli (Villa Cerna)
Castellina in Chianti, 53011 Siena.

Owner: The merchant house of Luigi Cecchi & Figli. Founded: 1893. DOC: Chianti, Chianti Classico. Other: Bianco della Lega, Galestro. Villa Cerna produces 40,000 cases of Chianti Classico from 150 acres. The Luigi Cecchi firm altogether produces 375,000–400,000 cases.

Castello di Cerreto
50122 Firenze

The estate near Castelnuovo Berardenga belongs to the dress designer Marchese Emilio Pucci. DOC: Chianti Classico. 11,000–13,500 cases. Pucci also owns the Granaiolo and Coiano estates in Chianti Colli Fiorentini.

Agricoltori del Chianti Geografico
Gaiole in Chianti, 53013 Siena.

The well-run cooperative of the southern half of the Classico zone. DOC: Chianti Classico. About 90,000 cases of a potential total of 225,000 are selected and bottled with the respected Geografico label.

Chianti Melini
Gaggiano di Poggibonsi, 53036 Siena.

Founded: 1705. Now part of the Swiss Winefood group. In the 1860s, Laborel Melini devised the strengthened Chianti flask which enabled shipping, thus becoming one of the best-known names abroad. DOC: Chianti, Chianti Classico, Orvieto, Vernaccia di San Gimignano, Vino Nobile di Montepulciano. Other: Lacrima d'Arno Bianco and Rosato, Spumante Brut, Vin Santo. Melini owns 5 vineyards of 400 acres though full production of about 600,000 cases derives mainly from bought-in grapes.

Tenuta La Chiusa
Magazzini di Portoferraio-Elba, 57037 Livorno.

Owner: (since 1973) Giuliana Foresi. DOC: Elba. 11 acres produce Elba's best wine, but only 1,000 cases.

Podere di Cignano
Bagnoro Montoncello, 52040 Arezzo.

Owner: (since 1965) Giovanni Bianchi. DOC: Chianti Colli Aretini. Other: Eburneo Bianco, Rory Rosato. An ancient property revived by its oenologist owner to make lively modern wines; in all 35,000 cases from 145 acres.

Poderi Emilio Costanti
Montalcino, 53024 Siena.

Owner: Emilio Costanti. DOC: Brunello di Montalcino, Chianti Colli Senesi. Other: Albatro (white), Vermiglio. A tiny 8.6-acre property, but its 1,100 cases include some of the grandest and longest-lived Brunello, wine of almost Piedmontese concentration that very slowly relaxes into a velvet mouthful for millionaires.

Castello di Fonterutoli
Castellina in Chianti, 53010 Siena.

Owners: The Mazzei family since 1435. DOC: Chianti Classico. Other: Bianco della Lega. Lapo Mazzei is president of the Classico Consortium, and a modest but wholly convincing champion of true Chianti. His 80 acres produce some 18,000 cases of distinctively elegant wine.

Marchesi de' Frescobaldi
50125 Firenze

Owners: the Frescobaldis since 1300, now 3 brothers: Vittorio (president), Ferdinando (manager for Italy), Leonardo (export manager). Wine maker: Luciano

Boarino. DOC: Chianti Rufina. Other: Galestro, Nuovo Fiore, Pomino Bianco, Villa di Corte Rosé, Vin Santo. Like the Antinoris, an ancient noble house leading the way for Tuscany with wines of outstanding quality, reliability, value and originality. All Frescobaldi wines come from their 8 estates east of Florence in Rufina, totalling 1,300 acres. Castello di Nipozzano is their most famous red (a superior selection is called Montesodi). Other estate Chiantis are Pomino and Poggio a Remole. Pomino Bianco is an excellent white seasoned with Chardonnay. Frescobaldi also manages Castelgiocondio at Montalcino.

Marchesi Incisa della Rocchetta (Sassicaia and Tenuta San Guido)

Bolgheri, 57020 Livorno.

Owner: Marchese Mario Incisa della Rocchetta. DOC: none. The Marchese planted Cabernet Sauvignon on his seaside estate near Bolgheri, Tenuta San Guido, in 1942. His Sassicaia emerged in the late 1960s as Italy's finest Cabernet. 11 acres produce only 2,000–3,000 cases, made and aged at Bolgheri and distributed by his cousins the Antinoris of Florence.

Monsanto

Barberino Val d'Elsa, 50021 Firenze.

Founded: 1962. Owner: Fabrizio Bianchi. DOC: Chianti Classico. A potential 40,000 cases of which 11,000 are selected as *riserva* and Il Poggio *riserva*, both fine aged Chiantis, from 125 acres.

Fattoria di Montagliari

Panzano, 50020 Firenze.

Owner: Giovanni Cappelli. DOC: Chianti Classico. Other: *bianco*, Vin Santo. A highly regarded estate in the same family since the 17th century, now making 20,000 cases. Cappelli's other estate, La Quercia, makes 33,000 cases.

Castello di Monte Antico e dell'Abbadia Ardenghesca

Civitella Marittima, 58045 Grosseto.

Owner: Giorgio Cabella. No DOC. Castello di Monte Antico Rosso, Ardenghesca Bianco. About 25,000 cases of first-class wine.

Fattoria di Montecarlo

Montecarlo, 55015 Lucca.

Founded 1890. Owner: Franca Mazzini-Franceschi. DOC: Montecarlo Bianco. One of the oldest and best producers of this smooth but lively white.

Monte Vertine

Radda, 53017 Siena.

Owner: Sergio Manetti. DOC: Chianti Classico. Other: Le Pergole Torte, Monte Vertine Bianco. A fastidiously tended little vineyard producing 2,000–3,000 cases of Chianti – and Le Pergole Torte, an oak-aged all-Sangiovese red of unusual quality and an interesting white.

Pagliarese

Castelnuovo Berardenga, 53033 Siena.

Owner: Alma Biasiotto Sanguineti. DOC: Chianti Classico. Other: Bianco della Lega, Vin Santo. A famous old estate, now making 17,000 cases of Chianti Pagliarese and 8,800 of Chianti Pigiatello from 74 acres and grapes from neighbouring farms.

Fattoria La Parrina

Albinia di Orbetello, 58010 Grosseto.

Owner: Maria Concetta Giuntini-Spinola and Franca Spinola. DOC: Parrina Bianco, Rosso. Other: Albinia Rosato. The principal producers of this dry white 'Vino Etrusco' from the coast near Orbetello. They make 75,000 cases from 150 acres.

Pile e Lamole

Greve in Chianti, 50022 Firenze.

Owners: The Tibaldi family. DOC: Chianti Classico. A small estate at Lamole near Greve, highly reputed for splendid old vintages.

Tenuta Il Poggione

Montalcino, 53024 Siena.

Founded: 1890. Owners: Clemente and Roberto Franceschi. Wine maker: Pierluigi Talenti. DOC: Brunello di Montalcino. Other: Moscadelletto di Montalcino, Rosso dei Vigneti di Brunello, Vin Santo. One of the biggest Montalcino estates. From 135 acres, half for Brunello, Talenti makes 10,000 cases of first-rate wine at reasonable prices, the Brunello intended for drinking young.

Fattoria La Querce

Impruneta, 50023 Firenze.

Owner: Gino Marchi and Grazia Montorselli. Wine maker: Attilio Pieri. DOC: Chianti. In some eyes (and some vintages) the best-made wine of Chianti, very carefully selected to make only 3,200 cases from 40 acres.

Barone Ricasoli (Castello di Brolio)

50123 Firenze.

Owners: The Ricasoli family since 1141; controlled by Seagram's since the mid-1970s. DOC: Chianti, Chianti Classico, Orvieto. Other: Arbia, Brolio Bianco, Galestro, Rosé, Torricella, Vin Santo. The great grim brickbuilt stronghold where the great grim Bettino Ricasoli, second Prime Minister of Italy in the 1850s, 'invented' Chianti – or at least the blend of grapes and method of production. Its former 'first-growth' reputation is in eclipse today as the pace becomes faster. More than 600 acres in Chianti Classico produce some 165,000 cases, besides other wines the firm buys and bottles.

Riecine

Gaiole, 53013 Siena.

Founded in 1971 by an Englishman, John Dunkley, and his wife Palmina Abbagnano. DOC: Chianti Classico. Other: Riecine Bianco. Dunkley proved himself a perfectionist from his first vintage. His attitude and his excellent, truly typical, Chianti have helped to make the British more attentive.

I. L. Ruffino

Pontassieve, 50065 Firenze.

Founded: 1877. Owners: The Folonari family. DOC: Chianti, Chianti Classico, Orvieto. Other: Galestro, Rosatello. The largest and perhaps the best-known of all Chianti houses. Part of the production is from 740 acres of company vines. Their holdings in Chianti Classico are the source of the respected Riserva Ducale.

Savignola Paolina

Greve, 50022 Firenze.

Owner-wine maker: Paolina Fabbri. DOC: Chianti Classico. Other: Bianco della Lega. The owner, in her 80s, is highly respected for the quality of her 1,000 cases a year.

Sellari Franceschini

Scansano, 58054 Grosseto.

Founded: 1877. Owner: Maria Grazia Sellari Franceschini. DOC: Morellino di Scansano. Other: Biondello dei Gaggioli. The principal producer of a promising new (1978) DOC for a Sangiovese dry red.

Conti Serristori (Antica Fattoria di Niccolò Machiavelli)

Sant'Andrea in Percussina, 50026 Firenze.

Now part of the Swiss Winefood group. DOC: Chianti, Chianti Classico, Orvieto, Vernaccia di San Gimignano. Other: Bianco and Rosato Toscano, Galestro, Vin Santo. The property includes the country house where Machiavelli lived in exile. The 67 acres of the estate produce 1,000 cases of Ser Niccolò, 8,300 of Machiavelli and 40,000 of Villa Primavera Chianti Classico. Total production is more than 125,000 cases.

Spalletti Valdisieve (Poggio Reale)

Rufina, 50068 Firenze.

Founded: 1912; owned since 1973 by Cinzano. DOC: Chianti, Orvieto, Vernaccia di San Gimignano. Growers and merchants, founded by the Spalletti family and based in the Villa Poggio Reale, designed by Michelangelo. Their own 125 acres produce 27,000 cases of Chianti Poggio Reale.

Guicciardini Strozzi (Fattoria di Cusona)

San Gimignano, 53037 Siena.

Owner: Girolamo Guicciardini Strozzi. DOC: Chianti, Vernaccia di San Gimignano. Other: Vin Santo. The leading producer of Vernaccia, dating back to the 16th century. 25,000 cases of Vernaccia and 20,000 of other wines from 125 acres.

Villa Terciona

Mercatale Val di Pesa, 50024 Firenze.

Owners: The Saccardi family. DOC: Chianti Classico. Other: Terciona Bianco. A lovely estate on the site of a 14th-century monastery. Recently, under Antinori influence, a crisp and toothsome white has joined the stately classical red.

Teruzzi & Puthod (Ponte a Rondolino)

San Gimignano, 53037 Siena.

Founded in 1975 by Enrico Teruzzi and Carmen Puthod. DOC: Chianti Colli Senesi, Vernaccia di San Gimignano. Other: Galestro. The estate is expanding; 15,000 cases of exemplary Vernaccia and wood-aged *riserva* from 50 acres. (Ex-ballerina) Carmen Puthod runs the Ponte a Rondolino restaurant, which serves the estate wines.

Fattoria di Tizzano

San Polo in Chianti, 50020 Firenze.

Owner: Filippo Pandolfini. DOC: Chianti Classico. 7,700 cases. The Pandolfinis bought the classical property in the last century. Their *riservas* have a considerable reputation.

Castello di Uzzano

Greve, 50022 Firenze.

Owner: Briano Castelbarco Albani Masetti, whose family has owned the property since the 17th century. DOC: Chianti Classico. One of the greatest names of Chianti, whose 14th-century cellars (the walls are 27 feet thick) slowly mature wines of sweet harmony and long life. They make about 27,000 cases of Castello di Uzzano, plus 11,000 cases under the labels Fattoria di Uzzano and Fattoria delle Lame from more than 300 acres of vines.

The ancient monastic estate of La Badia a Coltibuono.

Castello Vicchiomaggio
Greve, 50022 Firenze.

Owner: John Matta since 1968. DOC: Chianti Classico, Other: Paleo Bianco. A 9th-century castle in a superb site, now the scene of some excellent modern wine-making. They produce 4,400 cases of *riserva* and 7,200 of regular Chianti Classico from 62 acres.

Vignamaggio
Greve, 50022 Firenze.

Owner: Ranieri Sanminiatelli. DOC: Chianti Classico. The beautiful 15th-century villa where Mona Lisa probably lived, home of Michelangelo's biographer and one of the most prestigious Chiantis, though rather light in style.

Villa a Sesta
San Gusmè, 53010 Siena.

Owner: Emilio Bertoni. DOC: Chianti Classico. Villa a Sesta is a lovely hamlet near Brolio. The estate produces 6,000 cases of truly classical wine.

Castello di Volpaia
Radda, 53017 Siena.

Owner: Giovannella Stianti. DOC: Chianti Classico. Other: Bianco di Volpaia, Coltassala, Vin Santo. The medieval castle and its hamlet were high on the list of 15th-century *crus*. Its 100 acres now produce 16,500 cases of Chianti and 1,750 of other wines, including the new Coltassala of Sangiovese and Mammolo aged in *barriques*.

OTHER PRODUCERS

Fattoria della Aiola
Vagliagli, 53010 Siena. Owner: Giovanni Malagodi. DOC: Chianti Classico. 18,000 cases.

Altesino
Montalcino, 53024 Siena. Founded: 1971. Owner: Giulio Consonno. DOC: Brunello di Montalcino. Other: Bianco di Montosoli, Rosso dei Vigneti di Brunello. 44 acres in production.

Fattoria di Ama
Ama in Chianti, 53010 Siena. DOC: Chianti Classico. 8,000 cases.

Fattoria L'Amorosa
Sinalunga, 53046 Siena. Owners: Carlo and Livia Citterio. DOC: Chianti Colli Senesi. The house wine of the restaurant Locanda L'Amorosa.

Fattoria di Bacchereto
Bacchereto, 50040 Firenze. Owner: Carlo Bencini Tesi. DOC: Carmignano, Chianti. Other: Vin Ruspo.

Bertolli
Castellina Scalo, 53032 Siena. The family firm is known as Alivar S.p.A. DOC: Chianti, Chianti Classico. 75,000 cases of Chianti Classico, plus Chianti, Orvieto and other wines.

Palazzo al Bosco
La Romola, 50020 Firenze. Owner: Marcello Olivieri. DOC: Chianti Classico. Other: Bianco della Lega, Vin Santo. A 13th-century estate with 20 acres, making 4,500–5,500 cases of attractive Chianti. The owner also selects Brunello di Montalcino and white wine under the Olivieri label.

Camigliano
Montalcino, 53024 Siena. DOC: Brunello di Montalcino. Other: Bianco, Rosso dei Vigneti di Brunello. 11,000 cases of Brunello and 22,000 cases of the others from 170 acres (68 in Brunello).

Fattoria Casenuove
Panzano, 50020 Firenze. Owner: Pietro Pandolfini. DOC: Chianti Classico, 20,000 cases.

Castellare di Castellina
Castellina in Chianti, 53011 Siena. DOC: Chianti Classico. 4,400 cases.

Le Chiantigiane
Tavarnelle Val di Pesa, 50028 Firenze. A cooperative. DOC: Chianti Classico. Other: Galestro. Potentially 45,000 cases of Chianti.

Chigi Saracini (Azienda Agricola Madonna)
Castelnuovo Berardenga, 53033 Siena. DOC: Chianti Colli Senesi. The ancient estate was bequeathed to the Chigi Saracini musical academy of Siena by Conte Guido Chigi. 30,000 cases from 94 acres.

Col d'Orcia
Montalcino, 53024 Siena. A considerable estate bought by Cinzano in 1973. DOC: Brunello di Montalcino. Other: Rosso Col d'Orcia, Novembrino. Production is growing beyond 8,300 cases of Brunello and 3,300 of Rosso from 198 acres.

Cantine Riunite Mario Contucci
Montepulciano, 53045 Siena. DOC: Vino Nobile di Montepulciano.

Cantina Sociale di Cortona
Cortona, 52044 Arezzo. Cooperative. DOC: Bianco Vergine della Valdichiana.

Riccardo Falchini (Casale)
San Gimignano, 53037 Siena. Founded: 1965. DOC: Chianti, Vernaccia di San Gimignano. Other: Vin Santo. A principal producer of Vernaccia, with 12,000 cases from 50 acres. Also 3,300 of Chianti.

Adamo & Giuseppe Fanetti (Tenuta Sant'Agnese)
Montepulciano, 53045 Siena. DOC: Chianti Colli Senesi, Vino Nobile di Montepulciano.

Fassati
Pieve di Sinalunga, 53046 Siena. Founded 1913. Owned since 1969 by Fazi-Battaglia (*see* Marches). DOC: Chianti, Chianti Classico, Vino Nobile di Montepulciano. About 8,000 cases of Vino Nobile come from 30 acres.

Fortilizio Il Colombaio
Quercegrossa, 53010 Siena. Owner: Isabella Bonucci Ugurgieri della Berardenga. DOC: Chianti Classico. A 17th-century fortress with a rustic tavern and hotel in the grounds. It produces 5,500 cases under the Fortilizio Il Colombaio and Villa Colombaio labels.

Fossi
50133 Firenze. Owner: Duilio Fossi. DOC: Chianti Classico. A merchant who selects and ages about 5,500 cases. His reserves date back to 1958.

Dianella Fucini
Vinci, 50059 Firenze. Owner: Piero Billeri. DOC: Chianti. A potential 17,000 cases from 110 acres.

Castello di Gabbiano
Mercatale Val di Pesa, 50024 Firenze. DOC: Chianti Classico. Easily remembered by its colourful label of a mounted knight in armour. Some 27,000 cases of fine Chianti.

Fattorie Giannozzi
Marcialla, Barberino Val d'Elsa, 50021 Firenze. Founded: 1710. Owner: Luciano Giannozzi. DOC: Chianti. Other: Galestro. 20,000 cases from 85 acres.

Tenuta di Gracciano
Montepulciano Stazione, 53045 Siena. Owners: The Della Seta family. DOC: Vino Nobile di Montepulciano, Chianti Colli Senesi. Select Vino Nobile.

Grattamacco
Castagneto Carducci, 57022 Livorno. Owner: Piermario Meletti Cavallari. No DOC. Grattamacco Bianco, Rosso. A small estate making artisan wines.

Isole & Olena
Barberino Val d'Elsa, 50021 Firenze. Owned by the de Marchi family since 1954. Wine maker: Paolo de Marchi. DOC: Chianti Classico. 25,000 cases.

Leonardo
Vinci, 50059 Firenze. Founded: 1961. One of Tuscany's largest cooperatives. DOC: Chianti. The potential is about 400,000 cases from 1,200 acres.

Lilliano
Castellina in Chianti, 53011 Siena. Owner: Eleonora Berlingieri Ruspoli. DOC: Chianti Classico. 22,000 cases of distinguished wine.

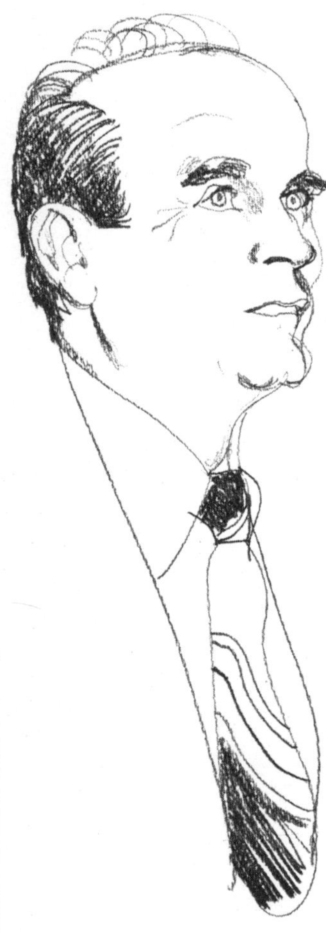

Ezio Rivella
As the wine director and chief oenologist for Villa Banfi, the largest exporters of Italian wine to the United States, Ezio Rivella (Piedmont-born, a man of startling competence and vitality) has fabulous resources at his disposal. His chief preoccupation is the vast new Banfi development at Montalcino in the south of Tuscany, where the company has acquired 700 acres for planting, partly with Brunello (as yet unmade) and partly with Muscatel for a lively Asti-type sweet *spumante* which is already proving excellent. Rivella's ambitions go much further. He is planting both Cabernet and Chardonnay (neither permitted DOC varieties in Montalcino) and will make the wines deliberately in the California style, aged in French oak, 'but better than Napa or Sonoma'.

Lisini
Montalcino, 53024 Siena. Owner: Elina Lisini. DOC: Brunello di Montalcino. Other: Rosso dei Vigneti di Brunello. 24 acres from which grapes are selected for less than 5,000 cases of opulent Brunello.

Fattoria delle Lodoline
Vagliagli, 53010 Siena. Owner: Pepita Radicati di Brozzolo. Wine maker: Hugh Hamilton. DOC: Chianti Classico. 5,500 cases of well-made wine.

Majnoni Guicciardini
Vico d'Elsa, 50050 Firenze. Owners: Stefano and Francesco Majnoni. DOC: Chianti. Other: Spareto (white). A 94-acre estate just to the west of the Classico zone. 40,000 cases of good Chianti.

La Mandria
Adine-Ama in Chianti, 53010 Siena. DOC: Chianti Classico. 22,000 cases from 100 acres

Montenidoli
San Gimignano, 53037 Siena. Owner: Elisabetta Fagiuoli. DOC: Chianti Colli Senesi.

Montepaldi
San Casciano Val di Pesa, 50026 Firenze. Owner: Marchesi Corsini. DOC: Chianti Classico. 27,000 cases.

Vecchia Cantina di Montepulciano
Montepulciano, 53045 Siena. A cooperative founded in 1937. DOC: Bianco Vergine della Valdichiana, Chianti, Vino Nobile di Montepulciano. A large producer of Montepulciano, but of no particular repute.

Morazzano
Montescudaio, 56040 Pisa. Owners: Andrea Mattei and Antonella Vigorelli Milanesi. DOC: none. Other: Da Morazzano. 250–400 cases of outstanding *rosato*.

Casavecchia di Nittardi
Castellina in Chianti, 53011 Siena. Owner: Anstalt Nittardi. DOC: Chianti Classico. 2,700 cases.

Nozzole
Greve, 50022 Firenze. Owner: I.L. Ruffino. DOC: Chianti Classico. Other: Nozzole Bianco. 250 acres of vines produce a well-known Chianti of regular commercial quality.

Fattoria Pagnana
Rignano sull'Arno, 50007 Firenze. DOC: Chianti. Other: Bianco, Vin Santo. A potential 60,000 cases from 170 acres.

Petroio alla Via della Malpensata
Radda, 53017 Siena. DOC: Chianti Classico.

Pian d'Albola
Radda, 53017 Siena. Owner: Principe Ginori Conti. DOC: Chianti Classico. 14,500 cases of reputable wine.

Le Pici
San Gusmè, 53030 Siena. Owner: Gunnar Lüneburg. DOC: Chianti Classico. 4,000 cases.

Fattoria di Pietrafitta
San Gimignano, 53037 Siena. DOC: Chianti, Vernaccia di San Gimignano. The venerable estate makes 11,000 cases of Vernaccia, 8,800 of Chianti.

Cantina Cooperativa di Pitigliano
Pitigliano, 58017 Grosseto. DOC: Bianco di Pitigliano. The cooperative includes most of Pitigliano's 800 registered growers.

Poggio alle Mura
Montalcino, 53024 Siena. Owners: The Mastropaolo family. DOC: Brunello di Montalcino, Chianti Colli Senesi. Other: Moscadello, Vin Santo. The huge property comprises a towering castle and 125 acres of vines.

Poggio al Sole
Sambuca Val di Pesa, 50020 Firenze. Owner: Aldo Torrini. DOC: Chianti Classico. Other: Vino della Signora, Vin Santo. 3,300–3,900 cases from 20 acres.

Il Poggiolo
Poggiolo di Monteriggioni, 53035 Siena. Owners: The Bonfio family. DOC: Chianti Colli Senesi. 2,500–4,000 cases from 25 acres.

Fattoria Il Poggiolo
Carmignano, 50042 Firenze. Owner: Giovanni Cianchi Baldazzi. DOC: Carmignano, Chianti Montalbano. Other: Vin Ruspo.

Castello di Poppiano
Montespertoli, 50025 Firenze. Owner: Ferdinando Guicciardini. DOC: Chianti Colli Fiorentini.

Castello di Querceto
Lucolena, 50020 Firenze. Manager-wine maker: Alessandro François. DOC: Chianti Classico. 10,000 cases.

Raccianello
San Gimignano, 53037 Siena. DOC: Chianti, Vernaccia di San Gimignano. Other: Galestro.

Castello di Rampolla
Panzano in Chianti, 50020 Firenze. DOC: Chianti Classico. About 3,300 cases.

Giorgio Regni
Castagnoli, 53010 Siena. DOC: Chianti Classico. 1,300 cases.

Castello di Rencine
Castellina in Chianti, 53011 Siena. DOC: Chianti Classico. 2,500–3,300 cases.

La Rinserrata
Casale Marittimo, 56040 Pisa. Owner: Annalisa Nahmias. DOC: Montescudaio Rosso. Other: *rosato*. 440 cases of hand-made wine.

Rocca delle Macie
Castellina in Chianti, 53011 Siena. Founded: 1974. DOC: Chianti Classico. Other: Galestro. A new and dynamic producer. Production is building to more than 80,000 cases from 220 acres.

Fattoria di Sammontana
Montelupo, 50056 Firenze. Owner: Massimo Dzieduszycki, whose noble Polish ancestors acquired the estate in 1870. DOC: Chianti. Potentially 35,000 cases from some 120 acres.

San Fabiano
52100 Arezzo. Owner: The Borghini Baldovinetti de Bacci family. DOC: Chianti. A potential 42,000 cases from 125 acres is sold partly in bottle, partly in bulk.

San Felice
San Gusmè, 53030 Siena. DOC: Chianti Classico. Other: Biancaccio, Fiamma, Santuccio. Production is surpassing 50,000 cases from 197 acres.

San Leonino
Castellina in Chianti, 53011 Siena. DOC: Chianti Classico. 33,000 cases from 130 acres.

Castello di San Polo in Rosso
Gaiole, 53013 Siena. Owner: Cesare Canessa. DOC: Chianti Classico. 8,300 cases.

Santa Lucia-Branca
Mercatale Val di Pesa, 50024 Firenze. DOC: Chianti Classico. Owner: Pierluigi Branca. More than 80,000 cases.

Savoia Aosta (Tenuta del Borro)
San Giustino Valdarno, 52034 Arezzo. Owner: Amedeo di Savoia Aosta. DOC: Chianti.

Villa La Selva
Bucine, 52020 Arezzo. The ancient estate is owned by the Carpini brothers. DOC: Chianti. Other: Ambra Bianco, Villa La Selva Riserva.

Selvapiana
Pontassieve, 50065 Firenze. Founded: 1840. Owner: Francesco Giuntini. DOC: Chianti Rufina. An old family property producing about 30,000 cases from 200 acres.

Fattoria di Selvole
Vagliagli, 53010 Siena. DOC: Chianti Classico, 8,800 cases.

Casa Sola
San Donato in Poggio, Barberino Val d'Elsa, 50021 Firenze. DOC: Chianti Classico, 12,000 cases.

Storiche Cantine
Radda, 53017 Siena. The Radda cooperative has 4 associated firms that market wines under separate labels: Castello di Meleto, Castello di San Donato in Perano, La Cerreta and La Pesanella-Monterinaldi. DOC: Chianti Classico. Total production: 220,000 cases. Meleto was formerly a property of the Ricasolis of Brolio.

Straccali
Castellina in Chianti, 53011 Siena. DOC: Chianti Classico. 11,000 cases.

Fattoria del Teso
Montecarlo, 55015 Lucca. DOC: Montecarlo Bianco.

Torre e Decima
Molino del Piano, 50065 Firenze. DOC: Chianti Colli Fiorentini. Other: Dolce Amore Bianco. A dramatic 13th-century castle built by the Pazzi family. 50,000 cases from 170 acres.

Fattoria I Tre Cancelli
Vallebuia, 55100 Lucca. DOC: Rosso delle Colline Lucchesi.

Fattoria dell'Ugo
Tavarnelle Val di Pesa, 50028 Firenze. Owner: Franco Amici Grossi. DOC: Chianti. 24,000 cases from 60 acres.

Val di Suga
Montalcino, 53024 Siena. Bought in 1981 by a Milanese group. Wine maker: Vittorio Fiore. DOC: Brunello di Montalcino. Other: Rosso del Merlot. A Brunello of emerging repute from 56 acres.

Castello di Verrazzano
Greve, 50020 Firenze. Owner: Luigi Cappellini. DOC: Chianti Classico. 3,500 cases. The castle where the explorer Giovanni da Verrazzano was born in 1485; the approach to New York is named after him.

Fattoria di Vetrice
Rufina, 50068 Firenze. Owner: Fratelli Grati. DOC: Chianti Rufina. Potential 70,000 cases from 220 acres.

Vigna Vecchia
Radda, 53017 Siena. Owner: Franco Beccari. DOC: Chianti Classico. 15,000 cases include a small quantity of sought-after *riserva*.

UMBRIA

If Umbria figured on a discerning wine buyer's shopping list in the past it was purely for Orvieto, its golden, gently sweet and occasionally memorable speciality. Today it is more likely to be for Rubesco, the noble red of Torgiano near Perugia, one of the best wines and best bargains in Italy. Orvieto has lost in personality what it has gained in volume.

If Torgiano can make such good wine, so surely can other hills in this inland region. New DOCs are appearing. They should allow for the maximum latitude in the choice of grapes, since those of the north and the south could both do well here, and there is no good reason for planting (say) Trebbiano if you could plant Sauvignon Blanc.

DOC AND OTHER WINES

Castello di Montoro

An individual red made at Montoro di Narni in the south of Umbria by the Marchesi Montoro (*see* Producers). Sangiovese is blended with Merlot, Barbera and Montepulciano to make a complex wine for 5 years' ageing.

Colli Altotiberini

DOC. Red and white wine. Province: Perugia. Villages: a wide sweep of country in northern Umbria, including Perugia, Gubbio, Citta di Castello. Grapes (red and *rosato*) Sangiovese 55–70%, Merlot 10–20%, Trebbiano and Malvasia 10%; (white) Trebbiano Toscano 75–90%, Malvasia up to 10%, others up to 15%. Max. crop: 77 hl/ha. Min. alch: 10.5° for white; 11.5° for red and *rosato*. Average production: no figures yet available. Price: 1,200–2,200 lire.

A new (1980) DOC for the hills of the upper Tiber. Production in the area is increasing. All its wines, including its dry red with Merlot, are intended for drinking young.

Colli Perugini

DOC. Red and white wine. Provinces: Perugia and Terni. Villages: Perugia and 6 other communes southwest of the city toward Todi. Grapes: (red and rosato) Sangiovese 65–85%, Montepulciano, Ciliegiolo, Barbera and/or Merlot 15–35% (but no more than 10% Merlot); (white) Trebbiano Toscano 65–85%, Grechetto, Verdicchio, Garganega and/or Malvasia del Chianti 15–35% (but no more than 10% Malvasia). Max. crop: 84 hl/ha (72 hl/ha rosato). Min. alch. 11% for red and rosato, 10.5% for white. No production figures yet available.

A 1982 DOC for the hill country which already makes good wine at Marscisno and Colli Marteni.

DR. GIORGIO LUNGAROTTI

The saturnine face of Dr. Giorgio Lungarotti masks one of Italy's most original wine makers, a man of extraordinary energy and sagacity who has pursued his vision of great wine independent of any historic reputation. His creation is now the DOC Torgiano. The little hill-town across the young Tiber from Perugia is the Lungarotti republic, from its modern winery to its excellent wine museum and its beautifully restored and greatly enlarged hotel, the Tre Vasselle (where each October the Umbrian government holds an all-Italian wine championship).

Lungarotti's red, Rubesco di Torgiano, is like a first-rate, unusually concentrated Chianti. Its *riserva* from the Monticcio vineyard even more so, deserving 10 years in bottle. Now he is experimenting with 25% Cabernet in a new *riserva* called San Giorgio. His traditional white, Torre di Giano, is Trebbiano enlivened with Grechetto to be crisp and fragrant. In 1981 he introduced a Chardonnay, and also has Gewürztraminer in his 500 acres of vineyards. His Soleone is one of Italy's rare sherry-style dry apéritif wines.

Colli del Trasimeno

DOC. White and red wine. Province: Perugia. Villages: 10 communes around Lake Trasimeno. Grapes: (white) Trebbiano Toscano 70%, Malvasia del Chianti, Verdicchio Bianco, Verdello and Grechetto up to 40%; (red) Sangiovese 60–80%, Gamay, Ciliegiolo or white grapes up to 40%. Max. crop: 87 hl/ha. Min. alch: 11° for white 11.5° for red. Average production: 278,000 cases. Price: 1,200–2,400 lire.

The red and white of this zone on the borders of Tuscany are both above average. Gamay and Ciliegiolo give spirit to the red and Grechetto gives the white a slight edge of acidity essential for freshness.

Grechetto or Greco

A 'Greek' white grape which plays an increasingly important role here and farther south. Unblended its wine is somewhat more fruity, firm and interesting than Trebbiano.

Montefalco and Sagrantino di Montefalco

DOC. Red wine. Province: Perugia. Villages: the commune of Montefalco and parts of 4 others. Grapes: Sangiovese 65–75%, Trebbiano Toscano 15–25%, Sagrantino 5–10%, others up to 15%; for Sagrantino: 100% with up to 5% Trebbiano. Max. crop: 91 hl/ha. Min. alch: 11.5° (12.5° for Sagrantino, 14° for *passito*). Production: figures not yet available. Prices: 1,300–2,300 lire, Sagrantino 1,800–5,000.

A new (1980) DOC for a small area south of Assisi where the local Sagrantino grape makes very dark red wine, described as tasting of blackberries. The true speciality is the sweet and strong *passito* version, a notable dessert wine. Dry it is tough and tannic but may yet command respect. Plain Montefalco red uses Sagrantino as seasoning in a less original but still smooth and agreeable wine.

Orvieto

DOC. White wine. Province: Orvieto. Villages: Orvieto and 15 other communes. 'Classico' is from Orvieto itself. Grapes: Trebbiano Toscano 50–65%, Verdello 15–25%, Grechetto, Drupeggio, Malvasia Toscana 20–30%. Max. crop: 71 hl/ha. Min. alch: 12°. Production: 667,000 cases. Price: 1,200–2,500 lire.

The simple and memorable name that used to mean golden, more or less sweet wine now suffers from the same identity crisis as many Italian whites. The taste for highly charged, then gently oxidized wines has gone. Modern vinification answers the problem with pale, clean but almost neuter ones. Not long ago (perhaps still) you could see huge barrels in Orvieto with their glass fermentation airlocks still occasionally breaking wind after 2 years or more. The wine, laboriously fermented dry, was then re-sweetened with a dried-grape *passito* to be *abboccato*. If you found a good one it was memorably deep and velvety, but probably none too stable – like Frascati, a poor traveller.

Modern Orvieto is nearly all pale, but should still have a hint of honey to be true to type. Much is dry and frankly dull. Chianti shippers put their names to several, Antinori to one of the better ones.

Torgiano

DOC. Red and white wine. Province: Perugia. Village: Torgiano. Grapes: (red) Sangiovese 50–70%. Canaiolo 15–30%, Trebbiano Toscano 10%, Ciliegiolo and/or Montepulciano 10%; (white) Trebbiano 50–70%, Grechetto 15–35%, Malvasia or Verdello up to 15%. Max. crop: 81 hl/ha. Min. alch: 12° for red, 11.5° for white. Average production: 117,000 cases. Price: 1,500–2,500 lire.

Virtually a one-man DOC, local tradition reshaped in modern terms by Dr. Giorgio Lungarotti (*see* above and Producers).

UMBRIA PRODUCERS

Fratelli Adanti

Arquata di Bevagna, 06031 Perugia.

DOC: Montefalco Rosso, Sagrantino. Others: Bianco d'Arquata, Rosato d'Arquata, Vin Santo. The Arquata estate is the quality leader for DOC Sagrantino di Montefalco. Its non-DOC Bianco d'Arquata shows signs of becoming one of central Italy's finest white wines.

Castello di Ascagnano

Pierantonio, 06015 Perugia.

DOC: Colli Altotiberini. Other: Merlot. The romantic summer hide-away of King Ludwig I of Bavaria is under the same direction as the Fattoria di Artimino in Tuscany. Only a select part of the 350,000-litre production of 89 acres is bottled.

Barberani

Orvieto, 05018 Terni.

Owner: Luigi Barberani. DOC: Orvieto Classico. Others: Lago di Corbara, Rosato Vallesanta. One of the best old firms in Orvieto, modernized and maintaining high standards. 22,000 cases of Orvieto, 6,500 cases of the others, from 75 acres. The superior Orvieto is called Le Cortone.

Luigi Bigi & Figlio

Ponte Giulio di Orvieto, 05018 Terni.

Founded: 1881. Now part of the Swiss Winefood group. DOC: Orvieto, Est! Est!! Est!!!, Vino Nobile di Montepulciano. Other: Rosso di Corbara. One of the best-known producers (with 220,000 cases) of several popular DOCs.

Decugnano dei Barbi

Corbara di Orvieto, 05018 Terni.

Owners: Casa Vinicola Barbi of Lombardy. DOC: Orvieto Classico. Others: Decugnano dei Barbi Brut *spumante*, Rosso Corbara. A conservative Orvieto maker but the wines are modern Orvieto's best.

La Fiorita (Lamborghini)

Macchie di Castiglione del Lago, 06060 Perugia.

Founded in 1970 by Ferruccio Lamborghini. DOC: Colli del Trasimeno. Other: Lamborghini Rosé. 27,500 cases of red Sangue di Miura, 22,000 of white Madonna del Busso, 5,500 cases of *rosato* from 370 acres. Lamborghini, better-known for his sports cars and tractors, has thrown himself with equal conviction into making wine.

Giorgio Lungarotti

Torgiano, 06089 Perugia.

Founded as a corporation in 1960. Owners: The Lungarotti family. DOC: Torgiano. Others: Cabernet Sauvignon di Miralduolo, Castel Grifone Rosato, Chardonnay, Rondo, Rosciano, Solleone. The creator of Torgiano as a DOC and one of Italy's greatest wine makers. Giorgio's daughter Teresa and oenologist Corrado Cantarelli now share the credit for continuing innovation. About 133,000 cases, or half the production of some 500 acres, is DOC Torgiano. The Rubesco Riserva Monticchio is the cream of this. Torre di Giano is the white. Cabernet (in a blend called San Giorgio) and Chardonnay are highly promising. Solleone is a sherry-style apéritif. *See also* DOC Torgiano and profile (opposite).

OTHER PRODUCERS

Belvedere
Villastrada Umbria, 06060 Perugia. Owner: Angelo Illuminati. DOC: Colli del Trasimeno.

Domenico Benincasa
Capro di Bevagna, 06031 Perugia. DOC: Sagrantino di Montefalco. Others: Capro Bianco, Rosso.

Centrale Cantine Cooperative
Orvieto, 05018 Terni. DOC: Orvieto.

Colle del Cardinale
Colle Umberto, 06070 Perugia. Colle del Cardinale Rosso.

Colle del Sole-Polidori
Pierantonio. 06015 Perugia. Owner: Carlo Polidori. DOC: Colli Altotiberini. Others: Rubino, Verdello. Polidori bottles an increasing proportion of a potential 33,000 cases from 100 acres of an area of growing interest.

Vincenzo Cotti
Castellunchio di Orvieto, 05018 Terni. DOC: Orvieto Classico. Other: Rosso dell'Umbria

CO.VI.P. (Consorzio Vitivinicolo Perugia)
Ponte Pattoli, 06080 Perugia. DOC: Colli del Trasimeno, Orvieto, Torgiano. Others: Bianco and Rosso d'Umbria. The consortium comprises 6 cooperatives with production of more than 2m. litres.

Enopolio di Foligno
Foligno, 06034 Perugia. Cooperative. DOC: Montefalco Rosso, Sagrantino. Other: Grechetto dell'Umbria.

Achille Lemmi
Montegabbione, 05010 Terni. DOC: Orvieto. Other: Montegiove.

Marchesi Patrizi Montoro (Castello di Montoro)
Montoro di Narni, 05020 Terni. DOC: none. Others: Castello di Montoro Bianco, Rosato and Rosso. The outstanding red is blended from Sangiovese, Merlot, Barbera and Montepulciano.

Silvio Nardi
Selci Lama, 06013 Perugia. DOC: Colli Altotiberini.

Papini
Allerona Scalo, 05010 Terni. DOC: Orvieto Classico.

Petrurbani
Orvieto, 05018 Terni. DOC: Orvieto Classico.

La Querciolana
Panicale, 06064 Perugia. Owner: Roberto Nesci. DOC: Colli del Trasimeno. Nesci sells his particularly good red under the name Grifo di Boldrino.

Fattoria San Littardo
Città della Pieve, 06062 Perugia. Owner: Ercole Lauro. DOC: Colli del Trasimeno.

Sasso Rosso
Assisi, 06082 Perugia. DOC: none. Other: Rosso di Assisi, a prize winner.

Adelio Tardioli
Campodonico di Spello, 06038 Perugia. DOC: Montefalco, Sagrantino. Others: Campodonico. Verdicchio dell'Umbria.

Cantina Sociale del Trasimeno
Castiglione del Lago, 06061 Perugia. Cooperative. DOC: Colli del Trasimeno. Other: Duca della Corgna Rosato.

Cantina Sociale Tudernum
Todi, 06059 Perugia. Cooperative. Greco di Todi, Tudernum Bianco, Rosso.

Tenuta Le Velette
Orvieto Stazione, 05019 Terni. DOC: Orvieto Classico. Other: Rosso Le Velette. A 16th-century estate restored and replanted in the 1960s; now making 65,000 cases, about two thirds Orvieto from 295 acres.

Ruggero Veneri
Spello, 06038 Perugia. No DOC. Other: Merlot. The best producer of unblended Merlot, which has a long tradition in Umbria. A warm, herb-scented wine, nicely soft after 5 years.

THE MARCHES

The central slice of the Adriatic coast, from the latitude of Florence to that of Orvieto, is probably even better known for its dry white Verdicchio than for the beaches and fishing boats that give the wine such a perfect context. The historic cities of Urbino in the north and Ascoli Piceno in the south of the region draw a proportion of its visitors inland, but the eastern flanks of the Apennines hardly rival the cultural crowd-pulling quality of Tuscany.

So the red wines of the Marches, potentially (sometimes actually) of Chianti quality, are less well known than they should be. The Montepulciano grape gives them a quality missing in most of those in Romagna to the north.

DOC AND OTHER WINES

Bianchello del Metauro

DOC. White wine. Province: Pesaro. Villages: valley of River Metauro. Grapes: Bianchello 95%, Malvasia 5%. Max. crop: 98 hl/ha. Min. alch: 11.5°. Average production: 94,500 cases. Price: 1,000–1,900 lire.

A pleasant sharp plain white from the north of the region, for drinking young with fish.

Bianco dei Colli Maceratesi

DOC. White wine. Provinces: Macerata and Ancona. Villages: Loreto and all of Macerata. Grapes: Trebbiano Toscano 50%, Maceratino 30–50%, Malvasia Toscana and Verdicchio 15%. Max. crop: 98 hl/ha. Min. alch: 11°. Average production: 31,000 cases. Price: 1,200–1,700 lire.

A minor DOC for another local dry seafood wine. Macerata is halfway from Ancona south to Ascoli Piceno.

Falerio dei Colli Ascolani

DOC. White wine. Province: Ascoli. Villages: all of province of Ascoli Piceno. Grapes: Trebbiano Toscano 80%, Passerina, Verdicchio, Malvasia Toscano, Pinot Bianco, Pecorino 20%. Max. crop: 98 hl/ha. Min. alch: 11.5°. Average production: 78,000 cases. Price: 1,000–2,000 lire.

Another of the local dry whites associated with restaurants on the beach.

Fontanelle

A Verdicchio of extra concentration and smoothness made by Tattà near Ascoli Piceno.

Montepulciano

Important in the Marches as a constituent grape of the best red wines, also sometimes sold unblended.

Rosso Cònero

DOC. Red wine. Province: Ancona. Villages: 5 communes in Ancona and part of 2 others. Grapes: Montepulciano 85%, Sangiovese 15%. Max. crop: 98 hl/ha. Min. alch: 11.5°. Average production: 190,000 cases. Price: 1,700–2,500 lire.

A full-strength, full-flavoured red from Monte Cònero, near the Adriatic just south of Ancona. One of the most flourishing of central and eastern Italy, with fruit to mellow and tannin to sustain it. Chianti methods are sometimes used to enrich and liven up the wine.

Rosso di Corinaldo

A particularly good Merlot and producer in the Verdicchio DOC area by the Cantina Sociale Val di Nevola (*see* Producers).

Rosso Piceno

DOC. Red wine. Provinces: Ancona, Ascoli Piceno, Macerata. Villages: a large number in the above provinces. Grapes: Sangiovese 60%, Montepulciano 40%. Max. crop: 98 hl/ha. Min. alch: 11.5°. *Superiore*, from a limited zone to the south, has 12°. Average production: 1.1m. cases.

The standard red of the southern half of the Marches, varying widely in quality from unremarkable to handmade and worth ageing, both in barrel and bottle. At its best it has Chianti-like weight and balance.

Sangiovese dei Colli Pesaresi

DOC. Red wine. Province: Pesaro. Villages: 30 communes and part of 6 others in and around Pesaro. Grapes: Sangiovese 85%, Montepulciano and/or Ciliegiolo 15%. Max. crop: 77 hl/ha. Min. alch: 11.5°. Average production: 167,000 cases.

A little-used DOC for a red of limited character. Sangiovese is frequently used for non-DOC reds.

Verdicchio dei Castelli di Jesi

DOC. White wine. Provinces: Ancona and Macerata. Villages: 17 communes and part of 5 others around the town of Jesi. Grapes: Verdicchio, Trebbiano Toscano and Malvasia. Max. crop: 105 hl/ha. Min. alch: 12°. Average production: 1m. cases.

The great commercial success of the Marches. Straightforward, dry, well balanced and clean; one of the earliest Italian whites to taste modern and international, thanks to the skill of its promoters, the firm of Fazi-Battaglia (*see* Producers). Their marketing flair produced the distinctive amphora-shaped bottle now seen among the fishnets in every Italian restaurant abroad. The Verdicchio is a tricky grape to grow but clearly has quality. The wine is short-lived, however, and bottles held too long in stock are often undrinkable. There is also a *champenoise* sparkling version.

Verdicchio di Matelica

DOC. White wine. Provinces: Macerata and Ancona. Villages: Matelica and 7 others. Grapes: Verdicchio, Trebbiano Toscano and Malvasia. Max. crop: 91 hl/ha. Min. alch: 12°. Average production: 67,000 cases.

Verdicchio from higher ground farther inland, said to be superior, but hardly ever seen abroad. Another (non-DOC) with a similar reputation is Verdicchio di Montanello.

Vernaccia di Serrapetrona

DOC. Red wine. Province: Macerata. Villages: Serrapetrona and part of Belforte del Chienti and San Severino Marche. Max. crop: 70 hl/ha. Min. alch: 11.5°. Average production: 11,000 cases. Price: 1,500–2,500 lire. (*méthode champenoise* 6,000–7,000).

A locally popular, normally sweet, sparkling red.

MARCHES PRODUCERS

M. Brunori & Figlio
Jesi, 60035 Ancona.

Owners: Mario and Giorgio Brunori. DOC: Verdicchio dei Castelli di Jesi. A few hundred cases of splendid Verdicchio from the tiny San Nicolò vineyard, planted in 1972.

Attilio Fabrini
Serrapetrona, 62020 Macerata.

DOC: Bianco dei Colli Maceratesi, Vernaccia di Serrapetrona *champenoise*. Others: Pian delle Mura Rosso, Verdicchio (still and *champenoise*). Fabrini began dedicating himself to wine in 1969. He now produces 4,000 cases of *champenoise* red and white and 4,500 of delicate still wines with the pride of a real craftsman.

Fazi-Battaglia Titulus
Castelplanio Stazione, 60032 Ancona.

Founded in 1949 by the Angelini family. DOC: Rosso Cònero, Rosso Piceno, Verdicchio dei Castelli di Jesi. Others: Rosato delle Marche, Sangiovese delle Marche. The house that devised the green amphora bottle that made Verdicchio famous. From 570 acres of company vines plus extra grapes bought in, Fazi-Battaglia makes 80% of the wine it sells; about 300,000 cases of Verdicchio and 33,000 cases of the others.

Garofoli
Loreto, 60025 Ancona.

Founded: 1871. Now run by 2 generations of Garofoli. Wine maker: Gaetano de Fusco. DOC: Rosso Cònero, Verdicchio dei Castelli di Jesi. A high-quality producer with 125 acres, supplemented to produce 133,000 cases, including a small amount of Verdicchio *champenoise*.

Monte Schiavo
Moie di Maiolati Spontini, 60032 Ancona.

DOC: Verdicchio dei Castelli di Jesi. The largest and most *avant-garde* Verdicchio producer concentrates quality on 24,000 cases from the 69-acre Colle del Sole vineyard.

Villa Pigna
Offida, 63035 Ascoli Piceno.

Founded about 1960. Owners: the Fratelli Rozzi. Wine maker: Rino Moretti. DOC: Falerio dei Colli Ascolani, Rosso Piceno. Others: Rosato, Villa Pigna Vellutato. With 150,000 cases from more than 600 acres of vines, Villa Pigna has quickly emerged as a model large-scale estate. A modern winery was built in 1979. Moretti also collaborates on a Verdicchio di Matelica sold under the Villa Pigna label.

Umani Ronchi
Osimo Scalo, 60028 Ancona.

Founded in 1960 by Gino Ronchi, now managed by the Bernetti brothers and part of the Swiss Winefood group. DOC: Rosso Cònero, Rosso Piceno, Verdicchio dei Castelli di Jesi. Others: Rosato delle Marche, Sangiovese delle Marche, Spumante Brut. One of the best-distributed brands of the Marches, producing 100,000 cases of good-quality estate-bottled wines from 180 acres of Verdicchio and 75 of Rosso Cònero. Other wines are made of bought-in grapes.

Cantina Sociale Val di Nevola
Corinaldo, 60013 Ancona.

Cooperative. DOC: Rosso Piceno, Verdicchio dei Castelli di Jesi. Others: Montepulciano, Rosato, Sangiovese and Trebbiano delle Marche, Rosso di Corinaldo, *spumanti*, table wines. The pride of this impressive cooperative is the non-DOC Rosso di Corinaldo, a very good Merlot. Price: 3,000 lire.

Villamagna
Contrada Montanello, 62100 Macerata.

Founded: 17th century. Owner and wine maker: Valeria Giacomini Compagnucci-Compagnoni. DOC: Bianco dei Colli Maceratesi, Rosso Piceno. Others: Rosato and Verdicchio di Montanello. The family company built new cellars in 1973 and has since made a name for some of the finest Rosso Piceno and Verdicchio on the market. About 2,200 cases of each wine are produced from 37 acres.

OTHER PRODUCERS

Anzilotti-Solazzi
Bonta di Saltara, 61030 Pesaro. Owners: Guglielmo Anzilotti and Giovanni Solazzi. DOC: Bianchello del Metauro, Sangiovese dei Colli Pesaresi.

Castelfiora
Loreto, 60025 Ancona. DOC: Rosso Cònero, Verdicchio dei Castelli di Jesi. Growing output of sound DOC wines.

Castellucci
Montecarotto, 60036 Ancona. Owners: Armando and Corrado Castellucci. DOC: Verdicchio dei Castelli di Jesi.

Cantina Sociale di Cupramontana
Cupramontana, 60034 Ancona. Cooperative. DOC: Rosso Piceno, Verdicchio dei Castelli di Jesi.

Italo Mattei
Matelica, 62024 Macerata. Owner: Mattei family. DOC: Verdicchio di Matelica. Other: Rosso Rubino di Matelica. About 4,000 cases.

La Monacesca
Civitanova Marche, 62012 Macerata. Owner: Casimiro Cifola. DOC: Verdicchio di Matelica.

Fattoria di Montesecco
Montesecco di Pergola, 61045 Pesaro. Owner-wine maker: Massimo Schiavi. No DOC. Other: Tristo di Montesecco. A unique, complex, dry, wood-aged white from Trebbiano, Malvasia, Riesling and Pinot Grigio.

Picenum (Consorzio Agrario Ascoli Piceno)
63100 Ascoli Piceno. Cooperative. DOC: Falerio dei Colli Ascolani, Rosso Piceno.

La Torraccia
Passo Sant'Angelo, 62020 Macerata. Owner: Piero Costantini. DOC: Bianco dei Colli Maceratesi, Rosso Piceno. Others: Bianco Anitori, Cabernet, Villa Saline.

Vallone
San Benedetto del Tronto, 63039 Ascoli Piceno. Owner: Vincenzo Vespasiani. DOC: Falerio dei Colli Ascolani, Rosso Piceno.

Vigna del Curato
Sappanico, 60100 Ancona. DOC: Rosso Piceno, Verdicchio dei Castelli di Jesi. Other: Moscato Nobile del Cònero. The vineyards and cellars of the ancient church, tended by Don Antonio Marinoni. His Rosso Piceno has finesse and charm.

Vinimar (Associazione Cantine Cooperative Marche)
Camerano, 60021 Ancona. A group of cooperatives bottling and selling all the region's DOC wines under the name Vinimar.

LATIUM

Rome can be compared with Vienna, as a capital city with wine so much in its veins that such artificial obstructions as bottles and corks have traditionally been foreign to it. The wine makers' taverns of Rome are slightly farther out of town than the *heurigen* of Vienna, but even more tempting as a summer outing, to the cool of the wooded Alban hills, or 'Castelli Romani' south of Rome. Frascati, the hub of the hills and their wine, has the air of a holiday resort. The spectacular Villa Aldobrandini and its beautiful gardens in the heart of Frascati show that the taste is patrician as well as popular.

Latium, both north and south of Rome, is pockmarked with volcanic craters, now placid lakes. The volcanic soil is highly propitious to the vine. The choice of grape varieties, presumably based on the Roman taste for soft young wines, has determined that they should remain local. The low acidity of the Malvasia, the grape that gives character to Frascati, makes it prone to disastrous oxidation once out of its cold damp cellar, without such modern tricks as pasteurization.

DOC AND OTHER WINES

Aleatico di Gradoli

DOC. Red wine. Province: Viterbo. Villages: Gradoli, Grotte di Castro, San Lorenzo Nuovo, Latera (in the hills above Lake Bolsena). Grape: Aleatico. Max. crop: 63 hl/ha. Min. alch: 12°. Average production: 4,400 cases.

A limited production of a local speciality: sweet red wine with a faintly Muscat aroma made at both normal strength and *liquoroso* (fortified to 17.5° alcohol).

Aprilia

DOC. Red, white and *rosato* wine. Provinces: Latina and Roma. Villages: Aprilia and Nettuno. Grapes: Merlot, Sangiovese or Trebbiano 95%. Max. crop: 90 hl/ha. Min. alch: 12°. Average production: 389,000 cases Price: 900–1,500 lire.

A vineyard area established by refugees from Tunisia after World War II. Merlot is reckoned its best product at 2 or 3 years of age. Although it was one of the first DOCs it still scarcely merits the dignity.

Bianco Capena

DOC. White wine. Province: Roma. Villages: Capena, Fiano Romano, Morlupo, Castelnuovo di Porto. Grapes: Malvasia di Candia, del Lazio and Toscana 55%, Trebbiano Toscano, Romagnolo and Giallo 25%, Bellone and Bombino up to 20%. Max. crop: 91 hl/ha. Min. alch: 11.5° (*superiore* 12°).

Similar white wine to that of the Castelli Romani (e.g. Frascati) but from just north of Rome instead of south.

Castel San Giorgio

Red and white table wines of above-average quality and value from the coastal plain near the mouth of the Tiber.

Castelli Romani

An umbrella (non-DOC) name for the verdant region, otherwise known as the Colli Albani, where Frascati and its peers are grown. Price: 1,000–1,300 lire.

Cerveteri

DOC. Red and white wine. Province: Roma. Villages: Cerveteri, Ladispoli, Santa Marinella, Civitavecchia, part of Allumiere, Rome, Tolfa and Tarquinia. Grapes: (red) Sangiovese and Montepulciano 60%, Cesanese Comune 25%, Canaiolo Nero, Carignano and Barbera 30%; (white) Trebbiano (Toscano, Romagnolo and Giallo) 50%, Malvasia 35%, Verdicchio, Tocai, Bellone and Bombino 15%. Max. crop: 108 hl/ha. Min. alch: 11.5° for white, 12° for red.

Sound standard dry wines from the country near the coast northwest of Rome.

Cesanese di Affile or Affile

DOC. Red wine. Province: Roma. Villages: Affile and Roiate, and part of Arcinazzo. Grapes: Cesanese di Affile and/or Cesanese Comune; Sangiovese, Montepulciano, Barbera, Trebbiano Toscano, Bombino Bianco 10%. Max. crop: 81 hl/ha. Min. alch: 12°. Average production: limited.

Neighbour and rival to Cesanese del Piglio.

Cesanese di Olevano Romano or Olevano Romano

DOC. Red wine. Province: Roma. Villages: Olevano Romano and part of Genazzano. Grapes: Cesanese di Affile and/or Cesanese Comune; Sangiovese, Montepulciano, Barbera, Trebbiano Toscano, Bombino Bianco 10%. Max. crop: 81 hl/ha. Min. alch: 12°. Average production: 11,000 cases.

A little closer to Rome but otherwise not to be distinguished from the other Cesaneses. All 3 were made DOCs in an excess of bureaucratic enthusiasm in 1973.

Cesanese del Piglio or Piglio

DOC. Red wine. Province: Roma. Villages: Piglio and Serrone, Acuto Anagni and Paliano. Grapes: Cesanese di Affile and/or Cesanese Comune: Sangiovese, Montepulciano, Barbera, Trebbiano Toscano or Bombino Bianco 10%. Max. crop: 81 hl/ha. Min. alch: 12°. Production: 50,000 cases.

Dry or sweet, still or sparkling red from a zone just to the left of the Autostrada del Sole, heading southeast 40 miles out of Rome, where ancient Anagni sits on its hilltop.

Colle Picchioni

Surprisingly good dry red of blended Merlot, Cesanese, Sangiovese and Montepulciano grapes, made in the traditionally white (i.e. Marino) country of the Castelli Romani. Price: 2,000 lire.

Colli Albani

DOC. White wine. Province: Roma. Villages: Ariccia and Albano, part of Rome, Pomezia, Castelgandolfo and Lanuvio. Grapes: Malvasia Rossa (or Bianca di Candia) 60%, Trebbiano Toscano, Verde and Giallo 25–50%, Malvasia del Lazio 15–40%. Max. crop: 108 hl/ha. Min. alch: 11.5° (*superiore* 12.5°). Average production: 444,000 cases. Price: 1,000–1,500 lire.

The local white of the Pope's summer villa (and that of the Emperor Domitian, too, on the same superb site with views west to the sea and east down to Lake Albano). Dry or sweet, still or fizzy.

Colli Lanuvini

DOC. White wine. Province: Roma. Villages: Genzano and part of Lanuvio. Grapes: Malvasia Bianca di Candia 70%, Trebbiano Toscano, Verde and Bianco 30%, Bellone and Bonvino 10%, Max. crop: 100 hl/ha. Min. alch: 11.5°. Average production: 167,000 cases.

A lesser-known but recommended dry white of the Castelli Romani. Genzano is on Lake Nemi, south of Lake Albano.

Cori

DOC. White and red wine. Province: Latina. Villages: Cisterna and Cori. Grapes (white) Malvasia di Candia 40–60%, Bellone 20–30%, Trebbiano Toscano 15–25%, Trebbiano Giallo 5–10%; (red) Montepulciano 40–60%, Nero Buono di Cori 20–40%, Cesanese 10–30%, Max. crop: 77 hl/ha. Min. alch: 11° for white, 11.5° for red. Average production: 4,450 cases.

Cori is south of the Castelli Romani where the country flattens towards the Pontine marshes. The red is soft and pleasant but rarely seen.

Est! Est!! Est!!!

DOC. White wine. Province: Viterbo. Villages: Montefiascone, Bolsena, San Lorenzo Nuovo, Grotte di Castro, Gradoli, Capodimonte and Marta. Grapes: Trebbiano Toscano 65%, Malvasia Bianca Toscana 20%, Rossetto 15%. Max. crop: 91 hl/ha. Min. alch: 11°. Average production: 111,000 cases. Price: 1,200–1,700 lire.

Large quantities of unpredictable wine take advantage of this, the earliest example of what is now called a fantasy name. The emphatic 'It is' was the first 3-star rating in history, antedating the Michelin guide by some 800 years. More recent inspectors have had less luck, but now modernization of techniques and taste is producing an acceptable, usually dry, white.

Falerno or Falernum

The most famous wine of ancient Rome, from the borders of Latium and Campania to the south. Then sweet and concentrated, now a good strong red of Aglianico and Barbera and a pleasant low-acid white. The red should really have a DOC.

Fiorano

The best of Rome's own wines, from one producer (*see* page 334) on the ancient Appian Way south of Rome. The red is Cabernet and Merlot like Bordeaux, the whites Malvasia di Candia and Sémillon. The wines are aged in wood and set a standard far above the local DOCs.

Frascati

DOC. White wine. Province: Roma. Villages: Frascati and part of Colonna, Montecompatri, Monteporzio Catone and Grottaferrata. Grapes: Malvasia Bianca di Candia, Malvasia del Lazio, Greco, Trebbiano Toscano, with up to 10% Bellone and Bonvino. Max. crop: 94 hl/ha. Min. alch: 11.5° (*superiore* 12°). Average production: 1.7m. cases. Price: 1,100–2,000 lire.

In legend and occasionally in fact the most memorable Italian white wine, though possibly the one that originated the notion of wines that 'do not travel', even the 20 miles to Rome. Malvasia on volcanic soil gives a splendid sensation of whole-grape ripeness, a golden glow to the wine, encouraged by fermenting it like red on its skins. The dry variety should be soft but highly charged with flavour, faintly nutty and even faintly salty. Sweeter (*amabile*) and sweeter still (*cannellino*) versions can be honeyed, too, but I would not count on it.

These are tasting notes made in a cool damp Frascati cellar. Notes on the bottled wine vary from neutral and sterile with no character to flat and oxidized to (occasionally) an approximation to the real thing. The best way to learn the difference between old-style and new-style Italian whites is to go to a restaurant in Frascati and order a bottle of a good brand, and also a jug of the house wine. Sadly the luscious qualities of the latter are the ones that do not travel. The best producers manage a very satisfactory compromise.

Marino

DOC. White wine. Province: Roma. Villages: Marino and part of Rome and Castelgandolfo. Grapes: Malvasia Rossa 60%, Trebbiano Toscano, Verde and Giallo 22–55%, Malvasia del Lazio 15–45%, Bonvino and Cacchione 10%. Max. crop: 108 hl/ha. Min. alch: 11.5° (*superiore* 12.5°). Average production: 611,000 cases. Price: 1,000–2,000 lire.

First cousin to Frascati, preferred by many Romans who dine out at Marino to drink it fresh and unbottled.

Montecompatri Colonna

DOC. White wine. Province: Roma. Villages: Colonna, part of Montecompatri, Zagarolo and Rocca Priora. Grapes: Malvasia 70%, Trebbiano 30%, Bellone, Bonvino 10%. Max. crop: 108 hl/ha. Min. alch: 11.5° (*riserva* 12.5°). Average production: 50,000 cases.

Another alternative to Frascati in the Castelli Romani.

Sangiovese di Aprilia

DOC. Red wine. Province: Latina. Villages: Aprilia, part of Cisterna, Latina and Nettuno. Grapes: Sangiovese 95%. Max crop: 84 hl/ha. Min. alch: 12°. Average production: included in Aprilia.

A strong dry *rosato*. *See* Aprilia.

Torre Ercolana

The highly recherché speciality of one producer (*see* Colacicchi) at Anagni (*see* Cesanese del Piglio). A red of Cesanese with Cabernet and Merlot, powerful in personality and maturing to outstanding quality. Price: 5,000–6,500 lire.

Trebbiano di Aprilia

DOC. White wine. Province: Latina. Villages: Aprilia, part of Cisterna, Latina and Nettuno. Grapes: Trebbiano 95%. Max. crop: 90 hl/ha. Min. alch: 12°. Average production: included in Aprilia.

Rather strong dull wine – *see* Aprilia.

Velletri

DOC. White and red wine. Province: Latina. Villages: Velletri, Lariano and part of Cisterna di Latina. Grapes: (white) Malvasia 70%, Trebbiano 30%, Bellone and Bonvino 10%; (red) Sangiovese 20–35%, Montepulciano 20–35%, Cesanese Comune 30%, Bombino Nero, Merlot and Ciliegiolo 10%. Max. crop: 100 hl/ha. Min. alch: 11.5° for white, 12° for red. Average production: 361,000 cases.

South of the Frascati zone of the Castelli Romani Velletri has a DOC for both its pleasant white and its mild red.

Zagarolo

DOC. White wine. Province: Roma. Villages: Zagarolo, Gallicano. Grapes: Malvasia 70%, Trebbiano 30%, Bellone and Bonvino up to 10%. Max. crop: 108 hl/ha. Min. alch: 11.5° (*superiore* 12.5°). Average production: 1,100 cases.

The smallest producer of the Frascati group, with similar white wine.

LATIUM PRODUCERS

Bruno Colacicchi

Anagni, 03012 Frosinone.

A family winery, made famous by the late Luigi Colacicchi, now run by his nephew Bruno. No DOC. Others: Romagnano (white), Torre Ercolana (red). The splendid red of Cabernet, Merlot and Cesanese, intense, long-lived and long on the palate, is one of Italy's rarest. Only about 200 cases are made from 4 acres.

Cantina Sociale Colli Albani (Fontana di Papa)

Cecchina, 00040 Roma.

Founded: 1959. A cooperative of 290 members with about 3,700 acres of vines and the potential to process about 20m. litres. DOC: Colli Albani. Others: Castelli Romani, Rosato, Rosso. Bottled wine is Fontana di Papa.

Fiorano

Divino Amore, 00134 Roma.

Founded in 1946 by Alberico Boncompagni Ludovisi, Principe di Venosa. No DOC. Others: Fiorano Bianco, Rosso. A perfectionist 5-acre estate which has proved that exceptional wine can be made in Rome. Fiorano Bianco is made of Malvasia di Candia grapes and Fiorano Rosso of Cabernet Sauvignon and Merlot. There is also a little Fiorano Sémillon. All are splendid but rare.

Fontana Candida

Monteporzio Catone, 00040 Roma.

DOC: Frascati. Part of the Swiss Winefood group, owning extensive vineyards, cellars and bottling plants in the Frascati DOC zone. It recently took over the Valle Vermiglia winery. The production of more than 350,000 cases includes a choice parcel of Vigneti Santa Teresa, one of the best of all Frascatis.

Cantina Produttori Frascati (San Matteo)

Frascati, 00044 Roma.

The central Frascati cooperative. DOC: Frascati. San Matteo is the label of the cooperative's selected wine sold in bottle – a reliable brand in the modern style.

Maccarese

Maccarese, 00057 Roma.

The vast estate adjacent to Rome's Fiumicino airport was owned by IRI, the state holding company, but was about to change hands after bankruptcy. No DOC. The wines are Castel San Giorgio Bianco, Rosso, Maccarese. The Rosso *riserva* is very good for a wine from the plain.

Paola di Mauro (Colle Picchioni)

Marino, 00040 Roma.

The small estate was bought by Paola di Mauro in 1968. DOC: Marino. Other: Colle Picchioni Rosso. From 7.5 acres, 1,800 cases of a remarkable traditional Marino and 400 cases of one of Rome's rare fine reds.

Italo Mazziotti

Bolsena, 01023 Viterbo.

An old family winery. DOC: Est! Est!! Est!!! di Montefiascone. Other: Bolsena Rosso. Mazziotti is a keen oenologist and grower. From his 60 acres he makes one of the rare Est! Est!! Est!!! worthy of exclamation marks.

OTHER PRODUCERS

Cantina Sociale di Aprilia (Enotria)
Aprilia, 04010 Latina. A huge cooperative with a plant capacity of 26.5m. litres or 3m. cases. DOC: Aprilia. Other: table wines. Aprilia Merlot, Sangiovese and Trebbiano are sold with the Enotria label.

Cantina Cenatiempo
Formia, 04023 Latina. No DOC. Others: Cecubo, Falerno, Falernum. The modern versions of the ancient wines.

Cantina Sociale Cesanese del Piglio
Piglio, 03010 Frosinone. Cooperative. DOC: Cesanese del Piglio.

Colli di Catone
Monteporzio Catone, 00040 Roma. DOC: Frascati.

Cantina Sociale Colli del Cavaliere
Aprilia, 04010 Latina. Cooperative. DOC: Aprilia. Others: Colli del Cavaliere Bianco, Rosso.

Colle Rubro
Genzano, 00045 Roma. Owner: Maurizio Ferdinandi. DOC: Colli Lanuvini.

CO.PRO.VI (Consorzio Produttori Vini Velletri)
Velletri, 00049 Roma. Cooperative. DOC: Velletri Bianco, Rosso. Other: Castelli Romani Rosato.

Cantina Sociale di Frascati (Colli di Tuscolo)
Frascati, 00044 Rome, Cooperative. DOC: Frascati. The Colli di Tuscolo brand is used for bottled Frascati.

Cantina Oleificio Sociale di Gradoli
Gradoli, 01010 Viterbo. Cooperative. DOC: Aleatico di Gradoli. Other: Greghetto.

Cantina Sociale Cooperative di Marino (Gotto d'Oro)
Frattocchie di Marino, 00040 Roma. Founded: 1945. A cooperative of more than 450 members with about 3,200 acres of vines. DOC: Frascati, Marino. Others: Rosato and Rosso Rubino dei Castelli Romani. Of a potential production of more than 2m. cases, about 250,000 cases are sold with the Gotto d'Oro label.

Fratelli Mennuni
Frascati, 00044 Roma. Owners: Michele and Giorgio Mennuni. DOC: Frascati. Other: table wines. Producers of more than 100,000 cases of good Frascati.

Monte Giove
Cecchina, 00040 Roma. Owner: Raimondo Moncada. DOC: Colli Lanuvini.

Cantina di Montefiascone
Montefiascone, 01027 Viterbo. Cooperative. DOC: Est! Est!! Est!!! di Montefiascone. Others: Colli Etrusco Bianco, Rosso.

Cantina Sociale di Monteporzio Catone
Monteporzio Catone, 00040 Roma. Cooperative. DOC: Frascati.

San Clemente
Velletri, 00049 Roma. DOC: Frascati, Velletri Bianco, Rosso. Others: San Clemente Bianco, Rosso, San Clemente Brut, Moscato Amabile.

La Selva
Paliano. 03018 Frosinone. Owners: The Ruffo di Calabria family. DOC: Cesanese del Piglio. Other: La Selva.

Società Lepanto CEPAI
Frattocchie, 00040 Roma DOC: Frascati, Marino. The Frascati is called Castel de' Paolis, the Marino Due Santi.

Conte Vaselli
Castiglione in Teverina, 01024 Viterbo. DOC: Orvieto Classico. Others: Rosso Castiglione, Santa Giulia del Poderaccio.

Conte Zandotti (Tenimento San Paolo)
00132 Roma. Owned by the Zandotti family since 1734. DOC: Frascati. Estate-bottled Frascati Superiore. 55 acres.

ABRUZZI

The Apennines rise to their climax in the 9,000-foot Gran Sasso d'Italia, which towers over L'Aquila ('The Eagle'), the capital of the Abruzzi. Mountains only subside close to the sea, where Pescara is the principal town. Close as it is to Rome, the Abruzzi is a backward region with simple ideas about wine. One of them, attachment to the red Montepulciano as chief grape, is a good one. Here and in the even more rural Molise to the south this grape makes wine of vigour and style, if not refinement. Whites at present are not remarkable, but only because the Trebbiano is the standard grape.

DOC WINES

Cerasuolo

See Montepulciano d'Abruzzo.

Montepulciano d'Abruzzo

DOC. Red wine. Provinces: Chieti, Aquila, Pescara, Teramo. Villages: many communes. Grapes: Montepulciano, plus Sangiovese up to 15%. Max. crop: 98 hl/ha. Min. alch: 12°. Average production: 2.2m. cases. Aged for 2 years or more is *vecchio*. Price: 1,500–2,500 lire.

The production zone for this excellent red stretches along most of the coastal foothills and back into the mountains along the valley of the river Pescara (where Sulmona has a particular reputation for its wine). Standards in this large area vary widely, but Montepulciano at its best is as satisfying, if not as subtle, as any Italian red – full of colour, life and warmth. Cerasuolo is the name for its DOC *rosato* – a pretty wine with plenty of flavour.

Trebbiano d'Abruzzo

DOC. White wine. Province: throughout the Abruzzi region. Villages: suitable (not too high) vineyards in the whole region. Grapes: Trebbiano d'Abruzzo, and/or Trebbiano Toscano; Malvasia Toscana, Coccociola and Passerina up to 15%. Max. crop: 98 hl/ha. Min. alch: 11.5°. Production: 333,000 cases.

A standard mild dry white, except in the case of Valentini (*see* Producers).

ABRUZZI PRODUCERS

Duchi di Castelluccio (Scali Caracciolo)

Scafa, 65027, Pescara.

Founded in 1971 by Francesco Scali. DOC: Montepulciano and Trebbiano d'Abruzzo. The winery has established a sterling reputation since its first vintage in 1974. Its 65,000 cases (from 98 acres plus 25 leased) are models of Abruzzi red and white; lively and satisfying wines. The red has more to say than the white.

Santoro Colella

Pratola Peligna, 67035 L'Aquila.

DOC: Montepulciano and Trebbiano d'Abruzzo. Others: Pinot Grigio, Riesling, Traminer, Veltliner. Colella is an innovative producer in the Val Peligna, high in the Apennines. His unusual whites are being watched with interest.

Emilio Pepe

Torano Nuovo, 64010 Teramo.

DOC: Montepulciano and Trebbiano d'Abruzzo. Pepe runs his family winery with almost eccentric devotion. 3,300 cases, crushed only by foot and aged only in bottle.

Scialletti

Cologna Paese di Roseto, 64020 Teramo.

Founded: 1884; run by Antonio Scialletti and his son Vincenzo. DOC: Montepulciano and Trebbiano d'Abruzzo. Others: Sammaro Bianco, Rosso. The best grapes from the family estate are selected for about 5,000 cases.

Casal Thaulero

Roseto degli Abruzzi, 64026 Teramo.

Cooperative. DOC: Montepulciano and Trebbiano d'Abruzzo. The winery, with a capacity of 1.7m. cases, bottles 35,000–40,000 of Montepulciano exemplary for sound quality on a large scale.

Edoardo Valentini

Loreto Aprutino, 65014 Pescara.

DOC: Montepulciano and Trebbiano d'Abruzzo. Valentini selects the best grapes from his 125 acres in the best years (selling the rest) to make 1,500–1,800 cases of artisan wine of the highest order, including a singular aged Trebbiano.

OTHER PRODUCERS

Nestore Bosco
56100 Pescara. DOC: Montepulciano and Trebbiano d'Abruzzo.

Vinicola Casacanditella (Rosso della Quercia)
Casacanditella, 66010 Chieti. Founded in 1975 by Giuseppe di Camillo and Ilio Mauro. DOC: Montepulciano d'Abruzzo. 35,000 cases of 'Rosso della Quercia' from selected grapes.

Barone Cornacchia
Torano Nuovo, 64010 Teramo. Owner: Piero Cornacchia. DOC: Montepulciano and Trebbiano d'Abruzzo.

Lucio di Giulio (Cantalupo)
Tocco di Casauria, 65028 Pescara. DOC: Montepulciano d'Abruzzo.

Dino Illuminati (Fattoria Nicò)
Controguerra, 64010 Teramo. DOC: Montepulciano and Trebbiano d'Abruzzo.

Vittorio Janni
67100 L'Aquila. DOC: Montepulciano and Trebbiano d'Abruzzo.

Camillo Montori
Controguerra, 64010 Teramo. DOC: Montepulciano and Trebbiano d'Abruzzo.

Tenuta Sant'Agnese
Città Sant'Angelo, 65013 Pescara. Owner: Nunzio Acciavatti. The red Rubino and white Spinello, though qualified to be Montepulciano and Trebbiano d'Abruzzo, are not DOC.

Cantina Sociale di Tollo
Tollo, 66010 Chieti. Cooperative. DOC: Montepulciano and Trebbiano d'Abruzzo.

CAMPANIA

The region of Naples and the Sorrento peninsula may have been cynical about the taste of tourists in the past, and left some of its visitors with a nasty taste in their mouths, but in many ways it is superbly adapted for wine-growing. Volcanic soils, the temperate influence of the sea and the height of its mountains give a range of excellent sites. Its own grapes have character and perform well. The red Aglianico (the name comes from Hellenico) and white Greco both refer in their names to the Greeks who presumably imported or at least adopted them in pre-Roman times. Quality wines are made at Ravello on the Sorrento peninsula, on the island of Ischia, and above all in the Irpinian hills north of Avellino, east of Naples, where the Mastroberardino winery has done more than anyone for the reputation of the region. Good wine is still very much in a minority, but it deserves recognition.

DOC AND OTHER WINES

Asprino

A light, sharp, low-alcohol, café white wine which comes as a surprise in this warm climate.

Biancolella

A white grape of the coast and its wine, especially from Ischia. Unblended it is almost astringently dry and refreshing: good with a squirt of soda.

Capri

DOC. White and red wine. Province: Sorrento. Area: the island of Capri and some nearby mainland vineyards. Grapes: (white) Falanghina and Greco, plus others up to 20%; (red) Piedirosso, plus others up to 20%. Max. crop: 84 hl/ha. Min. alch: 11° for white, 11.5° for red. Production: 6,100 cases.

A small supply of adequate dry white and a minute supply (550 cases) of light red to drink young are lucky enough to have this romantic name.

Falerno

The favourite wine of ancient Rome, as Falernum (*see under* Latium); now an Aglianico red made near the borders of the 2 regions. Price: 1,800–2,500 lire.

Fiano di Avellino

DOC. White wine. Province: Avellino. Villages: Avellino and surrounding communes. Grapes: Fiano di Avellino and up to 15% others. Max. crop: 70 hl/ha. Min. alch: 11.5°. Average production: 3,300 cases. Price: 5,500–6,000 lire.

One of the best white wines of the south, light yellow and nutty in scent and flavour with liveliness and length. It also goes by the name of Apianum, a Latin reference to bees, which apparently appreciated either its flowers or grapes – or juice.

Gragnano

A fruity, quite light, sometimes fizzy red from Gragnano near Ravello.

Gran Furor Divina Costiera

A perfectly dreadful red, white and *rosato*, but its resounding name and period-piece label make it unforgettable.

Greco di Tufo

DOC. White wine. Province: Avellino. Villages: Tufo and 9 other communes in the hills of Irpinia 40 miles east of Naples. Grapes: Greco di Tufo 80–100%, Coda di Volpe Bianco 20%. Max. crop: 70 hl/ha. Min. alch: 11.5°. Average production: 16,000 cases. Price: 4,000–5,000 lire.

White wine of positive character, a little neutral to smell but mouth-filling with a good 'cut' in the flavour which makes it highly satisfactory with flavoury food. Some bouquet develops with 2–3 years in bottle. It can also be made *spumante*.

Lacrimarosa d'Irpinia

A very pale coppery *rosato* of good quality, aromatic to smell, faintly underripe to taste, made of Aglianico by Mastroberardino (*see* Producers).

Ischia

DOC. Red and white wine. Province: the island of Ischia. Villages: throughout the island. Grapes: (red) Guarnaccia 50%, Piedirosso (alias Per'e Palummo) 40%, Barbera 10%; (white) Forastera 65%, Biancolella 20%, others 15%; (Bianco Superiore) Forastera 50%, Biancolella 40%, San Lunardo 10%. Max. crop: 72 hl/ha. Min. alch: 11° for white, 11.5° for red. Average production: 244,000 cases. Price: 1,200–2,000 lire.

The standard red and white of this green island in the Bay of Naples are made to drink young and fresh. The white should be sharp enough to quench thirst. Bianco Superiore is sometimes fermented in the old way on its skins and becomes substantial, dry, golden and rather striking. Don Alfonzo (*see* Perrazzo under Producers) is a good non-DOC brand from the island.

Lacryma Christi del Vesuvio

Probably the most famous name without DOC dignity, perhaps because nobody can pin it down. It comes in all colours, flavours and qualities, officially from the slopes of Mt. Vesuvius. Good examples (Mastroberardino's and Saviano's, for example) include a very dry full-coloured red of most agreeable structure and texture but no taste or smell to put a name to, and a light golden white with a promising southern richness of smell but a disappointingly flat taste. The *rosato* can be fruity.

Lettere

A DOC of the future for quite mild but well-made dry red from the Sorrento peninsula.

Per'e Palummo

The alternative name of the Piedirosso grape, meaning 'dove's foot', applied to one of Ischia's best reds, refreshingly tannic and a shade 'grassy' to smell.

Ravello

Surely a future DOC. Red, white and *rosato*, each good of its kind, from the terraced vineyards leading up to the ravishing hilltop town of Ravello. Sea mists, I suspect, keep the wines fresh. The Caruso family also provide the entrancing Hotel Belvedere in which to enjoy the wines.

Antonio Mastroberardino, who with his brother Walter has proved conclusively with their Taurasi, Greco di Tufo and Fiano di Avellino that Campania can make wines of distinct and excellent character

Solopaca

DOC. Red and white wine. Province: Benevento. Villages: Solopaca and 10 neighbouring communes. Grapes: (red) Sangiovese 45–50%, Aglianico 10–20%, Piedirosso 20–25%, Sciascinoso 10%; (white) Trebbiano Toscano 50–70%, Malvasia di Candia 40–20%, Malvasia Toscano and Coda di Volpe 10%. Max. crop: 105 hl/ha. Min. alch: 11.5° for red, 12° for white. Average production: 115,000 cases.

A little-known DOC zone north of Naples with decent red but rather dreary white.

Taurasi

DOC. Red wine. Province: Avellino. Villages: Taurasi and 16 other communes in the Irpinia hills east of Naples. Grapes: Aglianico about 80%, Piedirosso, Sangiovese and Barbera 30% max. Max. crop: 77 hl/ha. Min. alch: 12°. Aged for not less than 3 years, 4 for *riserva*. Average production: 10,000 cases. Price: 2,000–4,000 lire (*riserva* 4,000–6,000).

Possibly the best red of southern Italy, at least as made by Mastroberardino (*see* Producers). Aglianico ripens late in these lofty vineyards to make a firm wine of splendidly satisfying structure, still dark in colour even when mature at 5 years. It has a slightly roasted richness without being at all port-like. First class but impossible to pin down by comparisons.

CAMPANIA PRODUCERS

d'Ambra Vini d'Ischia

Panza d'Ischia, 80070 Napoli.

Founded in the late 19th century by Francesco d'Ambra; now part of the Swiss Winefood group. DOC: Ischia. Others: Amber Drops, Biancolella, Forastera, Per'e Palummo. The firm makes about 140,000 cases at 2 modern wineries on the island. Its 'tourist' wines include the dreadful 'Gran Furor Divina Costiera' (*see* wines).

P. Caruso

Ravello, 84010 Sorrento.

Founded: 1896; owned by the Caruso family. No DOC. Others: Gran Caruso Ravello Bianco, Rosato, Rosso. Well-made red and a 'fish' white of style made by the owners of the lovely Hotel Belvedere at Ravello.

Episcopio

Ravello, 84010 Sorrento.

Founded: 1860; owned by the Vuilleumier family. No DOC. Others: Episcopio Ravello Bianco, Rosato, Rosso. The most impressive wines of the Amalfi coast: the white crisp *rosato* full but refreshing.

Mastroberardino

Atripalda, 83042 Avellino.

Founded in 1878 as a continuation of a long-standing business; now run by Antonio and Walter Mastroberardino. DOC: Fiano di Avellino, Greco di Tufo, Taurasi. Others: Irpinia Bianco, Rosso, Lacrimarosa d'Irpinia, Lacryma Christi del Vesuvio. From 125 acres of family-owned vines and 173 acres of others under contract, Tonino Mastroberardino, the oenologist, makes 80,000 cases. The barrel-aged white Fiano and red Taurasi are the cream of their range, whose overall quality makes the firm the leading name in wine in the south of Italy.

Perrazzo Vini d'Ischia

Porto d'Ischia, 80077 Napoli.

Founded in 1880 by Don Alfonzo Perrazzo. DOC: Ischia. Others: Don Alfonzo Bianco, Rosato, Rosso. The Ischia Bianco Superiore is noteworthy.

Molise

Molise, a slice of central Italy stretching from the Apennines to the Adriatic, is a newcomer to Italy's wine map. Bottles, with labels on, are a relative novelty in a land of bulk production.

The first Molise DOCs date from 1983. They are Biferno, for red and white wine from 41 communes in the Biferno Valley; and Pentro, for red and white wines from 16 communes in the hills around Isernia. Both specify Montepulciano for red, in Biferno it is the dominant variety, in Pentro it is used half and half with Sangiovese. Both whites are based on Trebbiano Toscano. Both allow the addition of Bombino, in Biferno Malvasia Bianco may also be added.

One outstanding Molise winery, and one of the most modern in Italy, is **Masseria di Majo Norante** (Campomarino, 86023 Campobasso). The dynamic Luigi di Majo built the complex from scratch on his wife's family's vast seaside estates in the mid-1970s. His Montepulciano is as good as the best of Abruzzo, and Ramitello is a bargain in tasty everyday reds. He also makes Trebbiano del Molise, Rosato and Frizzante.

Other Molise producers include:

Sera Meccaglia

Pietracatella, 86040 Campobasso. Montepulciano, Sangiovese, Trebbiano and Vernaccia de Serra Meccaglia.

Colle Sereno

Petrella Tifernin, 86024 Campobasso. Tifernum Bianco, Rosato, Rosso. The red, of Sangiovese, Montepulciano and Aglianico, is the best.

Cantina Valbiferno

Guglioesi, 86024 Campobasso. Cooperative. Bianco and Rosso di Molise, Valbiferno. The region's largest winery, processing some 8m. litres a year.

APULIA

The heel and hamstrings of Italy are its most productive wine regions. Their historic role has been to supply strength and colour for more famous but frail wines in blending vats farther north. The reds are very red indeed, very strong and often inclined to portiness. The whites are the faceless background to vermouth. This is the one region where the best wines until recently were the rosés – or at least some of them.

The Salento Peninsula, the heel from Taranto southeastwards, is the hottest region. A few producers here are learning to moderate the strength and density of their reds to make good-quality winter-warming wines – though a bottle still goes a long way. Their grapes are the Primitivo (possibly California's Zinfandel) and the Negroamaro – 'bitter black'. North of Taranto the hills have well-established DOCs for dry whites, originally intended as vermouth base-wines, but with modern techniques increasingly drinkable as 'fish' wines on their own. As elsewhere in Italy the existence of a DOC is better evidence of tradition than of quality. There is more interest in the fact that even in this intemperate region successful spots have recently been found to plant superior northern grapes – even Chardonnay (*see* Favonio under Apulia Producers).

Much the best-known DOC is Castel del Monte, and this largely due to the crisp *rosato* of Rivera – for many years one of Italy's best. The list of producers shows that things are changing: Apulian reds are no longer ashamed of their origin.

DOC AND OTHER WINES

Aleatico di Puglia

DOC. Red wine. Provinces: Bari, Brindisi, Foggia, Lecce, Taranto. Area: the whole of Apulia. Grapes: Aleatico 85%, Negroamaro, Malvasia Nera and Primitivo 15%. Max. crop: 52 hl/ha. Min. alch: 13° plus 2° of sugar for *dolce naturale*; 16° plus 2.5° of sugar for *liquoroso*. Average production: *liquoroso* 670 cases, *dolce naturale* limited. Aged 3 years for *riserva*.

A dessert wine, approaching ruby port in its fortified (*liquoroso*) version. Of small supply and of local interest only.

Alezio

A very recent DOC for the red and *rosato* of the tip of Italy's heel, made from Negroamaro and Malvasia Rossa and every inch a southern red, dark and powerful. It is moot whether to try ageing it or to take it on the chin as it is. Like many Apulian *rosatos* the paler wine has more immediate appeal. Various names are used, including Doxi Vecchio, Portulano, Rosa del Golfo.

Brindisi

DOC. Red wine. Province: Brindisi. Villages: Brindisi and Mesagna, just inland. Grapes: Negroamaro, others up to 30%. Max. crop: 105 hl/ha. Min. alch: 12° (12.5° and 2 years' ageing for *riserva*). Average production: no figures yet available.

The local red of Brindisi, made DOC in 1980 and also available as a dry *rosato*.

Cacc'e Mmitte di Lucera

DOC. Red wine. Province: Foggia. Villages: communes of Lucera, Troia and Biccari. Grapes: Uva di Troia 35–65%, Montepulciano, Sangiovese and Nera Malvasia 25–35%, others 15–30%. Max. crop: 91 hl/ha. Min. alch: 11.5°. Average production: 4,450 cases.

Scholars tell us that the dialect name refers to a local form of '*governo*', in which fresh grapes are added to the fermenting must. The DOC is new, and little is made, so whether this fruity young red will become an international tongue-twister remains to be seen.

Castel Mitrano

An individual producer's (*see* Mitrano) well-made dry red, much improved by keeping.

Castel del Monte

DOC. Red, *rosato* and white wine. Province: Bari. Villages: Minervino Murge and parts of 9 other communes. Grapes: (red) Uva di Troia 70%, Bombino Nero, Montepulciano and Sangiovese 35%; (white) Pampanuto 70%, Trebbiano Toscano, Trebbiano Giallo, Bombino Bianco and Palumbo 35%, (*rosato*) Bombino Nero with up to 35% Uva di Troia and Montepulciano. Max. crop: 84 hl/ha. Min. alch: 11.5° for white and *rosato*, 12° for red. Aged 1 year in wood for *riserva*. Average production: 444,000 cases. Price: 1,500–2,000 lire.

Castel del Monte, the octagonal fortress of the medieval Hohenstaufens, lies 30 miles west of Bari near Minervino Murge. The leading DOC of Apulia takes its name for an outstanding red and famous *rosato*. The red has a fat, inviting smell and considerable depth and vitality, with a certain bite and long pruney finish. Rivera's Il Falcone is the best example. The pale *rosato* has long been popular all over Italy for balanced force and freshness.

Copertino

DOC. Red wine. Province: Lecce. Villages: Copertino and 5 other communes. Grapes: Negroamaro, plus others up to 30%. Max. crop: 98 hl/ha. Min. alch: 12° (12.5° and 2 years' ageing for *riserva*). Average production: 167,000 cases.

A warmly recommended red made in some quantity south of Lecce on Italy's heel. The *riserva* is said to be smooth with plenty of flavour and a bitter touch.

Donna Marzia

The next town to Copertino, Leverano, produces another good Negroamaro red and a surprisingly aromatic and ageable Malvasia white. The producer is Zecca (q.v.).

Favonio

One of the most revolutionary estates in the south of Italy, using California-style ideas to make fine-quality Pinot Bianco, Chardonnay, Cabernet Franc. The producer is Simonini (*See* Producers).

Five Roses

A powerful dry *rosato* from Leone de Castris (*see* Producers), so named by American soldiers who gave it one more rose than a famous Bourbon whiskey.

Gioia del Colle (or Primitivo di Gioia)

Gioia is halfway from Bari south to Taranto. The Primitivo gives a pretty brutal red in these hot hills. With age it becomes more politely overwhelming.

Gravina

DOC. White wine. Province: Bari. Village: Commune of Gravina near the border of Basilicata. Grape: Verdeca. No other details yet available.

Leverano

DOC. Red, *rosato*, white wine. Province: Lecce. Villages: commune of Leverano. Grapes: (red) Negroamaro, plus others up to 35%; (white) Malvasia Bianco, plus others up to 35%. Max. crop: 67 hl/ha. Min. alch: white 11°, *rosato* 11.5°, red 12° (12.5° aged 2 years is *riserva*). No other figures yet available.

One of the 1980 class of DOCs for Salento wines of so far unknown merit.

Locorotondo

DOC. White wine. Provinces: Bari and Brindisi. Villages: Locorotondo, Cisternino and part of Fasano. Grapes: Verdeca 50–65%; Bianco di Alessano 35–50%; Fiano, Bombino, Malvasia Toscana 5%. Max. crop: 91 hl/ha. Min. alch: 11°. Average production: 111,000 cases. Price: 1,200–1,600 lire.

Locorotondo is famous for its round stone dwellings. With Martina Franca it lies east of Bari at the neck of the Salento peninsula. Serious efforts are made to keep its white wine fresh and brisk. Burton Anderson strongly favours the output of the Cantina Sociale (cooperative).

Martina or Martina Franca

DOC. White wine. Provinces: Taranto, Bari and Brindisi. Villages: Martina Franca and Alberobello, and part of Ceglie Messapico and Ostuni. Grapes: Verdeca 50–65%, Bianco di Alessano 35–50%, Fiano Bombino and Malvasia Toscana 5%. Max. crop: 91 hl/ha. Min. alch: 11°. Average production: 78,000 cases.

Grapes and wine amount to much the same thing as Locorotondo.

Matino

DOC. *Rosato* and red wine. Province: Lecce. Villages: Matino and part of 7 other communes in the Murge Salentino, at the tip of Italy's heel. Grapes: Negroamaro 70%, Sangiovese and Malvasia Nera 30%. Max. crop: 78 hl/ha. Min. alch: 11.5° for *rosato* and red. Average production: 39,000 cases.

An early (1971) DOC but still obscure.

Moscato di Trani

DOC. White wine. Province: Bari. Villages: Trani and 11 other communes. Grapes: Moscato Bianco (or 'Reale'), plus other Muscats up to 15%. Max. crop: 52 hl/ha. Min. alch: 13° plus 2° of sugar for *dolce naturale*; 16° plus 2° of sugar for *liquoroso*. Average production: 5,500 cases.

Sweet golden dessert Muscats of good quality, fortified or not, from the north coast west of Bari. Other Apulian Muscats, particularly those of Salento, can also be very drinkable.

Negroamaro

One of the principal local black grapes (the name means 'bitter black') of Apulia. It seems to have certain inherent qualities – apart from blackness and bitterness – which make good wine possible. Some Salento wines are labelled with the name.

Ostuni and Ottavianello di Ostuni

DOC. White and red wine. Province: Brindisi. Villages: Ostuni, Carovigno, S. Vito dei Normanni, S. Michele Salentino and part of 3 other communes, including Brindisi. Grapes: (white) Impigno 50–85%, Francavilla 15–50%, Bianco di Alessandro and Verdeca 10%; Ottavianello: Ottavianello grapes. Max. crop: 77 hl/ha. Min. alch: 11° for Ostuni, 11.5° for Ottavianello. Average production: 24,400 cases.

The unusual white grapes give a very pale mild and dry 'fish' wine; Ottavianello is a cheerful cherry-red dry wine, pleasant to drink cool.

Primitivo di Manduria

DOC. Red wine. Provinces: Taranto, Brindisi. Villages: Manduria and 19 other communes along the south coast of Salento. Grape: Primitivo. Max. crop: 63 hl/ha. Min. alch: 14° for Primitivo di Manduria; 13° plus 3° of sugar for *dolce naturale*; 15° plus 2.5° of sugar for *liquoroso dolce naturale*; 16.5° plus 1.5° of sugar for *liquoroso secco*. Average production: 220,000 cases. Aged 2 years for *liquoroso* types.

The Primitivo, which may well be the same grape as California's Zinfandel, makes blackstrap reds here, some sweet and some even fortified, as though 14° were not enough. You may age them or not, depending on whether you appreciate full-fruit flavour or just full flavour.

Rosa del Golfo

A particularly good Alezio (q.v.) from Giuseppe Calò (*see* Producers).

Rosato del Salento

Rosatos are perhaps the best general produce of the Salento peninsula. It is not a DOC but this name is widely used. Price: 1,000–1,500 lire.

DOCG – Denominazione di Origine Controllata e Garantita

After several years of debate the new top level Denominazione for Italian wines was published in May 1982, though not signed by the President till the following year.

The first DOCs to be granted the additional distinction (and responsibilities) of being 'guaranteed' are Barolo, Barbaresco, Brunello di Montalcino, Vino Nobile di Montepulciano and Chianti (Classico and Putto). The first year the decree will have effect will be the 1983 vintage. The first DOCG wines to be sold will therefore be Chiantis of this vintage in 1985. DOCG *reserva* will first appear in 1987.

It can be assumed that the more stringent regulations concerning each stage of the process from vineyard to consumer will increase the prices of DOCG wines. Until they appear it is impossible to tell whether producers in these areas will be willing (or indeed able) to raise their standards correspondingly. For many the temptation must be to ignore the official regulations and follow the route of those who successfully make luxurious *vino da tavola* without restriction.

Rosso Barletta

DOC. Red wine. Provinces: Bari and Foggia. Villages: Barletta and 4 other communes. Grapes: Uva di Troia, plus others up to 30%. Max. crop: 105 hl/ha. Min. alch: 12°. Average production: 5,600 cases. '*Invecchiato*' if aged for 2 years. Price: 1,200–1,600 lire.

Some drink this relatively light red young and cool – others age it moderately and treat it like claret.

Rosso Canosa

DOC. Red wine. Province: Bari. Village: Canosa di Puglia. Grapes: Uva di Troia 65%, others 35%. Max. crop: 98 hl/ha. Min. alch: 12° (12.5° plus 2 years' ageing for *riserva*). Average production: no figures yet available.

Canosa, between Bari and Foggia, was the Roman Canusium (an alternative name for the wine). Its wine is in a similar style to Rosso Barletta.

Rosso di Cerignola

DOC. Red wine. Provinces: Foggia and Bari. Villages: Cerignola, Stornara, Stornarella, part of Ascoli Satriano (east of Foggia). Grapes: Uva di Troia 55%, Negroamaro 15–30%, Sangiovese, Barbera, Montepulciano, Malbec and Trebbiano Toscano 15%. Max. crop: 98 hl/ha. Min. alch: 12° (13° aged 2 years in wood is *riserva*). Average production: 3,300 cases.

A big dry heady red with faint bitterness.

Primitive harvesting methods in Apulia

Salice Salentino

DOC. Red and *rosato* wine. Provinces: Brindisi and Lecce. Villages: Salice Salentino and 5 other communes in the centre of the Salento peninsula. Grapes: Negroamaro plus up to 20% others. Max. crop: 98 hl/ha. Min. alch: 12.5° (*riserva* after 2 years), 12° for *rosato* (*invecchiato* after 1 year). Production: 220,000 cases. Price: 1,500–2,200 lire (*riserva* 3,000).

Typically big-scale southern reds with a porty undertone accompanied by a balancing measure of astringency. I have found this a rather clumsy wine, but I am prepared to believe I have been unlucky – other Salento reds are often nicely balanced with the astringent note giving them an attractively clean finish.

San Severo

DOC. White, red and *rosato* wine. Province: Foggia. Villages: San Severo, Torremaggiore, San Paolo Civitate and part of 5 other communes north of Foggia. Grapes: (white) Bombino Bianco and Trebbiano Toscano 40–60%, Malvasia Bianca and Verdeca up to 20%; (red and *rosato*) Montepulciano di Abruzzo 70–100% plus Sangiovese. Max. crop: 98 hl/ha. Min. alch: 11° for white, 11.5° for red and *rosato*. Average production: 400,000 cases. Price: 1,000–1,500 lire.

Inoffensive wines of no special qualities at present.

Squinzano

DOC. Red and *rosato* wine. Province: Lecce. Villages: Squinzano and 6 others. Grapes: Negroamaro plus 30% others. Max. crop: 98 hl/ha. Min. alch: 12.5° (13° aged 2 years is *riserva*). Average production: 36,700 cases.

Salento wines of moderate quality. The *rosato* is much less tiring to drink than the red.

Torre Quarto

A notable individual estate at Ceriguola east of Foggia, setting itself high standards for a red of Malbec, Uva di Troia and Negroamaro, intended for long ageing.

APULIA PRODUCERS

Vinicola Amanda

Sava, 74028 Taranto.

Owned by Vittorio Librale, who began selling bottled wine about 1965. DOC: Primitivo di Manduria. Others: Rosato and Rosso di Sava. A modern winery with increasing production, mainly from purchased grapes. Librandi's wines from Primitivo – of varying degrees of alcohol and sweetness – are not unlike their American cousin, California Zinfandel.

Giuseppe Calò

Alezio, 73011 Lecce.

The Calò family has been selling wine from its estate near Gallipoli since 1938. No DOC. Others: Portulano (Rosso del Salento), Rosa del Golfo (Rosato del Salento). Family and neighbouring vineyards produce 12,500 cases, two thirds of it Rosa del Golfo, one of Italy's most limpid and lovely *rosatos*. The wines will soon be DOC Alezio.

Leone de Castris

Salice Salentino, 73015 Lecce.

The ancient estate of the Leone de Castris family, now directed by Salvatore Leone de Castris. DOC: Locorotondo, Salice Salentino. Others: Albino, Blhiss Frizzante, Five Roses, Il Medaglione, Negrino, Primofiore, Rosato and Rosso del Salento, Spumanti, Ursi, Vini Novelli. Since 1929 the estate of 1,000 acres has bottled some of its (and Apulia's) best wine; rich and heady but not gross reds and (among others) Italy's first bottled *rosato*, Five Roses. 80% of their grapes are estate-grown and potential production is more than 1m. cases.

Centrale Cantine Cooperativa Riforma Fondiaria

Corato, 70033 Bari.

A network of cooperatives with plants in various parts of Apulia, Basilicata and Molise: a major producer of DOC and other wines. DOC: Aglianico del Vulture, Aleatico di Puglia, Cacc'e Mmitte di Lucera, Castel del Monte, Locorotondo, Martina Franca, Salice Salentino, San Severo. Other: Torre Alemanna.

Niccolò Coppola

Alezio, 73011 Lecce.

A family estate since 1460, now run by Carlo and Lucio Coppola. No DOC. Others: Alezio Rosato, Rosso.

Favonio (Attilio Simonini)

71100 Foggia

Founded in 1970 by Attilio Simonini. No DOC. Others: Favonio Cabernet Franc, Chardonnay, Pinot Bianco, Pinot Rosato, Trebbiano Toscano. Simonini has proved that such outsiders as Cabernet Franc, Chardonnay and Pinot Bianco can be made as attractive on the hot plains of Apulia as they are much farther north. His 40 acres of vines need drip irrigation but produce 25,000 cases of extraordinary wines. Prices: 1,500–2,500 lire.

Cantina Sociale Cooperativa di Locorotondo

Locorotondo, 70010 Bari.

Founded: 1932. A cooperative grouping 1,004 growers with 3,700 acres of vines. DOC: Locorotondo. Others: Rosso Rubino, Rosé de Rosé. Locorotondo DOC is selected and aged briefly in barrels into an impressive, crisp but by no means neutral white wine – possibly Apulia's best.

Baroni Malfatti

Veglie, 73010 Lecce.

The estate, in the family for generations, was split into 2 societies in 1980 – Vinicola Baroni Malfatti and Sviluppo Agricolo Salentino – both owned by Gioacchino Malfatti. DOC: Salice Salentino. Others: Bianco, Rosato and Rosso del Salento. A potential 140,000 cases from 370 acres. The best, bottled under the name Gloria del Salento, are outstanding for the region.

Rivera

Andria, 70031 Bari.

Founded by the De Corato family in the locality of Rivera. Bottling began in the early 1950s. Wine makers: Sebastiano and Carlo De Corato. DOC: Castel del Monte, Locorotondo, Moscato di Trani. Rivera makes about 90,000 cases of Castel del Monte from family vineyards and grapes from regular suppliers. The popularity of the lively *rosato* overshadows the quality of Il Falcone Riserva, one of Apulia's best-constructed reds.

Torre Quarto

Cerignola, 71042 Foggia.

Founded: 1847. Owners: Fabrizio Cirillo-Farrusi and his brothers. DOC: Rosso di Cerignola. Others: Torre Quarto Bianco, Rosato, Rosso. Torre Quarto in central Apulia was once one of Italy's greatest estates. From 150 acres and neighbouring vineyards it produces a potential 125,000 cases. Cerignola is the strong red of Negroamaro and Uva di Troia; the non-DOC Rosso is made of Malbec and is exceptionally long-lived – up to 10 years or more. Price: 1,500–2,500 lire.

Conti Zecca (Donna Marzia)

Leverano, 73043 Lecce.

Owner: Alcibiade Zecca. DOC: Leverano. Others: Donna Marzia Bianco, Rosso. The rich red and agreeable white are among the most admired wines of Salento.

OTHER PRODUCERS

Cantina Sociale Cooperativa Alberobello
Alberobello, 70011 Bari. DOC: Martina Franca.

Barone Bacile di Castiglione
73100 Lecce. Owner: Fabio Bacile di Castiglione. DOC: Copertino.

Cantina Sociale di Barletta
Barletta, 70051 Bari. Cooperative. DOC: Rosso Barletta.

Felice Botta
Trani, 70059 Bari. DOC: Aleatico di Puglia, Castel del Monte, Moscato di Trani.

Bruno
Minervino Murge, 70055 Bari. DOC: Castel del Monte.

Candido
Sandonaci, 72025 Brindisi. DOC: Aleatico di Puglia, Salice Salentino. Others: Bianco, Rosato and Rosso del Salento.

Albano Carrisi (Don Carmelo)
Cellino San Marco, 72020 Brindisi. Owner: the popular singer Albano Carrisi. DOC: Squinzano. Others: Don Carmelo Rosato, Rosso.

Chiddo Vini
Bitonto, 70032 Bari. DOC: Castel del Monte.

Distante Vini
Cisternino, 72014 Brindisi. DOC: Locorotondo. Others: Negroamaro, Rosato and Rosso del Salento.

Federico II
Lucera, 71036 Foggia. DOC: San Severo.

Lippolis
Alberobello, 70011 Bari. DOC: Aleatico di Puglia, Martina Franca.

Gennaro Marasciuolo
Trani, 70059 Bari. DOC: Castel del Monte, Moscato di Trani.

Vinicola Miali
Martina Franca, 74015 Taranto. DOC: Martina Franca. Others: Aglianico dei Colli Lucani, Apulia, Rosato.

Tenuta Mitrano
72100 Brindisi. Owner: Antonio Tarantini. DOC: Castel Mitrano.

Nuova Vinicola Picardi
Barletta, 70051 Bari. DOC: Aleatico di Puglia, Castel del Monte, Locorotondo, Moscato di Trani, Rosso Barletta.

Renna
Squinzano, 73018 Lecce. DOC: Salice Salentino, Squinzano. Others: Rosato and Rosso del Salento.

Cantina Riunite del Salento
73100 Lecce. Cooperative. Bianco, Rosato and Rosso del Salento.

Giovanni Soloperto
Manduria, 74024 Taranto. DOC: Primitivo di Manduria. Others: Bianco, Rosato and Rosso del Salento.

Cantina d'Alfonso del Sordo
San Severo, 71016 Foggia. DOC: San Severo.

Giuseppe Strippoli
70124 Bari. Strippoli selects and bottles an array of Apulian wines and sells them through the Supermercato del Vino at Saronno near Milan.

Cosimo Taurino (Notarpanaro)
Guagnano, 73010 Lecce. DOC: Brindisi, Salice Salentino. Others: Bianco, Rosato and Rosso di Salento, Notarpanaro Rosato, Rosso.

Fattoria Torricciola
Andria, 70031 Bari. DOC: Castel del Monte, Rosso Barletta.

CALABRIA

The vast mountainous peninsula that forms the toe of Italy has no famous wines, unless Cirò, with its athletic reputation, can be so called. The local red grape is the Gaglioppo, a variety of deep colour and potentially very high alcohol, but the spots where it is grown to best effect are (with the exception of Cirò) high enough in the Calabrian hills to cool its fiery temper.

The white is the Greco, which is used in the extreme south at Gerace to make a very good dessert wine which ages well and which goes for a high price.

With little established wine-making except of the most primitive kind, Calabria, like Sicily, is modernizing in a hurry. Its DOCs, though little known, represent wines that meet up-to-date criteria.

DOC AND OTHER WINES

Cirò

DOC. Red, white and *rosato* wine. Province: Catanzaro. Villages: Cirò, Cirò Marina, part of Melissa and Crucoli. Grapes: (red and *rosato*) Gaglioppo, plus 5% Trebbiano Toscano and Greco Bianco. Max. crop: 97 hl/ha. Min. alch: 13.5°. Average production: 244,000 cases. Aged 3 years for *riserva* (red only). Price: 1,200–1,800 lire (*riserva* 1,500–2,500).

Bruno Roncarati, himself an athlete, tells us that the Italian Olympic team maintain a 2,500-year-old tradition by training on this blockbuster of a wine from the heel of the toe of Italy. Red Cirò is certainly a full diet, but a soporific rather than a stimulating one. White Cirò, as modernized, is a decent standard dry white to drink young.

Donnici

DOC. Red and white wine. Province: Cosenza. Villages: 11 around and including Cosenza. Grapes: Gaglioppo 50%, Greco Nero 10–20%, Malvasia Bianca, Mantonico Bianco and Percorella 20%. Max. crop: 84 hl/ha. Min. alch: 12°. Average production: 22,000 cases.

A relatively light and fruity red to drink young and fairly cool, from the central western coastal hills of Calabria.

Greco di Bianco or Greco di Gerace

DOC. White wine. Province: Reggio Calabria. Village: commune of Bianco. Grape: Greco. Max. crop: 45 hl/ha. Min. alch: 14° plus 3° of sugar. Average production: expanding, but no detailed figures available. Aged 1 year. Price: 2,500–4,500 lire.

A new DOC for the smooth, juicy and intriguingly orange-scented sweet dessert wine made of Greco grapes at Bianco, where a few small vineyards make it their speciality. Bianco is on the south coast of the extreme toe of Italy. More vineyards are expanding production. Bianco also produces a drier, more lemony, barrel-aged dessert or apéritif white called (after its grapes) Mantonico.

Lamezia

DOC. Red wine. Province: Catanzaro. Villages: part of 10 communes around Lamezia Terme. Grapes: Nerello Mascalese and Nerello Cappuccio (either separately or together) up to 30–50%, Gaglioppo (known locally as Magliocco) 25–35%, Greco Nero (locally called Marsigliana) 25–35%. Max. crop: 84 hl/ha. Min. alch: 12°. Average production: no figures yet available.

A straightforward palish dry red from around the gulf of St. Eufemia on the west coast. Drink it young and cool. Lametina is the name of the local non-DOC sweet or dry white.

Melissa

DOC. White and red wine. Province: Catanzaro. Villages: Melissa and neighbours. Grapes: (white) Greco Bianco 80–95%, Trebbiano Toscano and Malvasia Bianca 5–20%; (red) Gaglioppo 75–95%, Greco Nero, Greco Bianco, Trebbiano Toscana, Malvasia Bianca. Max. crop: 84 hl/ha. Min. alch: 11.5° for white, 12.5° for red. Average production: no figures yet available.

The light, yellow, dry seafood wine of the heel of the toe of Italy, around the port of Crotone.

Pellaro

Powerful but light red or pink wines of imported Alicante vines grown on the Pellaro peninsula in the extreme south.

Pollino

DOC. Red wine. Province: Cosenza. Villages: Castrovillari, S. Basile, Saracena, Cassano Ionio, Civita and Frascineto. Grapes: Gaglioppo 60%, Greco Nero, Malvasia Bianca, Montonico Bianco and Guarnaccia Bianca 20%. Max. crop: 66 hl/ha. Min. alch: 12°. Average production: 67,000 cases. *Superiore* must be 2 years old. Price: 1,200–1,500 lire.

Monte Pollino is a 7,000-foot peak that divides northern Calabria from Basilicata. Its slopes produce a pale but powerful red.

Sant'Anna di Isola Capo Rizzuto

DOC. Red wine. Province: Catanzaro. Villages: Capo Rizzuto and parts of the communes of Crotone and Cutro. Grapes: Gaglioppo 40–60% with several others. Max. crop: 84 hl/ha. Min. alch: 12°. Average production: no figures yet available.

A pale red/*rosato* to drink young and cool, made on the easternmost cape (not an island) of the Calabrian coast.

Savuto

DOC. Red wine. Provinces: Cosenza and Catanzaro. Villages: 21 communes along the river Savuto south of Cosenza. Grapes: Gaglioppo 35–45%, Greco Nero, Nerello, Cappuccio, Magliocco Canino and Sangiovese 30–40%, and up to 25% Malvasia Bianca and Pecorino. Max. crop: 77 hl/ha. Min. alch: 12°. Average production: 39,000 cases. Aged for at least 2 years for *superiore*. Price: 1,200–2,000 lire.

A recommended red of moderate strength and some fragrance. Worth choosing the *superiore*.

Squillace

A locally popular fresh medium-dry white of Greco Bianco and Malvasia. Squillace is south of Catanzaro.

CALABRIA PRODUCERS

Pasquale Bozzo
Donnici Inferiore, 87030 Cosenza. DOC: Donnici. Others: Bianco, Malvasia, Rosato. A growing business in light young wines. Bozzo's 10 acres plus bought-in grapes produce 3,500 cases.

CACIB (Cooperativa Agricola Calabro Ionica Bianchese)
Bianco, 89032 Reggio Calabria. DOC: Greco di Bianco. Other: Mantonico del Bianco.

Caparra & Siciliani Cantina Sociale Cooperativa
Cirò Marina, 88072 Catanzaro. Founded: 1963. DOC: Cirò. A major Cirò producer. From 445 acres, potential production is 110,000 cases, but careful selection reduces the numbers.

Fratelli Caruso
88063 Catanzaro Lido. DOC: Cirò. Other: Villa Santelia Bianco.

Umberto Ceratti
Caraffa del Bianco, 89030 Reggio Calabria. DOC: Greco di Bianco. Other: Mantonico di Bianco. Minute production of the best dessert white of the south. (Mantonico is an apéritif.)

Vincenzo Ippolito
Cirò Marina, 88072 Catanzaro. Founded: 1845. Now run by Antonio and Salvatore Ippolito. DOC: Cirò. Potentially 60,000 cases, including a fine white Cirò, from 173 acres.

Librandi
Cirò Marina, 88072 Catanzaro. Founded in 1950 by Antonio Cataldo Librandi. DOC: Cirò. About 65,000 cases of widely admired wines from 123 acres. The red is best.

Cantina Sociale Vini di Pollino
Castrovillari, 87012 Cosenza. Cooperative. DOC: Pollino.

Cantina Sociale Sant'Anna
Isola di Capo Rizzuto. 88077 Catanzaro. Cooperative. DOC: Sant'Anna di Isola Capo Rizzuto.

Cantina Sociale Vini del Savuto (Giambattista Longo)
Savuto di Cleto, 87030 Cosenza. Cooperative. DOC: Savuto.

Cantina Sociale Cooperative Torre Melissa
Torre Melissa, 88070 Catanzaro. DOC: Cirò, Melissa.

BASILICATA

This mountainous region of the central south, almost entirely landlocked and chronically poor, would not feature on the wine list at all were it not for its romantically named Aglianico del Vulture, a close relation of Taurasi and one of the best reds of southern Italy.

Aglianico dei Colli Lucani
A worthwhile red, from the Apulia side of Basilicata. It is worth tasting any wine made from this grape.

Aglianico del Vulture
DOC. Red wine. Province: Potenza. Villages: 15 communes north of Potenza. Grape: Aglianico. Max. crop: 70 hl/ha. Min. alch: 11.5°. Average production: 61,000 cases. Aged 3 years, 2 in wood, is *vecchio*. Aged 5 years, 3 in wood, is *riserva*. Price: 1,200–2,000 lire, *riserva* 2,000–3,500.
Monte Vulture lies right in the north of Basilicata, not far from the Iripinia mountains where Campania's splendid Taurasi is made. The same grapes grown at high altitudes on volcanic soil give a well-balanced red of firm structure, sometimes offered young, sweet and fizzy, but more often as matured red with real quality and character.

Asprino or Asprinio
A welcome refresher; sharpish, fizzy white without pretensions: Naples' universal café wine.

BASILICATA PRODUCERS

Fratelli d'Angelo
Rionero, 85028 Potenza. Founded: 1944; now directed by oenologist Donato d'Angelo. DOC: Aglianico del Vulture. Others: Malvasia and Moscato del Vulture. The foremost winery of Basilicata. d'Angelo makes 8,500–12,500 cases of Aglianico from grapes purchased from high-altitude vineyards.

Botte
Barile, 85022 Potenza. Owner: Mario Botte. DOC: Aglianico del Vulture. Other: Moscato del Vulture.

Armando Martino
Rionero, 85028 Potenza. DOC: Aglianico del Vulture. Others: Malvasia and Moscato del Vulture.

Cantina Sociale di Metapontino
Metaponto, 75010 Matera. Cooperative. No DOC. Others Metapontum, Montepulciano di Basilicata.

Fratelli Napolitano
Rionero, 85028 Potenza. DOC: Aglianico del Vulture.

Paternoster
Barile, 85022 Potenza. DOC: Aglianico del Vulture. Others: Malvasia and Moscato del Vulture.

Italy in round figures

Italy holds first place in the world leagues of both wine production and consumption per head. The 1980 harvest, a record, produced 86,545,000 hectolitres of wine, or 961 million cases. The average total production of the years between 1977 and 1981 was 75,569,000 hectolitres or 840 million cases.

The province with the largest average production is Sicily. Next come Emilia-Romagna, Veneto and Apulia.

Total production by region, average of years 1977–81, in cases, was:

Piedmont	47,544,000
Valle d'Aosta	340,000
Lombardy	23,173,000
Trentino-Alto Adige	14,462,000
Veneto	114,020,000
Friuli-Venezia Giulia	14,913,000
Liguria	4,209,000
Emilia-Romagna	118,416,000
Tuscany	51,324,000
Umbria	9,798,000
Marches	26,524,000
Latium	65,515,000
Abruzzi	35,820,000
Molise	5,418,000
Campania	34,702,000
Apulia	111,064,000
Basilicata	463,000
Calabria	12,533,000
Sicily	118,876,000
Sardinia	26,380,000

DOC production made up 9.86% of the total in 1980. The DOC percentage reached a peak of 11.64 in 1979, after rising steadily from 1.5% in 1967. Of the regions, Veneto produced the largest amount of DOC wine, 18.8m. cases or 19.2% of the national total. The next largest contributors to the DOC totals are Friuli-Venezia Giulia, with 18.3m. cases (19%), Tuscany (16.6m. cases, 17%), Piedmont (9.7m. cases, 11.2%), Trentino-Alto Adige (7.9m. cases, 8.6%) and Emilia-Romagna (7.6m. cases, 8.4%). Only 15% of Veneto's crop was DOC, despite the province being the largest DOC producer. Trentino-Alto Adige had the highest proportion of DOC (49.6%).

SICILY

Of all the regions of Italy the island of Sicily has changed most in the past two decades. Twenty years ago it was an almost medieval land. The marriage of dignity and squalor was visible everywhere. Its unsurpassed Greek ruins lay apparently forgotten; Syracuse was still a small city commanding a bay of incredible beauty and purity where you could easily imagine the catastrophic defeat of the Athenian fleet 2,000 years before; Palermo was sleepy, violent, indigent but magnificent. As far as wine was concerned, there was Marsala, a name everyone knew but which nobody drank, and a few small aristocratic estates – the best-known on the ideal volcanic slopes of Mount Etna, and around Syracuse, from which there was a trickle of legendary sweet Moscato. But the general run of wine was almost undrinkable, and the best of it was exported northwards for blending.

An apparently well-directed regional development programme has changed all this. Palermo is now a great semi-modern city. Syracuse has all but disappeared among the most hideous disfigurements of industry in an ecological nightmare. But the wine industry has become the biggest in Italy and one of the most modern. Enormous new vineyards supply automated cooperatives, which churn out 'correct', clean and properly balanced, modern wines. Three quarters of the wine is white. Eighty per cent of the colossal total is made in the cooperatives. DOCs are almost irrelevant here; only five per cent qualifies. It is a table-wine industry, based not on local traditions but on choosing appropriate grapes, converting cornfields into mechanized vineyards, and making wine with cool efficiency (with the emphasis on cool). None of this could have been achieved without New World techniques of refrigeration – and huge government grants.

The industry has grown far faster than its market. Although fair quality, good reliability and modest prices have made one or two brands (above all Corvo) internationally famous, most Sicilian wine stays in bulk looking for a blender to turn it into something else – be it Vermouth or even an apparently German wine.

DOC AND OTHER WINES

Alcamo or Bianco Alcamo

DOC. White wine. Provinces: Palermo and Trapani. Villages: around the town of Alcamo. Grapes: Catarratto Bianco plus 20% Damaschino, Grecanico and Trebbiano Toscano. Max. crop: 84 hl/ha. Min. alch: 11.5°. Average production: 333,000 cases. Price: 1,200–2,000 lire.

A straight, fairly full-bodied dry white. Rapitalà is a much superior brand with some nuttiness and some astringency. Rincione Bianco is another similar brand.

Cerasuolo di Vittoria

DOC. Red wine. Provinces: Ragusa, Caltanissetta and Catania. Villages: 11 communes in southeastern Sicily. Grapes: Frappato 40%, Calabrese up to 60%, Grosso Nero and Nerello Mascalese up to 10%. Max. crop: 65 hl/ha. Min. alch: 13°. Production: figures not available. Price: 1,800–2,500 lire.

An unusual pale 'cherry' red of high strength which the critic Luigi Veronelli recommends keeping for as much as 30 years. Little is made, but its reputation is high.

Corvo

Perhaps the best known of all Sicilian wines today, a highly successful brand from Duca di Salaparuta at Casteldaccia near Palermo (*see* Producers). A green-labelled white is reasonably full-bodied but not over-strong and nicely in balance, a yellow-labelled one is very pale and delicate. The red is a brilliant piece of modern wine design; clean, warm and satisfying without leaving any clear memory of scent or flavour. There are also *spumante* and dry fortified Stravecchio Corvo wines.

Etna

DOC. White, red and *rosato*. Province: Catania. Villages: Milo and 20 other communes on the lower eastern slopes of Mt. Etna. Grapes: (white) Carricante 60%, Catarrato Bianco 40%, Trebbiano and Minella Bianca 15%; (red and *rosato*) Nerello Mascalese 80%, Nerello Mantellato 20%, other 10%. Max. crop: 63 hl/ha. Min. alch: 11.5° for white (12° from Milo with 80% Carricante is *superiore*); 12.5° for red and *rosato*. Average production: 172,000 cases. Price: 1,500–2,800 lire.

Until recently this was the only quality table-wine area in Sicily. The volcanic soil of the still-fiery volcano and the cool of its altitude allow both reds and whites of vigour and some refinement. The reds age well to a consistency not far from claret and the whites are brisk and tasty young. The leading estate is Villagrande (*see* Producers).

Faro

DOC. Red wine. Province: Messina. Villages: Messina and Ganzirri. Grapes: Nerello Mascalese 45–60%, Nerello Cappuccio 15–20%, Nocera 5–10%, others up to 15%. Max. crop: 70 hl/ha. Min. alch: 12°. Average production: figures not available.

Limited production of a distinctly superior red, best aged 3 years or so.

Malvasia delle Lipari

DOC. Dessert white wine. Province: Messina. Villages: islands of the Aeolian archipelago, especially Lipari. Grapes: Malvasia di Lipari 95%, Corinto Nero 8–9%. Max. crop: 63 hl/ha. Min. alch: 11.5° (18° plus 6° of sugar for *passito*, which must be 1 year old; 16° plus 6° of sugar for *liquoroso*). Average production: 2,750 cases. Price: 1,700–3,500 lire.

Well-known but scarcely exceptional wines (except in their lovely birthplace). There are many good dessert wines in Sicily; Moscato is much more interesting than Malvasia.

Racking wine in a traditional Sicilian cellar.

Marsala

DOC. Apéritif/dessert wine. Provinces: Trapani, Palermo and Agrigento. Villages: throughout the provinces but above all at Marsala. Grapes: Catarratto and/or Grillo, plus Inzolia up to 15%. Max. crop: 75 hl/ha. Min. alch: 17° by volume aged 4 months for *fine* (or Italia Particolare); 18° aged 2 years for *superiore* (or London Particular, or Superior Old Marsala, or Garibaldi Dolce, or Old Particular – or the appropriate initials); 18° by volume aged 5 years for *vergine*, and 18° by volume for *speciali*. Average production: 3.94m. cases.

An Englishman, John Woodhouse, started the Marsala industry in 1773. Nelson stocked his fleet with it. In a sense it is Italy's sherry, though without sherry's brilliant finesse or limitless ageing capacity. Its manufacture usually involves concentrated and/or 'muted' (stopped with alcohol) musts, known as *cotto* and *sifone* – but the best, *vergine*, is made with neither, simply by an ageing system similar to the soleras of sherry. *Fine* is normally sweet and rather nasty, *superiore* can be sweet or dry, with a strong caramel flavour; *vergine* is dry, with more barrel-wood flavour, *speciali* is a strange aberration – Marsala blended with eggs, or even coffee. A great deal of Marsala is used for making *zabaglione* (just as France buys volumes of Madeira for *sauce madère*).

Moscato di Noto

DOC. White dessert wine. Province: Siracusa. Villages: Noto, Rosolini, Pachino and Avola. Grape: Moscato Bianco. Max. crop: 81 hl/ha. Min. alch: 8° plus 3.5° of sugar for Moscato di Noto; 8° plus 5° of sugar for Moscato di Noto Spumante and 16° plus 6° of sugar for Moscato di Noto Liquoroso. Average production: limited.

Little of this delicious Moscato is made, but the *liquoroso* is a very good example of this sumptuous genre. The Greeks introduced the Muscat grape here 2,500 years ago.

Moscato di Pantelleria

DOC. White wine. Province: Trapani. Villages: the island of Pantelleria. Grapes: Zibibbo or Moscatellone. Max. crop: 49 hl/ha. Min. alch: 8° plus 4.5° of sugar for *naturale*; 14° plus 11° of sugar for Passito di Pantelleria. Average production: 110,000 cases. Price: 2,000–3,500 lire.

The island of Pantelleria is closer to Tunisia than Sicily. Moscato from its Zibibbo grapes has singular perfume, whether made as *spumante*, *naturale* or best of all *passito* (which can also be fortified). The best quality is known as Extra.

Moscato di Siracusa

DOC. White wine. Province: Siracusa. Village: Siracusa. Grape: Moscato Bianco. Max. crop: 45 hl/ha. Min. alch: 16.5° (14° plus 2° or more of sugar). Average production: limited.

The celebrated old Moscato vineyard of Syracuse, once the greatest city of the Greek world, home of Plato, Theocritus and Archimedes, is apparently extinct, like the matchless beauty of its bay before Sicily began to modernize. The fact will not stop a bar selling you a glass of sticky aromatic wine at a high price as 'Siracusa'.

Regaleali

The brand name of a good-quality range of wines, perhaps the island's best brand, from Conte Tasca d'Almerita (*see* Producers). The Riserva Rosso del Conte is as good as any Sicilian red; the white contains Sauvignon Blanc.

Settesoli

The acceptable handiwork of a Cantina Sociale at Menfi on the western south coast. Red and white are both well made, if not memorable.

SICILY PRODUCERS

Giuseppe Camilleri (Steri)
Naro, 92028 Agrigento.

Founded in 1966 by the oenologist Camilleri. No DOC. Others: Steri Bianco, Rosso and Rosso Riserva Speciale. More than 20,000 cases from 65 acres. The *riserva speciale* from Lambrusco and Barbera is unique in Sicily: an intense, high-flavoured and rich red.

Coria
Vittoria, 97019 Ragusa.

The ancient estate owned by Giuseppe Coria began bottling its own wine exclusively in 1968. DOC: Cerasuolo di Vittoria. Others: Moscato di Villa Fontane, Slicchiato, Villa Fontane, Villa Fontane Perpetuo. Coria is a former army officer, a dedicated wine maker, lecturer and author of books on Sicilian and Italian wines. From 7.4 acres he makes 1,175 cases of extraordinary wine, including a Cerasuolo Invecchiato (formerly known as Stravecchio Siciliano) aged 40 years in barrel, and Perpetuo, of which 500 bottles are filled annually from a large cask which is then topped up with new wine.

Corvo (Duca di Salaparuta)
Casteldaccia, 90014 Palermo.

Founded in 1824 by Edoardo Alliata di Villafranca, Duca di Salaparuta. The modern winery is owned by the region and run by Benedetto Migliore. Chief wine maker: Franco Giacosa. No DOC. Others: Corvo Ala, Bianco, Colomba Platino, Rosso, Spumante, Stravecchio di Sicilia. Corvo is the most famous brand of Sicilian wine. Production is about 650,000 cases, prevalently in Corvo Bianco and Rosso and the white Colomba Platino, from grapes bought in the hills of central and western Sicily.

Faustus (Azienda Vinicola Grotta)
90139 Palermo

Owner: Giuseppe Mazzetti. No DOC. Others: Faustus Bianco, Rosato, Rosso are 3 of Sicily's best table wines.

Florio
Marsala, 91025 Trapani.

Founded in 1883 by Vincenzo Florio. The firm was incorporated along with Ingham, Whitaker and Woodhouse as S.A.V.I. Florio & Co., part of the Cinzano group. DOC: Marsala. Florio was known in his day as 'the king of the historic Marsala'; now this rather lack-lustre company has no vines but makes more than 300,000 cases of Marsala, including about 4,000 of the fine *vergine* and *riserva* ACI and Egadi. Ingham, Whitaker and Woodhouse are sold under separate labels.

Agricoltori Associati di Pantelleria
Pantelleria, 91017 Trapani.

A cooperative of about 1,000 growers on the island of Pantelleria. Director: Vito Valenza. Wine maker: Fiorino Perletto. DOC: Moscato di Pantelleria. Others: table wines. Besides much ordinary wine the cooperative bottles about 50,000 cases of a notable dessert Moscato *passito extra* called Tanit and a growing amount of sparkling Solimano.

Diego Rallo & Figli
Marsala, 91025 Trapani.

Founded in 1860 by Diego Rallo. The large family winery is run by his descendants. DOC: Alcamo, Etna, Marsala. Others: Normanno Bianco, Rosso, Royal Club Spumante. Rallo makes about 90,000 cases of Marsala and 70,000 cases of other wines from 295 acres of company vines, supplemented by farmers. The best wine is Vergine 1860. Rallo also supplies table wines to the US market.

Rapitalà (Comte de la Gatinais)
Camporale, 90043 Palermo.

The name of the business is Adelkam S.p.A. The director is the French Comte Hugues de la Gatinais. DOC: Alcamo. Other: Rapitalà Rosso. An earthquake destroyed the winery in 1968. It was rebuilt in 1971. With nearly 500 acres it produces 55,000 cases of red and 166,000 of Alcamo white. Rapitalà adds unaccustomed lustre to the DOC with another dimension of balance and finesse.

Regaleali (Conte Tasca d'Almerita)
93010 Vallelunga Caltanissetta

A family estate founded in 1835. Owner: Giuseppe Tasca d'Almerita. No DOC. Others: Regaleali Bianco, Rosato, Rosso, Rosso del Conte. 400 acres of estate vineyards produce 110,000 cases of some of Sicily's finest dry wines, including 1,600 cases of the excellent Rosso del Conte. Price: 2,500–6,000 lire.

Tenuta Rincione dei Principi di Valdina
Calatafimi, 92013 Trapani.

Owner: Pietro Papè. DOC: Alcamo. Others: Rincione Bianco, Rosato. The best grapes are selected from 295 acres to make above-average Alcamo.

Samperi
Marsala, 91025 Trapani.

Owner: Marco de Bartoli. De Bartoli selects grapes from 37 acres for 1,250 cases of Vecchio Samperi, an outstanding apéritif wine, a superior virgin Marsala in all but DOC.

Cantina Sociale Settesoli
Menfi, 92013 Agrigento.

A cooperative founded in 1958, now with 1,275 members, 8,000 acres and a potential of 2m. cases. No DOC. Others: Settesoli Bianco, Rosato, Rosso. California techniques are evident in the light, surprisingly high-acid wines sold as Settesoli. 20% of production is sold in bottle, the rest in bulk.

Villagrande
Milo, 95010 Catania.

Owner: Paolo Nicolosi Asmundo, Barone di Villagrande, whose son, Carlo, a professor of oenology, makes the wine. DOC: Etna. A dignified old estate which made Etna wine respectable when little else in Sicily was. The red, aged in big old barrels, has almost claret-like texture and ages well; the *rosato* is crisp and the white full of ripeness balanced with good acidity. About 8,000 cases are produced from 75 acres. Only Villagrande makes Etna Bianco Superiore (80% Carricante grapes, 12° alcohol).

OTHER PRODUCERS

V. Giacalone Alloro
Marsala, 91025 Trapani. DOC: Malvasia delle Lipari, Marsala.
D'Angelo Vini (Gebbia)
Alcamo, 91011 Trapani. DOC: Alcamo.
Cooperativa Agricola Aurora
Salemi, 91018 Trapani. DOC: Alcamo. Others: Castelvecchio Bianco, Rosso.
Vito Curatolo Arini
Marsala, 91025 Trapani. Founded in 1875, the family firm is run by Roberto Curatolo. DOC: Marsala. Others: Marina Bianco, Rosso.
Cantina Sociale Enocarboj (Carboj)
Sciacca, 92019 Agrigento. Cooperative. No DOC. Others: Rosso di Sciacca,Trebbiano di Sicilia. Carboj is the brand name for some very drinkable wines.
Vignaioli Etnei (Berbero)
Linguaglossa, 95015 Catania. DOC: Etna. The trade name Berbero is used.
Fratelli Fici
Marsala, 91025 Trapani. Oenologist Nicolò Fici runs the family firm. DOC: Marsala.
Maccotta
Pantelleria, 97017 Trapani. Owner: F. Maccotta. DOC: Malvasia delle Lipari, Moscato di Pantelleria, Zibibbo.
Fratelli Marino di Simone
Marsala, 91025 Trapani. Nerello Siciliano, Verdello Siciliano.
Fratelli Martinez
Marsala, 91025 Trapani. DOC: Marsala.
Fratelli Montalto
Marsala, 91025 Trapani. DOC: Alcamo, Etna, Marsala. Others: Grecanico, Malvasia, Moscato, Nerello, Zibibbo.
Cantina Sociale Paladino
Alcamo, 91011 Trapani. Cooperative. DOC: Alcamo.
Carlo Pellegrino
Marsala, 91025 Trapani. Founded: 1880. DOC: Marsala. Others: Grecanico, Pignatello.
Cantina Sociale Sant'Antonio (Virzi)
Alcamo, 91011 Trapani. Cooperative. The label says Virzi.
Cooperativa Agricoltori Saturnia (Draceno)
Partanna, 91028 Trapani. Draceno Bianco, Rosato, Rosso.
Spinasanta
98100 Messina. DOC: Faro. Other: Mamertino.
Cantina Sociale Torrepalino
Solicchiata, 95030 Catania. Cooperative. DOC: Etna.
Fratelli de Vita
Marsala, 91025 Trapani. DOC: Marsala.
Cantina Sociale La Vite
Partanna, 91028 Trapani. Cooperative. Donzelle Bianco, Rosso.

SARDINIA

Sardinia is a strange, timeless island adrift in the centre of things and yet remote, without Sicily's innate drama, without Corsica's majestic mountains or sour social history.

The modern world comes and camps on the coastline of Sardinia, the jet set on the Costa Smeralda, the wine world on the opposite coast at Alghero, where one of Italy's most sophisticated and original wineries takes advantage of ideal natural conditions to break all the rules.

Sardinia's original wines are heroically strong, designed it seems by and for the supermen who built the round fortress houses of colossal stones that dot the island: the nuraghe.

The most characteristic wine of the island is Cannonau, an indigenous red with a minimum alcoholic degree of 13.5 and often much more. The traditional practice is to prevent all the sugar from converting to alcohol; to balance strength with sweetness in something faintly reminiscent of port. The sweet red is actually best *liquoroso*, fortified with brandy, when it goes all the way to a port-style dessert wine. The Anghelu Ruju of Sella & Mosca is the version of Cannonau most likely to appeal to untrained tastes. Two other grapes, Girò and Monica, make similar sweet and heady reds.

Nor are old-style Sardinian white wines any easier to cope with. Nasco, Malvasia and Vernaccia are three white grapes that all achieve formidable degrees, often tempered, like the reds, with unfermented sugar left to sweeten them.

Sweet Malvasia is a serious speciality that can reach very high quality. Vernaccia, on the other hand, is best fermented dry and aged in the same way as sherry. (It even develops the same *flor* yeast that allows it to oxidize to a nicely nutty maturity.) Old dry Vernaccia needs no apology.

The modern movement in Sardinia consists largely of cooperatives, but it is symbolized, and indeed led, by the Sella & Mosca winery at Alghero.

Italy's export trade
Italy's average exports of wine for the 3 years 1979–81 were 196m. cases, 23% of total national production. 31m. cases (or 16%) of this total were DOC. The total value of exports was 903,820m. lire. The value of DOC wine exports was 145,340m. lire, or 16% of the total.

France is the leading export customer in terms of quantity, taking an average of 81.5m. cases (1979–81). Of this, only 939,000 cases (1.2%) were DOC. Other major export markets are: West Germany 53.8m. cases, 10.9m. (20%) DOC; USA 32.6m. cases, 5.5m. (17%) DOC; UK 13.9m. cases, 2.4m. (17%) DOC.

However, the picture changes when the value of exports, rather than sheer volume, is considered. West Germany and the USA are the most important markets, followed by France.

DOC AND OTHER WINES

Campidano di Terralba or Terralba

DOC. Red wine. Provinces: Cagliari, Oristano. Villages: Terralba and district on the Campidano plain. Grapes: Bovale (others up to 20%). Max. crop: 105 hl/ha. Min. alch: 11.5°. Average production: 13,300 cases.

A lightish dry red, pleasantly soft and best served young and cool.

Cannonau di Sardegna

DOC. red and *rosato* wine. Province: whole of Sardegna. Grapes: Cannonau, plus 10% Bovale Grande Carignano, Pascale di Cagliari, Monica and Vernaccia di S. Gimignano. Max. crop: 71 hl/ha. Min. alch: 13.5° for Cannonau di Sardegna (1 year old: 3 years for *riserva*); 15° for *superiore naturalmente secco*; 15° for *superiore naturalmente amabile*, 13° for *superiore naturalmente dolce*; 18° for *vini liquorosi secco*; 16° for *vini liquorosi dolce naturale*. Average production: 89,000 cases. Price: 1,200–3,000 lire.

The complicated set of DOC rules means that much Cannonau is sold as Vino di Tavola (without the DOC qualification 'di Sardegna'), and is none the worse for a little less alcohol. It is the basic Sardinian red grape, traditionally both strong and sweet – in fact anything but refreshing, however rich (which it is) in flavour. The most famous old-style Cannonau is that of Oliena, near Nuoro in the eastern centre of the island.

Carignano del Sulcis

DOC. Red and *rosato* wine. Province: Cagliari. Villages: the islands of S. Antioco and S. Pietro on the southwest coast. Grapes: Carignano and up to 15% Monica, Pascale and Alicante-Bouschet. Max. crop: 104 hl/ha. Min. alch: 11.5°. Average production: 33,000 cases.

Both reasonable red and a quite smooth and fruity *rosato* are made of the French Carignan in this area of hilly islets and lagoons, known to the ancients as Sulcis. The red will take 1–2 years' ageing.

Girò di Cagliari

DOC. Red wine. Province: Cagliari. Villages: throughout the province. Grape: Girò. Max. crop: 72 hl/ha. Min. alch: 15.5° for *dolce naturale*; 15° for *secco*; 17.5° for *liquoroso dolce naturale* and *liquoroso secco*. Aged for at least 2 years for *riserva*. Average production: 1,350 cases.

Girò, like Cannonau, is a traditional red grape of formidable sugar content, most often seen as a sweet wine; impressive rather than attractive when it is made dry.

Malvasia di Bosa

DOC. White wine. Province: Nuoro. Villages: Bosa, Flussio, Magomadas, Modolo, Suni, Tinnura, Tresnuraghes – near the west coast south of Alghero. Grape: Malvasia di Sardegna. Max. crop: 56 hl/ha. Min. alch: 14.5° plus 0.5° of sugar for *secco*; 13° plus 2° of sugar for *dolce naturale*; 15° plus 2.5° of sugar for *liquoroso dolce naturale*; 16.5° plus 1.5° of sugar for *liquoroso secco*. Average production: 1,350 cases. Price: 4,000–10,000 lire.

The most highly prized of several Sardinian amber whites that can best be compared with sherry – at least in function. They go through a shorter and simpler ageing process but acquire smoothness and some depth of flavour, ending in a characteristically Italian bitter-almond note. Dry versions, served chilled, are good apéritifs.

Malvasia di Cagliari

DOC. White wine. Province: Cagliari. Villages: entire province. Grape: Malvasia di Sardegna. Max. crop: 71 hl/ha. Min. alch: as for Malvasia di Bosa. Average production: 11,000 cases. Aged for 1 year in wood for *liquoroso dolce* and *liquoroso secco riserva*.

Similar wines to the last but from less exclusive southern vineyards.

Mandrolisai

DOC. Red and white wine. Province: Nuoro. Village: Sorgono, in the centre of the island. Grapes: Cannonau, Bovale Sardo, Monica. Max. crop: 84 hl/ha. Min. alch: 11.5°. Average production: No figures yet available.

A new DOC for less than full-power Cannonau and *rosato* from modernized cooperatives.

Monica di Cagliari

DOC. Red wine. Province: Cagliari. Area: throughout the province. Grape: Monica. Max. crop: 71 hl/ha. Min. alch: 13° plus 2.5° of sugar for *dolce naturale*; 14.5° for *secco*; 15° plus 2.5° of sugar for *liquoroso dolce naturale*; 16.5° plus 1° of sugar for *liquoroso secco*. Aged for at least 2 years (of which 1 in wood) for *liquoroso dolce* and *secco riserva*. Average production: 11,100 cases.

The usual range of strengths and sweetnesses in lighter reds with less character than Cannonau.

Monica di Sardegna

DOC. Red wine. Province: the whole island. Grapes: Monica, plus 15% Pascale di Cagliari, Carignano, Bovale Grande and Bovale Sardo. Max. crop: 97 hl/ha. Min. alch: 12°. Average production: 278,000 cases. 1 year old is *superiore*.

A standard dry red table wine of acceptable quality, perhaps most enjoyable rather cool.

Moscato di Cagliari

DOC. White wine. Province: Cagliari. Villages: throughout the province. Grape: Moscato Bianco. Max. crop: 71 hl/ha. Min. alch: 13° plus 3° of sugar for *dolce naturale*; 15° plus 2.5° of sugar for *liquoroso dolce naturale* (fortified). Aged for 1 year for *riserva*. Average production: 5,560 cases.

The Muscat grape has a stronger tradition in Sicily than Sardinia. What is made here is reasonable local drinking. The fortified *liquoroso* is the most convincing.

Moscato di Sardegna

DOC. White wine. Province: the whole island. Grapes: Moscato Bianco plus 10% others. Max. crop: 91 hl/ha. Min. alch: 8° plus 3.5° of sugar. Average production: no figures yet available. Price: 2,000–3,000 lire.

A new DOC for low-strength sweet Muscat *spumante* – in fact the Asti of Sardinia. It can use the geographical term 'Tempio Pausania' or 'Tempio e Gallura' if the grapes are vinified at Gallura in the province of Sassari in the northwest.

Moscato di Sorso-Sennori

DOC. White wine. Province: Sassari. Villages: Sorso and Sennori, north of Sassari. Grape: Moscato Bianco. Max. crop: 54 hl/ha. Min. alch: 13° plus 2° of sugar. It can also be fortified to make a *liquoroso dolce*. Average production: 3,300 cases.

A local Muscat DOC for a strong sweet white, reputed better than that of Cagliari in the south.

Nasco di Cagliari

DOC. White wine. Province: Cagliari. Villages: throughout the province. Grape: Nasco. Max. crop: 65 hl/ha. Min. alch: 13° plus 2.5° of sugar for *dolce naturale*; 14.5° plus 0.5° of sugar for *secco*; 15° plus 2° of sugar for *liquoroso dolce naturale*; 16.5° plus 1° for *liquoroso secco*. Aged at least 2 years in wood for *liquoroso dolce naturale* and *secco riserva*. Average production: 4,450 cases.

Another rustic island white more appreciated sweet and strong by the locals, but in its modernized, lighter and drier versions by visitors. Sella & Mosca (*see* Producers) spurn the DOC to make the latter.

Nuragus di Cagliari

DOC. White wine. Provinces: Nuoro (part) and Cagliari. Grapes: Nuragus 85–95%, Trebbiano Toscano and Romagnolo, Vermentino, Clairette and Semidano 15%. Max. crop: 130 hl/ha. Min. alch: 11°. Average production: 111,000 cases.

A light and essentially neutral dry white wine, the standard resort of those who have been overwhelmed by Sardinia's more characteristic products.

Torbato di Alghero

The fruit of modern technology and intelligent market planning applied to a number of Sardinian white grapes by Sella & Mosca (*see* Producers). Not exactly a thrilling wine, but an extremely well-designed dry white of just-memorable personality, and just what is needed with the island's fish. In fact it is a bargain anywhere.

Vermentino di Gallura

DOC. White wine. Provinces: Sassari and Nuoro. Villages: 19 communes in the north of the island. Grape: Vermentino. Max. crop: 98 hl/ha. Min. alch: 12° (14° for *superiore*). Average production: 33,000 cases.

By tradition the sort of strong dry white with low acidity that does the opposite of quenching your thirst – epitomized by the 14° *superiore*.

Vernaccia di Oristano

DOC. White wine. Province: Cagliari. Villages: 15 communes in the south and west, including Oristano. Grape: Vernaccia di Oristano. Max. crop: 48 hl/ha. Min. alch: 15° (and 2 years in wood). Aged for 3 years in wood for *superiore*, 4 for *riserva*. Aged in wood for 2 years for *liquoroso* (which is fortified). Average production: 66,500 cases.

On first acquaintance I found this the most appealing of all Sardinian wines; a sort of natural first cousin to Spain's Montilla, or an unfortified sherry. The grapes are slightly shrivelled before fermentation, the natural strength slows down oxidation while subtle and distinct flavours develop – including the characteristic Italian bitterness lingering in the finish.

SARDINIA PRODUCERS

Attilio Contini

Cabras, 09072 Oristano.

Founded in the late 19th century. DOC: Vernaccia di Oristano. The most respected of Vernaccia producers.

Cantina Sociale Marmilla

Sanluri, 09055 Cagliari.

A huge cooperative founded in the early 1950s. Its 2,000 members have 13,000 acres of vines and a potential output of 3.5m. cases. DOC: Cannonau di Sardegna, Monica di Sardegna, Nuragus di Cagliari. Others: Malvasia, Nasco, Rosato. Run by oenologist and author Enzo Biondo.

Sella & Mosca

Alghero, 07041 Sassari.

Founded in 1899 by the Piedmontese Emilio Sella and Edgardo Mosca, now owned by the INVEST group. Chief wine maker: Mario Consorte. No DOC. Others: Anghelu Ruju, Cannonau di Alghero, I Piani, Monica, Nasco, Rosé di Alghero, Torbato di Alghero, Vermentino di Alghero. One of Europe's largest wine estates and a model of contemporary viticulture. 1,600 acres of vines have a potential production of 500,000 cases. The principal lines are Vermentino (150,000 cases), fine dry white Torbato (80,000 cases), Cannonau (25,000 cases) and the port-like Anghelu Ruju (10,000 cases).

OTHER PRODUCERS

Cantina Sociale Riforma Agraria
Alghero, 07041 Sassari. Cooperative. No DOC. Others: Aragosta, Le Bombarde. Aragosta is a good dry Vermentino (to go with lobsters).

Emilio & Gilberto Arru
Magomadas, 08010 Nuoro. No DOC. Other: Malvasia di Planargia. Small production of apéritif or dessert wine.

Cantina Sociale Cooperativa Dolianova (Parteolla)
Dolianova, 09041 Cagliari. DOC: Malvasia di Cagliari, Monica di Sardegna, Moscato di Cagliari, Nuragus di Cagliari. Others: Cannonau, Nasco, Sibiola Rosato and Rosso.

Cantina Sociale di Dorgali
Dorgali, 08022 Nuoro. Cooperative. DOC: Cannonau di Sardegna. Others: Bianco, Rosato and Rosso di Dorgali. One of the biggest and best producers of Cannonau.

Cantina Sociale Cooperativa Vitivinicola Jerzu
Jerzu, 08044 Nuoro. DOC: Cannonau di Sardegna. (The town of Jerzu, noted for Cannonau, may be given as a subdenomination.)

Mario Mereu
Tortoli, 08048 Nuoro. Perda Rubia. A good sweet port-like Cannonau.

Salvatore Deriu Mocci
Bosa, 08013 Nuoro. DOC: Malvasia di Bosa. 300–350 cases of a wine described and invoiced as 'liquid gold', from about 5 acres.

Cantina Sociale Il Nuraghe
Mogoro, 09050 Cagliari. Cooperative. DOC: Monica di Sardegna, Nuragus di Cagliari.

Josto Puddu
San Vero Milis, 09020 Oristano. DOC: Vernaccia di Oristano.

Cantina Sociale di Sant 'Antioco
Sant'Antioco, 09017 Cagliari. Cooperative. DOC: Carignano del Sulcis, Monica di Sardegna. Sardus Pater is the trademark of a notable red Carignano.

Vini Classici di Sardegna
09100 Cagliari. DOC: Girò, Malvasia, Moscato and Nuragus di Cagliari, Monica di Sardegna. Other: Vermentino.

Cantina Sociale della Vernaccia
09025 Oristano. Founded: 1953. The cooperative has about 900 members with some 2,000 acres of vines. DOC: Vernaccia di Oristano. The best of its Vernaccia is the brand Sardinian Gold.

Zedda Piras
09100 Cagliari. DOC: Girò, Malvasia, Monica di Cagliari.

SPAIN

To the majority of interested wine drinkers in other countries (South America excepted) Spanish wine is scarcely less of a novelty than Californian. Even Spain's finest export-quality table wine, Rioja, was almost unsaleable in fashionable markets 15 years ago. Sherry was the only Spanish wine with international acceptance. Sherry, and cheap strong wine of the most basic kind.

Inside Spain Rioja completely dominated the market for quality wine, not just in the north but nationwide. Not even sherry had the same coverage. Local wines were (as they still often are) offered in restaurants in carafes. Most visitors ignored them – not out of snobbery but from bitter experience. A great deal has changed in the last 10 years. First came the international discovery of Rioja. Then the rise of Penedès in Catalonia as its rival. A scattering of individual estates, some far from recognized wine regions, have made their names for wines which are extraordinary in every sense. Sherry, after a period of frenetic expansion, seems to have gone into a slow decline. But the general mood all over the country has been an awakening of local pride.

A slow succession of regions had since the 1920s formed local Consejos Reguladores to control and promote their products. In 1970 the Spanish government passed a statute which drew together the threads of wine law and established national minimum standards. In 1972 it instituted a central controlling body for *Denominacións de Origen*. There are now 26 regions with controls broadly analogous to French appellations and several more are on the drawing board. *See* pages 28–29.

Control, however, is not the same as quality. Only a small minority, even of *denominación* wine, is of international interest – and much of that only for its formidable strength combined with minimal character, as good blending material.

Modern cooperatives are now raising standards of essential technology and hygiene. There is still the problem of high strength to be overcome; much Spanish wine is simply too alcoholic for modern tastes. Better grape varieties and earlier picking can improve matters further if they are allowed to. But the great central Spanish well of wine, the region of La Mancha, south of Madrid, and its neighbours Jumilla, Yecla, Utiel-Requena, Almansa and Manchuela to the east, disposes of its potent produce without difficulty and seems likely to change its philosophy only slowly.

It is surprising to see in the statistics that Spain claims the highest acreage of vineyard in Europe – while coming only third in quantity produced. Spain's vineyards are still in the main old-fashioned, unmechanized and their soil relatively infertile. Crops are very small by French standards, except in the sherry region, where the clay soil allows production at an almost German rate. Average figures for some *denominación* regions in a recent year (1979) show how very little wine even the 'bulk' areas coax out of their land.

The vineyards of Spain are so widely scattered over the peninsula that only the broadest regional classification or grouping is strictly applicable. Only in one or two instances do the names of the old provinces evoke a style of wine: the *denominacións* and other wine areas follow a different logic.

The country can reasonably be divided into three broad latitudinal bands: the north for table wines of quality, or at least character; the centre for bulk wines with high alcohol as their dominant characteristic; the south for *vinos generosos*: apéritifs and dessert wines with sherry as their archetype.

A further, longitudinal, division finds the northwest alone in producing sharp 'green' wines in the manner of Portugal's better-known *vinho verde*; the centre north responsible for most of Spain's best-balanced red wines; and Catalonia in the northeast leading in white table and sparkling wines, with good reds rapidly gaining ground.

The same longitudinal division across the centre of Spain finds the wines at their rudest and most characterful in the west, very strong but sadly lacking in flavour in the centre, and even stronger but with more colour and body in the Levante, towards the Mediterranean.

This is as far as generalization can usefully go. But it gives us a framework for a progression from northwest to southeast.

Harvesting, Jerez

SPAIN IN ROUND FIGURES

Spain's vineyards cover just over 4m. acres, making her the country with the largest area under vines in the world (Italy is second, Soviet Russia third and France fourth). Both Italy and France, however, produce almost twice as much wine. The Spanish average of 33m. hectolitres (367m. cases) represents an average crop of only 20 hl/ha, which is extremely low by modern standards.

More than half Spain's vineyards, 2.55m. acres, are included in her system of Denominación de Origen. (In contrast only 10% of Italy's wine is DOC.) D.O. status therefore has little to do with quality.

The D.O. acres and their yield in hl/ha in 1980 are listed below:

	hl/ha
Alella	20
Alicante	13
Almansa	17.2
Ampurdán-Costa Brava	10.45
Cariñena	10
Huelva	33.45
Jerez-Xerez-Sherry	85.7
Jumilla	39
Málaga	12
Mancha	30.2
Manchuela	12
Méntrida	9
Montilla-Moriles	56.6
Navarra	22.25
Penedès	46.55
Priorato	3.3
Ribeiro	54
Rioja	44
Tarragona	23.87
Utiel-Requena	26
Valdeorras	63.88
Valdepeñas	38.45
Valencia	26
Yecla	10.64

Spain's exports average 73m. cases a year, but the total fluctuates widely with intermittent demand for bulk wine from the USSR and the other markets. The proportion being exported in bottle is steadily rising. In 1981 exports, in bottle and bulk, were as follows:

	cases
Table wine in bottle	7,382,000
Table wine in bulk	41,556,000
Sherry in bottle	611,678
Sherry in bulk	10,427,000
Other *vinos generosos* in bottle	744,000
Other *vinos generosos* in bulk	656,100

After sherry, Rioja is the most important export among D.O. wines. Total Rioja exports in 1981 in bulk and bottle, were more than 3m. cases.

The main export markets for sherry, in order of importance, are:

		cases
UK	In bottle:	1,060,000
	In bulk:	6,970,000
	Total:	**8,030,000**
Netherlands	In bottle:	2,470,000
	In bulk:	2,430,000
	Total:	**4,900,000**
W. Germany	In bottle:	1,080,000
	In bulk:	370,000
	Total:	**1,450,000**
USA	In bottle:	500,000
	In bulk:	3,750
	Total:	**503,750**

NORTHERN SPAIN

The Rioja region and its wines, much the most important for quality and consistency in Spain, have a section to themselves on pages 354–359. Recently wines of similar (in one case even better) quality have been developed in the regions to the northeast and southwest of Rioja.

Northeast is the old province of Navarra, which actually abuts on Rioja and can claim some of the vineyards of the Rioja Baja. Its limits are Catalonia in the east, the river Ebro in the south and the Pyrenees to the north. The province has some 75,000 acres of vineyard, using the same grapes as Rioja but with emphasis on the heavy, alcoholic Garnacha. The best lie just south of its capital, Pamplona, where the cooling influence of the Pyrenees can already be felt. The two most considerable bodegas are at Puente la Reina (Señorio de Sarria) and Las Campanas.

South of Navarra and the Ebro lies Aragón, whose climate tends more towards the Mediterranean. Aragón's one well-known *denominación*, Cariñena, is a byword for high-strength dark red wine with a rustic bite, though worth oak-ageing for two years to achieve a pleasantly smooth texture. The grape here is again largely Garnacha Tinta, despite the fact that the region gave its name to the great grape of France's Midi, the Carignan.

Cariñena lies in the south of the province of Zaragoza, with 54,000 acres of vineyard. A newer and small D.O., Campo de Borja (with 23,000 acres), lies halfway between Cariñena and the Rioja Baja. Borja (the origin of the Borgias) makes an

Racking in a Rioja bodega

even more rustic and alcoholic red, more in demand for blending than drinking. A third, still little known, lies round Huesca to the north of Zaragoza. Somontano, as it is called, feels the influence of mountain air and gives much lighter reds. Barbastro, east of Huesca, is its centre.

Catalonia, the quasi-independent province of the northeast, is described separately on page 361.

Surprisingly it is the very heart of the high plain of Old Castile, with some of the worst of Spain's savagely extreme climate, that is now producing wines of a quality seriously to challenge Rioja. Big hot-country wines that they are, the red table wines of the Portuguese upper Douro and the Spanish Ribera del Duero seem to be kindred in their fine engineering. They have the structure, the cleanness and 'cut' of a massive Bordeaux – something not found (as far as I know) elsewhere in Spain, although well known as the hallmark of Portugal's best wine.

Some of Spain's greatest reds, including her most expensive by far, grow along the Duero banks, the Ribera del Duero, just east of Valladolid towards Peñafiel. There are 6,000 acres in the *denominación*. Vega Sicilia, aged 10 years in cask, is the crown jewel, but even the *reservas* of the cooperative at Peñafiel echo the underlying quality of the region.

Farther upstream where the Duero flows through the province of Burgos at Aranda de Duero the Ribera de Burgos is a much bigger D.O. than the Ribera del Duero, with 27,000 acres. But its typical *claretes* lack the concentration and class of the Valladolid wines.

It is strange to find an up and coming white wine D.O. only 20 miles south of Valladolid, in the hot, parched country that breeds such massive reds. Rueda made its name with a sort of sherry, a strong *flor*-growing yellow wine of Verdejo, the local grape, grown on chalky clay not unlike the *albariza* of Jerez. Modern white-wine technology has revolutionized Rueda. First the Marqués de Riscal from Rioja, then other investors, have seen enough potential here to call in the best advice from France and invent a new Rueda: a full-bodied crisp dry white of the kind Spain chronically needs.

Every other wine in Old Castile is red. Toro is Rueda's nearest neighbour: a massive black wine for blending from the dusty Duero valley between Valladolid and Zamora. Cabreros, from over the mountains to the south between Avila and Madrid, makes powerful *claretes*. Cigales, just north of Valladolid, is another region of rough *clarete* – though pale in colour.

This sort of alcoholic dark rosé is met with all the way north to León, the capital of Castile's twin province. Benavente, with its castle-parador just south of León, is the centre for a bizarre sort of bodega burrowed in the ground. Among the vineyards of Los Oteros, along the shallow valley of the Tera river, and Valdevimbre nearer León, clusters of these extraordinary earthworks appear like ant cities. The city of León is now the commercial centre for the province. The great VILE bodega dominates the region and is turning its essentially peasant wine tradition to good account.

The last of the named wine areas of León, El Bierzo, lies west of the capital and over the mountains on the borders of cool Galicia. Vilafranca del Bierzo is the centre of a region of 24,000 acres, whose nearest wine-growing neighbour is the Galician *denominación* of Valdeorras. El Bierzo wines are correspondingly the lightest of León, with good acidity and not excessively strong. The Palacio de Arganza is perhaps the best producer of this region, whose future as a D.O. seems assured.

The geography and climate of Galicia make it more like a northern extension of Portugal than part of viticultural Spain. But whereas Portugal's Minho has turned its *vinho verde* into a significant export wine, Galicia's similarly 'green', acidic and more or less fizzy wines remain a local attraction. The best of them (as in the Minho) are made of the Albariño grape, which legend relates to the Riesling. The majority are made of a variety of local grapes adapted to much cooler and rainier conditions than anywhere else in Spain, except the Basque region. Yet even here, as in California, the degree of ocean influence varies widely from place to place with the incidence of coastal hills. Galicia's easternmost wine region, Valdeorras, shares the conditions of El Bierzo in León: moderate rain and a warm growing season. The main white grape is the Palomino; the red, Garnacha.

The other inland region, the *denominación* Monterrey, along the Portuguese border around Verín, shelters from the Atlantic behind the Sierra de Larouca with peaks of 5,000 and 6,000 feet. Monterrey wines are almost as sunbaked as those of León.

But these are the exceptions. The centre of Galician wine-growing is the D.O. Ribeiro, around Rivadavia between Orense and the coast at Vigo. Its cooperative is the biggest wine plant in Galicia, and its produce, particularly its red wines, in the eccentrically fizzy and rasping style of *vinho verde*.

Strangely, the best wines of Galicia come from the green coastal zone itself, despite its high rainfall. Pontevedra, the coastal province immediately north of Portugal (and containing the port of Vigo) grows the Albariño, notably in the Zona del Albariño round Cambados in the north, and the Condado del Salvatierra on the Portuguese border.

Northern producers are listed on pages 359–360.

RIOJA

As a wine region, Rioja claims a longer history than Bordeaux. Some French historians believe that the Romans may even have found the ancestor of the Cabernet in this part of Spain. Certainly the Romans followed the river Ebro up from the Mediterranean rather as they followed the Rhône, as a corridor of the climate and conditions they were accustomed to into a colder and more hostile land. High in the headwaters of the Ebro, over 2,000 feet up, round its little tributary Rio Oja, they found ideal conditions for wine of good quality – and possibly even the necessary grapes.

The postclassical history of Rioja was similar to that of all the Roman wine regions. Rapid decline (accelerated in Spain by the Moorish invasion), the dominance of the Church, a slow renaissance in the sixteenth century, but no real changes until the eighteenth or early nineteenth century. Then it was the influence of Bordeaux that reached Rioja, the new idea of barrel-ageing the best wines. It was first tried in 1787, was overruled by Luddite reaction, and was finally introduced by reforming aristocratic landowners – in much the same way and at the same time as Chianti was 'invented' by the Barone Ricasoli.

The first commercial bodegas of the modern age of Rioja were founded in the 1860s, by the Marqués de Riscal and the Marqués de Murrieta, with the Bordeaux château system very much in mind. Both used (and still use) grapes from their immediate districts. They sold their wine in bottle and spread the reputation of the region at a most opportune moment. Phylloxera was invading Bordeaux, and French capital and technology were looking for a new region to develop. Before the end of the century a dozen much bigger new bodegas had been built, drawing on grapes from a much wider area – the three regions of Rioja all contributed to their blends.

The railhead at Haro formed the nucleus for this boom, and the bodegas round it remain both physically and spiritually the embodiment of the late-Victorian technology. The cluster of huge, rather raffish buildings almost recalls Epernay, the Champagne capital that grew in the same lush decades.

Phylloxera reached Rioja in the early years of the twentieth century. The disruption, followed by World War I, then the Spanish Civil War, prevented the bodegas from capitalizing on the foreign markets they had successfully opened.

In 1926 Rioja became the first wine region of Spain to set up a Consejo Regulador to supervise its affairs. Among its regulations was a minimum size for a bodega before it was allowed to export: now expressed as a storage capacity of 7,500 hectolitres (about 83,000 cases), including at least 500 225-litre *barricas*. During this period the region was making and maturing superlative vintages (examples can still occasionally be found). Yet Rioja remained the staple of connoisseurs only in Spain and Latin America until the international wine boom of the 1970s.

The decade saw the founding of a new wave of bodegas, a flurry of takeovers, and a vast increase in planting and production. It also saw modifications in wine-making techniques which have added new styles to the already wide range produced in the region.

Long ageing in Bordeaux-type barrels is the hallmark of traditional Rioja. It gives the wines, whether red or white, an easily recognized fragrance and flavour related to vanilla. The best wines, with a concentrated flavour of ripe fruit, can support a surprising degree of this oaky overlay. Lesser wines become exhausted by it, losing their fruity sweetness and becoming dry and monotone. Spanish taste leans to emphasis on oak. International taste inclines to less oak-ageing for reds and little or none for whites. Many bodegas are therefore modifying their old practice of bottling the wine at what they consider full maturity. By replacing time in barrel with time in bottle they reduce the impact of the oak in favour of the more subtle bouquet of bottle-age.

The range offered by a typical Rioja bodega includes some or all of the following:

Vinos Blancos

White wines, either in Bordeaux-, burgundy- or German-shaped bottles. Normally very dry and gratifyingly low in alcohol (10-11%). Principally made of the Viura grape (alias Macabeo), with or without Malvasia and/or Garnacho Blanco. They have good acidity and resist oxidation well. Made in the old way they had little grape aroma but often very satisfying structure and balance. The style formerly sold as 'Chablis' was not aged in oak and was stony and austere at first, but responded rather well to four or five years in bottle. Some of these low-price wines may have been blended with strong neutral Valdepeñas. Examples still exist.

Better whites were formerly all aged in old oak barrels for between about three and anything up to 12 years – the best longest. Outstanding examples of these *reservas* remain pale lemon-yellow and keep an astonishing freshness, roundness and vigour beneath a great canopy of oaky fragrance. They can be compared with the best old vintages of white Graves.

Many bodegas now make all or some of their whites by long, slow fermentation followed by almost immediate bottling, the object being to capture primary grape aromas in all their freshness. The Viura makes delicious wine in this style, possibly benefiting from some bottle-age (though Bodegas Olarra make a white 'Reciente', which they recommend be consumed within months of the vintage). Most bodegas also make a compromise, semi-modern white, cold fermented and briefly oak-aged.

Sweet white Riojas are rarely a success. Noble rot is very rare in the dry upland atmosphere. Overripe grapes are simply half-raisined. But exceptional vintages have produced beautiful delicate and aromatic sweet wines of apparently limitless lasting power.

Vinos Rosados

Rosé wines, made in the customary way, normally dry and pale and not oak-aged.

Vinos Tintos

Many bodegas now call all their red wines *tinto*. The former custom was to divide them into *clarete*, light-coloured red wine of fairly low strength (10-11.5%) bottled in Bordeaux bottles, and *tinto* (sometimes called Borgogña) sold in burgundy bottles. *Tinto* in this sense is much darker in colour, more fruity, fuller in body and higher in alcohol. Both are made of a mixture of Tempranillo, the dominant red grape, with the luscious and aromatic Graciano and the alcoholic Garnacha Tinta (the Rhône Grenache), often with some Mazuelo, a cousin of the Carignan of the Midi. A little white Viura is also sometimes used in *claretes*. Both types are equally made up to the level of *reservas* or *gran reservas*, but Rioja's ultimate glories tend to be of the *tinto* type, which resists barrel-ageing better without growing thin and (although less fragrant) can grow marvellously velvety in the bottle.

All wines can be sold either as *sin crianza*, 'without ageing', or *con crianza*. A *vino de crianza* from Rioja is bottled at either three or four years old ('3°año' or '4°año'), of which at least one year must be in *barricas*, or 225-litre Bordeaux barrels. The rest will usually be in bigger oak containers. Wines of modest, medium and good quality are all handled like this. *Reservas* are wines at least five years old, of which two and a half years were in *barricas*. Now, however, any of the statutory period can be substituted by twice as long in bottle. White *reservas* have a minimum of six months in oak.

Gran reservas are wines of at least seven years old, with at least four years in *barricas*, or twice as long in bottle. Reputable bodegas will of course only select wines of fine quality to mature as *reservas* and top quality as *gran reservas* – although this is only implied, not required, by the regulations.

The regions

The Rioja district is divided into three regions, with a total vineyard area of some 110,000 acres, following the valley of the Ebro from the Conchas de Haro, the rocky gorge where it bursts through the Sierra Cantabrica, to its much wider valley at Alfaro, 60 miles east and nearly 1,000 feet lower in altitude.

The highest region, La Rioja Alta, has the city of Logroño as its capital, although the much smaller Haro is its vinous heart. Cenicero, Fuenmayor and Navarrete are the other towns with bodegas. Haro has 13 out of a total of 30. there are 42,000 acres of vineyards. The soils are a mixture of chalky clay, iron-rich clay and alluvial silt. The climate is cool here and the rainfall relatively high. The minimum required strength for Rioja Alta wine is only 10 degrees. Rioja Alta wines have the highest acidity but also the finest flavour and structure, finesse and 'grip' that sometimes allows them to age almost indefinitely.

The Rioja Alavesa, north of the Ebro, along the borders of the county of Alava, has more southern slopes and a more consistently chalky soil. Its 17,000 acres of vines are largely Tempranillo, which here gives particularly fragrant, smooth, almost lush light wine, tending to be pale and quick-maturing. The minimum strength is 11-11.5 degrees. A dozen bodegas are based in four villages: Labastida, Elciego, Laguardia and Oyon.

The Rioja Baja ('Lower Rioja') is the biggest of the three with much the warmest and driest climate. Its soil is silt and iron-rich clay, its principal grape the Garnacha Tinta and its wine stronger, broader and less fine, with a required minimum strength of 12-12.5 degrees. There are only six bodegas for ageing in the region, but nearly all bodegas buy some of their wine here, and several (notably Berberana) are planting the finer grapes in the highest parts of the region.

It is probably true to say that most red Riojas are blends of wines from all three regions, although the old-established bodegas draw most heavily on the areas in which they were founded, and a few in Rioja Alavesa make a particular point of the regional style of their wines.

RIOJA PRODUCERS

AGE Bodegas Unidas

Fuenmayor, Loggroño, Rioja Alta.

A large new bodega, but one with a long history. It was established in 1967 with the joining of Bodegas Romeral (founded in 1881 by Don Feliz Azpilicueta) and Las Veras (set up by Don Cruz García Lafuente in 1926) and it is now owned by the American firm of Schenley and the Banco Español de Credito. Since the new bodega was built in 1967, there has been continuous building and expansion to make this one of the largest and most automated bodegas of the region. Though they own vineyards, most grapes have to be bought in. The best of the reds are the traditional *reservas*, Marqués del Romeral, Fuentemayor and Siglo Saco, sold in a sacking wrapper. White wines, all made in the new fruity style and bottled at 5 months old, include Romeral, Siglo Saco, Pedregal and Esmerado. The policy is to give the red wines less barrel-age and more bottle-age than formerly. Sales now amount to 3.75m. cases a year.

Bodegas Berberana

Ctra Elciego, Cenicero, Rioja Alta.

Rumasa have recently bought this old company, founded in Ollauri in 1877 and run by the same family until 1970. The huge new bodega in Cenicero (with no less than 40,000 barrels) dates from 1970. About 43% of the grapes come from their own vineyards, which, unusually, are mostly in the Rioja Baja – 865 of the 1,235 acres are in an impressive pioneering plantation on high ground near Aldeanueva del Ebro. The classic Tempranillo of the Rioja Alta is thriving here. Preferido is their vigorous cheap *sin crianza* red, Carta de Plata is their big-selling 3° año, Carta de Oro the fuller-bodied 5° año. The *gran reservas* are big and velvety, while the new Berberana white is young and fruity without barrel-age. Sales of 1.8m. cases a year cover Europe and the Americas.

Bodegas Bilbainas

Particular del Norte 2, Bilbao 3 and at Haro.

The bodega was founded in 1901 and continues essentially as a family firm. 35% of their grapes are grown in their own 625 acres of vineyards in Haro (Rioja Alta) and Elciego and Leza in Alavesa. They sell 200,000 cases of still wines a year and over 29,000 cases of the champagne-method sparkling Royal Carlton, which they have been making since 1912. Their aim is a wide choice of wines rather than a strong house style, but all the wines are conservative; rather austere by modern standards. Viña Paceta is a dry white, Cepa de Oro a sweeter white and Brillante a golden dessert wine. Viña Zaco is a high-quality *clarete*, while Viña Pomal is its more full-bodied *tinto* complement. Pomal *reservas* are the biggest and longest-lived wines.

Bodegas Marqués de Cáceres

Union Viti-Vinicola, Carretera de Logroño, Cenicero, Rioja Alta.

Founded in 1970 by Enrique Forner (owner with his brother of Châteaux de Camensac and La Rose-Trintaudan in Bordeaux) and planned with the help of Professor Emile Peynaud. 70% of the wine comes from local growers, members of the Union Viti-Vinícola, together owning 1,500 acres of vines. The cooperative at Cenicero supplies the remaining 30%. Only white wine is made at the bodega. The red wines, made by the growers under supervision, spend no more than 18 months in wood and no less than 18 months in bottle. They emerge less oaky than traditional Rioja, but well balanced and fruity. The white Marqués de Cáceres was the first of the new-style whites and, with its fruit and freshness without excess acidity, probably still the best. Several brand names are used, among them Rivarey, Grandeza, Costanilla, Gran Vendema, Don Sebastian and E. Forner. 80% of the 200,000 cases sold annually are red wines; 14% are white.

Bodegas Campo Viejo

Poligono de Cascajos, Logroño, Rioja Alta.

One of the largest bodegas; owned by Savin and formed in 1963 by the amalgamation of 2 old firms. Capacity in the new premises, built in 1968 and extended in '71, is now 50m. litres. 70% of production is from wine bought from cooperatives and 26% is from grapes bought in for vinification. 4% comes from their own vineyards – 692 acres divided between Rioja Alta and Rioja Baja – which include, in addition to the traditional grape varieties, experimental quantities of Cabernet Sauvignon, Pinot Noir, Gamay, Merlot, Chenin Blanc, Sémillon and Chardonnay.

Annual sales amount to 2.5m. cases. On the domestic market Campo Viejo, Almenar, Castillo de San Asensio and Foncalada are among the most familiar trade marks, accounting for 25-30% of all Rioja sold in Spain. Campo Viejo 4° año is consistently good value among the less ethereal red Riojas. San Asensio is a robust un-aged red. Marqués de Villamagna (currently 1970) is the bodega's top *gran reserva*.

CVNE Compañia Vinícola del Norte de España

Calle Costa del Vino 1, Haro, Rioja Alta.

One of the top half-dozen Rioja houses, founded in 1879 by the Real de Asua brothers and still owned by this family. Though the home market is now their most important – accounting for 94% of annual sales of 333,300 cases – for the first 60 years they exported all they produced. Their own 694 acres under vine (583 acres in Rioja Alta and 111 in Rioja Baja) provide 46% of the grapes: another 24% comes from growers under contract. 2 bodegas are in Haro and Elciego. They make consistently good wines. Reds include the excellent, vigorous Cune 3°, 4° and 5° años, the velvety Imperial (a *reserva* from the Rioja Alta), and the notably full-bodied, spicy Viña Real from Alavesa (made at Elciego). A new-style no-oak white made from Viura grapes only, and marketed as Cune and Lanceros, has been well received, but CVNE is better known for its traditional oak-flavoured white in a Moselle bottle, Monopole.

Bodegas Faustino Martínez

Carretera de Logroño, Oyon, Alava.

Founded in 1860 and still family owned and run. All grapes come from around the Oyon area in Rioja Alavesa, 30% from their own 618 acres. They hope to increase this proportion to 50-60% within the next 10 years and already Faustino 1, the *gran reserva*, and Faustino V, an aromatic, lemony white in the new style, are made entirely from their own grapes from first-class vineyards.

The reds are given extra age in bottle rather than spending overlong in oak. Viña Faustino is a fruity 1-year-old Alavesa wine; Señor Burgues is 3 years old; Faustino V is the red *reserva*; Faustino I is the top wine. Total sales are 300,000 cases.

R. Lopez de Heredia Viña Tondonia

Avenida de Vizcaya 3 & 5, PO Box 8, Haro, Rioja Alta.

One of the great bastions of Rioja tradition. A family-owned, family-run bodega founded by Don Raphael Lopez de Heredia y Landeta in 1877 and now headed by his grandson, Don Pedro. The premises, on a railway siding at Haro, are a marvel of Art Nouveau design; the underground tasting-room Wagnerian in its lofty cobwebbed splendour; the cellars damp and chill. Half the grapes come from their own vineyards in Rioja Alta and most of the rest come from small local growers. All the wines are fermented and aged long in oak: the minimum is 3 years. Wines include Tondonia (fine red and white not less than 6° año), Bosconia (a bigger red, at best sumptuous) and Gravonia (an oaky white), and Cubillo, a red, and at 3° año their youngest wine. White wines are important, accounting for a quarter of their annual production of 1.2m. litres. A 1964 Tondonia Blanco was still brilliantly fresh in 1982. The domestic market is their biggest with annual sales of 67,000 cases, 25,000 cases are exported.

Bodegas Muga

Barrio de la Estacion, Haro, Rioja Alta.

A small family firm founded in 1926 by Don Isaac Muga. His son, Don Isaac Muga Caño, took over on his father's death in 1969 and 2 years later moved to a new bodega by the famous Haro railway station. Muga claim to be the only producers in Rioja to use American oak exclusively throughout fermentation and ageing. Their own 70 acres under vine provide 40% of their needs; the rest they buy from farmers in the Rioja Alta. Muga wines are almost alarmingly pale and ethereal but very fragrant. Much their best wine to my taste is the darker and richer Reserva Prado Enea, a wine with some of the velvet pungency of burgundy. They also make traditional white and a featherweight *méthode champenoise* with the new name of Conde de Haro. Though annual sales are only 33,000 cases, they export to both Europe and South America.

Marqués de Murrieta

Ygay, Logroño, Rioja Alta. PO Box 109, Logroño.

With Marqués de Riscal, one of the two noble houses of Rioja, the first 2 bodegas to be founded, still with a special cachet, and remarkably unchanged by time. Don Luciano de Murrieta y Garcia-Lemoine founded this, the second oldest, in 1870 and it remains in his family. Their own vineyards of 284 acres at Ygay near Logroño supply the majority of grapes and long-standing arrangements with neighbouring growers provide the rest. Wines are made by wholly traditional methods and reach a very high standard. The small range includes a fruity 4° año, Etiqueta Blanca, and their extremely rare and expensive Castillo Ygay – the 1934 vintage of which has recently been succeeded by the 1960. The current white Castillo Ygay vintage is 1950.

Bodegas Olarra

Logroño, Rioja Alta.

Founded 1972. The most stylish new bodega in Rioja, owned by a company headed by a Bilbao industrialist, Luis Olarra. The ultra modern winery, formed of 3 wings to symbolize Rioja's 3 regions, would look better in the Napa Valley than on an industrial estate outside Logroño. It owns no vines but has rapidly made a name for typical and stylish wines, red and white (the white very lightly oaked and ageing extremely well in bottle, viz. the '76 in 1982). Cerro Añon is the label of the fatter and darker *reservas*. Reciente is a new-wave white.

Bodegas Federico Paternina

Haro, Rioja Alta.

One of the largest bodegas, now owned by Rumasa. It was founded in Ollauri in 1898 by Don Federico Paternina Josue. Though they have 618 acres of Viura, Tempranillo and Garnacha in Rioja Baja, they buy in 80% of their grapes from cooperatives and growers. Wines include Banda Azul (a sound and popular young red), Viña Vial (full and fruity), a *gran reserva* and a *reserva especial* Conde de los Andes. The white Banda Dorada has recently changed from a traditional oaky style to one of the new no-oak whites. Annual sales are 790,000 cases.

La Rioja Alta

Haro, Rioja Alta.

One of the group of top-quality firms round the station at Haro. Founded in 1890 and still in the original family. Its 408 acres at Cenicero and Rodezno (Rioja Alta) and Tudelilla (Rioja Baja) provide 65% of total production. Of the long list, Metropol is an oaky white and Leonora a compromise between the old style and the new, touched with oak but rather lightweight. The reds are more distinguished. Viña Alberdi is the pleasant 3° año red, Viña Arana is a fine light red (and a rather dull white) and Viña Ardanza a sumptuous full red worth laying down. The top wine is the Reserva 904, selected for its depth of colour and flavour to withstand 7 or 8 years in American oak and emerge in perfect balance.

Anastasio Gutierrez of La Rioja Alta

Vinos de los Herederos Marqués de Riscal

Torrea 1, Elciego, Alava.

The oldest existing Rioja bodega, founded in 1860 by Don Camilo Hurtado de Amezaga, Marqués de Riscal. The bodega was designed by a Bordeaux *vigneron*, and most of the wines continue to have a light, elegant, almost claret-like character – the epitome of the Rioja Alavesa.

60% of the grapes come from their own vineyards, 49 acres of which are planted with Cabernet Sauvignon. Cabernet is used in a proportion of about 5% for most reds, but occasionally much more. A 1970 *reserva* had 60% and an astonishing 1938, still vigorous in 1982, had 80%. The wines are aged in barrel for up to 4 years, then in bottle for a minimum of 3, often 10 – and no maximum; though some *gran reservas* are barrelled for 3-4 years, then aged in bottle for 2, then decanted back into barrels for further ageing. Sales of 250,000 cases a year, including wines under the Riscalsa label, go to 82 countries.

Sociedad General de Viñas

Villabuena, Elciego, Alava.

Founded in the early '70s by the sherry house of Pedro Domecq and the Canadian giant, Seagram. When the two parted company in 1974, Domecq built a modern, vitrified-steel-equipped bodega and began planting new vineyards and buying old ones in Alavesa. They now claim to be the biggest growers in Rioja, with 988 acres in production, but still have to buy in 30% of their grapes. The low-priced Viña Eguia and the round, fruity Domecq Domain (labelled Privilegio Rey Sancho for the Spanish market) are their main brands. Other labels for *reservas* are Conde de Montijo and Marqués de Arienzo. Annual sales reach 250,000 cases.

Cooperativa Vinícola de Labastida

Rioja Alavesa

Founded 1956. The only growers' cooperative in Rioja to oak-age and bottle its own wine. Its 160-odd members are all in Rioja Alavesa with admirable vineyards, and their cooperative competes on equal terms with the best bodegas. The powerful reds range from the everyday Manuel Quintano and good-value Montebuena to very fine *reservas* and *gran reservas* called Gastrijo and Castillo Labastida (the top of the line). The white is un-oaked, in the modern manner, and one of the best of its sort.

OTHER RIOJA PRODUCERS

Lopez Agos y Cía
PO Box 9, Ctra de Logroño, Fuenmayor, Rioja Alta. Founded in 1972 by a group of businessmen with experience in Riojan bodegas. Half the grapes come from the company's own 99-acre site, the rest from farmers (all in Rioja Alta) under supervision. They market red *reservas* under the Señorio Agos and Viñas Tesos labels, a white *reserva*, Agos Oro, and a *sin crianza* range of red, white and rosé under the bodega name. Annual sales of 100,000 cases.

Bodegas Alavesas
Laguardia, Rioja Alavesa. Founded 1972. A family company owning 247 acres in Laguardia, planted with 90% Tempranillo and 10% Viura. They buy in 5 to 10 times their own production and make typically pale, light, fragrant Alavesa wines; 4 years old under the bodega name and 6- to 7-year-old *reservas* under Solar de Samaniego.

Bodegas Ramon Bilbao
Avda Santa Domingo, Haro, Rioja Alta. Founded in 1924; a family-owned company with vineyards in the Rioja Alta. Wines under the bodega name include Turzabella and Monte Llano. Another range goes under the name Rioja Ellauri.

Bodegas Corral
Navarrete, Rioja Alta. Owned by Don Florencio Corral Daroca (grandson of the founder) and a group of Riojan friends. Their own 99-acre Rioja Alta vineyard provides 19% of their grape needs, the rest comes from growers in the same area. Traditional methods produce distinctly oaky wines under the Don Jacobo and Corral labels. Sales of 100,000 cases.

Bodegas El Coto
Oyon, Alava, Rioja. A young bodega whose wines were first marketed commercially in 1975. The shareholders are growers with 445 acres of vineyards in Cenicero and Oyon, providing 70% of the Tempranillo for their red wines and 80% of the Viura for their whites. The remaining grapes come from small growers. Soft fruity reds, Coto de Imaz and El Coto, are made almost wholly from Tempranillo, while El Coto white is made in the new style almost entirely from Viura.

Bodegas Franco-Españolas
Cabo Noval 2, Logroño, Rioja Alta. A big bodega in the city of Logroño, owned by Rumasa, who bought and began modernizing the company in 1973. Its French and Spanish founders (hence the name) included Monsieur Anglade, a fugitive from phylloxera-devastated France. Their own vines, mostly Garnacha, are in Tudelilla (Rioja Baja); they buy in other varieties from Rioja Alta and Alavesa. Traditional oak-aged whites, Viña Soledad and Viña Sole, have now been joined by a young no-oak white Diamante. Traditional reds include a dark and flavoury (if rather coarse) bargain, Rioja Bordon, the Royal *reservas* and Excelso *gran reservas*. Annual exports of 208,000 cases to 65 countries supplement domestic sales of 670,000 cases.

Bodegas Gurpegui
PO Box 3, San Adrian, Navarra. One of the largest producers of wine to sell to other bodegas. Founded in 1872. Don Luis Gurpegui Muga is the third-generation proprietor. 10% of production comes from their own 250-acre vineyard, 90% from regular suppliers over many years. 2 of the well-known brands of well-made classic Riojas from this stable are Dominio de la Plana and Berceo (and Gonzalo de Berceo). Annual sales of 208,000 cases.

Martinez Lacuesta Hnos Lda
PO Box 45, Haro, Rioja Alta. A family firm founded in 1895 and now directed by Don Luis Martinez Lacuesta. All grapes, including an unusually high proportion of Garnacha, are bought in from cooperatives. Reds are a very pale and oaky *clarete* and a fuller, still oaky, Campeador (both to be found on Iberian Airlines). A white wine is called Viña Delys.

Bodegas Lan
Paraje de Buicio, Fuenmayor, Rioja Alta. Now owned by Rumasa; a large and very modern bodega founded in 1969. Tempranillo, Mazuelo and Viura from their own 173 acres in El Cortijo (Rioja Alta) provide 20% of their requirements. Most of the rest is bought from small growers, principally in Rioja Alavesa. The labels are Lan and Viña Lanciano (for *reservas*). Lambros is a good fresh white in the modern style.

Bodegas Muerza
Plaza Vera-Magallon, PO Box 1.44, San Adrian, Navarra, Rioja. A small bodega founded in 1882. It has changed hands several times and now belongs to a group from the south of Spain. All grapes are bought in from individual growers in all 3 regions, not from cooperatives. Reds are made in the traditional way, whites and rosés in the no-oak style. There are 2 brand names: Rioja Vega (now only for whites and rosés and, since 1980, Sẽnorial.

Bodegas Palacio-Coprimar
San Lazaro 1, Laguardia, Alava. Founded by Don Angel Palacio in 1894. Formerly famous for its splendid Glorioso. Now owned by the Seagram group. They have vineyards in Laguardia, where they grow Tempranillo and Viura for their Glorioso, Portil and Castillo red, white and rosé Riojas. The most important market for their 83,000-case annual sales is Switzerland.

Bodegas José Palacios
Poligono de Calabria, PO Box 1.152, Logroño, Rioja Alta. Founded by Don José Palacios Remondo in 1947 and still in the family. Grapes are bought in, mostly from Alfaro (Rioja Baja). Brands are Eral, Utrero, Copa Remondo and Herencia. Reds are traditional; whites unaged. Annual sales of 166,000 cases.

Bodegas Riojanas
Estacion, 1-21, Cenicero, Rioja Alta. A substantial and conservative bodega, conceived in 1890 as a sort of château in Spain, by families who still own and manage the company today. The original French staff stayed on until 1936. Some grapes are bought in, the rest come from their own 494-acre holding in Cenicero. Traditional methods, including some fermentation in open stone *lagos*, are used to produce the *reservas*, Viña Albina, and Monte Real, a most pungent and admirable red. Albina is a semi-sweet white, Medieval a dry one and Canchales a young red. Puerta Vieja and Bori are other brands. Annual sales are 83,000 cases, with Italy among the export markets.

Salceda
El Ciego (Alava) PO Box 8, Via Cenicero. founded in 1973. A red-wine-only bodega with 55 acres of its own vineyard, using modern methods to make good wine with a leaning to the soft Alavesa style. Viña Salceda is the 4-year-old quality; Conde de la Salceda the *reserva.*

Bodegas Carlos Serres
PO Box 4, Haro, Rioja Alta. Founded in 1896 by Charles Serres, who arrived in Haro from phylloxera-infected France. Now a limited company. All grapes are bought in from growers and cooperatives. Reds, whites and rosés are made by traditional methods with very modern equipment. The white *gran reserva* is an old-style Rioja, 2 years in vat and 2 in barrel. Red Carlomagno *reservas* (the top wines) are good; usually rather light in style.

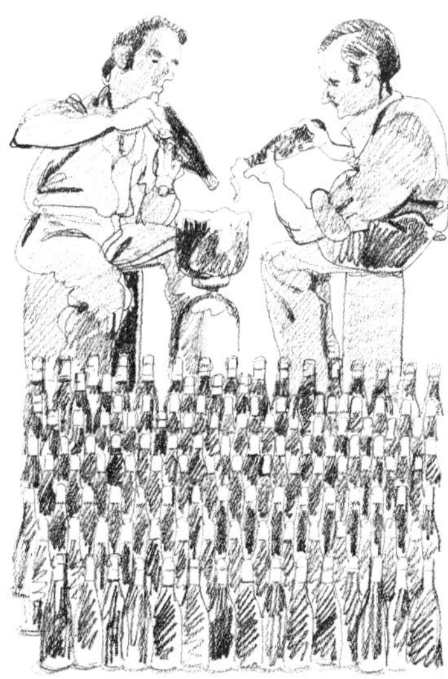

Adding wax capsules to bottles

Rioja exports

In 1981, 3.04m. cases of Rioja were exported, out of an average annual production of 15.5m. The main markets, in order of importance were:

UK	244,000 cases
Switzerland	229,000 ,,
Denmark	227,000 ,,
USA	223,000 ,,

Canada is also a large market, taking more white Rioja than red.

NORTHERN SPAIN PRODUCERS

Señorio de Sarria
Puente la Reina, *Navarra.*

The finest wine estate in Navarra, unique in the region (almost in Spain) for its château-style approach and almost Bordeaux-like results. The ancient estate was bought by a rich builder, Señor Huarte, in 1952. Since then he has rebuilt, landscaped, replanted vines and perfected cellarage. 247 acres of the 2,500-acre estate are vineyard, with Rioja vines in appropriate proportions (60% Tempranillo) and a little Cabernet Sauvignon. Its best *reservas* are better than most Riojas; even a light Cosecha (non-*reserva*) wine of '74 was very well balanced, Bordeaux-like to smell with a nice plummy flavour. A 3-year-old red is called Viña Ecoyen and a bigger, full-bodied red Viña del Perdon.

Bodegas Vega Sicilia
Valbuena de Duero, *Valladolid.*

The most prestigious wine estate in Spain: a legend for the quality (and the price) of its wines. It was founded in 1864 in limestone hills 2,400 feet above sea level on the south bank of the Duero. The founder imported Bordeaux grapes (Cabernet Sauvignon, Merlot and Malbec) to add to the local Tinto Aragonés (a form of Garnacha), Garnacha Tinta and Albillo. The yield is very low (only 10,500 cases from 296 acres) and the wine-making completely traditional. Only the unpressed *vin de goutte* is used, fermented for 15 days and matured in Bordeaux *barricas* for no less than 10 years (for the great *reserva* 'Unico' Vega Sicilia itself) and 3 or 5 for its younger brother Valbuena. The result is a wine combining immense power (13.5% alcohol with formidable fruit) and unmistakable 'breeding'. The raciness of the flavour is astonishing and the perfume intoxicating. Vega Sicilia is one of Europe's noble eccentrics, but if proof were needed of the potential of Rueda for fine reds of a more conventional kind Valbuena would be evidence enough.

OTHER NORTHERN SPAIN PRODUCERS

Albariño de Fefiñanes
Fefiñanes, Pontevedra, *Galicia*. The aristocrat of Galician wine, made by the Marqués de Figueroa in a small modern bodega in his palace of Fefiñanes, near Cambados. It is 100% Albariño, the best white grape of the region (and Portugal's Minho), aged for up to 6 years (for *reservas*) in oak. It bears no resemblance to *vinho verde* except in its remarkable freshness.

Albariño del Palacio
Fefiñanes, Pontevedra, *Galicia*. The brother of the Marqués de Figueroa makes this high-quality, typical fizzy young Albariño – but not in the palace.

Bodegas los Arcos
León, *Duero*. A small family-owned bodega in El Bierzo. Its Santo Rosado has a good reputation.

Bodegas Palacio de Arganza
Villafranca del Bierzo, León, *Duero*. Since 1805 the bodega that occupies the 15th-century palace of the Dukes of Arganza has been the most important in El Bierzo, the best wine area of León. It ages its potent *reservas* in oak casks. Almena del Bierzo is its considerable red, Vega Burbia a clean crisp white.

Bodegas Chaves
Cambados, Pontevedra, *Galicia*. A small family-run bodega offering typical sharp and fizzy Albariño to a good standard.

Bodegas Julián Chivite
Cintruenigo, *Navarra*. The largest private wine company in Navarra, founded in 1860, with vineyards and bodegas throughout the region and in Rioja and Aragón. Its Gran Feudo is a pleasant, rather thin, slightly oaky wine. Older *reservas*, Cibonero and the 10-year-old Parador, are fuller and more fruity. Chivite is a pleasant dry white.

Bodegas de Crianza de Castilla la Vieja
Rueda, *Valladolid*. Started in 1970 as a consortium of local growers to upgrade their wine. Their speciality was a *solera*-aged, sherry-style white. Since 1980 Emile Peynaud of Bordeaux has been engaged by new owners to make a small quantity (2,000 cases) of top-class modern white, carrying the name of the owner, Marqués de Griñon. The same nobleman has planted Bordeaux red grapes at Toledo.

Bodega la Magallonera
Magallon, Zaragoza, *Aragón*. A small family bodega in the D.O. Campo de Borja, founded in the 1950s by Andrés Ruberte, whose family are well-known wine makers. His typically alcoholic and full-bodied but also acidic red Pagos de Oruña is worth tasting.

Vinícola Navarra
Las Campanas, *Navarra*. A century-old company with French origins; the biggest exporter of Navarra wines, without great refinement but reliable and increasingly tasty in the better qualities. Las Campanas Extra is a stout plain red; Castillo de Olite is a clean, pleasantly fruity, faintly sweet red and dry white. Castillo de Tiebas is the full-bodied *reserva* with Rioja-like oaky notes.

Bodegas Ochoa
Olite, *Navarra*. A locally popular privately owned bodega in Olite, once the capital of the Kings of Navarre. The reds and rosés are soundly made.

Bodegas Sanz
Rueda, Valladolid, *Duero*. A substantial family-run bodega, founded in 1900. Its fresh young rosé is its best wine.

Bodegas Cayo Simon
Murchante, *Navarra*. A leading private bodega in the warm south of Navarra. Its powerful wines include Monte Cierzo and Viña Zarcillo.

Bodegas Joaquin Soria
Cariñena, Zaragoza, *Aragón*. A small family firm now over 150 years old, growing its own grapes for its benchmark Cariñena, Espigal *clarete*, made of Garnacha Tinta (Grenache Noir) and white Macabeo.

Vicente, Suso y Pérez
Cariñena (Zaragoza), *Aragón*. The biggest and best-known private bodega in Cariñena and the largest exporter. It buys grapes from growers, using oak to age the wines. Don Ramon is the standard red and rosé; *reservas* include Comendador and Duque de Sevilla.

VILE (Planta de Elaboracion y Embotellado de Vinos SA)
León, *Duero*. The unhappily named company is a private consortium growing and buying León wines on a big scale (it owns 2,500 casks) and with modern ideas. Its young Rey León red and white are well-made everyday wines. Older and *reserva* class wines include Palacio de Guzman, Catedral de León and Don Suero.

Vinos Blancos de Castilla
Rueda, *Duero*. A branch of the famous Rioja firm of Marqués de Riscal, founded in 1972 and built with advice from Emile Peynaud of Bordeaux. All the Riscal white wines are made here, largely of Verdejo grapes, cold fermented in stainless steel and matured only very briefly in oak to achieve maximum freshness.

Cooperativa Barco de Valdeorras
El Barco, *Orense*. A substantial coop bottling very adequate plain still red and white (D.O. Valdeorras) with the name El Barco ('The Boat').

Cooperativa de Monterrey
Verin, *Orense*. The only bottler of Monterrey wines, founded in 1963. Red and white are both bubble free; the best are labelled Castelo Monterrey.

Cooperativa del Ribeiro
Ribadavia, Orense, *Galicia*. Much the biggest cooperative in Galicia, with 1,600 members and very modern facilities, producing the equivalent of more than 750,000 cases a year. Its best white is crisp, clean and faintly fragrant, only slightly *pétillant*, like a Portuguese *vinho verde*. The red is fizzy, sharp and an acquired taste. The label for its top quality is Pazo.

Cooperativa de Ribeiro del Duero Peñafiel
Valladolid. A long-established cooperative with 230 members, producing red wines worthy of a more famous region, well above normal coop standards. Ribera Duero is their blackberryish red without oak ageing. Peñafiel is slightly oak-aged (they have 2,000 *barricas*) and Protos is a sensational *reserva*, deep in colour and in its oak and mulberry fragrance, at 10 years comparable to an excellent Rioja *tinto*; long, soft and delicious.

Cooperativa Vitícola San José de Aguaron
Aguaron – Cariñena (Zaragoza), *Aragón*. A 500-member cooperative founded in 1955. It ages its very sound wines in oak casks. Puente de Piedra is a typical Cariñena red.

Cooperativa San Roque
Murchante, *Navarra*. The best cooperative of southern Navarra, with powerful but clean reds typical of the warm and fertile region.

Cooperativa San Valero
Cariñena, Zaragoza, *Aragón*. A large cooperative with a wide market in Spain for its 'Don Mendo' and Monte Ducay wines.

Agricola Castellana Sociedad Cooperativa La Seca
Valladolid, *Duero*. An important cooperative, founded in 1935, producing from huge stocks both traditional *solera*-aged Rueda whites of Verdejo and Palomino (e.g. Campo Grande *fino* and Dorado 61) and a modern-style, unaged, fruity dry white, Verdejo Pallido.

CATALONIA

Your Catalan is only half a Spaniard. He is proud of the autonomy of his privileged province. He basks in a temperate, mild-winter climate without the extremes of most of Spain. Catalonia lies on the same latitude as Tuscany, sheltered from the north by the Pyrenees and their gradually rising foothills, facing southeast into the Mediterranean. It can be considered as a southward extension of the best wine area of France's Midi: the Côtes de Roussillon and their hinterland. They both have the capacity to produce ponderous and potent reds and elaborate luscious dessert wines – and also to surprise with the quality of their white grapes.

Historically most important have been the dessert wines of Tarragona, the warmest part of the Catalan coast. From Priorato, an inland enclave in the same area, came red wines of legendary colour and strength (but also quality) for blending. A century ago the Raventos family of Penedès realized the potential of their native white grapes, naturally high in acid, for the champagne treatment. Today Penedès produces 90 per cent of Spain's sparkling wine.

The latest development, but the most significant of all, has been the successful trial of the classic French and German grapes in the higher parts of Penedès. The Torres family, long-established wine makers of the region, have led the way with a judicious mixture of these exotics with the best of the well-tried Catalan varieties.

Among the native whites Parellada and Xarel-lo are crisply acidic with low alcoholic degrees, Malvasia is broadly fruity, with low acidity, and Macabeo (the Viura of Rioja) is admirably balanced and apt for maturing.

Catalonia shares the best red grapes of the rest of Spain, above all the Tempranillo (here called Ull de Llebre), the Garnacha Tinta and the deep and tannic Monastrell. The Cariñena (alias Carignan) is no more distinguished here than elsewhere.

Seven zones in Catalonia now have *Denominación de Origen* status. They are:

Alella
A coastal valley just north of Barcelona, now reduced to 1,000 acres of vines by urban sprawl. Almost all its many small growers take their grapes to the Alella cooperative.

Its best wine is a mildly fruity semi-sweet white made from the fruit of the southern slopes. The dry white is clean and acidic enough, but lacks character. The red is passable.

Ampurdán – Costa Brava
The northernmost D.O. centred round Perelada in the province of Gerona, behind the cliffs and beaches of the Costa Brava. The 12,000 acres produce mainly rosé, recently some *primeur*-style red called Vi Novell, and adequate whites, some made sparkling but without the quality of the best Penedès wines.

Conca de Barberá
A recently defined D.O. in the hills inland from Penedès, with 25,000 acres largely planted in white grapes for the Penedès sparkling-wine industry. It is to these cooler hills that the Torres company has looked for sites for classic French grapes.

Penedès
The biggest D.O. of Catalonia ranges from the coast at Sitges back into 2,000-foot limestone hills. Its centres are Vilafranca de Penedès, best known for its table-wine bodegas (among them Torres), and San Sadurní de Noya, 20 miles west of Barcelona, the capital of Spanish sparkling wine and headquarters of the vast firm of Codorníu.

The table wines of Penedès have been revolutionized in the last 20 years and can now rival Rioja. The reds are generally darker in colour and fruitier than Riojas, lacking the delicacy and refinement of Rioja at its best. But exceptional wines, especially those with a proportion of Cabernet, reach the best international standards. Modern methods have brought the white wines under total control. There is now a benchmark dry fruity Catalan white, highly satisfactory if not exactly exciting. Unlike the best Rioja whites it does not (at least to my taste) take kindly to ageing in oak. Possibly less concentrated fruit, partly the result of bigger crops, is to blame.

It may have been this characteristic leanness of body that inspired the creation of *cava* – the official term for champagne-method sparkling wine.

Certainly the Xarel-lo, Parellada and Viura produce high-acid musts of only slight flavour; ideal base material: the flavour of champagne yeast comes through distinctly with its richness and softness. Wines that were stored in wooden vats (some still are) also picked up a very faint tarry taste which added character.

The *cavas* of Penedès today range from the extremely deft and delicate to the fat and clumsy. The best can certainly be counted among the world's finest sparkling wines. It is only in the inevitable comparison with champagne that they lose. Where champagne finally triumphs is in the vigour of the flavours that it assembles so harmoniously.

Priorato

The long viticultural course of the river Ebro, starting near Haro in the Rioja Alta, might be said to end without shame in the western hills of Tarragona with this memorable wine. Priorato is a D.O. within the much greater *denominación* of Tarragona, applying to some 9,000 acres of steep volcanic hillside vines around the little Ebro tributary the Montsant. The fame of Priorato lies in the almost blackness of its wine, a brew of Garnacha and Cariñena that reaches 16 degrees alcohol, with the colour of crushed blackberries and something of their flavour. There is also amber-white Priorato deliberately oxidized to a *rancio* flavour.

Tarragona

The D.O. of Tarragona has the same vineyard area as Penedès spread over a wider region. The table wines are normally of blending quality without the extra distinction of Priorato. Its finest products are fortified dessert wines (*see* De Muller under Producers). But the great bulk of Tarragona's exports are of a more humble nature.

Terra Alta

A new D.O. continuing south from that of Tarragona beyond the river Ebro. Mora on the Ebro and Gandesa are the chief centres for the 40,000 acres of vines in the hills that rise to the mountainous province of Teruel. The wine is potent, vigorous and unpretentious, much used, like Tarragona, for blending.

CATALONIA PRODUCERS

Cavas del Ampurdan

Perelada, Gerona.

The sister company of Castillo de Perelada, producing very pleasant still red, white and rosé. The aged reds Tinto Cazador and Reserva Don Miguel are the top wines. 'Pescador' is a refreshing half-sparkling white. Sparkling wines are bulk produced by the *cuve close* method. The company was the defendant in a famous London court case in 1960 when the Champagne authorities succeeded in preventing it from using the term Spanish Champagne.

Masía Bach

Sant Estre Sesrovires, Barcelona.

Masía means farm. Bach was the name of 2 bachelor brothers who in 1920 used a fortune made clothing soldiers to build a Florentine folly in Penedès, with garages for 40 cars and a winery which grew in reputation and size until its 1,000 metres of cellars held 8,500 oak casks. It was recently bought by Codorníu (q.v.), but its old wine maker, Angel Escude, continues to make smooth red wines and the house speciality, an oak-flavoured sweet white called Extrísimo Bach.

René Barbier

San Sadurní de Noya, Barcelona.

An old-established bodega taken over by Rumasa. Its wines, both still and sparkling, are made in the cellars of Segura Viudas (q.v.). Kraliner is the fresh dry white. Reds are made fruity for everyday and oak-aged for Sundays.

Conde de Caralt

San Sadurní de Noya, Barcelona.

A famous old sparkling-wine bodega, now part of the Rumasa group and in the same cellars as Segura Viudas and René Barbier (qq.v.). The name now appears on a range of still wines, including delicate red *reservas*.

Castell del Remey

Penelles, Lerida.

A long-established firm on the inland fringes of Catalonia. Its vineyards include Cabernet Sauvignon and Sémillon and its wines have a good reputation.

Castillo de Perelada

Perelada, Gerona.

A celebrated *cava* concern in a picturesque castle dating back to the 14th century, now housing a fine library, collections of glass and ceramics and a wine museum – and a casino. Half the grapes come from the firm's vineyards. The best wine, Gran Claustro, is one of Catalonia's most satisfying *cavas*. Others are less notable. A sister company, Cavas de Ampurdan, produces the cheap and cheerful *cuve close* sparkling Perelada.

Codorníu.

San Sadurní de Noya, Barcelona.

The first Spanish firm to use the champagne method and now not only the biggest sparkling-wine house in Spain but apparently in the world. The Raventos family has made wine in Penedès since the 16th century. In 1872 Don José returned from Champagne to imitate its methods. The establishment is now monumental, its vast *fin-de-siècle* buildings, over 11 miles of cellars, lie in a green park with splendid cedars. They include a considerable wine museum and attract enormous numbers of visitors.

All the grapes are bought from 350 local growers, for total sales of some 3m. cases. The wines range from simple and fruity to highly refined – the apogee being the vintage Non Plus Ultra.

Coniusa

Raimat, Lerida.

A member of the Raventos family of Codorníu has replanted vineyards around the Castle of Raimat in inland Catalonia. The wines of Catalan grapes, light red Can Rius and heavier Can Clamor, are not extraordinary but a pure Cabernet Sauvignon, Clos Abbadia, shows promise.

Bodega José L. Ferrer

Binisalem, Majorca.

The one distinguished bodega of the Balearic islands. Señor Ferrer is a hotelier in Palma who owns 370 acres of vineyards in the centre of the island. The local Manto Negro grape makes lively reds. Autentico is the young Ferrer wine. *Reservas* can be extremely good. There is also a dry Blanc de Blancs.

Bodegas J. Freixadas

Vilafranca de Penedès, Barcelona.

A substantial bodega founded in 1897, owning 200 acres but buying the majority of its grapes for rather good sparkling wine and the Santa Marta range of Penedès table wines.

Freixenet

San Sadurní de Noya, Barcelona.

The second-biggest Spanish *cava* house, founded by the Bosch family in 1915 and rivalling Codorníu in everything but size. The top Freixenet wines are special vintage releases such as Cuvée D.S. 1969. Brut Nature is the best standard line; Cordon Negro is the best seller. Carta Nevada is a cheaper brand and La Sirena a fresh young dry wine. A range of still wines goes by the name of Viña Carossa. Freixenet also owns 50% of the big *cuve close* sparkling-wine firm L'Aixertell. Its partner is Savin.

Jean León.

Torrelavid, Barcelona.

A California transplant. León is the owner of La Scala Restaurant, Los Angeles. In 1964 he started to plant what is now 250 acres of Cabernet and 25 of Chardonnay in Penedès. The wines are first-rate, and excellent value. Most of the 16,000 cases of Cabernet and 800 of Chardonnay are sold in the USA.

Cavas Mascaro

Vilafranca de Penedès, Barcelona.

An old family bodega respected both for its *cava* sparkling wines and fine brandy. Antonio Mascaro has lately turned his hand to still wines. The lively unpretentious Viña Franca is a good start.

Marqués de Monistrol

San Sadurní de Noya, Barcelona.

A family firm with 740 acres of vines, making sparkling wines since 1882, recently bought by Martini & Rossi. Since 1974 they have added still wines, including an attractively lively 'Vin Natur Blanc de Blanc' and traditional-style red *reservas*, long-aged in oak and bottle.

De Muller

Tarragona

The great name in the classic tradition of sweet Tarragona wines. A family firm founded in 1851, now directed by the present Marqués de Muller y de Abadal, still in its old bodegas by the harbour with a vast capacity of oak storage. The pride of the house is its altar wines, supplied to (among others) the Vatican, and its velvety *solera*-aged Moscatel, Pajarete and other dessert wines. The firm has a Priorato bodega at Scala Dei, producing both the massive red of the area and a *solera*-aged dry apéritif, Priorato Rancio Dom Juan Fort. Standard-quality table wines are called Solimar.

Cellers de Scala Dei

Scala Dei, Tarragona.

Scala Dei was a great Carthusian monastery, now in ruins. The small modern bodega of Jaime Mussons is in an old stone building nearby, making 9,000 cases of high-quality oak-aged Priorato, deep, dark, strong (14.5°) but balanced with rich soft-fruit flavours. The label is Cartoixa Scala Dei.

Segura Viudas

San Sadurní de Noya, Barcelona.

The 3 *cava* companies owned by Rumasa all shelter in the same cellars. Segura Viudas is the prestige marque, made in a modern winery surrounded by a 270-acre vineyard that supplies part of its needs. Its best wine, Reserva Heredad, a very delicate production, comes in a horrifically vulgar bottle with a sort of built-in silvery coaster and other distractions. The Gonzales Byass sparkling wine Jean Perico also comes from the same cellars.

Viñedos Torres

Vilafranca de Penedès, Tarragona.

An old family company (founded 1870) which has changed the wine map of Spain in the last 10 years, putting Catalonia on a par with Rioja as a producer of really high-quality table wines. The family has 1,000 acres of vineyards, now planted with Chardonnay, Gewürztraminer, Riesling, Sauvignon Blanc, Muscat d'Alsace, Cabernets Sauvignon and Franc, Petite Syrah and Pinot Noir as well as the traditional Penedès varieties. White wines are cold-fermented, reds aged in oak for a mere 18 months, French style, then in bottle. Viña Sol is a fresh Parellada white; Gran Viña Sol a blend with Chardonnay. Green Label is Parellada and Sauvignon Blanc with a little oak age. Of the reds Tres Torres is a full-bodied blend of Garnacha and Cariñena (Carignan), Gran Sangre de Toro an older *reserva* of the same, Coronas a lighter blend of Monastrell and Ull de Llebra (Tempranillo), Gran Coronas Reserva the same with some Cabernet Sauvignon. Viña Magdala is a Pinot Noir blend. Gran Coronas Black Label, the top wine, is a blend of Cabernets Sauvignon and Franc with Monastrell. Other wines include a sweet Muscat/Gewürztraminer blend, Esmeralda, and a successful Riesling, Waltraud. (*See* page 364.)

Bodega Cooperativa Alella Vinícola

Alella, Barcelona.

The long-established (1906) cooperative of the dwindling Alella region, which is suffering building blight as Barcelona pushes north. There are 150-odd members. Its wines, in hock bottles, are labelled Alella Legitima Marfil ('Ivory'). The white *semisecco* is pleasant enough; the dry rather dull. The light red is just saved from ordinariness by a faint hint of incense – the smell of a vestry.

Cooperativa Agricola de Gandesa

Gandesa, Tarragona.

An old-established (1919) coop with 135 members now in the recent D.O. Terra Alta. Gandesa Blanc Gran Reserva is its most remarkable wine.

Cooperativa de Mollet de Perelada

Perelada, Gerona.

A considerable coop with a French-trained wine maker specializing in *primeur* red, white and rosé called Vi Novell – the red modelled on Beaujolais Nouveau. Their Garnacha Blanca dessert white is also attractive and their sparkling wine worth trying.

Union Agraria Cooperativa

Reus, Tarragona.

A federation of all 180 cooperatives in Tarragona, founded in 1962. Tarragona Union and Yelmo are their popular labels but most wine is sold in bulk. The best are *reservas* from the Cooperativa de Gratallops.

THE TORRES FAMILY

No single family of wine makers has made such an impact on the Spanish scene during the last decade as Manuel Torres and his son Miguel. In 1970 Catalonia was known only for blending wines and, within Spain, for its excellent sparkling *cavas*. Within 10 years the Torres Gran Coronas was being compared with Château Latour and the family operation, with father, son and daughter all deeply and enthusiastically involved, to the legendary Mondavis of California.

The Torres principle is to make uninhibited and innovative use of the wide range of growing conditions offered by the Catalonian coast and the mountains behind. Their base at Villa Franca de Penedès is the traditional centre of the industry, but higher altitudes have provided slower ripening and better conditions for trial lots of French grapes. They have not abandoned the regional varieties but rather improved their performance with careful growing and fermentation, modified the sometimes excessive local use of oak ageing, and when necessary added a seasoning of Cabernet or Chardonnay.

Torres marketing is done with the same uninhibited perfectionism. Manuel's daughter Marimar has demonstrated that Catalonia has nothing to learn from Madison Avenue. To create in 10 years a big-volume brand which is synonymous with quality, in the intensively competitive world of modern wine, is a tough assignment.

OTHER CATALONIA PRODUCERS

Alta Alella
Alella, Barcelona. A newcomer to the small Alella district, causing comment with a good fruity semi-sweet white.

Aquila Rossa
Vilafranca de Penedès, Barcelona. A century-old bodega known for its Montgros Penedès table wines and vermouths.

José Lopez Bertran y Cía
Tarragona. A long-established family business supplying such everyday wines as Vinate, Don Bertran and Corrida.

Bodegas Bosch-Guell
Vilafranca de Penedès, Barcelona. A family company founded in 1886, using the name Rómulo for a range of sound Penedès wines.

Gonzales y Dubosc
The sparkling-wine subsidiary of Gonzales Byass (*see* Sherry). Its wines are made by Segura Viudas (q.v.).

Cavas Hill
Moja, Vilafranca de Penedès. The English Hill family arrived in Penedès in 1660. In 1884 Don José Hill Ros established this commercial bodega, which now produces both *cava* and still wines. Labels include Viña San Manuel, and Gran Toc red *reservas*.

La Vinícola Iberica
Tarragona. A large old-established bodega in the bulk-buying and selling business.

Antonio Mestres Sagues
San Sadurní de Noya, Barcelona. A particularly good small family-owned *cava* house.

Bodegas Pinord
Vilafranca de Penedès, Barcelona. A family company with a wide range of labels: Chatel, Chateldon, Reynal and others.

Bodegas Robert
Sitges, Barcelona. A small company making the (now rare) traditional sweet white Sitges, from Moscatel and Malvasia.

Pedro Rovira
Mora la Nova, Tarragona. An old family firm producing *solera*-aged dessert Tarragona, 'Cream Solera' and 'Dry Solera', as well as strong everyday wines.

Vinos Jaime Serra
Alella, Barcelona. A small private bodega offering a range of wines as 'Alellasol'.

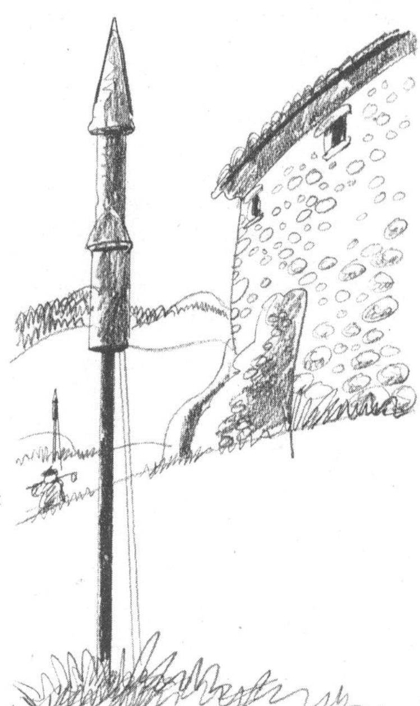

Rockets are used by Torres in Catalonia, among others, to disperse hail clouds

CENTRAL SPAIN

By far the greatest concentration of vineyards in Spain lies south and southeast of Madrid in a great block that reaches the Mediterranean at Valencia in the north and Alicante in the south. This central band, with scattered outposts farther west towards Portugal in Extremadura, contains no great names, no lordly estates, no pockets of perfectionism. Its wines combine various degrees of strength with various degrees of dullness – but in the main a generous helping of both.

Extremadura in the west has only one D.O., Tierra de Barros, around the town of Almendralejo in the province of Badajoz. Its 100,000-odd acres are largely planted with a common white grape, the Cayetana, giving dry low-acid but high-strength wines – the curse of Spain, in fact. Its rarer red wines, however, have some merit; particularly those of Salvatierra de Barros on the Portuguese border, and the eccentric Montánchez, from the northern province of Cáceres, which grows a *flor* yeast like sherry. The same is true of the white of Cañamero.

Toledo province, southwest of Madrid, contains the D.O. of Méntrida, an 80,000-acre spread of Garnacha vines supplying strong red wine.

By far the biggest wine region in the whole of Spain, demarcated or not, is La Mancha, the dreary plain of Don Quixote. It has no less than 1.2 million acres under vine, almost all a white variety called Airén, of which the best that can be said is that it has no flavour beyond that of its 13-14° of alcohol.

The one superior enclave of La Mancha is the D.O. Valdepeñas, 100 miles south of Madrid, where the tradition is to blend the Airén white with a small measure of very dark red, made of Tempranillo (here called Cencibel) and Garnacha. So dark is the red that a mere 10 per cent of it makes the wine – known as *aloque* – a *clarete* in colour, though it remains a soft rather spineless wine, low in acid and tannin. The old method is fermentation in the tall clay *tinajas* obviously descended from Roman or earlier vessels. A little is aged in barrel, but freshness and a certain light touch is the most one can hope for from Valdepeñas.

The sorry tale continues with the D.O. of Manchuela, east of La Mancha and making both white and red wine on its 20,000 acres.

The smaller D.O. of Almansa around Albacete concludes the uninspiring toll of the Castilian plain. Its 26,000 acres are planted in dark grapes.

The term Levante embraces five D.O.s of only very moderate interest at present, but some considerable potential as modern methods creep in. To the north on the coast is Valencia (and what was formerly called Cheste), liberal producers of alcoholic white wine and to a lesser degree red. Inland from Valencia lies Utiel-Requena, a hill region of black grapes (the principal one, the Bobal, as black as night) used expressly for colouring wine. The local technique is to ferment each batch of wine with a double ration of skins to extract the maximum colour and tannin: a brew called *vino de doble pasta*. Its by-product, the lightly crushed juice with barely any 'skin contact' or colour, surplus to the double brew, makes the second speciality of the region, a racy pale rosé more to the modern taste.

The D.O. Alicante covers both coastal vineyards producing sweet Moscatel and hill vineyards for red wines, *vino de doble pasta* and rosés. A little local white wine is (relatively) highly prized.

Behind Alicante in the province of Murcia there are two *denominacións*, Yecla and Jumilla, whose respective cooperatives are struggling with their inky material to teach it modern manners. So far Jumilla seems to be marginally more advanced.

Spanish prices

Ex-cellar prices for a bottle, for the basic qualities of Spanish wine, were as follows in late 1982:

	pesetas
Rioja *sin crianza*, red and white	100
Rioja *reserva*	125
Rioja *gran reserva*	208
Cava wines	150
Catalonia red and white	71
Vega Sicilia	1,250
Navarra *reserva*	150
Galician white	100
Valdepeñas	50
Alicante Moscatel	58
Sherry	116
Málaga *lágrima*	100
Montilla	63

CENTRAL SPAIN PRODUCERS

Ayuso
Villarobleda, Albacete. A family concern in Manchuela. Other labels are Armino and Estola.

Bodegas Bleda
Jumilla (Murcia). The son of the founder (in 1917) still runs this pioneer house for Jumilla wine. He matures his powerful reds, Castillo de Jumilla and Oro de Ley, in oak casks.

Casa de Calderon
Requena, Valencia. A small family vineyard and bodega making some of the best Requena. Their *generoso* has some of the flesh and grip of port.

Bodegas Miguel Carrion
Alpera, Almansa. The best producer of the D.O. Almansa to the east of La Mancha. A small company with a good soft strong Tinto Selecto, aged in oak.

Bodegas Cevisur
Tierra de Barros, Almendralejo, Badajoz. A family concern bottling the newly demarcated Tierra de Barros white, as Viña Extremeña.

Bodegas Galán
Montánchez, Badajoz. A little family bodega in a village near Mérida. Of interest because it makes a red wine called Trampal, growing *flor* and tasting like sherry. It has a following in Madrid.

Marqués de Griñon
Toledo. The recent enterprise of an ambitious landowner, advised by Emile Peynaud of Bordeaux. He is experimenting with Cabernet Sauvignon here in Garnacha country.

Luis Megia
Valdepeñas. A very modern mass-production wine factory.

Bodegas Morenito
Valdepeñas, Ciudad Real. The best-known bodega of Valdepeñas, a big family company bottling as much as 1m. cases a year. Fino Morenito and Seleccion '72 are aged in oak. The reds are best, with a certain bland appeal.

Bodegas Murviedro
Valencia. A long-established little bodega exporting above-average wines, including a reasonable white.

H.L. Garcia Poveda
Villena, Alicante. The 2 considerable bodegas of Alicante are both called Poveda. This is in the hills behind the town, family run and making a range of strong red, white and rosé with the names Costa Blanca and Marquesado.

Bodegas Salvador Poveda
Monavar, Alicante. Perhaps the best Alicante bodega, a family business known especially for its rich red Fonchillon. Other labels for its strapping wines are Doble Capa and Viña Vermeta.

Bodegas José Pulido Romero
Medellin, Badajoz. The biggest and best bodega of this obscure region of common reds and rosés. Its Castillo de Medellin is a fair if unexciting wine.

Bodegas Ruiz
Cañamero, Caceres. Unique bottlers of the roughish sherry-style Cañamero white, made of Palomino grapes and growing *flor* like sherry. It is the house wine of the Parador at Cañamero.

Bodega Sanchez Rustarazo
Valdepeñas, Cidad Real. A traditionalist family house founded in 1800 and still employing clay *tinajas* for fermentation. Their Solar de Hinojosa is aged in oak.

Bodegas Schenk
Valencia. The Spanish division of the biggest Swiss wine company, shipping from the Levante and La Mancha both blended (e.g. the well-known Don Cortez) and individual wines. Schenk's red Los Monteros, made entirely of the dark Monastrell, is one of the best of the region. Also a Valencian sweet Moscatel and a rosé from Utiel-Requena.

Bodegas Señorio del Condestable
Jumilla, Murcia. A member of the big Savin group of wine companies, best known for its red Condestable, a well-made everyday wine, light in colour and flavour but with a fresh almost cherry-like smell and pleasant texture.

Vinival
Valencia. A big bulk-wine shipping company founded in 1969. Its great vaulted brick bodega by the harbour handles the products of several producers under the label Torres de Serrano.

Visan
Santa Cruz de Mudela, Valdepeñas, Ciudad Real. Producer of the agreeable Castillo de Mudela and Viña Tito.

Cooperativa del Campo La Daimiel
Daimiel, Ciudad Real. One of the principal white wine producers of La Mancha. The brand is Clavileño.

Grupo Sindical de Colonizacion No. 795
Cebreros, Avila. Producers of a passable if powerful red, El Galago, in the undemarcated region west of Madrid.

Cooperativa La Invencible
Valdepeñas, Ciudad Real. The best cooperative of the region, making a clean *clarete*.

Cooperativa Nuestro Padre Jesus del Perdon
Manzanares, Ciudad Real. A large cooperative known particularly for its dry white. The brand name is Yuntero.

Cooperativa La Purisima
Yecla, Murcia. The major producer of Yecla wine. The huge bodega makes efforts to please the educated palate with wines of moderate strength (e.g. Viña Montana) but the result tends to mingle overripe and underripe flavours in rather thin wine.

Cooperativa de San Isidro
Jumilla, Murcia. The major Jumilla coop, with 2,500 members. All its wines are strong and heavy. Rumor is the best known. Some *reservas* are aged in oak (without achieving distinction).

Cooperativa Santa Rita
Fuenterobles, Valencia. A medium-sized modern cooperative turning out concentrated blending wine, *vino de doble pasta*, but also a remarkably fresh pale rosé, indicating what the region is capable of.

Cooperativa Virgen de la Viñas
Tormelloso, Ciudad Real. One of the bigger coops, known by its brand name Tomillar and its Reserva de Cencibel.

The solera system

A *solera* is the bodega's way of achieving complete continuity in its essential stock-in-trade: a range of wines of distinctive character. It is a 'fractional blending' system, in which wine is drawn for use from the oldest in a series of butts, which is then topped up from the next oldest, and so on down to young wine in the youngest *criadera* in the series, which in turn is supplied with young sherry as close in character to its elders as possible. The effect of withdrawing and replacing a portion (normally about a third) of a butt at a time is that each addition rapidly takes on the character of the older wine to which it is added. An incalculable fraction of the oldest wine in the *solera* always remains in the final butt (or rather butts, for the operation is on a big scale, and each stage may consist of 50). At the same time, so long as the *solera* is operating, the average age of the wine at every stage (except the new input) is getting gradually greater; thus the individuality of the *solera* more pronounced. Certain famous *soleras* in Jerez, those that produce Tio Pepe, for instance, or San Patricio, were started over a century ago.

Here the word 'produce', however, is misleading. It is more accurate to say 'give character to'. For *solera* wine is rarely, if ever, bottled 'straight'.

SHERRY

Sampling sherry

Sherry, like many Mediterranean wines, was first appreciated and shipped to the countries of northern Europe for its strength, its sweetness and its durability – all qualities that made it a radically different commodity from medieval claret. By Shakespeare's day, while spirits were still unknown, sack (as it was then called) was hugely popular as the strongest drink available. The warming effect of a 'cup of sack', at perhaps 17 per cent alcohol with considerable sweetness, was the addiction not just of Falstaff but of every tavern-goer. 'Sack' came from Málaga, the Canary Islands, and even from Greece and Cyprus. But the prince of sacks was 'sherris', named for the Andalucian town of Jerez de la Frontera.

Jerez has had an international trading community since the Middle Ages. Until the rise of Rioja it was unique in Spain for its huge bodegas full of stock worth millions. The refinement of its wine from a coarse product, shipped without ageing, to the modern elaborate range of styles began in the eighteenth century. Like champagne (which it resembles in more ways than one) it flowered with the wealth and technology of the nineteenth.

What its makers have done is to push the natural adaptability of a strong but not otherwise extraordinary, indeed rather flat and neutral, white wine to the limit. They have exploited its potential for barrel-ageing in contact with oxygen – the potentially disastrous oxidation – to produce flavours as different in their way as a lemon and a date. And they have perfected the art of blending from the wide spectrum in their paintbox to produce every conceivable nuance in between – and to produce it unchanging year after year.

The making of sherry today, folklore apart, differs little from the making of any white wine. A fairly light wine is rapidly pressed and fermented. Its acidity is adjusted upwards, traditionally by adding gypsum or plaster. It is traditionally fermented in new oak barrels (with a violence in the early stages that sends fountains of froth high into the air). Eventually it reaches a natural strength of between 12 and 16 degrees. At this point it is fortified with spirit to adjust the strength to either 15 or 18 degrees, depending on its quality and characteristics. This is where sherry's unique ageing process begins.

It is the wayward nature of sherry that different

barrels (500-litre 'butts') of wine, even from the same vineyard, can develop in different ways. The essential distinction is between those that develop a growth of floating yeast, called *flor*, and those that do not. All the young wines are kept in the 'nursery' in butts filled four fifths full. The finest and most delicate wines, only slightly fortified to maintain their finesse, rapidly develop a creamy scum on the surface, which thickens in spring to a layer several inches deep. This singular yeast has the property of protecting the wine from oxidation and at the same time reacting with it to impart subtle hints of maturity. These finest wines, or *finos*, are ready to drink sooner than heavier sherries. They remain pale because oxygen is excluded. They can be perfect at about five years old. But their precise age is irrelevant because, like all sherries, they are blended for continuity in a *solera* (see page 366).

Young wines of a heavier, clumsier and more pungent style grow less *flor*, or none at all. A stronger dose of fortifying spirit discourages any *flor* that may appear. This second broad category of sherry is known, if it shows potential quality, as *oloroso*, if not as *raya*. These wines are barrel-aged without benefit of *flor*, in full contact with the air. Their maturing is therefore an oxidative process, darkening their colour and intensifying their flavour.

A third, eccentric, class of sherry is also found in this early classifying of the crop – one that combines the breadth and depth of a first-class *oloroso* with the fragrance, finesse and 'edge' of a *fino*. This rarity is known as a *palo cortado*.

These three are the raw materials of the bodega – naturally different from birth. It is the bodega's business to rear them so as to accentuate these differences, and to use them in combinations to produce a far wider range of styles. A *fino* which is matured beyond the life span of its *flor* usually begins to deepen in colour and broaden in flavour, shading from straw to amber to (at great age) a rich blackish brown. Every bodega has one or more *soleras* of old *finos* which have been allowed to move through the scale from a fresh *fino*, to a richer, more concentrated *fino-amontillado*, to an intensely nutty and powerful old *amontillado*.

Commercially, however, such true unblended *amontillados* are very rare. In general usage the term has been more or less bastardized to mean any 'medium' sherry, between dry *fino* and creamy old *oloroso* in style but rarely with the quality of either. All sherries in their natural state, maturing in their *soleras*, are bone dry. Unlike port, sherry is never fortified until fermentation is completely over – all sugar used up. Straight unblended sherry is therefore an ascetic, austere taste, a rarity in commerce. The only exception is *dulce* – concentrated wine used for sweetening blends.

As it ages in the bodega, evaporation of water increases both the alcohol content and the proportion of flavouring elements. Very old sherries still in wood often become literally undrinkable in their own right – but priceless in the depth of flavour they can add to a blend. Classic sherry-blending is very much the art of the shipper, but anyone can try it for himself by acquiring, say, a bottle of a very old dry sherry such as Domecq's Rio Viejo or Valdespino's Tio Diego, and simply adding one small glassful of it to a carafe of an ordinary 'medium' sherry. The immediate extra dimension of flavour in the everyday wine is a revelation.

The former custom was for every wine merchant to have his own range of blends made in Jerez to his

Sherry glossary

Almacenista a wholesaler or stockholder of wines for ageing; also used for the individual old unblended wines he sells which are occasionally offered as collectors' items.

Amontillado literally 'a wine in the style of Montilla'. Not at all so in fact, but a well-aged *fino* that has developed a nutty flavour with maturity in oak. Also loosely used for any medium sherry.

Amoroso the name of a vineyard famous for *oloroso* sherry. Literally 'amorous': not a bad description of the sweet *oloroso* sold under the name.

Añada the wine of one year, kept as such in a butt until (or instead of) becoming part of a *solera*.

Arroba the working measure in a sherry bodega. The standard 500-litre butt holds 30 *arrobas*.

Arrope a *vino de color*: wine reduced by boiling to one fifth of its original volume, intensely sweet and treacly black, used only for colouring and sweetening blends. *Sancocho* is similar.

Bristol the historic centre of the sherry trade in Britain, a name much used on labels to imply quality, but not a reference to any particular style of wine.

Brown sherry sweet sherry blended from *olorosos* and *rayas* to be sweeter and darker than a 'cream'.

Cream sherry a blend of sweetened *olorosos*, with or without *vino de color*. Harvey's Bristol Cream was the original. Croft's introduced the idea of a pale (uncoloured) 'cream' in the 1970s.

Dulce apagado intensely sweet wine made by stopping the fermentation of must by adding brandy. Used only for sweetening 'medium' sherries.

Dulce de almibar a mixture of young wine and invert sugar used for sweetening pale sherries without darkening them.

Dulce pasa dark sweetening wine made by leaving ordinary sherry grapes in the sun to concentrate the sugar, then stopping their fermenting must with brandy. Used for sweetening good-quality 'cream'.

East India now a fanciful name for a sweet, usually Brown, sherry. It derives from the former custom of sending sherry (like madeira) to the Indies and back as ship's ballast to speed its maturity.

Entre fino the classification of a young wine which shows *fino* character but not the required quality for the finest *soleras*.

Fino the lightest, most delicate, and literally finest of sherries. It naturally develops a growth of *flor* yeast, which protects its pale colour and intensifies its fresh aroma.

own specification, and label them with brand names from his own imagination. In practice this meant that there were far too many indistinguishable (and often undistinguished) blended wines on the market. The more rational modern trend is for the shippers in Jerez to promote their own brands. The best of these will be the produce of a single prized *solera*, usually slightly sweetened with special treacly sweetening wine. A touch of near-black but almost tasteless *vino de color* may be needed to adjust the colour. Possibly a little younger wine in the same style will be added to give it freshness.

A common commercial blend, on the other hand, will consist largely of low-value, minimally aged *rayas* or *entre finos* (the term for second-grade wine in the *fino* style). A small proportion of wine from a good *solera* will be added to improve the flavour, then a good deal of sweetening wine to mask the faults of the base material. It is, unfortunately, wines made to this sort of specification that have given sherry the image of a dowdy drink of no style.

The sad result is that the truly great wines of Jerez, wines that can stand comparison in their class with great white burgundy or champagne, are absurdly undervalued. There is no gastronomic justification for the price of Montrachet being four times that of the most brilliant *fino* – nor, at the other end of sherry's virtuoso repertoire, of the greatest *olorosos* selling at a fraction of the price of their equivalent in madeira.

The sherry region

Jerez lies 10 miles inland from the bay of Cádiz in southwest Spain. Its vineyards surround it on all sides, but all the best of them are on outcrops of chalky soil in a series of dune-like waves to the north and west, between the rivers Guadalete and Guadalquivir. The Guadalquivir, famous as the river of Seville, from which Columbus set out to discover America and Pizarro to conquer Peru, forms the northern boundary of the sherry region. Its port, Sanlúcar de Barrameda, Jerez and Puerto are the three sherry towns. The land between them is the zone known as Jerez Superior, the heart of the best sherry country.

There are three soil types in the sherry region, but only the intensely white *albariza*, a clay consisting of up to 80 per cent pure chalk, makes the best wine. It has high water-retaining properties that resist summer drought and the desiccating wind, the 'Levante', that blows from Africa. It also reflects sunlight up into the low-trained bush vines, so that the grapes bask in a slow oven as they ripen.

Barro, a brown chalky clay, is more fertile but produces heavier, coarser wine. *Arena*, or sand, is little used now for vineyards at all.

The distinct, low vineyard hills each has a name: Carrascal, Macharnudo, Añina, Balbaina are the most famous of the *pagos*, as they are called, surrounding Jerez in an arc of *albariza* to the north and west. A separate outbreak of excellent soil gives rise to the *pagos* south and east of Sanlúcar, 14 miles from Jerez, of which the best-known name is Miraflores.

The regulations of the Consejo Regulador, the governing body of Jerez, stipulate that every bodega buys a certain proportion of its wine from the Superior vineyards – a rule scarcely necessary today, since 85 per cent of the whole region is Superior: outlying low-quality vineyards have fallen out of use. The present total area of sherry vineyards is 37,000 acres. In 1970 it was 28,652.

Fino-amontillado a *fino* on the way to maturing as an *amontillado*.

Fino viejo, viejissimo occasionally an old *fino* declines to enter middle age as an *amontillado* and simply intensifies its aristocratic finesse, growing formidably powerful, dusty dry and austere while remaining straw-pale.

Jerez quinado a cordial or apéritif made by mixing quinine with sherry.

Macharnudo the most famous of the *pagos*, vineyard districts, northwest of Jerez; sometimes mentioned on labels.

Manzanilla the speciality of Sanlúcar de Barrameda. Sherries matured in its bodegas by the sea take on a singular sharp and even salty tang that makes them the most appetizing of all. Removed to bodegas elsewhere they revert to normal wines. Most *manzanilla* is drunk as pale and unsweetened *fino*. With age it becomes *pasada*, darker and slightly nutty with an almost buttery richness. Eventually it becomes a deeply nutty *Manzanilla amontillado*; one of the most vivid and intense of all sherries.

Moscatel sweetening wine made of sun-dried Moscatel grapes for giving added sugar and fruity flavour to certain sweet blends.

Oloroso in its natural state, full-bodied dry sherry without the delicacy, fragrance or piquancy of *fino* but with extra richness and depth. It does not develop *flor* to the same extent but picks up colour and oak flavours in the butt. Old unblended *olorosos* are astonishingly dark, pungent and so concentrated that they almost seem to burn your mouth. In practice nearly all *oloroso* is used as the base for sweet sherries, particularly 'creams'.

Palma a classification for a particularly delicate and fragrant *fino*. Tres Palmas is the brand name of a very fine one.

Palo Cortado an aberrant sherry which shows the good characters of both *fino* and *oloroso* at the same time. A highly prized rarity nearly always kept apart and bottled as an unblended *solera* wine with only a little sweetening.

Pata de galina an *oloroso* which in its natural state shows signs of sweetness, derived from glycerine. Occasionally bottled as such, when it is incomparable.

Paxarete an alternative name for *vinos de color*.

Raya the classification for an *oloroso*-type wine of secondary quality; the makeweight in most middle-range blends.

Vino de color colouring wine, e.g. *arrope*.

Vino de pasto 'table wine' light medium-dry sherry of uncertain quality, now rarely seen.

SHERRY PRODUCERS

Antonio Barbadillo

c/Luis de Eguilaz 11, PO Box 25, Sanlúcar de Barrameda.

The biggest bodega in Sanlúcar, with a near-monopoly of the *manzanilla* business and some wonderful old wines. It was founded in 1821 by Don Benigno Barbadillo. 5 generations later, the firm is run by Antonio Barbadillo, a respected poet and wine writer. Offices (in the former bishops' palace) and the original bodegas are in the town centre. In the surrounding *albariza* areas of Cádiz, Balbaina, San Julian, Carrascal and Gibaldin, they own 2,000 acres of vines, producing a wide range of *manzanillas* and other sherries: Solear, Eva, Pastora, Tio Rio, Pedro Rodriguez, Principe, La Caridad, Ducado de Sanlúcar and Villareal. Recently they have pioneered with dry white table wines from Palomino grapes called Castillo de San Diego and Gibalbino (the name of a vineyard company they own jointly with Harvey's). Turnover is some 1,000m. pesetas a year.

Don José Ignacio Domecq, head of the oldest sherry firm

Hijos de Agustín Blázquez

PO Box 540, Carretera de la Cartuja.

A relatively small high-quality bodega founded in 1795 by the Paul family, now part of the Pedro Domecq group, operated independently under its own name, with 3 vineyards, 2 in the Balbaina district, one in Macharnudo. Stocks are 20,000 butts. Its best-known products are a well-aged *fino*, Carta Blanca, Carta Roja *oloroso* and Felipe II brandy. In smaller quantities, they make a *palo cortado* called Capuchino and a noble old *amontillado*, Carta Oro. They have recently introduced a new range in Spain under the name Balfour. Sales of 1m. cases a year of sherry and brandy go to the Americas, Holland and Italy.

Croft Jerez

Rancho Croft, Carretera Madrid, Jerez.

The port shippers (founded 1768) gave their name to the sherry division (formerly Gilbeys) of International Distillers and Vintners in 1970. Rancho Croft is an ambitious development from Gilbeys' simple old bodegas; a huge complex of traditional-style buildings housing the most modern plant and 90,000 butts (45 m. litres) of sherry. Crofts have planted 865 acres of *albariza* land in Los Tercios and Cuartillos. Market research led them to launch the first pale cream sherry, Croft Original. Croft Particular is a pale *amontillado*, classic medium-dry, and Delicado a true *fino*. They also make a *palo cortado* and a brandy called Gourmet. Exports (to 65 countries) are 1.5m. cases a year.

Díez-Merito

Diego Fernández Herrera 16, PO Box 7, Jerez.

An important high-quality bodega specializing in supplying 'buyers' own brands'. It was founded in France in 1875 as Díez Hermanos and is still wholly owned by the Díez family. The name was changed in 1979 when they took over the old house of Merito. Since 1972 expansion has been rapid. Stocks are now about 35,000 butts. They have 500 acres of vines in the Jerez Superior area, with a huge new bodega in Jerez and one at Puerto de Santa Maria. Their own brands include Palma and Lolita *finos*, Fino Imperial (a very old *amontillado*), a splendid *oloroso* Victoria Regina, Primo Paco *amontillado*, Favorito cream and Alhambra pale cream. Sales are now about 1m. cases a year.

Pedro Domecq

Bodegas Pedro Domecq, Jerez de la Frontera, Cadiz.

Founded 1730. The oldest, largest and one of the most respected shipping houses, founded by Irish and French families and including in its history (as English agent) John Ruskin's father. It owns 2 acres of vines and no less than 73 bodegas all over the region. The present head of the firm, Don José Ignacio Domecq, is recognized worldwide both literally and figuratively as 'the nose' of sherry. The finest wines, apart from some superb *solera* rarities, are the gentle Fino La Ina, Rio Viejo, a dark, rich but bone-dry *oloroso*, Celebration Cream and the luscious Double Century. Domecq also owns La Riva (q.v.).

Duff Gordon

Fernan Caballero 2, El Puerto de Santa Maria.

Founded in 1768 by the British Consul in Cádiz, Sir James Duff, and his nephew Sir William Gordon. It remained in the family for more than a century, before being bought in 1872 by Thomas Osborne, who had been a partner in the firm since 1833. The Osborne company (owners of 618 acres of vines) continue to market the Duff Gordon sherries and brandies for export, but do not sell them in Spain. Their most popular brands are Fino Feria, El Cid *amontillado* and Santa Maria cream.

Garvey

Bodegas de San Patricio, Divina Pastora, Jerez.

One of the great bodegas, founded in 1780 in Sanlúcar de Barrameda by an Irishman, William Garvey, who built what for many years remained the grandest bodega in Spain: 558 feet long. Since 1979, when it was taken over by Rumasa, a new winery and new maturing bodegas have been built on the outskirts of Jerez and the original family mansion has been carefully restored. Garvey's have 740 acres under vine in the *albariza* areas of Maribe, Balbaina, Macharnudo, Carrascal, Montegil and Campix, producing consistently good wines. San Patricio (named after the patron saint of Ireland), a full-flavoured *fino*, is their best-known sherry. Others include Tio Guillermo *amontillado*, Ochavico dry *oloroso*, Long Life medium-dry *oloroso*, La Lidia *manzanilla*, Lanza cream and Bicentenary pale cream. 1,076,800 cases were sold on the domestic market in 1981 and about 367,000 cases were exported.

Gonzalez Byass

Manuel M. Gonzalez 12, Jerez.

One of the greatest sherry houses, founded in 1835 by Don Antonio Gonzalez y Rodriguez, whose London agent, Robert Blake Byass, became a partner in 1855. The company is still owned and directed entirely by descendants of these two men. They own nearly 15% of the vineyards in the Jerez area. In addition to the world's biggest-selling *fino*, Tio Pepe, La Concha *amontillado*, Alfonso dry *oloroso*, San Domingo pale cream and Nectar cream are exported throughout the world. In 1979 they sold 1,889,000 cases of sherry and 3,731,000 cases of brandy (mainly Soberano and Lepanto). Other interests include Bodegas Beronia in Rioja and Gonzalez y Dubosc in Catalonia.

Bodegas Internacionales

PO Box 300, Carr M-Cádiz.

A public company founded in 1974 by Rumasa and said to be the largest bodegas in the world, covering 50,000 square metres and holding stocks of 42.5m. litres. These house, in addition to their own Duke of Wellington and B.E.S.T. sherries and Primado, Solaron and Dickens brandies, the wines and *soleras* of the Varela, Bertola and Marqués de Misa companies which have all been taken over by Rumasa. Rumasa-owned vineyards in the Añina district supply a proportion of Bodegas Internacionales' wines. Annual sales, including those of the affiliate companies, amount to 1.399m. pesetas.

Harvey's of Bristol

John Harvey & Sons (España), Alvar Nuñez, PO Box 494, Jerez.

The famous Bristol shippers were founded in 1796. In 1822 the first John Harvey joined the firm. In 1968 it was taken over by Allied Breweries, though John Harvey's great-grandson, Michael McWatters, is the present managing director. Another John Harvey, fifth of the name, heads the company's fine-wine business. The firm became famous as blenders of 'Bristol' sweet sherries, above all Bristol Cream, now the world's biggest-selling brand with a reported 20% of the British market and a huge export business. Not until 1970, when they bought McKenzie & Co., did they own their own bodegas or vineyards. Now they have 1,735 acres, all in fine *albariza* land. Bristol Cream, once the ultimate luxury sherry, is now merely good. Other brands are Bristol Milk (not in the UK), Club Amontillado, Bristol Dry (which is medium) and Luncheon Dry, a dry *fino*.

Emilio Lustau

PO Box 193, Plaza del Cubo 4, Jerez.

Founded in 1896, one of the largest independent family-owned producers making top-quality sherries under their own and customers' labels. Tomás Abad is a subsidiary company. Their best wines include Dry Lustau *oloroso*, Jerez Lustau *palo cortado* and a selection of rare *almacenista* reserve sherries from small private stockholders. One of their two vineyards, Nuestra Señora de la Esperanza in the Carrascal district, was noted by Richard Ford in his travel journal in 1845. The bodegas, just outside the Jerez city walls, include one cellar with a high, vaulted dome, believed to have been the headquarters of the Guard during the Moorish occupation. Sales are 500,000 cases a year, exported to North and South America and Europe.

Osborne y Cía

Calle Fernan Caballero 3, El Puerto de Santa Maria.

A large and expanding, entirely family-owned and run bodega founded in 1772 by Don Tomás Osborne y Mann. The head of the family today is the Conde de Osborne. In 1872 Osborne took over Duff Gordon. Today, it is also co-owner of Jonas Torres y Cía (founded in 1980), Osborne de Portugal (founded in 1967) and Osborne de Mexico (founded in 1971), owner of Bodegas Montecillo in Rioja, Coivisa and Osborne Distribuidora. Among their sherry brands are Quinta *fino*, Coquinero *amontillado*, Bailen *oloroso* and Osborne Cream. Their important brandy portfolio includes Veterano, Magno, Independencia and Conde de Osborne. The turnover in 1981 was 11,000 m. pesetas.

Palomino & Vergara

Colon 1-25, Jerez.

One of the oldest big bodegas in Jerez, founded in 1765. Taken over by Rumasa in 1963. Its offices and bodegas (capacity 40,000 butts) in the centre of Jerez are housed in an extraordinary glass-domed building still equipped with the original mahogany and gilt counters. Palomino & Vergara is a name on the domestic market, but is less important in the export field, with no UK distributor at present. Tio Mateo *fino* is their most important sherry. Others include Buleria *amontillado*, Los Flamencos *oloroso* and 1865 Solera cream. Their brandies are also important, especially Fabuloso (3° año) and Eminencia (5° año). The oldest is Gran Reserva.

Zoilo Ruiz-Mateos

PO Box 140 La Atalaya, Cervantes 3, Jerez.

Founded in 1857 by Zoilo Ruiz-Mateos and today run by a descendant of the same name, who is also vice-president of Spain's largest private holding company, Rumasa. (Rumasa, under the presidency of Don Zoilo's brother, José Maria, since 1962, owns banks, hotels, department stores, 17 sherry firms, Rioja bodegas and various overseas wine concerns.) The Don Zoilo company has 556 acres of vineyards in the best *albariza* areas of Añina and produces an extremely high-quality (and expensive) Don Zoilo range of *fino*, *amontillado* and cream sherry, and one of Spain's best brandies, Gran Duque de Alba. The bodegas in Jerez contain 200,000 butts of 500 litres each.

Sandeman Hermanos y Cía

Calle Pizarro 10, Jerez.

One of the great port and sherry shippers, founded in London in 1790 by George Sandeman, a Scot from Perth, to import wine. It now belongs to the Seagram group, but a descendant, David Sandeman, is chairman. After shipping sherries from other firms for many years, Sandeman's founded their own bodega and now have 15 vineyards, totalling 988 acres, all on *albariza* soil. They use traditional methods to produce some very fine sherries: Fino Apitiv, Dry Don Amontillado, Armada Cream and a *palo cortado,* Royal Ambrosante.

Williams & Humbert

Nuno de Canas 1, PO Box 23, Jerez.

Founded in 1877 by Alexander Williams. His partner was his brother-in-law, Arthur Humbert. Bought in 1972 by Rumasa. The firm quickly became one of the most important in Jerez and continues to be a major exporter, with markets in North and South America, Europe, Japan and the Far East. Vineyards on *albariza* soils in Carrascal, Balbaina and Los Tercios produce good wines. The best known is Dry Sack *amontillado.* Pando is an excellent fresh *fino-amontillado*, a big-selling wine in Spain. Other brands are Canasta Cream, Walnut Brown, A Winter's Tale, As You Like It and Cedro. The bodegas in the centre of Jerez are exceptionally handsome.

OTHER SHERRY PRODUCERS

Tomás Abad
PO Box 337, Muro de la Merced 28, Jerez. A small bodega on a hill overlooking the harbour of Puerto de Santa Maria. It is affiliated to the Jerez Superior Cooperative of Nuestra Señora de las Angustias and sells, in addition to the Tomás Abad and Don Tomás brands, fine *almacenista* reserve sherries. Stocks are about 2,000 butts.

Herederos de Manuel Baron
Banda Playa 21, PO Box 39, Sanlúcar de Barrameda. A small family firm dating back over 300 years; now comprising Bodegas Tartaneros, Regina, Monlinillo, Trabajadero and Carretería, and owning 346 acres of *albariza* vineyards at Viña Atalaya and Martin Miguel. They make a range of sherries under names such as Baron, Atalaya, Pinoviejo, Malva, Lider, Jorge III and Marqués de Casa Trevino.

Bodegas Bertola
PO Box 15, Carretera de Sanlúcar, Jerez. Of the 3 Bertola sherries, the best known is the cream, which is aimed at the British palate and sells especially well in Scotland.

Luis Caballero
Puerto de Santa Maria. Founded 1830. A family-owned firm amalgamated in 1932 with the famous English house of Burdon and continuing to ship Burdon Fino, Bristol Milk, etc., under the Burdon label, as well as their own *fino* Don Guiso, *fino* Benito and other good-quality wines.

Cuvillo y Cía
Puerto de Santa Maria. Founded 1783. A fine independent bodega of medium size with excellent wines to offer; notably its 'Fino C' Trabajadero dry *oloroso* and a model *palo cortado.*

Delgado Zuleta
PO Box 4, Carmen 32, Sanlúcar de Barrameda. An independent family firm founded in 1744. Their best-known wine is La Goya, a *manzanilla pasada.* Other wines include a range under the Zuleta name, a *fino* called Don Tomás and a range of brandies under the Mateagudo label.

Francisco Garcia de Velasco
Sebastian Elcano 2, Sanlúcar de Barrameda. A relatively small bodega founded in 1803 by Francisco Garcia de Velasco and now owned by Bodegas Barcena. Los 48 *manzanilla* is their most important product, but they make several other sherries under various labels, including El Padre, Los Angeles Diplomatico, Tia Anita and Tres Cañas.

Luis G. Gordon
PO Box 48, Jerez. One of the oldest sherry companies, founded by a Scot, Arthur Gordon, in 1754. Brands include Alexander Gordon, Gordon & Rivero, Marqués de Irun, Doz y Cía. Specialities are Manola *fino* and Royal, an old brandy.

Emilio M. Hidalgo
Clavel 29, PO Box 221, Jerez. A family firm based in the old town of Jerez, now in the fourth generation of the Hidalgo family since it was founded in 1874. They have 346 acres of *albariza* in Añina and Carrascal and have been vinifying their own grapes since 1926. Stocks stand at 8,000 butts. Their principal brands, in addition to the bodega name, are Rodil and Privilegio.

Vinícola Hidalgo y Cía
Banda Playa 24, Sanlúcar de Barrameda. A small bodega founded in 1800 and still owned and run by the Hidalgo family. They have 494 acres of *albariza* vineyards in Balbaina and Miraflores, stock 6,000 butts and sell 30,000 cases a year on the home market. Their principal brands are the fine La Gitana *manzanilla*, Jerez Cortado Hidalgo and Napoleon *amontillado.*

Bodegas de los Infantes de Orleans-Borbon
Sanlúcar de Barrameda. Torre Breva, the 543-acre vineyard owned by this company, was turned over to vines in 1886 by Don Antonio de Orleans, Duke of Montpensier, who had until then used it as a shooting estate. Bodegas Infantes was founded much later, in 1943. It now has stocks of 8,000 butts. Their principal sherries are Torre Breva and La Ballena *manzanillas*, Alvaro *fino*, Orleans cream and Fenicio *oloroso.*

Lacave & Cía
Avda A. Alvaro Domecq 9, PO Box 519, Jerez. Founded in Cádiz in 1810; bought and moved to Jerez by Rumasa in 1972. They have 370 acres of *albariza* land in the Jerez Superior area and produce a range of 3 sherries and a brandy under the Lacave name.

B. M. Lagos
Carretera de Sanlúcar, PO Box 440, Jerez. Founded in 1910. From stocks of 5,000 butts they sell 178,000 cases a year; 111,000 of these to Britain. (They have connections with Harvey's.) Their own brands include Señero and Tio Cani *finos*, Las Flores *manzanilla*, Gran Cartel *oloroso* and a range of brandies.

José Medina & Cía
Banda de la Playa 46/50, Sanlúcar de Barrameda. A traditional family firm with 15,000 butts of sherry in its bodegas in Sanlúcar and vineyards in Carrascal.

Rafael O'Neale
Jerez de la Frontera. Founded 1724. The earliest of the several houses founded by Irishmen and still independent. The present director is Señora Casilda O'Neale de la Quintana. The vineyards have been in the female line since 1264. Modest in size but fine in quality. Its labels are Wild Geese, Spanish Arch, Casilda Cream and a good *manzanilla.*

Luis Paez
Jardinillo 2, PO Box 545, Jerez. A small family firm with 6,000 butts of stock in Jerez and Sanlúcar, but no vineyards. Brand names are Conqueror, Rey de Oro, Primavera, Verano, Otoño and Invierno.

Hijos de Rainera Pérez Marin, 'La Guita'
Banda de la Playa 28, PO Box 89, Sanlúcar de Barrameda. A small company known for its first-class *manzanillas,* especially Guita, the name by which the bodega is often known. Other wines include Hermosilla *manzanilla* and Bandera *fino.*

Herederos de Marqués del Real Tesoro
Calle Pajarete 3 & 5. PO Box 27, Jerez. A respected small family firm founded towards the end of the 19th century by the Marqués del Real Tesoro. From fine stocks of 10,000 butts they produce a range of sherries under the bodega name, including the fresh and fragrant Ideal *fino*, and a range under the label Bodegas M. Giles.

La Riva SA
Alvar Nunez 44, Jerez de la Frontera. An old-established small bodega with some of the finest *soleras* in Jerez, bought in the 1970s by Pedro Domecq but still operated independently for its lovely *fino* Tres Palmas, *amontillado* Guadalupe and old *olorosos* and *palo cortados* of superlative quality. Vineyards 130 acres and stocks 2,773 butts.

Felix Ruiz y Ruiz
Calle Cristal 4, 6 & 8, Jerez. A small firm founded in 1809; now owning 3 bodegas and selling over 222,000 cases of sherry and brandy each year from stocks of 10,000 butts. They sell 2 ranges of sherries, Don Felix and Ruiz, each with 3 styles (dry, medium and cream) plus brandies of the same names.

Bodegas Sanchez de Alva
Carretera de Arcos Km 2, PO Box 26, Jerez. Founded in 1935 by Manuel Gil Luque and taken over by the Cantarero group in 1978, since when turnover has increased considerably, particularly in export. Stocks are now over 10,000 butts, plus a wide range of brandies and liqueurs. Their main sherry names are Deportivo and Alba *finos*, Don Quijote *oloroso* and a range of 5 styles under the Sanchez de Alva label.

Sanchez Romate Hnos
Calle Lealos 26-30, PO Box 5, Jerez. A respected small bodega, founded in 1781 by Juan Sanchez de la Torre, a well-known businessman and philanthropist. It remains an independent company owning 200 acres in 4 vineyards. One in Balbaina and 2 in Macharnudo are on *albariza* and the fourth, in the Cuartillo district, is on *barros* soil. Stocks are some 8,000 butts. Brands include Marismeño and Cristal *finos*; Viva la Pepa and Petenera *manzanillas*; NPU (Non Plus Ultra) *amontillado*; Iberia cream and Doña Juana *oloroso*. Mendoza brandy (called Cardinal for the USA) is made in limited quantities.

José de Soto
M. A. Jesus Tirado 6, PO Box 29, Jerez. Founded towards the end of the 18th century by Francisco de Soto, who acquired Viña Santa Isabel (which still remains in the company) at the same time. They own 6 vineyards covering 370 acres of *albariza* in the finest districts of Balbaina and Macharnudo. Stocks of 10,000 butts go to make Soto and Camper *finos*, Don Jaime and La Uvita *amontillados* and La Espuela *oloroso*. The firm is probably most famous for making the first *ponche* (a sherry-based liqueur) – and still one of the best.

Fernando A. de Terry
Puerto de Santa Maria. Founded 1883. Originally the foundation of an Irish family, and better known for their Centenario brandy than their sherries. In 1981 they were bought by a bank and now have ultramodern premises housing over 50,000 butts. Camborio is their label in Spain. In the UK they supply Marks & Spencer's own-label sherries.

Valdespino SA
Jerez de la Frontera. Still the property of the Valdespino family. Their Ynocente, named from a single Macharnudo vineyard, is a classic *fino* and Tio Diego one of the driest dark and masculine *amontillados*.

Bodegas Varela
C/Albareda 4, Puerto de Santa Maria, Jerez. Founded in 1850 by Ramón Jiménez Varela and bought from his descendants by Rumasa in 1960. The *amontillado* and cream are the best known of the 5 Varela sherries.

Wisdom & Warter Ltd.
Pizarro 7, Jerez. Wisdom and Warter, although apparently a short-cut recipe for bargain sherry, were the two Englishmen who founded the company in 1854. It owns a 173-acre *albariza* vineyard, La Bodogonera, in Los Tercios. The main brands are Olivar *fino*, Royal Palace *amontillado*, Wisdom's Choice cream, Merecedor *oloroso* and a range under the Wisdom label.

Delgado Zuleta
PO Box 4, Carmen 32, Sanlúcar de Barrameda. An independent family firm founded in 1744. Their best-known wine is La Goya, a *manzanilla pasada*. Other wines include a range under the Zuleta name, a *fino* called Don Tomás and a range of brandies under the Mateagudo label.

C.A.Y.D.
Sanlúcar de Barrameda. The trading name of the important Sanlúcar cooperative, with 1,000 members and a stock of 30,000 butts. Its speciality is such *manzanillas* as Bajo de Guia and Sanluqueña.

SOUTHERN SPAIN

The great fame and success of sherry were achieved to some degree at the expense of the other regions of Andalusia. From their long-established trading base, the sherry makers were able to buy the best from their neighbours to add to their own stock. Sherry may be the best *vino generoso* of Andalucia, but it is not the only one. Montilla can compete with very similar wines, and Málaga with worthwhile alternatives.

Málaga

Málaga, on the Costa del Sol, is strictly an entrepôt rather than a vineyard centre. The grapes that make its sweet (occasionally dry) brown wines are grown either in the hills 25 miles to the east or the same distance to the north. East are the coastal vineyards of Axarquia, where the grape is the Moscatel. North around Mollina (in fact towards Montilla) it is the Pedro Ximénez. The rules require that all the grapes are brought to Málaga to mature in its bodegas. Various methods are used to sweeten and concentrate the wines, from sunning the grapes to boiling down the must to *arrope*, as in Jerez. The styles of the finished wine range from a dry white of Pedro Ximénez not unlike a Montilla *amontillado* to the common dark and sticky *dulce color*, thickly laced with *arrope*. The finest quality, comparable in its origin to the *essencia* of Tokay, is the *lagrima* the 'tears' of uncrushed grapes. The difference is that noble rot concentrates Tokay; in Málaga it is the sun. Other Málagas are Pajarete, a dark semi-sweet apéritif style, the paler semi-*dulce* and the richly aromatic Moscatel. The finer wines are made in a *solera* system like sherry, with younger wine refreshing older. A great rarity, a century-old vintage Málaga from the Duke of Wellington's estate, bottled in 1875, was a superlative, delicate, aromatic and still-sweet dessert wine in 1982.

Montilla-Moriles

Montilla's wines are close enough to sherry to be easily confused with (or passed off as) its rivals. The soil is the same *albariza* but the climate is harsher and hotter and the Pedro Ximénez, grown here in preference to the Palomino, yields smaller crops, producing wines of a higher degree and slightly lower acidity. The wines are fermented in tall clay *tinajas*, like giant amphoras, and rapidly develop the same *flor* yeast as sherry. They fall into the same classifications: *fino*, *oloroso* or *palo cortado* – the *finos* from the first light pressing. With age *fino* becomes *amontillado*, 'in the style of Montilla'. Unfortunately, however, the sherry shippers have laid legal claim in Britain (the biggest export market for Montilla) to the classic terms. Instead of a Montilla *fino*, *amontillado* or *oloroso*, a true and fair description, the label must use 'dry', 'medium' or 'cream'.

Montilla has much to recommend it as an alternative to sherry. Its *finos* in particular have a distinctive dry softness of style, with less 'attack' but no less freshness. A cool bottle disappears with gratifying speed as a partner to *hors d'oeuvre*.

Last of the Andalusian *denominacións*, and most deeply in the shadow of Jerez, is the coastal region of Huelva near the Portugese border. Huelva (known in Chaucer's time as 'Lepe') has exported its strong white wines, with or without the refinements of *flor* and *soleras*, for 1,000 years. The commercial power of Jerez has effectively kept it in obscurity. Until the 1960s its wine was blended and shipped as sherry. Now that it has to compete with its old paymaster times are not easy.

SOUTHERN SPAIN PRODUCERS

Alvear

Maria Auxiliadora 1, Montilla, Cordoba.

An independent firm founded by the Alvear family in 1729. Today it is jointly owned and managed by Alvaro de Alvear and his cousin Fernández. They have 358 acres under vine in Montilla-Moriles, much of it in the superior Sierra district, and 17,000 butts of maturing wine in their bodegas. Fermentation in *tinajas* and ageing through the *solera* system are carried out according to the traditions of Montilla, but bottling is done with very modern equipment, producing wines of high quality. Fino CB is their biggest seller and is No. 3 *fino* (behind 2 sherries) in volume terms in Spain. Festival is a slightly fuller *fino* and other names and styles include El Capote, La Muleta, Brindis, Aurora and Conde La Cortina. They also have a Jerez subsidiary, Portalto, in Puerto de Santa Maria.

Scholtz Hermanos

Málaga

The leading bodega in Málaga, founded in 1807 and owned for many years by the German family whose name it bears (though it is now Spanish owned). The wines are made at Mollina in the hills north of Málaga, but matured (as the Consejo requires) in the city, in a modern plant that produces some 220,000 cases a year. Half is exported. The company's most famous wine is Solera Scholtz 1885 It is a light brown dessert wine of 18°, forming a slight 'crust' in its bottle, neither quite like an *oloroso* nor a tawny port, pungent and long-flavoured, starting sweet and finishing dry. I find it slightly more at home before a meal than after one. There are a score of other Scholtz brands of similar quality from dry to sweet; the driest Seco Añejo 10 years old, the sweetest *lagrima* 10 years old.

OTHER PRODUCERS

Hijos de Antonia Barcelo
Málaga. A family firm founded in 1876, now a major exporter, also branching out into Rioja and Rueda in the north of Spain. The brand name is Bacarles, covering a wide range of typical Málaga styles, including old Moscatel and a very sweet Pedro Ximénez, Gran Málaga Solera Vieja.

Carbonell y Cía
Córdoba. A substantial Montilla producer, equally well known for its olive oil. The bodegas are in the Moorish city of Córdoba. Some fine old *soleras* produce 3 *finos*, Moriles, Serranio and Monte Corto. Moriles Superior is a *fino amontillado* (used for once in the literal sense). Flor de Montilla is an *amontillado pasado*, an older and nuttier wine. 'Nectar' is a fair description of both the *oloroso* and the dark Pedro Ximénez.

Gracias Hermanos
Montilla, Córdoba. A family-run bodega with high standards. Their *fino*, Kiki, is a typically light and refreshing one.

Larios
Málaga. Better known for its gin in Spain, but a Málaga bodega with an excellent sweet Moscatel, Colmenares.

Bodegas Mazaga
Lanzarote, Canary Islands. The one serious bodega in the Canaries, once famous for 'sack'. Its Malvasia Seco of white Malvasia grapes is well made, aged briefly in oak and longer in bottle, in cellars cut in the lava rock. A pleasant apéritif wine.

Bodegas Monte Cristo
Montilla, Córdoba. Large exporters of Montilla, now part of the Rumasa group. They have 60% of exports to the UK, Montilla's biggest export market.

Bodegas Perez Barquero
Montilla, Córdoba. Another Rumasa company. Brand name: Don Roger.

Perez Teixera
Málaga. A Málaga bodega making a true *lagrima* wine from the 'tears' of the uncrushed overripe grapes.

Bodegas Miguel Salas Acosta
Bollullos del Condado, Huelva. A family-run company known for above-average sherry-style Huelva wines.

Hijos de Francisco Vallejo
Bollullos del Condado, Huelva. A Huelvan family bodega with good sherry-style wines.

Bodega Cooperativa Vinícola del Condado
Bollullos del Condado, Huelva. The main cooperative of Huelva, responsible for large quantities of brandy, some table wines and some good *solera*-aged sherry-style *generosos*.

PORTUGAL

Portugal, conservative as she is, was the first country in modern times to invent a new style of wine for export, and to get it so spectacularly right that it is now, 25 years later, among the biggest-selling brands on earth. The wine, of course, is Mateus Rosé. With its competitors it now accounts for the greater part of Portugal's wine exports – twice as much as port, her traditional tribute to foreign taste.

Mateus is simply an imaginative development of a peasant tradition: *vinho verde*, the sharp and fizzy 'green wine' of the country's northern province, the Minho. It is the measure of Portuguese conservatism that neither the Mateus style, nor even port, has ever caught on in a big way in their home country. Portugal continues to drink old-fashioned wines. Yet this is no little backwater. Portugal is sixth in the league of wine-producing nations and third in the league of consumption per head. The Portuguese drink three quarters of the 10 million hectolitres they produce; the remaining quarter constitutes their largest single export item.

Conservative they may be, but the Portuguese were the first to establish the equivalent of a national system of *appellation contrôlée* – 25 years before France instituted her appellation laws, Portugal had legally defined boundaries, grapes, techniques and standards for all of what were then her better wines.

For many years, unfortunately, these have sat heavily on progress, leading to a distorted picture of where the best wines were really being grown. It is more realistic today to ignore the original list of demarcated regions for all except historical purposes and to consider the regional names in use as being of equal validity.

The snag is that during the long period while the regional system was out of date, many of Portugal's better wine companies took to using brand names without indication of origin. Several of Portugal's most distinguished and reliable wines still come from 'somewhere in Portugal'. Portugal is the only country where a brand without any further clues may lead to the best available wine. This will change with entry to the European Common Market, and already the ground is being staked out for a geographical system for all superior wines.

The ascendancy of merchant companies, rather than the primary producers, is another Portuguese peculiarity. Big wine estates are almost unknown, except in the port country where shippers have planted or accumulated considerable vineyards. Only 13 per cent of Portugal's 180,000 growers make more than 1,000 cases a year, and only 4 per cent as much as 3,000 cases or their equivalent. Forty per cent take their grapes to the country's 113 cooperative cellars. Most of the rest who have wine to spare after supplying their families and friends sell it to merchants. Merchants and their brands rather than growers' names are therefore the key to Portuguese wine. Most of the bigger and better merchants buy and bottle wine from each of the major areas: there is little regionality at this level either.

The Portuguese practice is to divide all wines into two categories: *verde* or *maduro*. *Vinho verde* is unaged wine, and the use of the term now legally limited to the northern province, the Minho. Sparkling rosés, not much used in Portugal, would however logically fit into this category. *Maduro* means mature. It implies long ageing in barrel and bottle. It is the natural, indeed the essential, treatment for wines, red or white, made in the traditional manner of every part of Portugal except the Minho. For the Portuguese grow thick-skinned grapes, pick them fully ripe, ferment them stalks and all at a high temperature, and then admire the concentration, the colour, the tannin and the strength rather than looking for fruitiness or finesse in their handiwork.

The very real virtue of Portuguese wine made this way is its structure: it is engineered to last for decades, slowly evolving from gum-withering astringency to the most satisfying texture, when firmness is rounded out to velvet smoothness without losing the feel of the iron fist within. Its vice is lack of flavour, and often only the shyest fragrance for such a potent wine.

Earlier picking, destemming the bunches and cooler fermentation are among the manoeuvres that more modern wine makers are adopting to catch the flavour of their admirable fruit. But in Portugal the old habits die hard.

A peculiar piece of terminology is used for selected and long-aged wines. The word *garrafeira* has much of the meaning of *reserva* but with the added implication that it is the merchant's 'private' best wine, aged for several years in bottle as well as in barrel to be ready for drinking when it is sold.

PORTUGUESE TABLE WINES

The wines of Portugal (excluding port) are described here in a progress as nearly as possible from north to south. For port *see* pages 380–385.

The Minho

The single most important table-wine region, accounting for a quarter of the country's harvest, is the northern province of the Minho from Oporto to the Spanish border. Its name is synonymous with *vinho verde*, Portugal's most original and successful contribution to the world's cellar.

What is green about *vinho verde* is not its colour (70% is red and the white is like lemon-stained water). It is its salad-days freshness, which seems to spring straight from the verdant pergolas where it grows in promiscuous polyculture with maize and vegetables. The vines hang in garlands from tree to tree, or are trained on pergolas of granite post and chestnut lintel. Growing the grapes so high above the ground has several advantages: it slows their ripening and produces the desired sugar/acid balance; it counteracts the tendency to fungus diseases in a cool and rainy climate; it also allows for other cultivation below and between.

The principle of making *vinho verde* is to encourage an active malolactic fermentation. The cool climate, the grapes cultivated (*see* pages 28 and 29), and their elevated training result in very high levels of malic acid. The natural bacterial conversion of malic to lactic acid takes the rasp out of the acidity and adds the tingle of its by-product, carbon dioxide. In country inns the jug wine from barrels is not unlike very dry, fizzy and rather cloudy cider. In a modern winery the process is controlled to rack and clean the wine first, and then to achieve the final stages of malolactic fermentation in the bottle. The obvious short cut adopted by the biggest wineries is to finish the wine to complete bacterial stability and then to bottle it with an injection of carbon dioxide to arrive at approximately the same result. The last method also gives the wine maker the option of sweetening his wine (with unfermented must) without the danger of it refermenting. The total dryness and distinct sharpness of 'real' *vinho verde* is not to everyone's taste. In the red version, fermented stalks and all, it contrives with high tannin to make an alarmingly astringent drink which foreigners rarely brave a second time.

The merchants' brands of *vinho verde* do not normally specify which part of the wide region they come from. Of the eight subregions, Amarante and Peñafiel, just inland from Oporto, produce the highest proportion of white wine. Braga, the centre of the Minho, has good-quality fresh red and white. Lima, along the river of the same name north of Braga, specializes in fuller-bodied reds. Monção, along the river Minho on the Spanish border in the north, is most famous for its single-variety white, its Alvarinho, much the most expensive wine of the region but only by courtesy, if at all, a *vinho verde*. Alvarinho is smooth and still, aged in wood and softly fragrant of apricots or freesias, rather than brisk and tinglingly fruity.

Dão

The region of Dão, centred on the old cathedral city of Viseu, 50 miles south of the Douro, is much the biggest and most prosperous producer of *vinhos maduros* under a seal of origin. It is pine-forested country along the valleys of three rivers, the Alva,

The traditional means of transporting port down the Douro was by flat-bottomed boats, the barcos rabelos

the Mondego and the Dão, cut through hills of granite boulders and sandy soil. The vast majority of its 45,000 acres of vineyard is planted with black grapes (several of which it has in common with the Douro). White Dão, however, seems to have as much potential for quality: modern methods are finding in it very pleasant fruit flavours along with a dry firmness vaguely reminiscent of Chablis.

The profile of a red Dão remains, despite the care and skill of several of the merchants who mature it, a rather dry, hard wine reluctant to 'give', excellent palate cleansing with rich food, smooth and inviting to swallow, yet strangely lacking in bouquet or lingering sweetness.

The reason is that nobody (except the 10 local cooperatives) may make Dão except from his own grapes; the vineyards belong to small farmers, and there is, astonishingly, only one estate-grown Dão on the market – that of the Conde de Santar. The merchant bottlers must make the best of what the farmers and cooperatives provide them with.

Bairrada

Although it remained undemarcated until 1979, some 70 years after the Dão region, Bairrada is a real rival to the Dão in the quality of its wines. The name applies to an area between Dão and the Atlantic north of Coimbra and south of Oporto, with the towns of Mealhada and Anadia as its main centres. Its low hills of heavy lime-rich soil have a slightly greater vineyard area than Dão, and the same overwhelming preponderance of red grapes (90%) over white. But its climate is more temperate, its grape varieties different and its *adegas* more individual.

Two local grapes not found elsewhere have outstanding qualities. The red Baga is a late-ripening variety high in tannin and acid that gives real authority and 'cut' to a blend. As the dominant variety it needs 15 to 20 years' ageing, but eventually achieves the *poumada* (the Portuguese for pomade; a term for great fragrance) of a fine claret.

The aromatic local white grape is the Bical, which seems to have an outstanding balance of acidity and extract, aromatic of apricots, brisk and long-flavoured. Bical forms the basis of the sparkling-wine industry of Bairrada, which now has some very palatable products.

Garrafeira wines from almost any Portuguese merchant may contain or be based on Bairrada wines. The following firms are in the area and make good examples: Aliança, Barrocão, Imperio, Messias, São João.

The Douro

The mythology of the Douro reports that it was its terrible table wine that forced merchants to lace it with brandy and create port. It may have been so, but today the Douro produces the admirable table wines drunk daily by most port shippers, a number of well-known merchants' *garrafeiras*, and, in the shape of Barca Velha (*see* the entry for A. A. Ferreira under Port Producers on page 383), a great red wine of international stature to put beside Spain's Vega Sicilia, from 100 miles farther up the same river.

Both Tràs-os-Montes, north of the Douro, and Beira Alta to its south have well-balanced, not over-strong red wines to offer. Lafões is a recently regulated region in the wetter west of the Beira Alta; Beiras is farther east, between Dão and the border of Spain.

The Centre and South

Of the four historic wine regions, demarcated with *selos de origen*, clustering round Lisbon, the capital, two are reduced to relics with only a single remaining producer, one is still substantial but dwindling, and only the fourth, Setúbal, across the Tagus estuary, has escaped the attrition of housing development to prosper under modern conditions.

Carcavelos is nearest to extinction. Indeed I have still never managed to find the remaining vineyard that produces 3,000 cases a year. The sprawling resort of Estoril seems to have swallowed it up. But the quality of the wine justifies the search. It is a light amber, velvety, not oversweet, slightly fortified dessert or apéritif wine like a soft, nutty and buttery Verdelho or Bual madeira.

More is heard of Bucelas, whose 450 acres of vineyards 10 miles due north of Lisbon continue to produce 74,000 cases of a very pleasant, if not very original, dry white of moderate strength, in my experience rather lacking in aroma and not improved by the age in barrel it is often subjected to.

Still more is heard of Colares, not because there is any quantity – 26,000 cases is the average – but because it is a true original, and one of Portugal's most sought-after red wines. Its vineyards are an unplottable sprawl in the sand dunes of the Atlantic coast west of Lisbon, between Sintra and the sea. They grow the Ramisco, a tiny, bloomy dark-blue bullet of a grape whose thick skin would tan an oxhide. Grown in pure sand (the plants have to be planted at the bottom of deep pits, which are then progressively filled in) it makes wine of quite unreasonable inkiness and astringency. Grafting is unnecessary: phylloxera is baffled by sand.

Much the biggest Lisbon area lies across the Tagus, between the bridge and Setúbal on the far side of the Arrabida peninsula, a region with nearly 50,000 acres of vineyards divided between good plain red wine and the sumptuously aromatic

Muscat of Setúbal. Setúbal in this form was apparently the creation of the firm of José-Maria da Fonseca of Azeitão, in the middle of the region, who have a quasi-monopoly in the area. It is a 'muted' wine, its fermentation stopped by the addition of spirit, in which the skins of more Muscat grapes, themselves highly aromatic, are steeped and macerated to give it the precise fragrance of a ripe dessert grape. The wine is barrel-aged and drunk, without further ageing in bottle, either at six years (when it is still amazingly fresh and grapey) or at 25 or more (when it has taken on more piquant notes of fragrance and developed the tobacco hue and satin texture of a fine tawny port).

The biggest undemarcated wine region of Portugal is the central coastal area, north of Lisbon, where Wellington held the famous lines of Torres Vedras. From here eastwards to the far banks of the Tagus beyond Santarem, Ribatejo is bulk-wine country, yet bulk wine which a stranger can drink with pleasure; not over-alcoholic like its equivalent from Spain. How good it can be is demonstrated by Serradayres, the standard produce of Carvalho, Ribeiro and Ferreira, the most prestigious merchant of the region. The Ribatejo concentrates on white wine, but its red has more interest.

The vast area south of the Tagus, the Alentejo, has never been considered a wine region. Its brown hills are covered with the dark cork oaks that furnish the world with its best-quality corks. Nevertheless the names of certain areas are establishing themselves for good workaday red wine: notably Portalegre near the Tagus, Vidigueira near Evora, and Redondo and Borba towards Elvas (of the famous preserved plums). These regions are almost neighbours of the Spanish Extremadura and their wines correspondingly high in alcohol. So are those of the newly demarcated Algarve, the south coast, of which only a coarse sherry-style white has any reputation.

Rosés

The fabulous success of Mateus and subsequent Portuguese semi-sweet, semi-sparkling rosés was achieved by applying the idea (not the traditional technique) of *vinho verde* to red grapes from a region where the wine had no particular reputation: the hills north of the Douro round the town of Vila Real. It did not matter that this was not a demarcated region; rather the reverse: it meant that when the local grapes ran out supplies could be found in other areas. Today, rosés are made of grapes from almost anywhere in Portugal.

It is a process, then, and not a regional identity that characterizes these wines. They are made in the usual rosé fashion, of red grapes with a very short period of skin contact after crushing to extract the pink tinge, then fermented like white wine, the fermentation stopped while about 18 grams per litre of original grape sugar remain intact. This is done by adding sulphur dioxide and removing the yeast with a centrifuge pump. The wine is then blended for consistency and bottled with the addition of carbon dioxide under pressure.

TABLE-WINE PRODUCERS

Caves Aliança – Vinícola de Sangalhos

Sangalhos, 3783 Anadia. Founded 1920. Visits.

One of Portugal's principal table- and sparkling-wine producers. A public company controlled by the Neves family, based in the Bairrada but offering *vinho verde* (the good dry Casal Mendes), Dão, and Douro rosé as well as its admirable Bairrada red Alianca Tinto Velho, and very passable *méthode champenoise* sparkling wine, one of Portugal's best.

Arealva Limitada

P. Minicipio 20, 1100 Lisbon. No visits.

A family company making and 'elaborating' table wines from Estremadura, Dão and the Minho. Their lodges at the Quinta de Arealva on the Tagus have 25 acres of vines. Brands are Arealva and Tagus Rosé. J. Serra and the Sociedade Vinícola Sul de Portugal are associated companies.

Borges & Irmão SARL

Avenida da Republica 796, 4401 Vila Nova de Gaia. Founded 1884. Visits.

A substantial company in both the table wine and port trades with a major winery in the Minho. Their best-known brands are Gatão, a rather sweet 'commercial' *vinho verde*, Trovador, a ditto rosé, Gamba, a dry *vinho verde* and Dão wines under the label Meia Encosta, of which the white is a fruity, modern-style wine. They have also shipped 11 vintages of port since 1905, the latest in 1970. Total sales (1981) were 552,000 cases in Portugal, 134,000 abroad.

Carvalho, Ribeiro & Ferreira

Avenida da Republica 19, 1000 Lisbon. Founded 1898.

An important table-wine merchant without vineyards or press house but ageing and bottling such excellent wines as Serradayres (a claret-weight red and dry white from the Ribatejo), Ravel *vinho verde* and the only single-estate Dão, that from the lovely 'château' of the Conde de Santar. Some of their old *garrafeira* wines are anonymous in origin but splendid in quality.

J. M. da Fonseca

Largo do Corpo Santo 6, 1200 Lisbon. Founded 1834. Visits: week days.

One of the leading wine companies of Portugal both for quantity and quality, famous both as (almost) the sole producers of the great Moscatel de Setúbal and as the makers of Lancers pink *vinho verde*. Lancers in a sweetened and carbonated form is a best-seller in the USA. In Portugal it is much drier.

Faisca, another Fonseca brand, is a pale rosé, more like

a traditional *vinho verde*. In Portugal Fonseca (no relation to the port firm) is equally well known for its regular red table wine Periquita, made, like the Moscatel, at Azeitão. Its finest reds are Camarate (from a 250-acre *quinta* of this name at Palmela nearby, planted with Periquita, Cabernet and Merlot grapes) and the Terras Altas Dãos. The firm is still run by a member of the founding family, António Soares Franco.

Palace Hotel do Buçaco

3050 Mealhada

The cellars of this extravagant hotel mature one of Europe's most unusual wines. The hotel's 37-acre vineyards are near Luso on the fringes of the Bairrada region and grow its typical grapes. They are trodden (both red and white) in a 5,000-litre stone *lagar* and their wine made exactly in the manner of the last century; fermented in casks, then only racked; the red bottled at 4-5 years, the white at 2-3. Average production is 5,500 cases of red, 3,300 of white and a little dry rosé. Vintages available in the hotel go back to 1944 white and 1927 red, both still well preserved. The best vintages (e.g. white: 1966, '65, '56; red: 1963, '60, '58, '53) have an exquisite hand-made quality, great fragrance and depth.

Real Companhia Vinícola do Norte de Portugal

Vila Nova de Gaia

The old monopoly company of the port trade is now better known for its wide range of popular table wines, including the *vinho verde* Lagosta, Cabido Dãos, one of the few brands of Colares, Evel reds from the Douro (with good *garrafeiras*) and a sweet white, Grandjó, from the same area. The company was nationalized during the revolution of the early 1970s but is now again in the control of its tycoon proprietor, Senhor da Silva Reis. (*See* also under port producers.)

SOGRAPE-Vinhos de Portugal SARL

Rua Sá da Bandeira 819, 4000 Porto. Founded 1942. Visits.

Portugal's biggest wine company, the makers of Mateus Rosé, with total sales of over 3.5m. cases. The founding Guedes family still control the firm and its subsidiary, Vinícola do Vale do Dão, which makes one of the best Dão brands, Grão Vasco. Mateus Rosé is made of Bastardo, Touriga, Alverelhão and Tinta Pinheira, red grapes of the Douro and Dão regions, though most come from north of the Douro. It has a little-known, similarly semi-sweet, white counterpart made of Arinto, Malvasia, Esgana Cão and Cercial also grown north of the Douro, around Vila Real, and picked early to keep the alcohol as low as 10° (the rosé is 11°). Sogrape *garrafeira* is an excellent mature Douro red.

Caves Velhas – Companhia Portuguesa de Vinhos de Marca Lda

Rua Fernão Lopes 9, Lisbon. Founded 1939. Visits.

The trading name of Adegas Camilo Alves (founded 1881), the sole remaining producers of Bucelas wine. The firm owns 26 of the 81 acres remaining in Bucelas and buys the grapes from the rest. Bucellas *garrafeira* is aged 3 years in cask in their grand old barn of an *adega*. Romeira is the name used for red and rosé wines from the Ribatejo; Caves Velhas for their equally well-made Dãos.

OTHER PRODUCERS

Quinta da Aveleda Lda
PO Box 121, 4002 Porto. Founded 1947. Visits by appt. Makers of the most famous traditional dry *vinho verde*, Casal Garcia, the rather sweeter Aveleda, and a fine, delicate and dry estate *vinho verde*, Quinta da Aveleda. The extremely beautiful estate of the Guedes family, in colourful gardens near Porto, makes the wine principally from 3 family-owned *quintas*: Aveleda, Lavandeira and Fiães. The same family controls SOGRAPE.

Caves do Barrocão Lda
Fogueila, PO Box 1, Sangalhos, 3780 Anadia. Founded 1920. Visits. A family firm in the Bairrada, specializing in *méthode champenoise* wines (for which it has the largest champagne-style cellar in Portugal). Diamante Azul is the principal brand. Other Bairrada whites and reds and Dão wines, including some very long-lived *garrafeiras*, are also labelled Barrocão. *Vinho verde* is labelled Diamante Verde.

Caves do Casalinho Lda
R. Duque de Saldanha 182, 4300 Porto. A rapidly growing family-owned (the Camelo and Costa families) table-wine company with several *quintas* in the Minho and one (rented) in the Douro. Casalinho is their best brand of dry *vinho verde*, others are Três Marias, Montemar and 5 Cidades. Casalinho Rosé is a look-alike of Mateus. Their Dão brand, Alexandre Magno, can be impressive.

I may have been prejudiced against their prestige line, Ouro Velho, by its absurd fake-dusty lop-sided bottle. I found the red *garrafeira* muddy and the white like oily sherry.

Raul Ferreira & Filho Lda
Quinta do Barão, Carcavelos 2775 Parede, Praia. The only remaining producer of the luscious Madeira-like Carcavelos, whose vineyards have almost disappeared among villas. Production is now down to 3,000 cases.

Gonçalves Monteiro & Hos. Lda
PO Box 8, Valadares, 4408 Vila Nova de Gaia. Founded 1918. No visits. A substantial family-owned table-wine company with 3 brands: Magriço, a good traditional dry *vinho verde*, 3 Cavaleiros, a Mateus-type Douro rosé, and Catedral Dão.

Vinhos de Monção Lda
4950 Monção. Diminutive producers of the famous (and expensive) Alvarinho white, Cepa Velha, a potential *vinho verde* fermented and aged in wood to achieve a totally different result.

Palacio de Brejoeira
4950 Monção. Minho. The most prestigious producer of the rare Alvarinho white.

Abel Pereira da Fonseca SARL
Rua Amorim – 12, Poço do Bispo, 1900 Lisbon. Founded 1907. Visits. General wine merchants best known for their brand of Dão wines: Viriatus.

Caves de Raposeira
5100 Lamego. Producers of some of Portugal's best *méthode champenoise* sparkling *bruto*, in the region between Dão and Douro. Recently taken over by Seagram's of Canada.

Ribeiro & Irmão
Makers of one of the crisper and better *vinhos verdes*, Ribeiros.

C. da Silva (Vinhos) SARL
247 Rua Felizardo de Lima, 4401 Vila Nova de Gaia. Founded 1930. Shippers of both port and table wines, including the good-quality Dom Silvano *vinhos verdes*, Isabel Rosé, Dalva Dãos and Douro Fathers table wines. Port brands are Dalva, Presidential and Player's.

Adega Regional de Colares
Colares, 2710 Sintra. The only producer of real Colares, although most of its produce is matured and bottled by several firms, including Real Companhia Vinícola and Colares Chita.

Adega Cooperativa de Monção
4950 Monção. The growers' cooperative of Monção makes, besides much *vinho verde*, some 2,000 cases of the rare still white Alvarinho.

PORT

What the English have long known as port, and the Portuguese and other nations as porto, belongs with champagne and sherry in the original trinity of great 'processed' wines. Each is an elaboration on the natural produce of its region to enhance its latent quality. Being capital intensive, requiring the holding of big stocks for long periods, their trade has become concentrated in the hands of shippers. Single-vineyard ports, and even single-vintage ports, are the exceptions in an industry which lives day to day on long-established, unchanging blends.

Unlike champagne and sherry, port was the child of political pressure. In the late seventeenth century the British were obliged by their government to find alternatives to the French red wines they preferred. They turned to Portugal, an old and useful ally, for a convenient substitute for claret. Finding nothing to their liking in the existing vineyards (which is surprising: Lisbon had good wine, if Oporto did not) the enterprising traders pushed inland from Oporto up the valley of the Douro into the rugged hinterland. What they tasted there that made them persevere is hard to imagine. They could hardly have chosen a more difficult and inaccessible place, with a more extreme climate, to develop as a major new wine area. They started around Regua, about 60 miles (or three mule-days) upstream from Oporto where the river Corgo joins the main stream. Gradually, finding that the higher they went the better the wine became, they built terraces up the almost impossible mountains surrounding the Douro and its tributaries: the Távora, the Torto, the Pinhão, the Tua. They dotted the mountainsides with white-walled *quintas* or farms, and demonstrated that once cultivated, the thin arid soil of granite and schist became extraordinarily fertile. Today not just the grapes but the nuts, oranges, almonds and even vegetables of the Douro are famous.

The first port was apparently a strong dry red wine, made even stronger with 'a bucket or two' of brandy to stabilize it for shipping. It got a very cold reception from British claret lovers, who complained bitterly. The shippers tried harder, and at some time in the eighteenth century hit on the idea of stopping the fermentation with brandy while the wine was still sweet and fruity. History is unclear on when this became the standard practice, since as late as the 1840s the most influential British port shipper of all time, James Forrester (created a Portuguese Baron for his services), was urging a return to unfortified (therefore dry) wines. Sweet or dry, however, port was much the most-drunk wine in Britain from the early eighteenth century to the early twentieth.

Today port is one of the most strictly controlled of all wines. A series of statutory authorities regulate and oversee every stage of its making. Every one of 85,000 vineyards, totalling 62,000 acres, is individually classified for quality on an eight-point scale by the 'Casa de Douro', taking into account its situation, altitude, soil, inclination, grape varieties, standard of cultivation, fertility and the age of its vines. It is then given an annual quota. Only 40 per cent on average of the total Douro crop may be turned into port, the rest is just red wine. The maximum yield, allowed for vineyards classified A on the eight-point scale, is 700 litres to 1,000 vines.

At harvest time, late September in the Douro, bureaucracy seems remote enough. The grinding labour of picking and carrying the crop from the steep terraces to the press-houses is carried on with amazingly cheerful, even tuneful, energy by gangs of villagers who often walk miles over the mountains for their annual 'holiday'. On remote little farms, and with the best-quality grapes at some of the largest *quintas*, the crop is still trodden barefoot by lamplight in open granite *lagars*, then fermented in the *lagars* until it is ready to be 'stopped' with brandy. Much the greater proportion today though is machine crushed and fermented in closed concrete fermenting tanks of a kind introduced from Algeria, with a simple percolating system, operated by the natural build-up of carbon dioxide, to keep the juice constantly churning over the skins.

With either method the moment comes when about half the grape sugar is fermented into alcohol. This is when the half-made wine is run off into barrels one quarter full of brandy. Fermentation stops instantly.

The great majority of the port is moved, after its first racking off its gross lees, to the shippers' lodges to mature. The lodges are huddled together in the Oporto suburb of Vila Nova de Gaia, facing the steep streets of the city across the Douro and linked to it by a remarkable double-decker bridge. The down-river journey can no longer be made by the beautiful Viking-style *barcos rabelos* since the river was dammed for hydroelectric power. What was once a picturesque if perilous river highway is now a series of placid lakes, dotted with windsurfers and occasionally furrowed by water-skiers. Today port travels by truck.

Once in the shipper's lodge, port, like sherry, is classified by tasting and its destiny decided by its quality and potential for improvement. Most ports join a sort of perpetual blending system whose object is an unchanging product.

Simple, fruity and rather light wines without great concentration are destined to become ruby, aged for up to about two years in wood and bottled while their bright red colour and full sweetness show no sign of maturity. This is the cheapest category, very popular in France as an apéritif. It makes a stimulating rather than a satisfying or complex drink.

Young wines with more aggressive characters and greater concentration, some outstandingly good, some of only moderate quality, are set aside to develop into tawnies – so-called from their faded colour after many years in wood. Tawnies include some of the greatest of all ports, the shippers' own favourite blends, kept for up to 40 years in cask, then (usually) refreshed with a little younger wine of the highest quality. Tawnies also include some very ordinary mixtures with scarcely any of the character of barrel-age, made by blending young red and white ports. Their price varies accordingly. The best tawnies have an indication of age on the label. Twenty years is old enough for most of them – the high premium for a 30- or 40-year-old wine is seldom worth it. Styles among top tawnies vary from the intensely luscious (e.g. Ferreira's Duque de Bragança) to refinement and dry finish (e.g. Taylor's Finest Old Tawny).

The great majority of port falls into one or other of the above categories, which together are known as 'wood ports'; their whole maturing process takes place in wood.

Vintage port, by contrast, is the product of one of the three or four vintages in a decade which come close to the shipper's idea of perfection – which have so much flavour and individuality that to make them anonymous as part of a continuing blend would be a waste of their potential. Whether or not a shipper 'declares' a vintage is entirely his own decision. It is very rare that all do so in the same year. The Douro is too varied in its topography and conditions.

Vintage ports are blended in the particular style the shipper has developed over many years, using the best lots of wine from his regular suppliers – including invariably his own best vineyards. They are matured for a minimum of 22 and a maximum of 31 months in cask for their components to 'marry', then bottled 'in Oporto' (i.e. in Vila Nova de Gaia) while they are still undrinkably tannic, aggressive and concentrated in flavour. Almost all their maturing therefore happens in the airless 'reductive' conditions of a black-glass bottle with a long cork, designed to protect the wine for decades

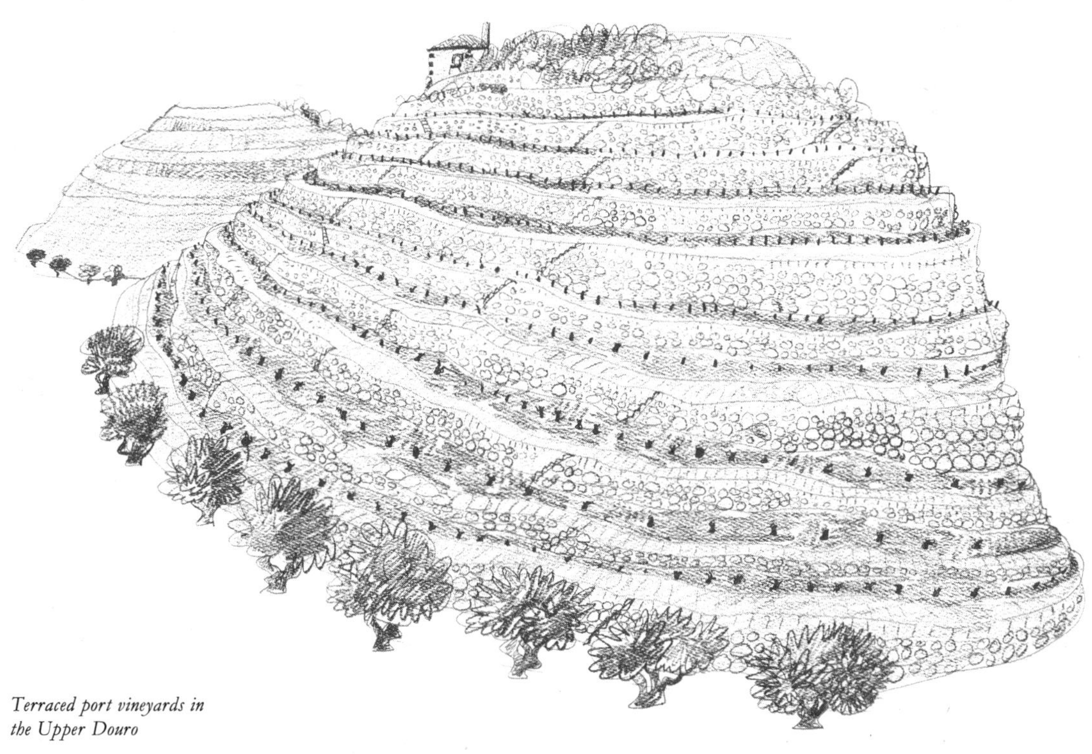

Terraced port vineyards in the Upper Douro

while it slowly feeds on itself. Its tannins and pigments react to form a heavy skin-like 'crust' that sticks to the side of the bottle. Its colour slowly fades – far more slowly than if it were in wood – and its flavour evolves from violently sweet and harsh to gently sweet, perfumed and mellow. Yet however mellow, vintage port is designed to have 'grip', a vital ingredient in some wine which will never lose its final bite even in old age.

Between the clear-cut extremes of wood port and vintage port come a number of compromises intended to offer something closer to vintage port without the increasingly awkward need to cellar the wine for between 10 and 30 years. Vintage character (or vintage reserve) is effectively top-quality ruby port whose ingredient wines were almost up to vintage standards, but kept for four or five years in cask. These potent and tasty wines are 'ready' when bottled, but will continue to develop, and even to form a slight 'crust' in bottle if they are kept. The term crusted or crusting port is sometimes used for the same style (though not officially recognized in Portugal).

Late-bottled vintage is similar, but is made of the wine of one 'vintage' year, kept twice as long as vintage port in barrel: i.e. from three and a half to six years. The label 'L.B.V.' carries both the date of the vintage and the bottling, is lighter in colour and flavour than vintage port but should have some of its firmness. It may or may not form a deposit in bottle according to its maturity on bottling and the degree to which the shipper has chilled and filtered it for stability.

An increasingly popular compromise with some of the best shippers is single-*quinta* vintage port. In years that are not generally up to vintage standard some wine of excellent quality is often made in the best sites. In several famous cases these belong to eminent shippers. In vintage years they are the backbone of the blend. In less-than-perfect years the shippers sometimes bottle them unblended, with the vintage date. They will mature sooner than classic vintages but often have distinct and charming character. Being bottle-matured they will of course form a crust and need decanting. Some of the best-known single-*quinta* wines occasionally offered are Taylor's Quinta de Vargellas, Graham's Quinta dos Malvedos, Croft's Quinta da Roêda, Cálem's Quinta da Foz.

White port is made in the same way as red port but of white grapes, usually fermented further towards dryness before being fortified with brandy. It is intended as an apéritif rather than a dessert wine, but never achieves the quality or finesse of, say, a *fino* sherry. Its underlying heaviness needs to be enlivened, at least with a lump of ice, and it can be even more enjoyable as a long drink with tonic water, ice and a slice of lemon.

PORT PRODUCERS

A. A. Cálem & Filho Ltd.

Rua de Reboleira 7, 4000 Porto. Stock: 15,500 pipes. Vintages: 1935, '50, '54, '58, '60, '63, '70, '75, '77, and '78. Visits. Prices: 10-year-old tawny, 300 escudos; vintage '77, 400 escudos.

Founded in 1859 by a family already long in the trade, and who still own the firm. The Cálems own the excellent Quinta da Foz and 3 others, in total 45 acres of vineyards, at Pinhão, where they still tread the grapes. They make other ports from bought grapes by 'autovinification'. Their Cálem and da Costa ports are well known in France, Germany, the Netherlands and the UK.

Cockburn Smithes & Cia Lda

Rua das Coradas 13, Vila Nova de Gaia. Stocks (including Martinez): 32,000 pipes. Vintages: 1900, '04, '08, '12, '27, '35, '47, '50, '55, '60, '63, '67, '70 and '75.

Founded 1815. Visits. Prices: Director's Reserve, 750 escudos.

One of the greatest names in port, owned by Allied Breweries but still run by descendants of its Scottish founders. Cockburn vineyard properties are the Quintas do Tua (60 acres), da Santa Maria near Regua (40 acres) and do Val do Coelho and do Atayde near Tua where they are planting 500 acres. 60% of the *quinta* wines is still trodden. Cockburn's wines have a distinctive dry finish, or 'grip'. Their best tawny, Director's Reserve, with Special Reserve Tawny and Fine Old Ruby, make up 38% of port sales in the UK. Martinez Gassiot (q.v.) is an associated company.

Croft & Ca Lda

Largo Joaquim Magalhães 23, 4401 Vila Nova de Gaia. Stock: 30,000 pipes. Vintages: Croft – 1900, '04, '08, '12, '17, '20, '22, ,24, '27, '35, '42, '45, '50, '55, '60, '63, '66, '70, '75 and '77. Quinta da Roêda – 1967, '78 and '80. Morgan – 1900, '04, '08, '12, '20, '22, '24, '27, '42, '48, '55, '60, '63, '66, '70 and '77. Founded 1678. Visits by appt.

Perhaps the oldest port firm, originally known as Phayre and Bradley, now owned by International Distillers & Vintners (*see also* Sherry). Owners of the superb Quinta da Roêda with 247 acres at Pinhão, responsible for the distinctive floweriness of their vintage wines – regularly among the finest of all. Other wines include the excellent Distinction Tawny, and the sister brands Delaforce (q.v.) and Morgan.

Delaforce Sons & Co.

Rua das Coradas 72, Vila Nova de Gaia. Stock: 15,000 pipes. Vintages: 1908, '17, '20, '21, '22, '27, '35, '45, '47, '50, '55, '58, '60, '63, '66, '70, '75 and '77. Quinta da Corte: '78; '80. Founded 1868. Visits by appt.

Still family run by the Delaforces, although since 1968 a subsidiary (like Crofts, q.v.) of I.D.V. The firm's finest wines, with great freshness and elegance, come from the contracted Quinta da Corte in the Rio Torto valley. His Eminence's Choice is a superbly succulent 16-year-old tawny.

Dow's *see* Silva & Cosens Ltd.

A. A. Ferreira

91-103 Rua da Carvalhosa, 4400 Vila Nova de Gaia. Stocks: 15,000–20,000 pipes. Vintages: 1945, '55, '58, '60, '63, '66, '70, '75, '77 and '78. Founded 1761.

A historic Portuguese house, in the mid-19th century the richest in the Douro, then ruled over by the famous Dona Antonia, who built the magnificent Quintas do Vesuvio and do Vale de Meão, colossal establishments in the remotest high Douro. They still own, between the company and members of the family, no less than 4,000 acres of vineyard. Today Ferreira sells more bottled port in Portugal than any other house, and none in wood. Sales in 1982 were 3m. bottles. Their vintage wines (though fine) are less well known than their tawnies, Superior, Dona Antonia and above all the superlative Duque de Bragança, largely made of wines from the great Quinta do Roriz above Pinhão.

Hunt, Roope is a subsidiary company, which in turn ships Tuke, Holdsworth vintage ports. Another close link is with MacKenzie & Co. Ferreira also make, in the cavernous *lagars* at the Quinta do Vale de Meão, almost on the Spanish frontier, some 4,000 cases of one of the finest Portuguese table wines, their Ferreirinha, in its best years (e.g. '65, '66, '78, '79, '80) christened Barca Velha.

Fonseca *see* Guimaraens

W. & J. Graham & Co.

Rua Rei Ramiro 514, 4401 Vila Nova de Gaia. Stocks: 9,000 pipes. Vintages: 1904, '08, '12, '17, '20, '24, '27, '35, '42, '45, '48, '55, '60, '63, '66, '70, '75 and '77.
Founded 1820. Visits by appt.

A shipper renowned for some of the richest and sweetest vintage ports, now part of the empire of the Symington family (with Warre, Silva & Cosens etc. qq.v). Graham's Quinta dos Malvedos on the Douro near Tua provides exceptionally ripe fruit for vintage port of great colour, body and guts which mellows to a singularly sumptuous wine. Part of the crop is still trodden. Malvedos is also issued as a single-*quinta* wine (e.g. in 1965). Tawny and late-bottled vintage follow the full-bodied, luscious style.

Guimaraens Vinhos SARL

Quinta Dom Prior, 4401 Vila Nova de Gaia. Stock: 5,000 pipes. Vintages: 1904, '08, '12, '20, '22, '27, '34, '45, '48, '55, '60, '63, '66, '70, '75 and '77.
Founded 1822. Visits.

Shippers of Fonseca ports, and despite their name an English family business for over a century, now linked to Taylors. Their vineyards of Quinta do Cruzeiro (160 acres) and Quinta Santo Antonio (100 acres), both in the Val de Mendiz near Alijo, are splendidly sited and still make all their best wines by treading. Fonseca is regularly one of the finest and richest vintage ports and their Bin '27 an admirable youngish tawny.

Gould, Campbell *see* Smith, Woodhouse

C. N. Kopke & Co.

Rua Serpa Pinto 183-191, 4400 Vila Nova de Gaia. Vintages: 1934, '35, '44, '45, '52, '55, '58, '60, '63, '66, '70, '74, '75, '77, '78, '79 and '80. Founded 1636.

In name at least the oldest of all the port firms, founded by a German. It now belongs to Barros Almeida (q.v.). Kopke has 500 acres of vines and uses the names Quinta São Luiz for vintages, Old World for tawny and Bridge for ruby. Colheita 1937 is a very old tawny.

Sociedade Agricola e Comercial dos Vinhos Messias SARL

3050 Mealhada, 4401 Vila Nova de Gaia. Stocks: port 8,500 pipes; table and sparkling wines 200,000 cases. Vintages: 1955, '60, '63, '65, '66, '67, '70, '75, '77, '78, '79 and '80.
Founded 1926. Visits.

A Portuguese family-run company owning substantial port vineyards, notably the Quinta do Cachão near San João da Pesqueira (250 acres). The *quinta* crops are trodden for vintage and vintage-style wines, which are reputed to have a faint almond flavour. For table wines Messias have a lodge at Mealhada in the Bairrada in central Portugal.

Quinta do Noval

Rua Cândido dos Reis 575, 4401 Vila Nova de Gaia. Stock: 6,000 pipes. Vintages: 1904, '08, '12, '17, '20, '24, '27, '31, '34, ('41 & '42), '45, '50, '55, '58, '60, '63, '66, '70, '75 and '78.
Founded 1813. Visits.
Prices: 20-year-old tawny, 650 escudos; vintage '78, 540 escudos.

Perhaps the most famous, and one of the most beautiful, *quintas* on the Douro, perched high above Pinhão. It belongs to the Van Zeller family, who also own the firm of A. J. da Silva. A tragic fire in 1982 destroyed the historic records of the company and part of the stock. Old Noval vintages were some of the most magnificent of all ports. The '31 is legendary and the '27 was even better. A small plot of ungrafted vines still occasionally makes an astoundingly concentrated 'Nacional' vintage. Most Noval wines have recently been in a lighter, more feminine, very charming style. Noval late-bottled wines, tawnies and white ports are good, though they are not single-*quinta* wines. Quinta do Silval is another property.

Offley Forrester (Vinhos) Lda

Rua do Choupelo 260, 4401 Vila Nova de Gaia. Stock: 13,000 pipes.
Founded 1737. No visits.

The firm of the great genius of the port trade, Baron Forrester (d.1862); now jointly owned by Sandeman and St. Raphael. The famous Quinta do Boa Vista in the hills above the Rio Corgo near Regua supplies the bulk of their vintage wines. Total vineyards, including the Quinta do Cachucha near Pinhão, add up to 200 acres. Other wines include the Duke of Oporto, Porto Rei, Boa Vista L.B.V., and Baron de Forrester Reserves.

Manoel D. Poças Junior, Lda

Rua Visconde das Devesas 186, 4401 Vila Nova de Gaia. Stock: 7,000 pipes. Vintages: 1960, '63, '64, '67, '70, '75, '77 and '78.
Prices: 20-year-old tawny, 696 escudos; vintage '78, 350 escudos.

An independent family company founded in 1918, owning 2 Douro properties, the Quintas das Quartas and Santa Barbara, run on traditional lines. Their brands Poças Junior, Pousada, Terras, Almiro and Pintão have recently doubled in sales, particularly in Belgium and France, winning them the government export award.

Quarles Harris & Co. Lda

Tr. Barão de Forrester 4401 Vila Nova de Gaia. Stock: 4,000 pipes. Vintages: 1908, '12, '20, '27, '34, '45, '47, '50, '55, '58, '60, '63, '66, '70, '75 and '77.
Founded 1680. Visits by appt.

Together with Warre, Graham, Dow, etc. (qq.v), now part of the remarkable stable of the Symington family;

there are no vineyards, but old contacts with good growers along the Rio Torto maintain a style of very intense full vintage port with a powerful bouquet. Only a small proportion is still trodden. Harris (not Quarles) is the brand for tawnies, ruby and white ports.

Adriano Ramos-Pinto

Avenida Ramos-Pinto 380, 4401 Vila Nova de Gaia. Stock: 8,000 pipes. Vintages: 1924, '27, '35, '45, '52, '63, '70 and '77. Visits.

Prices: tawny '37, 2,250 escudos; vintage '77, 469 escudos.

Founded in 1880 and one of the most distinguished Portuguese-owned houses. Their properties include the famous Quinta Bom-Retiro with 112+ acres in the Rio Torto valley, the 90-acre Quinta Santa Maria and the smaller San Domingos. Tawnies (including a fine '1937') are their specialities and Brazil their traditional market, although France, Switzerland and Germany are now important.

Real Companhia Vinícola do Norte de Portugal

Rua Azevedo Magalhães 314, 4401 Vila Nova de Gaia. Vintages: 1908, '41, '43, '44, '45, '47, '54, '55, '58, '60, '62, '63, '67, '70, '77, '78, '79 and '80.

Founded 1889. Visits.

Prices: Old Tawny, 450 escudos; vintage '80, 370 escudos.

Founded in 1756 by the Marquis de Pombal to control the port trade, the company now belongs to Senhor da Silva Reis. Its interests are now half in port and half in other wines (of which half are sparkling). Its port Quintas do Corval and do Sibio (near Tua) provide part of its needs for a stock of 8,000 pipes. *See* also under table-wine producers.

Robertson Bros. & Co. Lda

Rua Dr. António Granjo 207, 4400 Vila Nova de Gaia. Stocks: 3,600 pipes.

Founded 1881. No visits.

Prices: Imperial, 574 escudos; vintage '77, 800 escudos.

Now a subsidiary of Sandeman. Shippers of Rebello Valente vintage ports, notably robust, tannic and fruity wines still trodden in *lagars*, largely at the Quinta de la Rosa at Pinhão. Robertsons also pioneered new-method vinification for their tawnies: Game Bird, Privateer, Pyramid, Izaak Walton and the splendid Imperial.

Sandeman & Co. Lda

Largo Miguel Bombarda, 3, 4400 Vila Nova de Gaia. Stocks: 39,000 pipes. Vintages: 1904, '08, '11, '12, '17, '20, '27, '34, '35, '42, '45, '47, '50, '55, '58, '60, '63, '66, '67, '70, '75 and '77.

Founded 1790. Visits.

Prices: Imperial tawny, 937 escudos; vintage '77, 830 escudos.

One of the biggest shippers of both port and sherry, now a subsidiary of Seagrams but still chaired by David Sandeman, a direct descendant of George Sandeman, the founder, a friend of the Duke of Wellington. The firm's vineyards are the Quintas de Confradeiro and de Celeirós (118 acres on the Pinhão river). Quinta das Laranjeiras (528 acres at Moncorvo) is a big new development in the highest Douro near Spain. Another 60 acres at Vale de Mendiz near Pinhão are rented. Sandeman's view is that their vintage wines are on the dry side, which is not borne out by my experience. I find them fruity, if not as rich as (say) Graham. Their tawnies are nice and nutty. Associated companies are Robertson, Offley Forrester, Diez Hermanos and Rodriguez Pinho.

Silva & Cosens Ltd. (Dow's Port)

Tr. Barão de Forrester, 4401 Vila Nova de Gaia. Stock: 15,000 pipes. Vintages: 1904, '08, '12, '20, '24, '27, '34, (42 & '44), '45, '47, '50, '55, '60, '63, '66, '70, '72, '75 and '77.

Founded 1798. Visits by appt.

The proprietors of Dow's brand, named after a Victorian partner. Since 1912 a sister company of Warre, under the control of the ubiquitous Symingtons. The family Quinta do Bomfim at Pinhão is one of the finest on the Douro. Supported by the Quinta Santa Madalena nearby up the Rio Torto it gives mightily tannic and concentrated vintage port, recognized by its dry finish in maturity. Most is now made by 'autovinification'. Dow also sell 'Boardroom' and 30-year-old tawny, and ruby and white ports.

Smith, Woodhouse & Co. Lda

Rua Rei Ramiro 514, 4401 Vila Nova de Gaia. Stock: 4,000 pipes. Vintages: 1904, '08, '12, '17, '20, '24, '27, '35, '45, '47, '50, '55, '60, '70, '75 and '77.

Founded 1784. Visits by appt.

Together with Dow, Warre, etc. (qq.v.), now part of the Symington family property (which altogether stocks some 40,000 pipes). Smith, Woodhouse also ship Gould, Campbell vintage ports. Both come largely from the Rio Torto (Vale Dona Maria). Gould, Campbell vintages are big, dark, powerful and very long-lasting wines; the Smith, Woodhouse style is more fragrant and fruity and their tawnies notably so. Part of the crop for both is still trodden.

Taylor Fladgate & Yeatman

Rua do Choupelo 250, 4401 Vila Nova de Gaia. Stocks: 12,000 pipes. Vintages: 1904, '06, '08, '12, '17, '20, '24, '27, '35, '38, '40, '42, '45, '48, '55, '60, '63, '66, '67, '70, '75, '77.

Founded 1692. Visits.

One of the oldest and consistently one of the best shippers, still owned by descendants of the Yeatman family (Chairman, Alistair Robertson). The style of their tremendous vintage wines, of unrivalled ripeness, depth and every other dimension, is largely derived from their famous Quinta de Vargellas (630 acres), high on the upper Douro above São João de Pesqueira. In 1973 they also bought the Quintas do Panascal at Tabuaço and de Terrafeita at Celeiros up the Pinhão valley. Each has 400 acres. Their vintage ports are still trodden by foot, although they are experimenting with stainless steel fermenters at their vinification centre for ruby ports near Regua. In occasional second-quality vintages Vargellas wine is shipped unblended under its own label. Fonseca is an associate company. Taylor's tawnies are no less exceptional.

Warre & Co. Lda

Travessa Barão de Forrester, 4401 Vila Nova de Gaia. Stock: 13,000 pipes. Vintages: 1904, '08, '12, '20, '22, '24, '27, '34, ('42), '45, '47, '50, '55, '58, '60, '63, '66, '70, '75 and '77.

Founded 1670. Visits.

Possibly the oldest English port firm, now one of the largest firms in the group owned by the Symington family. The vintage wines are based on their Quinta da Cavadinha near Pinhão, produced by modern methods. The style is extremely fruity with a fresh, almost herbal bouquet and a firm 'grip' at the finish. Some recent vintages have been beautifully balanced and lingering. Warrior is a good vintage-character wine and Nimrod a tawny. Cintra is a label for France.

OTHER PRODUCERS

Barros Almeida
4400 Vila Nova de Gaia. A family-owned substantial shipper of medium-quality ports, largely in bulk. Also proprietors of Kopke, the oldest brand of all, Feuerheerd (qq.v.), the Douro Wine Shippers Association and several other companies.

J. W. Burmester & Co.
Rua de Belomonte 39, 4000 Porto. Founded in 1750. No visits. A small family-owned, now Portuguese, house of English and German foundation. No vineyards, but well-chosen wines from Pinhão go to make their Tordiz tawny and vintages. Other names used are Jems and Southam's. Stocks: 4,500 pipes. Vintages: 1900, '10, '20, '22, '27, '29, '34, '35, '37, '40, '44, '48, '50, 55, '58, '60, '63, '75, '77.

Diez Hermanos Lda
Rua Guilherme Braga 38, 4401 Vila Nova de Gaia. No Visits. A small subsidiary of Offley Forrester (q.v.). Stock: 6,000 pipes.

Feuerheerd Bros. & Co.
4400 Vila Nova de Gaia. Founded 1815. The formerly British-owned company now belongs to Barros Almeida (q.v.).

Martinez Gassiot & Co. Ltd
Rua das Coradas 13, Vila Nova de Gaia. Founded 1790. Visits. The company was bought by Harvey's in 1961 and is now a subsidiary of Allied Breweries; thus allied to Cockburn (q.v.). Its speciality is fine tawnies rather than ruby or vintage-character wines. Stocks: *see* Cockburn. Vintages: 1900, '04, '08, '11, '12, '19, '22, '27, '31, '34, '45, '55, '58, '60, '63, '67, '70 and '75. Prices: Director's Tawny, 800 escudos.

Niepoort & Co. Ltd
Rua Serpa Pinto 278, Villa Nova de Gaia. Founded 1842. No visits. A small Dutch family-owned company, unusual in storing its vintage port before bottling in glass demijohns in a cellar, rather than pipes in a lodge.

Rozes Lda
Rua do Choupelo 250, Vila Nova de Gaia. Founded 1853. No visits. A shipper jointly owned by Möet Hennessy and Taylor, Fladgate and Yeatman, specializing in the French market for its tawny, ruby and white ports. Stocks: 6,000 pipes. Vintages: 1963, '67 and '77.

Wiese & Krohn
4401 Vila Nova de Gaia. Founded 1866. No visits. A small independent company, originally German, without vineyards. Shipped the vintages of 1957, '58, '60, '61, '63, '65, '67, '70, '75, '78.

MADEIRA

The very existence of madeira has been touch and go for a century. No famous wine region has suffered so much the combined onslaught of pests, diseases, disillusioned growers and public neglect. It is doubtful whether any other would have survived as more than a footnote.

What has kept madeira alive is the unique quality its old wines have of going on getting better and better. The remaining bottles of madeira from before its troubles began are proof that the island can make the longest-lived wines in the world. At a century old they have concentrated their flavours into a pungency that would be overwhelming were it not so fresh. They leave the mouth so cleanly and gracefully as you swallow that water could not be more reviving. Harmony between sweetness and acidity can go no further.

Madeira is the largest of three small islands 400 miles west of the coast of Morocco. It was discovered early in the fifteenth century by an eloping Bristol sea captain, who died there with his bride. Their crew sailed on, to be captured by corsairs. In a Moroccan dungeon they told their tale to a Spanish navigator, who in 1420 piloted a Portuguese ship to the island.

It flourished as a Portuguese colony. Prince Henry the Navigator ordered the sweet Malvasia grapes of Greece to be planted, as well as sugar cane from Sicily. Later, with the discovery of the West Indies, bananas became an important part of the island's harvest. The crops were, and still are, grown in a garden-like mixture on steep terraces that rise half-way up the 6,000-foot island-mountain. As in the north of Portugal the vines are trained on pergolas to allow other crops beneath. With its warm climate Madeira was a natural producer of 'sack', like Jerez and the Canaries. What settled its destiny was a piece of English legislation of 1665, forbidding the export of European wines to British colonies except through British ports and in British ships. Madeira was presumably deemed to be in Africa; at all events it became the regular supplier for American vessels heading west. By the end of the seventeenth century the American and West Indian British colonists used madeira as their only wine.

Far from being spoilt by the long hot voyage across the mid-Atlantic, the wine proved better as a result. Later, with growing British interests in the Far East, it was discovered to benefit even more from a voyage to India. So fine was their sea-matured madeira that casks were shipped as ballast to India and back to give connoisseurs in Europe a yet finer wine. It was during the eighteenth century that brandy was increasingly added, as it was to port, to sweeten and stabilize it.

In America the appreciation of old madeira became a cult – southern gentlemen would meet to dine simply on terrapin and canvas-back duck before 'discussing' several decanters of ancient wine, named sometimes for their grapes, sometimes for the ship that brought them over, sometimes for the families in whose cellars they has rested and become heirlooms. Thus a Bual might be followed by a Constitution, and that by a Francis, a Butler or a Burd. One popular pale blend, still sometimes seen, is known as Rainwater – because, apparently, of a similarity of taste. Almost the same reverence was paid to its qualities in England – and still is, by the few who have tasted such wines.

Quantities became far too great to transport through the tropics as a matter of course. In the 1790s Napoleon's navy also put difficulties in the way of merchantmen. A practical substitute was found in heating the wines to 45°C (113°F) in hot stores (Portuguese *estufas*) for up to six months: the cheaper wines in large pipe-heated vats; the best wines in casks in the warm space above them.

Four principal grape varieties and three or four others were grown to provide different styles of wine. The original, the Malvasia or Malmsey, made the richest: the Bual a less rich, more elegant but equally fragrant wine; Verdelho a soft, much drier wine with a faintly bitter finish, the Sercial (a clone of Riesling) a fine light wine with a distinct acid 'cut'. Tinta Negra Mole, reputedly a form of Pinot Noir, was planted to make the strong red wine once known as 'Tent'. Bastardo, Terrantez and Moscatel were also grown in smaller quantities.

Madeira was at the peak of prosperity when a double disaster struck. In the 1850s came oidium, the powdery mildew. In 1873 phylloxera arrived. Six thousand acres of vineyard were destroyed, and only 1,200 replaced with true madeira vines. To save grafting the remainder were replanted (if at all) with French-American hybrids whose wine has no claim to be called madeira at all.

Since then, Madeira has lived on its reputation, kept alive by memories, by a meagre trickle of high-quality wines, and by the convenient French convention of *sauce madère*, which is easily enough satisfied with any wine that has been cooked. Half the wine from the island today is destined for sauce-making with no questions asked. Unfortunately even the replanting of the original European vines, the four classics, was neglected in favour of the obliging Tinta Negra Mole. Today 80 per cent of the crop (hybrids apart) is Tinta. It has to do service for the Malmsey, Bual, Verdelho and Sercial (respectively 3.5, 2, 2 and 1.5 per cent of the crop) in all except the most expensive brands. Tinta, in fact, is picked earlier or later, fortified during or after fermentation, 'stoved' more or less, coloured and sweetened more or less, according to whether it is destined to be sold as Sercial, Verdelho, Bual or Malmsey.

Portugal's entry to the E.E.C. will stop this practice. Its regulations require 85 per cent of a wine to be of the grape variety named. 'Malmsey' can no longer be simply a style: it will have to be genuine Malvasia. Taking note of this, the islanders are busy regrafting vines, 100,000 of them a year, to the classic varieties.

It is their only hope. They cannot thrive on cheapness and low quality. They have no cash crop of 'instant' wine; it all needs ageing. The *estufas* are expensive to run (on imported coal). Happily the Madeira shippers have never lost sight of their traditions. Despite all odds they have gone on feeding fine old *soleras* (as in Jerez) with the rare classic wines, and even occasionally declaring a vintage – always a rarer occurrence with madeira than with port, and taking place not immediately after the vintage but some 30 years later. Vintage madeira is kept in cask for 20 years, then in glass 20-litre demijohns for another 2 years before bottling – when it is deemed ready to drink. In reality it is still only a young wine at this stage; it needs another 20 to 50 years in bottle to achieve sublimity.

Noël Cossart, the fifth generation of the old firm of madeira shippers Cossart Gordon, counsels 'never to buy a cheap Sercial or Malmsey; these grapes are shy growers and must consequently be expensive; whereas Bual and Verdelho are prolific and develop faster and may be both cheaper and good.'

Vintages

The most famous madeira vintages up to 1900, bottles of which are still occasionally found, were 1789, 1795 (esp. Terrantez), 1806, 1808 (Malmsey), 1815 (esp. Bual), 1822, 1836, 1844, 1846 (esp. Terrantez and Verdelho), 1851, 1862, 1865, 1868, 1870 (Sercial), 1880 (esp. Malmsey).

Since 1900 some 13 vintages have been shipped: 1900 (the last year Moscatel was made), 1902 (esp. Verdelho and Bual), 1905 (esp. Sercial), 1906 (esp. Malmsey), 1907 (esp. Verdelho and Bual), 1910, 1914 (Bual), 1915 (Bual and Sercial), 1916, 1920, 1926 (esp. Bual), 1934 (Verdelho), 1940, 1941 (esp. Bual), 1950, 1954 (esp. Bual), 1956.

Shippers

In 1925 a number of shippers in the beleaguered trade formed themselves into The Madeira Wine Association to pool their resources. They are Blandy's (founded 1811), Cossart Gordon & Co (1745), Rutherford & Miles Lda (1814), Leacock & Co (1754) and Lomelino Lda (1820). The association supplies wines from central stocks to furnish the individual blends of each house. It also stores some old wines exclusively for the member firms that made them. Altogether about 100 different brands are produced by the Association.

In addition there are still four independent firms: Barbeito (the last entirely family-owned independent), H.M. Borges, Companhia Vinícola de Madeira and Henriques & Henriques.

SWITZERLAND

So rare are Swiss wines outside their own country that it is easy to assume that they fall short of international standards and remain the special taste of a blinkered culture.

But the Swiss are a critical, wine-conscious people with money to spare. They are massive importers of foreign wines (Burgundy in particular). The cost of land and the expense of culture of their cliff-hanging vineyards are startlingly high. To justify inevitably high prices there is every pressure on them to concentrate on high quality.

One hundred and fifty years ago the emphasis was on red wines, and the best of them came from the Grisons or Graubünden in the German-speaking east. The best whites came from the north shore of Lac Léman between Lausanne and Montreux, where the steep south slopes ripened the local Fendant to perfection. The upper Rhône valley above the lake, the Valais, was a remote mountain area planted (if at all) with outlandish grapes chosen for their potential sweetness and strength in the dry and sunny alpine climate.

The modern industry began to take shape when the Fendant spread up the Rhône valley, when pressure for the sunny lake slopes as building sites drove half the vines out of the Vaud, and when selected forms of the Pinot Noir and Gamay began to penetrate from France, via Geneva and then eastwards. Meanwhile the Müller-Thurgau, bred by a Swiss scientist in Germany, began to invade the eastern cantons (where, strangely enough, his name is forgotten, and his plant mistakenly labelled Riesling-Sylvaner). At the same time the Ticino in the Italian-speaking south adapted the Merlot of Bordeaux to improve its red wine.

In the last 100 years the total vineyard area has diminished by three quarters, with the cantons of Ticino, Zurich and the Vaud losing most and only two cantons, the Valais and Geneva, increasing their acreage.

The essential information on the often rather taciturn, though highly coloured, Swiss wine label depends on the canton and its laws and traditions. Some German-Swiss labels use terms with no international validity – but then they never travel abroad. Italian-Swiss wine labels are simplicity itself: there are essentially only two types of wine.

The principal wine cantons of the Valais, the Vaud and Geneva each have their own terms for what are really the same kinds of wine – Chasselas white and Pinot/Gamay red.

The maker's name is the second piece of essential information. This is often in small print, while pride of place is given to a brand name or estate name. It is not always easy to tell which. The term Premier Cru can only be used for estate wines and is sometimes the only indication.

All Swiss wines can be assumed to be dry or fairly dry unless a specific caution is included on the label in the phrase *Avec sucre residuel* or *Légèrement doux*.

THE FRENCH-SPEAKING CANTONS

All the principal vineyards of the Suisse Romande lie along the south-facing right bank of the Rhône, from its emergence into the Valais, a suntrap sheltered on all sides by towering Alps, to its departure through Geneva into France.

The Lake of Geneva is simply an enormous widening of the Rhône in an arc that offers ideal steep south-facing vineyard sites basking in reflected sunlight from the surface of the lake. Three quarters of all Swiss wine is grown here; 80 per cent of it white. To the north the little region of Neuchâtel takes advantage of a similar lake-shore.

The Valais

The Valais has Switzerland's driest and sunniest climate – so dry that on its steeper vineyards, terraced on arid mountain slopes, irrigation is essential: wooden channels known as *bisses* are the traditional method. The centre of the Valais is the town of Sion, which gives its name to a simple appellation for the white Fendant of its surrounding villages. Sierre to the east is the upper limit of intensive wine-growing (although far higher, the village of Visperterminen, on the way up to Zermatt, has what are said to be Europe's highest vineyards at 3,700 feet). The principal villages round Sion are Conthey, Vétroz, Ardon, Leytron and Chamason. There is little notion of crus here: the Domaine du Mont d'Or probably has the best site, but many vineyards will ripen the Fendant in good years almost to excess. Its wine (50 per cent of the total) becomes broad, low in acidity and high in alcohol but impressive in its texture and essential cleanness. The Sylvaner, known here as Johannisberger, makes an even broader, almost sticky dry wine. Riesling (though rare) ripens to a singular concentration and can be very fine.

The real specialities of the Valais are old varieties that hover on the brink of becoming liquorous and sometimes cross it: Marsanne (its wine called Ermitage) is big, usually dry and often a shade bitter; Malvoisie (alias Pinot Gris) is 'stiff' and mouthfilling; Amigne is often even heavier and tastier and Arvine becomes a wine for heroes. There are still more: white Humagne, perhaps the oldest variety of all, making golden semi-sweet to sweet wines; Païen, apparently a form of Traminer grown in the highest vineyards; and Rèze, unknown elsewhere but giving acidic wine of brilliant vigour and concentration, pale amber in colour, traditionally aged for years in a 'solera system' in small casks in the cold of the high Val d'Anniviers, and known as *vin du glacier*.

One third of Valais wine is red, and two thirds of the red vineyard Pinot Noir, which makes as good wine in the Valais as anywhere in Switzerland – though that is still a thin product by good Burgundian standards. The general practice is to blend it with Gamay (of which the Valais has half as much) and to call the composition Dôle. The appellation demands 12 per cent alcohol and a tasting test. However, chaptalization is taken for granted: the Swiss permit it up to a remarkable five per cent in red wines, and three per cent in whites. Of antique red grapes there remains only the Humagne Rouge, or Alter Landroter, making a simple, pleasantly tannic and appetizing country wine.

The Vaud

The canton of Vaud includes all the vineyards of the north shore of the Lake of Geneva and the Rhône valley, as high up as its dogleg at Martigny, where the Valais begins; a 50-mile arc of southern slopes. It is divided into three main zones: Chablais, the right bank of the Rhône between Martigny and the Lake; Lavaux, the central section between Montreux and Lausanne, and La Côte, from Lausanne round to Nyon near Geneva.

Chablais is centred on the town of Aigle and its neighbours Yvorne and Ollon, all with good southwest slopes above the Rhône, but without either the dry heat of Sion or the tempering effect of the lake below. Its northern extremity is at Villeneuve and its southern at Bex. Chablais Chasselas is drier and more stony, still soft but less fleshy than Fendant from the Valais, at its best a good compromise between the elegant austerity of Lavaux and the fatness of Sion. A carafe of Aigle in a restaurant should be pale yellow with a very faint *spritz*, softly dry and yet refreshing. Aigle from a top vineyard can have real vigour, ripeness and length (a quality rare in Chasselas wines).

Lavaux is certainly Switzerland's most scenic vineyard, piled high in toppling terraces above the lakeside villages. The view from among the vines is superb: the mountains of Savoie a great dark jagged-topped bulk against the sun opposite, the lake surface below gleaming grey, wrinkled by white paddle-steamers gliding from village pier to village pier. Erosion is a serious problem: a brown stain in the lake after a night's heavy rain is a vineyard lost.

The culmination of Lavaux is the slope called Dézaley, above the villages of Rivaz and Treytorrens and below Epesses on the higher road. Dézaley and its subsection Marsens have their own appellation and have been considered for centuries the high point of Swiss white wine. The Chasselas takes on a liveliness and an almost aromatic quality on these upper slopes which distinguishes it from the more austere dryness of the lower vineyards. Each village, however, has its committed supporters and the names of Vevey, Epesses, St. Saphorin, Rivaz, Cully, Villette, Lutry, Chardonne and others are printed in bigger letters than the appellation Dorin, which is the Vaudois equivalent of Fendant. A wine labelled simply Dorin (with a trademark) is a blend without the style of a single village.

Eighty per cent of the Vaud vineyard is Dorin, or Chasselas, a very small part Pinot Gris and Pinot Noir, and 15 per cent Gamay. Vaudois red (Gamay or Gamay-and-Pinot) passing a statutory test is sold as Salvagnin. It rarely reaches the quality of Dôle.

La Côte from Lausanne to Nyon, with gentler southeast slopes over the lake, is in turn divided into La Bonne Côte, its central part with half a dozen well-known wine villages, and its less distinguished extremities at Morges and Nyon. The best-known names of La Bonne Côte are Féchy, Perroy, Mont-sur-Rolle, Tartegnin, Vinzel and Luins.

Côte wines are rarely as vigorous or flavoury as those of Lavaux but make lightly fruity, introductory drinking.

Geneva

The canton of Geneva has increased its vineyards steadily with the introduction of forms of the Gamay that suit its conditions and the taste of its inhabitants. The Chasselas (here known as 'Perlan') is no more than half its vineyard, its wine here so light and dry that it is usually bottled with a slight bubble to give it some character. A little Müller-Thurgau is grown in the canton in the hopes of something better.

The canton is divided into three wine districts. Mandement, to the north on the right bank of the Rhône, is much the biggest. Its centre, Satigny, is the seat of the huge cooperative Vin-Union-Genève, which handles three quarters of the grapes of the whole canton. South of the city and the river, Arve-et-Rhône and Arve-et-Lac each has only 500-odd acres of scattered vineyards compared with the 1,750 acres of Mandement.

All their slopes are gentle and mechanical harvesting, impossible in most Swiss vineyards, is a practicality. Almost all the consumption is local, with prices as low as half those of other cantons.

Neuchâtel

The Lake of Neuchâtel, lying in the shelter of the Jura to the north of Geneva, softens the seasons in the limestone hills to its north and west, which in turn seem to bring out some of the distinction of the Pinot Noir. Although the canton is planted with three quarters Chasselas it is Pinot Noir that gives its best wine, particularly as pale *oeil de perdrix* and even paler Blanc de Noir. There is no Gamay in the canton: all Neuchâtel reds can be assumed to be Pinot Noir, and be expected to have some distinction. The best-known village name is Cortaillod, on the lakeshore south of Neuchâtel. Vaumarcus lies on the lake at the southern tip of the canton – farther south an enclave of the Vaud, the Coteaux du Jura, shares similar conditions in its wine villages of Concise, Bonvillars, Corcelles and Champagne. The Chasselas of Neuchâtel is light, very dry and given to a natural prickle, particularly when bottled *sur lie*. The well-known sparkling-wine industry of Neuchâtel emphasizes this character, but it is also practised on Pinot Noir, and even on wines imported from other parts of Switzerland to be 'champagnized'.

Bern

Very much the same conditions as in Neuchâtel produce similar but featherweight wines along the north shore of the Lac de Bienne, the Bielersee, following the same line as Lake Neuchâtel a few miles north. The villages of the north shore have the same proportions of Chasselas (75%) and Pinot Noir (20%). The names of Schafis and Twann are the best known; since 1948 they have been used interchangeably as Schafiser or Twanner for all the pale faintly fizzy whites of the lake – to their great commercial advantage.

Schloss Aigle, in the Chablais district of the Vaud, is now a wine museum

VALAIS PRODUCERS

Chs. Bonvin Fils

1951 Sion, Valais. Founded 1858. Owners: The Bonvin family. 62 acres.

Among the best-known and respected Valais houses, especially for 4 qualities of Fendant: Sans Culotte, La Gachette, Château Conthey and Brûlefer (a powerful wine from a single vineyard) and Dôle Clos du Château.

Les Fils de Charles Favre

CH 1950 Sion, Valais. Founded 1944. Owners: Mme Hanny Favre and Jean-Pierre Favre (mother and son). 6.25 acres.

The slogan of the house is 'La Petite Maison des Grands Vins'. It buys from 400 small growers to make an ideal, very dry, clean Fendant, Dame de Sion, an outstanding Dôle, Hurlevent, a good *oeil de perdrix* and one of the best Arvines: Réserve de Tous Vents. Mme Favre is the treasurer of the Academie Internationale du Vin.

Maurice Gay

Sion. Founded 1883. Owners: Schenk S.A. Director: Jean-Pierre Rollier. 35 acres.

A long-established house which supplements the crop from its own terraced vineyards by buying from 500-odd local growers. Total production is almost 10 times that of the estate. 60% is Chasselas and Johannisberg, 30% Pinot and Gamay; 10% 'specialities', of which the Muscat is best known. The Réserve Fendant (from the estate) and late-picked Amigne are outstanding. The establishment is 'very open' to visitors. Prices: 6.90–14.90 francs.

Domaine Château Lichten

Vinicole de Sierre, 3953 Loeche. Founded 1908. Owner: Arnaud Tavelli. 54 acres.

The Tavelli family, related to the historic owners, bought the estate (apparently Switzerland's largest single vineyard) in 1970. Strenuous efforts in both wine-making and publicity have established its name for the usual range of Valais wines (some of them rather lightweight). The most distinguished wine is Dôle Selection Or: very well made, vigorous but rounded. Prices: 8.50–12.50 francs.

Domaine du Mont d'Or

1962 Pont de la Morge. Founded 1848. Owners: Schenk S.A. Director: M. D. Favre. 52 acres.

The most famous property of Sion, established on a steep, dry, sheltered hill by a soldier from the Vaud, one Sergeant-Major Masson, who installed irrigation by *bisses* and discovered the potential of the arid soils. It was bought by Schenk in 1978. The domaine is now best known for rich, almost thick Johannisbergs (especially the late-picked St. Martin and Goût du Conseil), magnificent Arvine, and strong tannic and alcoholic Dôle. Fendant tends to be too heavy for refreshment, lacking acidity, but since 1980 has been made rather lighter. Prices: 12.60–28.00 francs.

Nouveau Sierre, Caves de Riondaz

3960 Sierre, Valais. Founded 1943. Director: M. A. Schneiter.

An attractive and welcoming establishment using bought grapes to make Fendant, Johannisberg, Ermitage, Malvoisie, Amigne, Arvine, Payen, Humagne Blanc and Rouge, Muscat, Pinot Noir, Pinot Blanc and the rare Rèze. The house specializes in mature old vintages which are sometimes remarkable. Even Fendant is available up to 6 years old. A visit (by appointment) is an excellent introduction to Valais traditions.

Alphonse Orsat

1920 Martigny, Valais. Founded 1874. Joint directors: Jacques-Alphonse Orsat and Philippe Orsat. 86.5 acres.

The biggest privately owned Swiss wine company, buying grapes from 3,500 growers in the Valais to boost its production to 120,000 hl (1,110,000 cases). The wines (60% Fendant and Johannisberg; 35% Pinot Noir and Gamay) are reliable and true to type. The remaining 5% of 'specialities' includes some fine wines, particularly Ermitage du Prévot. Pinot Noir Römer Blut is also notable. Muzak in the tasting room is an unfortunate distraction. Prices: 7.50–12.50 francs.

Provins

Federation des Caves de Producteurs de Vins du Valais, 1951 Sion, Valais. Founded 1930. Director: Jean Actis.

The enormous central cooperative of the Valais, uniting 5,000 growers, produces very acceptable wines under its well-known brand name, Provins. Pierrafeu Fendant is reliable; Provins Dôle is well regarded. Their sparkling 'Apricot Cocktail' is less well known.

Louis Vuignier & Fils

1961 Grimisuat, Valais. Founded 1957. Owners: Three Vuignier brothers. 84 acres at Clavoz near Sion and Ollon in Chablais.

A second-generation firm with modern equipment and methods and high ambitions (including wine-making in New Mexico). Half their production is Fendant with the ideal bright freshness (the best from Clavoz); one third is Pinot Noir. The really exceptional wines are the 'specialities': a buttery dry Malvoisie, concentrated Petite Arvine, very clean Johannisberg and warm fruity red Humagne. The Ollon Blanc and Pinot Noir are both notable. Prices: 7.10–11.50 francs.

Traditional signs

VAUD PRODUCERS

Henri Badoux

1860 Aigle, Vaud. Founded 1908. Owners: Marcel Bacca and André Parachini. 123.5 acres.

A substantial second-generation, family-owned business producing 10,000 cases from their own vines in Aigle, Yvorne, Ollon, Villeneuve, St. Saphorin, Féchy, Vinzel and Mont-sur-Rolle. Their pride is Aigle Les Murailles from a fine terraced vineyard (the label, showing a lizard, is a classic): also an Aigle Pinot Gris with strength and style. Pinot Noir is rather tannic and pale but well made, also made into sparkling rosé, Casanova.

Bolle & Cie

1110 Morges, Vaud. Founded 1842. Family owned. 25 acres.

The fifth generation of the family control the wine-making at 7 separate estates besides their own, bottling a total of over 90,000 cases from Morges, Chizony, Mont-sur-Rolle, Luins, Vinzel, Bouchy and Féchy (on 'La Bonne Côte'), Dézaley, Lausanne and St. Saphorin in Lavaux and Aigle in Chablais. The wines are reliably made from particularly good vineyards. Dorin Domaine du Château de Vufflens (just above Morges) is notable value. Dézaley 'Grotte des Moines' and the Abbaye du Mont of Lausanne (which belongs to the City) are twice the price. The house has adopted screw-caps because of problems with corks. Prices: 8.50–19.00 francs.

Les Frères Dubois & Fils

Le Petit Versailles, 1096 Cully, Vaud. Founded 1928. Owner: M. and C. Dubois. 15 acres.

One of the most impressive small houses of Lavaux. This Dézaley vineyard, La Tour de Marsens, is superbly situated, growing excellent Dorin but also Pinot Noir, Pinot Gris and Riesling-Sylvaner; all the whites combining concentration with fresh liveliness. Dorin Braise d'Enfer from Epesses is slightly lighter and more stony. Other Dorins (e.g. L'Ecu d'Or, Caves du Petit Versailles, Puidoux) from bought grapes are all well made. Total production is about 28,000 cases. Prices: 11–20 francs.

Hammel

1180 Rolle, Vaud. Founded 1920. Director: Gilbert Hammel Rolaz. 62 acres.

The third generation runs this leading domaine and merchant house of La Côte, with a score of tributary domaines supplying high-quality wines from all parts of the Vaud. At Mont-sur-Rolle, Domaines Les Pierrailles and la Bigaire are both well known for soft, dry Dorin. Domaine de Riencourt at Bougy is outstanding. In Chablais Clos du Chatelard at Villeneuve produces stiffer, more alcoholic but less fruity wine, the Clos de la George at Yvorne (in my notes) is more fruity, richer and riper. Hammel's whites are all very pale but distinctively intense in bouquet, well made for maturing. A 1961 Pierrailles was excellent in 1982. Prices: 9.50–18.20 francs.

Robert Isoz

1853 Yvorne, Vaud. Founded 1929. Owner: Robert Isoz. 11 acres.

A small third-generation family estate making some of the very best wine of Chablais: the white confusingly called Portes Rouges, the Pinot Noir Ave Maria; also excellent Pinot Gris and Gewürztraminer. The style is simple but the wine is drunk at Girardet, Switzerland's best restaurant. Prices: 12.50–14.50 francs.

La Commune de Lausanne

Vaud

Owns vineyards at: Abbaye de Mont (3.25 acres); Allaman (0.65 acres); Burignon (1.30 acres); Dézaley, Clos des Abbayes (1.15 acres); Dézaley, Clos des Moines.

Obrist

Avenue Reller 26, 1800 Vevey, Vaud. Founded 1854. Owners: The Schenk group. Director: Dr. J. Schenker. 100 acres.

One of the largest growers of typical Swiss Chasselas whites. Total production is about 33,000 cases.

Société Vinicole de Perroy

1166 Perroy, Vaud. Founded 1938. President: Pierre Chessex.

A company uniting 200 vignerons of La Côte. Wines include Chasselas from Féchy, Vinzel, Mont-sur-Rolle and Perroy, Gamay called Clavignon and Folamour, light and *friand*, more substantial Salvagnin called Croix du Val and Grand Veneur, and their best wine which is Château d'Allaman, a Pinot/Gamay blend. Prices: white wine 9–11 francs; red 8–11 francs.

Gérard Pinget

1812 Rivaz, Vaud. Founded 1884. 3.7 acres. Administrator: C. Pinget.

A wholly traditional little estate growing only Chasselas but doing its own thing supremely well. The top wine is Dézaley Renard (the label shows a fox), then St. Saphorin, then a more modest blend, Soleil de Lavaux. All are models of their type. Prices: 9.50–15.70 francs.

Schenk

1180 Rolle, Vaud. Founded 1893. Owner: Pierre Schenk. 568 acres.

The famous fourth-generation business, founded by a cooper, now the largest vineyard owner and wholesaler of Swiss wines. Its principal estates are Château Maison Blanche at Yvorne, Château de Chatagnéréaz, Domaine de Haute Cour and Domaine de Autecour at Mont-sur-Rolle, Château de Vinzel at Vinzel and Domaine du Martheray at Féchy. These domaine wines are all of a high standard. With its subsidiaries (which include Obrist at Vevey and Gay and Mont d'Or at Sion, qq.v.) Schenk controls nearly 10% of the market in Swiss wines and over 50% of the market in grape juice.

Production in 1980 was 3.5m. cases. Foreign subsidiaries include Henri de Villamont in Burgundy and Schenk companies in the Midi, Spain, northern Italy, Belgium and the USA.

Jean & Pierre Testuz

1096 Treytorrens-Cully. Founded 1845. Directors: J. and P. Testuz. 494 acres.

The Testuz family date their wine-growing from the 16th century. In 1865 they sold the first bottled wine in Switzerland. Their premises are actually in Dézaley. The Dézaley domaine, L'Arbalète, contests with the Renard of Gerard Pinget as the finest of the area. Other Lavaux wines include fine St. Saphorin Roche Ronde and Epesses. Chablais wines include Aigle Les Cigales and Yvorne Haute-Combe. Lavaux and Côte wines both include some from the vineyards of the City of Lausanne. Reds from the same sites as the whites are good though less distinguished. The red label is Grand Croix. Prices: 8.40–28.00 francs.

NEUCHÂTEL PRODUCERS

Samuel Chatenay

2017 Boudry. Founded 1796. Directors: J. C. von Buran, F. Bonderet, R. Felix. 100 acres (half owned, half managed).

The best-known house of Neuchâtel, owners since 1931 of the sparkling-wine firm Bouvier Frères (founded 1811). The Chatenay estate is 75% Chasselas, 25% Pinot Noir. Red, white and *oeil de perdrix* domaine wines from the Château de Vaumarcus near St. Aubin on the north shore of the lake and Dorin from the Domaine de la Lance at Bonvillars on the south (Vaud) shore are some of the best of the region. Total production is about 33,000 cases.

André Ruedin

La Grillette, 2088 Cressier. Founded 1884. Owner: André Ruedin. 20 acres.

A third-generation family house with particularly good Chasselas from its own vines and those of 32 small growers, making up another 20 acres. 65% is Chasselas, 25% Pinot Noir, 8% Chardonnay. André Ruedin is also responsible for the 26-acre vineyard of the Hôpital de Pourtalés at Neuchâtel, a charity founded in 1823 on the lines of the Hospices de Beaune. Prices: for Ruedin 8.80–12.50 francs; Hôpital approx. 13–17 francs.

GENEVA PRODUCERS

Claude & Gilbert Dupraz

8 Che. de Placet, 1249 Soral, Geneva. Founded 1945. Owners: C. and G. Dupraz. 29.5 acres.

A mixed farm as well as a wine estate, in the Arve-et-Rhône district, growing 45% Chasselas, 40% Gamay and 15% Pinot Noir and Müller-Thurgau (Riesling-Sylvaner). Its Perlan Coteau de Rougemont is one of the best of the canton. Prices: 5.80–7.20 francs.

Leyvraz & Stevens

1242 Peissy-Satigny, Geneva. Founded 1905. Owners: Eric Leyvraz and Donald Stevens. 125 acres.

One of Switzerland's biggest private wine estates and the leading house of the Mandement region. 40% is Gamay, 30% Chasselas, 15% Riesling-Sylvaner, 14% Pinot Noir and 1% Pinot Gris and Gewürztraminer. Chasselas Etoile de Peissy is light and *pétillant*, Gamay Les Velours light and fruity, Pinot Noir Le Vieux Clocher remarkably full and long lived. All are notable value for money. Prices: 5.30–6.00 francs.

Pierre Villard

40 rue Central, 1247 Anières, Geneva. Founded 1955. Owner: Pierre Villard. 7.5 acres.

A notable example of the more-than-competent small traditional producer offering good Pinot Noir and Chardonnay as well as the standard Chasselas and Gamay of Geneva. Anières is on the south bank of the lake in the Arve-et-Lac district. Prices: 4.80–6.50 francs.

Vin-Union-Genève

1242 Satigny. President: Jean Revaclier. Director: Jean Sinard.

A federation of 3 cooperative cellars whose 365 members own some 2,500 acres, or 83% of the canton's vineyards. Gamay and Pinot Noir reds range from very light to fairly heavy and alcoholic. Grand Comtal would pass for a fair Beaujolais. Perlans from the Mandement are the most substantial of Geneva, but all are very light and dry with little acidity, leaning on fizz for freshness. Le Goût du Prieur is an adequate Müller-Thurgau.

THE GERMAN-SPEAKING CANTONS

Eastern (which includes northern) Switzerland shares the wine tastes and habits of its neighbours in Baden in southern Germany. It has what seems a perverse weakness for the Pinot Noir (here called Blauburgunder) however soft, pale and nerveless its wine. It grows the Gutedel (German name for the Chasselas, also the favourite of the Markgräflerland across the Rhine). Nowadays it is increasingly taking to the Müller-Thurgau.

There are no less than eight wine-growing cantons in German Switzerland; their vineyards widely scattered so that no clear pattern emerges, save the inevitable concentrations around lakes and along rivers. The Rhine is the dominant presence, flowing north through the Graubünden (better known as the Grisons) on the borders of Lichtenstein, up through the canton of St. Gallen to the Bodensee, then west through the little Untersee (canton of Thurgau) and along the borders of Schaffhausen (with its famous falls) and Aargau cantons. The tributary river Aare, flowing north from the Bielersee, also contributes its vineyards. Finally, the northern lakeshore of Zurich and a few vines around Basel add to the total.

Historically the best known of these areas is the Graubünden, whose warmer autumn climate ripens Blauburgunder to real substance, with colour and a velvet touch. Ninety-nine per cent of its vines are Blauburgunder, but in addition one village of the 'Herrschaft', just south of Lichtenstein, called Malans, grows a mysterious white grape called the Completer. Completer ripens to a splendid natural 15 per cent potential alcohol, making it very much an Auslese and a very expensive rarity.

The most productive cantons today are Zurich (70% Pinot Noir, with a small amount of good Pinot Gris; Wädenswil on the Zurich lake and Winterthur in the 'Weinland' farther north are the principal centres) and Schaffhausen (80% Pinot Noir, with Hallau as its principal wine town).

The story of eastern Switzerland, in fact, is of local demand scarcely satisfied by the small supply of wine made to the local taste. As a result prices are quite out of proportion to intrinsic quality.

ZURICH AND GRISONS PRODUCERS

Grundbacher Schlosskellerei Thun

Burgstrasse 4–8, 3601 Thun, Zurich. Founded 1790. Owner: Château de Thun S.A. 18.5 acres.

A private lakeside estate planted with 70% Müller-Thurgau, 30% Pinot Noir, making light wines. A *vin mousseux* is made for the firm in Neuchâtel.

Weinbaugenossenschaft Lohningen

8224 Lohningen. Founded 1950. Director: Jak. Walter.

Small cooperative press-house (the wine is finished by USEGO in Winterthur). Pinot Noir (sold as Lohninger Clevner) is very light; Müller-**Thurgau** is extremely dry.

Rimuss-Kellerei, Rahm & Co.

8215 Hallau. Founded 1945. Directors: E. and R. Rahm (brothers). 45 acres.

One of the largest wine houses in German Switzerland, supplementing their 45 acres (80% Pinot Noir, 20% Müller-Thurgau) with bought grapes to make 200,000 cases (including large quantities of grape juice). Hallauer Blauburgunder Graaf von Spiegelberg 'Beerliwein' is round, full-coloured (the must is heated) but very soft. Müller-Thurgau is sold as Adelheid von Randenburg 'Riesling-Sylvaner'. Prices: 8–9 francs.

Hans Schlatter

8215 Hallau, Zurich. Founded 1931. Owner: Hans Schlatter. 27 acres.

One of the best growers and merchants of German Switzerland, particularly for late-picked Hallauer Blauburgunder 16-Fahre-Wy and Tokayer (Pinot Gris). Total production is 55,000 cases. Prices: 9.00–10.50 francs.

Verband Ostschweizer Landwirtschaftl. Genossenschaften (VOLG)

Weinabteilung, Winterthur. Founded 1886. Director: F. Rottermann.

A major agricultural cooperative with a chain of stores. Vineyards producing 270,000 cases are in Hallau, Winterthur and the Grisons, including an estate of 74 acres planted with 75% Blauburgunder, 20% 'Riesling-Sylvaner' and 5% 'specialities'. The wines are light but very clean and well made. Hallauer Blauburgunder appears to have some keeping qualities.

THE ITALIAN-SPEAKING CANTON

In happy contrast to the intricacies of eastern Switzerland, the Ticino is a simple smiling vineyard making nothing but red wine, and increasingly making it to international standards and at a reasonable price.

Its secret is the steady replacement of mixed Italian varieties by Merlot, introduced from Bordeaux at the end of the nineteenth century. The early ripening but rot-prone variety thrives in the dry sunny alpine air, its harvest over before the autumn rains in October.

Merlot of 12 per cent alcohol, submitted for tasting, carries the term VITI as a guarantee of its quality – an effective promotional device. The term Nostrano covers the rump of miscellaneous red grapes blended into everyday table wine.

TICINO PRODUCERS

Istituto Agrario

Cantonale Mezzana, 6828 Balerna. Founded 1912. Owned by the canton. Director: Sandro Guarneri. 17 acres.

The agricultural institute of the canton occupies an 18th-century palace built by Sardinian royalty with magnificent gardens and views. It sells small quantities of good Merlot and a less interesting white wine, as well as honey. Prices: 7.20–8.50 francs.

Figli fu Alberto Daldini

Lugano-Crocefisso. Founded 1883. Director: Leandro Daldini. 20 acres.

An attractive little family business in a handsome house and grotto cellar, set in a pretty garden. The fourth generation makes one of the best Merlots of Ticino, second only to Roncobello of Valsangiacomo. Prices: 7.20–9.20 francs a litre.

Vassalli Della Gada

6825 Capolago. Founded 1870. Directors: G. and E. Luisoni. 8.5 acres.

The Luisoni family bought the property of Vassalli in 1935. They produce 2 quality Merlots, Cantinetta under the Luisoni label and St. Abbondio under the Vassalli label. Both are good, serious wines and good value. Prices: 6–8 francs.

Cantina Sociale Giubiasco

6512 Giubiasco. Founded 1928. Cooperative.

A well-equipped cooperative producing 90,000 cases. Wines are cheap Nostrano in litres, standard Merlot, a more full-bodied VITI Merlot called Alba and a good Riserva Speciale. Prices: 4.20–9.00 francs a litre.

Cantina Sociale Mendrisio

Via G. Vernasconi, 6850 Mendrisio. Founded 1950. Director: E. Crivelli. 62 acres.

The growers' cooperative of Mendrisio farms the 62-acre Tenuta Montalbano in Stabio to make a rather light Merlot of high quality as well as a standard Merlot, a Nostrano and a *rosato*. Prices: 4.70–8.90 francs.

Fratelli Valsangiacomo fu Vittore

C.S. Gottardo 107, 6830 Chiasso. Founded 1831. Director: Cesare Valsangiacomo. 35 acres.

The most distinguished house of the Ticino, 5 generations in the family, producing the outstanding wine of the region, Merlot Roncobello di Morbio Inferiore. The firm buys grapes to make up a total of 30,000 cases, including a small quantity of this excellent full-bodied wine. Almost all their wine is Merlot, including good-value fruity wine in litres. Only the *rosato* is, like most Ticino rosés, rather disappointing. Prices: 7.00–11.50 francs.

AUSTRIA

Harvesting in the Danube Valley

Austria's entry into the international wine community is so recent that the star quality of her best wines is still unrecognized. Her image is only slowly changing from that of the land of operetta taverns where the wine goes round in jugs. Vienna's *heurigen,* the new-wine taverns of her wine-growing suburbs, and their country cousins the *buschenschenken*, are still major and characteristic elements in Austria's wine economy.

The change started in 1971, with a government that realized what a chance was being missed. Under the old happy-go-lucky regime Austria's name was being widely abused, appearing on wines from eastern Europe *en route* for the west.

The new German wine law made Austria sit up and think. In 1972 she passed a wine law similar in many respects to the German. The principal differences arose from the warmer climate which makes Austrian wine generally riper and stronger than German, and the national taste for dry wines. To achieve the Austrian equivalent of German Prädikatswein (unsugared wine) status the must weight, or ripeness, has to be higher, and Süssreserve is not allowed. *See* page 398.

The country has 147,000 acres of vineyards, concentrated entirely in the east, with the regions of Niederösterreich (Lower Austria, north and south of Vienna) and the Burgenland (on the Hungarian border, southeast of Vienna) much the most important for quality and quantity. Niederösterreich has 87,000 acres, or more than half the nation's wines, Burgenland 51,500, Steiermark 6,500 acres and Vienna some 2,000 acres.

The finest wines, still astonishingly undervalued both internationally and even by their producers, come from the Burgenland. Sauternes is the nearest equivalent: an area with frequent (here regular) sunny but misty autumns, the mists of Burgenland arising from the shallow mere of the Neusiedler See on the Hungarian border. Noble rot is a routine occurrence, and sweet wines of Beerenauslese to Trockenbeerenauslese level are made in industrial quantities even by the cooperatives. The principal vines are the Welschriesling, Grüner Veltliner,

Müller-Thurgau and Muskat-Ottonel, but superb wines are also made of Rheinriesling, Gewürztraminer, Weissburgunder and Neuburger. The most famous wines are those of Rust, Donnerskirchen and Eisenstadt (where the Esterhazy family still has a palace and cellars) on the west of the lake. Their Weissburgunder and Muskat-Ottonel in particular are among the world's greatest dessert wines.

The sandy district of the Seewinkel on the eastern shore has less of a great tradition, but the wines made by Lenz Moser (among others) at Apetlon are supremely aromatic and pungent, lacking perhaps only the extraordinary balance (and potential long life) of the other shore.

The sprawling region of Niederösterreich can most conveniently be surveyed using its traditional division into the Donauland (Danube) region, the Südbahn or southern railway out of Vienna, and the Weinviertel or Wine Quarter, which stretches from the Danube north to the Czech border. The last is now divided into Falkenstein-Matzen to the east and Retz to the west (including the important vineyards of Röschitz and Mailberg). This is overwhelmingly Grüner Veltliner country and its wine is light, dry: the very opposite of Burgenland's potent produce. Falkenstein has been chosen, largely for its beauty, as the spokestown and label for large quantities of very adequate and slightly aromatic dry white wine.

Of the Danube regions much the most memorable is the Wachau, where the river suddenly looks almost like the Rhine washing the Lorelei rocks. The steep north bank from Weissenkirchen past Dürnstein to Krems is pocked with laborious plots of Grüner Veltliner and Rheinriesling, here making wine as good as any in Austria, ranging from finely tart and harmonious to peppery and full of fire according to the season and the exposure of their 'Ried'.

The word Ried is the Austrian for a vineyard, and used to have the standing of an Einzellage in Germany. It is far from clear today, though, when a true Ried name is being used, as cooperatives in particular (and the Wachau is dominated by the great Dürnstein coop) make up their own fantasy names for blended wines which are indistinguishable from genuine Rieds.

The town of Krems, with fine sites facing the river, is linked by the little valley of the Kamp to its northern neighbour, Langenlois. They are officially separate districts from each other and from the Wachau, but make similar wine. Langenlois in particular, from the soft, deep loess (half rock, half soil) of the Kamp valley, makes extremely good Rheinrieslings and even reds of deep colour and a certain firmness. A few miles west of Krems the otherwise unremarkable village of Rohrendorf is on the itinerary of every wine tourist in Austria as the headquarters of the Moser family. Lenz Moser was the father of the high-culture system of training vines and its tireless advocate, a man whose personal conviction changed the system of viticulture not just in Austria but among believers all over the world. His sons continue with one of the country's most progressive estates.

The rest of Lower Austria's viticulture is all so interwoven with the capital and its suburbs that it can be listed in one north–south catalogue. Overlooking Vienna from the north are the vineyards of Klosterneuburg with its great baroque palace-abbey, the Chorherrenstift, Austria's largest individual wine estate.

Few of the wines of Vienna's own vineyards escape the clutches of its citizens and their guests. There are some 1,000 *heurigen* in the district to dispense them either in the form of *sturm*, the fermenting juice before it even becomes wine, after November 11th as new wine, incredibly lively and dashing, and for older and wiser customers the '*alte*' wine of the previous year. Sievering, Grinzing, Neustift, Nüssdorf are the principal resorts of the thirsty. The *heurige* is a facet of wine that everyone should experience.

The Südbahn runs south from Vienna, its trains stopping at a series of spas-cum-wine-towns of varying charm and reputation. Much the most famous is Gumpoldskirchen, a very pretty resort. The best of its wines, notably from Thallern, are refreshing Rheinrieslings and a piquant, full-bodied speciality blending lively Zierfändler and heavier Rotgipfler. Baden and its neighbour Bad Vöslau are specialists in red wines, principally of Blauer Portugieser, which gives good dark colour but a rather soft bland taste. Vöslau, with chalky soil, also produces white sparkling wines.

The last of Austria's wine provinces, least known in the world's markets, is Steiermark or Styria, the southeastern boundary province with Slovenia (now part of Yugoslavia). This corner of the Alpine foothills has few natural advantages for the vine. The soil is stony on the steep slopes, and although rainfall is high, vines often suffer from drought. South Styria with its capital Leibnitz is the most fertile region, growing Welschriesling, Rheinriesling, Sauvignon Blanc ('Muskat-Sylvaner') and the mild Morillon, a local form of Weissburgunder. East Styria specializes in Gewürztraminer and Ruländer, making more pungent wines on red volcanic soil.

AUSTRIA PRODUCERS

Weingut Bründlmayer

3550 Langenlois. Founded 1581. Family owned. 86 acres; 10,750 cases. Grape var: Rheinriesling, Grüner Veltliner, Ruländer, Müller-Thurgau.

Traditional producer – no chemicals used – specializing in dry Kabinett wines which are kept in acacia casks. Best site: Zobinger Heiligenstein (Rheinriesling).

Weingut Elfenhof

7071 Rust, Burgenland. Owners: Johannes and Elfriede Holler. Founded 1680. 37 acres in Ruster Vogelsang (Grosslage), with plots in Rust's best Riede. 13,000 cases. Grape var: various, 80% white.

Old concern re-formed in 1969 and now with the most modern cellar in Rust. Half of the production is exported.

Esterhazy'sche Schlosskellerei

700 Eisenstadt, Burgenland. 106 acres, 75% white; 27,500 cases. Grape var: Welschriesling, Rheinriesling, Grüner Veltliner, Ruländer.

The ancient princely family of Esterhazy, patrons of Haydn and tamers of the Turks, have been making some of the best wine in the Burgenland since the 17th century. Vineyards include experimental plots run with Klosterneuberg college. Commercial vineyards in Rust, St. Georgen, St. Margaretten, Grosshöflein and Eisenstadt itself. 140 great casks line the cellars beneath the castle. The wines they hold are traditional, full and rich in extract. Some of the best dessert wines of the Burgenland carry the Esterhazy label.

Schlossweingut Freiherr von Geymüller

3132 Krems. A family property, founded 1811. 59 acres (47 in Ried Kleedorf) produce 13,000 cases of Grüner Veltliner, Rheinriesling, Müller-Thurgau, etc.

Traditional methods and wood-ageing make this a locally respected conservative house. Exports 12%.

Weingut Karl Graber – Sepp Schierer

2500 Sooss, Gumpoldskirchen. Founded 1950. 30 acres, plus grapes bought in, giving 28,000 cases. Grape var: 60-40 red–white

Consistent medal winner with typical Gumpoldskirchner wines up to Trockenbeerenauslese standard.

Schlosskellerei Halbturn

7131 Halbturn, Burgenland. Owners: F. Pieroth & Co. (West Germany). 138 acres: 17 in Jois (red), 79 in Halbturn-Wittmanshof (white), 42 in Halbturn-Klaylehof (Weissburgunder, Blauburgunder).

A former summer residence of the Empress Maria Theresa, now the centre of a major estate, owned by the German giant Pieroth since 1979. High-culture vineyards, modern cellar techniques, stress on red wines, also Sekt. Exports through Pieroth to West Germany.

Weingut Franz Hirtzberger

3620 Spitz, Wachau. 17 acres; 4,200 cases. Grape var: Grüner Veltliner (10 acres), Rheinriesling, Müller-Thurgau.

Franz Hirtzberger, Bürgermeister of Spitz, is the fourth generation to own this old-established, traditionally minded property, well-known locally for typical dry Wachau Grüner Veltliner from the noted Rotes Tor and Tausandeimerberg Riede. His 14th-century cellars, with a 300-year-old working press, are the oldest still in use in Austria.

Weingut Sepp Hold

7001 St. Georgen, Burgenland. Owner: Frau Eva Hold. Founded 1947. Merchant with 32 acres in St. Georgen.

Large modern premises producing local Tafelwein, QbA and QmP wines; also bottles wine from other Austrian regions and abroad. The late Sepp Hold started the business selling wine from a trailer towed by a bicycle. His widow now runs the firm, which produces a wide range including attractive Ausleses. Exports to West Germany, UK, USA.

Weingut Josef Jamek

3610 Joching, Wachau. Founded 1912. 45 acres, plus grapes bought in; 14,000 cases of estate wines. Grape var: Grüner Veltliner, Rheinriesling, Weissburgunder, Müller-Thurgau and red varieties.

Pioneer of totally dry Wachau wines – up to Spätlese quality they contain only 1 or 2 grams of sugar a litre, which makes them pungent drinking. The Auslese has a maximum of 15 grams of sugar a litre. The vineyards include plots in the best Riede of Joching (Klaus, Hochrain, Achleiten). The Jamek family also run a good restaurant in the village.

Johann Kattus

Vienna

Major Vienna merchant with wines from all over Austria, specializing in Sekt under the Hochriegel brand. Specialities include Gewürztraminer from Nussdorf – in the Vienna suburbs.

Kelleramt Chorherrenstift Klosterneuburg

3400 Klosterneuburg. Founded 1108. Monastery. 247 acres: Klosterneuburg (84 acres), Kahlenbergerdorf (84 acres) and Tattendorf (79 acres). Grape var: various, 60-40 white–red.

The Augustines of Klosterneuburg have made wine for nearly 9 centuries, but the operation is now a commercial company wholly owned by the monastery. Grapes from the extensive vineyards are augmented by supplies from small producers in Burgenland and Niederösterreich. Weissburgunder and Rheinriesling are wood-aged, late-bottled, and can be distinguished, especially in QmP qualities. Grüner Veltliner (brand name 'Klostergarten') is weightier than other comparable wines. Reds – Klosterneuburg has the largest red-grape vineyard in the country – are typical. All wines use the characteristic squat bottle. Sekt – including a pink one – can be delicious. Exports: 15-20%. The UK is the largest market. Also West Germany, Switzerland, USA.

The enormous 3-level cellars harbour 3m. bottles, including the Austrian State Wine Archive. Visitors are shown the tidemark a metre above the floor where wine flowed after Russian looters smashed all the casks in 1945.

Klosterneuburg also controls the ancient Deutsch-Ordens-Schlosskellerei in Gumpoldskirchen.

Prinz Liechtenstein'sches Weingut

8522 Gross St. Florian, Steiermark. Owners: E. and M. Müller. Growers and merchants. Founded 1813, bought by the Müllers in 1936. 13.5 acres in Riede Burgegg and Deutschlandsberg. Grape var: Blauer Wildbacher (for Schilcher), Welschriesling, Gewürztraminer, Zweigelt, etc. Grapes are also bought in to make a total of 85,000 cases.

The leading producers of the Schilcher rosé of Steiermark, plus whites and reds, all of QbA standard. Exports 12% of production, mostly by direct sales.

Weingut Josef Lust

2054 Haugsdorf, Retz. 44 acres. Grape var: mostly red.

Pioneer of high-quality, wood-aged, estate-bottled reds, which can develop a surprisingly un-Austrian quality in bottle. If Austria produces any serious red wines, they are made by Lust. Exports 40% of production to Denmark, Switzerland, West Germany, USA.

Weingut Mantlerhof

3494 Gedersdorf bei Krems. Founded 1814. 27 acres; 16,500 cases. Grape var: Grüner Veltliner 50%, Roter Veltliner 20%, Rheinriesling 15%, Müller-Thurgau 10%.

Traditional methods. Kabinett quality, dry wines. The rare and delicious dry Roter Veltliner is a Mantler speciality. Exports 15%. Widely distributed in Tirol hotels.

Weingut Franz Mayer

1190 Vienna. Founded 1683. 62 acres, yielding 13,000 cases in Nussberg, Grinzing and Alsegg. Grape var: Grüner Veltliner, Rheinriesling, Müller-Thurgau, Gewürztraminer, Weissburgunder, red varieties.

Mayer is Vienna's largest grower and owns the Beethovenhaus, probably the best known of all the *heurigen*. His modern cellar produces wines from Heuriger to Spätlese. Exports 15%.

Alois Morandell & Sohn

6300 Wörgl, Tirol. Founded 1926.

One of Austria's better-known merchants. Wines from 300 small growers in all parts of the country, at all price levels. Their Ruster Weissburgunder Auslese was the top wine at the 1981 Krems Wine Fair.

Lenz Moser

3495 Rohrendorf bei Krems. Founded 1929, family owned. Vineyards at Rohrendorf (148 acres); Mailberg, Retz (148 acres); and Seewinkelhof, Apetlon, Burgenland (136 acres). Grape var: many, including Cabernet Sauvignon at Mailberg, Sauvignon Blanc at Seewinkelhof. Brands: Schluck (Grüner Veltliner), Blue Danube.

The 2 sons of Dr. Lenz Moser (d. 1978) run the business. Dr. Moser developed a system of growing vines on high trellises much used in Austria and other wine countries. Wines from Lenz Moser's own estate (particularly at Apetlon) include Beeren- and Trockenbeeerenausleses of fabulous quality, sometimes reaching a pitch of concentration almost painful to taste. All their wines are well made and most are extremely good value. The estate at Mailberg formerly belonged to the Maltese knights. Exports 40% of production, to 50 countries. Austria's largest exporter.

Winzerhof Paul

2464 Goettlesbrunn, Klosterneuburg. Founded 1884. 30 acres. Grape var: Grüner Veltliner, Rheinriesling, Müller-Thurgau, Weissburgunder, Gewürztraminer, Muskat-Ottonel, Blaufränkisch.

A modern cellar, producing 10,000 cases of estate wines and more from bought-in local grapes. QbA wines for bottling are kept 1 year in wood.

Weingut Franz Prager

3610 Weissenkirchen, Wachau. Founded 1715. 25 acres; 16,000 cases. Grape var: Grüner Veltliner 40%, Rheinriesling 40%, others 20%. Holdings in Reide Steinriegl, Hinter der Burg, Ritzling, Durnsteiner Grünchen, Kollmitzberg.

A proud maker of Kabinett wines (Spätlese in good years) by traditional methods. All his wines are dry.

The baroque monastery of Klosterneuburg, atop three tiers of ancient cellars

Weingut Romerhof

7051 Markt Grosshoflein, Burgenland. Owner: Anton Kollwentz. Founded 1775. 30 acres of the southwest end of the Leithagebirge hills, west of Rust.

Good unblended dry wines (even his Spätleses). Reds keep well. No exports.

Weingut Robert Schlumberger

2540 Bad Vöslau. Founded 1842.

Robert Schlumberger, son of a branch of the Alsace family, made Austria's first *méthode champenoise* Sekt in 1842 after learning his trade in Champagne (he rose to be manager of Ruinart) and marrying the daughter of a Vöslau grower. Today the family firm makes respected reds from 34 acres. The Sekt business was sold to Underberg in 1973 and is still carried on, making high-quality wines that are unfortunately little exported. The Bad Vöslau reds are made from St. Laurent (60%), Cabernet Sauvignon, Merlot and Blauer Portugieser. Stress is on Bordeaux-style wines made by classic methods.

Weingut Schwamberg

2352 Gumpoldskirchen. 99 acres; 320,000 cases. Grape var: Rotgipfler, Neuburger, Zierfandler, plus purchased grapes.

One of the major growers and merchants of Gumpoldskirchen, founded in 1780. Automated production. Exports 28% to Germany, Switzerland and USA.

Klosterkeller Siegendorf

7011 Siegendorf, Burgenland. Founded 1860. Owners: The Patzenhofer family. Wine maker and manager: Jost Hopler. Visits by appointment. 79 acres, plus grapes and wine bought in from the locality; 80,000 cases. Grape var: the usual.

An ancient monastic estate which has expanded to become one of the Burgenland's largest private firms. The wine maker has worked in France, Germany and Australia. His wines have distinct varietal character. Cold fermentation, but Weissburgunder, Gewürztraminer and reds age in wood for up to 2 years. Exports to West Germany, UK and USA.

Freigut Thallern

2352 Gumpoldskirchen. Founded 1141, owned and farmed since by the Cistercians of Heiligenkreuz. 237 acres at Gumpoldskirchen and Burgenland, usual varieties.

Holdings include land in Ried Wiege, one of Austria's best sites, producing lively, fresh Rieslings and legendary Zierfandler that ages for decades. Wine-maker Günther Pozdina uses traditional techniques, all wines are aged in wood. Long-lived, complex-structured (and good-value) wines results, leading Austria in the field of traditional wine-making.

Ladislaus Torok

7071 Rust, Burgenland. Founded 1626. 15 acres; 8,000 cases. Grape var: the usual reds and whites.

Seventh-generation family concern produces full range from Neuburger diabetic wine to Trockenbeerenausleses, including a red from St. Laurent grapes. High-culture vineyards; a synthesis of modern and traditional techniques. The firm was selling to the Baltic in the 17th century, and now exports 30% of production.

Schlosskellerei Uhlheim

8262 Ilz, Steiermark. Owner: Dr. Karl Maier. 7 acres in Klöch, Steiermark. 116,000 cases, of which 2,100 cases are estate wines. Grape var: Welschriesling, Müller-Thurgau, Sauvignon Blanc.

Merchant dealing in the wines of Styria and other Austrian districts, exporting 15% of production. Notable wines in a quality range are Rheinriesling from Retz and a gold-medal St. Laurent from the best red-wine district of Austria, Vöslau.

Weingut Undhof, Fritz Saloman

3504 Stein, Wachau. Owner: Fritz Saloman. Founded 1792. 40 acres, plus grapes bought in; 12,000 cases. Grape var: Rheinriesling, in Riede Kögl and Steiner Pfaffenberg, Grüner Veltliner in Riede Undhof-Wieden and Wachtberg, Müller-Thurgau in Riede Steiner Goldberg. Also Weissburgunder (vines brought from Meursault before the war).

One of the first Austrian estates to bottle its own wine. Saloman makes completely dry, powerful, balanced whites which age well. A benchmark of quality in Austria. Exports 15% to USA, West Germany.

Weingut & Sektkellerei R. Zimmerman

3400 Klosterneuburg. Founded 1920. 7.5 acres in Grinzing, 10 in Klosterneuburg (Ried Buchberg) plus grapes bought in. Grape var: Rheinriesling, Weissburgunder, Grüner Veltliner, Müller-Thurgau, St. Laurent.

Grower, Sekt producer and owner of a popular *heurige* in the Vienna village of Grinzing. Exports 20% to W. Germany, Hong Kong, Mexico.

Verband Niederösterreichischen Gebietswinzergenossenschaften

1110 Vienna. Director: Josef Weissböck.

Union of 16 growers' coops in Lower Austria, with two large plants in Vienna and at Walkersdorf. The union has a total of 10,000 members farming 17,250 acres, and also owns the 45-acre Gut Türkenweg in Baden. Brands include Dukatenwein. Exports mostly to West Germany, also UK.

The qualities of wine
The sugar content ('must weight') of grapes is expressed in degrees KMW (Klosterneuburger Mostwaage), which measure the percentage of sugar in the juice: e.g. the minimum for Qualitätswein is 15° KMW (15% sugar), which equals 73° Oechsle on the German scale (based on specific gravity). *See* the table on page 229 for German requirements: 73° Oechsle would be a Rheingau Kabinett. The approximate conversion factor is Oechsle = 5 × KMW.

Categories
Tafelwein/Tischwein/Normalwein is from 13° to 15° KMW.
Qualitätswein must be 15° KMW but may be 'enriched' with sugar as concentrated must. Minimum alcohol must be 9.5°. It must state its geographical origin.
Kabinett Wein must be 17° KMW (= Rheingau Spätlese) and may not be 'enriched'. Higher categories are described as 'Besonderer Reife und Leseart'. They must not only have higher degrees but taste extra ripe.
Spätlese must be 19° KMW (= Baden Spätlese or Mosel Auslese).
Auslese must be 21° KMW from selected fully ripe grapes.
Beerenauslese must be 25° KMW (= Rheingau Beerenauslese).
Ausbruch must be 27° KMW and made from nobly rotten and dry grapes.
Trockenbeerenauslese must be 30° KMW (the same as the German requirement).
Eiswein must be from frozen grapes and 22° KMW.

OTHER PRODUCERS

Weingut Feiler
Rust, Burgenland. Traditionalist with 37 high-class acres in Rust, making noted Trockenbeerenauslese. In good years half the harvest can attain this quality. Exports to West Germany and USA.

Weingut Gunter Haimer
2170 Poysdorf, Falkenstein. Founded 1860. 30 acres. Grape var: Grüner Veltliner (25 acres), Rheinriesling, Müller-Thurgau, Gewürztraminer. Traditionally made Grüner Veltliner, up to Spätlese quality.

Weingut Heidebodenhof, Seigfried Tschida
Pamhagen, Burgenland. 40 acres in the Seewinkel, also merchant, buying grapes from the Rust region. A prolific medal winner with modern techniques. Exports to West Germany, USA, Scandinavia.

Franz & Maria Heiss
Illmitz, Burgenland. 22 acres in the Seewinkel villages of Illmitz and Apetlon. Mixed varieties. All qualities up to Eiswein, leaning towards the modern, lighter Burgenland style.

Weingut Marienhof
Rust. Owner: Franz Just. 25 acres in Rust, most in Ried Umriss, on the slopes away from the lake.

Weingut Nikolaihof
3512 Mautern, Wachau, Owners: Nickolaus and Christine Sachs. 25 acres; 8,000 cases. Grape var: Grüner Veltliner, Rheinriesling. Traditionally made wine, all sold locally.

Weingut Sattlerhof
8462 Samlitz, Steiermark. Founded 1887. 12 acres. Grape var: Welschriesling, Muskat, Weissburgunder, Ruländer, Sauvignon Blanc, Müller-Thurgau.

Franz Schwartz
3492 Eltsdorf-Walkersdorf, Krems. Grower and merchant. 62 acres; 19,000 cases from own vineyards.

Alexander Unger
St. Margarethen, Burgenland. Grower (32 acres) and merchant, also using names Weingut Moorhof and Weingut Hubertshof. Complete range of colours and styles from rosé to Eiswein. Exports 60% of production to European markets and Japan.

COOPERATIVES

Burgenlandischer Winzerverband
Rust, Burgenland. A 'mother coop' heading 28 smaller organizations, founded in 1957. About 6,000 members with a total vineyards area of 17,300 acres. Total storage capacity of the group is 500,000 hl. Wines up to Trockenbeerenauslese quality. Exports to West Germany, Sweden, USA.

Winzergenossenschaft Gumpoldskirchen
Founded 1907. 350 members. Brands include Gold and Königswein. Austria's oldest active coop, with a name for quality. Exports 20-30%.

Winzergenossenschaft Krems
3500 Krems. Founded 1938. 2,800 members. 4,000 acres in Krems, Langenlois and Klosterneuberg; 2.5m. cases. Grape var: the usual; 92% white, 8% red. Largest independent coop in Austria and a consistent medal winner. Exports 30%.

Winzergenossenschaft Dinstlgut Loiben
3601 Unter Loiben, Wachau. Founded as a coop 1936, previously privately owned ex-monastic cellars, founded in 1002. 2,960 acres. Grape var: Grüner Veltliner, Rheinriesling, Müller-Thurgau, Weissburgunder. Brands: Loibner Kaiserwein, Schütt, Burgstall, Rotternberg Rheinriesling Spätlese. Exports 17%.

Winzergenossenschaft St. Martinus
7082 Donnerskirchen, Burgenland. Chairman: Stefan Leeb. 317 members with 4,900 acres in Donnerskirchen, Purbach, Breitenbrunn and Schutzen. 77,500 cases. Grape var: Grüner Veltliner 40%, Welschriesling 25%, Muskat-Ottonel 10%, Weissburgunder, Gewürztraminer, Bouvier, Blaufränkisch (5% each). The largest quality-wine producer in Burgenland, founded in 1953, taking over the 14th-century cellars of the noble family of Windisch-Graetz. The first Burgenland Trockenbeerenauslese was made here, and called *Lutherwein* by a fanatical Protestant proprietor.

St. Martinus goes far to prove that size need not mean loss of quality – half the production is of Kabinett standard. Exports to West Germany (40%), USA, UK and Japan.

Winzergenossenschaft Wachau
3601 Durnstein. Founded 1938. 850 members; 350 acres. Grape var: Grüner Veltliner, Rheinriesling, Müller-Thurgau. Brandy also made. A traditionally minded coop whose members own some of the best vineyards in the Wachau and whose best wines are not to be despised. Above the cellars is the 1714 Kellerschloss, a miniature baroque château beautifully decorated with frescoes and carvings.

Winzergenossenschaft Wolkersdorf
Founded 1938. Members own 2,200 acres, mostly Grüner Veltliner. 500,000 cases. Brands: Roseneck (Grüner Veltliner QbA), Katzensteiner (Weissburgunder QbA). Makes the altar wine for the Archdiocese of Vienna. Exports through the Lower Austria coops union.

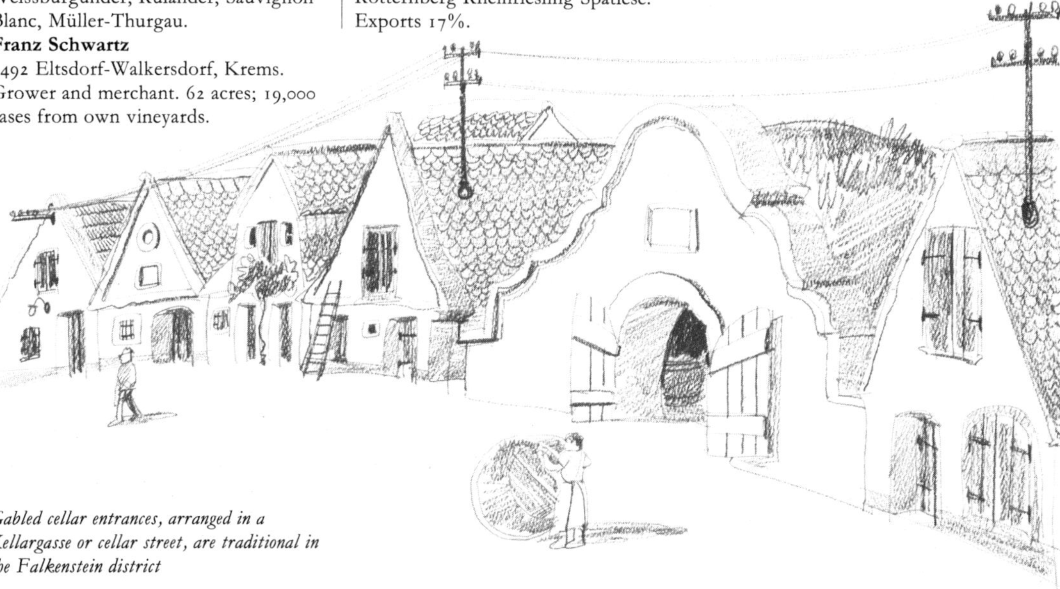

Gabled cellar entrances, arranged in a Kellargasse or cellar street, are traditional in the Falkenstein district

HUNGARY

The true Hungarian words of appreciation for the country's traditional wines sum up their character and appeal. They call a good white wine 'fiery' and 'stiff' – masculine terms which promise a proper partner for the paprika in the cooking.

Such wines can occasionally still be found in the historical sites of Hungarian viticulture, the hill regions which dot the country from the southwest northwards, skirt the long Lake Balaton, then run up the Czech border from near Budapest to Tokay.

Unfortunately the predictable result of growing efficiency in the huge state farms has been a vast increase in harvests and loss of this highly desirable concentration. Use of the traditional Hungarian grapes ensures that the wines are still very much individuals, but even within the last 10 years they seem to me to have become milder, less male, Magyar and memorable.

Hungary is rich in indigenous grapes of character that could contribute splendid wines to the world scene but have hardly been tried elsewhere. The most notable of all is the vigorous Furmint, the dominant grape of Tokay, which not only rots nobly but in its dry form gives strongly sappy, velvety and high-flavoured wine. The Hárslevelü or 'lime-leaf' is scarcely less notable: an excellent dry-climate late ripener with abundant crops and good acid levels, resistant to fungus diseases – a model grape for South Africa, Australia or California.

Szürkebarát or 'grey friar' is more familiar than it sounds: it is a form of Pinot Gris (German Ruländer) grown to splendid effect on the volcanic Mt. Badacsonyi. But the Kéknyelü ('blue-stalk') of the same vineyards is purely indigenous, a modest producer of concentrated and complex golden-green wines for the fish course. More widespread are three other white Hungarians (at least by adoption), Ezerjó ('thousand blessings'), which is a good bulk-producer on the Great Plain, making fine wine only at Mor in the north, Leányka ('little girl') whose delicate dry white is probably the best wine of Eger, again in the northern hills, and Mezesfeher ('white honey'), an archetypal description of the national view of a good glass of wine.

Most widespread of all is the international Italian (here 'Olasz') Riesling. The Great Plain makes most of its white from it, and on Mt. Badacsonyi it rises to its maximum flavour and concentration.

The great Hungarian red grape is the Kadarka, which flourishes equally producing light wine with a slight but convincing 'cut' on the Great Plain, and big stiff spicy red for ageing at Eger and Szekszárd. The Kékfrankos (Austrian Blaufränkisch, a relation of Gamay), is planted more and more. Pinot Noir (Nágyburgundi) is as good in south Hungary around Vilányi as anywhere in Europe outside Burgundy. Merlot (bizarrely called 'Médoc Noir') is equally successful in the north.

Added to these admirable grapes are others whose names are easily recognizable: Szilváni, Cabernet, Rajnairizling, Traminí, Muskat Ottonel.

Each of Hungary's notable wines is called by a simple combination of place and grape name. The place name has the suffix '-í'. Thus Ezerjó from Mor is Morí Ezerjó.

Hungary has 400,000 acres of vines. Production is dominated by seven huge regional '*combinats*', run as individual enterprises but owned by the state, and the separately and centrally controlled state farms organization, Agker, founded in 1947 and operating 108 farms with 77,000 acres of vines. The state farms seem to have a larger share of the finest land,

The classes of Tokay

Tokay Szamorodni

This is Tokay 'as it comes' – i.e. the basic wine, sweeter or drier according to the vintage.

Tokay Aszu

Aszu is the term for grapes infected with noble rot (*Botrytis cinerea*). Destalked hand-picked Aszu grapes are stored 6–8 days, then kneaded to a pulp which is added to base Tokay wine, or to must, by the *puttony* (hod of 20–25 kilos). The eventual sweetness depends on the number of *puttonyos* added to 136–140 litres of base wine – usually 3, 4 and 5 *puttonyos*. 6 is exceptional. The sequence then is:

– maceration and stirring for 24–48 hours
– settling and racking the must
– fermentation period depending on number of *puttonyos*
– racking, fining and filtering
– ageing in oak for not less than 3 years
– filtering prior to bottling
– if binned in Tokay cellars bottles are not laid on their sides but stood upright, corks changed every 15–20 years.

Tokay Aszu Essencia

Only individually hand-selected Aszu grapes. Only produced in exceptional years from the best vineyards. Method as for Tokay Aszu, but:

– quality cannot be measured by number of *puttonyos* as sugar content is higher than for 6 *puttonyos*
– fermentation takes several years (special yeast is used – Tokaj 22)
– minimum of 10 years' ageing in oak.

Tokay Essence

Destalked hand-picked Aszu grapes. While grapes are being stored (*see* Tokay Aszu) the pressure of their own weight produces a minute amount of highly concentrated juice at the bottom of the tub (one *puttonyo* yields only 142 millimetres of this Essence). The juice is then allowed to ferment extremely slowly for many years in oak casks.

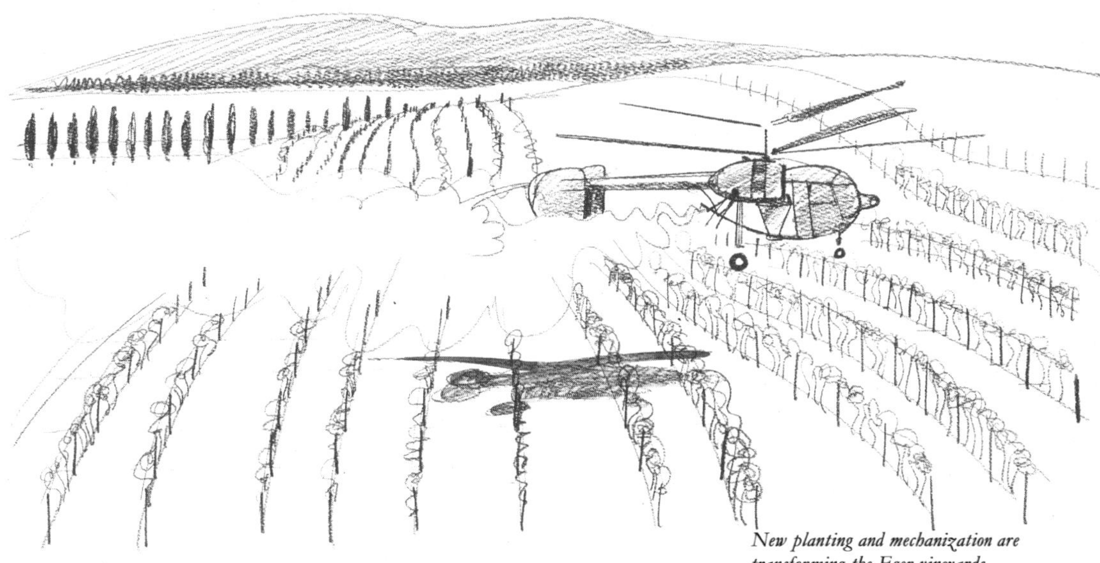

New planting and mechanization are transforming the Eger vineyards

e.g. all Tokay; although some 'peasant' holdings still exist in classic areas. Hungarovin, although relatively small as a producer with only 3,000 acres, acts as a major merchant or négociant within the system and owns the larger part of the great centre of the Hungarian wine trade, Budafok, near Budapest; a historic warren of cellars. All exports, from whatever source, are handled by one agency, Monimpex. A monopolistic filtering system thus ensures that relatively few wines of the vast variety are exported, and those in a standardized form.

The Danube divides Hungary almost down the middle. All the old wine regions are either to the west of the river or along the Czech border. East of the Danube lies the sandy Pannonian or Great Plain, a dreary steppe which has found its first useful purpose in this century with the planting of vines. Half Hungary's wine now comes from there.

A single awesome '*combinat*' at Kecskemet has no less than 62,000 acres making one million hectolitres (11 million cases) a year. They are light white wines from Ezerjó, Olaszrizling and Müller-Thurgau with a little Kékfrankos light red. Another at Szeged near the Yugoslav border in the south has 28,000 acres making heavier and sweeter wines of a wider range of grapes: Olaszrizling, Leányka, Kövidinka (a common white), Muskat Ottonel and also Cabernet Franc and Merlot. Other growers' cooperatives on the plain tend to grow Kadarka for their red and Olaszrizling for their white, both low-strength everyday wines which they sell to their local *combinat*. Until recently half the vines of the Alföld, the Great Plain, were Kadarka and much of its wine pink 'Siller' for instant drinking.

The historic wine regions start across the Danube in the south at Siklos and Vilányi where, on hills of stiff loess, the Pinot Noir (with or without some Kékfrankos) gives unmistakably Burgundian wine. Four or five years' bottle-age give Vilányi Burgundi the velvet touch. They continue a little to the north at Pecs in the Mecsék region, producer of very respectable off-dry Olaszrizling, and Pinot Blanc that deserves three years' bottle-age. Farther north again Szekszárd has a historic reputation for a Kadarka red (Vörös) with strength and astringency, traditionally likened to Bordeaux. The Szekszárdi from the State farm is known as Nemes Kadar.

Lake Balaton lies across the heart of western, trans-Danubian, Hungary, in the centre of the country's finest white-wine region. The north shore of the 50-mile-long lake has ideal southern slopes on the basalt stumps of very dead volcanoes. The most famous of these, Mt. Badacsonyi, is the source of Hungary's best full-bodied whites, neither fully dry nor very sweet. Dryish Kéknyelü is perhaps the best of all; Szürkebarát is denser and stickier. Badacsonyi and the nearby hills have 6,000 acres of vines.

On the same shore 20 miles east red-sand soil and a slightly warmer microclimate give wines with more roundness and less 'nerve'. This area of 5,000 acres is known as Balatonfüred-Csopak. Olaszrizling and Furmint make notable wines here. The remainder of the Balaton area goes by the simple name of the lake alone, its wines standing in relation to Badacsonyi as, say, other Palatinate wines stand in relation to the Mittelhaardt. The south side of the lake has a major state farm at Balatonboglár, specializing in white wines, Szilváni, Leányka, Tramini, Muskotaly, sparkling Csabagyöngye and table grapes. The wines are much less attractive than the north-shore collection. But Hajos, 20 miles west, has a name for surprisingly good Cabernet.

Three widely separated hills north of Balaton are considered 'classic' areas. Somló, with a mere 1,000 acres, today largely of Furmint and Olaszrizling, used to have a reputation second only to Tokay, not only for flavour but for restorative properties.

Sopron, far north on the border of Austria's Burgenland, is a red-wine district growing Kékfrankos and claiming kinship with Beaujolais, though the resemblance is remote.

Mor, north towards the hills of the Czech border, conjures qualities out of the Ezerjó which are not found elsewhere: aroma and body in a dry wine which is usually neutral. The credit goes to steep quartz-rich soil on a limestone base which continues north into the newer area of Barsönyös-Csaszar.

Hungary's greatest concentration of quality vineyards stretches east from here along the hilly border country with Czechoslovakia as far as Tokay. The biggest delimited area surrounds the 'historic' wine-town of Debró, whose Hárslevelü remains one of the country's best medium-sweet aromatic wines. It is now buried in the Mátraalya (or Matravidek) region, of 22,000 acres, including its neighbour Gyöngyös-Visonta. A wide variety of the commoner grapes, including Chasselas for the table, are grown in the shelter of these hills.

Mátraalya leads on into the district of Eger to the east. The baroque city of Eger is the centre of 36,000 acres of both red grapes for its famous Bull's Blood, or Bikavér, and white for its less-known but equally good Leányka, Muskotaly and Olaszrizling. Another 7,000 acres wait to be planted.

Eger's impressive tufa-quarried state cellars are lined with vast red-hooped casks in which even the white wines are sometimes kept for up to five years without losing freshness. Tufa appears to be the secret of Egri quality. The red grapes for Bull's Blood are Kadarka 70%, Kékfrankos 15% and 'Médoc Noir' (Merlot) 15%. To my surprise the cellar master (in big boots, *gris de travail* and a little military cap) preferred the Médoc Noir straight, with a high degree of unfermented sugar. Bull's Blood built its reputation on potency which it no longer displays. It has become a mere middle-of-the-road red with a memorable name. But one quality it has not entirely lost is its longevity. Full-strength Kadarka benefits enormously from bottle-age, and Bull's Blood ought to be kept at least four years for its warm, almost Italian, character to emerge.

Tokay remains Hungary's one wine still hand-made by ancient painstaking methods to capture a character found nowhere else: a sort of eastern Yquem. It is now all made in the cellars of the state farm of Tokajhegyaljai at Satoraljaujhely. The vineyards amount to 15,000 acres in the worn-down, loess-covered, once volcanic hills on the Soviet border. Its twin secrets are the Furmint grape and the late autumn sun alternating with mist that provokes *Botrytis cinerea*, or noble rot. There are many degrees of sweetness and quality, as there are of rottenness in the grapes. Much confusion has been caused by the cellar techniques which build up the different qualities from whatever the harvest brings. They are most clearly explained in tabular form (*see* page 400).

CZECHOSLOVAKIA

With 133,000 acres, or a third as many vines as Hungary, Czechoslovakia is no dabbler in wine-making, little as her produce is seen in the West. Such wines as I have seen have lacked the superficial graces of good bottles and well-designed labels, and suffered from tiny corks, but have nonetheless been the well-made product of a modern and competent wine industry in the Austro/German style. Slovakia, the eastern half of the country lying along the northern border of Hungary, is the chief producer, with 94,000 acres. In the Czech system of classifying grape varieties 20 per cent of this is planted with First Class 'A' white varieties: Rhine Riesling, Pinot Blanc, Gewürztraminer, Sauvignon Blanc, Muscat Ottonel. Half is planted with First Class 'B' whites (of which Wälschriesling, Grüner Veltliner and Müller-Thurgau are much the most important). About a quarter is red, with Limberger the leading grape and the whole list having an Austrian air – save for some 1,500 acres of Cabernet Sauvignon. Limberger is known as Frankovka, and the state farm at Rača, just north of Bratislava, produces Slovakia's best-known red under this name.

Slovakia's other special pride is in possessing a small corner of the Tokay vineyard on the Hungarian border, growing 65 per cent Furmint, 25 per cent Hărslevelü and 10 per cent Muscat de Frontignan to produce her own Tokay.

The vineyards of Moravia, the central section of the country, lie between Brno and the Austrian border – a natural extension of Austria's 'Weinwiertel'. The 37,000 acres are largely planted in 'B' varieties: Müller-Thurgau first, then Grüner Veltliner.

Bohemia, the western province with Prague at its heart, has a mere 2,500 acres. A little Rhine Riesling of good quality is grown here, but none exported.

YUGOSLAVIA

The six republics and two autonomous regions that make up Yugoslavia are all in the wine business: some more traditionally and interestingly than others but all with considerable and growing competence and professionalism. Three are major exporters: Slovenia in the northwest for white wines, Kosovo in the south for red and Serbia in the east for a wide variety of both.

Yugoslavia comes tenth among the world's wine countries and tenth among exporters: a respectable position for a country which had to build its wine industry almost from scratch after World War II. Its roots are as old as Italy's, but long occupation by the Turks removed the sense of continuity. The recent reconstitution of the industry combines the Germanic Austro-Hungarian traditions of the north, the Italian influence down the coast and some truly Balkan traditions in the east and south, with a general move towards adopting the internationally known grapes in place of indigenous characters.

The wine industry is state controlled but consists almost half-and-half of small independent growers and state-owned farms. The small growers normally take their crops to the local cooperatives. These in turn supply the larger regional organizations, which act as négociants, blenders and distributors.

SERBIA

The republic of Serbia was formerly the whole of the eastern, landlocked, third of Yugoslavia from Hungary to Macedonia. Now its northern section, north of the Danube, is the autonomous region of Vojvodina, and a significant southern slice, adjacent to Albania, is also autonomous as Kosovo or Kosmet. Both are important wine areas.

Serbia is second to Croatia in vineyard area with 181,000 acres (30% of the national total). Vojvodina has 44,000 (7%) and Kosovo 20,000 (3.3%).

Serbia has been relatively conservative in its grape varieties, with the dark Prokupac as its chief red grape and Smederevka (Smederevo is near Belgrade) as its white. Its oldest and most famous vineyard is Župa, 80 miles south of the capital between Svetozarevo and Kruževac. Župsko Crno ('Župa red') is a Prokupac blend with the lighter Plovdina. Prokupac is also widely used for rosé ('Ružica'). More and more Cabernet, Merlot and Gamay is being planted, but not so far with results as good as those farther south. The Royal Serbian Cellars makes a rather disappointing Cabernet. Farthest east of all, the region of Timok and Krajina (adjoining Bulgaria) plants mainly Gamay.

Vojvodina has a history of red-wine making (of which Carlowitz was once a famous example). Today a wide range of mainly white grapes is producing nicely aromatic and balanced wines, the best of them in the Fruška Gora hills by the Danube north of Belgrade. Gewürztraminer and Sauvignon Blanc are particularly tasty, though I fear less widely planted than Laski Riesling. Farther north and east, Subotiča and Banat are the area bordering on Hungary and Romania, both with sandy Great Plain soils and light wines; Subotiča growing the Hungarian red Kadarka and white Ezerjó.

Kosmet (or Kosovo) is extraordinarily successful for a relatively new region. Its Pinot Noir, made sweet for the German taste and labelled Amselfelder, is one of Yugoslavia's largest exports. Its Cabernet, exported to Britain simply as 'Cabernet from Kosovo', takes bottle-age extremely well. It is a light wine but at six years still retains fresh and faintly exotic aromas of the grape – though oddly enough not recognizably Cabernet: I have found a touch of the apricot smell of Žilavka which makes me wonder whether its lightness is a clever piece of blending. Žilavka is also grown in Kosovo.

SLOVENIA AND DALMATIA

Slovenia, tucked into the Italian–Austrian–Hungarian northwest corner of the country, makes Yugoslavia's best white wines. Its principal grape is the Italian (here 'Laski') Riesling, also called the Graševina. The 47,000 acres of vineyards (8% of the national total) reach their highest quality at Ljutomer, Maribor, Ptuj and Ormož in the extreme north, between the valley of the Mura (which forms the border in places with Austria and Hungary) and the Drava. The combined influences of the Adriatic, the Alps and the Hungarian plain make the climate moderate, while limestone subsoils favour white wine. The hills between Lutomer and Ormož, only 50 miles from the west end of Lake Balaton, bear a vineyard almost as famous as Mt. Badacsonyi, known by the name of Jerusalem from crusader connections. The majority of the exports from this admirable region are unfortunately of Laski Riesling, although Pinots Blanc and Gris, Gewürztraminer, Sylvaner and Rhine Riesling are also grown. It seems a pity to waste a first-rate vineyard on what is essentially a second-rate grape, however satisfactory its performance – and some of its late-picked wines here are more than satisfactory. Its wines are usually made dry for the domestic market but sweetened for export.

South of the Drava the Haloze hills produce a similar range of white wines. South again the Sava valley, continuing into Croàtia and on to its capital, Zagreb, makes light red Cviček of local grapes.

At the western end of Slovenia on the Italian border four small viticultural regions with a total of 12,000 acres have a mild Mediterranean climate. Their best-known wine is a vigorous but not heavy red called Kraški Teran. Teran is the Italian Refosco and Kraški signifies that it is grown on the rugged limestone 'karst' that stretches up the coast.

Vipava, between Ljublana and Trieste, grows Cabernet, Merlot, Barbera and dry white Rebula. The tiny part of Istria that is Slovenia's brief sea coast makes some rich Malvasias and Muscats for local consumption, using the same red grapes as Vipava. Slovin of Ljubljana, the country's biggest exporter, is the main Slovenia producer.

CROATIA

The old kingdom of Croatia musters the most vineyards of any of the republics, 198,000 acres or very nearly a third (32.5%) of the national total. It falls into two distinct and very different parts: Slavonia, the continental north between Slovenia and Serbia, between the Drava and the Sava rivers, and the coast, from the Istrian peninsula in the north all the way south to Montenegro, including all Dalmatia and its lovely islands.

Slavonia has half the grape acreage, but its wines have neither the appeal of Slovenia's whites, close though they are, nor of some of the new wines of Vojvodina to the east. Wine shipped as Yugoslav Laski Riesling without further particulars (e.g. by Slovin) comes from here.

Croatia's best wines come from Istria and Dalmatia. Istria grows the same grapes as western Slovenia: Merlot, Cabernet, Pinot Noir and Teran for reds – the Merlot particularly good. The whites include rich Muscats and Malvasias, and Pinot Blanc, which is the base of the local sparkling wine.

Dalmatia has Yugoslavia's richest array of original characters – mainly red. Plavac Mali (there seems to be no translation) is the principal grape, supported by Plavina, Vranac, Babić, Cabernet, Merlot and 'Modra Frankija'. Plavac has its moments of glory. One is Postup, a concentrated sweet red, aged for years in oak, produced on the Pelješac peninsula north of Dubrovnik. A 15-year-old Postup is still bright red, a strange sort of half-port with more than a hint of retsina, a big (14.2°) well-balanced and structured wine that would appeal to those who like Recioto from Valpolicella. Dingač is very similar. Another is Faros from the island of Hvar, a degree lighter than Postup and softly dry rather than sweet; a full-bodied, warmly satisfying wine without coarseness. The regular quality of coastal red is simply called Plavac. Some find Babić, when aged three or four years, a better wine. The dry rosé of the coast, made from several grapes, is called Opol.

White Dalmatian wines are in a minority but in greater variety than red. The Maraština is the most widespread white variety and has its own appellation at Čara Smokvica. Grk is the oxidized, sherry-like speciality of the island of Korčula. Pošip (which some equate with Šipon/Furmint) makes heavy but

Yugoslavia's other regions

Macedonia's 96,000 acres make up 16 per cent of the national total. The best wines are reds from Vranac, Prokupac, Merlot, Kratosija and some Cabernet and Pinot Noir. Macedonija Vino of Skopje controls 7 big wineries in the republic.

Bosnia, largely Muslim in tradition, has only 13,500 acres. The most notable wine, a full dry white, is made from the aromatic Zilavka. Kombinat Hepok at Mostar is the principal producer.

Montenegro produces mostly red Vranac wines from 10,000 acres. The chief producer is Agrokombinat 13 Jul, Titograd.

Wine prices in Yugoslavia are very modest – producers sell at between 30 and 45 dinars a litre.

USSR

The Soviet Union is the world's third-largest wine producer, with more than 3m. acres of vines. The country is also a considerable net importer. The Western World therefore sees few, if any, Soviet wines. Samples confirm that almost all are made sweet, (exceptions being the worthwhile table wines of Georgia – notably Tsinandali and Gurdzhaani dry whites, and Saperavi and Napareuli reds). Some of the sweet wines of the Crimea are of high quality, but since further information is academic, elusive and suspect it is omitted here.

not flat wine. Bogdanuša, especially on the islands of Hvar and Brač, can be surprisingly light, crisp and aromatic. Vugava, grown on the remote island of Vis, is similar. Sometimes they are presented as separate varieties, sometimes in blends. It is hard to discover, in fact, whether some are different names for the same grape. But they certainly have old-style character to balance against the predictable correctness of Laski Riesling.

Dalmatia's dessert wines, whether of red or white grapes or both, are known as Prošek. The best Prošek tends to be a family matter, nursed in a little cask and given to guests in a thick tumbler with absolutely appropriate pride.

BULGARIA

Of all the Soviet-dominated countries of Eastern Europe Bulgaria has been most adept at reprogramming its wine industry to earn Western currency. Since the mid-1970s Bulgarian wine has not been an occasional exotic excursion, but standard fare in several Western markets. Today it offers some of the world's best value for money in familiar flavours – above all in rich Cabernet Sauvignon, which satisfies palates accustomed to red Bordeaux. Bulgaria, according to official figures, has four times as much vineyard planted in Cabernet Sauvignon as California.

Wine is a major preoccupation of the whole country. Over 400,000 acres, or 4% of the land area, is vineyard. Red and white varieties are evenly balanced. Of the red vineyard 55% (about 90,000 acres) is Cabernet, 20% Merlot, 11% Pamid, most of the rest such other traditional varieties as Gamza (the Hungarian Kadarka) and Mavrud, and a little Pinot Noir and Gamay.

The white vineyard is much more traditional: almost half is Rkatziteli, Red Misket 14%, Dimiat (or Smederevka) 13%, Muscat Ottonel 11% with so far only developing plantings of Chardonnay, Riesling, Aligoté and Ugni Blanc alongside small acreages of Tamianka, Gewürztraminer and Sauvignon Blanc. Nobody can doubt, however, from their progress to date, that the better varieties will be long in taking over. Chardonnay is beginning to show its natural superiority, even without expensive ageing in oak.

Wine-growing Bulgaria is divided into four main regions. The northern and southern regions, divided by the narrow spine of the Stara Planina, the Balkan Mountains, each produce one third of the country's red and white wines. But conditions are cooler, and quality generally higher, to the north. Five official subregions in the northern zone concentrate on Cabernet Sauvignon, Gamza, Pinot Noir and Gamay. The state wineries of Suhindol, Pleven and Pavlikeni in particular produce good Cabernets. Sparkling wine is another speciality of the region, benefiting from its relatively high acid levels. Iskra is the national 'champagne'; Donau Perle a dry white of Feteasca, a grape more common in Romania.

The southern region also grows Cabernet and some Pinot Noir and Merlot, but concentrates more on traditional varieties: Pamid, which makes a rather pallid everyday wine, and Mavrud, which makes the opposite, Bulgaria's pride, a substantial dark Rhône-like wine needing four years' ageing.

The winery at Asenovgrad near Plovdiv has a reputation for Mavrud. Karlovo, in the Valley of Roses (the source of attar of roses) specializes in Muscats – Hemus is the brand name – and has recently been succeeding in trials with Chardonnay, Gewürztraminer and Sauvignon Blanc.

The eastern region, between the mountains and the Black Sea, has 30 per cent of the vineyards and specializes in white wines, sparkling wines and brandy. Shumen in the north makes the best Chardonnay to date, along with Riesling (usually a blend of Rhine and Italian), Gewürztraminer and Dimiat. Dimiat gives a sweet wine popular in Germany under the name Klosterkeller. Farther south in the sandy coastal zone the wines grow sweeter: Sungurlare, inland from Burgas, has a name for sweet Muscats and is the source of the popular Sonnenküste, made of Dimiat and Rkatsiteli for the German market.

A fourth, very small and distinct, region lies on the Yugoslav border across the Rhodope Mountains in the southwest of the country. Bulgarians have the greatest respect for Melnik, its red wine, which they say is so concentrated that you can carry it in a handkerchief.

From 1982 onwards 18 subregions have been officially recognized as appellations, each for one or more grape varieties. The new rules do not in several cases coincide with labels that have become familiar. It remains to be seen whether, for example, the excellent Cabernet of Pavlikeni will disappear because the region is only recognized now for Gamza. All Bulgarian wines are sold by the state marketing organization, Vinimpex.

Prices in Bulgaria vary from 1.2 to 3.2 leva (75 cents US) a bottle.

ROMANIA

The long-established quality and individuality of Romanian wine has suffered sadly in the socialist era. The country speaks a Latin-based tongue and has both cultural and climatic affinities with France. Once the wines of Moldavia were drunk in Paris. Today little Romanian wine is seen in Western countries. Samples of Cabernets, Chardonnays and other international grapes appear to have been made for the Russian taste: heavy and sweet.

Romania's vineyards surround the central Carpathian mountains. The main centres are Tirnave, at 1,600 feet on the Transylvanian plateau to the north, Cotnari to the northeast in Moldavia, Vrancea (including the once-famous Odobeşti and Nicoreşti) to the east, Dealul Mare to the southeast and Murfatlar in the extreme southeast by the Black Sea, and in the south Stefaneşti, Dragasani and Segarcea. In the west, part of the sandy Banat plain round Minis is planted with both Hungarian and international grapes. The rest of the vineyards are stocked with a mixture of international varieties and Romania's own white Fetească, Grasă and Tămîioasă and red Băbească and Fetească Neagră.

Cotnari is the best and most individual wine: a pale dessert wine like a distant cousin of Sauternes. Tirnave produces a reasonable white blend called Perla de Tirnave and more interesting 'varietal' Fetească, Rulander, Gewürztraminer, Riesling and Muscat Ottonel. Vrancea's most notable wine is the brisk red Băbească of Nicoreşti. Dealul Mare specializes in Cabernet, Merlot and Pinot Noir – in the Russian style. The state experimental station at Valea Călugărească is the country's most modern, with a wide range including a fairly dry Riesling.

Murfatlar is traditionally a white and dessert wine area. Its Muscat is of good quality, but Chardonnay from here is too heavy for Western palates. In the southern vineyards Stefaneşti and Drăgăşani are better known for whites and Segarcea and Sadova for reds – particularly Cabernet and a rosé.

On the whole the white wines of Romania are more acceptable than the red. The whites of Tirnave have the highest standard, but at present Cotnari is the only wine to be sought out for its own sake.

GREECE

The ancient Greeks colonized the Mediterranean and the Black Sea with the vine, exporting their wines in exchange for Egyptian grain, Spanish silver and Caucasian timber. In the Middle Ages the Peloponnese and Crete were valued sources of Malmsey sack for northern Europe. The largely alkaline (in places, volcanic) soils and multifarious microclimates of Greece make her a natural country of the vine. With 257,000 acres of wine grapes she is a major producer – but on a level of sophistication far lower than, say Yugoslavia. Only in the last decade, with entry into the E.E.C. imminent, has there been a move towards varieties and systems of control that will lead to fine wine. So far only 12 per cent of the crop qualifies for the national appellation quality seal, but there are signs of rapid progress.

Under primitive conditions, with hot fermentations, the best qualities that could be produced were all sweet wines. The Athenian taste remained faithful to what appears to be an ancient tradition of adding pine-resin during fermentation to make retsina. Eighty per cent of the wine of Attica (almost all white) is resinated. It goes too well with Greek cooking to be ignored.

At present Greek wine can usefully be divided into national brands (usually blends), retsina and other traditional and country wines for uncritical first-year drinking, and wines from defined areas now controlled by an appellation system in accordance with E.E.C. law. There are 26 such areas.

The Peloponnese has more than half of Greece's vineyards (162,000 acres) and produces more than a third of her wine. Patras at the mouth of the Gulf of Corinth is the main wine centre, with four appellations: Muscat, Muscat of Rion, Mavrodaphne and plain Patras. Mavrodaphne can be the most notable of these: a sweet dark red wine of up to 16 per cent alcohol, something in the style of a Recioto of Valpolicella, much improved by long maturing. Plain Patras red is for drinking young. Two other appellations of the Peloponnese are better: the region of Nemea for strong red made of the Agiogiorgitiko (St. George) grape and Mantinia for a reasonable, though rather flat, white. The main Nemea producer is the cooperative, which uses the name Hercules (the conqueror of the dreaded Nemean lion). Their Rhoditis rosé is adequate.

The 45,000 acres of vines in the north of Greece, from Thrace in the east through Macedonia to

Epirus, appear to have most potential for quality. Its appellations are Naoussa (west of Thessaloniki) for potent though balanced and nicely tannic red, Aminteion, at 2,000 feet in the mountains of Macedonia, producing lighter red, Sitsa (near Joannina in Epirus) for a light mountain white of Debina grapes, and Metsovo in Epirus, which was replanted after phylloxera with Cabernet Sauvignon. But the most important new development in the country is the planting of the Sithonian peninsula, the middle one of the three fingers of Khalkidhiki, with Cabernet and other grapes, by the firm of Carras.

The island of Crete is second to the Peloponnese in acreage, but only third in production (Attica has far more productive vineyards). Crete has four local appellations, all for dark and more or less heavy and sweet reds: Daphnes, Archanes, Sitia and Peza – Peza being the seat of the island's biggest producer, its cooperative. The grapes are Kotsiphali, Mandilari and Liatico, old Cretan strains sometimes just called Mavro Romeiko.

Attica (including mainland Boetia and the island of Euboea) is Greece's most productive area, but overwhelmingly for retsina. Experiments with fine grapes on Euboea have not yet materialized. Delphi has a certain reputation for its red Mavroudi.

Next in importance for acreage and quality comes Cephalonia, which with the other Ionian (western) islands musters 25,000 acres. Cephalonia is known for its dry white Robola (also grown in Slovenia), its red Mavrodaphne, and its Muscat. Zakinthos to the south makes a white Verdea and red Byzantis (which have no appellation, but perhaps merit one).

The central mainland region of Thessaly also has 25,000 acres of vineyards, but only one appellation, Rapsani, a middle-weight red from Mt. Olympus.

The wines of the Aegean islands, the Dodecanese and the Cyclades, have more renown, notably the pale gold Muscat of Samos, the luscious Vino Santo and a curious semi-sparkling white of the volcanic Santorini, the red and the Muscat of Lemnos and the sweet Malvasia and Muscat of Rhodes. (Rhodes ordinary dry wine, sold as Lindos, is not in the appellation class.)

Malvasia is grown on many islands and is often their best product. Other island wines with esoteric reputations are the very dark Mavro of Paros and the Santa Mavra of Levkas, whose grape, the Vertzani, is unknown elsewhere.

Greece is modernizing her wine industry to take advantage of membership of the E.E.C.

GREEK PRODUCERS

Beso
Patras. A well-known merchant house.

Botrys
(Société Hellenique des Vins et Spiritueux) Athens.
Négociant specializing in Attic wines, plus those of Peza in Crete, the Peloponnese and Paros (the noted red Mavro).

J. Boutari
Salonika.
Merchant in Macedonian wines, specializing in Naoussa reds. His top red is Grande Réserve Boutari; also a pleasant white Le Lac aux Roches.

Andrew P. Cambas
PO Box 885, Athens. Founded 1869.
Major producers, bottlers and distillers with 2 big wineries at Kantza (Athens) and Mantinia, with a wide range of table and sparkling wines, ouzo and brandy. Domaine de Kantza is a dry white and Pendeli a good standard red from Cambas' 200 acres at Kantza. Mantinia is a fresh white and Cava Cambas a matured one.

Achaia Clauss
PO Box 35, Patras. 2m. cases. 20% exported.
The biggest and most famous Greek wine house, founded in 1861 by Gustav Clauss, a Bavarian, now owned by the Antonopoulos Company. Its imposing castellated buildings are unmistakable in Patras. The best-known wines are Demestica red and white, reliable blends, Castel Danielis red, Château Clauss (a barrel-aged red), the admirable Santa Helena, a 'hock-style' dry white of Roditis and Savatiano (the retsina grapes), Mavrodaphne of Patras, Santa Rose rosé and Muscatel. The firm has vineyards in the Peloponnese and Crete.

D. Courtakis
Athens. Founded 1895. 540,000 cases. A family merchant house. Brand names are Apollo, Apelia (full, dry white from Attic and Boetian grapes) and Courtakis, a dark, oaky Nemean red.

Oinoexagogiki Kalligas & G.E.P.E.
53 Patr. Loakim, Athens.
A firm with modern marketing ideas, specializing in well-above-average wines from the island of Cephalonia. Their winery there produces dry white Robola Kalliga, red Monte Nero and Kalliga's Rosé.

Karelas & Son
Patras. Merchant with a pale dry red called Aeolos.

Marcopoulo Cooperative
Attica. Founded 1914.
Dry whites Château Marco and Cava Mapko, from Savatiano and Fileri grapes, are aged 1 year before bottling. The Marco red, blended dark and soft for the German taste, is more pleasant than the oxidized, heavy white.

Minos, Miliarkis Brothers
Peza-Pediados, Crete. Exports.
Winery specializing in wines from the vineyards once cultivated by the Minoan civilization. Castello is the *reserva* red. Other wines are Minos Cava (dry white), Minos white and rosé, and Candia white and red.

Peza Cooperative
Iraklion, Crete. Est. 1933. The biggest Cretan coop, with 2,750 members, 8,650 acres. Exports to UK and elsewhere. Table wines under the name Logardo, from Liatiko and Mandilari grapes, Ekacri retsina and Mantiko superior 12.5° red.

Domaine de Porto Carras
Sithonia, Khalkidhiki. 100,000 cases.
The single most important new development in Greece: 4,500 acres planted by the arms tycoon John Carras on the middle prong of the Khalkidhiki peninsula with advice from Professor Peynaud of Bordeaux. Bordeaux varieties are mixed with Greek ones. Five 'Côtes de Méliton' wines are made: Blanc de Blancs (light and dry; Sauvignon predominating); Grand Vin Blanc (darker, heavier); Grand Vin Rouge; Château Carras (Bordeaux aspirations – 18–20 months in *barriques*, 2 years in bottle); and a rosé. The Château Carras 1977 had ripe, even rich aromas of Bordeaux with an extravagantly tannic finish that seems to need considerable bottle age.

Union des Cooperatives Vincoles de Samos
Kortaxis Street 2, Samos. Founded 1934. 670,000 plus cases. Exports to UK, USA, W. Europe.
40 member coops represent about 300 growers, producing Muscat de Samos in various grades of sweetness. Also Samena dry white from Muscat grapes, Retsina and rosé.

E. Tsantalis
Agios Paulos, Khalkidhiki. 275,000 cases.
A second-generation Macedonian merchant house which made its name with Olympic ouzo. 210 acres of vines including Cabernet and Sauvignon Blanc provide 20% of the grapes for a wide range of sound wines. These include wines made by the monks of Mt. Athos. Cava Tsantalis is matured in small barrels for 3 years. Other wines are Naoussa, Imiglykos and Muscat of Patras. Dr. Georg Tsantalis has hopes for good Greek Cabernets.

CYPRUS

It was the close connection of Cyprus with Britain that put the farthest east of the Mediterranean islands firmly into the business of making wine for export. Not only has she ancient and honourable wine traditions that centuries of Islamic rule somehow failed to extinguish, but British government from 1878 brought stability and a market.

Cyprus has no great range of wines to offer, but what she does she does well: produce low-cost sherries modelled on the Spanish, smooth dry red and white table wines and her own extremely luscious liqueur-wine, Commandaria. Commandaria is to Cyprus what Constantia was to South Africa or Tokay is to Hungary – except that it still tends mysteriously to be missed out of the roll-call of great dessert wines.

Cyprus has until very recently been intensely conservative about grape varieties. Having never been afflicted with phylloxera, and intending to stay untainted, she spurned new-fangled introductions and planted only three grapes: Mavron the black, Xynisteri the white, and Muscat of Alexandria. There is also a traditional red grape called Ophthalmo. Today there are promising experiments with superior grapes that suggest that the Troodos Mountains could be a mini-California.

All the island's quality vineyards lie on the south slopes of the Troodos Mountains, between 1,000 and 2,500 feet. Grape acreage has increased in 10 years by 25%, to 124,000 acres, creating a great inland sea of vines on the high plateaux and every pocket of hill-top soil. Some of the best vineyards are on almost pure red sand; others on grey chalk.

The best Commandaria is grown on the south slopes just north of Limassol. One famous village, Khalokhorio, makes it from pure Xynisteri – a light brown wine of considerable finesse which can be drunk young. Others, notably Zoopiyi and Yerasa, use Mavron and Ophthalmo to make a dark tawny wine, superb after five or more years in barrel. The grapes are simply sun-dried for 10 days in the vineyard, then pressed. No fortification is used and the wine reaches 15–16° alcohol. The commercial brands tend to be largely youngish Mavron. All the Khalokhorio wine, made in one cooperative, is bought for blending by one firm, Keo.

Four concerns dominate the Cyprus trade, three Limassol-based merchants (all very well equipped and modern) and the Sodap Cooperative. Etko/Haggipavlu, founded in 1844, produces Emva Cream sherry and some of the Hirondelle table wines for the British Bass Charrington, which owns 35% of the company. Their Semeli is a classic Cyprus red. Keo, founded in 1926, makes the smooth traditional Othello red, Aphrodite dry white, St. Pantaleimon sweet white and the pale, slightly fizzy Bellapais. Domaine d'Ahera is a prestige red of lighter character. Mosaic, their brand of sherries, includes a good very dry wine. Their St. John is perhaps the best commercial Commandaria.

Loel is the maker of the fine Negro red and a very clean Palomino dry white as well as Amathus (alias Kykko) table wines, Command sherries and Alasia Commandaria. Sodap is a group of cooperatives, with Afames as its flagship Mavron red and Arsinoe its traditional dry white. Salamis and Kolossi are other table-wine brands, St. Barnabas its Commandaria and Lysander its sherry.

TURKEY

If Noah's vineyard on the slopes of Mount Ararat was really the first, Turkey can claim to be the original home of wine. Hittite art of 4000 BC is possibly better evidence that Anatolia (central Turkey) used wine in highly cultivated ways. In relation to such a time span the long night of Islam has been scarcely more of an interruption than Prohibition was in the United States. For since the 1920s Turkey has again been making good wines; much better than her lack of a reputation leads us to expect. One of the most surprising bottles of fine wine I have ever drunk was a 1929 Turkish red – at a friend's house in Bordeaux. I took it for a Bordeaux of that famous vintage.

Turkey's vineyards are the fifth largest on earth (more than twice as great as Argentina's), but only a fraction of their produce is made into wine. Kemal Ataturk founded the twentieth-century wine industry in his drive to modernize the country. The state monopoly, Tekel, is much the biggest producer, with 21 wineries handling wines from all regions and dominating exports, particularly with popular bulk wines to Scandinavia. But there are 118 private wineries, two with very high standards.

The main wine regions are Trakya, the Thrace–Marmara region on the European side of the Bosphorus, the Aegean coast around Izmir, central Anatolia around Ankara and eastern Anatolia.

The majority of the grapes are local varieties whose names are unknown in the West, except in Trakya, where Cinsaut and Gamay and Sémillon (supported by Clairette) make the best-known red and white. A Gamay red, Hosbag (from Tekel), is not remarkable, but Trakya Kirmisi, made of the Turkish Papazkarasi and Adakarasi, is a good vigorous wine. *Kirmisi* is Turkish for red and *Beyaz* for white; *Sarap* for wine. Trakya Beyaz (dry Sémillon) is one of the most popular exports.

Kutman's Villa Doluca at Mürefte on the Sea of Marmara is the most distinguished independent local producer. Founded in 1926 (the first in modern Turkey) they now make two qualities of red: Doluca of Cinsaut and Papazkarasi and Villa Doluca of Gamay, Papazkarasi and Cabernet Sauvignon. In my experience this is the best Turkish red. Doluca also make oak-aged Sémillon, unaged Sémillon and some 'Johannisberg Riesling'.

The Aegean region counts Cabernet and Merlot (known, I believe, as 'Bordo') among its reds, along with Carignan and Calkarasi. Most of the white is made of Sultanye, the seedless table grape with no real wine-making potential. Some Sémillon and Muscat is grown – the Muscat probably the best.

Central Anatolia makes dry white Urgup from Emir grapes and sweet white Narbag from Narince, grown at Tokat. Eastern Anatolia is the home of the best known of Turkish reds, the heavy and powerful Buzbag, made of Bogazkarasi near Elâzig. This is the produce of Tekel, the state enterprise. Its private enterprise rivals includeYakut and Dikmen, reds aged respectively for four and two years from the largest independent firm, Kavaklidere (who are based in Ankara, but use grapes from as far apart as Thrace and eastern Anatolia). Yakut is said to contain some Cabernet as well as native varieties.

THE LEVANT AND NORTH AFRICA

Lebanon

What wine might be in the Levant, were it not for the followers of the Prophet, is a tantalizing topic. In 1840 Cyrus Redding had heard tell (he certainly had not been there) that 'Syria makes red and white wine of the quality of Bordeaux'.

But now we have current evidence that the eastern Mediterranean can make great wine. Noah's ancient land of Canaan, now the Bekaa valley, 3,000 feet above sea level at the foot of Mt. Lebanon, emerged in the 1970s as a producer to be compared with Bordeaux, just as Redding had reported.

During the early nineteenth century its reputation was for dry white *'vin d'or'* preserved in amphoras. In 1875 the Jesuits founded a vast underground winery at Ksara, with more than a mile of barrel-filled natural tunnels. This establishment, secularized in 1973, now dominates the local market, though the quality of its arrack is more celebrated than its wine.

The estate which suddenly fluttered the dovecots of the wine trade is Château Musar, at Ghazir, 16 miles north of Beirut. In the 1930s Gaston Hochar founded the property, with vineyards in the Bekaa valley 15 miles to the east. In 1959 his son Serge, after training in Bordeaux, became wine maker. Bottles started appearing in London. In 1982 he showed a range of vintages going back to the 1940s which demonstrated beyond doubt that the region can produce extraordinarily fine and long-lived reds based on Cabernet Sauvignon with some Cinsaut and Syrah, aged in *barriques* – not at all unlike big Bordeaux of ripe vintages. White wines are well made but less fine, clearly needing the coming introduction of better grape varieties.

Other Bekaa valley properties with aspirations are Domaine de Tournelles, Naquad and Kefraga.

Israel

The wine industry of Israel was a gift to the state by Baron Edmond de Rothschild, who founded the wineries at Richon-le-Zion near Tel Aviv and Zichron-Jacob on Mount Carmel near Haifa at the end of the nineteenth century. From their original aim of making sweet sacramental wine they have long since developed dry table and sparkling wines, principally with Carignan, Grenache and Sémillon, but latterly experimenting with all the classic varieties. Today there are some 7,000 acres of wine grapes in Israel, divided between the hills of Upper Galilee (an expanding area), Lower Galilee near Nazareth, Samaria, the coast between Haifa and Tel Aviv, Judea (Richon), Jerusalem and the Negev. Carmel is the established brand name on the international Kosher market, but recently some adequate Cabernet from Galilee and (better) Petite Syrah from Samson have been sold under the name Société Cooperative Vigneronne des Grandes Caves. 'The President's' sparkling wine is also well made.

Tunisia

The institution of an Office du Vin in 1970 marked the start of Tunisia's coordinated plan to make wines of export quality. Her vineyard area has been reduced from 124,000 to some 61,000 acres, all in the vicinity of Tunis (and ancient Carthage) on the north coast. There are now 13 state-owned, 13 cooperative and 10 private cellars offering a dozen wines for export. Muscats are the most characteristic wines of the country, as they are of the Sicilian islands lying not far off-shore. Reds, rosés and whites are made of French Midi-type grapes, in many cases using modern methods. As in Algeria the pale rosés are often the most attractive.

The biggest producer is the Union des Cooperatives Viticoles de Tunisie (route de Mornag, Djebel Djelloud). The union makes an unusual dry white Muscat, Muscat de Kelibia, from vineyards at the tip of Cap Bon to the northeast. It is highly aromatic, not overstrong at 11.8° but nonetheless a difficult wine to enjoy with a meal. Its best-quality red is Magon, from Tébourba in the valley of the river (Oued) Medjerdah, west of Tunis. Cinsaut and Mourvèdre in this 12° wine give it both roundness and more personality than the standard 11.5° Coteaux de Carthage. Other Union wines are Château Mornag (both red and rosé) from the Mornag hills east of Tunis, a pale dry Gris de Tunisie of Grenache and Cinsaut from the same region, and a dry Muscat-scented rosé called Sidi Rais.

The most notable wines of the state-owned Office des Terres Domaniales are the red Château Thibar, from the hills 85 miles west of Tunis up the Medjerdah valley, and Sidi Salem from Kanguet, near Mornag. Other producers to note are the Société Lomblot for their 12° red Domaine Karim from the Coteaux d'Utique, near the sea north of Tunis, Château Feriani for one of Tunisia's tastiest red wines from the same area, Héritiers René Lavau for their Koudiat, another strong red from Tébourba, and Société des Vins Tardi at Aïn Ghellal, north of Tébourba, for their Royal Tardi, which contains a touch of Pinot Noir. Perhaps better than any of these are the strong sweet dessert Muscats with the appellation Vin Muscat de Tunisie. What is lacking is good white wine.

Algeria

The biggest and most intensely planted of France's former North African colonies has reduced her wine-grape vineyard from 900,000 acres, its total of the 1960s, to not much more than 378,000 today – and her productivity by an even greater proportion. Most of this has been done by converting the fertile plains to cereals and concentrating on the hill vineyards which produced superior wine in French days. A dozen 'Crus' were indeed given VDQS status before independence.

Seven regions are recognized by the Office Nationale de Commercialization des Produits Viticoles as quality zones. They are all in the hills about 50 miles inland in the two western provinces of Oran and Alger. Oran has always been the bulk producer, with three quarters of Algeria's vines. The ONCV has standard labels that reveal nothing about the origin of the wine except its region – and in the case of its prestige brand, Cuvée le Président, not even that. Le Président is a matured faintly claret-like wine I have not found as good as the best regional offerings.

The western quality zone, the Coteaux de Tlemcen, lies close to the Moroccan border, covering north-facing sandstone hills at 2,500 feet. Red, rosé and white wines are all well made: strong, very dry but soft in the style the Algerians have mastered. The rosés and whites in particular have improved enormously with cool fermentation.

The Monts du Tessalah at Sidi-bel-Abbès to the northeast seem rather less distinguished; certainly less so than the Coteaux de Mascara, whose red wines in colonial days were frequently passed off as burgundy. Mascara reds are powerful and dark with real body, richness of texture and, wood-aged as they are sold today, a considerable aroma of oak and spice. A certain crudeness marks the finish. This I have not found in the Mascara white, dry though it is; it would be creditable in the South of France: pleasantly fruity, not aromatic but smooth and individual – probably as good as any white wine made in North Africa.

At Dahra the hills approach the sea. The former French VDQS Crus of Robert, Rabelais and Renault (now known as Taughrite, Aïn Merane and Mazouna) make smooth, dark and full-bodied reds and a remarkable rosé with a fresh almost cherry-like smell, light and refreshing to drink – a skilful piece of wine-making. Farther east and farther inland, in the province of Alger, the capital, the Coteaux du Zaccar makes slightly lighter, less fruity wines. Again the rosé, though less fruity than the Dahra, is well made. South of Zaccar and higher, at 4,000 feet, the Medea hills are cooler, and finer varieties are grown along with the standard Cinsaut, Carignan and Grenache. Cabernet and Pinot Noir go into Medea blends, which have less flesh and more finesse than Dahra or Mascara. The easternmost of the quality zones is Aïn Bessem Bouira, making relatively light (11.5°) reds and what some consider Algeria's best rosés.

Morocco

Morocco has the smallest wine-grape acreage of the North African wine countries (56,000 acres) but the tightest organization and the highest standards. The few wines that are 'AOG' (Appellation d'Origine Garantie') have similar controls to French appellation wines, strictly applied. They are produced by a central organization, SODEVI, which includes the important cooperative union of Meknès, and are bottled and sold by a Moroccan company in Brussels, the Comptoir des Vins du Maroc (Avenue des Arts 20, 1040 Bruxelles).

Four regions of Morocco produce fair wines, but by far the best and biggest is the Fez/Meknès area at 1,500–2,000 feet in the northern foothills of the middle Atlas mountains, where the regions of Sais, Beni Sadden, Zerkhoun, Beni M'Tir and Guerrouane are designated. The last two have achieved remarkable reds of Cinsaut, Carignan and Grenache, respectively sold abroad as Tarik and Chantebled (and in Morocco as Les Trois Domaines). Tarik is the bigger and more supple of the two, but both are smooth, long and impressive. Guerrouane also specializes in an AOG *vin gris*, a very pale dry rosé of Cinsaut and Carignan, which substitutes well for the white wines Morocco lacks. SODEVI at Meknès makes sound non-AOG red and rosé under the name Aïn Souala.

A little wine, but none of consequence, is made in the Berkane/Oujda area to the east near the Algerian border. The other principal areas are around Rabat, on the coastal plain, in the regions of Gharb, Chellah, Zemmour and Zaer. The brand names Dar Bel Amri, Roumi and Sidi Larbi, formerly used for pleasant soft reds from these zones, have been abandoned in favour of the regional names.

Farther south down the coast the Casablanca region has three wine zones: Zennata, Sahel and Doukkala. The first produces a solid 12° red marketed as Ourika. South of Casablanca the firm of Sincomar makes the standard drinking of every thirsty visitor, the Gris de Boulaouane. Boulaouane is the archetypal North African refresher: very pale, slightly orange, dry, faintly fruity, extremely clean and altogether suited to steamy Casablanca nights.

CALIFORNIA

The 1970s was the decade when California decisively took up her position in the world of wine. She had had what proved to be a false start, though a very promising one, a century earlier. An adolescent America was not ready for what she (and wine in general) had to offer. The generation of wine makers that followed the repeal of Prohibition did indispensable groundwork for an industry that appeared to be remarkably friendless. Hardly anyone was prepared for the impact when in the late 1960s Americans started to change their habits, to look outwards for new ideas, to start thinking about their environment, their diet and their health, and to discover that they had a well of the world's most satisfactory beverage in their own back yard.

From the early 1970s on, growth has been so rapid and change so breathless that one of the observers and critics closest to the scene in California, Bob Thompson, has compared an attempt to follow it to 'taking a census in a rabbit warren'. The figures hardly express the changes. In 1970 there were 220 wineries; in 1982, 540. In 1970 there were 170,000 acres of wine grapes; in 1982, 343,000. But beneath these figures, impressive as they are, everything was in ferment: grapes, men, priorities, areas, tanks and philosophy. They still are.

Predictably the other-drink businesses – brewers, distillers and, latterly, soft-drink manufacturers – have moved in to control what they can of the mass-production end of the market. Although Gallo, the company that has done most for wine in America, and sells an almost unbelievable proportion – one bottle in three – of American wine, is still run personally by the brothers who started it.

At the other extreme, in what rapidly and rather unkindly became known as boutique wineries, fashion has rocketed about from one winery to another as drinkers even newer to wine than the wine makers tried to make up their minds what they liked, at the same time as discovering who made it – or if he made it again the following year. There are enduring landmarks, but they are few and far between. Essentially this is an industry with no structure and very few rules.

There are four approaches to finding what you want in California, and you need them all. There is no escaping the dominance of the brand name. The grape variety is the only firm information available about what is in the bottle. The area of production is a good clue to the style of the wine, if not its quality. And the vintage date at least tells you how old it is – and often considerably more.

Access to the essentials in this chapter is therefore organized into three alphabetical directories: of brands, of grapes (and wine types) and of areas.

How good are the wines, and where do they fit into an international comparison?

In the last five years the top class of handmade wines have proved that they can outshine in blind tastings the very European wines they emulate. The reason why they do this with almost monotonous predictability is inherent in their nature. It is the fully ripe grape, a comparative rarity in France and Germany, that makes California wines comparable with the great vintages and the best vineyards of Europe – the only places where those flavours occur.

There is also, however, the rate of ripening and the question of soil to consider. Both of these have more bearing on the long-term quality of wine than California is at present inclined to allow. The concomitant disadvantage of the super-ripe grape is the relentless force of flavour that it gives. The taste tends to be so emphatic that a little goes a long way.

Heartiness suits Americans – at least the Americans of today. It suits many wine drinkers everywhere. But it is an important sign of the maturity of the California wine maker that today he is talking in terms of toning it down. A year or two ago the terms of highest praise were 'impressive fruit', 'heaps of varietal character', 'distinct notes of French oak'. Today 'delicacy', 'balance', 'harmony' and 'elegance' are becoming fashionable terms of approval. Americans now have less assertive wines from the Pacific northwest to compare with those of California. With what may be an over-reaction, some of the big California wineries have even started marketing extremely low-alcohol 'soft' wines.

California should not try to be all things to all men. It should make its own style of wine with all the formidable skill and sensitivity it can muster. It has nothing to fear from comparison – but nor has it as much to gain from it as it sometimes thinks.

Personal taste is the final arbiter – as I was reminded when I rashly asked a gathering in New York if they would really like all red Bordeaux to have the character of the great champion of modern vintages, 1961. 'Of course,' they said. What a fool I must be, not to want the most concentrated, the most overwhelmingly full-flavoured (but the least refreshing) of all wines with every meal.

THE CLIMATE

California's climate can only be understood in terms of the Pacific Ocean alongside and the effect of the long chain of 2,000-foot mountains that follows the coast. The prevailing northwest sea winds cause currents that bring very cold water from the depths to the surface close inshore. Sea-warmed air passing over the cold water vapourizes. The effect is dense fog just offshore all summer long.

Behind the mountains it is hot and dry. Every day in summer the Central Valley reaches 80° or 90°F (26° or 32°C) its hot air rises and draws colder air in from the sea to take its place. Every gap or pass in the coast range becomes a funnel for the coastal fog to seep inland.

Everyone who has been to San Francisco in spring or autumn has marvelled at the white blanket stealing under the Golden Gate by lunchtime, and by early evening mounting its towers and creeping in wisps over the surrounding hills. In summer the city is often shrouded in fog all day.

The same phenomenon happens far down the coast to the south, and its moderating influence is felt in places many miles inland. The exhilarating air of San Francisco Bay not only cools the Carneros vineyards at the mouth of the Napa Valley to the north. It penetrates, via the flats of the Sacramento River delta, as far inland as Lodi in the Central Valley.

Each coastal valley from Mendocino in the north to Santa Barbara in the south receives its regular draught of clammy air. At Monterey, where the Salinas Valley opens invitingly to the ocean, the chill prevents some grape varieties from ripening at all.

In other words topography, rather than latitude, is the determining factor in the climate of California. Its emerging vineyard areas therefore have to be studied and experimented with individually – a process that in many cases is still only at the beginning of its development.

THE CLIMATE REGION SYSTEM

The complexities of California's climate have led the Department of Viticulture at the Davis campus of the University of California to devise a climate zone system, to help growers plant grapes suitable to their area.

The basis of the system is 'heat-summation', which is a measure of the total number of 'degree-days' when a vine will be in active growth. The degree-days are arrived at by averaging each day's temperature between 1 April and 31 October, then subtracting 50°F (the temperature at which a vine becomes active).

For example, if the average temperature for ten days was 80°F, the heat summation would be 80–50=30×10=300 degree-days.

The state has been divided into five regions, which are mapped on page 31.

Region 1
The coolest, has 2,500 degree-days or less, the equivalent of such northern European vineyards as Champagne, the Côte d'Or and the German Rhine. Chardonnay, Riesling, Sauvignon Blanc, Cabernet and Pinot Noir are recommended. Region 1 only exists where the influence of the ocean is paramount.

Region 2
Has between 2,500 and 3,000 degree-days – an average temperature similar to Bordeaux. Most Region 1 grapes are also recommended for Region 2, although not so emphatically.

Region 3
Has between 3,000 and 3,500 degree-days, a total comparable to the Rhône valley. Recommended varieties include Sauvignon Blanc, Semillon, Carignane and Ruby Cabernet. Zinfandel does well but only has a qualified recommendation.

Region 4
With 3,500 to 4,000 degree-days, is comparable to the south of Spain and is therefore dessert-wine country, with the exception of Emerald Riesling, Barbera and Ruby Cabernet. Port grapes grow well.

Region 5
Has more than 4,000 degree-days. Souzão, Tinta Madera and Verdelho are highly recommended varieties in this North African-type climate.

The regions are built into the California system and are constantly referred to (e.g. in the notes on grapes that follow). Like all generalizations, however, they are riddled with qualifications and exceptions. California has just as many microclimates as equivalent parts of Europe. And in the ripening of grapes the average temperature may not be nearly so important as the timing of periods of unusual heat or cold. For example, the North Coast tends to grow warmer and less foggy towards vintage time, when in Bordeaux the chance of rain increases. The final spurt towards ripeness is therefore normally more rapid – which has a distinct effect on the style of the wine.

THE REGIONS

California is in the process of working out a system of designated viticultural areas, which will be referred to informally as appellations.

They should in no way be confused with French appellations, which include strict control of grape types, quantities produced and every other aspect of wine-making. California's are purely geographical. The rule is simply that 85 per cent of the grapes in the bottle must come from the viticultural area named on the label.

The broadest area is 'California' – used either for wine from an unprestigious grape-growing region, or for a blend of wines or grapes from several (which may, of course, be of the highest quality).

More specific are the counties. Their boundaries may or may not have viticultural significance, but at present their names are the only officially recognized areas that cover the whole state.

Areas under discussion and being gradually agreed will be both more and less specific: as unspecific, for example, as 'North Coast' and as pinpointed as Knight's Valley (a part of Sonoma affecting only one winery). 'North Coast' causes an argument because it is broad but carries an inference of quality. (It sounds cool.) One lobby wants six counties included; another only Napa, Sonoma and Mendocino. Surprisingly, it does not seem to have occurred to the folk of Sonoma that Napa is not a coast county at all.

An early decision was taken on the limits of the 'Napa Valley' – virtually the whole of Napa County, minus a rocky fraction on the borders of Lake County. 'Sonoma Valley' is quite different: a tightly drawn area in the south of the county. This is because other parts of Sonoma farther north, notably the Alexander, Dry Creek and Russian River valleys, all intend to acquire their own appellations.

In San Luis Obispo County the Edna Valley was soon designated as a precise area. Other appellations are under review. The following list includes all the counties with wineries, and grape-growing areas with some claim to being considered individual (and, by implication, above average quality) whose names are used on labels, whether legislation has defined them or not.

The Napa Valley. Until quite recently, the deep, fertile soil of the valley floor was cultivated in preference to the rocky slopes. Frost is a danger here: hence the oil heaters and windmills to disperse cold air.

CALIFORNIA'S SOIL

You hear surprisingly little about soil in California. With all the official stress on climate, it has been left to individuals to discover the characteristics of their own land – a startling contrast to France, where soil differences are given pride of place.

The assumption here is that any reasonably fertile and well-drained land will produce a good crop of grapes. Fertility is generally high because the land is new to agriculture – at least by European standards – and much of it is volcanic in origin. Drainage is rarely a problem because hardly any rain falls in the growing season. The deep soil of the valley floors can therefore be profitably used – though leaching of minerals by winter rains is proving a problem in some bottom-land vineyards.

The chief argument for planting in more difficult places, the rocky hillsides with their thin topsoil, is that the vine under stress, its crop limited by scarcity of water and nutrients, produces a smaller quantity of more concentrated juice that makes better wine.

Soil temperatures are also higher on the gravelly loam of the hills than on the heavier alluvial land of the valley floor. Whether this, or faster drainage, or better air circulation or any of several other factors is the most important, it is assumed that it is the physical rather than the chemical properties of the soil that determine quality. Chalk soil (such as produces the white wines with the utmost finesse in Europe, notably in Champagne and the sherry country) is rare in California – but at least one vineyard, Chalone, has been planted in an almost inaccessible and waterless spot for the sake of its alkaline properties.

Now more and more perfectionist growers are moving higher and higher into the hills, especially around the Napa Valley. Besides the search for more strenuous soil conditions, the higher they go, the cooler the growing season and the less the chance of early leafing followed by disastrous frost – an annual threat in the valley.

The years to come will bring more discussion of soils and more distinctions between vineyards. Already one winery, Diamond Creek, has three Cabernets distinguished as coming from Red Rock Terrace, Volcanic Hill and Gravelly Meadow.

APPELLATIONS, COUNTIES AND DISTRICTS OF CALIFORNIA

Alameda. East of San Francisco Bay, climate region 3, with 2,000 acres of vineyards. The Livermore Valley, best known for white wine, is its main district.

Alexander Valley. *See* Sonoma.

Amador. In the Sierra foothills 100 miles east of San Francisco. Regions 4-5. 1,000 acres, mainly Zinfandel. Shenandoah Valley is the principal vineyard area.

Anderson Valley. *See* Mendocino.

Arroyo Seco. *See* Monterey.

Calaveras. The county south of Amador. Regions 4-5. 60 acres.

Calistoga. *See* Napa.

Carmel Valley. *See* Monterey.

Carneros. *See* Napa.

Central Coast. At present an inexact term for counties between San Francisco and Santa Barbara.

Central Valley. A general term for the hot inland region often referred to as the San Joaquin Valley.

Chiles Valley. *See* Napa.

Cloverdale. *See* Sonoma.

Contra Costa. The county south of Alameda. Region 3. 900 acres. (No winery listed.)

Cucamonga. *See* Riverside.

Dry Creek Valley. *See* Sonoma.

Edna Valley. *See* San Luis Obispo.

El Dorado. Sierra foothill county north of Amador. Gold country. Regions 3-4. 225 acres.

Fresno. Central San Joaquin Valley. County with 39,000 acres of wine grapes and far more of table. Regions 4-5. Mainly Thompson Seedless, Barbera, French Colombard.

Geyserville. *See* Sonoma.

Greenfield. *See* Monterey.

Guerneville. *See* Sonoma.

Hecker Pass. *See* Santa Clara.

Healdsburg. *See* Sonoma.

Humboldt. On the coast north of Mendocino. 1 winery but no recorded vineyards.

Kenwood. *See* Sonoma.

Kern. Southern San Joaquin Valley. 38,000 acres of wine grapes in region 5 heat. Mainly Thompson Seedless, Barbera, Chenin Blanc, French Colombard.

Knight's Valley. *See* Sonoma.

La Cienega. *See* San Benito.

Lake. North of Napa, east of Mendocino. Region 3. 2,500 acres, mainly Cabernet Sauvignon, Zinfandel and Gamay. 5 wineries.

Livermore Valley. *See* Alameda.

Lodi. *See* San Joaquin.

Los Angeles. 4 wineries but no recorded vineyards.

Madera. Central San Joaquin Valley. Region 5. 32,000 acres of wine grapes, mainly Thompson Seedless, Barbera, Carignane, French Colombard. 3 wineries.

Marin. Just north of San Francisco across the Golden Gate. Region 1. 300 acres and 5 wineries.

McDowell Valley. *See* Mendocino.

Mendocino. The northernmost wine county, on the coast, ranging from region 1-3. A dozen wineries and 10,000 acres, still largely old plantations of Carignane and French Colombard but increasingly Cabernet and Zinfandel, Chardonnay, Pinot Noir and Johannisberg Riesling. Emerging viticultural areas are Anderson Valley near the coast, cool region 1, Ukiah Valley, region 3, and adjacent McDowell, Redwood and Potter valleys, regions 2-3.

Merced. Central San Joaquin Valley. Regions 4 and 5. 13,500 acres of wine grapes, mainly Thompson Seedless, Chenin Blanc, French Colombard, Barbera.

Modesto. *See* Stanislaus.

Monterey. The most important vineyard county of the Central Coast, with 32,000 acres and 10 wineries, chiefly in the Salinas Valley, region 1 at the ocean end, to Soledad, then warming to 3 at King City. (The Greenfield and Arroyo Seco areas come between the two.) Also Carmel Valley, region 1, and The Pinnacles (*see* Chalone Vineyards). All the best varieties are grown, led by Cabernet with 4,400 acres (though it can have difficulty ripening).

Mount Veeder. *See* Napa.

Napa. The most concentrated and prestigious vineyard county, with 26,000 acres ranging from region 1 in the south (Carneros, just north of San Francisco Bay) to 3 at Calistoga in the north. Now has about 100 wineries. Unofficially recognized appellations or sub-areas include Carneros, Mount Veeder, Yountville, Oakville, Rutherford (famous for Cabernet), St Helena, Spring Mountain and Calistoga on the western side, and Stag's Leap, Silverado Trail and Chiles Valley on the east, with Pope Valley tucked away up in the hills northeast. All the best grape varieties are grown: Cabernet leading with 5,000 acres, Chardonnay 3,000, Pinot Noir, 2,300, Zinfandel 1,900, Chenin Blanc 1,600, Johannisberg Riesling 1,400, Gamay 1,100, Gewürztraminer 400.

North Coast. At present an inexact term for the counties north of San Francisco Bay.

Oakville. *See* Napa.

Paicines. *See* San Benito.

Paso Robles. *See* San Luis Obispo.

The Pinnacles. *See* Monterey.

Placer. Sierra foothills county, north of El Dorado. Regions 3 and 5. 130 acres of wine grapes.

Pope Valley. *See* Napa.

Potter Valley. *See* Mendocino.

Redwood Valley. *See* Mendocino.

Riverside. The principal wine county of Southern California, east of Los Angeles, with 14,000 acres, mainly Thompson Seedless, but significant new acreages of good varieties at Temecula, led by Johannisberg Riesling despite being regions 3-4. There are 6 wineries at present.

Russian River Valley. *See* Sonoma.

Rutherford. *See* Napa.

Sacramento. Inland county northeast of San Francisco Bay, regions 4-5, with 3,000 acres, mainly of Zinfandel, Chenin Blanc, Cabernet and Gamay, and 2 wineries.

St. Helena. *See* Napa.

Salinas Valley. *See* Monterey.

San Benito. County inland from Monterey, region 3, with 4,600 acres, almost all planted by Almadén in Chardonnay, Cabernet, Pinot Noir, etc. Paicines and La Cienega are local names sometimes cited on labels.

San Bernardino. Largely desert (region 5) county east of Los Angeles with over 7,000 acres of Zinfandel, Mission, Grenache, Palomino, etc. Cucamonga is the wine district, with 5 wineries.

San Diego. Southernmost coast county, regions 4-5, with 240 acres of mixed vines and 3 wineries.

San Francisco. No vineyards, but at least 2 wineries recorded, 1 of them on a pier in the harbour.

San Joaquin. The northern county of the central San Joaquin Valley with 37,000 acres of wine grapes. Most is region 5, but the Lodi area is region 4 and specializes in Zinfandel, some 11,000 acres of it. Carignane, Petite Sirah and French Colombard are the other principal grapes. The dozen wineries in the county include the huge Franzia and Guild.

San Luis Obispo. The coastal county south of Monterey, relatively new to wine-growing but with 4,700 acres in 3 areas, Paso Robles/Templeton (region 3), Shandon and the cooler Edna Valley running south from San Luis Obispo city. Cabernet, Zinfandel, Chardonnay and Sauvignon Blanc are the main grapes being grown. There are 17 wineries.

San Mateo. The county immediately south of San Francisco has 6 recorded acres of vines and 3 wineries.

Santa Barbara. The southern central coast county, with 2 valleys in regions 2-3 mustering 7,000 acres, mostly of Johannisberg Riesling, Cabernet, Chardonnay and Pinot Noir. The Santa Maria and Santa Ynez valleys are up-and-coming appellations with 19 wineries.

Santa Clara. South of San Francisco Bay but sheltered from the coast by the Santa Cruz Mountains. The Hecker Pass in south Santa Clara is region 3, the Santa Cruz Mountain vineyards region 1. The 1,600 acres are divided between Zinfandel and cool-climate varieties. 30 wineries include the giant Almaden and Paul Masson and many small country ones.

Santa Cruz. Central Coast county, south of San Mateo. Only 94 acres of wine grapes, but 12 wineries.

Santa Maria Valley. *See* Santa Barbara.

Santa Ynez Valley. *See* Santa Barbara.

Shenandoah Valley. *See* Amador.

Silverado Trail. *See* Napa.

Sonoma. Large, varied and important county between Napa and the ocean, its 29,000 acres of vines distinctly divided into: Sonoma Valley, just north of the Bay, region 1 warming up to region 2 at Kenwood; Russian River Valley, long and diverse, region 1 at the ocean end near Guerneville, to region 3 farther north and inland near Cloverdale; Dry Creek Valley, an offshoot northwest from the centre of the Russian River Valley near Healdsburg, regions 2-3; Alexander Valley, the centre of the Russian River Valley between Healdsburg and Geyserville, also regions 2-3; Knight's Valley, east of Alexander Valley and a shade warmer. Sonoma has the biggest plantings in the state of Gewürztraminer, Pinot Noir and high-quality Zinfandel, and important ones of Cabernet and Chardonnay. There are 94 wineries.

Sonoma Valley. *See* Sonoma.

Spring Mountain. *See* Napa.

Stag's Leap. *See* Napa.

Stanislaus. Central San Joaquin Valley county with 19,000 acres, mostly region 5 and largely Carignane, French Colombard, Chenin Blanc, Grenache and Ruby Cabernet. The one winery, Gallo, at Modesto, is the world's biggest.

Temecula. *See* Riverside.

Templeton. *See* San Luis Obispo.

Tulare. Southern San Joaquin, region 5, with 17,000 acres, largely Barbera, Carignane and French Colombard.

Ukiah Valley. *See* Mendocino.

Ventura. Coastal county just north of Los Angeles with 7 acres and 1 winery.

Winery Lake. A much-cited source of high-quality, cool-climate grapes in the Carneros region of Napa.

Yolo. County east of Napa, region 4, with 700 acres, mainly Chenin Blanc, and 1 winery.

Yountville. *See* Napa.

California wine prices

Prices are given in the California entries for a large cross-section of the wines. These were the prices prevailing in retail stores in San Francisco in March 1982. Nothing is less stable than a retail price and they can be considered as nothing more than an indicator of the values put on the wines in question by the market at the time. They do not tell us which were selling well and which were overpriced and sticking. Nor do they necessarily agree with prices in other cities or states. But they do record how the wineries viewed their own products in relation to their competitors.

To draw any useful conclusions one would have to repeat the exercise at intervals over at least 10 years.

Varietals and varieties

The useful word 'varietal' was coined in California as shorthand for a wine that is either made entirely from, or derives its character from, one named grape variety. Up to 1983 the law required that the named variety be 51% of the total. From 1983 the requirement is 75%. Most high-quality varietals have long been closer to 100%.

On a semantic note, varietal is an epithet describing a wine. It is not a noun meaning a specific sort of grape. That noun is variety. The Chardonnay grape is a variety; its wine is a varietal wine.

GRAPES AND GENERIC WINE NAMES

Angelica

A fortified sweet wine traditional to California, usually made from the old Mission grape. Heitz makes the best-known example.

Barbera

The Italian red variety has good acidity in hot regions; used mainly for blending in California. Increasing acreage in the Central Valley. Recommended for climate regions 3 and 4. Produces 5 to 8 tons an acre.

Burgundy

An accepted term for any red wine, with the vague implication that it should be dark and full-bodied (unlike real burgundy). California burgundy is usually slightly sweet. But it is not all low quality; some reputable firms use the term for good wine.

Cabernet Sauvignon (Cab. Sauv.)

Makes California's best red: fruity, fragrant, tannic, full-bodied. Needs maturing in oak, and at least 4 years in bottle. Also makes very pretty rosé. Highly recommended for region 1 and recommended for 2. Crop is 4 to 6 tons an acre. The best Cabernets come from the central Napa Valley, parts of Sonoma and certain parts of the Central Coast. Total acreage has increased from 6,600 in 1977 to 26,000 in 1982.

Carignane (Carig.)

A high-yield – 8 to 12 tons an acre – red blending grape recommended for region 3 and little seen as a 'varietal'.

Carnelian (Carn.)

A new red grape produced at Davis to give Cabernet-flavoured wines in hot regions.

Chablis

Despite justified French protests that this is a part of France, it remains the uninformed American's term for (relatively) dry white wine from California, or anywhere else.

Champagne

Until some imaginative new name for California sparkling wine appears, the name of the French region will continue to be used – although not by the French.

Charbono

Little-used Italian red grape produced by two Napa wineries.

Chardonnay (Chard.)

California's most successful white grape, capable of great wines in the Burgundian tradition with age, and sometimes fermentation, in oak. Nice judgement is needed not to produce overintense, ponderous wines (especially in Napa). Parts of Sonoma and the Central Coast (Monterey) tend to have a lighter touch. The best examples age for 10 years or more in bottle. Highly recommended for region 1, recommended for region 2, but surprisingly now also rather good in Central Valley region 3. Acreage has increased from 3,000 to 17,000 acres in 10 years and more is needed. Yield is 4 to 6 tons an acre.

Chenin Blanc (Ch. Bl.)

A surprisingly popular, usually rather dull white grape recommended for region 1 but adequate in regions 2 and 3, appreciated for its high crop – 6 to 10 tons – and clean, adaptable flavour, pleasant when semi-sweet (although best dry); good in blends; not needing age. Acreage in the state has increased in 10 years from 9,600 to 32,000.

Chianti

The Italian name still unfortunately used as a 'generic' for sweetish reds of moderate to poor quality.

Emerald Riesling (Em. Ries.)

An original Davis University white grape (Riesling × Muscat) recommended for enormous crops (6 to 12 tons) and fruity flavours in warm region 4. Scarcely an improvement on (e.g.) French Colombard for popular cheap whites.

Flora

Another Davis-bred white derived from Gewürztraminer, moderately recommended for regions 1 and 2. Crops 4 to 7 tons an acre. Makes tolerable sweetish wine.

French Colombard (Fr. Col.)

Very popular white blending grape recommended for regions 3 and 4, where it gives 6 to 10 tons an acre and maintains good fresh acidity. Also used for sparkling wine and sometimes as a 'varietal', although 'weedy' describes its flavour rather well. Acreage has doubled to 44,000 acres in 10 years.

Fumé Blanc (Fumé Bl.)

See Sauvignon Blanc.

Gamay Beaujolais (Gamay Beauj.)

Not the Beaujolais grape but a form of Pinot Noir, productive in cool regions but not recommended anywhere.

Gamay (Napa Gamay)

The Beaujolais grape, or something very like it. Moderately recommended for regions 1 and 2. Crops well, 6 to 9 tons an acre. Some recent Napa versions have been good enough to encourage its use. Acreage has risen from 1,400 to 5,400 over 10 years.

Gewürztraminer (Gewürz.)

After a hesitant start, a great success in California, where its wine is oddly softer and less spicy than in Alsace. Recommended for region 1. Crops 4 to 6 tons an acre. 10 years have seen acreage rise from 650 to 3,600 acres. More is needed.

Golden Chasselas

An alias of the Palomino, the best sherry grape. Produces 6 to 10 tons an acre in region 5.

Gray Riesling (Gray Ries.)

Not a Riesling but a minor French grape, Chauché Gris, related to the Trousseau of the Jura. Adequate white table wine, not recommended by Davis. There are some 2,400 acres.

Green Hungarian

A minor white grape, reasonably fruity and acidic, not recommended but offered by a few wineries.

Grenache (Gren.)

The pale red blending and pink-wine grape of the south of France, recommended for region 2. Crops 5 to 9 tons. High sugar content makes it popular for dessert wines in warmer regions.

Grignolino (Grig.)

Non-recommended red grape, presumably from Italy, used by 1 or 2 wineries in cool regions to make off-beat red or rosé, sometimes distinctly Muscat flavoured.

Johannisberg Riesling (or White Riesling) (J.R.)

Commonly called 'J.R.' for short. The real Rhine Riesling, surprisingly a great success in California's coolest areas (highly recommended in region 1, recommended in 2). The dry equivalents of German Kabinetts are rarely as good as the sweet or very sweet wines. Late-picking with botrytis ('noble rot') is triumphant.

California's faster ripening also seems to hasten the maturing of the wine, which tastes fully developed in 2 or 3 years – much sooner than in Germany. The crop is 4 to 6 tons an acre (much lower than in Germany). There are 10,000 acres.

Malbec

The Bordeaux blending grape. There is very little in California but more is being planted.

Malvasia Bianca

The common Italian grape, recommended for dessert wines in regions 4 and 5 but capable of pleasant, soft table wine in cooler areas.

Merlot

The Pomerol grape; a coming thing in California both for blending with Cabernet and as a 'varietal'. It is better blended. Acreage is 10 times the 300 acres of 10 years ago (mainly in Napa, Sonoma and Monterey). Not officially recommended, but best in region 1.

Mission

The coarse old grape of the Franciscan missionaries. Some 4,000 acres are left in regions 4 and 5. Crops 6 to 12 tons an acre, used in dessert wines (*see* Angelica)!

Muscat or Moscato

The best is Muscat de Frontignan or Moscato Canelli, recommended for white table wines in regions 2 and 3; for dessert wines in hotter areas. Crop 4 to 6 tons an acre. Its best production is a very sweet, low-alcohol wine so unstable that it must be kept refrigerated. There are only 1,400 acres in the state. Muscat of Alexandria is a hot-climate grape grown mainly for eating.

Nebbiolo

Piedmont's noble grape, never yet given a fair chance in California, although fog is the very thing it likes best.

Petite Sirah (Pet. Sir.)

California's name for a low-grade French grape, Duriff. Useful for giving colour and tannin to blends. Recommended for region 2 (4 to 8 tons an acre). Most is grown in Monterey and (oddly) the San Joaquin Valley.

Pinot Blanc (P.Bl.)

Like a low-key Chardonnay, recommended for region 1 but little planted.

Pinot Noir (P.N.)

Burgundy's red grape is widely regarded as the last great hurdle for California's wine makers – early results were over-strong, heavy and dull. The late 1970s have seen intermittent but increasing success. Recommended for region 1 but only 3 to 4 tons an acre. The 11,000 acres are 3 times the figure of 10 years ago.

Pinot St. George (P.St.Geo.)

A minority speciality of very few wineries. Most of the 700 acres are in Monterey. Never exciting wine.

Port

A 'generic' name taken from the Old World for sweet dessert wine which rarely resembles the Portuguese original – although it may well have qualities of its own.

Rkatsiteli

A (white) Russian variety occasionally seen. In cool regions it makes adequate, quite lively dry wine.

Ruby Cabernet (Ruby Cab.)

A Davis-bred Cabernet × Carignane with really useful qualities: a high yield – 6 to 8 tons – of Cabernet-flavoured red from regions 3 and 4, too hot for Cabernet. There are some 17,000 acres, mainly in the San Joaquin Valley.

Sauvignon Blanc (Sauv. Bl.)

Newly fashionable, but always potentially excellent in California. Its best wine is closer to white Graves than Pouilly Fumé, although its frequent alias of Fumé Blanc suggests the Loire. It can be light and 'herbaceous' or oak-aged, solid and of Chardonnay quality. Highly recommended for region 1, recommended for regions 2 and 3. Crops 4 to 7 tons an acre. There are still only about 7,000 acres, but success in Sonoma, Monterey and Central Coast counties will encourage more.

Semillon (Sem.)

Bordeaux's sweet-wine and Australia's dry-wine grape, little exploited yet in California. Recommended for regions 2 and 3 (1 might be better). Crops 4 to 6 tons an acre. There are some 3,000 acres.

Sherry

California 'sherry' has never achieved the standard of imitation of the Spanish original found in South Africa. There are some tolerable sweet dessert wines under the name.

Souzão

One of the Portuguese port grapes used for some of California's best sweet dessert wines.

Sylvaner (Sylv.)

Once more popular than it is today for poor man's Riesling. Recommended for region 2, though much the best I have had came from Monterey in region 1. Crops 4 to 6 tons. Only 1,400-odd acres.

Syrah

The splendid red of the Rhône and Australia is a newcomer to California with a tiny acreage. Regions 2 and 3 may suit it. The first, from Phelps, was excellent.

Thompson Seedless

A neutral white table, dessert and distilling wine grape never mentioned on the label, but present in many jug whites and perhaps sparklers. One third of the State's total of 250,000 acres (all in the San Joaquin Valley) is crushed for wine.

Zinfandel (Zin.)

California's own red grape, possibly of Italian origin, immensely successful and popular for all levels of wine from cheap blends to fresh light versions and to galumphing sticky blackstrap. The best have excellent balance, a lively raspberry flavour and seem to mature indefinitely. Recommended for region 1 but grown everywhere – 30,000 acres of it. Crops 4 to 6 tons an acre.

CALIFORNIA WINERIES

It is a dull (and unusual) week in California when another new winery (or wineries) does not announce itself. The yeast of romance and experiment is so active that any list is out of date before it comes back from the printers.

Like the rest of this book, therefore, the following survey of the California wineries is a record of a moment in history: the autumn of 1982, with as much hard fact as the wineries cared to make known about themselves and as much explanatory or critical comment as experience and space allows.

Specifically, each entry states (if the information was available) the location of the winery, its ownership, date of foundation, the name of the wine maker (a key figure in determining quality and style), vineyards owned (if any) and the principal wines produced. In many cases, one or two sample prices are given for comparison. A note on these prices appears on page 417. The most striking feature is the number of wineries founded in 1979 and since. Clearly, any critical evaluation on the basis of two or three vintages is extremely tentative: there simply has not been enough time for consistency – or lack of it – to make itself felt. So there are many entries which belong here as a matter of record, but where evaluation must wait.

The basic facts were collected in a survey that was made by the Wine Institute of California in 1982. As to the critical opinion, it is my own unless I specify otherwise.

The Rhine House at the Beringer/Los Hermanos winery in St. Helena reflects the origins and the aspirations of a pioneer German wine-making family a century ago

Acacia

Napa, *Napa*. Founded 1979.
Partners: Mike Richmond and Jerry Goldstein. Up to 15,000 cases. 50 acres in Carneros, Napa. Wines: Chard., P.N.
Prices: Carneros Chard. '80, $14.00; P.N. '79, $15.00.

The '79 Pinot Noir from this infant enterprise had exciting qualities of freshness, the berry smell of Pinot Noir and the soft texture of burgundy (and almost its price) – clear indication that the Carneros district is right for the variety.

Adler Fels

Santa Rosa, *Sonoma*. Founded 1980.
5,000 cases. Wines: J.R., Gewürz., Cab.

d'Agostini

Near Plymouth, Shenandoah Valley, *Amador*. Founded 1856.
Owners: The d'Agostini family. Visits. 125 acres of Zin., Carig., Moscato Canelli, etc.

They make traditional rustic wines for locals.

Ahern Winery

San Fernando, *Los Angeles*. Founded 1978.
Wine maker: Jim Ahern. 3,500 cases. Wines: Sauv.Bl., Chard., Zin., P.N.

Ahlgren Vineyard

Boulder Creek, *Santa Cruz*. Founded 1976.
Wine maker: Dexter Ahlgren. 1,000 cases of Chard., Sem., Cab.Sauv., Zin.

Ahlgren's '78 Cabernet was rapturously received by the critics.

Alexander Valley Vineyards

Healdsburg, *Sonoma*. Founded 1964.
Owners: The Wetzel family. Wine maker: Hank Wetzel. Visits by appt. 12,500 cases plus. 240 acres in Alexander Valley, Sonoma. Wines: Chard., Ch.Bl., J.R., Gewürz., Cab.Sauv.
Prices: J.R. '80, $4.99; Gewürz. '80, $6.25.

Dry Burgundian-style Chardonnay with life and length, accepted in England as one of California's best and an indication of the ideal climate of the Alexander Valley.

Almadén Vineyards

San Jose, *Santa Clara*. Founded 1852.
Owners: National Distiller & Chemical Corporation.
President: John P. McClelland. Wine maker: Klaus Mathes. Visits. 13.5 m. cases. 6,766 acres in Monterey and San Benito. Wines: about 60 different wines under Almadén, Charles LeFranc and Le Domaine labels.
Prices: Chard. $5.49; Cab. $5.49; Jug $2.87.

One of the historic names, a pioneer of quality after Prohibition and of the move south down the Central Coast with huge plantings in San Benito in the 1960s. Now the third or fourth largest wine company in America and the largest so-called 'premium' one. Its only wines that get any critical attention are a pleasant, sweetish Gewürztraminer, a very decent light Cabernet and some quite good sparkling wine, especially the pale pink, fruity Pinot Noir Eye of the Partridge. The Charles LeFranc (the founder) label is used for higher-priced varietals. A new joint venture with Laurent Perrier makes a Blanc de Blanc modelled on Coteaux Champenois.

Alta Vineyard Cellar

Calistoga, *Napa*. Founded 1878, refounded 1979.
Owners: Benjamin and Rose Falk. Visits by appt. 2,100 cases. 7 acres in Napa Valley. Wines: Chardonnay only.

The original winery (next door to Schramsberg) was visited by Robert Louis Stevenson. The new one is to be a Chardonnay specialist.

Amador Foothill Winery

Plymouth, *Amador*. Founded 1980.
Wine maker: Ben Zeitman. 3,000 cases. Wines: Wh.Zin., Zin., Ch.Bl., Cab.Sauv., Sauv.Bl.

Small Shenandoah Valley vineyard. The winery is excavated in the ground for natural cooling.

Anderson Wine Cellars

Exeter, *Tulare*. Founded 1980.
Wine maker: Don Anderson. 2,000 cases of Ruby Cab., Ch.Bl.

S. Anderson Vineyard

Yountville, *Napa*. Vineyard founded 1971, winery 1979.
Owner and wine maker: Stanley B. Anderson Jr. Visits. 2,100 cases. 22 acres in Yountville. Wines: Chard. and sparkling wine only.

Argonaut Winery

Ione, *Amador*. Founded 1976.
Wine maker: Neal Overboe. 2,100 cases. Wines: Zin. and Barbera.

Arroyo-Sonoma Winery

see The California Wine Company.

Baldinelli Vineyards

Plymouth, *Amador*. Founded 1972.
Wine maker: Edward Baldinelli. 2,100 cases. Wines: Cab. Sauv., Zin.

Ballard Canyon Winery

Solvang, *Santa Barbara*. Founded 1978.
Owner: Gene Hallock. Wine maker: Robert Indelicato. Visits by appt. 5,000-6,000 cases. 40 acres in Santa Ynez Valley, Santa Barbara. Wines: Cab.Sauv. (red and white), Chard., J.R. and late-harvest.

Balverne Winery and Vineyards

Windsor, *Sonoma*. Founded 1980.
President: B. J. Bird. Wine maker: Douglas Nalle. No visits. 20,000 cases. 200 acres in Chalk Hill area of Sonoma County. Wines: Chard., J.R., Scheurebe, Gewürz., Sauv.Bl., Cab.Sauv., Zin.

The vineyards look excellent. A winery to watch.

Bandiera Winery

see The California Wine Company.

Barengo Winery

Acampo, nr. Lodi, *San Joaquin*. Founded 1934.
Owner: Berdugo Hills Inc. 800,000 cases, 640 acres at Lodi, Modesto, Fresno.

A wide range of good-value generics and some modest varietals, including Ruby Cabernet.

Beau Val Wines

Plymouth, *Amador*. Founded 1979.
Wine maker: D. D. Cobb. 1,250-5,000 cases. Wines: oak-aged Zin., Pet.Sir., Sauv.Bl., etc.
Price: Zin. '79, $5.25.

Beaulieu Vineyard

Rutherford, *Napa*. Founded 1900.
Owners: Heublein, Inc. President: Legh Knowles. Wine maker: Thomas Selfridge. 250,000 cases. Vineyards at Rutherford and in the Carneros region. Wines: Cab.Sauv., Chard., Sauv.Bl., J.R., P.N., Rosé, burgundy, Muscat de Frontignan.
Prices: Chard. $10.00; Cab. $7.99; Jug $3.50.

The foundation of a French family, the de Latours, which set the pace for the Napa Valley throughout the 1940s, '50s and '60s under a wine maker of genius, the Russian-born André Tchelistcheff. Tchelistcheff retired in 1973 and is now consultant to many wineries. At Beaulieu he pioneered small-barrel ageing and malolactic fermentation for reds, cold fermentation for whites (the basis of most California practice today) and discovered the virtues of the Carneros region south of Napa for cool-climate varieties.

Tchelistcheff's masterpiece (or the one that has lasted best) is the Georges de Latour Private Reserve Cabernet. Bottles from the 1950s and '60s are excellent, and the tradition is continued by his successors. The grapes are grown on Rutherford land still owned by the founding family. Pinot Noir (a Tchelistcheff passion) has never quite reached this standard, but Chardonnays have been brilliant, the standard Cabernet and the Napa burgundy are very good, and there was once a sparkling Pinot Noir rosé I still dream about.

Beringer/Los Hermanos Vineyards

St. Helena, *Napa*. Founded 1876.
Owners: Nestlé. Wine maker: Myron Nightingale. Visits. 140,000 cases. 800 acres of vineyards in Carneros, Napa Valley and Knight's Valley, Sonoma. Most table wine varieties plus port, sherry, dessert malvasia and brandy.
Prices: Chard. $9.42; Cab. $7.83; Jug $3.75.

One of the great old stone-built wineries of Napa, with coolie-cut tunnels into the hills as its original cellars. Under the Beringers it declined, was bought in 1971 by Nestlé, who fixed it on an upward course. Nightingale is particularly skilful with white wines; his Fumé Blanc, Riesling (especially late-harvest from Sonoma) and Chardonnay are setting the pace. There is good report of his latest Cabernets.

Los Hermanos is the second label.

Bernardo Winery

San Diego, *San Diego*. Founded 1889.
Owner/wine maker: Ross Rizzo. 4,000 cases. Table and dessert wines.

Boeger Winery

Placerville, *El Dorado*. Founded 1973.
Wine maker: Greg Boeger. 9,000 cases. 20 acres plus. Wines: Cab. Sauv., Zin., J.R., Ch.Bl., Chard., Sauv.Bl. Also 'Sierra Blanc' and 'Hangtown Red'.

Bogle Vineyards Winery

Clarksburg, *Yolo*. Founded 1979.
Wine maker: Richard Vierra. 15,000 cases of Ch.Bl., Pet.Sir. (red and rosé).

Borra's Cellar

Lodi, *San Joaquin*. Founded 1975.
Wine maker: Steve Borra. 500 cases of Barbera and Carignane.

Bouchaine Vineyards

Napa, *Napa*. Founded 1924, refounded 1981.
Managing partner: David Pollak Jr. Wine maker: Jerry Luper. 80,000 cases Private label, 17,000 Bouchaine label. Wines: Chard., P.N., Sauv.Bl.

The first bonded winery in the Carneros district, bought by Beringer in 1955 and the present partners in 1981. The appointment of Jerry Luper (from Chateau Montelena) as wine maker indicates high ambitions.

Brander

Santa Ynez. *Santa Barbara*. Founded 1979.

Fred Brander makes 3,000 cases of outstanding Sauvignon Blanc.

Brookside Vineyard Company

Guasti, *San Bernardino*. Founded 1832 in Monterey, moved to Guasti 1916.
Owners: Beatrice Foods. President: René Biane. Wine maker: William Wieland. Visits. 835,000 cases. Grapes mainly from Cucamonga and Temecula for a range of over 100 wines under labels including Brookside, Biane, Guasti, E. Vache and (for the better varietals including Zin. and Pet.Sir.) Assumption Abbey.

One of the oldest firms in California, until recently only distributed there but now nationally and in Canada, Central America and Japan.

David Bruce Winery

Los Gatos, *Santa Clara*. Founded 1964.
Principal: David Bruce. Wine maker: Steve Millier. Visits. 16,500 cases. 25 acres in the Santa Cruz Mountains. Wines: Chard., P.N., Cab.Sauv., Zin., Pet.Sir., J.R.
Prices: Zin. '79, $7.50; Chard. '79, $10.00; P.N. '78, $12.00.

The owner believes in wine on a heroic scale from very ripe grapes. The results can impress or oppress, according to taste.

Buehler Vineyards

St. Helena, *Napa*. Founded 1978.
Wine maker: John Buehler Jr. 7,500 cases. Wines: Cab.Sauv., Zin., Musc.Bl., P.Bl.

Buena Vista Winery and Vineyards

Sonoma, *Sonoma*. Founded 1857, refounded 1943.
Owner: A. Racke. Wine maker: Don Harrison. Visits. 73,000 cases. 600 acres in Carneros and Napa. Many table and dessert wines.
Prices: Chard. $7.98; Cab. $7.65; Jug $4.15.

Historically important as the winery of Agoston Haraszthy, 'the father of California wine'. Restarted in 1943 by Frank Bartholomew, who was ahead of his time but never made great wine here. Now with German owners (since 1979) and new vineyards, the prospects seem good. At present the whites (Fumé Blanc) and Zinfandel are the wines to try.

Burgess Cellars

St. Helena, *Napa*. Founded 1972.
Owner: Tom Burgess. Wine maker: Bill Sorenson. Visits. 30,000 cases. 70 acres in Napa County. Wines: Zin., Cab.Sauv., Chard., J.R. (late-harvest).

This was the original little Souverain winery where Lee Stewart made great Cabernet in the 1960s. It was bought and rebuilt by an ex-pilot in the 1970s and is best known for Cabernet Sauvignon Vintage Select, barrel-fermented Chardonnay and heady Zinfandel.

Bell Canyon Cellars is a second label.

The Buena Vista winery at Sonoma was the scene of Agoston Haraszthy's epoch-making experiments with European grape varieties

Davis Bynum Winery

Healdsburg, *Sonoma*. Founded 1975.
Wine maker: Davis Bynum. 20,000 cases. Wines: Chard., Fumé Bl., Gewürz., Cab.Sauv., P.N., Zin.

Cache Cellars

Davis, *Solano*. Founded 1978.
Wine maker: Charles Lowe. 2,500 cases of Chard., Cab.Sauv., Zin., P.N.

Cadenasso Winery

Fairfield, *Solano*. Founded 1906.
50,000 cases of Grig., Cab.Sauv., Zin., Ch.Bl.

Cadlolo Winery

Lodi, *San Joaquin*. Founded 1913.
100,000 cases (mostly in bulk) of generic and dessert wines.

Cakebread Cellars

Oakville, *Napa*. Founded 1973.
Owner: Jack Cakebread. Wine maker: Bruce Cakebread. Visits by appt. 15,000 cases. 22 acres in Napa Valley. Wines: Cab.Sauv., Zin., Sauv.Bl., Chard.
Prices: Chard. '80, $12.50; Zin. '79, $10.00.

Specialists in dry Sauvignon Blanc from their own vines. Also dry Chardonnay, but rich pungent reds including a 14° Zinfandel from Beatty Ranch grapes.

Calera Wine Company

Hollister, *San Benito*. Founded 1975.
Owners: Josh and Jeanne Jensen. Wine maker: Steve Doerner. Visits by appt. 6,250 cases. 24 acres of lime-rich hill in San Benito. Wines: Zin. and P.N.
Prices: P.N. '79, $18.00; Zin. '79, $7.50.

Specialists in estate-bottled Pinot Noirs and distinct named-vineyard Zinfandels from San Benito, San Luis Obispo and Butte counties. Also botrytis-infected dessert Zinfandel Essence for the curious.

California Growers

Tulare, *Tulare*. Founded 1936.
Owner: Robert Setrakian. 600,000 cases. Wines: Sherries, Ruby Cab., Fr.Col., Ries., Cab.Sauv., J.R. from vineyards in Sierra foothills southeast of Fresno.

The cooperative-sounding name California Growers owns several brands, none of them much above run-of-the-mill. They include Growers, L. le Blanc, Bounty and Setrakian (which has a recommended brandy).

The California Wine Company

Cloverdale, *Sonoma*. Founded 1937, refounded 1975 as Bandiera Winery.
Owners: The California Wine Company. President: Adolph Mueller II. Visits. 100,000 cases. Wines: Cab.Sauv., P.N., Zin., Chard., J.R., Gray Ries., Sauv.Bl., Col.

A new grouping around the still-new Bandiera Winery; identity yet to be established. Brand names are Arroyo Sonoma, Potter Valley, Bandiera Wines.

Callaway Vineyard and Winery

Temecula, *Riverside*. Founded 1974.
Owners: Hiram Walker and Sons. President: Ely Callaway. Wine maker: Stephen O'Donnell. Visits. 75,000 cases. 150 acres of vineyards at Temecula of Chard., Sauv.Bl., Ch.Bl., J.R., Cab.Sauv., Pet.Sir., Zin.

The most considerable pioneer of varietal table wine in Southern California. Best known for whites, including bizarre 'botrytized' 'Sweet Nancy' Chenin Blanc. Zinfandel is dark, pruney – very southern.

Cambiaso Vineyards

Healdsburg, *Sonoma*. Founded 1934.
Director: Somchai Likitprakong. Wine maker: Robert Fredson. Visits. 170,000 cases of various generic and varietal table wines from Sonoma and other grapes.

A name long associated with good cheap jug wines. New Thai owners have (slightly) higher ambitions.

CHAPPELLET

Donn Chappellet was the second man to build a new winery for the new age of California wine. He started in 1968, two years after Robert Mondavi. The scope of Mondavi's success in combining quality with quantity has no parallel. But the Chappellet property was the prototype for many newcomers. (Chappellet himself was in industrial catering before he heard the call.)

The aim is a limited range of top-class wines made as far as possible from estate-grown grapes. The capacity of the winery matches the size of the vineyard – though both have room for gradual expansion up to perhaps another 10,000 cases a year.

An artist friend designed the strange, church-like, triangular-pyramid winery to sit high on Pritchard Hill east of St. Helena, above the Napa Valley but at the foot of its own steep ramp of vines out of the reach of valley frosts. The roof is of steel protected by its own warm-brown rust, almost the same colour as the iron-rich soil around. One corner of the triangle is full of large and small stainless steel tanks, all with temperature-control jackets, for fermenting, storing and blending. The second corner is stacked with French oak barrels. The third is for bottled wine – while the centre space is free for whatever work is in progress.

Caparone
Paso Robles, *San Luis Obispo*. Founded 1980.
Wine maker: Dave Caparone. 3,000 cases. 8 acres of Zin. and Nebbiolo planted. Wines: Cab.Sauv., Merlot.

J. Carey Cellars
Solvang, *Santa Barbara*. Founded 1977.
Wine maker: Richard Longoria. 4,000 cases. 43 acres of Cab.Sauv., Merlot, Sauv.Bl., Chard. in the Santa Ynez Valley.

The 1979 Upper Vineyard Cabernet is a good beginning.

Carneros Creek Winery
Napa, *Napa*. Founded 1972.
President: Balfour C. Gibson. Wine maker: Francis Mahoney. Visits by appt. 15,000 cases. Vineyards in Napa Valley, Carneros and Sonoma. Wines: P.N., Chard., Cab.Sauv., Sauv.Bl.

Winery at the south end of the Napa Valley that caused a sensation with its first Pinot Noir. The '77 was the best I had tasted in California, with the combined velvet and carpentry of very good burgundy. The Chardonnay and Zinfandel have the same conviction. Apparently the named-vineyard Cabernets are equally fine.

Casa Nuestra
St. Helena, *Napa*. Founded 1980.
Wine maker: Tom Cottrell. 1,000 cases. Wine: Ch.Bl.

Cassayre-Forni Cellars
Rutherford, *Napa*. Founded 1976.
Owner: James L. Cassayre. Wine maker: Mike Forni. Visits by appt. 6,250 cases plus. Wines: Zin., Cab.Sauv., Ch.Bl., Chard.
Prices: Cab. Sauv. '79, $10.75; Zin. '79, $7.50.

Two third-generation Napa families started in leased space with good dry Chenin Blanc. All Napa Valley appellation wines except Zinfandel from Dry Creek Valley, Sonoma.

The '79 was a model of the lively, soft-fruity red that Zinfandel can be if it is not overdone.

Caymus Vineyards
Rutherford, *Napa*. Founded 1972.
President and wine maker: Charles Wagner. Visits by appt. 18,000 cases. 70 acres in Rutherford. Wines: Cab.Sauv., P.N., Zin., Fumé Bl., Chard.
Prices: Cab.Sauv. '78, $12.00; Chard. '78, $7.00.

Chappellet's wines have an austere, built-to-last style quite different from the Napa norm. His Chenin Blanc is the best in California: dry, firm, long-flavoured and truly appetizing. His Chardonnay, fermented partly in barrels, partly in steel, is impressively reined-in – his Riesling less so; perhaps his least successful variety. He makes his Cabernet with Château Latour in mind; serious and tannic,

balanced for long maturing. Ten per cent of Merlot is blended in, and surplus Merlot occasionally sold separately (he will replace some of his Merlot with Cabernet in the vineyard to get the balance right). At the 1981 Napa Valley wine auction, an annual event in June, a jeroboam of Chappellet's 1969 Cabernet fetched $6,000 – the highest price for a California wine.

Wagner's finest wine is his juicy, even flowery Cabernet. His white wine from Pinot Noir, the palest 'partridge eye', really tastes of the grape. The excellent-value second label is Liberty School.

Chalone Vineyard

Soledad, *Monterey*. Vines planted 1920; current owners since 1964 (first vintage '69). Owners: Gavilan Vineyards, Inc. President: Richard Graff. Wine maker: Peter Watson-Graff. Visits by appt. 12,000 cases. 120-acre estate. Wines: Chard., P.Bl., Ch.Bl., P.N., Cab.Sauv.
Price: P.N. '79, $12.00.

For 50 years a lonely outpost of viticulture on a droughty limestone hilltop near the Pinnacles National Monument, where all water had to be brought up by truck. Then the Graffs stunned California with Pinot Noir successfully modelled on great Côte d'Or burgundies and Chardonnay maturing to the smoky fragrance of the great white wines of the northern Rhône. The '77 was uncannily close to the luxurious Viognier.

In 1973-75 the Graffs expanded production tenfold without lowering their sights. New ideas include Cabernet Sauvignon and wine-making entirely without SO_2.

Chamisal Vineyard

San Luis Obispo, *San Luis Obispo*. Vineyard founded 1972, winery 1980.
Wine maker: Scott Boyd. 1,600 cases. Wines: Chard., Cab.Sauv., sparkling wines to come.

Channing Rudd Cellars

Alameda, *Alameda*. Founded 1976.
Wine maker: Channing Rudd. 625 cases (planting 60 acres in Lake County). Wines: various.

Chappellet

St. Helena, *Napa*. Founded 1968.
President: Donn Chappellet. Wine maker: Cathy Corizon. No visits. 25,000 cases, 110 acres of vineyard in Napa Valley. Wines: Cab.Sauv., Chard., J.R.., Ch.Bl., Merlot.
Prices: Chard. $14.00; Cab. $12.50. *See* profile, left.

Chateau Cheure

Yountville, *Napa*. Founded 1973.
Wine maker: Gerald Hazen. 2,000 cases. Wine: Merlot.

Chateau Chevalier Winery

St. Helena, *Napa*. Founded 1891, refounded 1969.
Owners and wine makers: Gregory and Kathleen Bissonette. Visits by appt. 11,000 cases. 60 acres in Napa Valley. Wines: Cab.Sauv., Chard., P.N., Merlot, Zin.

Chevalier was the original founder's name. The splendid mountainside vineyard on Spring Mountain Road, west of St. Helena, makes formidable concentrated Cabernet.

Chateau De Leu Winery

Suisun, *Solano*. Founded 1981.
Wine maker: Larry Waro. 20,000 cases of Chard., Fumé Bl., Ch.Bl., Fr.Col., Gam., Pet.Sir.

Chateau Montelena

Calistoga, *Napa*. Founded 1881, refounded 1969.
President: Jim Barrett. Wine maker: James P. 'Bo' Barrett. 30,000 cases. 90 acres (mainly Cab.Sauv.) near the winery. Wines: Chard., Cab.Sauv., Ries., Zin.
Prices: Napa Chard. '79, $16.00; Cab.Sauv. '77, $12.00.

Old stone winery north of Calistoga, at the foot of Mt. St. Helena, now has a 10-year record of some of the best California Chardonnays and Cabernets from the estate vineyard and grapes bought in from Napa, Sonoma and Santa Barbara. The Napa wines tend to be richer – and so do their drinkers. Two distinguished wine makers have set the style: Mike Grgich up to 1974, Jerry Luper up to 1981 – the first known for elegant discretion, the second for heaps of flavour. The '74 was a model of Cabernet.

Chateau St. Jean

Kenwood, *Sonoma*. Founded 1974.
Owners: Robert and Edward Merzoian, Ken Sheffield. Wine maker: Richard Arrowood. Visits. 84,000 cases. 80 acres in Sonoma. Wines: Chard., Sauv.Bl., J.R., Gewürz., P.Bl., Cab.Sauv., Moscato Canelli and sparkling Blanc de Blanc Brut.
Prices: Chard. '80, $10.00; J.R. (I.D.B.S.L.) '78, $25.00.

A showplace new winery specializing in white wines of the sort of subtropical ripeness more often associated with the Napa Valley. Robert Young Vineyard Chardonnay is the biggest and lushest of all. I often prefer the more easily drinkable regular bottling. Arrowood also makes formidable sweet, late-harvest Rieslings up to Trockenbeerenauslese quality and price.

A new sparkling wine facility will soon double the winery's total capacity.

At the Christian Brothers' Greystone winery, an archway is covered with a colossal old grapevine

Christian Brothers

Mount La Salle, *Napa*. Founded 1920s.
Owners: The Catholic teaching Order of La Salle. Principal: Brother Timothy. 4m. cases. 1,250 acres in Napa Valley; 1,200 acres in Fresno. Wines: a full range of table and dessert wines and brandy.
Prices: Chard. $10.25; Cab. $8.13; Jug $2.75.

Apart from their hilltop showpiece, the stone-built Mount La Salle winery, the Brothers own the huge old Greystone winery, two others in the Napa Valley, and two more in the San Joaquin Valley. Their massive production is known for consistency, value for money, and the personal touch of their modest but exceptionally experienced and perceptive wine maker. Until recently Brother Timothy refused to vintage-date any wine, preferring to use his acute palate to design ideal wines by blending. I have endless tasting notes that show how rewarding the results have been. My favourites are Napa Fumé Blanc (ripe, dry, slightly oaked, mature at 1 year); Chardonnay ('79: firm, dry and satisfying – no exaggerated fruit or oak); Cabernet (the non-vintage light by Napa standards, but not simple; the vintage bigger with the structure to last); Gamay Noir (sweetly fruity to smell; enjoyable gummy finish). Others include (to me rather dull) red Pinot St. George, sweet Pineau de la Loire (Chenin Blanc) and very sweet Muscat Chateau La Salle, and a Charmat-process sparkler. Tinta Madeira port and XO brandy are outstanding of their kind.

Cilurzo & Piconi

Temecula, *Riverside*. Founded 1978.
4,000 cases of Cab.Sauv., Pet.Sir., Ch.Bl. Wines: Cab.Sauv., Pet.Sir., plus a rosé from Pet.Sir. and Ch.Bl. called 'Chenite'.

Clos du Bois

Healdsburg, *Sonoma*. Founded 1974.
Principal: Frank Woods. 40,000 cases. Partners own a total of 1,200 acres in Dry Creek and Alexander Valley. Wines: Chard., Gewürz., J.R., Cab.Sauv., P.N.
Price: Chard. '80, $7.99.

Clos du Bois wines (made at Souverain) were well established before there was a winery. The best are boldly winey Gewürztraminer and an easily drinkable claret-style Cabernet. I have found the Riesling rather feeble and diffuse but the Chardonnay lively, long and dry, with a hint of green (in both colour and flavour) that seems to spell Alexander Valley. Wines are only sold when they are judged to have enough bottle-age.

Clos du Val Wine Co.

Yountville, *Napa*. Founded 1973.
Principal: Bernard Portet. 25,000 cases. Vineyards in the Stag's Leap area, east of Yountville. Wines: Cab.Sauv., Zin., Chard.
Prices: Chard. '80, $12.50; Cab.Sauv. '79, $12.50.

Portet was brought up at Château Lafite, where his father was manager. As in Bordeaux, he blends Merlot with Cabernet. His wines are reckoned soft and supple by Napa standards but they are still deep-coloured, juicy, and long on the palate. The '76 was ideal for drinking in 1982, but I would confidently keep it another 5 years. His Zinfandel is as strapping as they come. Like all good examples of this grape, they can be drunk young, sweet and heady, or kept virtually for ever. Taltarni in Victoria, Australia, has the same owners.

Colony

The shortened brand name is all that is left of the once-proud Italian Swiss Colony winery of Asti, Mendocino. It was bought by Heublein Inc. and moved to Madera, where it is part of United Vintners, making jug wines and low-price varietals.

Concannon Vineyard

Livermore, *Alameda*. Founded 1883.
Owner: Augustin Huneeus. President: James Concannon. Visits. 52,000 cases. 180 acres in Livermore Valley. A wide range of table wines.
Prices: Chard. $8.38; Cab. $9.51; Jug $3.95.

Founded to make altar wine in the same year as the other great Livermore Valley winery, Wente Bros., and still estate-bottling some Livermore wine, although also buying grapes in Clarksburg (Yolo County, the Sacramento River delta) and Amador, for 'selected vineyard' bottlings. Specialities include California's first Petite Sirah (from Livermore: a big soft wine) and perhaps its only Rkatsiteli, a crisp white Russian. The Sauvignon Blanc is now dry in style. A vigorous company with one of the steadiest reputations in California.

Congress Springs Vineyards

Saratoga, *Santa Clara*. Founded 1892, refounded 1976.
Owner: Vic Erickson. Wine maker: Daniel Gehrs. Visits. 5,000 cases. 70 acres in Santa Cruz Mountains. Various vintage varietal table wines.

Well-made Sauvignon Blanc (a drier version is called Fumé Blanc) and dry Semillon lead the whites and Zinfandel the reds.

Conn Creek

St. Helena, *Napa*. Founded 1974.
Principal: W. D. Collins Jr. Wine maker: Daryl Eklund. Visits by appt. 21,000 cases. Vineyards east of Yountville and north of St. Helena. Wines: Cab.Sauv., Chard., Zin.
Prices: Cab.Sauv. '78, $12.50; Chard. '80, $6.00.

A reputation built mainly on stylish Cabernet, distinctly oak-tinged with both plummy and more ascetically herbaceous notes. What I have tasted of the Chardonnay was rather blunt and the Zinfandel meaty with a certain astringency. Among the partners is the owner of Château La Mission-Haut-Brion. Chateau Maja is a second label.

R. & J. Cook

Clarksburg, *Yolo*. Founded 1978.
Wine maker: Bruce McGuire. 40,000 cases. Big-scale grape farmer in the Sacramento River delta.
Price: Ch.Bl. '80, $5.75.

Their first 'Steamboat' Cabernet was astonishingly fruity.

Cordtz Brothers Cellars

Cloverdale, *Sonoma*. Founded 1906, refounded 1980.
Wine maker: David Cordtz. 16,000 cases. Wines: Sauv.Bl., Gewürz., Chard., Cab.Sauv., Zin.

H. Coturri & Sons Ltd

Glen Ellen, *Sonoma*. Founded 1979.
Wine maker: Anthony Coturri. 2,000 cases. Various varietals.

Crescini Wines

Soquel, *Santa Cruz*. Founded 1980.
Wine maker: Richard Crescini. 650 cases. Various varietals.

Cresta Blanca

Formerly an important Livermore, Alameda, winery. Now part of Guild Wineries, operating at Ukiah, Mendocino, using coop members' grapes for 100,000 cases of a wide range of varietal and table wines.

Cronin Vineyards

Woodside, *San Mateo*. Founded 1980.
400 cases. Wines: Chard., Cab.Sauv., P.N., Zin.

Cuvaison Vineyard

Calistoga, *Napa*. Founded 1970.
Principal: Christoph Weber. Visits. 10,500 cases. 400 acres in Napa Valley. Wines: Chard., Cab.Sauv., Zin.
Prices: Chard. $12.00; Cab. $10.00; Jug $7.50.

Swiss owned, with its style set by Swiss-born wine maker Philip Togni (who left in 1982). Togni believes in powerful and austere, even hard wines that need considerable bottle-age, but deserve it. The style may change. Calistoga Vineyards is a second brand name.

Deer Park Winery

Deer Park, *Napa*. Founded 1979.
Wine maker: David Clark. 4,200 cases. Wines: Sauv.Bl., Zin., Chard.
Price: Sauv.Bl. '80, $7.50.

Dehlinger Winery

Sebastopol, *Sonoma*. Founded 1975.
Owner and wine maker: Tom Dehlinger. Visits by appt. 8,000 cases. 14 acres in Sonoma County. Wines: Chard., P.N., Cab.Sauv., Zin.
Price: Zin. '79, $7.00.

Highly regarded little winery, offering wines that taste distinctly of the grape, not overstrong or overpriced.

Delicato Vineyards

Manteca, *San Joaquin*. Founded 1924.
Owners: The Indelicato family. Visits by appt. 5.8m. cases (mainly in bulk). Many generics and some varietals from 'Northern California'.

DeLoach Vineyards

Santa Rosa, *Sonoma*. Founded 1975 (winery built 1979).
Owner and wine maker: Cecil O. DeLoach. Visits. 13,500 cases. 123 acres in Russian River Valley in Sonoma County. Wines: Zin. (red and white), P.N., Fumé Bl., Chard., Gewürz.
Prices: Zin. '79, $7.00; Chard. '80, $10.00.

The '79 Pinot Noir, the one product I have tasted, was deep in colour and flavour, excellent in youth and apparently fit to age.

Devlin Wine Cellars

Soquel, *Santa Cruz*, Founded 1978.
Wine maker: Charles Devlin. 2,000 cases of Chard., Cab.Sauv., Zin., Sauv.Bl.
Price: Zin. P.R. '79, $5.50.

Diablo Vista

Venicia, *Solana*. Founded 1977.
Wine maker: Leon Borowski. 3,500 cases of Cab. and Zin.

Diamond Creek Vineyards

Calistoga, *Napa*. Founded 1972.
Owner: Al Brounstein. No visits. 3,500 cases. 20 acres west of Calistoga, Napa. Wines: Cab.Sauv. only.
Price: Cab.Sauv. '79, $15.00.

Cabernet from 3 small vineyards, Volcanic Hill, Red Rock Terrace and Gravelly Meadow, reflects 3 different soils and situations – a subject little enough studied in California. They are all big, tough wines designed for long ageing.

Dolan Vineyards

Redwood Valley, *Mendocino*. Founded 1980.
Wine maker: Paul Dolan. 800 cases. Wines: Chard., Cab.Sauv.

Domaine Chandon

Yountville, *Napa*. Founded 1973; winery opened 1977.
Owners: Moët-Hennessy (Paris). Wine maker: Dawnine Sample. Consultant: Edmond Maudière. Visits. In 1981: 150,000 cases; by 1983, 250,000 cases. 800 acres in Napa Valley. Wines: Chandon Napa Valley Brut, Chandon Blanc de Noirs, Still White, Pinot Noir Blanc and Panache, a sweet apéritif. The second label is Fred's Friends.
Price: Napa Brut, $11.95.

The spearhead of France's invasion of California, a characteristically stylish and successful outpost of Champagne (but you must not use the word). A wine factory and an entertainment at the same time, with a first-class fashionable restaurant. Both sparkling wines are excellent, the Blanc de Noirs considerably heftier, and marvellous value for money. Out of context, in England, the sheer fruitiness of the Napa grapes makes the wines taste distinctly sweet, technically Brut though they may be.

Domaine Laurier

Forestville, *Sonoma*. Founded 1978.
Owners: Jacob and Barbara Shilo. Wine maker: Stephen Test. Visits by appt. 5,500 cases. 30 acres in Russian River Valley, Sonoma. Wines: Chard., Sauv.Bl., J.R., P.N., Cab.Sauv.
Price: P.N. '78, $7.99.

Donna Maria Vineyards

Healdsburg, *Sonoma*. Founded 1974.
Owner: Frederick P. Furth. Wine maker: Charles Illgen. No visits. 10,500 cases. 150 acres in Sonoma County. Wines: Chard., Gewürz., P.N., Cab.Sauv.

An established grower just starting to make his own wine.

Dry Creek Vineyard

Healdsburg, *Sonoma*. Founded 1972.
President and wine maker: David Stare. Visits by appt. 37,500 cases. 45 acres in Dry Creek, Sonoma. Wines: Ch.Bl., Fumé Bl., Chard., Zin., Cab.Sauv., Gewürz.
Prices: Ch.Bl. '80, $5.75; Chard. '80, $10.00.

Maker of one of California's best dry Sauvignon Blancs (Fumé Blanc) with other whites in the same balanced, vital but not-too-emphatic style.

Duckhorn Vineyards

St. Helena, *Napa*. Founded 1976.
Owner: Daniel Duckhorn. Wine maker: Thomas Rinaldi. No visits. 3,000 cases. 6.5 acres at St. Helena, newly planted with Sauv.Bl. and Sem. Wines: Napa Merlot and Cab.Sauv.
Price: Merlot '79, $12.50.

One of the wineries provoking great interest in Merlot.

Durney Vineyard

Carmel, *Monterey*. Vineyards founded 1968, winery 1977.
Owners: W. W. and D. K. Durney. Wine maker: John Estell. No visits. 10,000 cases. 70-acre estate in Carmel Valley. Wines: Ch.Bl., J.R., Gam.Beauj., Cab.Sauv.

Carmel's only vineyard, on steep slopes not far from the ocean. The Cabernet is ripe, deep and impressive, the Chenin Blanc equally well made.

East Side Winery

Lodi, *San Joaquin*. Founded 1934.
A growers' cooperative with 8m. gallons' storage, bottling perhaps 1m. cases under Conti Royale, Royal Host and Gold Bell labels.

Conti Royale is the label for some worthy varietals, dessert wines and brandies.

Edmeades Vineyards

Philo, *Mendocino*. Founded 1968.
President: Deron Edmeades. Wine maker: Jed Steele. Visits by appt. 20,000 cases. 35 acres in Anderson Valley, Mendocino. Wines: Chard., Cab.Sauv., Gewürz., Zin., P.N., P.Bl., Fr.Col., 'Rain Wine' and apple wine.
Prices: Rain '80, $4.95; Chard. '79, $8.95.

Originally a grape grower for Parducci, since 1974 a winery proud of being (at only 25 miles from the Pacific) in California's rainiest wine region. Hence the name of their generic white. In 1977 they made California's first ice wine, a sweet Colombard from frozen grapes. All this damp and cold, says Steele, produces intense 'varietal character'. 'DuPratt' Zinfandel is also in high demand.

Edna Valley Vineyard

San Luis Obispo, *San Luis Obispo*. Founded 1979.
Owners: Chalone Vineyard and Paragon Vineyard. Wine maker: Gary Mosby. Visits. 20,000 cases. Vineyards in Edna Valley, San Luis Obispo County, planted with Chard., P.N.

Have already supplied grapes for very good Hoffmann Mountain Ranch and Felton Empire wines.

Enz Vineyards

Hollister, *San Benito*. Vineyards founded 1895, winery 1973.
3,500 cases. Wines: Zin., P.St. George, Fumé Bl., Fr.Col.

Estrella River Winery

Paso Robles, *San Luis Obispo*. Founded 1973.
President: Clifford R. Giacobine.
Visits. 66,000 cases. 700 acres in San Luis Obispo County, planted with Cab.Sauv., Zin., Syrah, Barbera, Chard., Ch.Bl., Sauv.Bl., Musc., J.R.
Price: Cab.Sauv. (NV), $3.99.

A considerable estate in the making. Early wines have been promising.

Evensen Vineyards & Winery

Oakville, *Napa*. Founded 1979.
Wine maker: Richard Evensen. 800 cases. 20 acres between Rutherford and Oakville. Wine: Gewürz.

Far Niente Winery

Oakville, *Napa County*. Founded 1979.
Wine maker: Chuck Ortman. Production: to be 30,000 cases. Wines: Chard., Cab.Sauv.

A famous pre-Prohibition name being reborn in its original stone building in Oakville with its old vineyard replanted, but not yet bearing. The first Chardonnay has been highly praised.

Felton-Empire Vineyards

Felton, *Santa Cruz*. Founded 1976.
President and wine maker: Leo P. McCloskey. Visits. 18,000 cases. 45 acres of vineyards in Santa Cruz. Wines: J.R., Gewürz., Ch.Bl., Cab.Sauv., P.N., Zin.
Prices: J.R. '80, $7.50; P.N. '79, $7.50.

The speciality is Riesling (some from far northern Mendocino) made with aseptic precision that tends to leave me as cold as the fermentation must have been. The sweet versions with echoes of noble rot are first class. McCloskey also advises at Ridge (q.v.).

Fenestra Winery

Livermore, *Alameda*. Founded 1976.
Wine maker: Larry Replogle. 2,000 cases. Wines: Ch.Bl., Chard., Sauv.Bl., Cab.Sauv., Pet.Sir., Zin.

Fenton Acres Winery

Healdsburg, *Sonoma*. Founded 1979.
Wine makers: 3 partners. 1,400 cases. Wines: P.N., Chard.

Fetzer Vineyards

Redwood Valley, *Mendocino*. Founded 1968.
President: Bernard Fetzer. Wine maker: Paul Dolan. Visits. 350,000 cases. 200 acres in Redwood Valley, planted mainly in Cab.Sauv., Sauv.Bl. and Sem.
Price: Cab.Sauv. '78, $7.50.

A family business with a mixed reputation, making some outstanding Petite Sirah, Zinfandels of distinct styles from named Mendocino and Lake County vineyards, equally various Rieslings, estate Cabernet Sauvignon and most of the usual varieties. Attractive jug wines include Fetzer Premium and a second label, Bel Arbres. Generally very good value for money.

Ficklin Vineyards

Madera, *Madera*. Founded 1946.
President: David Ficklin. Wine makers: David and Peter Ficklin. Visits by appt. 10,000 cases. Family vineyards grow Portuguese port varieties.

California's most respected specialists in port-style wine, neither vintage nor tawny in character but ages indefinitely like vintage. Like vintage, it needs careful, often early, decanting.

Field Stone Winery

Healdsburg, *Sonoma*. Founded 1976.
Owner: Mrs Marion Johnson. Visits by appt. 8,750 cases.
140 acres in Alexander Valley, Sonoma.
Wines: J.R., Ch.Bl., Gewürz., Pet.Sir., Cab.Sauv.
Price: Table White, $3.79.

A gem of a winery, burrowed in the ground among the vineyards, designed by the late Wallace Johnson, who made picking machines. The grapes for white and rosé are crushed in the vineyard. They include a ravishingly pretty, pale pink 'Spring Cabernet', perhaps California's best picnic wine. Also good Riesling and Petite Sirah.

J. Filippi Vintage Co.

Mira Loma, *San Bernardino*. Founded 1922.
Wine maker: Joseph Filippi. 200,000 cases. Wines: table, dessert and 'special natural' distributed in S. California.

Filsinger Vineyards and Winery

Temecula, *Riverside*. Founded 1980.
Wine maker: Mike Menghini. 8,000 cases of Chard., Sauv.Bl., Em.Ries., Zin., Pet.Sir., Gam.

The Firestone Vineyard

Los Olivos, *Santa Barbara*. Founded 1973.
Principal: A. Brooks Firestone. Wine maker: Tony Austin. Visits. 73,000 cases. 300 acres in Santa Ynez Valley planted in Cab.Sauv., J.R., Chard., P.N., Merlot, Gewürz., Sauv.Bl.
Prices: P.N. Res. '77, $15.00; Chard. $9.50; Cab. $15.00; Jug $4.00.

Firestone (of the tyres) in partnership with Suntory, the Japanese distillers, have pioneered the relatively cool Santa Ynez Valley with a handsome Napa-style wooden winery. The conditions suit Riesling and Gewürztraminer particularly well; also Chardonnay and Pinot Noir. Merlot is preferred to Cabernet by many (although not by me). Ambassador's Vineyard (sweet) Riesling is outstanding and all wines are modestly priced for the quality, which over the range is as high as any to be found in California.

Fisher Vineyards

Santa Rosa, *Sonoma*. Founded 1974.
Wine maker: Fred Fisher. 4,000 cases. Wines: Chard., Cab.Sauv.

Flora Springs Wine Co.

St. Helena, *Napa*. Founded 1978.
Owners: The Komes and Garvey families. Wine maker: Ken Deis. Visits by appt. 4,200 cases. 250 acres in Napa Valley.
Wines: Chard., Cab.Sauv., Sauv.Bl., Ch.Bl., J.R.
Price: Chard. '80, $11.00

A new winery in an old stone barn used by Louis Martini to store wine during Prohibition. First-release Chardonnay ('79) won a gold medal at the Los Angeles County Fair. The equipment is all there.

L. Foppiano Wine Co.

Healdsburg, *Sonoma*. Founded in 1896.
Owner: Louis J. Foppiano. Wine maker: Rod Foppiano. Visits. 200,000 cases. 200 acres in Sonoma County.
Many wines.

One of the oldest family-owned wineries, recently refurbished and raising its already respectable standards. Good-value generics (especially white burgundy) and varietals (especially Petite Sirah).

ANDRE TCHELISTCHEFF

The California wine world has silently and unanimously bestowed the title of its 'dean' on André Tchelistcheff. His career has spanned the whole history of the industry since Prohibition, for 36 years (1937–73 as wine maker at Beaulieu vineyard and since, from his home in St. Helena, as consultant to many of the best wineries all over California and beyond. Tchelistcheff was born in Russia and trained in Burgundy. He was chosen to make their wine by the French de Latour family, founders of Beaulieu and for many years the royal family of the Napa Valley. In the early 1940s he introduced the idea of ageing red wine in small oak barrels. His reserve Cabernet from the best Rutherford vineyards, named as a memorial to Georges de Latour, has served as a model for California wine makers ever since. Cold fermentation of white wine, malolactic fermentation ... many of the house rules of California were written by Tchelistcheff and his advice continues to point new directions today.

Among the many wine makers who owe at least part of their training to him are such masters as Joe Heitz, Mike Grgich of Grgich Hills, Warren Winiarski of Stag's Leap, Richard Peterson of Monterey Vineyards and Theo Rosenbrand of Sterling.

Forman Winery (now Newton Vineyard)

St. Helena, *Napa*. Founded 1980.
Principal wine maker: Ric Forman. 8,000 cases. 60 acres on Spring Mountain, St. Helena. Wines: Cab.Sauv., Merlot, Sauv.Bl.

A dramatically ambitious venture up into the hills. Forest was cleared for the vineyard and the winery is topped by a gazebo overlooking an elaborate boxwood parterre – on top of the cellars. Forman's track record (at Sterling) includes very fine Sauvignon Blanc. He looks for 'giddy fruit' by fermenting it in steel. His 1981 had exciting acidity. A 1980 blend of Cabernet Sauvignon 60%, Cabernet Franc 20%, Merlot 20% was a good start, middleweight with 'nerve' and balance. Ric Forman left the winery in 1983.

Fortino Winery

Gilroy, *Santa Clara*. Founded 1970.
Wine maker: Ernest Fortino. 10,000 cases of various varietals and generic wines.

Franciscan Winery

St. Helena, *Napa*. Founded 1973.
Owners: Peter Eckes Co. Wine maker: Tom Ferrell. Visits. 175,000 cases. 250 acres at Oakville, Napa; 200 acres in Alexander Valley, Sonoma. Wines: sparkling wines, Cab.Sauv., Zin., Merlot., Chard., J.R.
Prices: Chard. $8.99; Cab. $7.99, Jug $3.49.

A major new enterprise, founded by the ebullient Justin Meyer and now German owned. Successes so far are sweetish Riesling, oaky Napa Chardonnay, different Cabernets from Napa and Sonoma vineyards and a good burgundy blend, all at fair prices.

Franzia Brothers Winery

Ripon, *San Joaquin*. Founded 1906.
Owners: The Coca-Cola Bottling Company of New York. Visits. 9.6m. (about half in bulk), from 4,000 acres of vineyards.

Many generics and a few varietal wines under various names, all traceable by the Ripon address on the label. Franzia French Colombard recalls Gallo Chablis Blanc, but slightly fizzy.

Jas. Frasinetti & Sons

Sacramento, *Sacramento*. Founded 1897.
Owners: Gary and Howard Frasinetti. 40,000 cases. Various table and dessert wines and wine cocktails.

Chris A. Fredson Winery

Geyserville, *Sonoma*. Founded 1885.
100,000 cases. Wines: Zin. and others for the Charles Krug winery (q.v.).

Freemark Abbey Winery

St. Helena, *Napa*. Founded 1895, refounded 1967.
Principal: Charles A. Carpy. Wine maker: Larry Langbehn.
Visits. 25,000 cases. Vineyard in Napa Valley. Wines: Chard., Cab.Sauv., J.R.
Prices: Chard. '79, $12.25; J.R. '80 $6.50; Cab.Sauv. '77, $12.50 (Bosché).

Perfectionist winery just north of St. Helena. Three of the partners (Messrs. Carpy, Jaeger and Wood) are leading Napa grape growers. Another (Brad Webb) made history with barrels at Hanzell (q.v.) in the late 1950s. Their Chardonnay is often the best in the valley. My notes on the '79 read: 'generous and complex, round and silky but with good grip and sweet, clean finish.' In 1973 they pioneered sweet botrytis-rotten Riesling, now labelled 'Edelwein'. Cabernet from a Rutherford grower called Bosché (and so labelled) is outstandingly concentrated and balanced, even better than their splendid regular bottling. Nobody has yet seen a fully mature Freemark Cabernet Bosché.

*Newton Vineyard (*see *under Forman winery) has broken entirely new ground, bulldozing forest high on Spring Mountain above the Napa Valley. Mountain vineyards escape destructive late frosts, benefit from alternating hot days and cool nights in the ripening season. Their shallow rocky soil 'stresses' the vine, intensifying the flavour of the grapes*

Fretter Wine Cellars

Berkeley, *Alameda*. Founded 1977.
Wine maker: Travis Fretter. 850 cases. Wines: Chard., Cab., P.N., Merlot, Gam., Gam.Rosé., Sem., Sauv.Bl.

Frick Winery

Santa Cruz, *Santa Cruz*. Founded 1977.
Wine maker: William Frick. 1,500–3,000 cases of P.N., Chard., Pet.Sir., Zin.
Price: Pet.Sir. '79, $6.99.

Galleano Winery

Mira Loma, *Riverside*. Founded 1927.
Wine maker: Nino Galleano. 84,000 cases of red and white generic wines and Zinfandel.

Labels

Two pieces of information included on the label of many good California wines give a helpful indication of what to expect in the bottle.

Alcohol content is measured in degrees or percentage by volume (the two are the same). Traditional wines vary between about 11.5° and 14° – enough to make a substantial difference to taste and effect. New-style 'soft' wines go down to 7.5°. But the law allows the labeller a remarkable latitude of 1.5° from the truth. As a practical tip, if you find a he-man Napa Chardonnay, for example, too powerful for you at 13.5°, there is no law against adding a drop of water. Perrier refreshes clumsy wines beautifully.

Residual sugar is most commonly reported on labels of Riesling and Gewürztraminer. It is the unfermented sugar left (or kept) in the wine at bottling. Below 0.5% by weight sugar is undetectable: the wine is fully dry. Above about 1.5% it would be described as 'medium sweet', above 3% as 'sweet' and above 6% as 'very sweet'. A 'selected bunch late harvest' might have 14% and a 'selected berry late harvest' as much as 28%. Measurement in grams per 100 millilitres is the same as measurement in percentages.

California's range

One of the most impressive (and confusing) things about visiting a California winery is the range of products. To a European accustomed to the specialization of old wine areas, it is bewildering to be asked to sample the equivalent of claret, burgundy (red or white), German wines and Italian wines too, with possibly sparkling and dessert wines as well – all in the same tasting. And yet it is hard to tell a wine maker that you are only interested in his Cabernet, or his Riesling – at least on that occasion. Tasting at wineries demands a prodigious effort of concentration.

E. & J. Gallo Winery

Modesto, *Stanislaus*. Founded 1933.
Principals: Ernest and Julio R. Gallo. Wine maker: Julio R. Gallo. No visits. 250,000 cases *a day*. Grapes from Healdsburg–Sonoma area, Napa, Fresno, Modesto, Livingston.
Prices: Chard. $6.90; Cab. $3.56; Jug $2.42.

The world's biggest wine maker, still run by the brothers who founded it. Everything about Gallo is stupendous. They own the world's 2 biggest wineries to supply their incredible tank farm, which has a capacity of 265 m. gallons, including a 1m. gallon storage tank and a 25-acre warehouse. The bottling line starts with a glass factory. And the whole operation is still growing fast.

Farmers in most parts of California (including the best) supply grapes. The wines are patiently and thoroughly designed for their huge markets.* The long-running favourites are Chablis Blanc (well structured, fragrant, not quite dry, if anything more German than French in style) and Hearty Burgundy (which is more Italian in feeling). In fact, both comparisons are backward looking: they are the archetypes for California. Gallo sparkling wine, sweet sherry and E & J brandy are all equally well designed and good value. The late 1970s saw the introduction of Gallo varietals: Colombard, Barbera, Ruby Cabernet, Zinfandel, Sauvignon Blanc, followed later by Gewürztraminer, Riesling, Cabernet and Chardonnay. Sauvignon Blanc is generally reckoned the best (and very good value). I enjoyed the Colombard, Barbera and Ruby Cabernet rather more than what I have seen of the later arrivals (especially the very dry Riesling).

*Brand names are: The Wine Cellars of Ernest & Julio Gallo, Gallo, Paisano, Thunderbird, Carlo Rossi, Ripple, Boone's Farm, Madria-Madria, Tyrolia, Spanada, Night Train Express, Brandy: E & J.

Gemello Winery

Mountain View, *Santa Clara*. Founded 1934.
President: Louis C. Sarto. Wine maker: Mario Gemello. Visits by appt. 8,500 cases of Cab.Sauv., P.N., Zin. (red and white), Pet.Sir., Chard., Ch.Bl., P.N. (white).

This winery is best known for Italian-style Zinfandel.

Geyser Peak Winery

Geyserville, *Sonoma*. Founded 1880.
Owners: the Triore family. Wine maker: Armand Bussane. Visits. 2.5 m. cases (most sold in bulk). 600 acres in Sonoma County. Many table and sparkling wines.

An old bulk-selling winery bought in 1972 by Schlitz Brewery and sold again a decade later. Gewürztraminer and Fumé Blanc are the top choices in a range without peaks. The jug wines are called 'Summit'.

Gibson Wine Company

Sanger, *Fresno*. Founded 1939.
A 6m. gallon growers' cooperative making bulk table and dessert wines.

Girard Winery

Oakville, *Napa*. Founded 1974.
Wine maker: Fred Payne. 10,000 cases. 42 acres. Wines: Chard., Ch.Bl., Cab.

Giumarra Vineyards Corporation

Bakersfield, *Kern*. Founded 1946.
Owners: The Giumarra and Corjaro families. Wine makers: Bill Nakata and Dale Anderson. Visits. 3.5m. cases. Own 4,000-acre estate in south San Joaquin Valley.

Enormous vineyard acreage produced bulk wines until 1973, when the Giumarra label appeared on good-value generic lines and some vintage-dated varietal reds, under the brand names of Giumarra Vineyards, Breckinridge and Ridgecrest.

Glen Ellen Winery

Glen Ellen, *Sonoma*. Founded 1982.
Wine maker: Patrick Flynn. 1,200 cases. Wine: Cab.Sauv.

Glen Oak Hills Winery

Temecula, *Riverside*. Founded 1978.
Wine maker: Hugo Woerdemann. 650 cases of various wines.

Grand Cru Vineyards

Glen Ellen, *Sonoma*. Founded 1886, refounded 1971.
Wine maker: Robert Magnini. Visits by appt. 40,000 cases. Vineyards in Alexander and Dry Creek valleys and Yolo County. Wines: Ch.Bl., Gewürz., Sauv.Bl., Zin., Cab.Sauv.
Prices: Cab. $16.00; Jug $5.75.

Primarily known for one of the county's best Gewürztraminers from Gardon Creek Ranch, Alexander Valley – a slightly sweet, very spicy one. Also a syrupy 'botrytized' version. Chenin and Sauvignon Blancs are both highly professional.

Grand Pacific Vineyard Co.

San Anselmo, *Marin*. Founded 1975.
Wine maker: Richard Dye. 8,500 cases. Wines: Chard., Merlot.

Green and Red Vineyard

St. Helena, *Napa*. Founded 1977.
Wine maker: J. Heminway. 2,500 cases plus. Wine: Estate Zinfandel. Price: '78, $6.50.

Greenwood Ridge Vineyards

Philo, *Mendocino*. Founded 1972.
Wine maker: Allan Green. 2,000 cases from 8-acre estate. Wines: J.R., Cab.Sauv.

Grgich Hills Cellar

Rutherford, *Napa*. Founded 1977.
Owners: Austin Hills and Mike Grgich. Visits by appt. 10,000 cases. 140 acres in Napa Valley. Wines: Chard., J.R., Fumé Bl., Zin., Cab.Sauv.
Prices: Chard. '79, $16.25, Fumé Bl. $10.00.

Hills grows the grapes, Grgich (formerley at Chateau Montelena, q.v.) has enhanced his reputation for vigorous, balanced wines with more fruit than weight. Chardonnay Riesling (especially late-harvest) and Fumé Blanc have led the way. Cabernet is promised soon.

Grover Gulch Winery

Soquel, *Santa Cruz*. Founded 1979.
626 cases of Pet.Sir., Zin., Cab.Sauv., Carig.

Emilio Guglielmo Winery

Morgan Hill, *Santa Clara*. Founded 1925.
Wine maker: George Guglielmo. 40,000 cases of various varietals, 'Emile's' generic wines.

Guild Wineries and Distilleries

San Francisco, *San Francisco*. Founded 1937.
President: Robert M. Ivie. 6m. cases.

1,000-member growers' cooperative with 3 main wineries: Guild at Lodi, B. Cribari & Sons at Fresno and Cresta Blanca at Ukiah. A huge range under these names and Winemaster, Roma, Tavola and Cook's.

Gundlach Bundschu

Vineburg, *Sonoma*. Founded 1856, refounded 1973.
Principal and wine maker: Jim Bundschu.
Visits by appt. 16,500 cases. 350 acres in Sonoma Valley.
Wines: Cab.Sauv., P.N., Merlot, Zin., Chard., Gewürz., J.R., Kleinberger.
Prices: Chard. $11.25; Cab. $11.50; Jug $3.00.

A famous San Francisco wine business destroyed by the 1906 earthquake. Grapes from the old vineyards were sold until 1973, when the winery reopened in a small way with Zinfandel. An ex-dairyman partner installed stainless steel milk tanks for fermentation. The range is very promising, especially Cabernet and Merlot and a crisp, refreshing Gewürztraminer like an Alsace wine.

Hacienda Wine Cellars

Sonoma, *Sonoma*. Founded 1973.
President: Crawford Cooley. Wine maker: Steven MacRostie.
Visits by appt. 18,500 cases. 50 acres at Sonoma, 60 at Russian River, Sonoma. Wines: Chard., Gewürz., J.R., Ch.Bl., Cab.Sauv., P.N., Zin.
Prices: P.N. '79, $12.00; Zin. '79, $6,99; Chard. '80 $10.50; Cab.Sauv. '78, $10.00.

Part of Haraszthy's original vineyard (*see* Buena Vista), still owned by Frank Bartholomew, has made a new reputation for Chardonnay (not too strong) and particularly Gewürztraminer. I have been less impressed with Hacienda's Pinot Noir.

Hanzell Vineyards

Sonoma, *Sonoma*. Founded 1956.
Owner: Barbara de Brye. Wine maker: Robert Sessions. Visits by appt. 625 cases. 34 acres on Sonoma Mountain. Wines: Chard., P.N., Cab.Sauv. (to come).
Prices: Chard. '79, $16.00; P.N. '77, $14.00.

Scene of revolutionary wine-making in the late 1950s, when James D. Zellerbach set out to make burgundy-style wines in small French oak barrels. His first Pinot Noir is still magnificent. The steep south-facing vineyard gives high alcohol but the concentration and balance of both the Chardonnay and the Pinot Noir still makes them among California's most impressive, demanding long maturing. The winery is (vaguely) a miniature Château du Clos de Vougeot. An additional vineyard has been planted in Cabernet.

J. J. Haraszthy & Son

Sonoma, *Sonoma*. Founded 1978.
Wine maker: Val Haraszthy (a descendant of Agoston H.).
6,250 cases. Wines: Zin., Chard., J.R., Gewürz.

THE GALLO BROTHERS

The brothers Ernest and Julio Gallo have done more to determine the direction and rate of growth of wine drinking in America than anybody else in history. By far the biggest wine producers in America, and probably the world, they still personally, entirely and privately own and direct their company.

The sons of an Italian immigrant grape farmer, they were brought up in Modesto in the heart of the Central Valley, where they still live and work. They started making wine in 1933, when Ernest was 24 and Julio 23. Julio made the wine and Ernest sold it.

They built their first winery in 1935 where the present vast plant now stands, and in 1940 started planting vineyards to experiment with better grapes. They realized the limitations of Central Valley grapes and bought from growers in Napa and Sonoma. They were prepared to outbid rivals. Today they are said to grow or buy one wine-grape in three in California.

In the 1950s the Gallos started a craze for flavoured 'pop' wines with the fortified Thunderbird, to be followed by a series of such enormously advertised and vastly popular gimmicks as fizzy Ripple and Boone's Farm apple wine. In 1964 they launched Hearty Burgundy which, with Chablis Blanc, set a new standard for California jug wines.

The Gallo trend has been slowly but steadily up-market, taking America with it. In 1974 they introduced their first varietal wines, which were much better than they were given credit for at the time. Their first generation of varietals, which included such compromises as Ruby Cabernet and Barbera, was replaced by a second, going all the way with wood-ageing for Chardonnay and Cabernet. In the process they made a two-acre cellar to house some two million gallons in oak.

When the day comes to inscribe a Gallo memorial, the word I would choose for it would be Consistency.

Harbor Winery

Sacramento, *Sacramento*. Founded 1972.
Owner and wine maker: Charles H. Myers. No visits. 1,250 cases. Grapes from Napa Valley and Amador County. Wines: Cab.Sauv., Chard., Mission del Sol.

A university professor's hobby and his friends' delight, especially Napa Chardonnay and Amador Zinfandel.

Hart Winery

Temecula, *Riverside*. Founded 1980.
Wine maker: Joe T. Hart. 1,700 cases of Pet.Sir., Gam.Beauj., Cab.Sauv., Merlot, Sauv.Bl.

Haywood Nursery

Sonoma, *Sonoma*. Founded 1980.
Wine maker: Charles Tolbert. 6,650 cases. 100 acres of Chard., J.R., Cab.Sauv., Zin.

Healdsburg Wine Company

Healdsburg, *Sonoma*. Founded 1979.
Wine maker: Julia Iantoska. 4,000 cases of Cab.Sauv., Chard., P.N.

Hecker Pass Winery

Gilroy, *Santa Clara*. Founded 1972.
Owners: Mario and Frances Fortino (wine maker). Visits by appt. 3,500 cases. 14 acres in Santa Clara. Wines: Pet.Sir., Zin., Carig., Ruby Cab., Gren., Chablis, Fr.Col., sherry.

Heitz Wine Cellars

St. Helena, *Napa*. Founded 1961.
Owners: Joe and Alice Heitz. Wine makers: Joe and David Heitz. Visits by appt. Separate tasting room every weekday. 33,500 cases. 40 acres in Napa Valley. Wines: Cab.Sauv., Chard., P.N., Grig., Gewürz., Barbera, Chablis, burgundy, port, sherry, sparkling wine and Angelica.
Prices: Grig.Rosé $3.99; Cab.Sauv. '77, $17.50.

Heitz is known worldwide for his Cabernet, more locally for his Chardonnay and Riesling, and very locally for his surprisingly long list of other wines. Yet they all reflect the man; a sometimes gruff original whose palate has its own logic. The Heitz's white house and old stone barn in an eastern side-valley still have an early-settler feeling among far more sophisticated neighbours. Most of the grapes are bought from friends, one of whom, Martha May, has already passed into legend as the name on 'Martha's Vineyard', Heitz's flagship Cabernet – a dense and gutsy wine of spicy, cedary and gumtree flavours, somehow unmistakably the Mouton of the Napa Valley even at the teeth-staining stage. Bella Oaks vineyard looks set to follow in its path. Young Heitz Chardonnay (his first was from Hanzell, q.v., in 1962) stands out in tastings as strong and dry, its fruit flavour held in check. It needs keeping for sumptuous richness and length to emerge. Riesling (since ceased) I have found rather rough and ragged. Grignolino is a surprising, sweet, Muscat-flavoured red. Angelica is a California tradition you would expect Joe Heitz to respect.

William Hill Winery

Napa, *Napa*. Founded 1976.
Owner and wine maker. William H. Hill. No visits. 7,000 cases (100,000 planned). 700 acres around Atlas Mountain and Mt. Veeder in Napa Valley. Wines: Cab.Sauv., Chard.
Price: Cab.Sauv. '78, $15.00.

One of Napa's biggest vineyard holdings, on high ground promising fine wine, judging by the opening Cabernet. Whatever happens will be worth watching.

Hoffman Mountain Ranch

Paso Robles, *San Luis Obispo*. Owner: Dr Stanley Hoffman. Wine maker: Michael Hoffman. 30,000 cases, largely from 120-acre estate. P.N., Chard, Cab.Sauv., J.R.
Prices: Chard. $10.00; Cab. $8.25; Jug $4.75.

Vineyards on limey soil above 1,000 feet (as at Chalone, q.v.) give Chardonnay and Pinot Noir of more than the usual dimensions. The Riesling I have tasted (from, I think, Edna Valley grapes) was feeble and disappointing in comparison.

Hop Kiln Winery

Healdsburg, *Sonoma*. Founded 1975.
Wine maker: Martin Griffin. 6,650 cases. 200 acres in Russian River Valley of Fr.Col., Chard., Gewürz., J.R. and late-harvest reds.

Horizon Winery

Santa Rosa, *Sonoma*. Founded 1977.
Wine maker: Paul Gardner. 1,045 cases of Zinfandel.

Hultgren & Samperton

Healdsburg, *Sonoma*. Founded 1978.
Wine maker: Ed Samperton. 20,000 cases of Cab.Sauv., Chard., Pet.Sir., Gam.
Price: Gam. '80, $4.50.

Husch Vineyards

Philo, *Mendocino*. Founded 1968.
Wine maker: Hugo Oswald. 6,500 cases. From Anderson and Ukiah valleys. Wines: Chard., Gewürz., P.N., Sauv.Bl., Cab.Sauv.

Inglenook Vineyards

Rutherford, *Napa*. Founded 1881.
Owners: United Vintners, subsidiary of Heublein Inc. 1.5m. cases. Vineyards in Napa Valley and elsewhere. Many wines.
Prices: Chard. $7.50; Cab. $6.50; Jug $3.00.

Inglenook was one of the handful of vineyards to survive Prohibition. A family property with a tradition of memorable, if not subtle, wines until John Daniel, grand-nephew of the founder, sold it to United Vintners in 1964. There is still an Inglenook Napa estate, but the name is also a brand for wines of all classes (except the top). The estate wines are led by tannic, Cask Cabernets, Charbono (lumbering in youth, enjoyable with age) and a good Gewürztraminer. Inglenook Vintage label wines are 'North Coast' in origin: a range of varietals and some generics (of which the burgundy is said to be best). The third label (and often best value) is Inglenook Navalle – especially French Colombard. The original stone winery on the west slopes of the valley is a historic landmark.

Iron Horse Vineyard

Sebastopol, *Sonoma*. Founded 1979.
Principal: Audrey Sterling. Wine maker: Forrest Tancer. No visits. 14,000 cases. 110 acres in Russian River. 20 acres in Alexander Valley. Wines: P.N., Cab.Sauv., Chard., Sauv.Bl.
Prices: Chard. $10.00; Cab. $12.00; Jug $5.00.

I took an instant liking to Iron Horse Cabernet, tannic to start, ripely sweet to finish, like good claret. The Sauvignon Blanc is more like burgundy than Bordeaux. There will soon be sparkling Iron Horse.

Jade Mountain

Cloverdale, *Sonoma*. Founded 1974.
Wine maker: Douglas Cartwright. 800 cases of Cab.Sauv., J.R.

Hop Kiln winery is a conversion from a 19th-century hop-drying plant in the Russian River Valley. Wine has ousted beer

Jekel Vineyard

Greenfield, *Monterey*. Vineyard founded 1972, winery 1978. Owners: Bill and Gus Jekel. Wine maker: Dan Lee. Visits. 30,000 cases. 140 acres in Arroyo Seco, Monterev, are Chard. and Ries. (40 acres each), P.N. and Cab.Sauv. (20 acres each). Price: Chard '80, $10.00.

The whites (especially Riesling) are among the best of the region, ripe but not heavy. Cabernet Sauvignon has recently been a huge critical success.

Johnson's Alexander Valley

Healdsburg, *Sonoma*. Founded 1975. Owners: Tom, Jay and Will Johnson. Wine maker: Tom Johnson. Visits. 9,000 cases. 45 acres in Alexander Valley, Sonoma. Wines: Chard., J.R., Gewürz., Pinot (red and white), Zin., Cab.Sauv. and Pear wine.

The Cabernet and white Pinot Noir are apparently the best wines. I am curious about the Pear.

Johnson Turnbull Vineyards

Oakville, *Napa*. Founded 1979. Wine maker: Lawrence Wara. 2,000 cases. Wine: Cab.Sauv.

Jordan Vineyard and Winery

Healdsburg, *Sonoma*. Vineyard founded 1972, winery 1976. Owner: Thomas N. Jordan. Wine maker: Robert Davis. Visits by appt. 52,000 cases. 300 acres in Alexander Valley, Sonoma. Wines: Cab.Sauv. (with Merlot), Chard. Prices: Cab.Sauv. '77, $14.00; Chard. '79, $12.00.

At least in folklore the most extravagant tycoon's chateau-in-California yet: a Bordeaux-style mansion and winery deliberately set on producing claret like the Médoc, in a setting of dark oaks and rolling golden grassland beautiful even by Sonoma standards. The first vintage, '76, made in barrels from Château Lafite, was light but very stylish. From 1978 the red will be aged 5 years before release. Judging by the first two it should then drink well.

Kalin Cellars

Novato, *Marin*. Founded 1977. Wine maker: Terence Leighton. 3,000 cases. Wines: Chard., Cab.Sauv., P.N., Ries., Sem., Merlot, from Sonoma, Mendocino and Santa Barbara grapes.

Robert Keenan Winery

St. Helena, *Napa*. Founded 1977. Owner: Robert H. Keenan. Wine maker: Joe Cafaro. Visits by appt. 7,100 cases. 45 acres of new vineyard in Napa Valley. Wines: Chard., Cab.Sauv. Prices: Chard. '80, $14.00; Cab.Sauv. '79, $12.00.

The first wines from this new winery high on Spring Mountain Road were from bought-in grapes, but showed the sure hand of the ex-Chappellet wine maker. Mountain-grown grapes should add firmness to richness.

Kathryn Kennedy Winery

Saratoga, *Santa Clara*. Founded 1973. Wine maker: Bill Anderson. 2,000 cases of Cab.Sauv., P.N. Rosé.

Also called Saratoga Cellars.

Kenwood Vineyards

Kenwood, *Sonoma*. Founded 1906 as Pagani Bros; renamed 1970. President: John Sheela. Wine maker: Bob Kozlowski. Visits. 50,000 cases. 20 acres in Sonoma Valley. Wines: Cab.Sauv., P.N., Zin., Chard., Sauv.Bl., J.R., Gewürz. Prices: Sauv.Bl. '80, $7.50; Cab.Sauv. $3.95.

An informal, not physically impressive winery but an interesting producer of especially individualistic reds, Artist's label and Jack London Ranch Cabernets.

Kenworthy Vineyards

Plymouth, *Amador*. Founded 1978. Wine maker: John Kenworthy. 1,000 cases. Wines: Cab.Sauv., Zin. and Chard.

Kirigin Cellars

Gilroy, *Santa Clara*. Founded 1976.
Wine maker: Nikola Kirigin Chargin. 17,000 cases of various varietals.

This was formerly the Bonesio winery.

Kistler Vineyards

Glen Ellen, *Sonoma*. Founded 1978.
Wine maker: Stephen Kistler. 5,000 cases. 40 acres in the Mayacamas Mountains. Wines: Chard., P.N., Cab.Sauv.
Prices: Chard. '80, $16.00; Cab.Sauv. '79, $18.00.

Highly fashionable – though to me the Chardonnay is too potent to drink.

Konocti Cellars Winery

Kelseyville, *Lake*. Founded 1974.
Owners: Parducci 60%, Lake County Vintners 40%. Visits. 21,000 cases and growing. 27 Lake County growers with 10 to 20 acres each. Wines: Cab.Sauv., Zin., Sauv.Bl., J.R. and whites from Cab. and Gam., but the emphasis is on reds.

F. Korbel and Bros.

Guerneville, *Sonoma*. Founded 1882.
President: Adolf L. Heck. Wine maker: Jim Huntsinger. Visits. 600,000 cases. 600 acres in Russian River Valley, Sonoma County. Wines: sparkling, brandy and table wines.
Price: Brut NV $8.99.

Until Domaine Chandon came on the scene this was the first choice in widely available California 'Champagne'. It is still a reliable bargain, especially the extremely dry Natural. Recent additions are Blanc de Blancs and Blanc de Noirs. The winery is a lovely old place in coastal redwood country.

Hanns Kornell Champagne Cellars

St. Helena, *Napa*. Founded 1952.
President and wine master: Hanns J. Kornell. Visits. 100,000 cases. No vineyards. Wines are all *méthode champenoise* sparkling: Sehr Trocken, Brut, Extra Dry, Demi Sec, Rosé, Rouge and Muscat of Alexandria.
Prices: S.T. NV $13.35; Brut NV $10.25.

If Domaine Chandon is France's invasion of Napa, this is Germany's. Germany no longer makes Sekt like Kornell's Sehr Trocken, with burly dry Riesling-and-yeast flavours. His fruity, faintly sweet Brut is more in the refreshing modern Sekt style.

Charles Krug Winery

St. Helena, *Napa*. Founded 1861.
President: Peter Mondavi. Visits. 625,000 cases (plus twice as much 'C.K.'). 1,200 acres in Napa Valley. Wines: a wide range, including the second label, 'C.K.'.
Prices: Chard. $12.50; Cab. $12.50; Jug $2.10.

C. Mondavi & Sons is the company name at the oldest of Napa's historic wineries. The other son is Robert, who left in 1966 to start his own winery, with spectacular success. The Krug reputation is largely for whites. They led the field with Chenin Blanc as a semi-sweet varietal. Their Chardonnay is Napa at its least reticent – what Bob Thompson calls 'buttered asparagus'. Krug Cabernets also have a fine pedigree; the standard one is lightish and ready-matured but the Cesare Mondavi Selection is the typical deep-flavoured, ripe-fruit-and-dust sort from the Rutherford/Oakville foothills.

Thomas Kruse

Hecker Pass, *Santa Clara*. Founded 1971.
3,000 cases of Fr.Col., Sauv.Bl., Cab.Sauv., Zin.

The Czech Korbel brothers built their red brick winery by the Russian River in northern Sonoma in 1886. The 'brandy tower' stands as a symbol for the produce of one of California's most consistent companies

La Crema Vinera

Petaluma, *Sonoma*. Founded 1979.
Wine maker: Rod Berglund. 7,000 cases of P.N. and Chard. Other labels are Petaluma Cellars, Sonoma Mountain Cellars.

The 1979 Ventana Vineyard (Monterey) Pinot Noir has greatly impressed the critics.

Lakespring Winery

Napa, *Napa*. Founded 1980.
Wine maker: Randy Mason. 15,000 cases. Wines: Chard., Ch. Bl., Sauv.Bl., Merlot, Cab.Sauv.

Ronald Lamb Winery

Morgan Hill, *Santa Clara*. Founded 1976.
840 cases of Gam.Beauj., Zin., J.R.
Grapes from Monterey, Sonoma and Amador. Most wines from specified vineyards.

Lambert Bridge

Dry Creek Valley, *Sonoma*. Founded 1975.
Principal: Gerard Lambert. 10,000 cases. 80 acres in Dry Creek Valley. Wines: Cab.Sauv., Chard.
Price: Cab.Sauv. '79, $7.99.

Critics approve Lambert's oaky Chardonnay but are less certain about his full-blooded Cabernet.

LaMont Winery

Di Giorgio, *Kern*. Founded 1978.
(Previously Bear Mountain Winery.) A subsidiary of John Labatt Ltd. Wine maker: Charles Feaver. Visits. 8.5m. cases. Many different table, dessert and sparkling wines under the M. LaMont and Mountain Gold labels.

Mostly low-price generic wines, LaMont brand varietals are fair. Sweet, strong Muscat Black Monukka is fine.

Landmark Vineyards

Windsor, *Sonoma*. Founded 1974.
Wine maker: William R. Mabry III. 15,000 cases. 80 acres of Chard., Cab.Sauv., Zin., J.R.

Laurel Glen Vineyards

Santa Rosa, *Sonoma*. Founded 1980.
Wine maker: Patrick Campbell. 4,200 cases of Cab.Sauv.

Lawrence Winery

Edna Valley, *San Luis Obispo*. Founded 1979.
President and wine maker: James S. Lawrence. Visits. 300,000 cases. Vineyards in San Luis Obispo and Santa Barbara counties. Wines: Many (mostly sold in bulk).

A remarkably big-scale launch in the new Edna Valley region, where Chardonnay and Riesling are dominant.

Leeward Winery

Oxnard, *Ventura*. Founded 1978.
Wine makers: Chuck Brigham and Chuck Gardner. 3,340 cases of Chard., Cab.Sauv., Zin.
Price: Chard. Ven. '80, $12.50.

Ventura (Monterey) Chardonnay has been a promising beginning for this coastal winery.

Live Oaks Winery

Gilroy, *Santa Clara*. Founded 1912.
Wine maker: Peter Scagliotti. 17,000 cases of old-style generic wines.

Livermore Valley Cellars

Livermore, *Alameda*. Founded 1978.
Wine maker: Chris Lagiss. 4,000 cases. Wines: P.Bl., Fr.Col., Golden Chasselas.

Llords and Elwood Winery

Fremont, *Alameda*. Founded 1955.
17,000 cases. Wines: Chard., J.R., Rosé of Cab., P.N., Cab.Sauv., champagne, 3 sherries, 1 port.

This winery is best known for Great Day Dry Sherry.

Long Vineyards

St. Helena, *Napa*. Founded 1968.
Owner and wine maker: Robert B. Long Jr. Visits by appt. 1,100 cases. 20 acres on Pritchard Hill, Napa. Wines: Chard., Ries., Cab.Sauv.
Price: Chard. $7.99.

The husband of the celebrated ex-Mondavi wine maker at Simi (q.v.) made notably stylish opening Chardonnay and Riesling.

Lower Lake Winery

Lower Lake, *Lake*. Founded 1977.
Wine maker: Dr Daniel Stuermer. 3,500 cases. Wines: Cab.Sauv., Sauv.Bl.

Lake County's pioneer post-Prohibition winery.

The Lucas Winery

Lodi, *San Joaquin*. Founded 1978.
Wine maker: David Lucas. 625 cases of Zin., light dry and sweet late-harvest.

Lytton Springs Winery

Healdsburg, *Sonoma*. Founded 1977.
Principal and wine maker: Bura W. Walters. Visits. 10,000 cases. 50 acres at Valley Vista, Russian River, Sonoma.
Price: '79, $7.50.

Old vines, formerly the source of a well-regarded Ridge (q.v.) wine, now make one of Sonoma's biggest (and most expensive) Zinfandels. I find it metallic, fierce and hot, but many love such things.

Madrona Vineyards

Camino, *El Dorado*. Founded 1973.
Wine maker: Richard Bush. 8,300 cases. Wines: Cab.Sauv., Merlot, Zin., Wh.Ries., Gewürz.

Maniar Vineyards

Napa, *Napa*. Founded 1980.
Wine maker: Jeff Libarle. 20,000 cases. Wines: Fumé Bl., J.R., Chard., Cab.Sauv. The label is Diamond Oaks Vineyard.

Marietta Cellars

Healdsburg, *Sonoma*. Founded 1980.
Wine maker: Chris Bilbro. 5,500 cases of Zin., Cab.Sauv.

Markham Winery

St. Helena, *Napa*. Founded 1975.
President: H. Bruce Markham. Wine maker: Robert Foley Jr. Visits by appt. 18,000 cases. 300 acres in Napa Valley. Wines: Chard., Chen.Bl., J.R., Musc., Gam.Beauj., Cab.Sauv., Merlot.

Production based on 3 vineyards, near Calistoga, Yountville and Napa, should give a good range of wines. At first they were sold in bulk. In 1978 Markham bought an old stone building in St. Helena and in 1979 launched his Chardonnay. Vin Mark is a second label.

Mark West Vineyards

Forestville, *Sonoma*. Founded 1972.
Owners and wine makers: Bob and Joan Ellis. Visits. 12,000 cases. 62 acres in Russian River Valley in Sonoma County.
Wines: Chard., Gewürz., J.R., P.N. (red and white).

Relatively cool vineyard producing white wines with good fruity acidity.

Louis M. Martini

St. Helena, *Napa*. Founded 1922.
President: Louis P. Martini. Wine makers: Louis P. and Michael R. Martini. Visits. 350,000 cases. 850 acres in Napa and Sonoma counties. Wines: Cab.Sauv., P.N., Merlot, Zin., Barbera, Gam.Beauj., Chard., J.R., Ch.Bl., Folle Blanche, Gewürz., Mountain red and white, sherries and Moscato Ambile (sold only at the winery).
Prices: Cab.Sauv. '68, $21.50; '78, $5.30.

Two generations of Louis Martinis have their name on the short list of California's great individual wine makers. Martini Cabernets of the 1960s rank alongside Beaulieu in quality, but in a different style which, as Bob Thompson has noted, appeals strongly to Englishmen weaned on claret. Martini continues to go less for guts than good manners in his wine. His Special Selection Cabernets are best, but all are well-balanced. Pinot Noir (from Carneros) is only modestly fruity, but again hauntingly well-finished. Barbera and Zinfandel are true to type. Of whites the best are dry and spicy Gewürztraminer and a ravishing sweet, low-strength Moscato Amabile.

Martini & Prati Wines

Santa Rosa, *Sonoma*. Founded 1951.
Wine maker: Frank Vanucci. 625,000 cases (90% in bulk) of various generic varietal and dessert wines. The varietals are labelled Fountaingrove.

Paul Masson Vineyards

Saratoga, *Santa Clara*. Founded 1852.
Owners: Seagrams & Sons. President: Elliott A. Fine. Wine maker: Joe Stillman. Visits. 7.5m. cases. 4,500 acres in Monterey, San Benito and Santa Clara counties. A wide range of table, dessert and sparkling wines.
Prices: burgundy $1.95; Chard. $8.15; Cab. $5.95; Jug $3.10.

Saratoga is still the headquarters of this historic firm, with a huge sparkling wine and bottling plant and visitor facilities, but the main wineries are now at Soledad, Monterey (for table wines), and in the San Joaquin Valley (for dessert wines). Their pleasant 'Carafe' wines are the best-known product. Varietals, however, remain distinctly good value. The standard Chardonnay is recognizable and not oversweet; the 'Pinnacles Selection' is remarkably good. The Pinnacles Chardonnay, Fumé Blanc and Gewürztraminer come from Masson's own vineyards in Monterey, which also supply the grapes for their Johannisberg Riesling Champagne. Zinfandel and Gewürztraminer are honourable. Emerald Dry is an enjoyable everyday white, rather sweet but sufficiently tart, and Brut Champagne is very fair. Much the most memorable wine is Rare Souzao port – and not only for its awful heart-shaped bottle. A new development is light (7.1% alcohol) Chablis.

Mastantuono

Paso Robles, *San Luis Obispo*. Founded 1980.
2,500 cases. Wines: Zin., Gren., P.N., Carig.
Price: Zin. '79, $9.25.

The most concentrated of Zinfandels, from Templeton Vineyards, planted in 1925.

Matanzas Creek Winery

Santa Rosa, *Sonoma*. Founded 1977.
Owner: Sandra P. MacIver. Wine maker: Merry Edwards. Visits by appt. 4,000 cases. 50 acres in Bennett Valley, Sonoma.

Very good things are expected from this property. The wine maker was previously at Mt. Eden Vineyards (q.v.). The Chardonnay made a splendid London début, the Gewürztraminer is winey and substantial and the Pinot Blanc a good Chardonnay-like example of this variety.

Mayacamas Vineyards

Miles up in the hills above Napa, *Napa*. Founded 1889, refounded 1941.
Owners: Bob and Nonie Travers. Visits by appt. 5,000 cases. 50 acres in Napa. Wines: Chard., Cab.Sauv., Sauv.Bl., P.N., Zin.
Prices: Chard. '78, $13.00; Cab.Sauv. '74, $48.00.

Mayacamas is the name of the mountains between Napa and Sonoma. If it were the Indian word for 'white man's strongest medicine' it would not be far wrong. The Travers' predecessors, the Taylors, planted Chardonnay and Cabernet in the 1940s in a spectacular natural amphitheatre 1,000 feet up. The sun, the fogs, the winds, the cold and the rocks of the hills conspire to concentrate grape flavour into something you can chew. The hot autumn of 1978 made the Chardonnay almost treacly. Travers' Cabernets are awe-inspiring in colour and bite for the first 5 years at least. Late-harvest Zinfandel he makes from bought grapes when they are tasty enough.

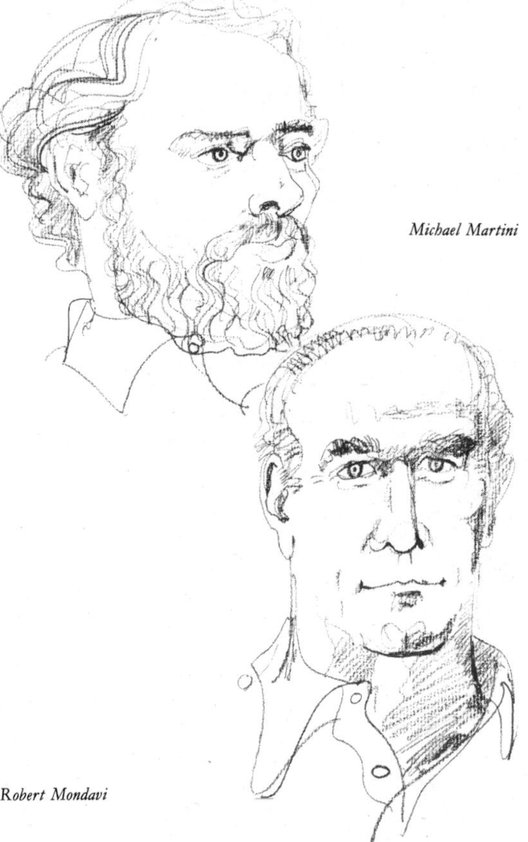

Michael Martini

Robert Mondavi

McDowell Valley Vineyards

Hopland, *Mendocino*. Founded 1978.
Owners: Richard and Karen Keehn. Wine maker: George Bursick. Visits. 46,000 cases. 360 acres in McDowell Valley, Mendocino. Wines: Chard., Ch.Bl., Sauv.Bl., Fr.Col., Gren., Cab.Sauv., Pet.Sir., Zin.

Ambitious, indeed visionary, venture to re-establish this forgotten little vineyard valley in S. Mendocino with a futuristic winery, using solar energy, deep cellars and nocturnal harvesting. Over 2,000 acres – the whole valley – could be planted.

McHenry Vineyards

Santa Cruz, *Santa Cruz*. Founded 1980.
Wine maker: Henry McHenry. 625 cases of P.N. and Chard.

McLester

Inglewood, *Los Angeles*. Founded 1979.
Wine maker: Cecil McLester. 1,250 cases. Wines: Cab.Sauv., Zin. from named vineyards in San Luis Obispo County.

Milano Winery

Hopland, *Mendocino*. Founded 1977.
Wine maker: Jim Milone. 8,500 cases. Wines: Chard., Sauv.Bl., Ch.Bl., Cab.Sauv., Zin., Pet.Sir., Gam.Beauj.

Mill Creek Vineyards

Healdsburg, *Sonoma*. Founded 1974.
President: Chas. W. Kreck. Wine maker: Bob Kreck. Visits. 10,000 cases. 65 acres in Russian River Valley, Sonoma. Wines: Chard., Cab.Sauv. (and Rosé), P.N., Merlot, Gam.Beauj., Gewürz.
Price: Merlot '79, $7.50.

Soft and agreeable rather than competition wines.

Mirassou Vineyards

San Jose, *Santa Clara*. Founded 1854.
Owners: The Mirassou family. Wine maker: Don Alexander. Visits by appt. 365,000 cases. 1,500 acres in Monterey and Santa Clara. A wide range of table and sparkling wines.
Prices: Chard. $9.00; Cab. $9.00; Jug $3.50.

The fifth generation of Mirassous run an enterprising company with panache. Being squeezed out of increasingly urban San Jose, most of their vines are now in the Salinas Valley, Monterey, where they pioneered field-crushing. Their wines were more exciting 10 years ago. Soft, aromatic Gewürztraminer, fruity Gamay Beaujolais, above-average Chardonnay, Zinfandel and Cabernet and below-average Chenin Blanc are my recent experience. 'Home Ranch' wines from San Jose, 'Harvest' from Salinas.

Robert Mondavi Winery

Oakville, *Napa*. Founded 1966.
Principal: Robert Mondavi. Wine maker: Tim Mondavi. Visits. 500,000 cases. 1,000 acres in the Napa Valley. Wines: Cab.Sauv., Pet.Sir., P.N., Napa Gam., Zin., Chard., Ch.Bl., Fumé Bl., J.R., Gam. Rosé., red, white and rosé table wines.
Prices: Fumé Bl.Res. '79, $15.25; Cab.Sauv. '78, $12.00; Chard '79, $12.99.

Mondavi's energy and his enquiring mind took less than 10 years to produce the most important development in the Napa Valley since Prohibition. He fits the standard definition of a genius better than anyone I know. His aim is top quality on an industrial scale. Inspiration and perspiration have taken him there.

The winery is (in the local jargon) state-of-the-art. The art includes not only advanced analysis and every shiny gadget but a personal knowledge of every French barrel maker worth a hoop. Each vintage is like a frontier with the Mondavi family cheering each other on to reach it – and something new always develops.

His best wine is his Cabernet Sauvignon Reserve; a gentle titan you can drink after dinner with relish but would do well to keep for 20 years. His regular Cabernet is a model of balance between berries and barrels. Each vintage his Pinot Noir grows more velvetly satisfying. Among whites he is best known for Fumé Blanc, Sauvignon and Semillon with the body and structure (and barrel-age) of first-class Chardonnay. His Chardonnay (notably the Reserve) can be compared with the best. The '78 had incredible richness and nerve. The Riesling is rather sweet, but crisp and refreshing and I suspect will age well. Late-harvest, botrytis-rotten Riesling is golden treacle. Red and white table wines keep up the good work. Only the Chenin Blanc disappoints me. The world awaits Moutondavi, or whatever they christen the forthcoming coproduction of two great impresarios, Bob and Baron Philippe de Rothschild.

Montclair Winery

Piedmont, *Alameda*. Founded 1975.
Wine maker: R. K. Dove. 1,250 cases. Grapes from Dry Creek, Sonoma. Wines: Zin., Fr.Col., Cab.Sauv., Pet.Sir.

Monterey Peninsula Winery

Monterey, *Monterey*. Founded 1974.
President and wine maker: Dr Roy Thomas. Visits by appt. 16,000 cases. Wines: mainly Zin. and Cab.Sauv. Second brand: Monterey Cellars.
Price: Zin. '78, $5.99.

Red wine specialist, using grapes from Amador, San Luis Obispo and Monterey counties to make many different one-vineyard Zinfandels and Cabernets, generally dense and heady, probably at their best quite young. Also Chardonnay in the same robust spirit.

The Monterey Vineyard

Gonzales, *Monterey*. Founded 1973.
Owners: The Coca-Cola Company. Wine maker: Dr Richard Peterson. Visits. 150,000 cases, plus wine for Taylor California Cellars (q.v.).
Prices: Chard. $7.00; Cab. $5.00; Jug $4.25.

Grapes from Monterey and San Luis Obispo counties go into a wide range of table wines, including 'soft' Riesling. Strong-flavoured Monterey grapes have had most success in white varietals, especially Riesling, Sauvignon Blanc, Gewürztraminer and Sylvaner. Late harvesting produces 'Thanksgiving' Riesling (wonderful at 5 years) and 'December' Zinfandel, a splendid concentrated dry red. High hopes for the winery (the first in the area and an impressive building with lovely stained-glass windows) have somehow not yet been entirely fulfilled.

Monteviña Wines

Plymouth, *Amador*. Founded 1970.
President: Jeff Runquist, oenologist. 180 acres plus Gott Vineyard in Amador. Wines: Zin., Barbera, Ruby Cab., Sauv.Bl., Chard.
Price: Zin.Ama. '79, $5.99.

Some of the most powerful Zinfandels, red or white, and equally strong Sauvignon Blanc.

Mont St. John Cellars

Napa, *Napa*. Founded 1979.
Wine maker: Andrea Bartolucci. 20,000 cases. Wines: various table wines.

J. W. Morris Wineries

Concord, *Alameda*. Founded 1975.
Principals: Neal Davidson and J. W. Morris. Wine maker: Jim Olsen. Visits by appt. 30,000 cases. Vineyards in Black Mountain, Sonoma; La Reina, Monterey; St. Amant, Amador County. Wines: port, Sauv.Bl., Chard., Zin., P.N., Cab., Angelica.
Prices: P.N. '78, $8.99; Chard. '80, $5.99.

At first charmingly known as 'J. W. Morris Port Works'. Vintage and Founder's Ruby are specialities. Also very sweet Amador Angelica from Mission grapes.

Mountain House Winery

Cloverdale, *Mendocino*. Founded 1980.
Wine maker: Ron Lipp. 2,500 cases. Wines: Chard., Cab.Sauv., late-harvest Zin., from Mendocino, Sonoma and Amador county grapes.

The Mountain View Winery

Mountain View, *Santa Clara*. Founded 1980.
Wine maker: Patrick Ferguson. 300–600 cases of Chard. and Zin.

Mount Eden Vineyards

Santa Clara, *Santa Clara*. Founded 1975.
Wine maker: Richard White. 1,500 cases. 22 acres of vineyard in the Santa Cruz Mountains. Wines: Chard., P.N., Cab.Sauv.
Prices: Cab.Sauv. '78, $25.00; Chard. '80, $12.00.

Richard Graff of Chalone (q.v.) directs the making of these wines on land that belonged to Martin Ray (q.v.). The Chardonnay is a rich, soft, spicy wine (in German terms, Pfalz-style), Pinot Noir deep and rich (but the '78 spoilt, for me, by a metallic flavour like Zinfandel). Cabernet is tannic and gutsy. Wines made from bought grapes are labelled MEV.

Mount Palomar Winery

Temecula, *Riverside*. Founded 1975.
Wine maker: Joseph Cherpin. 12,500 cases. 150 acres of Sauv.Bl., Ch.Bl., J.R., Zin., Pet.Sir., Cab.Sauv. and sherry. Other brands are Rancho Temecula and Long Valley Vineyards.

Mt. Veeder Winery

Mt. Veeder, *Napa*. Founded 1973, vineyard since 1965.
Owner: Michael Bernstein. 4,000 cases. 20 acres on Mt. Veeder. Wines: Cab.Sauv., Ch.Bl., Zin.
Price: Cab.Sauv. '78, $12.75.

Rocky vineyard known for concentrated, earthy, gummy, tannic Cabernets. The '78 still tasted new in 1982. Bernstein Vineyard is a second label.

Napa Cellars

Yountville, *Napa*. Wine maker: Aaron Mosely. 10,000 cases of Chard., Cab.Sauv., Gewürz.
Price: Chard '79, $11.50.

Big strong reds and whites with a soft, dry Gewürztraminer a favourite.

Napa Creek Winery

St. Helena, *Napa*. Founded 1980.
Wine maker: Eric Peterson. 17,000 cases. Wines: Chard., Cab.Sauv., J.R., Gewürz., Sauv.Bl., Ch.Bl.

Napa Valley Cooperative Winery

St. Helena, *Napa*. Founded 1934.
Wine maker: David M. Perez. No visits. 1.1m. cases. Vineyards in Napa Valley. Dry wines.

The whole production is sold to E. & J. Gallo (q.v.).

Napa Vintners

Napa, *Napa*. Founded 1978.
Wine maker: Donald Ross. 10,000 cases. Wines: Chard., Sauv.Bl., Cab.Sauv., Zin.
Price: Sauv.Bl. '79, $6.50.

Navarro Vineyards

Philo, *Mendocino*. Founded 1975.
Principal and wine maker: Edward T. Bennett. Visits by appt. 6,250 cases from 30 acres of vineyards in Anderson Valley and Mendocino of Chard., Gewürz., Wh.Ries., Cab.Sauv., P.N.

A grower taking advantage of a relatively foggy area to make fresh wines, notably Gewürztraminer.

Nichelini Vineyard

St. Helena, *Napa*. Founded 1890.
Wine maker: James Nichelini. 6,250 cases. 200 acres. Wines: Ch.Bl., Sauv.Vert, Zin., Gam., Pet.Sir., Cab.Sauv.

Niebaum Coppola Estate

Rutherford, *Napa*. Founded 1978.
Wine maker: Russ Turner. 5,000 cases. Wines: Cab.Sauv. with Cab.Fr., Merlot and Chard.

The property of the film producer Francis Ford Coppola.

A. Nonini Winery

Fresno, *Fresno*. Founded 1936.
Wine makers: Reno and Tom Nonini. 40,000 cases. Wines: various generic and varietal table wines, especially earthy reds, from the family's 200 acres.

Novitiate

Los Gatos, *Santa Clara*. Founded 1888.
Owner: Society of Jesus. Wine maker: Brother Lee Williams, Society of Jesus. Visits. 35,000 cases of commercial table and dessert wines.

Not many years ago I watched a horse hoeing the Novitiate's vines. They now buy their grapes, but make more effort in the winery. Sweet, coarse Black Muscat was the most memorable wine. Now their Pinot Blanc and Flor Dry Sherry are cited as fair or better.

Obester Winery

Half Moon Bay, *San Mateo*. Founded 1977.
Wine maker: Paul Obester. 4,000 cases. Wines: Sauv.Bl., J.R., Cab.Sauv. from Mendocino, Sonoma and Monterey grapes.
Price: Sauv.Bl. '80, $7.99.

Orleans Hill Vinicultural Association

Woodland, *Yolo*. Founded 1980.
Wine maker: Jim Lapsley. 590 cases of Zin. (red and white).

Pacheco Ranch Winery (alias RMS Cellars)

Ignacio, *Marin*. Founded 1979.
Wine maker: Jamie Meves. 650 cases. Wines: Cab.Sauv., Cab.Rosé.

Page Mill Winery

Santa Cruz Mountain, *Santa Clara*. Founded 1976.
1,500 cases of Ch.Bl., Chard., Cab.Sauv.

Papagni Vineyards

Madera, *Madera*. Founded 1920, winery 1975.
President: Angelo Papagni. Wine master: John Daddino. Visits by appt. 130,000 cases. Vineyards are the Clovis and Bonita ranches, Madera; many varieties.
Prices: Chard. $6.50; Cab. $5.25; Jug $3.85.

A grape grower turned wine maker with such success that he has made critics reassess the qualities of the San Joaquin Valley. First with light Alicante Bouschet red and sweet Moscato d'Angelo; then with crisp and concentrated Chardonnay aged 6 months in French oak.

Parducci Wine Cellars

Ukiah, *Mendocino*. Founded 1933.
Principal: John A. Parducci. Wine makers: Joe and Tom Monostori. Visits. 250,000 cases. 400 acres in Mendocino planted mainly in Cab.Sauv. and other reds.
Prices: Fr.Col. $3.75; 'Cellar Master' Cab.Sauv., Merlot '78, $9.95.

The first Mendocino winery, now run by the fourth generation, consistent in offering hearty big-scale reds (Cabernet Sauvignon, Petite Sirah, Zinfandel, Carignane and others). Their whites have been led by sweetish French Colombard and Chenin Blanc, and latterly Mendocino Riesling. Grapes come from the family's home, Talmage and Largo ranches and growers in Mendocino and Lake counties.

Parson's Creek

Near Ukiah, *Mendocino*. Founded 1979.
Owners: Jesse Tidwell and Hal Doran. Up to 10,000 cases. Grapes from Ukiah, Anderson and Alexander valleys. Wines: Chard., Gewürz., J.R.

Pastori Winery

Geyserville, *Sonoma*. Founded 1975.
Wine maker: Frank Pastori. 10,000 cases of Cab.Sauv. and Zin.

Pat Paulsen Vineyard

Cloverdale, *Sonoma*. Founded 1980.
Wine maker: James Meves. A small supply of Russian River Valley Sauv.Blanc.
Price: Sauv.Bl. '80, $7.50.

Robert Pecota Winery

Calistoga, *Napa*. Founded 1978.
Owners: Robert and Susan Pecota. Visits by appt. 6,500 cases (12,000 in 1986). 40 acres in Napa Valley. Wines: Cab., Sauv.Bl., Fr.Col., Gam.Beauj.
Price: Gam.Beauj. '81, $5.50.

Modern techniques, waiting for a replanted vineyard to catch up, include carbonic maceration of Gamay to make a wine Georges Duboeuf (of Beaujolais) greatly admired.

Pedrizzetti Winery

Morgan Hill, *Santa Clara*. Founded 1919.
Wine maker: Ed Pedrizzetti. 85,000 cases of various table wines, also called Crystal Springs or Morgan Hill Cellars.

J. Pedroncelli Winery

Geyserville, *Sonoma*. Founded 1904.
Owners: John and James Pedroncelli. Wine maker: John Pedroncelli. Visits by appt. 125,000 cases. 135 acres in Sonoma. Wines: many generic and varietal table wines.
Prices: Chard. $7.50; Cab. $5.50; Jug $2.59.

An old reliable for local country jug wines, more recently making Zinfandel, Gewürztraminer, Chardonnay, to a higher standard.

Pendleton Winery

San Jose, *Santa Clara*. Founded 1977.
Wine maker: Brian Pendleton. 6,250 cases of Chard., Cab.Sauv., P.N., Zin., Ch.Bl. from Napa and Monterey grapes.

Perelli-Minetti Winery

Delano, *Kern*. Founded 1894 (as the California Wine Association).
Owners: Perelli-Minetti family and others. About 6m. cases.
Prices: Chard. $8.50; Cab. $8.50; Jug $4.00.

A tangled web in which the wine-making Perelli-Minetti family took over their distributors (in 1971). They now produce several brands, including Guasti, Ambassador, Eleven Cellars and Greystone, mostly used for high-volume lines. The Perelli-Minetti name is used for selected wines from coastal regions (of which I have had a creditable Pinot Noir).

What the jargon means

References to California wine in current literature, on labels and from winery tour guides are full of racy jargon. Some of the less self-explanatory terms are:

Botrytized (pronounced with the accent on the first syllable). Grapes or wine infected, naturally or artificially, with *botrytis cinerea*, the 'noble rot' of Sauternes: hence normally very sweet.

Brix. The American measure of sugar content in grapes, also known as Balling, approximately equal to double the potential alcohol of the wine if all the sugar is fermented. 19.3 Brix is equivalent to 10% alcohol by volume.

Cold stabilization. A near-universal winery practice for preventing the formation of (harmless) tartaric acid crystals in the bottle. The offending tartaric acid is removed by storing wine near freezing point for about 15 days.

Crush. A California term for the vintage; also the quantity of grapes crushed, measured in tons an acre.

Field-grafting. A method much used recently for converting established vines from one variety to another – usually red to white. The old vine top is cut off near the ground and a bud of the new variety grafted on.

Free-run juice. The juice that flows from the crushed grapes 'freely' before pressing. By implication, superior. Normally mixed with pressed juice.

Gas chromatograph. An expensive gadget for analysing a compound (e.g. wine) into its chemical constituents.

Gondola. A massive hopper for carrying grapes from vineyard to crusher, behind a tractor or on a truck.

Jug wines. Originally, wines collected from the winery in a jug for immediate use – therefore of ordinary quality. Now standard wines sold in large bottles.

Ovals. Barrels of any size with oval, rather than round, ends, kept permanently in one place and not moved around the cellar – the German rather than the French tradition.

Polish filtration. Nothing to do with Poland; a final filtration through a very fine-pored filter to 'polish' the wine to gleaming brilliance.

Pomace. The solid matter – skins, pips and stems – left after pressing.

Skin contact. Alas not that, but a reference to leaving the juice mixed with the skins before separating them. All red wines must have maximum skin contact. Some white wines gain good flavours from a few hours' 'maceration' with their skins before fermentation. For the 'cleanest', most neutral wine, a wine maker would avoid any skin contact.

Pesenti Winery

Templeton, *San Luis Obispo*. Founded 1934.
Wine maker: Frank Nerelli. 33,000 cases. Wines: Zin., Zin.Bl., Cab.Sauv., Cab.Sauv.Bl., Cab.Rosé.

Joseph Phelps Vineyards

St. Helena, *Napa*. Founded 1972.
Owner: Joseph Phelps. Wine maker: Walter Schug. No visits. 50,000 cases. 170 acres in Napa Valley. Wines: Chard., Sauv.Bl., Gewürz., P.N., Cab.Sauv., Zin., Syrah., J.R. Prices: Syr. '77, $7.75; Chard. '79, $12.00; J.R. '80, $6.25; Cab.Sauv. '78, $10.75.

An ex-builder with an unerring sense of style built his beautiful redwood barn in the choppy foothills east of St. Helena near the Heitz place. His achievement is like a scaled-down Robert Mondavi's; all his many wines are good and several are among the best. My favourites are Riesling, distinctly Germanic (whether dry or late-harvest) and beautiful with bottle-age; Gewürztraminer – dry but joyous like a yellow balloon; Syrah – real Rhône Syrah, the '75 sweet and nutty in 1981; Cabernets – far from obvious but inspiring confidence. The Insignia label is for a Cabernet/Merlot blend on Bordeaux lines not qualifying as 'varietal' by the rules. Phelps Chardonnay is also restrained at first, but secretly rich: the '77 in 1982 rang as true as a bell; the '76 had opened into a golden glow. Le Fleuron is a second label.

Pine Ridge Winery

Napa, *Napa*. Founded 1978.
Principal and wine maker: R. Gary Andrus. Visits. 14,600 cases. 119 acres in Carneros, Rutherford, Stag's Leap and Big Ranch, all in Napa Valley. Wines: Cab.Sauv., Chard., Ch.Bl. Price: Cab.Sauv. '79, $8.99.

Another old winery revived to make Chardonnay of Carneros and Stag's Leap grapes, Cabernet from Rutherford.

Piper-Sonoma

Windsor, *Sonoma*. Founded 1980.
A joint enterprise between Piper-Heidsieck and Sonoma Vineyards. Consultant wine maker: Michel Lacroix. Visits. 100,000 cases plus of Brut, Blanc de Noirs and Tête de Cuvée.

The second Champo-California venture. At birth (first wine 1982) it shows signs of vigour to match Domaine Chandon, the first.

Pommeraie Vineyards

Sebastopol, *Sonoma*. Founded 1979.
Wine maker: Ken Dalton. 2,000 cases of Cab.Sauv. and Chard.

Pope Valley Winery

Pope Valley, *Napa*. Founded 1972.
Wine maker: James McDevitt. 12,000 cases. Wines: Chard., Cab.Sauv., Zin., Ch.Bl., J.R., Sauv.Bl., Pet.Sir.

Prager Winery & Port Works

St. Helena, *Napa*. Founded 1980.
Wine maker: James Prager. 1,500 cases. Wines: Cab.Sauv., Chard., ports.

Preston Vineyards

Healdsburg, *Sonoma*. Founded 1975.
Owner and wine maker: Louis D. Preston. No visits. 4,000 cases (growing). 80 acres in Dry Creek Valley, Sonoma. Wines: Sauv.Bl., Zin., Gam., Ch.Bl.

One of Sonoma's best Sauvignons of the leaves-and-all school and a similarly vivid, not heavy, Zinfandel.

Quady

Madera, *Madera*. Founded 1977.
Principal and wine maker: Andrew Quady. Visits by appt. 1,250 cases. Wines: vintage port, Essensia dessert wine.

Quady uses Zinfandel from Amador County but has the classic Portuguese varieties planted there for future use. The handsome 'artist's label' is for wine to buy for ageing.

Quail Ridge

Napa, *Napa*. Founded 1978.
Owner and wine maker: Elaine Wellesley. Visits by appt. 6,000 cases – increasing to 10,000 cases. Napa Valley Chard., Fr.Col.

The first Chardonnay, 1978, barrel fermented, was a triumph.

Rafanelli Winery

Dry Creek Valley, *Sonoma*. Founded 1974.
Wine maker: Fred Peterson. 2,500 cases of Cab.Sauv. and Zin. Much respected by some who know.

Ranchita Oaks Winery

San Miguel, *San Luis Obispo*. Founded 1979.
President: Ron Bergstrom. Wine maker: John Scott. Visits. 4,000 cases. 44 acres in San Miguel, San Luis Obispo County. Wines: Cab.Sauv., Pet.Sir., Zin., Chard.

Rancho de Philo

Alta Loma, *San Bernardino*. Founded 1975.
Wine maker: Philo Biane. A few hundred cases. Wine: 'Triple' Cream Sherry, 16 years old, made as a retirement pursuit by the ex-President of Brookside (q.v.).

Rancho Sisquoc Winery

Santa Maria, *Santa Barbara*. Founded 1972, winery 1978.
Wine maker: Harold Pfeiffer. 2,000 cases. 194 acres. Wines: Cab.Sauv., Chard., Sauv.Bl., J.R., Sylvaner in Santa Maria Valley. (Part of the 38,000-acre James Flood Ranch.)

Ravenswood

San Francisco, *San Francisco*. Founded 1976.
Wine maker: Doel Peterson. 2,500–4,000 cases. Wines: Zin., Cab.Sauv., Merlot.

Martin Ray Vineyards

Saratoga, *Santa Clara*. Founded 1946.
Principal: Peter M. Ray. Visits by appt. 5,000 cases. Vineyard in Santa Cruz Mountains. Wines: Chard., P.N., Cab.Sauv., Merlot, J.R. and *méthode champenoise* sparkling wines.

Martin Ray was a friend of Paul Masson, a gifted wine maker but temperamentally the only one in step. His wines were outrageously expensive and frequently out of condition, but the good bottles were memorable. His original taste is illustrated by the fact that he drank his Pinot Noir at 80°F (27°C). Litigation (rarely far away) split his vineyard. Part is now Mt. Eden (q.v.). His son continues to make controversial wines, principally Chardonnay, incredibly expensive sparkling and varietals from bought-in grapes under the La Montana label.

Raymond Winery and Vineyards

St. Helena, *Napa*. Founded 1974.
Principal: Ray Raymond Sr. 25,000 cases from 905 acres of Chard., Cab.Sauv., Zin., Gamay, Ch.Bl., Sauv.Bl.

A family-run affair considered to give good value with typical oaky Napa Chardonnay, Cabernet in the same vein and a good example of a late-harvest Riesling.

Ridge Vineyards

Cupertino, *Santa Clara*. Founded 1959.
President: Dave Bennion. Wine maker: Paul Draper. Visits. 30,000 cases. Vineyards near the winery plus grapes bought elsewhere (see below). Wines: Cab.Sauv., Zin., Pet.Sir. (and small quantities of Ruby Cab., Chard. and Merlot).
Prices: Zin. York '79, $8.99; Cab.Sauv. '78, $12.00.

One of California's accepted first-growths, isolated on a mountain-top south of San Francisco in an atmospheric old stone building that is cooled by a natural spring. The adjacent vineyard produces Montebello Cabernet but Cabernet and Petite Sirah are also bought at York Creek, Napa, and Zinfandel from Geyserville, Sonoma, and Fiddletown, Amador.

All the wines have a reputation for darkness, intensity and needing long ageing. My notes record that the '78 York Creek Cabernet is heavier and more concentrated than the excellent, elegant and lingering Montebello. The Amador Zinfandel '78 is no overripe monster, but admirably fruity, clean and long. The '74 Zinfandel from Geyserville smells of honey, a beautiful wine. The '75 Montebello Cabernet is delicate, but very good quality. The '72 has taken 10 years to lose a mean bite and become a very fine bottle of claret.

Ritchie Creek

St. Helena, *Napa*. Founded 1974.
Wine maker: Peter Minor. 350 cases plus from 6 acres of steep vineyard in the Mayacamas Mountains. Wine: Cab.Sauv. All sold locally.

River Oaks

A corporation with a total of 700 acres in Sonoma producing some 100,000 cases of good commercial generic and varietal wines. The wine is made at the Clos du Bois winery (q.v.).

River Road Vineyards

Forestville, *Sonoma*. Founded 1977.
Wine maker: Gary Mills. 3,000 cases from 120 acres of Chard., J.R., Fumé Bl., Zin.

River Run Vintners

Watsonville, *Monterey*. First harvest 1978.
Owners: William and Terra Hangen. 2,500 cases. Wines: Zin., Cab.Sauv., Chard., P.N., Wh.Ries.

Roddis Cellar

Calistoga, *Napa*. Founded 1979.
Wine maker: William Roddis. 210 cases from vineyard on Diamond Mountain. Wine: Cab.Sauv.

Rosenblum Cellars Winery

Oakland, *Alameda*. Founded 1978.
1,450 cases. Wines: Chard., J.R., Ch.Bl., Gewürz., Cab.Sauv., Zin., Pet.Sir.

Ross-Keller

Buellton, *Santa Barbara*. Founded 1980.
Wine maker: William Fluck. 3,500 cases of various generic and varietal wines from Santa Ynez Valley grapes. Brand names are San Carlos de Jonata, Zaca Creek.

Roudon-Smith Vineyards

Santa Cruz, *Santa Cruz*. Founded 1972.
Owners: Bob and Annamaria Roudon, Jim and June Smith. Wine maker: Bob Roudon. Visits. 10,000 cases. Grapes from Santa Cruz, Monterey, Sonoma and Mendocino. Wines: Chard., Cab.Sauv., Zin., Pet.Sir.

A 2-family affair, children and all, with outstanding Chardonnay, balanced between firm and smooth like a 1974 Meursault. The Cabernet matches it well in style; the Zinfandel is more burly. The second label is MacKenzie Creek.

Round Hill Cellars

St. Helena, *Napa*. Founded 1978.
President: Charles Abela. Wine maker: Doug Manning. Visits. 75,000 cases. Many wines from Napa, Sonoma and North Coast grapes.
Price: Zin. Napa '78, $4.50.

Not all new Napa wineries aim at Montrachet. Round Hill supplies a wider market with good-value versions of distinct variety-plus-region character, notably Napa Gewürztraminer and Fumé Blanc; Sonoma Cabernet. Rutherford Ranch is a second label.

Rutherford Hill Winery

St. Helena, *Napa*. Founded 1972.
Partners: Bill Jaeger and Chuck Carpy. Wine maker: Phil Baxter. Visits. 100,000 cases. The partners own some 600 acres in the valley. Wines: Chard., Gewürz., J.R., Zin., P.N., Merlot, Cab.Sauv., Sauv.Bl.
Prices: Gewürz. '79, $5.25; Cab.Sauv. '78, $7.99.

Compare the partners with Freemark Abbey. Here they use their nicknames and relax. The winery was built for Souverain but sold to the present owners in 1976. Now the idea is true fruity varietals with a light touch for restaurant-drinking and the better class of picnic – which in California is saying a lot.

Rutherford Vintners

Rutherford, *Napa*. Founded 1976.
Owners: Bernard and Evelyn Skoda. Visits. 14,500 cases. 30 acres in Napa Valley. Wines: Cab.Sauv., J.R., P.N., Chard., Muscat.

The former manager of Louis M. Martini (q.v.) aims for delicacy and succeeds in balancing his wines without excess of alcohol or oak. His Chardonnay comes from Alexander Valley, Sonoma. Chateau Rutherford and Rutherford Cellars are other registered names.

St. Clement Vineyards

St. Helena, *Napa*. Founded 1975.
Owner: William J. Casey. Wine maker: Dennis Johns. No visits. 7,500 cases. Vineyard in Napa. Wines: Cab.Sauv., Chard., Sauv.Bl.
Price: Chard. '80, $13.00.

A small and specialized producer; a great success with critics at the outset, though I have been unlucky with a badly oxidized Chardonnay ('77). The '79 is an example of the (to me) oversized style: too fiercely alcoholic for its fruit.

St. Francis Winery

Kenwood, *Sonoma*. Founded 1979.
Wine maker: Bob Robertson. 12,000 cases plus (all estate wine) from 100 acres of Chard., J.R., Gewürz., Merlot, and P.N.
Prices: Gewürz. '79, $6.50; Cab.Sauv. '79, $12.00.

San Antonio Winery

Los Angeles. Owners: The Riboli family. 300,000 cases of various types from Central Coast and other grapes for local L.A. sales.

Sanford & Benedict Vineyards

Lompoc, *Santa Barbara*. Founded 1975.
Principal and wine maker: Michael Benedict. Visits by appt. 8,500 cases. 112 acres in Santa Ynez Valley, Santa Barbara, planted in P.N., Chard., Cab.Sauv., Merlot.
Prices: Chard. $12.50; Cab. $10.00; Jug $5.95.

At the ocean end of the Santa Ynez Valley, a simple, almost primitive little winery, specializing in estate Pinot Noir and Chardonnay. Pinot Noir is dark, rich-flavoured, tannic and true to type. Chardonnay is neat and clean. Not so the ('79) Cabernet I have tasted.

San Martin Winery

San Martin, *Santa Clara*. Founded 1908.
Owners: Somerset Wine Co. No visits. 585,000 cases (some sold in bulk). Grapes from the Central Coast and Central Valley. Many table wines.
Prices: Chard. $7.50; Cab. $7.75; Jug $3.95.

An inventive, technically excellent and bargain-priced winery shaking off a scruffy image to emerge as the leader in 'soft' (i.e. about German-strength) white wines made to taste of the grape. Riesling, Sauvignon Blanc and Chardonnay do so. Petite Sirah, Zinfandel and late-harvest wines are also good buys.

San Pasqual Vineyards

Escondido, *San Diego*. Founded 1974.
Wine maker: Kerry Damskey. 25,000 cases. Wines: Ch.Bl., Fumé Bl., Gam., Pet.Sir., Moscato Canelli from 100 acres in San Pasqual Valley.

Pleasant Sauvignon Blanc and Gamay and sweet, light-weight Muscat Canelli.

Santa Barbara Winery

Santa Barbara, *Santa Barbara*. Founded 1962.
Wine maker: Pierre Lafond. 10,000 cases of Ch.Bl., Ries., Zin., Cab.Sauv. and sherry from Santa Ynez Valley grapes.

Santa Cruz Mountain Vineyard

Santa Cruz, *Santa Cruz*. Founded 1974.
Principal and wine maker: Ken D. Burnap. 3,125 cases from 12 acres of vineyards in Santa Cruz Mountains of P.N., Cab.Sauv., Chard.

A locally respected specialist in powerful Pinot Noir.

Santa Ynez Valley Winery

Santa Barbara, *Santa Barbara*. Founded 1969.
Owners: The Bettencourt, Davidge and Brander families. Wine maker: Fred Brander. Visits. 10,000 cases. 140 acres in Santa Ynez Valley, Santa Barbara, planted in Sauv.Bl., Chard., Ries., Gewürz., Cab.Sauv., Merlot.
Price: Sauv.Bl. '80, $7.50.

A white wine specialist celebrated from birth for marvellously confident and vital Sauvignon-Blanc (1977).

Santino Wines

Plymouth, *Amador*. Founded 1979.
President: Nancy Santino. Wine maker: Scott Harvey. 8,500 cases. Wines: Zin. (red and white), Cab.Sauv., Sauv.Bl.

Emerging as the best winery of the area; hefty Zinfandels include a sweetish near-white one rather like a South German *Weissherbst*.

Sarah's Vineyard

Gilroy, *Santa Clara*. Founded 1978.
Wine maker: Marilyn Otteman. 1,500 cases of Chard., Cab.Sauv., Merlot, J.R. and Zin.

Sarah's Chardonnay already has a high reputation.

V. Sattui Winery

St. Helena, *Napa*. Founded 1885, refounded 1975 (by the same family).
Owner and wine maker: Daryl Sattui. Visits. 8,500 cases. Wines. Cab.Sauv., Zin., Chard., J.R., 'Madeira'.

Respectable Napa and Mendocino Rieslings and about average Amador County Zinfandel.

Sausal Winery

Healdsburg, *Sonoma*. Founded 1973.
Principal and wine maker: Dave Demostene. No visits. 29,000 cases. 125 acres in Alexander Valley, Sonoma. Wines: Zin., P.N., Gam., Chard., Cab.Sauv.Bl.
Prices: Cab.Sauv. '78, $7.50; Chard. '80, $8.50.

A former supplier of grapes and bulk wines launched (1979) with above-average Zinfandel and others.

Scharffenberger Cellars

Ukiah, *Mendocino*. Founded 1981.
Wine maker: Robert Porter. 4,000 cases. Wines: Brut (sparkling wine).

Schramsberg Vineyards

Calistoga, *Napa*. Founded 1862 by Jacob Schram, 1965 by Jack Davies.
Owners: Jack and Jamie Davies. Wine maker: Gregory Fowler. Visits by appt. 20,000 cases. 40 acres in Napa Valley. Wine: bottle-fermented sparkling wines.
Price: Cuv.Pinot '78, $12.65.

Robert Louis Stevenson drank 'bottled poetry' at Schram's ornate white, verandahed house. So have I, many times, under the Davies regime. Jack has visited just about every sparkling-wine cellar on earth and learned something in all of them. He practises his mystery in shiny steel, in old coolie-driven rock tunnels, and in his forest-clearing vineyard. His Blanc de Blancs is California's subtlest and driest, most age-worthy 'champagne', the Blanc de Noirs juicier and more generous, the Cuvée de Pinot a dry 'partridge-eye' pink and the Crémant a sweet, subtly Muscat, less fizzy party wine.

Schug Cellars

Calistoga, *Napa*. Founded 1980 by Walter Schug and Jerry Seps.
1,800 cases Pinot Noir in 1982, with others to come.

A new enterprise by the brilliant wine maker of Joseph Phelps (q.v.) using rock cellars cut in 1880 for the Jacob Grimm Winery. Seps also owns Storybook Mountain.

Seaview Winery

Casadero, *Sonoma*. Founded 1980.
Wine maker: Dan Wickham. 5,000 cases of P.N. from a 10-acre estate 3 miles from the ocean. Also Zin., Sauv.Bl.

Sebastiani Vineyards

Sonoma, *Sonoma*. Founded 1904.
Owner: Sam J. Sebastiani. Wine maker: Jim Carter. Visits. 750,000 cases (total sales 3.5m. cases). 400 acres in Sonoma Valley. Many wines.
Prices: Chard. $7.50; Cab. $6.25; Jug $3.35.

A name intimately connected with the historic little city of Sonoma (which even has a turn-of-the-century Sebastiani Theatre) but now a brand drawing wines from less distinguished regions for huge low-price sales. The original hearty Italian style is still seen in Barbera and perhaps Zinfandel. 'Mountain' generics are fair enough. I have had an excellent bottle of fruity dry 'Eye of the Swan' Pinot Noir.

Schramsberg, high in the hills near Calistoga, where Robert Louis Stevenson drank 'bottled poetry' with Jacob Schram, and Jack Davies now makes splendid sparkling wine

Sequoia Grove Vineyards
Napa, *Napa*. Founded 1980.
Wine maker: James Allen. 4,200 cases. Wines: Estate Chard., Cab.Sauv.

Shafer Vineyards
Napa, *Napa*. Founded 1979.
Principal: John R. Shafer. Wine maker: Nikko Schoch. Visits by appt. 8,500 cases. Wines: Chard., Cab.Sauv., Zin. from 40 acres at Stag's Leap, Napa.

Charles F. Shaw Vineyard and Winery
St. Helena, *Napa*. Founded in 1979.
Owner: Charles F. Shaw Jr. No visits. 12,500 cases. 47 acres in Napa County. Wines: Gam., Zin.

The Shaws live in their vineyard and for their Gamay. With carbonic maceration, then oak ageing, they aim to produce Napa's equivalent of a Beaujolais Cru – a Fleurie or Chénas, a 2- or 3-year wine. A second label, Bale Mill Cellars, offers a Chenin Blanc.

Shenandoah Vineyards
Plymouth, *Amador*. Founded 1977.
Wine maker: Len Sobon. 6,250 cases. Wines: Zin., Ch.Bl., Mission, Muscat.

Unusual rich wines that bespeak the Sierra foothills.

Sherrill Cellars
Woodside, *Santa Clara*. Founded 1973.
Wine maker: Nat Sherrill. 2,000–3,000 cases from Central Coast of Pet.Sir., Cab.Sauv., Zin.; also called Skyline.

Shown & Sons Vineyards
Rutherford, *Napa*. Founded 1971.
Wine maker: Tom Cottrell. 14,500 cases. Wine: Estate Ch.Bl., J.R., Cab.Sauv.
Price: Cab.Sauv. '78, $8.00.

Sierra Vista Winery
Placerville, *El Dorado County*. Founded 1977.
Wine maker: John McReady. 2,000 cases. Wines: Zin., Cab.Sauv., Ch.Bl., Chard., Sauv.Bl., Fumé Bl., Pet.Sir.

Silver Mountain Vineyards
Los Gatos, *Santa Cruz*. Founded 1979.
Wine maker: Gerald O'Brien. 1,250 cases from 12 acres of Chard., Zin.

Silver Oak Cellars
Oakville, *Napa*. Founded 1972.
Partners: Justin Meyer and Raymond Duncan. Visits by appt. 6,250 cases of Cab.Sauv. from Alexander Valley, Sonoma, grapes.

100% Cabernet Sauvignon aged 3 years in wood and 2 in bottle before release. Appreciated for forthright style.

Simi Winery
Healdsburg, *Sonoma*. Founded 1876.
President: Michael G. D. Dixon. Wine maker: Zelma Long. Visits. 125,000 cases. Vineyard in Alexander Valley and Medocino County. Wines: Chard., Gewürz., Ch.Bl., Gam.Beauj., P.N., Zin., Cab.Sauv., Cab.Rosé.
Prices: Chard. $10.00; Cab. $9.00; Jug $4.00.

Simi 1935 Zinfandel is one of the very few antique California wines to have survived in any quantity. It is marvellous. The impressive old stone winery has had several changes of owner and policy but seems to have settled for a fairly unemphatic but fruity style of reds that goes down well in Britain. It now belongs to Moët-Hennessy.

Alexander Valley Chardonnay is pretty pungent; Mendocino is quieter. Gewürztraminer is both fresh and racy. I have also tasted a remarkable Beaujolais-style Pinot Noir and a fine Merlot, but they were not, I think, commercially available.

Sky Vineyards

Mayacamas Mountains, *Sonoma*. Founded 1979.
Wine maker: Lore Olds. 4,000 cases of Zin. from 20 acres at 2,000 feet.

Smith-Madrone

St. Helena, *Napa*. Founded 1971.
Owner and wine maker: Stuart Smith. Visits by appt. 3,000 rising to 6,000 cases from 50 acres on Spring Mountain, Napa.
Wines: J.R., Chard., P.N., Cab.Sauv.
Price: Chard. '79, $8.99.

Vineyards at 1,700 feet and total hard-working dedication are making remarkable wines in a simple cellar. Sweet, lemony Riesling; dark, waxy young Pinot Noir; Cabernet '78, 31 months in new barrels and still fruity. Stew Smith even has a few of the rare Viognier vines from the Rhône.

Smothers (Vine Hill Wines, Inc.)

Santa Cruz, *Santa Cruz*. Founded 1977.
Owner: Dick Smothers. Wine maker: William Arnold. No visits. 3,500 cases of Gewürz., Chard., J.R., Zin., Cab.Sauv. from vineyards in Santa Cruz and Sonoma County.

A comedian's hobby. Incredibly scented late-harvest Gewürztraminer is my only experience of his wine.

Soda Rock Winery

Healdsburg, *Sonoma*. Founded 1980.
Wine maker: Charles Tomka. A potential 50,000 cases plus of Zin., Cab.Sauv., Ch.Bl., J.R.

Sommelier

Mountain View, *Santa Clara*. Founded 1976.
Wine maker: Dick Keezer. 3,750 cases of Chard., Cab.Sauv., Pet.Sir., Zin.

Sonoma Vineyards

Windsor, *Sonoma*. Founded 1959.
Chairman: Kenneth J. Kwit. Wine maker: Rodney D. Strong. Visits. 585,000 cases. 1,200 acres in Sonoma County. Wines: Cab.Sauv., J.R., Zin., Chard. and others.
Prices: Chard. $9.00; Cab. $12.00; Jug $3.29.

The business started as a mail-order house in Tiburon on San Francisco Bay, moved to Windsor in 1970 and now controls a great deal of good vineyards. The standard wines are good value. The high points are Alexander's Crown Estate Cabernet and River West Estate Chardonnay. *See* Piper-Sonoma.

Sotoyome Winery

Healdsburg, *Sonoma*. Founded 1973.
Wine maker: William Chaikin. 2,500 cases of Chard., Cab.Sauv., Pet.Sir., Zin.

Souverain Cellars

Geyserville, *Sonoma*. Founded 1973.
Owners: California North Coast Grape Growers Assn. Wine maker: Bob Mueller. Visits. 520,000 cases. Many wines under the general appellation 'North Coast'.
Prices: Chard. $7.38; Cab. $7.38; Jug $2.63.

A very grand edifice for a growers' cooperative, explained by a complicated history in which the link with the once-renowned Napa Souverain of Lee Stewart was broken. Look out for Cabernet, Chardonnay, Colombard Blanc, Gamay Beaujolais and Moscato Canelli.

The town of Sonoma, briefly the capital of California, is the most historic and best preserved of the wine centres. At its Franciscan Mission, priests planted the first grapes in the region

Spring Mountain Vineyards

St. Helena, *Napa*. Founded 1968 (since 1976 on present site).
President: Michael Robbins. Wine maker: John Williams.
Visits. 25,000 cases. 125 acres in Spring Mountain and Rutherford. Wines: Cab.Sauv., Chard., Sauv.Bl., P.N.
Prices: Cab.Sauv. '78, $12.50; Chard. '79, $13.50.

Spring Mountain Road climbs the hills west of St. Helena to several splendid vineyards. Robbins' Victorian house and faintly French-looking winery ('Falconcrest' of a T.V. serial) stand on the first slopes. Robbins' whole aim is elegance and finesse. Chardonnay and Cabernet are both among the best from the newer small wineries, clearly designed to age rather than win medals in their first year. In the mid-1970s a non-vintage Cabernet, Les Trois Cuvées, appeared. It was still young in 1982.

Stag's Leap Wine Cellars

Napa, *Napa*. Founded 1972.
Owners: Warren and Barbara Winiarski. Visits by appt.
15,000–20,000 cases. 40 acres in Napa Valley. Wines: Cab.Sauv., Chard., J.R., Gam.Beauj., Merlot, Pet.Sir.
Price: Cab.Sauv. '78, $15.00.

Winiarski is a professor of Greek turned wine maker, whose Cabernets have startled the French with their resemblance to great Bordeaux. My notes are full of 'harmony, elegance, feminine, finesse'. Compared with Bordeaux they age relatively soon. At 8 years the '74 was complete, with consistent sweetness from lips to throat. At 9 years the '73 was lovely, but beginning to weaken. Stag's Leap Merlot and Chardonnay get equally good reviews, although my favourite remains the Cabernet.

Stags' Leap Winery

Napa, *Napa*. Founded 1972.
Wine maker: Randle Johnson. 10,000 cases from 100 acres.
Wines: Pet.Sir., Ch.Bl., Cab.Sauv., Merlot, P.N.
Price: Cab.Sauv. '78, $7.50.

P. and M. Staiger

Boulder Creek, *Santa Cruz*. Founded 1973.
Wine maker: Paul Staiger. 500 cases of Chard., Cab.Sauv.

Robert Stemmler Winery

Healdsburg, *Sonoma*. Founded 1977.
Principal and wine maker: Robert Stemmler. Visits by appt.
4,000 cases. Small vineyard in Dry Creek Valley, Sonoma.
Wines: Chard., Fumé Bl., Sauv.Bl., Cab.Sauv.

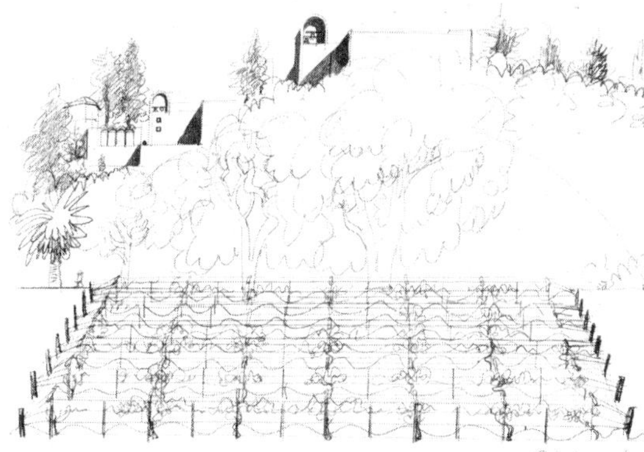

Sterling Vineyard crowns a knoll in the Napa Valley

Sterling Vineyards

Calistoga, *Napa*. Founded 1964.
Owners: The Coca-Cola Company. President: M. P. W. Stone.
Wine maker: Theo Rosenbrand. Visits. 75,000 cases. 350 acres in Napa Valley. Wines: Cab.Sauv., Merlot, P.N., Zin., Chard., Sauv.Bl., Gewürz.
Prices: Sauv.Bl. '80, $9.10; Merlot '78, $9.50.

The long white building like a Greek monastery hugs the top of a lump in the valley floor big enough to need cable cars to get up it. British money built it in the 1960s; Coca-Cola bought it in 1978. Ric Forman, now with his own winery, designed the Sterling style of original, serious wines. The wine boss is now Theo Rosenbrand, who worked at Beaulieu for many years. The Sterling specialities have been austere Cabernet with a daring level of volatile acidity, similar intense Merlot and strong, dry Sauvignon Blanc which can come as a relief after some of the more tropical-fruit flavours of the valley. Chardonnay follows the same lines.

Stevenot Winery

Murphys, *Calaveras*. Founded 1978.
Principal: Barden Stevenot. Wine maker: Julia Iantosca. Visits.
11,000 cases. 20 acres of estate vineyard. Wines: Ch.Bl., Zin.Bl., Pet.Sir., Chard., Ries.

Ambitious winery well launched with Chenin Blanc and Zinfandel.

Stone Creek

A San Francisco distributor's label for wines made at Souverain (q.v.), Sonoma, including a very pleasant brambly Zinfandel.

Stonegate

Calistoga, *Napa*. Founded 1973.
Owners: James and Barbara Spaulding. Wine makers: David Spaulding and Michael Fallow. Visits by appt. 13,500 cases. Vineyard in Napa Valley plus grapes from Sonoma. Wines: Cab.Sauv., Merlot, P.N., Chard., Sauv.Bl., Fr.Col. Price: Merlot '77, $8.50.

Estate wines are high-flavoured but not always in good condition.

Stoneridge

Sutter Creek, *Amador*. Founded 1975.
Wine maker: Gary Porteous. 830 cases. Wines: Zin. (red and white), Ruby Cab.

A small cellar that uses only local grapes.

Stony Hill Vineyard

St. Helena, *Napa*. Founded 1951.
Owner: Eleanor W. McCrea. Wine maker: Michael Chelini. Visits by appt. 4,000 cases. 35 acres in Napa Valley. Wines: Chard., J.R., Gewürz., Sweet Semillon de Soleil.

Fred McCrea was the first of the flood of men from busy offices who realized that the Napa Valley offered something better. He planted white grapes in the 1940s and made 25 vintages of his own understated style of wine. Neither the variety nor the maturation grabs your attention; the point seems to be boundless vigour and depth without an obvious handle. At a 1980 tasting of all the Chardonnay vintages of the 1960s, the '62 was best, in fact fabulous, but not markedly older than the '69. Eleanor McCrea has inherited her late husband's total integrity of purpose. Inevitably there is a waiting list for something so special.

Stony Ridge Winery

Pleasanton, *Alameda*. Founded 1887, refounded 1975.
Wine maker: Bruce Rector. 17,000 cases. Vineyards in Livermore Valley. Wines: Chard., Sem., Ch.Bl., Fumé Bl., Cab., P.N., Zin., Barbera.

Sullivan Vineyards Winery

Rutherford, *Napa*. Founded 1979.
Wine maker: James Sullivan. 4,000 cases. Wines: Estate Cab.Sauv., Ch.Bl., Chard., Zin.

Summerhill Vineyards

Gilroy, *Santa Clara*. Founded 1917.
40,000 cases of various wines (including fruit wines).

Sunrise Winery

Santa Cruz, *Santa Cruz*. Founded 1976.
Wine maker: Keith Hohlfeldt. 2,000 cases of P.N., Cab.Sauv., Chard. and Zin.

Sutter Home Winery

St. Helena, *Napa*. Founded 1874, refounded 1946 (by the Trincheros).
President and wine maker: Louis 'Bob' Trinchero. Visits. 100,000 cases. Wines: Zin., Muscat Amabile.

A family operation (named after another, pre-Prohibition family) that shows the virtue of specialization – oddly rare in California. 85% of the wine is Zinfandel of the gutsy kind from Amador County grapes, balanced in flesh and spirit to be worth laying down for 10 years or more. Also rich-flavoured, not-quite-white Zinfandel.

Joseph Swan Vineyards

Forestville, *Sonoma*. Founded 1969.
Owner and wine maker: Joseph Swan. 2,000 cases. 10 acres in Russian River Valley, Sonoma. Wines: Zin., Chard., P.N.

Swan's Zinfandel is a waiting-list wine for those whose cigar-scarred palates are looking for a perceptible flavour.

Sycamore Creek Vineyards

Morgan Hill, *Santa Clara*. Founded 1976.
Wine maker: Terry Parks. 3,000 cases from 16 acres of Chard., Gewürz., J.R., Zin., Cab.Sauv.

Taylor California Cellars

Gonzalez, *Monterey*. Founded 1979.
Owner: The Coca-Cola Company. Wine maker: Dr Richard Peterson. 5.4m. cases. Wines: Cab.Sauv., Chard., Sauv.Bl., Ch.Bl., Ries. and generic table wines.

A huge new winery; its initial colossal success based on the wide reputation of Taylor's New York State wines. The Monterey Vineyard (q.v.), where the blends are made, produces 15%. The rest is made by Franzia, Sierra, Bronco, Noble and others. The varietals are very well received in their price range.

Topolos at Russian River Vineyard

Forestville, *Sonoma*. Founded 1969, refounded 1980.
Wine maker: Michael Topolos. 6,250 cases of Chard., Cab.Sauv., P.N., Zin., Gewürz., Pet.Sir.

Toyon Winery and Vineyards

Healdsburg, *Sonoma*. Founded 1972.
Wine maker: Donald Holm. 5,000 cases of Cab.Sauv., Zin., Chard. and Gerwürz.

The 'bear flag' of the short-lived California Republic flies over the winery tower of Spring Mountain, built in 1979 in the style of the last century. Behind the façade is a rock tunnel; cellars dug for Tiburcio Parrot 100 years ago

Trefethen Vineyards

Napa, *Napa*. Founded 1886, refounded 1973.
Owners: The Trefethen family. President: John Trefethen.
Wine maker: David Whitehouse Jr. Visits by appt. 33,500 cases. 600 acres in Napa Valley. Wines: J.R., Chard., P.N., Cab.Sauv., red and white 'Eshcol'.
Prices: Esch. Red NV $4.25; Chard. '79, $12.00; Cab.Sauv. '78, $10.00.

The Trefethens bought the former 'Eshcol' vineyards, in mid-valley near Napa, in 1968, leased their grand old wooden barn to Moët-Hennessy for their first vintage of Domaine Chandon (for which they grew many of the grapes), then started using their best grapes to make their own wine. The whole line is highly polished and professional (and good value). Chardonnay attracted most notice at first, but the clean mid-weight Cabernet, the dry Riesling with no lush or melony touches and a Pinot Noir that shows the nervous nature of this thoroughbred make a classy stable. Blended 'Eshcol' table wines are some of the best value in the state. Eshcol was the valley where the monster grape cluster grew (Numbers XIII v. 23). So is this.

Trentadue Winery and Vineyards

Geyserville, *Sonoma*. Founded 1969.
Owners and wine makers: Leo and Evelyn Trentadue. 25,000 cases from 200 acres of many varieties. Big dry wines without finesse.

Tudal Winery

St. Helena, *Napa*. Founded 1974.
Wine maker: Arnold Tudal. 1,500 cases. Wines: Estate Cab.Sauv., Chard.

Tulocay Winery

Napa, *Napa*. Owners and wine makers: W. C. and Barbara Cadman. Founded 1975.
Visits by appt. 2,000 cases. Wines: Cab.Sauv., P.N., Zin., Chard., all from Napa Valley grapes.

A small operation making full-flavoured reds designed for laying down.

Turgeon & Lohr

San Jose, *Santa Clara*. Founded 1974.
Partners: Jerry Lohr and Bernie Turgeon. Wine maker: Barry Gnekow. Visits by appt. 100,000 cases. 280 acres in Salinas Valley, Monterey. Wines: J.R., Ch.Bl., Fumé Bl., P.Bl., Chard., Gam., P.N., Cab.Sauv., Zin., Pet.Sir.

Riesling from Monterey is the best-regarded wine. Cabernet Rosé and Gamay are useful light reds. The labels are J. Lohr and Jade.

Turner Winery

Lodi, *San Joaquin*. Founded 1979.
10,000 cases from 580 acres in Lake County, of J.R., Cab.Sauv., Gam.Beauj., Zin., Chard., Ch.Bl., Sauv.Bl.

Tyland Vineyards

Ukiah, *Mendocino*. Founded 1979.
Owners: Dick and Judy Tijsselin. Wine maker: Miles Karakasevich. Visits. 6,000 cases. 35 acres south of Ukiah. Wines: Chard., Ch.Bl., Gewürz., J.R., Cab.Sauv., Zin., Gam.Beauj.

United Vintners

A subsidiary of Heublein, Inc., operating many big wineries, including Inglenook and Colony.

Valley of the Moon

Sonoma, *Sonoma*. Founded 1944.
90,000 cases, mainly jug wines. Also Fr.Col., Sem., Zin., P.N.

Vega Vineyards Winery

Buellton, *Santa Barbara*. Vineyards planted 1971, winery founded 1979.
Wine maker: Bill Mosby. 4,000 cases of Wh.Ries., Gewürz., Chard., P.N., Cab.Sauv., Pet.Sir., from own vineyards in Santa Ynez Valley.

Ventana Vineyards Winery

Soledad, *Monterey*. Founded 1978.
Owners: J. Douglas and Shirley Meador. Wine maker: Ken Wright. Visits by appt. 30,000 cases. 300 acres on the west side of Salinas Valley. Many wines.

A grower who also supplies half a dozen wineries with grapes for named-vineyard wines, especially Chardonnay. Ventana's own range has good Chardonnay, Pinot Blanc, Riesling, Chenin Blanc, a 'botrytis' Sauvignon Blanc and as many reds.

Vichon Winery

Oakville, *Napa*. Founded 1980.
Partner and wine maker: George Vierra. 12,500 cases plus. Wines: Chard., Cab.Sauv., Sem.

A new winery in the foothills above Oakville showing a distinct sense of style and restraint with moderately oaky, nicely racy Chardonnay (first, 1980) and Chernier, an elegant, dry, well-balanced half-and-half blend of Sauvignon Blanc and Semillon. Cabernet Sauvignon is not yet released. Production, now 25,000 cases, will rise to 40,000.

Villa Armando

Pleasanton, *Alameda*. Founded 1962.
Principal: Anthony Scotto. 150,000 cases. Wines: various, especially sweet reds.

Villa Bianchi

Fresno, *Fresno*. Founded 1974.
Producers of light jug wines.

Villa Mt. Eden

Oakville, *Napa*. Founded 1881, refounded 1970.
Owners: James K. McWilliams and Anne McWilliams. Wine maker: Nils Venge. Visits by appt. 13,000 cases. 87 acres in Oakville, Napa. Wines: Cab.Sauv., Chard., P.N., Chen.Bl., Gewürz., Gam.

A historic vineyard replanted has rapidly made a name for beautifully made dry wines, first Gewürztraminer, then one of the best Chenin Blancs, since 1975 Chardonnay and Cabernet of intensity but balance. Bob Finigan chooses the Chardonnay as one of the longest keepers of all. The grapes are picked by hand but crushed in the vineyard to lose no freshness.

Vina Vista

Cloverdale, *Sonoma*. Founded 1971.
Wine maker: Keith Nelson. 3,000 cases of Cab.Sauv., Chard., J.R., Pet.Sir., Zin.

Vose Vineyards

Napa, *Napa*. Founded 1970.
Wine maker: Hamilton Vose III. 5,000 cases. Wines: Estate Wh.Zin., Cab.Sauv., Chard., Zin., Sauv.Bl.

Walker Wines

Los Altos Hills, *Santa Clara*. Founded 1979.
Wine maker: Russ Walker. 850 cases of Chard., Pet.Sir., Gam., Cab.Sauv., Barbera.

Weibel Champagne Vineyards

Mission San Jose, *Santa Clara*. Founded 1945.
President: Fred E. Weibel. Wine maker: Rick Casqueiro. Visits. 1.4m. cases. 400 acres in Mendocino. Many wines, including sparkling wines.

The speciality is sparkling wine, mostly sold under other merchants' labels. Recently north-coast varietals have been introduced at a new winery at Ukiah, Mendocino.

Wente Bros.

Livermore, *Alameda*. Founded 1883.
Owners: The Wente family (Eric, President; Philip and Jean). Visits. 1.25m. cases. 800 acres in Livermore Valley and 600 acres at Arroyo Seco, Monterey County; produce most varieties of table wine.
Price: J.R. '80, $4.39.

One of the greatest wine dynasties of America. The founder, Carl, started with Charles Krug in the Napa Valley and moved to the stony Livermore Valley because land was cheaper. His sons Herman (wine maker and marketer, d.1961), Ernest (grape grower, d.1981) and Ernest's son Karl (d.1977) are greatly respected names. Karl was a bold innovator, the first in California to build steel fermenting tanks outdoors and a pioneer of Monterey vineyards. The fourth generation have bought 600 more potential vineyard acres (old Cresta Blanca and ranching land) in Livermore to plant in 1982–83. They are also building a sparkling winery at Greenfield, Monterey.

White wines made their name. In the early 1960s their Sauvignon Blanc was my favourite; bold, sappy, old Bordeaux style. Now it and Chardonnay are good, fresh but less distinctive. Arroyo Seco Riesling is unusually sweet but well-balanced. Bob Thompson strongly recommends their dry Semillon.

Whitehall Lane Winery

St. Helena, *Napa*. Founded 1980.
Wine maker: Arthur Finkelstein. 1,500 cases. Wines: Sauv.Bl., Chard., Cab.Sauv. (Second label Jacabels Cellars.)

Willow Creek Winery

McKinleyville, *Humboldt*. Founded 1975.
Wine maker: Dean Williams. 3,000–4,000 cases. Wines: Cab.Sauv., Chard., Gewürz., Zin. red and white., Pet.Sir., Green Hungarian and Chablis.

Willowside Vineyards

Santa Rosa, *Sonoma*. Founded 1970.
Wine maker: Berle Beliz. 3,000 cases of estate Chard., Gewürz., P.N. and Zin.

Wine and the People

Berkeley, *Alameda*. Founded 1970.
Principals: Peter and Fay Brehm. Wine maker: John Tierney. Visits. 6,250 cases. Wines: Cab.Sauv., P.N., Chard.

Specialities are Chardonnay from Winery Lake Vineyard and bulk wines for the restaurant trade under brand names of Berkeley Wine Cellars and Wine and the People.

Winters Winery

Winters, *Yolo*. Founded 1980.
Wine maker: David Storm. 6,250 cases of Zin., Sauv.Bl., Pet.Sir., P.N., Ch.Bl. (also called Storm Cellars).

Woodbury Winery

San Rafael, *Marin*. Founded 1977.
Owner and wine maker: Russell T. Woodbury. Visits by appt. 4,000 cases. Grapes from Sonoma County. Wines: ports.

Woodbury uses Zinfandel, Petite Sirah, Pinot Noir and Cabernet from old vines with pot-still brandy to make port for ageing.

Woodside Vineyards

Woodside, *San Mateo*. Founded 1960.
Wine maker: Robert Mullen. 650 cases. Wines: Cab.Sauv., P.N., Chard., Zin.

Yerba Buena

San Francisco, *San Francisco*. Founded 1977.
Wine maker: Brian Whipple. Wines of various sorts are made in small quantities inside Pier 33 on the harbour.

York Mountain Winery

Templeton, *San Luis Obispo*. Founded 1882.
Wine maker: Steve Goldman. 3,500 cases. Wines: Chard., P.N., Cab.Sauv., Zin., Chen.Bl., Ries.

Old winery now owned by the oenologist Max Goldman.

Yverdon Vineyards

St. Helena, *Napa*. Founded in 1970.
Owner: Fred Aves. 5,000 cases. 92 acres on Spring Mountain and at Calistoga. Wines: Ch.Bl., J.R., Cab.Sauv., Napa Gam.

Zaca Mesa Winery

Los Olivos, *Santa Barbara*. Vineyards planted 1973.
President: Louis Marshall. Wine maker: Ken Brown. Visits. 50,000 cases. 220 acres of vineyards in Santa Ynez Valley, planted in Sauv.Blanc, Chard., Ries., Cab.Sauv., P.N., Zin.

With Firestone (q.v.) one of the first to plant in the Santa Ynez Valley. Pioneer vineyards on the 1,500-foot flat-topped 'mesa' (former cow country) are phylloxera-free and ungrafted. Chardonnay and Riesling were the first two successes. There are high hopes for Pinot Noir, reinforced by the '79 vintage. 'Cool' as the region is, a warm summer can produce blowsy and overstrong wines.

ZD Wines

Napa, *Napa*. Founded 1969.
Partners and wine makers: Norman de Leuze and Gino Zepponi. Visits by appt. 10,000 cases. Grapes bought in Napa, Sonoma, Santa Barbara and St. Louis Obispo for Chard., P.N., Cab.Sauv., Merlot, Zin., J.R.

Pinot Noir and Chardonnay are the focus; the philosophy is to find the right grapes in any part of California.

Classification

The American wine trade has begun to see the advantages of some system of classification to help consumers through the jungle of California wine names. The first publicized attempt was made in 1982 by Ronald Kapon of the magazine *Liquor Store*, in association with *Les Amis du Vin* magazine, by asking 39 of the nation's leading retailers and restaurateurs to classify the best Cabernets of California in a fashion, and to a number, modelled on the 1855 classification of Bordeaux. No doubt later models of a classification, if the idea persists, will modify this arbitrary limit on numbers. It should also be remembered that the short track record of most of these wines bears no resemblance to the tightknit group of Médoc châteaux over a century of trading. Nonetheless the list has some historic value.

The 'first-growths' were Beaulieu Private Reserve, Chappellet, Chateau Montelena, Heitz Martha's Vineyard, Mayacamas, Robert Mondavi Reserve, Stag's Leap Wine Cellars and Sterling Reserve.

The 'second-growths' were Burgess, Burgess 'Vintage Selection', Caymus, Clos du Val, Diamond Creek 'Red Rock Terrace', Diamond Creek 'Volcanic Hill', Jordan, Robert Mondavi, Joseph Phelps 'Insignia', Ridge 'Montebello', Ridge 'York Creek', Spring Mountain, Trefethen, Villa Mt. Eden.

An old water pump marks the Oakville Vineyards of Villa Mt. Eden

THE PACIFIC NORTHWEST

If, in the early 1970s, America was waking up to superlative quality from Napa and Sonoma, by the end of the decade the *avant-garde* were preaching the Pacific Northwest as the coming wine region, with strong hints that the new area would make something closer to the European model: wines less overbearing than the California champions.

It was apparently a visit to Washington in 1967 by André Tchelistcheff, the dean of the Napa Valley, that gave the tentative wine makers of the northwest the confidence to start operating on a commercial scale. He tasted a Gewürztraminer, a variety that had not up to then performed well in California, and recognized the potential of more northerly growing conditions for grapes that tend to overripen in a warm climate. In fact, the previous year David Lett, a California-trained wine maker, had shown his conviction by planting Pinot Noir, another problem grape in California, in the Willamette Valley south of Portland, Oregon.

Fifteen years have been ample time to justify their hopes. In fact it took only nine. In 1979, Lett's 1975 Pinot Noir was placed second in a competitive blind tasting in Paris organized by Robert Drouhin of Beaune and won by his own 1959 Chambolle-Musigny. The Oregon climate, as uncertain as that of Burgundy, seems ideal for this most temperamental grape.

But why the great leap over hundreds of miles of northern California to grow grapes so much farther north than Mendocino County, which already has cool and foggy areas? The answer seems to lie in the configuration of the coastal hills. North of Mendocino the barrier to ocean fog and rain clouds dies away in more broken terrain. Not until north of the Oregon border does the Coast Range reassert itself as a rain catcher, sheltering in the south the Umpqua, then farther north the Willamette Valley. The rainfall is a reasonable 40 inches, and the latitude just that of Bordeaux.

In complete contrast the vineyards of Washington have been planted two ranges back from the ocean, east of the much higher Cascade Mountains, in an area with a mere ten inches in a wet year – the Columbia River Basin and in particular the Yakima Valley. This former semi-desert has been reclaimed for agriculture by irrigation. Its first vines were the American Concord, grown for jelly-making. But its deep sandy soil, long summer daylight and hot sunshine have proved ideal for wine grapes. There are now about 15,000 acres, and suitable south slopes for perhaps 12,000 more. The indications are that the latitude – 100 miles farther north than the Willamette Valley – and the continental extremes of temperature (very cold in winter and surprisingly chilly even on a summer night) are most suited for white grapes. They ripen well while keeping remarkably high acidity, with consequent intensity and length of flavour. Another recent unlooked-for bonus has been a generous top dressing of free fertilizer: ash from the eruption of Mount St. Helens.

Thus the Pacific Northwest is not one area but two, very distinct in conditions and style. What is confusing at present is that Oregon, which has more established wineries, has less vineyards; a mere 2,000 acres. Many Oregon wines therefore contain Washington-grown grapes. Happily, though, Oregon has state wine laws that should put California to shame. The label must say where the grapes were grown. What is more, the old 'generic' terms (Chablis, Burgundy, etc.) are banned. And 'varietal' wines must contain 90 per cent of the grape variety named, with the sensible exception of Cabernet Sauvignon, where other Bordeaux varieties may make up 25 per cent of the blend.

Three regional designations are permitted on Oregon labels: Willamette Valley (nine counties from Portland 100 miles south to Eugene); Umpqua Valley (Douglas county, centred on Roseburg, another 50 miles south); and Rogue Valley (Jackson and Josephine counties, centred on Grant's Pass, 50 miles south again).

Washington's vineyards are concentrated in the Yakima Valley, but its established wineries are centred around Seattle. Up to now the grapes have been transported the 150 miles over the Cascades between the two, but several companies have recently started building near the vineyards, between the ridges of such unvinous-sounding ranges as the Rattlesnake and the Horse Heaven hills.

Many Washington wineries are so new that no wine has yet emerged, but their number represents what can only be described as an explosion and for the first time the state now has more *vinifera* wineries than Oregon. Among the established wineries, the proportion of grapes trucked to Oregon and to Washington wineries that have no significant plantings accounts for the discrepancy, in a number of instances, between the annual production figures and the acreages owned or bearing. Neighbouring Idaho has two wineries, at Caldwell and Wilder, on the latitude of central Oregon (but without its rain).

OREGON WINERIES

Adelsheim Vineyard

Newberg, OR 97132. Willamette Valley.
Owners: David and Virginia Adelsheim. Wine maker: David Adelsheim. 4,000 cases. 18 acres Chard., P.N., J.R., Sauv.Blanc.

The winery first crushed in 1978, using mainly Washington grapes. Recent Chardonnay, Sauvignon and Riesling have been well made.

Amity Vineyards

Amity, OR 97101. Willamette Valley.
Owners: Myron and Ione Redford, Janis Checchia. Wine maker: Myron Redford. 5,000 cases, 70 acres, mainly Chard., Gewürz., P.N., J.R.

An established winery, best so far for Pinot Noir, blended from Oregon and Washington grapes, both barrel-aged and 'Nouveau'. Redford Cellars is a second label, for Cabernet and Merlot. Solstice Blanc is a white blend.

Elk Cove Vineyards

Gaston, OR 97119. Willamette Valley.
Owners and wine makers: Joe and Pat Campbell. 5,000 cases. 24 acres, 22 currently bearing Chard., P.N., J.R.

Uses only local grapes for increasingly good Riesling (crisp and racy), Chardonnay and Pinot Noir. Wines from three vineyards are bottled separately.

The Eyrie Vineyards

Dundee, OR 97115. Willamette Valley.
Owners: David and Diana Lett. Wine maker: David Lett. 5,000 cases. 26 acres, 16 currently bearing Chard., Muscat Ottonel, P.Gris, P.Meunier, P.N.

The pioneer of Pinot Noir in Oregon, equally successful with Chardonnay, fermented in the barrel. His Pinot Gris and Meunier are apparently unique in America; he looks to them for a more economic return than Pinot Noir.

Hillcrest Vineyard

Roseburg, OR 97470. Umpqua Valley.
Owner and wine maker: Richard Sommer. 10,000 cases. 30 acres Cab. Sauv., P.N., J.R.

The first post-Prohibition winery in Oregon, founded in 1961. Sommer specializes in Riesling, particularly late-harvest wines with decided sweetness and some noble rot. Umpqua is marginally warmer than Willamette – enough to encourage Cabernet and round out Pinot Noir.

Knudsen Erath Winery

Dundee, OR 97115. Willamette Valley.
Owners: C. Calvert Knudsen and Richard Erath. Wine maker: Richard Erath. 20,000 cases. 100 acres, 80 currently bearing Chard., P.N., J.R.

Oregon's biggest winery, founded 1975, now well established in Yamhill County. Best regarded for Pinot Noir and Riesling, which are notable value for money. Sparkling wine is planned.

Ponzi Vineyards

Beaverton, OR 97007. Willamette Valley.
Owners: Richard and Nancy Ponzi. Wine maker: Richard Ponzi. 4,200 cases. 11 acres owned, 35 leased; 8 owned and 25 leased bearing Chard., P.Gris, P.N., J.R.

A small family operation but highly regarded, especially for dry Riesling and Chardonnay, and a house blend, 'Oregon Harvest'. Rather blunt, solid Pinot Noir.

Sokol Blosser Winery

Dundee, OR 97115. Willamette Valley.
Owners: The Sokol and Blosser families. Wine maker: Dr. Robert McRitchie. 20,000 cases. 45 acres, 30 currently bearing Chard., P.N., J.R.

One of the larger Oregon wineries with a wide range of products including Merlot, Sauvignon Blanc and Müller-Thurgau, as well as the more typical Willamette Valley grapes. Also two blends, Bouquet Blanc and Rosé. Pinot Noir, Merlot and slightly sweet Riesling are all successes with the critics. Yamhill County Chardonnay is particularly promising.

Tualatin Vineyard

Forest Grove, OR 97116. Willamette Valley.
Owners: Bill Malkmus and William Fuller. Wine maker: William Fuller. 17,000 cases. 85 acres, 65 currently bearing Chard., Gewürz., P.N., J.R.

One of the most consistent northwest wineries, specializing in white wines largely from Washington grapes. Home-grown wines are designated 'estate-bottled'. Riesling, dry Muscat and Gewürztraminer have been particular successes. Estate-bottled Pinot Noir seems to have surprising potential considering the youth of the vines. Bill Fuller did a stint with the Louis Martini winery in the Napa Valley.

Blind tastings

The principal trial ground of the northwest at present is the annual blind tasting staged by the North-West Enological Society in Seattle. Gold medals from this contest are good coinage in a region where the grammar is still being written. Some critics, however, point to the fact that Washington and Oregon wines are too different to compete on equal terms. The intense flavours generated by the climate of extremes in eastern Washington have the same effect in a blind tasting as California wines do on French. They are unreturnable aces. Certainly many Oregon wineries win medals with Washington-grown grapes. One important source is the leading grower, Sagemoor Farms near Pasco in the extreme east of Washington. A certain fresh 'grassy' flavour may often be traced to Sagemoor-grown wines. But there seem to be contrasts within the Yakima Valley: some of Ste. Michelle's Grandview wines, originating farther west, taste more firmly and roundly ripe. There is clearly endless room for experiment.

Grape varieties

For abbreviations and descriptions *see* California, pages 418 and 419.

Prices

Prices for wines from the Pacific Northwest range at present from about \$3.00 to \$13.00 for Oregon and from \$2.50 to \$10.00 for Washington. Eyrie Vineyards: Sauvignon Blanc \$8.50, Pinot Noir and Chardonnay \$13.00. Ch. Ste. Michelle Cabernet \$8.00. Ch. Ste. Michelle Cabernet Reserve \$10.00. Hillcrest Cabernet \$6.00. 'Cascade' (jug) wines a magnum (1.5 litres) \$5.50–\$9.00.

Laboratory analysis plays its part in developing the Northwest's wines

OTHER PRODUCERS

Alpine Vineyards
Alpine (Willamette). Owners: Dan and Christine Jepsen. Wine maker: Dan Jepson. 1,000 cases. 20 acres, 14 bearing. Cab.Sauv., Chard., Gewürz., P.N., J.R.

Arterberry Ltd.
McMinnville. Maker of sparkling cider, but a first *méthode champenoise* Chardonnay in 1982 was excellent.

Bjelland Vineyards
Roseburg (Umpqua). Owners and wine makers: Paul and Mary Bjelland. 1,260 cases. 22 acres, 7 bearing. Cab.Sauv., Chard., Gewürz., Sauv.Bl., Sem., J.R.

Century Home Wines
Newberg (Willamette). Owners: The Mave family. Wine maker: David Mave. 420 cases. 2 acres P.N., J.R.

Chateau Benoit
Carlton (Willamette). Owners: Fred and Mary Benoit. Wine maker: Rich Cushman. 5,500 cases. 40 acres, 10 bearing. Chard., M.-Thurgau, P.N., J.R.

Chehalem Mountain Winery
Newberg (Willamette). Owners: Zane and Pat Mulhausen. Wine maker: Zane Mulhausen. 2,500 cases. 20 acres, 15 bearing, 40 more planned. Chard., P.N., good Ries., some Sylv.

Côte des Colombe Vineyard
Banks (Willamette). Owners: Joseph Coulombe, Barbara and Don Hauge. 1,200 cases. 5 acres, 2 bearing. Cab.Sauv., Chard., P.N. Early wines uneven.

Ellendale Vineyards
Dallas (Willamette). Owners: Robert and Ella Mae Hudson. Wine maker: Robert Hudson. 1,000 cases. 13 acres, 2 bearing. Cab.Franc, Chard., Merlot, P.N., J.R.

Forgeron Vineyard
Elmira (Willamette). Owners: George and Linda Smith. Wine maker: George Smith. 2,200 cases. 20 acres, 14 bearing. Cab.Sauv., Chard., P.Gris, P.N., J.R. particularly good.

Henry Winery
Umpqua. Owners: Scott and Sylvia Henry. Wine maker: Scott Henry. 6,300 cases. 28 acres, 14 bearing. Chard., Gewürz., P.N.

Hidden Springs Winery
Amity (Willamette). Owners: The Byard and Alexanderson families. Wine makers: Don Byard and Alvin Alexanderson. 2,500 cases. 28 acres, 12 bearing. Chard., P.N., J.R.

Hinman Vineyards
Eugene (Willamette). Owners and wine makers: Doyle Hinman and David Smith. 3,000 cases. 20 acres. Gewürz., P.N., J.R. and good Cabernet from Washington grapes.

Hood River Vineyards
Hood River (on the Columbia River east of Portland). Owners: Cliff and Eileen Blanchette. Wine maker: Cliff Blanchette. 1,200 cases. 12 acres, 5 bearing. Chard., Gewürz., P.N., J.R.

Oak Knoll Winery
Hillsboro (Willamette). Owners: Ron and Marjorie Vuylsteke and John R. Kobbe. Wine maker: Ron Vuylsteke. 5,000 cases. No acreage. Principal wines: Chard., Gewürz., P.N., J.R.

Serendipity Cellars Winery
Monmouth (Willamette). Owners: Glen and Cheryl Longshore. 420 cases. 3 acres, none currently bearing. Cab.Sauv., Chard., P.Gris, P.N.

Shafer Vineyard Cellars
Forest Grove (Willamette). Owner and wine maker: Harvey Shafer. 1,500 cases. 20 acres, 19 bearing, 14 more planned. Chard., Gewürz., P.N., Sauv.Blanc, J.R.

Siskiyou Vineyards
Cave Junction (Rogue). Owners: Chuck and Suzi David. Wine maker: Bill Nelson. 1,260 cases (6,000 projected for 1983). 12 acres. Cab.Sauv., Gewürz., P.N.

Valley View Vineyard
Jacksonville (Rogue). Owner: Anna Wishnovsky. Wine maker: John Eagle. 6,300 cases. 25 acres. Cab.Sauv., Chard. Early examples are admirable.

WASHINGTON WINERIES

Associated Vintners

Bellevue, WA 98004.

A privately owned corporation with 25 stockholders. Wine maker: David Lake MW. 30,000 cases. No vineyards. Principal wines: Gewürz., Cab.Sauv., Chard., P.N., Sem., J.R.

The rather unexciting name and label disguise one of the pioneers of the northwest, originally (1962) a group of professors at the University of Washington. Since 1976 it has been a fully commercial operation using Yakima Valley grapes and directed by a British Master of Wine, who worked with David Lett in Oregon. Their best-known wine is a very dry Gewürztraminer of spicy character, their Semillon and Chardonnay are remarkable and the blended 'Cascade Red' and 'Valley White' are excellent value for money.

Chateau Ste. Michelle

Woodinville, WA 98072.

Owner: United States Tobacco Company. President: Wallace Opdycke. Wine maker: Peter Bachman. 250,000 cases (500,000 by 1985). 2,600 acres, 1,200 currently bearing. Cab.Sauv., Chard., Ch.Bl., Gren., Merlot., Sauv.Bl., Sem., J.R.

Much the biggest northwest winery, and with its top wines among the best. André Tchelistcheff has advised from the start in 1967. The winery, 15 miles northeast of Seattle, is a spectacular evocation of a French château full of ultra-modern equipment. Its grapes come from 2 areas of the Columbia basin, Cold Creek (where 600 acres are proving very successful for Cabernet and Merlot) and Grandview, which seems to be more white-wine territory. Hahn Hill is a single-vineyard Grandview Riesling.

Up to now grapes have been transported to Seattle for fermentation, but the company has now restored an old winery at Grandview and is building one at Paterson, where half its total of vineyards is situated, particularly Sauvignon Blanc and Chardonnay. 'Chateau Reserve' Cabernet is aged 20 months in French oak barrels and up to 4 years in bottle. Pinot Noir is used only for sparkling wine, unblended, and spending 4 years on its yeast.

E. B. Foote Winery

Seattle, WA 98118.

Owner and wine maker: Eugene B. Foote. 2,500 cases. No vineyard. Cab.Sauv., Chard., Ch.Bl., Gewürz., P.N., J.R.

A critical success in recent competitions, with gold medals for Yakima Valley Gewürz and Chardonnay.

Hinzerling Vineyards

Prosser, WA 99350.

Owners: Wallace family. Wine maker: Michael Wallace. 5,000 cases. 24 acres. Cab.Sauv., Chard., Gewürz., Merlot, J.R.

A pioneer winery, started in 1971. Specialities include a sweet 'Botrytized' Gewürztraminer, Die Sonne.

Mont Elise Vineyards

(formerly Bingen Wine Cellars) Bingen, WA 98605.

Owners: The Henderson family. Wine maker: Charles Henderson. 5,000 cases. 35 acres, 15 currently bearing Chard., Gamay Beauj., Gewürz., P.N.

A winery (founded 1974) in a converted cold-storage plant. The promisingly named Bingen is on the Columbia River near the Dalles, east of Portland, Oregon.

Preston Wine Cellars

Pasco, WA 99301. Yakima Valley.

Owners: Bill and Joann Preston. Wine maker: Rob Griffin. 58,000 cases. 181 acres. Cab.Sauv., Chard., Ch.Bl., Gamay Beauj., Gewürz., Merlot, Muscat of Alexandria, Royalty, Sauv.Bl., J.R.

Washington's second-largest winery, founded in 1976 and producing some of the best, as well as the widest range, of the state's wines. Pasco is on the Columbia River at the eastern end of the Yakima Valley.

Manfred Vierthaler Winery

Sumner, WA 98390.

Owners: Manfred and Ingeborg Vierthaler. Wine maker: Manfred Vierthaler. 4,200 cases. 5 acres owned, 15 leased, all currently bearing M.-Thurgau and J.R.

Founded in 1976 and as German-oriented as its name. Vierthaler alone has planted in western Washington for Germanic cool-climate wines. The winery includes a restaurant.

Yakima River Winery

Prosser, WA 99350. Yakima Valley.

Owners: John and Louise Rauner. Wine maker: John Rauner. 3,800 cases. 2.5 acres Chard., J.R.

A tiny affair in the heart of the Yakima Valley vineyards. So far, good white wines.

IDAHO WINERIES

Ste. Chapelle Vineyards

Caldwell, ID 83605.

Owners: Bill Broich and the Symms family. Wine maker: Bill Broich. 55,000 cases. 420 acres, 115 currently bearing Chard., J.R.

Until 1982 the only winery in Idaho, drawing on grapes from both Washington and Oregon to add to its own crop. Ste. Chapelle Merlot has won a gold medal, Riesling and Gewürztraminer bronzes, but it seems to be the Chardonnay that has attracted most critical attention.

Facelli Vineyards

Wilder, ID 83676.

Owner and wine maker: Lou Facelli. 420 cases (1,000 projected for 1982). 5.5 acres Chard., J.R., none bearing yet.

OTHER PRODUCERS

The following wineries are either brand new or extremely small:

Bainbridge Island Winery, Winslow
Baquila Wines, Seattle
Cedar Ridge Vintners, Snohomish
Haviland Vintners, Lynnwood
Hoodsport Winery, Hoodsport
Kiona Cellars, West Richland
Franz Wilhelm Langguth Winery, Mattawa. A big-scale German investment in the Yakima Valley, launched in 1982. The intention is to make about 250,000 cases of Germanic generics a year.
Leonetti Cellars, Walla Walla
Lost Mountain Winery, Sequim
Mount Baker Vineyards, Deming
Mount Rainier Vineyards, Puyallup
Neuharth Winery, Sequim
Quail Run Winery, Zillah
Another considerable current building project. 6 growers are collaborating in what will be a big Yakima Valley winery.
Salishan Vineyards, La Center
Snohomish Valley Winery, Marysville
Spokane River Winery, Spokane
Paul Thomas Wines, Bellevue
Mostly excellent dry fruit wines; a little *vinifera*.
Tucker Cellars, Sunnyside
Woodward Canyon Winery, Lowden
Worden's Washington Winery, Spokane

OTHER REGIONS OF THE USA

The experience of centuries has seemed to show that the true wine-vine, *Vitis vinifera*, cannot successfully be grown in the climate of most of North America. The problems are extremes of cold in the north and centre and of heat and humidity in the south. The cold simply kills the vines in winter. Humidity brings rampant mildew; the heat of southern summers, a general malfunction of the vine (instead of respiring at night and building up sugar the plant continues to grow; the sugar is used in excessive foliage and the grapes, despite months of broiling heat, are scarcely ripe). The south, moreover, is plagued with a bacterial malady of the vine called Pierce's disease, transmitted by leaf-hoppers.

Two regions, the northeast (led by New York State) and the southeast, have strong wine traditions of their own based on native grapes which are adapted to their local climate. The New York industry is seeing a great revival (*see* pages 457–459). In the south the grape is the Muscadine, or Scuppernong, a plant very unlike the classic wine-vine (its grapes are like clusters of marbles with tough skins that slip off the flesh). The powerful flavour of its sweet wine was once immensely popular in America in a famous brand called Virginia Dare. Scuppernong still flourishes but bears no relation to the wines of the rest of the world.

But now almost every state of the Union outside these areas has hopeful wine makers – hopeful of seeing their industry, fledgling or a century old, as some of them are, establish itself as part of the American wine boom.

A number of long-established wineries have distinct local markets. These tend, however, to be a disincentive to experimenting with new grapes. When it has been assumed for so long that *Vitis vinifera* cannot be grown, it is a brave wine maker who does more than dip a toe in the water with an acre or two of experimental planting.

With modern knowledge more and more dippers are reporting success. There are certainly odd spots, and probably quite large areas, where the microclimate makes *vinifera* a practicable proposition after all. Isle St. George in Lake Erie, for example, now has 50 acres of *vinifera* vines which have survived winters with temperatures down to −17°C – but only by dint of being buried, as the Russians bury their vines, under 16 inches of earth for the winter. There is also a new race of hybrid vines, crosses between *vinifera* and American natives, which show the hardiness of the natives without their peculiar flavours. These French-American hybrids have established themselves as the mainstay of the northeastern wine industry and many believe that their wine, unexciting up to now, can be greatly improved. The problem is that their names at present have little consumer appeal.

The wine boom is being led from the metropolitan areas of America, which have latched like lightning on to the varietal names of California. Riesling, Chardonnay, Cabernet Sauvignon have become household words within a decade. Seyval Blanc, Chelois, de Chaunac and half a dozen other hybrids have a long way to go. At present, in fact, wine growers in the eastern and central states are looking three ways at once: at the old American varieties of *Vitis labrusca*, the exciting but risky *viniferas*, and the hybrids between the two.

New York State has the biggest and best-established wine industry, but there is really no reason to think that it has overwhelming natural advantages. What the other regions lack is a bold entrepreneur to interpret their increasing range of wines to the critical metropolitan public.

NEW YORK STATE

The wine industry in New York State, long-established around the Finger Lakes south of Lake Ontario, has up to now been considered a maverick backwater by most wine lovers. Basing its wine-making on varieties and chance hybrids of the native *Vitis labrusca*, its characteristic wines have the peculiar scented *labrusca* character known as 'foxiness'. Most also have high acidity, usually masked by considerable sweetness.

Over the last 40 years the non-foxy French-American hybrids have become accepted by all but the most conservative wineries. While their wine has not yet proved exciting by European/California standards, it is usually acceptable and occasionally very good. There are now several companies in New York, as elsewhere in the east, who see it as the mainstream future for their industry. At present about a quarter of New York wine is 'hybrid'.

Since the mid-1950s, however, there has been a vocal minority, led by Dr. Konstantin Frank, dedicated to proving that *vinifera* vines can successfully be grown in the Finger Lakes area. Their successes, at least with white wines, have convinced many (though the hard winter of 1980 was a serious setback to this faith). There are now, therefore, three parallel and often interwoven wine cultures in New York. The notes on the wineries below show which way the different companies are inclined.

America's wine boom started to affect New York in the mid-1970s. First Seagram and then Coca-Cola decided that the industry could be expanded. Seagram bought Gold Seal, the most forward-looking of the big wineries. Coca-Cola bought Taylors and Great Western. In 1976 the State law was changed to encourage 'farm wineries', lowering the licence fee for firms producing less than 50,000 gallons (about 21,000 cases) a year and easing restrictions on their sales.

The result was the rapid start-up of exactly the sort of small, open-minded enterprises New York needed to improve its image. Some three dozen small wineries were born or reborn, mainly in the Finger Lakes but also in the Hudson River Valley above New York City – which has a long history of nearly being a wine region – and on Long Island, where the maritime climate is much kinder than upstate.

NEW YORK STATE WINERIES

Benmarl Wine Company

Marlboro, N.Y. 12542. Founded 1971.
Owners: Mark and Dene Miller. 42 acres (95% hybrids, 5% *vinifera*).

The restoration of a historic vineyard site in the Hudson River Valley where the hybrid Dutchess was raised in the 19th century. The Millers run it as a cooperative of some 400 wine lovers, the Société des Vignerons, who help finance, pick and drink their range of varietal Seyval, Baco Noir and Chardonnay and blended Cuvée du Vigneron. Their wines are all highly regarded in New York.

Bully Hill Vineyards

Hammondsport, N.Y. 14840. Founded 1970.
Owner: Walter S. Taylor. About 25,000 cases.

The only member of the Taylor family still making wine – on the original family property on Lake Keuka. Wines are both *labrusca* and hybrids, well thought of as some of the best of the old school, and 'Champagne'.

Canandaigua Wine Company, Inc.

Canandaigua, N.Y. 14424.
A public company. Some 6 m. cases. No vineyards.

Producers of *labrusca* wines under the brand names Richards (Wild Irish Rose) and J. Roget.

Casa Larga

Fairport, N.Y. 14450. Founded 1976.
Owners: The Colaruotolo family. 12 acres, mostly Chardonnay.

Glenora Wine Cellars, Inc.

Glenora-on-Seneca, Dundee, N.Y. 14837. Founded 1977.
Owners: E Beers, E. Pierce, H. Kimball, E. Dalrymple. 15,000 cases. 500 acres (60% *labrusca*, not used for wine production; 30% hybrids; 10% *vinifera*, Chard. and Riesling).

One of the best-regarded smaller wineries of the Finger Lakes, specializing in German-style whites. Early issues of Chardonnay are also successful.

Gold Seal Vineyards, Inc.

Hammondsport, N.Y. 14840. Founded 1865.
Owners: Seagram Corporation. About 600,000 cases (75% of grapes are bought under contract). 500 acres (63% *labrusca*, 15% hybrids, 22% *vinifera*).

The most enterprising and quality-oriented of the big long-established Finger Lakes wineries, thanks to the work of Charles Fournier, its former President, a skilled champagne maker and pioneer (with Dr. Frank) of *vinifera* vines in New York State. Charles Fournier is the label of their best sparkling wines, which many consider New York's best (especially the Blanc de Blancs). Henri Marchant is a cheaper line, using *labrusca* grapes. Most of the table wines are generics, although in the Charles Fournier Superieur range *vinifera* is blended with hybrids. More *vinifera* wines will be forthcoming as the vines recently planted begin to bear.

Great Western, The Pleasant Valley Wine Company

Hammondsport, N.Y. 14840. Founded 1860.
Owner: The Wine Spectrum, a subsidiary of The Coca-Cola Company.

Great Western is the Wine Spectrum's smarter New York label (the other is Taylor). The best wines made at Pleasant Valley, the state's oldest winery, are 'Champagne' and hybrid varietals, particularly Baco Noir, Verdelet, Aurora, de Chaunac. Others are *labrusca* and hybrid generics. Great Western 'Champagne' with orange juice makes a tolerable Buck's Fizz. The sparkling wines are fermented in bottle but disgorged and clarified by the transfer process, as are many New York 'Champagnes'.

Canada

The last decade has seen Canada emerge as a producer of some very adequate table wines to replace her formerly very poor dessert wines.

Only two provinces are involved: British Columbia, with some 4,000 acres of vines, on the latitude of the Rhine, but with a wet maritime climate, and Ontario, where the Niagara peninsula is on the latitude of Rome, but suffers bitter continental winters. Each has a dozen wineries.

In British Columbia, the principal white grape is the 'Okanagan Riesling', of unknown parentage but possibly Hungaro-American. The reds (50% of total) are the hybrids de Chaunac and Marechal Foch. The biggest winery is Calona, at Kelowna, owned by Nabisco and producing the German-style Schloss Laderheim. The best is probably Claremont, at Peachland, with 22 acres of Pinots Blanc and Noir, Foch, Gewürztraminer and Chenin Blanc.

In Ontario the same red hybrids and the white Seyval Blanc predominate. The best wines are made by Charal (100 acres at Blenheim, good Seyval Blanc), Chateau des Charmes (150 acres at Niagara-on-the-Lake; Riesling, Aligoté and Chardonnay, including *méthode champenoise*) and the pioneering Inniskillin (68 acres at Niagara: Foch, Riesling, Chardonnay, Gewürztraminer). The biggest are Andres, Bright's and Chateau Gai.

Hargrave Vineyard

Cutchogue, Long Island, N.Y. Founded 1973.
Owners: Alexander and Louisa Hargrave. 55 acres, all *vinifera* (40% Chard., 20% each Cab. Sauv., P.N., Sauv. Blanc).

One of New York's great surprises. The Hargraves have ideal conditions for *vinifera* vines on the North Fork of Long Island, 70 miles east of New York city with the ocean close by on three sides. Their Chardonnay and Sauvignon Blanc can easily be confused with top-rank California or Oregon wines. Cabernet and Pinot Noir are aged for 3 and 2 years respectively in new American oak barrels without losing a fine flavour of ripe fruit. 1980 and 1981 were particularly good years. Not surprisingly, neighbours are planting too.

Heron Hill Vineyards, Inc.

Hammondsport, N.Y. 14840. Founded 1977.
Owners: John Ingle and Peter Johnstone. 8,300 cases. 40 acres (35% each Chard. and Riesling; 12% each Aurora and Seyval Blanc; 5% Ravat 51).

One of the successful new generation of wineries inclining New York towards *vinifera* wines. All their wines are crisp and 'Germanic', showing the influence of a cool ripening season, but even the Chardonnay is true to character.

Hudson Valley Wine Co.

Highland, N.Y. 12528. Founded 1907.
Owner: Herbert Feinberg. 100,000 cases. 150 acres planted out of 325. Mainly *labrusca* (Catawba, Iowna, Delaware, Concord, Chelois) with some Baco Noir and Warden.

Producers of generic-labelled chablis, burgundy, 'Champagne', etc., and varietal dry red Chelois.

Monarch Wine Co. Inc.

Brooklyn, N.Y. 11232.
Owners: Leo Star and Meyer H. Robinson. About 20 m. cases.

The producers of the famous Kosher wine, Manischewitz, principally from Concord grapes. Also of Pol d'Argent, Le Premier Cru and Chateau Laurent New York State 'Champagnes' and importers of low-price European wines.

Plane's Cayuga Vineyard

Ovid, N.Y. 14521. Founded 1981.
Owners: Bob and Mary Plane.
50 acres including hybrids, *labrusca* (Dutchess) and *vinifera* (Riesling and Chardonnay).

The Taylor Wine Company Ltd.

Hammondsport, N.Y. 14840. Founded 1880.
Owner: The Wine Spectrum, a subsidiary of The Coca-Cola Company. 1,134 acres of *labrusca* and hybrids.

Producers of Taylor and Lake County brands of 'Champagnes', sherries and generics. Taylor's were the company that introduced French-American hybrids to New York; they have not yet shown interest in *vinifera* vines.

Vinifera Wine Cellars

Hammondsport, N.Y. 14840. Founded 1962.
Owners: Dr. Konstantin D. Frank & Sons. Only about 6,000 cases, since much of the vineyard is experimental. 100 acres of Chard., Riesling, Gewürz., Sauv., P.N., Gamay.

The enthusiast who, with Charles Fournier, proved that *vinifera* vines will grow in upper New York State. Since 1965 he has made good, fine and sometimes brilliant white wine, including selected late-harvest Riesling, but less successful reds.

Wagner Vineyards

Lodi, N.Y. 14860.
Owner: Bill Wagner. About 40,000 cases. 125 acres (20% *vinifera* inc. Chard. and Riesling; 70% hybrids, de Chaunac, Aurora, Seyval, Rougeon, Ravat; 10% *labrusca*, Delaware).

An attractive little Finger Lakes winery. 85% of production is dry varietal table wines.

Widmer Wine Cellars, Inc.

Naples, N.Y. 14512. Founded 1888.
Owners: R. T. French Co. (Reckitt & Colman). About 400,000 cases. 237 acres of *labrusca* and hybrids (35% Niagara, 11% Foch, 8% Delaware; also Vincent, Catawba, Elvira, Rosette, Cayuga, Concord, de Chaunac, Aurora, Moore's Diamond, Ventura, Vidal, Seyval, etc.).

Best known for wood-aged sherries, Lake Niagara sweetish *labrusca* wines and Widmer-brand hybrids, mostly with generic names.

Herman J. Wiemer Vineyard

Dundee, N.Y. 14837. Founded 1979.
Owner: Herman J. Wiemer. 35 acres (24 Riesling, 11 Chardonnay).

The Bernkastel-born ex-wine maker of Bully Hill has had striking success with Riesling (including late-harvest) and now Chardonnay fermented in new French barrels – a departure for New York. He credits Seneca Lake, the biggest and deepest of the Finger Lakes, for the favourable Dundee microclimate. He is trying Pinot Noir, but Gewürztraminer suffers from bud injury in the winter cold. An extension of 25 more acres is planned for 1983/4.

Charles Fournier, a pioneer of vinifera vines in New York State

OTHER NEW YORK STATE WINERIES

Cagnasso Winery
Marlboro, N.Y. 12542. Founded 1977. Owner: Joseph Cagnasso. 10 acres (80% hybrids, 20% *labrusca*). A new Hudson River winery aiming at 'Italian'-style full reds and smooth, very dry whites.

Cascade Mountain Vineyards
Amenia, N.Y. 12501. Owners: The Wetmore family. About 6,000 cases. 45 acres hybrids (30% each Seyval and Leon Millot; 10% each Foch, Aurora, Vidal; 5% each Baco Noir and Chancellor). Careful producers of crisp, dry whites and rosé and fresh young reds, described as 'Spring' wines. Also an aged Reserved Red.

Johnson Estate
Westfield, N.Y. 14787. Founded 1962. Owner: Frederick S. Johnson. About 10,000 cases. 125 acres *labrusca* (Delaware, Ives, Chelois, Catawba) and hybrids (Chancellor, Seyval, Aurora, Cascade). Good-quality estate-bottled wines, including a dry white Delaware.

Merritt Estate Winery Inc.
Forestville, N.Y. 14062. Owners: The Merritt family. 62 acres hybrids, principally Aurora, de Chaunac and Foch; 8% *labrusca*, Niagara. A family estate making popular wines ranging from dry to very sweet, including bottled Sangria and ready-spiced mulled wine for serving hot to cold skiers.

North Salem Vineyard, Inc.
North Salem, N.Y. 10560. founded 1980. Owner: Dr. George W. Naumberg. 18 acres hybrids, principally Seyval Blanc, Foch. A new Hudson River winery aiming to make fresh, light whites and reds for drinking young.

Royal Kedem Winery
Milton, N.Y. 12547. Owners: The Herzog family. 168 acres (72% Concord and other *labruscas*; 28% hybrids, Aurora, Seyval and de Chaunac).

Valley Vineyards
Walker Valley, N.Y. 12588. Founded 1979. Owner: Gary Dross. 25 acres (55% white hybrids, 20% red hybrids, 15% Riesling, 10% Chard). A new farm winery 20 miles west of Marlboro. Aim is European-style wines, including a November-released 'Nouveau'.

Woodbury Vineyards
Dunkirk, N.Y. 14048. Founded 1979. Owners: The Woodbury family. 14,000 cases. 43 acres (50% Dutchess and Niagara, 24% Chard., 16% de Chaunac, 6% Riesling, 3% Gewürz., 1% Cab. Sauv.). An old farming family of the district who were the first (in 1970) to plant *vinifera* vines in Chautauqua County, on a gravel ridge overlooking Lake Erie. Success has encouraged them to plant more.

East Coast vine varieties

Aurora (Seibel 5279). Early-ripening, pinky gold hybrid popular in the Finger Lakes for still and sparkling white wine, slightly peppery in taste.

Baco Noir (Baco No.1). One of the better red French hybrids for short-season regions. Dark colour, good sugar and high acid; makes slightly jammy wine capable of maturing.

Cascade (Seibel 13053). Very early, rather pale French hybrid, best for very light red or rosé.

Catawba. Famous old American variety still much grown for sparkling wine. Definitely foxy.

Cayuga. A recent white French hybrid with slightly lemony character.

Chambourcin (Joannès-Seyve 26205). A mid-season red bred in the Rhône valley, apparently very promising for quality.

Chancellor (Seibel 7053). A dark red French hybrid from the Rhône valley. Rich dark wine but disease-prone in humid areas.

Chelois (Seibel 10878). One of the best red French hybrids, healthy and widely grown for 'burgundy-style' wine.

Colobel (Seibel 8357). Intensely red-juiced blending grape.

Concord. The dark purple, powerfully foxy American grape used for jelly and sweet wines. Still the most planted.

Cynthiana (alias **Norton**, alias **Virginia Seedling**). American red grape used in the midwest for heavy foxy wines.

De Chaunac (Seibel 9549). Very hardy French red popular in Ontario and elsewhere for well-balanced wine.

Delaware. Old American pink grape, only slightly foxy, one of the standards for eastern 'Champagne'.

Dutchess. Similar to Delaware; even less foxy but also less healthy; bred in Dutchess County near the Hudson.

Elvira. A second-rate foxy old American white, dying out.

Isabella. Very foxy dark red old American variety.

Ives. Concord-style old American red, now rare.

Léon Millot (Kuhlmann 1922). Good-quality, Alsace-bred early red hybrid, similar to Maréchal Foch.

Maréchal Foch (or **Foch**) **(Kuhlmann 1882).** One of the best red hybrids for the north; well-balanced fruity wine with moderate acid. It has Gamay genes.

Moore's Diamond. An old American white, not too foxy for moderately dry wine.

Niagara. Very foxy American white used for sweet wines.

Ravat 51. (alias **Vignoles**). A hybrid of Chardonnay being tried in the east, especially for 'Champagne'.

Ravat Noir. A French Pinot hybrid being grown experimentally.

Rayon d'Or (Seibel 4986). Healthy white French hybrid for warmer areas; well-balanced wine.

Rougeon (Seibel 5898). A red hybrid from the Rhône being tested by some growers.

Seibel (*see* the names given to the numbered crosses of this prolific Rhône-valley breeder).

Seyval Blanc (Seyve-Villard 5276). Bland but productive and healthy white hybrid rapidly becoming the most popular as a 'varietal'.

Seyve-Villard. The French breeder of Seyval Blanc and the crosses known as Villard.

Verdelet (Seibel 9110). Hardy white hybrid for the north, including Canada. Also a table grape.

Vidal Blanc (Vidal 256). Good-quality white hybrid for warmer areas. Has Trebbiano genes.

Villard Blanc (Seyve-Villard 12375). Well-established healthy heavy cropper; the Seyval Blanc of warmer areas.

Villard Noir (Seyve-Villard 18315). Red equivalent of the last; for warm areas.

NEW ENGLAND

Wine-making in New England is still on a small experimental scale, with opinions divided, as they are farther south, about the relative merits of hybrid and *vinifera* vines. *Vinifera* varieties will grow, at least right down by the coast where the ocean moderates the winters. Islands offer the best chance.

Martha's Vineyard, off the Massachusetts coast, now very properly has a patch of *vinifera* vines, at Chicama Vineyards, which grows Chardonnay, Riesling and Cabernet Sauvignon.

The state of Rhode Island, deeply invaded by ocean inlets, has half a dozen small vineyards; the biggest, Sakonnet, growing both hybrid and *vinifera* vines. Prudence Island Vineyards, on that island in Naragansett Bay, has 20 acres of *vinifera* vines, the best being Chardonnay and Gewürztraminer.

Connecticut's first winery, Haight Vineyards at Litchfield, west of Hartford, manages to grow both *vinifera* (Chardonnay and Riesling) and the hybrid Maréchal Foch despite being many miles inland.

But there are also those who believe that the regional character of the northeast should be asserted by developing the best of the hybrids alone. The little Commonwealth Winery in Plymouth, Massachusetts, makes wines of Finger Lakes grapes: clean whites of Seyval and Vidal Blanc and a new US-bred cross called Cayuga with a faint citrus flavour, and reds of Foch and de Chaunac.

New Hampshire also has at least one winery, White Mountain Vineyards, which since 1969 has encouraged farmers, even as far afield as Vermont and Maine, to plant hybrids for its wine-making.

THE MID-ATLANTIC

There is a growing feeling that the mid-Atlantic states of Virginia and Maryland, southern Pennsylvania and perhaps a belt stretching inland into West Virginia, Kentucky and Tennessee may have a promising future in wine-growing. It is a well-publicized fact that Thomas Jefferson had no luck, but modern vines, sprays and know-how have started to change the situation.

In the 1940s Philip Wagner made history at Boordy Vineyards, near Ryderwood in Maryland, by planting the first French-American hybrids in America. These vines had been bred by the French to bring phylloxera-resistance to France, but ironically it was to be America that appreciated their virtues of hardiness and vigour. Boordy Vineyards continues to produce hybrid wines, although it has been overtaken in ambition by others who are showing that *vinifera* is a possibility. The leader in these experiments has been Hamilton Mowbray of Montbray Wine Cellars at Westminster, northwest of Baltimore, who planted Chardonnay and Riesling in 1966 and Cabernet Sauvignon in 1972, and has been delighted with the results. A recent run of exceptionally cold winters has done some damage. Late-September Atlantic storms, coinciding with hurricanes, are another threat. But early October is usually fine and dry and Mowbray compares his Cabernet to Bordeaux petits châteaux, his Riesling to Alsace and his Chardonnay, aged one year in American oak, to a delicate white burgundy. Although there are still only 20 acres of *vinifera* vines in Maryland, the reception of the wine in Washington, D.C., is encouraging more planting. Even Mowbray, however, hedges his bets with hybrids. He has made a 'varietal' Seyve-Villard (alias Seyval Blanc) since 1966 in two styles, one young and fruity 'like a Loire wine' and the other oak-aged.

The Virginians are still wary of *vinifera*. Archie Smith of Meredyth Vineyards at Middleburg, who has been one of the leaders, was initially entirely sceptical and planted only hybrids, but has started to come round to Riesling and Chardonnay. Although they take more maintenance, are less reliable and produce smaller crops, he is encouraged by results, especially with Riesling. Much depends on the effectiveness of antirot treatments. Fungus infections develop immunity to one chemical and must be sprayed with another. Can the chemists produce enough alternatives? Most of the Meredyth wines are still hybrids.

Foreign investors have more confidence. It made a great stir in 1976 when Zonin, a big wine company from the Veneto in Italy, bought 700 acres at Barboursville and started to plant *vinifera* vines. Since then a German investor, Dr. Gerhard Guth, has planted 160 acres which are said to be producing reasonable 'but light' wines. More Virginia wineries, Shenandoah, Farfelu and others, have *vinifera* trials going. The two deciding factors are going to be the health of the vines and the prices the public will pay. *Vinifera* wine is bound to be more expensive.

Meanwhile the southeast corner of Pennsylvania apparently has much in common with Maryland. Soils and climates are very variable; there are certainly good vineyard sites among them. Frank Mazza, who abandoned *vinifera* trials at the other end of Pennsylvania on Lake Erie when 18 acres were wiped out, is happy with his south Pennsylvania Chardonnay and Riesling. He seems to be even happier with his white hybrids, which do exceptionally well in this climate.

John Crouch of Allegro Vineyards has 12 acres of Chardonnay and Cabernet Sauvignon. Richard Naylor, at York near the Maryland border, is happy with Chardonnay, Riesling and Cabernet Sauvignon but more at ease with Vidal, Seyval, de Chaunac, Chambourcin and a host of other hybrids.

Everybody believes there is room for both schools. It is a toss-up between natural conditions and customers' reactions which comes out on top.

THE MIDWEST

Lake Michigan provides the heat storage to make life bearable for vines in parts of the northern midwest bordering the lake. Michigan is the state with most vineyards and wineries, the majority grouped not far from Chicago at the lake's southeast corner. Bronte, St. Julian and Warner, the biggest companies, the first at Hartford and the second two at Paw Paw, concentrate on hybrid vines. Bronte, in 1953, was the first company to produce a hybrid 'varietal', its red Baco.

Chateau Grand Travers is much farther north on the lakeshore, where the big bay called Grand Traverse produces a tolerable winter microclimate which has encouraged trial planting of Riesling and Chardonnay, with some success.

Michigan's most surprising vineyard, however, is at Buchanan, near the lake and the Indiana border in the south. At Tabor Hill a small acreage of Riesling and Chardonnay is now more than ten years old and steadily producing good-quality wine. Production is supplemented by grapes grown at Sagemoor Farms in Washington State and transported in refrigerated trucks – and also, as in all the eastern and midwestern wineries, by such hybrids as Vidal and Seyval Blanc and Baco Noir which carry no risk.

Wineries of the other states of the northern midwest are in Indiana, Illinois, Wisconsin and even Minnesota. Ohio's Lake Erie shore has promising *vinifera* vineyards.

The states of Missouri and Arkansas would seem improbable places to plant vines, but both have long-established vineyards. Missouri, indeed, enjoyed the distinction of having the first official appellation granted to a viticultural area in the United States, in 1980 when the Bureau of Alcohol, Tobacco and Firearms declared Augusta, just west of St. Louis, a designated region. Its first vines were planted in hills above the Missouri in the 1830s.

It is far too cold here for *vinifera* vines. Lucian Dressel, of Mount Pleasant Vineyards at Augusta, the leading wine maker of the region, makes his best white wines of the hybrids Seyval and Vidal Blanc and his reds of Cynthiana, which makes a full-bodied 'Rhône-type' wine, Münch, which is light 'like Beaujolais', and Cordon Rouge, or Couderc 7120, which is closer to claret. Dressel feels that Missouri wines can improve. At the moment the whites are better; compared with Finger Lakes hybrids they are less fruity and more full-bodied.

Arkansas to the south has one unexpected outcrop of *vinifera* growing in the peculiar microclimate of a spot called Altus, identified and settled in the 1870s by immigrants from Switzerland, Austria and Bavaria who understood mountains. Altus lies on a plateau between 1,000 and 2,000 feet, sheltered from the north by the Ouachita range.

According to Al Wiederkehr, whose Swiss family founded its winery in 1880, thermal inversion currents produce a very tolerable climate in which Riesling, Chardonnay, Sauvignon Blanc, Muscat Ottonel, Cabernet, Pinot Noir and Gamay are all more or less at home. The majority of his considerable acreage – 575 acres – will soon be planted in these grapes, although he is not burning his boats with hybrids.

THE SOUTHWEST

Prospects look positive for *vinifera* vines in certain parts of the southwest. The biggest vineyards are in West Texas, where the State University has planted some 700 acres in conditions akin to California's Central Valley. Much of the state is too humid and subject, like the deep south, to Pierce's disease. The most promising area at present seems to be a high plateau at 3,600 feet near Lubbock, in a cool but dry climate, about California Region 3.

The McPherson family and their partners are the pioneers with 160 acres of *vinifera* vines on the Llano Estacado ('Staked Plains') ranch. They are successfully growing Cabernet, Sauvignon Blanc, Chenin Blanc, Riesling and Chardonnay (first vintage, 1982) using California-style techniques, including wood-ageing. Their premium wines are drawing attention to the Lubbock area, while others are experimenting in parts of Arizona and New Mexico.

Meanwhile several small wineries are successfully growing hybrids in the more difficult areas. A tolerable Vidal Blanc from La Buena Vida at Springtown, near Fort Worth, shows what can be achieved.

AUSTRALIA

It comes as a real surprise to visitors to Australia to discover how important wine is in the country's life; how knowledgeable and critical many Australians are; how many wineries, wine regions and 'styles' (the favourite Australian wine word) this country, with a total population only one quarter that of California, can profitably support. Extraordinarily little of the buzz of Australian winemanship penetrates overseas – largely because her best wines are made in vast variety but small quantities, and partly, I believe, because lack of any kind of central direction makes Australian labels a pathless jungle.

Even more of a surprise is how excellent the best Australian wines are: different in flavour from California's best but not a jot inferior, and presenting a wider range of types. In Australia Shiraz, Semillon and Rhine Riesling have been excellently grown for decades. A new generation of first-class Cabernet and Chardonnay has now joined them – while California's very best wines are limited to Cabernet, Chardonnay, Riesling and arguably Sauvignon Blanc. In both cases Pinot Noir is still only on the threshold of success.

The whirlwind of change and innovation is no less strong in Australia than in California but the establishment through which it blows is far older. An astonishing number of wineries still belong to the families that founded them over a century ago. They have powerful traditions. Although most of their turnover today is in bulk wines sold in 'cask', or 'bag-in-box', they continue to make small high-quality lots from their best grapes. Medium-sized and little 'boutique' wineries are also proliferating in direct competition with these established classics, adding to the alarming number of good wines there are to choose from. Australia long ago lost any inhibitions (if she ever had any) about blending wines from different grapes and different regions – even as much as 1,000 miles apart. In these circumstances it takes a dedicated amateur to keep track of the new 'releases'. Labels carry the names of grapes, growers, makers, districts, vineyards, vintage dates and 'bin numbers' (a strange way of indicating a 'style' to the initiated). The facts (we assume) are all in good faith. But they seem to have been compiled precisely to frighten away the honest, simple drinker.

It helps if we understand the traditions underlying the confusion. Until the recent boom, Australia's four wine-growing states had only half a dozen quality areas of any importance. New South Wales had the (then almost moribund) Hunter River Valley, north of Sydney. Victoria had Rutherglen and its neighbourhood in the northeast, Great Western in the west (and the lonely Chateau Tahbilk in the middle). South Australia, throughout this century much the greatest producer, had the Barossa Valley, Southern Vales and Clare, all grouped round Adelaide, and Coonawarra in the remote south. Western Australia had the Swan Valley at Perth.

In addition the Murray River, flowing between the three eastern states, irrigated large areas dedicated to low-quality wine, most of which was distilled.

Each of these areas had four grapes at most which it grew well for fine wines. And each was dominated by at most four or five considerable producers – a manageable number of permutations, even given the bin-number habit.

Once these producers began to cross regional lines, to buy grapes, vineyards, or their competitors, the pattern was blurred. Now new vineyards have been developed in a score of districts which are either entirely new to the vine but promise cooler growing conditions, or which (like many parts of Victoria) flourished as vineyards a century ago. It is still just possible to group these developments into rough geographical zones (*see* pages 463–464) – but certainly not yet to give each zone a regional character. Southeastern Australia from Adelaide to Sydney is starting to look on the map like one great wine area. Soon, it seems, the same will be true of the southwest. This does not stop your Australian enthusiast from trying to follow the 'quality of the fruit' through the maze of wine-makers' foibles.

Until Australia begins to develop an appellation system (Western Australia has made the first move) the only means of selection will be through the maker's name. The following pages start with a list of the wine regions and their principal wineries. The main listing that follows is of the wineries, with as much information as possible about the sources of their wines. With the accompanying tasting notes and commentaries a picture begins to emerge – of one of the world's most exciting wine countries in late, difficult and protracted adolescence.

Chateau Tahbilk, Victoria, was established in 1860

THE REGIONS

VICTORIA

Central Victoria The most diffuse region, around the old gold-mining towns of Ballarat and Bendigo 100 miles north by west of Melbourne. There are no big or long-established wineries, but excellent indications from, e.g., Balgownie.
Wineries: Balgownie, Best's Concongella. Chateau Le Amon. Knights. Mt. Avoca. Taltarni. Virgin Hills. Yellowglen.
Geelong A new small area just west of Melbourne's Port Phillip Bay. Cool conditions.
Wineries: Anakie. Prince Albert.
Goulburn Valley An important old though small area on the Hume Highway 100 miles north of Melbourne. Marsanne, Riesling, Cabernet and Shiraz are excellent at e.g. Chateau Tahbilk.
Wineries: Chateau Tahbilk. Mitchelton.
Great Western and Avoca The west-central area, some 140 miles west of Melbourne, includes the famous old sparkling winery of Seppelts and some of the most ambitious new ventures, several for sparkling wine.
Wineries: Mt. Avoca. Best's Concongella.
Murray Valley Long-established, mainly irrigated area along the Murray River to the northwest, including Echuca, Swan Hill, Robinvale and Mildura. Echuca (150 miles north of Melbourne) is producing fine table wines; farther down-river to the west is dessert-wine country (with some outstanding sherries).
Wineries: Lindeman's. Mildara. Tisdall.
Northeast Victoria The most illustrious area, between Milawa and Rutherglen on the New South Wales border, famous in history for superb dessert wines, especially Muscats, and the heaviest of Hermitage. Milawa is now also a centre for fine white-wine making, led by Brown Bros.
Wineries: All Saints. Baileys. Brown Bros. Campbells. Chambers. Morris. St. Leonard's. Stanton & Killeen.
Yarra Valley Thirty miles east of Melbourne, an old vineyard area turned over to sheep and fruit but now reviving with some of the best 'cool-climate' wines from boutique wineries. Outstanding Riesling, Chardonnay, Cabernet, Gewürztraminer, Pinot Noir.
Wineries: Chateau Yarrinya. Fergusson. Mount Mary. St. Huberts. Seville Estate. Wantirna. Yarra Yering. Yeringberg.

SOUTH AUSTRALIA

Adelaide The Mount Lofty ranges on the outskirts of Adelaide were formerly important, but now only for Penfold's relic Grange vineyard at Magill.
Wineries: A. Norman & Sons. Penfolds. Petaluma. Seppelt. Tolley.
Barossa Valley The oldest and most important region, 35 miles from Adelaide, settled by Germans in the 1840s and a good all-round producer, most famous for dessert wines on the valley floor round Nuriootpa and Rieslings in the 1,800-foot eastern hills (Eden Valley, Pewsey Vale). Reds tend to be stern and tannic. 22,000 acres.
Wineries: Basedow. Wolf Blass. Chateau Yaldara. Hamilton's. Henschke. Kaiser Stuhl. Krondorf. Orlando. Penfolds. Saltram. Seppelt. Smith's Yalumba. Tollana (Tolley, Scott & Tolley). Woodley. Wynn's.
Clare/Watervale A smaller area 40 miles north of Barossa with almost as long a history. 1,300-foot hills give it a cooler season in which Rhine Riesling gives fine wine but Shiraz and Cabernet are also strong-boned and long-lived. 'Clare Riesling' is actually Crouchen, a Semillon-like grape known in South Africa as Cape Riesling. 5,000 acres.
Wineries: Enterprise. Lindeman's. Mitchells. Quelltaler. Sevenhill. Stanley. Wendouree.
Coonawarra A remote area 250 miles south of Adelaide on an eccentric flat carpet of red earth over limestone with a high water table. Its latitude makes it

relatively cool; its soil is absurdly fertile. The result is some of Australia's best, most claret-like, Cabernet, middle-weight Shiraz and excellent Rhine Riesling. Attempts to extend the region northwards at Padthaway and Keppoch have produced both a wide range of whites with a rapidly growing reputation and some adequate reds. *Wineries*: Bowen Estate. Brand's Laira. Katnook Estate. Leconfield. Lindeman's. Mildara Wines. Redman.

Langhorne Creek A tiny historic area 25 miles southeast of Adelaide. Dessert wines and big reds.
Wineries: Bleasdale.

McLaren Vale Now the major vineyard area of the Southern Vales, the country immediately south of Adelaide. Many new small wineries have opened recently in a warm area best known for full-blooded reds and good dessert wines, and have raised more than a few eyebrows with some very interesting Rieslings and Chardonnays. The southern Mt. Lofty ranges to the east offer some cooler spots.
Wineries: Coriole, D'Arenberg. Fern Hill. Thomas Hardy. Kay Brothers. Maxwell Wines. Piramimma. Wirra Wirra.

The Riverland The course of the Murray River northeast of Adelaide is dotted from Mildura to Morgan with bulk-producing irrigated vineyards for fortified wines and brandy. Coops at Renmano, Berri, Waikerie and Loxton are the main producers. Like the Riverina area in New South Wales they are now making good-value table wines from all manner of grapes.
Wineries: Angoves Pty. Ltd. Berri Estate and Renmano. Renmano.

Southern Vales *See* McLaren Vale
Wineries Clarendon. Coolawin. Marienberg. Reynella.

NEW SOUTH WALES

Corowa Adjacent to the great northeast Victoria dessert wine area of Rutherglen. New South Wales' most southern vineyards.

Cowra A small new district 200 miles west of Sydney with moderate conditions at 1,800 feet. Excellent Chardonnay has been used by Brown Bros. and Petaluma.

Hunter Valley The Lower Hunter, round Pokolbin, near Cessnock, 100 miles north of Sydney, is long-established as a producer of serious Shiraz reds and Semillon ('Riesling') whites which age superbly. Cloud cover mitigates the extreme summer heat but rain often dampens the vintage. More recently Cabernet and Chardonnay have been planted with great success, Pinot Noir more doubtfully.
Wineries: Arrowfield. Brokenwood. Chateau Francois. Drayton's Bellevue. Elliot's Oakvale. Hungerford Hill. Lake's Folly. Lindeman's. McWilliams Mount Pleasant. Robson. Rosemount. Rothbury. Saxonvale. Tulloch. Tyrrells. Wollundry. Wyndham Estate.

Mudgee An old-established small area 100 miles west of the Hunter Valley and 1,200 feet higher, with a sunnier but later season. Mudgee growers have a self-imposed appellation system and take great pride in their extremely full-flavoured wines. Chardonnay has been grown here for many years, albeit in tiny quantities.
Wineries: Botobolar. Craigmoor. Huntington. Miramar. Montrose.

Riverina or Murrumbidgee Irrigation Area (M.I.A.) Richly fertile flat irrigated fruit-growing land round Griffith, 300 miles west of Sydney. Almost any vine seems to flourish here, giving excellent value if not great keeping qualities. McWilliams is much the biggest exploiter of the area.

Rooty Hill A remnant area in the outskirts of Sydney.
Wineries: Richmond Estate.

WESTERN AUSTRALIA

Great Southern area (Mount Barker, Frankland) A sprawling region of diverse topography and soil with 12 operating wineries and innumerable small vineyards in the course of establishment. Very cool, slow ripening conditions the common factor. *Wineries (at Frankland)*: Alkoomi.

Margaret River Recently established as the major new quality-wine region of the state. Two hundred miles south of Perth on a promontory with a markedly oceanic climate. The early results have varied from encouraging to sensational for all the classic grape varieties.
Wineries: Capel Vale. Cape Mentelle. Cullen's. Evans & Tate. Leeuwin. Leschenault. Moss Wood. Peel Estate. Vasse Felix. Wrights.

Mount Barker A hilly region in the extreme south, recently graduated from experiment to exciting producer, especially of Rhine Riesling.
Wineries: Chateau Barker. Conteville. Forest Hill. Plantagenet.

Swan Valley The traditional Western Australian vineyard, on the eastern outskirts of Perth. Long experience of its warm climate has brought mastery of the light full-bodied white burgundy style, skilful light dry Verdelhos, very good Cabernets and some noble dessert wines.
Wineries: Bassenden. Evans & Tate. Olive Farm. Plantagenet. Sandalford. Vignacourt. Westfield.

QUEENSLAND

Wineries: Robinsons Family Winery.

TASMANIA

Following the search for a cooler climate to its logical conclusion, a number of growers have planted French and German vines near Launceston in the north and Hobart in the (cooler) south. Early results show the north better, with similar intense fruit flavours and good acidity to Mount Barker in Western Australia.
Wineries: Heemskerk. Moorilla. Pipers Brook.

Principal grape varieties

Shiraz (alias Hermitage) Makes big, dark and tasty reds varying from deep, raisiny and tannic with salty mineral flavours (e.g. south of Adelaide and in northeast Victoria) to smooth, soft and relatively delicate in the Hunter Valley. With barrel-age (e.g. Grange Hermitage) it can become as glorious a wine here as in the Rhône valley. Also makes excellent port and blends superbly with Cabernet Sauvignon.

Cabernet Sauvignon Makes less well-balanced wine than Shiraz, tending to harshness and hollowness, and is improved by blending. Exceptions only in Coonawarra and parts of Victoria until Max Lake reintroduced it and small barrels to the Hunter Valley in the 1960s. Now it is widely successful, though still not at its best in South Australia except in the cooler Coonawarra area.

Semillon At its best, in the Hunter Valley (as 'Hunter Riesling'), is a total triumph: a light, dry, soft wine, Chablis-green when young and lively, ageing superbly for up to 20 years. Also good as 'Clare Riesling' in South Australia.

Rhine Riesling Modern methods have largely improved this superbly adaptable German grape – but sometimes filleted it too. The best today are excitingly flowery, just off-dry, satisfyingly acid and well worth several years' ageing.

Secondary grape varieties

Chardonnay Recently introduced but sweeping the board almost everywhere.

Chenin Blanc Is used mainly as a blending grape.

AUSTRALIA PRODUCERS

Alkoomi

Winge Ballup Road, Frankland, *WA*. Est. 1971. 4,000 cases rising to 7,000. Visits by appt. Owners: Mervyn and Judith Lange. Vineyards: about 30 acres of Cab.Sauv., Rhine Ries., Shiraz, Malbec, Sauv.Bl., some Merlot and Sem. Wines: Cab., Malbec, Shiraz, Rhine Ries., 'Vintage Port', etc. Prices: $4–5.

The pace-setter for the new Frankland area, best in dense, full-flavoured Cabernet and clean tannic Shiraz. Riesling is light and sweetish in the finish.

Allandale

Pokolbin, *NSW*. Est. 1977. 7,500 cases rising. Visits. Owners: Villa Villetini Pty. Ltd. Wine maker: Ed Joualt. Vineyards: 12 acres of P.N., Sem. and Chard. Prices: $3.50–6.50.

A new departure for the Hunter; a small winery set up largely to process small lots of grapes from named specialist growers, e.g. Leonard Vineyards Chardonnay, Cabernet and Semillon and Dawson Chardonnay. Joualt's Chardonnays fetch good prices. Sales largely by mail.

All Saints Winery

All Saints Road, Wahgunyah, *Victoria*. Est. 1864. Approx. 60,000 cases. Visits. Owners: The Sutherland Smith family. Vineyards: 260 acres, principally Shiraz, with Cab.Sauv., P. Meunier, P.N., Palomino, Marsanne, Rhine Ries., etc. and a little Crouchen and Chard.
Prices: $3.50 up to $10 for old dessert wines.

A conservative family affair run with aplomb by George Sutherland Smith in what he hopes looks like a Scottish castle. Honest if unsubtle wines include the popular Lyre Bird White Burgundy, Spätlese Frontignac (light sweet Muscat) and Shiraz/Cabernet blend. Dessert wines are best, especially Old Tawny Port, Very Old Madeira and Mature Muscat.

Anakie (Hickinbotham Winemakers)

Stroughton Vale Road, Geelong, *Victoria*. Est. 1968. 2,500 cases. Visits weekends. Owners: Ian Hickinbotham and son Stephen. Vineyards: 20 acres, being grafted over to Chard., Cab.Sauv. and Franc, Merlot, Rhine Ries. At present Riesling and a Bordeaux-style blend are the main wines.
Prices: $4.50–9.00.

The winery was leased in 1981 by the Hickinbothams, skilled and original wine makers. Early wines, all stylish and well made, have included excellent Germanic 'Meadowbank' Riesling from Hobart, Tasmania, an attractive light carbonic maceration Shiraz/Grenache, Cabernets from both Anakie and Tasmania and a first-rate late-picked Anakie Auslese. (*See* also Clarendon.)

Angoves

Bookmark Ave., Renmark, *SA*. Founded 1910. Approx. 300,000 cases. Visits. Owners: The Angove family. Vineyards: 500 acres, recently concentrating on Rhine Ries., Sauv.Bl., Ch.Bl. and Gewürz.
Prices: $3–4.

A conservative old family company in the Riverland irrigated area. Tregrehan claret and Bookmark Riesling have long been well-known low-price lines. Since 1979 new-look whites have changed the firm's image: all simple, fruity, lightweight, well made and cheap.

Arrowfield

Jerry's Plains, Upper Hunter District, *NSW*. Est. 1969. 30,000 cases. Visits. Owners: W. R. Carpenter Pty. Ltd. Vineyards: 690 acres of Sem., Cab., Rhine Ries., Shiraz, Gewürz. and Chard. Prices: $3–5.

After an overambitious start and some difficulties with 1,200 acres, the firm is now establishing a name for very good value. Best are a light spicy Cabernet Sauvignon and a big California-style Chardonnay.

Baileys Vineyards

Glenrowan, *Victoria*. Est. 1870. 30,000 cases. Visits. Owners: Davies Consolidated Industries (since 1972). Wine maker: Harry Tinson. Vineyards: 100 acres of Muscat, Tokay, Shiraz, Cab.Sauv., some whites.
Prices: $3.50–5.50 for Bundarra; $9 Tokay; $14 Muscat.

The famous makers of heroic Bundarra Hermitage, a caricature Aussie wine with a black and red label like a danger signal. A thickly fruity wine which ages 20 years to improbable subtlety. Even better (and amazing value) are their dessert Muscats and Tokays, profoundly fruity, intensely sweet and velvety. The best selections have the initials HJT.

Balgownie

Hermitage Lane, Maiden Gulley, nr. Bendigo, *Victoria*. Est. 1969. 4,000–5,000 cases. Visits. Owner: Stuart Anderson. Vineyards: 30 acres, 17 of Cab.Sauv., 8 Shiraz, the rest P.N. and Chard. Prices: $4.50–7.00.

A modest ex-pharmacist who studied French methods and established one of the best names in Australia for Cabernet Sauvignon built like Château Latour. In 1982 the '74 was ready, the '76 still very tannic. His Hermitage is variable, at its best as aromatic as Christmas cake. Chardonnay and Pinot Noir are developing well. The vineyard was the first in its area, in a forest clearing.

Cinsaut (alias Oeillade) Common in the Barossa Valley, for blending and for ports.
Crouchen A strain of Semillon grown in Clare and Barossa as Clare Riesling. Can be good, but not up to 'Hunter Riesling' Semillon standards.
Doradillo Bulk white grape of the irrigation areas, used for distilling, sherry and 'cask' wines.
Durif A Shiraz-like grape used occasionally in northeast Victoria for interesting dark wine.
Frontignac The brown Muscat used in northeast Victoria for superbly luscious dessert and 'liqueur' wines.
Lexia (alias Gordo Blanco) A white Muscat used in the irrigation areas and Swan Valley to make a good light wine.
Marsanne Occasionally used in Victoria for long-lived big whites, and Swan Valley for blending.
Mataro Minor blending red, especially in the Barossa Valley.
Merlot A recent success in rounding out harsh Cabernets.
Muscadelle Used to good effect for rich sweet or dry wines in South Australia and northeast Victoria.
Pinot Noir A blending grape in the past, just now coming into its own.
Riesling Rhine (German) Riesling is always so-called. Riesling alone means either Semillon or Crouchen.
Trebbiano Sometimes called White Hermitage or Ugni Blanc. Chiefly used for blending.
Verdelho An essential component of Australia's 'white burgundy' style of full, soft but agreeable wine.
Zinfandel Tried with some success in Margaret River, Western Australia.

Basedow Wines

Barossa Valley, *SA*. Est. 1895. About 2,500 cases. Owners: since 1971 a group of Adelaide businessmen – now a public company.

A small but sometimes excellent Barossa winery, best known for its reds and dessert wines, including claret, Special Dry Red and various ports. In the late 1970s its Shiraz reached real heights of richness and complexity. The vineyards were sold in 1982, and grapes are now bought locally.

Bassenden Estate

147 West Road, Bassenden, Perth, *WA*. Est. 1951. 3,000 cases. Visits. Owners: Laurie and Moira Nicoletto. Vineyards: 5 acres, mainly Grenache. Prices: $3–4.

A conservative producer of typical soft and full-flavoured Swan Valley 'burgundies' which occasionally surprise (and delight) show judges with their elegance.

Berri Estate and Renmano

Berri, *SA*. Est. 1918. Berri 1.5m. cases; Renmano 0.5m. Visits. Prices: $2.50–4.00.

The huge Riverland coops, merged as Consolidated Cooperatives, have a rising profile. Berri's Rhine Riesling was always creditable; now their Cabernet blends with oak age are winning medals. Renmano blends Ruby Cabernet with Cabernet Sauvignon to achieve a sweetly fruity wine, and offers clean Sauvignon Blanc and Rieslings. Much of their production goes into 'casks'.

Best's Concongella

Great Western, *Victoria*. Est. 1866. 6,500 cases. Visits. Owners: The Thomson family since 1920. Vineyards: about 50 acres, largely Shiraz. Wines include P. Meunier, Rhine Ries., Chard., Chasselas and sparkling. Prices: $3–5; sparkling $7.

A famous old name in Victoria, conservative and highly picturesque in its original stone buildings. Great Western Hermitage No.0 is their best-known wine: not overweight but tannic enough for balance. Pinot Meunier is also very long-lived. Recent Chardonnay is matured in wood and promises well. Carbonated sparkling wine from Irvine's White (alias Ondenc) is their best-seller.

Wolf Blass Wines

Sturt Highway, Nuriootpa, Barossa Valley, *SA*. Est. 1973. Owner: Wolf Blass. Prices: $5.00–9.50.

A winery built round the tasting, blending and marketing talents of a German whom nobody would describe as modest or quiet spoken. Blass grows very little, but blends popular ready-to-drink wines of strong varietal character, ignoring regions but making full use of new oak. His labels include Eaglehawk ('Bilyara'), Yellow Label, Grey Label and Black Label on an ascending price scale – none of them a bargain. Yellow Label Rhine Riesling is a huge seller. No company in Australia has a better record of medals in shows.

Bleasdale Vineyards

Langhorne Creek, *SA*. Est. 1860. 30,000 cases. Visits. Owners: The Potts family. Vineyards: about 100 acres. Wines: an astonishing variety. Prices: $2–4.

The third generation of the pioneering Potts family operates this working slice of Australian history (it still has the huge old red-gum beam press). In this arid area the vineyards are irrigated by flooding through sluices from the Bremer River. The wines are cheap and very drinkable. A 15-year-old sweet Verdelho was excellent.

Botobolar

Botobolar Lane, Mudgee, *NSW*. Est. 1970. 11,000 cases (half red). Visits. Owners: Gil and Vincie Wahlquist. Vineyards: 62 acres, principally Shiraz, Crouchen, Chard., Rhine Ries., Trebbiano, Sem.

An engagingly personal winery run on ecological principles. Some products (e.g. Cabernet) are wholly successful, others (e.g. white Crouchen) a matter of taste and one or two (e.g. Budgee Budgee, a sweet white of Muscat and Shiraz) decidedly eccentric.

Bowen Estate

Coonawarra, *SA*. Est. 1972. 2,600 cases. Visits. Owners: Doug and Joy Bowen. Vineyards: 40 acres, largely Cab.Sauv. and Shiraz with some Rhine Ries. and recent plantings of Merlot and Chard. Prices: $7–9.

An ex-Lindeman's wine maker, Doug Bowen offers a near-model Coonawarra Cabernet. Riesling and Shiraz are also good examples of the area. He built a handsome new winery in 1980 and plans sparkling Chardonnay.

Brand's Laira

Coonawarra, *SA*. Est. 1966. 14,000 cases. Visits. Owners: The Brand family. Vineyards: 56 acres of Shiraz, Cab.Sauv., Malbec and a little Gren. Prices: $3.50–6.00.

Eric Brand started what has become like a modest Médoc Château, at first with fairly primitive methods. But his grapes are excellent, and from 1972 I have followed his Cabernets as some of Coonawarra's richest and best, needing 10 years to reach their peak. The Shiraz is very good but not so interesting; to my taste the blend of the two is better. Laira rosé is light and pretty.

Brokenwood

MacDonald's Road, Bacalbon, Hunter Valley, *NSW*. Est. 1971. 7,000 cases (rising). Visits. Owners: a partnership, including wine author James Halliday. Wine maker: Iain Riggs. Vineyards: 45 acres, mainly Cab. and Herm., with some Malbec, Merlot, Chard. and P.N. Prices: $7–10.

An apparently amateurish operation to start with, but its partners have good palates. They pick early for 'cleanness' of structure, sometimes adding a big Coonawarra Cabernet for richness. The results are not typical of the Hunter Valley but have their own considerable harmony. A new (1983) winery is now producing barrel-fermented Semillon and Chardonnay from bought-in grapes.

Brown Bros.

Milawa, *Victoria*. Est. 1889. 80,000 cases. Visits. Owners: The Brown family. Vineyards: 300 acres at Milawa and Mystic Park, new plantings at 2,500 ft at Whitelands. Also grapes on contract from 100 acres in King Valley (from '84 vintage). Prices: $3–6, with dessert wines up to $15.

Perhaps the closest approximation in Australia to the phenomenon of Robert Mondavi in California. In this case the third generation has furnished 4 able brothers to expand their father's remarkable work. New ideas are everywhere and growth almost alarming. New hill-top vineyards are providing excellent white grapes. The range is very wide: dry white Muscat, Late Harvest Rhine Riesling, Chardonnay, Pinot Noir, Merlot, Cabernet and old Shiraz have all given me great pleasure. Perhaps most of all the traditional Liqueur Muscat of the area.

Campbells

Murray Valley Highway, Rutherglen, *Victoria*. Est. 1870. 25,000 cases. Visits. Owners: The Campbell family. Wine maker: Colin. Grape grower: Malcolm. Vineyards: 100 acres;

Muscat, Tokay, Rhine Ries., Shiraz, Malbec, P.X.

Traditionally a producer of luscious dessert wines and Shiraz, since 1980 active in dry whites and a modern clean-cut Cabernet/Malbec blend. But Muscat, Tokay and port are still their backbone.

Capel Vale

Capel, nr. Bunbury, *WA*. Est. 1974. Visits. Owners: Peter and Elizabeth Pratten. Vineyards: about 22 acres of Shiraz, Cab.Sauv., Chard., Rhine Ries. and Gewürz.

A promising young winery. Its short track record suggests that its reds will be decidedly fruity, not over-oaky and rather elegant in general effect.

Cape Mentelle

Margaret River, *WA*. Est. 1969. 6,000–7,000 cases. Visits. Owners: a partnership, including the wine maker David Hohnen. Vineyards: 42 acres of Cab.Sauv., Rhine Ries., Shiraz, Zin., some Sem. and Ch.Bl. Prices: $5–7.

A much-discussed producer of very fruity and big-flavoured California-influenced wines; massive Cabernet and a rare example of Zinfandel in Australia.

Chambers Rosewood

Rutherglen, *Victoria*. Est. 1860. Visits. Owners: The Chambers family. Vineyards: about 100 acres at Rosewood, plus more family-owned vines. Many varieties. Wines: many.

Bill Chambers is a veteran wine maker, respected most of all for his old liqueur Muscat and Tokay. As always in Rutherglen the rich dry reds are better than the whites.

Chateau Barker

Mount Barker, Albany Highway, *WA*. Est. 1973. 4,800 cases. Visits. Owners: David and Margaret Cooper. Vineyard: 38 acres of Rhine Ries., Cab.Sauv. and smaller lots of Gewürz., Sem., Malbec, Merlot, Shiraz and P.N.

A convincing small family-run winery. Quondyp Riesling and Gewürztraminer are crisp, Germanic and almost too light. Pyramup is a good red blend. Pinot Noir is at the experimental stage.

Chateau Francois

Broke Road, Pokolbin District, *NSW*. Est. 1970. No visits. Owner: Dr. Don Francois. Prices: about $4.

A very small vineyard of Semillon, Shiraz, Pinot Noir. A weekend wine maker who does well in shows, especially with a Pinot Noir/Shiraz blend.

Chateau Le Amon

Beek Hill, Bendigo, *Victoria*. Est. 1973. 2,500 cases. Visits. Owners: Philip and Alma Leamon. Vineyards: 10 acres of Cab.Sauv., Shiraz, Sem. and Rhine Ries.

One of Victoria's successful small wineries, best known for powerful and deep Cabernet. A Shiraz/Cabernet blend has more finesse, if less depth. Semillon and Riesling are blended.

Chateau Tahbilk

Tabilk, *Victoria*. Est. 1860. 35,000 cases. Visits. Owners: The Purbrick family. Vineyards: 125 acres of Rhine Ries., Cab.Sauv., Chard., Shiraz, Marsanne and a little Sem. and Ch.Bl. Prices: $3.50–7.00.

Victoria's most historic and attractive winery and one of Australia's best. The old farm with massive trees stands by the Goulburn River in lovely country, its barns and cellars like a film set of early Australia. English-born Eric Purbrick has recently ceded the wine-making to his grandson Alister. Dry white Marsanne, starting life light but ageing to subtle roundness, is the main production. Riesling is crisp but full of flavour and also ages well. Special Bin reds (either Cabernet or Shiraz) are selected for maturing in 4,500-litre casks and only released at 6–7 years. A '64 Cabernet was perfection in 1982.

Chateau Yaldara

Lyndoch, Barossa Valley, *SA*. Est. 1947. Visits. Owner: Hermann Thumm.

A showplace for tourists: a sort of vinous Disneyland with sweet still and sparkling wine as its product.

Chateau Yarrinya

Pinnacle Lane, Dickson's Creek, Yarra Valley, *Victoria*. Est. 1971. 5,000 cases. Visits. Owners: Denise and Graeme Miller, Dan and Don Hall. Wine maker: Graeme Miller. Vineyards: 35 acres with 100 more to plant. Cab.Sauv., Shiraz, P.N., Rhine Ries., Gewürz. Prices: $5–8.

The winner of the 1980 Jimmy Watson Trophy for the best one-year-old red, with a king-size Cabernet which impressed everyone at the time. The Shiraz is lighter; Riesling and Gewürztraminer are blended into a rather sticky mixture.

Clarendon Estate

Tortilla, Clarendon 5157, *SA*. Est. 1970. Owners: The Hickinbotham family (*see* Anakie). Vineyards: 103 acres of Cab.Sauv., Shiraz, Chard., Ries., Gewürz. and Merlot.

The first Clarendon Shiraz, in 1976, was superb. Since then wines have been unpredictable; the best excellent.

Conteville

Wanneroo Road, Wanneroo, *WA*. Est. 1966. 6,000 cases. Visits. Wine maker: Paul Conti. Vineyards: 50 acres of Rhine Ries., Cab.Sauv., Gewürz. and some Merlot and Chard. Prices: $4–6.

A (stylistically) leading Swan Valley producer, also producing Mt. Barker wines from Forest Hill (q.v.) under a joint-venture agreement.

Coolawin Estate

Clarendon, *SA*. Est. 1969. 18,000 cases. Visits. Owners: Light & Sons Pty. Ltd. Wine maker: Brian Light. Vineyards: about 50 acres, at Clarendon and Murray Bridge. Rhine Ries., Cab.Sauv., Shiraz, Sem., Malbec. Prices: $3.00–4.50.

An underrated winery. Their Riesling is clean and good; Cabernet Sauvignon generous and soft; Shiraz 'Fine Hermitage', oak-aged, vivid, ripe and alive. Vintage and tawny ports are another speciality. Prices are modest.

Coriole

Chaffeys Road, McLaren Vale, *SA*. Est. 1967. 5,000–7,000 cases. Visits. Owners: The Lloyd family. Vineyards: about 30 acres of Cab.Sauv., Shiraz, Ch.Bl., Rhine Ries. and Touriga. Prices: $4–5.

Shiraz and blended Cabernet/Shiraz are the specialities of this good, small estate. Both have spicy ripeness.

Craigmoor

Mudgee, *NSW*. Est. 1858. 22,500 cases. Visits. Owners: Cyrille and Jocelyn Van Heyst (since 1980). Vineyards: about 130 acres, mainly Chard. and Sem. Also Shiraz, Cab., P.N., Gewürz., Sauv.Bl. Prices: $3.50–7.00.

The oldest-established Mudgee vineyard, long owned by the Roth family; a pioneer of a dry blend of Semillon and Chardonnay. The range of wines is wide, formerly made with a fairly heavy hand; recently more 'elegant'. Shiraz port matured in rum casks is a tradition.

Cullen's

Willyabrup, Cowaramup, Margaret River, *WA*. Est. 1971. 5,500 cases. Visits. Owners: Dr. Kevin and Diana (the wine maker) Cullen. Vineyards: 52 acres, mainly Cab.Sauv., with Rhine Ries., Sem., Sauv.Bl., Chard. and some Malbec, P.N. and Gewürz. Prices: $4.50–8.50.

Cabernet, both straight and blended with Merlot and Malbec, have made their reputation. It is dense, tannic and so far more accessible in the blend. A fairly gentle Sauvignon Blanc has been a recent success and a 'Fumé Cabernet' (rosé) another. Also Rhine Riesling Auslese in very small quantities.

D'Arenberg

McLaren Vale, *SA*. Est. 1928. Up to 50,000 cases. Visits. Owners: The Osborne family. Vineyards: 150 acres of Shiraz, Cab.Sauv., Gren., Palomino, Crouchen, Rhine Ries. and P.X. Prices: $2.50–5.00.

D'Arry Osborne is an experienced wine maker with old-fashioned tastes; his best standard red is 'burgundy' (75% Grenache, 25% Shiraz) with a rustic spiciness that grows on you (and ages well). Hearty Cabernet, soft, juicy but dry white Palomino and soft sweet vintage port are equally characteristic.

Drayton's Bellevue

Pokolbin, Hunter Valley, *NSW*. Founded 1850. Visits. Owners: The Drayton family. Vineyards: about 150 acres on Bellevue, Ivanhoe, Lambkin and Mangerton estates, principally Sem. and Shiraz. Prices: $2.50–7.00.

An old-fashioned company whose wines are increasingly well made and always good value. A 1979 Chardonnay fermented in wood and full of racy flavour showed them to be well up with more modern Hunter companies. An Ivanhoe 1978 Hermitage 'Pressings' was an excellent ripe but vigorous Rhône-style wine.

Elliott's Oakvale

Pokolbin, Hunter Valley, *NSW*. Founded 1893. Owners: The Elliott family.

An old family company with several famous vineyards (Belford, Fordwich, Tallawanta and Oakvale). After becoming part of Hermitage Estate in the 1970s (*see* Wyndham) they are again independent and making weighty Oakvale and lighter Belford Semillons, a traditional big Shiraz and a passable Chardonnay.

Enterprise Wines

2 Pioneer Ave., Clare, *SA*. Est. 1976. 10,000 cases. Visits. Owners: The Knappstein family. Wine maker: Tim. Vineyards: 90 acres of Rhine Ries., Cab.Sauv., Shiraz, Sauv.Bl. and Gewürz.; also Chard., Merlot. 45 acres being planted in the (cooler) Adelaide hills. Prices: $4.00–5.50.

The young former wine maker of Stanley Wines now practises his fanaticism for himself with convincing results. Flowery Rhine Riesling is one passion; densely fruity Cabernet another. All the wines are well made; more subtlety will come with maturing ideas (and vines).

Evans & Tate

Bakers Hill and Gnangara, Swan Valley; Redbrook Vineyard, Willyabrup, Margaret River, *WA*. Est. 1972. 6,000 cases to rise to 16,000. Visits. Owners: John Evans, John Tate and their wives. Vineyards: 68 acres – 52 at Redbrook (Margaret River), 11 at Gnangara, 5 at Bakers Hill. Largely Shiraz or Cab.Sauv., with some Chard., Sem., Merlot, Rhine Ries., Gewürz., Sauv.Bl., Price: $5.

The old and new of Western Australia are combined in a winery that grows grapes in Swan Valley and the Margaret River, making and barrel-ageing wine at Gnangara. Shiraz from Gnangara is softer and fuller than the reds from Redbrook but a house style is emerging, using new oak and aiming for moderation in ripeness.

Fern Hill Estate

Ingoldby Flat, McLaren Flat, *SA*. Est. 1975. 2,500 cases. Visits. Owners: Wayne and Patricia Thomas. Vineyards: 2.5 acres of Cab.Sauv. (most grapes bought locally).

Rich, mouth-filling Shiraz is the most impressive wine so far from an unusual little operation intending to use the cream of the local crop. Rhine Riesling has also been a critical success.

Forest Hill

Mt. Barker, *WA*. Owners: Betty and Tony Pearse.

The first vineyard in the Mount Barker area, established by the state government for research and still making some of its best wines, notably very intense-flavoured Cabernet Sauvignon and Riesling, both oak-aged and showing every sign of developing well in bottle. The wines are made at the Conteville winery, Wanneroo, near Perth (q.v.)

Hamilton's Ewell Vineyards

Glenelg (Adelaide), *SA*. Est. 1840. Owners: Mildara (q.v.). Vineyards: 120 acres in Eden Valley, 75 at Springton, 550 at Nildottie (Murray Valley), 150 at Swan Hill, Victoria.

One of the oldest firms, now best known for their light sweet Ewell Moselle and Springton Rhine Riesling. Their wines are all light, popular and mostly good value. Mildara Wines bought the company in 1982 and is making big changes.

Thomas Hardy

Willunga Road, McLaren Vale, *SA*. Est. 1857. 750,000 cases. Visits. Owners: The Hardy family. Vineyards: Keppoch – 320 acres of Rhine Ries., 225 of Shiraz, 95 Cab., 15 P.N., 20 Chard., 15 Gewürz., 5 Malbec; McLaren Vale – 85 of Shiraz for port. Bought grapes account for two thirds of production. Prices: $3–4 ('Eileen Hardy' $10).

An Adelaide family dynasty in its fifth generation and still growing. Its origins were in McLaren Vale, where it still makes some of Australia's best fortified wines. In the 1970s plantings were largely moved south to the cooler Keppoch area. Table wines have traditionally been skilful blends (e.g. St. Thomas Burgundy and the gutsy Nottage Hill Claret). In the 1970s with Brian Croser as consultant some outstanding wines emerged, especially reds labelled Eileen Hardy. Old Castle (Barossa) Riesling is their most famous white; Siegersdorf a rather finer and drier blend of Barossa and Keppoch grapes; Keppoch Riesling drier still. Eden Moselle is sweet.

Hardy's have recently taken over both Houghton in Western Australia and Reynella in Southern Vales, South Australia (the estate where the first Tom Hardy had his first job). Both companies appear to be blossoming as a result.

Heemskerk

Pipers Brook, Launceston, *Tasmania*. Est. 1966. 3,500 cases to rise to 7,000. No visits. Owner: Fesq, Haselgrove, Wiltshire & Co. Pty. Ltd. Vineyards: about 50 acres, with more to plant. Largely Cab.Sauv., with Gewürz., Chard., P.N. Price: $8.

In a remote and lovely spot on red soil within sight of the north coast. Cabernet so far has been a shade green but very promising.

Henschke

Keyneton, Barossa Valley, *SA*. Est. 1850s. 30,000 cases. Visits. Owners: The Henschke family. Vineyards: 250 acres in the Eden Valley of Shiraz, Rhine Ries. plus Cab.Sauv., Malbec, Sem., etc. Prices: $4.00–5.50.

A fifth-generation family firm (Stephen is wine maker) with 2 famous brands of Shiraz: Hill of Grace (deep austere wine from ancient vines) and Mount Edelstone (easier, more elegant red). Other wines include a crisp, dry and delicate Rhine Riesling. Fashion has swung back to their staunch conservative approach.

Houghton/Valencia

Dale Road, Swan Valley, *WA*. Est. 1859. 165,000 cases (plus bulk wine). Visits. Owner: Thomas Hardy and Sons. Vineyards: 800 acres, large blocks at Houghton and Valencia in the Swan Valley and Moondah Brook north of Perth, and a smaller property in the Frankland River area near Mt. Barker far to the south. Mostly Ch.Bl., Tokay, Verdelho, Shiraz, Gren., Cab.Sauv., Malbec. Prices: $4.50–5.00.

The most famous name in Western Australia. For 50 vintages it was made by the legendary Jack Mann. From 1950–1976 Emu Wines owned the company. Now under Hardy's its lustre has revived. White Burgundy is a little lighter and more polished, Cabernet excellent and the whole range honest and good value.

Hungerford Hill

Hunter Valley, *NSW*. Est. 1967. About 50,000 cases. Visits. Owner: Hungerford Hills Holdings Ltd. Wine maker: Ralph Fowler. Vineyards: 250 acres in the Hunter Valley of Chard., Shiraz and Sem., plus Rhine Ries., Gewürz., Cab., Malbec and P.N.; 345 acres at Coonawarra of Rhine Ries., Cab.Sauv., Shiraz, plus P.N. and Chard. Prices: $12.50, $6.00–7.50, $4.00.

Two widely separated vineyards, some of whose best wines are blended together. After early problems they are concentrating on Hunter Chardonnay and Coonawarra Cabernet and Riesling. Best wines, 'Show Reserves', have included Hunter and Coonawarra Chardonnays. 'Collection Series' is the next level and 'Black Label' the everyday line. Also some Coonawara Chardonnay 'Champagne'.

Huntington Estate

Cassilis Road, Mudgee, *NSW*. Est. 1969. 13,000 cases. Visits. Owners: Bob and Wendy Roberts. Vineyards: 101 acres of Shiraz, Cab.Sauv., Chard., Sem., P.N., Merlot and Sauv.Bl. Prices: $3–5.

Cabernets from this little family estate have been some of Mudgee's best, particularly those with a proportion of Merlot. The Shiraz is bigger and plainer. It also leads Mudgee in Chardonnay.

Kaiser Stuhl *see* Penfolds.

Katnook Estate

Coonawarra, *SA*. Wines since 1979. 10,000 cases. Visits by appt. Owners: Coonawarra Machinery Ltd. Vineyards: more than 500 acres of Chard., Cab.Sauv., Rhine Ries., Gewürz., Sauv.Bl. Prices: $9–12.

The small lots of fine wine recently released by this big grape-ranch have been supervised by Australia's most advanced and fashionable consultants, Brian Croser and Tony Jordan. They include very intense and powerful Chardonnay, Riesling along similar lines, lighter Gewürztraminer and some rather jammy Cabernet (1980) – all wines that speak more of beautiful ripe grapes than subtlety in the cellar.

Kay Brothers

Amery Vineyards, McLaren Vale, *SA*. Est. 1890. Visits. Owners: The Kay family. Vineyards: 125 acres.

An old firm making sound wines, including Sauvignon Blanc and typically full McLaren Vale Shiraz.

Krondorf

Krondorf Road, Barossa Valley, *SA*. Est. 1960s. 45,000 cases. Visits. Owners: Grant Burge and Ian Wilson, since 1978. Vineyards: about 90 acres, but three quarters of the grapes are bought in. Prices: $3.50–5.00.

A thriving new company using the same policy as the biggest: buying grapes widely and blending regions without qualms. Main wines are a Barossa Rhine Riesling, a nice light Chardonnay, and several reds, of which the Barossa Cabernet is the best.

Lake's Folly

Broke Road, Pokolbin, Hunter Valley, *NSW*. Est. 1963. 3,500 cases. Visits by appt. Owners: The Lake family. Wine maker: Stephen. Vineyards: 74 acres of Cab.Sauv., Chard., Shiraz, also some Malbec, etc. Price: $100 a dozen mixed.

At first the hobby, then the passion of a distinguished surgeon from Sydney, Max Lake. He started the first new Hunter winery in 40 years, ignoring tradition to prove that Cabernet can be the same splendid thing under Hunter skies as elsewhere. Then he did the same with Chardonnay, making vibrantly lively wines. Both can be among Australia's best.

Leconfield

The Main Penola Road, Coonawarra, *SA*. Est. 1970. 5,000 cases. Visits. Owner: Dr. Richard Hamilton. Prices: $6–10.

The retirement hobby of a professional wine maker, Syd Hamilton, bought in 1980 by his nephew, who also owns Willanga. Big-scale Cabernets and dry Rhine Riesling aged in oak have been the outcome so far.

Max Lake (right) and Len Evans: two champions of the Hunter.

Leeuwin

Gnarawary Road, Margaret River, *WA*. Est. 1974. Will be 40,000 cases. Visits. Owner: Denis Horgan. Vineyards: 222 acres of Rhine Ries., Chard., P.N., Cab.Sauv., plus some Shiraz, Malbec, Sauv.Bl. and Gewürz.
Prices: $8–17 (for Chardonnay).

One of the most important recent enterprises in Australia; a substantial very modern winery built with advice from Robert Mondavi in the green hills and woods of the Margaret River (the ocean only a jog away). The first Chardonnays have been sensational, with aromas, liveliness, richness and grip to outdo anything in Australia and most in California. Rieslings have varied from excitingly steely ('79) to melon-rich ('82 Reserve), with an excellent Auslese. Gewürztraminer is light, dry and long. Hermitage '79 tasted like Zinfandel. Pinot Noir succeeded well in '82. The first Cabernet is a rich but not overripe wine, considered highly promising.

Lindeman's and Leo Buring

Nyrang Road, Lidcombe, *NSW*. Founded 1870 as Ben Ean, bought by Lindeman's in 1912. Leo Buring founded 1945, bought by Lindeman's 1962. Rouge Homme bought 1965. 600,000 cases. Owners: The Philip Morris Co. (since 1971). Vineyards: Corowa, NSW: 277 acres in 2 main blocks, Southern Cross and Felton, mainly for dessert wines. Watervale and Clare, SA: 76 acres of Rhine Ries., Barossa Valley: 90 acres (for Leo Buring). Lower Hunter, NSW: 370 acres. Karadoc, Victoria: 395 acres in Sunraysia district for cask wines. Coonawarra: 500 acres (including the Rouge Homme winery). Padthaway, SA: 1,432 acres.

Australia's third biggest wine company. In addition to the grapes they grow, Lindeman's buy vast quantities, particularly in the Barossa and Hunter valleys and Coonawarra. They are Australia's master blenders with some 400 different labels and a major share of the 'cask' market. Yet they maintain excellent individual wines from their own estates. These include: Rhine Rieslings, both Lindeman's Watervale and Leo Buring's more austere Barossa. Also Rouge Homme Coonawarra and Padthaway Auslese. Semillon: Ben Ean Hunter Valley whites (and reds) are superb with bottle age. So is Porphyry 'Sauternes'. Cabernet: best from Rouge Homme, Coonawarra (q.v.). Chardonnay and Pinot Noir: very good from Padthaway. Dessert wines: excellent Corowa Muscats and Macquarie port. Among popular wines Ben Ean Moselle is said to be Australia's biggest-selling bottled wine.

McWilliams

Bulwara and Pyrmont Ridge Roads, Pyrmont, Sydney, *NSW*. Est. 1880. 2.2m. cases. Visits. Owners: The McWilliam family. Vineyards: 642 acres – 442 in the Hunter Valley (Mount Pleasant) and 200 near Griffith in the Riverina irrigated area (where they also buy large quantities and have 3 wineries: Hanwood, Yenda and Beelbangera).
Prices: $3.50–8.00

A single-minded and conservative family business with a large and loyal following, entirely in New South Wales (except for an offshoot in New Zealand). Their flagships are Mt. Pleasant Elizabeth Riesling and Philip Hermitage, both of which have honourable histories and maintain high standards. Wines from Griffith are lighter commercial stuff, but always well made. The full range at Griffith includes good dessert wines, Mark View 'Champagne' and much bulk and flagon wine.

Marienberg

Coromandel Valley, Clarendon, *SA*. Est. 1966. Visits. Owners: The Pridham family. Wine maker: Ursula. Vineyards: 15 acres at Clarendon, more at Bettany, east of McLaren Vale. Rhine Ries., Shiraz, Cab.Sauv. Prices: $4–5.

Australia's best-known woman wine maker has a fairly uninhibited way with oak. Her Schiraz [*sic*] is perhaps her best wine. The Riesling is hard to recognize except in the late-picked examples. Individual and not expensive.

Maxwell Wines

24 Kangarilla Road, McLaren Vale, *SA*. Est. 1979. 3,500 cases. Owners: The Maxwell family. Wine maker: Ken. No vineyards. Main wines are Cab.Sauv. and Ch.Bl. blended with Rhine Ries.

A small but technically impressive enterprise making deep and tannic Cabernet for laying down, and an original aromatic full-bodied white.

Mildara Wines

Merbein, nr. Mildura, *Victoria*. Est. 1891. Visits. Owner: a public company. Vineyards: 600 acres of Cab., Shiraz, Rhine Ries. at Coonawarra, 75 at Irymple, Mildura. Most Mildura grapes bought in. Prices: $3–7.

A name famous for some of Australia's better sherries from Mildura on the Murray River, and equally good Coonawarra table wines – the best of these are their Cabernets, outstanding since '79. Overall wine quality transformed since '78 following management changes at Coonawarra.

Miramar

Henry Lawson Drive, Mudgee, *NSW*. Est. 1974. About 6,000 cases. Visits. Owners: Iain Macrae and 3 partners. Vineyards: 37 acres at Miramar, 42 nearby, with P.N., Shiraz, Cab.Sauv., Merlot, Sem., Rhine Ries., Chard., etc.
Prices: $2.50–7.50.

One of the most competent wineries in Mudgee, bringing out powerful characteristics in each variety, especially Chardonnay, a Chardonnay/Semillon blend, Cabernet and Shiraz. Also a clean rosé and 'vintage port'.

Mitchells

Hugh's Park Road, Seven Hill, Clare Valley, *SA*. Est. 1975. 6,000 cases. Visits. Owners: Andrew and Jane Mitchell. Vineyards: 60 acres – 30 of Rhine Ries. at Watervale; 20 of Cab.Sauv., and 10 of Rhine Ries. at Seven Hill.

One of the most promising new wineries in Clare. Best wines so far are from Seven Hill.

Mitchelton

Mitchells Town, Nagambie, *Victoria*. Est. 1969. 20,000 cases. Visits. Owner: Dorado Wine Co. of Melbourne. Vineyards: 250 acres of Cab.Sauv., Shiraz, Rhine Ries., Trebbiano, Marsanne, Sem. Grapes also come from Coonawarra.
Prices: $3.50–5.00.

An extraordinary edifice like a 1970's monastery on the banks of the lovely Goulburn River. A lookout tower, aviary and restaurant were built to attract tourists. But the wines are another matter. The Mitchelton label is used for estate wines: excellent Marsanne, aged in cask, and distinctly aromatic for this grape, wood-matured Semillon, well-made Riesling and slightly dull Cabernet. 'Winemakers' Selection' is used for Coonawarra or blended wines; a fine velvety Coonawarra/Nagambie Cabernet and more highly flavoured Rieslings, some with noble rot. Thomas Mitchell is the second-quality label, e.g. Trebbiano 'chablis'. A very good range at modest prices.

Montrose

Henry Lawson Drive, Mudgee, *NSW*. Est. 1974. 30,000 cases. Visits. Owners: Carlo Salteri and Franco Belgiorno Nettis (both engineers). Vineyards: 111 acres of Chard., Cab., Rhine Ries., Shiraz, Gewürz., P.N. and a few Italian varieties – Sangiovese, Nebbiolo and Barbera.
Prices: $4–5.

A leading Mudgee winery with an Italian tilt towards light, sweetish, rather earthy reds and big sweet Chardonnay. Montrose Brut is a bargain tank-fermented sparkler.

Moorilla Estate

655 Main Road, Berridale, Hobart, *Tasmania*. Est. 1970. 2,500–3,000 cases. Visits by appt. Owner: Claudio Alcorso. Vineyards: 20 acres of Cab.Sauv., P.N. and Rhine Ries., kept 'like a garden'. Prices are high.

One of the first bold souls to look for quality in Tasmania, and in a cool corner at that. Frost, birds and underripeness are persistent problems. Riesling does best to give Moselle-like flavours. Cabernet, though made with love and care, tends to distinct greenness. The locals say it tastes of coffee. Pinot Noir is also a wraith. Alcorso is a textile man and gives his bottles cloth labels.

Morris Wines

Mia Mia Vineyard, Rutherglen, *Victoria*. Est. 1859. 15,000 cases. Visits. Owners: Orlando Wines (Reckitt & Colman). Wine maker: Mick Morris. 2 vineyards: Mia Mia in Victoria – 104 acres of Muscat; and Balldale in NSW with Tokay, Sem., Chard., Durif, Shiraz, Cab.Sauv.
Prices: $4–5 for table wines, $8–9 for Liqueur Muscat and Tokay, up to $30 for rare antiques.

Morris's Liqueur Muscat is Australia's secret weapon: an aromatic silky treacle that draws gasps from sceptics. The old tin winery building is a treasure-house of ancient casks of Muscats and Tokays, so concentrated by evaporation that they need freshening with young wine before bottling. The dark red Cabernet and Durif are impressive but hard wines; Semillon and Chardonnay surprisingly good since Orlando's came under the same ownership.

Moss Wood

Willyabrup, Metricup Road, Margaret River, *WA*. Est. 1969. Visits. Owners: Dr. Bill and Sandra Pannell. Vineyards: 22 acres of Cab., Sem., P.N. and Chard.
Prices: $7.50 for Cab., $8.50 for Pinot, $15 for Chard.

The winery that put the Margaret River among Australia's top-quality areas. Moss Wood Cabernet seems to define the style of the region: sweetly clean, faintly grassy, intensely deep and compact – almost thick, in fact, but without the clumsiness that implies. Definitely for very long ageing. Chardonnay and Pinot Noir are clearly going to be up to the same standard – the '81 Pinot Noir may be Australia's best yet.

Mount Avoca

Moate Lane, Avoca, *Victoria*. Est. 1970. Visits. Owners: John and Arda Barry. Vineyards: 40 acres of Cab., Shiraz and small parcels of Sem. and Trebbiano. New plantings of Chard. and Sauv.Bl. in 1981.

A mid-Victorian estate making rather full-bodied Cabernet and Shiraz wines with the rich, rather heavy, mint character which is the hallmark of the region. Also a well-regarded claret, a blend of the two.

Mount Mary

Coldstream West Road, Lilydale, Yarra Valley, *Victoria*. Est. 1971. No visits. Owners: Dr. John and Mary Middleton. Vineyards: 12 acres of Cab., Cab.Franc, Merlot, Chard., Pinot and some Gewürz.

A near-fanatical doctor's pastime which has become very serious indeed. His 1980 'Cabernets' blend (Cab.Sauv. 50%, Cab.Franc and Merlot 22.5% each and Malbec 5%) is like a classic Bordeaux; mid-weight, complex and intensely fruity without any 'burn'. 1978 Pinot Noir was equally remarkable; this grape clearly needs 3 or 4 years to show its form. Mount Mary Chardonnays are strong, rich and golden; new-oak fermented.

A. Norman & Sons

Underdale, Adelaide, *SA*. Est. 1859. 15,000 cases. Visits. Owners: The Norman family. Vineyards: 140 acres at Angle Vale of Gewürz., P.N., Ch.Bl., Cab.Sauv., Shiraz.
Prices: $3.50–4.50.

Still family-run after 120 years, and still fertile in good ideas. In 1973 the Normans produced South Australia's first Gewürztraminer. This, their Chenin Blanc and Pinot Noir are all original and well made. A Cabernet/Shiraz blend is very oaky.

Olive Farm

77 Great Eastern Highway, South Guildford, Perth, *WA*. Est. 1829. Visits. Owners: V. & J. Yurisich & Son. Vineyards: 7.5 acres being replanted with Cab.Sauv. Most grapes (Cab.Sauv., Ch.Bl., Chard. and Muscat) are bought in. Prices: $3–4.

Possibly the oldest winery in uninterrupted use and family ownership in Australia. Bargain well-made flagon wine is most of the business, but 3,000 cases are bottles of considerable quality – especially the Cabernet. Prices are very modest.

Orlando

Rowland Flat, Barossa, *SA*. Est. 1847 by Johann Gramp. Visits. Owner: Reckitt & Colman. Vineyards: about 260 acres spread over Barossa and in Eden and surrounding hills. Cab.Sauv., Cab.Franc, Rhine Ries., Frontignac, Sem., Merlot, Chard., P.N., Muscadelle. 136 acres in Eden Valley, Barossa, mainly Rhine Ries. and Gewürz. 148 acres at Ramco Riverland: Muscat Gordo, Frontignac, Chard., Ruby Cab., Sauv.Bl. In addition very large quantities of fruit are bought in. Prices: $4.50–17.00 (for best Ausleses).

One of the biggest and most technically advanced firms. Their best wines are white, especially Rhine Rieslings, of which their rare Steingarten has often been Australia's best in the steely style. Spätleses and Ausleses are exceptionally well made. Their leading red is Jacob's Creek Claret, a well-mannered beautifully packaged middleweight, Australia's biggest-selling bottled dry red. Its white sister wine is a remarkably good value $5 Chardonnay. Different wines are labelled William Jacob for export markets. Malbecs are also big and age-worthy. Eden Valley Gewürztraminer is softly spicy.

Peel Estate

Fletcher Road, Baldivis, nr. Mandurah, *WA*. Est. 1974. 2,000 cases, rising. Visits. Owners: Will and Helen Nairn and an English syndicate. Vineyard: 32 acres of Cab.Sauv., Chard., Ch.Bl., Shiraz, Verdelho and Zin.

Strong California influence shows in this blossoming estate. Chenin Blanc aged in oak is modelled on the lovely Chappellet Napa wine, California's best. Zinfandel is clean and aromatic, Shiraz with 15 months in French and American oak seems to be a wine for long ageing.

Penfolds

Nuriootpa Winery, Barossa Valley, *SA*. Est. 1844. Visits. Owner: Tooth & Co. Brewing Group of NSW. Vineyards: the acreage is not released, but large plantings in the Barossa Valley (at least 1,000 acres), Coonawarra and at Morgan, SA. Smaller plantings in the Hunter Valley and a historic remnant at the original site, Magill, Adelaide. All varieties are both grown and bought in.

Prices: $2–22 (for Grange Hermitage, $26 for Grandfather).

Penfolds was founded by a doctor and run by his descendants until 1962. Tooth's took over in 1976. It remains the most esteemed red-wine company in Australia, above all for its brilliant Grange Hermitage, the one true first-growth of the southern hemisphere. Grange, although Shiraz, tastes more like Bordeaux than Rhône wine. St. Henri claret, Private Bin reds, Bin 707 Cabernet, Bin 389 Cabernet Shiraz, Bin 128 Coonawarra Shiraz are all among the best of their class. The house style, using American oak, is almost as important as the origin of the grapes. Estate names in South Australia are Kalimna, Auldana, Koonunga Hill and Modbury; in New South Wales, Dalwood in the Hunter Valley (for cheaper lines) and Minchinbury and Rooty Hill (for sparkling wines). White wines have never been Penfolds' strong point: Pinot Riesling from the Hunter Valley is perhaps best. Ports are excellent: Magill a bargain and Grandfather a legend.

Penfolds recently bought Kaiser Stuhl, the Barossa Valley Cooperative, which has a 20-year reputation for outstanding Rhine Rieslings and very good Shiraz and Cabernet. Individual vineyard (Green, Gold and Purple Ribbon) Rieslings are some of Australia's best, at moderate prices.

Petaluma

Piccadilly, Adelaide, *SA*. Est. 1976. 5,000 cases Chard., 8,000 Rhine Ries., 4,000 Cab.Sauv. No visits. Owners: Len Evans, Denis Horgan and Brian Croser.

Prices: $10 Chard., $12.50 Cab.Sauv. (rising).

The name to conjure with in small new luxury wineries. Brian Croser started the idea of buying small batches of the best grapes to process either at the College at Riverina, where he was senior lecturer, or in borrowed facilities. His first wine was a notable late-picked Rhine Riesling. In 1977 he made Australia's most impressive Chardonnay to date with grapes from Cowra, New South Wales. Now with partners he has established a winery and small vineyard at Piccadilly near Adelaide. Both Chardonnay (now from Coonawarra) and Riesling (from Clare) have memorable impact, concentrated aromas and sheer class. Cabernet (launched 1982) seems set to follow the pattern.

Pipers Brook

Launceston, *Tasmania*. Est. mid-1970s. 4,000 cases. Visits by appt. Owners: 17 shareholders. Wine maker: Dr. Andrew Pirie (the largest shareholder). Vineyards: 25 acres of Cab., Chard., Pinot, Rhine Ries., Gewürz., Merlot, Cab.Franc.

Prices: $6–8.

The bold enterprise of an eclectic mind in search of ideal conditions: cool but not too cool. Dr. Pirie stresses that vines work most efficiently where evaporation is not too high – 'when the grass stays green'. His hill-top vineyard within sight of the north coast (and reach of sea winds) has already made superb dry Riesling and austere Chardonnay, very characteristic Pinot Noir and Cabernet with lively and intense flavours promising great things.

Max Schubert, for many years chief wine maker at Penfolds

Piramimma

Johnston Road, McLaren Vale, *SA*. Est. 1892. 70,000 cases. Visits. Owners: The Johnston family. Wine maker: Geoff Johnston. Vineyard: 250 acres of Cab.Sauv., Shiraz, Mataro, Rhine Ries., Palomino and other lesser varieties. Prices: $2.50–6.00.

Long-established but recently much improved estate, still making bulk wine but scoring high points for clean blackberryish Cabernet, aromatic Riesling, a soft light Shiraz and a bigger oak-aged one. Also good gutsy vintage ports.

Plantagenet Wines

Mount Barker, *WA*. Est. 1968. 4,500 cases. Visits. Owners: 3 partners; 2 Australian and 1 English. Wine maker: Robert Bowen. Vineyards: 75 acres at Mt. Barker, mainly Rhine Ries., with Cab.Sauv., Shiraz, Sauv.Bl., Merlot, some Chard. Also Ch.Bl. from Swan Valley. Prices: $5–6.

The senior winery at Mount Barker. Their triumph to date is exceptional Rhine Riesling of powerful Spätlese style with a beautifully long dry finish. Cabernet and Shiraz are less distinguished but could hardly be more.

Quelltaler

Clare-Watervale, Clare Valley, *SA*. Est. 1865 by the Sobels family. Visits. Owners: Rémy Martin of France. Vineyards: 617 acres of Cab.Sauv., Rhine Ries., Shiraz, also P.X., Grenache, some Mataro. Prices: $7–12 for top wines.

A famous old name for reliable basic hock and claret, recently revolutionized by French owners. Suddenly cool Rieslings, interesting Cabernets and experiments with *macération carbonique* have changed the scene – and pushed up the prices.

Redman

Coonawarra, *SA*. Est. 1966. 25,000 cases. Visits. Owner: Owen Redman. Vineyards: 89 acres of Cab.Sauv., Shiraz. Prices: $5–7.

Redman's father gave his name to what is now Lindeman's Rouge Homme. Owen's breeding in Coonawarra has given him a style of his own: claret that seems light at first but stays the course. Long bottle age is essential. Shiraz claret accounts for 17,500 cases, the balance straight Cabernet of great class.

Renmano

Riverland, *SA*. Est. 1919. Visits. A consolidated coop. Prices: $3.50–4.00.

Formerly a mere bulk-producer, now marketing good dry Rhine Riesling (Bin 604) and sweet (654), Sauvignon Blanc and a remarkably good Chairman's Selection Cabernet – a real bargain.

Reynella

Southern Vales, *SA*. Owner: Thomas Hardy & Sons Pty. Ltd. (q.v.). Wine maker: Geoff Merrill.

A famous old name particularly for ports and red wines, with a historic cellar and vineyards just south of Adelaide. Fewer notable wines have appeared in the last 10 years, despite a takeover by Rothman's in 1976. In 1982 Thomas Hardy & Sons bought the firm; it now appears to be in good shape. Grapes are bought under contract in Coonawarra for a wide range, of which very good Cabernet and Rhine Riesling are the best. Wines from the Southern Vales vineyards are labelled Chateau Reynella. 'Vintage port' is a notable example.

Richmond State

Gadds Road, Sydney Basin, North Richmond, nr. Sydney, *NSW*. Est. 1967. Visits. Owner: Gary Bracken. Vineyards: 22 acres, half Shiraz, half Cab., a little Malbec and Merlot. Prices: $3.50–4.00. A bargain for very good wines.

A surgeon's solace: making wine (Shiraz especially) to pick up gold medals at shows.

Robinsons Family Winery

Lyra Church Road, Ballandean, *Queensland*. 3,500 cases. Visits. Owner and wine maker: John Robinson. Vineyards: 26 acres of Cab., Chard., P.N., Gewürz., Shiraz and a bit of Rhine Ries. Prices: $4–5.

A great rarity in Queensland, but only just north of the New South Wales border. Very well made, if inevitably stout red wines. Oak-age gives them surprising structure. Whites are less convincing.

Robson Vineyard

Mount View Road, Hunter Valley, *NSW*. Est. 1972. 5,000 cases. Visits. Owner: Murray Robson. Vineyards: 10 acres of Chard., Cab., Gewürz., Merlot, Malbec, P.N. and Sauv.Bl. Prices: $6–8.

A highly personal, even faintly precious aura pervades this miniature winery. Robson even signs every label himself. Biggest and most successful production is of Shiraz, modern, oaky and elegant, needing 5–6 years to integrate. Chardonnay is leanish, Cabernet also rather austere. Semillon grapes are brought in to make a good Hunter example and also a sweet one.

Rosemount Estate

Denman, Upper Hunter District, *NSW*. Est. 1969. 150,000 cases. Visits. Owner: Anco Pty. Ltd. 3 vineyards: Rosemount – 300 acres; Roxburgh – 300 acres; Penfolds' old Wybong vineyard – 300 acres. Prices: $4.00–7.50.

An ambitious large-scale venture which came to prominence in 1975 with gold medals for aromatic Rhine Riesling and Gewürztraminer – still their specialities. Wood-matured Semillon and Chardonnay have followed. They still make light 'Melon Creek' but also impressive wines from Coonawarra grapes. Hot off the press is an astonishing '82 Riesling Trockenbeerenauslese.

Rothbury Estate

Broke Road, Pokolbin, Hunter Valley, *NSW*. Est. 1968. 90,000 cases. Visits. Owners: a large syndicate of shareholders. Wine maker: David Lowe. Vineyards: 550 acres in the Hunter Valley of Shiraz, Sem., Cab., Chard. and P.N., 85 acres in Cowra of Cab., Chard., Gewürz., Sem. and Sauv.Bl. Prices: $4.50–7.50.

The brainchild of Len Evans, Australia's foremost wine author, judge and good companion. Several hundred shareholders own the impressive winery and banquet regularly in its dramatic 'cask-hall', buying the wines by mail order. Long-lived Semillon in the true old Hunter style made its reputation. Hermitage backed it up. Spicy high-flavoured Chardonnays from Cowra and Hunter (the latter finer) are a new attraction. Cabernet and Pinot Noir are still almost experimental, but promise well. Top wines have a black Individual Paddock label.

St. Huberts

Maroondah Highway, Coldstream, Yarra Valley, *Victoria*. Est. 1968. 6,000 cases. Visits. Owner: a syndicate. Wine maker: Peter Connolly. Vineyards: 40 acres of Cab., Shiraz, Rhine Ries., P.N., Chard. and Trebbiano. Prices: $6–17.

A rather shambolic winery with some excellent wines and

others disappointing. Riesling is their best wine; the 1977 at 5 years old is one of Australia's most vital and lovely. Chardonnay '81 and '82 were poor. Shiraz '81 was soft, smooth and earthy. Cabernet '80 had a metallic, Zinfandel-like flavour; the '81 was good, concentrated, sweet and simple with a hint of Bordeaux.

St. Leonard's Winery

Wahgunyah, *Victoria*. Est. 1860. Visits. Owner: Brown Brothers and Syndicate. Prices: $4–6.

An old northeast Victoria winery name revived in the 1970s for a replanted vineyard in collaboration with Brown Bros. of Milawa, who make the wines. Semillon, Orange Muscat, Chardonnay, Cabernet and Shiraz are all successful – the whites particularly so.

Saltram

Angaston Road, Barossa Valley, *SA*. Est. 1859. Visits. Owner: Seagrams. Vineyards: about 250 acres, mainly white, but great majority of grapes bought in.

A winery with a complicated history and an uncertain future. It was bought from the original Salter family with its neighbour Stonyfell in 1972 by Dalgety's the graziers. In 1978 Seagrams took charge. Over the last 20 years the wines were made by Peter Lehmann, whose Mamre Brook (Barossa) Cabernet became a classic. Metala Cabernet/Shiraz also survives his moving on. Brian Croser (*see* Petaluma) was subsequently consulted and a good-value Chardonnay is one of the principal attractions.

Sandalford

Caversham, Swan Valley, *WA*. Est. 1840. Visits. Owner: The Inchcape Group. Wine maker: Dorham Mann. 2 vineyards: Margaret River – 358 acres, mainly Rhine Ries., Verdelho, Sem. and Shiraz. Swan Valley – 100 acres of Cab., Ch.Bl., Shiraz, Muscat and Grenache. Prices: $4–6.

An atmospheric old property on the Swan River near Perth, next door to Houghtons (q.v.). Dorham Mann's father Jack started the 'white burgundy' style – he continues it at Sandalford, using Chenin Blanc, Semillon, Muscadelle and Verdelho to make a rich aromatic dry wine which ages 7 years to real character. He also makes a crisp Chenin Blanc from Swan vineyards. Top Margaret River wines are Riesling Auslese, an unusual, slightly sweet but clean and fine Verdelho, and soft fruity Cabernet. Sandalera is delectable old 'madeira-style' dessert wine of Pedro Ximénez aged 7 years in small casks.

Saxonvale

Fordwich, Broke Road, Hunter Valley, *NSW*. Founded 1971. Visits. Owner: Stanlee Pty. Ltd. Vineyards: over 800 acres in Fordwich and Pokolbin, mostly Chard., Cab., Sem. and Shiraz. Prices: $3.50–10.00.

An energetic young company with the technology to make a wide range well. Chardonnay and Semillon are their 2 best wines.

Seppelt

181 Flinders Street, Adelaide, *SA*. Est. 1851. Visits. Owners: a public company. Vineyards: 500 acres at Great Western, Victoria, of Ondenc, Rhine Ries., Chasselas, P.N., Chard., Shiraz and Cab.Sauv.; 484 acres at Keppoch, SA, of Rhine Ries., Sylv., Chard., Frontignan Bl., Cab.Sauv., Shiraz and P.N.; 276 acres at Seppeltsfield, Barossa Valley, SA, of Palomino, Grenache, Rhine Ries., Shiraz, Cab.Sauv.; 313 acres at Drumborg, Victoria, of Rhine Ries., Ondenc, Muscadelle, Sylv., Gewürz., Chard., P.N., P.Meunier and Cab.Sauv.; 101 acres at Rutherglen, Victoria, of Chard., P.N., Muscat, Cab.Sauv.; 306 acres at Barooga, NSW, near Rutherglen, of Chard., Ondenc, Ch.Bl., P.N., Muscat and Trebbiano; 383 acres at Qualco, SA, near Renmark, of Chard., Muscadelle, Rhine Ries., Colombard, Cab.Sauv. and Ch.Bl.; 462 acres at Partalunga in the Adelaide hills, SA, newly planted with Rhine Ries., Chard. and Gewürz.

Prices: $2.00–16.50 (for Para Liqueur). Best table wines and 'Champagne' about $7.

This vast acreage only supplies one third of Seppelt's needs for a kaleidoscope of wines. They dominate the sparkling market with Great Western 'Champagne'. Whites and reds range from such standards as Arawatta Riesling, Moyston Claret, Chalambar Burgundy to Reserve bins and their top wines: Black Label (Cabernet, Shiraz and Rhine Riesling). 'District varietals' are new show-winning releases. One of Australia's most impressive companies and apparently on top form, winning innumerable prizes. Their Barossa H.Q. has vast stocks of fine old dessert wines, including some of Australia's best sherries and their legendary Para Liqueur port.

Sevenhill

Clare Valley, *SA*. Est. 1852. 12,500 cases. Visits. Prices: $3–4.

An old Jesuit holding with its church and winery, principally making altar wine for many other Jesuit churches throughout Australia. They make a very good vintage port, and some long-lived reds, especially Shiraz/Cabernet.

Seville Estate

Linwood Road, Seville, *Victoria*. Est. 1962. 1,000 cases. Visits by appt. Owners: Dr. Peter McMahon and family. Price: $6.50 upwards.

A tiny, exceptionally beautiful estate ranked as one of Australia's very best. Cabernet is gently juicy like Pomerol, Chardonnay also low key but deep flavoured, Shiraz at 4 years spicy and almost honeyed – all taste (and are) luxuriously handmade. Most extraordinary are Riesling Beerenausleses, comparable with California's luscious best.

Smith's Yalumba

Eden Valley Road, Angaston, Barossa Valley, *SA*. Est. 1863. 45,000 cases. Visits. Owners: The Hill-Smith family. Vineyards: about 600 acres in the Barossa area, largely up at Pewsey Vale; 600 acres near Waikerie on the Murray River. Almost all the grapes come from their own vineyards. Main varieties: Rhine Ries., Cab.Sauv., Chard., Gewürz., Merlot, Shiraz.

Prices: $3–7; best port $14.

The sixth generation of the Hill-Smith family is active in this distinctively upper-crust winery with an air of the turf about it. Their finest wines in the past were 'ports', but since the planting of higher and cooler land in the 1960s, their Pewsey Vale Rhine Rieslings have been very good and hugely popular. The drier Carte d'Or Riesling is one of the best-value whites in Australia today. Wood-matured Semillon is good; Yalumba Chardonnay is expected soon. Sparkling wines are also successful.

Reds in the past have been rather tough and dull, like many in Barossa. Galway Claret is a reliable mid-weight, but recently the Signature series of reds has included some very good Cabernet/Shiraz and Cabernet/Malbec blends. Stocks of fine barrel-aged reds are now the biggest in Australia. Galway Pipe tawny is perhaps their best port, followed by a very rich Vintage.

Stanley (Leasingham)

Dominic Street, Clare, *SA*. Est. 1894. Visits. Owner: H. J. Heinz. Prices: $2.50–7.00.

The leading winery of the Clare district. It buys most of its grapes. Once it sold its wine to Lindeman's, then with Tim Knappstein as wine maker (*see* Enterprise Wines) made first-class Leasingham Cabernet (esp. Bin 49), Cabernet/Malbec (Bin 56) and Rhine Rieslings (Bins 5 – sweetish, and 7 – dry).

Stanton & Killeen

Rutherglen, *Victoria*. Est. 1925. 6,000 cases. Visits. Owners: The Stanton and Killeen families. Wine maker: Chris Killeen. Prices: $3–4 for reds.

A small old family winery revitalized since 1970. Its Moodemere reds, both Cabernet and Shiraz, are now among the best in northeast Victoria. Gracerray dessert Muscats and ports are luscious in the regional tradition.

Taltarni

Moonambel, nr. Stawell, *Victoria*. Est. 1972. 25,000 cases. Visits. Owners: Red Earth Nominees Pty. Ltd. (John Goelet). Wine maker: Dominique Portet. Vineyards: 250 acres, shallow gravel over clay, of Rhine Ries., Chard., Sauv.Bl., Ch.Bl., Hermitage Bl., Cab.Sauv., Cab.Merlot, Malbec, Shiraz.

The brother winery to Clos du Val in the Napa Valley: extremely modern and well equipped without extravagance. Taltarni needs time to rival Clos du Val, but already its reds are imposing. 1977 and 1979 Special Reserve Cabernets are demonstrations of intent: enormous dark wines, including pressings, built to last 20 years. Shiraz is made much lighter. A 1982 Merlot was fleshy but pleasantly tannic. Whites are less sure-footed.

Tisdall

Cornelia Creek Road, Echuca, *Victoria*. Est. 1979. About 30,000 cases (Rosbercon); 15,000 cases (Mt. Helen); plus bulk wines. Visits. Owner: Dr. Peter Tisdall. Wine maker: John Ellis. 2 vineyards: Rosbercon (Echuca) – 200 acres of Colombard, Ch.Bl., Rhine Ries., Sem., Merlot, Cab.Sauv., Shiraz; Mt. Helen in Strathbogie Ranges, central Victoria – 100 acres of Cab.Sauv., Merlot, P.N., Rhine Ries., Chard., Sauv.Bl., Gewürz.
Prices: $3.50–4.00 (Mt. Helen $8–9).

A substantial new company making good commercial wines from Echuca (Murray Valley) grapes. Merlot is the best. In the same winery John Ellis vinifies a different class of wine from young vineyards planted in the cool Strathbogie hills in central Victoria. His Cabernet (with and without Merlot), Chardonnay, Pinot Noir and Rhine Riesling (also late harvest) are making Mt. Helen one of the most carefully watched labels in Australia.

Tollana (Tolley, Scott & Tolley)

Barossa Valley, *SA*. Est. 1888. Visits. Owners: The Distillers Company Ltd. Vineyards: Woodbury Estate, Eden Valley, 250 acres Rhine Ries., Cab.Sauv., Gewürz., Shiraz; Qualco, near Waikerie, 1,000 acres (500 for distilling wine).
Prices: $4–6.

An old Barossa brandy company taken over in 1961, was jerked into prominence in the late 1960s by the young Wolf Blass, who made some splendid wines and said outrageous things about them. Since then Tollana has become a reliable name for very fruity and well-balanced Rhine Riesling, good Eden Valley Shiraz, Cabernet/Shiraz blended and Gewürztraminer.

Douglas A. Tolley

30 Barracks Road, Hopes Valley, nr. Adelaide, *SA*. Est. 1892. 2.5m. cases. Visits. Owners: The Tolley family. Vineyards: Barossa Valley; Qualco, Murray River. Prices: $3–4.

One of Australia's largest family-owned wineries, long based on bulk wines but now changing gear with the advice of Tony Jordan and Brian Croser. The name Pedare is now used for their premium wines, of which a crisp, cold-fermented Rhine Riesling, delicately spicy Gewürztraminer, good Shiraz, Semillon, rosé and excellent ports are most remarkable. A name to watch.

Tulloch

De Beyers Road, Pokolbin, Hunter Valley, *NSW*. Est. 1893. Visits. Owner: Gilbeys (Australia) Pty. Ltd. Wine maker: Pat Auld. Vineyards: Pokolbin and Fordwich, Sem., Chard., Shiraz, Cab.Sauv., Verdelho. Prices: $3–7.

The Hunter Valley side of a business bought by Gilbeys in 1974, consisting of the old Tulloch family winery and Ryecroft in McLaren Vale, SA. They produce Hunter Riesling, Pokolbin dry red, and the premium White Label range which is doing well with Chardonnay, Semillon, a Semillon/Verdelho blend, and notably Hermitage and Cabernet.

Tyrrells, 'Ashman's'

Broke Road, Pokolbin, Hunter Valley, *NSW*. Est. 1858. 50,000 cases. Visits. Owners: The Tyrrell family. Vineyard: 100 acres in Hunter Valley, plus grapes from Ch. Douglas, Upper Hunter. Prices: $2.50–9.00.

Murray Tyrrell has been one of the main architects of the Hunter Valley revival of the 1970s, building on a traditional Semillon and Shiraz base but startling Australia with his well-calculated, not overstressed Chardonnays. His 'Bin 47' really led the way for Chardonnay in Australia. Pinot Noir has been much more variable (with '79 and '81 very good). 'Old Winery' is a premium commercial range of good character. 'Pinot Riesling' is a 50/50 Chardonnay/Semillon blend. Long Flat Red and Short Flat White are serious (!) everyday wines. On the whole Tyrrell's whites are more exciting than his reds.

Vasse Felix

Cowaramup, Margaret River, *WA*. Est. 1967. Visits. Owners: Dr. Cullity and David and Anne Gregg. Vineyard: 20 acres, Rhine Ries., Cab.Sauv., Shiraz.

The pioneer winery of Margaret River, and still level with the best, especially for very dark, firm and undoubtedly long-lived Cabernet. Late-picked Riesling and Gewürztraminer have both been very successful.

Vignacourt

Toodyay Road, Swan Valley, *WA*. Est. 1955. 6,000 cases plus bulk wines. Visits. Vineyards: 17 acres of Shiraz, Cab.Sauv., Ch.Bl., Verdelho, Rhine Ries., Frontignac and Malbec. Other grapes are bought. Prices: $4–6.

A small but significant Swan Valley producer, often winning Perth medals with Chenin Blanc and late-harvest Frontignac from the Swan Valley and Cabernet from the Frankland River.

Virgin Hills

Kyneton, *Victoria*. Est. 1968. No visits. Owner: Marcel Gilbert. Wine maker: Tom Lazar. Vineyards: 45 acres of Cab.Sauv., Malbec, Shiraz, P.N.

Lazar believes he has made the best Australian wine ever. Certainly small crops and great concentration made his '76 and '79 huge wines for a distant future.

Wantirna Estate

Wantirna South, *Victoria*. Est. 1963. 2,000 cases. No visits. Owners: Reg and Tina Egon. Vineyards: 10 acres of Cab., Chard., P.N., Merlot, Rhine Ries. Prices: $6–7.

A tiny estate in the suburbs of Melbourne, producing a Pinot Noir some consider Australia's best yet, a most gentlemanly Cabernet/Merlot blend and tiny quantities of other well-made wines. There is a waiting list for the mailing list.

Wendouree

Clare, *SA*. Est. 1895. Visits. Owner: Tony Brady. Prices: $4–5.

The late owner, Roly Burkes, was one of the great conservative Aussie wine makers who made massive reds, largely used for blending by other wineries. The style is maintained by the new owner, especially in his Cabernet/Malbec/Shiraz; deep, dark, oak-scented. The Clare Riesling is also a fat, full-bodied wine. 'Vintage ports' are splendidly vigorous.

Westfield

Baskerville, Swan Valley, *WA*. Est. 1922. 3,000 cases. Visits. Owner: John Kosovich. Vineyard: 4 acres Cab.Sauv., Shiraz, Malbec, Rhine Ries., Verdelho, Sem., Ch.Bl. Prices: $3.50–5.00.

A Swan Valley miniature, notable for exceptional Semillon, good Cabernet and 'vintage port' with great depth rather than great sweetness.

Wirra Wirra

Mcmurtrie Road, McLaren Vale, *SA*. Est. 1894. 6,000 cases. Visits. Owners: Greg and Roger Trott. Vineyards: 7.5 acres of Cab.Sauv., Shiraz, Grenache, Rhine Ries., P.N., Merlot, Chard., Sauv.Bl.

The resurrection (in 1969) of a fine old bluestone winery to make lighter and more graceful wines than the usual macho McLaren Vale style. Rieslings are most remarkable. 'Church Block' is a Shiraz/Grenache blend.

Woodley Wines

Glen Osmond (Adelaide), *SA*. Est. 1856. Owners: Crooks National Holdings Pty. Ltd. Prices: $3–6.

A historic winery with cellars in a former silver mine. The elegant Queen Adelaide label is used for indifferent bought-in Barossa Riesling and McLaren Vale Cabernet/Shiraz claret.

Wrights

Cowaramup, Margaret River, *WA*. Est. 1974. 2,500 cases. Visits by appt. Owners: Henry and Maureen Wright. Vineyards: 22 acres of Cab.Sauv., Rhine Ries. and Shiraz, some Sem. and Chard. not yet bearing. Prices: $5–7.

An unpretentious but quietly impressive winery. Dense, slightly earthy Cabernet, strongly flavoured Hermitage, broadly fruity, almost white-burgundy Riesling are clear expressions of Margaret River's exceptionally tasty grapes.

Wyndham Estate

Dalwood, Branxton, *NSW*. Est. 1928. 270,000 cases. Visits. Owners: a syndicate. Manager: Brian McGuigan. Vineyards: Hollydene – 500 acres; Hermitage Estate – 200 acres; Richmond Grove – (all white varieties) 250 acres. Prices: $3.00–6.50.

The old Wyndham Estate and the new Hollydene, Hermitage Estate and Richmond Grove are all part of one very large and proficient group under the leadership of an ex-Penfolds' wine maker. Standards range from popular sweet whites – Riesling, Gewürztraminer, Sauvignon Blanc, to traditional dry Hunter Riesling and some fairly long-lived reds: Bin 444 Cabernet and 555 Burgundy. Chardonnays look promising. Other wines include a 'Seafood Riesling' made specially for Pete Doyle's famous Sydney restaurants and a number unforgivably labelled White Bordeaux, Graves, Sauterne, Chablis, Moselle and other names to which they have not the remotest right (or resemblance).

Wynn Winegrowers

9–19 Rooks Road, Nunawading, *Victoria*. Est. 1918. No visits. Owners: Castlemaine Tooheys Ltd. Vineyards: Coonawarra – 1,718 acres of Cab.Sauv., Shiraz, Rhine Ries., Chard., P.N.; 'High Eden' (Barossa) – 1,000 acres; Southern Vales – 1,000 acres; Padthaway – 680 acres.

Wynn's most famous wines are Coonawarra Cabernet and Hermitage and a blend of the two; the Cabernet particularly successful. Coonawarra Rhine Rieslings (made at Glenloth) are less outstanding. Their bulk wines (and their rather good 'Samuel' port) come from Murrumbidgee grapes processed at another winery at Yenda. The name Seaview Champagne Cellars is given to Wynn's old Romalo (Adelaide) operation (Australia's only purely *méthode champenoise* cellar).

Yarra Yering

Yarra Yering Road, Coldstream, Yarra Valley, *Victoria*. Est. 1969. 2,500 cases. Visits. Owner: Dr. Bailey Carrodus. Vineyards: 30 acres, Bordeaux and Côtes du Rhône varieties. Prices: $5–7.

An individualist who not only initiated the wine revival of the Yarra Valley but apparently ignores the fashion for 'varietal' labelling. A Bordeaux-type blend is called Dry Red No.1, a Rhône-type Dry Red No.2. Both are widely admired for harmonious composition. 'Dry White' is his third wine. But Pinot Noir he makes straight and less successfully.

Yellowglen

White's Road, Smythesdale, nr. Ballarat, *Victoria*. Est. 1971. 4,000 cases soon. Visits. Owners: Ian Home and Dominique Landragin (wine maker). Vineyards: 30 acres at Smythesdale of P.N. and Chard. 60 to be planted. Grapes also from Sulky near Creswick, and Dalwhinnie near Avoca. Prices: $6.75–9.75.

Home and Landragin are determined to make Australia's best sparkling wine. Landragin learnt his trade with Lanson and Deutz in Champagne before becoming the wine maker for Seppelt's Great Western. The first fruits are extremely promising – particularly a Blanc de Pinot Noir. Other wines include a remarkable lightweight burgundy-like Pinot Noir red, an elegant and aromatic Shiraz and a gentle, Chinon-like Cabernet.

Yeringberg

Coldstream, Yarra Valley, *Victoria*. Est. 1969. 800 cases – 200 each of Cab., Chard., Pinot and Marsanne. Visits by appt. Owner: Guillaume de Pury. Vineyards: 4 acres of Cab., Merlot, Malbec, P.N., Chard. and Marsanne. Prices: $5–6.

The remnant of a wonderful old country estate near Melbourne, rather tentatively making some excellent wines. Riesling alas has been pulled up, but the 1980 Pinot Noir was a charming and delicate wine and the Cabernet/Merlot/Malbec of the same vintage very good, dark, berry-like and nicely astringent.

NEW ZEALAND

While almost every Australian settler, it seems, planted vines for wine, the new New Zealanders did little to exploit the temperate climate and fertile soils of their islands. No wine industry, beyond isolated missions and private estates, existed until Dalmatian and Lebanese Kauri-gum workers started to provide for their own needs in the Auckland area early in the twentieth century. Their products were crude, from poor vines unsuited to the warm humidity of Auckland. Phylloxera forced them to plant hybrids. Most of the wine was fortified and probably deserved its label of 'Dally plonk'. Nor did the small and strait-laced Anglo-Saxon community provide an encouraging marketplace.

In 1960 almost half of the total of 958 acres was in the Auckland area, and most of the rest in Hawkes Bay on the central east coast of the North Island. The '60s saw a trebling of the Auckland acreage and the development of Waikato, 40 miles south. It saw the Hawkes Bay vineyards double in size and an important new area spring up at Poverty Bay near Gisborne, north of Hawkes Bay. These two east-coast areas are the ones that flourished in the 1970s, quintupling their acreage while Auckland's slightly shrank. But the '70s also saw the vine move to the South Island – by 1980 Marlborough, at its northern tip, had nearly 2,000 acres and experimental planting had moved as far south as Canterbury. Most of this new planting is in wide rows intended for mechanized cultivation, harvesting and possibly pruning – a technological vineyard. The 1981 total was 14,000 acres.

Climatic conditions are quite different in these four main areas. Auckland is almost subtropical with considerable cloud cover and frequent autumn rain. Hawkes Bay lies in the rain shadow of the volcanic mountain centre of the island, with dry summers and autumns, and largely deep, free-draining soils which sometimes call for irrigation. Gisborne and Poverty Bay have a climate between the two, with a tendency for autumn rains to force the harvest forward. Marlborough is the sunniest of all, but cooler in the autumn from its southerly latitude. It has very low rainfall (irrigation is essential, at least for young vines). Wind is a problem: young leaves are burned by perpetual strong breezes across flat, open plantations. Rows of poplars would undoubtedly help matters.

Despite this variety, New Zealanders have been convinced that their climate is akin to Germany's, and accordingly planted huge areas of Müller-Thurgau (which they call Riesling Sylvaner). The resulting mild dry or semi-sweet wines are pleasant enough, but give little clue to the real potential of their vineyards. To me their natural affinity seems to be with certain parts of France: the east coast and Marlborough vineyards conjure vivid flavours out of Chardonnay, Gewürztraminer and Cabernet. If Germany is to be invoked, it should be on the South Island, which can produce good sunny late-ripening conditions for real Riesling.

At present it appears that the fruit-growing Huapai area north of Auckland, with heavy soils, has good potential for red grapes. Gisborne is a fine white-grape area with the drawback of autumn rain (and also active phylloxera, which is causing almost total replanting). Hawkes Bay has a glorious mixture of soils; silt, shingle and clay, where rivers drain its umbrella of mountains. These and its sunshine give it enormous potential for red and white grapes. Marlborough is already showing that its climate gives extremely well-flavoured fruit.

New Zealand's natural gift is what the wine makers of Australia and California are constantly striving for: the growing conditions that give slowly ripened, highly aromatic rather than super-ripe grapes. It is too soon to judge yet just how good her eventual best wines will be, but the signs so far suggest that they will have the strength, structure and delicacy of wines from (for example) the Loire, possibly the Médoc, possibly Champagne. New Zealanders are wisely determined to develop their own styles of wine-making. So far almost all the emphasis has been on white wines. There is enough demand and enough small and technically proficient wineries now to experiment with every likely looking grape, blend and technique.

NEW ZEALAND PRODUCERS

Babich Wines Ltd.

Babich Road, Henderson, Auckland. Est. 1916.
Owners: The Babich family.
Vineyards: 80 acres of sloping loam-on-clay. Cab.Sauv., P.N., Müller-Thurgau, Chard., Palomino, Pinotage.

A well-established, thoroughly modernized winery making firm and fruity whites and wood-aged reds. Their Müller-Thurgau, Chenin Blanc, Pinot Noir and Cabernet have all scored high in competition and have been appreciated in England.

Collard Brothers Ltd.

303 Lincoln Road, Henderson, Auckland. Est. 1946.
Owners: Bruce and Geoffrey Collard.
Vineyards: 30 acres of the rolling Sutton Baron estate (Ries., Müller-Thurgau, Gewürz., Sylv., Cab.Sauv., Merlot). 25 acres at Waimauku, 14 miles northwest, newly planted with classic white varieties.

A small family company bent on perfecting the regional style of the North Island; in other words fruity 'Germanic' whites and reds based on Bordeaux grapes and methods, including French oak. But weather is unpredictable and dry years will make full-bodied dry whites.

Cooks New Zealand Wine Co. Ltd.

PO Box 12–417, Penrose, Auckland. Founded 1968. Visits.
Owners: Public company. Wine maker: Kerry Hitchcock.
Vineyards: 170 acres at the winery at Te Kauwhata, 40 miles south of Auckland (Cab.Sauv., Cab.Franc, Merlot, Ch.Bl., P. Gris, P. Meunier, P.N., Müller-Thurgau, Flora, Ries., Sauv.Bl.). 90 acres at Fernhill, Hawkes Bay (Cab.Sauv., Müller-Thurgau, Ch. Bl., Chard., Gewürz.) on river silt. 130 acres at River Head, Hawkes Bay (Cab.Sauv., Cab.Franc, Merlot, Ch.Bl., Grey Ries., Sylv., Sauv.Bl., and Dr.Hogg Muscat on volcanic loam). Grapes are also bought in Gisborne and Hawkes Bay.

A young company with a very modern winery; the most active in exports to Britain and hence largely responsible for the instant acceptance of NZ wine by international critics. The top of their range is oak-aged Chardonnay of great charm, a light but vividly fruity Cabernet, firm and lively Gewürztraminer with some sweetness and appley sweet Chenin Blanc not unlike a Coteaux du Layon wine. Sauvignon Blanc shows promise. Müller-Thurgaus are popular but need drinking very young. New plantings in the hills round Hawkes Bay hold out hopes for bigger reds.

Corbans Wines Ltd.

426–448 Great North Road, Henderson, Auckland. Est. 1902. Visits.
Owners: Rothmans Industries Ltd.
Vineyards: 950 acres in Auckland, Gisborne and Tolaga Bay, and a progressive expansion at Blenheim, Marlborough, South Island. Major grapes: Ries., Müller-Thurgau, Ch.Bl., Chard., Gewürz., Sauv.Bl., Cab.Sauv., Merlot. Also contract growers.

Founded by a Lebanese family and now NZ's biggest exporter – mainly to Canada. Corbans have a winery at Gisborne as well as Auckland and are building one at Marlborough. The emphasis is on white wines, but a Tolaga Chenin Blanc, Gisborne Gewürztraminer and Henderson Müller-Thurgau Auslese shown in London were not as crisp and clean as the best NZ whites. The names Robard and Butler and Riverlea are used for premium wines.

Delegat's Vineyard Ltd.

Hepburn Road, Henderson, Auckland. Est. 1947. Visits.
Owners: The Delegat family.
Vineyards: about 50 acres in Huapai, mainly Cab.Sauv.

Good whites from Gisborne grapes include gold-medal-winning Chardonnay, Pinot Gris and a notable sweet Müller-Thurgau Auslese. Huapai Cabernet, though immature, seems big and 'wild', with real potential.

Glenvale Vineyards Ltd.

Bay View, Napier, Hawkes Bay. Est. 1933. Visits by appt.
Owners: The Bird family.
Vineyards: 160 acres of flat silt and loam in Eskdale. Cab.Sauv., Pinotage, Merlot, Seibel 5455, Müller-Thurgau, Chasselas, Palomino, Seyve-Villard. 70 more being added with Gewürz., Merlot and Sauv.Blanc.

A third-generation business best known for dessert wines, not yet exporting but gearing up with premium varieties.

McWilliams Wines (NZ) Ltd.

Church Road, Taradale, Hawkes Bay. Est. 1944. Visits.
Owners: A private company partly owned by McWilliams of Australia (q.v.).
Vineyards: 900 acres at Hawkes Bay plus a similar area under contract. Mostly flat; some silt, some clay. Müller-Thurgau ('Cresta Dore'), Chasselas, Chard., Palomino, P.X., Cab.Sauv., Gren., Gamay, P.N., Gewürz., Merlot, red hybrids ('Bakano').

The major producer of the Hawkes Bay area, second largest in New Zealand, long famous for its Cresta Dore and Bakano but also, with Tom McDonald as wine maker in the 1960s, for the first NZ Cabernets: remarkable wines which are still in good heart. Recent reds have not been up to this standard. Chardonnay is the current success.

Matawhero Wines

Riverpoint Road, Gisborne. Est. 1975. Mail order only.
Owners: The Irwin family.
Vineyards: 86 acres of river loam, Gewürz., Ch.Bl., Chard., Müller-Thurgau, Sauv.Blanc. Half the grapes are sold; half vinified.

A small-scale family operation whose hand-made wines have attracted as much critical attention as anything in NZ. Their Gewürztraminer is notably dry, aromatic and lingering. A blend of Gewürz and Müller-Thurgau is a huge improvement on Müller-Thurgau alone.

Matua Valley Wines Ltd.

Waikoukou Road, Waimauku, Kumeu, Auckland. Est. 1974. Visits and restaurant.
Owners: Ross and Bill Spence.
Vineyards: 60 acres of rolling, red sandy loam. Cab.Sauv., Shiraz., P.N., P'tage, Malbec, Sem., Chard., Muscat Bl., Sauv.Bl., Flora, Gewürz., Ch.Bl., Grey Ries.

A new California-style winery just north of Auckland. Ross Spence is an uninhibited wine maker looking for original tastes. His best early efforts are Muscat Blanc, clean and long-flavoured, a convincing Chardonnay and a 'vintage port' of Cabernet Sauvignon. A man to watch.

Mission Vineyards

Church Road, Greenmeadows, Taradale, Hawkes Bay. Est. 1851. 25,000 cases.
Owners: The Catholic Society of Mary.
Vineyards: 110 acres of varied soils on flat land plus 25 under contract. Cab.Sauv., Sem., Sauv.Bl., Merlot, Gewürz., Müller-

Thurgau, P. Gris, Chasselas, Chard., P.N., Dr. Hogg Muscat.

A historic and beautiful spot at the foot of grassy hills, seemingly old-fashioned but making remarkable white wines, including outstanding Sauvignon Blanc (some blended with Semillon) and a subtle half-sweet Tokay d'Alsace (Pinot Gris). Reds are not yet up to this level.

Montana Wines Ltd.

PO Box 18–293, Glen Innes, Auckland 6. Est. 1961. Owners: A public company (40% Seagrams). No visits.
Vineyards: 1,400 acres, mainly at Marlborough, also at Mangatangi, south of Auckland, and Gisborne, plus a similar area under contract. Müller-Thurgau, Chard., Ries., Gewürz., Sauv.Bl., Dr. Hogg Muscat, Cab.Sauv., Pinotage, P.N.

New Zealand's biggest wine company, started by the Dalmatian Ivan Yukich, was extremely successful in expanding through the 1970s, when it pioneered the new Marlborough region, labelling most of its best 'varietal' wines 'Marlborough'. Other proprietary names are Benmorven (Riesling/Muscat), Blenheimer, Ormond, Fairhall River and Lindauer sparkling. 85% of the whites are semi-sweet. Montana whites have 50% of the total home market. The Marlborough wines include a very dry Sauvignon Blanc, slightly spicy Riesling with good acidity, and a rather pale but firm Cabernet, with a Médoc-like 'cut'. Gisborne produces very good Chardonnay, not aged in oak.

Nobilo Vintners Ltd.

Station Road, Huapai Valley, Auckland. Est. 1943. Visits. Owners: A family-run private company.
Wine maker: Nick Nobilo. Vineyards: 212 acres on rolling land of mixed clay and volcanic ash: 90 acres Cab.Sauv., 52 Pinotage, 29 P.N., 16 Merlot and 16 Malbec.

The Nobilos came from the Dalmatian island of Korcula. After problems with corporate shareholders the family have reconstituted their business and their vineyard to concentrate on red varieties that ripen well in the warm damp Auckland climate. White grapes are brought from Gisborne. Nick Nobilo is a passionate traditional wine maker looking for distinction and delicacy, not obvious 'varietal' tastes. His whites are light and refreshing but age well. Pinot Noir made by *macération carbonique*, then aged 2 years in French oak, is light but full of character. Private Bin Claret includes Pinotage in a most satisfying blend.

San Marino Vineyards Ltd.

Main Road, Kumeu, Auckland.
Owners: The Brajkovich family.
Vineyards: 34 acres of Chard., Cab.Sauv., Müller-Thurgau, Gewürz., Palomino.

A small Yugoslav family winery north of Auckland beginning to make firm, balanced Cabernet with real finesse. The whites are fresh and modern. 'Trinity' is a tasty blend of Müller-Thurgau, Gewürztraminer and Riesling.

Te Mata Estate

PO Box 335, Havelock North, Hawkes Bay. Est. 1896. To 30,000 cases. Visits by appt.
Owners: John Buck and Michael Morris (since 1978).
Vineyards: 80 acres on north slopes with limestone and shingle subsoil, newly planted with Cab.Sauv., Cab.Franc, Merlot, Chard., Sauv.Bl., Müller-Thurgau, Furmint and Gewürz.

The oldest winery in New Zealand, just restored and already making the country's best Cabernet/Merlot blend; a very fine wine. This and Chardonnay are wood-aged.

Maori harvester

Müller-Thurgau and Fumé Blanc are medium-dry, Furmint sweet with high acidity. The owners see the conditions as similar to Sonoma, California, and aim to make long-lived wines with plenty of acid backbone.

Totara Vineyards

Main Road, Thames (south of Auckland). Est. 1950.
Owners: The Chan family.
Vineyards: 18 acres at Thames, 15 near Kumeu, plus grapes from Gisborne.

A Chinese-owned winery making Fu Gai, a Muscat-flavoured white blend for Chinese cooking, and prize-winning Chenin Blanc, Müller-Thurgau and Chasselas.

Vidal Wine Producers Ltd.

119 St. Aubyn's Street, Hastings, Hawkes Bay. Est. 1908. Visits and restaurant.
Owner: George Fistonich. Wine maker: Warwick Orchiston.

An atmospheric yet technically advanced winery offering very aromatic Gewürztraminer, restrained Chardonnay, a burgundy that tastes like claret, and a Cabernet with beautifully sweet and lively flavours, from a grower with old vines on shingle at Takaupau to the south. Most novel and exciting, a 100% Cabernet Sauvignon 'red blend' sparkling wine, fresh, yeasty, dry and deep – daring to imitate Krug. All this plus a barrel-lined restaurant with excellent food.

Villa Maria

5 Kirkbride Road, Mangere, Auckland. Est. 1961. Owner: George Fistonich.
Vineyards: 12 acres of light volcanic soil at Mangere south of Auckland with old Cab. and young Gewürz., Chard. and Ries. Most grapes grown on contract in Gisborne and Hawkes Bay.

A modern winery (NZ's fourth largest) making full-flavoured, if not very aromatic, whites and light reds, aged briefly in oak. Future emphasis will be on premium white wines. Camberley Dry is a dry blend, Brookvale a medium-sweet Müller-Thurgau. Gewürztraminer and Müller-Thurgau are also blended in a sweet wine. Vidal Wines at Hawkes Bay also belongs to Fistonich.

SOUTH AFRICA

South Africa entered the new-world fine-wine league in the mid-1970s – a decade later than California and Australia. She has not so far caught up with them, partly for self-imposed reasons. Government has purposely limited both the supply of good grapevines and the land to grow them on. Nonetheless there are those who argue that the natural conditions of the Cape for the vine are as good as any on earth. The essential grape varieties are now at last planted and coming into bearing. It is presumably a matter of a very few years before we see wines as excellent as Australia's bearing the bizarre Dutch names of the lovely estates of Stellenbosch and Franschoek.

The natural advantages of the Coastal Region of the Cape are impressive. Ideal slopes can be found facing every point of the compass. There is an eight-month growth period; never any frost, never any hail, no autumn rain, very few of the diseases that plague other vineyards. The soil is so fertile that the normal ration of fertilizer is one tenth that of Europe's long-worked vineyards.

An important quality factor is the wide range of temperatures: cool nights between hot days, the Cape pattern, reduce night-time respiration from the vine leaves. The plant, unable to consume sugars accumulated during the day, stores more of them.

None of these conditions is a guarantee of good wine, but taken together, with intelligent handling, they encourage optimism.

What has been lacking in Cape history has been a demand for fine table wines. The one historically famous wine was the dessert Muscat of Constantia (which in Napoleon's time fetched prices as high as any wine in the world). Britain, the principal export market, has been more interested in Cape sherry than Cape claret. South Africans were the world's thirstiest brandy drinkers. It is only with gradual liberalization (non-white prohibition ended in 1962; grocers could sell wine from 1966) and legislation aimed at quality control (Wines of Origin were implemented in 1973) that conditions have been created for a healthy domestic table-wine market: the essential spring-board for exports.

Another problem has been the apparently benevolent presence of the KWV, an organization founded by the government in 1918 to protect grape farmers from low wine prices by fixing a minimum price and distilling the surplus. The KWV has been a bastion of protection and conservatism: the very thing a new wine industry can do without. Licences to plant vines are only granted to established growers. At the same time the State has enforced crippling quarantine regulations on new vines, effectively holding up for over a decade the importation of the finest varieties. With such millstones round its neck even California would still be where it was in the 1950s.

The evidence that very fine wine is on the way is recent, but it is convincing. At present the finest wines of the Cape are its sherries and fortified wines in the manner of port, its rare naturally sweet dessert wines affected by noble rot, and a few of its estate reds made of Cabernet Sauvignon, formerly blended with Cinsaut but increasingly with the noble varieties Merlot and Cabernet Franc. There are also beginnings of great promise with the newly planted noble white varieties. And underpinning the whole industry, of inestimable value, there is South Africa's fortunate inheritance of the Steen as its everyday white grape. It is a lucky country that will never go short of good cheap white wine.

South Africa in round figures
South Africa is the tenth largest wine producer, with 1.8% of total world production. Domestic wine consumption is 9.09 litres per head a year (USA 7.64 litres). Wine production has risen from 44m. cases in 1960 to 83.5m. in 1981, with 1980 producing the largest harvest of 91.5m. cases.

In 1982 just over half of the total wine production was distilled. Of the 48% of the crop sold as wine, 71% was natural and sparkling, 29% fortified. 30% of the distilled wine went into exports and the buffer stock held by the KWV and other wholesalers.

There are 71 cooperatives producing 75% of the crop. The balance is produced by the 6,000 individual wine farmers and estates, the producer-wholesalers and the KWV.
Exports rose from 3.95m. rand in 1970 to 17.67m. rand in 1980, falling back to 11.84m. rand in 1981. Natural wine contributed half of this, with fortified and sparkling wine and brandy making up the total.

The Nederburg auction
The key social and commercial event in the Cape wine calendar is the Nederburg auction, held at vintage time in March since 1975. In 1975 six participants entered 12,500 cases of 15 different wines. In 1981 there were 84 wines – 2,500 people attended the auction, including buyers from Europe and the Americas. The auction has helped to make the name of Nederburg Edelkeur, which regularly sets price records (*see* page 485).

GRAPES AND STYLES OF WINE

Blanc Fumé

As in California, a term used for Sauvignon Blanc (or a blend in which it strikes its characteristic smoky sparks).

Bukettraube (B.)

A new German grape introduced to South Africa for its good acidity and aroma of Muscat, a useful contributor to popular blends but rarely offered alone.

Cabernet Sauvignon (Cab. Sauv.)

As in California and Australia, the supremely adaptable Cabernet has long made the Cape's best red wines. The cool Coastal Region gives the best results. A tradition of big blunt wines needing very long ageing is rapidly being modified for more sophisticated tastes. Cabernet now occupies about 7,000 acres, 2.7% of the total South African vineyard.

Cape Riesling (C. Ries.)

See Riesling.

Cabernet Franc (Cab. Franc)

Recently planted by growers anxious to liven up the formerly stodgy Cabernet Sauvignon in emulation of Bordeaux.

Chardonnay (Chard.)

A very recent arrival. No conclusive results yet, but high hopes.

Chenin Blanc (Ch. Bl.)

Grown and nearly always sold as Steen (q.v.). The most important quality white grape in South Africa at present.

Cinsaut (Cin.)

The most widely grown red for table wines, sometimes labelled Hermitage. As in France, it is a heavy producer, lacking character on its own, but it has merit in lightening blends. 33,000 acres.

Clairette

The neutral white grape of the Midi plays a part in many blends. 9,000 acres (3.5% of total).

Colombard (Col.)

Increasingly popular white for fresh table wines, though formerly mostly for brandy. 11,000 acres (4% of total).

Gamay (Gam.)

The Beaujolais grape is grown without cultural problems in South Africa, but so far without distinction either.

Gewürztraminer (Gewürz.)

It is hard to judge the potential from the mixed results of a few plantings. The best are very good; the worst awful.

Grand Cru

A widely used term (without a shred of justification) generally understood to mean a bone dry white wine.

Hanepoot

Local name for the popular Muscat of Alexandria, capable of making excellent fortified dessert wines but a coarse low-quality white when made dry.

Hermitage

Archaic alias for Cinsaut.

Kerner (K.)

The new German Riesling substitute shows promise for aromatic whites.

Late Harvest

A common term for semi-sweet white wines. When qualified by the word 'Special' the residual sugar must be natural. 'Noble Late Harvest' is reserved for 'botrytis' wines.

Merlot

Only recently introduced to South Africa, but great hopes are pinned on its ability to mollify the stern Cabernet and add to its complexity, rather than simply attenuate it as does Cinsaut.

Müller-Thurgau (M-T.)

Tentatively planted but unlikely to be of interest, unless for sweet wines. It has been labelled Sylvaner!

Palomino (Fransdruif)

The Spanish sherry grape is oddly known as the French White. Used for sherries, brandy and low-grade white blends. 40,000 acres.

Pinotage (P'age)

A South African cross between Pinot Noir and Cinsaut ('Hermitage'); an unfortunate distraction from growing better grapes. Its wines are sweetish when young with a curious greasy fatness which lingers even when they mature (as they will) to dry wines with some bouquet. 7,500 acres.

Pinot Noir (P.N.)

A recent introduction to commerce in South Africa and still only a very small acreage. Early results with this awkward grape have been disappointingly thin and light, but it should have potential in the right sites.

Rhine Riesling (Rh. Ries.)

Also called Weisser Riesling. Surprisingly, a recent introduction. It has immediately shown its superiority to the local 'Riesling'.

Riesling (Ries.)

Almost a synonym for white wine in South Africa despite the fact that the local variety so-called is no relation of the true Riesling. It is apparently the obscure French Crouchen, a Semillon-like variety which also goes under the name Clare Riesling in South Australia. As both South Africa and South Australia have amply demonstrated, it can make more-than-adequate dry white wine, though not as good as the Steen.

Semillon (Sem.)

Uncommon in South Africa although both the Greengrape and Riesling are similar and possibly related. 7,000 acres.

Sauvignon Blanc (Sauv. Bl.)

A recent arrival that has caused a great stir by promising first results – possibly, one suspects, the excitement of a new easily recognizable 'varietal' aroma in a land long starved of them.

Shiraz

The Rhône grape must have great potential, although it is not often seen in South Africa unblended. One estate makes a fine fruity light Shiraz. 1,800 acres.

Steen

The workhorse white of South Africa (possibly a selection of the Chenin Blanc of the Loire), which proves more than satisfactory for everything from sparkling wine to sherry, and even gives unambitious off-dry whites a spark of vigour and interest. Its full-bodied wine with a good clean 'attack' must be capable of greatness. 72,000 acres.

Sylvaner (Syl.)

Grown in very small quantities in Overgaauw, although the name has also been wrongly used for Müller-Thurgau.

Tinta Barocca (T.B.)

A port variety sometimes used in the Coastal Region to make an adequate red table wine.

Vin Fumé

A coinage for a blended dry white, not necessarily of Sauvignon Blanc (as the name implies).

Weisser Riesling (W.R.)

See Rhine Riesling.

Zinfandel (Zin.)

Tentative trials with the California red grape have encouraged some.

REGIONS OF ORIGIN

Acreages are area under vine in 1980.

Benede-Orange The most northerly demarcated Region of Origin. Irrigated vineyards along the Orange River producing mainly wine for distilling.

Boberg An appellation for fortified wines grown in the Paarl and Tulbagh districts (qq.v.).

Bonnievale *See* Robertson

Breede River Valley The appellation for fortified wines grown in the Worcester, Robertson and Swellendam districts (qq.v.), east of the Drakenstein Mountains.

Coastal Region An appellation that may be given to wines made from grapes from Stellenbosch, Durbanville, Paarl, Constantia and Tulbagh Wine of Origin districts (qq.v.).

Constantia Once the world's most famous Muscat wine, from the Cape. Now the southernmost and coolest Region of Origin, producing quality wines. 1,025 acres.

Durbanville A small Wine of Origin district just north of Cape Town. 3,300 acres.

Eilandia *See* Robertson

Goree *See* Robertson

Klein (Little) Karoo The easternmost Wine of Origin district. Very little rainfall and all irrigated vineyards. Good only for dessert wine and brandy. 9,400 acres.

Olifantsrivier Northerly Wine of Origin district, with a warm dry climate. Mostly wine for distilling from irrigated vineyards. 17,300 acres.

Overberg Southern coastal Wine of Origin district. Contains Walker Bay ward, with some of the coolest vineyards. 3,700 acres.

Paarl South Africa's wine capital, 50 miles northeast of Cape Town. Its surrounding region is among the best in the country, particularly for white wine and sherry. Most of its wine is made by cooperatives. 54,000 acres.

Piquetberg A small western Wine of Origin district north of Tulbagh, towards the Olifants River. A warm dry climate gives mainly dessert wine and wine for distilling. 4,800 acres.

Riverside *See* Robertson

Robertson A small Wine of Origin district to the east of the Cape, and inland. Irrigated vineyards along the Kopmanskloof and Breede rivers provide some high-quality white and red table wines as well as fine fortified wines. Contains Eilandia, Goree, Riverside, Bonnievale and Vinkrivier wards. 21,700 acres.

Stellenbosch The beautiful old Cape Dutch town and its demarcated region 30 miles east of Cape Town, extending south to the ocean at False Bay. Most of South Africa's best estates, especially for red wine, are in the mountain foothills of the region. 39,200 acres.

Swartland A warm Wine of Origin district around Malmesbury and Riebeek-Wes, between Tulbagh and the west coast. Most growers supply cooperatives. 40,700 acres.

Swellendam The easternmost Wine of Origin district of the Breede River Valley. Produces mainly distilling wine. 1,360 acres.

Tulbagh A demarcated district sheltered in the hills north of Paarl, best known for the white wines of its 3 famous estates, Montpellier, Theuniskraal and Twee Jongegezellen. *See also* Boberg. 10,800 acres.

Worcester Demarcated wine region round the Breede and Hex river valleys, east of Paarl. North of Worcester, up to Tulbagh, rainfall is high enough for good table wines, southeast to Swellendam irrigation is necessary. Many cooperative cellars make mainly dry white and dessert wines. 45,900 acres.

The traditional Cape Dutch architecture adds distinction to many of the estates

MAJOR PRODUCERS

Allesverloren

Riebeek West, *Swartland*. Founded 1974. Owner and wine maker: Fanie Malan. 395 acres. Wines: Cab.Sauv., port., Swartland Rood, T.B. Prices: Cab.Sauv., '78, R3.50; Swartland Rood '77, R2.50; port, R5.00.

A specialist in port and recently full dry reds. A warm dry site gives very ripe, soft, sometimes rather raisin-flavoured Cabernet.

Alto

Stellenbosch. Founded 1920. Owners: Pieter du Toit and Distillers Corporation. 247 acres on the western slopes of the Helderberg, Stellenbosch. Wines: Cab.Sauv., Rouge. Prices: Cab.Sauv., '76, R7.00; Alto Rouge '79, R3.50.

A superbly sited vineyard running straight up a mountainside near the sea for a mile and a half (in which it rises nearly 1,000 feet). The estate only makes red wine. Cabernet, Cinsaut, Shiraz and Pinot Noir are planted at appropriate altitudes to take advantage of the widely different temperatures and ripening conditions. The Cabernet has been a good but typically sturdy traditional Cape wine; Alto Rouge is a lighter, though still solid, blend. Both need considerable ageing. 5% of the crop is exported.

Backsberg

Simondium, *Paarl*. Founded 1969. Owners: Michael and Sydney Back. Visits. 395 acres. Wines: Cab.Sauv., Chard., Ch.Bl., P'age, Sauv.Bl., Shiraz, Special Late Harvest, Steen. Prices: Cab.Sauv. '80, R2.50; Shiraz '80, R2.50.

On the north-facing slopes of Kanonkop, Backsberg has planted white varieties on higher ground than the reds. Sydney Back was one of the pioneers of the return to high-density planting in the Cape. He is justified by very good red and, particularly, white wines. Local critics rated the '82 Chardonnay, Sauvignon Blanc and Chenin Blanc some of the best young dry wines yet produced in this area. The Chardonnay is aged 2 years in cask and bottle before release.

The Bergkelder

Stellenbosch. Member of the Oude Meester Group. Chief Executive: Dr. Julius Laszlo. Wine maker: Hoffie Hoffman. Wines: Fleur du Cap, Grünberger and Stellenryk ranges, plus many estate wines bottled by The Bergkelder. Prices: Cab.Sauv. '79, R4.00; Shiraz '79, R3.00; Stein, R2.00.

The second largest Stellenbosch merchant, buying wines from 17 top estates and making some very good wines from grapes bought in Stellenbosch and Paarl. Although the scale is enormous, the firm is a pioneer in improving Cape wines. Dr. Laszlo (a Hungarian) was formerly head of the Romanian state wine industry and brings provocative ideas to what he considers the world's finest area for grapes. Experiments with Sauvignon Blanc, Chardonnay and Gewürztraminer all show real promise. The '79 Fleur du Cap Cabernet Sauvignon is one of the Cape's top reds. Grünberger Steen remains a stimulating, good-value everyday white.

Blaauwklippen

Stellenbosch. Founded 1972. Owner: Graham Boonzaier. Wine maker: Walter Finlayson. Visits. 18,000 cases. 295 acres on the lower slopes of the Stellenboschberg. Wines: Cab.Sauv., Ch.Bl., Rh.Ries., C.Ries., Sauv.Bl., several blends. Prices: Cab.Sauv. '79, R4.00; Sauv.Bl. '82, R3.00.

One of the pioneers of lighter, fruity reds. Also known for delicate dry and rich semi-sweet whites. Overall quality is consistent and improving. The '79 Cabernet Sauvignon is a generous wine with good depth of flavour. The '80 is bigger, with a creamy richness.

Le Bonheur

Muldersvlei, *Stellenbosch*. Founded 1973. Owners: Distillers Corp. & Michael Woodhead. 5,000 cases. 173 acres. Wines: Cab.Sauv. rosé, Blanc Fumé. Prices: Blanc Fumé '82, R3.00.

On the generally north-facing slopes of the Klapmutskop, these vineyards have been given the benefit of Woodhead's soil science background and are expected to produce some of the Cape's top whites. The '82 Sauvignon Blanc is mouth-filling, with striking style.

Boschendal

Groot Drakenstein, *Paarl*. Founded 1977. Owner: RFF (Pty) Ltd. Wine maker: Achim von Arnim. Visits. 617 acres, and up to 740 more being planted, on the eastern slopes of Simonsberg. Varieties: Cab.Sauv., C.Ries., Chard., Ch.Bl., Gewürz., Merlot, P.Gris, P.N., Sauv.Bl., Sem., Shiraz, W.Ries. Wines: varietals plus blends. Prices: Lanoy (Cab. Sauv.-based blend), R3.00; Ries., R2.00.

A large estate producing a wide range, chiefly whites, from shaded vineyards stretching for 8 miles along the side of Simonsberg. 'Our philosophy,' says von Arnim, 'is that wine is grown in the vineyard and not made in the cellar. Grapes picked at ideal ripeness look after themselves.' The vines are cropped lightly by Cape standards, aiming at 65hl/ha. The Cabernet-based Lanoy is light, fragrant and very fruity, an unusual style for the Cape.

Delheim

Simonsberg, *Stellenbosch*. Founded 1941. Owners: The Hoheisen family. Chief Executive: Spatz Sperling. Wine maker: Kevin Arnold. Visits. 60,000 cases. 124 acres on the southwestern Simonsberg slopes and 185 acres east-facing below Klapmutskop. Wines: Cab.Sauv., Gewürz, Heerenwyn (100% Steen), Noble Late Harvest, P'age, P.N., port, Sauv.Bl., Shiraz, sparkling, W. Ries., various semi-sweet whites. Prices: Cab.Sauv. '80, R2.50; P.N. '81, R3.00.

With the produce of vineyards 3 miles apart and bought-in grapes from neighbours, Delheim (not a registered estate) is able to produce a wide range. Soft reds for early drinking and rich-flavoured semi-sweet whites have been traditional, with delicate and fuller dry whites now added. The '80 Cabernet Sauvignon is full, rich and soft; the '82 Sauvignon Blanc a good balance of grassy grape character and wood. Limited exports, mostly to West Germany.

Fairview

Suider Paarl, *Paarl*. Founded 1974. Owner: Cyril Back. Wine maker: Charles Back. Visits. 300 acres on the southwest slopes of the Paarl Mountain. Wines: Cab.Sauv., Shiraz, P'age, P.N., Ch.Bl., Sauv.Bl., B., blended reds and whites. Prices: Cab.Sauv. '79, R3.50: Shiraz '80, R3.00; Ch.Bl., R2.00.

An estate with a reputation for very powerful and full-bodied reds, especially Shiraz, and unusual broad dry whites. The reds seem more elegant since the recent introduction of fermentation in closed steel tanks.

Gilbey's

Stellenbosch. Founded 1950. Owned by IDV (UK) and the Rembrandt South African Corporation. Wine maker: Dr. Arnold Schickerling. 240 acres at Kleine Zalze and 540 acres in Devon Valley. Wines: Bertrams, Valley, Festival ranges,

Director's Reserve Zinfandel. Prices: Cab.Sauv. '79, R3.50; Ries. '82, R2.50; Shiraz '79, R3.00.

Two farms supplemented by grapes bought from Stellenbosch growers make a wide spectrum of wines. The Bertrams range has highly regarded reds, winners of many prizes in young-wine shows. The '79 Cabernet is, at 3 years, deep-bodied and tannic. Valley and Festival are lower-priced wines for the mass market. Gilbey's also own Montagne Estate (q.v.) and sell Vredenburg. 7% of production is exported to UK, West Germany, Holland, USA and Switzerland.

Douglas Green

Milnerton, *Cape Town*. Founded 1942. Part of the Rennie's group. Wines: Douglas Green range, Côte de Rosé, Côte de Blanc, Fransteter, St. Augustine, St. Raphael, Valais Rouge. Prices: from R1.50–R3.00.

A wholesaler without production facilities, buying wines from the KWV, private cellars and coops. Standards are a little uneven, but wines such as Douglas Green Cabernet Sauvignon are of good quality.

Groot Constantia

Constantia, *Cape Town*. Founded 1685. Refounded 1975. Owners: Groot Constantia Control Board. Wine maker: Pieter du Toit. Visits. 30,000 cases. 284 acres on the southern slopes of Constantiaberg. Wines: Cab.Sauv., Ch.Bl., Heerenrood (blend of Shiraz, Cab.Sauv. and port varieties), P'age, Sauv.Bl., Shiraz, W.Ries. and blended reds, whites and rosé. Prices: Cab.Sauv. '80, R4.00; Heerenrood '79, R4.00.

The most famous estate of the Cape; source of the legendary Constantia Muscat of the early 19th century. The beautiful Cape Dutch farm was a mere museum until the 1970s, when a new administration took over. All the vineyards have been replanted and clean fresh reds are now being made. The whites are adding a new dimension to the traditional light Cape style. Sauvignon Blanc '82, first from a new vineyard, is extremely promising. Weisser Riesling, from older vines, has had several vintages that have matured into full and wholesome wines. 12% is exported to the USA, UK, Holland, Belgium, Italy and West Germany.

Hamilton-Russell Vineyards

Hemel-en-Aarde Valley, Walker Bay, *Overberg*. Founded 1974. 138 acres, 7,000 cases. Wines: Cab.Sauv., Chard., P.N., Sauv.Bl.

The southernmost estate in Africa, in a coastal valley behind Hermanus, averaging 2 degrees cooler than Stellenbosch.

Hamilton-Russell's aim is to blend a Bordeaux-type red and crack the secret of Pinot Noir. Small crops, all hand-picking and new French barrels indicate his resolve. The danger is underripe grapes, but his first wines have been eagerly received.

Kanonkop

Muldersvlei, *Stellenbosch*. Founded 1973. Owner: Jannie Krige. Wine maker: Beyers Truter. Visits. 12,000 cases. 320 acres. Wines: Cab.Sauv., P'age., Paul Sauer Fleur, Rh.Ries., Sauv.Bl., blended white and red. Prices: Paul Sauer Fleur '81, R4.50; Cab.Sauv. '81, R4.50; Sauv.Bl. '82, R2.00.

An outstanding estate specializing in classic-style reds. The 1981 Cabernet is superbly fruity, well balanced and has a clean, slightly astringent finish. One of the Cape's first Bordeaux-style blends, Paul Sauer Fleur, is 40% Cabernet Sauvignon, 40% Cabernet Franc and 20% Merlot.

The KWV (Kooperative Wijnbouwers Vereniging)

Paarl. Founded 1918.

The State cooperative to which all grape-farmers are obliged to belong (It has 6,000 members). It was founded to protect them from low prices but has long since had a policing function over the whole industry. It fixes an annual minimum price for 'good wine' and another for 'distilling wine', and declares an annual percentage surplus, determined by the size of the crop and the state of the market. All growers must deliver this percentage of their crop (often about one third) to the cooperative – the object being to prevent an oversupply. The KWV is not allowed to resell wine in South Africa except to other wineries. It sells brandy on the home market, and for many years had a near-monopoly of South African wine on the export market.

The KWV has 5 wineries at Paarl (its magnificent HQ), Stellenbosch, Worcester, Robertson and Montagu and 1 estate, Laborie at Paarl. 60 local cooperatives collect and crush grapes for it. Its principal products are brandies, sherries and port-style tawnies and rubies.

Its best sherries (the Cavendish Cape range) are of very high quality, approaching close to their Spanish models. Tawnies and 'vintage character' are another very successful product. Table wines (not available in South Africa, at least under these names) include the very reliable and good-value KWV Chenin Blanc, a pleasantly *spritzig* Riesling, a slightly sweet Weisser Riesling and a very sweet Special Late Harvest Steen. The best-known red is a blend called Roodeberg, of Pinotage, Shiraz, Cinsaut and Tinta Barocca, mainly from Paarl, Durbanville and Swartland. Recently, however, some of the best suppliers of red grapes have been 'poached' by the big rival wineries. The KWV also sells a few estate wines, particularly Vergenoegd.

Laborie

Suider Paarl, *Paarl*. Founded 1972. Owner: KWV. Wine maker: Willier Hacker. Visits. 10,000 cases. 69 acres. Wines: Laborie (red); Blanc de Noirs (transfer-method sparkling); Ries. Prices: Blanc de Noirs, R4.00; Laborie, R3.00.

A very attractive estate on the northeast slopes of the Paarl Mountain, owned by the KWV and used as a guesthouse. Wine-making is new, with first-rate facilities, but the first efforts are a pretty rather than exciting sparkling wine mostly from Pinotage and a full-blooded blended red that will probably gain with some extra age.

Landskroon

Suider Paarl, *Paarl*. Founded 1974. Owner: Paul de Villiers. Wine maker: Paul de Villiers jnr. Visits. 543 acres on the southwest slopes of Paarl Mountain. Wines: Cab.Sauv., Cab.Franc, Shiraz, P'age., P.N., T.B., Cin., Bouquet Rouge, blended white, port. Prices: Cab.Sauv. '79, R3.00.

The eighth generation of a Huguenot family who have made wine at the Cape for 3 centuries. Recently the first estate to make significant quantities of Cabernet Franc. The 2 Cabernets are not blended but sold separately. The Cabernet Franc is soft and early maturing. The '80 Pinot Noir has deep colour and flavour. All the reds are ripe and robust in the style that spells Paarl to Cape connoisseurs.

Meerlust

Faure, *Stellenbosch*. Owner: Nico Myburgh (whose family bought Meerlust in 1776). Wine maker: Georgio della Cia. 25,000 cases. 570 acres on western and southern slopes within 3 miles of False Bay. Wines: Cab.Sauv., P.N., Rubicon (Cab.Sauv./Cab.Franc/Merlot blend). Prices: Rubicon '80, R6.50; Cab.Sauv. '78, R5.00; P.N. '80, R5.00.

One of the oldest farms in the Cape: a beautiful white manor house where vines have been grown for 290 years. Now a red-wine estate, which under Nico Myburgh's guidance has broken away from the hearty style of Cape reds and is producing a blend aimed squarely at the Médoc. Myburgh started planting Cabernet Sauvignon in the 1960s. Merlot, Cabernet Franc and Pinot Noir have been added in the last 8 years. Myburgh's Bordeaux-style Rubicon blend is a courageous break with the prevailing 'varietal' orthodoxy. He makes the point for visitors by blending from the cask and contrasting the result with his 'straight' Cabernet. Rubicon and the Pinot Noir have not had time yet to show their quality at maturity, but the Cabernet was South African champion in 1980, a year when Meerlust won top-estate and Myburgh top wine-maker awards. The '75 and '76 Cabernet were the first to show the Meerlust potential, with the '78 and '80 also fine. No Cabernet was bottled in '77 or '79, vintages that Myburgh felt were not up to his standards. Wines are matured in wood in the estate cellars but are bottled and marketed by The Bergkelder. 5 per cent is exported.

Montagne

Bottelary, *Stellenbosch*. Founded 1958. Owner: Gilbey's. Wine maker: Danie Truter. 6,000 cases. 320 acres. Wines: Cab.Sauv., Shiraz, blended white.

Due to a dispute involving the estate's name and the Cape's complicated Wine of Origin rules, Montagne will soon have to change its name. In recent years the wines have been solid, not inspiring.

Montpellier

Tulbagh. Founded in 1970. Principal: De Wet Theron. Wine maker: Jan Theron. Visits. 35,000 cases. 370 acres of vineyards on alluvial soils astride the Klein Berg River. Wines: Ch.Bl., W.R., C.Ries., Gewürz., sparkling. Prices: Ch.Bl. '82, R1.50; W.R. '82, R2.50.

Like its neighbour Twee Jongegezellen, a specialist in white wines, for which the relatively warm Tulbagh has a surprising reputation. Montpellier pioneered Gewürztraminer in the Cape with some success, making a soft round wine, but has been hampered by the limitations of Cape Riesling and Steen. The Montpellier dry wines have tended to flatness for lack of acidity. 'Special Late Harvest' and sweet Tuinwingerd Rhine Riesling are better balanced.

Muratie

Simonsberg, *Stellenbosch*. Founded 1926. Owner: Anne-Marie Canitz. Wine maker: Ben Prins. Visits. 110 acres. Wines: Cab.Sauv., P.N., C.Ries., Steen, blended whites and reds, port. Prices: Cab. Sauv., R2.00; P.N., R3.00.

One of the Cape's original estates, this south-facing mountainside farm has been producing Cabernet Sauvignon and Pinot Noir wines for decades and has a small but loyal following. The old cellar and techniques give uneven quality but at best, very good wines.

Nederburg

Paarl. Founded 1936. Owner: Nederburg Wines (Pty) Ltd. Part of the Stellenbosch Farmers Winery. Cellar master; Günther Brözel. Visits. 1,850 acres in Paarl and Groot Drakenstein valleys. Wines: wide range including the famous Edelkeur sweet wines. Prices: Cab.Sauv. '79, R3.50; Paarl Ries. '82, R2.50; Edelkeur '80, R18.00.

The Cape's largest quality cellar, and scene of the now famous annual wine auction in March. Nederburg grows grapes in Paarl and buys from throughout the Coastal Region. The standard of the wines is high and improving. Some old Cabernets, notably '66, '68, '74, '76, have matured well.

The '79 Cabernet Sauvignon has been made in a new style; lighter, fresher and fruitier. Baronne, a Cabernet-based blend, is oak-aged for 15 months and can be impressive. Paarl Riesling is reliable and the sparkling wine (Charmat process) clean and good value. Recent introductions of Gewürztraminer and Muscat Ottonel have been very encouraging. Brözel's speciality is the lusciously rich, raisiny Edelkeur – an outstanding dessert wine by any standards, made of Steen and sometimes Riesling infected with noble rot. Edelkeur is intensely sweet at first and deserves several years ageing.

Günter Brözel, cellar master at Nederburg, is perhaps best known for his Edelkeur, a new star in the world's cast-list of dessert wines

Neethlingshof

Vlottenburg, *Stellenbosch*. Owner: Jannie Momberg. Wine maker: Schalk van der Westhuizen. Visits. 5,000 cases. 690 acres on southern slopes facing the Eerste River Valley. Wines: Cab.Sauv., P'age, Cin., W.R., Gewürz., B., K.

Very sound Cabernet Sauvignon and for 2 years crisp Weisser Riesling have brought this big estate to the fore recently. Very little of its wine is estate bottled at present.

L'Ormarins

Groot Drakenstein, *Paarl*. Founded 1969. Owner: Anthony Rupert. Wine maker: Nico Vermeulen. 333 acres on the eastern slopes of Groot Drakenstein. Wines: Ries., Rh.Ries., Sauv.Bl.

Extensive newly planted vineyards, high on contoured slopes. This mountainside farm has been planted with all the classic varieties, with heavy emphasis on whites, in a determined effort to produce outstanding wines. The first results have recognizable varietal flavour and are fresh and readily drinkable. Exports are planned.

Overgaauw

Stellenbosch Kloof, *Stellenbosch*. Founded 1906, on a farm owned by the family since 1783. Owners: David and Braam (son) van Velden. Visits. 10,000 cases. 160 acres. Planted with Cab.Sauv., Cin., Merlot, P'age and port varieties; Ch.Bl., Clairette, Col., K. and M-T., Cab.Franc and Sauv.Bl. being planted. Prices: Cab.Sauv. '78, R5.50; port, R6.00.

One of the first Cape growers of Merlot in vineyards on south slopes in the Stellenbosch Kloof Overgaauw, is at present producing a blend of Cabernet Sauvignon, Merlot and Cinsaut called Tria Corda. When newly planted Cabernet Franc vines are bearing the Cinsaut will be phased out. The first few vintages have not measured up to the estate's pure Cabernet Sauvignon, which is a good 10-year wine. The van Veldens bottle only 10% of their production, feeling this is all they can do justice to while staying a family business. The Müller-Thurgau (marketed as Sylvaner) can be extremely agreeable.

Rust-en-Vrede

Helderberg, *Stellenbosch*. Founded 1979. Owner and wine maker: Jannie Engelbrecht. Visits. 8,000 cases. Wines: Cab.Sauv., Shiraz, blended red.

North-facing mountainside vineyards, just below Alto, producing ambitious reds which already win medals. Both Cabernet and Shiraz are given long, slow fermentation, producing deep, tannic wines that are designed to last for years. Early efforts look very promising. Pinot Noir and Merlot will soon be added.

Schoongezicht Rustenberg

Simonsberg, *Stellenbosch*. Founded 1913. Owner: Pam Barlow. Wine maker: Etienne le Riche. Visits. 15,000 cases. 198 acres. Wines: Cab.Sauv., P.N., W.Ries., rosé, blended red and white. Prices: Rustenberg '80, R3.00; Rustenberg P.N. '82, R2.50; blended red Cab.Sauv. '80, R3.00.

Perhaps the most beautiful estate in the Cape; low white Dutch buildings shaded by enormous trees. A long-established and highly regarded producer of red wines with extensive vineyards on south-facing mountain slopes. Rustenberg Dry Red of good vintages ('73, '70 were remarkable) is a light wine worth maturing. Cabernet Sauvignon (excellent in '75) has established itself among the best of the Cape. Pinot Noir has had a promising beginning. White wines (sold as Schoongezicht) are agreeable. New cellars have recently been added to increase production.

Simonsig

Koelenhof, *Stellenbosch*. Founded 1968. Owner: Frans Malan. Wine maker: Johann Malan. Visits. 100,000 cases. Wines: B., Cab.Sauv., Ch.Bl., Col., Gewürz., K., P'age, Ries., Shiraz., W.Ries. plus Noble Late Harvest, Kaapse Vonkel (100% Ch.Bl.) *méthode champenoise* sparkling, Vin Fumé blended white and other red, white and rosé blends. Prices: Cab.Sauv. '79, R3.50; Gewürz. '82, R4.50; Vin Fumé '82, R2.50; *méthode champenoise* '80, R7.00.

With both northeast- and southeast-facing vineyards on gentle slopes, Simonsig has tended to concentrate on white wines. After early emphasis on varietals, Frans Malan and his 3 sons have a runaway success with a blended white (Vin Fumé) matured in wood. This innovative family were the first in the Cape to make a true *méthode champenoise* wine.

Simonsvlei Cooperative

Suider Paarl, *Paarl*. Founded 1945. 78 members. Wine maker: Johan Rossouw. Wines: Late Vintage, B., Ch.Bl., Grand Cru, Dry Steen, Syl., Late Harvest, Ries., Cin., P'age., Cab.Sauv.

This large cellar, drawing grapes from all corners of the Paarl Valley, is a consistent prize winner. The wines are often very fruity and fragrant and are best bought and drunk young.

Spier

Lynedoch, *Stellenbosch*. Founded 1969. Owner: Niel Joubert. Chief Executive: Chris Joubert. Wine maker: B.W. Myburgh. Visits. 60,000 cases. 680 acres of vineyard on mostly southern slopes, facing the Eerste River Valley. Wines: P'age., Ries., Col., Steen, several blended reds, whites, rosé. Prices: P'age., R3.00; Col., R2.00.

A big estate with a wide variety of microclimates, producing a range of medium- to fine-quality wines, mostly white. Dry and semi-sweet Colombard and Chenin Blanc have a great deal of flavour. The Pinotage is consistently one of the Cape's better wines from this grape.

Stellenbosch Farmers' Wineries

Stellenbosch. Founded 1935. Owner: Cape Wine and Distillers Ltd. Production Director: Duimpie Bailey. Visits. Wines: Zonnebloem, Oude Libertas, Kellerprinz, Autumn Harvest, Virginia, Taskelder ranges, Château Libertas, Lanzerac Rosé, La Gratitude, Capenheimer and several other blends. Monis dessert wines. Prices: Zonnebloem Cab.Sauv. '80, R3.50; Late Harvest, R3.00; Oude Libertas Dry Steen, '82, R2.00; Lanzerac Rosé, R2.00.

The Cape's largest cellar presses some grapes, but buys large volumes of wine from private and coop cellars, blending to produce dry and semi-sweet products in all price ranges. Nederburg (q.v.) is their most prestigious product. Zonnebloem reds also have a well-founded reputation gong back many years; Shiraz and Cabernet are both big wines with good colour, texture and length, fit to mature for a decade.

Theuniskraal

Tulbagh. Founded 1962. Partners: Rennie and Kobus Jordaan. 45,000 cases. 395 acres on alluvial soils along the Klein Berg River. Wines: Gerwürz., Late Harvest, Ries., Sem., Steen. Prices: Ries. '82, R3.00; Gewürz. '82, R4.00.

A consistent, award-winning estate specializing in dry whites. Cape tasters rate the Riesling, a blend of Cape Riesling and Rhine Riesling, as fragrant, fresh and well balanced. The Gewürztraminer is full, rich, spicy and slightly sweet. A small percentage is exported to the UK and Holland.

Twee Jongegezellen

Tulbagh. Founded 1950, on a farm in the Krone family for 200 years. Principal: N.C. Krone. Wine maker: Nicky Krone (son). 617 acres on the southern slopes of the Obiekwa mountain. Wines: Gewürz., Rh.Ries., Sauv.Bl., Schanderl, TJ 39, Ries., Steen, red and white blends. prices: Rh.Ries. '82, R3.00; Sauv.Bl. '82, R3.00; Gewürz., R3.00; Schanderl '82, R2.50; TJ 39 '82, R3.00.

Twee Jongegezellen (abbreviated to 'TJ' by owners and aficionados) was one of the pioneers of quality white wines in the Cape. The Krones have experimented ceaselessly with everything from clonal selection to pruning techniques. In 1982, 90% of the grapes were harvested at night, giving the wines new vitality and grape character. Wines include Schanderl, a white blend based on a red clone of Frontignac isolated and bred in the estate's nurseries. This unlikely starting point leads to a wine of intense, fruity and altogether novel character. TJ 39, another blend, is based upon Riesling. The Sauvignon Blanc, one of Nicky Krone's 'target' varieties, is full bodied, with lots of 'grassy' flavour. 14% of the estate's production is exported, via Gilbey's.

Uiterwyk

Stellenbosch Kloof, *Stellenbosch*. Founded 1946. Owner: Danie de Waal. Wine maker: Chris de Waal. Visits. 3,000 cases of estate-bottled wine. 295 acres. Wines: Cab.Sauv., P'age., Col., C.Ries. Prices: Cab.Sauv. '79, R4.00; Ries. '82, R2.00.

A beautiful estate bottling a small quantity of its best wines in a traditional cellar. The Cabernet Sauvignon, lighter than most, is one of the Cape's best.

Uitkyk

Muldersvlei, *Stellenbosch*. Founded 1973. Owner: Gerry Bouwer. Wine maker: Dr. Harvey Illing. Potentially 100,000 cases. 400 acres on the western slopes of the Simonsberg planted with Cab.Sauv., Ch.Bl., Clairette Blanche, Cin., P'age., P.Gris, Rh.Ries., C.Ries., Sauv.Bl., Shiraz. Wines: Carlonet Cab.Sauv., Carlsheim (Ch.Bl./Sauv. Bl. blend), Ries., Shiraz, Late Harvest Chenin Blanc. Prices: Carlonet '78, R4.00; Carlsheim '82, R2.50.

A large estate on the mountain slopes above a dignified 1788 mansion. The great expectations that followed the planting of vineyards high on the exposed mountainside have yet to be fully realized. Enigmatic microclimates have forced replanting of Cabernet on lower slopes and some whites to be cautiously moved higher. Local tasters report that the '82 Carlsheim (mostly Chenin Blanc with a dash of Sauvignon Blanc) has a clean, broad flavour that sets new standards for Cape whites. Future planting plans include Chardonnay, and Rhine Riesling in the highest, coldest vineyards. Dr. Illing aims for the styles of Burgundy and Loire with his whites. The Cabernet, he claims, 'is already comparable to a good Bordeaux'. Bottling and marketing are carried out by The Bergkelder (q.v.). Exports to UK, West Germany, Belgium, Switzerland, Hong Kong.

Union Wine

Wellington, *Paarl*. Founded 1964. Part of the Picardi Group. Wine maker: Johan Schreuder. 750,000 cases. 237 acres in Groot Drakenstein. Wines: Bellingham and Culemborg ranges. Prices: Premier Grand Cru, R2.50; Shiraz '79, R3.00.

A merchant buying grapes in the Paarl Valley and wines throughout the Cape to swell production from the vineyards they own. Overall quality is improving. Bellingham is full, soft and easy to drink. 2% is exported.

Vergenoegd

Faure, *Stellenbosch*. Founded 1969. Owners: Jac and Brand Faure. Visits. 3,000 cases, 319 acres. Wines: Cin., Cab. Sauv., P'age., Shiraz, T.B. Prices: Cab.Sauv. '79, R4.00.

Vineyards are on level ground separated from False Bay by sand dunes and marshes. The sea lowers the temperature, though humidity is high except for the first 3 months of the growing season, when a southeast wind sweeps across the farm almost daily. Vines are grown on low trellises and produce intense, almost tarry red wines. The Cabernet can be too soft; Shiraz from old vines has been excellently deep and firm. Selected wines are bottled at the property, with most of the production going to the KWV. Estate Cabernet and Shiraz get 3 years in old wood, 6 months in bottle before release.

Villiera

Koelenhof, *Paarl*. Founded 1975. Owner: Helmut Rats. Wine maker: Josef Kramer. 10,000 cases. 257 acres of level vineyard. Wines: Ch.Bl., Sauv.Bl., Rh.Ries., Rubiner, blended wines.

An Austrian-owned property making unusual very light reds and a good Steen called Operette, sold in Austria.

Vriesenhof

Stellenbosch. Founded 1981. Owner: Jan Boland Coetzee. Visits. 3,000 cases. 27 acres of south-sloping vineyards on the Stellenboschberg. Wine: Cab.Sauv.

Jan Boland, previously in charge of Kanonkop, made the first wine from his small established vineyard of Cabernet in 1981. Will be pure Cabernet Sauvignon until Merlot and Cabernet Franc are bearing. Chardonnay is planned.

Welgemeend

Klapmuts, *Paarl*. Founded 1974. Owner: Billy Hofmeyr. 3,000 cases. 30 acres of vineyards on gravelly soil. Wines: Welgemeend, Amade, Vin Rouge.

A tiny estate by South African standards, but an influential pioneer of red wines made in the style and by the methods of Bordeaux. Hofmeyr (a land surveyor, wine writer and now farmer) has demonstrated the merits of picking early, blending the 2 Cabernets with Merlot, Malbec and Petit Verdot, and maturing for up to 18 months in small, new oak barrels. His wines are rarely more than 12% alcohol and sometimes as low as 10.5% but with good tannin and clean-cut flavours. Amade is an early maturing blend of Pinotage, Grenache and Shiraz.

De Wetshof

Robertson. Founded 1974. Owner: J.J. de Wet. Wine maker: Danie de Wet. 153 acres of level vineyard beside the Breede River. Wines: Chard., Sauv.Bl., Rh.Ries. Prices: Chard. '82, R6.50; Sauv.Bl. '82, R3.00; Rh.Ries. '82, R3.00.

Danie de Wet was trained in Germany and brought back boundless enthusiasm for white wines of styles not then found in South Africa. His experimental work with Rhine Riesling, Sauvignon Blanc and Chardonnay, and with his noble-rot sweet wine, Edeloes, has shaken old ideas about the Robertson area, and about South African whites in general. One of the most influential estates in the Cape.

Zandvliet

Ashton, *Robertson*. Founded 1975. Owner: Paul de Wet. Wine maker: Paul de Wet, jnr. 556 acres of alluvial vineyard on both sides of the Kogmanskloof River. Wine: Shiraz.

A considerable reputation based on a light but vigorous and tasty Shiraz, which over its 5 vintages has been certified as Superior 5 times. Cabernet and Pinot Noir have also been planted.

CHILE

Chile has the potential for wines of really outstanding quality; as good as California's. The fruit of her vineyards is some of the finest in the world. The fact has been accepted by authorities for generations, yet the truly great wines of Chile have yet to be made. There is still a certain clumsiness about even her most prestigious products. The missing element is the marketplace. Chile's domestic market is relatively unsophisticated, lacking the means to buy and compare the best European and Californian wines. Her principal export markets are in Latin America. North America, another important market, tends to appreciate the low price rather than the exciting quality of Chilean imports. However frequent, and however true, the travellers' tales of exceptional old bottles of Cabernet, the signal for a quality wine industry will have to come from Chile herself.

Wine has been made in Chile since missionaries introduced it in the mid-sixteenth century. Their grape, the Pais (the equivalent of California's Mission grape), is still widely grown for peasant wine and brandy. The quality wine industry started in 1851, when a number of landowners and entrepreneurs introduced the grapes and methods of Bordeaux. They chose the moment just before the twin scourges of phylloxera and oidium appeared in Bordeaux. Their stock was absolutely clean and has never been affected: isolation by the Andes and the Pacific means that Chile still has an entirely pre-phylloxera vineyard: a viticulturist's paradise.

Unfortunately both grape grower and wine maker have been hampered by politics. Under the government that ended in 1973 there was neither the incentive nor the means to invest in quality. Conditions are now much improved and the wines are reliable again. The next stage of experimentation, of enterprises willing to take the expensive steps towards great wine, is only now beginning.

Chile is divided into six viticultural regions with a total of 272,000 acres of wine grapes, approximately half red and half white. Only one region, the central valley zone, is of interest for top-quality wine. With 109,000 acres it produces almost half the national total, using irrigation to achieve an average crop of 60 hectolitres a hectare. It starts in the north on the Aconcagua River near the capital, Santiago, and runs south through the provinces of Santiago, Valparaiso, O'Higgins, Colchagua, Curicó and Talca; a distance of some 160 miles. The rivers Maipo, Cachapoal, Tinguiririca, Lontué and Maule, fed by Andean glaciers, carved the valleys and furnish the irrigation for all Chile's best vineyards.

Rainfall is low everywhere, increasing in the south, where conditions are marginally cooler, but summer rain is unknown. In the dry atmosphere rot is rare and the ungrafted vines are extraordinarily healthy. The Maipo valley has the finest reputation, but there is evidence that the cooler conditions and higher rainfall of the Maule and Lontué valleys in Talca can produce more lively and delicate wines.

Cabernet Sauvignon is much the most successful red grape, supported by Merlot and Malbec. Pinot Noir has not yet produced fine wine in Chile. Riesling is the best white grape, although much outnumbered by the Sauvignon and Semillon of Bordeaux. Chardonnay is rare. So far none of the white wines has reached the class of the best reds.

The only official classification of Chilean wines is by age: Special is two years old, Reserve four and Gran Vino at least six – which in many cases involves too long in barrel for modern tastes. My most successful experience has been with a Cabernet bottled at three years old and bottle-aged for eight. It resembled a rather rustic Médoc Cru Bourgeois of a splendidly full-flavoured vintage.

CHILE PRODUCERS

José Canepa

Camino Lo Sierra 1500, Maipú. Founded 1930. Family owned. Visits by appt. 1,225 acres. Production: 500,000 cases.

A large modern winery with reliable and sometimes excellent wines. Vineyards are in Isla de Maipo, Curicó and Lontué in Talca province to the south. The claret-weight Gran Brindis Cabernet is excellent; so is the young Gran Brindis Semillon white. Finissimo is much bigger, good but without such style. 'Pinot Noir' (in 1975) was 65% Cabernet, 35% Semillon. There is also a so-called Pommard. A semi-sweet Moscatel/Semillon blend is clean, long and well made.

Concha y Toro

Fernando Lazcano 1220, Puente Alto. Founded 1883. Public company. 3,950 acres. Production: 1.1m. cases. Visits.

The biggest and best-known Chilean bodega, with spacious and beautiful estates, based at Pirgue, south of Santiago (and much visited by tourists). Their best-known brands are Marqués de Casa Concha and Casillero del Diablo; principal wines are Cabernet Sauvignon (the Marqués is more powerful than refined), Chilean Burgundy, rosé, Riesling and Sauvignon Blanc. 300 acres of new white varieties (Chardonnay, Riesling, Chenin Blanc and Gewürztraminer) have recently been planted with California stock. A new bodega has been opened in Maipú, run by the German wine maker Goetz von Gerzdorf.

Cousiño Macul

Quilin con Canal San Carlos, Santiago. Founded 1882. Family owned. 925 acres, 300,000 cases, no grapes bought. Visits by appt.

A serenely beautiful old family estate on the outskirts of Santiago, criss-crossed with tall avenues of English oak against the vast backdrop of the Andes. Two thirds of the wines are red: light Don Luis and dark, substantial Don Matias and Antiguas Reservas Cabernets (aged 3 years in cask, 2 in bottle). The very dry rather 'green' whites are Semillon, Palacio Cousiño, Doña Isidora Riesling/Semillon and a little Chardonnay. The estate grows Merlot and Petit Verdot as well as Cabernet. After passing through an unhappy patch in the mid-1970s it is once again the 'first-growth' of Chile.

Viña Linderos

Maipo valley. Founded 1865. Family owned. 250 acres, Cab. Sauv. 70%, Sem. 20%, Ries. 5%, Chard. 5%. Visits.

Brands include the excellent Cabernet Linderos Para Guarda (to be kept at least 6 months in bottle after buying); Subterráneo XII red, white and rosé. Most wine is sold directly to private clients, mainly in Chile. Principal export markets are Colombia, Ecuador, Venezuela and the United Kingdom.

Viña Manquehue

Vicuña Mackenna 2289, Santiago. Founded 1927. Family company. 600 acres. Visits by appt.

Run by the founder's son, José Rabat Comella, on the edge of Santiago, with vineyards on the Manquehue hill. José Rabat is the label of their better wines: Premium, Alcalde Jufré and Reservado Rabat; Cabernet, Sauvignon Blanc and Semillon, mainly sold in South America.

San Pedro

Molina, VI Region. Founded 1865. Private company. 1,000 acres in Talca province, 60% Sauv. Bl., 40% Cab., 450,000 cases. No visits.

A well-known old company (now controlled by the Spanish giant Rumasa) whose Gato Blanco is one of Chile's most popular better-than-average whites. Gato Negro is a similar, rather plain red. Brands are Castillo de Moline, Llava de Oro and Las Encinas.

Santa Carolina

Rodrigo de Araya 1431, Santiago. Founded 1875. Private company. Visits by appt.

One of the biggest and most popular bodegas in Chile, though discreet about its vineyard holdings and claiming improbably high sales figures. Their Cabernet (with Merlot and Cot), Semillon, Sauvignon and a little Chardonnay are very reasonably priced.

Santa Rita

Buin. Founded 1880. Private company. 250 acres. Visits by appt.

One of the best-respected old family firms. Their most famous brand is '120', so-called because Bernardo O'Higgins (the liberator of Chile) and 120 men hid in the Santa Rita cellars after the battle of Rancagua. Other brands are Casa Real (the best), Real Audiencia and Gran Libertador. Exports are over 100,000 cases a year, mainly within South America.

Tarapacá Ex Zavala

Rojas Magallanes con Canal San Carlos, La Florida, Santiago. Founded 1874. Private company. 173 acres. 67,000 cases a year. Visits.

One of the smaller bodegas and, apart from Cousiño Macul, the only one to grow all its own grapes. Brands are: Embajador, Canciller, Gran Canciller Cosecha, Borgoña, Chablis, Gran Tarapaca and Gran Reserva. Exports are mainly within South America.

Tocornal

Fundo San José de Puente Alto. Founded 1875. Private company. 360 acres, mainly Cab. Sauv. 55,000 cases. Visits by appt.

A 'small' estate now under the aegis of Concha y Toro. Brands are Grande Cave and Fond de Cave. Main export markets are in South America.

Undurraga

Camino Melipilla, Santiago. Founded 1885. Private company. 617 acres (P.N., Pinot Blanc, Cab., Ries., Sem.). 450,000 cases. Visits.

A famous family-owned firm in the central Maipo valley, maintaining an air of gracious colonialism with its (iron-roofed) old country house in lavish gardens. Traditional oak-aged wines are labelled Viejo Roble (old oak) but modern fresh wines are also made, among them 'champagnes'. Undurraga is now alone in using the once-common Chilean *caramayola*, a 700-centilitre flagon like the German *Bocksbeutel*. Chileans rate their wines reliable and good value. One third is exported.

Brazil

The immense domestic market of South America's largest country has led some of the biggest names in the international drinks industry – Cinzano, Domecq, Heublein, Martini & Rossi, Moët & Chandon and National Distillers – to invest in Brazilian vineyards.

The 175,000 acres of vineyards are concentrated in the southernmost states of Rio Grande do Sul and to a lesser extent Santa Catarina. Southern Rio Grande do Sul, between Uruguay and the Atlantic, lies on the latitude of Mendoza in Argentina. But here a warm wet oceanic climate makes grape-growing far more problematical. Until recently American and hybrid non-*vinifera* vines dominated.

In 1969 a subsidiary of the American Heublein Corporation, Dreher, introduced Cabernet. Barbera and other Italian varieties were already showing that *vinifera* could cope in well-chosen sites. One of the most promising is Bage, 700 feet up, 125 miles from the Atlantic and near the Uruguay border, chosen on the advice of the University of California and equated with California Region III. National Distillers' Brazilian subsidiary has a stake here and early results are good.

Most of Brazil's vines are 300 miles farther north around Caxias do Sul, Garibaldi and Bento Gonçalves, towns founded by Italians a century ago. The biggest company, Vinicola Riograndense, produces wines under the Granja Uniào label at Caxias, and Dreher, the pioneer with quality vines, is at Bento Gonçalves.

A 1981 Brazilian 'wine Olympiad' named the country's four best wines as: Champagne M. Chandon (Profivín), white Lejon (Dreher/Heublein), rosé Moscato Adega Medieval (Viamão) and red Vinho Velho do Museu (Vinhos finos Santa Rosa – Chateau Lacave).

ARGENTINA

Argentina's own brand of vintage festival

There can be little doubt that a politically stable Argentina will one day re-establish itself as one of the world's most important sources of good every-day wines. Her wine industry has 750,000 acres of wine grapes. It is a century old, yet modern – far more modern than Chile's – with massive industrial wineries the rule. So far there has been little place for the pursuit of excellence, but a massive turnover of agreeable wines in a style that owes more to Italy than France or even (with the exception of sherry types) Spain. Unfortunately due to the recurrent financial and other crises since 1977 precise information is scarce.

The centre of the industry is the province of Mendoza, in the rain shadow of the Andes on the same latitude as (and only 150 miles away from) Santiago in Chile. Mendoza alone has two and a half times as many wine vines as Chile and half of all those in South America. The whole area is irrigated and immensely productive; its basic workhorse grapes the old native Criolla and Malbec for red wine and the Palomino and Torrontes for white.

The strong Italian influence is evident: Barbera, Lambrusco, Nebbiolo, Sangiovese and Bonarda give character to the standard blends. The French red grapes planted recently, Cabernets Sauvignon and Franc, Merlot, Syrah and Pinot Noir, have so far scarcely improved on the best reds from the well-established Malbec. The tradition is to age red wines in oak for years.

The superior white grapes are Semillon, Sylvaner (which is called 'Riesling'), Ugni Blanc, Chenin Blanc (usually called 'Pinot Blanc') and Chardonnay. Unblended one-variety wines are the exception. Some very good Chardonnay has been made recently. Oxidized sherry-style wines made of Palomino, Pedro Ximénez and Torrontes are popular. Sparkling wine has been remarkably perfected by Proviar, a subsidiary of Moët & Chandon.

The province of San Juan, north of Mendoza and hotter and drier, has 150,000 acres of irrigated vines, 90 per cent white for sherries, for export as concentrate or for distilling.

Neuquen and Rio Negro, south of Mendoza, have a climate more akin to that of Europe, though still deprived of rain by the Andean barrier. 44,000 acres here are planted with Malbec, Barbera and increasingly white grapes, since their acid balance makes them the crispest in Argentina. In the long run this may well be the best quality region.

ARGENTINA PRODUCERS

Bianchi
San Rafael, Mendoza. Founded 1927. A Seagram subsidiary with 250 acres. Their best wine is Cabernet Particular. Don Valentin is a good standard. Bianchi Borgogna (Barbera and Malbec) is the country's top-selling 'fine red'.

Crillon
Godoy Cruz, Mendoza. Founded 1927. A Seagram subsidiary. No vineyards. Specialists in sparkling Crillon (20,000 cases) and Monitor (130,000). Embajador is their still-wine label.

Esmeralda
Cordoba. Large growers of Cabernet, Malbec, Sauvignon, Sylvaner, etc. St. Felicien Cabernet is their best brand.

Flichman
5500 Mendoza. Good Merlot and Syrah and a white 'Caballero de la Cepa'.

Angel Furlotti
Maipú, Mendoza. An important bodega with 2,500 acres, known for a blend of Cabernet, Merlot and Lambrusco. In financial trouble recently.

Giol
Paraguay 4902, 1414 Buenos Aires. A huge cooperative run by the state of Mendoza. Canciller is the principal brand. Financial problems here, too.

Goyenechea
Alsina 1970, 1090 Buenos Aires. A family-owned estate of 740 acres. Aberdeen Angus is their heavy-duty label; Marqués del Nevado more modern.

Bodegas Lopez
Godoy Cruz 2000, Buenos Aires. An old company with 2,500 acres, famous for its consistent Chateau Montchenot (exported as Don Federico). Merlot and Malbec are reckoned the best of their wood-aged reds. Cabernet Chateau Vieux is exported as Casona Lopez.

Norton
Suarez 2857, 1284 Buenos Aires. An old-established company with 1,250 acres, best known for oak-aged Perdriel Cabernet but also making some fresh whites of Riesling, Chardonnay, etc.

Orfila
San Martin, Mendoza. A family estate of 680 acres. Sauvignon, Chardonnay and Cabernet are the main grapes. Cautivo is their top label.

Peñaflor
Av.J.B. Justo 1015, Buenos Aires. The country's biggest wine company, owned by the Pulenta family, with 4 modern bodegas and a huge range of wines, including the popular Andean brand, designed for export.

Proviar
Florida 378, 4°, 1351 Buenos Aires. The Argentine arm of Moët & Chandon, producing Champaña (Baron B is the top quality), a smooth light Castell Chandon white of Sauvignon, Semillon and Ugni Blanc, Valmont of Malbec and Cabernet Sauvignon and Valtour of Pinot Noir. All very competently done.

Bodegas La Rural
Maipú 5501, Mendoza. A bodega with 620 acres, still wood-ageing reds lavishly but making Riesling and Gewürztraminer with a lighter touch.

Santa Ana
Guaymallen, Mendoza. A small family property of 95 acres largely planted with Barbera and Bonarda, but also Syrah.

San Telmo
A large new concern making good variental wines in the California manner.

Suter
San Rafael, Mendoza. A Seagram subsidiary with 2,400 acres. Their Etiqueta Maron 'Pinot Blanc' is the brand leader in 'fine whites'.

Michel Torino, Bodega La Rosa
Cordoba 366, Salta 4400. An 870-acre property, 75% white Torrontes for a heavily fruity white 'Don David'. Cabernet is potent but well made.

Pascual Toso
San Jose, Mendoza. A small family concern best known for one of Argentina's best Cabernets.

Trapiche
Part of the Peñaflor group, 775 acres of the best varieties making some of Argentina's freshest wines.

Weinert
Parana 720, 1017 Buenos Aires. A modern winery without vineyards. Fresh and fruity wines, especially a Chardonnay without ageing in wood.

Mexico

Mexico is the oldest producer of wine in the Americas, with winery buildings going back to the sixteenth century. Only recently, though, has the Mexican market demanded anything better than peasant wine and brandy (which still uses 90 per cent of the wine grapes grown). Progress towards quality has come in four main areas: Baja California, which benefits from cold Pacific currents, and dotted along the high mountain chain of the Sierra Madre, San Juan del Rio (100 miles north of the capital); Aguascalientes (250 miles north); and Saltillo, Parras and Torreon, 500 miles north, to the west of Monterrey. Of these, Parras is the oldest and Baja California and Aguascalientes the most advanced. The noble grape varieties are newcomers, but investments by international companies are encouraging.

Mexico producers

Marqués de Aguayo SA
Ramos Arizpe No. 195, Hacienda el Rosario, Parras, Coahuila. The oldest winery in the Americas, founded in 1593, it now makes only brandy.

Cía. Vinicola de Aguascalientes
Av. Copilco No. 164, Col. Oxtopulco C.U., Mexico 20.
Mexico's biggest wine company. The main product of its 15,000 acres is brandy. San Marcos is the table-wine brand, Champ d'Or the sparkling wine. The company also owns the Alamo brand and Cía-Vin. de Vergel at Gomez Palacio in Durango province, with its Tinto Noblejo, Blanco Verdizo, Tinto Viña Santiago, etc.

Industrias Vinicolas Domecq
Av. Mexico No. 91, Mexico 21.
Largely brandy, but also the highly regarded Los Reyes table wines from Guadalupe in Baja California.

Formex-Ybarra
Valle de Guadalupe, Mpio. de Ensenada, Baja California.
800 acres in Baja California produce the well-known Terrasola table wine. Other brands: Urbinon, Trevere, Oncala.

Casa Madero
Bodegas de San Lorenzo, Parras, Coahuila. A historic and beautiful bodega founded in 1626, the second oldest in the Americas. 1,000 acres, brand name San Lorenzo.

Cavas de San Juan
San Juan del Rio, Queretaro.
Mexico's southernmost and highest winery at 6,100 feet. 625 acres include Cabernet, Chardonnay and Pinot Noir Hidalgo, and (sparkling) Carte Blanche.

Bodegas de Santo Tomas
Av. Miramar No. 666, Ensenada, B.C.
Owned by Elias Pando. Fame arrived with Dmitri Tchelistcheff, son of the renowned André of Beaulieu Vintners, who brought noble vines from the Napa Valley. Most of the vines are still such compromise varieties as Chenin Blanc, Carignan, Grenache, but plantings of Chardonnay, Cabernet and Pinot Noir have had some success.

Productos de Uva de Aguascalientes
PO Box 350, Aguascalientes, Ags.
The Cetto family's main winery, producing Valle Redondo wines from 300 acres. They also own modern vineyards at Tecate, Tijuana, producing Calafia and F. Chauvenet brands.

ENGLAND

The fact that England and Wales are at the farthest northern limit of the zone where grapes will ripen has not discouraged some 700 landowners, farmers and gardeners from planting vineyards of from half an acre up to 30 acres. The revival of English wine-growing (it was widespread in the Middle Ages) started slowly in the 1950s and accelerated rapidly in the 1970s. The excellent summer of 1976 encouraged many to think that wine-growing could be more than a hobby and part-time job. In spite of a succession of dismal harvests in the late '70s, with vintage rain a regular occurrence, the little industry has consolidated its position. There are now some 1,000 acres of vineyards scattered across southern England and Wales, with concentrations in the traditional fruit-growing areas of Kent and Sussex, Essex and Suffolk, along the south coast through Hampshire as far as Devon and north through Berkshire, Wiltshire and Somerset as far as Worcester.

It is too early to say that any regional styles have emerged. English wine is and presumably always will be a light, refreshing, slightly tart summer drink. The qualities it achieves best are floweriness, delicate fruitiness and a crisp clean freshness. Its acidity should be noticeable and matched with a gentle sweetness. A little *spritz* is often a good idea.

In the cool climate with uncertain summers and autumns, early ripening and resistance to rot are two of the major factors governing the choice of grapes. The official E.E.C. recommendations for Britain are Müller-Thurgau, Pinot Meunier (sometimes called Wrotham Pinot) and Auxerrois – which is successful in Luxembourg. Growers have concentrated on white grapes, above all Müller-Thurgau and the non-recommended French-American hybrid Seyval Blanc, whose wine is reliable, if neutral in character. They have also taken advantage of the new German aromatic crossings to give character and lift to their wine. Huxelrebe, Reichensteiner, Madeleine Angevine, Bacchus and Schönburger all have marked characters. Too marked, some feel, to produce very agreeable wine without a less aromatic element in the blend.

The industry's regulatory body, founded in 1967, is the English Vineyard Association. Since 1978 it has been empowered to grant a certificate seal to wines submitted for its inspection, analysis and tasting. So far few growers have submitted their wines.

An annual competition to find the 'English Wine of the Year', however, attracts some 50 entries.

ENGLAND PRODUCERS

Adgestone, Sandown, Isle of Wight. Owner: K. Barlow. 8.5. acres.
Barton Manor, East Cowes, Isle of Wight. Owner: A. Goddard. 4.5.acres.
Beaulieu Vineyards, Palace House, Beaulieu, Hampshire. Owner: Lord Montagu 4.5 acres.
Biddenden, Ashford, Kent. Owner: R. Barnes. 14 acres.
Bruisyard St. Peter, Saxmundham, Suffolk. Owner: I.H. Berwick. 10 acres.
Cavendish Manor, Sudbury, Suffolk. Owner: B. Ambrose, 10 acres.
Carr Taylor Vineyards, Westfield, Hastings, Sussex. Owner: D. Carr-Taylor. 21 acres.
Chickering, Eye, Suffolk. Owner: P. Day. 2 acres.
Chilford Hundred, Linton, Cambs. Owner: S. Alper. 18 acres.
Chilsdown Vineyard, Singleton, Chichester, Sussex. Owner; Paget Brothers. 10 acres.
Elmham Park, Dereham, Norfolk. Owner: R. Don. 7.5 acres.
Felstar, Felsted, Essex. Owners: J.G. & I.M. Barrett. 9 acres.
Gamlingay, Sandy, Bedfordshire. Owner: G. Reece. 8.5 acres.
Hambledon, Hants. Owner: Maj. Gen. Sir Guy Salisbury-Jones. 7 acres.
Heywood, Diss, Norfolk. Owner: R.C. Aikman. 2 acres.
Highwaymans, Bury St. Edmunds, Suffolk. Owners: Macrae Farms. 25 acres.
Lamberhurst Priory, Lamberhurst, Nr Tunbridge Wells, Kent. Owner: K. McAlpine. 32 acres. Also 8 acres, Horam Manor, Heathfield, Sussex.
New Hall, Purleigh, Maldon, Essex. Owner: S.W. Greenwood. 20 acres.
Pilton Manor Vineyard, Shepton Mallet, Somerset. Owner: N. Godden. 6 acres.
Rock Lodge Vineyard, Haywards Heath, Sussex. Owner: N. Cowderoy. 3 acres.
St. Etheldreda, Isle of Ely Vineyard, Cottenham, Cambs. Owner: N.J. Sneesby. 2 acres.
Spots Farm, Small Hythe, Tenterden, Kent. Owner: S. Skelton. 10 acres.
Staple Vineyards, Staple, Canterbury, Kent. Owner: W. Ash. 7 acres.
Thakeham, Thakeham, Sussex. Owner: J. Rice. 10 acres.
Three Choirs, Newent, Glos. Owner: A.A. McKechnie. 17.5 acres.
Westbury, Purley, Reading, Berks. Owner: B Theobald. 12.5 acres.
Wootton, Shepton Mallett, Somerset. Owner: Major C.L.B. Gillespie. 6 acres.
Wraxall Vineyards, Shepton Mallet, Somerset. Owner: A. Holmes. 6 acres.

Wine is becoming part of rural England

Enjoying Wine

It is the inquisitive who enjoy wine most. The essence of the game is variety; you could taste a different wine every day of your life and yet not learn it all. Each wine evolves with time. There will always be new wines to taste, and new combinations of wine with food to try. There will always be more to learn about yourself, your palate and its reactions, too.

No single attitude or set of rules can apply to a commodity that can be either a simple foodstuff as basic as bread and cheese, or one of the most recherché of luxuries, or anywhere in between. There are enamel-mug wines and Baccarat-crystal wines, and there is no point in pretending that one is the other.

This chapter is concerned with choosing, buying, storing, serving and appreciating wine that is above the ordinaire or jug level. Once a wine has a named origin (as opposed to being an anonymous blend) it reflects a particular soil, climate, culture and tradition. For better or worse it has some character.

The mastery of wine consists in recognizing, bringing out and making the most of that character. I cannot improve on André Simon's definition of a connoisseur: 'One who knows good wine from bad, and appreciates the distinctive merits of different wines.' Thank heaven all white wines are not Moselles, however fresh, flowery and fragrant, or all reds great thumping Cabernets.

It is a crucial (but also a common) misunderstanding of the nature and variety of wine to say that a Barolo, for example, is better than a Rioja, or a Napa Cabernet than a Pauillac. The secret is to learn to understand and enjoy each of them for what it is.

There is only one essential I would press on you, if you are going to spend more than a bare minimum and buy wines above the jug level. Make a conscious act of tasting. Become aware of the messages your nose and mouth are sending you – not just about wine, but about all food and drink. Seek out new tastes and think about them.

By far the greater part of all fine wine, and even – perhaps especially – of the best, is thrown away by being used as a mere drink. A great bottle of wine is certainly wasted if nobody talks about it, or at least tries to pinpoint in his own consciousness the wonderful will-o'-the-wisp of fragrance and flavour.

BUYING WINE

To buy wine and get exactly what you expect is the exception rather than the rule. Wine is a moving target; a kaleidoscope of vintners and vintages that never stands still. If this bothers you, there is a solution – stick to a brand. But you will be sacrificing the great fascination of wine; its infinite variety. Not to mention the fun of the chase: the satisfaction of finding a winner (and the chagrin of backing a dud).

There are few cardinal rules in such an open field, where one day you may be buying from the corner store, the next by mail-order and the third direct from the producer. But the first rule is absolute. Always buy ahead of your needs; never drink the bottle you have just bought. There are very good reasons for this rule. To start with you need time to think. If you go shopping knowing that you must bring home some wine, the chances are that what you buy will be unsuitable and you will probably pay more than you really want to.

Nobody can take in all the offerings of a well-stocked store at a glance. Do your wine buying when you are in the mood and have time to browse, to compare prices, to make calculations, to use reference books. By far the best place to do this is at home, by comparing the price lists of alternative suppliers. Avoid traders who have no list and rely on you to fall for this week's 'special'.

Your wine needs time to rest. Although many modern white and light-red wines are so stable that you could play skittles with them and do them no harm, all mature red wines need a settling period of at least several days after being moved. Your chances of serving a wine at its best are far greater if you can prepare it calmly at home.

Given time you can make an order that qualifies for a discount. Buying by the case is cheaper than buying by the bottle. Assuming you have a cupboard with a lock, and a reasonable resistance to temptation, you will use no more wine, and pay less.

An investment in pleasure

An investment in future pleasure is often one of the most profitable of all. Inflation aside, when you come to drink the wine, now better than when you bought it, the expenditure will be a thing of the past; the pleasure will seem a gift from the gods.

In fact, very little money is needed to convert you from a bottle-by-bottle buyer to the proud possessor of a 'cellar'. Calculate what you spend on wine in three months, or two months, or at a pinch only one month – and spend it all at once in a planned spree. Lock the wine away. Then continue to buy the same quantity as before but use it to replenish your stock, instead of for instant

In the past, only the grandest producers were capable of maturing and bottling their wine satisfactorily, and marketing was an idea unknown to them. The key to what the consumer wanted was held by the merchants, who blended wine to the customers' tastes. Today, buying wine direct from the maker has largely changed the shape of the wine trade.

It is the broker's job to know his region in the finest detail, to be a sort of family doctor to the small grower's wine, to advise him on its condition, choose samples with him and take them to the right merchant. To the merchant the broker is a valued talent spotter who can gather and submit the right samples. The merchant's traditional function is to finance the wine while it is maturing, to make sure it suits the customers' tastes, then to bottle and ship it. In many cases he and his agents create both the wine and the market. His agents provide the link with the wholesalers, who are stockholders for retailers. The possible permutations of the system are endless. Its advantages are that each aspect of the chain from grower to table has its highly experienced expert, whether in knowing the right time to bottle or the turnover of a nightclub's refrigerator.

The wine trade

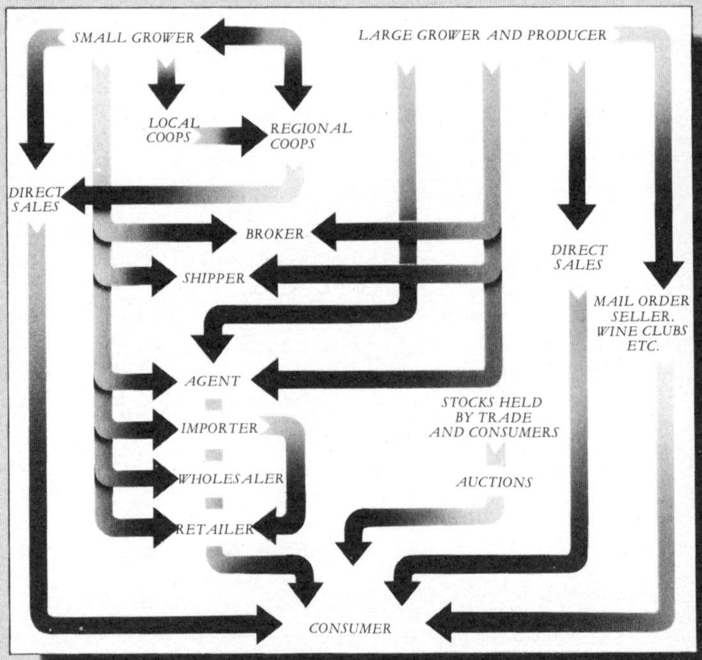

drinking. All you have done is to borrow three, two or one month's wine money and the interest on that is your only extra expenditure. Your reward is wine you have chosen carefully and kept well, ready when you want it, not when you can get to the shops.

Make an effort to be clear headed about what you really need. Do not spend more than you can comfortably afford. Think twice before buying unknown wines as part of a package. Do not buy a quantity of wine you have never tasted and may not like. Consider whether home delivery is really practicable: will there be someone at home to answer the door? Can you easily lift the 40 or 50 pounds that a case of wine weighs?

One of the wiliest ways of broadening your buying scope is to join with a small group of like-minded people to form a syndicate. A syndicate can save money by buying bigger lots of everyday wine. It can spread risks. It can also bring within reach extraordinary bottles at prices that would make you, on your own, feel guilty for months. Three or four friends who have never tasted Château Lafite or Romanée-Conti will enjoy them more if they buy and open them together, sharing their opinions (and their guilt). While there may be laws that prevent an unlicensed citizen from selling wine, even to a friend, there is nothing to stop them sharing its cost.

The wine trade

The structure of the wine trade has changed radically in recent years from a fairly rigid pattern of brokers, shippers, agents, wholesalers and retailers to an intricate but fluid mixture of ingredients, some old and some new. It is not surprising that such a pleasant vocation has more volunteers than the army. The great growth areas have been in 'experts', writers and consultants, and in ingenious methods of selling with or without a shop.

In America the period has seen wine change from a minority – even a faintly suspect minority – interest to a national pastime. The wine trade has recruited regiments of specialists at every level. Locally the retailers are the most prominent; nationally the marketing men. But what remains sovereign (and to the foreigner most bizarre) is the changing legislation from state to state. Scarcely two are alike. New York, California, Texas, Florida and a few more states are relatively free to benefit from all the rich possibilities; the rest are more or less inhibited by local legislation. Even individual counties can stick their oar in and say what you may and may not drink. Seen from across the Atlantic it looks as though the Constitution is in mortal peril.

In Britain the changes started in the 1960s with the ponderous tread of the brewers, fearful that a growing taste for wine would erode their sales of beer, buying scores of traditional local wine shops and replacing them with chains tied to national brand-marketing ideas.

Whatever the merits of the old merchants (and many of them were excellent) the new shops were generally dismal, and the rising generation of vocational wine merchants – as opposed to accountants – wanted nothing to do

The alcohol in wine

The amount of alcohol in wine varies considerably. While alcohol provides much of the 'body' in many wines, it needs to be balanced by the flavouring elements: sugar, acidity, tannin and extract. These, combined with the alcohol, give richness of flavour. Alcohol alone makes a wine fierce and unpleasant. Typical alcoholic strengths, per cent by volume, are:

Wine	%	Wine	%
German Kabinett	*8–9*	Chianti	*12–13*
German Tafelwein	*8–11*	Barolo	*12–14*
French vin de table	*9–12*	Sauternes	*12–15*
German Auslese	*10–10.5*	California Zinfandel	*12–16*
Beaujolais-Villages	*10–10.5*	Chambertin	*12.4*
Alsace Riesling	*10.5–11.5*	Rioja Reserva	*12.5*
Chablis Premier Cru	*10.5–12.7*	Montrachet	*12.6*
Red Bordeaux	*10.5–13*	Châteauneuf-du-Pape	*12.6+*
California Chardonnay	*10.5–14*	German Beerenauslese	*12.8–14*
Bordeaux Cru Classé	*11–12*	Château Yquem	*13.5–16*
Beaune	*11–14*	Australian Shiraz	*13.8*
California Cabernet	*11.44–14.2*	Fino sherry	*18–20*
Valpolicella	*11.7*	Oloroso sherry	*18–20*
Muscadet	*12*	Vintage port	*19–20*

The price of wine and the price of food

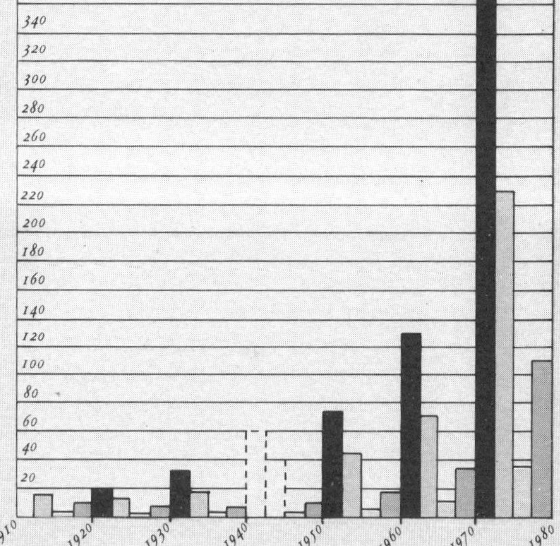

The graph (right) shows the facts of inflation as far as they can be measured. It compares the prices of a loaf of bread and a pound of rib beef in London between 1912 and 1980 with the prices of a bottle of plain red Bordeaux and (from 1924) of a minor classed growth (fifth-growth Médoc). After long stability prices rose during World War II only to steady and rise very slightly in the 1950s. Since 1974 wine has kept pace with inflation.

with them. They found it easy to reinvent the old individualistic wine trade for the new generation of better travelled and more knowledgeable (if less wealthy) wine lovers. Some of them specialized in particular areas or styles of wine. Gerald Asher in London was the first, shipping the 'lesser' wines of France – names like Touraine and Roussillon, which today are considered almost classic. The old trade, weaned on Bordeaux and burgundy, had never heard of them and the brewers (most of them) preferred a simple life with tank trucks of a Spanish blend. Today there is a specialist for almost every area of the wine-growing world and it must be said that the brewers now employ some of the best.

Other wine merchants offer the old virtues of personal service, delivery to your door and credit (at a price). Personal service consists largely of word-of-mouth recommendations based on a regular customer's known tastes and resources. A very few firms, including some of the oldest and one or two of the youngest, are prepared to become as involved as family solicitors, keeping track of what a customer has in his cellar and reminding him to drink it when it has reached its best. Such firms are skilful at offering the best wines of a new vintage early, while they are still in their makers' cellars and long before they are even bottled, at 'opening' prices that rarely fail to rise once the wines come on the general market.

At the opposite extreme, making wine available and tempting to every shopper, are the supermarkets, offering a rather simple and limited range, sometimes under their own brand names. These are nearly always the cheapest places to buy single bottles, which are usually good value for money, if rarely memorable. In their early days of selling wine most supermarkets left a lot to be desired, particularly by way of explanation and description, but more recently helpful labels and even in some cases trained staff have appeared.

Learn while you drink

Mail-order wine merchants prosper on the proposition that the calm customer, reference book and calculator to hand, is likely to aim true and be satisfied. Wine clubs and societies, often offering a great deal of information about the wines they sell, and usually setting up periodic tastings for members, feed the urge to learn while you drink.

Discount stores doing cash-and-carry business appeal to bargain hunters. Magazines can be highly persuasive about their mixed case of the month. There has even been a wine investment programme linked to a life insurance policy. All in all, the efforts of marketing men make a subject which is already confusing a great deal more so.

The world's wine list

Although there is no such thing as a universal wine list, it has proved an interesting exercise to compile one. Prices of individual and generic wines are given in local currency for comparison through most sections of this book. The object here is to relate the prices of the broad categories of wine to each other. The wine and prices are chosen from London lists of 1982 with the relevant excise and other taxes removed. The figure in brackets is the factor by which each wine exceeds the basic 'commodity' wine price – in so far as there is one. The figure chosen for this was the price of London's cheapest jug wines, less taxation. It is approximately the same as the least you can pay for table wine in the United States in 1982: $1.50 a 75 cl. bottle. Thus a bottle of fine sherry costs 3.5 times the base price, while a bottle of first-growth claret costs 18 times the standard factor.

Below £0.85 (1)

Valdadige
Italian Vino Rosso/Bianco
French Vin de Pays
Corbières AOC
California jug wine

£1.15–£1.40 (1)

Coteaux d'Aix-en-Provence
Yugoslav Riesling
Retsina
Bulgarian Cabernet

£1.40–£1.65 (1)

Valpolicella
Côtes de Roussillon
Coteaux du Languedoc
Minervois
Soave
Côtes-du-Rhône
Bull's Blood
Lambrusco
Argentinian red & white
Grüner Veltliner
Yugoslav Traminer
Sauvignon de Touraine
Cabernet d'Anjou

£1.65–£1.90 (2)

Entre-Deux-Mers
Vinho Verde
Young red and white Rioja
Bordeaux Rouge (brand or Petit Château)
Cuve close sparkling wine
Liebfraumilch

£1.90–£2.15 (2)

Muscadet
Frascati
Dão
1980 Beaujolais
Fino and Amontillado sherry
Piesporter Michelsberg
Young Chianti Classico
Popular brand California varietals

£2.15–£2.40 (2.5)

Verdicchio
Sylvaner d'Alsace
Barbera d'Asti
Saumur-Champigny

£2.40–£2.65 (2.5)

Riesling d'Alsace
Mâcon-Villages
Chinon

£2.65–£2.90 (2.5)

Ruby and Tawny port
Australian Rhine Riesling
1977 Chilean Cabernet, estate bottled
Vouvray
Cahors

£2.90–£3.15 (3.5)

Cava (Spanish sparkling wine)
Bonnezeaux
Gewürztraminer d'Alsace
Australian Sémillon
Bordeaux Cru Bourgeois
Barbaresco
Malmsey and Sercial Madeira
Manzanilla

£3.15–£3.65 (3.5)

Vino Nobile di Montepulciano
Australian Rhine Riesling
1972 Château Musar
Chianti Classico Riserva
Sancerre
Brouilly
Beringer Zinfandel
Crémant de Loire
Pouilly Blanc Fumé

£3.65–£4.15 (3.5)

Australian Cabernet Sauvignon
Palo Cortado
Muscat de Beaumes de Venise
Crozes-Hermitage
1979 Hochheimer Holle Riesling Kabinett
Barolo
Savennières

In the last few years auctions have come to epitomize both the scholarship and the showmanship of wine. Michael Broadbent at Christie's, followed by Colin Fenton and then Patrick Grubb at Sotheby's, have become wine's ringmasters and at the same time the repositories of esoteric vinous knowledge. Auctions are now regularly used in the United States, Germany, South Africa and many countries besides Britain to sell and publicize at the same time. But the London auction houses have another role, simply to turn over private cellars, surplus stocks and awkward small amounts of wine that complicate a wine merchant's life. There is a steady flow of mature wine, young wine and sometimes good but unfashionable wine at absurdly low prices. Anyone can buy, but the real bargains are often in lots larger than an individual may want. It is common practice to form syndicates to buy and divide such lots.

Speculating in blue chips

The auction houses established a flourishing market in old wines whose value had been unknown before. In their wake a new class of, so to speak, second-hand wine merchants has sprung up. The first was Andrew Low in Suffolk. Their business can be compared with antiquarian booksellers, finding rare wines on behalf of collectors – for collectors there certainly are today, as there never were in the spacious days when a gentleman filled his cellars with first-growth claret as a matter of course.

Those who buy such blue-chip wines in quantity these days are more likely to be engaged in the less gentlemanly game of speculation. Wine is a commodity susceptible to buying cheap and selling dear – but happily with no certainty of success. In 1974, overconfident speculators in wine lost millions.

The more expensive the wine the greater the chance of its appreciation. But other factors come into it, too: the vintage and its reputation (which will shift, not always predictably, as time goes on); the general financial climate; the popularity of the château or grower in question; perhaps most of all the proven ability of the wine to age. It is the classed growths of Bordeaux and vintage port that are known or presumed to have the longest potential life span; therefore the biggest spread of opportunity for reselling at a profit. Modern burgundies and German wines are considered relatively poor risks, with or without justification. The very best Italian and Spanish wines, and such rarities as Tokay Essence, have a certain following. Some fine California wines undoubtedly will have a considerable following, once they have proved their ability to age.

£4.15–£4.65 (5)

1979 Wehlener Sonnenuhr Riesling Spätlese
Mature Rioja
Prestigious '78 Bordeaux Cru Bourgeois
Côtes de Beaune-Villages
Chablis
1975 Cru Bourgeois
Sauternes

£4.65–£5.15 (5)

1976 Givry
Châteauneuf-du-Pape

£5.15–£6.15 (7)

1974 Ch. Gruaud-Larose
Quarts de Chaume
1978 Bordeaux classed growths begin
1979 Robert Mondavi Cabernet Sauvignon
Brunello di Montalcino
Australian Chardonnay
1979 Hattenheimer Mannberg Riesling Spätlese

£6.15–£7.15 (7)

Côte Rôtie
Hermitage
1er Cru Chablis
Pouilly-Fuissé
1975 Croft port
1978 Ch. Talbot
Coulée de Serrant

£7.15–£8.15 (9.4)

Grand Cru Chablis
1978 Trefethen Chardonnay
1973 Ch. Beychevelle
1972 Puligny Montrachet Les Folatières
1978 Ch. Beychevelle
1977 Croft port
1978 Sassicaia

£8.15–£9.15 (9.4)

NV Champagne
1977 Puligny Montrachet Les Folatières
1975 Torres Gran Coronas Black Label

£9.15+ (10.75)

1967 Ch. Gruaud-Larose
Ch. Grillet
1972 Pommard 1er Cru Rugiens

£10.15+ (10.75)

1970 Croft port
1977 Pommard, 1er Cru Rugiens
1978 Puligny Montrachet Les Folatières

£11.15+ (13)

1976 Aloxe Corton Domaine Louis Latour
1970 Ch. Talbot
1978 Pommard 1er Cru Rugiens
1969 Puligny Montrachet Les Folatières

£12.15+ (13)

Vintage champagne
1976 Bernkasteler Badstube Riesling Beerenauslese
1971 Pommard 1er Cru Rugiens

£14.15+ (13)

1960 and 1963 Croft port
1966 Ch. Talbot
1969 Pommard 1er Cru Rugiens

£15.15+ (18)

1970 Ch. Beychevelle

£17.15+ (18)

1979 Corton Charlemagne Comtes de Grancey
1975 Heitz Cabernet Sauvignon, Martha's Vineyard
1976 First-growth Bordeaux
1976 Bonnes Mares

£19.15+ (22.5)

1966 Ch. Beychevelle
1978 Ch. Haut Brion

£24.15+ (22.5)

1955 Croft port
1971 Dom Perignon
1977 Le Montrachet

£29.15+ (34)

1978 Le Montrachet
1975 Ch. d'Yquem

£34.15+ (40)

1979 Niersteiner Spiegelberg Müller Thurgau Trockenbeerenauslese
1961 Ch. Talbot
1978 Ch. Latour

£39.15+ (40)

1961 Ch. Beychevelle
1969 Le Montrachet
1978 Ch. Pétrus

£49.15+ (61)

1955 Ch. d'Yquem

A rarity at auction

1 Imperial of 1928 Ch. Mouton-Rothschild
£525 a bottle (617)

CHOOSING WINE

One of the many advantages of living in wine-making country is the way it simplifies your choice. You drink the local wine, preferably made by friends. You tend to suit your diet to it; if the wine is delicate you will go easy on the seasoning; if it is strapping you will make meals of garlic and peppers. All bets are off in California, where your friends may make anything from a fragile Chenin Blanc to a galumphing Zinfandel, but most wine regions arrived at a balanced food and wine regime years ago.

In a country or region with no such traditions things are more complicated. In Britain, or the eastern United States, where the shops offer every wine there is, it is hardest of all to know where to start. Our wonderful variety makes a wonderfully difficult choice.

The realistic starting point, of course, is the price. The poorer you are the easier your choice will be. Together with the price goes the company and the occasion. If your companions are as interested in wine as you are you will want to seize the opportunity of discussing a good bottle with them. If they are indifferent, no matter how much you love them, remember that the wine itself is an occasion; it does not have to be fascinating too – unless to save you from death by boredom.

A moment in the limelight

In short, before you choose a wine, decide whether it is going to have even a moment in the limelight – and who, besides yourself, will be drinking it. Test yourself with your reaction to the behaviour of Voltaire, who habitually gave his guests Beaujolais while he drank the finest burgundies himself.

Whether you give priority to the food or the wine is the next question. Ideally they should share the stage as harmonious equals – no more rivals than a hero and heroine. In a restaurant the menu and the wine list should be offered to you at the same time.

In practice the proposition is probably either 'what shall we drink with the lamb tonight?' or 'what shall we eat with this bottle of Pomerol?' You need, in fact, a two-way frame of reference; a mental image of the flavours of both food and wine so that you can match them.

It is surprising how often I am asked 'You don't have to drink red wine with meat and white wine with fish, do you?', usually with a sort of indignation that implies that this simple piece of lore is a savage attack on liberty and the constitution. Of course you don't have to. You may please yourself. But if you want to please yourself you could do worse than follow such sensible guidelines, based on sound reasons and centuries of practice.

The reasons are both chemical and aesthetic. The appetizing, refreshing quality of white wine is provided by acids that enhance the flavour of fish, while the saltiness of fish in turn emphasizes the fruity grape flavours of the wine. By contrast, the 'edge' of a red wine is not acidity but tannin, which reacts disastrously with the salt, which makes it bitter, and the fishy oils, which leave a lasting metallic tang in your mouth.

Of course there are exceptions. Certain fish (and, best of all, lampreys) are cooked in red wine to make a dish that goes excellently with a full-flavoured red – not Beaujolais but St-Emilion. Some people like cool, light-red wine with fresh poached salmon.

But on the aesthetic side the association of white wine with pale fish, and for that matter pale meat, is no accident either. Each foodstuff has its appropriate colour. The eye tells the brain what kind of flavour to expect. And the eye finds it natural to associate pale drink with pale food.

Some of the traditional associations have even simpler reasons. We drink dry white wine with goat cheese, for example, because the cheese's salty dryness makes us thirsty. Some associations are simply negative: we do not drink red wine with sweets because sugar, like salt, makes tannin taste bitter.

Strong, savoury, protein-rich meat and game dishes are the natural partners of vigorous red wines; their tannin finds a match, and so does their colour. But light grapey reds ask for a less strenuous marriage with poultry or veal or pale lamb.

What the French so evocatively call 'la cuisine douce', such rich things of gentle savour as foie gras, sweetbreads, quenelles and cream cheeses, has a similar affinity for sweet, or at least fat and unctuous, white wines.

Clearly there are broad classes of wine that are more or less interchangeable. They can be matched with similar classes of dishes to achieve satisfactory harmonies, if not perfect ones. There are other dimensions of taste that have to be taken into account, too.

Intensity is one: a powerful flavour, however appropriate, will annihilate a bland or timid one. Unfortunately this is the effect many strong cheeses have, even on splendid full-scale red wines. Style is another: there are hearty rustic tastes and pronounced urbane ones; garlic, if you like, and truffles. The wine and the food should belong to the same culture. Peasant and aristocrat rarely show one another off to advantage; neither will bread and cheese and great claret.

The total context of the meal is important. Is it leisurely or hurried? Fine wine deserves time. Is the day hot or cold? Even air conditioning fails to make big red wines a good idea in tropical heat.

There are a few dishes that destroy the flavour of wine entirely. The commonest is salad dressed with vinegar. Surprisingly, even some of France's best restaurants serve violently acetic salads. Vinegar is best avoided altogether;

A dinner with old friends to drink exceptional wines in their prime is the ultimate pleasure that wine offers. The dinner on this menu never (alas) took place, but is composed of wines and notes from several dinners at about the same period.

The scene is a London club. There are 12 guests. The food is simple and rich. The talk is unashamedly centred on the wines, with suitable excursions into reminiscence, poetry, flirtation and the rest.

I always scribble my tasting notes on the menu card. Remember that they were written in the heat of the moment, not the cool of a morning tasting – but this is what their makers made the wines for.

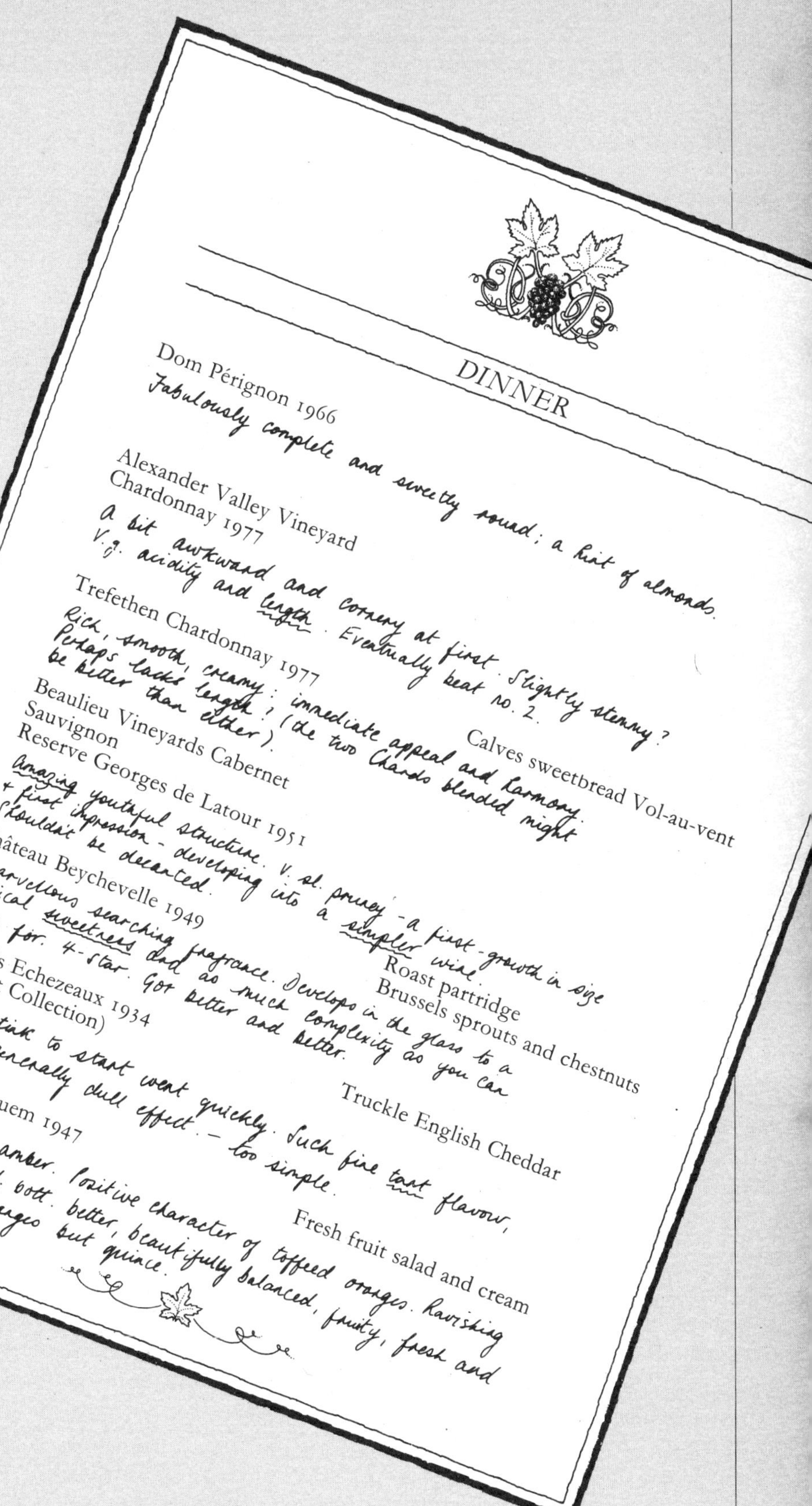

DINNER

Dom Pérignon 1966
Fabulously complete and sweetly round; a hint of almonds.

Alexander Valley Vineyard
Chardonnay 1977
A bit awkward and cornery at first. Slightly stemmy? V.g. acidity and length. Eventually beat no. 2.

Trefethen Chardonnay 1977
Rich, smooth, creamy; immediate appeal and harmony. Perhaps lacks length; (the two Chards blended might be better than either).

Calves sweetbread Vol-au-vent

Beaulieu Vineyards Cabernet
Sauvignon
Reserve Georges de Latour 1951
Amazing youthful structure. V. sl. pruney – a first-growth in size + first impression – developing into a simpler wine. Shouldn't be decanted.

Château Beychevelle 1949
Marvellous searching fragrance. Develops in the glass to a typical sweetness and as much complexity as you can hope for. 4-star. Got better and better.

Roast partridge
Brussels sprouts and chestnuts

Grands Echezeaux 1934
(Barolet Collection)
Foul stink to start went quickly. Such fine taut flavour, then a generally dull effect. – too simple.

Truckle English Cheddar

Château Yquem 1947
Full light amber. Positive character of toffeed oranges. Ravishing but odd. 2nd. bott. better, beautifully balanced, fruity, fresh and long. Not oranges but quince.

Fresh fruit salad and cream

lemon juice makes a better salad dressing in any case. Salad dressings with vinegar include the red 'cocktail sauce' of American restaurants, too.

Chocolate is another flavour that dominates and spoils the taste of any wine. In my view, most desserts are better served without wine; creamy highly perfumed concoctions fight wine rather than complement it. So do syrupy, fruity ones. Citrus fruit is particularly guilty. Where a very rich gâteau is on the menu I sometimes drink a glass of madeira or even brandy with it. On the other hand raspberries and strawberries, and particularly wild strawberries, are a wonderful match for fine red wine. In Bordeaux they pour claret rather than cream over them.

There are times when no single wine will fill the bill. It happens in a restaurant where everyone is eating something different: one shellfish, another game, a third a dish with a creamy sauce. The cop-out answer is a neutral wine that will offend nobody. Liebfraumilch and Portuguese rosés have made fortunes by offering themselves as the safe bet. A more swashbuckling (if less digestible) choice is champagne. My suggestion is to start with a bottle of white wine that will match almost any hors d'oeuvre, and then (if it is a party of four or more) continue with both white and red. There is no good reason not to have both on the table at the same time.

The structure of a more formal meal with a succession of wines is the great opportunity of gastronomy. To achieve a graduated harmony of successive flavours it is worth taking pains. The ground rules are simple: follow lighter and more delicate with heavier and more pungent – both in wine and food. The fresh and hungry palate is susceptible to the subtlest flavours. Feeding fatigues it. It needs more powerful stimuli as the meal proceeds.

Occasionally the best way to bring out the singularity of a wine is to serve it concurrently with another which is similar but distinct; either slightly younger or from a neighbouring property.

Wine divided into ten basic styles

I have risked a rather arbitrary division of the infinite variety of wine into ten categories, and associated each category with a selection of dishes, as a guide to where to start to look, whether your starting point is the wine or the food.

No such generalization can be defended in every particular, but it is true to say that certain criteria of flavour, age and quality can be applied across the board. Some wines could appear equally in two different categories, but for the sake of clarity I have put them firmly where, in my judgement, they most often belong.

Dry white wines of neutral, simply 'winey' flavour

Among the cheapest wines, generally useful but too plain to be exciting, or to be particularly pleasant as apéritifs without the addition of extra flavour (such as blackcurrant or grenadine syrup).

These wines are better with simple food, especially with strong-flavoured or highly seasoned dishes, e.g. hors d'oeuvre (antipasto), aïoli or fish stew, mussels, herrings and mackerel (which need a rather acid wine to cut their oil), salad niçoise, red mullet, grilled sardines, terrines and sausages, curry or Chinese food (both of these are better for a little sweetness in the wine, e.g. Yugoslav Riesling). All should be served very well chilled (about 46°F/8°C).

Examples are: most branded 'jug' whites; Entre-Deux-Mers, Gaillac, Muscadet (Gros Plant du Pays Nantais or Aligoté for more acidity); southern French whites; many Swiss whites; most standard Italian whites (including Soave, Verdicchio, Orvieto Secco, Frascati, Pinot Bianco, Trebbiano, Sardinian and Sicilian wines); most standard Spanish and Portuguese whites; central and east European 'Welsch' Rieslings (i.e. Hungarian, Yugoslav, Bulgarian, etc.); California jugs ('Chablis') and many Chenin Blancs; South African 'Grands Crus'.

Light, fresh, grapey white wine with fruity and sometimes flowery aromas

This is the category of wine which has grown most in recent years, at the expense of the dry whites. Modern techniques, especially cold fermentation, capture whatever flavour the grape has (some have much more than others) and add as little as possible. The very aromatic German-style grapes are nearly always in this or the sweet white wine category.

All these wines make good apéritifs or refreshing between-meal or evening drinks, most of all in summer. Those with relatively high acidity are good with many first courses, but are dominated by seriously savoury dishes and lack the substance to be satisfying throughout a meal. Suitable dishes include: poached trout, crab salad, cold chicken. They need slightly less chilling than the previous category.

Wines include: German Tafelwein, Qualitätswein, most Kabinetts and some Spätleses; light French Sauvignons from the Dordogne and Touraine; Savoie whites (Crépy, Apremont); Portuguese vinho verde; certain California Chenin Blancs and French Colombards; Australian 'moselles'; New Zealand and English Müller-Thurgaus and Seyval Blancs; Austrian Grüner Veltliners.

White wines with body and character, aromatic from certain grapes or with the bouquet of maturity

The fine French dry whites all come into this category. High flavour often makes them taste rich even when they are fully dry.

Without food, these wines can be too assertive; they are best matched with a savoury dish which is also rich in flavour and pale in colour, e.g. oysters, clams, lobsters and prawns, smoked fish, frogs' legs, snails, onion or leek tart, ballotines, prosciutto, salmon, turbot and other rich fish in butter, hollandaise or other rich sauces, scallops, poultry, sweetbreads, hard Swiss cheeses. Wines should only be lightly chilled (50°-55°F/10°-13°C).

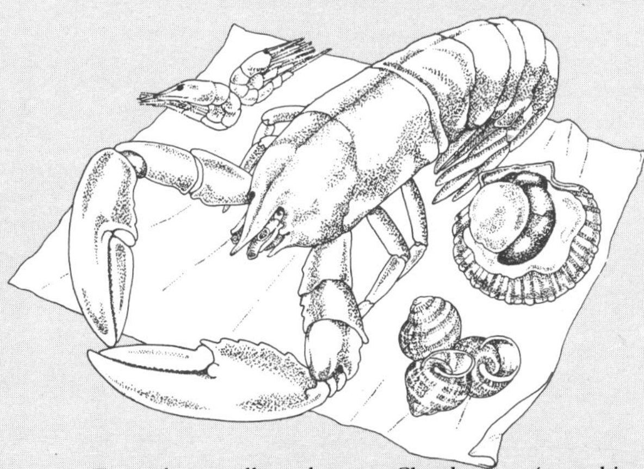

Examples are: all good mature Chardonnays (e.g. white burgundies after two or more years depending on their quality); their equivalents from California and Australia; Alsace Riesling, Gewürztraminer and Pinot Gris; Sancerre and Pouilly Fumé and Savennières from the Loire; fine white Graves; mature white Rhône wines (e.g. Hermitage Blanc) and young Condrieu; exceptional Italian whites (the best examples of Frascati, Soave Classico, Pinot Grigio, Cortese di Gavi, Montecarlo, Pomino, Traminer, etc.); best-quality mature Rioja and Penedès whites from Spain, manzanilla sherry or montilla fino; Hungarian Szürkebarát, Kéknelyü and Furmint; Austrian Rotgipfler, and Ruländer from either Austria or Baden; Australian Sémillons and dry Barossa and Coonawarra Rieslings with three or four years in bottle; California Johannisberg Riesling.

Sweet white wines

Varying from delicately fruity and lightly sweet to overwhelmingly luscious, these wines are to be sipped slowly by themselves and are rarely improved by food.

Very rich and highly flavoured desserts, however delicious, tend to fight sweet wines. Chocolate and coffee ones are fatal. If you want anything at all, the best choice is a dessert such as French apple or raspberry tart, crème brûlée, plain sponge cake or such fruit as peaches or apples. Sweet white wines are usually drunk after meals, but in France often as apéritifs, too. They are normally served very well chilled.

The finest natural sweet wines are produced by the action of 'noble rot'. These include Sauternes and Barsac and the best qualities of Ste-Croix-du-Mont and Monbazillac, which are the most potent, Vouvray and Anjou whites of certain years, late-gathered wines of Alsace and Austria, and the rare and expensive very late-harvested wines of Germany, Beerenausleses and Trockenbeerenausleses (which have recently been imitated with real success in California). German wines offer every gradation between the light flowery whites and the intensely sweet ones with the same delicately acid flavour. None of them is really a mealtime wine.

Sweet Muscats are found in most wine countries; the best 'natural' (not fortified) ones are made in the south of France at Beaumes de Venise and at Asti in northern Italy, where the very low-strength base wine for Spumante is delicious. Heavier brown Muscats are made in Languedoc and Roussillon, several parts of Italy (especially Sicily), on the east coast of Spain, at Setúbal in Portugal, in Greece and Russia and (perhaps the best) in northeast Victoria, Australia.

Rosé wines

Rosés are usually workhorse, compromise wines of adequate quality, made by fermenting the juice of red grapes very briefly with the skins, then separating it and making it like white wine. The great exception is pink champagne, which is made by adding still red wine to normal white champagne. Few things are more delicious. Rosés divide broadly into two camps: the light, pale purply pink, usually faintly sweet Loire style, and the drier, more orange-pink, stronger and more sunburnt Provençal variety. Portuguese-carbonated fizzy rosés fit into the first category. Tavel from the Rhône and most rosés from Spain and Italy are stronger and drier. Some of Italy's best are called Chiaretto and are really very light reds. A third group that can be classed as rosé are *vins gris*, red-grape white wines merely shaded with colour, more grey than pink, and a fourth, *pelure d'oignon* ('onion skin'), which are very pale orange-brown. Both are usually made very dry; the *gris* more fruity and the onion skin more alcoholic. *Vin gris* has recently become popular in California under such names as 'Eye of the Swan' as a way of using surplus red grapes, often Pinot Noir or even Cabernet, to make white wine.

Rosés are best in summer with salads and on picnics, and the Provençal style with oily and garlicky or even oriental dishes. They have possibilities with such hors d'oeuvre as artichokes, crudités, salami or taramasalata. Pink wines need to be served really cold; colder than most whites. If this is difficult to arrange on a picnic choose a light red wine instead.

Grapey young reds with individuality, not intended to mature

Beaujolais is the archetype of a light red wine made to be drunk young while it is still lively with fresh grape flavour. Beaujolais-Villages is a better, stronger and tastier selection. Simple young Bordeaux, burgundy and Rhône reds, Cabernet from Anjou and Mondeuse from Savoie should have the same appeal. Similar wines are now made in the Midi (Corbières, Minervois, Roussillon, St-Chinian) by the Beaujolais technique of carbonic maceration but of grapes with less distinct flavour.

Italy's Valpolicella and Bardolino, Barbera and Dolcetto and even Chianti can be freshly fruity if they are caught young enough – which is not often. Fizzy red Lambrusco is a sort of caricature of the style. Spain provides few examples, although Valdepeñas has possibilities and no doubt will be made fresher in the future. Portugal's red vinho verde is an extreme example not to everyone's taste. California, Australia, South Africa and South America have been slow to master this style of wine. Light Zinfandels and Gamays from California sometimes achieve it.

In its liveliness and vigour this is perhaps the safest and best all-round class of red wine for mealtimes; appetizing with anything from pâté to fruit and often better than a more 'serious' or older wine with strong cheese, in mouthfuls rather than sips. For the same reason it is the easiest red wine to drink without food. It is always best served cool.

Ideal dishes include: pâtés and terrines (including those made from vegetables), quiches, salads, hamburgers, liver, ham, grilled meats, many cheeses, raspberries, plums, peaches or nectarines.

Plain everyday or 'jug' reds

These are unpretentious and anonymous blended wines with little body or flavour. French ordinaires in particular are often mere refreshment; dry, thin and frankly watery. Whether you prefer them or the usually softer and stronger Italian or Spanish style is a matter of taste. California's 'jug' reds have more body and are often rather sweet.

Most inexpensive imports from southern, central and eastern Europe, North Africa, Argentina, Chile, South Africa and Australia are in this class. Exceptions are specifically mentioned in the classes that follow.

Like the 'neutral' cheap whites these are essentially wines for mealtimes, a healthy and stimulating accompaniment to almost any homely food. They are always best served rather cool. As drinks on their own they are improved by being iced in summer (as Sangria, with orange juice added) and 'mulled' on the stove with sugar and spices in winter.

The term 'table wine' has been adopted by the E.E.C. as denoting the lowest category of quality; wines without a specific origin (i.e. this group). The commissioners in their wisdom have ignored its English meaning, which is any wine you drink at table, including the best. They have also bracketed all wines that do not conform to national laws of appellation regardless of the reason. This produces total absurdity, for example, in Italy, where several of the country's finest wines are nontraditional, therefore outside the DOC system, therefore vino da tavola, therefore officially relegated to jug-wine status.

Mature reds of light to medium strength and body

This category includes most of the world's finest red wines, epitomized by claret (red Bordeaux) and most of the typical wines of Burgundy and the Rhône, although some of the greatest fall into the next class, depending on the ripeness of the vintage. These wines need more care in serving than any others since they often throw a deposit in maturing.

They are wines for meat and game dishes with the best ingredients and moderate seasoning. Lamb, beef, veal (also sweetbreads and tongue), chicken, duck, partridge, grouse, pheasant are all ideal, although very gamey birds may need wines from the next category. Only mild cheeses should be served with these relatively delicate wines. They need to be served at a temperature of between 60°F and 65°F (15° and 18°C) to bring out their flavour.

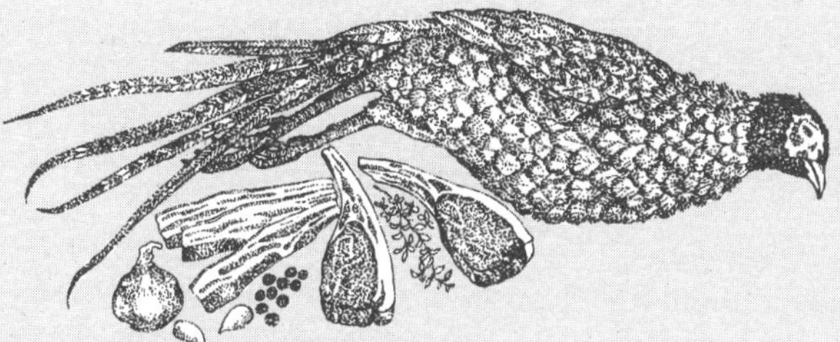

Wines in this category (apart from French) include the best of Rioja and Penedès from Spain; Chianti Riservas, Torgiano, Sassicaia and Tignanello, Carmignano, Venegazzú; Portuguese garrafeiras from Dão, Douro and Bairrada; top California, Oregon and Washington Cabernets and Pinot Noirs with the exception of a few mentioned in the next category; Coonawarra, Western Australian and some Hunter Valley reds (but above all Penfold's Grange Hermitage); top South African estates; Chilean Cabernet; Château Musar from the Lebanon and Cook's Cabernet from New Zealand.

Exceptionally concentrated, full-flavoured and powerful reds, usually but not always needing to mature

In Europe this category depends more on the vintage than the producer. Wines that achieve this status fairly regularly include Château Pétrus in Pomerol, Chambertin and Corton in Burgundy, Hermitage and Châteauneuf-du-Pape (Côte Rôtie is more often in the previous category), exceptional Roussillons (not for maturing); Barolo and Barbaresco, Brunello di Montalcino, Recioto and Recioto Amarone from Valpolicella; Spanish Vega Sicilia (and on a humbler level Priorato); Portuguese Barca Velha; Yugoslav Posip and Postup; Bulgarian Cabernet. Occasional vintages such as 1961 in Bordeaux and 1971 in Burgundy produce many such wines.

California, Australia and South Africa find it hard not to make such big reds. Most of their best wines are carefully restrained in ripeness, but in California many wines are made with maximum extract to be larger than life. Australia makes many such wines, especially in Victoria (e.g. Bailey's, Balgownie, Château Tahbilk) and the Southern Vales in South Australia. South African examples include estate wines from Alto, Meerendal, Allesverloren and Vergenoegd.

Well-hung game and strong cheeses are the obvious candidates for these wines, although those in the appropriate price bracket are also excellent with barbecues and on picnics, when someone else is driving.

Fortified wines

Wines whose natural strength is augmented with added alcohol, either during the fermentation to preserve the natural sweetness (as in port) or after they have fermented to dryness, as a preservative (as in sherry). Since the role of these wines is largely determined by their sweetness, which is at their makers' discretion, all that can usefully be said is that dry versions (whether of port, sherry, madeira or their regional equivalents) are intended as apéritifs, while sweet ones are used either before or after meals according to local taste and custom. The French, for example, prefer sweet apéritifs, the Italians bitter ones and the British, who divide everything along class lines, some sweet and some dry. In all cases smaller glasses are needed because the alcoholic strength is between five and ten per cent higher than that of table wine.

They also have their uses with certain foods. Dry sherry is always drunk in Spain with tapas, which are infinitely various savoury snacks. It is one of the best wines for smoked eel. Old oloroso sherry, whether dry or with added sweetness, is very good with cake, nuts and raisins. Port, both vintage and tawny, is often drunk with cheese. Madeira has a cake especially designed for it.

Other wines in this category include Spanish Malaga and Tarragona, Sicilian Marsala, Cypriot Commandaria, French Vins Doux Naturels (e.g. Banyuls), Hungarian Tokay and a host of wines, usually with borrowed names, in the New World.

STORING WINE

The greatest revolution in the history of wine was the discovery that if air could be excluded from wine its life span was increased enormously. And, even better, that it could take on an undreamed-of range of flavours and a different, less grapey and infinitely more subtle and interesting smell.

The invention that made airtight storage possible was the cork, which came into use some time in the seventeenth century. It is possible that the ancient Greeks knew the secret, but all through the Middle Ages and up to the seventeenth century the premium was on new wine, not old. The latest vintage often sold for twice as much as the remnants of the previous one, which stood a good chance of having become vinegar. The only exceptions were the class of high-strength and possibly sweet wines generally known as sack, products of hot sunshine in the eastern Mediterranean, southern Spain and later the Canary Islands. Their constitution allowed them to age in barrels in contact with air and take on the nuttiness and warmth of flavour we associate with sherry.

Ageing in bottles under cork is a totally different process. Instead of oxidizing, or taking in oxygen, the wine is in a state of 'reduction' – in other words what little oxygen it contains (absorbed in the cellars, while being 'racked' from one cask to another, and in being bottled) is being used up (reduced) by the life processes within it. So long as it lives – and wine is a living substance with a remarkable life span – it is the battleground of bacteria, the playground of pigments, tannins, enzymes . . . a host of jostling wildlife preying on each other. No air gets through a good cork as long as it is kept wet, in contact with the wine, so that there is no risk of the vinegar process starting.

Whether the reduction process is beneficial, and for how long, is the determining factor in deciding when a bottled wine will be at its best.

Which wines to store

The great majority of wines are made with the intention of being ready to drink as soon as possible. This is true of all bulk wines, most white wines except very sweet and particularly full-bodied ones, nearly all rosés and the whole class of red wines that can be compared with Beaujolais – whose character and charm lie in a direct flavour of the grape. Reduction spoils their simple fruitiness. The only table wines that benefit from storage are a minority of sweet or very concentrated, intensely flavoury whites and those reds specifically made, by long vatting with their skins and pips, to take up pigments and tannins as preservatives – which include, of course, all the world's best.

Precisely how much of these elements combines with

Purpose-built private cellars are rare today, but they exist, in some cases with a degree of sophisticated planning undreamt of in the past. The cellar illustrated here is based on that of Tawfiq Khoury, a wine collector in San Diego, California. It has a total capacity of 40,000 bottles, with allowance for storage of every bottle size up to 8-bottle Imperials. It is air conditioned to 52°F (11°C) and is also used as a tasting room for small private parties, a wine book library and a museum of rare old bottles and glasses.

All the shelves have a slope of one sixteenth of an inch to the back to keep any sediment at the bottom of the bottle.

The whole cellar is air conditioned to a constant 52°F (11°C) – perfect serving temperature for white wine and maturing temperature for reds. It is chilly for mere human beings: they have to wear an extra sweater.

A roll-top desk for keeping accounts and writing notes. Records of the stock are kept in a card-index system. The volume and complexity actually justifies a small computer.

Random storing

The best way to make use of a limited number of pigeonholes in a storage rack is to put new acquisitions into whatever holes are empty, regardless of order – even if it means scattering a dozen bottles in random ones and twos. All that is needed is a clear grid reference system and an entry in your cellar book or card index for each pigeonhole you have used. This is the only way to avoid wasting space.

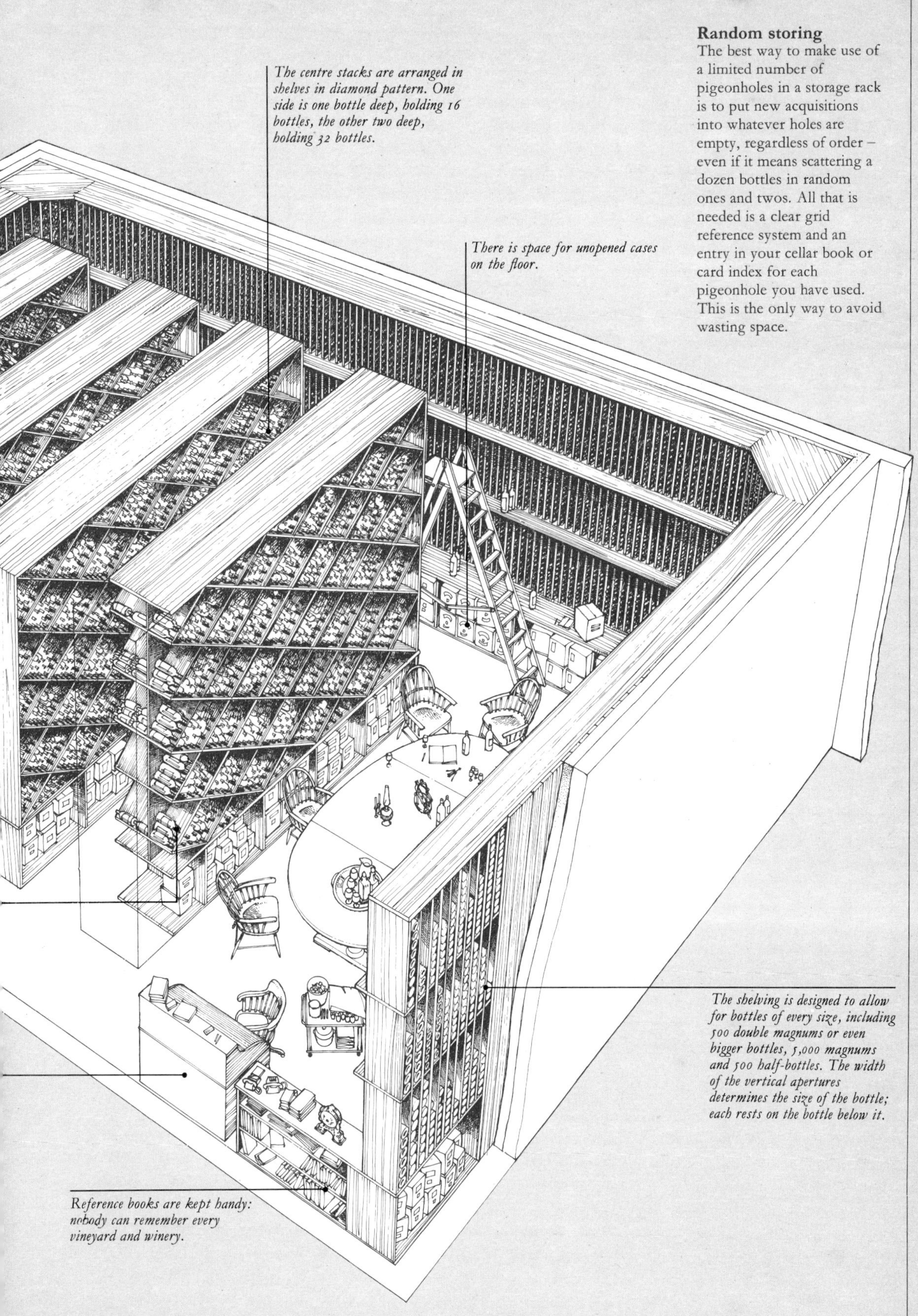

The centre stacks are arranged in shelves in diamond pattern. One side is one bottle deep, holding 16 bottles, the other two deep, holding 32 bottles.

There is space for unopened cases on the floor.

The shelving is designed to allow for bottles of every size, including 500 double magnums or even bigger bottles, 5,000 magnums and 500 half-bottles. The width of the vertical apertures determines the size of the bottle; each rests on the bottle below it.

Reference books are kept handy: nobody can remember every vineyard and winery.

the juice and how well they act as preservatives is only partly in the hands of the wine maker. The overriding decisive factor is the vintage. And no two vintages are exactly alike. The analysis of the grapes at harvest time may be similar, but each crop has stood out in the fields through a hundred different days since the vine flowers opened. The number and size of the grapes, the formation of the bunches, the thickness of the skins, the yeasts they gathered will always be subtly different. No two vintages develop in the same way or at precisely the same speed. But the better wines of each vintage will always last longer and mature further, to more delicious flavours, than the less good.

Thus laying down wines for maturing is always an exploratory business. Experts will give their opinion that the 1978 Bordeaux need from 5 to 15 years to reach their best, depending on their quality. Such a margin will be safe enough, although it is scarcely a very helpful guide. They will also tell you that, based on their assessment of the style of the 1979 vintage, which has less tannin and concentration (it was a record-size crop), its wines will be at their best before the 1978s. (But they may be wrong.)

Is it time to try?

Happily there are always plenty of other people opening bottles of every vintage and adding to a general pool of information about it, transmitted through wine books and magazines and catalogues. You will never have to look very far for an indication of whether it is time to try the wine you are storing. You can even tell a certain amount about the maturity of red wine without opening the bottle by holding its neck up to a strong light: the depth and quality of colour are quite readable through the glass.

The more difficult decision, assuming you intend to lay

Cellar log book

The Wine Society Cellar Book

DISTRICT Burgundy NAME Volnay, Cuvée General Muteau (Hospices) VINTAGE 1962

RECEIVED				OPENED		
Source	*Cost*	*Date*	*Qty*	*Date*	*Qty*	*Remarks*
Berry Bros.	15/-	4·66	12	9·66	1	Dark, firm, great depth & future.
(bottled by)				4·68	2	With R.A.C., D.D. Still dark, round,
						lovely texture. A big volnay. Keep
				10·69	1	Marvellous balance, depth. Delicious "
				9·70	2	Developing well - sweetness with fine
						'strike'. With B.J. (Roast grouse)
				7·72	1	Colour still deep, full, firm, fragrant.
						Ideal. With M.B.
				11·72	3	With Ralphs. A dream - but one
						bottle poor, sl. corky.

The reason for methodically entering tasting notes in a cellar book is to keep an orderly biography of each wine you buy. It would be wrong to pretend I am always as methodical as this specimen page implies. Most of my tasting notes are muddled in pocket notebooks and on the sheets provided at organized tastings. But this page reminds me of what the wine cost and from whom it came. What it first tasted like and how it has developed. Who it was shared with and even with what food. Everyone can devise his own cellar book. In practice, I find there is no need for so many columns as above. The identity of the wine, the bottler, the price and date of acquisition can all go to the top, leaving more room for notes below.

down some wine, is how much of which vintages to buy. It is probably a mistake to plunge too heavily for one vintage – you never know whether the next one will be better. It is more sensible to buy regularly as good vintages turn up, which in Bordeaux in recent years has been about two years out of three, in Burgundy one out of three, in the Rhône valley (well worth putting in your cellar) two out of three and in California, for the sort of reds we are talking about, the same.

Since there is rarely enough space (and never enough money) it is worth making a calculation of how much dinner-party wine you are likely to use, which in turn depends on how many of your friends share your passion. Let us suppose that you give an average of one dinner party a month for eight people, and each time use four bottles of mature wine (in addition to such current items as young white wines and possibly champagne). Your annual consumption will be about 48 bottles. Perhaps you use another bottle a week on family occasions (or alone). That makes about eight dozens a year.

The theoretically ideal stock is arrived at by multiplying the annual consumption by the number of years it stays in the cellar. Since this number varies from perhaps two, for fine white wines, to ten or more for the best reds, a finer calculation is needed. Let us say that two of the eight dozens are two-year wines, four are five-year wines and two are ten-year wines. The total is $2 \times 2 + 4 \times 5 + 2 \times 10 = 44$ cases.

Besides table wines two other kinds of wine are worth laying down: champagne and vintage port. Champagne is a relatively short-term proposition. Vintage champagne almost invariably gains a noticeable extra depth of flavour over two or three years. Lovers of old champagne will want to keep it far longer, up to 10 or even 20 years, until

Storage systems

The commonest form of permanent wine rack is made of wooden bars joined with galvanized metal strips in a modular system which can be any shape or size. The wooden cases of the grander château wines are ideal storage. A new idea is a modular spiral system building up into a flight of steps.

CHATEAU ROHAN 1982

Maturity comparisons

Beaujolais 1979 — Optimum — Nouveau — Fleurie — Vintage — Months 12 18 24 30 36 42 48

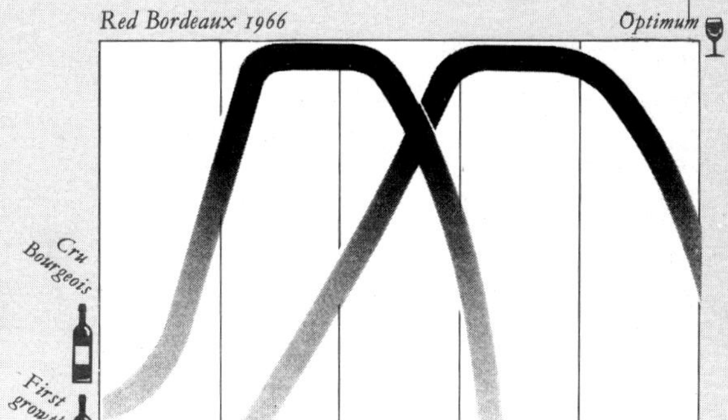

Red Bordeaux 1966 — Optimum — Cru Bourgeois — First growth — Vintage — Years 5 10 15 20 25

White Burgundy 1971 — Optimum — Mâcon-Viré — Montrachet — Vintage — Years 10 15 20

Every bottle proceeds at its own pace towards maturity with almost incredible differences between the fastest and the slowest, between even similar types from the same regions, varieties and seasons.

It is interesting to plot the life span of a range of wines in a graphic form. In these diagrams I have assumed a notional (and unmeasurable) 'optimum' for each wine; the time when all its potential is realized. The better the wine the longer this 'plateau of perfection' is likely to be. The 'drinkability' of each wine up to the optimum is the vertical dimension of each diagram. For clarity it assumes that all wines are equally 'perfect' at some stage of their lives. The horizontal scale shows time measured from the vintage in years (or months, as indicated).

its colour deepens and its bubbles quieten. In Britain it is worth keeping non-vintage champagne for a year or two as well, but I have found that in America it is usually mature (sometimes overmature) by the time it reaches the customer.

Vintage port is an entirely different matter. The way the wine goes through almost its whole life cycle in the bottle is explained in the section on port. It needs cellaring longer than any other wine – except the almost unobtainable vintage madeira. All good vintages need 20 years or more to reach their hour of glory.

The practical arrangements for storing wine are a challenge to most householders. The ideal underground cellar is even more remote than its ideal contents. But the storage conditions that make an underground cellar ideal are relatively easy to reproduce upstairs (at least in temperate climates) if the space is available.

The conditions required are darkness, freedom from vibration, fairly high humidity and a reasonably even temperature. Darkness is needed because ultraviolet light penetrates even green glass bottles and hastens ageing prematurely. Vibration is presumed to be bad (on what evidence I am not sure; it would have to be pretty violent to keep any normal sediment in suspension). Humidity helps the corks to stay airtight; but much more important is that the wine remains in contact with the corks inside the bottle. It is essential to store all wine horizontally, even if you only expect to keep it for a month or two. Excess humidity is a serious nuisance: it rapidly rots cardboard boxes and soon makes labels unreadable. My own answer to the label problem is to give each one a squirt of scentless hair lacquer before storing it away.

Temperature and time

Temperature is the most worrisome of these conditions. The ideal is anything between a steady 45°F and 65°F (7° and 18°C). A 50°F (10°C) cellar is best of all, because the white wines in it are permanently at or near the perfect drinking temperature. It is probable that wines in a cold cellar mature more slowly and keep longer than wines in a relatively warm one, but the excellent Mirabelle restaurant in London keeps all its red wines – even the very old ones – permanently at serving temperature, about 65°F (18°C), and I have heard no complaints of premature ageing.

Chemists point out that chemical reaction rates double with each 10 degrees centigrade (18 degrees Fahrenheit) increase in temperature. If the maturing of wine were simply a chemical reaction this would mean that a wine stored in a cellar at 68°F (19°C) would mature twice as fast

Bottle size, shape and capacity

Bordeaux
Vintage Port
German wine bottle
Champagne
Beaujolais
Cubitainer
Sherry
Franconian

Each European wine region has a long-established traditional bottle shape which helps to preserve an identity in the public mind. In most cases the New World wines based on the same grape varieties are also sold in the appropriately shaped bottles to help identify the style of their wineries.

Colour of glass is as important as shape. All Rhine wines are bottled in brown glass, all Moselles in green. White Bordeaux is in clear glass, red Bordeaux is in green.

For table wines whose origin is not important the 'cubitainer' or 'bag-in-box' is a useful invention. The wine is in a plastic foil bag in a cardboard box. As it is drawn off through a tap the bag collapses, protecting the wine from harmful contact with air.

The diagram below gives the contents of the usual standard-sized bottles and gives a conversion chart from fluid ounces to litres and vice versa.

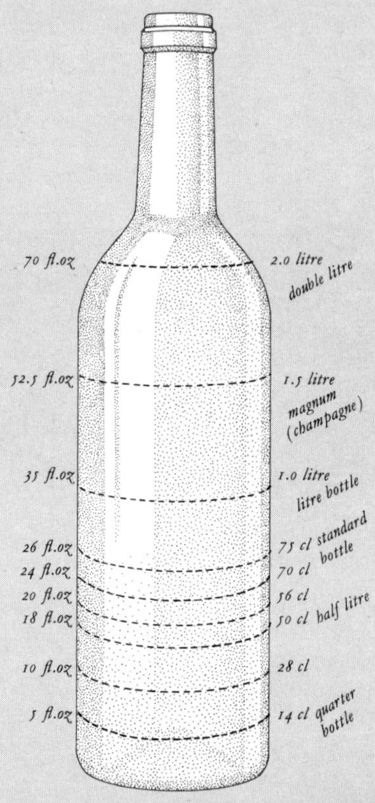

as one in a 50°F (10°C) cellar. But it is not so simple; wine is alive. Its ageing is not just chemical but a whole life process.

One should not exaggerate the effects of fluctuation, either. My own (underground) cellar moves gradually from a winter temperature of about 48°F (8°C) to a summer one of over 60°F (15°C) without the wine suffering in any detectable way. The most common difficulty arises in finding a steadily cool place in a house or apartment heated to 70°F (21°C) or more in winter, when the outside temperature can range from 60°F (15°C) plus to well below freezing. The answer must be in insulating a small room or large cupboard near an outside wall. In practice fine wines are successfully stored in blocked-up fireplaces, in cupboards under the stairs, in the bottoms of wardrobes . . . ingenuity can always find somewhere satisfactory.

The same applies to racks and 'bins'. A bin is a large open shelf (or space on the floor) where a quantity of one wine is laid bottle on bottle. In the days when households bought very few wines, but bought them a barrel at a time, the bin was ideal. For collections of relatively small quantities of many different wines racks are essential. They can either be divided into single-bottle apertures (one or two bottles deep) or into a diamond pattern of apertures large enough to take several bottles – a half-dozen or a dozen depending on the quantities you usually buy. I find it convenient to have both single-bottle and dozen-bottle racks.

Red Bordeaux comes in several sizes. The bigger the bottle the longer the wine keeps, the slower it matures and the better it will become.

Champagne is the only other wine with the same range of bottle sizes – but in this case for celebratory reasons.

A much more complex problem, as a collection grows, is keeping track of the bottles. It is difficult not to waste space if you deplete your stock in blocks. Where space is limited you want to be able to use every slot as it becomes vacant. This is the advantage of the random storage system. But its efficaciousness depends entirely on dedicated book-keeping. If this is not your line you are likely to mislay bottles just when you want them.

Very fine wines – most classed-growth Bordeaux, for instance – are shipped in wooden packing cases, which are perfect storage while the wine matures. If you do buy such wines by the complete case there is no point in unpacking it until you have reason to think the wine will be nearing maturity.

If possible make allowance in your storage arrangements for bigger-than-normal bottles. The 75-centilitre (26-fluid ounce) bottle has been accepted by generations as the most convenient regular size – although whether it was originally conceived as being a portion for one person or two is hard to say. But bigger bottles keep wine even better. Length of life, speed of maturity and level of ultimate quality are all in direct proportion to bottle size. Half-bottles are occasionally convenient, particularly for such powerful and expensive sweet wines as great Sauternes, where a little goes a long way. Otherwise, bottles are better, and magnums better still. Double magnums begin to be difficult to handle (and how often can you assemble enough like-minded friends to do justice to one?). The counsel of perfection is to lay down 6 magnums to every 12 bottles of each wine on which you pin really high hopes.

The reference section of this book gives typical examples of the potential life span of each class of wine. It is not necessarily only expensive wines that are worth laying down. Many Australian reds, for example, will evolve from a muscle-bound youth into a most satisfying maturity. One of my greatest successes was a barrel of a three-year-old Chilean Cabernet which I bottled in my amateurish way in my own cellar. It reached its quite delectable peak ten years later.

Experiment, therefore, with powerful, deep-coloured and tannic reds from whatever source. Be much more circumspect with white wines. Most of those that have proved that cellaring improves them beyond a year or two are expensive already: the better white burgundies, the best Chardonnays, Sauternes of the best châteaux and outstanding German Ausleses – which probably provide the best value for money today.

The neglected areas to add to these are Anjou and Vouvray from the Loire, top-quality Alsace wines, and what was once considered the longest lived of all white wines, the rare white Hermitage of the Rhône.

GLASSES

Each wine region has its own ideas about the perfect wineglass. Most are based on sound gastronomic principles that make them just as suitable for the wines of other regions, too. Perhaps the most graceful and universally appropriate is the shape used in Bordeaux. A few are flamboyantly folkloric – amusing to use in their context but as subtle as a dirndl at a dinner party. The traditional *römer* of the Rhine, for instance, has a thick trunk of a stem in brown glass ornamented with ridges and excrescences. It dates from the days when Rhine wine was preferred old and oxidized, the colour of the glass, and presumably when Rhinelanders wanted something pretty substantial to thump the table with. The Mosel, by contrast, serves its wine in a pretty shallow-bowled glass with a diamond-cut pattern that seems designed to stress the wine's lightness and grace. Alsace glasses have very tall green stems which reflect a faint green hue into the wine. Glasses like these are pleasant facets of a visit to the wine region, adding to the sense of place and occasion, but you do not need them at home.

The International Standards Organization has pre-empted further discussion by producing specifications for the perfect wine-tasting glass. Its narrowing-at-the-top shape is designed as a funnel to maximize the smell of the wine for the taster's nose. For ordinary table use this feature can be less pronounced. In all other respects it has the characteristics that any good glass should have: it is clear, unornamented, of rather thin glass with a stem long enough for an easy grip and an adequate capacity.

Capacity is important. A table wineglass should never be filled more than half full. A size which is filled to only one third by a normal portion (about 4 fl.oz/11 cl or an eighth of a bottle) is best of all. Anything larger is merely ostentatious.

Displaying the bubbles

Sparkling wines are best served in a slightly smaller but relatively taller glass filled to about three quarters of its capacity, giving the bubbles a good way to climb – one of the prettiest sights wine has to offer. They should never

Types of glasses

under any circumstances be served in the shallow 'coupes' sometimes used by ignorant caterers.

Dessert wines, being stronger, are served in smaller portions in smaller glasses, usually filled to between a half and two thirds of their capacity. Their scents are more pungent than table wines; to plunge your nose into a wide bowl of port fumes would be almost overpowering.

When several wines are being served at the same meal it saves confusion if each has a slightly different glass. In any case guests should be told that the order of pouring is from left to right (i.e. the first wine is poured into the left-hand glass and so on in order). I imagine this tradition is for the practical reason that a right-handed drinker is less likely to knock over his first glass in reaching for his second. As a further precaution against confusion (if two or more similar wines are being poured) it is a simple matter to slip a little rubber band around the stem of one of the glasses.

Wineglasses should be as clean as you can possibly make them – which is unfortunately beyond the capacity of any dishwasher. Detergents inevitably leave a coating on the glass which may or may not have a taste or smell, but is always detectable to the touch, and even affects the fizz of champagne. There is only one way of achieving a perfectly clean, polished, brilliant glass. After washing with soap or detergent to remove grease it should be thoroughly rinsed in clean hot water, then not drained but filled with hot water and only emptied immediately before it is dried. Practice shows that a clean linen or cotton cloth polishes a warm wet glass perfectly (and very quickly) whereas it leaves smears and fluff on a cold one.

The best place to keep glasses is in a closed cupboard, standing right way up. On an open shelf they collect dust. Upside down on a shelf they pick up odours of wood or paint. An alternative to a closed cupboard is a rack where they hang upside down, but dust on the outside of a glass is no better than dust on the inside.

You can argue that there is only one perfect wineglass, equally ideal for all table wines. But there is also a case for enjoying the traditional, sometimes fanciful, shapes adopted by different regions to promote the identity of their products.

Here a range of the most distinctive glasses is displayed with a carousel, which is a traditional German way of offering wines for tasting. At cafés in the Palatinate or the Black Forest you can order as many as a dozen different 'open' house wines which will be brought in a sort of dumbwaiter with numbered holes. All the guests can then taste and discuss all the wines, while keeping them in order for reference.

The traditional white-wine glass of Alsace has a green stem to reflect colour into the bowl.

The Trier glass, intended for Mosel. The engraving catches the light, making the green-gold wine look even more appetizing.

The traditional Rhine-wine or hock glass. The thick brown stem is designed to reflect colour into the wine.

Anjou's traditional white-wine glass, with long stem and in-turned bowl.

SERVING WINE

The no-nonsense approach to serving wine takes up very little space or time. The cork is out before discussion starts. There are times, and wine, for this can-of-beans attack which it would be pretentious to deny. But here I put the case for taking trouble to make the most of every bottle. On the basis that anticipation is a part of every great pleasure I argue that you should enjoy reading the label, be aroused by handling the bottle, relish removing the capsule, feel stirred by plunging in the corkscrew.

Sensuous enjoyment is the entire purpose of wine. The art of appreciating it is to maximize the pleasure of every manoeuvre, from choosing to swallowing. The art of serving wine is to make sure that it reaches the drinker with all its qualities at their peak.

No single factor is as important to success or failure as temperature. The characteristic scent and flavour of wine consists of infinitely subtle volatile compounds of different molecular weights, progressively heavier from 'light' white wines to 'heavy' reds. It is the temperature that controls their volatility – the point at which they vaporize and come to meet your sense of smell.

Each grape variety seems to behave differently in this respect. The Riesling scent is highly volatile: a Moselle sends out its flowery message even when it is too cold to drink with pleasure. Champagne's powerful fragrance of grapes and yeasts can hardly be suppressed by cold (although I have known people who seem to try). The Sauvignon Blanc is almost as redolent as the Riesling; the Chardonnay much less so – less so, in fact, than the Gamay; Beaujolais is highly volatile at low temperatures. The Pinot Noir vaporizes its ethereal sapidity even in a cool Burgundian cellar, whereas the Cabernets of Bordeaux hold back their aromas, particularly when they are young. In a Bordeaux *chai* it tends to be the oak you smell more than the wine. California and other warm-climate Cabernets are often more forthcoming.

Are aromas everything?

It will be seen that these observations tally more or less with the generally accepted norms of serving temperatures shown opposite. Not that aromas are everything. We expect white wines to be refreshingly cool; we expect red wines to awaken our palates with other qualities of vigour and completeness. It is fascinating to test how much your appreciation is affected by temperature. Taste, for instance, a good mature Meursault and a Volnay of the same quality (they are the white and red wines of the same vineyards, made of grapes with much in common) at precisely the same fairly cool temperature and with your eyes shut. You will find they are almost interchangeable.

It is time to forget the misleading word 'chambré' to describe the right temperature for red wines. Whatever the temperature of dining-rooms in the days when it was coined (and it must have varied from frigid to a fire-and-candle-heated fug) the chances of arriving at the right temperature by simply standing the bottle in the room where it is to be drunk are slight. An American dining-room at 70°F (21°C) plus is much too warm for wine. At that temperature the alcohol becomes unpleasantly heady. Mine, at 60°F (15°C), is good for burgundy but too cold for Bordeaux.

Everybody has, in his refrigerator, a cold place at a

Cooling vessels

Failing the ideal arrangement of storing white wine permanently at the perfect drinking temperature – that of a cool cellar – the most efficient way to chill it rapidly is by immersing the entire bottle in ice-cold water. A refrigerator takes up to 10 times as long as an ice-bath to achieve the same effect. Ice-cubes or crushed ice alone are inefficient. Ice must be mixed with cold water for rapid conduction of heat from the bottle. The perfect ice bucket is deep enough to immerse the whole bottle, neck and all: otherwise you have to put the bottle in upside down to start with to cool the neck. On the right is a new idea: a sort of open-ended Thermos flask which keeps an already chilled bottle cool by maintaining a wall of cold air around it.

Ice buckets

Decorative antique champagne bucket

Insulated plastic cylinder

The wineometer

Nothing makes or mars any wine so much as its temperature. The thermometer illustrated was specially designed for wine. It has the obvious disadvantage that it can only be used once the bottle is open. (Another kind clips around the outside of the bottle.) Experience soon makes any such gadget unnecessary. Here it serves to show the ideal temperatures for each category of wine. It is wrong, however, to be too dogmatic. Some people enjoy red wines several degrees warmer than the refreshing temperature I suggest for them here, and some like their white wines considerably colder than the moderate chill I advocate for the best appreciation of scent and flavour.

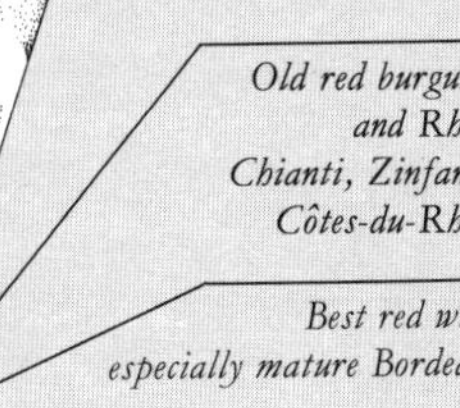

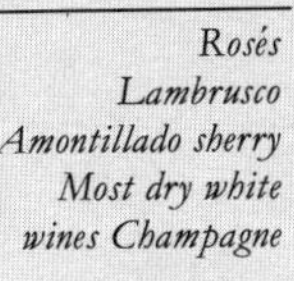

Opening sparkling wine

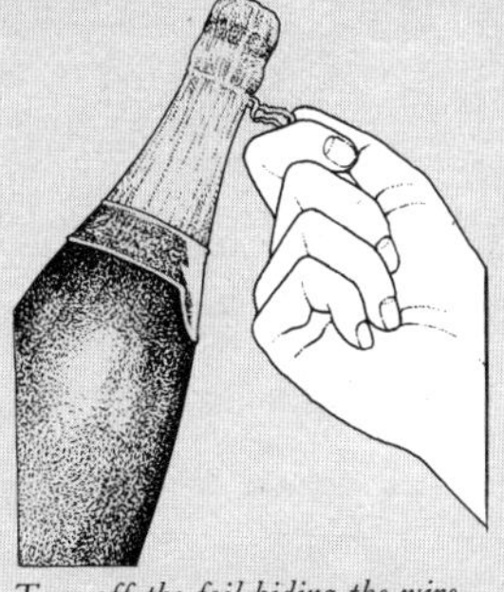

Tear off the foil hiding the wire 'muzzle' to uncover the 'ring'. Tilt the bottle and untwist the ring, being careful not to point the bottle at anyone.

Remove the muzzle. Tilt the bottle, holding the cork down firmly with your thumb. Ease the cork sideways and upwards with the other thumb.

When the cork feels loose, grasp it firmly and twist, keeping the bottle tilted, with a glass beside you to take the first foam.

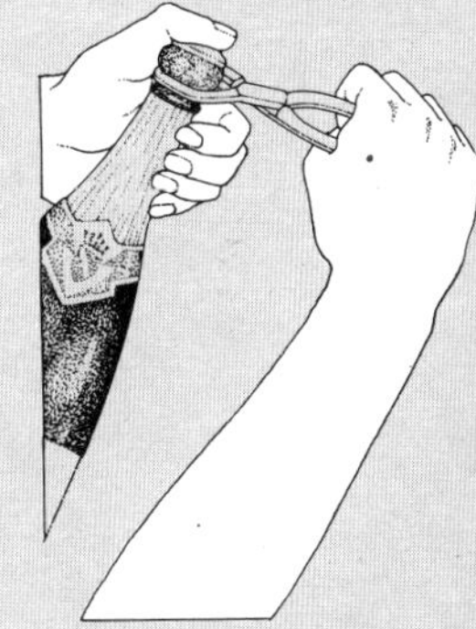

Specially made pliers are sometimes used when a champagne cork is very stiff, or when opening a number of bottles.

Butlers in the great champagne houses pour champagne by holding the bottle with a thumb in the indentation known as the 'punt', and their fingers supporting the weight. With practice this becomes the most comfortable and stylish way to do it.

Retaining the sparkle

Sparkling wines should be spur-of-the-moment celebratory drinks. When opening expensive bottles, it is a good idea to have a stopper that will keep the fizz intact if the celebration should be short-lived. The two models illustrated will keep partly filled bottles of méthode champenoise wines in good bubble for at least 24 hours.

constant temperature that can be used for cooling white wine. Nobody I have met has a 63°F (16°C) oven. On the other hand since an ice bucket is a perfectly acceptable (in fact by far the most efficient) way of chilling wine, why not a warm-water bucket for red? Water at 70°F (21°C) will raise the temperature of a bottle from 55°F to 65°F (13°-18°C) in about eight minutes, which is the same time as it would take to lower the temperature of a bottle of white wine from 65°F to 55°F (18°-13°C) in a bucket of icy water. (Ice without water is much less efficient in cooling.) In a fridge, incidentally, where air rather than water is the cooling medium, the same lowering of temperature would take about one hour.

Bold spirits who have accustomed themselves to microwave ovens will no doubt have experimented with them on red wine. I am told that the time it takes to warm a bottle from 55°F to 65°F is something under 20 seconds.

Bear in mind that the prevailing temperature affects the wine not only before it is poured out but while it is in your glass as well. Serve white wine on a hot day considerably colder than you want to drink it. Never leave a bottle or glass in the sun; improvise shade with a parasol, the menu, a book, under your chair ... anywhere. At one sumptuous outdoor buffet in South Africa the white wine was admirably cold but the red wine was left on the table in the sun. Not only was it ruined beyond recognition but I nearly burnt my tongue on it. There are circumstances where the red wine needs an ice bucket too.

Do you decant?

Wine lovers seem to find a consensus on most things to do with their subject, but decanting is a divisive issue. There is one school of thought, the traditional, that holds that wine needs to 'breathe' for anything from a few minutes to a few hours, or even days, to reach its best. Its opponents, armed with scientific evidence, proclaim that it makes no difference or (a third view) that it is deleterious. Each is right about certain wines, and about its own taste. But they are all mistaken to be dogmatic.

There are three reasons for decanting. The most important is to clean the wine of sediment. A secondary one is the attraction of the plump, glittering, glowing-red decanter on the table. The third is to allow the wine to breathe. Nobody argues with the first two. The debate revolves around when the operation should take place.

The eminent Professor Peynaud, whose contribution to gastronomy in general and Bordeaux in particular should make us listen carefully, writes (in *Le Goût du Vin*), 'If it is necessary to decant [at all], one should always do it at the last possible moment, just before moving to

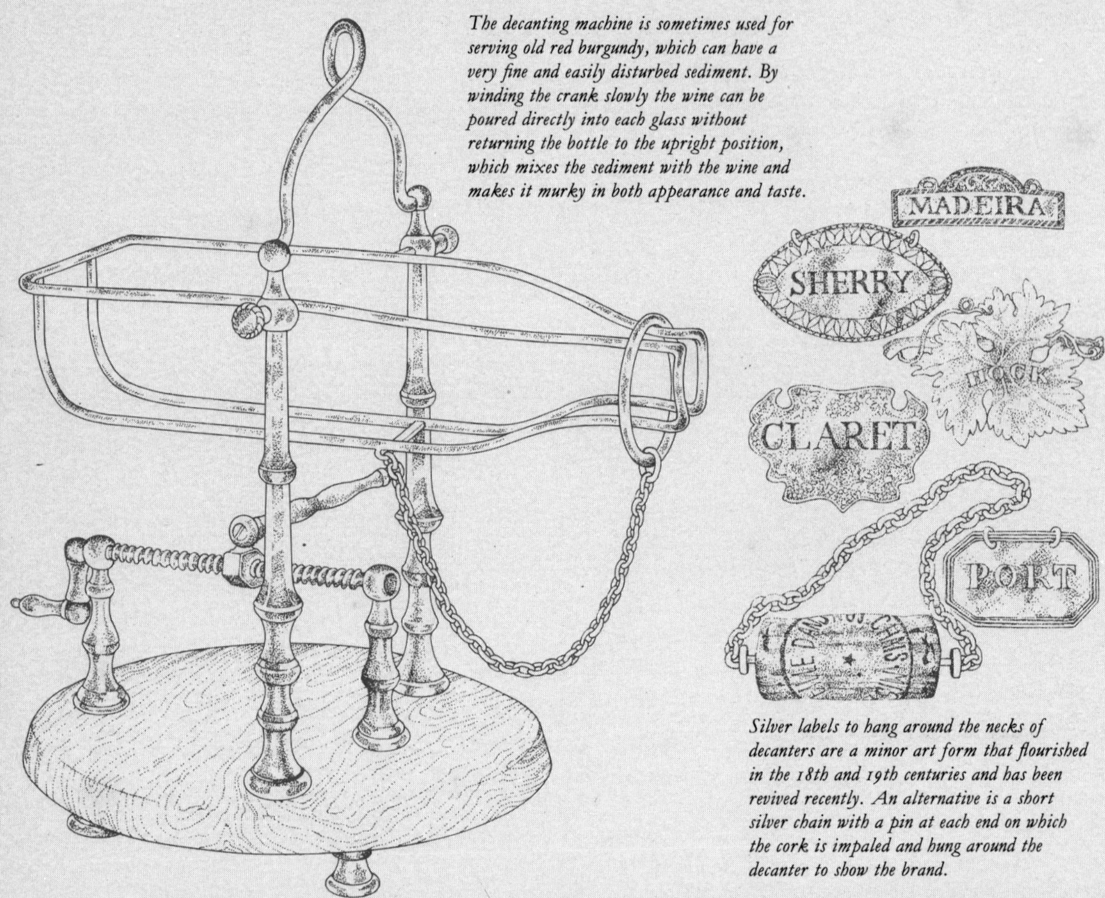

The decanting machine is sometimes used for serving old red burgundy, which can have a very fine and easily disturbed sediment. By winding the crank slowly the wine can be poured directly into each glass without returning the bottle to the upright position, which mixes the sediment with the wine and makes it murky in both appearance and taste.

Silver labels to hang around the necks of decanters are a minor art form that flourished in the 18th and 19th centuries and has been revived recently. An alternative is a short silver chain with a pin at each end on which the cork is impaled and hung around the decanter to show the brand.

the table or just before serving [the wine]; never in advance.' The only justification Peynaud sees for aeration, or letting the wine breathe, is to rid it of certain superficial faults that sometimes arise, such as the smell of slight refermentation in the bottle. Otherwise, he says, decanting in advance does nothing but harm; it softens the wine and dulls the brilliance of its carefully acquired bouquet.

Scientifically minded Americans have come to much the same conclusions, although their consensus seems to be that decanting makes no difference that can in any way be reliably detected.

My own experience is that almost all wines change perceptibly in a decanter, but whether that change is for the better or worse depends partly on the wine and partly on personal taste.

There are wine lovers who prefer their wine softened and dulled; vintage port in particular is often decanted early to soothe its fiery temper: its full 'attack' is too much for them. They equate mellowness with quality. The Spanish equate the taste of oak (as in Rioja) with quality. Who can say they are wrong about their own taste?

The English have always had strong ideas about how their wine should taste. A hundred years ago they added Rhône or Spanish wine to claret; it was altogether too faint for them without it. There are surely some people who preferred the burgundies of the days before the strict application of the appellation laws to the authentic straight-from-the-grower burgundy we drink today. The Californians, too, have their own taste. They love direct, strong-flavoured wines that often seem as though the transition from fruit juice was never fully completed. It is not surprising that ideas about decanting differ.

There are certain wines that seem to curl up when you open the bottle like woodlice when you turn over a log. The deeply tannic Barolo of Piedmont shows nothing but its carapace for an hour or sometimes several. If you drink it during that time you will have nothing to remember but an assault on your tongue and cheeks. But in due course hints of a bouquet start to emerge, growing stronger until eventually you are enveloped in raspberries and violets and truffles and autumn leaves.

The standard French restaurant practice is not to decant burgundy. If it is true that the Pinot Noir is more volatile than the Cabernet the practice makes sense: the contact with the air when pouring from bottle to carafe wakes the Bordeaux up; the burgundy does not need it.

Those who believe in decanting would give several hours' airing to a young wine, one or two to a mature wine (these terms being relative to the expected maturing time), and treat an old wine as an invalid who should be kept out of draughts. Yet strange to say it is an often repeated experience of those who have tasted very old and very great wines (Château Lafite 1803 was a case in point) that they can add layer upon layer of bouquet and flavour hour after hour – even, in some cases, tasting better than ever the following day. I regularly finish bottles the

Decanting

There is much debate about whether and when to decant wine; whether 'breathing' is a good thing or not. Modern 'scientific' opinion tends to be against it. Certainly its effects are hard to predict, but if a rule of thumb is called for I suggest that:

Vigorous young ('young' in this context relates to the vintage – a great vintage is young at 10 years, a poor one up to 4 or 5) red Bordeaux, Cabernets, Rhône reds, Barolo and Barbaresco, heavy Zinfandels, Australian Shiraz, Portuguese reds and other similar tannic wines: decant at least 1 hour before drinking, and experiment with periods of up to 6 hours.

'Young' red burgundy, Pinot Noirs and Spanish wines: decant just before serving.

Fully mature wines of all kinds: decant just before serving. *But* do not finish the decanter precipitately unless the wine is obviously fading. If it seems to hold back, give it as long as it needs.

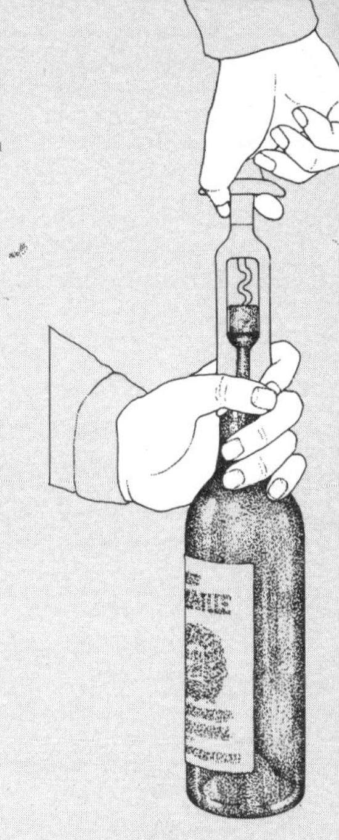

The best way to prepare red wine for decanting is to stand it upright for several days in advance. The corkscrew being used here is the Screwpull, which draws the cork up into itself with almost infallible ease.

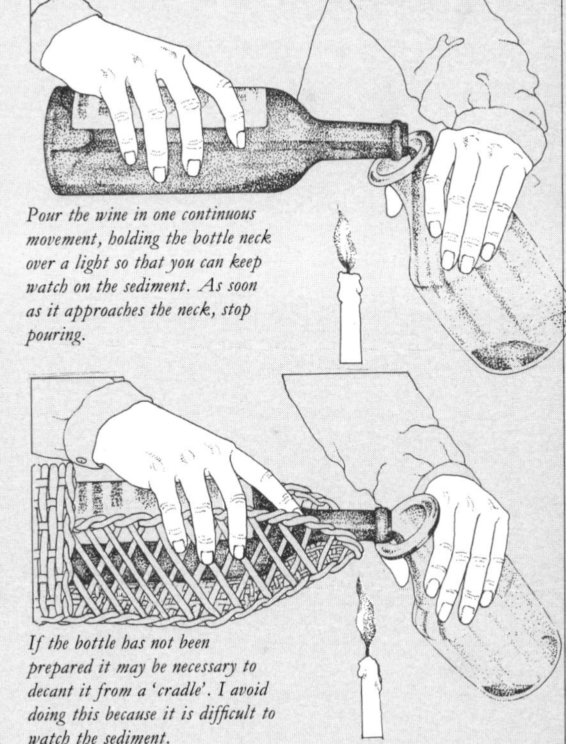

Pour the wine in one continuous movement, holding the bottle neck over a light so that you can keep watch on the sediment. As soon as it approaches the neck, stop pouring.

If the bottle has not been prepared it may be necessary to decant it from a 'cradle'. I avoid doing this because it is difficult to watch the sediment.

Opening vintage port

Bottles of vintage port older than about 20 years often present a special problem: the cork becomes soft and crumbly and disintegrates in the grip of a corkscrew.

Spongy corks are almost impossible to remove. The answer is to cut the top off the bottle, which can be done in either of 2 ways shown below.

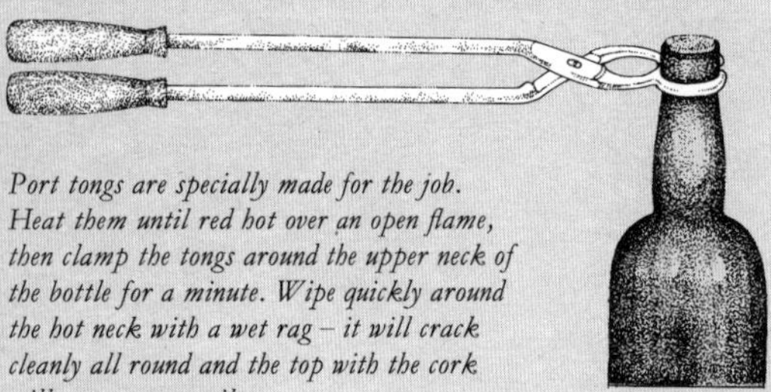

Port tongs are specially made for the job. Heat them until red hot over an open flame, then clamp the tongs around the upper neck of the bottle for a minute. Wipe quickly around the hot neck with a wet rag – it will crack cleanly all round and the top with the cork will come away easily.

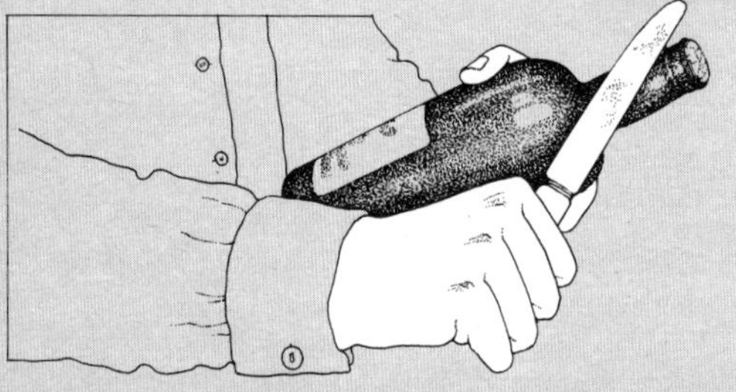

An equally effective and more spectacular way of opening an old bottle of port is to grasp it firmly in one hand and take a heavy carving knife in the other. Run the back of the knife blade up the neck of the bottle to give a really sharp blow to the 'collar'. The neck will crack cleanly. Practise before making your début at a dinner party. Confidence is all.

If a port cork crumbles into the bottle it is possible to filter the wine through a clean muslin-lined glass or plastic funnel, or to use one of the handsome old-fashioned silver funnels which has a built-in strainer.

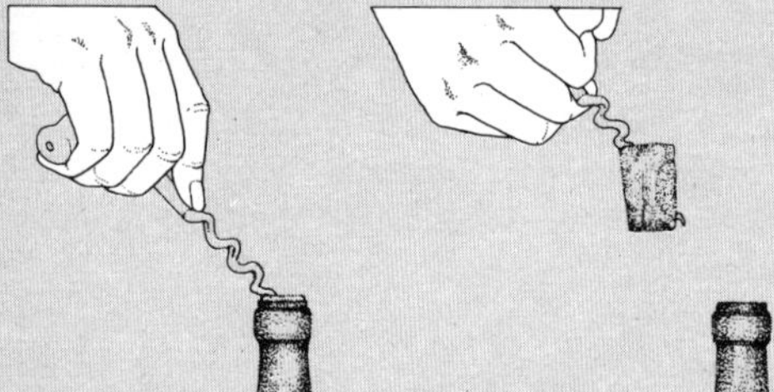

If a cork shows signs of weakness, or breaks in half when you pull it, the situation can sometimes be retrieved by inserting the corkscrew into the remainder of the cork diagonally, and pushing towards the opposite side of the neck.

evening after opening them. The only general rule I have found is that the better the wine, taking both origin and vintage into account, the more it benefits from prolonged contact with the air. Sometimes a wine that is a distinct disappointment on opening changes its nature entirely. A bottle of Château Pontet-Canet 1961 (in 1982) had a poor, hard, loose-fitting cork and, on first tasting, a miserable timid smell and very little flavour at all (although the colour was good). Twenty-four hours later it seemed to have recharged its batteries; it opened up into the full-blooded, high-flavoured wine I had expected. The moral must be to experiment and keep an open mind.

The pros and cons of decanting are much more long winded than the process itself. The aim is simply to pour the wine, but not its sediment, into another receptacle (which can be a decanter, plain or fancy, or another bottle, well rinsed).

If there is enough advance warning take the bottle gently from its rack at least two days before you need it and stand it upright. Two days (or one at a pinch) should be long enough for the sediment to slide to the bottom. If you must decant from a bottle that has been horizontal until the last minute you need a basket or cradle to hold the bottle as near its original position as possible but with the wine just below cork level.

Cut the capsule right away. Remove the cork gently with a counter-pressure corkscrew. Then, holding the decanter in the left hand, pour in the wine in one smooth movement until you see the sediment advancing as a dark arrow towards the neck of the bottle. When it reaches the shoulder, stop pouring.

It makes it easier to see where the sediment is if you hold the neck of the bottle over a candle-flame or a torch, or (I find best) a sheet of white paper or a napkin with a fairly strong light on it. Vintage port bottles are made of very dark glass (and moreover are usually dirty), which makes it harder to see the sediment. If the port has been lying in one place for years its sediment is so thick and coherent that you can hardly go wrong. If it has been moved recently it can be troublesome, and may even need filtering. Clean damp muslin is the best material; I have found that coffee filter papers can give wine a detectable taste.

The French way with burgundy

Serving burgundy, if you follow the French practice and do not decant it, presents more of a problem. Restaurants often serve it from a cradle; the worst possible system because each time the bottle is tipped to pour and then tipped back the sediment is stirred into the remaining wine. The Burgundian answer to this is the splendid engine that tips the bottle continuously, as in the motion of decanting, but straight into the guests' glasses. Without such a machine I decant burgundies at the last minute – but only when they have sediment. Unless they are very old they are often clear to the last drop.

CORKS AND CORKSCREWS

The first corks must have been like stoppers, driven only halfway home. There is no known illustration of a corkscrew until 100 years after corks came into use.

Although screw-caps and crown closures now offer cheaper and simpler ways of keeping the wine in and the air out, cork remains the way fine wine is sealed.

What makes cork so ideal as a wine plug? Certainly its lightness, its cleanness, and the simple fact that it is available in vast quantities. It is almost impermeable. It is smooth, yet it stays put in the neck of the bottle. It is unaffected by temperature. It very rarely rots. It is extremely hard to burn. Most important of all it is uniquely elastic, returning, after compression, to almost exactly its original form. Corking machines are based on this simple principle: you can squeeze a cork enough to slip it easily into the neck of a bottle and it will immediately spring out to fill the neck without a cranny to spare.

As for its life span, it very slowly goes brittle and crumbly, over a period of between 20 and 50 years. Immaculately run cellars (some of the great Bordeaux châteaux, for example) recork their stocks of old vintages approximately every 25 years, and one or two send experts to recork the château's old wines in customers' cellars. But many corks stay sound for half a century.

The only thing that occasionally goes wrong with a cork is a musty smell that develops unaccountably. Corks are carefully sterilized in manufacture, but sometimes one or two of the many cells that make up the cork (there are 20 to 30 in a square millimetre) are infected with fungus. When these cells are in contact with wine the wine picks up the smell and becomes 'corky' or 'corked'. The problem is rare (one champagne house calculates the risk at 1.3:1,000) but when it happens it is instantly noticeable – and naturally disappointing. There is nothing to be done but to open another bottle.

Good-quality corks produce no other problems. Poor

Producing Cork

Cork is the thick outer bark of the cork oak, *Quercus suber*, a slow-growing evergreen tree which has evolved this spongy substance for protection and insulation, particularly against fire. The world supply of cork is concentrated in the western Mediterranean area and the neighbouring Atlantic coasts. Portugal, above all, furnishes half of the total, and almost all of the top-grade cork for use with wine.

The bark is cut into sheets from mature trees every 9 or 10 years between the months of June and August. (Each tree has a productive life of 165 years.) The sheets are stacked to dry for 3 months, then boiled in vats with fungicides. After several more months' storage in a dark, cold cellar, the corks are cut as plugs from the thickness of the bark.

The longest (up to 57 mm) and best-quality corks are graded for the best wine. Dust and scraps from the process are agglomerated to make cheap corks. For specialized use by champagne makers extra large corks are made of 3 layers glued together. A normal wine cork is 24 mm in diameter, compressed into an 18 mm neck. For champagne a 31 mm cork is compressed into a 17.5 mm neck, with the upper third protruding in the characteristic bulging mushroom shape.

Champagne corks (below) before and after bottling. Note the layers, with the best-quality cork at the base, in contact with the wine.

Brands on corks (below) indicate authenticity of the wine, showing producer and vintage, but phrases such as 'mise en bouteille dans nos chais' or 'caves' mean nothing. The shorter corks are for white wines.

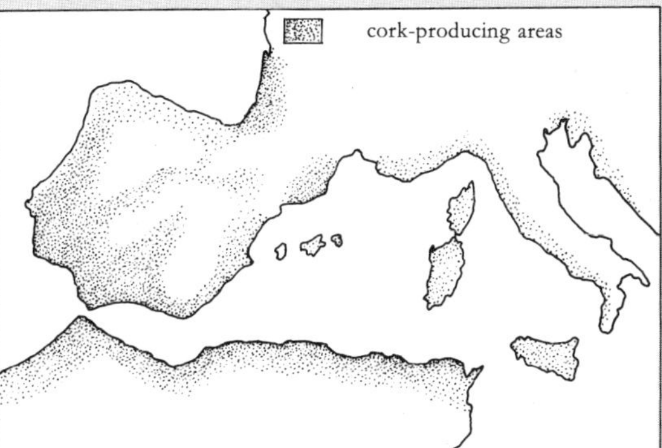

ones do. Many Italian wine bottles have very hard, small, low-grade corks in necks that are narrower than the norm. They make it extremely tough going for the corkscrew, which sometimes pushes the cork in instead of pulling it out. If you have wiped the top of the cork clean with a damp cloth before starting to open the bottle, no harm is done. A gadget made of three parallel lengths of thick wire with a wooden handle is made for fishing for lost corks. It is reasonably effective, but a simpler answer is to leave the cork in and pour the wine out, holding the cork down with a knife or a skewer until it floats clear of the neck.

The quality of your corkscrew is most important. Enormous ingenuity has been expended on the engineering of corkscrews. The simple screw-with-a-handle has long since been improved on by designs that use counter-pressure against the bottle. The straight pull is strictly for the young and fit: it can take the equivalent of lifting 80 pounds to get a cork out.

Various dodges are used to provide leverage, but the most important factor of all is the blade – the screw – that pierces and grips the cork. At all costs avoid narrow gimlets on the one hand and open spirals of bent wire on the other. The gimlet will merely pull out the centre of a well-installed cork; the bent wire will simply straighten if it meets with resistance. A good corkscrew blade is a spiral open enough to leave a distinct chimney up the middle, and made like a flattened blade with a sharp point and two cutting edges on its horizontal sides. The fine points of corkscrew design are illustrated below.

Types of corkscrew

Endless ingenuity has been applied to the mechanical problem of grasping a cork in a bottle and pulling it out without exertion. A straight pull with the bottle between your knees is neither dignified nor necessary: all you need is some sort of leverage against the rim of the bottle. Out of a catalogue of thousands of devices, these are some of the most popular and effective in current use.

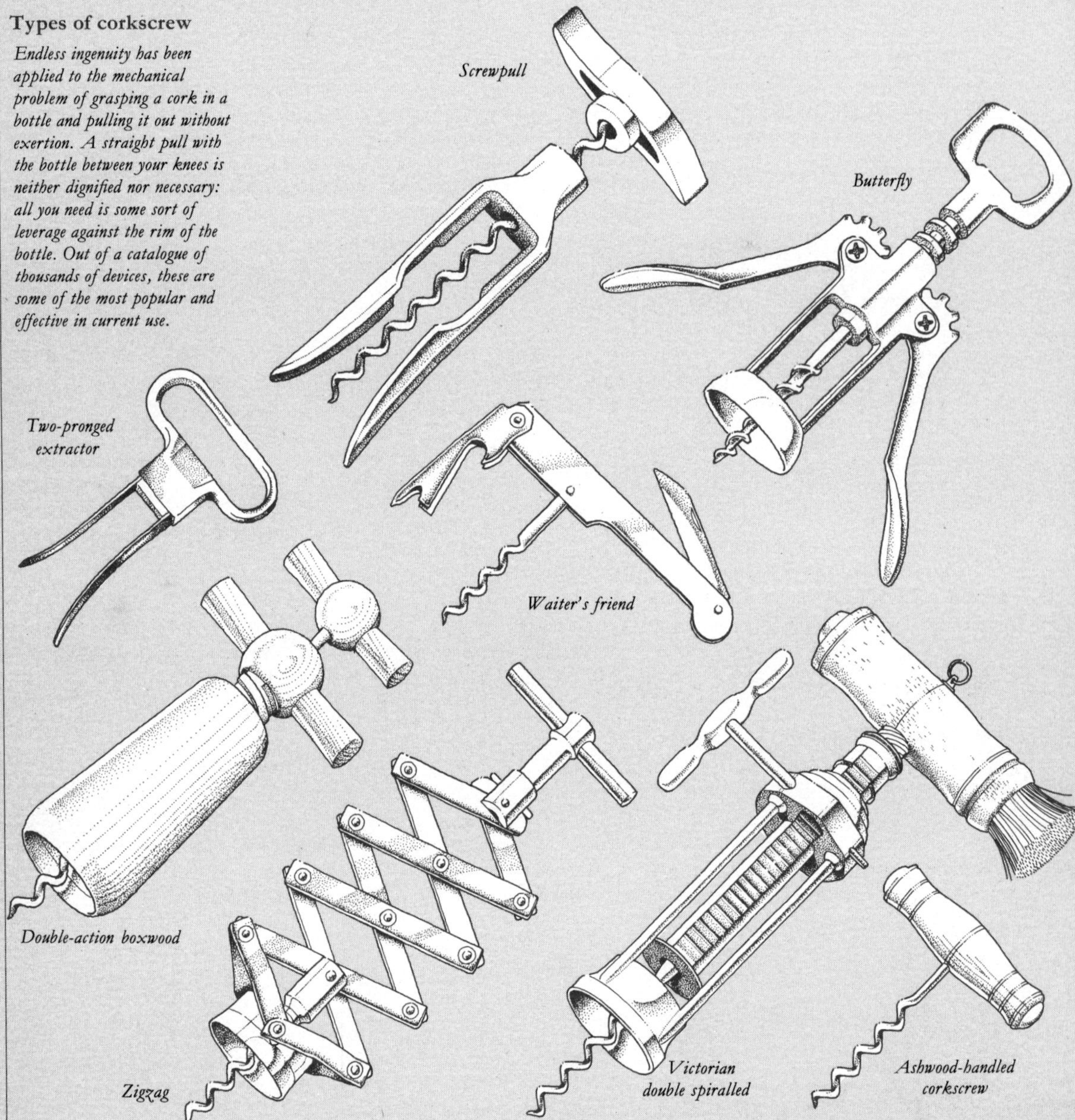

TASTING WINE

There are wine tastings on every level of earnestness and levity, but to taste wine thoroughly, to be in a position to give a considered opinion, demands wholehearted concentration. A wine taster, properly speaking, is one who has gone through a professional apprenticeship and learned to do much more than simply enjoy what he tastes. He is trained to examine every wine methodically and analytically until it becomes second nature. Although I am by no means a qualified professional taster I often find myself, ridiculously, putting a glass of tap water through its paces as though I were judging it for condition and value. If I do not actually hold it up to the light I certainly sniff it and hold it in my mouth for a moment while I see how it measures up to some notional yardstick of a good glass of water. Then naturally I spit it out.

Whether or not you have any desire to train your palate (it has its disadvantages too; it makes you less tolerant of faulty or boring wines) it makes no sense to pay the premium for wines of character and then simply swallow them. It is one of the commonest misunderstandings about wine that if it is 'better' it will automatically give more pleasure. To appreciate degrees of quality you need conscious, deliberate awareness. You need to know what sort of quality you are looking for. And you need a method to set about finding it.

Pierre Poupon, one of the most eloquent of Burgundians, has written: 'When you taste don't look at the bottle, nor the label, nor your surroundings, but look directly inwards to yourself, to observe sensations at their birth and develop impressions to remember.' He even suggests shutting your eyes to concentrate on the messages of your nose and mouth.

Before dinner parties become like prayer meetings let me say that there is a time and place for this sort of concentration. But if you apply it at appropriate moments it will provide you with points of reference for a more sociable approach.

What, to start with, are you tasting for? A very basic wine tasting for beginners might consist of five wines to show the enormous variety that exists: a dry white and a sweet one; a light young red and a fine mature one, and a glass of sherry or port. The point here is that the wines have nothing in common at all. Another very effective elementary tasting is to compare typical examples of the half-dozen grape varieties that have very marked and easily recognized characters.

Most tastings are intended to compare wines with an important common factor, either of origin, age or grape variety. A tasting of Rieslings from a dozen different countries is an excellent way of learning to identify the common strand, the Riesling taste, and judge its relative success in widely different soils and climates. A variant of this, more closely focused, would be to take Rieslings of the same category of quality (Kabinett or Spätlese) from the four principal wine regions of Germany.

Vertical and horizontal tastings

Tastings of the same wine from different vintages are known in the jargon as 'vertical'; those of different wines (of the same type) in a single vintage are known as 'horizontal'.

Professional tastings concerned with buying are nearly always horizontal. The important thing here is that they should be comparing like with like. It is of no professional interest to compare Bordeaux with burgundy, or even Chablis with Meursault; if the Chablis is a good Meursault it is a bad (because untypical) Chablis. A Médoc that tasted like a Napa Valley wine would be a poor Médoc – although it might be hard to convince a Napa grower that the converse was true.

Most of us, of course, drink most of our wine with meals. We judge it, therefore, partly by how well it goes with the sort of food we like. Professional and competitive tasters always judge wine either by itself or in company with other wines, which gives them a different, and clearer, point of view. It is clearest of all when you are hungry and not tired; the end of the morning is the time most professionals prefer.

The ideal conditions, in fact, are rather unattractively clinical; a clean well-lit place without the suggestive power of atmosphere, without the pervasive smell of wine barrels, without the distraction of friendly chatter – and above all without the chunks of cheese, the grilled sausages and home-made bread that have sold most of the world's second-rate wine since time immemorial.

Whether you should know what you are tasting, or taste 'blind' and find out afterwards, is a topic for endless debate. The power of suggestion is strong. It is very difficult to be entirely honest with yourself if you have seen the label; your impressions are likely to reflect, consciously or otherwise, what you think you should find rather than simply what your senses tell you – like a child's picture of both sides of a house at once.

If I am given the choice I like to taste everything blind first. It is the surest method of summoning up concentration, forcing you to ask yourself the right questions, to be analytical and clear minded. I write a note of my opinion, then ask what the wine is or look at the label. If I have guessed it right I am delighted; I know that my mental image of the wine (or memory, if I have tasted it before) was pretty close to reality. If (which is much more frequent) I guess wrong, or simply do not know, this is my chance to get to know the wine, to taste it again carefully and try to understand why that grape, in that vineyard, in that year, produced that result. This is the time to share impressions with other tasters.

It is always interesting to find out how much common ground there is between several people tasting the same wine. So little is measurable, and nothing is reproducible, about the senses of smell and taste. Language serves them only lamely, leaning on simile and metaphor for almost everything illuminating that can be said.

The convenient answer, normally used at competitive tastings, is the law of averages. Ask a group of tasters to quantify their enjoyment, and reduce their judgement to scores, and the wine with the highest average score must be the 'best'. The disadvantage of averaging is that it hides the points of disagreement, the high and low scores given to the same wine by different tasters who appreciate or dislike its individual style, or one of whom, indeed, is a better judge than another. At a well-conducted tasting the chairman will therefore consider an appeal against an averaged score and encourage a verbal consensus as well, especially where gold medals hang on the result.

This is as close to a final judgement on wine quality as fallible beings can get. But at best it represents the rating by one group of one bottle among the wines they tasted that day. It takes no account of other wines that were not tasted on the same occasion. All one can say about medal winners is that they are good of their sort.

For competitive tastings, taster against taster, 'blindness' is the whole point of the exercise. The individual (or team) with the widest experience and the best memory for tastes should win. For competitive tastings, wine against wine, it is the only fair method. But it can nonetheless produce misleading results. It tends to favour impact at the expense of less obvious but ultimately more important qualities. When California Cabernets are matched against red Bordeaux of similar age the Californians almost always dominate. They are like tennis players who win by serving ace after ace.

The grand tour

The act of tasting has been anatomized by many specialists. To me there are five aspects of wine that convey information and help me gauge its quality, origin, age, the grape varieties involved and how long it will keep (and whether it will improve). They constitute the grand tour of its pleasures, the uplift excepted. To take them in order they are its appearance, smell, the first impression the wine makes in your mouth, its total flavour as you hold it there, and the taste it leaves behind.

I take each of these into account, note each separately (writing a note is not only an *aide-mémoire*, it forces you to make up your mind) and then draw a general conclusion. Tasting is a demanding discipline, quite distinct from the mere act of drinking. It sometimes has to be a quick and private little ceremony at a party where wine is not an accepted priority. Yet to contract the habit and apply a method of one kind or another is the only way to get full value out of your wine.

There is more to appearance than simply colour. Fine wine is brilliantly clear. Decanting should make sure that even old wine with sediment has the clarity of a jewel, capturing and reflecting light with an intensity that is a pleasure in itself.

Wine is more or less viscous, at one extreme forming heavy, slow-moving 'legs' on the walls of the glass, at the other instantly finding its own level like water. The more dense it is the more flavour-giving 'extract' and/or sugar it contains – which of course is neither good nor bad in itself; it must be appropriate to the kind of wine. On the other hand a deposit of crystals in white wine is (if anything) an indication of good quality; it is certainly not under any circumstances a fault.

'Colour [I quote Professor Peynaud] is like a wine's face. From it you can tell age, and something of character.' That is, you can if you have certain other information about the wine, which the smell will soon provide.

The best way to see its colour clearly is to hold the glass against a white surface – a piece of paper will do – and to

Tasting wine

The secret of getting the maximum pleasure out of wine is to remember that we smell tastes: it is our noses and the nerves high in the brain behind the nasal cavity that distinguish nuances of flavour – not our tongues, lips or palates. The mouth detects what is sweet, sour, salt, bitter, burning, smooth, oily, astringent. But the colour and character of a flavour lie in its volatile compounds, which need the nose to apprehend them. Thus the procedure for tasting wine pivots around the moment of inhalation: the crucial first sniff.

To taste, first look carefully at the precise colour, clarity and visual texture of the wine.

Swirl wine to volatilize its aroma while you concentrate; then sniff. First impressions are crucial.

Take a generous sip, a third of a mouthful, and 'chew' it so that it reaches all parts of your mouth.

The final judgement comes when the volatile compounds rise into the upper nasal cavity.

tip it slightly away from yourself so that you are looking through the rim of the liquid. Shallow silver tasting cups are used in dark cellars, where it is hard for light to penetrate the depth of wine in a glass.

White wines grow darker as they age; reds go through a slow fading process from purplish through red to a brickish reddy brown (which can be seen even through the green glass of the bottle by looking at the neck against a light). In young wines the colour in the glass is almost uniform from edge to edge (making allowance, that is, for greater density where you are looking through more wine). In older wines the rim is usually decidedly paler. A browning rim is a sure sign of maturity in red wines.

Sheer redness is an indicator of quality rather than a virtue in its own right. The famous 1961 Bordeaux vintage can often be recognized across the room by its extraordinary glowing darkness – even in maturity a colour of pregnancy and promise. A Priorato from Spain might well manage to be even darker still, without being fit to be on the same table.

Burgundy rarely has the same deep tints, and never precisely the same hue as Bordeaux. Chianti is rarely deep red because of the proportion of white grapes in it. Rioja is also generally rather pale, but because it has been aged for so long in cask. Beaujolais is light coloured in a different way; more the translucent purple of grape juice. In general hot-country wines of good grape varieties, the Cabernets, for example, of Australia, California and South Africa, have more intensity of colour than their cool-country equivalents. Vintage port is deep purple-red, ruby port a much lighter, more watery colour, and tawny port, aged in wood for many years, anything from the brown-red of old claret to a clear light amber when it is very old – the most extreme example of a red wine fading.

White wine has scarcely less variety than red. Chablis has a green light in its pale gold which is uncommon in other white burgundies. Moselles also have a touch of green, with less of the gold, while Rhine wines tend to a straw colour, deepening almost to orange in old sweet examples. Sherry is coloured by oxidation; young finos only very slightly, old olorosos to a mahogany brown. When great sweet Sauternes ages, it goes through all the tints of gold to arrive at a deep golden brown.

Hold your nose

You have only to hold your nose while you sip to realize that it is the organ that does most of the serious work of tasting. Unfortunately our sense of smell is our least cooperative, least stable faculty. While taste, like hearing and sight, is constantly awake, the sense of smell rapidly wearies. If you sniff more than half a dozen times in rapid succession at the same glass (or the same rose) its message becomes dimmed. Your nose needs a different stimulus.

For this reason wine tasters place a great deal of faith in their first impression. They swirl the wine once or

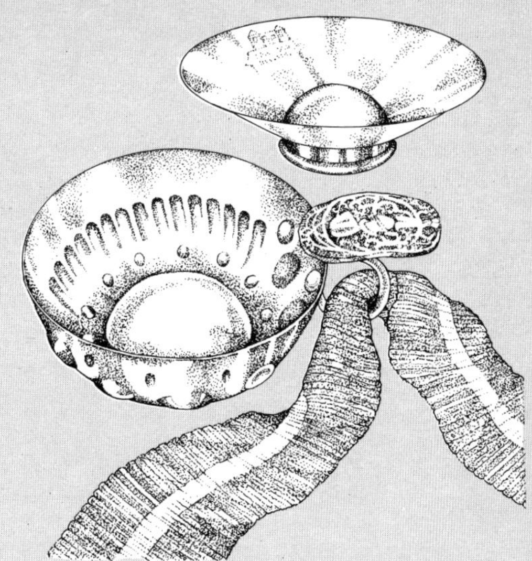

Silver tasting cups are common in parts of France – particularly Burgundy – where wine is kept in dark cellars. It is easier to judge the colour of red wine in a shallow layer over the brightly reflecting silver than in a glass, where it is in a greater mass. The 'tastevin' worn on a ribbon around the neck has become the ceremonial symbol of Burgundy. The plainer version was made for Château Lafite Rothschild in Bordeaux.

An ideal tasting glass, to the specifications of the International Standards Organization, is about 6 inches (152 mm) high and would hold 7 fl. oz (215 ml). For tasting purposes it is usually only filled to about one fifth of capacity. The tall funnel shape is designed to capture the aroma, or bouquet, for the taster's nose. It needs a long enough stem to keep the hand away from the bowl. (Professional tasters often hold their glass by its foot.) The thinner the glass, within reason, the better. Wine is tasted more vividly from thin glass.

twice to wet the sides of the glass and volatilize as much of the smell as possible. Then they exclude all other thoughts and sniff. The nerves of smell have instant access to the memory (their immediate neighbour in the brain). The first sniff should trigger recognition; possibly the memory of the identical wine tasted before. If the smell is unfamiliar it will at least give this piece of negative information, and suggest where in the memory-bank partially similar smells are to be found.

The smell will be the first warning sign if there is something wrong with the wine: a slight taint of vinegar, the burning sensation of too much sulphur, a mouldy smell from an unsound cork or an unclean barrel. Nowadays obvious faults like these are relatively rare. Most wines have a more or less agreeable but simple compound smell of grapes and fermentation, and in some cases barrel-wood; the smell we recognize as 'winey'. The better the wine, the more distinctive and characteristic this smell, the more it attracts you to sniff again.

At this stage certain grape varieties declare themselves. The 'classics' all set a recognizable stamp on the smell of their wine. Age transmutes it from the primary smell tasters call the 'aroma' to a more complex, less definable and more rewarding smell. This scent of maturity is known, by analogy with the mixed scents of a posy of flowers, as the bouquet.

The essence of a fine bouquet is that you cannot put your finger on it. It seems to shift, perhaps from cedar-wood to wax to honey to wildflowers to mushrooms. Mature Riesling can smell like lemons and petrol, Gewürztraminer like grapefruit, Chardonnay like butter – or rather, they can fleetingly remind you of these among many other things.

By the time the glass reaches your lips, then, you have already had answers, or at least clues, to most of the questions about wine: its overall quality, its age, perhaps its grape (and by deduction possibly its origin).

If all is well the taste will confirm the smell like the orchestra repeating the theme introduced by a soloist, adding the body of sound, the tonal colours that were missing. Only at this stage can you judge the balance of sweetness and acidity, the strength of the alcohol and whether it is counterpoised by the intensity of fruity flavours, and the quantity and quality of tannin.

Each wine has an appropriate combination of these elements; its quality is judged on whether they harmonize in a way that is both pleasant in itself and typical of its class. In fact, typical comes before pleasant. A young red wine may be disagreeably tannic and astringent; the taster's job is to judge it for the latent fruitiness that in time will combine with the tannins.

Different parts of your mouth pick up different facets of flavour. It is the tip of your tongue that recognizes sweetness, so sweetness is the first taste you become aware of. Acidity and saltiness are perceived by taste buds along the sides of your tongue and palate, bitterness by the soft back part of your tongue.

The tastes switch off in the same order: sugar after a mere two seconds or so; salt and acid after rather longer. Bitterness, which you notice last, lingers – a quality the Italians appreciate; many of their red wines (Valpolicella is an example) have a slightly bitter aftertaste.

Science can measure many (not all) of the chemical constituents that provide these sensations. It has identified more than 400 in wine up to now. But our perception of them is entirely personal. A few tasters, like a few musicians, may have 'perfect pitch', but most people probably have slight blind spots. Someone who takes three spoonfuls of sugar in coffee must have a high threshold of perception for sweetness. If you need to

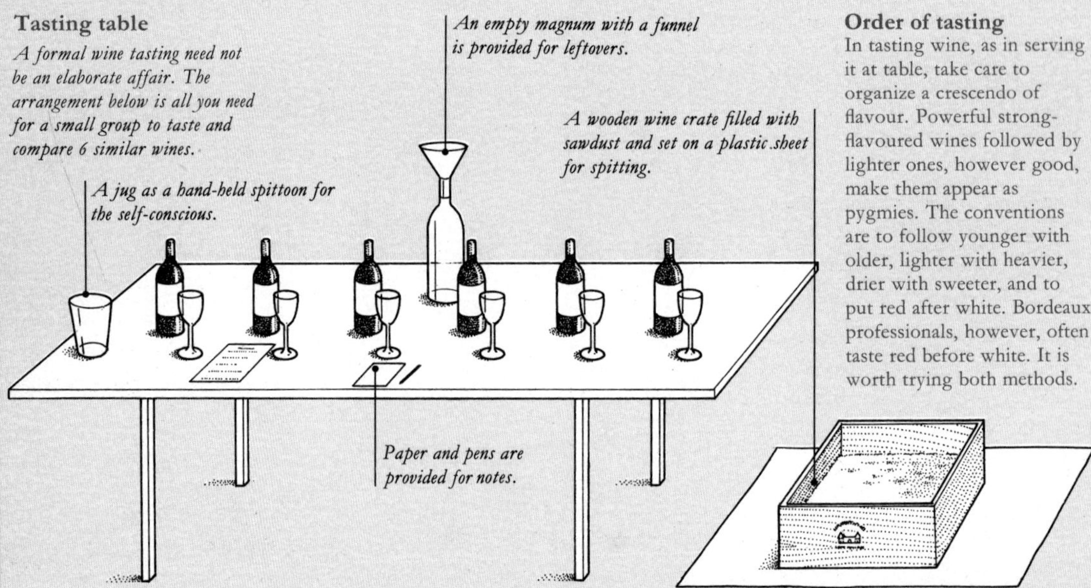

Tasting table

A formal wine tasting need not be an elaborate affair. The arrangement below is all you need for a small group to taste and compare 6 similar wines.

Order of tasting

In tasting wine, as in serving it at table, take care to organize a crescendo of flavour. Powerful strong-flavoured wines followed by lighter ones, however good, make them appear as pygmies. The conventions are to follow younger with older, lighter with heavier, drier with sweeter, and to put red after white. Bordeaux professionals, however, often taste red before white. It is worth trying both methods.

smother your food with salt you will hardly pick up the subtle touches of saltiness in wine.

Sweet, sour, salt and bitter in any case hardly start to express the variety of sensations that evolve in your mouth between sipping and swallowing. The moment of maximum flavour is when the wine reaches the soft palate and you start to swallow. Its vapour mounts directly to the olfactory nerves through the channels that link mouth and nose. At a serious tasting, where it is essential to spit the wine out to keep a clear head, this moment can be maximized by holding a small quantity in the very back of the mouth and breathing in through it between slightly parted lips. The grimace and the gurgling are a small price to pay for the redoubled concentration of flavour.

Red wines contain more or less tannin, the substance that turns hide to leather. Very tannic wine is so astringent (like walnut or broad-bean skins) that your mouth can begin to feel leathery and further tasting can be difficult. Tannin varies in taste and quality, too, from fully ripe, agreeable astringence, or the mouth-drying astringence of oak, to unripe green harshness.

Acids vary from harsh to delicately stimulating – not just in their concentration, or their power (measured in pH), but in their flavours. Of the wine acids malic is green-appley, citric is fresh and lemony, tartaric is harsh. Acetic is vinegary, lactic is mild, and succinic is a chemical cousin of glutamic acid. We owe much of the lip-smacking, appetizing taste of wine to tiny traces of succinic acid generated as a by-product of fermentation.

As for the alcohol itself, in low concentrations it merely has a faintly sweet taste, but at about 11 per cent by volume it begins to give the mouth the characteristic feeling of winey warmth known as 'vinosity'. (German wines at eight or nine per cent lack this feeling.)

Add the ability of your tongue to differentiate between (more or less) fluid or viscous, to pronounce that one liquid feels like satin, another like velvet, and the permutations begin to be impressive. Finally, add the all-important element of persistence – the length of the final flavour. Really great wines have more to offer at the beginning, in the beauty of the bouquet, and at the end, in the way they haunt your breath for minutes after they have gone. Logical in all things, French scholars have even invented a unit of persistence; one second of flavour after swallowing is known as a 'caudalie'. According to one theory the hierarchy of the wines of Burgundy is in direct proportion to their caudalie-count.

A tasting scorecard produced by Michael Broadbent and myself in 1975 – but never a great success, because it tried to embody both descriptive and qualitative terms, and a scoring system. Many scorecard systems have been elaborated, most notably in California, where the Davis campus is the world headquarters of what it pleases them to call organoleptic evaluation. The high priests of the discipline have a long list of proscribed descriptive words which should be avoided because they are not sufficiently accurate, or are positively misleading. Unfortunately it includes most of my vinous vocabulary. The virtues of this card are that it helps you to analyse a wine methodically, reminding you of each aspect to think about in turn.

Name of Wine Ch. Giscours · Vintage 1966 District/type Margaux · Date purchased 1969 Merchant/bottler J. Morgan Furze / C.B · Price £2.00 ?	DATE OF TASTING 15 · 1 · 82
SIGHT Score (Maximum 4) 4 CLARITY: cloudy, bitty, dull, clear, brilliant DEPTH OF COLOUR: watery, pale, medium, deep, dark COLOUR: (White wines) green tinge, pale yellow, yellow, gold, brown (Red wines) purple/red, red, red/brown VISCOSITY: slight sparkle, watery, normal, heavy, oily	Comments Col. still deep & strong with sl. whitening at edge.
SMELL Score (Maximum 4) 3 GENERAL APPEAL: neutral, clean, attractive, outstanding, off (e.g. yeasty, acetic, oxidized, woody, etc) FRUIT AROMA: none, slight, positive, identifiable (e.g. Riesling) BOUQUET: none, pleasant, complex, powerful	Starts earthy / mineral stones, wood – hessian? Develops to sweetness, growing more high-pitched, near violets but with undercurrent of ripe fruit.
TASTE Score (Maximum 9) 7 SWEETNESS: (White wines) bone dry, dry, medium dry, medium sweet, very sweet TANNIN: (Red wines) astringent, hard, dry, soft ACIDITY: flat, refreshing, marked, tart BODY: very light and thin, light, medium, full bodied, heavy LENGTH: short, acceptable, extended, lingering BALANCE: unbalanced, good, very well balanced, perfect	Still, powerful and warm; excellently crisp & clear (typical Margaux). Essentially dry, a shade astringent. Long firm finish. V.V.G.
OVERALL QUALITY Score (Maximum 3) 2½ Coarse, poor, acceptable, fine, outstanding	HOW TO USE THIS CHART Wine appeals to three senses: sight, smell and taste. This card is a guide to analysing its appeal and an *aide-mémoire* on each wine you taste. Tick one word for each factor in the left-hand column and any of the descriptive terms that fit your impressions. Then award points according to the pleasure the wine gives you.
SCORING Total Score (out of 20) 16½	

INDEX

Properties and wines entitled Château are indexed under their names.

D

E

F

Mc

M

N

Q

R

U

V

ACKNOWLEDGMENTS

In addition to the people named on page 4, and the many wine lovers whose assistance has been invaluable in writing this book, the author particularly acknowledges help given by the following, whether written, spoken or in their printed work. John Adams, Richard Allen, Dr. Hans Ambrosi, Colin Anderson, M.W., Marquis d'Angerville, Marchese Dot. Piero Antinori, Gerald Asher, David Balls, Jean Barbet, Mr. and Mrs. Graham Barrett, Antony Barton, Lilian Barton, Professor Dr. Becker, Diana Beevers, Katie Benjce, Professor Harold Berg, Alexis Bespaloff, Tim Bleach, Jean-Eugène Borie, Professor Roger Boulton, Gordon Brown, Ross Brown, Sheila Cavanagh-Bradbury, Don Chappellet, Tim Clarke, Michael Cliff, M.W., Bruce Coleman, Deeta Colvin, Professor James E. Cook, David Cossart, Alain de Courseulles, Henry Damant, Jean Demolombe, Professor A. Dinsmoor Webb, Beltram Domecq, Georges Duboeuf, Diana Durant, Evelyn Ellis, The English Vineyards Association, Jorge Erasodis, Charles Eve, M.W., Jorge Ferreira, Geoffrey Francom, Fromm & Sichell, Inc., Diana Furness, Janet Furze, Anthony Goldthorp, Richard Goodman, Dick Graff, Peter Hasslacher, Serge Hochar, Denis Horgan, The late Dr. G. Horney, Jean Hugel, V. Ishpekov, Gérard Jaboulet, Alan Johnson-Hill, Andrew Jones, A. N. Kasimatis, Tawfiq Khoury, Mark Kliewer, Matt Kramer, Professor Ralph E. Kunkee, Anthony Lacey, Daniel Lawton, John Lipitch, Nina Lobanov, Catherine Manac'h, Pierre Maufoux, Malcolm McIntyre, Jean Miailhe, Dr. Franz Werner Michel, Dr. Eric Minarić, Janel Minors, Robert Mondavi, Christian Moueix, Alain Mozés, Mario B. Neves, Professor Ann Noble, Richard O'Quinn, David Peppercorn, M.W., Professor Emile Peynaud, Andrew Pirie, Dr. Desiderius Pongracz, Michel Pons, Pierre Poupon, Bruno Prats, Q.E.D. Publishing, Jean Quénard, Alain and Sheila Querre, David Rayment, Michael Rayment, Mrs. Belle Rhodes, Dr. Bernard Rhodes, M. Jean Rière, Bertrand de Rivoyre, Geoffrey Roberts, André Roux, Hamilton Russell, David Rutherford, Henry Ryman, Jean-Pierre Saboye, Brian St. Pierre, Raymond le Sauvage, Mark Savage, Walter Schug, Debbie Scott, Peter Sichel, Joanna Simon, Professor Vernon L. Singleton, Cornelia Smith-Bauer, Kerry Brady Stewart, Serena Sutcliffe, M.W., David Thomas, M. Thomas, Helen Thompson, Miguel and Marimar Torres, Dip. Ing. Traxler, John and Janet Trefethen, Ugurlu Tunali, Michel Villedey, Tony Willis, Grant Willoughby, James Earl Wilson, Robin Yapp.

Illustrators: Russell Barnett, Lindsay Blow, Bob Chapman, Edwina Keene, Aziz Khan, James Robins, John Woodcock.

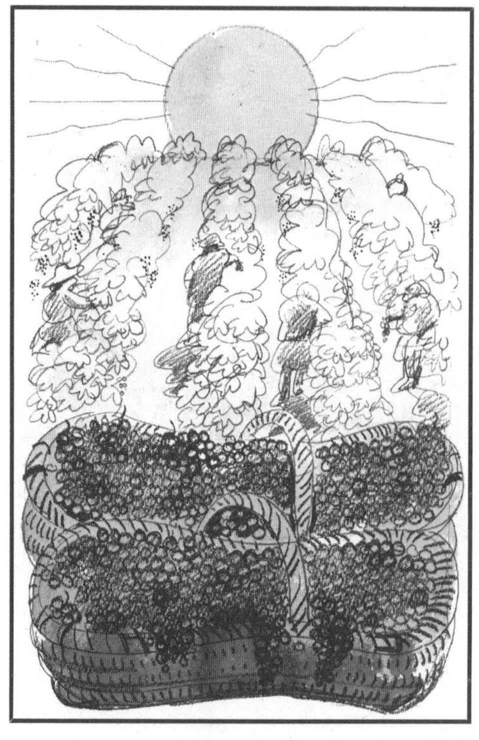